D0985927

THE NEW
COLLINS
COMPACT
DICTIONARY
OF THE
ENGLISH
LANGUAGE

THE NEW
COLLINS
COMPACT
DICTIONARY
OF THE
ENGLISH
LANGUAGE

Managing Editor
William T. McLeod

Editorial Staff
Danielle McGrath, Alice Truten

Marian Makins, Diana Adams, Michael Munro

Collins
London & Glasgow

First Published 1984
Latest Reprint 1990
© Wm. Collins Sons & Co. Ltd. 1984
ISBN 0 00 433149-4

Computer typeset by C. R. Barber & Partners
Wrotham, England

Printed and bound in Great Britain
by William Collins Sons & Co. Ltd.
P.O. Box, Glasgow G4 0NB.

Arrangement of Entries

All main entries are given in a single alphabetical listing that includes abbreviations, foreign words, and prefixes and suffixes (combining forms). These last enable the reader to construct for himself the meanings of hundreds of additional terms.

Within each main entry different meanings are clearly marked off from each other by bold numbers. After the meanings of the main headword come *derived* words as subentries in smaller bold type, in alphabetical order. These in turn are followed by *compounds* (if any) and then by *phrases*, again in alphabetical order within the paragraph.

Words that can function as more than one part of speech are printed out only once, the change of function being shown by a second (or subsequent) part-of-speech label, thus: **advance** (əd'vɑ:ns) *vt.* **1.** bring forward. . .—*vi.* **5.** go forward. . .—*n.* **7.** forward movement. . .—*a.* **11.** (*with* of) ahead in time. . . In the case of very short, simple entries, two parts of speech may be combined, thus: **agape** (ə'geɪp) *a. /adv.* open-mouthed. . . Spelling of verb parts is indicated as necessary in brackets after the definition of the verb, thus: **jab**. . . stab abruptly (-**bb**-)

Pronunciation Key

The symbols used in the pronunciation transcriptions are those of the International Phonetic Alphabet. The following consonant symbols have their usual English values: *b*, *d*, *f*, *h*, *k*, *l*, *m*, *n*, *p*, *r*, *s*, *t*, *v*, *w*, *z*. The remaining symbols and their interpretations are listed below.

English Sounds

ɑː	as in *father* ('fɑ:ðə), *alms* (ɑ:mz)		ɔɪ	as in *void* (vɔɪd), *boy* (bɔɪ)
æ	as in *act* (ækt), *plait* (plæt)		ʊ	as in *pull* (pʊl), *good* (gʊd), *should* (ʃʊd)
aɪ	as in *dive* (daɪv), *aisle* (aɪl), *guy* (gaɪ)		uː	as in *zoo* (zu:), *do* (du:), *queue* (kju:)
aɪə	as in *fire* (faɪə), *buyer* ('baɪə), *liar* ('laɪə)		ʊə	as in *poor* (pʊə), *skewer* ('skjʊə)
aʊ	as in *out* (aʊt), *bough* (baʊ)		ə	as in *potter* ('pɒtə), *alone* (ə'ləʊn)
aʊə	as in *flour* (flaʊə), *cower* ('kaʊə)		ɜː	as in *fern* (fɜ:n), *burn* (bɜ:n), *fir* (fɜ:)
ɛ	as in *bet* (bɛt), *ate* (ɛt), *bury* ('bɛrɪ)		ʌ	as in *cut* (kʌt), *flood* (flʌd), *rough* (rʌf)
eɪ	as in *paid* (peɪd), *day* (deɪ), *deign* (deɪn)		ʃ	as in *ship* (ʃɪp), *election* (ɪ'lɛkʃən)
ɛə	as in *bear* (bɛə), *dare* (dɛə), *prayer* (prɛə)		ʒ	as in *treasure* ('trɛʒə), *azure* ('æʒə)
g	as in *get* (gɛt), *give* (gɪv), *ghoul* (gu:l)		tʃ	as in *chew* (tʃu:), *nature* ('neɪtʃə)
ɪ	as in *pretty* ('prɪtɪ), *build* (bɪld)		dʒ	as in *jaw* (dʒɔ:), *lodge* (lɒdʒ)
iː	as in *see* (si:), *aesthete* ('i:sθi:t)		θ	as in *thin* (θɪn), *strength* (strɛŋθ)
ɪə	as in *fear* (fɪə), *beer* (bɪə), *mere* (mɪə)		ð	as in *these* (ði:z), *bathe* (beɪð)
j	as in *yes* (jɛs), *onion* ('ʌnjən)		ŋ	as in *sing* (sɪŋ), *finger* ('fɪŋgə)
ɒ	as in *pot* (pɒt), *botch* (bɒtʃ), *sorry* ('sɒrɪ)		ə	indicates that the following consonant (*l* or *n*) is syllabic, as in *bundle* ('bʌndəl) and *button* ('bʌtən).
əʊ	as in *note* (nəʊt), *beau* (bəʊ), *hoe* (həʊ)			
ɔː	as in *thaw* (θɔ:), *broad* (brɔ:d)			

PRONUNCIATION KEY

Foreign Sounds

Certain common foreign sounds require additional symbols, as follows:

a *a* in French *ami*, German *Mann*, Italian *pasta*: a sound between English /æ/ and /ɑ:/.

e *é* in French *été*, *eh* in German *sehr*, *e* in Italian *che*: similar to the Scottish vowel in *day*.

i *i* in French *il*, German *Idee*, Spanish *filo*, Italian *signor*: similar to English /i:/, but shorter.

ɔ *o* in Italian *no*, French *bonne*, German *Sonne*: a vowel resembling English /ɒ/, but with a higher tongue position and more rounding of the lips.

o *o* in French *rose*, German *so*, Italian *voce*: similar to the Scottish vowel in *so*.

y *u* in French *tu*, *ü* in German *über*: similar to English /i:/ made with closely rounded lips.

ø *eu* in French *deux*, *ö* in German *schön*: similar to /e/ made with closely rounded lips.

œ *eu* in French *œuf*, *ö* in German *zwölf*: similar to English /ɛ/ made with open rounded lips.

~ above a vowel indicates nasalization, as in French *un* (œ̃), *bon* (bɔ̃), *vin* (vɛ̃), *blanc* (blã).

x *ch* in Scottish *loch*, German *Buch*.

ç *ch* in German *ich*: similar to the first sound in *huge*.

β *b* in Spanish *Habana*: similar to /v/ but made by the two lips.

ʎ *ll* in Spanish *llamar*, *gl* in Italian *consiglio*: similar to the /lj/ sequence in *million*.

ɥ *u* in French *lui*: a short /y/.

ŋ *gn* in French *vigne*, Italian *gnocchi*, *ñ* in Spanish *España*: similar to the /nj/ sequence in *onion*.

γ *g* in Spanish *luego*: a weak /g/ made with voiced friction.

Length

The symbol : is shown with certain vowel symbols when the vowels are typically long.

Stress

The main stress is shown by ', immediately *before* the stressed syllable.

Notes

(i) Though words like *castle*, *path*, *fast* are shown as pronounced with an /ɑ:/ sound, many speakers use an /æ/. Such variations are acceptable and are to be assumed by the reader.

(ii) The letter "r" in some positions is not sounded in the speech of Southern England and elsewhere. However, many speakers in other areas do sound the "r" in such positions. Again, such variations are to be assumed.

(iii) Though the widely received pronunciation of words like *which*, *why* is with a simple /w/ sound and is so shown in the dictionary, many speakers, in Scotland and elsewhere, preserve an aspirated sound: /hw/. Once again this variation is to be assumed.

Abbreviations used in the Dictionary

a.	adjective	*Gram.*	Grammar
abbrev.	abbreviation	*Her.*	Heraldry
Acc.	Accounting	*Hist.*	History
adv.	adverb	*Hort.*	Horticulture
Aeron.	Aeronautics	*ie*	that is
Afr.	Africa(n)	*impers.*	impersonal
Amer.	America(n)	*ind.*	indicative
Anat.	Anatomy	*inf.*	informal
Archaeol.	Archaeology	*interj.*	interjection
Archit.	Architecture	It.	Italian
Arith.	Arithmetic	k	kilogram(s)
Astrol.	Astrology	km	kilometre(s)
Astron.	Astronomy	l	litre(s)
Aust.	Australia(n)	Lat.	Latin
Biochem.	Biochemistry	*Linguis.*	Linguistics
Biol.	Biology	lit.	literally
Bot.	Botany	*Lit.*	Literary, Literature
Brit.	Britain, British	m	metre(s)
Bus.	Business	*masc.*	masculine
Canad.	Canada, Canadian	*Maths.*	Mathematics
cent.	century	*Mech.*	Mechanics
Ch.	Church	*Med.*	Medicine
Chem.	Chemistry	*Met.*	Meteorology
Cine.	Cinema	*Mil.*	Military
Class. lit.	Classical literature	*Min.*	Mineralogy
Class. myth.	Classical mythology	mm	millimetre(s)
cm.	centimetre(s)	*Mus.*	Music
Comm.	Commerce	*Myth.*	Mythology
comp.	comparative	*n.*	noun
Comp.	Computers	N	North
conj.	conjunction	*Naut.*	Nautical
cu.	cubic	*N.T.*	New Testament
dial.	dialect	*N.Z.*	New Zealand
dim.	diminutive	*obs.*	obsolete, obsolescent
E	East	*offens.*	offensive
Eccles.	Ecclesiastical	oft.	often
Ecol.	Ecology	orig.	originally
Econ.	Economics	*O.T.*	Old Testament
Educ.	Education	*Pathol.*	Pathology
eg	for example	*pers.*	person
Elec.	Electricity	pert.	pertaining
Electron.	Electronics	*Philos.*	Philosophy
esp.	especially	*Phonet.*	Phonetics
fem.	feminine	*Photog.*	Photography
fig.	figuratively	*Phys.*	Physics
Fin.	Finance	*Phys. Ed.*	Physical Education
Fr.	French	*Physiol.*	Physiology
g	gram(s)	*pl.*	plural
Geog.	Geography	*pl.n.*	plural noun
Ger.	German	*Poet.*	Poetic, Poetry
Gr.	Greek	*Pol.*	Politics

ABBREVIATIONS

poss.	possessive	*sl.*	slang
pp.	past participle	*Sociol.*	Sociology
prep.	preposition	Sp.	Spanish
pres.t.	present tense	sq.	square
Print.	Printing	*St.Ex.*	Stock Exchange
pron.	pronoun	*sup.*	superlative
pr.p.	present participle	*Surg.*	Surgery
Psych.	Psychiatry	*Surv.*	Surveying
Psychoanal.	Psychoanalysis	*Theat.*	Theatre
Psychol.	Psychology	*Trig.*	Trigonometry
pt.	past tense	*T.V.*	Television
Rad.	Radio	*usu.*	usually
R.C.	Roman Catholic	*v.*	verb
refl.	reflexive	*v.aux.*	auxiliary verb
Rel.	Religion	*Vet.*	Veterinary Medicine
S	South	*vi.*	intransitive verb
Sc.	Science	*vt.*	transitive verb
Scot.	Scottish	W	West
sing.	singular	*Zool.*	Zoology

R	Registered Trade Mark
A	Australian
C	Canadian
NZ	New Zealand
SA	South African
UK	United Kingdom
US	United States

A

a *or* **A** (eı) *n.* **1.** first letter of English alphabet **2.** any of several speech sounds represented by this letter, as in *take, calm* **3.** first in series, *esp.* highest mark (*also* **'alpha**) (*pl.* **a's, A's,** *or* **As**) —**from A to Z** from start to finish

a (ə; *emphatic* eı) *a.* the indefinite article meaning one; *an* is used before vowel sounds, and sometimes before unaccented syllables beginning with *h* aspirate

A 1. *Mus.* sixth note of scale of C major; major or minor key having this note as its tonic **2.** human blood type of ABO group **3.** UK major arterial road **4.** UK formerly, (film) certified for viewing by all age groups **5.** ampere **6.** absolute (temperature) **7.** area **8.** alto **9.** (*comb. form*) atomic, as in *A-bomb, A-plant*

Å angstrom unit

a. 1. acre **2.** adjective **3.** answer **4.** are

a-¹ *or* **before vowel an-** (*comb. form*) not; without; opposite to, as in *atonal, asocial, anaesthetic*

a-² (*comb. form*) **1.** on; in; towards, as in *aground, aback* **2.** in state of, as in *afloat, asleep*

A1, A-1, *or* **A-one** (eɪ'wʌn) *a.* **1.** physically fit **2.** *inf.* first-class; excellent **3.** (of vessel) in first-class condition

AA 1. Alcoholics Anonymous **2.** anti-aircraft **3.** Automobile Association **4.** UK formerly, (film) that may not be shown to child under fourteen

A.A.A. 1. UK Amateur Athletic Association **2.** US Automobile Association of America

aardvark ('ɑːdvɑːk) *n.* nocturnal Afr. mammal which feeds on termites

A'asia Australasia

AB Alberta

A.B. able-bodied seaman·

ab-¹ (*comb. form*) away from; opposite to, as in *abnormal*

ab-² (*comb. form*) cgs unit of measurement in electromagnetic system, as in *abampere, abvolt*

aback (ə'bæk) *adv.* —**taken aback** startled

abacus ('æbəkəs) *n.* **1.** counting device of beads on wire frame **2.** flat tablet at top of column

abaft (ə'bɑːft) *Naut. adv./a.* **1.** towards stern of vessel —*prep.* **2.** behind; aft of

abalone (æbə'ləʊnı) *n.* edible shellfish, yielding mother-of-pearl

abandon (ə'bændən) *vt.* **1.** desert **2.** give up altogether —*n.* **3.** freedom from inhibitions *etc.* —**a'bandoned** *a.* **1.** deserted, forsaken **2.** uninhibited **3.** wicked —**a'bandonment** *n.*

abase (ə'beɪs) *vt.* humiliate, degrade —**a'basement** *n.*

abash (ə'bæʃ) *vt.* (*usu. passive*) confuse, make ashamed —**a'bashment** *n.*

abate (ə'beɪt) *v.* make or become less, diminish —**a'batement** *n.*

abattoir ('æbətwɑː) *n.* slaughterhouse

abbé ('æbeɪ) *n.* **1.** French abbot **2.** title used in addressing any French cleric

abbess ('æbɪs) *n.* female superior of convent

abbey ('æbɪ) *n.* **1.** dwelling place of community of monks or nuns **2.** church of an abbey

abbot ('æbət) *n.* head of abbey or monastery (**'abbess** *fem.*) —**'abbacy** *n.* office, rights of abbot

abbr., abbrev. abbreviation

abbreviate (ə'briːvɪeɪt) *vt.* shorten, abridge —**abbrevi'ation** *n.* shortened form of word or phrase

ABC *n.* **1.** (*oft. pl. in Amer.*) the alphabet **2.** (*pl. in Amer.*) rudiments of subject **3.** alphabetical guide

abdicate ('æbdɪkeɪt) *v.* formally give up (throne *etc.*) —**abdi'cation** *n.*

abdomen ('æbdəmən) *n.* belly —**abdominal** (æb'dɒmɪnəl) *a.*

abduct (æb'dʌkt) *vt.* carry off, kidnap —**ab'duction** *n.*

abeam (ə'biːm) *adv.* abreast, in line

abele (ə'biːl, 'eıbı) *n.* white poplar

Aberdeen Angus ('æbədiːn 'æŋgəs) breed of cattle, *orig.* Scottish

aberration (æbə'reɪʃən) *n.* **1.** deviation from what is normal **2.** flaw **3.** lapse —**a'berrant** *a.*

abet (ə'bɛt) *vt.* assist, encourage, *esp.* in doing wrong —**a'better** *or* **a'bettor** *n.*

abeyance (ə'beɪəns) *n.* condition of not being in use or action

abhor (əb'hɔː) *vt.* dislike strongly, loathe —**ab'horrence** *n.* —**ab'horrent** *a.* hateful

abide (ə'baɪd) *vt.* **1.** endure, put up with —*vi.* **2.** *obs.* stay, reside (**a'bode** *or* **a'bided** *pt./pp.*, **a'biding** *pr.p.*) —**abide by** obey

ability (ə'bɪlɪtɪ) *n.* **1.** competence, power **2.** talent

ab initio (æb ɪ'nɪʃɪəʊ) *Lat.* from the start

abject ('æbdʒɛkt) *a.* **1.** humiliated, wretched **2.** despicable —**ab'jection** *or* **'abjectness** *n.*

abjure (əb'dʒʊə) *vt.* give up by oath, renounce —**abju'ration** *n.*

ablation (æb'leɪʃən) *n.* **1.** surgical removal of organ or part **2.** *Astrophysics* melting or wearing away of part **3.** wearing away of rock or glacier

ablative ('æblətɪv) *n.* case in (*esp.* Latin) nouns indicating source, agent, instrument of action

ablaut ('æblaut) *n.* vowel change within word, indicating modification of use, *eg* sink, sank, sunk

ablaze (ə'bleɪz) *a.* burning

able ('eɪbəl) *a.* capable, competent —'**ably** *adv.* —**able-bodied** *a.* —**able-bodied seaman** seaman, *esp.* one in merchant navy, trained in certain skills (*also* **able seaman**)

-able (*a. comb. form*) **1.** capable of or deserving of (being acted upon as indicated), as in *enjoyable, washable* **2.** inclined to; able to; causing, as in *comfortable, variable* —**ably** (*adv. comb. form*) —**ability** (*n. comb. form*)

ablution (ə'bluːʃən) *n.* (*usu. pl.*) act of washing (oneself)

ABM antiballistic missile

abnegate ('æbnɪgeɪt) *vt.* give up, renounce —**abne'gation** *n.*

abnormal (æb'nɔːməl) *a.* **1.** irregular **2.** not usual or typical **3.** freakish, odd —**abnor'mality** *n.* —**ab'normally** *adv.*

aboard (ə'bɔːd) *adv.* on board, on ship, train or aircraft

abode (ə'bəʊd) *n.* **1.** home **2.** dwelling —*v.* **3.** *pt./pp.* of ABIDE

abolish (ə'bɒlɪʃ) *vt.* do away with —**abo'lition** *n.* —**abo'litionist** *n.* one who wishes to do away with something, *esp.* slavery

A-bomb *n.* atomic bomb

abominate (ə'bɒmɪneɪt) *vt.* detest —**a'bominable** *a.* —**a'bominably** *adv.* —**abomi'nation** *n.* **1.** loathing **2.** the object loathed —**abominable snowman** large legendary apelike creature said to inhabit the Himalayas

Aboriginal (æbə'rɪdʒɪnəl) *a.* **1.** of, relating to the Aborigines of Aust. **2.** (**a-**) indigenous, earliest —*n.* **3.** Aborigine

Aborigine (æbə'rɪdʒɪnɪ) *n.* **1.** one of race of people inhabiting Aust. when European settlers arrived **2.** (**a-**) original inhabitant of country *etc.*

abort (ə'bɔːt) *v.* **1.** (cause to) end prematurely (*esp.* pregnancy) —*vi.* **2.** give birth to dead foetus **3.** fail —**a'bortion** *n.* **1.** operation to terminate pregnancy **2.** something deformed —**a'bortionist** *n.* one who performs abortion, *esp.* illegally —**a'bortive** *a.* unsuccessful —**a'bortively** *adv.*

abound (ə'baʊnd) *vi.* **1.** be plentiful **2.** overflow —**a'bounding** *a.*

about (ə'baʊt) *adv.* **1.** on all sides **2.** nearly **3.** up and down **4.** out, astir —*prep.* **5.** round **6.** near **7.** concerning —**about to** ready to —**about-turn** *n.* reversal, complete change

above (ə'bʌv) *adv.* **1.** higher up —*prep.* **2.** over **3.** higher than, more than **4.** beyond

abracadabra (æbrəkə'dæbrə) *n.* supposedly magic word

abrade (ə'breɪd) *vt.* rub off, scrape away

abrasion (ə'breɪʒən) *n.* **1.** place scraped or worn by rubbing (*eg* on skin) **2.** scraping, rubbing —**a'brasive** *n.* **1.** substance for grinding, polishing *etc.* —*a.* **2.** causing abrasion **3.** grating

abreast (ə'brɛst) *adv.* side by side —**abreast of** keeping up with

abridge (ə'brɪdʒ) *vt.* cut short, abbreviate —**a'bridgment** *or* **a'bridgement** *n.*

abroad (ə'brɔːd) *adv.* **1.** to or in a foreign country **2.** at large

abrogate ('æbrəʊgeɪt) *vt.* cancel, repeal —**abro'gation** *n.*

abrupt (ə'brʌpt) *a.* **1.** sudden **2.** blunt **3.** hasty **4.** steep —**a'bruptly** *adv.* —**a'bruptness** *n.*

abscess ('æbsɛs) *n.* gathering of pus in any part of the body

abscissa (æb'sɪsə) *n. Maths.* distance of point from the axis of coordinates (*pl.* **-s,** **-sae** (-siː))

abscond (əb'skɒnd) *vi.* leave secretly, *esp.* having stolen something

abseil ('æbsaɪl) *vi.* descend vertical slope by means of rope

absent ('æbsənt) *a.* **1.** away **2.** not attentive —*vt.* (æb'sɛnt) **3.** keep away —'**absence** *n.* —**absen'tee** *n.* one who stays away, *esp.* habitually —**absen'teeism** *n.* persistent absence from work *etc.* —'**absently** *adv.* —**absent-minded** *a.*

absinthe *or* **absinth** ('æbsɪnθ) *n.* potent aniseed-flavoured liqueur

absolute ('æbsəluːt) *a.* **1.** complete **2.** not limited, unconditional **3.** pure (as **absolute alcohol**) —*n.* **4.** something that is absolute —**abso'lutely** *adv.* **1.** completely —*interj.* **2.** certainly —**absoluteness** *n.* —**absolutism** *n.* political system in which unrestricted power is vested in dictator *etc.*; despotism —**absolutist** *n.* —**absolute zero** lowest temperature theoretically attainable

absolve (əb'zɒlv) *vt.* free, pardon, acquit —**absolution** (æbsə'luːʃən) *n.*

absorb (əb'sɔːb) *vt.* **1.** suck up, drink in **2.** engage, occupy (attention *etc.*) **3.** receive (impact) —**ab'sorbent** *n.* —**ab'sorption** *n.* —**ab'sorptive** *a.*

abstain (əb'steɪn) *vi.* (*usu. with* from) keep (from), refrain (from drinking alcohol, voting *etc.*) —**ab'stainer** *n.* —**abstention** (əb'stɛnʃən) *n.* —**abstinence** ('æbstɪnəns) *n.* —**abstinent** ('æbstɪnənt) *a.*

abstemious (əb'stiːmɪəs) *a.* sparing in food or *esp.* drink, temperate —**ab'stemiously** *adv.* —**ab'stemiousness** *n.*

abstract ('æbstrækt) *a.* 1. existing only in the mind 2. not concrete 3. not representational —*n.* 4. summary, abridgment —*vt.* (æb'strækt) 5. draw (from), remove 6. deduct —**ab'stracted** *a.* preoccupied —**ab'straction** *n.* —**'abstractly** *adv.*

abstruse (əb'struːs) *a.* obscure, difficult to understand, profound —**ab'strusely** *adv.*

absurd (əb'sɜːd) *a.* contrary to reason —**ab'surdity** *n.* —**ab'surdly** *adv.*

abundance (ə'bʌndəns) *n.* great amount —a'**bundant** *a.* plentiful —a'**bundantly** *adv.*

abuse (ə'bjuːz) *vt.* 1. misuse 2. address rudely —*n.* (ə'bjuːs) 3. improper use 4. insulting speech —a'**busive** *a.* —a'**busively** *adv.* —a'**busiveness** *n.*

abut (ə'bʌt) *vi.* adjoin, border (on) (-tt-) —a'**butment** *n.* support, *esp.* of bridge or arch

abuzz (ə'bʌz) *a.* noisy, busy with activity *etc.*

abysmal (ə'bɪzməl) *a.* 1. immeasurable, very great 2. *inf.* extremely bad —a'**bysmally** *adv.*

abyss (ə'bɪs) *n.* very deep gulf or pit

Ac *Chem.* actinium

AC 1. aircraftman 2. alternating current

a/c account

acacia (ə'keɪʃə) *n.* gum-yielding tree or shrub

academy (ə'kædəmɪ) *n.* 1. society to advance arts or sciences 2. institution for specialized training 3. secondary school —**aca'demic** *a.* 1. of academy 2. belonging to University *etc.* 3. theoretical —**aca'demically** *adv.* —**acade'mician** *n.*

acanthus (ə'kænθəs) *n.* 1. prickly plant 2. architectural ornament like leaf of acanthus plant (*pl.* **-es, -thi** (-θaɪ))

ACAS ('eɪkæs) Advisory Conciliation and Arbitration Service

acc. 1. accompanied 2. account 3. accusative

accede (æk'siːd) *vi.* (*usu.* *with* to) 1. agree, consent 2. attain (office, right *etc.*)

accelerando (ækselə'rændəʊ) *a./adv.* *Mus.* becoming faster

accelerate (æk'seləreɪt) *v.* (cause to) increase speed, hasten —**accele'ration** *n.* —**ac'celerative** *a.* —**ac'celerator** *n.* mechanism to increase speed, *esp.* in car

accent ('æksənt) *n.* 1. stress or pitch in speaking 2. mark to show such stress 3. local or national style of pronunciation 4. particular attention or emphasis —*vt.* (æk'sent) 5. stress 6. mark with accent

accentor (æk'sentə) *n.* sparrowlike songbird

accentuate (æk'sentjʊeɪt) *vt.* stress, emphasize —**ac'centual** *a.* —**accentu'ation** *n.*

accept (ək'sept) *vt.* 1. take, receive 2. admit, believe 3. agree to —**accepta'bility** *n.* —**ac'ceptable** *a.* —**ac'ceptably** *adv.* —**ac'ceptance** *n.* —**accep'tation** *n.* common or accepted meaning of word *etc.* —**ac'cepter** *n.* —**ac'ceptor** *n.* 1. *Comm.* person or organization on which bill of exchange is drawn 2. *Electron.* impurity added to semiconductor to increase its p-type conductivity

access ('ækses) *n.* 1. act, right or means of entry —*vt.* *Comp.* 2. obtain or retrieve (information) from storage device 3. place (information) in storage device —**accessi'bility** *n.* —**ac'cessible** *a.* easy to approach —**ac'cessibly** *adv.* —**access time** *Comp.* time required to retrieve stored information

accessary (ək'sesərɪ) *see* ACCESSORY

accession (ək'seʃən) *n.* 1. attaining of office, right *etc.* 2. increase, addition

accessory (ək'sesərɪ) *n.* 1. additional or supplementary part of motorcar, woman's dress *etc.* 2. person inciting or assisting in crime —*a.* 3. contributory, assisting

accidence ('æksɪdəns) *n.* the part of grammar dealing with changes in the form of words

accident ('æksɪdənt) *n.* 1. event happening by chance 2. misfortune or mishap, *esp.* causing injury 3. nonessential quality —**acci'dental** *a.* —**acci'dentally** *adv.*

acclaim (ə'kleɪm) *vt.* 1. applaud, praise —*n.* 2. applause —**acclamation** (æklə'meɪʃən) *n.* —**ac'clamatory** (ə'klæmətərɪ) *a.*

acclimatize *or* **-tise** (ə'klaɪmətaɪz) *vt.* accustom to new climate or environment —**acclimati'zation** *or* **-ti'sation** *n.*

accolade ('ækəleɪd) *n.* 1. praise, public approval 2. award, honour 3. token of award of knighthood

accommodate (ə'kɒmədeɪt) *vt.* 1. supply, *esp.* with board and lodging 2. oblige 3. harmonize, adapt —**ac'commodating** *a.* obliging —**accommo'dation** *n.* 1. lodgings 2. agreement 3. adjustment of lens of eye 4. loan —**accommodation address** address on letters *etc.* that is not permanent or actual address

accompany (ə'kʌmpənɪ) *vt.* 1. go with 2. supplement 3. occur with 4. provide a musical accompaniment for (**-panied, -panying**) —**ac'companiment** *n.* that which accompanies, *esp.* in music, part which goes with solos *etc.* —**ac'companist** *n.*

accomplice (ə'kɒmplɪs, ə'kʌm-) *n.* one assisting another in criminal deed

accomplish (ə'kɒmplɪʃ, ə'kʌm-) *vt.* 1. carry out 2. finish —**ac'complished** *a.* 1. complete, perfect 2. proficient —**ac'complishment** *n.* 1. completion 2. personal ability

accord (ə'kɔːd) *n.* 1. agreement, harmony (*esp.* *in* **in accord with**) —*v.* 2. (cause to) be in accord —*vt.* 3. grant —**ac'cordance** *n.* —**ac'cordant** *a.* —**ac'cordingly** *adv.* 1. as the circumstances suggest 2. therefore —**according to** 1. in proportion to **2.** as stated by **3.** in conformity with

accordion (ə'kɔːdɪən) *n.* portable musical instrument with keys, metal reeds and a bellows —**ac'cordionist** *n.* —**piano accordion** accordion in which right hand plays piano-like keyboard

accost (ə'kɒst) *vt.* approach and speak to, ask question *etc.*

account (ə'kaʊnt) *n.* **1.** report, description **2.** importance, value **3.** statement of moneys received, paid or owed **4.** person's money held in bank **5.** credit available to person at store *etc.* —*vt.* **6.** reckon **7.** judge —*vi.* **8.** give reason, answer (for) —**accounta'bility** *n.* —**ac'countable** *a.* responsible —**ac'countancy** *n.* keeping, preparation of business accounts, financial records *etc.* —**ac'countant** *n.* one practising accountancy —**ac'counting** *n.* skill or practice of keeping and preparing business accounts

accoutre *or U.S.* **accouter** (ə'kuːtə) *vt.* equip —**accoutrements** *or U.S.* **accouterments** (ə'kuːtrəmənts, ə'kuːtər-) *pl.n.* **1.** equipment, *esp.* military **2.** trappings

accredit (ə'krɛdɪt) *vt.* **1.** ascribe, attribute **2.** give official recognition to **3.** certify as meeting required standards **4.** (*oft. with* at, to) send (envoy *etc.*) with official credentials; appoint as envoy *etc.* **5.** believe —**ac'credited** *a.*

accretion (ə'kriːʃən) *n.* **1.** growth **2.** something added on

accrue (ə'kruː) *vi.* **1.** be added **2.** result

acct. account

acculturate (ə'kʌltʃəreɪt) *vi.* assimilate traits of another cultural group —**accultur'ation** *n.*

accumulate (ə'kjuːmjʊleɪt) *v.* **1.** gather, become gathered in increasing quantity **2.** collect —**accumu'lation** *n.* —**ac'cumulator** *n.* type of rechargeable battery, as in car

accurate (ə'ækjərɪt) *a.* exact, correct, without errors —**'accuracy** *n.* —**'accurately** *adv.*

accursed (ə'kɜːsɪd, ə'kɜːst) *or* **accurst** (ə'kɜːst) *a.* **1.** under a curse **2.** hateful, detestable

accuse (ə'kjuːz) *vt.* **1.** charge with wrongdoing **2.** blame —**accu'sation** *n.* —**ac'cusative** *a.* grammatical case indicating the direct object —**ac'cusatory** *a.* —**ac'cuser** *n.*

accustom (ə'kʌstəm) *vt.* make used (to), familiarize —**ac'customed** *a.* **1.** usual **2.** used (to) **3.** in the habit (of)

ace (eɪs) *n.* **1.** the one at dice, cards, dominoes **2.** *Tennis* winning serve, *esp.* one untouched by opponent **3.** very successful fighter pilot **4.** *inf.* person expert at anything —*a.* **5.** *inf.* excellent

-aceous (*comb. form*) relating to, having the nature of, or resembling, as in *herbaceous*

acerbate ('æsəbeɪt) *vt.* **1.** make worse **2.** make sour, bitter —**a'cerbity** *n.* **1.** severity, sharpness **2.** sourness, bitterness

acetaldehyde (æsɪ'tældɪhaɪd) *n.* colourless volatile pungent liquid used as solvent

acetate ('æsɪteɪt) *n.* salt of acetic acid —**acetate rayon** synthetic textile fibre

acetic (ə'siːtɪk) *a.* derived from or having the nature of vinegar —**acetic acid** colourless pungent liquid used in manufacture of plastics *etc.* (*see also* VINEGAR)

aceto- *or before vowel* **acet-** (*comb. form*) containing acetyl group or derived from acetic acid, as in *acetone*

acetone ('æsɪtəʊn) *n.* colourless liquid used as solvent

acetylene (ə'sɛtɪliːn) *n.* colourless, flammable gas used *esp.* in welding metals

acetylsalicylic acid (æsɪtaɪlsælɪ'sɪlɪk) *Chem.* aspirin

ache (eɪk) *n.* **1.** continuous pain —*vi.* **2.** be painful **3.** be in pain —**'aching** *a.*

achieve (ə'tʃiːv) *vt.* **1.** accomplish, perform successfully **2.** gain —**a'chievement** *n.* something accomplished

Achilles heel (ə'kɪliːz) small but fatal weakness

Achilles tendon fibrous cord that connects muscles of calf to heelbone

achromatic (ækrə'mætɪk) *a.* free from or not showing colour, as of a lens, colourless

acid ('æsɪd) *a.* **1.** sharp, sour —*n.* **2.** sour substance **3.** *Chem.* one of a class of compounds which combines with bases (alkalis, oxides *etc.*) to form salts —**a'cidic** *a.* —**a'cidify** *v.* (**-fied**, **-fying**) —**a'cidity** *n.* —**a'cidulate** *vt.* make slightly acid —**a'cidulous** *a.* —**acid rain** rain acidified by atmospheric pollution —**acid test** conclusive test of value

ack-ack ('ækæk) *n.* anti-aircraft guns or gunfire

acknowledge (ək'nɒlɪdʒ) *vt.* **1.** admit, own, recognize **2.** say one has received —**ac'knowledgment** *or* **ac'knowledgement** *n.*

aclinic (ə'klɪnɪk) *a.* without inclination, said of the magnetic equator, on which the magnetic needle has no dip

acme ('ækmɪ) *n.* highest point

acne ('æknɪ) *n.* pimply skin disease

acolyte ('ækəlaɪt) *n.* follower or attendant, *esp.* of priest

aconite ('ækənaɪt) *n.* **1.** genus of plants related to the buttercup, including monkshood **2.** drug, poison obtained from such

acorn ('eɪkɔːn) *n.* nut or fruit of the oak tree

acoustic (ə'kuːstɪk) *or* **acoustical** *a.* pert. to sound and to hearing —**a'coustics** *pl.n.* **1.** (*with sing. v.*) science of sound **2.** features of room or building as regards sounds heard within it

acquaint (ə'kweɪnt) *vt.* make familiar, inform

—ac'quaintance *n.* **1.** person known **2.** personal knowledge —ac'quaintanceship *n.*

acquiesce (ækwɪ'ɛs) *vi.* agree, consent without complaint —acqui'escence *n.* —acqui'escent *a.*

acquire (ə'kwaɪə) *vt.* gain, get —ac'quirement *n.* —acquisition (ækwɪ'zɪʃən) *n.* **1.** act of getting **2.** material gain —acquisitive (ə'kwɪzɪtɪv) *a.* desirous of gaining —acquisitiveness (ə'kwɪzɪtɪvnɪs) *n.* —acquired immunodeficiency syndrome disease that breaks down the body's natural immunity, oft. resulting in fatal infection

acquit (ə'kwɪt) *vt.* **1.** declare innocent **2.** settle, discharge, as a debt **3.** behave (oneself) (-tt-) —ac'quittal *n.* declaration of innocence in court —ac'quittance *n.* discharge of debts

acre ('eɪkə) *n.* **1.** measure of land, 4840 square yards —*pl.* **2.** lands, estates *3. inf.* large area or plenty —'acreage *n.* extent of land in acres

acrid ('ækrɪd) *a.* **1.** pungent, sharp **2.** irritating —a'cridity *n.*

acrimony ('ækrɪmənɪ) *n.* bitterness of feeling or language —acri'monious *a.*

acrobat ('ækrəbæt) *n.* one skilled in gymnastic feats, *esp.* as entertainer in circus *etc.* —acro'batic *a.* —acro'batics *pl.n.* (*with sing. v.*) any activity requiring agility

acronym ('ækrənɪm) *n.* word formed from initial letters of other words, *eg* UNESCO, ANZAC, NATO

acrophobia (ækrə'fəʊbɪə) *n.* abnormal fear of being at great height

acropolis (ə'krɒpəlɪs) *n.* citadel, *esp.* in ancient Greece

across ('ækrɒs) *adv./prep.* **1.** crosswise **2.** from side to side **3.** on or to the other side —get (or put) something across explain something, make something understood

acrostic (ə'krɒstɪk) *n.* word puzzle in which the first, middle, or last letters of each line spell a word or words

acrylic (ə'krɪlɪk) *n.* variety of synthetic materials, *esp.* textiles, derived from an organic acid —acrylic resin any of group of polymers of acrylic acid, its esters or amides, used as paints, plastics *etc.*

act (ækt) *n.* **1.** thing done, deed **2.** doing **3.** law, decree **4.** section of a play —*v.* **5.** perform, as in a play —*vi.* **6.** exert force, work, as mechanism **7.** behave —'acting *n.* **1.** performance of a part —*a.* **2.** temporarily performing the duties of another —'action *n.* **1.** operation **2.** deed **3.** gesture **4.** expenditure of energy **5.** battle **6.** lawsuit —'actionable *a.* subject to lawsuit —'activate *vt.* **1.** make active, put into operation **2.** make radioactive **3.** make chemically active —acti'vation *n.* —'activator

n. —'active *a.* **1.** moving, working **2.** brisk, energetic —'actively *adv.* —'activism *n.* —'activist *n.* one who takes (direct) action to achieve political or social ends —ac'tivity *n.* —'actor *n.* one who acts in a play, film *etc.* (-'tress *fem.*) —action painting type of abstract painting characterized by smeared or spattered paint (*also* 'tachisme) —action replay rerunning of section of television film or tape of match *etc.*, oft. in slow motion —action stations *pl.n.* **1.** *Mil.* positions manned instantly in preparation for battle —*interj.* **2.** *Mil.* command to take up such positions **3.** *inf.* warning to get ready for something —activated sludge aerated sewage added to untreated sewage to hasten bacterial decomposition —active list *Mil.* list of officers available for full duty —Act of God *Law* unavoidable occurrence, such as earthquake, caused by natural forces

A.C.T. Australian Capital Territory

actinide series ('æktɪnaɪd) series of 15 radioactive elements with increasing atomic numbers from actinium to lawrencium

actinism ('æktɪnɪzəm) *n.* chemical action of sun's rays —ac'tinic *a.*

actinium (æk'tɪnɪəm) *n.* radioactive element occurring as decay product of uranium

actual ('æktʃʊəl) *a.* **1.** existing in the present **2.** real —actu'ality *n.* —'actually *adv.* really, indeed

actuary ('æktʃʊərɪ) *n.* statistician who calculates insurance risks, premiums *etc.* —actu'arial *a.*

actuate ('æktʃʊeɪt) *vt.* **1.** activate **2.** motivate —actu'ation *n.*

acuity (ə'kjuːɪtɪ) *n.* keenness, *esp.* in vision or thought

acumen ('ækjʊmɛn, ə'kjuːmən) *n.* sharpness of wit, perception, penetration

acupuncture ('ækjʊpʌŋktʃə) *n. orig.* Chinese medical treatment involving insertion of needles at various points on the body —'acupuncturist *n.*

acute (ə'kjuːt) *a.* **1.** keen, shrewd **2.** sharp **3.** severe **4.** less than 90° —*n.* **5.** accent (´) over a letter to indicate the quality or length of its sound, *eg* abbé —a'cutely *adv.* —a'cuteness *n.*

ad (æd) *n.* advertisement —'adman *n. inf.* man who works in advertising

A.D. anno Domini

ad- (*comb. form*) **1.** to; towards, as in *adverb* **2.** near; next to, as in *adrenal*

adage ('ædɪdʒ) *n.* much-used wise saying, proverb

adagio (ə'dɑːdʒɪəʊ) *a./adv./n. Mus.* leisurely, slow (passage) (*pl.* -s)

Adam ('ædəm) *a.* in neoclassical style made

popular by Robert Adam, Scottish architect and furniture designer

adamant ('ædəmənt) a. very hard, unyielding —**ada'mantine** a.

Adam's apple projecting part at front of the throat, the thyroid cartilage

adapt (ə'dæpt) v. l. alter for new use 2. fit, modify 3. change —**adapta'bility** n. —**a'daptable** a. —**adap'tation** n. —**a'dapter** or **a'daptor** n. esp. appliance for connecting two parts (eg electrical)

A.D.C. l. aide-de-camp 2. analogue-digital converter

add (æd) v. l. join 2. increase by 3. say further —**ad'dition** n. —**ad'ditional** a. —**'additive** n. something added, esp. to foodstuffs

addendum (ə'dɛndəm) n. thing to be added (pl. **-da** (-də)) —**'addend** n. any of set of numbers that form sum

adder ('ædə) n. small poisonous snake

addict ('ædɪkt) n. l. one who has become dependent on something, eg drugs (drug addict) —vt. (ə'dɪkt) 2. (usu. passive) cause to become dependent (on something, esp. drug) —**a'dicted** a. —**ad'diction** n. —**ad'dictive** a. causing addiction

addle ('æd°l) v. make or become rotten or muddled

address (ə'drɛs) n. l. direction on letter 2. place where one lives 3. speech —pl. 4. courtship —vt. 5. mark destination on 6. speak to 7. direct 8. dispatch —**addres'see** n. person addressed

adduce (ə'djuːs) vt. offer as proof 2. cite —**ad'ducible** a. —**adduction** (ə'dʌkʃən) n.

-ade (comb. form) sweetened drink made of fruit, as in lemonade

adenoids ('ædɪnɔɪdz) pl.n. tissue at back of nose —**ade'noidal** a.

adept (ə'dɛpt) a. l. skilled —n. ('ædɛpt) 2. expert

adequate ('ædɪkwɪt) a. l. sufficient, enough, suitable 2. not outstanding —**'adequacy** n. —**'adequately** adv.

à deux (a 'dø) Fr. of or for two persons

adhere (əd'hɪə) vi. l. stick 2. be firm in opinion etc. —**ad'herent** n./a. —**ad'hesion** n. —**ad'hesive** a./n.

ad hoc (æd 'hɒk) l. for a particular occasion only 2. improvised

ad hominem (æd 'hɒmɪnɛm) Lat. directed against person rather than his arguments

adieu (ə'djuː) interj. l. farewell —n. 2. act of taking leave (pl. **-s, adieux** (ə'djuːz))

ad infinitum (æd ɪnfɪ'naɪtəm) Lat. endlessly

ad interim (æd 'ɪntərɪm) Lat. for the meantime

adipose ('ædɪpəʊs) a. of fat, fatty

adit ('ædɪt) n. almost horizontal entrance into a mine

adj. l. adjective 2. adjourned 3. adjutant

adjacent (ə'dʒeɪsənt) a. lying near, next (to) —**ad'jacency** n.

adjective ('ædʒɪktɪv) n. word which qualifies or limits a noun —**adjectival** (ædʒɪk'taɪvəl) a. of adjective

adjoin (ə'dʒɔɪn) v. l. be next (to) 2. join —**ad'joining** a. next (to), near

adjourn (ə'dʒɜːn) vt. l. postpone temporarily, as meeting —vi. 2. inf. move elsewhere —**ad'journment** n.

adjudge (ə'dʒʌdʒ) vt. l. declare 2. decide 3. award —**ad'judgment** or **ad'judgement** n.

adjudicate (ə'dʒuːdɪkeɪt) v. l. try, judge —vi. 2. sit in judgment —**adjudi'cation** n. —**ad'judicator** n.

adjunct ('ædʒʌŋkt) a. l. joined, added —n. 2. person or thing added or subordinate —**ad'junctive** a.

adjure (ə'dʒʊə) vt. beg, entreat earnestly —**adju'ration** n.

adjust (ə'dʒʌst) v. l. make suitable, adapt 2. alter slightly, regulate —**ad'justable** a. —**ad'juster** n. —**ad'justment** n.

adjutant ('ædʒətənt) n. military officer who assists superiors —**'adjutancy** n. his office, rank

ad-lib (æd'lɪb) v. l. improvise, speak etc. without previous preparation —n. 2. such speech etc. —a. 3. improvised —**ad lib** without preparation; freely

ad libitum (æd 'lɪbɪtəm) Mus. at performer's discretion

Adm. l. Admiral 2. Admiralty

admin ('ædmɪn) n. inf. administration

administer (əd'mɪnɪstə) vt. l. manage, look after 2. dispense, as justice etc. 3. apply —**ad'ministrate** v. manage (business, institution, government department etc.) —**admini'stration** n. —**ad'ministrative** a. —**ad'ministrator** n. (-**atrix** fem.)

admiral ('ædmərəl) n. naval officer of highest sea rank (also **admiral of the fleet**) —**Admiralty (Board)** department in charge of Royal Navy

admire (əd'maɪə) vt. l. look on with wonder and pleasure 2. respect highly —**admirable** ('ædmərəbəl) a. —**admirably** ('ædmərəblɪ) adv. —**admiration** (ædmə'reɪʃən) n. —**ad'mirer** n. —**ad'miringly** adv.

admit (əd'mɪt) vt. l. confess 2. accept as true 3. allow 4. let in (**-tt-**) —**ad'missible** a. —**ad'missibly** adv. —**ad'mission** n. l. permission to enter 2. entrance fee 3. confession —**ad'mittance** n. permission to enter —**ad'mittedly** adv. willingly conceded

admixture (əd'mɪkstʃə) n. 1. mixture 2. ingredient —ad'mix vt.

admonish (əd'mɒnɪʃ) vt. 1. reprove 2. advise 3. warn 4. exhort —admo'nition n. —ad'monitory a.

ad nauseam (æd 'nɔːzɪæm) Lat. to a boring or disgusting extent

ado (ə'duː) n. fuss

adobe (ə'dəʊbɪ) n. sun-dried brick

adolescence (ædə'lɛsəns) n. period of life just before maturity —ado'lescent n. 1. a youth —a. 2. of adolescence 3. immature

Adonis (ə'dəʊnɪs) n. a beautiful youth beloved of Venus

adopt (ə'dɒpt) vt. 1. take into relationship, esp. as one's child 2. take up, as belief, principle, resolution —a'doption n. —a'doptive a. due to adoption

adore (ə'dɔː) vt. 1. love intensely —v. 2. worship —a'dorable a. —ado'ration n. —a'dorer n. lover

adorn (ə'dɔːn) vt. beautify, embellish, deck —a'dornment n. ornament, decoration

A.D.P. automatic data processing

ad rem (æd 'rɛm) Lat. to the point

adrenal (ə'driːnəl) a. near the kidney —adrenal gland —adrenaline or adrenalin (ə'drɛnəlɪn) n. 1. hormone secreted by adrenal glands 2. this substance used as drug

adrift (ə'drɪft) a./adv. 1. drifting free 2. inf. detached 3. inf. off course

adroit (ə'drɔɪt) a. 1. skilful, expert 2. clever —a'droitly adv. —a'droitness n. dexterity

adsorb (æd'sɔːb) v. (of gas, vapour) condense and form thin film on surface —ad'sorbent a./n. —ad'sorption n.

adulation (ædjʊ'leɪʃən) n. flattery —'adulate vt. flatter —'adulator n. —'adulatory a.

adult ('ædʌlt, ə'dʌlt) a. 1. grown-up, mature —n. 2. grown-up person 3. full-grown animal or plant

adulterate (ə'dʌltəreɪt) vt. make impure by addition —a'dulterant n./a. —a'dulterated a. —adulter'ation n. —a'dulterator n.

adultery (ə'dʌltərɪ) n. sexual unfaithfulness of a husband or wife —a'dulterer n. (a'dulteress fem.) —a'dulterous a.

adumbrate ('ædʌmbreɪt) vt. 1. outline 2. give indication of —a'dumbrant or a'dumbrative a. —adum'bration n.

adv. 1. adverb(ial) 2. advertisement

ad valorem (æd və'lɔːrəm) Lat. in proportion to the value of goods in question

advance (əd'vɑːns) vt. 1. bring forward 2. suggest 3. encourage 4. pay beforehand —vi. 5. go forward 6. improve in position or value —n. 7. forward movement 8. improvement 9. loan —pl. 10. personal approach(es) to gain favour etc. —a. 11. (with) ahead in time or position

—ad'vanced a. 1. at a late stage 2. not elementary 3. ahead of the times —ad'vancement n. promotion —Advanced level formal name for A LEVEL

advantage (əd'vɑːntɪdʒ) n. 1. superiority 2. more favourable position or state 3. benefit —advan'tageous a. —advan'tageously adv.

advent ('ædvɛnt, -vənt) n. 1. a coming, arrival 2. (A-) the four weeks before Christmas —'Adventist n. one of number of Christian sects believing in imminent return of Christ —the Advent the coming of Christ

adventitious (ædvɛn'tɪʃəs) a. 1. added, artificial 2. accidental, occurring by chance

adventure (əd'vɛntʃə) n. 1. risk 2. bold exploit 3. remarkable happening 4. enterprise 5. commercial speculation —v. 6. (take) risk —ad'venturer n. 1. one who seeks adventures 2. one who lives on his wits (ad'venturess fem.) —ad'venturism n. recklessness, esp. in politics and finance —ad'venturous a. —ad'venturously adv. —ad'venturousness n. —adventure playground UK playground for children that contains building materials etc., used to build with, climb on etc.

adverb ('ædvɜːb) n. word added to verb, adjective or other adverb to modify meaning —ad'verbial a. —ad'verbially adv.

adverse ('ædvɜːs) a. 1. opposed 2. hostile 3. unfavourable, bringing harm —'adversary n. enemy —ad'versative a. —'adversely adv. —ad'versity n. distress, misfortune

advert¹ (əd'vɜːt) vi. 1. turn the mind or attention 2. refer —ad'vertence n. —ad'vertently adv.

advert² ('ædvɜːt) n. inf. advertisement

advertise or U.S. (sometimes) -tize ('ædvətaɪz) vt. 1. publicize 2. make known 3. give notice of, esp. in newspapers etc. —vi. 4. make public request (for) —advertisement or U.S. (sometimes) -tizement (əd'vɜːtɪsmənt) n. —'advertiser or U.S. (sometimes) -tizer n. —'advertising or U.S. (sometimes) -tizing a./n.

advice (əd'vaɪs) n. 1. opinion given 2. counsel 3. information 4. (formal) notification

advise (əd'vaɪz) vt. 1. offer advice 2. recommend a line of conduct 3. give notice (of) —ad'visable a. expedient —ad'vised a. considered, as in well-advised —advisedly (əd'vaɪzɪdlɪ) adv. —ad'viser or ad'visor n. —ad'visory a.

advocaat ('ædvəʊkɑː) n. liqueur with raw egg base

advocate ('ædvəkɪt) n. 1. one who pleads the cause of another, esp. in court of law 2. barrister —vt. ('ædvəkeɪt) 3. uphold, recommend —'advocacy n. —advo'cation n.

advowson (ədˈvauzən) n. English eccles. law right of presentation to vacant benefice

advt. advertisement

adze or U.S. **adz** (ædz) n. carpenter's tool, like axe, but with arched blade set at right angles to handle

A.E.A. Atomic Energy Authority

aegis or U.S. (sometimes) **egis** (ˈiːdʒɪs) n. sponsorship, protection (orig. shield of Zeus)

aegrotat (ˈaɪɡrəʊtæt, -iː-) n. in British university, exemption esp. from final examinations because of illness

-aemia, -haemia, or U.S. **-emia, -hemia** (comb. form) blood, esp. specified condition of blood in diseases, as in leukaemia

Aeolian (iːˈəʊlɪən) a. acted on by the wind, as Aeolian harp

aeon or U.S. **eon** (ˈiːən, ˈiːɒn) n. 1. age, very long period of time 2. eternity

aerate (ˈeəreɪt) vt. 1. charge liquid with gas, as effervescent drink 2. expose to air —**aeriation** n. —ˈaerator n. apparatus for charging liquid with gas

aerial (ˈeərɪəl) a. 1. of the air 2. operating in the air 3. pertaining to aircraft —n. 4. part of radio etc. receiving or sending radio waves —ˈaerialist n. chiefly US trapeze artist

aerie (ˈeərɪ) n. see EYRIE

aero-, aeri-, or before vowel **aer-** (comb. form) air or aircraft, as in aero engine

aerobatics (eərəʊˈbætɪks) pl.n. stunt flying

aerodrome (ˈeərədrəʊm) n. UK airfield

aerodynamics (eərəʊdaɪˈnæmɪks) pl.n. (with sing. v.) study of air flow, esp. round moving solid bodies

aero engine engine for powering aircraft

aerofoil (ˈeərəʊfɔɪl) n. surfaces of wing etc. of aircraft designed to give lift

aerogram or **aerogramme** (ˈeərəɡræm) n. air-mail letter form (also **air letter**)

aerolite (ˈeərəlaɪt) n. meteoric stone

aerometry (eəˈrɒmɪtrɪ) n. measurement of weight or density of gases

aeronaut (ˈeərənɔːt) n. pilot or navigator of lighter-than-air craft —**aeroˈnautical** a. —**aeroˈnautics** pl.n. (with sing. v.) science of air navigation and flying in general

aeroplane (ˈeərəpleɪn) or U.S. **airplane** (ˈeəpleɪn) n. heavier-than-air flying machine

aerosol (ˈeərəsɒl) n. (substance dispensed as fine spray from) pressurized can

aerospace (ˈeərəspeɪs) n. 1. earth's atmosphere and space beyond —a. 2. of missiles, space vehicles etc.

aerostatics (eərəˈstætɪks) pl.n. (with sing. v.) 1. study of gases in equilibrium and bodies held in equilibrium in gases 2. study of lighter-than-air craft

aesthetic (iːsˈθɛtɪk, ɪs-), **aesthetical** or U.S. (sometimes) **esthetic, esthetical** a. relating to principles of beauty, taste and art —aesˈthetics or U.S. (sometimes) esˈthetics pl.n. (with sing. v.) study of art, taste etc. —aesthete or U.S. esthete (ˈiːsθiːt) n. one who affects extravagant love of art —aesˈthetically or U.S. (sometimes) esˈthetically adv. —aesˈtheticism or U.S. esˈtheticism n.

aestivate or U.S. **estivate** (ˈiːstɪveɪt) vi. spend the summer, esp. in dormant condition —**aestival** or U.S. **estival** (iːˈstaɪvəl) a. rare of summer —aestiˈvation or U.S. estiˈvation n.

aether (ˈiːθə) n. see ETHER

aetiology or U.S. **etiology** (iːtɪˈɒlədʒɪ) n. study of causes, esp. inquiry into origin of disease —aetioˈlogical or U.S. etioˈlogical a.

a.f. audio frequency

afar (əˈfɑː) adv. from, at, or to, a great distance

A.F.C. 1. Air Force Cross 2. Association Football Club 3. automatic frequency control

affable (ˈæfəbəl) a. easy to speak to, polite and friendly —affaˈbility n. —ˈaffably adv.

affair (əˈfɛə) n. 1. thing done or attended to 2. business 3. happening 4. sexual liaison —pl. 5. personal or business interests 6. matters of public interest

affect (əˈfɛkt) vt. 1. act on, influence 2. move feelings of 3. make show, pretence of 4. assume 5. make liking for —affecˈtation n. show, pretence —afˈfected a. 1. making a pretence 2. moved 3. acted upon —afˈfectedly adv. —afˈfecting a. moving the feelings of —afˈfectingly adv. —afˈfection n. fondness, love —afˈfectionate a. —afˈfectionately adv.

afferent (ˈæfərənt) a. bringing to, esp. describing nerves which carry sensation to the brain

affiance (əˈfaɪəns) vt. betroth —afˈfianced a./n. (one) promised in marriage

affidavit (æfɪˈdeɪvɪt) n. written statement on oath

affiliate (əˈfɪlɪeɪt) vt. (with to or with) 1. connect, attach (with larger body, organization) 2. adopt —affiliˈation n. —**affiliation order** Law order that putative father of illegitimate child contribute towards its maintenance

affinity (əˈfɪnɪtɪ) n. 1. natural liking 2. resemblance 3. relationship by marriage 4. chemical attraction —afˈfinitive a.

affirm (əˈfɜːm) v. 1. assert positively, declare 2. maintain (statement) —vi. 3. make solemn declaration —afˈfirˈmation n. —afˈfirmative a. 1. asserting —n. 2. word of assent —afˈfirmatively adv.

affix (əˈfɪks) vt. 1. fasten 2. attach, append —n. (ˈæfɪks) 3. addition, esp. to word, as suffix, prefix

afflatus (əˈfleɪtəs) n. impulse of creative power or inspiration

afflict (əˈflɪkt) vt. 1. give pain or grief to, distress 2. trouble, vex —af'fliction n. —af'flictive a.

affluent (ˈæfluənt) a. 1. wealthy 2. abundant —n. 3. tributary stream —'affluence n. wealth, abundance

afford (əˈfɔːd) vt. 1. be able to buy 2. be able to spare (the time etc.) 3. produce, yield, furnish

afforest (əˈfɒrɪst) vt. turn into forest, plant trees on —affores'tation n.

affray (əˈfreɪ) n. fight, brawl

affront (əˈfrʌnt) vt. 1. insult openly —n. 2. insult 3. offence

aficionado (əˌfɪsjəˈnɑːdəʊ) n. 1. ardent supporter or devotee 2. devotee of bullfighting (pl. -s)

afield (əˈfiːld) adv. 1. away from home 2. in or on the field

afire (əˈfaɪə) adv. on fire

aflame (əˈfleɪm) adv. burning

afloat (əˈfləʊt) adv. 1. floating 2. at sea 3. in circulation

A.F.M. Air Force Medal

afoot (əˈfʊt) adv. 1. astir 2. on foot

afore (əˈfɔː) prep./adv. before, usu. in compounds —a'forementioned a. chiefly in legal documents stated or mentioned before —a'forethought a. premeditated (esp. **in malice aforethought**)

a fortiori (eɪ fɔːtɪˈɔːraɪ) adv. for a stronger reason

afoul (əˈfaʊl) a./adv. into difficulty

Afr. Africa(n)

afraid (əˈfreɪd) a. 1. frightened 2. sorry

afresh (əˈfreʃ) adv. again, anew

African (ˈæfrɪkən) a. 1. belonging to Africa —n. 2. native of Africa —**Afri'cana** pl.n. objects of cultural or historical interest of southern Afr. origin —**African lily** S Afr. plant with funnel-shaped flowers —**African violet** house plant with pink or purple flowers and hairy leaves

Africander (æfrɪˈkændə, æf-) n. breed of humpbacked S Afr. cattle

Afrikaans (æfrɪˈkɑːns, -ˈkɑːnz, æf-) n. language used in S Afr., derived from 17th-cent. Dutch —**Afri'kaner** n. White native of S Afr. with Afrikaans as mother tongue

Afro (ˈæfrəʊ) n. fuzzy, bushy hairstyle

Afro- (comb. form) Africa or African, as in Afro-Asiatic

afrormosia (æfrɔːˈməʊzɪə) n. hard teaklike wood obtained from tropical Afr. tree

aft (ɑːft) adv. towards stern of ship

after (ˈɑːftə) adv. 1. later 2. behind —prep. 3. behind 4. later than 5. on the model of 6. pursuing —conj. 7. at a later time than that at which —a. 8. nearer ship's stern —'afters pl.n. inf. course after main course; dessert —'afterwards or 'afterward adv. later

afterbirth (ˈɑːftəbɜːθ) n. membrane expelled after a birth

aftercare (ˈɑːftəkɛə) n. care, esp. medical, bestowed on person after period of treatment, and esp. after childbirth

aftereffect (ˈɑːftərɪfɛkt) n. subsequent effect of deed, event etc.

afterglow (ˈɑːftəɡləʊ) n. light after sunset

afterlife (ˈɑːftəlaɪf) n. life after death or at later time in person's lifetime

aftermath (ˈɑːftəmæθ) n. result, consequence, esp. difficult one

afternoon (ɑːftəˈnuːn) n. time from noon to evening

afterpains (ˈɑːftəpeɪnz) pl.n. pains caused by contraction of uterus after childbirth

aftershave (lotion) (ˈɑːftəʃeɪv) n. lotion applied to face after shaving

afterthought (ˈɑːftəθɔːt) n. idea occurring later

Ag Chem. silver

again (əˈɡɛn, əˈɡeɪn) adv. 1. once more 2. in addition 3. back, in return 4. besides

against (əˈɡɛnst, əˈɡeɪnst) prep. 1. in opposition to 2. in contact with 3. opposite 4. in readiness for

agape (əˈɡeɪp) a./adv. open-mouthed as in wonder etc.

agar (ˈeɪɡə) n. gelatinous carbohydrate obtained from seaweeds, used as culture medium for bacteria in food etc. (also **agar-agar**)

agaric (ˈæɡərɪk) n. 1. any of various fungi, eg mushroom —a. 2. fungoid

agate (ˈæɡɪt) n. coloured, semiprecious, decorative form of quartz

agave (əˈɡeɪvɪ) n. plant native to tropical Amer.

age (eɪdʒ) n. 1. length of time person or thing has existed 2. time of life 3. period of history 4. maturity 5. long time —v. 6. make or grow old —**aged** (ˈeɪdʒɪd) a. 1. old —pl.n. 2. old people —'**ageless** a. —**age-old** a.

-age (comb. form) 1. collection, set or group, as in baggage 2. process or action or result of action, as in breakage 3. state or relationship, as in bondage 4. house or place, as in orphanage 5. charge or fee, as in postage 6. rate, as in dosage

agenda (əˈdʒɛndə) pl.n. (with sing. v.) 1. things to be done 2. programme of business meeting

agent (ˈeɪdʒənt) n. 1. one authorized to carry on business or affairs for another 2. person or thing producing effect 3. cause 4. natural force —'**agency** n. 1. instrumentality 2. business, place of business of agent

agent provocateur (a'ʒɑ̃ prɔvɔka'tœːr) *Fr.* police spy who tries to provoke persons to act illegally

agglomerate (ə'glɒməreɪt) *v.* **1.** gather into a mass —*n.* (ə'glɒmərɪt, -reɪt) **2.** confused mass **3.** rock consisting of volcanic fragments —*a.* (ə'glɒmərɪt, -reɪt) **4.** formed into a mass —**agglomer'ation** *n.* —**agglomerative** *a.*

agglutinate (ə'gluːtɪneɪt) *vt.* **1.** unite with glue *etc.* **2.** form (words) into compounds —*a.* (ə'gluːtɪnɪt, -neɪt) **3.** united, as by glue —**aggluti'nation** *n.* —**ag'glutinative** *a.*

aggrandize *or* **-dise** (ə'grændaɪz) *vt.* make greater in size, power or rank —**aggrandizement** *or* **-disement** (ə'grændɪzmənt) *n.*

aggravate ('ægrəveɪt) *vt.* **1.** make worse or more severe **2.** *inf.* annoy —**aggravating** *a.* —**aggra'vation** *n.*

aggregate ('ægrɪgeɪt) *vt.* **1.** gather into mass —*a.* ('ægrɪgɪt) **2.** gathered thus —*n.* ('ægrɪgɪt, -geɪt) **3.** mass, sum total **4.** rock consisting of mixture of minerals **5.** mixture of gravel *etc.* for concrete —**aggre'gation** *n.*

aggression (ə'grɛʃən) *n.* **1.** unprovoked attack **2.** hostile activity —**ag'gress** *vi.* —**ag'gressive** *a.* —**ag'gressiveness** *n.* —**ag'gressor** *n.*

aggrieve (ə'griːv) *vt.* pain, injure —**ag'grieved** *a.*

aggro ('ægrəʊ) *n. sl.* aggression

aghast (ə'gɑːst) *a.* overcome with horror or amazement

agile ('ædʒaɪl) *a.* **1.** nimble **2.** active **3.** quick —'**agilely** *adv.* —**agility** (ə'dʒɪlɪtɪ) *n.*

agin (ə'gɪn) *prep. inf., dial.* against

agitate ('ædʒɪteɪt) *vt.* **1.** disturb, excite **2.** keep in motion, stir, shake up **3.** trouble —*vi.* **4.** stir up public opinion (for or against something) —**agi'tation** *n.* —**'agitator** *n.*

agitprop ('ædʒɪtprɒp) *n.* political agitation and propaganda, *esp.* of Communist nature

agley (ə'gleɪ, ə'gliː, ə'glaɪ) *a. Scot.* awry

aglitter (ə'glɪtə) *a.* sparkling; glittering

aglow (ə'gləʊ) *a.* glowing

A.G.M. Annual General Meeting

agnostic (æg'nɒstɪk) *n.* **1.** one who holds that we know nothing of things outside the material world —*a.* **2.** of this theory —**ag'nosticism** *n.*

Agnus Dei ('ægnʊs 'deɪɪ) **1.** figure of a lamb emblematic of Christ **2.** part of Mass beginning with these words

ago (ə'gəʊ) *adv.* in the past

agog (ə'gɒg) *a.* eager, astir

agony ('ægənɪ) *n.* extreme suffering of mind or body, violent struggle —'**agonize** *or* **-ise** *vi.* **1.** suffer agony **2.** worry greatly —'**agonizing** *or* **-ising** *a.* —**agony column** *n.* magazine feature offering advice to readers on personal problems

2. *inf.* newspaper column containing personal messages *etc.*

agoraphobia (ægərə'fəʊbɪə) *n.* fear of open spaces

AGR advanced gas-cooled reactor

agrarian (ə'grɛərɪən) *a.* of agriculture, land, or its management —**a'grarianism** *n.*

agree (ə'griː) *v.* **1.** be of same opinion **2.** consent **3.** harmonize **4.** determine, settle **5.** suit (**a'greed**, **a'greeing**) —**agrea'bility** *n.* —**a'greeable** *a.* **1.** willing **2.** pleasant —**a'greeableness** *n.* —**a'greeably** *adv.* —**a'greement** *n.* **1.** concord **2.** contract

agriculture ('ægrɪkʌltʃə) *n.* art, practice of cultivating land —**agri'cultural** *a.* —**agri'culturist** *n.*

agrimony ('ægrɪmənɪ) *n.* yellow-flowered plant with bitter taste

agronomy (ə'grɒnəmɪ) *n.* study of management of land and scientific cultivation of crops —**a'gronomist** *n.*

aground (ə'graʊnd) *adv./a.* (of boat) touching bottom

agt. agent

ague ('eɪgjuː) *n. obs.* **1.** malarial fever with periodic attacks of chills and sweating **2.** fit of shivering

ah (ɑ) *interj.* exclamation of pleasure, pain *etc.*

A.H. (indicating years in Muslim system of dating, numbered from Hegira (622 A.D.)) anno Hegirae

aha (ɑː'hɑː) *interj.* exclamation of triumph, surprise *etc.*

ahead (ə'hɛd) *adv.* **1.** in front **2.** onwards

ahem (ə'hɛm) *interj.* clearing of throat to attract attention *etc.*

ahoy (ə'hɔɪ) *interj.* shout used at sea for hailing

A.I. 1. artificial insemination **2.** artificial intelligence

aid (eɪd) *vt.* **1.** to help —*n.* **2.** help, support, assistance

A.I.D. artificial insemination by donor

aide (eɪd), **aide-de-camp**, *or* **aid-de-camp** ('eɪd də 'kɒŋ) *n.* military officer personally assisting superior (*pl.* **aides(-de-camp)** *or* **aids-de-camp**)

AIDS (eɪdz) acquired immuno-deficiency syndrome

aigrette *or* **aigret** ('eɪgrɛt) *n.* **1.** long plume worn on hats or as headdress, *esp.* one of egret feathers **2.** ornament in imitation of plume of feathers

aiguille (eɪ'gwiːl) *n.* **1.** sharp, slender peak **2.** blasting drill

A.I.H. artificial insemination by husband

ail (eɪl) *vt.* **1.** trouble, afflict, disturb —*vi.* **2.** be ill —'**ailing** *a.* sickly —'**ailment** *n.* illness

aileron ('eɪlərən) *n.* movable section of wing of aircraft which gives lateral control

aim (eɪm) *v.* 1. give direction to (weapon *etc.*) 2. direct effort (towards) —*n.* 3. direction 4. object, purpose —'**aimless** *a.* without purpose

ain't (eɪnt) *nonstandard* 1. am not 2. is not 3. are not 4. has not 5. have not

air (ɛə) *n.* 1. mixture of gases we breathe, the atmosphere 2. breeze 3. tune 4. manner —*pl.* 5. affected manners —*vt.* 6. expose to air to dry or ventilate —'**airily** *adv.* —'**airiness** *n.* —'**airing** *n.* time spent in the open air —'**airless** *a.* stuffy —'**airy** *a.* —**air bag** 1. bag in car, that inflates automatically in accident and prevents passengers from being thrown forwards 2. inflatable bag for restraining loads in partly filled containers —**air base** —**air bed** —'**airborne** *a.* flying, in the air —**air brake** 1. brake worked by compressed air 2. method of slowing down an aircraft —'**airbrick** *n. chiefly UK* brick with holes in it, for ventilation —'**airbus** *n.* airliner operated over short distances —**air commodore** —**air-condition** *vt.* —**air conditioner** —**air conditioning** system for controlling temperature and humidity of air in building —'**aircraft** *n.* 1. collective name for flying machines 2. aeroplane —**aircraft carrier** —**air curtain** air stream across doorway to exclude draughts *etc.* —**air cushion** 1. pillow which can be inflated 2. pocket of air supporting hovercraft —'**airfield** *n.* landing and taking-off area for aircraft —**air force** strength of country in military aircraft —**air gun** gun discharged by force of compressed air —**air hostess** stewardess on aircraft —**air letter** air-mail letter, aerogram —'**airlift** *n.* transport of goods *etc.* by aircraft —'**airline** *n.* company operating aircraft —'**airliner** *n.* large passenger aircraft —'**airlock** *n.* 1. air bubble obstructing flow of liquid in pipe 2. airtight chamber —**air mail** —'**airman** *n.* —**air pocket** less dense air where aeroplane drops suddenly —'**airport** *n.* airfield for civilian aircraft —**air pump** machine to extract or supply air —**air raid** attack by aircraft —**air rifle** rifle discharged by compressed air —**air sac** any of air-filled extensions of lungs of birds —'**airscrew** *n.* propeller of any aircraft —**air shaft** passage for air into a mine *etc.* —'**airship** *n.* lighter-than-air flying machine with means of propulsion —'**airsickness** *n.* nausea caused by motion of aircraft in flight —'**airspeed** *n.* speed of aircraft relative to air —'**airstrip** *n.* small airfield with only one runway —'**airtight** *a.* not allowing passage of air —**air-to-air** *a.* operating between aircraft in flight —**air trap** device to prevent escape of foul gases —**air valve** —'**airway** *n.* 1. regular aircraft route 2. passage for ventilation, *esp.* in mine —'**airworthiness** *n.* —'**airworthy** *a.* fit for service in air

Airedale ('ɛədeɪl) *n.* large rough-coated terrier dog

aisle (aɪl) *n.* passageway separating seating areas in church, theatre *etc.*

aitch (eɪtʃ) *n.* letter *h* or sound represented by it

aitchbone ('eɪtʃbəʊn) *n.* 1. rump bone in cattle 2. cut of beef from rump bone

ajar[1] (ə'dʒɑː) *a./adv.* partly open

ajar[2] (ə'dʒɑː) *a.* not in harmony

AK Alaska

akimbo (ə'kɪmbəʊ) *adv.* with hands on hips and elbows outwards

akin (ə'kɪn) *a.* 1. related by blood 2. alike, having like qualities

Al *Chem.* aluminium

AL Alabama

-al[1] (*a. comb. form*) of; related to, as in *functional, sectional*

-al[2] (*n. comb. form*) act or process of, as in *renewal*

-al[3] (*n. comb. form*) 1. aldehyde, as in *salicylal* 2. pharmaceutical product, as in *phenobarbital*

à la (ɑː lɑː) 1. in the manner of 2. as prepared in, by or for

alabaster ('æləbɑːstə) *n.* soft, white, semi-transparent stone —**ala'bastrine** *a.* of, like this

à la carte (ɑː lɑː 'kɑːt) *Fr.* selected freely from menu

alack (ə'læk) *or* **alackaday** (ə'lækədeɪ) *interj. obs., poet.* cry of sorrow

alacrity (ə'lækrɪtɪ) *n.* quickness, briskness, readiness

à la mode (ɑː lɑː 'məʊd) *Fr.* in fashion

alarm (ə'lɑːm) *n.* 1. sudden fright 2. apprehension 3. notice of danger 4. bell, buzzer 5. call to arms —*vt.* 6. frighten 7. warn of danger —a'**larming** *a.* —a'**larmist** *n.* one given to prophesying danger or exciting alarm *esp.* needlessly —**alarm clock** clock which sounds a buzzer or bell at a set time, as to wake someone up

alas (ə'læs) *interj.* cry of grief

alate ('eɪleɪt) *a.* having wings

alb (ælb) *n.* long white priestly vestment, worn at Mass

albacore ('ælbəkɔː) *n.* tunny occurring *esp.* in warm regions of Atlantic and Pacific

albatross ('ælbətrɒs) *n.* large oceanic bird of petrel family

albeit (ɔːl'biːt) *conj.* although

albert ('ælbət) *n.* watch chain usu. attached to waistcoat

albino (æl'biːnəʊ) *n.* person or animal with white skin and hair, and pinkish eyes, due to lack of colouring matter (*pl.* **-s**) —**albinism** ('ælbɪnɪzəm) *n.*

Albion ('ælbɪən) *n. obs., poet.* **1.** Britain **2.** England

album ('ælbəm) *n.* **1.** book of blank leaves, for photographs, stamps, autographs *etc.* **2.** one or more longplaying gramophone records

albumen ('ælbjumɪn) *n.* egg white

albumin *or* **albumen** ('ælbjumɪn) *n.* constituent of animal and vegetable matter, found nearly pure in white of egg —**al'bumin ous** *a.*

alchemy ('ælkəmɪ) *n.* medieval chemistry, *esp.* attempts to turn base metals into gold and find elixir of life —**'alchemist** *n.*

alcohol ('ælkəhɒl) *n.* **1.** intoxicating fermented liquor **2.** class of organic chemical substances —**alco'holic** *a.* **1.** of alcohol —*n.* **2.** one addicted to alcoholic drink —**'alcoholism** *n.* (disease caused by) habitual heavy consumption of alcoholic drink

alcove ('ælkəʊv) *n.* recess

aldehyde ('ældɪhaɪd) *n.* one of a group of organic chemical compounds

alder ('ɔːldə) *n.* tree related to the birch

alderman ('ɔːldəmən) *n.* formerly, member of governing body of a municipality —**alder'man ic** *a.*

ale (eɪl) *n.* fermented malt liquor, type of beer, *orig.* without hops —**'alehouse** *n. obs.* public house

aleatory ('eɪlɪətərɪ) *or* **aleatoric** (eɪlɪə'tɒrɪk) *a.* **1.** dependent on chance **2.** *Mus.* involving elements chosen at random

alembic (ə'lɛmbɪk) *n.* **1.** formerly, retort used for distillation **2.** anything that distils or purifies

alert (ə'lɜːt) *a.* **1.** watchful **2.** brisk, active —*n.* **3.** warning of sudden attack or surprise —*vt.* **4.** warn, *esp.* of danger **5.** draw (someone's) attention to something —**a'lertness** *n.* —**on the alert** watchful

A level UK 1. advanced level of General Certificate of Education **2.** pass in subject at A level

Alexandrine (ælɪg'zændraɪn) *n.* verse of six iambic feet

alexandrite (ælɪg'zændraɪt) *n.* green chrysoberyl used as gemstone

alexia (ə'lɛksɪə) *n.* impaired ability to read

alfalfa (æl'fælfə) *n.* plant of Europe and Asia used as fodder (*also* **lu'cerne**)

alfresco (æl'frɛskəʊ) *adv./a.* in the open air

alg. algebra

algae ('ældʒiː) *pl.n.* various water plants, including seaweed (*sing.* **alga** ('ælgə))

algebra ('ældʒɪbrə) *n.* method of calculating, using symbols to represent quantities and to show relations between them, making a kind of abstract arithmetic —**algebraic(al)** (ældʒɪ'breɪk(əl)) *a.* —**algebraist** (ældʒɪ'breɪst) *n.*

-algia (*n. comb. form*) pain in part specified, as in *neuralgia* —**-algic** (*a. comb. form*)

algid ('ældʒɪd) *a. Med.* chilly, cold

ALGOL ('ælgɒl) computer programming language designed for mathematical and scientific purposes

algorism ('ælgərɪzəm) *n.* **1.** Arabic or decimal system of counting **2.** skill of computation **3.** algorithm

algorithm ('ælgərɪðəm) *n.* procedural model for complicated calculations

alias ('eɪlɪəs) *adv.* **1.** otherwise —*n.* **2.** assumed name (*pl.* **-es**)

alibi ('ælɪbaɪ) *n.* **1.** plea of being somewhere else when crime was committed **2.** *inf.* excuse (*pl.* **-s**)

alien ('eɪlɪən) *a.* **1.** foreign **2.** different in nature **3.** repugnant —*n.* **4.** foreigner —**aliena'bility** *n.* —**'alienable** *a.* able to be transferred to another owner —**'alienate** *vt.* **1.** estrange **2.** transfer —**alie'nation** *n.* —**'alienist** *n.* US psychiatrist who specializes in legal aspects of mental illness

alight¹ (ə'laɪt) *vi.* **1.** get down **2.** land, settle

alight² (ə'laɪt) *a.* **1.** burning **2.** lit up

align (ə'laɪn) *vt.* bring into line or agreement —**a'lignment** *n.*

alike (ə'laɪk) *a.* **1.** like, similar —*adv.* **2.** in the same way

aliment ('ælɪmənt) *n.* something that nourishes or sustains body or mind —**ali'mentary** *a.* of food —**alimentary canal** food passage in body

alimony ('ælɪmənɪ) *n.* allowance paid under court order to separated or divorced spouse

aline (ə'laɪn) *vt. rare see* ALIGN —**a'linement** *n.*

A-line ('eɪlaɪn) *a.* (of garments) flaring out slightly from waist or shoulders

aliped ('ælɪpɛd) *a.* **1.** wing-footed —*n.* **2.** animal, like the bat, whose toes are joined by membrane that serves as wing

aliphatic (ælɪ'fætɪk) *a.* (of organic compound) not aromatic, *esp.* having open chain structure

aliquant ('ælɪkwənt) *a. Maths.* of quantity or number) that is not exact divisor of given quantity or number

aliquot ('ælɪkwɒt) *a. Maths.* of or signifying an exact divisor of a quantity or number

alive (ə'laɪv) *a.* **1.** living **2.** active **3.** aware **4.** swarming

alizarin (ə'lɪzərɪn) *n.* brown-to-red crystalline solid used as dye

alkali ('ælkəlaɪ) *n.* substance which combines with acid and neutralizes it, forming a salt; potash, soda *etc.* are alkalis (*pl.* **-s, -lies**) —**'alkaline** *a.* —**alkalinity** (ælkə'lɪnɪtɪ) *n.* —**'alkalize** *or* **-ise** *vt.* —**'alkaloid** *n./a.*

Alkoran or **Alcoran** (ælkɒˈrɑːn) n. see KORAN

all (ɔːl) a. **1.** the whole of, every one of —adv. **2.** wholly, entirely —n. **3.** the whole **4.** everything, everyone —**All Black** member of international Rugby Union football team of N.Z. —**all found** (of accommodation charges) inclusive of meals, heating etc. —**all fours** hands and feet —**all in** exhausted —**all-in** a. Wrestling of style of professional wrestling with no internationally agreed set of rules —**all out** inf. to one's maximum capacity —**all-out** a. inf. using one's maximum powers —**all right** a. **1.** adequate; satisfactory **2.** unharmed; safe —adv. **3.** very well **4.** satisfactorily **5.** without doubt (also (nonstandard) **al'right**) —**all-right** a. US sl. acceptable; reliable (also (nonstandard) **al-'right**) —**all-round** a. **1.** efficient in all respects, esp. in sport **2.** comprehensive; many-sided —**all-rounder** n. person with ability in many fields —**All Saints' Day** Christian festival celebrated on Nov. 1st to honour all saints —**All Souls' Day** R.C.Ch. day of prayer (Nov. 2nd) for the dead in purgatory

alla breve ('ælə 'breɪvɪ) Mus. a./adv. **1.** with two beats to the bar —n. **2.** formerly, time of two or four minims to the bar

Allah ('ælə) n. Moslem name for the Supreme Deity

allay (ə'leɪ) vt. lighten, relieve, calm, soothe

allege (ə'lɛdʒ) vt. **1.** state without or before proof **2.** produce as argument —**allegation** (ælɪ'geɪʃən) n. —**al'leged** a. —**allegedly** (ə'lɛdʒɪdlɪ) adv.

allegiance (ə'liːdʒəns) n. duty of a subject to his sovereign or state, loyalty

allegory ('ælɪɡərɪ) n. **1.** story with a meaning other than literal one **2.** description of one thing under image of another —**alle'goric(al)** a. —**alle'gorically** adv. —**'allegorist** n. —**allego-rize** or -**rise** vt.

allegretto (ælɪ'grɛtəʊ) adv./a./n. Mus. lively (passage) but not so quick as allegro

allegro (ə'leɪɡrəʊ, -'lɛɡ-) adv./a./n. Mus. fast (passage)

alleluia (ælɪ'luːjə) interj. praise the Lord

allergy ('ælədʒɪ) n. abnormal sensitivity to some food or substance innocuous to most people —**'allergen** n. substance capable of inducing an allergy —**aller'genic** a. —**al'lergic** a. **1.** having or caused by an allergy **2.** inf. having an aversion (to)

alleviate (ə'liːvɪeɪt) vt. **1.** ease, lessen, mitigate **2.** make light —**allevi'ation** n. —**al'leviator** n.

alley ('ælɪ) n. **1.** narrow street **2.** walk, path **3.** enclosure for skittles **4.** fine marble (pl. -s)

Allhallows (ɔːl'hæləʊz) n. see **All Saints' Day** at ALL.

alliance (ə'laɪəns) n. **1.** state of being allied **2.** union between families by marriage, and states by treaty **3.** confederation

alligator ('ælɪɡeɪtə) n. animal of crocodile family found in Amer.

alliteration (əlɪtə'reɪʃən) n. beginning two or more words in close succession with same sound, eg Sing a Song of Sixpence —**al'literate** v. —**al'literative** a.

allocate ('æləkeɪt) vt. **1.** assign as a share **2.** place —**allo'cation** n.

allocution (ælə'kjuːʃən) n. formal address

allogamy (ə'lɒɡəmɪ) n. cross-fertilization

allomorphism (ælə'mɔːfɪzəm) n. **1.** variation of form without change in essential nature **2.** variation of crystalline form of chemical compound

allopathy (ə'lɒpəθɪ) n. **1.** orthodox practice of medicine **2.** opposite of homeopathy

allot (ə'lɒt) vt. **1.** distribute as shares **2.** give out (-tt-) —**al'lotment** n. **1.** distribution **2.** portion of land rented for cultivation **3.** portion allotted

allotropy (ə'lɒtrəpɪ) or **allotropism** n. property of some elements of existing in more than one form, eg carbon in the form of diamond and graphite —**'allotrope** n. —**allo-'tropic** a.

allow (ə'laʊ) vt. **1.** permit **2.** acknowledge **3.** set aside —vi. (usu. with for) **4.** take into account —**al'lowable** a. —**al'lowably** adv. —**al'lowance** n. —**al'lowedly** (ə'laʊdlɪ) adv. **1.** by general agreement **2.** admittedly

alloy ('ælɔɪ, ə'lɔɪ) n. **1.** mixture of two or more metals —vt. (ə'lɔɪ) **2.** mix (metals) to form an alloy **3.** debase by mixing with something inferior

allspice ('ɔːlspaɪs) n. **1.** berry of W Indian tree **2.** spice made from this berry

allude (ə'luːd) vi. **1.** mention lightly, hint (at), make indirect reference (to) **2.** refer (to) —**al'lusion** n. —**al'lusive** a. —**al'lusively** adv.

allure (ə'lʊə) vt. **1.** entice, win over, fascinate —n. **2.** attractiveness —**al'lurement** n. —**al'lur-ing** a. charming, seductive —**al'luringly** adv.

alluvial (ə'luːvɪəl) a. deposited by rivers —**al'luvion** n. land formed by washed-up deposit —**al'luvium** n. water-borne matter deposited by rivers, floods etc. (pl. -s, -via (-vɪə))

ally (ə'laɪ) vt. **1.** join in relationship by treaty, marriage or friendship etc. (**al'lied**, **al'lying**) —n. ('ælaɪ) **2.** state or sovereign bound to another by treaty **3.** confederate (pl. 'allies') —**allied** ('ælaɪd, 'æləɪd) a. —**Allies** pl.n. **1.** (in World War I) powers of the Triple Entente (France, Russia and Britain) together with nations allied with them **2.** (in World War II) countries that fought against the Axis, esp.

Britain and Commonwealth countries, Amer., Soviet Union and France

alma mater ('ælmə 'mɑːtə, 'meɪtə) *Lat.* one's school, university, or college

almanac ('ɔːlmənæk) *n.* yearly calendar with detailed information on year's tides, events *etc.*

almighty (ɔːl'maɪtɪ) *a.* 1. having all power, omnipotent 2. *inf.* very great —**the Almighty** God

almond ('ɑːmənd) *n.* 1. edible kernel of the fruit of a tree related to the peach 2. tree bearing this fruit

almoner ('ɑːmənə) *n.* **UK** in hospitals, formerly, trained social worker dealing with patients' welfare

almost ('ɔːlməʊst) *adv.* very nearly, all but

alms (ɑːmz) *pl.n.* gifts to the poor —'**almshouse** *n.* **UK** privately supported house offering accommodation to the needy

aloe ('æləʊ) *n.* 1. genus of plants of medicinal value —*pl.n.* (*with sing. v.*) 2. bitter drug made from plant

aloft (ə'lɒft) *adv.* 1. on high 2. overhead 3. in ship's rigging

alone (ə'ləʊn) *a.* single, solitary —*adv.* 2. separately, only

along (ə'lɒŋ) *adv.* 1. in a line 2. together with one 3. forward —*prep.* 4. over the length of one —**along'side** *adv./prep.* beside (something)

aloof (ə'luːf) *a.* 1. withdrawn 2. distant 3. uninvolved —**a'loofness** *n.*

alopecia (æləʊ'piːʃɪə) *n.* baldness

aloud (ə'laʊd) *adv.* 1. loudly 2. audibly

alp (ælp) *n.* high mountain —'**alpine** *a.* 1. of the Alps 2. of high mountains —*n.* 3. mountain plant —'**alpinist** *n.* mountain climber —'**alpenstock** *n.* iron-shod staff used by climbers —**the Alps** high mountain range in S central Europe

alpaca (æl'pækə) *n.* 1. Peruvian llama 2. its wool 3. cloth made from this

alpha ('ælfə) *n.* 1. first letter in Greek alphabet (A, α) 2. **UK** highest grade or mark, as in examination —*a.* 3. involving helium nuclei; denoting isomeric or allotropic form of substance —**alpha particle** helium nucleus emitted during some radioactive transformations —**alpha ray** ionizing radiation consisting of stream of alpha particles —**alpha and omega** the first and last

alphabet ('ælfəbet) *n.* the set of letters used in writing a language —**alpha'betic(al)** *a.* in the standard order of the letters —**alpha'betically** *adv.* —'**alphabetize** *or* -**ise** *vt.* 1. arrange in alphabetical order 2. express by alphabet

alphanumeric (ælfənjuː'mɛrɪk) *or* **alphameric** (ælfə'mɛrɪk) *a.* consisting of alphabetical and numerical symbols

already (ɔːl'rɛdɪ) *adv.* 1. before, previously 2. sooner than expected

alright (ɔːl'raɪt) *adv. nonstandard see* **all right** at ALL

Alsatian (æl'seɪʃən) *n.* large dog of wolfhound breed, German shepherd dog

also ('ɔːlsəʊ) *adv.* 1. as well, too 2. besides, moreover —**also-ran** *n.* 1. contestant *etc.* failing to finish among first three 2. *inf.* loser

alt. 1. alternate 2. altitude 3. alto

Alta. Alberta

altar ('ɔːltə) *n.* 1. raised place, stone *etc.*, on which sacrifices are offered 2. in Christian church, table on which priest consecrates the Eucharist —**altar boy** serving as an acolyte —'**altarcloth** *n.* —'**altarpiece** *n.*

alter ('ɔːltə) *v.* change, make or become different —**altera'bility** *n.* —'**alterable** *a.* —'**alterably** *adv.* —**alte'ration** *n.* —'**alterative** *a.*

altercation (ɔːltə'keɪʃən) *n.* dispute, wrangling, controversy —'**altercate** *vi.*

alter ego ('æltər 'iːgəʊ, 'ɛgəʊ) *Lat.* 1. second self 2. close friend

alternate (ɔːl'tɜːnɪt) *v.* 1. occur or cause to occur by turns —*a.* (ɔːl'tɜːnɪt) 2. one after the other, by turns —al'**ternately** *adv.* —alter'**nation** *n.* —al'**ternative** *n.* 1. one of two choices —*a.* 2. presenting choice, *esp.* between two possibilities only 3. (of two things) mutually exclusive 4. denoting lifestyle *etc.* regarded as preferable to that of contemporary society because it is less conventional, materialistic or institutionalized —al'**ternatively** *adv.* —'**alternator** *n.* electric generator for producing alternating current —**alternating current** electric current that reverses direction with a frequency independent of characteristics of circuit —**alternative society** group of people who agree in rejecting traditional values of society around them

althorn ('ælthɔːn) *n.* a tenor saxhorn

although (ɔːl'ðəʊ) *conj.* despite the fact that

altimeter (æl'tɪmɪtə, 'æltɪmiːtə) *n.* instrument for measuring height

altitude ('æltɪtjuːd) *n.* height, eminence, elevation, loftiness

alto ('æltəʊ) *n. Mus.* 1. male singing voice or instrument above tenor 2. contralto (*pl.* -s) —**alto clef** clef that establishes middle C as being on third line of staff

altogether (ɔːltə'gɛðə, 'ɔːltəgɛðə) *adv.* 1. entirely 2. on the whole 3. in total

altruism ('æltruːɪzəm) *n.* principle of living and acting for good of others —**altru'istic** *a.* —**altru'istically** *adv.*

alum ('æləm) *n.* mineral salt, double sulphate of

aluminium and potassium **—aluminous** (əˈluːmɪnəs) a.

aluminium (æljuˈmɪnɪəm) or U.S. **aluminum** (əˈluːmɪnəm) n. light silvery nonrusting metal **—alumina** (əˈluːmɪnə) n. oxide of aluminium **—aluminize** or **-ise** (əˈluːmɪnaɪz) vt. coat with aluminium **—aluminous** (əˈluːmɪnəs) a.

alumnus (əˈlʌmnəs) or (fem.) **alumna** (əˈlʌmnə) n. US graduate of college (pl. **-ni** (-naɪ) or **-nae** (-niː))

always (ˈɔːlweɪz) adv. 1. ˆt all times 2. for ever

alyssum (ˈælɪsəm) n. garden plant with small yellow or white flowers

am (æm; unstressed əm) first person sing. pres. ind. of BE

Am Chem. americium

AM or **am** amplitude modulation

Am. America(n)

a.m. or **A.M.** ante meridiem

Amadhlozi or **Amadlozi** (æmæˈhlɔʒi) pl.n. SA ancestral spirits

amah (ˈɑːmə) n. in East, esp. formerly, nurse or maidservant

amain (əˈmeɪn) adv. obs., poet. with great strength or haste

amalgam (əˈmælɡəm) n. 1. compound of mercury and another metal 2. soft, plastic mixture 3. combination of elements

amalgamate (əˈmælɡəmeɪt) v. mix, combine or cause to combine **—amalgaˈmation** n.

amanuensis (əmænjuˈɛnsɪs) n. 1. person employed to take dictation 2. copyist 3. secretary (pl. **-ses** (-siːz))

amaranth (ˈæmərænθ) n. 1. imaginary purple everlasting flower 2. genus of flowering plants **—amaˈranthine** a. never fading

amaryllis (æməˈrɪlɪs) n. lilylike plant

amass (əˈmæs) vt. collect in quantity **—aˈmassable** a.

amateur (ˈæmətə) n. 1. one who carries on an art, study, game etc. for pleasure rather than for financial gain 2. unskilled practitioner **—a.** 3. not professional or expert **—ˈamateurish** a. imperfect, untrained **—ˈamateurishly** adv. **—ˈamateurism** n.

amatol (ˈæmətɒl) n. high explosive consisting of ammonium nitrate and trinitrotoluene (TNT)

amatory (ˈæmətərɪ) or **amatorial** (æməˈtɔːrɪəl) a. relating to love

amaze (əˈmeɪz) vt. surprise greatly, astound **—aˈmazement** n. **—aˈmazing** a. **—aˈmazingly** adv.

Amazon (ˈæməzˀn) n. 1. female warrior of legend 2. tall, strong woman **—Amaˈzonian** a.

ambassador (æmˈbæsədə) n. senior diplomatic representative sent by one state to another

(amˈbassadress fem.) **—ambassaˈdorial** a. **—amˈbassadorship** n.

amber (ˈæmbə) n. 1. yellowish, translucent fossil resin **—a.** 2. made of, coloured like amber

ambergris (ˈæmbəɡriːs, -ɡriːs) n. waxy substance secreted by the sperm whale, used in making perfumes

ambi- (comb. form) both, as in ambidextrous, ambivalence

ambiance (ˈæmbɪəns) n. see AMBIENCE

ambidextrous (æmbɪˈdɛkstrəs) a. able to use both hands with equal ease **—ambidexˈterity** n.

ambience or **ambiance** (ˈæmbɪəns) n. atmosphere of a place

ambient (ˈæmbɪənt) a. surrounding

ambiguous (æmˈbɪɡjʊəs) a. 1. having more than one meaning 2. obscure **—ambiˈguity** n. **—amˈbiguously** adv.

ambit (ˈæmbɪt) n. 1. circuit 2. compass

ambition (æmˈbɪʃən) n. 1. desire for power, fame, honour etc. 2. the object of that desire **—amˈbitious** a. **—amˈbitiously** adv. **—amˈbitiousness** n.

ambivalence (æmˈbɪvələns) or **ambivalency** n. simultaneous existence of two conflicting desires, opinions etc. **—amˈbivalent** a.

amble (ˈæmbl) vi. 1. move along easily and gently 2. move at an easy pace **—n.** 3. this movement or pace **—ˈambler** n.

ambrosia (æmˈbrəʊzɪə) n. 1. Myth. food of the gods 2. anything smelling or tasting particularly good

ambulance (ˈæmbjʊləns) n. conveyance for sick or injured

ambulatory (ˈæmbjʊˌleɪtərɪ) a. 1. of or for walking 2. not fixed 3. able to walk (also **ˈambulant**) **—n.** 4. place for walking, such as cloister

ambuscade (æmbəˈskeɪd) n. 1. act of hiding to launch surprise attack 2. ambush

ambush (ˈæmbʊʃ) n. 1. act of lying in wait **—vt.** 2. waylay, attack from hiding, lie in wait for

ameliorate (əˈmiːljəreɪt) v. make better, improve **—amelioˈration** n. **—aˈmeliorative** a.

amen (eɪˈmɛn, ɑːˈmɛn) interj. 1. surely, so let it be

amenable (əˈmiːnəbl) a. easy to be led or controlled **—amenaˈbility** or aˈmenableness n. **—aˈmenably** adv. **—amenable to** 1. likely to respond to 2. answerable to

amend (əˈmɛnd) vt. 1. correct 2. improve 3. alter in detail, as bill in parliament etc. **—aˈmendment** n. **—aˈmends** pl.n. reparation

amenity (əˈmiːnɪtɪ) n. (oft. pl.) useful or pleasant facility or service

amenorrhoea or esp. U.S. **amenorrhea**

(æmɛnəˈrɪə, eɪ-) *n.* abnormal absence of menstruation

American (əˈmɛrɪkən) *n./a.* (native or inhabitant) of the American continent or the U.S.A.

americium (æməˈrɪsɪəm) *n.* white metallic transuranic element artificially produced from plutonium

amethyst (ˈæmɪθɪst) *n.* bluish-violet semi-precious stone

Amharic (æmˈhærɪk) *n.* **1.** official language of Ethiopia —*a.* **2.** denoting this language

amiable (ˈeɪmɪəbᵊl) *a.* friendly, kindly —**ami'a'bility** *or* **'amiableness** *n.* —**'amiably** *adv.*

amicable (ˈæmɪkəbᵊl) *a.* friendly —**amica'bil'ity** *n.* —**'amicably** *adv.*

amicus curiae (æˈmiːkʊs ˈkjʊəriiː) *Law* person, not directly engaged in case, who advises court (*pl.* **amici curiae** (æˈmiːkaɪ))

amid (əˈmɪd) *or* **amidst** *prep.* in the middle of, among

amidships (əˈmɪdʃɪps) *adv.* near, towards middle of ship

amino acid (əˈmiːnəʊ) organic compound found in protein

amiss (əˈmɪs) *a.* **1.** wrong —*adv.* **2.** faultily, badly —**take amiss** to be offended by

amity (ˈæmɪtɪ) *n.* friendship

ammeter (ˈæmmiːtə) *n.* instrument for measuring electric current

ammo (ˈæməʊ) *n. inf.* ammunition

ammonia (əˈməʊnɪə) *n.* pungent alkaline gas containing hydrogen and nitrogen —**am'moniac** *or* **ammoniacal** (æməˈnaɪəkᵊl) *a.* —**am'moniated** *a.* —**am'monium** *n.*

ammonite (ˈæmənaɪt) *n.* whorled fossil shell like ram's horn

ammunition (æmjʊˈnɪʃən) *n.* **1.** any projectiles (bullets, rockets *etc.*) that can be discharged from a weapon **2.** any means of defence or attack, as in argument

amnesia (æmˈniːzɪə, -ˈniːzjə, -ˈniːʒə) *n.* loss of memory

amnesty (ˈæmnɪstɪ) *n.* **1.** general pardon —*vt.* **2.** grant amnesty to

amnion (ˈæmnɪən) *n.* innermost of two membranes enclosing embryonic reptile, bird or mammal (*pl.* **-s, amnia** (ˈæmnɪə)) —**amni'otic** *a.* —**amniotic** fluid surrounding baby in womb

amoeba *or U.S.* **ameba** (əˈmiːbə) *n.* microscopic single-celled animal able to change its shape, found in ponds *etc.* (*pl.* **-s, -bae** (-biː))

amok (əˈmʌk, əˈmɒk) *adv. see* AMUCK

among (əˈmʌŋ) *or* **amongst** *prep.* mixed with, in the midst of, of the number of, between

amoral (eɪˈmɒrəl) *a.* nonmoral, having no moral qualities —**amo'rality** *n.*

amorous (ˈæmərəs) *a.* **1.** inclined to love **2.** in love —**'amorously** *adv.* —**'amorousness** *n.*

amorphous (əˈmɔːfəs) *a.* without distinct shape —**a'morphism** *n.*

amortize *or* **-tise** (əˈmɔːtaɪz) *vt.* pay off (a debt) by a sinking fund

amount (əˈmaʊnt) *vi.* **1.** come (to), be equal (to) —*n.* **2.** quantity **3.** sum total

amour (əˈmʊə) *n.* (illicit) love affair

amour-propre (amuːr ˈprɔpr) *Fr.* self-respect

amp. **1.** amperage **2.** ampere

ampere (ˈæmpɛə) *n.* unit of electric current —**amperage** (ˈæmpərɪdʒ) *n.* strength of electric current measured in amperes

ampersand (ˈæmpəsænd) *n.* the sign & (and)

amphetamine (æmˈfɛtəmiːn) *n.* synthetic liquid used medicinally mainly for its stimulant action on central nervous system

amphi- (*comb. form*) **1.** on both sides; at both ends; of both kinds, as in *amphipod, amphibious* **2.** around, as in *amphibole*

amphibious (æmˈfɪbɪəs) *a.* living or operating both on land and in water —**am'phibian** *n.* **1.** animal that lives first in water then on land **2.** vehicle able to travel on land or water **3.** aircraft that can alight on land or water

amphitheatre *or U.S.* **amphitheater** (ˈæmfɪθɪətə) *n.* building with tiers of seats rising round an arena

amphora (ˈæmfərə) *n.* two-handled jar of ancient Greece and Rome (*pl.* **-rae** (-riː), **-s**)

ample (ˈæmpᵊl) *a.* **1.** big enough **2.** large, spacious —**'amply** *adv.*

amplify (ˈæmplɪfaɪ) *vt.* **1.** increase **2.** make bigger, louder *etc.* (**-fied, -fying**) —**amplifi'cation** *n.* —**'amplifier** *n.*

amplitude (ˈæmplɪtjuːd) *n.* spaciousness, width, magnitude —**amplitude modulation** *Rad.* method of transmitting information in which amplitude of carrier wave is varied

ampoule (ˈæmpuːl, -pjuːl) *or* (*esp. U.S.*) **ampule** *n.* container for hypodermic dose

ampulla (æmˈpʊlə) *n.* **1.** *Anat.* dilated end part of duct or canal **2.** *Christianity* vessel for wine and water used at the Eucharist; small flask for consecrated oil **3.** Roman two-handled bottle (*pl.* **ampullae** (-ˈpʊliː))

amputate (ˈæmpjʊteɪt) *v.* cut off (limb *etc.*) —**ampu'tation** *n.*

amuck (əˈmʌk) *or* **amok** *adv.* —**run amuck** rush about as in murderous frenzy

amulet (ˈæmjʊlɪt) *n.* something carried or worn as a charm

amuse (əˈmjuːz) *vt.* **1.** divert **2.** occupy pleasantly **3.** cause to laugh or smile —**a'musement** *n.* entertainment, pastime —**a'musing** *a.* —**a'musingly** *adv.*

amylase ('æmıleız) *n.* enzyme that hydrolyses starch and glycogen to simple sugar

amylum ('æmıləm) *n. see* STARCH

an (æn; *unstressed* ən) *see* A

an- *or before consonant* **a-** (*comb. form*) not; without, as in *anaphrodisiac*

-an, -ean, *or* **-ian** (*comb. form*) **1.** belonging to; coming from; typical of; adhering to, as in *European, Elizabethan, Christian* **2.** person who specializes or is expert in, as in *dietician*

Anabaptist (ænə'bæptıst) *n.* member of Protestant movement that rejected infant baptism and insisted adults be rebaptized

anabolism (ə'næbəlızəm) *n.* metabolic process in which complex molecules are synthesized from simpler ones with storage of energy —**ana'bolic** *a.* —**anabolic steroid** any of various hormones that encourage muscle and bone growth

anabranch ('ænəbrɑ:ntʃ) *n.* stream that leaves a river and re-enters it further downstream

anachronism (ə'nækrənızəm) *n.* **1.** mistake of time, by which something is put in wrong historical period **2.** something out of date —**anachro'nistic** *a.*

anacoluthon (ænəkə'lu:θɒn) *n.* a sentence or words faulty in grammatical sequence (*pl.* **-tha** (-θə))

anaconda (ænə'kɒndə) *n.* large snake which kills by constriction

anadromous (ə'nædrəməs) *a.* (of salmon *etc.*) migrating up rivers to breed

anaemia *or U.S.* **anemia** (ə'ni:mıə) *n.* deficiency in number of red blood cells —**a'naemic** *or U.S.* **a'nemic** *a.* suffering from anaemia **2.** pale, sickly, lacking vitality

anaerobe ('ænɛərəʊb) *or* **anaerobium** (ænəə'rəʊbıəm) *n.* organism that can live without free oxygen (*pl.* **-obes** *or* **-obia** (-'əʊbıə)) —**anaer'obic** *a.*

anaesthetic *or U.S.* **anesthetic** (ænıs'θɛtık) *n./a.* (drug) causing loss of sensation —**anaesthesia** *or U.S.* **anesthesia** (ænıs'θi:zıə) *n.* loss of sensation —**anaes'thetically** *or U.S.* **anes'thetically** *adv.* —**anaesthetist** *or U.S.* **anesthetist** (ə'ni:sθətıst) *n.* expert in use of anaesthetics —**anaesthetize, anaesthetise,** *or U.S.* **anesthetize** (ə'ni:sθətaız) *vt.*

Anaglypta (ænə'glıptə) *n.* **R** thick, embossed wallpaper

anagram ('ænəgræm) *n.* word or words made by arranging in different order the letters of another word or words, *eg* *ant* from *tan* —**anagram'matical** *a.* —**ana'grammatist** *n.*

anal ('eınəl) *a. see* ANUS

analects ('ænəlɛkts) *or* **analecta** (ænə'lɛktə)

pl.n. selected literary passages from one or more works

analgesia (ænəl'dʒi:zıə) *or* **analgia** (æn'ældʒıə) *n.* absence of pain —**anal'gesic** *a./n.* (drug) relieving pain

analogue *or U.S.* (*sometimes*) **analog** ('ænəlɒg) *n.* **1.** something analogous to something else **2.** *Biol.* analogous part or organ —*a.* **3.** using analogue (such as dial and pointer) to represent data or information —**analogue computer** computer that uses voltages to represent numbers of physical quantities

analogy (ə'nælədʒı) *n.* **1.** agreement or likeness in certain respects **2.** correspondence —**ana-'logical** *a.* —**ana'logically** *adv.* —**a'nalogist** *n.* —**a'nalogize** *or* **-gise** *v.* explain by analogy —**a'nalogous** *a.* **1.** similar **2.** parallel —**a'nalogously** *adv.*

analysis (ə'nælısıs) *n.* separation of something into its elements or components (*pl.* **-yses** (-ısi:z)) —**'analyse** *or U.S.* **-lyze** *vt.* **1.** examine critically **2.** determine the constituent parts of —**'analyst** *n.* one skilled in analysis, *esp.* chemical or psychiatric analysis —**ana'lytic(al)** *a.* **1.** relating to analysis **2.** capable of or given to analysing —**ana'lytically** *adv.*

anapaest *or* **anapest** ('ænəpɛst, -pi:st) *n.* metrical foot of two short syllables followed by one long

anaphora (ə'næfərə) *n.* **1.** *Rhetoric* repetition of word or phrase at beginning of successive clauses **2.** *Gram.* use of word such as pronoun to avoid repetition

anarchy ('ænəkı) *n.* **1.** lawlessness **2.** lack of government in a state **3.** confusion —**an'archic(al)** *a.* —**an'archically** *adv.* —**l'anarchism** *n.* —**'anarchist** *n.* one who opposes all forms of government

anastigmat (æ'næstıgmæt, ænə'stıgmæt) *n.* lens corrected for astigmatism —**anastig'matic** *a.* (of lens) not astigmatic

anastomosis (ənæstə'məʊsıs) *n.* interconnection of veins, arteries *etc.* (*pl.* **-ses** (-si:z))

anat. **1.** anatomical **2.** anatomy

anathema (ə'næθəmə) *n.* **1.** anything detested, hateful **2.** ban of the church **3.** curse —**a'nathematize** *or* **-tise** *v.*

anatomy (ə'nætəmı) *n.* **1.** science of structure of the body **2.** detailed analysis **3.** the body —**ana'tomical** *a.* —**ana'tomically** *adv.* —**a'natomist** *n.* —**a'natomize** *or* **-mise** *vt.*

-ance *or* **-ancy** (*comb. form*) action, state or condition, or quality, as in *utterance, resemblance*

ancestor ('ænsɛstə) *n.* **1.** person from whom another is descended **2.** early type of later form or product —**an'cestral** *a.* —**'ancestry** *n.*

anchor ('æŋkə) *n.* **1.** heavy (*usu.* hooked)

implement dropped on cable, chain *etc.* to bottom of sea to secure vessel **2.** source of stability or security —*vt.* **3.** fasten by or as by anchor —'**anchorage** *n.* act of, place of anchoring —**anchor man 1.** *Sport* end member of tug-of-war team; last runner in relay team **2.** in broadcasting, compere who links different parts of programme —**weigh anchor** haul up anchor and set sail

anchorite ('æŋkəraɪt) *n.* hermit, recluse ('**anchoress** *fem.*)

anchovy ('æntʃəvɪ) *n.* small savoury fish of herring family

anchusa (æŋ'kjuːsə) *n.* plant with hairy leaves and blue flowers

ancien régime (ãsjɛ̃ reˈʒim) *Fr.* political and social system of France before the Revolution of 1789 (*pl.* **anciens régimes** (ãsjɛ̃ reˈʒim))

ancient ('eɪnʃənt) *a.* **1.** belonging to former age **2.** old **3.** timeworn —*n.* **4.** (*oft. pl.*) one who lived in an earlier age —'**anciently** *adv.* —**ancient monument** notable building or site preserved as public property

ancillary (æn'sɪlərɪ) *a.* subordinate, subservient, auxiliary

-ancy (*comb. form*) condition or quality, as in *poignancy* (*also use* **-ance**)

and (ænd; *unstressed* ənd, ən) *conj.* connecting word, used to join words and sentences, to introduce a consequence *etc.* —**and/or** *conj.* used to join terms when either one or other or both is indicated

andante (æn'dæntɪ) *Mus. a./adv.* **1.** at moderately slow tempo —*n.* **2.** passage or piece performed in this manner

andantino (ændæn'tiːnəʊ) *Mus. a./adv.* **1.** slightly faster or slower than andante —*n.* **2.** passage or piece performed in this manner (*pl.* **-s**)

andiron ('ændaɪən) *n.* iron bar or bracket for supporting logs in fireplace

andro- *or before vowel* **andr-** (*comb. form*) **1.** male; masculine **2.** in botany, stamen or anther

androgen ('ændrədʒən) *n.* steroid that promotes development of male sexual characteristics

androgynous (æn'drɒdʒɪnəs) *a.* **1.** *Bot.* having male and female flowers in same inflorescence **2.** hermaphrodite

android ('ændrɔɪd) *n.* **1.** in science fiction, robot resembling human being —*a.* **2.** resembling human being

anecdote ('ænɪkdəʊt) *n.* very short story dealing with single incident —**anec'dotal** *or* **anec'dotic** *a.*

anemia (ə'niːmɪə) *n. US see* ANAEMIA

anemograph (ə'nɛməʊɡrɑːf) *n.* self-recording anemometer

anemometer (ænɪ'mɒmɪtə) *n.* instrument for recording force and direction of wind —**anemo'metric** *a.* —**ane'mometry** *n.*

anemone (ə'nɛmənɪ) *n.* flower related to buttercup —**sea anemone** plantlike sea animal

anent (ə'nɛnt) *prep. obs.* concerning

aneroid ('ænərɔɪd) *a.* denoting a barometer which measures atmospheric pressure without the use of mercury or other liquid

aneurysm *or* **aneurism** ('ænjərɪzəm) *n.* swelling out of a part of an artery

anew (ə'njuː) *adv.* afresh, again

angel ('eɪndʒəl) *n.* **1.** divine messenger **2.** ministering or attendant spirit **3.** person with the qualities of such a spirit, as gentleness, purity *etc.* —**angelic** (æn'dʒɛlɪk) *a.* —**angelically** (æn'dʒɛlɪkəlɪ) *adv.* —**angel cake** *or esp. U.S.* **angel food cake** light sponge cake made without egg yolks —'**angelfish** *n.* **1.** small tropical marine fish which has brightly coloured body **2.** S Amer. freshwater fish which has large dorsal and anal fins **3.** shark with flattened pectoral fins (*pl.* **-fish, -fishes**)

angelica (æn'dʒɛlɪkə) *n.* **1.** aromatic plant **2.** the candied stalks of this plant used in cookery

Angelus ('ændʒɪləs) *n.* devotional service in R.C. Church in memory of the Incarnation, said at morning, noon and sunset

anger ('æŋɡə) *n.* **1.** strong emotion excited by a real or supposed injury **2.** wrath **3.** rage —*vt.* **4.** excite to wrath **5.** enrage —'**angrily** *adv.* —'**angry** *a.* **1.** full of anger **2.** inflamed

angina pectoris (æn'dʒaɪnə 'pɛktərɪs) severe pain accompanying heart disease

angiosperm ('ændʒɪəʊspɜːm) *n.* any plant having a seed vessel

angle[1] ('æŋɡəl) *vi.* fish with hook and line —'**angler** *n.* **1.** fisherman **2.** sea fish with spiny dorsal fin (*also* **angler fish**) —'**angling** *n.*

angle[2] ('æŋɡəl) *n.* **1.** meeting of two lines or surfaces **2.** sharp corner **3.** point of view **4.** *inf.* devious motive —*vt.* **5.** bend at an angle —**angle of incidence 1.** angle of line or beam of radiation to line perpendicular to surface at point of incidence **2.** angle between chord line of aircraft wing or tailplane and longitudinal axis

Anglican ('æŋɡlɪkən) *a./n.* (member) of the Church of England —'**Anglicanism** *n.*

anglicize *or* **-cise** ('æŋɡlɪsaɪz) *vt.* express in English, turn into English form —'**Anglicism** *n.* English idiom or peculiarity

Anglo ('æŋɡləʊ) *n.* C English-speaking Canadian (*pl.* **-s**)

Anglo- ('æŋɡləʊ-) (*comb. form*) English, as in *Anglo-American*

Anglo-French *a.* **1.** of England and France **2.** of Anglo-French —*n.* **3.** Norman-French language of medieval England

Anglo-Norman *a.* 1. relating to Norman conquerors of England or their language —*n.* 2. Norman inhabitant of England after 1066 3. Anglo-French language

Anglophile ('æŋgləʊfıl, -faıl) *or* **Anglophil** *n.* person having admiration for England or the English

Anglophobia (æŋgləʊ'fəʊbıə) *n.* dislike of England *etc.*

Anglo-Saxon *n.* 1. member of West Germanic tribes that settled in Britain from 5th century A.D. 2. language of these tribes (*see* Old English *at* OLD) 3. White person whose native language is English 4. *inf.* plain blunt English —*a.* 5. forming part of Germanic element in Modern English 6. of Anglo-Saxons or Old English language 7. of White Protestant culture of Britain and Amer.

angora (æŋ'gɔːrə) *n.* (*sometimes* A-) 1. goat with long white silky hair which is used in the making of mohair 2. cloth or wool made from this hair —**angora cat** *or* **rabbit** varieties of cat and rabbit with long, silky fur

angostura bitters (æŋgə'stjʊərə) R (*oft.* A-) bitter tonic, used as flavouring in alcoholic drinks

angstrom ('æŋstrəm) *n.* unit of length for measuring wavelengths of electromagnetic radiation

anguish ('æŋgwıʃ) *n.* great mental or physical pain

angular ('æŋgjʊlə) *a.* 1. (of people) bony, awkward 2. having angles 3. measured by an angle —**angu'larity** *n.*

anhydrous (æn'haıdrəs) *a.* (of chemical substances) free from water

anil ('ænıl) *n.* leguminous West Indian shrub (*also* '**indigo**)

aniline ('ænılın, -liːn) *n.* product of coal tar or indigo, which yields dyes

animadvert (ænımæd'vɜːt) *vi.* (*usu. with on or upon*) criticize, pass censure —**animad'version** *n.* criticism, censure

animal ('ænıməl) *n.* 1. living creature, having sensation and power of voluntary motion 2. beast —*a.* 3. of, pert. to animals 4. sensual —**ani'malcular** *a.* —**ani'malcule** *n.* very small animal, esp. one which cannot be seen by naked eye —'**animalism** *n.* —'**animally** *adv.* —**animal husbandry** science of breeding and rearing farm animals —**animal magnetism** 1. quality of being attractive, esp. to opposite sex 2. *obs.* hypnotism

animate ('ænımeıt) *vt.* 1. give life to 2. enliven 3. inspire 4. actuate 5. make cartoon film of —'**animated** *a.* 1. lively 2. in form of cartoons —**ani'mation** *n.* 1. life, vigour 2. cartoon film —'**animator** *n.*

animato (ænı'mɑːtəʊ) *a./adv. Mus.* lively; animated

animism ('ænımızəm) *n.* belief that natural effects are due to spirits or that inanimate things have spirits —'**animist** *n.* —**ani'mistic** *a.*

animosity (ænı'mɒsıtı) *n.* hostility, enmity

animus ('ænıməs) *n.* 1. intense dislike; hatred 2. animosity

anion ('ænaıən) *n.* ion with negative charge

anise ('ænıs) *n.* plant with aromatic seeds, which are used for flavouring

aniseed ('ænısiːd) *n.* liquorice-flavoured seed of anise

ankle ('æŋkəl) *n.* joint between foot and leg —'**anklet** *n.* ornamental chain *etc.* worn around ankle

ankylosis *or* **anchylosis** (æŋkı'ləʊsıs) *n.* abnormal adhesion or immobility of bones in joint

anna ('ænə) *n.* formerly, Indian coin worth one sixteenth of rupee

annals ('ænəlz) *pl.n.* historical records of events —'**annalist** *n.*

anneal (ə'niːl) *vt.* 1. toughen (metal or glass) by heating and slow cooling 2. temper (determination, will *etc.*) —**an'nealing** *n.*

annelid ('ænəlıd) *n.* one of class of invertebrate animals, including the earthworm *etc.*

annex (æ'nɛks) *vt.* 1. add, append, attach 2. take possession of (*esp.* territory) —**annex'ation** *n.*

annexe *or esp. U.S.* **annex** ('ænɛks) *n.* 1. supplementary building 2. something added

annihilate (ə'naıəleıt) *vt.* reduce to nothing, destroy utterly —**annihi'lation** *n.* —**an'nihilative** *a.* —**an'nihilator** *n.*

anniversary (ænı'vɜːsərı) *n.* 1. yearly recurrence of a date of notable event 2. celebration of this

anno Domini ('ænəʊ 'dɒmınaı, -niː) *Lat.* in the year of our Lord

annotate ('ænəʊteıt, 'ænə-) *vt.* provide notes for (literary work *etc.*), comment —**anno'tation** *n.* —'**annotator** *n.*

announce (ə'naʊns) *vt.* make known, proclaim —**an'nouncement** *n.* —**an'nouncer** *n.* broadcaster who announces items in programme, introduces speakers *etc.*

annoy (ə'nɔı) *vt.* 1. vex 2. make slightly angry 3. tease —**an'noyance** *n.*

annual ('ænjʊəl) *a.* 1. yearly 2. of, for a year —*n.* 3. plant which completes its life cycle in a year 4. book published each year —'**annually** *adv.*

annuity (ə'njuːıtı) *n.* sum or grant paid every year —**an'nuitant** *n.* holder of annuity

annul (əˈnʌl) vt. make void, cancel, abolish (-ll-) —an'nulment n.

annular (ˈænjulə) a. ring-shaped —'annulate a. having or marked with rings —'annulated a. formed in rings —annu'lation n. —'annulet n. small ring or fillet

Annunciation (ənʌnsɪˈeɪʃən) n. 1. angel's announcement to the Virgin Mary 2. (a-) announcing —an'nunciate vt. proclaim, announce

anode (ˈænəʊd) n. Elec. the positive pole, or point of entry of current —'anodize or -dise vt. cover metal object with protective film by using it for anode in electrolysis

anodyne (ˈænədaɪn) a. 1. relieving pain, soothing —n. 2. pain-relieving drug

anoint (əˈnɔɪnt) vt. 1. smear with oil or ointment 2. consecrate with oil —a'nointment n. —the Anointed the Messiah

anomalous (əˈnɒmələs) a. irregular, abnormal —a'nomaly n. 1. irregularity 2. deviation from rule

anomie or **anomy** (ˈænəʊmɪ) n. Sociol. lack of social or moral standards

anon (əˈnɒn) adv. obs. 1. in a short time, soon 2. now and then

anon. anonymous

anonymous (əˈnɒnɪməs) a. nameless, esp. without an author's name —ano'nymity n. —a'nonymously adv.

anopheles (əˈnɒfɪliːz) n. genus of the malarial mosquito

anorak (ˈænəræk) n. lightweight, warm, waterproof, usu. hooded jacket

anorexia (ænəˈrɛksɪə) n. loss of appetite —anorexia nervosa (nɜːˈvəʊsə) psychological condition characterized by refusal to eat

another (əˈnʌðə) pron./a. 1. one other 2. a different (one) 3. one more

ans. answer

anserine (ˈænsəraɪn) a. 1. of or like goose 2. silly

answer (ˈɑːnsə) v. 1. reply (to) 2. be accountable (for, to) —vt. 3. solve; reply correctly 4. meet 5. match 6. satisfy, suit —n. 7. reply 8. solution —'answerable a. accountable

ant (ænt) n. small social insect, proverbial for industry —ant bear see AARDVARK —'anteater n. animal which feeds on ants by means of long, sticky tongue —ant hill mound raised by ants

-ant (comb. form) causing or performing action or existing in certain condition, as in pleasant, deodorant, servant

antacid (æntˈæsɪd) n. 1. substance used to treat acidity, esp. in stomach —a. 2. having properties of this substance

antagonist (ænˈtæɡənɪst) n. opponent, adversary —an'tagonism n. —antago'nistic a.

—antago'nistically adv. —an'tagonize or -nise vt. arouse hostility in

antalkali (æntˈælkəlaɪ) n. substance that neutralizes alkalis (pl. -s, -lies)

Antarctic (æntˈɑːktɪk) a. 1. of south polar regions —n. 2. region round South Pole —Antarctic Circle imaginary circle around earth at latitude 66° 32′ S

ante (ˈæntɪ) n. 1. player's stake in poker —v. 2. place stake

ante- (comb. form) before, as in antechamber. Such words are not given here where the meaning may easily be inferred from the simple word

antecedent (æntɪˈsiːdənt) a./n. (event, person or thing) going before

antedate (æntɪˈdeɪt) vt. 1. be or occur at earlier date than 2. affix or assign date to (document etc.) earlier than actual date 3. cause to occur sooner —n. 4. earlier date

antediluvian (æntɪdɪˈluːvɪən) a. 1. before the Flood 2. ancient

antelope (ˈæntɪləʊp) n. deerlike ruminant animal, remarkable for grace and speed

ante meridiem (məˈrɪdɪəm) Lat. before noon

antenatal (æntɪˈneɪtəl) a. of care etc. during pregnancy

antenna (ænˈtɛnə) n. 1. insect's feeler 2. aerial (pl. -ae (-iː))

antepenultimate (æntɪpɪˈnʌltɪmɪt) a. 1. third last —n. 2. anything third last

anterior (ænˈtɪərɪə) a. 1. to the front 2. earlier

anteroom (ˈæntɪruːm, -rʊm) n. room giving entrance to larger room, oft. used as waiting room

anthem (ˈænθəm) n. 1. song of loyalty, esp. to a country 2. Scripture passage set to music 3. piece of sacred music, orig. sung in alternate parts by two choirs

anther (ˈænθə) n. sac in flower, containing pollen, at top of stamen —'antheral a.

anthology (ænˈθɒlədʒɪ) n. collection of poems, literary extracts etc. —an'thologist n. maker of such —an'thologize or -gise vt. include (poem etc.) in anthology

anthracene (ˈænθrəsiːn) n. colourless crystalline solid used in manufacture of chemicals etc.

anthracite (ˈænθrəsaɪt) n. hard coal that burns slowly almost without flame or smoke

anthrax (ˈænθræks) n. 1. malignant disease in cattle, communicable to man 2. sore caused by this

anthropo- (comb. form) man, human, as in anthropology

anthropocentric (ænθrəpəʊˈsɛntrɪk) a. regarding man as central factor in universe

anthropoid (ˈænθrəpɔɪd) a. 1. like man —n. 2. ape resembling man

anthropology (ænθrə'pɒlədʒɪ) *n.* scientific study of origins, development of human race —**anthropo'logical** *a.* —**anthro'pologist** *n.*

anthropomorphize *or* -**ise** (ænθrəpə'mɔːfaɪz) *vt.* ascribe human attributes to (God or an animal) —**anthropo'morphic** *a.* —**anthropo'morphism** *n.* —**anthropo'morphous** *a.* shaped like human being

anti ('æntɪ) *inf. a.* 1. opposed to party *etc.* —*n.* 2. opponent

anti- (*comb. form*) against, as in *anti-aircraft, antispasmodic.* Such words are not given here where meaning may easily be inferred from simple word

antibiosis (æntɪbaɪ'əʊsɪs) *n.* association between two organisms that is harmful to one of them

antibiotic (æntɪbaɪ'ɒtɪk) *n.* 1. any of various chemical, fungal or synthetic substances, *esp.* penicillin, used against bacterial infection —*a.* 2. of antibiotics

antibody ('æntɪbɒdɪ) *n.* substance in, or introduced into, blood serum, which counteracts growth and harmful action of bacteria

Antichrist ('æntɪkraɪst) *n.* 1. *Bible* the antagonist of Christ 2. (*sometimes* a-) an enemy of Christ or Christianity

anticipate (æn'tɪsɪpeɪt) *vt.* 1. expect 2. take or consider beforehand 3. foresee 4. enjoy in advance —**antici'pation** *n.* —**an'ticipative** *or* **an'ticipatory** *a.*

anticlerical (æntɪ'klɛrɪkl) *a.* 1. opposed to influence of clergy, *esp.* in politics —*n.* 2. supporter of anticlerical party

anticlimax (æntɪ'klaɪmæks) *n.* 1. disappointing conclusion to series of events *etc.* 2. sudden descent to the trivial or ludicrous

anticline ('æntɪklaɪn) *n.* formation of stratified rock folded into broad arch so that strata slope down on both sides from common crest

antics ('æntɪks) *pl.n.* absurd or grotesque movements or acts

anticyclone (æntɪ'saɪkləʊn) *n.* system of winds moving round centre of high barometric pressure

antidote ('æntɪdəʊt) *n.* counteracting remedy

antifreeze ('æntɪfriːz) *n.* liquid added to water to lower its freezing point, as in car radiators

antigen ('æntɪdʒən, -dʒɛn) *n.* substance stimulating production of antibodies in the blood

antihero ('æntɪhɪərəʊ) *n.* central character in novel *etc.,* who lacks traditional heroic virtues

antihistamine (æntɪ'hɪstəmiːn, -mɪn) *n.* drug used *esp.* to treat allergies

antiknock (æntɪ'nɒk) *n.* compound added to petrol to reduce knocking in engine

antilogarithm (æntɪ'lɒgərɪðəm) *n.* number whose logarithm is the given number (*also* **'antilog**)

antimacassar (æntɪmə'kæsə) *n.* cover to protect chairs from macassar oil

antimatter ('æntɪmætə) *n.* hypothetical form of matter composed of antiparticles

antimony ('æntɪmənɪ) *n.* brittle, bluish-white metal

antinomy (æn'tɪnəmɪ) *n.* 1. opposition of one law *etc.* to another 2. *Philos.* contradiction between two apparently indubitable propositions

antinovel ('æntɪnɒvl) *n.* prose fiction in which conventional novelistic elements are rejected

antiparticle ('æntɪpɑːtɪkl) *n.* any of group of elementary particles that have same mass as corresponding particle but have charge of equal magnitude but opposite sign

antipasto (æntɪ'pɑːstəʊ, -'pæs-) *n.* course of hors d'œuvres in Italian meal (*pl.* -**s**)

antipathy (æn'tɪpəθɪ) *n.* dislike, aversion —**antipa'thetic** *a.*

antiperspirant (æntɪ'pɜːspərənt) *n.* substance used to reduce sweating

antiphon ('æntɪfən) *n.* 1. composition in which verses, lines are sung alternately by two choirs 2. anthem —**an'tiphonal** *a.*

antipodes (æn'tɪpədiːz) *pl.n.* countries, peoples on opposite side of the globe (oft. refers to Aust. and N.Z.) —**an'tipodal** *or* **antipo'dean** *a.*

antipope ('æntɪpəʊp) *n.* pope elected in opposition to the one regularly chosen

antipyretic (æntɪpaɪ'rɛtɪk) *n./a.* (remedy) effective against fever

antique (æn'tiːk) *n.* 1. relic of former times, usu. piece of furniture *etc.* that is collected —*a.* 2. ancient 3. old-fashioned —**antiquary** ('æntɪkwərɪ) *or* **antiquarian** (æntɪ'kwɛərɪən) *n.* student or collector of old things —**antiquated** ('æntɪkweɪtɪd) *a.* out-of-date —**antiquity** (æn'tɪkwɪtɪ) *n.* 1. great age 2. former times

antirrhinum (æntɪ'raɪnəm) *n.* genus of plants including snapdragon

antiscorbutic (æntɪskɔː'bjuːtɪk) *n./a.* (agent) preventing or curing scurvy

anti-Semitic *a.* discriminating against Jews —**anti-Semitism** (-'sɛmɪtɪzəm) *n.*

antiseptic (æntɪ'sɛptɪk) *n./a.* 1. (substance) preventing infection —*a.* 2. free from infection

antisocial (æntɪ'səʊʃəl) *a.* 1. avoiding company of other people; unsociable 2. contrary to interests of society in general

antistatic (æntɪ'stætɪk) *a.* (of textile *etc.*) retaining sufficient moisture to provide conducting path, thus avoiding effects of static electricity

antithesis (æn'tɪθɪsɪs) *n.* 1. direct opposite 2.

contrast **3.** opposition of ideas (*pl.* **-eses** (-ɪsiːz)) —**anti'thetical** *a.* —**anti'thetically** *adv.*

antitoxin (æntɪ'toksɪn) *n.* serum used to neutralize disease poisons

antitrades ('æntɪtreɪdz) *pl.n.* winds blowing in opposite direction from and above trade winds

antitrust (æntɪ'trʌst) *a.* chiefly **US** regulating or opposing trusts or similar organizations

antitype ('æntɪtaɪp) *n.* **1.** person or thing foreshadowed or represented by type or symbol **2.** opposite type

antivenin (æntɪ'venɪn) *n.* antitoxin to counteract specific venom, *eg* of snake or spider

antler ('æntlə) *n.* branching horn of certain deer —**'antlered** *a.*

antonym ('æntənɪm) *n.* word of opposite meaning to another, *eg cold* is an antonym of *hot*

antrum ('æntrəm) *n. Anat.* natural cavity or sinus, *esp.* in bone (*pl.* **-tra** (-trə))

anuresis (ænjʊ'riːsɪs) *n.* inability to urinate

anus ('eɪnəs) *n.* the lower opening of the bowels —**'anal** *a.* of or near the anus

anvil ('ænvɪl) *n.* heavy iron block on which a smith hammers metal into shape

anxious ('æŋkʃəs, 'æŋʃəs) *a.* **1.** troubled, uneasy **2.** concerned —**anxiety** (æŋ'zaɪɪtɪ) *n.* —**'anxiously** *adv.*

any ('enɪ) *a./pron.* **1.** one indefinitely **2.** some **3.** whatever, whichever —**'anybody** *pron.* —**'anyhow** *adv.* —**any more** or *esp. U.S.* **any'more** *adv.* any longer; still; nowadays —**'anyone** *pron.* —**'anything** *pron.* —**'anyway** *adv.* —**'anywhere** *adv.*

Anzac ('ænzæk) *a.* **1.** of Australian-New Zealand Army Corps in WWI —*n.* **2.** soldier of that corps, Gallipoli veteran —**Anzac Day** Apr. 25th, public holiday in Aust. and N.Z. commemorating Anzac landing at Gallipoli in 1915

ANZUS ('ænzəs) Aust., N.Z. and U.S., with reference to security alliance between them

a.o.b. or **A.O.B.** any other business

aorist ('eɪərɪst, 'ɛərɪst) *n. Gram.* tense of verb, *esp.* in classical Greek, indicating past action without reference to whether action involved was momentary or continuous

aorta (eɪ'ɔːtə) *n.* great artery rising from left ventricle of heart —**a'ortal** *a.*

apace (ə'peɪs) *adv.* swiftly

Apache (ə'pætʃɪ) *n.* **1.** member of N Amer. Indian people of SW U.S. and N Mexico (*pl.* **-s**, **A'pache**) **2.** language of this people

apart (ə'pɑːt) *adv.* **1.** separately, aside **2.** in pieces

apartheid (ə'pɑːtheɪt, -heɪt) *n. esp.* in S Afr., official government policy of racial segregation

apartment (ə'pɑːtmənt) *n.* **1.** room **2.** *esp.* US a flat —*pl.* **3.** lodgings

apathy ('æpəθɪ) *n.* **1.** indifference **2.** lack of emotion —**apa'thetic** *a.* —**apa'thetically** *adv.*

apatite ('æpətaɪt) *n.* common mineral consisting basically of calcium fluorophosphate

ape (eɪp) *n.* **1.** tailless primate (*eg* chimpanzee, gorilla) **2.** coarse, clumsy person **3.** imitator —*vt.* **4.** imitate —**'apish** *a.* —**'apishly** *adv.* —**'apeman** *n.* apelike primate thought to have been forerunner of modern man

aperient (ə'pɪərɪənt) *a.* **1.** mildly laxative —*n.* **2.** any mild laxative

aperiodic (eɪpɪərɪ'ɒdɪk) *a. Elec.* having no natural period or frequency

apéritif (əperɪ'tiːf) *n.* alcoholic appetizer

aperture ('æpətʃə) *n.* opening, hole

apex ('eɪpeks) *n.* **1.** top, peak **2.** vertex (*pl.* **-es**, **'apices**) —**'apical** *a.* of, at, or being apex

APEX ('eɪpeks) **1.** Advanced Purchase Excursion (reduced airline fare, paid for at least 30 days before departure) **2.** Association of Professional, Executive, Clerical and Computer Staff

aphasia (ə'feɪzɪə) *n.* dumbness or loss of speech control, due to disease of brain

aphelion (æp'hiːlɪən, ə'fiː-) *n.* point of planet's orbit farthest from sun (*pl.* **-lia** (-lɪə))

aphis ('eɪfɪs) *n.* any of various sap-sucking insects (*pl.* **aphides** ('eɪfɪdiːz)) —**'aphid** *n.* an aphis

aphorism ('æfərɪzəm) *n.* maxim, pithy saying —**'aphorist** *n.* —**apho'ristic** *a.*

aphrodisiac (æfrə'dɪzɪæk) *a.* **1.** exciting sexual desire —*n.* **2.** substance which so excites

apiary ('eɪpɪərɪ) *n.* place where bees are kept —**api'arian** or **'apian** *a.* —**'apiarist** *n.* beekeeper —**'apiculture** *n.* breeding and care of bees

apices ('æpɪsiːz, 'eɪ-) *n., pl. of* APEX

apiece (ə'piːs) *adv.* for each

aplomb (ə'plɒm) *n.* self-possession, coolness, assurance

apo- or **ap-** (*comb. form*) **1.** away from; off, as in *apogee* **2.** separation of, as in *apocarpous*

apocalypse (ə'pɒkəlɪps) *n.* **1.** prophetic revelation, *esp.* of St. John **2.** (A-) last book of New Testament —**apoca'lyptic** *a.* —**apoca'lyptically** *adv.*

apocrypha (ə'pɒkrɪfə) *n.* religious writing of doubtful authenticity —**a'pocryphal** *a.* spurious —**the Apocrypha** collective name for 14 books orig. in Old Testament

apodosis (ə'pɒdəsɪs) *n.* consequent clause in conditional sentence, as distinct from protasis or *if* clause (*pl.* **-oses** (-əsiːz))

apogee ('æpədʒiː) *n.* **1.** point of moon's or satellite's orbit farthest from the earth **2.** climax

apolitical (eɪpə'lɪtɪkəl) a. politically neutral

apologia (æpə'ləʊdʒɪə) n. written defence of one's beliefs, conduct etc.

apologue ('æpəlɒg) n. allegory, moral fable

apology (ə'pɒlədʒɪ) n. 1. acknowledgment of offence and expression of regret 2. written or spoken defence 3. (with for) poor substitute —**apolo'getic** a. —**apolo'getically** adv. —**apolo'getics** pl.n. (with sing. v.) branch of theology charged with defence of Christianity —a'**polo- gist** n. —a'**pologize** or -**gise** vi.

apophthegm or **apothegm** ('æpəθem) n. terse saying, maxim —**apophthegmatic** or **apothegmatic** (æpəθeg'mætɪk) a.

apoplexy ('æpəpleksɪ) n. loss of sense and oft. paralysis caused by broken or blocked blood vessel in brain —apo'**plectic** a.

apostasy (ə'pɒstəsɪ) n. abandonment of one's religious or other faith —a'**postate** n./a.

a posteriori (eɪ pɒsterɪ'ɔːraɪ, -rɪ, ɑː) 1. denoting form of inductive reasoning which arrives at causes from effects 2. empirical

apostle (ə'pɒsəl) n. 1. (oft. A-) one sent to preach the Gospel, esp. one of the first disciples of Jesus 2. founder of Christian church in a country 3. leader of reform —a'**postleship** n. —apostolic(al) (æpə'stɒlɪk(əl)) a. —**Apostles' Creed** concise statement of Christian beliefs —**Apostolic See** see of pope

apostrophe (ə'pɒstrəfɪ) n. 1. mark (') showing omission of letter or letters in word 2. digression to appeal to someone dead or absent —a'**postrophize** or -**phise** v.

apothecary (ə'pɒθɪkərɪ) n. old name for one who prepares and sells drugs, now chemist —**apothecaries' measure** system of liquid volume measure used in pharmacy in which 20 fluid ounces equal 1 pint

apothegm ('æpəθem) n. see APOPHTHEGM

apothem ('æpəθem) n. perpendicular from centre of regular polygon to any of its sides

apotheosis (əpɒθɪ'əʊsɪs) n. deification, act of raising any person or thing to status of a god (pl. -**ses** (-siːz)) —a'**potheosize** or -**ise** vt. 1. deify 2. glorify, idealize

appal or U.S. **appall** (ə'pɔːl) vt. dismay, terrify (-**ll**-) —ap'**palling** a. dreadful, terrible

appanage or **apanage** ('æpənɪdʒ) n. 1. land or other provision granted by king for support of esp. younger son 2. customary perquisite

apparatus (æpə'reɪtəs, -'rɑːtəs) n. 1. equip- ment, instruments, for performing any experi- ment, operation etc. 2. means by which something operates

apparel (ə'pærəl) n. 1. clothing —vt. 2. clothe (-**ll**-)

apparent (ə'pærənt) a. 1. seeming 2. obvious 3.

acknowledged, as in heir apparent —ap'**parent- ly** adv.

apparition (æpə'rɪʃən) n. appearance, esp. of ghost

appeal (ə'piːl) vi. 1. make earnest request 2. be attractive 3. refer, have recourse 4. apply to higher court —n. 5. request 6. reference 7. supplication —ap'**pealable** a. —ap'**pealing** a. 1. making appeal 2. pleasant, attractive —ap'**peal- ingly** adv. —ap'**pellant** n. one who appeals to higher court —**appellate** (ə'pelɪt) a. of appeals

appear (ə'pɪə) vi. 1. become visible or present 2. seem, be plain 3. be seen in public —ap'**pearance** n. 1. an appearing 2. aspect 3. pretence

appease (ə'piːz) vt. pacify, quiet, allay, satisfy —ap'**peasable** a. —ap'**peasement** n.

appellant (ə'pelənt) n. see APPEAL

appellation (æpɪ'leɪʃən) n. name —ap'**pella- tive** a./n.

append (ə'pend) vt. join on, add —ap'**pendage** n.

appendix (ə'pendɪks) n. 1. subsidiary addition to book etc. 2. Anat. projection, esp. small worm- shaped part of intestine (pl. -**dices** (-dɪsiːz), -**es**) —**appendi'ectomy** or **appen'dectomy** n. surgical removal of any appendage, esp. vermiform appendix —**appendi'citis** n. inflam- mation of vermiform appendix

apperception (æpə'sepʃən) n. 1. perception 2. apprehension 3. the mind's perception of itself as a conscious agent —apper'**ceive** vt.

appertain (æpə'teɪn) vi. belong, relate, be appropriate

appetence ('æpɪtəns) or **appetency** n. 1. desire, craving 2. sexual appetite —'**appetent** a.

appetite ('æpɪtaɪt) n. desire, inclination, esp. desire for food —ap'**petitive** a. —'**appetizer** or -**iser** n. something stimulating to appetite —'**appetizing** or -**ising** a. —'**appetizingly** or -**isingly** adv.

applaud (ə'plɔːd) v. 1. express approval (of) by hand-clapping —vt. 2. praise; approve —ap'**plauder** n. —ap'**plause** n. loud approval

apple ('æpəl) n. 1. round, firm, fleshy fruit 2. tree bearing it —**apple-pie bed** UK way of making bed to prevent person from entering it —**apple-pie order** inf. perfect order —**apple of one's eye** person or thing very much loved

appliance (ə'plaɪəns) n. piece of equipment, esp. electrical

appliqué (æ'pliːkeɪ) n. 1. ornaments, embroi- dery etc., secured to surface of material —vt. 2. ornament thus

apply (ə'plaɪ) vt. 1. utilize, employ 2. lay or place on 3. administer, devote —vi. 4. have reference (to) 5. make request (to) (-**lied**, -**lying**) —**applicability** (æplɪkə'bɪlɪtɪ) n. —**appli-**

cable (ˈæplɪkəbəl, əˈplɪkə-) a. relevant —**applicably** (ˈæplɪkəblɪ, əˈplɪkə-) adv. —**applicant** (ˈæplɪkənt) n. —**application** (æplɪˈkeɪʃən) n. **1.** applying something for a particular use **2.** relevance **3.** request for job etc. **4.** concentration, diligence —**applicator** (ˈæplɪkeɪtə) n. device, such as spatula, for applying medicine, glue etc. —**apˈplied** a. (of skill, science etc.) put to practical use

appoint (əˈpɔɪnt) vt. **1.** name for, assign to job or position **2.** fix, settle **3.** equip —**apˈpointment** n. **1.** engagement to meet **2.** (selection for a) job —pl. **3.** fittings

apportion (əˈpɔːʃən) vt. divide out in shares —**apˈportionment** n.

appose (əˈpəʊz) vt. **1.** place side by side **2.** place (something) near or against another thing

apposite (ˈæpəzɪt) a. suitable, apt —**appositely** a. —**appositeness** n. —**appoˈsition** n. **1.** proximity **2.** the placing of one word beside another

appraise (əˈpreɪz) vt. set price on, estimate value of —**apˈpraisable** a. —**apˈpraisal** or **apˈpraisement** n. —**apˈpraiser** n.

appreciate (əˈpriːʃɪeɪt, -sɪ-) vt. **1.** value at true worth **2.** be grateful for **3.** understand **4.** enjoy —vi. **5.** rise in value —**apˈpreciable** a. **1.** estimable **2.** substantial —**apˈpreciably** adv. —**appreciˈation** n. —**apˈpreciative** or **apˈpreciatory** a. capable of expressing pleasurable recognition —**apˈpreciator** n.

apprehend (æprɪˈhend) vt. **1.** seize by authority **2.** take hold of **3.** recognize, understand **4.** dread —**apprehensiˈbility** n. —**appreˈhensible** a. —**appreˈhension** n. **1.** dread, anxiety **2.** arrest **3.** conception **4.** ability to understand —**appreˈhensive** a.

apprentice (əˈprentɪs) n. **1.** person learning a trade under specified conditions **2.** novice —vt. **3.** bind as apprentice —**apˈprenticeship** n.

apprise or -**ize** (əˈpraɪz) vt. inform

appro (ˈæprəʊ) inf. approval

approach (əˈprəʊtʃ) v. **1.** draw near (to) —vt. **2.** set about **3.** address request to **4.** approximate to —n. **5.** a drawing near **6.** means of reaching or doing **7.** approximation **8.** (oft. pl.) friendly overture(s) —**approachaˈbility** n. —**apˈproachable** a.

approbation (æprəˈbeɪʃən) n. approval

appropriate (əˈprəʊprɪeɪt) vt. **1.** take for oneself **2.** put aside for particular purpose —a. (əˈprəʊprɪɪt) **3.** suitable, fitting —**apˈpropriately** adv. —**apˈpropriateness** n. —**appropriˈation** n. **1.** act of setting apart for purpose **2.** parliamentary vote of money —**apˈpropriative** a. —**apˈpropriator** n.

approve (əˈpruːv) vt. **1.** think well of, commend **2.** authorize, agree to —vi. **3.** (usu.

with of) take favourable view —**apˈproval** n. —**apˈprover** n. —**apˈprovingly** adv.

approx. approximate(ly)

approximate (əˈprɒksɪmɪt) a. **1.** very near, nearly correct **2.** inexact, imprecise —vt. (əˈprɒksɪmeɪt) **3.** bring close **4.** be almost the same as —vi. (əˈprɒksɪmeɪt) **5.** come near —**apˈproximately** adv. —**approxiˈmation** n. —**apˈproximative** a.

appurtenance (əˈpɜːtɪnəns) n. **1.** less significant thing or part **2.** accessory

Apr. April

après-ski (æpreɪˈskiː) n. social activities after day's skiing

apricot (ˈeɪprɪkɒt) n. **1.** orange-coloured stone-fruit related to plum —a. **2.** of the colour of the fruit

April (ˈeɪprəl) n. fourth month —**April fool** victim of practical joke performed on Apr. 1st (**April Fools' Day** or **All Fools' Day**)

a priori (eɪ praɪˈɔːraɪ, ɑː prɪˈɔːrɪ) a. **1.** denoting deductive reasoning from general principle to expected facts or effects **2.** denoting knowledge gained independently of experience

apron (ˈeɪprən) n. **1.** cloth, piece of leather etc., worn in front of body to protect clothes, or as part of official dress **2.** in theatre, strip of stage before curtain **3.** on airfield, tarmac area where aircraft stand, are loaded etc. **4.** fig. any of a variety of things resembling these —**tied to someone's apron strings** dominated by one's mother or wife

apropos (æprəˈpəʊ) adv. **1.** to the purpose **2.** by the way —a. **3.** apt, appropriate —**apropos of** concerning

apse (æps) n. arched recess, esp. in church —**apsidal** a.

apsis (ˈæpsɪs) n. either of two points lying at extremities of eccentric orbit of satellite etc. (pl. **apsides** (æpˈsaɪdɪːz)) (also **apse**)

apt (æpt) a. **1.** suitable **2.** likely **3.** prompt, quick-witted **4.** dexterous —**aptitude** n. capacity, fitness —**aptly** adv. —**aptness** n.

APT Advanced Passenger Train

apteryx (ˈæptərɪks) n. see KIWI (sense 1)

aqua (ˈækwə) n. **1.** water (pl. **aquae** (ˈækwiː), -s) —a. **2.** see AQUAMARINE (sense 2)

aqualung (ˈækwəlʌŋ) n. breathing apparatus used in underwater swimming

aquamarine (ækwəməˈriːn) n. **1.** variety of beryl used as gemstone —a. **2.** greenish-blue, sea-coloured

aquanaut (ˈækwənɔːt) n. person who works or swims underwater

aquaplane (ˈækwəpleɪn) n. **1.** plank or boat towed by fast motorboat —vi. **2.** ride on aquaplane **3.** (of car) be in contact with water on road, not with road surface —'**aquaplaning** n.

aquarium (ə'kwεərıəm) n. tank or pond for keeping aquatic animals or plants (pl. -s, -ria (-rıə))

Aquarius (ə'kwεərıəs) n. (the water-bearer) 11th sign of zodiac, operative c. Jan. 20th–Feb. 18th

aquatic (ə'kwætık) a. living, growing, done in or on water —a'**quatics** pl.n. water sports

aquatint ('ækwətınt) n. etching, engraving imitating drawings etc.

aqua vitae ('vıːtaı, 'vaıtiː) Lat. obs. brandy

aqueduct ('ækwıdʌkt) n. 1. artificial channel for water, esp. one like bridge 2. conduit

aqueous ('eıkwıəs) a. of, like, containing water —**aqueous humour** Physiol. fluid between cornea and lens of eye

aquilegia (ækwı'liːdʒıə) n. columbine

aquiline ('ækwılaın) a. 1. relating to eagle 2. hooked like eagle's beak

Ar Chem. argon

AR Arkansas

ar. 1. arrival 2. arrive(s)

Ar. 1. Arabic 2. Aramaic

Arab ('ærəb) n. 1. native of Arabia 2. general term for inhabitants of Middle Eastern countries 3. Arabian horse (small breed used for riding) —**Arabian** (ə'reıbıən) a. 1. of Arabia —n. 2. Arab —'**Arabic** n. 1. language of Arabs —a. 2. of Arabia or Arabs —**Arabic numeral** one of numbers 1,2,3,4,5,6,7,8,9,0

arabesque (ærə'bεsk) n. 1. classical ballet position 2. fanciful painted or carved ornament of Arabian origin —a. 3. (in style) of arabesque

arabis ('ærəbıs) n. low-growing garden plant with white, pink or lilac flowers

arable ('ærəb°l) a. suitable for ploughing or planting crops

Araby ('ærəbı) n. obs., poet. Arabia

arachnid (ə'ræknıd) n. one of the Arachnida (spiders, scorpions and mites) —a'**rachnoid** a. —arach'**nology** n.

arak ('ærək) n. see ARRACK

Aramaic (ærə'meıık) n. 1. ancient Semitic language of Middle East —a. 2. of, relating to or using this language

Aran ('ærən) a. (of sweaters etc.) made with naturally oily, unbleached wool, oft. with complicated pattern

arbiter ('ɑːbıtə) n. judge, umpire (-tress fem.) —ar'**bitrament** n. —'**arbitrarily** adv. —'**arbitrary** a. 1. not bound by rules, despotic 2. random —'**arbitrate** vt. 1. decide (dispute) 2. submit to, settle by arbitration —vi. 3. act as umpire —arbi'**tration** n. hearing, settling of disputes, esp. industrial and legal, by impartial referee(s) —'**arbitrator** n.

arbor ('ɑːbə) n. 1. rotating shaft in machine on which grinding wheel is fitted 2. rotating shaft

arboreal (ɑː'bɔːrıəl) a. relating to trees —**arbo'rescent** a. having characteristics of tree —**arbo'retum** n. place for cultivating specimens of trees (pl. -s, -ta (-tə)) —'**arboriculture** n. forestry, cultivation of trees

arbour ('ɑːbə) n. leafy glade etc., sheltered by trees

arbutus (ɑː'bjuːtəs) n. shrub having evergreen leaves and strawberry-like berries (pl. -es)

arc (ɑːk) n. 1. part of circumference of circle or similar curve 2. luminous electric discharge between two conductors —vi. 3. form an arc (**arced**, '**arcing** or **arcked**, '**arcking**) —**arc lamp** —**arc light**

arcade (ɑː'keıd) n. 1. row of arches on pillars 2. covered walk or avenue, esp. lined by shops

Arcadian (ɑː'keıdıən) a. 1. of idealized Arcadia of pastoral poetry 2. rustic, bucolic —n. 3. person who leads simple rural life

arcane (ɑː'keın) a. 1. mysterious 2. esoteric

arch[1] (ɑːtʃ) n. 1. curved structure in building, supporting itself over open space by pressure of stones one against the other 2. any similar structure 3. curved shape 4. curved part of sole of foot —v. 5. form, make into, an arch —**arched** a. —'**archway** n.

arch[2] (ɑːtʃ) a. 1. chief 2. experienced, expert 3. superior, knowing; coyly playful —'**archly** adv. —'**archness** n.

arch. 1. archaic 2. architecture

arch- or **archi-** (comb. form) chief, as in archangel, archenemy. Such words are not given here where the meaning may easily be inferred from the simple word

-arch (comb. form) leader; ruler; chief, as in patriarch, monarch

archaeology or **archeology** (ɑːkı'ɒlədʒı) n. study of ancient times from remains of art, implements etc. —**archaeo'logical** or **archeo'logical** a. —**archae'ologist** or **arche'ologist** n.

archaeopteryx (ɑːkı'ɒptərıks) n. extinct bird of Jurassic times, with teeth, long tail and well-developed wings

archaic (ɑː'keıık) a. old, primitive —ar'**chaically** adv. —'**archaism** n. obsolete word or phrase

archbishop ('ɑːtʃ'bıʃəp) n. chief bishop —'**arch'bishopric** n.

archdeacon ('ɑːtʃ'diːkən) n. chief deacon, clergyman next to bishop —'**arch'deaconry** n. —**archidiaconal** (ɑːkıdaı'ækən°l) a.

archdiocese ('ɑːtʃ'daıəsiːs) n. diocese of archbishop

archduke ('ɑːtʃ'djuːk) n. duke of specially high rank ('**arch'duchess** fem.) —'**arch'ducal** a. —'**arch'duchy** n.

archery ('ɑːtʃərɪ) *n.* skill, sport of shooting with bow and arrow —'**archer** *n.*

archetype ('ɑːkɪtaɪp) *n.* **1.** prototype **2.** perfect specimen —'**archetypal** *a.*

archfiend (ɑːtʃ'fiːnd) *n.* (*oft.* **A-**) the devil; Satan

archiepiscopal (ɑːkɪɪ'pɪskəpəl) *a.* of archbishop —**archie'piscopate** *n.*

archipelago (ɑːkɪ'pɛləgəʊ) *n.* **1.** group of islands **2.** sea full of small islands, *esp.* Aegean (*pl.* **-es**) —**archipelagic** (ɑːkɪpɪ'lædʒɪk) *a.*

architect ('ɑːkɪtɛkt) *n.* **1.** one qualified to design and supervise construction of buildings **2.** contriver —**architec'tonic** *a.* of or resembling architecture —**archi'tectural** *a.* —'**architecture** *n.*

architrave ('ɑːkɪtreɪv) *n. Archit.* **1.** lowest division of entablature **2.** ornamental band round door or window opening

archives ('ɑːkaɪvz) *pl.n.* **1.** collection of records, documents *etc.* about institution, family *etc.* **2.** place where these are kept —**ar'chival** *a.* —**archivist** ('ɑːkɪvɪst) *n.*

archpriest ('ɑːtʃ'priːst) *n.* **1.** formerly, chief assistant to bishop **2.** senior priest

Arctic ('ɑːktɪk) *a.* **1.** of northern polar regions **2.** (**a-**) very cold —*n.* **3.** region round North Pole —**Arctic Circle** imaginary circle around earth at latitude 66° 32′ N

ardent ('ɑːdənt) *a.* **1.** fiery **2.** passionate —'**ardency** *n.* —'**ardently** *adv.* —'**ardour** or *U.S.* '**ardor** *n.* **1.** enthusiasm **2.** zeal

arduous ('ɑːdjʊəs) *a.* **1.** hard to accomplish, difficult **2.** strenuous; laborious —'**arduously** *adv.* —'**arduousness** *n.*

are¹ (ɑː; *unstressed* ə) *pres. ind. pl. of* BE

are² (ɑː) *n.* unit of measure, 100 square metres

area ('ɛərɪə) *n.* **1.** extent, expanse of any surface **2.** two-dimensional expanse enclosed by boundary (**area** of square, circle *etc.*) **3.** region **4.** part, section **5.** subject, field of activity **6.** small sunken yard

areca ('ærɪkə, ə'riːkə) *n.* genus of palms, including betel palm

arena (ə'riːnə) *n.* **1.** enclosure for sports events *etc.* **2.** space in middle of amphitheatre or stadium **3.** sphere, scene of conflict

arenaceous (ærɪ'neɪʃəs) *a.* **1.** composed of sand **2.** growing in sandy soil

aren't (ɑːnt) **1.** contraction of are not **2.** *inf.*, *chiefly UK* (used in interrogative sentences) contraction of am not

areola (ə'riːələ) *n.* **1.** *Biol.* space outlined on surface, such as area between veins on leaf **2.** *Anat.* any small circular area, such as pigmented ring around human nipple (*pl.* **-lae** (-liː), **-s**)

arête (ə'reɪt) *n.* sharp ridge that separates glacial valleys

argent ('ɑːdʒənt) *n.* **1.** silver —*a.* **2.** silver, silvery-white, *esp.* in heraldry

argon ('ɑːgɒn) *n.* a gas, inert constituent of air

argosy ('ɑːgəsɪ) *n. Poet.* large richly-laden merchant ship

argot ('ɑːgəʊ) *n.* slang

argue ('ɑːgjuː) *vi.* **1.** quarrel, dispute **2.** offer reasons —*vt.* **3.** prove by reasoning **4.** discuss —'**arguable** *a.* —'**arguably** *adv.* as can be argued —'**arguer** *n.* —'**argument** *n.* **1.** quarrel **2.** reasoning **3.** discussion **4.** theme —**argumen'tation** *n.* —**argu'mentative** *a.*

Argus ('ɑːgəs) *n.* fabulous being with a hundred eyes —**Argus-eyed** *a.* watchful

aria ('ɑːrɪə) *n.* air or rhythmical song in cantata, opera *etc.*

arid ('ærɪd) *a.* **1.** parched with heat, dry **2.** dull —a'**ridity** *n.*

Aries ('ɛəriːz) *n.* (the ram) 1st sign of zodiac, operative c. Mar. 21st-Apr. 21st

aright (ə'raɪt) *adv.* rightly

arise (ə'raɪz) *vi.* **1.** come about **2.** get up **3.** rise (up), ascend (a'**rose**, **arisen** (ə'rɪzʰn), a'**rising**)

aristocracy (ærɪ'stɒkrəsɪ) *n.* **1.** nobility **2.** upper classes **3.** government by the best in birth or fortune —**a'ristocrat** *n.* —**aristo'cratic** *a.* **1.** noble **2.** elegant —**aristo'cratically** *adv.*

arithmetic (ə'rɪθmətɪk) *n.* **1.** science of numbers **2.** art of reckoning by figures —**arith'metic(al)** *a.* —**arith'metically** *adv.* —**arithme'tician** *n.* —**arithmetic mean** average value of set of terms or quantities, expressed as their sum divided by their number (*also* '**average**) —**arithmetic progression** sequence, each term of which differs from succeeding term by constant amount

ark (ɑːk) *n.* Noah's vessel

Ark (ɑːk) *n. Judaism* **1.** most sacred symbol of God's presence among Hebrew people, carried in their journey from Sinai to Promised Land (*also* **Ark of the Covenant**) **2.** receptacle for the scrolls of the Law (*also* **Holy Ark**)

arm¹ (ɑːm) *n.* **1.** limb extending from shoulder to wrist **2.** anything projecting from main body, as branch of sea, supporting rail of chair *etc.* **3.** sleeve —'**armlet** *n.* band worn round arm —'**armchair** *n.* —'**armful** *n.* —'**armhole** *n.* —'**armpit** *n.* hollow under arm at shoulder

arm² (ɑːm) *vt.* **1.** supply with weapons, furnish **2.** prepare (bomb *etc.*) for use —*vi.* **3.** take up arms —*n.* **4.** weapon **5.** branch of army —*pl.* **6.** weapons **7.** war, military exploits **8.** official heraldic symbols —'**armament** *n.*

armada (ɑː'mɑːdə) *n.* large number of ships or aircraft

armadillo (ɑːmə'dɪləʊ) *n.* small Amer.

burrowing mammal protected by bands of bony plates (*pl.* **-s**)

Armageddon (ɑːməˈgedən) *n.* **1.** *Bible* place designated as scene of final battle at end of world **2.** catastrophic and extremely destructive conflict

armature (ˈɑːmətjʊə) *n.* part of electric machine, *esp.* revolving structure in electric motor, generator

armistice (ˈɑːmɪstɪs) *n.* truce, suspension of fighting —**Armistice Day** anniversary of signing of armistice that ended World War I (*see also* **Remembrance Day** *at* REMEMBER)

armoire (ɑːmˈwɑː) *n.* large cabinet, orig. used for storing weapons

armour *or U.S.* **armor** (ˈɑːmə) *n.* **1.** defensive covering or dress **2.** plating of tanks, warships *etc.* **3.** armoured fighting vehicles, as tanks —**arˈmorial** *a.* relating to heraldic arms —**ˈarmourer** *or U.S.* **ˈarmorer** *n.* —**ˈarmoury** *or U.S.* **ˈarmory** *n.* —**armour plate** tough heavy steel oft. hardened on surface, used for protecting warships *etc.*

army (ˈɑːmɪ) *n.* **1.** large body of men armed for warfare and under military command **2.** host, great number

arnica (ˈɑːnɪkə) *n. Bot.* genus of hardy perennials. A tincture of *Arnica montana* is used for sprains and bruises

aroma (əˈrəʊmə) *n.* **1.** sweet smell, fragrance **2.** peculiar charm —**aroˈmatic** *a.* —**aˈromatize** *or* **-tise** *vt.*

arose (əˈrəʊz) *pt. of* ARISE

around (əˈraʊnd) *prep.* **1.** on all sides of **2.** somewhere in or near **3.** approximately (of time) —*adv.* **4.** on every side **5.** in a circle **6.** here and there, nowhere in particular **7.** *inf.* present in or at some place

arouse (əˈraʊz) *vt.* **1.** awaken **2.** stimulate

arpeggio (ɑːˈpedʒɪəʊ) *n. Mus.* **1.** notes sounded in quick succession, not together **2.** chord so played (*pl.* **-s**)

arquebus (ˈɑːkwɪbəs) *or* **harquebus** (ˈhɑː-) *n.* portable gun dating from 15th century

arr. 1. arranged **2.** arrival **3.** arrive(d)

arrack *or* **arak** (ˈærək) *n.* coarse spirit distilled from rice *etc.*

arraign (əˈreɪn) *vt.* accuse, indict, put on trial —**arˈraigner** *n.* —**arˈraignment** *n.*

arrange (əˈreɪndʒ) *vt.* **1.** set in order **2.** arrive at agreement about **3.** plan **4.** adapt, as music **5.** settle, as dispute —**arˈrangement** *n.*

arrant (ˈærənt) *a.* downright, notorious —**ˈarrantly** *adv.*

arras (ˈærəs) *n.* tapestry

array (əˈreɪ) *n.* **1.** order, *esp.* military order **2.** dress **3.** imposing show, splendour —*vt.* **4.** set in order **5.** dress, equip, adorn

arrears (əˈrɪəz) *pl.n.* amount unpaid or undone

arrest (əˈrest) *vt.* **1.** detain by legal authority **2.** stop **3.** catch (attention) —*n.* **4.** seizure by warrant **5.** making prisoner —**arˈresting** *a.* attracting attention, striking —**arˈrestor** *n.* **1.** person who arrests **2.** mechanism to stop or slow moving object

arrière-pensée (arjɛrpɑ̃ˈse) *Fr.* hidden meaning or purpose

arris (ˈærɪs) *n.* sharp ridge or edge

arrive (əˈraɪv) *vi.* **1.** reach destination **2.** (*with* at) reach, attain **3.** *inf.* succeed —**arˈrival** *n.*

arrivederci (arriveˈdɛrtʃi) *It.* goodbye

arriviste (æriːˈviːst) *n.* person who is unscrupulously ambitious

arrogance (ˈærəgəns) *n.* aggressive conceit —**ˈarrogant** *a.* **1.** proud **2.** overbearing —**ˈarrogantly** *adv.*

arrogate (ˈærəgeɪt) *vt.* **1.** claim for oneself without justification **2.** attribute to another without justification

arrow (ˈærəʊ) *n.* pointed shaft shot from bow —**ˈarrowhead** *n.* **1.** head of arrow **2.** any triangular shape

arrowroot (ˈærəʊruːt) *n.* nutritious starch from W Indian plant, used as a food

arsenal (ˈɑːsənˈl) *n.* magazine of stores for warfare, guns, ammunition

arsenic (ˈɑːsnɪk) *n.* **1.** soft, grey, metallic element **2.** its oxide, a powerful poison —**arˈsenical** *a.* —**arsenious** (ɑːˈsiːnɪəs) *a.*

arson (ˈɑːsən) *n.* crime of intentionally setting property on fire

art (ɑːt) *n.* **1.** skill **2.** human skill as opposed to nature **3.** creative skill in painting, poetry, music *etc.* **4.** any of the works produced thus **5.** profession, craft **6.** knack **7.** contrivance, cunning, trick **8.** system of rules —*pl.* **9.** certain branches of learning, languages, history *etc.*, as distinct from natural science **10.** wiles —**ˈartful** *a.* wily —**ˈartfully** *adv.* —**ˈartfulness** *n.* —**ˈartist** *n.* **1.** one who practises fine art, *esp.* painting **2.** one who makes his craft a fine art —**arˈtiste** *n.* professional entertainer, singer, dancer *etc.* —**arˈtistic** *a.* —**arˈtistically** *adv.* —**ˈartistry** *n.* —**ˈartless** *a.* natural, frank —**ˈartlessly** *adv.* —**ˈartlessness** *n.* —**ˈarty** *a.* ostentatiously artistic

art. 1. article **2.** artificial

artefact *or* **artifact** (ˈɑːtɪfækt) *n.* something made by man, *esp.* by hand

arteriosclerosis (ɑːtɪərɪəʊsklɪˈrəʊsɪs) *n.* hardening of the arteries (*pl.* **-ses** (-sɪːz))

artery (ˈɑːtərɪ) *n.* **1.** one of tubes carrying blood from heart **2.** any main channel of communications —**arˈterial** *a.* **1.** pert. to an artery **2.** main, important, as in *arterial road*

artesian well (ɑː'tiːzɪən) deep well in which water rises by internal pressure

arthritis (ɑː'θraɪtɪs) n. painful inflammation of joint(s) —**arthritic** (ɑː'θrɪtɪk) a./n.

arthropod ('ɑːθrəpɒd) n. animal with jointed limbs and segmented body, eg insect, spider

artic (ɑː'tɪk) inf. articulated lorry

artichoke ('ɑːtɪtʃəʊk) n. 1. thistlelike perennial 2. its edible flower —**Jerusalem artichoke** sunflower with edible tubers like potato

article ('ɑːtɪkəl) n. 1. item, object 2. short written piece 3. paragraph, section 4. Gram. words the, a, an 5. clause in contract 6. rule, condition —vt. 7. bind as apprentice

articular (ɑː'tɪkjʊlə) a. of joints or structural components in joint

articulate (ɑː'tɪkjʊlɪt) a. 1. able to express oneself fluently 2. (of speech) clear, distinct —vt. (ɑː'tɪkjʊleɪt) 4. joint 5. utter distinctly —vi. (ɑː'tɪkjʊleɪt) 6. speak —**articulated** a. jointed —**ar'ticulately** adv. —**ar'ticulateness** n. —**articu'lation** n.

artifice ('ɑːtɪfɪs) n. 1. contrivance 2. trick 3. cunning; skill —**ar'tificer** n. craftsman —**artificial** a. 1. manufactured, synthetic 2. insincere —**artifici'ality** n. —**arti'ficially** adv. —**artificial respiration** method of restarting person's breathing after it has stopped

artillery (ɑː'tɪlərɪ) n. 1. large guns on wheels 2. troops who use them

artisan ('ɑːtɪzæn, ɑːtɪ'zæn) n. craftsman; skilled mechanic; manual worker

artiste (ɑː'tiːst) n. see ART

Art Nouveau ('ɑː nuː'vəʊ; Fr. ar nu'vo) style of art and architecture of 1890s, characterized by sinuous outlines and stylized natural forms

arum lily ('ɛərəm) plant with large white flower

-ary (comb. form) 1. of; related to; belonging to, as in cautionary 2. person or thing connected with, as in missionary, aviary

Aryan ('ɛərɪən) a. relating to Indo-European family of nations and languages

as (æz, əz) adv./conj. denoting 1. comparison 2. similarity 3. equality 4. identity 5. concurrence 6. reason

As Chem. arsenic

AS 1. Anglo-Saxon (also **A.S.**) 2. antisubmarine

A.S.A. 1. UK Amateur Swimming Association 2. US American Standards Association

asafoetida or **asafetida** (æsə'fetɪdə) n. bitter resin with unpleasant smell, obtained from roots of some umbelliferous plants

asap as soon as possible

asbestos (æs'bestɒs) n. fibrous mineral which does not burn —**asbestosis** (æsbes'təʊsɪs) n. lung disease caused by inhalation of asbestos fibre

ascend (ə'sɛnd) vi. 1. climb, rise —vt. 2. walk up, climb, mount —as'cendancy or as'cendency n. control, dominance —as'cendant or as'cendent a. rising —as'cension n. —as'cent n. rise

Ascension Day (ə'sɛnʃən) 40th day after Easter, when Ascension of Christ into heaven is celebrated

ascertain (æsə'teɪn) vt. get to know, find out, determine —ascer'tainable a. —ascer'tainment n.

ascetic (ə'sɛtɪk) n. 1. one who practises severe self-denial —a. 2. rigidly abstinent, austere —as'cetically adv. —as'ceticism n.

ascorbic acid (ə'skɔːbɪk) vitamin C, present in green vegetables, citrus fruits etc.

ascribe (ə'skraɪb) vt. attribute, impute, assign —as'cribable a. —ascription (ə'skrɪpʃən) n.

aseptic (ə'sɛptɪk, eɪ-) a. germ-free —a'sepsis n.

asexual (eɪ'sɛksjʊəl) a. without sex

ash¹ (æʃ) n. 1. dust or remains of anything burnt —pl. 2. ruins 3. remains, eg of cremated body —'ashen a. 1. like ashes 2. pale —'ashy a. —**ash can** US dustbin (also garbage can, ash bin, trash can) —'ashtray n. receptacle for tobacco ash, cigarette butts etc. —**Ash Wednesday** first day of Lent —**the Ashes** symbol of victory in cricket test-match series between England and Australia

ash² (æʃ) n. 1. deciduous timber tree 2. its wood —'ashen a.

ashamed (ə'ʃeɪmd) a. affected with shame, abashed

ashlar or **ashler** ('æʃlə) n. hewn or squared building stone

ashore (ə'ʃɔː) adv. towards or on shore

ashram ('æʃrəm) n. religious retreat or community where Hindu holy man lives

Asian ('eɪʃən, 'eɪʒən) a. 1. pert. to continent of Asia —n. 2. native of Asia or descendant of one —Asi'atic a.

aside (ə'saɪd) adv. 1. to or on one side 2. privately —n. 3. words spoken in an undertone not to be heard by some person present

asinine ('æsɪnaɪn) a. of or like an ass, silly —asininity (æsɪ'nɪnɪtɪ) n.

ask (ɑːsk) vt. 1. request, require, question, invite —vi. 2. make inquiry or request

askance (ə'skæns) or **askant** (ə'skænt) adv. 1. sideways, awry 2. with a side look or meaning —**look askance** view with suspicion

askew (ə'skjuː) adv. awry

aslant (ə'slɑːnt) adv. on the slant, obliquely, athwart

asleep (ə'sliːp) a. sleeping, at rest

ASLEF ('æzlɛf) Associated Society of Locomotive Engineers and Firemen

asocial (eɪˈsəʊʃəl) a. 1. avoiding contact 2. unconcerned about welfare of others 3. hostile to society

asp (æsp) n. small venomous snake

asparagus (əˈspærəgəs) n. plant whose young shoots are a table delicacy

aspect (ˈæspekt) n. 1. look 2. view 3. appearance 4. expression

aspen (ˈæspən) n. type of poplar tree

asperity (æˈsperɪtɪ) n. 1. roughness 2. harshness 3. coldness

aspersion (əˈspɜːʃən) n. 1. (usu. in pl.) malicious remarks 2. slanderous attack

asphalt (ˈæsfælt) n. black, hard bituminous substance used for road surfaces etc. —asˈphaltic a.

asphodel (ˈæsfədel) n. plant with clusters of yellow or white flowers

asphyxia (æsˈfɪksɪə) n. suffocation —asˈphyxiate v. —asˈphyxiated a. —asphyxiˈation n.

aspic (ˈæspɪk) n. 1. jelly used to coat meat, eggs, fish etc. 2. Bot. species of lavender

aspidistra (æspɪˈdɪstrə) n. plant with broad tapered leaves

aspire (əˈspaɪə) vi. 1. desire eagerly 2. rise to great height —aspirant (ˈæspɪrənt) n. 1. one who aspires 2. candidate —aspirate (ˈæspɪreɪt) vt. pronounce with full breathing, as 'h' —aspiration (æspɪˈreɪʃən) n. —aspirator (ˈæspɪreɪtə) n. device employing suction, such as jet pump or one for removing fluids from body cavity —asˈpiring a. —asˈpiringly adv.

aspirin (ˈæsprɪn) n. (a tablet of) drug used to allay pain and fever

ass (æs) n. 1. quadruped of horse family 2. stupid person

assagai (ˈæsəgaɪ) n. see ASSEGAI

assail (əˈseɪl) vt. attack, assault —asˈsailable a. —asˈsailant n.

assassin (əˈsæsɪn) n. 1. one who kills, esp. prominent person, by treacherous violence 2. murderer —asˈsassinate vt. —assassiˈnation n.

assault (əˈsɔːlt) n. 1. attack, esp. sudden —vt. 2. attack —assault and battery Law threat of attack to person followed by actual attack

assay (əˈseɪ) v. 1. test (esp. proportions of metals) in alloy or ore —n. (əˈseɪ, ˈæseɪ) 2. analysis, esp. of metals 3. trial, test —asˈsayer n.

assegai or **assagai** (ˈæsəgaɪ) n. slender spear of S Afr. tribes

assemble (əˈsembəl) v. 1. meet, bring together 2. collect —vt. 3. put together (of machinery etc.) —asˈsemblage n. —asˈsembly n. 1. gathering, meeting 2. assembling —asˈsembly line sequence of machines, workers in factory assembling product

assent (əˈsent) vi. 1. concur, agree —n. 2. acquiescence, agreement, compliance

assert (əˈsɜːt) vt. 1. declare strongly 2. insist upon —asˈsertion n. —asˈsertive a. —asˈsertively adv.

assess (əˈses) vt. 1. fix value of 2. evaluate, estimate, esp. for taxation 3. fix amount of (tax or fine) 4. impose tax or fine on (a person etc.) —asˈsessable a. —asˈsessment n. —asˈsessor n.

asset (ˈæset) n. 1. valuable or useful person, thing —pl. 2. property available to pay debts, esp. of insolvent debtor —asset-stripping n. Comm. practice of taking over a company at low price and then selling assets piecemeal

asseverate (əˈsevəreɪt) vt. assert solemnly —asseveˈration n.

assiduous (əˈsɪdjʊəs) a. persevering, attentive, diligent —assiˈduity n. —asˈsiduously adv.

assign (əˈsaɪn) vt. 1. appoint to job etc. 2. allot, apportion, fix 3. ascribe 4. transfer —n. 5. assignee —asˈsignable a. —assignation (æsɪgˈneɪʃən) n. 1. secret meeting 2. appointment to meet —assignee (æsɪˈniː) n. Law person to whom property etc. is transferred —asˈsignment n. 1. act of assigning 2. allotted duty —assignor (æsɪˈnɔː) n.

assimilate (əˈsɪmɪleɪt) vt. 1. learn and understand 2. make similar 3. absorb into the system —asˈsimilable a. —assimiˈlation n. —asˈsimilative a.

assist (əˈsɪst) v. 1. give help 2. work as assistant (to) —asˈsistance n. —asˈsistant n. helper

assizes (əˈsaɪzɪz) pl.n. formerly, law court held in each area or county of England and Wales

assn. association

assoc. 1. associated 2. association

associate (əˈsəʊʃɪeɪt, -sɪ-) vt. 1. link, connect, esp. as ideas in mind 2. join —vi. 3. keep company 4. combine, unite —n. (əˈsəʊʃɪɪt) 5. companion, partner 6. friend, ally 7. subordinate member of association —a. (əˈsəʊʃɪɪt) 8. affiliated —associˈation n. society, club —association football 1. see SOCCER 2. A Australian Rules played in football association rather than league

assonance (ˈæsənəns) n. 1. likeness in sound 2. rhyming of vowels only —ˈassonant a.

assort (əˈsɔːt) vt. 1. classify, arrange —vi. 2. match, agree, harmonize —asˈsorted a. mixed —asˈsortment n.

ASSR Autonomous Soviet Socialist Republic

asst. assistant

assuage (əˈsweɪdʒ) vt. 1. soften, pacify 2. soothe —asˈsuagement n.

assume (əˈsjuːm) vt. 1. take for granted 2. pretend to 3. take upon oneself 4. claim

—**assumption** (ə'sʌmpʃən) n. —**assumptive** (ə'sʌmptɪv) a.

assure (ə'ʃʊə) vt. 1. tell positively, promise 2. make sure 3. insure against loss, esp. of life 4. affirm —**as'surance** n. —**as'sured** a. sure —**assuredly** (ə'ʃʊərɪdlɪ) adv.

A.S.T. US, C Atlantic Standard Time

astatic (æ'stætɪk, eɪ-) a. Phys. having no tendency to take fixed position

astatine ('æstətiːn) n. radioactive element that occurs naturally in minute amounts and is artificially produced by bombarding bismuth with alpha particles

aster ('æstə) n. 1. plant with starlike flowers 2. Michaelmas daisy

asterisk ('æstərɪsk) n. 1. star (*) used in printing —vt. 2. mark thus —**'asterism** n.

astern (ə'stɜːn) adv. 1. in or towards the stern 2. backwards

asteroid ('æstərɔɪd) n. 1. small planet —a. 2. star-shaped

asthma ('æsmə) n. illness in which one has difficulty in breathing —**asth'matic** a./n. —**asth'matically** adv.

astigmatism (ə'stɪɡmətɪzəm) or **astigmia** (ə'stɪɡmɪə) n. inability of lens (esp. of eye) to focus properly —**astig'matic** a.

astilbe (ə'stɪlbɪ) n. plant with ornamental pink or white flowers

astir (ə'stɜː) a. 1. on the move 2. out of bed 3. in excitement

A.S.T.M.S. Association of Scientific, Technical, and Managerial Staffs

astonish (ə'stɒnɪʃ) vt. amaze, surprise —**a'stonishing** a. —**a'stonishment** n.

astound (ə'staʊnd) vt. 1. astonish greatly 2. stun with amazement —**a'stounding** a. startling

astraddle (ə'strædəl) a. 1. with a leg on either side of something —prep. 2. astride

astrakhan (æstrə'kæn) n. lambskin with curled wool

astral ('æstrəl) a. of the stars or spirit world —**astral body**

astray (ə'streɪ) adv. 1. off the right path 2. in error

astride (ə'straɪd) adv. 1. with the legs apart —prep. 2. straddling

astringent (ə'strɪndʒənt) a. 1. severe, harsh 2. sharp 3. constricting (body tissues, blood vessels etc.) —n. 4. astringent substance —**as'tringency** n.

astro- (comb. form) indicating star or star-shaped structure

astrol. astrology

astrolabe ('æstrəleɪb) n. instrument used by early astronomers to measure altitude of stars etc.

astrology (ə'strɒlədʒɪ) n. 1. foretelling of events by stars 2. medieval astronomy —**as'trologer** n. —**astro'logical** a.

astrometry (ə'strɒmɪtrɪ) n. determination of apparent magnitudes of fixed stars

astron. astronomy

astronaut ('æstrənɔːt) n. one trained for travel in space —**astro'nautics** pl.n. (with sing. v.) science and technology of space flight

astronomy (ə'strɒnəmɪ) n. scientific study of heavenly bodies —**as'tronomer** n. —**astro'nomical** a. 1. very large 2. of astronomy —**astronomical unit** unit of distance used in astronomy equal to the mean distance between the earth and the sun

astrophysics (æstrəʊ'fɪzɪks) n. the science of the chemical and physical characteristics of heavenly bodies —**astro'physical** a. —**astro'physicist** n.

astute (ə'stjuːt) a. perceptive, shrewd —**as'tutely** adv. —**as'tuteness** n.

asunder (ə'sʌndə) adv. 1. apart 2. in pieces

asylum (ə'saɪləm) n. 1. refuge, sanctuary, place of safety 2. old name for home for care of the unfortunate, esp. of mentally ill

asymmetry (æ'sɪmɪtrɪ, eɪ-) n. lack of symmetry —**asym'metric(al)** a.

asymptote ('æsɪmtəʊt) n. straight line that continually approaches a curve, but never meets it

asyndeton (æ'sɪndɪtən) n. omission of conjunctions between parts of sentence (pl. -deta (-dɪtə)) —**asyn'detic** a. without conjunctions or cross-references

at (æt) prep./adv. denoting 1. location in space or time 2. rate 3. condition or state 4. amount 5. direction 6. cause

At Chem. astatine

at. 1. atmosphere 2. atomic

ataraxia (ætə'ræksɪə) or **ataraxy** ('ætəræksɪ) n. calmness, emotional tranquillity

atavism ('ætəvɪzəm) n. appearance of ancestral, not parental, characteristics in human beings, animals or plants —**ata'vistic** a.

ataxia (ə'tæksɪə) or **ataxy** (ə'tæksɪ) n. lack of muscular coordination

A.T.C. 1. air traffic control 2. UK Air Training Corps

ate (ɛt, eɪt) pt. of EAT

-ate¹ (comb. form) 1. having appearance or characteristics of, as in fortunate 2. chemical compound, esp. salt or ester of acid, as in carbonate 3. product of process, as in condensate 4. forming verbs from nouns and adjectives, as in hyphenate

-ate² (comb. form) office, rank or group having certain function, as in episcopate

atelier ('ætəljeɪ) n. workshop, artist's studio

atheism ('eɪθɪɪzəm) n. belief that there is no God —'**atheist** n. —**athe'istic(al)** a.

athenaeum or U.S. **atheneum** (æθɪ'niːəm) n. 1. institution for promotion of learning 2. building containing reading room or library

atherosclerosis (æθərəʊsklɪə'rəʊsɪs) n. degenerative disease of arteries characterized by thickening of arterial walls, caused by deposits of fatty material (pl. **-oses** (-əʊsɪz))

athlete ('æθliːt) n. 1. one trained for physical exercises, feats or contests of strength 2. one good at sports —**athletic** (æθ'lɛtɪk) a. —**athletically** (æθ'lɛtɪkəlɪ) adv. —**athleticism** (æθ'lɛtɪsɪzəm) n. —**athletics** (æθ'lɛtɪks) pl.n. (with sing. v.) sports such as running, jumping, throwing etc. —**athlete's foot** fungal infection of skin of foot, esp. between toes and on soles

at-home n. 1. social gathering in person's home 2. occasion when school etc. is open for inspection by public (also **open day**)

athwart (ə'θwɔːt) prep. 1. across —adv. 2. across, esp. obliquely

Atlantic (ət'læntɪk) n. 1. (short for **Atlantic Ocean**) world's second largest ocean —a. 2. of or bordering Atlantic Ocean 3. of Atlas or Atlas Mountains

Atlantis (ət'læntɪs) n. in ancient legend, continent said to have sunk beneath Atlantic west of Gibraltar

atlas ('ætləs) n. volume of maps

atm. 1. atmosphere 2. atmospheric

atmosphere ('ætməsfɪə) n. 1. mass of gas surrounding heavenly body, esp. the earth 2. prevailing tone or mood (of place etc.) 3. unit of pressure in cgs system —**atmospheric** (ætməs'fɛrɪk) a. —**atmospherics** (ætməs'fɛrɪks) pl.n. noises in radio reception due to electrical disturbance in the atmosphere

at. no. atomic number

atoll ('ætɒl) n. ring-shaped coral island enclosing lagoon

atom ('ætəm) n. 1. smallest unit of an element which can enter into chemical combination 2. any very small particle —a'**tomic** a. of, arising from atoms —ato'**micity** n. number of atoms in molecule of an element —'**atomize** or **-ise** vt. reduce to atoms or small particles —'**atomizer** or **-iser** n. instrument for discharging liquids in fine spray —**atom bomb** or **atomic bomb** bomb whose immense power derives from nuclear fission or fusion, nuclear bomb —**atomic energy** nuclear energy —**atomic number** the number of protons in the nucleus of an atom —**atomic pile** see **reactor** at REACT —**atomic theory** 1. any theory in which matter is regarded as consisting of atoms 2. current concept of atom as entity with definite structure —**atomic weight** the weight of an atom of an element relative to that of carbon 12

atonality (eɪtəʊ'nælɪtɪ) n. 1. absence of or disregard for established musical key in composition 2. principles of composition embodying this

atone (ə'təʊn) vi. 1. make reparation, amends 2. give satisfaction —a'**tonement** n.

atonic (eɪ'tɒnɪk, æ-) a. unaccented

atop (ə'tɒp) adv. 1. at or on the top —prep. 2. above

atrocious (ə'trəʊʃəs) a. 1. extremely cruel or wicked 2. horrifying 3. inf. very bad —a'**trociously** adv. —**atrocity** (ə'trɒsɪtɪ) n. wickedness

atrophy ('ætrəfɪ) n. 1. wasting away, emaciation —vi. 2. waste away, become useless

atropine ('ætrəpɪn) n. poisonous alkaloid obtained from deadly nightshade

att. 1. attention 2. attorney

attach (ə'tætʃ) v. 1. join, fasten 2. unite 3. be connected 4. attribute 5. appoint 6. seize by law —at'**tached** a. (with to) fond (of) —at'**tachment** n.

attaché (ə'tæʃeɪ) n. specialist attached to diplomatic mission (pl. **-s**) —**attaché case** small leather hand-case for papers

attack (ə'tæk) vt. 1. take action against (in war, sport etc.) 2. criticize 3. set about with vigour 4. affect adversely —n. 5. attacking action 6. bout

attain (ə'teɪn) vt. 1. arrive at 2. reach, gain by effort, accomplish —attaina'**bility** n. —at'**tainable** a. —at'**tainment** n. esp. personal accomplishment

attainder (ə'teɪndə) n. Hist. loss of rights through conviction of high treason

attar ('ætə), **otto** ('ɒtəʊ), or **ottar** ('ɒtə) n. fragrant oil made esp. from rose petals

attempt (ə'tɛmpt) vt. 1. try, endeavour —n. 2. trial, effort

attend (ə'tɛnd) vt. 1. be present at 2. accompany —vi. (with to) 3. take care (of) 4. give the mind (to), pay attention (to) —at'**tendance** n. 1. an attending 2. presence 3. persons attending —at'**tendant** n./a. —at'**tention** n. 1. notice 2. heed 3. act of attending 4. care 5. courtesy 6. alert position in military drill —at'**tentive** a. —at'**tentively** adv. —at'**tentiveness** n.

attenuate (ə'tɛnjʊeɪt) v. 1. weaken or become weak 2. make or become thin —at'**tenuated** a. —attenu'**ation** n. reduction of intensity

attest (ə'tɛst) vt. bear witness to, certify —atte'**station** n. formal confirmation by oath etc. —at'**tested** a. UK (of cattle etc.) certified free from disease, esp. tuberculosis

attic ('ætɪk) n. space within roof where ceiling follows line of roof

Attic ('ætɪk) a. 1. of Attica, esp. its dialect 2. classically pure

attire (ə'taɪə) vt. 1. dress, array —n. 2. dress, clothing

attitude ('ætɪtjuːd) n. 1. mental view, opinion 2. posture, pose 3. disposition, behaviour —**atti'tudinize** or **-nise** vi. assume affected attitudes

attorney (ə'tɜːnɪ) n. one legally appointed to act for another, esp. a lawyer (pl. **-s**)

attract (ə'trækt) vt. 1. draw (attention etc.) 2. arouse interest of 3. cause to come closer (as magnet etc.) —**at'traction** n. 1. power to attract 2. something offered so as to interest, please —**at'tractive** a. —**at'tractively** adv. —**at'tractiveness** n.

attribute (ə'trɪbjuːt) vt. 1. regard (with with to) as belonging (to) or produced (by) —n. ('ætrɪbjuːt) 2. quality, property or characteristic of anything —**at'tributable** a. —**attri'bution** n. —**at'tributive** a. —**at'tributively** adv.

attrition (ə'trɪʃən) n. 1. wearing away of strength etc. 2. rubbing away, friction

attune (ə'tjuːn) vt. 1. tune, harmonize 2. make accordant

A.T.V. UK Associated Television

at. wt. atomic weight

atypical (eɪ'tɪpɪkəl) a. not typical

Au Chem. gold

aubergine ('əʊbəʒiːn) n. edible, purple fruit of the eggplant

aubrietia or **aubretia** (ɔː'briːʃə) n. trailing plant with purple flowers

auburn ('ɔːbən) a. 1. reddish-brown —n. 2. this colour

au courant (o ku'rā) Fr. 1. up-to-date 2. acquainted

auction ('ɔːkʃən) n. 1. public sale in which bidder offers increase of price over another and what is sold goes to one who bids highest —vt. 2. (oft. with off) sell by auction —**auctio'neer** n. —**auction bridge** card game —**Dutch auction** auction in which price starts high and is reduced until purchaser is found

audacious (ɔː'deɪʃəs) a. 1. bold 2. daring, impudent —**audacity** (ɔː'dæsɪtɪ) n.

audible ('ɔːdɪbəl) a. able to be heard —**audi'bility** n. —'**audibly** adv.

audience ('ɔːdɪəns) n. 1. assembly of hearers 2. act of hearing 3. judicial hearing 4. formal interview

audio- (comb. form) relating to sound or hearing

audio frequency ('ɔːdɪəʊ) frequency in audible range of 50 hertz to 20 000 hertz

audiometer (ɔːdɪ'ɒmɪtə) n. instrument for testing hearing

audiotypist ('ɔːdɪəʊtaɪpɪst) n. typist trained to type from dictating machine

audiovisual (ɔːdɪəʊ'vɪzjʊəl) a. (esp. of teaching aids) involving, directed at, both sight and hearing, as film etc.

audit ('ɔːdɪt) n. 1. formal examination or settlement of accounts —vt. 2. examine (accounts) —'**auditor** n.

audition (ɔː'dɪʃən) n. 1. screen or other test of prospective performer 2. hearing —v. 3. conduct or be tested in such a test —**audi'torium** n. 1. place where audience sits 2. hall (pl. **-s**, **-ia** (-ɪə)) —'**auditory** a. pert. to sense of hearing

A.U.E.W. Amalgamated Union of Engineering Workers

au fait (o 'fɛ) Fr. 1. fully informed 2. expert

auf Wiedersehen (auf 'viːdərzeːən) Ger. goodbye

Aug. August

Augean (ɔː'dʒiːən) a. extremely dirty

auger ('ɔːgə) n. carpenter's tool for boring holes, large gimlet

aught or **ought** (ɔːt) Lit., obs. n. 1. anything —adv. 2. UK dial. to any extent

augment (ɔːg'mɛnt) v. increase, enlarge —**augmen'tation** n. —**aug'mentative** a. increasing in force

au gratin (o gra'tɛ̃) Fr. with browned breadcrumbs and sometimes cheese

augur ('ɔːgə) n. 1. among the Romans, soothsayer —v. 2. be a sign of future events, foretell —**augural** ('ɔːgjʊrəl) a. —**augury** ('ɔːgjʊrɪ) n.

august (ɔː'gʌst) a. majestic, dignified

August ('ɔːgəst) n. eighth month

Augustan (ɔː'gʌstən) a. 1. of Augustus, the Roman Emperor 2. classic, distinguished, as applied to a period of literature

auk (ɔːk) n. northern web-footed seabird with short wings used only as paddles

au lait (əʊ 'leɪ) with milk

auld lang syne ('ɔːld læŋ 'saɪn) times past, esp. those remembered with nostalgia

au naturel (o naty'rɛl) Fr. 1. naked; nude 2. uncooked or plainly cooked

aunt (ɑːnt) n. 1. father's or mother's sister 2. uncle's wife —'**auntie** or '**aunty** n. 1. inf. aunt 2. (A-) sl. British Broadcasting Corporation —**Aunt Sally** UK 1. figure used as target in fairground 2. person who is target for insults or criticism

au pair (əʊ 'pɛə) young foreigner who receives free board and lodging in return for housework etc.

aura ('ɔːrə) n. 1. quality, air, atmosphere considered distinctive of person or thing 2. medical symptom warning of impending epileptic fit etc.

aural ('ɔːrəl) a. of, by ear —'**aurally** adv.

aureate ('ɔːrɪɪt) a. 1. covered with gold; gilded

2. (of style of writing or speaking) excessively elaborate

aureole ('ɔːrɪəʊl) *or* **aureola** (ɔː'rɪːələ) *n.* **1.** gold disc round head in sacred pictures **2.** halo

au revoir (o rə'vwaːr) *Fr.* goodbye

auricle ('ɔːrɪkᵊl) *n.* **1.** outside ear **2.** upper cavity of heart —**au'ricular** *a.* **1.** of the auricle **2.** aural

auricula (ɔː'rɪkjʊlə) *n.* **1.** widely cultivated alpine primrose with leaves shaped like bear's ear (*also* **bear's ear**) **2.** *Biol.* ear-shaped part (*also* **auricle**) (*pl.* **-lae** (-liː), **-s**)

auriferous (ɔː'rɪfərəs) *a.* gold-bearing

aurochs ('ɔːrɒks) *n.* species of wild ox, now extinct

aurora (ɔː'rɔːrə) *n.* **1.** lights in the atmosphere seen radiating from regions of the poles. The northern is called **aurora borealis** and the southern, **aurora australis 2.** *Poet.* dawn (*pl.* **-s**)

auscultation (ɔːskəl'teɪʃən) *n.* listening to movement of heart and lungs with stethoscope —**'auscultator** *n.* —**aus'cultatory** *a.*

auspice ('ɔːspɪs) *n.* **1.** omen, augury —*pl.* **2.** patronage —**aus'picious** *a.* of good omen, favourable —**aus'piciously** *adv.*

Aussie ('ɒzɪ) *n./a. inf.* Australian

austere (ɒ'stɪə) *a.* **1.** harsh, strict, severe **2.** without luxury —**aus'terely** *adv.* —**austerity** (ɒ'stɛrɪtɪ) *n.*

austral ('ɔːstrəl) *a.* southern

Australasian (ɒstrə'leɪʒən) *a./n.* (native or inhabitant) of Australasia (Australia, New Zealand and adjacent islands)

Australian (ɒ'streɪlɪən) *n./a.* (native or inhabitant) of Australia —**Australian Rules** game resembling rugby football, played in Aust. between teams of 18 men each on oval pitch, with ball resembling large rugby ball

Austro-¹ (*comb. form*) southern, as in *Austro-Asiatic*

Austro-² (*comb. form*) Austrian, as in *Austro-Hungarian*

autarchy ('ɔːtɑːkɪ) *n.* despotism, absolute power, dictatorship

autarky ('ɔːtɑːkɪ) *n.* (*esp.* of political unit) policy of economic self-sufficiency

auth. 1. author **2.** authority **3.** authorized

authentic (ɔː'θɛntɪk) *a.* **1.** real, genuine, true **2.** trustworthy —**au'thentically** *adv.* —**au'thenticate** *vt.* **1.** make valid, confirm **2.** establish truth, authorship *etc.* of —**authenti'cation** *or* **authenticity** (ɔːθɛn'tɪsɪtɪ) *n.*

author ('ɔːθə) *n.* **1.** writer of book **2.** originator, constructor (**-ess** *fem.*) —**'authorship** *n.*

authority (ɔː'θɒrɪtɪ) *n.* **1.** legal power or right **2.** delegated power **3.** influence **4.** permission **5.** expert **6.** (*oft. pl.*) body or board in control —**authori'tarian** *a.* **1.** favouring or character-

ized by strict obedience to authority or government by small elite **2.** dictatorial —*n.* **3.** person who favours or practises authoritarian policies —**au'thoritative** *a.* —**au'thoritatively** *adv.* —**authori'zation** *or* **-ri'sation** *n.* —**'authorize** *or* **-rise** *vt.* **1.** empower **2.** permit, sanction —**Authorized Version** English translation of the Bible published in 1611 under James I (*also* **King James Version**)

autistic (ɔː'tɪstɪk) *a.* withdrawn and divorced from reality

auto- *or sometimes before vowel* **aut-** (*comb. form*) self, as in *autograph, autosuggestion.* Such words are not given here where the meaning may easily be inferred from the simple word

autobahn ('ɔːtəbɑːn) *n.* German motorway

autobiography (ɔːtəʊbaɪ'ɒɡrəfɪ) *n.* life story of person written by himself —**autobi'ographer** *n.* —**autobio'graphical** *a.* —**autobio'graphically** *adv.*

autochthon (ɔː'tɒkθən) *n.* primitive or original inhabitant —**au'tochthonous** *a.*

autocrat ('ɔːtəkræt) *n.* **1.** absolute ruler **2.** despotic person —**au'tocracy** *n.* —**auto'cratic** *a.* —**auto'cratically** *adv.*

autocross ('ɔːtəʊkrɒs) *n.* motor-racing sport over rough course

auto-da-fé (ɔːtəʊdə'feɪ) *n.* **1.** *Hist.* ceremony of Spanish Inquisition including pronouncement and execution of sentences passed on heretics **2.** burning to death of people condemned as heretics by Inquisition (*pl.* **autos-da-fé**)

autoeroticism (ɔːtəʊɪ'rɒtɪsɪzəm) *or* **autoerotism** (ɔːtəʊ'ɛrətɪzəm) *n.* self-produced sexual arousal

autogamy (ɔː'tɒɡəmɪ) *n.* self-fertilization

autogenous (ɔː'tɒdʒɪnəs) *a.* self-generated

autogiro *or* **autogyro** (ɔːtəʊ'dʒaɪrəʊ) *n.* aircraft like helicopter using horizontal airscrew for vertical ascent and descent

autograph ('ɔːtəɡrɑːf) *n.* **1.** handwritten signature **2.** person's handwriting —*vt.* **3.** sign —**auto'graphic** *a.*

autogyro (ɔːtəʊ'dʒaɪrəʊ) *n. see* AUTOGIRO

autointoxication (ɔːtəʊɪntɒksɪ'keɪʃən) *n.* poisoning of tissues of the body as a result of the absorption of bodily waste

automat ('ɔːtəmæt) *n.* vending machine

automate ('ɔːtəmeɪt) *vt.* make (manufacturing process *etc.*) automatic

automatic (ɔːtə'mætɪk) *a.* **1.** operated or controlled mechanically **2.** done without conscious thought —*a./n.* **3.** self-loading (weapon) —**auto'matically** *adv.* —**automation** (ɔːtə'meɪʃən) *n.* use of automatic devices in industrial production —**au'tomatism** *n.* involuntary action —**au'tomaton** *n.* self-acting machine, *esp.* simulating a human being (*pl.* **-ata**

(-ətə)) —**automatic transmission** transmission system in motor vehicle, in which gears change automatically

automobile ('ɔːtəməbiːl) n. motor car —**automo'bilist** n. motorist

automotive (ɔːtə'məʊtɪv) a. 1. relating to motor vehicles 2. self-propelling

autonomy (ɔː'tɒnəmɪ) n. self-government —**au'tonomous** a.

autopsy ('ɔːtɒpsɪ, 'ɔːtəp-) n. 1. post-mortem examination to determine cause of death 2. critical analysis —**au'toptic(al)** a.

autoroute ('ɔːtəuruːt) n. French motorway

autostrada ('ɔːtəustraːdə) n. Italian motorway

autosuggestion (ɔːtəusə'dʒestʃən) n. process of influencing the mind (towards health etc.), conducted by the subject himself

autumn ('ɔːtəm) n./a. (typical of) the season after summer —**autumnal** (ɔː'tʌmnəl) a. typical of the onset of winter —**autumnally** (ɔː'tʌmnəlɪ) adv.

aux. auxiliary

auxiliary (ɔːg'zɪljərɪ, -'zɪlə-) a. 1. helping, subsidiary —n. 2. helper 3. something subsidiary, as troops 4. verb used to form tenses of others

av. average

A.V. Authorized Version (of the Bible)

avail (ə'veɪl) v. 1. be of use, advantage, value (to) —n. 2. benefit (esp. in of no avail, to little avail) —**availa'bility** n. —**a'vailable** a. 1. obtainable 2. accessible —**avail oneself of** make use of

avalanche ('ævəlɑːntʃ) n. 1. mass of snow, ice, sliding down mountain 2. sudden overwhelming quantity of anything

avant-garde (ævɒŋ'gɑːd) a. markedly experimental or in advance

avarice ('ævərɪs) n. greed for wealth —**ava'ricious** a. —**ava'riciously** adv.

avast (ə'vɑːst) interj. stop

avatar ('ævətɑː) n. 1. Hinduism manifestation of deity in human or animal form 2. visible manifestation of abstract concept

avaunt (ə'vɔːnt) interj. obs. go away, depart

avdp. avoirdupois

Ave. or **ave.** Avenue

Ave Maria ('ɑːvɪ mə'riːə) R.C.Ch. prayer to Virgin Mary, based on salutations of angel Gabriel and Elisabeth to her

avenge (ə'vendʒ) vt. take vengeance on behalf of (person) or on account of (thing) —**a'venger** n.

avenue ('ævɪnjuː) n. 1. wide street, oft. lined with trees 2. approach 3. double row of trees

aver (ə'vɜː) vt. affirm, assert (-rr-) —**a'verment** n.

average ('ævərɪdʒ, 'ævrɪdʒ) n. 1. the mean value or quantity of a number of values or

quantities —a. 2. calculated as an average 3. medium, ordinary —vt. 4. fix or calculate an average of —vi. 5. exist in or form a mean

averse (ə'vɜːs) a. disinclined, unwilling —**a'version** n. (usu. with to or for) dislike, person or thing disliked —**aversion therapy** Psychiatry way of suppressing undesirable habit by associating unpleasant effect, such as electric shock, with it

avert (ə'vɜːt) vt. 1. turn away 2. ward off

aviary ('eɪvjərɪ) n. enclosure for birds —**'aviarist** n.

aviation (eɪvɪ'eɪʃən) n. 1. art of flying aircraft 2. design, production and maintenance of aircraft —**'aviator** n.

avid ('ævɪd) a. 1. keen, enthusiastic 2. (oft. with for) greedy —**a'vidity** n.

avocado (ævə'kɑːdəu) n. 1. tropical tree 2. its green-skinned edible fruit

avocation (ævə'keɪʃən) n. 1. vocation 2. employment, business

avocet or **avoset** ('ævəset) n. wading bird of snipe family with upward-curving bill

avoid (ə'vɔɪd) vt. 1. keep away from 2. refrain from 3. not allow to happen —**a'voidable** a. —**a'voidance** n.

avoirdupois or **avoirdupois weight** (ævədə'pɔɪz) n./a. (of) system of weights used in many English-speaking countries based on pounds and ounces

avouch (ə'vautʃ) vt. obs. affirm, maintain, attest, own —**a'vouchment** n.

avow (ə'vau) vt. 1. declare 2. admit —**a'vowable** a. —**a'vowal** n. —**a'vowed** a. —**avowedly** (ə'vauɪdlɪ) adv.

avuncular (ə'vʌŋkjulə) a. of or resembling an uncle, genial

await (ə'weɪt) vt. 1. wait or stay for 2. be in store for

awake (ə'weɪk) v. 1. emerge or rouse from sleep 2. become or cause to become alert (**a'woke** or **a'waked**, **a'woken** or **a'waked**, **a'waking**) —a. 3. not sleeping 4. alert —**a'wakening** n.

award (ə'wɔːd) vt. 1. give formally (esp. prize or punishment) —n. 2. prize 3. judicial decision

aware (ə'wɛə) a. informed, conscious —**a'wareness** n.

awash (ə'wɒʃ) a. 1. level with surface of water 2. filled or overflowing with water

away (ə'weɪ) a. 1. absent, apart, at a distance, out of the way —n. 2. Sport game played on opponent's ground

awe (ɔː) n. dread mingled with reverence —**'awesome** a.

aweigh (ə'weɪ) a. Naut. (of anchor) no longer hooked into bottom; hanging by its rope or chain

awful ('ɔːful) a. 1. very bad, unpleasant 2. obs.

impressive 3. *inf.* very great —'**awfully** *adv.* **1.** in an unpleasant way **2.** *inf.* very much

awhile (ə'waɪl) *adv.* for a time

awkward ('ɔːkwəd) *a.* **1.** clumsy, ungainly **2.** difficult **3.** inconvenient **4.** embarrassed —'**awkwardly** *adv.* —'**awkwardness** *n.*

awl (ɔːl) *n.* pointed tool for boring wood, leather *etc.*

awn (ɔːn) *n.* any of bristles growing from flowering parts of certain grasses and cereals

awning ('ɔːnɪŋ) *n.* (canvas) roof or shelter, to protect from weather

awoke (ə'wəʊk) *pt.* of AWAKE —a'**woken** *pp.* of AWAKE

A.W.O.L. *or* **AWOL** (*when acronym* 'eɪwɒl) absent without leave

awry (ə'raɪ) *adv.* **1.** crookedly **2.** amiss **3.** at a slant —*a.* **4.** crooked, distorted **5.** wrong

axe *or U.S.* **ax** (æks) *n.* **1.** tool with sharp blade for chopping **2.** *inf.* dismissal from employment *etc.* —*vt.* **3.** *inf.* dismiss, dispense with

axel ('æksəl) *n.* Skating jump of one and a half turns, taking off from forward outside edge of one skate and landing on backward outside edge of other

axes[1] ('æksiːz) *n., pl.* of AXIS

axes[2] ('æksɪz) *n., pl.* of AXE

axil ('æksɪl) *n.* upper angle between branch or leaf stalk and stem

axiom ('æksɪəm) *n.* **1.** received or accepted principle **2.** self-evident truth —**axio'matic** *a.*

axis ('æksɪs) *n.* **1.** (imaginary) line round which body spins **2.** line or column around which parts of thing, system *etc.* are arranged (*pl.* '**axes**) —'**axial** *a.* —'**axially** *adv.* —'**Axis** *n.* coalition of Germany, Italy and Japan, 1936–45

axle ('æksəl) *n.* rod on which wheel turns

axolotl ('æksəlɒtl) *n.* aquatic salamander of N Amer.

ay *or* **aye** (eɪ) *adv. Poet., obs.* always

ayah ('aɪə) *n.* in parts of former British Empire, native maidservant or nursemaid

ayatollah (aɪə'tɒlə) *n.* one of class of Islamic religious leaders

aye *or* **ay** (aɪ) *adv.* **1.** yes —*n.* **2.** affirmative answer or vote —*pl.* **3.** those voting for motion

AZ Arizona

azalea (ə'zeɪljə) *n.* genus of shrubby flowering plants, allied to rhododendron

azimuth ('æzɪməθ) *n.* **1.** vertical arc from zenith to horizon **2.** angular distance of this from meridian

Aztec ('æztɛk) *a./n.* (member) of Indian race ruling Mexico before Spanish conquest

azure ('æʒə, 'eɪ-) *n.* **1.** sky-blue colour **2.** sky —*a.* **3.** sky-blue

B,b

b *or* **B** (biː) *n.* **1.** second letter of English alphabet **2.** speech sound represented by this letter, as in *bell* **3.** second in series, class or rank (*also* '**beta**) (*pl.* **b's, B's,** *or* **Bs**)

B **1.** *Mus.* seventh note of scale of C major; major or minor key having this note as its tonic **2.** less important of two things **3.** human blood type of ABO group **4.** *UK* secondary road **5.** *Chem.* boron **6.** magnetic flux density **7.** *Chess* bishop **8.** (of pencils) black **9.** *Phys.* bel (*also* b) **10.** *Phys.* baryon number

b. *or* **B. 1.** *Mus.* bass; basso **2.** (on maps *etc.*) bay **3. (B.)** Bible **4.** book **5.** born **6. (b.)** *Cricket* bowled; bye **7.** breadth

Ba *Chem.* barium

B.A. Bachelor of Arts

B.A.A. British Airports Authority

baa (bɑː) *vi.* **1.** make cry of sheep; bleat ('**baaing, baaed**) —*n.* **2.** cry made by sheep

baas (bɑːs) *n.* SA boss

baba ('bɑːbɑ) *n.* small cake, usu. soaked in rum

babble ('bæbl) *vi.* **1.** speak foolishly, incoherently, or childishly —*n.* **2.** foolish, confused talk —'**babbler** *n.* **1.** one who babbles **2.** tropical bird with incessant song —'**babbling** *n./a.*

babe (beɪb) *n.* **1.** *old-fashioned* baby **2.** guileless person

babel ('beɪbəl) *n.* confused noise or scene, uproar

baboon (bə'buːn) *n.* large monkey of Afr. and Asia —ba'**boonish** *a.*

baby ('beɪbɪ) *n.* very young child, infant —'**babyhood** *n.* —'**babyish** *a.* —**baby grand** small grand piano —**baby-sit** *vi.* —**baby-sitter** *n.* one who cares for children when parents are out

baccarat ('bækərɑː, bækə'rɑː) *n.* gambling card game

bacchanal ('bækənl) *n.* **1.** follower of Bacchus **2.** (participant in) drunken, riotous celebration

bacchanalia (bækə'neɪlɪə) *pl.n.* **1.** (*oft.* **B-**) orgiastic rites associated with Bacchus **2.** drunken revelry —**baccha'nalian** *a./n.*

bacchant ('bækənt) *or* (*fem.*) **bacchante** (bə'kæntɪ) *n.* **1.** priest or priestess of Bacchus **2.** drunken reveller

baccy ('bækɪ) *n. UK inf.* tobacco

bachelor ('bætʃələ, 'bætʃlə) *n.* **1.** unmarried man **2.** holder of lowest university degree **3.** *Hist.* young knight —'**bachelorhood** *or* '**bachelorship** *n.* —**bachelor girl** young unmarried woman, *esp.* one who is self-supporting

bacillus (bə'sıləs) *n.* minute organism sometimes causing disease (*pl.* **-cilli** (-'sılaı)) —**ba'cilliform** *a.*

back (bæk) *n.* 1. hinder part of anything, *eg* human body 2. part opposite front 3. part or side of something further away or less used 4. (position of) player in ball games behind other (forward) players —*a.* 5. situated behind 6. earlier —*adv.* 7. at, to the back 8. in, into the past 9. in return —*vi.* 10. move backwards —*vt.* 11. support 12. put wager on 13. provide with back or backing —'**backer** *n.* 1. one supporting another, *esp.* in contest 2. one betting on horse, *etc.* in race —'**backing** *n.* 1. support 2. material to protect the back of something 3. musical accompaniment, *esp.* for pop singer —'**backward** *a.* 1. directed towards the rear 2. behind in education 3. reluctant, bashful —*adv.* 4. backwards —'**backwardness** *n.* —'**backwards** *adv.* 1. to the rear 2. to the past 3. into a worse state (*also* '**backward**) —'**back'bencher** *n.* Brit. or Aust. member of Parliament not holding office in government or opposition —'**backbite** *v.* slander (absent person) —'**backbiter** *n.* —'**backbiting** *n.* —'**backboard** *n.* 1. board that is placed behind something to form or support its back 2. board worn to support back, as after surgery 3. *Basketball* flat upright surface under which basket is attached —**back boiler** tank or series of pipes at back of fireplace for heating water —'**backbone** *n.* 1. spinal column 2. strength of character —'**backbreaking** *a.* exhausting —'**backchat** *n. inf.* impudent answer —'**backcloth** *or* '**backdrop** *n.* painted cloth at back of stage —'**backcomb** *v.* comb under layers of (hair) towards roots to add bulk to hair style (*also* **tease**) —**back'date** *vt.* make effective from earlier date —**back door** 1. door at rear or side of building 2. means of entry to job *etc.* that is secret or obtained through influence —**back'fire** *vi.* 1. ignite at wrong time, as fuel in cylinder of internal-combustion engine 2. (of plan, scheme *etc.*) fail to work, *esp.* to the cost of the instigator 3. ignite wrongly, as gas burner *etc.* —'**backgammon** *n.* game played with draughtsmen and dice —'**background** *n.* 1. space behind chief figures of picture *etc.* 2. past history of person —'**backhand** *n. Tennis etc.* stroke with hand turned backwards —**back-'handed** *a.* (of compliment *etc.*) with second, uncomplimentary meaning —'**backhander** *n.* 1. blow with back of hand 2. *inf.* a bribe —'**backlash** *n.* sudden and adverse reaction —'**backlog** *n.* accumulation of work *etc.* to be dealt with —**back marker** competitor who is at back of field in race —**back number** 1. issue of newspaper *etc.* that appeared on a previous date 2. *inf.* person or thing considered old-fashioned —**back pack** *n.* 1. type of knapsack

—*vi.* 2. travel with knapsack —**back-pedal** *vi.* 1. turn pedals of bicycle backwards 2. retract previous opinion *etc.* —**back room** place where important and usu. secret research is done —**back seat** 1. seat at back, *esp.* of vehicle 2. *inf.* subordinate or inconspicuous position (*esp. in* **take a back seat**) —**back-seat driver** *inf.* 1. passenger who offers unwanted advice to driver 2. person who offers advice on matters that are not his concern —**back'side** *n.* rump —'**backslide** *vi.* fall back in faith or morals —**back'stage** *adv.* 1. behind part of theatre in view of audience —*a.* 2. situated backstage —'**back'stairs** *pl.n.* 1. secondary staircase in house —*a.* 2. underhand (*also* '**back'stair**) —'**backstroke** *n. Swimming* stroke performed on the back —'**backtrack** *vi.* 1. return by same route by which one has come 2. retract or reverse one's opinion *etc.* —'**backup** *n. chiefly US* 1. support; reinforcement 2. reserve; substitute —'**backwash** *n.* 1. water thrown back by ship's propellers *etc.* 2. a backward current 3. a reaction —'**backwater** *n.* still water fed by back flow of stream —'**backwoods** *pl.n.* remote forest areas —**back yard** yard at back of house *etc.* —**back up** 1. support 2. (of water) accumulate 3. *Comp.* make copy of (data file) —**in one's own back yard** close at hand

bacon ('beıkən) *n.* cured pig's flesh

Baconian (beı'kəunıən) *a.* 1. pert. to English philosopher Francis Bacon or his inductive method of reasoning —*n.* 2. follower of Bacon's philosophy

bacteria (bæk'tıərıə) *pl.n.* microscopic organisms, some causing disease (*sing.* **-rium** (-rıəm)) —**bac'terial** *a.* —**bacteri'ologist** *n.* —**bacteri'ology** *n.* study of bacteria

Bactrian camel ('bæktrıən) two-humped camel, used in deserts of central Asia

bad (bæd) *a.* 1. (of poor quality) 2. faulty 3. evil 4. immoral 5. offensive 6. severe 7. rotten, decayed (**worse** *comp.*, **worst** *sup.*) —'**badly** *adv.* —'**badness** *n.* —**bad blood** feeling of intense hatred or hostility; enmity —**bad debt** debt which is not collectable

bade (bæd, beıd) *or* **bad** *pt. of* BID

badge (bædʒ) *n.* distinguishing emblem or sign

badger ('bædʒə) *n.* 1. carnivorous burrowing mammal, about the size of a fox —*vt.* 2. pester, worry

badinage ('bædınɑːʒ) *n.* playful talk, banter

badminton ('bædmıntən) *n.* game like tennis, played with shuttlecocks over high net

baffle ('bæfəl) *vt.* 1. check 2. frustrate 3. bewilder —'**baffler** *n.* —'**baffling** *a.* —**baffle plate** device to regulate or divert flow of liquid, gas, soundwaves *etc.*

bag (bæg) *n.* 1. sack, pouch 2. measure of

quantity **3.** woman's handbag **4.** *offens.* unattractive woman —*pl.* **5.** *inf.* lots (of) —*vi.* **6.** swell out **7.** bulge **8.** sag —*vt.* **9.** put in bag **10.** kill as game *etc.* (**-gg-**) —**'bagging** *n.* cloth —**'baggy** *a.* loose, drooping —**'bagman** *n.* commercial traveller

bagasse (bə'gæs) *n.* sugar cane refuse

bagatelle (bægə'tɛl) *n.* **1.** trifle **2.** game like pinball played with nine balls and cue on a board

baggage ('bægɪdʒ) *n.* **1.** suitcases *etc.*, packed for journey **2.** *offens.* woman

bagpipes ('bægpaɪps) *pl.n.* musical wind instrument, of windbag and pipes —**'bagpiper** *n.*

bah (bɑː, bæ) *interj.* expression of contempt or disgust

Bahaism (bə'hɑːɪzəm) *n.* religious system founded in 1863, emphasizing value of all religions and spiritual unity of mankind —**Ba'haist** *or* **Ba'haite** *a./n.*

bail¹ (beɪl) *n.* **1.** *Law* security given for person's reappearance in court **2.** one giving such security —*vt.* **3.** release, or obtain release of, on security —**bail out** *inf.* help (person, firm *etc.*) out of trouble

bail² (beɪl) *n.* **1.** *Cricket* crosspiece on wicket **2.** bar separating horses in stable

bail³ *or* **bale** (beɪl) *vt.* empty out (water) from boat —**bail out** leave aircraft by parachute

bailey ('beɪlɪ) *n.* outermost wall of castle

Bailey bridge ('beɪlɪ) bridge composed of prefabricated sections

bailie ('beɪlɪ) *n. Scot.* municipal magistrate

bailiff ('beɪlɪf) *n.* **1.** land steward, agent **2.** sheriff's officer

bailiwick ('beɪlɪwɪk) *n.* jurisdiction of bailiff

bain-marie (bɛ̃ma'ri) *Fr.* vessel for holding hot water, in which sauces *etc.* are gently cooked or kept warm (*pl.* **bains-marie** (bɛ̃ma'ri))

bairn (bɛən) *n. Scot.* infant, child

bait (beɪt) *n.* **1.** food to entice fish **2.** any lure or enticement —*vt.* **3.** set a lure for **4.** annoy, persecute

baize (beɪz) *n.* smooth woollen cloth

bake (beɪk) *vt.* **1.** cook or harden by dry heat —*vi.* **2.** make bread, cakes *etc.* **3.** be scorched or tanned —**'baker** *n.* —**'bakery** *or* **bakehouse** *n.* —**'baking** *n.* —**baked beans** haricot beans, baked and tinned in tomato sauce —**baker's dozen** thirteen —**baking powder** raising agent containing sodium bicarbonate *etc.* used in cooking

Bakelite ('beɪkəlaɪt) *n.* **R** hard nonflammable synthetic resin, used for dishes, trays, electrical insulators *etc.*

baksheesh *or* **backsheesh** ('bækʃiːʃ) *n.* in some Eastern countries, *esp.* formerly, money given as tip

Balaclava helmet (bælə'klɑːvə) close-fitting woollen helmet covering head and neck

balalaika (bælə'laɪkə) *n.* Russian musical instrument similar to guitar

balance ('bæləns) *n.* **1.** pair of scales **2.** equilibrium **3.** surplus **4.** sum due on an account **5.** difference between two sums —*vt.* **6.** weigh **7.** bring to equilibrium —**balance of payments** difference over given time between total payments to and receipts from foreign nations —**balance of power** distribution of power among countries so that no nation can seriously threaten another —**balance sheet** tabular statement of assets and liabilities —**balance wheel** regulating wheel of watch

balcony ('bælkənɪ) *n.* **1.** railed platform outside window **2.** upper seats in theatre

bald (bɔːld) *a.* **1.** hairless **2.** plain **3.** bare —**'balding** *a.* becoming bald —**'baldly** *adv.* —**'baldness** *n.*

balderdash ('bɔːldədæʃ) *n.* idle, senseless talk

baldric ('bɔːldrɪk) *n.* shoulder-belt for sword *etc.*

bale¹ (beɪl) *n.* **1.** bundle or package —*vt.* **2.** make into bundles or pack into cartons —**'baler** *n.* machine which makes bales of hay *etc.*

bale² (beɪl) *vt. see* BAIL³

baleen (bə'liːn) *n.* whalebone

baleful ('beɪlful) *a.* menacing —**'balefully** *adv.*

balk *or* **baulk** (bɔːk, bɔːlk) *vi.* **1.** swerve, pull up —*vt.* **2.** thwart, hinder —*n.* **3.** hindrance **4.** square timber, beam —**balk at 1.** recoil from **2.** stop short at

Balkan ('bɔːlkən) *a.* of or denoting large peninsula in SE Europe, its inhabitants, countries *etc.*

ball¹ (bɔːl) *n.* **1.** anything round **2.** globe, sphere, *esp.* as used in games **3.** *Cricket* ball as delivered **4.** bullet —*vi.* **5.** clog, gather into a mass —**ball-and-socket joint** *Anat.* joint in which rounded head fits into rounded cavity —**ball bearings** steel balls used to lessen friction on bearings —**ball boy** *esp.* in tennis, person who retrieves balls that go out of play —**ball cock** device for regulating flow of liquid into cistern *etc.*, consisting of floating ball and a valve —**ball game 1.** any game played with a ball **2.** US game of baseball **3.** US *inf.* any activity —**ball-park figure** rough estimate; guess —**'ballpoint** *or* **ballpoint pen** *n.* pen with tiny ball bearing as nib (*also* **'Biro**)

ball² (bɔːl) *n.* assembly for dancing —**'ballroom** *n.*

ballad ('bæləd) *n.* **1.** narrative poem **2.** simple song

ballade (bæ'lɑːd) *n.* **1.** short poem with refrain and envoy **2.** piece of music

ballast ('bæləst) *n.* **1.** heavy material put in ship to give steadiness **2.** that which renders anything steady —*vt.* **3.** load with ballast, steady

ballet ('bæleɪ, bæ'leɪ) *n.* theatrical presentation of dancing and miming —**balle'rina** *n.* female ballet dancer

balletomania (bælɛtəʊ'meɪnɪə) *n.* enthusiasm for ballet —**bal'letomane** *n.*

ballista (bə'lɪstə) *n.* ancient catapult for hurling stones *etc.* (*pl.* -**tae** (-tiː)) —**bal'listic** *a.* moving as, or pertaining to motion of a projectile —**bal'listics** *pl.n.* (*with sing. v.*) scientific study of ballistic motion —**ballistic missile** missile that follows ballistic trajectory when propulsive power is discontinued

balloon (bə'luːn) *n.* **1.** large, airtight bag that rises when filled with air or gas —*vi.* **2.** puff out —**bal'looning** *n.* —**bal'loonist** *n.*

ballot ('bælət) *n.* **1.** method of voting secretly, usu. by marking ballot paper and putting it into box —*v.* **2.** vote or elicit a vote from —**ballot box 1.** sealed receptacle for completed ballot papers **2.** *fig.* the democratic process

ballyhoo (bælɪ'huː) *n.* **1.** noisy confusion or uproar **2.** vulgar, exaggerated publicity or advertisement

balm (bɑːm) *n.* **1.** aromatic substance obtained from certain trees, used for healing or soothing **2.** anything soothing —'**balminess** *n.* —'**balmy** *a.*

baloney *or* **boloney** (bə'ləʊnɪ) *n. inf.* foolish talk; nonsense

BALPA ('bælpə) British Airline Pilots' Association

balsa ('bɔːlsə) *n.* Amer. tree with light but strong wood

balsam ('bɔːlsəm) *n.* **1.** resinous aromatic substance obtained from various trees and shrubs **2.** soothing ointment —**bal'samic** *a.*

Baltic ('bɔːltɪk) *a.* **1.** denoting or relating to the Baltic Sea or the states bordering it **2.** of or characteristic of Baltic as a group of languages

baluster ('bæləstə) *n.* short pillar used as support to rail of staircase *etc.* —'**balustrade** *n.* row of short pillars surmounted by rail

bamboo (bæm'buː) *n.* large tropical treelike reed

bamboozle (bæm'buːzəl) *vt.* **1.** mystify **2.** hoax

ban (bæn) *vt.* **1.** prohibit, forbid, outlaw (-**nn**-) —*n.* **2.** prohibition **3.** proclamation —**bans** *or* **banns** *pl.n.* proclamation of marriage

banal (bə'nɑːl) *a.* commonplace, trivial, trite —ba'**nality** *n.*

banana (bə'nɑːnə) *n.* **1.** tropical treelike plant **2.** its fruit —**banana republic** *inf.* small country,

esp. in Central Amer., that is politically unstable and has economy dominated by foreign interest

band[1] (bænd) *n.* **1.** strip used to bind **2.** range of values, frequencies *etc.*, between two limits —'**bandage** *n.* strip of cloth for binding wound —**band saw** power-operated saw consisting of endless toothed metal band running over two wheels

band[2] (bænd) *n.* **1.** company, group **2.** company of musicians —*v.* **3.** (*with* together) bind together —'**bandmaster** *n.* —'**bandsman** *n.* —'**bandstand** *n.*

bandanna *or* **bandana** (bæn'dænə) *n.* coloured silk or cotton handkerchief

b. and b. bed and breakfast

bandbox ('bændbɒks) *n.* light box of cardboard for hats *etc.*

bandeau ('bændəʊ) *n.* band, ribbon for the hair (*pl.* -**deaux** (-dəʊz))

bandicoot ('bændɪkuːt) *n.* ratlike Aust. marsupial

bandit ('bændɪt) *n.* **1.** outlaw **2.** robber, brigand (*pl.* -**s**, **banditti** (bæn'dɪtɪ))

bandoleer *or* **bandolier** (bændə'lɪə) *n.* shoulder belt for cartridges

bandwagon ('bændwægən) *n.* —**climb, jump, get on the bandwagon** join something that seems assured of success

bandy ('bændɪ) *vt.* **1.** beat to and fro **2.** toss from one to another ('**bandied**, '**bandying**) —'**bandy** *or* **bandy-legged** *a.* having legs curving outwards

bane (beɪn) *n.* person or thing causing misery or distress —'**baneful** *a.* —'**banefully** *adv.*

bang[1] (bæŋ) *n.* **1.** sudden loud noise, explosion **2.** heavy blow —*vi.* **3.** make loud noise —*vt.* **4.** beat, strike violently **5.** slam —'**banger** *n.* UK **1.** *sl.* sausage **2.** old decrepit car **3.** firework that explodes loudly

bang[2] (bæŋ) *n.* fringe of hair cut straight across forehead

bangle ('bæŋgəl) *n.* ring worn on arm or leg

banian ('bænjən) *n. see* BANYAN

banish ('bænɪʃ) *vt.* **1.** condemn to exile **2.** drive away **3.** dismiss —'**banishment** *n.* exile

banisters ('bænɪstəz) *pl.n.* railing and supporting balusters on staircase

banjo ('bændʒəʊ) *n.* musical instrument like guitar, with circular body (*pl.* -**s**, -**es**) —'**banjoist** *n.*

bank[1] (bæŋk) *n.* **1.** establishment for keeping, lending, exchanging *etc.* money **2.** any supply or store for future use, as blood bank —*vt.* **3.** put in bank —*vi.* **4.** transact business with bank —'**banker** *n.* —'**banking** *n.* —**bank account** account created by deposit of money at bank by customer —'**bankbook** *n.* book held by depositor, in which bank enters record of deposits, withdrawals *etc.* (*also* '**passbook**) —**bank card** *or* **banker's card** card guaranteeing payment of cheques by bank up to an agreed amount —**bank holiday** day(s), usu. public holiday(s), when banks are closed by law —**bank note** written promise of payment —**bank rate** (*sometimes* **B- R-**) minimum rate by which central bank is obliged to rediscount bills of exchange —**bank on** rely on

bank² (bæŋk) *n.* 1. tier 2. row of oars

bank³ (bæŋk) *n.* 1. mound or ridge of earth 2. edge of river, lake *etc.* 3. rising ground in sea —*vt.* 4. enclose with ridge —*v.* 5. pile up 6. (of aircraft) tilt inwards in turning

bankrupt ('bæŋkrʌpt, -rəpt) *n.* 1. one who fails in business, insolvent debtor —*a.* 2. financially ruined —*vt.* 3. make, cause to be, bankrupt —'**bankruptcy** *n.*

banksia ('bæŋksɪə) *n.* genus of Aust. shrubs with dense, usu. yellow, cylindrical heads of flowers

banner ('bænə) *n.* 1. long strip with slogan *etc.* 2. placard 3. flag used as ensign

bannisters ('bænɪstəz) *pl.n. see* BANISTERS

bannock ('bænək) *n.* round flat cake orig. in Scotland, made from wheat or barley

banns *or* **bans** (bænz) *pl.n. see* BAN

banquet ('bæŋkwɪt) *n.* 1. feast —*vi.* 2. hold or take part in banquet —*vt.* 3. treat with feast —'**banqueter** *n.*

banquette (bæŋ'kɛt) *n.* 1. raised firing step behind parapet 2. US upholstered bench

banshee ('bænʃiː, bæn'ʃiː) *n.* Irish fairy with a wail portending death

bantam ('bæntəm) *n.* dwarf variety of domestic fowl —'**bantamweight** *n.* 1. professional boxer weighing 112-118 lbs. (51-53.5 kg); amateur boxer weighing 112-119 lbs. (51-54 kg) 2. wrestler weighing usu. 115-126 lbs. (52-57 kg)

banter ('bæntə) *v.* 1. speak or tease lightly or jokingly —*n.* 2. light, teasing language

Bantu ('bæntuː) *n.* 1. collective name for large group of related native tribes in Afr. 2. family of languages spoken by Bantu peoples

bantubeer ('bæntubɪə) *n.* SA malted drink made from sorghum

banyan *or* **banian** ('bænjən) *n.* Indian fig tree with spreading branches which take root

baobab ('beɪəubæb) *n.* Afr. tree with thick trunk and angular branches

bap (bæp) *n.* UK soft bread roll

baptise *or* **-ize** (bæp'taɪz) *vt.* 1. immerse in, sprinkle with water ceremoniously 2. christen —'**baptism** *n.* —**bap'tismal** *a.* —**bap'tismally** *adv.* —'**Baptist** *n.* member of Protestant Christian denomination believing in necessity of baptism by immersion, *esp.* of adults —'**baptistry** *or* '**baptistery** *n.* place where

baptism is performed —**baptism of fire** 1. soldier's first experience of battle 2. any initiating ordeal

bar¹ (baː) *n.* 1. rod or block of any substance 2. obstacle 3. bank of sand at mouth of river 4. rail in law court 5. body of lawyers 6. counter where drinks are served, *esp.* in hotel *etc.* 7. unit of music —*vt.* 8. fasten 9. obstruct 10. exclude (-**rr**-) —*prep.* 11. except —'**barring** *prep.* excepting —**bar code** arrangement of parallel lines, readable by computer, printed on, and giving details of, merchandise in shop *etc.* —**bar graph** graph consisting of bars whose lengths are proportional to quantities —'**barmaid** *n.* —**bar sinister** 1. (*not in heraldic usage*) *see* **bend sinister** at BEND 2. condition of being of illegitimate birth —'**bartender** *n.*

bar² (baː) *n.* unit of pressure

bar. 1. barometer 2. barrel 3. barrister

barb (baːb) *n.* 1. sharp point curving backwards behind main point of spear, fish hook *etc.* 2. cutting remark —**barbed** *a.* —**barbed wire** fencing wire with barbs at close intervals

barbarous ('baːbərəs) *a.* 1. savage, brutal 2. uncivilized —**barbarian** (baː'bɛərɪən) *n.* —**barbaric** (baː'bærɪk) *a.* —'**barbarism** *n.* —**barbarity** (baː'bærɪtɪ) *n.* —'**barbarously** *adv.*

Barbary ape ('baːbərɪ) tailless macaque that inhabits NW Afr. and Gibraltar

barbecue ('baːbɪkjuː) *n.* 1. meal cooked outdoors over open fire 2. fireplace or grill used for this —*vt.* 3. cook (meat *etc.*) in this manner (-**cued, -cuing**)

barbel ('baːbəl) *n.* 1. spine or bristle that hangs from jaws of certain fishes 2. any of several European fishes resembling carp

barbell ('baːbel) *n.* metal rod to which heavy discs are attached at each end used for weightlifting exercises

barber ('baːbə) *n.* one who shaves beards and cuts hair

barberry ('baːbərɪ) *n.* 1. any spiny Asian shrub, having yellow flowers and orange or red berries 2. fruit of these plants

barbican ('baːbɪkən) *n.* 1. outwork of fortified place, *esp.* to defend drawbridge 2. watchtower projecting from fortification

barbiturate (baː'bɪtjʊrɪt, -reɪt) *n.* derivative of barbituric acid used as drug —'**barbitone** *or* U.S. '**barbital** *n.* —**barbituric acid** crystalline solid used in preparation of barbiturate drugs

barcarole *or* **barcarolle** ('baːkərəʊl, -rɒl; baːkə'rəʊl) *n.* gondolier's song

bard (baːd) *n.* 1. formerly, Celtic poet 2. wandering minstrel —'**bardic** *a.* —**the Bard** Shakespeare

bare (bɛə) *a.* 1. uncovered 2. naked 3. plain 4. scanty —*vt.* 5. make bare —'**barely** *adv.* only just, scarcely —'**bareness** n. —'**barebacked** a. on unsaddled horse —'**barefaced** a. shameless

bargain ('bɑːgɪn) n. 1. something bought at price favourable to purchaser 2. contract, agreement —vi. 3. haggle, negotiate 4. make bargain

barge (bɑːdʒ) n. 1. flat-bottomed freight boat 2. state or pleasure boat —vi. inf. 3. (with into or in) interrupt 4. (with into) bump (into), push —bar'gee or U.S. 'bargeman n. —'bargepole n. long pole used to propel barge —**not touch with a bargepole** inf. refuse to have anything to do with

baritone ('bærɪtəʊn) n. 1. (singer with) second lowest adult male voice —a. 2. written for or possessing this vocal range

barium ('bɛərɪəm) n. white metallic element —**barium meal** preparation of barium sulphate, which is opaque to x-rays, swallowed by patient before x-ray of upper part of alimentary canal

bark¹ (bɑːk) n. 1. sharp loud cry of dog etc. —v. 2. make, utter with such sound —'**barker** n. crier outside fair booth etc.

bark² (bɑːk) n. 1. outer layer of trunk, branches of tree —vt. 2. strip bark from 3. rub off (skin), graze (shins etc.)

bark³ (bɑːk) n. see BARQUE

barley ('bɑːlɪ) n. grain used for food and in making malt —'**barleycorn** n. 1. (grain of) barley 2. obs. unit of length equal to a third of an inch —**barley sugar** sweet originally made with barley —**barley water** drink made from infusion of barley

barm (bɑːm) n. 1. obs. yeast 2. froth —'**barmy** a. inf. silly, insane

bar mitzvah (bɑː ˈmɪtsvə) (sometimes B- M-) Judaism 1. ceremony marking 13th birthday of boy, who then assumes full religious obligations 2. the boy himself

barn (bɑːn) n. farm building, used to store grain, hay etc. —**barn dance** (party with) country dancing —**barn owl** owl with pale brown and white plumage —'**barnstorm** vi. chiefly US tour rural districts putting on shows or making speeches in political campaign —'**barnstormer** n. —'**barnyard** n. farmyard

barnacle ('bɑːnəkəl) n. shellfish which adheres to rocks and ships' bottoms —**barnacle goose** N European goose that has black-and-white head and body

barney ('bɑːnɪ) inf. n. 1. noisy argument 2. fight —vi. 3. argue or fight

barograph ('bærəʊgrɑːf, -græf) n. recording barometer

barometer (bəˈrɒmɪtə) n. instrument to measure pressure of atmosphere —baro'metric a. —ba'rometry n.

baron ('bærən) n. 1. member of lowest rank of peerage (-ess fem.) 2. powerful businessman —'**baronage** n. —ba'**ronial** a. —'**barony** n. —**baron of beef** cut of beef consisting of double sirloin joined at backbone

baronet ('bærənɪt, -nɛt) n. lowest British hereditary title, below baron but above knight —'**baronetage** n. —'**baronetcy** n.

baroque (bəˈrɒk, bəˈrəʊk) a. extravagantly ornamented, esp. in architecture and art

baroscope ('bærəskəʊp) n. any instrument for measuring atmospheric pressure —**baroscopic** (bærəˈskɒpɪk) a.

barouche (bəˈruːʃ) n. four-wheeled carriage with folding top over rear seat

barque (bɑːk) n. sailing ship, esp. large, three-masted one —'**barquentine** n. small barque

barrack¹ ('bærək) n. 1. (usu. pl.) building for lodging soldiers 2. huge bare building

barrack² ('bærək) inf. vi. 1. (usu. with for) encourage by cheering, esp. at sporting events —vt. 2. criticize loudly —v. 3. jeer —'**barracking** n.

barracouta (bærəˈkuːtə) n. type of large, elongated, predatory fish, mostly tropical

barrage ('bærɑːʒ) n. 1. heavy artillery fire 2. continuous and heavy delivery, esp. of questions etc. 3. dam across river —**barrage balloon** one of number of tethered balloons with cables or net suspended from them, used to deter low-flying air attack

barratry or **barretry** ('bærətrɪ) n. 1. fraudulent breach of duty by master of ship 2. stirring up of law suits —'**barrator** n. —'**barratrous** a.

barre (bɑː) Fr. rail used for ballet practice

barrel ('bærəl) n. 1. round wooden vessel, made of curved staves bound with hoops 2. amount that barrel can hold (also 'barrelful) 3. anything long and hollow, as tube of gun etc. —vt. 4. put in barrel (-ll-) —'barrelled a. —**barrel organ** instrument consisting of cylinder turned by handle, having pins that interrupt air flow to certain pipes or pluck strings, thereby playing tunes —**barrel vault** Archit. vault in form of half cylinder

barren ('bærən) a. 1. unfruitful, sterile 2. unprofitable 3. dull —'**barrenness** n. —**Barren Grounds** sparsely inhabited tundra region in N Canada

barricade (bærɪˈkeɪd, 'bærɪkeɪd) n. 1. improvised fortification, barrier —vt. 2. protect by building barrier 3. block

barrier ('bærɪə) n. fence, obstruction, obstacle, boundary —**barrier cream** cream to protect skin —**barrier reef** coral reef lying parallel to shore

barrister ('bærɪstə) n. advocate in the higher law courts

barrow¹ ('bærəʊ) n. 1. small wheeled handcart 2. wheelbarrow

barrow² ('bærəʊ) n. 1. burial mound 2. tumulus

Bart. Baronet

barter ('bɑːtə) v. 1. trade by exchange of goods —n. 2. practice of bartering

baryon ('bærɪɒn) n. Phys. elementary particle of matter

baryta (bə'raɪtə) n. 1. barium oxide 2. barium hydroxide

barytes (bə'raɪtiːz) n. barium sulphate

basalt ('bæsɔːlt) n. dark-coloured, hard, compact, igneous rock —ba'saltic a.

bascule ('bæskjuːl) n. 1. lever apparatus 2. drawbridge on counterpoise principle

base¹ (beɪs) n. 1. bottom, foundation 2. starting point 3. centre of operations 4. fixed point 5. Chem. compound that combines with an acid to form a salt 6. medium into which other substances are mixed 7. Maths. number that when raised to a certain power has logarithm equal to that power —vt. 8. found, establish —'basal a. of base —'baseless a. —'baseline n. 1. Surv. measured line through survey area from which triangulations are made 2. line at each end of tennis court that marks limit of play —'basement n. lowest storey of building

base² (beɪs) a. 1. low, mean 2. despicable —'basely adv. —'baseness n. —'baseborn a. illegitimate

baseball ('beɪsbɔːl) n. game, orig. Amer., played with bat and ball

bases ('beɪsiːz) n., pl. of BASIS

bash (bæʃ) inf. vt. 1. strike violently —n. 2. blow 3. attempt

bashful ('bæʃfʊl) a. shy, modest —'bashfully adv. —'bashfulness n.

basic ('beɪsɪk; Austral. also 'bæsɪk) a. 1. relating to, serving as base 2. fundamental 3. necessary —basic slag slag produced in steel-making, containing calcium phosphate

BASIC ('beɪsɪk) Comp. Beginners' All-purpose Symbolic Instruction Code

basil ('bæzəl) n. aromatic herb

basilica (bə'zɪlɪkə) n. type of church with long hall and pillars —ba'silican a.

basilisk ('bæzɪlɪsk) n. legendary small fire-breathing dragon

basin ('beɪsən) n. 1. deep circular dish 2. harbour 3. land drained by river

basis ('beɪsɪs) n. 1. foundation 2. principal constituent (pl. 'bases)

bask (bɑːsk) vi. lie in warmth and sunshine —basking shark large plankton-eating shark

basket ('bɑːskɪt) n. vessel made of woven cane, straw etc. —'basketry or 'basketwork n. —'basketball n. ball game played by two teams —basket chair wickerwork chair —basket

weave weave of yarns, resembling that of basket

basque (bæsk) n. tight-fitting bodice for women

Basque (bæsk, bɑːsk) n. 1. one of race from W Pyrenees 2. their language

bas-relief (bɑːrɪ'liːf, 'bæsrɪliːf) n. sculpture with figures standing out slightly from background

bass¹ (beɪs) n. 1. lowest part in music 2. bass singer or voice —a. 3. relating to or denoting the bass —bass clef clef that establishes F a fifth below middle C on fourth line of staff

bass² (bæs) n. any of large variety of fish, esp. sea perch

basset ('bæsɪt) n. type of smooth-haired dog

basset horn obsolete woodwind instrument

bassinet (bæsɪ'nɛt) n. wickerwork or wooden cradle or pram, usu. hooded

bassoon (bə'suːn) n. woodwind instrument of low tone —bas'soonist n.

bast (bæst) n. fibrous material obtained from phloem of jute, flax etc. used for making rope etc.

bastard ('bɑːstəd, 'bæs-) n. 1. child born of unmarried parents 2. inf. person, as in lucky bastard —a. 3. illegitimate 4. spurious —'bastardize or -ise vt. 1. debase 2. declare illegitimate —'bastardy n.

baste¹ (beɪst) vt. 1. moisten (meat) during cooking with hot fat 2. beat with stick —'basting n.

baste² (beɪst) vt. sew loosely, tack

bastinado (bæstɪ'neɪdəʊ) n. 1. beating with stick, esp. on soles of feet (pl. -es) —vt. 2. inflict a bastinado on (-doing, -doed)

bastion ('bæstɪən) n. 1. projecting part of fortification, tower 2. strong defence or bulwark

bat¹ (bæt) n. 1. any of various types of club used to hit ball in certain sports, eg cricket, baseball —v. 2. strike with bat or use bat in sport (-tt-) —'batting n. performance with bat —'batsman n.

bat² (bæt) n. nocturnal mouselike flying animal

bat³ (bæt) vt. flutter (one's eyelids) (-tt-)

batch (bætʃ) n. group or set of similar objects, esp. cakes etc. baked together

bated ('beɪtɪd) a. —with bated breath anxiously

bath (bɑːθ) n. 1. vessel or place to bathe in 2. water for bathing 3. act of bathing —pl. 4. place for swimming —v. 5. wash —bath cube cube of soluble scented material for use in bath —'bathrobe n. loose-fitting garment of towelling, for wear before or after bath or swimming —'bathroom n. room containing bath and usu. washbasin and lavatory 2. US lavatory —bath salts soluble scented salts for use in bath

Bath chair (bɑːθ) invalid chair

bathe (beɪð) vi. 1. swim —vt. 2. apply liquid to —v. 3. wash 4. immerse or be immersed in water (**bathed**, '**bathing**) —n. 5. a swim or paddle —'**bather** n.

bathometer (bə'θɒmɪtə) n. instrument for measuring depth of water —**batho'metric** a.

bathos ('beɪθɒs) n. ludicrous descent from the elevated to the ordinary in writing or speech

bathyscaph ('bæθɪskæf), **bathyscaphe** ('bæθɪskeɪf, -skæf), or **bathyscape** n. vessel for deep-sea observation

bathysphere ('bæθɪsfɪə) n. strong steel deep-sea diving sphere, lowered by cable

batik or **battik** ('bætɪk) n. dyeing process using wax

batiste (bæ'tiːst) n. fine plain-weave cotton

batman ('bætmən) n. military officer's servant

baton ('bætɒn) n. 1. slender stick used by conductor of an orchestra 2. policeman's truncheon 3. staff serving as symbol of office

batrachian (bə'treɪkɪən) n. any amphibian, esp. frog or toad

battalion (bə'tæljən) n. military unit consisting of three or more companies

batten[1] ('bætən) n. 1. narrow piece of board, strip of wood —vt. 2. (esp. with down) fasten, make secure

batten[2] ('bætən) vi. (usu. with on) thrive, esp. at someone else's expense

'**batter** ('bætə) vt. 1. strike continuously —n. 2. mixture of flour, eggs, milk, used in cooking —**battered baby** young child who has sustained serious injuries through violence of parent or other adult —**battering ram** esp. formerly, large beam used to break down fortifications

battery ('bætərɪ) n. 1. connected group of electrical cells 2. any electrical cell or accumulator 3. number of similar things occurring together 4. Law assault by beating 5. number of guns 6. place where they are mounted 7. unit of artillery 8. large number of cages for rearing poultry etc.

batting ('bætɪŋ) n. cotton fibre, used as stuffing

battle ('bætəl) n. 1. fight between armies, combat —vi. 2. fight 3. struggle —'**battlement** n. wall, parapet on fortification with openings or embrasures —**battle-axe** n. inf. domineering woman —**battle cruiser** high-speed heavily armed warship of battleship size but with light armour —**battle dress** ordinary uniform of soldier —**battle fatigue** mental disorder characterized by anxiety and depression, caused by stress of warfare —'**battlefield** or '**battleground** n. place where battle is fought —**battle royal** 1. fight involving more than two combatants 2. long violent argument —'**battleship** n. heavily armed and armoured fighting ship

battledore ('bætəldɔː) n. 1. ancient racket game 2. light racket used in this game (also **battledore and shuttlecock**)

batty ('bætɪ) a. inf. crazy, silly

bauble ('bɔːbəl) n. showy trinket

baulk (bɔːk) see BALK —**baulk line** or **balk line** Billiards straight line across table behind which cue balls start game

bauxite ('bɔːksaɪt) n. clay yielding aluminium

bawd (bɔːd) n. 1. prostitute 2. brothel keeper —'**bawdy** a. obscene, lewd

bawl (bɔːl) v. 1. cry 2. shout —n. 3. loud cry or shout

bay[1] (beɪ) n. 1. wide inlet of sea 2. space between two columns 3. recess —**bay window** —'**sickbay** n. room for sick people in ship, school etc.

bay[2] (beɪ) n. 1. bark 2. cry of hounds in pursuit —vi. 3. bark —**at bay** 1. cornered 2. at a distance

bay[3] (beɪ) n. 1. laurel tree —pl. 2. honorary crown of victory —'**bayberry** n. tropical Amer. tree that yields oil —**bay rum** aromatic liquid, used in medicines etc., orig. obtained by distilling leaves of bayberry tree with rum

bay[4] (beɪ) a. reddish-brown

bayonet ('beɪənɪt) n. 1. stabbing weapon fixed to rifle —vt. 2. stab with this ('**bayoneted**, '**bayoneting**)

bazaar or **bazar** (bə'zɑː) n. 1. market, esp. in Orient 2. sale of goods for charity

bazooka (bə'zuːkə) n. antitank rocket launcher

B.B. 1. Boys' Brigade 2. (of pencils) double black

B.B.C. British Broadcasting Corporation

BC British Columbia

B.C. before Christ

BCG Bacillus Calmette-Guérin (anti-tuberculosis vaccine)

B.Com. or **B.Comm.** Bachelor of Commerce

B.D. Bachelor of Divinity

B/D bank draft

B.D.S. Bachelor of Dental Surgery

be (biː; unstressed bɪ) vi. 1. live 2. exist 3. have a state or quality (**I am**, **he is**; we, you, they **are**, pr. ind. —**was**, pl. **were**, pt. —**been** pp. —'**being** pr.p.)

Be Chem. beryllium

be- (comb. form) 1. surround; cover, as in befog 2. affect completely, as in bedazzle 3. consider as; cause to be, as in befriend 4. at, for, against, on, or over, as in bewail, berate

B.E. 1. bill of exchange 2. Bachelor of Engineering

beach (biːtʃ) n. 1. shore of sea —vt. 2. run (boat) on shore —'**beachcomber** n. one who habitually searches shore debris for items of value —'**beachhead** n. 1. area on beach captured from enemy 2. base for operations

beacon ('biːkən) n. 1. signal fire 2. lighthouse, buoy 3. (radio) signal used for navigation

bead (biːd) n. 1. little ball pierced for threading on string of necklace, rosary etc. 2. drop of liquid 3. narrow moulding —'**beaded** a. —'**beading** n. —'**beady** a. small and bright

beadle ('biːdəl) n. Hist. church or parish officer

beagle ('biːgəl) n. small hound

beak (biːk) n. 1. projecting horny jaws of bird 2. anything pointed or projecting 3. sl. magistrate

beaker ('biːkə) n. 1. large drinking cup 2. glass vessel used by chemists

beam (biːm) n. 1. long squared piece of wood 2. ship's cross timber, side, or width 3. ray of light etc. 4. broad smile 5. bar of a balance —vt. 6. aim (light, radio waves etc.) in a certain direction —vi. 7. shine 8. smile benignly —**on her beam-ends** (of vessel) heeled over through angle of 90° —**on one's beam-ends** out of resources; destitute

bean (biːn) n. any of various leguminous plants or their seeds —n. inf. celebration —'**beanbag** n. 1. small cloth bag filled with dried beans and thrown in games 2. large cushion filled with foam rubber or polystyrene granules and used as seat —'**beanfeast** n. UK inf. 1. annual dinner given by employers to employees 2. any festive occasion —**full of beans** inf. lively

bear[1] (beə) vt. 1. carry 2. support 3. produce 4. endure —vi. 5. (with upon) press (upon) (bore pt., born or borne pp., '**bearing** pr.p.) —'**bearable** a. endurable; tolerable —'**bearer** n.

bear[2] (beə) n. 1. heavy carnivorous quadruped 2. other bearlike animals, eg Aust. koala bear —**bear garden** scene of tumult —**bear hug** 1. wrestling hold in which arms are locked round opponent's chest and arms 2. any similar tight embrace —'**bearskin** n. Guards' tall fur helmet

beard (biəd) n. 1. hair on chin —vt. 2. oppose boldly

bearing ('beəriŋ) n. 1. support or guide for mechanical part, esp. one reducing friction 2. relevance 3. behaviour 4. direction 5. relative position 6. device on shield

beast (biːst) n. 1. animal 2. four-footed animal 3. brutal man —'**beastliness** n. —'**beastly** a.

beat (biːt) vt. 1. strike repeatedly 2. overcome 3. surpass 4. stir vigorously with striking action 5. flap (wings) 6. make, wear (path) —vi. 7. throb 8. sail against wind (**beat** pt., '**beaten** pp.) —n. 9. stroke 10. pulsation 11. appointed course 12. basic rhythmic unit in piece of music —a. 13. sl. exhausted —'**beater** n. 1. instrument for beating 2. one who rouses game for shooters

beatify (bi'ætifai) vt. 1. make happy 2. R.C.Ch. pronounce in eternal happiness (first step in

canonization) (-**fied, -fying**) —**bea'tific** a. —**beatifi'cation** n. —**be'atitude** n. blessedness

beatnik ('biːtnik) n. 1. member of Beat Generation of 1950s, rebelling against conventional attitudes 2. inf. person with long hair and shabby clothes

beau (bəʊ) n. suitor (pl. **-s, beaux** (bəʊ, bəʊz))

Beaufort scale ('bəʊfət) system of indicating wind strength (from 0, calm, to 17, hurricane)

beaujolais ('bəʊʒəlei) n. (sometimes B-) red or white wine from southern Burgundy, France

beauty ('bjuːti) n. 1. loveliness, grace 2. beautiful person or thing —'**beauteous** a. —**beau'tician** n. one who works in beauty parlour —'**beautiful** a. —'**beautifully** adv. —'**beautify** vt. —**beauty parlour** or **salon** establishment offering hairdressing, manicure etc. —**beauty sleep** inf. sleep, esp. before midnight —**beauty spot** 1. small dark-coloured patch worn on lady's face as adornment 2. mole or similar natural mark on skin 3. place of outstanding beauty

beaver ('biːvə) n. 1. amphibious rodent 2. its fur —**beaver away** work hard

bebop ('biːbɒp) n. see BOP (sense 1)

B.Ec. Bachelor of Economics

becalmed (bi'kɑːmd) a. (of ship) motionless through lack of wind

became (bi'keim) pt. of BECOME

because (bi'kɒz, -'kəz) conj. since —**because of** on account of

béchamel sauce (beiʃə'mel) thick white sauce

bêche-de-mer (beiʃdə'meə) n. edible sea slug

beck[1] (bek) n. —**at someone's beck and call** subject to someone's slightest whim

beck[2] (bek) n. stream

beckon ('bekən) v. (sometimes with to) summon or lure by silent signal

become (bi'kʌm) vi. 1. come to be —vt. 2. suit (be'**came** pt., be'**come** pp., be'**coming** pr.p.) —be'**coming** a. suitable to 2. proper

becquerel (bekə'rel) n. SI unit of activity of radioactive source

bed (bed) n. 1. piece of furniture for sleeping on 2. garden plot 3. place in which anything rests 4. bottom of river 5. layer, stratum —vt. 6. lay in a bed 7. plant (**-dd-**) —'**bedbug** n. —'**bedbug** n. any of several bloodsucking wingless insects infesting dirty houses —'**bedclothes** pl.n. sheets, blankets, and other bed coverings —**bedding plant** immature plant that may be planted out in garden bed —**bed linen** sheets, pillowcases etc. —'**bedpan** n. container used as lavatory by bedridden people —'**bedridden** a. confined to bed by age or sickness —'**bedrock** n. —'**bedroom** n. —'**bedsitter** n. one-roomed flat —'**bedsore** n. chronic ulcer on skin of bedridden person, caused by prolonged pressure —'**bedspread** *n.* top cover on bed —'**bedstead** *n.* —**bed and breakfast** *chiefly UK* in hotel, boarding house *etc.*, overnight accommodation and breakfast

B.Ed. Bachelor of Education

bedaub (bɪ'dɔːb) *vt.* **1.** smear with something thick, sticky or dirty **2.** ornament in gaudy or vulgar fashion

bedeck (bɪ'dɛk) *vt.* cover with decorations; adorn

bedevil (bɪ'dɛvəl) *vt.* **1.** confuse **2.** torment —be'**devilment** *n.*

bedew (bɪ'djuː) *vt.* wet as with dew

bedizen (bɪ'daɪzən, -'dɪzən) *vt. obs.* dress gaudily or tastelessly —be'**dizenment** *n.*

bedlam ('bɛdləm) *n.* noisy confused scene

Bedlington terrier ('bɛdlɪŋtən) woolly-coated terrier with convex head profile

Bedouin *or* **Beduin** ('bɛduɪn) *n.* **1.** member of nomadic Arab race **2.** *n.* nomadic

bedraggle (bɪ'dræɡəl) *vt.* dirty by trailing in wet or mud —be'**draggled** *a.*

Beds. (bɛdz) Bedfordshire

bee[1] (biː) *n.* insect that makes honey —**bee-eater** *n.* insect-eating bird —'**beehive** *n.* —'**beeline** *n.* shortest route —'**beeswax** *n.* wax secreted by bees —'**beeswing** *n.* filmy crust of tartar that forms in some wines after long keeping in bottle

bee[2] (biː) *n. chiefly US* social gathering for specific purpose, as to carry out communal task

Beeb (biːb) *n. inf.* the B.B.C.

beech (biːtʃ) *n.* **1.** European tree with smooth greyish bark and small nuts **2.** its wood —'**beechen** *a.*

beef (biːf) *n.* **1.** flesh of cattle raised and killed for eating **2.** *inf.* complaint —*vi.* **3.** *inf.* complain —'**beefy** *a.* fleshy, stolid —**beeves** *pl.n.* cattle —'**beefburger** *n. see* HAMBURGER —'**beefeater** *n.* **1.** yeoman of the guard **2.** warder of Tower of London —**beef tea** drink made by boiling pieces of lean beef

Beelzebub (bɪ'ɛlzɪbʌb) *n.* Satan or any devil

been (biːn, bɪn) *pp. of* BE

beep (biːp) *n.* **1.** short, loud sound of car horn *etc.* —*vi.* **2.** make this sound

beer (bɪə) *n.* fermented alcoholic drink made from hops and malt —'**beery** *a.* —**beer parlour** C licensed place where beer is sold to the public —**beer and skittles** *inf.* enjoyment or pleasure

beestings, biestings, *or U.S.* **beastings** ('biːstɪŋz) *pl.n.* (*with sing. v.*) first milk secreted by cow or similar animal after giving birth

beet (biːt) *n.* any of various plants with root used for food or extraction of sugar —'**beetroot** *n.* variety of beet that has bulbous dark red root that may be eaten as vegetable

beetle[1] ('biːtəl) *n.* class of insect with hard upper-wing cases closed over the back for protection —**beetle-browed** *a.* with prominent brows

beetle[2] ('biːtəl) *vi.* **1.** overhang; jut —*a.* **2.** overhanging; prominent

befall (bɪ'fɔːl) *v.* happen (to) (be'**fell,** be'**fallen**)

befit (bɪ'fɪt) *vt.* be suitable to (-tt-) —be'**fittingly** *adv.*

befog (bɪ'fɒɡ) *vt.* perplex, confuse (-ɡɡ-)

before (bɪ'fɔː) *prep.* **1.** in front of **2.** in presence of **3.** in preference to **4.** earlier than —*adv.* **5.** earlier **6.** in front —*conj.* **7.** sooner than —be'**forehand** *adv.* previously

befoul (bɪ'faʊl) *vt.* make filthy

befriend (bɪ'frɛnd) *vt.* make friend of

befuddle (bɪ'fʌdəl) *vt.* **1.** confuse **2.** make stupid with drink —be'**fuddlement** *n.*

beg (bɛɡ) *vt.* **1.** ask earnestly, beseech —*vi.* **2.** ask for or live on alms (-ɡɡ-) —'**beggar** *n.* —'**beggarly** *a.*

began (bɪ'ɡæn) *pt. of* BEGIN

beget (bɪ'ɡɛt) *vt.* produce, generate (be'**got,** be'**gat** *pt.,* be'**gotten,** be'**got** *pp.,* be'**getting** *pr.p.*) —be'**getter** *n.*

begin (bɪ'ɡɪn) *vi.* **1.** (cause to) start —*vt.* **2.** originate **3.** initiate (be'**gan,** be'**gun,** be'**ginning**) —be'**ginner** *n.* novice —be'**ginning** *n.*

begone (bɪ'ɡɒn) *interj.* go away

begonia (bɪ'ɡəʊnjə) *n.* genus of tropical plant

begot (bɪ'ɡɒt) *pt./pp. of* BEGET

begrudge (bɪ'ɡrʌdʒ) *vt.* grudge, envy someone the possession of

beguile (bɪ'ɡaɪl) *vt.* **1.** charm, fascinate **2.** amuse **3.** deceive —be'**guiler** *n.*

beguine (bɪ'ɡiːn) *n.* **1.** dance of S Amer. origin **2.** music in rhythm of this dance

begum ('beɪɡəm) *n. esp.* in India, Muslim woman of high rank

begun (bɪ'ɡʌn) *pp. of* BEGIN

behalf (bɪ'hɑːf) *n.* favour, benefit, interest (*esp. in* on behalf of)

behave (bɪ'heɪv) *vi.* act, function in particular way —be'**haviour** *or U.S.* be'**havior** *n.* conduct —be'**haviourism** *or U.S.* be'**haviorism** *n.* school of psychology that regards observable behaviour as the only valid subject for study —**behave oneself** conduct oneself (well)

behead (bɪ'hɛd) *vt.* cut off head of

beheld (bɪ'hɛld) *pt./pp. of* BEHOLD

behemoth (bɪ'hiːmɒθ) *n.* **1.** *Bible* gigantic beast described in Job **2.** huge person or thing

behest (bɪ'hɛst) *n.* charge, command

behind (bɪ'haɪnd) *prep.* **1.** further back or earlier than **2.** in support of —*adv.* **3.** in the rear —be'**hindhand** *a./adv.* **1.** in arrears **2.** tardy

behold (bɪ'həʊld) vt. watch, see (**be'held** pt., **be'held, be'holden** pp.) —**be'holder** n.

beholden (bɪ'həʊldən) a. bound in gratitude

behove (bɪ'həʊv) vt. (only impers.) be fit, necessary for

beige (beɪʒ) n. 1. undyed woollen cloth 2. its colour

being ('biːɪŋ) n. 1. existence 2. that which exists 3. creature —v. 4. pr.p. of BE

bejewel (bɪ'dʒuːəl) vt. decorate as with jewels (-ll-)

bel (bɛl) n. unit for comparing two power levels

belabour or U.S. **belabor** (bɪ'leɪbə) vt. beat soundly

belated (bɪ'leɪtɪd) a. 1. late 2. too late

belay (bɪ'leɪ) vt. fasten (rope) to peg, pin etc.

belch (bɛltʃ) vi. 1. void wind by mouth —vt. 2. eject violently 3. cast up —n. 4. emission of wind etc.

beldam or **beldame** ('bɛldəm) n. obs. old woman

beleaguer (bɪ'liːgə) vt. besiege

belfry ('bɛlfrɪ) n. bell tower

Belial ('biːlɪəl) n. the devil, Satan

belie (bɪ'laɪ) vt. 1. contradict 2. misrepresent (**be'lied** pt./pp., **be'lying** pr.p.)

believe (bɪ'liːv) vt. 1. regard as true or real —vi. 2. have faith —**be'lief** n. —**be'lievable** a. credible —**be'liever** n. esp. one of same religious faith

Belisha beacon (bə'liːʃə) flashing light in orange globe marking a pedestrian crossing

belittle (bɪ'lɪt'l) vt. regard, speak of, as having little worth or value —**be'littlement** n.

bell (bɛl) n. 1. hollow metal instrument giving ringing sound when struck 2. electrical device emitting ring or buzz as signal —**bell-bottomed** a. —**bell-bottoms** pl.n. trousers that flare from knee —**'bellboy** n. pageboy in hotel —**bell jar** bell-shaped glass cover to protect flower arrangements etc. or to cover apparatus in experiments (also **bell glass**) —**bell metal** alloy of copper and tin, used in casting bells —**'bellwether** n. 1. sheep that leads flock, oft. bearing bell 2. leader, esp. one followed blindly

belladonna (bɛlə'dɒnə) n. deadly nightshade

belle (bɛl) n. beautiful woman, reigning beauty

belles-lettres (Fr. bɛl'lɛtr) pl.n. (with sing. v.) literary works, esp. essays and poetry —**bel'letrist** n.

bellicose ('bɛlɪkəʊs, -kəʊz) a. warlike

belligerent (bɪ'lɪdʒərənt) a. 1. hostile, aggressive 2. making war —n. 3. warring person or nation —**bel'ligerence** n.

bellow ('bɛləʊ) v. 1. roar like bull 2. shout —n. 3. roar of bull 4. any deep cry or shout

bellows ('bɛləʊz) pl.n. instrument for creating stream of air

belly ('bɛlɪ) n. 1. part of body which contains intestines 2. stomach —v. 3. swell out (**'bellied, 'bellying**) —**belly ache** inf. stomachache —**'bellyache** vi. sl. complain repeatedly —**'bellybutton** n. inf. navel (also **tummy button**) —**belly dance** sensuous dance performed by women, with undulating movements of abdomen —**belly-dance** vi. perform belly dance —**belly flop** dive into water in which body lands horizontally —**belly-flop** vi. perform belly flop —**'bellyful** n. 1. as much as one wants or can eat 2. sl. more than one can tolerate —**belly laugh** inf. hearty laugh

belong (bɪ'lɒŋ) vi. 1. (with to) be the property or attribute (of) 2. (with to) be a member or inhabitant (of) 3. have an allotted place 4. pertain —**be'longings** pl.n. personal possessions

beloved (bɪ'lʌvɪd, -'lʌvd) a. 1. much loved —n. 2. dear one

below (bɪ'ləʊ) adv. 1. beneath —prep. 2. lower than

belt (bɛlt) n. 1. band 2. girdle 3. zone or district —vt. 4. surround, fasten with belt 5. mark with band 6. inf. thrash

beluga (bɪ'luːgə) n. large white sturgeon

belvedere ('bɛlvɪdɪə, bɛlvɪ'dɪə) n. building, such as summerhouse, sited to command fine view

B.E.M. British Empire Medal

bemoan (bɪ'məʊn) vt. grieve over (loss etc.)

bemuse (bɪ'mjuːz) vt. confuse, bewilder

ben[1] (bɛn) Scot. n. 1. inner room in cottage —prep./adv. 2. in; within; inside

ben[2] (bɛn) n. Scot., Irish mountain peak

bench (bɛntʃ) n. 1. long seat 2. seat or body of judges etc. —vt. 3. provide with benches —**bench mark** fixed point, criterion

bend (bɛnd) v. 1. (cause to) form a curve (**bent** pt./pp.) —n. 2. curve —pl. 3. decompression sickness —**'bender** n. inf. drinking bout —**bend sinister** Her. diagonal line on shield, typically indicating bastard line

beneath (bɪ'niːθ) prep. 1. under, lower than —adv. 2. below

Benedictine (bɛnɪ'dɪktiːn, -taɪn) n. 1. monk or nun of order of Saint Benedict 2. (bɛnɪ'dɪktiːn) liqueur first made at Benedictine monastery

benediction (bɛnɪ'dɪkʃən) n. invocation of divine blessing

benefit ('bɛnɪfɪt) n. 1. advantage, favour, profit, good 2. money paid by a government etc. to unemployed etc. —vt. 3. do good to —vi. 4. receive good (**'benefited, 'benefiting**) —**ben-e'faction** n. —**'benefactor** n. 1. one who helps or does good to others 2. patron (**'benefactress** fem.) —**'benefice** n. an ecclesiastical living —**be'neficence** n. —**be'neficent** a. 1. doing good 2. kind —**be'neficently** adv. —**bene'ficial**

a. advantageous, helpful —**bene'ficially** *adv.* —**bene'ficiary** *n.* —**benefit society** US *see* **friendly society** *at* FRIEND

benevolent (bɪ'nevələnt) *a.* **1.** kindly **2.** charitable —**be'nevolence** *n.* —**be'nevolently** *adv.*

Bengali (bɛn'gɔːlɪ, bɛŋ-) *n.* **1.** member of people living chiefly in Bangladesh and West Bengal **2.** their language —*a.* **3.** of Bengal, Bengalis or their language

benighted (bɪ'naɪtɪd) *a.* ignorant, uncultured

benign (bɪ'naɪn) *a.* **1.** kindly **2.** mild **3.** favourable **4.** *Pathol.* (of tumour *etc.*) not malignant —**benignancy** (bɪ'nɪgnənsɪ) *n.* —**be'nignant** (bɪ'nɪgnənt) *a.* —**benignantly** (bɪ'nɪg-nəntlɪ) *adv.* —**benignity** (bɪ'nɪgnɪtɪ) *n.* —**be-'nignly** *adv.*

benison ('bɛnɪzən, -sən) *n.* *obs.* blessing

bent (bɛnt) *v.* **1.** *pt./pp. of* BEND —*a.* **2.** curved **3.** resolved (on) **4.** *inf.* corrupt **5.** *inf.* deviant **6.** *inf.* crazy —*n.* **7.** inclination, personal propensity —'**bentwood** *n.* wood bent in moulds after being heated by steaming

bent grass low-growing perennial grass which has spreading panicle of tiny flowers

benumb (bɪ'nʌm) *vt.* make numb, deaden

Benzedrine ('bɛnzɪdriːn, -drɪn) *n.* R amphetamine

benzene ('bɛnziːn) *n.* one of group of related flammable liquids used in chemistry and as solvents, cleaning agents *etc.*

benzoin ('bɛnzəʊɪn, -zəʊɪn) *n.* gum resin obtained from various tropical Asian trees, used in ointments, perfume *etc.*

bequeath (bɪ'kwiːð, -'kwiːθ) *vt.* leave (property *etc.*) by will —**bequest** (bɪ'kwɛst) *n.* **1.** bequeathing **2.** legacy

berate (bɪ'reɪt) *vt.* scold harshly

Berber ('bɜːbə) *n.* **1.** member of Caucasoid Muslim people of N Afr. **2.** language of this people —*a.* **3.** of this people or their language

berberis ('bɜːbərɪs) *n.* shrub with red berries

berceuse (*Fr.* bɛr'søz) *n.* **1.** lullaby **2.** instrumental piece suggestive of this

bereave (bɪ'riːv) *vt.* (*usu. with of*) deprive (of), *esp.* by death (-'**reaved**, -'**reft** *pt./pp.*) —**be'reavement** *n.* loss, *esp.* by death

beret ('bɛreɪ) *n.* round, closefitting hat

berg (bɜːg) *n.* **1.** large mass of ice **2.** SA mountain

bergamot ('bɜːgəmɒt) *n.* **1.** type of pear with strong flavour **2.** type of orange **3.** fragrant oil produced from this, used in perfumery

beriberi (bɛrɪ'bɛrɪ) *n.* tropical disease caused by vitamin B deficiency

berk (bɜːk) *n.* UK *sl.* stupid person

berkelium (bɜː'kiːlɪəm, 'bɜːklɪəm) *n.* radioactive transuranic element

Berks. (bɑːks) Berkshire

Bermuda shorts (bə'mjuːdə) close-fitting shorts that come down to knees

berry ('bɛrɪ) *n.* **1.** small juicy stoneless fruit —*vi.* **2.** look for or pick berries

berserk (bə'zɜːk, -'sɜːk) *a.* frenzied

berth (bɜːθ) *n.* **1.** ship's mooring place **2.** place to sleep in ship or train —*vt.* **3.** moor

beryl ('bɛrɪl) *n.* variety of crystalline mineral including aquamarine and emerald

beryllium (bɛ'rɪlɪəm) *n.* corrosion-resistant toxic metallic element

beseech (bɪ'siːtʃ) *vt.* entreat, implore (**be-'sought** *pt./pp.*)

beset (bɪ'sɛt) *vt.* assail, surround with danger, problems (**be'set, be'setting**)

beside (bɪ'saɪd) *prep.* **1.** by the side of, near **2.** distinct from —**be'sides** *adv./prep.* in addition (to)

besiege (bɪ'siːdʒ) *vt.* surround (with armed forces *etc.*)

besmirch (bɪ'smɜːtʃ) *vt.* **1.** make dirty; soil **2.** reduce brightness of **3.** sully

besom ('biːzəm) *n.* broom, *esp.* one made of bundle of twigs tied to handle

besotted (bɪ'sɒtɪd) *a.* **1.** drunk **2.** foolish **3.** infatuated

besought (bɪ'sɔːt) *pt./pp. of* BESEECH

bespangle (bɪ'spæŋgəl) *vt.* cover with or as if with spangles

bespatter (bɪ'spætə) *vt.* **1.** splash, as with dirty water **2.** defile; besmirch

bespeak (bɪ'spiːk) *vt.* engage beforehand (**be'spoke** *pt.*, **be'spoke, be'spoken** *pp.*) —**be'spoke** *a.* **1.** (of garments) made to order **2.** selling such garments

Bessemer process ('bɛsɪmə) process for producing steel by blowing air through molten pig iron in refractory-lined furnace to remove impurities

best (bɛst) *a./adv.* **1.** *sup. of* GOOD *and* WELL —*vt.* **2.** defeat —**best man** (male) attendant of bridegroom at wedding —**best seller 1.** book or other product that has sold in great numbers **2.** author of one or more such books *etc.*

bestial ('bɛstɪəl) *a.* like a beast, brutish —**besti'ality** *n.*

bestiary ('bɛstɪərɪ) *n.* moralizing medieval collection of descriptions of real and/or mythical animals

bestir (bɪ'stɜː) *vt.* rouse to activity

bestow (bɪ'stəʊ) *vt.* give, confer —**be'stowal** *n.*

bestrew (bɪ'struː) *vt.* scatter over (surface)

bestride (bɪ'straɪd) *vt.* **1.** sit or stand over with legs apart **2.** mount (horse) (**be'strode, be'stridden, be'striding**)

bet (bɛt) *v.* **1.** agree to pay (money *etc.*) if wrong (or win if right) in guessing result of contest *etc.* (**bet** *or* '**betted** *pt./pp.,* '**betting** *pr.p.*) —*n.* **2.** money risked in this way

beta ('biːtə) *n.* **1.** second letter in Gr. alphabet (B or β) **2.** second in group or series

betake (bı'teık) *vt.* —**betake oneself** go; move

beta particle electron or positron emitted by nucleus during radioactive decay

betatron ('biːtətrɒn) *n.* particle accelerator for producing high-energy beams of electrons by magnetic induction

betel ('biːtəl) *n.* species of pepper, chewed in parts of Asia as a narcotic —**betel nut** the nut of the areca palm

bête noire (bɛt 'nwaːr) *Fr.* pet aversion

bethink (bı'θıŋk) *obs., dial. v.* **1.** cause (oneself) to consider or meditate —*vt.* **2.** (*oft. with of*) remind (oneself)

betide (bı'taıd) *v.* happen (to)

betimes (bı'taımz) *adv. obs.* **1.** in good time; early **2.** soon

betoken (bı'təukən) *vt.* be a sign of

betony ('bɛtənı) *n.* plant with reddish-purple flower spike

betray (bı'treı) *vt.* **1.** be disloyal to, *esp.* by assisting an enemy **2.** reveal, divulge **3.** show signs of —be'**trayal** *n.* —be'**trayer** *n.*

betroth (bı'trəuð) *vt.* promise to marry —be'**trothal** *n.* —be'**trothed** *n./a.*

better ('bɛtə) *a./adv.* **1.** *comp.* of GOOD and WELL —*v.* **2.** improve —'**betterment** *n.*

between (bı'twiːn) *prep./adv.* **1.** in the intermediate part, in space or time **2.** indicating reciprocal relation or comparison

betwixt (bı'twıkst) *prep./adv. obs.* between

bevel ('bɛvəl) *n.* **1.** surface not at right angle to another **2.** slant —*vi.* **3.** slope, slant —*vt.* **4.** cut on slant (-**ll**-) —*a.* **5.** slanted —**bevel gear** gear having teeth cut into conical surface

beverage ('bɛvərıdʒ, 'bɛvrıdʒ) *n.* drink

bevy ('bɛvı) *n.* flock or group

bewail (bı'weıl) *vt.* lament

beware (bı'wɛə) *v.* be on one's guard (against), be wary (of)

bewilder (bı'wıldə) *vt.* puzzle, confuse —be'**wildering** *a.* —be'**wilderingly** *adv.* —be'**wilderment** *n.*

bewitch (bı'wıtʃ) *vt.* **1.** cast spell over **2.** charm, fascinate —be'**witching** *a.* —be'**witchingly** *adv.*

bey (beı) *n.* **1.** in Ottoman Empire, title given to provincial governors **2.** in modern Turkey, title of address, corresponding to *Mr.* (*also* **beg**)

beyond (bı'jɒnd) *adv.* **1.** farther away **2.** besides —*prep.* **3.** on the farther side of **4.** later than **5.** surpassing, out of reach of

bezel ('bɛzəl) *n.* **1.** sloping face adjacent to working edge of cutting tool **2.** oblique faces of

cut gem **3.** grooved ring or part holding watch crystal *etc.*

bezique (bı'ziːk) *n.* **1.** card game for two or more players **2.** in this game, queen of spades and jack of diamonds declared together

b.f. 1. UK *inf.* bloody fool **2.** *Print.* bold face

B/F *or* **b/f** brought forward

BFPO British Forces Post Office

bhang *or* **bang** (bæŋ) *n.* preparation of leaves and flower tops of Indian hemp, much used as narcotic in India

b.h.p. brake horsepower

Bi *Chem.* bismuth

bi- *or* *sometimes before vowel* **bin-** (*comb. form*) **1.** two; having two, as in *bifocal* **2.** occurring every two, as in *biennial* **3.** on both sides *etc.*, as in *bilateral* **4.** occurring twice during, as in *biweekly* **5.** indicating acid salt of dibasic acid, as in *sodium bicarbonate*

biannual (baı'ænjuəl) *a.* occurring twice a year —bi'**annually** *adv.*

bias ('baıəs) *n.* **1.** slant **2.** personal inclination or preference **3.** one-sided inclination (*pl.* **-es**) —*vt.* **4.** influence, affect (**-s-, -ss-**) —'**biased** *a.* prejudiced —**bias binding** strip of material cut on bias, used for binding hems or for decoration

biaxial (baı'æksıəl) *a.* (*esp.* of crystal) having two axes

bib (bıb) *n.* **1.** cloth put under child's chin to protect clothes when eating **2.** top of apron or overalls

bibcock ('bıbkɒk) *or* **bibb** (bıb) *n.* tap with nozzle bent downwards

bibelot ('bıbləu) *n.* attractive or curious trinket

bibl. 1. bibliographical **2.** bibliography

Bibl. Biblical

Bible ('baıb'l) *n.* the sacred writings of the Christian religion —**biblical** ('bıblık'l) *a.* —**biblicist** ('bıblısıst) *n.*

biblio- (*comb. form*) book or books, as in *bibliography*

bibliography (bıblı'ɒgrəfı) *n.* **1.** list of books on a subject **2.** history and description of books —bibli'**ographer** *n.* —biblio'**graphical** *a.*

bibliomania (bıblıəu'meınıə) *n.* extreme fondness for books —biblio'**maniac** *n./a.*

bibliophile ('bıblıəfaıl) *or* **bibliophil** ('bıblıəfıl) *n.* lover, collector of books —bibli'**ophily** *n.*

bibulous ('bıbjuləs) *a.* given to drinking

bicameral (baı'kæmərəl) *a.* (of legislature) consisting of two chambers —bi'**cameralism** *n.*

bicarb ('baıkɑːb) *n.* bicarbonate of soda

bicarbonate (baı'kɑːbənıt, -neıt) *n.* chemical compound releasing carbon dioxide when mixed with acid —**bicarbonate of soda** sodium bicarbonate, *esp.* as medicine or raising agent

bicentenary (baısɛn'tiːnərı) *or U.S.* **bicen-**

tennial (baɪsɛnˈtɛnɪəl) n. 1. two hundredth anniversary 2. its celebration

biceps ('baɪsɛps) n. two-headed muscle, esp. muscle of upper arm

bicker ('bɪkə) vi./n. quarrel over petty things —'**bickering** n.

bicolour ('baɪkʌlə), **bicoloured** or U.S. **bicolor, bicolored** a. two-coloured

bicuspid (baɪˈkʌspɪd) or **bicuspidate** (baɪˈkʌspɪdeɪt) a. 1. having two points —n. 2. bicuspid tooth; premolar

bicycle ('baɪsɪkəl) n. vehicle with two wheels, one in front of other, pedalled by rider —'**bicyclist** n.

bid (bɪd) vt. 1. offer 2. say 3. command 4. invite (**bad, bade** or **bid, 'bidden**) —n. 5. offer, esp. of price 6. try 7. Cards call —'**biddable** a. 1. having sufficient value to be bid on 2. docile; obedient —'**biddableness** n. —'**bidder** n. —'**bidding** n.

biddy ('bɪdɪ) n. dial. chicken or hen

bide (baɪd) vi. 1. remain 3. dwell —vt. 3. await ('**bided** or **bode**, '**bided**) —'**biding** n.

bidet ('biːdeɪ) n. low basin for washing genital area

biennial (baɪˈɛnɪəl) a. 1. happening every two years 2. lasting two years —n. 3. plant living two years —bi'**ennially** adv.

bier (bɪə) n. frame for bearing dead to grave

biff (bɪf) sl. n. 1. blow with fist —vt. 2. give (someone) such a blow

bifid ('baɪfɪd) a. divided into two lobes by median cleft —bi'**fidity** n.

bifocal (baɪˈfəʊkəl) a. having two different focal lengths —bi'**focals** pl.n. spectacles having bifocal lenses for near and distant vision

bifurcate ('baɪfəkeɪt) vi. 1. divide into two branches —a. ('baɪfəkeɪt, -kɪt) 2. forked or divided into two branches —bifur'**cation** n.

big (bɪg) a. of great or considerable size, height, number, power etc. ('**bigger** comp., '**biggest** sup.) —'**bigness** n. —**Big Brother** person or organization that exercises total dictatorial control —**big dipper** (in amusement parks) narrow railway with open carriages that run swiftly over route of sharp curves and steep inclines —**big end** UK larger end of connecting rod in internal-combustion engine —**big shot** sl. important person —**big stick** inf. force or threat of force —**big time** sl. highest level of profession, esp. entertainment —**big-timer** n. —**big top** inf. 1. main tent of circus 2. circus itself —'**bigwig** n. sl. important person

bigamy ('bɪgəmɪ) n. crime of marrying a person while one is still legally married to someone else —'**bigamist** n. —'**bigamous** a.

bight (baɪt) n. 1. curve or loop in rope 2. long curved shoreline or water bounded by it

bigot ('bɪgət) n. person intolerant or not

receptive to ideas of others, esp. on religion etc. —'**bigoted** a. —'**bigotry** n.

bijou ('biːʒuː) n. 1. something small and delicately worked (pl. -**joux** (-ʒuːz)) —a. 2. oft. ironic small but tasteful

bike (baɪk) n. 1. bicycle 2. motor bike

bikini (bɪˈkiːnɪ) n. woman's brief two-piece swimming costume

bilateral (baɪˈlætərəl) a. two-sided

bilberry ('bɪlbərɪ) n. small European moorland plant with edible blue berries

bile (baɪl) n. 1. fluid secreted by the liver 2. anger, ill-temper —'**biliary** ('bɪlɪərɪ) a. of bile, ducts that convey bile, or gall bladder —**bilious** ('bɪlɪəs) a. nauseous, nauseating —'**biliousness** ('bɪlɪəsnɪs) n.

bilge (bɪldʒ) n. 1. bottom of ship's hull 2. dirty water that collects in vessel's bilge (also **bilge water**) 3. inf. nonsense —vi. 4. spring a leak

bilingual (baɪˈlɪŋgwəl) a. speaking, or written in, two languages —bi'**lingualism** n.

bilk (bɪlk) vt. 1. balk; thwart 2. (oft. with of) cheat, deceive 3. escape from; elude —n. 4. swindle, cheat 5. person who swindles or cheats —'**bilker** n.

bill¹ (bɪl) n. 1. written account of charges 2. draft of Act of Parliament 3. poster 4. commercial document —vt. 5. present account of charges to 6. announce by advertisement —'**billing** n. degree of importance, esp. in theatre etc. —'**billboard** n. chiefly US see HOARDING —'**billposter** or '**billsticker** n. person who sticks advertising posters to walls etc. —'**billposting** or '**billsticking** n. —**bill of exchange** document instructing third party to pay stated sum at designated future date or on demand —**bill of fare** menu —**bill of lading** document containing full particulars of goods shipped —**clean bill of health** inf. 1. good report of one's physical condition 2. favourable account of person's or company's financial position

bill² (bɪl) n. 1. bird's beak —vi. 2. touch bills, as doves 3. caress

bill³ (bɪl) n. 1. tool for pruning 2. hooked weapon —'**billhook** n. hatchet with hook at end of cutting edge

billabong ('bɪləbɒŋ) n. A pool in intermittent stream

billet¹ ('bɪlɪt) n. 1. civilian quarters for troops 2. resting place —vt. 3. quarter, as troops

billet² ('bɪlɪt) n. 1. chunk of wood, esp. for fuel 2. small bar of iron or steel

billet-doux ('bɪlɪ'duː) Fr. love letter

billiards ('bɪljədz) n. game played on table with balls and cues

billion ('bɪljən) n. million millions (U.S., France thousand millions)

billow ('bɪləʊ) *n.* 1. great swelling wave —*pl.* 2. the sea —*vi.* 3. surge 4. swell out

billy ('bɪlɪ) *or* **billycan** ('bɪlɪkæn) *n.* can with wire handle used for boiling water on open fire —**billy goat** male goat

biltong ('bɪltɒŋ) *n.* **SA** thin strips of meat dried in sun

B.I.M. British Institute of Management

bimetallism (baɪ'mɛtəlɪzəm) *n.* use of two metals, *esp.* gold and silver, in fixed relative values as standard of value and currency

bimonthly (baɪ'mʌnθlɪ) *adv./a.* 1. every two months 2. twice a month

bin (bɪn) *n.* 1. receptacle for corn, refuse *etc.* 2. one particular bottling of wine

binary ('baɪnərɪ) *a.* 1. composed of, characterized by, two 2. dual —**binary star** double star system containing two associated stars revolving around common centre of gravity

bind (baɪnd) *vt.* 1. tie fast 2. tie round, gird 3. tie together 4. oblige 5. seal 6. constrain 7. bandage 8. unite 9. put (book) into cover —*v.* 10. (cause to) cohere (**bound** *pt./pp.*) —**'binder** *n.* one who, or that which binds —**'bindery** *n.* 1. cover of book 2. tape for hem *etc.* —**'binding** *n.* 1. cover of book 2. tape for hem *etc.* —**'bindweed** *n.* convolvulus

bine (baɪn) *n.* climbing or twining stem of any of various plants, such as bindweed

binge (bɪndʒ) *n. inf.* 1. excessive indulgence in eating or drinking 2. spree

bingo ('bɪŋɡəʊ) *n.* game of chance in which numbers drawn are matched with those on a card

binnacle ('bɪnəkəl) *n.* box holding ship's compass

binocular (bɪ'nɒkjʊlə, baɪ-) *a.* seeing with, made for both eyes —**bi'noculars** *pl.n.* telescope made for both eyes

binomial (baɪ'nəʊmɪəl) *a./n.* (denoting) algebraic expression consisting of two terms —**binomial theorem** general formula that expresses any power of binomial without multiplying out

bio- *or before vowel* **bi-** (*comb. form*) life, living, as in *biochemistry*. Such words are not given here where the meaning may easily be inferred from the simple word

bioastronautics (baɪəʊæstrə'nɔːtɪks) *pl.n.* (*with sing. v.*) study of effects of space flight on living organisms

biocoenosis (baɪəʊsiː'nəʊsɪs) *n.* relationships between animals and plants subsisting together

biodegradable (baɪəʊdɪ'ɡreɪdəbəl) *a.* capable of decomposition by natural means

bioengineering (baɪəʊendʒɪ'nɪərɪŋ) *n.* 1. design and manufacture of aids to rectify defective body functions 2. design, manufacture and maintenance of engineering equipment used in biosynthetic processes —**bioengi'neer** *n.*

biog. 1. biographical 2. biography

biogenesis (baɪəʊ'dʒɛnɪsɪs) *n.* principle that living organism must originate from similar parent organism —**bioge'netic(al)** *a.*

biography (baɪ'ɒɡrəfɪ) *n.* story of one person's life —**bi'ographer** *n.* —**bio'graphical** *a.* —**bio'graphically** *adv.*

biol. 1. biological 2. biology

biology (baɪ'ɒlədʒɪ) *n.* study of living organisms —**bio'logical** *a.* —**bio'logically** *adv.* —**bi'ologist** *n.* —**biological control** control of destructive organisms by nonchemical means —**biological warfare** use of living organisms or their toxic products as weapon of war

biomedicine (baɪəʊ'mɛdɪsɪn) *n.* medical and biological study of effects of unusual environmental stress

bionics (baɪ'ɒnɪks) *pl.n.* (*with sing. v.*) study of relation of biological and electronic processes —**bi'onic** *a.* having physical functions augmented by electronic equipment

biophysics (baɪəʊ'fɪzɪks) *pl.n.* (*with sing. v.*) physics of biological processes and application of methods used in physics to biology —**bio'physical** *a.* —**biophysicist** (baɪəʊ'fɪzɪsɪst) *n.*

biopsy ('baɪɒpsɪ) *n.* examination of tissue removed surgically from a living body

biorhythm ('baɪəʊrɪðəm) *n.* complex repeated pattern of physiological states, believed to affect physical, emotional, or mental states

bioscope ('baɪəskəʊp) *n.* **SA** cinema

bioscopy (baɪ'ɒskəpɪ) *n.* examination of body to determine whether it is alive

biosphere ('baɪəsfɪə) *n.* part of earth's surface and atmosphere inhabited by living things

biosynthesis (baɪəʊ'sɪnθɪsɪs) *n.* formation of chemical compounds by living organisms —**biosynthetic** (baɪəʊsɪn'θɛtɪk) *a.*

biotin ('baɪətɪn) *n.* vitamin of B complex, abundant in egg yolk and liver

bipartisan (baɪpɑːtɪ'zæn, baɪ'pɑːtɪzæn) *a.* consisting of or supported by two political parties

bipartite (baɪ'pɑːtaɪt) *a.* consisting of two parts or parties

biped ('baɪpɛd) *n.* two-footed animal —**bipedal** (baɪ'piːdəl, -'pɛdəl) *a.*

biplane ('baɪpleɪn) *n.* aeroplane with two pairs of wings

bipolar (baɪ'pəʊlə) *a.* 1. having two poles 2. of North and South Poles 3. having two opposed opinions *etc.*—**bipo'larity** *n.*

birch (bɜːtʃ) *n.* 1. tree with silvery bark —*vt.* 2. flog —**'birchen** *a.* —**the birch** rod made of birch twigs used, *esp.* formerly, for punishment

bird (bɜːd) n. 1. feathered animal 2. sl. young woman or girl —'**birdlime** n. 1. sticky substance smeared on twigs to catch small birds —vt. 2. smear with birdlime —**bird of paradise** any of various songbirds of New Guinea and neighbouring regions, males having brilliantly coloured plumage —**bird of passage** 1. bird that migrates seasonally 2. transient person —**bird's-eye** a. 1. seen from above; summarizing (esp. in **bird's-eye view**) 2. having markings resembling birds' eyes

birdie ('bɜːdɪ) n. Golf score of one stroke under par for hole 2. inf. bird, esp. small bird

biretta or **berretta** (bɪ'rɛtə) n. square cap worn by Catholic clergy

Biro ('baɪrəʊ) n. R ballpoint pen

birth (bɜːθ) n. 1. bearing, or the being born, of offspring 2. parentage, origin 3. noble descent —**birth control** limitation of childbearing usu. by artificial means —'**birthday** n. —'**birthmark** n. blemish, usu. dark, formed on skin before birth —**birth rate** ratio of live births in specified area etc. to population, usu. expressed per 1000 population per year —'**birthright** n. 1. privileges that person is entitled to as soon as he is born 2. privileges of first-born son 3. inheritance —'**birthstone** n. precious or semiprecious stone associated with month or sign of zodiac and thought to bring luck if worn by person born in that month

biscuit ('bɪskɪt) n. dry, small, thin variety of cake

bisect (baɪ'sɛkt) vt. divide into two equal parts —bi'**sector** n.

bisexual (baɪ'sɛksjʊəl) a. 1. sexually attracted to both men and women 2. of both sexes

bishop ('bɪʃəp) n. 1. clergyman governing diocese 2. chess piece —'**bishopric** n. diocese or office of a bishop

bismuth ('bɪzməθ) n. reddish-white metal used in medicine etc.

bison ('baɪsən) n. 1. large wild ox 2. Amer. buffalo

bisque¹ (bɪsk) n. thick rich soup made from shellfish

bisque² (bɪsk) n. 1. pink to yellowish tan colour 2. earthenware or porcelain that has been fired but not glazed

bistre or U.S. **bister** ('bɪstə) n. 1. transparent water-soluble brownish-yellow pigment made by boiling soot of wood 2. yellowish-brown to dark brown colour

bistro ('biːstrəʊ) n. small restaurant

bit¹ (bɪt) n. 1. fragment, piece 2. biting, cutting part of tool 3. mouthpiece of horse's bridle —'**bitty** a. 1. lacking unity; disjointed 2. containing bits, sediment etc.

bit² (bɪt) pt./pp. of BITE

bit³ (bɪt) n. Comp. smallest unit of information

bitch (bɪtʃ) n. 1. female dog, fox or wolf 2. offens. sl. spiteful woman 3. inf. complaint —vi. 4. inf. complain —'**bitchy** a.

bite (baɪt) vt. 1. cut into, esp. with teeth 2. grip —vi. 3. rise to bait —v. 4. (of corrosive material) eat away or into (**bit** pt., **bit**, '**bitten** pp., '**biting** pr.p.) —n. 5. act of biting 6. wound so made 7. mouthful —'**biter** n. —'**biting** a. 1. piercing; keen 2. sarcastic; incisive —'**bitingly** adv.

bitter ('bɪtə) a. 1. sharp, sour tasting 2. unpleasant 3. (of person) angry or resentful 4. sarcastic —'**bitterly** adv. —'**bitterness** n. —'**bitters** pl.n. essence of bitter herbs —**bitter end** final extremity —'**bittersweet** n. 1. N Amer. climbing plant 2. woody nightshade —a. 3. being a mixture of bitterness and sweetness 4. pleasant but tinged with sadness

bittern ('bɪtən) n. wading bird like heron

bitumen ('bɪtjʊmɪn) n. viscous substance occurring in asphalt, tar etc. —bi'**tuminous** a.

bivalent (baɪ'veɪlənt, 'bɪv-) a. 1. Chem. see DIVALENT 2. (of homologous chromosomes) associated together in pairs —bi'**valency** n.

bivalve ('baɪvælv) a. 1. having a double shell —n. 2. mollusc with such shell

bivouac ('bɪvʊæk, 'bɪvwæk) n. 1. temporary encampment of soldiers, hikers etc. —vi. 2. pass the night in temporary camp ('**bivouacked**, '**bivouacking**)

biz (bɪz) n. inf. business

bizarre (bɪ'zɑː) a. unusual, weird

Bk Chem. berkelium

bk. 1. bank 2. book

B.L. 1. Bachelor of Laws 2. Bachelor of Letters 3. Barrister-at-Law 4. British Library

blab (blæb) v. 1. reveal (secrets) —vi. 2. chatter idly (-**bb**-) —n. 3. telltale 4. gossip —'**blabber** n. 1. person who blabs 2. idle chatter —vi. 3. talk without thinking; chatter

black (blæk) a. 1. of the darkest colour 2. without light 3. dark 4. evil 5. sombre 6. dishonourable —n. 7. darkest colour 8. black dye, clothing etc. 9. (B-) person of dark-skinned race —vt. 10. boycott (specified goods etc.) in industrial dispute —'**blacken** v. —'**blacking** n. substance used for blacking and cleaning leather etc. —'**blackamoor** n. obs. Negro or other person with dark skin —**black-and-blue** a. 1. (of skin) discoloured, as from bruise 2. feeling pain, as from beating —**black-and-white** n. photograph etc. in black, white, and shades of grey rather than in colour —**black art** black magic —'**blackball** vt. vote against, exclude —**black belt** Judo, karate black belt worn by instructor or expert; person entitled to wear this —'**blackberry** n. plant with thorny stems and dark juicy berries, bramble —'**blackbird**

common European songbird —**blackboard** n. dark-coloured surface for writing on with chalk —**black book** book containing names of people to be punished, blacklisted etc. —**black box** inf. flight recorder —**blackcap** n. type of warbler —**blackcock** n. male of the black grouse —**black'currant** n. 1. N temperate shrub having edible black berries 2. its fruit —**black eye** inf. bruising round eye —**blackhead** n. dark, fatty plug blocking pore in skin —**black hole** Astron. region of space resulting from collapse of star, and surrounded by gravitational field that neither matter nor radiation could escape from —**blackleg** n. 1. one who works during strike 2. disease of cattle —**blacklist** n. 1. list of people, organizations considered suspicious, untrustworthy etc. —vt. 2. put on blacklist —**black magic** magic used for evil purposes —**blackmail** vt. 1. extort money from (a person) by threats —n. 2. act of blackmailing 3. money extorted thus —**blackmailer** n. —**Black Maria** (mə'raɪə) police van for transporting prisoners —**black mark** indication of disapproval etc. —**black market** illegal buying and selling of goods —**black mass** travesty of Christian Mass performed by practitioners of black magic —**blackout** n. 1. complete failure of electricity supply 2. sudden cutting off of all stagelights 3. state of temporary unconsciousness 4. obscuring of all lights as precaution against night air attack —**Black Power** social, economic, and political movement of Black people to obtain equality with Whites —**black pudding** sausage made from minced pork fat, pig's blood etc. (also **blood pudding**) —**black sheep** person regarded as disgrace or failure by his family or group —**Blackshirt** n. member of fascist organization, esp. It. Fascist party before and during World War II —**blacksmith** n. smith who works in iron —**black spot** dangerous place, esp. on a road —**blackthorn** n. shrub with black twigs —**black tie** 1. black bow tie worn with dinner jacket —a. 2. denoting occasion when dinner jacket should be worn —**black widow** highly poisonous Amer. spider —**black out** 1. obliterate or extinguish (lights) 2. create a blackout in (a city etc.) 3. lose consciousness, vision or memory temporarily —**in black and white** in print or writing; in extremes —**in someone's black books** inf. out of favour with someone —**the Black Country** heavily industrialized West Midlands of England —**the Black Death** form of bubonic plague pandemic in Europe and Asia during 14th cent. (see BUBONIC PLAGUE)

blackguard ('blæɡɑːd, -ɡəd) n. 1. scoundrel —a. 2. unprincipled, wicked —vt. 3. revile —**blackguardism** n. —**blackguardly** a.

bladder ('blædə) n. membranous bag to contain liquid, esp. urinary bladder

blade (bleɪd) n. 1. edge, cutting part of knife or tool 2. leaf of grass etc. 3. sword 4. obs. dashing fellow 5. flat of oar

blain (bleɪn) n. 1. inflamed swelling 2. pimple, blister

blame (bleɪm) vt. 1. censure 2. culpability —vt. 3. find fault with 4. censure —**blamable** or **blameable** a. —**blameless** a. —**blameworthy** a.

blanch (blɑːntʃ) vt. 1. whiten, bleach, take colour out of 2. (of foodstuffs) briefly boil or fry —v. 3. turn pale

blancmange (blə'mɒnʒ) n. jellylike dessert made with milk

bland (blænd) a. 1. devoid of distinctive characteristics 2. smooth in manner

blandish ('blændɪʃ) vt. 1. coax 2. flatter —**blandishments** pl.n.

blank (blæŋk) a. 1. without marks or writing 2. empty 3. vacant, confused 4. (of verse) without rhyme —n. 5. empty space 6. void 7. cartridge containing no bullet —**blankly** adv. —**blank cheque** 1. cheque that has been signed but on which amount payable has not been specified 2. complete freedom of action —**blank verse** unrhymed verse, esp. in iambic pentameters

blanket ('blæŋkɪt) n. 1. thick (woollen) covering for bed 2. concealing cover —vt. 3. cover with blanket 4. cover, stifle —**blanket stitch** strong reinforcing stitch for edges of blankets and other thick material

blare (bleə) v. 1. sound loudly and harshly —n. 2. such sound

blarney ('blɑːnɪ) n. flattering talk

blasé ('blɑːzeɪ) a. 1. indifferent through familiarity 2. bored

blaspheme (blæs'fiːm) v. show contempt for (God or sacred things, esp. in speech) —**blas'phemer** n. —**blasphemous** ('blæsfɪməs) a. —**blasphemously** ('blæsfɪməslɪ) adv. —**blasphemy** ('blæsfɪmɪ) n.

blast (blɑːst) n. 1. explosion 2. high-pressure wave of air coming from an explosion 3. current of air 4. gust of wind or air 5. loud sound 6. sl. reprimand —vt. 7. blow up 8. remove, open etc. by explosion 9. blight 10. ruin —**blasted** a. 1. blighted, withered 2. damned —**blast furnace** furnace for smelting ore, using preheated blast of air —**blastoff** n. 1. launching of rocket 2. time at which this occurs —**blast off** be launched

blatant ('bleɪt²nt) a. obvious —**blatancy** n.

blather ('blæðə) vi. 1. speak foolishly —n. 2. foolish talk; nonsense

blaze¹ (bleɪz) n. 1. strong fire or flame 2.

brightness **3.** outburst —*vi.* **4.** burn strongly **5.** be very angry

blaze² (bleɪz) *v.* **1.** mark (trees) to establish trail —*n.* **2.** mark on tree **3.** white mark on horse's face

blaze³ (bleɪz) *vt.* **1.** proclaim, publish (as with trumpet) —*n.* **2.** wide publicity

blazer ('bleɪzə) *n.* type of jacket, worn *esp.* for sports

blazon ('bleɪzᵊn) *vt.* **1.** make public, proclaim **2.** describe, depict (arms) —*n.* **3.** coat of arms

bleach (bliːtʃ) *v.* **1.** make or become white —*n.* **2.** bleaching substance —**bleaching powder** white powder consisting of chlorinated calcium hydroxide (*also* **chloride of lime, chlorinated lime**)

bleak¹ (bliːk) *a.* **1.** cold and cheerless **2.** exposed —'**bleakly** *adv.*

bleak² (bliːk) *n.* small, silvery fish

bleary ('blɪərɪ) *a.* with eyes dimmed, as by tears or tiredness —**bleary-eyed** *or* **blear-eyed** *a.* having bleary eyes

bleat (bliːt) *vi.* **1.** cry, as sheep —*v.* **2.** say, speak plaintively —*n.* **3.** sheep's cry

bleed (bliːd) *vi.* **1.** lose blood —*vt.* **2.** draw blood or liquid from **3.** extort money from (**bled** *pt./pp.*)

bleep (bliːp) *n.* short high-pitched sound —'**bleeper** *n.* small portable electronic signalling device

blemish ('blemɪʃ) *n.* **1.** defect **2.** stain —*vt.* **3.** make (something) defective, dirty *etc.* —'**blemished** *a.*

blench (blentʃ) *vi.* start back, flinch

blend (blend) *vt.* **1.** mix —*n.* **2.** mixture —'**blender** *n.* one who, that which blends, *esp.* electrical kitchen appliance for mixing food

blende (blend) *n.* **1.** a zinc ore **2.** any of several sulphide ores

blenny ('blenɪ) *n.* small fish with tapering scaleless body

blesbok *or* **blesbuck** ('blesbʌk) *n.* S Afr. antelope

bless (bles) *vt.* **1.** consecrate **2.** give thanks to **3.** ask God's favour for **4.** (*usu. pass.*) endow (with) **5.** glorify **6.** make happy (**blessed, blest** *pp.*) —**blessed** ('blesɪd, blest) *a.* **1.** made holy **2.** worthy of deep reverence **3.** *R.C.Ch.* (of person) beatified by pope **4.** characterized by happiness **5.** bringing great happiness **6.** damned —**blessedness** ('blesɪdnɪs) *n.* —'**blessing** *n.* **1.** (ceremony asking for) God's protection, aid **2.** short prayer **3.** approval **4.** welcome event, benefit

blether ('bleðə) *n.* nonsense, gossip (*also* '**blather**)

blew (bluː) *pt. of* BLOW¹

blight (blaɪt) *n.* **1.** plant disease **2.** harmful influence —*vt.* **3.** injure as with blight

blighter ('blaɪtə) *n. inf.* fellow, person

Blighty ('blaɪtɪ) *n.* **UK** *sl.* **1.** Britain; home **2.** *esp.* in World War I, wound that causes recipient to be sent home to Britain (*also* **blighty one**)

blimey ('blaɪmɪ) *interj.* **UK** *sl.* exclamation of surprise or annoyance

blimp (blɪmp) *n.* small, nonrigid airship used for observing

blind (blaɪnd) *a.* **1.** unable to see **2.** heedless, random **3.** dim **4.** closed at one end **5.** *sl.* very drunk —*vt.* **6.** deprive of sight —*n.* **7.** something cutting off light **8.** window screen **9.** pretext —'**blindly** *adv.* —'**blindness** *n.* —**blind alley 1.** alley open at one end only; cul-de-sac **2.** *inf.* situation in which no further progress can be made —**blind date** *inf.* social meeting between man and woman who have not met before —**blind flying** navigation of aircraft by use of instruments alone —'**blindfold** *vt.* **1.** cover the eyes of, so as to prevent vision —*n.* **2.** piece of cloth *etc.* used to cover eyes —**blindman's buff** game in which one player is blindfolded —**blind spot 1.** small area of retina, where optic nerve enters, in which vision is not experienced **2.** area where vision is obscured **3.** subject about which person is ignorant or prejudiced

blink (blɪŋk) *vi.* **1.** wink **2.** twinkle **3.** shine intermittently —*n.* **4.** gleam —'**blinkers** *pl.n.* leather flaps to prevent horse from seeing to the side —**blink at** see, know about, but ignore —**on the blink** *inf.* not working (properly)

blip (blɪp) *n.* repetitive sound or visible pulse, *eg* on radar screen

bliss (blɪs) *n.* perfect happiness —'**blissful** *a.* —'**blissfully** *adv.* —'**blissfulness** *n.*

blister ('blɪstə) *n.* **1.** bubble on skin **2.** surface swelling, *eg* on paint —*v.* **3.** form blisters (on) —'**blistering** *a.* (of verbal attack) bitter —**blister pack** package for goods with hard, raised, transparent cover

blithe (blaɪð) *a.* happy, gay —'**blithely** *adv.* —'**blitheness** *n.*

blithering ('blɪðərɪŋ) *a.* **1.** talking foolishly; jabbering **2.** *inf.* stupid; foolish

B.Litt. *or* **B.Lit. 1.** Bachelor of Letters **2.** Bachelor of Literature

blitz (blɪts) *n.* sudden, concentrated attack —**blitzkrieg** ('blɪtskriːg) *n.* intensive military attack designed to defeat opposition quickly

blizzard ('blɪzəd) *n.* blinding storm of wind and snow

bloat (bləʊt) *v.* **1.** puff or swell out —*n.* **2.** distension of stomach of cow *etc.* by gas —'**bloated** *a.* swollen —'**bloater** *n.* smoked herring

blob (blɒb) n. 1. soft mass, esp. drop of liquid 2. shapeless form

bloc (blɒk) n. (political) grouping of people or countries

block (blɒk) n. 1. solid (rectangular) piece of wood, stone etc., esp. Hist. that on which people were beheaded 2. obstacle 3. stoppage 4. pulley with frame 5. large building of offices, flats etc. 6. group of buildings 7. area enclosed by intersecting streets —vt. 8. obstruct, stop up 9. shape on block —'**blockage** n. obstruction —**block and tackle** hoisting device in which rope or chain is passed around pair of blocks containing one or more pulleys —'**blockbuster** n. inf. 1. large bomb used to demolish extensive areas 2. very forceful person, thing etc. —'**blockhead** n. derogatory fool, simpleton —'**blockhouse** n. 1. formerly, wooden fortification with ports for defensive fire etc. 2. concrete structure strengthened for protection against enemy fire, with apertures for defensive gunfire 3. building constructed of logs or squared timber —**block letters** written capital letters —**block release** UK release of trainees from work for study at college for several weeks at a time —**block vote** see **card vote** at CARD —**block in** sketch in

blockade (blɒ'keɪd) n. 1. physical prevention of access, esp. to port etc. —vt. 2. subject to blockade

bloke (bləʊk) n. inf. fellow, chap

blond (blɒnd) a. 1. (of hair) light-coloured —n. 2. someone with blond hair (**blonde** fem.)

blood (blʌd) n. 1. red fluid in veins 2. race 3. kindred 4. parental heritage 5. temperament 6. passion —vt. 7. initiate (into hunting, war etc.) —'**bloodily** adv. —'**bloodless** a. —'**bloody** a. 1. covered in blood 2. slaughterous —a./adv. 3. sl. common intensifier —vt. 4. make bloody —**blood bank** (institution managing) store of human blood preserved for transfusion —**blood bath** indiscriminate slaughter; massacre —**blood count** determination of number of red and white blood corpuscles in sample of blood —'**bloodcurdling** a. terrifying; horrifying —**blood group** any of various groups into which human blood is classified (also **blood type**) —'**bloodhound** n. breed of large hound noted for its keen powers of scent —**blood-letting** n. 1. therapeutic removal of blood 2. bloodshed, esp. in feud —**blood money** 1. compensation paid to relatives of murdered person 2. money paid to hired murderer —**blood poisoning** disease in which blood contains poisonous matter (also **septi'caemia**) —**blood pressure** pressure exerted by blood on inner walls of arteries —**blood relation** or **relative** person related by birth —'**bloodshed** n. slaughter, killing —'**bloodshot** a. (of eyes) inflamed —**blood sport** sport in which animals are killed, eg fox-hunting —**blood stream** flow of blood through vessels of living body —'**bloodsucker** n. 1. parasite (eg mosquito) living on host's blood 2. parasitic person —**blood test** examination of sample of blood —'**bloodthirsty** a. murderous, cruel —**blood transfusion** transfer of blood from one person to another —**blood vessel** artery, capillary or vein —**bloody-minded** a. UK inf. deliberately obstructive and unhelpful —**in cold blood** cruelly and ruthlessly; deliberately and calmly —**make one's blood boil** cause to be angry —**make one's blood run cold** fill with horror

bloom[1] (bluːm) n. 1. flower of plant 2. blossoming 3. prime, perfection 4. glow 5. powdery deposit on fruit —vi. 6. be in flower 7. flourish —'**blooming** a.

bloom[2] (bluːm) n. rectangular mass of metal obtained by rolling or forging cast ingot

bloomer ('bluːmə) n. inf. ludicrous mistake

bloomers ('bluːməz) pl.n. wide, baggy knickers

blossom ('blɒsəm) n. 1. flower 2. flower bud —vi. 3. flower 4. develop

blot (blɒt) n. 1. spot, stain 2. disgrace —vt. 3. spot, stain 4. obliterate 5. detract from 6. soak up (ink etc.) from (-tt-) —**blotting paper** absorbent paper, used esp. for soaking up surplus ink

blotch (blɒtʃ) n. 1. dark spot on skin —vt. 2. make spotted —'**blotchy** a.

blotto ('blɒtəʊ) a. sl. unconscious, esp. through drunkenness

blouse (blaʊz) n. light, loose upper garment

blouson ('bluːzɒn) n. loosely fitting but tight-waisted jacket

blow[1] (bləʊ) vi. 1. make a current of air 2. pant 3. make sound by blowing 4. (of whale) spout —vt. 5. drive air upon or into 6. drive by current of air 7. sound 8. fan 9. sl. squander (**blew, blown**) —n. 10. blast 11. gale —'**blower** n. —'**blowy** a. windy —**blow-by-blow** a. explained in great detail —**blow-dry** vt. 1. style (hair) after washing, using hand-held hair dryer —n. 2. this method of drying hair —'**blowfly** n. fly which infects food etc. (also '**bluebottle**) —'**blowhole** n. 1. nostril of whales, situated far back on skull 2. hole in ice through which seals etc. breathe 3. vent for air or gas —'**blowlamp** n. small burner with very hot flame, for removing paint etc. (also **blow torch**) —**blow-out** n. 1. sudden puncture in tyre 2. uncontrolled escape of oil or gas from well 3. sl. large meal —'**blowpipe** n. dart tube —**blow out** 1. extinguish 2. (of tyre) puncture suddenly 3. (of fuse) melt —**blow up** 1. explode 2. inflate 3. enlarge (photograph) 4. inf. lose one's temper

blow² (bləʊ) n. 1. stroke, knock 2. sudden misfortune, loss

blown (bləʊn) pp. of BLOW¹

blowzy or **blowsy** ('blaʊzɪ) a. 1. slovenly, sluttish 2. red-faced

blubber ('blʌbə) vi. 1. weep —n. 2. fat of whales 3. weeping

bludgeon ('blʌdʒən) n. 1. short thick club —vt. 2. strike (as) with bludgeon 3. coerce

blue (bluː) a. 1. of colour of sky or shades of that colour 2. depressed 3. indecent —n. 4. the colour 5. dye or pigment 6. indigo powder used in laundering —vt. 7. make blue 8. dip in blue liquid (**blued** pt./pp.) —**blues** pl.n. inf. (oft. with sing. v.) 1. depression 2. form of Amer. Negro folk song in slow tempo, employed in jazz music —'**bluish** a. —**blue baby** baby born with bluish skin caused by heart defect —'**bluebell** n. wild spring flower —'**blueberry** n. N Amer. shrub with blue-black edible berries —**blue blood** royal or aristocratic descent —'**bluebook** n. UK government publication bound in blue cover —'**bluebottle** n. blowfly —**blue-collar** a. denoting manual industrial workers —**blue-eyed boy** inf., chiefly UK favourite of person or group —**blue-pencil** vt. alter, delete parts of, esp. to censor —**blue peter** signal flag of blue with white square at centre, displayed by vessel about to leave port —'**blueprint** n. 1. copy of drawing 2. original plan —**blue ribbon** 1. UK badge of blue silk worn by members of Order of the Garter 2. badge awarded as first prize in competition —'**bluestocking** n. scholarly, intellectual woman —'**bluetit** n. common European tit having blue crown, wings, and tail, and yellow underparts —**blue whale** largest mammal: bluish-grey whalebone whale

bluff¹ (blʌf) n. 1. cliff, steep bank 2. C clump of trees —a. 3. hearty 4. blunt 5. steep 6. abrupt

bluff² (blʌf) v. 1. deceive (someone) by pretence of strength —n. 2. pretence

blunder ('blʌndə) n. 1. clumsy mistake —vi. 2. make stupid mistake 3. act clumsily

blunderbuss ('blʌndəbʌs) n. obsolete short gun with wide bore

blunt (blʌnt) a. 1. not sharp 2. (of speech) abrupt —vt. 3. make blunt —'**bluntly** adv. —'**bluntness** n.

blur (blɜː) v. 1. make, become less distinct (-rr-) —n. 2. something vague, indistinct —'**blurry** a.

blurb (blɜːb) n. statement, advertising or recommending book etc.

blurt (blɜːt) vt. (oft. with out) utter suddenly or unadvisedly

blush (blʌʃ) vi. 1. become red in face 2. be ashamed 3. redden —n. 4. this effect —'**blusher** n. cosmetic applied to cheeks to give rosy colour

bluster ('blʌstə) vi./n. (indulge in) noisy, aggressive behaviour —'**blustering** or '**blustery** a. (of wind etc.) noisy and gusty

B.M. British Museum

B.M.A. British Medical Association

B.Mus. Bachelor of Music

B.N.O.C. British National Oil Corporation

B.O. 1. inf. body odour 2. box office

boa ('bəʊə) n. 1. large, nonvenomous snake 2. long scarf of fur or feathers —**boa constrictor** very large snake of tropical Amer. and W Indies, that kills prey by constriction

boar (bɔː) n. 1. male pig 2. wild pig

board (bɔːd) n. 1. broad, flat piece of wood 2. sheet of rigid material for specific purpose 3. table 4. meals 5. group of people who administer company 6. governing body 7. thick, stiff paper —pl. 8. theatre, stage 9. C wooden enclosure where ice hockey, box lacrosse is played —vt. 10. cover with planks 11. supply with regular meals 12. enter (ship etc.) —vi. 13. take daily meals —'**boarder** n. —**boarding house** lodging house where meals may be had —**boarding school** school providing living accommodation for pupils —'**boardroom** n. room where board of company meets —**above board** beyond suspicion —**on board** into or onto ship

boast (bəʊst) vi. 1. speak too much in praise of oneself, one's possessions etc. —n. 2. something boasted (of) —'**boaster** n. —'**boastful** a. —'**boastfully** adv. —'**boastfulness** n. —**boast of** 1. brag of 2. have to show

boat (bəʊt) n. 1. small open vessel 2. ship —vi. 3. sail about in boat —'**boater** n. flat straw hat —'**boating** n. —'**boathook** n. —'**boathouse** n. —'**boatman** n. —'**boatswain** ('bəʊsⁿn) n. ship's officer in charge of boats, sails etc. —**boat train** train scheduled to take passengers to or from particular ship

bob (bɒb) vi. 1. move up and down —vt. 2. move jerkily 3. cut (hair) short (**-bb-**) —n. 4. short, jerking motion 5. short hair style 6. weight on pendulum etc. 7. inf. formerly, shilling —**bobbed** a.

bobbejaan ('bɒbəjɑːn) n. SA baboon

bobbin ('bɒbɪn) n. cylinder on which thread is wound

bobble ('bɒbᵊl) n. small, tufted ball for decoration

bobby ('bɒbɪ) n. inf. policeman

bobcat ('bɒbkæt) n. Amer. wild cat, bay lynx

bobolink ('bɒbəlɪŋk) n. Amer. songbird

bobsleigh ('bɒbsleɪ) n. 1. racing sledge for two or more people, with steering mechanism —vi. 2. ride on bobsleigh (also (esp. US) **bobsled** ('bɒbslɛd))

bobtail ('bɒbteɪl) n. 1. docked or diminutive tail 2. animal with such tail —a. 3. having tail cut short (*also* 'bobtailed) —*vt.* **4.** dock tail of **5.** cut short; curtail

BOC British Oxygen Company

bode¹ ('bəud) *vt.* be an omen of

bode² *pt. of* BIDE

bodega (bəu'di:gə) *n.* shop selling wine, *esp.* in Spanish-speaking country

bodge (bɒdʒ) *vt. inf.* make mess of; botch

bodice ('bɒdɪs) *n.* upper part of woman's dress

bodkin ('bɒdkɪn) *n.* **1.** large blunt needle **2.** tool for piercing holes

body ('bɒdɪ) *n.* **1.** whole frame of man or animal **2.** main part of such frame **3.** corpse **4.** main part of anything **5.** substance **6.** mass **7.** person **8.** number of persons united or organized **9.** matter, opposed to spirit —'**bodiless** *a.* —'**bodily** *a./adv.* —'**bodyguard** *n.* escort to protect important person —**body politic** people of nation or nation itself considered as political entity —**body stocking** one-piece undergarment, usu. of nylon, covering torso —'**bodywork** *n.* shell of motor vehicle

Boer (buə) *n.* a S Afr. of Dutch or Huguenot descent —**boerbul** ('buəbəl) *n.* SA crossbred mastiff —**boerewors** ('buərəvɔːs) *n.* SA mincemeat sausage —**boerperd** ('buəpɜːt) *n.* S Afr. breed of horse

boet (but) *or* **boetie** *n.* SA *inf.* friend

boffin ('bɒfɪn) *n. inf.* scientist, technical research worker

bog (bɒg) *n.* **1.** wet, soft ground **2.** *sl.* lavatory —'**boggy** *a.* marshy —**bog down** stick as in a bog

bogan ('bəugən) *n.* C sluggish side stream

bogey *or* **bogy** ('bəugɪ) *n.* **1.** evil or mischievous spirit **2.** standard golf score for good player —'**bogeyman** *n.*

boggle ('bɒgl) *vi.* stare, be surprised

bogie *or* **bogy** ('bəugɪ) *n.* **1.** low truck on four wheels **2.** pivoted undercarriage, as on railway rolling stock

bogus ('bəugəs) *a.* sham, false

Bohemian (bəu'hi:mɪən) *a.* **1.** unconventional —*n.* **2.** (*oft.* b-) one who leads an unsettled life —Bo'**hemianism** *n.*

boil¹ (bɔɪl) *vi.* **1.** change from liquid to gas, *esp.* by heating **2.** become cooked by boiling **3.** bubble **4.** be agitated **5.** seethe **6.** *inf.* be hot **7.** *inf.* be angry —*vt.* **8.** cause to boil **9.** cook by boiling —*n.* **10.** boiling state —'**boiler** *n.* vessel for boiling —**boiler suit** garment covering whole body —**boiling point** temperature at which boiling occurs (100°C for water)

boil² (bɔɪl) *n.* inflamed suppurating swelling on skin

boisterous ('bɔɪstərəs, -strəs) *a.* **1.** wild **2.** noisy **3.** turbulent —'**boisterously** *adv.* —'**boisterousness** *n.*

bold (bəuld) *a.* **1.** daring, fearless **2.** presumptuous **3.** striking, prominent —'**boldly** *adv.* —'**boldness** *n.*

bole (bəul) *n.* trunk of tree

bolero (bə'lɛərəu) *n.* **1.** Spanish dance **2.** short loose jacket

boll (bəul) *n.* seed capsule of cotton, flax *etc.*

bollard ('bɒlɑːd, 'bɒləd) *n.* **1.** post on quay or ship to secure mooring lines **2.** short post in road or footpath as barrier or marker

Bolshevik ('bɒlʃɪvɪk) *n.* violent revolutionary —'**bolshie** *or* '**bolshy** *a. inf.* **1.** rebellious, uncooperative **2.** left-wing

bolster ('bəulstə) *vt.* **1.** support, uphold —*n.* **2.** long pillow **3.** pad, support

bolt¹ (bəult) *n.* **1.** bar or pin, *esp.* with thread for nut **2.** rush **3.** discharge of lightning **4.** roll of cloth —*vt.* **5.** fasten with bolt **6.** swallow hastily —*vi.* **7.** rush away **8.** break from control

bolt² *or* **boult** (bəult) *vt.* **1.** pass (flour *etc.*) through sieve **2.** examine and separate —'**bolter** *n.*

bomb (bɒm) *n.* **1.** explosive projectile **2.** any explosive device **3.** *sl.* large amount of money —*vt.* **4.** attack with bombs —bom'**bard** *vt.* **1.** shell **2.** attack (verbally) —bombar'**dier** (bɒmbə'dɪə) *n.* artillery noncommissioned officer —bom'**bardment** *n.* —'**bomber** *n.* aircraft capable of carrying bombs —'**bombshell** *n.* **1.** shell of bomb **2.** surprise **3.** *inf.* very attractive girl —**the bomb** nuclear bomb

bombast ('bɒmbæst) *n.* **1.** pompous language **2.** pomposity —bom'**bastic** *a.*

Bombay duck (bɒm'beɪ) fish eaten dried with curry dishes as savoury (*also* '**bummalo**)

bombazine *or* **bombasine** (bɒmbə'zi:n, 'bɒmbəzi:n) *n.* twilled fabric, *esp.* one of silk and worsted

bona fide ('bəunə 'faɪdɪ) *Lat.* **1.** genuine(ly) **2.** sincere(ly) —**bona fides** ('faɪdi:z) good faith, sincerity

bonanza (bə'nænzə) *n.* sudden good luck or wealth

bonbon ('bɒnbɒn) *n.* sweet

bond (bɒnd) *n.* **1.** that which binds **2.** link, union **3.** written promise to pay money or carry out contract —*vt.* **4.** bind **5.** store (goods) until duty is paid on them —'**bonded** *a.* **1.** placed in bond **2.** mortgaged —'**bondsman** *n.* **1.** person bound by bond to act as surety for another **2.** serf, slave (*also* '**bondservant**)

bondage ('bɒndɪdʒ) *n.* slavery

bone (bəun) *n.* **1.** hard substance forming animal's skeleton **2.** piece of this —*pl.* **3.** essentials —*vt.* **4.** remove bones from —*vi.* **5.** *inf.* (with up) study hard —'**boneless** *a.* —'**bony** *a.* —**bone china** porcelain containing bone ash —**bone-dry** *a. inf.* completely dry —'**bonehead**

n. inf. stupid person —**bone meal** dried and ground animal bones, used as fertilizer or in stock feeds —'**boneshaker** *n.* **1.** early type of bicycle having solid tyres **2.** *sl.* any rickety vehicle

bonfire ('bɒnfaɪə) *n.* large outdoor fire

bongo ('bɒŋɡəʊ) *n.* small drum, usu. one of pair, played with fingers (*pl.* **-s, -es**)

bonhomie ('bɒnəmiː) *Fr.* good humour, geniality

bonkers ('bɒŋkəz) *a. sl.* crazy

bon mot (*Fr.* bɔ̃ 'mo) clever and fitting remark (*pl.* **bons mots** (bɔ̃ 'mo))

bonnet ('bɒnɪt) *n.* **1.** hat with strings **2.** *cap* **3.** cover of motor vehicle engine

bonny ('bɒnɪ) *a.* beautiful, handsome —'**bonnily** *adv.*

bonsai ('bɒnsaɪ) *n.* (art of growing) dwarf trees, shrubs

bontebok ('bɒntɪbʌk) *n.* S Afr. antelope

bonus ('bəʊnəs) *n.* extra (unexpected) payment or gift

bon vivant (bɔ̃ vi'vɑ̃) *Fr.* person who enjoys luxuries, *esp.* good food and drink (*pl.* ***bons vivants*** (bɔ̃ vi'vɑ̃))

bon voyage (*Fr.* bɔ̃ vwa'jaːʒ) phrase used to wish traveller pleasant journey

bonze (bɒnz) *n.* Chinese or Japanese Buddhist priest or monk

boo (buː) *interj.* **1.** expression of disapproval or contempt **2.** exclamation to surprise *esp.* child —*v.* **3.** make this sound (at)

boob (buːb) *n. sl.* **1.** foolish mistake **2.** female breast

booby ('buːbɪ) *n.* **1.** fool **2.** tropical marine bird —**booby prize** mock prize for poor performance —**booby trap 1.** harmless-looking object which explodes when disturbed **2.** form of practical joke

boodle ('buːd°l) *n. US sl.* money

boogie-woogie ('buɡɪ'wuɡɪ, 'buːɡɪ'wuːɡɪ) *n.* kind of jazz piano playing, emphasizing a rolling bass in syncopated eighth notes

book (bʊk) *n.* **1.** collection of sheets of paper bound together **2.** literary work **3.** main division of this —*v.* **4.** reserve (room, ticket *etc.*) —*vt.* **5.** charge with legal offence **6.** enter name in book —'**booking** *n.* reservation —'**bookish** *a.* studious, fond of reading —'**booklet** *n.* —'**bookbinder** *n.* —'**bookcase** *n.* —**book club** club that sells books at low prices to members —**book end** one of pair of ornamental supports for holding row of books upright —**book-keeping** *n.* systematic recording of business transactions —'**bookmaker** *n.* person whose work is taking bets (*also* (*inf.*) '**bookie**) —'**bookmark** *or* '**bookmarker** *n.* strip of material put between pages of book to mark

place —'**bookplate** *n.* label bearing owner's name and design, pasted into book —**book value 1.** value of asset of business according to its books **2.** net capital value of enterprise as shown by excess of book assets over book liabilities —'**bookworm** *n.* great reader

boom[1] (buːm) *n.* **1.** sudden commercial activity **2.** prosperity —*vi.* **3.** become active, prosperous

boom[2] (buːm) *vi./n.* (make) loud, deep sound

boom[3] (buːm) *n.* **1.** long spar, as for stretching the bottom of a sail **2.** barrier across harbour **3.** pole carrying overhead microphone *etc.*

boomerang ('buːməræŋ) *n.* **1.** curved wooden missile of Aust. Aborigines, which returns to the thrower —*vi.* **2.** recoil **3.** return unexpectedly **4.** backfire

boon (buːn) *n.* something helpful, favour

boor (bʊə) *n.* rude person —'**boorish** *a.*

boost (buːst) *n.* **1.** encouragement, help **2.** upward push **3.** increase —*vt.* **4.** encourage, assist or improve —'**booster** *n.* person or thing that supports, increases power *etc.* —**booster shot** *inf.* supplementary injection of vaccine given to maintain immunization

boot[1] (buːt) *n.* **1.** covering for the foot and ankle **2.** luggage receptacle in car **3.** *inf.* kick —*vt.* **4.** *inf.* kick —'**booted** *a.* —'**bootee** *n.* baby's soft shoe

boot[2] (buːt) *n.* profit, use —'**bootless** *a.* fruitless, vain —**to boot** in addition

booth (buːð, buːθ) *n.* **1.** stall **2.** cubicle

bootleg ('buːtleɡ) *v.* **1.** make, carry, sell (illicit goods, *esp.* alcohol) (**-gg-**) —*a.* **2.** produced, distributed or sold illicitly —'**bootlegger** *n.*

booty ('buːtɪ) *n.* plunder, spoil

booze (buːz) *n./vi. inf.* (consume) alcoholic drink —'**boozer** *n. inf.* **1.** person fond of drinking **2.** bar, pub —'**boozy** *a. inf.* inclined to or involving excessive consumption of alcohol —**booze-up** *n. inf.* drinking spree

bop (bɒp) *n.* **1.** form of jazz characterized by rhythmic and harmonic complexity (*also* '**bebop**) —*vi.* **2.** *inf.* dance to pop music (**-pp-**) —'**bopper** *n.*

borage ('bɒrɪdʒ, 'bʌrɪdʒ) *n.* Mediterranean plant with star-shaped blue flowers

borax ('bɔːræks) *n.* white soluble substance, compound of boron —**boracic** (bə'ræsɪk) *a.*

Bordeaux (bɔː'dəʊ) *n.* any of several red, white or rosé wines produced around Bordeaux in SW France —**Bordeaux mixture** *Hort.* fungicide consisting of solution of copper sulphate and quicklime

border ('bɔːdə) *n.* **1.** margin **2.** frontier **3.** limit **4.** strip of garden —*vt.* **5.** provide with border **6.** adjoin —'**borderline** *n.* **1.** border; dividing line **2.** indeterminate position between two conditions

—*a.* **3.** on edge of one category and verging on another

bore[1] (bɔː) *vt.* **1.** pierce —*vi.* **2.** make a hole —*n.* **3.** hole **4.** calibre of gun —'**borer** *n.* **1.** instrument for making holes **2.** insect which bores holes

bore[2] (bɔː) *vt.* **1.** make weary by repetition *etc.* —*n.* **2.** tiresome person or thing —'**boredom** *n.* —'**boring** *a.*

bore[3] (bɔː) *n.* tidal wave which rushes up river estuary

bore[4] (bɔː) *pt. of* BEAR[1]

born (bɔːn) *pp. of* BEAR[1] —**born again** having undergone a conversion, *esp.* to new spiritual life

borne (bɔːn) *pp. of* BEAR[1] —**be borne in on** *or* **upon** (of fact *etc.*) be realized by

boron ('bɔːrɒn) *n.* chemical element used in hardening steel *etc.* —'**boric** *a.* of or containing boron (*also* bo'**racic**) —**boric acid** white weakly acid crystalline solid, used as mild antiseptic (*also* **orthoboric acid**)

borough ('bʌrə) *n.* town

borrow ('bɒrəʊ) *vt.* **1.** obtain on loan or trust **2.** appropriate —'**borrower** *n.*

borsch, borsh, (bɔːʃ), **borscht** (bɔːʃt), *or* **borshch** (bɔːʃtʃ) *n.* Russian and Polish soup based on beetroot

borstal ('bɔːstəl) *n.* reformatory for young criminals

borzoi ('bɔːzɔɪ) *n.* breed of tall hound with long, silky coat

bosh (bɒʃ) *n. inf.* nonsense

bo's'n ('bəʊsən) *n. Naut. see* **boatswain** *at* BOAT

bosom ('bʊzəm) *n.* **1.** human breast **2.** seat of passions and feelings

boss[1] (bɒs) *n.* **1.** person in charge of or employing others —*vt.* **2.** be in charge of **3.** be domineering over —'**bossy** *a.* overbearing

boss[2] (bɒs) *n.* **1.** knob or stud **2.** raised ornament —*vt.* **3.** emboss

bosun ('bəʊsən) *n. Naut. see* **boatswain** *at* BOAT

bot. **1.** botanical **2.** botany **3.** bottle

botany ('bɒtənɪ) *n.* study of plants —bo'**tani-c(al)** *a.* —'**botanist** *n.*

botch (bɒtʃ) *vt.* (*oft. with* up) spoil by clumsiness

botfly ('bɒtflaɪ) *n.* fly, larvae of which are parasites of man, sheep and horses

both (bəʊθ) *a./pron.* **1.** the two —*adv./conj.* **2.** as well

bother ('bɒðə) *vt.* **1.** pester **2.** perplex —*vi./n.* **3.** fuss, trouble —**bothe'ration** *n.* **1.** state of worry, trouble, or confusion —*interj.* **2.** *chiefly* UK exclamation of slight annoyance —'**bothersome** *a.* causing bother; troublesome

bo tree (bəʊ) *see* PEEPUL

bottle ('bɒtəl) *n.* **1.** vessel for holding liquid **2.** its

contents **3.** UK *sl.* courage; nerve; initiative —*vt.* **4.** put into bottle —'**bottler** *n.* —'**bottlebrush** *n.* cylindrical brush for cleaning bottle —'**bottle-neck** *n.* narrow outlet which impedes smooth flow of traffic or production of goods —**bottle party** party to which guests bring drink —**bottle up 1.** restrain (powerful emotion) **2.** *inf.* keep (army or other force) contained or trapped

bottom ('bɒtəm) *n.* **1.** lowest part of anything **2.** bed of sea, river *etc.* **3.** buttocks —*vt.* **4.** put bottom to **5.** base **6.** get to bottom of —'**bottomless** *a.* —**bottom drawer** UK young woman's collection of linen, cutlery *etc.* made in anticipation of marriage —**bottom line** last line of financial statement that shows net profit or loss of company *etc.* —**bottom out** reach lowest point

botulism ('bɒtjʊlɪzəm) *n.* type of food poisoning

bouclé ('buːkleɪ) *n.* looped yarn giving knobbly effect

boudoir ('buːdwɑː, -dwɔː) *n.* **1.** lady's private sitting-room **2.** bedroom

bouffant ('buːfɒŋ) *a.* **1.** (of hair style) having extra height through back combing **2.** (of skirts *etc.*) puffed out

bougainvillea (buːgən'vɪlɪə) *n.* (sub)tropical climbing plant with red or purple bracts

bough (baʊ) *n.* branch of tree

bought (bɔːt) *pt./pp. of* BUY

bouillabaisse (buːjə'bes) *n.* rich stew or soup of fish and vegetables

bouillon ('buːjɒn) *n.* plain unclarified broth or stock

boulder ('bəʊldə) *n.* large weatherworn rounded stone —**boulder clay** unstratified glacial deposit consisting of fine clay, boulders, and pebbles

boulevard ('buːlvɑː, -vɑːd) *n.* broad street or promenade

boult (bəʊlt) *vt. see* BOLT[2]

bounce (baʊns) *v.* **1.** (cause to) rebound (repeatedly) on impact, as a ball —*n.* **2.** rebounding **3.** quality in object causing this **4.** *inf.* vitality, vigour —'**bouncer** *n. sl.* man, *esp.* one employed at club *etc.* to evict undesirables (forcibly) —'**bouncing** *a.* vigorous, robust —'**bouncy** *a.* lively

bound[1] (baʊnd) *n./vt.* limit —'**boundary** *n.* —'**bounded** *a.* —'**boundless** *a.*

bound[2] (baʊnd) *vi./n.* spring, leap

bound[3] (baʊnd) *a.* on a specified course, as *outward bound*

bound[4] (baʊnd) *v.* **1.** *pt./pp. of* BIND —*a.* **2.** committed **3.** certain **4.** tied

bounden ('baʊndən) *a.* morally obligatory (*obs. except in* **bounden duty**)

bounder ('baʊndə) *n. old-fashioned* **UK** *sl.* morally reprehensible person; cad

bounty ('baʊntɪ) *n.* **1.** liberality **2.** gift **3.** premium —'**bounteous** *or* 'bountiful *a.* liberal, generous

bouquet (buː'keɪ) *n.* **1.** bunch of flowers **2.** fragrance of wine **3.** compliment —**bouquet garni** ('buːkeɪ gɑː'niː) bunch of herbs tied together and used for flavouring stews *etc.* (*pl.* **bouquets garnis** ('buːkeɪz gɑː'niː))

bourbon ('bɜːbən) *n.* **US** whiskey made from maize

bourgeois ('bʊəʒwɑː) *n./a. oft. disparaging* **1.** middle class **2.** smugly conventional (person) —**bourgeoi'sie** *n.* **1.** middle classes **2.** in Marxist thought, capitalist ruling class

bourn¹ *or* **bourne** (bɔːn) *n. obs.* **1.** destination; goal **2.** boundary

bourn² (bɔːn) *n. chiefly S Brit.* stream

Bourse (bʊəs) *n.* stock exchange of continental Europe, *esp.* Paris

bout (baʊt) *n.* **1.** period of time spent doing something **2.** contest, fight

boutique (buː'tiːk) *n.* small shop, *esp.* one selling clothes

bouzouki (buː'zuːkɪ) *n.* Greek stringed musical instrument

bovine ('bəʊvaɪn) *a.* **1.** of the ox or cow **2.** oxlike **3.** stolid, dull

bow¹ (bəʊ) *n.* **1.** weapon for shooting arrows **2.** implement for playing violin *etc.* **3.** ornamental knot of ribbon *etc.* **4.** bend, bent line **5.** rainbow —*v.* **6.** bend —**bow-legged** *a.* bandy —**bow tie** tie tied in bow —**bow window** window with outward curve

bow² (baʊ) *vi.* **1.** bend body in respect, assent *etc.* **2.** submit —*vt.* **3.** bend downwards **4.** cause to stoop **5.** crush —*n.* **6.** bowing of head or body

bow³ (baʊ) *n.* **1.** fore end of ship **2.** prow **3.** rower nearest bow —**bowline** ('bəʊlɪn) *n. Naut.* **1.** line for controlling weather leech of square sail when vessel is close-hauled **2.** knot for securing loop —**bowsprit** ('bəʊsprɪt) *n.* spar projecting from ship's bow

bowdlerize *or* **-ise** ('baʊdləraɪz) *vt.* expurgate

bowel ('baʊəl) *n.* (*oft. pl.*) **1.** part of intestine (*esp.* with reference to defecation) **2.** inside of anything

bower ('baʊə) *n.* **1.** shady retreat **2.** inner room —'**bowerbird** *n.* Aust. bird that hoards decorative but useless things

bowie knife ('bəʊɪ) stout hunting knife with short hilt and guard for hand

bowl¹ (bəʊl) *n.* **1.** round vessel, deep basin **2.** drinking cup **3.** hollow

bowl² (bəʊl) *n.* **1.** wooden ball —*pl.* **2.** game played with such balls —*v.* **3.** roll or throw (ball)

in various ways —'**bowler** *n.* —'**bowling** *n.* **1.** game in which heavy ball is rolled down alley at group of wooden pins **2.** game of bowls **3.** *Cricket* delivering ball to batsman —**bowling alley** —**bowling green**

bowler ('bəʊlə) *n.* man's low-crowned stiff felt hat

bowser ('baʊzə) *n.* fuel tanker

box¹ (bɒks) *n.* **1.** (wooden) container, usu. rectangular with lid **2.** its contents **3.** small enclosure **4.** any boxlike cubicle, shelter or receptacle, *eg* letter box —*vt.* **5.** put in box **6.** confine —**box girder** girder that is hollow and square or rectangular in shape —**Boxing Day UK** first weekday after Christmas —**box junction UK** road junction having yellow cross-hatching on road surface —**box lacrosse C** indoor lacrosse —**box number** number given to newspaper advertisements to which replies may be sent —**box office 1.** office at theatre *etc.* where tickets are sold **2.** public appeal of actor or production —**box pleat** double pleat made by folding under fabric on either side of it —'**boxroom** *n.* small room or large cupboard —**the box UK** *inf.* television —**box the compass** make complete turn

box² (bɒks) *v.* **1.** fight with fists, *esp.* wearing padded gloves —*vt.* **2.** strike —*n.* **3.** blow —'**boxer** *n.* **1.** one who boxes **2.** breed of large dog resembling bulldog —'**boxing** *n.* art or profession of fighting with fists

box³ (bɒks) *n.* evergreen shrub used for hedges

boy (bɔɪ) *n.* **1.** male child **2.** young man —*interj.* **3.** exclamation of surprise —'**boyhood** *n.* —'**boyfriend** *n.* male friend with whom person is romantically or sexually involved —**boy scout** see SCOUT (sense 2)

boycott ('bɔɪkɒt) *vt.* **1.** refuse to deal with or participate in —*n.* **2.** act of boycotting

boysenberry ('bɔɪz²nbərɪ) *n.* **1.** type of bramble, cross of loganberry, various blackberries and raspberries **2.** edible fruit of this plant

B.P. 1. British Petroleum **2.** British Pharmacopoeia

Br *Chem.* bromine

B.R. British Rail

br. 1. branch **2.** bronze **3.** brother

Br. 1. Breton **2.** Britain **3.** British

bra (brɑː) *n. short for* BRASSIERE

brace (breɪs) *n.* **1.** tool for boring **2.** clasp, clamp **3.** pair, couple **4.** strut, support —*pl.* **5.** straps worn over shoulders to hold up trousers —*vt.* **6.** steady (oneself), as before a blow **7.** support, make firm —'**bracelet** *n.* **1.** ornament for the arm —*pl.* **2.** *sl.* handcuffs —'**bracing** *a.* invigorating —**brace and bit** tool for boring holes, consisting of cranked handle and drilling bit

brachiopod ('breɪkɪəpɒd, 'bræk-) n. any marine invertebrate animal having ciliated feeding organ and shell consisting of dorsal and ventral valves

bracken ('brækən) n. large fern

bracket ('brækɪt) n. 1. support for shelf etc. 2. group —pl. 3. marks [ ], ( ) used to enclose words etc. —vt. 4. enclose in brackets 5. connect

brackish ('brækɪʃ) a. (of water) slightly salty

bract (brækt) n. small scalelike leaf

brad (bræd) n. small nail —**bradawl** n. small boring tool

brae (breɪ) n. Scot. hill(side); slope

brag (bræg) vi. 1. boast (-gg-) —n. 2. boastful talk —**braggart** n.

braggadocio (brægə'dəʊtʃɪəʊ) n. 1. vain empty boasting 2. braggart (pl. -s)

Brahma ('brɑːmə) n. 1. Hindu god, the Creator 2. Hinduism ultimate and impersonal divine reality of universe (also '**Brahman**)

Brahman ('brɑːmən) n. 1. member of priestly Hindu caste (also esp. (formerly) '**Brahmin**) 2. breed of beef cattle

braid (breɪd) vt. 1. interweave 2. trim with braid —n. 3. length of anything interwoven or plaited 4. ornamental tape

Braille (breɪl) n. system of printing for blind, with arrangements of raised dots instead of letters

brain (breɪn) n. 1. mass of nerve tissue in head 2. intellect —vt. 3. kill by hitting on head —'**brainless** a. —'**brainy** a. —'**brainchild** n. invention —**brain death** irreversible cessation of respiration due to irreparable brain damage —**brain drain** inf. emigration of scientists, academics etc. —'**brainstorm** n. sudden mental aberration —**brains trust** group of knowledgeable people who answer questions in panel games, quizzes etc. —'**brainwash** vt. change, distort ideas or beliefs of —**brain wave** sudden, clever idea

braise (breɪz) vt. stew in covered pan

brake[1] (breɪk) n. 1. instrument for retarding motion of wheel on vehicle —vt. 2. apply brake to —**brake horsepower** rate at which engine does work, expressed in horsepower, measured by resistance of applied brake —**brake shoe** curved metal casting to which brake lining is riveted in drum brake

brake[2] (breɪk) n. 1. fern 2. bracken 3. thicket 4. brushwood

bramble ('bræmbəl) n. 1. prickly shrub 2. blackberry —'**brambly** a.

brambling ('bræmblɪŋ) n. type of finch

bran (bræn) n. sifted husks of corn

branch (brɑːntʃ) n. 1. limb of tree 2. offshoot or subsidiary part of something larger or primary —vi. 3. bear branches 4. diverge 5. spread —**branched** a. —'**branchy** a.

brand (brænd) n. 1. trademark 2. class of goods 3. particular kind, sort 4. mark made by hot iron 5. burning piece of wood 6. sword 7. mark of infamy —vt. 8. burn with iron 9. mark 10. stigmatize —**brand-new** a. absolutely new

brandish ('brændɪʃ) vt. flourish, wave (weapon etc.)

brandy ('brændɪ) n. spirit distilled from wine —**brandy snap** crisp, sweet biscuit

brash (bræʃ) a. bold, impudent

brass (brɑːs) n. 1. alloy of copper and zinc 2. group of brass wind instruments forming part of orchestra or band 3. inf. money 4. inf. (army) officers —a. 5. made of brass —'**brassy** a. 1. showy 2. harsh —**brass hat** UK inf. top-ranking official, esp. military officer —**brass tacks** inf. basic realities; hard facts (esp. in **get down to brass tacks**)

brasserie ('bræsərɪ) n. restaurant specializing in food and beer

brassica ('bræsɪkə) n. plant of cabbage and turnip family

brassiere ('bræsɪə, 'bræz-) n. woman's undergarment for supporting the breasts

brat (bræt) n. disparaging child

bravado (brə'vɑːdəʊ) n. showy display of boldness

brave (breɪv) a. 1. bold, courageous 2. splendid, fine —n. 3. warrior —vt. 4. defy, meet boldly —'**bravely** adv. —'**bravery** n.

bravo (brɑː'vəʊ) interj. well done

bravura (brə'vjʊərə, -'vʊərə) n. 1. display of boldness or daring 2. Mus. passage requiring great spirit and skill by performer

brawl (brɔːl) vi. 1. fight noisily —n. 2. noisy disagreement or fight —'**brawler** n.

brawn (brɔːn) n. 1. muscle 2. strength 3. pickled pork —'**brawny** a. muscular

bray (breɪ) n. 1. donkey's cry —vi. 2. utter this sound 3. give out harsh or loud sounds

braze[1] (breɪz) vt. decorate with or make of brass

braze[2] (breɪz) vt. make joint between (two metal surfaces) by fusing layer of high-melting solder between them —'**brazer** n.

brazen ('breɪzən) a. 1. of, like brass 2. impudent, shameless —vt. 3. (usu. with out) face, carry through with impudence —'**brazenness** n. effrontery

brazier[1] or **brasier** ('breɪzɪə) n. brassworker

brazier[2] or **brasier** ('breɪzɪə) n. pan for burning charcoal or coals

brazil nut (brə'zɪl) 1. tropical S Amer. tree producing globular capsules, each containing several triangular nuts 2. its nut

B.R.C.S. British Red Cross Society

breach (briːtʃ) n. 1. break, opening 2. breaking of rule, duty etc. 3. quarrel —vt. 4. make a gap in —breach of promise Law formerly, failure to carry out promise to marry

bread (brɛd) n. 1. food made of flour or meal and then baked 2. food 3. sl. money —'**breadfruit** n. breadlike fruit found in Pacific Islands —'**breadline** n. queue for free food —'**breadwinner** n. person supporting dependants by his earnings —**bread and butter** inf. means of support or subsistence; livelihood —**on the breadline** inf. living at subsistence level

breadth (brɛdθ, brɛtθ) n. 1. extent across, width 2. largeness of view, mind

break (breɪk) vt. 1. part by force 2. shatter 3. burst, destroy 4. fail to observe 5. disclose 6. interrupt 7. surpass 8. make bankrupt 9. relax 10. mitigate 11. accustom (horse) to being ridden 12. decipher (code) —vi. 13. become broken, shattered, divided 14. open, appear 15. come suddenly 16. crack, give way 17. part, fall out 18. (of voice) change in tone, pitch (**broke,** '**broken**) —n. 19. fracture 20. gap 21. opening 22. separation 23. interruption 24. respite 25. interval 26. inf. opportunity 27. dawn 28. Billiards consecutive series of successful strokes 29. Boxing separation after a clinch 30. Cricket deviation of a ball on striking the pitch —'**breakable** a. —'**breakage** n. —'**breaker** n. 1. one that breaks, eg electrical circuit breaker 2. wave beating on rocks or shore —'**breakaway** n. loss or withdrawal of group of members from association, club etc. —'**breakdown** n. 1. collapse, as nervous breakdown 2. failure to function effectively 3. analysis —**breakfast** ('brɛkfəst) n. first meal of the day —**break-in** n. illegal entering of building, esp. by thieves —'**breakneck** a. dangerous —**break-out** n. escape, esp. from prison —'**breakthrough** n. important advance —**break-up** n. 1. separation or disintegration 2. in Canad. north, breaking up of ice on body of water that marks beginning of spring 3. this season —'**breakwater** n. barrier to break force of waves —**break away** (oft. with from) 1. leave hastily; escape 2. withdraw, secede —**break out** 1. begin suddenly 2. make escape, esp. from prison 3. (with in) (of skin) erupt (in rash etc.) —**break up** 1. (cause to) separate 2. put an end to (a relationship) or (of a relationship) to come to an end 3. dissolve or cause to dissolve 4. sl. lose control of emotions

bream (briːm, Austral. brim) or Austral. **brim** (brim) n. broad, thin fish

breast (brɛst) n. 1. human chest 2. milk-secreting gland on chest of human female 3. seat of the affections 4. any protuberance —vt. 5. face, oppose 6. reach summit of —'**breastbone** n. thin flat structure of bone to which most

of ribs are attached in front of chest (also 'sternum) —**breast-feed** v. feed (baby) with milk from breast —'**breastplate** n. piece of armour covering chest —'**breaststroke** n. stroke in swimming —'**breastwork** n. temporary defensive work, usu. breast-high

breath (brɛθ) n. 1. air used by lungs 2. life 3. respiration 4. slight breeze —**breathe** (briːð) vi. 1. inhale and exhale air from lungs 2. live 3. pause, rest —vt. 4. inhale and exhale 5. utter softly, whisper —**breather** ('briːðə) n. short rest —'**breathing** ('briːðɪŋ) n. —'**breathless** a. —'**breathtaking** a. causing awe or excitement —**breath test** UK chemical test of driver's breath to determine amount of alcohol he has consumed

Breathalyser or **-lyzer** ('brɛθəlaɪzə) n. R device that estimates amount of alcohol in breath —'**breathalyse** or **-lyze** vt.

bred (brɛd) pt./pp. of BREED

breech (briːtʃ) n. 1. buttocks 2. hinder part of anything, esp. gun —**breeches** ('brɪtʃɪz, 'briː-) pl.n. trousers —**breech delivery** birth of baby with feet or buttocks appearing first —**breeches buoy** ring-shaped life buoy with support in form of pair of breeches —'**breechloader** n.

breed (briːd) vt. 1. generate, bring forth, give rise to 2. rear —vi. 3. be produced 4. be with young (**bred** pt./pp.) —n. 5. offspring produced 6. race, kind —'**breeder** n. —'**breeding** n. 1. producing 2. manners 3. ancestry —**breeder reactor** nuclear reactor that produces more fissionable material than it consumes

breeze (briːz) n. gentle wind —'**breezily** adv. —'**breezy** a. 1. windy 2. jovial, lively 3. casual

breeze block light building brick made of ashes bonded by cement

Bren gun ('brɛn) air-cooled gas-operated submachine gun, used by Brit. in World War II

brent (brɛnt) or esp. U.S. **brant** (brænt) n. small goose that has dark grey plumage and short neck and occurs in most northern coastal regions (also **brent goose**)

brethren ('brɛðrɪn) n., pl. of BROTHER, obs. except in religious contexts

Breton ('brɛtən) n. 1. of Brittany, its people or their language —n. 2. native or inhabitant of Brittany

breve (briːv) n. long musical note

breviary ('briːvjərɪ, 'brɛv-) n. book of daily prayers of R.C. Church

brevity ('brɛvɪtɪ) n. 1. conciseness of expression 2. short duration

brew (bruː) vt. 1. prepare (liquor, as beer) from malt etc. 2. make (drink, as tea) by infusion 3. plot, contrive —vi. 4. be in preparation —n. 5. beverage produced by brewing —'**brewer** n. —'**brewery** n. —'**brewing** n.

briar[1] *or* **brier** ('braɪə) *n.* prickly shrub, *esp.* the wild rose

briar[2] *or* **brier** ('braɪə) *n.* European shrub —**briar pipe** tobacco pipe made from its root

bribe (braɪb) *n.* 1. anything offered or given to someone to gain favour, influence —*vt.* 2. influence by bribe —**'briber** *n.* —**'bribery** *n.*

bric-a-brac ('brɪkəbræk) *n.* miscellaneous small objects, used for ornament

brick (brɪk) *n.* 1. oblong mass of hardened clay used in building —*vt.* 2. build, block *etc.* with bricks —**'brickbat** *n.* 1. piece of brick *etc., esp.* used as weapon 2. *inf.* blunt criticism —**'bricklayer** *n.*

bride (braɪd) *n.* woman about to be, or just, married —**'bridal** *a.* of, relating to, a bride or wedding —**'bridegroom** *n.* man about to be, or just, married —**'bridesmaid** *n.*

bridge[1] ('brɪdʒ) *n.* 1. structure for crossing river *etc.* 2. something joining or supporting other parts 3. raised narrow platform on ship 4. upper part of nose 5. part of violin supporting strings —*vt.* 6. make bridge over, span —**'bridgehead** *n.* advanced position established on enemy territory —**bridging loan** loan to cover period between two transactions, such as buying of another house before sale of first is completed

bridge[2] ('brɪdʒ) *n.* card game

bridle ('braɪd[ə]l) *n.* 1. headgear of horse harness 2. curb —*vt.* 3. put bridle on 4. restrain —*vi.* 5. show resentment —**bridle path** path suitable for riding horses

Brie (briː) *n.* soft creamy white cheese

brief (briːf) *a.* 1. short in duration 2. concise 3. scanty 4. summary of case for counsel's use 5. papal letter 6. instructions —*pl.* 7. underpants 8. panties —*vt.* 9. give instructions —**'briefly** *adv.* —**'briefness** *n.* —**'briefcase** *n.* hand case for carrying papers

brier ('braɪə) *n. see* BRIAR[1], BRIAR[2]

brig (brɪg) *n.* two-masted, square-rigged ship

Brig. 1. Brigade 2. Brigadier

brigade (brɪ'geɪd) *n.* 1. subdivision of army 2. organized band —**briga'dier** *n.* high-ranking army officer, usu. in charge of a brigade

brigand ('brɪgənd) *n.* bandit, *esp.* member of gang in mountainous areas

brigantine ('brɪgəntiːn, -taɪn) *n.* two-masted vessel with square-rigged foremast and fore-and-aft mainmast

bright (braɪt) *a.* 1. shining 2. full of light 3. cheerful 4. clever —**'brighten** *v.* —**'brightly** *adv.* —**'brightness** *n.*

Bright's disease (braɪts) chronic inflammation of kidneys; chronic nephritis

brill (brɪl) *n.* European food fish

brilliant ('brɪljənt) *a.* 1. shining 2. sparkling 3. splendid 4. very clever 5. distinguished —**'brilliance** *or* **'brilliancy** *n.* —**'brilliantly** *adv.*

brilliantine ('brɪljəntiːn) *n.* perfumed hair oil

brim (brɪm) *n.* margin, edge, *esp.* of river, cup, hat —**brim'ful** *a.* —**'brimless** *a.* —**'brimming** *a.*

brimstone ('brɪmstəʊn) *n.* sulphur

brindled ('brɪnd[ə]ld) *a.* spotted and streaked

brine (braɪn) *n.* 1. salt water 2. pickle —**'briny** *a.* 1. very salty —*n.* 2. *inf.* the sea

bring (brɪŋ) *vt.* 1. fetch 2. carry with one 3. cause to come (**brought** *pt./pp.*)

brink (brɪŋk) *n.* 1. edge of steep place 2. verge, margin —**'brinkmanship** *n.* practice of pressing dangerous situation, *esp.* in international affairs, to limit of safety in order to win advantage

briquette *or* **briquet** (brɪ'kɛt) *n.* block of compressed coal dust

brisk (brɪsk) *a.* active, vigorous —**'briskly** *adv.* —**'briskness** *n.*

brisket ('brɪskɪt) *n.* joint of meat from breast of animal

brisling ('brɪslɪŋ) *n. see* SPRAT

bristle ('brɪs[ə]l) *n.* 1. short stiff hair —*vi.* 2. stand erect 3. show temper —**'bristliness** *n.* —**'bristly** *a.*

Brit (brɪt) *n. inf.* British person

Brit. 1. Britain 2. Britannia 3. British

Britannia (brɪ'tænɪə) *n.* 1. female warrior carrying trident, personifying Great Britain or British Empire 2. in ancient Roman Empire, southern part of Great Britain —**Britannia metal** alloy of tin with antimony and copper, used for decorative purposes and for bearings

Britannic (brɪ'tænɪk) *a.* of Britain; British (*esp. in* His *or* Her Britannic Majesty)

britches ('brɪtʃɪz) *pl.n. see* **breeches** *at* BREECH —**too big for one's britches** *inf.* overconfident; arrogant

British ('brɪtɪʃ) *a.* 1. of Great Britain or the British Commonwealth 2. relating to English language as spoken in Britain —*n.* 3. natives or inhabitants of Britain —**'Briton** *n.* native or inhabitant of Britain —**British thermal unit** unit of heat equal to 1055 joules

brittle ('brɪt[ə]l) *a.* 1. easily broken, fragile 2. curt, irritable —**'brittleness** *n.*

broach (brəʊtʃ) *vt.* 1. pierce (cask) 2. open, begin —*vi.* 3. *Naut.* turn beam-on to wind and waves

broad (brɔːd) *a.* 1. wide, spacious, open 2. plain, obvious 3. coarse 4. general 5. tolerant 6. (of pronunciation) dialectal —**'broaden** *v.* —**'broadly** *adv.* —**'broadness** *n.* —**broad bean** 1. Eurasian plant cultivated for its large edible seeds 2. its seed —**'broadcast** *v.* 1. transmit (broadcast) by radio or television —*vt.* 2. make widely known 3. scatter, as seed —*n.* 4. radio or television programme —'**broadcaster** n. —'**broadcloth** n. **1.** fabric woven on wide loom **2.** closely woven fabric of wool etc. with lustrous finish —**broad-minded** a. **1.** tolerant **2.** generous —'**broadsheet** n. **1.** newspaper with large format **2.** ballad or popular song printed on one side of sheet of paper, esp. in 16th-cent. England (also **broadside (ballad)**) —'**broadside** n. **1.** discharge of all guns on one side of ship **2.** strong (verbal) attack —'**broadsword** n. broad-bladed sword for cutting rather than stabbing

B-road n. secondary road in Britain

brocade (brəʊ'keɪd) n. rich woven fabric with raised design

broccoli ('brɒkəlɪ) n. type of cabbage

brochure ('brəʊʃjʊə, -ʃə) n. pamphlet, booklet

broderie anglaise ('brəʊdərɪ ɑːŋ'gleɪz) open embroidery on white cotton etc.

brogue (brəʊg) n. **1.** stout shoe **2.** dialect, esp. Irish accent

broil¹ ('brɔɪl) n. noisy quarrel

broil² (brɔɪl) vt. **1.** cook over hot coals **2.** grill —vi. **3.** be heated

broke (brəʊk) v. **1.** pt. of BREAK —a. **2.** inf. penniless —'**broken** pp. of BREAK —**broken chord** see ARPEGGIO —**broken-down** a. **1.** worn out, as by age; dilapidated **2.** not in working order —**broken'hearted** a. overwhelmed by grief or disappointment

broker ('brəʊkə) n. **1.** one employed to buy and sell for others **2.** dealer —'**brokerage** n. payment to broker

brolly ('brɒlɪ) n. inf. umbrella

bromide ('brəʊmaɪd) n. chemical compound used in medicine and photography —**bromide paper** photographic printing paper, treated with silver bromide

bromine ('brəʊmiːn, -mɪn) n. liquid element used in production of chemicals —'**bromic** a.

bronchus ('brɒŋkəs) n. either of two main branches of trachea (pl. **bronchi** ('brɒŋkaɪ)) —'**bronchial** a. —**bron'chitis** n. inflammation of bronchi

bronco or **broncho** ('brɒŋkəʊ) n. half-tamed horse (pl. **-s**)

brontosaurus (brɒntə'sɔːrəs) or **brontosaur** ('brɒntəsɔː) n. very large herbivorous dinosaur

bronze (brɒnz) n. **1.** alloy of copper and tin —a. **2.** made of, or coloured like, bronze —vt. **3.** give appearance of bronze to —**bronzed** a. **1.** coated with bronze **2.** sunburnt —**Bronze Age** era of bronze implements

brooch (brəʊtʃ) n. ornamental pin or fastening

brood (bruːd) n. **1.** family of young, esp. of birds **2.** tribe, race —vi. **3.** sit, as hen on eggs **4.** meditate, fret —'**broody** a. moody, sullen

brook¹ (brʊk) n. small stream —'**brooklet** n.

brook² (brʊk) vt. put up with, endure, tolerate

broom (bruːm, brum) n. **1.** brush for sweeping **2.** yellow-flowered shrub —'**broomstick** n. handle of broom

bros. or **Bros.** brothers

brose (brəʊz) n. Scot. porridge made by adding boiling liquid to meal, esp. oatmeal

broth (brɒθ) n. thick soup

brothel ('brɒθəl) n. house of prostitution

brother ('brʌðə) n. **1.** son of same parents **2.** one closely united with another —'**brotherhood** n. **1.** relationship **2.** fraternity, company —'**brotherliness** n. —'**brotherly** a. —**brother-in-law** n. **1.** brother of husband or wife **2.** husband of sister

brougham ('bruːəm, bruːm) n. **1.** four-wheeled horse-drawn closed carriage having raised open driver's seat in front **2.** obs. early electric car

brought (brɔːt) pt./pp. of BRING

brouhaha (bruː'hɑːhɑː) n. loud confused noise; uproar

brow (braʊ) n. **1.** ridge over eyes **2.** forehead **3.** eyebrow **4.** edge of hill —'**browbeat** vt. bully

brown (braʊn) a. **1.** of dark colour inclining to red or yellow —n. **2.** brown colour, pigment, or dye—v. **3.** make, become brown —'**brownie** n. **1.** in folklore, elf said to do helpful work at night, esp. household chores **2.** chiefly US flat, nutty, chocolate cake —**Brownie Guide** or '**Brownie** n. junior Girl Guide —**brown rice** unpolished rice —**brown study** mood of deep absorption; reverie —**brown sugar** unrefined or partially refined sugar —**browned off** inf. bored, depressed

browse (braʊz) vi. **1.** look (through book, articles for sale etc.) in a casual manner **2.** feed on shoots and leaves

brucellosis (bruːsɪ'ləʊsɪs) n. infectious disease of cattle, goats, and pigs, caused by bacteria and transmittable to man (also **undulant fever**)

bruin ('bruːɪn) n. name for a bear, used in children's tales etc.

bruise (bruːz) vt. **1.** injure without breaking skin —n. **2.** contusion, discoloration caused by blow —'**bruiser** n. strong, tough person

brumby ('brʌmbɪ) n. Aust. wild horse

brunch (brʌntʃ) n. inf. breakfast and lunch combined

brunette (bruː'nɛt) n. **1.** woman of dark complexion and hair —a. **2.** dark brown

brunt (brʌnt) n. **1.** shock of attack, chief stress **2.** first blow

brush (brʌʃ) n. **1.** device with bristles, hairs, wires etc. used for cleaning, painting etc. **2.** act, instance of brushing **3.** brief contact **4.** skirmish, fight **5.** bushy tail **6.** brushwood **7.** (carbon) device taking electric current from moving to stationary parts of generator etc. —vt. **8.** apply, remove, clean, with brush —v. **9.** touch lightly —'**brushoff** n. inf. **1.** dismissal **2.** refusal **3.** snub **4.** rebuff —**brush-up** n. UK act or instance of tidying one's appearance (esp. in **wash and brush-up**) —'**brushwood** n. **1.** broken-off branches **2.** land covered with scrub —**brush up** inf. **1.** (oft. with on) refresh one's knowledge, memory of (subject) **2.** make person or oneself clean or neat as after journey

brusque (bru:sk, brusk) a. rough in manner, curt, blunt

Brussels sprout ('brʌsəlz) **1.** variety of cabbage, having stem with heads resembling tiny cabbages **2.** head of this plant, eaten as vegetable

brute (bru:t) n. **1.** any animal except man **2.** crude, vicious person —a. **3.** animal **4.** sensual, stupid **5.** physical —'**brutal** a. —bru'**tality** n. —'**brutalize** or -**ise** vt. —'**brutally** adv. —'**brutish** a. bestial, gross

bryony or **briony** ('braɪənɪ) n. wild climbing hedge plant

bryophyte ('braɪəfaɪt) n. any moss or liverwort —**bryophytic** (braɪə'fɪtɪk) a.

BS British Standard(s)

b.s. 1. balance sheet **2.** bill of sale

B.Sc. Bachelor of Science

B.S.C. 1. British Steel Corporation **2.** British Sugar Corporation

BSI British Standards Institution

B.S.T. British Summer Time

Bt. Baronet

btu or **B.Th.U.** British Thermal Unit

bubble ('bʌbəl) n. **1.** hollow globe of liquid, blown out with air **2.** something insubstantial, not serious **3.** transparent dome —vi. **4.** rise in bubbles **5.** make gurgling sound —'**bubbly** a. —**bubble and squeak** UK dish of cabbage and potatoes fried together —**bubble gum** chewing gum that can be blown into bubbles

bubonic plague (bju:'bɒnɪk) acute infectious disease characterized by swellings and fever

buccaneer (bʌkə'nɪə) n. pirate, searover —**bucca'neering** a.

buck[1] (bʌk) n. **1.** male deer, or other male animal **2.** act of bucking **3.** US, A sl. dollar —vt. **4.** (of horse) attempt to throw rider by jumping upwards etc. **5.** resist, oppose —**buckshot** n. lead shot in shotgun shell —'**buckskin** n. **1.** skin of male deer **2.** strong greyish-yellow leather, orig. made from deerskin but now usu. made from sheepskin **3.** starched cotton cloth **4.** strong satin-woven woollen fabric —'**buckteeth** pl.n. projecting upper teeth

buck[2] (bʌk) n. Poker marker in jackpot to remind winner of some obligation when his turn to deal —**pass the buck** inf. shift blame or responsibility

buckboard ('bʌkbɔ:d) n. US open four-wheeled horse-drawn carriage with seat attached to flexible board between front and rear axles

bucket ('bʌkɪt) n. **1.** vessel, round with arched handle, for water etc. **2.** anything resembling this —vt. **3.** put, carry, in bucket —'**bucketful** n. —**bucket seat** seat with back shaped to occupier's figure —**bucket shop** chiefly UK firm specializing in cheap airline tickets —**bucket down** rain very hard

buckle ('bʌkəl) n. **1.** metal clasp for fastening belt, strap etc. —vt. **2.** fasten with buckle —vi. **3.** warp, bend —'**buckler** n. shield —**buckle down** start work

buckram ('bʌkrəm) n. coarse cloth stiffened with size

Bucks. (bʌks) Buckinghamshire

buckshee (bʌk'ʃi:) a. sl. free

bucolic (bju:'kɒlɪk) a. rustic

bud (bʌd) n. **1.** shoot or sprout on plant containing unopened leaf, flower etc. —vi. **2.** begin to grow —vt. **3.** graft (-**dd**-)

Buddhism ('bʊdɪzəm) n. religion founded in India by the Buddha —'**Buddhist** a./n.

buddleia ('bʌdlɪə) n. shrub with mauve flower spikes

buddy ('bʌdɪ) n. chiefly US sl. mate, chum

budge (bʌdʒ) v. move, stir

budgerigar ('bʌdʒərɪgɑ:) n. small Aust. parakeet (also '**budgie**)

budget ('bʌdʒɪt) n. **1.** annual financial statement **2.** plan of systematic spending —vi. **3.** prepare financial statement —v. **4.** plan financially

buff[1] (bʌf) n. **1.** leather made from buffalo or ox hide **2.** light yellow colour **3.** bare skin **4.** polishing pad —vt. **5.** polish

buff[2] (bʌf) n. inf. expert on some subject

buffalo ('bʌfələʊ) n. any of several species of large oxen (pl. -**es**, -**s**, -**lo**)

buffer[1] ('bʌfə) n. contrivance to lessen shock of concussion —**buffer state** small, usu. neutral state between two rival powers

buffer[2] ('bʌfə) n. UK inf. stupid or bumbling man (esp. in **old buffer**)

buffet[1] ('bʊfeɪ) n. **1.** refreshment bar **2.** meal at which guests serve themselves **3.** ('bʌfɪt, 'bʊfeɪ) sideboard —**buffet car** railway coach where light refreshments are served

buffet[2] ('bʌfɪt) n. **1.** blow, slap **2.** misfortune —vt. **3.** strike with blows **4.** contend against —'**buffeting** n.

buffoon (bə'fu:n) n. **1.** clown **2.** fool —buf'**foonery** n. clowning

bug (bʌg) n. **1.** any small insect **2.** inf. disease, infection **3.** inf. concealed listening device —vt.

inf. **4.** install secret microphone *etc.* in **5.** irritate (**-gg-**)

bugbear ('bʌgbɛə) *n.* **1.** object of needless terror **2.** nuisance

bugger ('bʌgə) *n.* **1.** sodomite **2.** *vulg. sl.* unpleasant person or thing —*vt. sl.* **3.** tire **4.** (*with* up) ruin, complicate

buggy ('bʌgɪ) *n.* light horse-drawn carriage having two or four wheels

bugle ('bjuːgəl) *n.* instrument like trumpet —'**bugler** *n.*

bugloss ('bjuːglɒs) *n.* shrub with blue flower clusters

build (bɪld) *v.* **1.** make, construct, by putting together parts or materials (**built** *pt./pp.*) —*n.* **2.** make, form —'**builder** *n.* —'**building** *n.* —**building society** cooperative banking enterprise financed by deposits on which interest is paid and from which mortgage loans are advanced on homes —**build-up** *n.* **1.** progressive increase in number *etc.* **2.** extravagant publicity or praise **3.** *Mil.* process of attaining required strength of forces and equipment —**built-in** *a.* **1.** made as integral part **2.** essential; inherent —*n.* **3.** A built-in cupboard —**built-up** *a.* having many buildings —**build up 1.** construct gradually **2.** increase, *esp.* by degrees **3.** improve health of **4.** prepare for climax, as in story

bulb (bʌlb) *n.* **1.** modified leaf bud emitting roots from base, *eg* onion **2.** anything resembling this **3.** globe surrounding filament of electric light —'**bulbous** *a.*

bulbul ('bulbul) *n.* tropical songbird

bulge (bʌldʒ) *n.* **1.** swelling, protuberance **2.** temporary increase —*vi.* **3.** swell out —'**bulginess** *n.* —'**bulgy** *a.*

bulk (bʌlk) *n.* **1.** size **2.** volume **3.** greater part **4.** cargo —*vi.* **5.** be of weight or importance —'**bulkiness** *n.* —'**bulky** *a.*

bulkhead ('bʌlkhɛd) *n.* partition in interior of ship

bull¹ (bul) *n.* **1.** male of cattle **2.** male of various other animals —'**bullock** *n.* castrated bull —'**bulldog** *n.* thickset breed of dog —'**bulldoze** *vt.* —'**bulldozer** *n.* powerful tractor with blade for excavating *etc.* —'**bullfight** *n.* traditional Spanish spectacle in which matador baits and usu. kills bull in arena —'**bullfighter** *n.* —'**bullfighting** *n.* —'**bullfinch** *n.* **1.** European finch, male of which has bright red throat and breast **2.** any of similar finches —**bull-headed** *a.* blindly obstinate; stupid —'**bullring** *n.* arena for bullfighting —**bull's-eye** *n.* middle part of target —**bull terrier** breed of terrier developed by crossing bulldog with English terrier

bull² (bul) *n.* papal edict

bull³ (bul) *n. sl.* nonsense

bullet ('bulɪt) *n.* projectile discharged from rifle, pistol *etc.*

bulletin ('bulɪtɪn) *n.* official report

bullion ('buljən) *n.* gold or silver in mass

bully ('bulɪ) *n.* **1.** one who hurts, persecutes, or intimidates weaker people —*vt.* **2.** intimidate, overawe **3.** ill-treat ('**bullied**, '**bullying**) —**bully beef** corned beef

bully-off *n. Hockey* method of starting play, in which two players strike sticks together and against ground three times before trying to hit ball (*also* 'bully) —**bully off** *Hockey* start play with bully-off (*also* '**bully**)

bulrush ('bulrʌʃ) *n.* tall reedlike marsh plant with brown velvety spike

bulwark ('bulwək) *n.* **1.** rampart **2.** any defence or means of security **3.** raised side of ship **4.** breakwater

bum (bʌm) *sl. n.* **1.** buttocks, anus **2.** US loafer, scrounger —*vt.* **3.** get by scrounging —*a.* **4.** useless —**bum'bailiff** *n.* UK *derogatory* formerly, officer employed to collect debts and arrest debtors

bumble ('bʌmbəl) *vi.* speak or proceed clumsily —'**bumbler** *n.*

bumblebee ('bʌmbəlbiː) *or* **humblebee** *n.* large bee

bump (bʌmp) *n.* **1.** heavy blow, dull in sound **2.** swelling caused by blow **3.** protuberance **4.** sudden movement —*vt.* **5.** strike or push against —'**bumper** *n.* **1.** horizontal bar at front and rear of motor vehicle to protect against damage **2.** full glass —*a.* **3.** full, abundant —**bump off** *sl.* murder

bumph *or* **bumf** (bʌmf) *n. inf.* useless documents, information *etc.*

bumpkin ('bʌmpkɪn) *n.* rustic

bumptious ('bʌmpʃəs) *a.* offensively self-assertive

bun (bʌn) *n.* **1.** small, round cake **2.** round knot of hair

bunch (bʌntʃ) *n.* **1.** number of things tied or growing together **2.** cluster **3.** tuft, knot **4.** group, party —*vt.* **5.** put together in bunch —*vi.* **6.** gather together —'**bunchy** *a.*

bundle ('bʌndəl) *n.* **1.** package **2.** number of things tied together **3.** *sl.* lot of money —*vt.* **4.** tie in bundle **5.** send (off) without ceremony

bundu ('bundu) *n.* SA wild uninhabited country

bung (bʌŋ) *n.* **1.** stopper for cask **2.** large cork —*vt.* **3.** stop up, seal, close **4.** *inf.* throw, sling —'**bunghole** *n.*

bungalow ('bʌŋgələʊ) *n.* one-storeyed house

bungle ('bʌŋgəl) *vt.* **1.** do badly from lack of skill, botch —*vi.* **2.** act clumsily, awkwardly —*n.* **3.** blunder, muddle —'**bungled** *a.* —'**bungler** *n.* —'**bungling** *a./n.*

bunion ('bʌnjən) *n.* inflamed swelling on foot or toe

bunk[1] (bʌŋk) *n.* narrow, shelflike bed —**bunk bed** one of pair of beds constructed one above the other

bunk[2] (bʌŋk) *n. sl.* hasty departure

bunk[3] (bʌŋk) *n. see* BUNKUM

bunker ('bʌŋkə) *n.* 1. large storage container for oil, coal *etc.* 2. sandy hollow on golf course 3. (military) underground defensive position

bunkum *or* **buncombe** ('bʌŋkəm) *n.* nonsense

bunny ('bʌnɪ) *n. inf.* rabbit

Bunsen burner ('bʌnsən) gas burner, producing great heat, used for chemical experiments

bunting[1] ('bʌntɪŋ) *n.* material for flags

bunting[2] ('bʌntɪŋ) *n.* bird with short, stout bill

buoy (bɔɪ, *U.S.* 'buːɪ) *n.* 1. floating marker anchored in sea 2. lifebuoy —*vt.* 3. mark with buoy 4. keep from sinking 5. support —'**buoyancy** *n.* —'**buoyant** *a.*

BUPA ('bjuːpə, 'buːpə) British United Provident Association

bur (bɜː) *n.* head of plant with prickles or hooks (*also* **burr**)

burble ('bɜːb²l) *vi.* 1. gurgle, as stream or baby 2. talk idly

burden[1] ('bɜːd²n) *n.* 1. load 2. weight, cargo 3. anything difficult to bear —*vt.* 4. load, encumber —'**burdensome** *a.*

burden[2] ('bɜːd²n) *n.* 1. chorus of a song 2. chief theme

burdock ('bɜːdɒk) *n.* plant with prickly burs

bureau ('bjuərəu) *n.* 1. writing desk 2. office 3. government department (*pl.* **-s, -reaux** (-rəuz)) —**bureaucracy** (bjuə'rɒkrəsɪ) *n.* 1. government by officials 2. body of officials —'**bureaucrat** *n.* —bureau'**cratic** *a.*

burette *or* **buret** (bju'rɛt) *n.* graduated glass tube with stopcock on one end, for dispensing known volumes of fluids

burgee (bɜː'dʒiː) *n.* small nautical flag

burgeon *or* **bourgeon** ('bɜːdʒən) *vi.* 1. bud 2. develop rapidly

burgess ('bɜːdʒɪs) *n.* inhabitant of borough, *esp.* citizen with full municipal rights

burgh ('bʌrə) *n.* Scottish borough —**burgher** ('bɜːgə) *n.* citizen

burglar ('bɜːglə) *n.* one who enters building to commit crime, *esp.* theft —'**burglary** *n.* —'**burgle, 'burglarize** *or* **-ise** *vt.*

burgundy ('bɜːgəndɪ) *n.* name of various red or white wines produced in the Burgundy region of France

burin ('bjuərɪn) *n.* chisel of tempered steel used for engraving metal, wood, or marble

burlap ('bɜːlæp) *n.* coarse canvas

burlesque (bɜː'lɛsk) *n.* 1. (artistic) caricature 2. ludicrous imitation —*vt.* 3. caricature

burly ('bɜːlɪ) *a.* sturdy, stout, robust —'**burliness** *n.*

burn[1] (bɜːn) *vt.* 1. destroy or injure by fire —*vi.* 2. be on fire (*lit.* or *fig.*) 3. be consumed by fire (**burned** *or* **burnt** *pt./pp.*) —*n.* 4. injury, mark caused by fire —'**burner** *n.* 1. part of stove *etc.* that produces flame 2. apparatus for burning fuel, refuse *etc.* —'**burning** *a.* —**burning glass** convex lens for concentrating sun's rays to produce fire

burn[2] (bɜːn) *n.* small stream

burnish ('bɜːnɪʃ) *vt.* 1. make bright by rubbing 2. polish —*n.* 3. gloss, lustre —'**burnisher** *n.*

burnoose, burnous, *or* **burnouse** (bɜː'nuːs, -'nuːz) *n.* long circular cloak with hood, worn *esp.* by Arabs

burnt (bɜːnt) *v.* 1. *pt./pp.* of BURN[1] —*a.* 2. affected as if by burning; charred

burp (bɜːp) *n./v. inf.* (esp. of baby) belch

burr[1] (bɜː) *n.* soft trilling sound given to letter *r* in some dialects

burr[2] (bɜː) *n.* rough edge left after cutting, drilling *etc.*

burro ('burəu) *n.* donkey (*pl.* **-s**)

burrow ('bʌrəu) *n.* 1. hole dug by rabbit *etc.* —*v.* 2. make holes in (ground) —*vt.* 3. bore 4. conceal

bursar ('bɜːsə) *n.* official managing finances of college, school *etc.* —'**bursary** *n.* scholarship

burst (bɜːst) *vi.* 1. fly asunder 2. break into pieces 3. rend 4. break suddenly into some expression of feeling —*vt.* 5. shatter, break violently (**burst** *pt./pp.*) —*n.* 6. bursting 7. explosion 8. outbreak 9. spurt

bury ('bɛrɪ) *vt.* 1. put underground 2. inter 3. conceal (**buried, 'burying**) —'**burial** *n./a.*

bus (bʌs) *n.* 1. large motor vehicle for passengers (*orig.* omnibus) —*v.* 2. travel or transport by bus (**bused** *or* **bussed** *pt.*, '**busing** *or* '**bussing** *pr.p.*) —**busman's holiday** *inf.* holiday spent doing same as one does at work

bus. business

busby ('bʌzbɪ) *n.* tall fur hat worn by certain soldiers

bush[1] (buʃ) *n.* 1. shrub 2. woodland, thicket 3. A, SA *etc.* uncleared country, backwoods, interior —**bushed** *a.* 1. tired out 2. A lost, bewildered —'**bushy** *a.* shaggy —'**bushbaby** *n.* tree-living, nocturnal Afr. animal —**bush fire** widespread destructive fire in the bush —**bush jacket** SA shirtlike jacket with patch pockets —**bush line** C airline operating in bush country —'**Bushman** *n.* member of hunting and gathering people of southern Afr. —**bush pilot** —**bush telegraph** *inf.* means of spreading rumour *etc.* —**bushveld** ('buʃfɛlt) *n.* **SA** bushy countryside

bush² (buʃ) n. 1. thin metal sleeve or tubular lining serving as bearing —v. 2. fit bush to (casing etc.)

bushel ('buʃəl) n. dry measure of eight gallons

business ('bɪznɪs) n. 1. profession, occupation 2. commercial or industrial establishment 3. commerce, trade 4. responsibility, affair, matter 5. work —'**businesslike** a. —'**businessman** n. person engaged in business, esp. as owner or executive ('**businesswoman** fem.)

busker ('bʌskə) n. one who makes money by singing, dancing etc. in the street —**busk** vi.

buskin ('bʌskɪn) n. 1. formerly, sandal-like covering for foot and leg, reaching calf 2. thick-soled laced half boot worn esp. by actors of ancient Greece 3. (usu. with the) tragic drama

bust¹ (bʌst) n. 1. sculpture of head and shoulders of human body 2. woman's breasts

bust² (bʌst) inf. v. 1. burst 2. make, become bankrupt —vt. 3. raid 4. arrest —a. 5. broken 6. bankrupt —n. 7. police raid or arrest

bustard ('bʌstəd) n. large swift-running bird

bustle¹ ('bʌsl) vi. 1. be noisily busy, active —n. 2. fuss, commotion

bustle² ('bʌsl) n. Hist. pad worn by ladies to support back of skirt

busy ('bɪzɪ) a. 1. actively employed 2. full of activity —vt. 3. occupy ('**busied**, '**busying**) —'**busily** adv. —'**busybody** n. meddler —**busy lizzie** ('lɪzɪ) house plant

but (bʌt, unstressed bət) prep./conj. 1. without 2. except 3. only 4. yet 5. still 6. besides

butane ('bjuːteɪn, bjuː'teɪn) n. gas used for fuel

butch (butʃ) a./n. sl. markedly or aggressively masculine (person)

butcher ('butʃə) n. 1. one who kills animals for food, or sells meat 2. ruthless or brutal murderer —vt. 3. slaughter, murder 4. spoil (work) —'**butchery** n.

butler ('bʌtlə) n. chief male servant

butt¹ (bʌt) n. 1. the thick end 2. target 3. object of ridicule 4. bottom or unused end of anything —v. 5. lie be placed end-on to

butt² (bʌt) vt. 1. strike with head 2. push —n. 3. blow with head, as of sheep —**butt in** interfere, meddle

butt³ (bʌt) n. large cask

butter ('bʌtə) n. 1. fatty substance made from cream by churning —vt. 2. spread with butter 3. flatter —**butter bean** lima bean with large pale edible seeds —'**butterfingered** a. —'**butter-fingers** n. inf. person who drops things inadvertently —'**buttermilk** n. milk that remains after churning —'**butterscotch** n. kind of hard, brittle toffee

buttercup ('bʌtəkʌp) n. plant with glossy, yellow flowers

butterfly ('bʌtəflaɪ) n. 1. insect with large wings 2. inconstant person 3. stroke in swimming —**butterfly nut** see wing nut at WING

buttery ('bʌtərɪ) n. storeroom for food or wine

buttock ('bʌtək) n. (usu. pl.) rump, protruding hinder part

button ('bʌtn) n. 1. knob, stud for fastening dress 2. knob that operates doorbell, machine etc. —vt. 3. fasten with buttons —'**buttonhole** n. 1. slit in garment to pass button through as fastening 2. flower, spray worn on lapel etc. —vt. 3. detain (reluctant listener) in conversation

buttress ('bʌtrɪs) n. 1. structure to support wall 2. prop —vt. 3. support (wall) with buttress

buxom ('bʌksəm) a. 1. full of health, plump, gay 2. large-breasted

buy (baɪ) vt. 1. get by payment, purchase 2. bribe (**bought** pt./pp.) —'**buyer** n.

buzz (bʌz) vi. 1. make humming sound —n. 2. humming sound of bees 3. inf. telephone call —'**buzzer** n. any apparatus that makes buzzing sound

buzzard ('bʌzəd) n. bird of prey of hawk family

B.V.M. Beata Virgo Maria (Lat., Blessed Virgin Mary)

bwana ('bwɑːnə) n. in E Afr., master, oft. used as form of address corresponding to sir

by (baɪ) prep. 1. near 2. along 3. across 4. past 5. during 6. not later than 7. through use or agency of 8. in units of —adv. 9. near 10. away, aside 11. past —by and by soon, in the future —by and large 1. on the whole 2. speaking generally —come by obtain

by- or **bye-** (comb. form) subsidiary, incidental, out-of-the-way, near, as in bypath, by-product, bystander

bye (baɪ) n. 1. Sport situation where player, team, wins by default of opponent 2. Cricket run scored off ball not touched by batsman

by-election or **bye-election** n. parliamentary election caused by death or resignation of member

bygone ('baɪgɒn) a. 1. past, former —n. 2. (oft. pl.) past occurrence 3. small antique

bylaw or **bye-law** ('baɪlɔː) n. law, regulation made by local subordinate authority

by-line n. 1. line under title of newspaper or magazine article giving author's name 2. see touchline at TOUCH

bypass ('baɪpɑːs) n. road for diversion of traffic from crowded centres

by-play n. diversion, action apart from main action of play

byre (baɪə) n. cowshed

Byronic (baɪ'rɒnɪk) a. of, like, or characteristic of Byron, his poetry, or his style

bystander ('baɪstændə) n. person present but not involved; spectator

byte (bait) *n. Comp.* sequence of bits processed as single unit of information

byway ('baiwei) *n.* 1. secondary or side road 2. area, field of study *etc.* that is of secondary importance

byword ('baiwɜːd) *n.* well-known name, saying

Byzantine (bi'zæntain, -tiːn, bai-; 'bizəntiːn, -tain) *a.* 1. of Byzantium or Byzantine Empire 2. of Orthodox Church 3. of style of architecture developed in Byzantine Empire, characterized by domes, mosaics *etc.* 4. complicated —*n.* 5. inhabitant of Byzantium

---

C,c

c or **C** (siː) *n.* 1. third letter of English alphabet 2. speech sound represented by this letter, usu. either as in *cigar* or as in *case* 3. third in series, *esp.* third highest grade in examination 4. something shaped like C (*pl.* **c's, C's** or **Cs**)

C 1. *Mus.* first degree of major scale containing no sharps or flats (**C major**); major or minor key having this note as tonic; time signature denoting four crotchet beats to bar (*see also* ALLA BREVE (sense 2), **common time** *at* COMMON) 2. *Chem.* carbon 3. capacitance 4. heat capacity 5. cold (water) 6. *Phys.* compliance 7. Celsius 8. centigrade 9. Conservative 10. century, as in *C20* 11. Roman numeral, 100

c. 1. carat 2. cent 3. circa 4. copyright

Ca *Chem.* calcium

CA California

ca. circa

C.A. chartered accountant

C.A.A. UK Civil Aviation Authority

cab (kæb) *n.* 1. taxi 2. driver's enclosed compartment on locomotive, lorry *etc.* —**'cabman** or **'cabby** *n.*

cabal (kə'bæl) *n.* 1. small group of intriguers 2. secret plot

cabaret ('kæbərei) *n.* floor show at nightclub or restaurant

cabbage ('kæbidʒ) *n.* vegetable with large head of green or reddish leaves

cabbala, cabala, kabbala or **kabala** (kə'bɑːlə) *n.* 1. ancient Jewish mystical tradition 2. any secret or occult doctrine —**'cabbalist, 'kabbalist** or **'kabalist** *n.* —**cabba'listic, caba'listic, kabba'listic** or **kaba'listic** *a.*

caber ('keibə) *n.* heavy wooden pole tossed as trial of strength at Highland games

cabin ('kæbin) *n.* 1. hut, shed 2. small room, *esp.* in ship —*vt.* 3. cramp, confine —**cabin boy** boy who waits on officers and passengers of ship

—**cabin cruiser** power boat with cabin, bunks *etc.*

cabinet ('kæbinit) *n.* 1. piece of furniture with drawers or shelves 2. outer case of television, radio *etc.* 3. (*oft.* C-) committee of politicians governing country 4. *obs.* small room —**cabinetmaker** *n.* craftsman who makes fine furniture

cable ('keibəl) *n.* 1. strong rope 2. wire or bundle of wires conveying electric power, telegraph signals *etc.* 3. message sent by this 4. nautical unit of measurement (100-120 fathoms) —*v.* 5. telegraph by cable —**cable car** passenger car on cable railway, drawn by strong cable operated by motor —**'cablegram** *n.* cabled message

caboodle (kə'buːdəl) *n. inf.* —**the whole caboodle** the whole lot

caboose (kə'buːs) *n.* 1. ship's galley 2. US guard's van on train

cabriolet (kæbriəʊ'lei) *n.* early type of hansom cab

cacao (kə'kɑːəʊ, -'keiəʊ) *n.* tropical tree from the seeds of which chocolate and cocoa are made

cachalot ('kæʃəlɒt) *n.* sperm whale

cache (kæʃ) *n.* 1. secret hiding place 2. store of food *etc.*

cachet ('kæʃei) *n.* 1. mark, stamp 2. mark of authenticity 3. prestige, distinction

cachinnate ('kækineit) *vi.* laugh loudly —**cachin'nation** *n.*

cachou ('kæʃuː, kæ'ʃuː) *n.* 1. lozenge eaten to sweeten breath 2. substance obtained from certain tropical plants and used in medicine *etc.* (*also* **'catechu, cutch**)

cack-handed (kæk'hændid) *a. inf.* 1. left-handed 2. clumsy

cackle ('kækəl) *vi.* 1. make chattering noise, as hen —*n.* 2. cackling noise or laughter 3. empty chatter —**'cackler** *n.*

caco- (*comb. form*) bad, unpleasant, incorrect, as in *cacophony*

cacoethes (kækəʊ'iːθiːz) *n.* uncontrollable urge or desire

cacophony (kə'kɒfəni) *n.* 1. disagreeable sound 2. discord of sounds —**ca'cophonous** *a.*

cactus ('kæktəs) *n.* spiny succulent plant (*pl.* **-es, cacti** ('kæktai))

cad (kæd) *n.* UK *inf., old-fashioned* dishonourable, unchivalrous person —**'caddish** *a.*

cadaver (kə'deivə, -'dɑːv-) *n.* corpse —**cadaverous** (kə'dævərəs) *a.* 1. corpselike 2. sickly-looking 3. gaunt

caddie or **caddy** ('kædi) *n.* 1. golfer's attendant —*vi.* 2. act as caddie

caddis fly ('kædis) small mothlike insect having two pairs of hairy wings —**caddis worm** or **'caddis** *n.* aquatic larva of caddis fly, which constructs protective case around itself made of silk *etc.* (*also* **'caseworm, 'strawworm**)

caddy ('kædı) *n.* small box for tea

cadence ('keɪd⁽ə⁾ns) *or* **cadency** *n.* fall or modulation of voice in music or verse

cadenza (kə'dɛnzə) *n. Mus.* elaborate passage for solo instrument or singer

cadet (kə'dɛt) *n.* youth in training, *esp.* for officer status in armed forces

cadge (kædʒ) *v.* get (food, money *etc.*) by sponging or begging —**'cadger** *n.* sponger

cadi *or* **kadi** ('kɑːdɪ, 'keɪdɪ) *n.* judge in Muslim community (*pl.* **-s**)

cadmium ('kædmɪəm) *n.* metallic element

cadre ('kɑːdɪ) *n.* nucleus or framework, *esp.* skeleton of regiment

caduceus (kə'djuːsɪəs) *n.* **1.** *Class. myth.* winged staff entwined with two serpents carried by Hermes (Mercury) **2.** insignia resembling this, used as emblem of medical profession (*pl.* **-cei** (-sɪaɪ))

caecum *or U.S.* **cecum** ('siːkəm) *n. Anat.* pouch, *esp.* at beginning of large intestine (*pl.* **-ca** (-kə))

Caenozoic (siːnəʊ'zəʊɪk) *see* CAINOZOIC

Caerphilly (keə'fɪlɪ) *n.* creamy white mild-flavoured cheese

Caesarean, Caesarian, *or U.S.* **Cesarean, Cesarian** ('sɪ'zɛərɪən) *a.* **1.** of any of Caesars, *esp.* Julius Caesar —*n.* **2.** (*sometimes* **c-**) *Surg.* Caesarean section —**Caesarean section** surgical incision through abdominal wall to deliver baby

caesium *or U.S.* **cesium** ('siːzɪəm) *n.* ductile silvery-white element of alkali metal group, used in photocells *etc.*

caesura (sɪ'zjʊərə) *n.* **1.** in modern prosody, pause, *esp.* for sense, usu. near middle of verse line **2.** in classical prosody, break between words within metrical foot (*pl.* **-s, -rae** (-riː))

café ('kæfeɪ, 'kæfɪ) *n.* small or inexpensive restaurant serving light refreshments —**caf-e'teria** *n.* restaurant designed for self-service

caff (kæf) *n. sl.* café

caffeine *or* **caffein** ('kæfiːn) *n.* stimulating alkaloid found in tea and coffee plants

caftan ('kæftæn, -tɑːn) *n. see* KAFTAN

cage (keɪdʒ) *n.* **1.** enclosure, box with bars or wires, *esp.* for keeping animals or birds **2.** place of confinement **3.** enclosed platform of lift, *esp.* in mine —*vt.* **4.** put in cage, confine —**'cagey** *or* **'cagy** *a.* wary, not communicative

cagoule (kə'guːl) *n.* lightweight, usu. knee-length type of anorak

cahoots (kə'huːts) *pl.n. sl.* partnership (*esp. in* **in cahoots with**)

caiman ('keɪmən) *n. see* CAYMAN

Cainozoic (kaɪnəʊ'zəʊɪk, keɪ-), **Cenozoic** *or* **Caenozoic** *a.* **1.** of most recent geological era

characterized by development and increase of mammals —*n.* **2.** Cainozoic era

cairn (kɛən) *n.* heap of stones, *esp.* as monument or landmark —**cairn terrier** small rough-haired terrier orig. from Scotland

cairngorm ('kɛəngɔːm) *n.* yellow or brownish-coloured gem

caisson (kə'suːn, 'keɪs⁽ə⁾n) *n.* **1.** chamber for working under water **2.** apparatus for lifting vessel out of water **3.** ammunition wagon

caitiff ('keɪtɪf) *obs. n.* **1.** mean, despicable fellow —*a.* **2.** base, mean

cajole (kə'dʒəʊl) *vt.* persuade by flattery, wheedle —**ca'jolement** *n.* —**ca'joler** *n.* —**ca'jolery** *n.*

cake (keɪk) *n.* **1.** baked, sweetened, breadlike food **2.** compact mass —*vt.* **3.** make into cake —*vi.* **4.** harden (as of mud) —**'cakewalk** *n.* **1.** dance orig. performed by Amer. Negroes for prize of cake **2.** piece of music for this dance

cal. 1. calendar **2.** calibre **3.** (small) calorie

Cal. (large) Calorie

calabash ('kæləbæʃ) *n.* **1.** tree with large hard-shelled fruit **2.** this fruit **3.** drinking, cooking vessel made from gourd

calaboose ('kæləbuːs) *n.* US *inf.* prison

calamine ('kæləmaɪn) *n.* pink powder used medicinally in soothing ointment

calamity (kə'læmɪtɪ) *n.* **1.** great misfortune **2.** deep distress, disaster —**ca'lamitous** *a.*

calceolaria (kælsɪə'lɛərɪə) *n.* Amer. plant with speckled, slipper-shaped flowers

calces ('kælsiːz) *n., pl. of* CALX

calciferol (kæl'sɪfərɒl) *n.* fat-soluble steroid, found *esp.* in fish-liver oils and used in treatment of rickets (*also* **vitamin D₂**)

calcium ('kælsɪəm) *n.* metallic element, the basis of lime —**calcareous** (kæl'kɛərɪəs) *a.* containing lime —**cal'ciferous** *a.* producing salts of calcium, *esp.* calcium carbonate —**'calcify** *v.* convert, be converted, to lime —**'calcine** *vt.* reduce to quicklime **2.** burn to ashes —**'calcite** *n.* crystalline calcium carbonate —**calcium carbonate** white crystalline salt occurring in limestone, chalk *etc.*

calculate ('kælkjʊleɪt) *vt.* **1.** estimate **2.** compute —*vi.* **3.** make reckonings —**'calculable** *a.* —**'calculated** *a.* **1.** undertaken after considering likelihood of success **2.** premeditated —**'calculating** *a.* **1.** able to perform calculations **2.** shrewd, designing, scheming —**calcu'lation** *n.* —**'calculator** *n.* electronic device for making calculations —**'calculus** *n.* **1.** branch of mathematics **2.** stone in body (*pl.* **calculi** ('kælkjʊlaɪ))

caldron ('kɔːldrən) *n. see* CAULDRON

calèche (*Fr.* ka'lɛʃ) *n.* C horse-drawn carriage for taking tourists around

Caledonian (kæli'dəʊnɪən) a. 1. relating to Scotland —n. 2. *Lit.* native of Scotland

calendar ('kælɪndə) n. 1. table of months and days in the year 2. list of events, documents, register —vt. 3. enter in list 4. index

calender ('kælɪndə) n. 1. machine in which paper or cloth is smoothed by passing between rollers —vt. 2. subject to such process

calends or **kalends** ('kælɪndz) pl.n. first day of each month in ancient Roman calendar

calendula (kə'lɛndjʊlə) n. marigold

calf¹ (kɑːf) n. 1. young of cow and of other animals 2. leather made of calf's skin (*pl.* **calves**) —**calve** vi. give birth to calf —**calf love** infatuation of adolescent for member of opposite sex

calf² (kɑːf) n. fleshy back part of leg below knee (*pl.* **calves**)

calibre or *U.S.* **caliber** ('kælɪbə) n. 1. size of bore of gun 2. capacity, character —'**calibrate** vt. mark (scale of measuring instrument) so that readings can be made in appropriate units —cali'**bration** n.

calices ('kælɪsiːz) n., *pl. of* CALIX

calico ('kælɪkəʊ) n. cotton cloth

californium (kælɪ'fɔːnɪəm) n. transuranic element artificially produced from curium

caliper ('kælɪpə) n. *US see* CALLIPER

caliph, calif or **khalif** ('keɪlɪf, 'kæl-) n. *Islam* title of successors of Mohammed as rulers of Islamic world —**caliphate, califate** or **khalifate** ('keɪlɪfeɪt) n. office or reign of caliph

calix ('keɪlɪks, 'kæ-) n. cup; chalice (*pl.* '**calices**)

calk¹ (kɔːk) vt. *see* CAULK

calk² (kɔːk) or **calkin** ('kɔːkɪn, 'kæl-) n. 1. metal projection on horse's shoe to prevent slipping —vt. 2. provide with calks

call (kɔːl) vt. 1. speak loudly to attract attention of 2. summon 3. (*oft. with* up) telephone 4. name —vi. 5. shout 6. pay visit —n. 7. shout 8. animal's cry 9. visit 10. inner urge, summons, as to be priest *etc.* 11. need, demand —'**caller** n. —'**calling** n. vocation, profession —**call box** kiosk for public telephone—**call girl** prostitute with whom appointments are made by telephone —**call up** 1. summon to serve in army 2. imagine

calligraphy (kə'lɪgrəfɪ) n. handwriting, penmanship —calli'**graphic** a.

calliper or *U.S.* **caliper** ('kælɪpə) n. 1. metal splint for leg —pl. 2. instrument for measuring diameters

callisthenics or **calisthenics** (kælɪs'θɛnɪks) pl.n. light gymnastic exercises —**callis-** '**thenic** or **calis'thenic** a.

callosity (kə'lɒsɪtɪ) n. 1. hardheartedness 2. callus

callous ('kæləs) a. hardened, unfeeling —'**callously** adv. —'**callousness** n.

callow ('kæləʊ) a. 1. inexperienced 2. immature

callus ('kæləs) n. area of thick, hardened skin

calm (kɑːm) a. 1. still 2. quiet 3. tranquil —n. 4. stillness 5. tranquillity 6. absence of wind —v. 7. become, make, still or quiet —'**calmly** adv. —'**calmness** n.

calomel ('kæləmɛl, -məl) n. colourless, tasteless powder used medicinally, *esp.* as cathartic

Calor Gas ('kælə) R butane gas liquefied under pressure in portable containers for domestic use

calorie or **calory** ('kælərɪ) n. 1. unit of heat 2. unit of energy obtained from foods —ca'**loric** a. 1. of heat or calories —n. 2. *obs.* hypothetical elastic fluid, embodiment of heat —calo'**rific** a. heat-making —calo'**rimeter** n.

calumet ('kæljumɛt) n. 1. tobacco pipe of N Amer. Indians 2. pipe of peace

calumny ('kæləmnɪ) n. slander, false accusation —ca'**lumniate** vt. —calumni'**ation** n. —ca'**lumniator** n. —ca'**lumnious** a.

Calvary ('kælvərɪ) n. place outside walls of Jerusalem where Jesus was crucified (*also* Gol'**gotha**)

calves (kɑːvz) n., *pl. of* CALF¹, CALF²

Calvinism ('kælvɪnɪzəm) n. theological system of Calvin, characterized by emphasis on predestination and justification by faith —'**Calvinist** n./a. —Calvin'**istic(al)** a.

calx (kælks) n. 1. powdery metallic oxide formed when ore or mineral is roasted 2. calcium oxide (*pl.* -es, '**calces**)

calypso (kə'lɪpsəʊ) n. W Indian improvised song on topical subject

calyx ('keɪlɪks, 'kælɪks) n. covering of bud (*pl.* -es, **calyces** ('kælɪsiːz, 'keɪlɪ-))

cam (kæm) n. device to change rotary to reciprocating motion —'**camshaft** n. in motoring, rotating shaft to which cams are fixed to lift valves

camaraderie (kæmə'rɑːdərɪ) n. spirit of comradeship, trust

camber ('kæmbə) n. 1. convexity on upper surface of road, bridge *etc.* 2. curvature of aircraft wing

Cambrian ('kæmbrɪən) a. 1. of first 100 million years of Palaeozoic era 2. of Wales —n. 3. Cambrian period or rock system 4. Welshman

cambric ('keɪmbrɪk) n. fine white linen or cotton cloth

Cambs. ('kæmbz) Cambridgeshire

came (keɪm) pt. *of* COME

camel ('kæməl) n. animal of Asia and Afr., with humped back, used as beast of burden —**camel's**

hair or **'camelhair** n. 1. hair of camel, used in rugs etc. 2. soft cloth made of this hair, usu. tan in colour —a. 3. (of painter's brush) made from tail hairs of squirrels

camellia (kəˈmiːliə) n. ornamental shrub

camelopard (ˈkæmɪləpɑːd, kəˈmɛl-) n. obs. giraffe

Camembert (ˈkæməmbɛə) n. soft creamy cheese

cameo (ˈkæmɪəʊ) n. 1. medallion, brooch etc. with profile head or design carved in relief 2. single brief scene or appearance in film etc. by (well-known) actor

camera (ˈkæmərə) n. apparatus used to take photographs —**'cameraman** n. photographer, esp. for television or cinema —**camera obscura** (ɒbˈskjʊərə) darkened chamber in which views of surrounding country are shown on sheet by means of lenses —**in camera** (of legal proceedings etc.) conducted in private

camiknickers (ˈkæmɪnɪkəz) pl.n. women's knickers attached to camisole top

camisole (ˈkæmɪsəʊl) n. underbodice

camomile or **chamomile** (ˈkæməmaɪl) n. aromatic creeping plant, used medicinally

camouflage (ˈkæməflɑːʒ) n. 1. disguise, means of deceiving enemy observation, eg by paint, screen —vt. 2. disguise

camp (kæmp) n. 1. (place for) tents of hikers, army etc. 2. cabins etc. for temporary accommodation 3. group supporting political party etc. 4. SA field, pasture —a. inf. 5. homosexual 6. consciously artificial —vi. 7. form or lodge in camp —**'camper** n. 1. person who lives or temporarily stays in tent etc. 2. US vehicle equipped for camping out —**'camping** n. —**camp follower** 1. civilian, esp. prostitute, who unofficially provides services to military personnel 2. nonmember who is sympathetic to group etc.

campaign (kæmˈpeɪn) n. 1. series of coordinated activities for some purpose, eg political or military campaign —vi. 2. serve in campaign —cam**'paigner** n.

campanile (kæmpəˈniːlɪ) n. esp. in Italy, bell tower, not usu. attached to another building

campanology (kæmpəˈnɒlədʒɪ) n. art of ringing bells musically

campanula (kæmˈpænjʊlə) n. plant with blue or white bell-shaped flowers

camphor (ˈkæmfə) n. solid essential oil with aromatic taste and smell —**'camphorated** a. —**cam'phoric** a. —**camphorated oil** liniment consisting of camphor and peanut oil, used as counterirritant

campion (ˈkæmpɪən) n. white or pink wild flower

campus (ˈkæmpəs) n. grounds of college or university

can¹ (kæn; unstressed kən) vi. 1. be able to 2. have the power to 3. be allowed to (**could** pt.)

can² (kæn) n. 1. container, usu. metal, for liquids, foods —vt. 2. put in can (-**nn**-) —**canned** a. 1. preserved in can 2. (of music, programmes etc.) previously recorded —**'cannery** n. factory where food is canned

Can. 1. Canada **2.** Canadian

Canadian (kəˈneɪdɪən) n./a. (native) of Canada —**Ca'nadianize** or **-ise** v. make, become Canadian —**Canada balsam** (ˈkænədə) 1. yellow transparent resin obtained from balsam fir 2. balsam fir —**Canada Day** Jul. 1st, anniversary of day in 1867 when Canad. received dominion status —**Canada goose** large greyish-brown N Amer. goose —**Canadian Shield** wide area of rock extending over most of E and Central Canad.: rich in minerals (also **Laurentian Shield**)

canaille (kaˈnɑːj) Fr. masses; mob; rabble

canal (kəˈnæl) n. 1. artificial watercourse 2. duct in body —**canali'zation** or **-li'sation** n. —**'canalize** or **-ise** vt. 1. convert into canal 2. direct (thoughts, energies etc.) into one channel

canapé (ˈkænəpɪ, -peɪ) n. small piece of toast etc. with savoury topping

canard (kæˈnɑːd) n. 1. false report; rumour, hoax 2. aircraft in which tailplane is mounted in front of wing

canary (kəˈnɛərɪ) n. yellow singing bird

canasta (kəˈnæstə) n. card game played with two packs

cancan (ˈkænkæn) n. high-kicking (orig. Fr. music-hall) dance

cancel (ˈkænsəl) vt. 1. cross out 2. annul 3. call off (-**ll**-) —**cancel'lation** n.

cancer (ˈkænsə) n. malignant growth or tumour —**'cancerous** a.

Cancer (ˈkænsə) n. 1. (crab) 4th sign of zodiac, operative c. Jun. 21st–Jul. 21st 2. constellation —**tropic of Cancer** parallel of latitude 23½° N of the equator

candela (kænˈdiːlə, -ˈdeɪlə) n. basic SI unit of luminous intensity

candid (ˈkændɪd) a. 1. frank, open 2. impartial —**'candidly** adv. —**'candidness**, **'candour** or U.S. **'candor** n. frankness —**candid camera** small camera used to take informal photographs of people

candidate (ˈkændɪdeɪt) n. 1. one who seeks office, appointment etc. 2. person taking examination or test —**'candidacy** or **'candidature** n.

candle (ˈkændəl) n. 1. stick of wax with wick 2. light —**candelabrum** (kændɪˈlɑːbrəm) n. large, branched candle holder (pl. -**bra** (-brə))

—'**candlepower** n. unit for measuring light —'**candlestick** n. —'**candlewick** n. cotton fabric with tufted surface

Candlemas ('kændᵊlməs) n. Christianity Feb. 2nd, Feast of Purification of Virgin Mary and presentation of Christ in Temple

candy ('kændɪ) n. **1.** crystallized sugar **2.** US confectionery in general —vt. **3.** preserve with sugar —vi. **4.** become encrusted with sugar ('**candied**, '**candying**) —'**candied** a. —'**candy-floss** n. UK light fluffy confection made from coloured spun sugar, usu. held on stick

candytuft ('kændɪtʌft) n. garden plant with clusters of white, pink or purple flowers

cane (keɪn) n. **1.** stem of small palm or large grass **2.** walking stick —vt. **3.** beat with cane —**cane sugar 1.** sucrose obtained from sugar cane **2.** see SUCROSE

canine ('keɪnaɪn, 'kæn-) a. like, pert. to, dog —**canine tooth** one of four sharp, pointed teeth, two in each jaw

canister ('kænɪstə) n. container, usu. of metal, esp. for storing dry food

canker ('kæŋkə) n. **1.** eating sore **2.** thing that eats away, destroys, corrupts —vt. **3.** infect, corrupt —vi. **4.** decay —'**cankered** or '**cankerous** a. —'**cankerworm** n.

canna ('kænə) n. tropical flowering plant

cannabis ('kænəbɪs) n. **1.** hemp plant **2.** drug derived from this

cannel coal or **cannel** ('kænᵊl) n. dull coal burning with smoky luminous flame

cannelloni or **canneloni** (kænɪ'ləʊnɪ) pl.n. tubular pieces of pasta filled with meat etc.

cannibal ('kænɪbᵊl) n. **1.** one who eats human flesh —a. **2.** relating to this practice —'**cannibalism** n. —**cannibal**'**istic** a. —'**cannibalize** or **-ise** vt. use parts from (one machine etc.) to repair another

cannon¹ ('kænən) n. large gun (pl. **-s**, '**cannon**) —**canno**'**nade** n./vt. attack with cannon —'**cannonball** n. —**cannon bone** horse's leg bone —**cannon fodder** men regarded as expendable in war because they are part of huge army

cannon² ('kænən) n. **1.** billiard stroke, hitting both object balls with one's own —vi. **2.** make this stroke **3.** rebound, collide

cannot ('kænɒt, kæ'nɒt) negative form of CAN¹

canny ('kænɪ) a. **1.** shrewd **2.** cautious **3.** crafty —'**cannily** adv.

canoe (kə'nuː) n. very light boat propelled with paddle or paddles —ca'**noeist** n.

canon¹ ('kænən) n. **1.** law or rule, esp. of church **2.** standard **3.** body of books accepted as genuine **4.** list of saints —**canoni**'**zation** or **-i**'**sation** n. —'**canonize** or **-ise** vt. enrol in list of saints

canon² ('kænən) n. church dignitary, member of cathedral chapter —ca'**nonical** a. —ca'**nonicals** pl.n. vestments worn by clergy when officiating —**canon**'**istic** a. —**canonical hour 1.** R.C.Ch. one of seven prayer times appointed for each day by canon law **2.** Ch. of England any time at which marriages may lawfully be celebrated —**canon law** body of laws enacted by supreme authorities of Christian Church

canoodle (kə'nuːdᵊl) vi. (oft. with with) sl. kiss and cuddle

canopy ('kænəpɪ) n. **1.** covering over throne, bed etc. **2.** any overhanging shelter —vt. **3.** cover with canopy (**-opied, -opying**)

can't (kɑːnt) v. cannot

cant¹ (kænt) n. **1.** hypocritical speech **2.** whining **3.** language of a sect **4.** technical jargon **5.** slang, esp. of thieves —vi. **6.** use cant

cant² (kænt) vt. **1.** tilt, slope **2.** bevel —n. **3.** inclination from vertical or horizontal plane

Cantab. (kæn'tæb) Cantabrigiensis (Lat., of Cambridge)

cantabile (kæn'tɑːbɪlɪ) Mus. a./adv. **1.** singing —n. **2.** piece or passage performed in this way

Cantabrigian (kæntə'brɪdʒɪən) a. **1.** of Cambridge or Cambridge University —n. **2.** member or graduate of Cambridge University **3.** inhabitant or native of Cambridge

cantaloupe or **cantaloup** ('kæntəluːp) n. variety of muskmelon

cantankerous (kæn'tæŋkərəs) a. ill-natured, quarrelsome

cantata (kæn'tɑːtə) n. choral work like, but shorter than, oratorio

canteen (kæn'tiːn) n. **1.** place in factory, school etc. where meals are provided **2.** small shop in military camp **3.** case of cutlery **4.** mess tin

canter ('kæntə) n. **1.** easy gallop —v. **2.** move at, make to canter

Canterbury bell ('kæntəbərɪ) cultivated campanula

cantharides (kæn'θærɪdiːz) pl.n. diuretic and urogenital stimulant prepared from dried bodies of Spanish fly (sing. '**cantharis**) (also **Spanish fly**)

canticle ('kæntɪkᵊl) n. short hymn

cantilever ('kæntɪliːvə) n. beam, girder etc. fixed at one end only

canto ('kæntəʊ) n. division of poem (pl. **-s**)

canton ('kænton, kæn'ton) n. division of country, esp. Swiss federal state

Cantonese (kæntə'niːz) n. **1.** Chinese language spoken in Canton etc. **2.** native or inhabitant of Canton (pl. **-ese**) —a. **3.** of Canton or Chinese language spoken there

cantonment (kən'tuːnmənt) n. quarters for troops

cantor ('kæntɔː) n. **1.** Judaism leading singer in

synagogue liturgy **2.** *Christianity* leader of singing in church choir

Canuck (kə'nʌk) *n./a.* C *inf.* Canadian

canvas ('kænvəs) *n.* **1.** coarse cloth used for sails, painting on *etc.* **2.** sails of ship **3.** picture —**under canvas** in tents

canvass ('kænvəs) *vt.* **1.** solicit votes, contributions *etc.* from **2.** discuss, examine —*n.* **3.** solicitation

canyon *or* **cañon** ('kænjən) *n.* deep gorge

caoutchouc ('kautʃuk) *n. see* RUBBER[1] (sense 1)

cap (kæp) *n.* **1.** covering for head **2.** lid, top or other covering —*vt.* **3.** put cap on **4.** outdo **5.** select for a team (-**pp**-)

cap. **1.** capacity **2.** capital **3.** capitalize **4.** capital letter

capable ('keɪpəb²l) *a.* **1.** able, gifted **2.** competent **3.** having the capacity, power —**capa'bility** *n.*

capacity (kə'pæsɪtɪ) *n.* **1.** power of holding or grasping **2.** room **3.** volume **4.** character **5.** ability, power of mind —**capacious** (kə'peɪʃəs) *a.* roomy —**ca'pacitance** *n.* (measure of) ability of system to store electric charge —**ca'pacitor** *n.*

caparison (kə'pærɪsən) *n.* **1.** ornamental covering, equipment for horse —*vt.* **2.** adorn thus

cape[1] (keɪp) *n.* covering for shoulders

cape[2] (keɪp) *n.* point of land running into sea, headland —**Cape Coloured SA** *see* **Coloured** (sense 2) *at* COLOUR —**Cape pigeon** pied petrel of southern oceans —**Cape salmon SA** geelbek —**Cape sparrow** common S Afr. bird

caper[1] ('keɪpə) *n.* **1.** skip **2.** frolic **3.** escapade —*vi.* **4.** skip, dance

caper[2] ('keɪpə) *n.* pickled flower bud of Sicilian shrub

capercaillie *or* **capercailzie** (kæpə'keɪlɪ) *n.* large black grouse

capillary (kə'pɪlərɪ) *a.* **1.** hairlike **2.** of capillarity —*n.* **3.** tube with very small bore, *esp.* small blood vessel —**capil'larity** *n.* phenomenon caused by surface tension and resulting in elevation or depression of surface of liquid in contact with solid (*also* **capillary action**)

capital ('kæpɪt²l) *n.* **1.** chief town **2.** money, stock, funds **3.** large-sized letter **4.** headpiece of column —*a.* **5.** involving or punishable by death **6.** serious **7.** chief **8.** leading **9.** excellent —**'capitalism** *n.* economic system which is based on private ownership of industry —**'capitalist** *n.* **1.** owner of capital **2.** supporter of capitalism —*a.* **3.** run by, possessing, capital —**'capitalize** *or* **-ise** *vt.* **1.** convert into capital —*vi.* **2.** (*with* on) turn to advantage —**'capitally** *adv.* —**capital gain** amount by which selling

price of financial asset exceeds cost —**capital levy** tax on capital or property as contrasted with tax on income —**capital punishment** punishment of death for crime; death penalty —**capital stock 1.** par value of total share capital a company is authorized to issue **2.** total physical capital existing in economy at any time —**capital transfer tax UK** tax payable on total of gifts of money or property made during donor's lifetime or after his death

capitation (kæpɪ'teɪʃən) *n.* **1.** tax or grant per head **2.** census

Capitol ('kæpɪt²l) *n.* **1.** U.S. Congress House **2.** a U.S. state legislature building **3.** temple of Jupiter in Rome

capitulate (kə'pɪtjuleɪt) *vi.* surrender on terms, give in —**capitu'lation** *n.*

capo ('kæpəu) *n.* device fitted across all strings of guitar *etc.* to raise pitch of each string simultaneously (*pl.* -**s**) (*also* **capo tasto** ('tæstəu))

capon ('keɪpən) *n.* castrated cock fowl fattened for eating —'**caponize** *or* **-ise** *vt.*

cappuccino (kæpu'tʃiːnəu) *n.* coffee with steamed milk

caprice (kə'priːs) *n.* whim —**capricious** (kə'prɪʃəs) *a.* —**capriciousness** (kə'prɪʃəsnɪs) *n.*

Capricorn ('kæprɪkɔːn) *n.* **1.** (sea-goat) 10th sign of zodiac, operative c. Dec. 21st–Jan. 19th **2.** constellation —**tropic of Capricorn** parallel of latitude 23½° S of the equator

capriole ('kæprɪəul) *Dressage n.* **1.** upward but not forward leap made by horse with all four feet off ground —*vi.* **2.** perform capriole

caps. **1.** capital letters **2.** capsule

capsicum ('kæpsɪkəm) *n.* tropical vegetable with mild peppery flavour, sweet pepper

capsize (kæp'saɪz) *vt.* **1.** (of boat) upset —*vi.* **2.** be overturned —**cap'sizal** *n.*

capstan ('kæpstən) *n.* machine to wind cable, *esp.* to hoist anchor

capsule ('kæpsjul) *n.* **1.** gelatin case for dose of medicine or drug **2.** any small enclosed area or container **3.** seed vessel of plant —'**capsulize** *or* **-ise** *vt.* **1.** state in highly condensed form **2.** enclose in capsule

Capt. Captain

captain ('kæptɪn) *n.* **1.** commander of vessel or company of soldiers **2.** leader, chief —*vt.* **3.** be captain of

caption ('kæpʃən) *n.* heading, title of article, picture *etc.*

captious ('kæpʃəs) *a.* **1.** ready to find fault **2.** critical **3.** peevish —'**captiously** *adv.* —'**captiousness** *n.*

captive ('kæptɪv) *n.* **1.** prisoner —*a.* **2.** taken, imprisoned **3.** unable to avoid speeches *etc.*

—'**captivate** vt. fascinate —'**captivating** a. delightful —**cap**'**tivity** n.

capture ('kæptʃə) vt. 1. seize, make prisoner —n. 2. seizure, taking —'**captor** n.

Capuchin ('kæpjutʃın, -ʃın) n. friar belonging to branch of Franciscan Order

capybara (kæpı'bɑːrə) n. largest rodent, found in S Amer.

car (kɑː) n. 1. self-propelled road vehicle 2. passenger compartment, as in cable car 3. railway carriage of specified type —**car park** area, building where vehicles may be left for a time —'**carport** n. shelter for car usu. consisting of roof supported by posts

carabineer or **carabinier** (kærəbı'nıə) n. see carbineer at CARBINE

caracal ('kærəkæl) n. 1. lynxlike feline mammal inhabiting deserts of N Afr. and S Asia, having smooth coat of reddish fur 2. this fur

caracole ('kærəkəʊl) or **caracol** ('kærəkɒl) Dressage n. 1. half turn to right or left —vi. 2. execute half turn

caracul ('kærəkʌl) n. 1. black, loosely curled fur from skins of newly born lambs of caracul sheep (also **Persian lamb**) 2. sheep of Central Asia with coarse dark hair (also '**karakul**)

carafe (kə'ræf, -'rɑːf) n. glass water bottle for table, decanter

caramel ('kærəml) n. 1. burnt sugar for cooking 2. type of confectionery

carapace ('kærəpeıs) n. thick hard shield that covers part of body of tortoise etc.

carat ('kærət) n. 1. small weight used for gold, diamonds etc. 2. proportional measure of twenty-fourths used to state fineness of gold

caravan ('kærəvæn) n. 1. large enclosed vehicle for living in, pulled as trailer by car etc. 2. company of merchants travelling together for safety in the East —**caravanserai** (kærə'vænsəraı) or **caravansary** (kærə'vænsərı) n. in some Eastern countries, large inn enclosing court-yard, providing accommodation for caravans

caravel ('kærəvel) or **carvel** n. two- or three-masted sailing ship in 15th and 16th centuries

caraway ('kærəweı) n. plant of which the seeds are used as spice in cakes etc.

carbide ('kɑːbaıd) n. compound of carbon with an element, esp. calcium carbide

carbine ('kɑːbaın) n. short rifle —**carbineer** (kɑːbı'nıə), **carabi'neer** or **carabi'nier** n. formerly, soldier equipped with carbine

carbo- or before vowel **carb-** (comb. form) carbon, as in carbohydrate, carbonate

carbohydrate (kɑːbəʊ'haıdreıt) n. any of large group of compounds containing carbon, hydrogen and oxygen, esp. sugars and starches as components of food

carbolic acid (kɑː'bɒlık) disinfectant derived from coal tar —'**carbolated** a. containing carbolic acid

carbon ('kɑːbən) n. nonmetallic element, substance of pure charcoal, found in all organic matter —**carbo'naceous** a. of, resembling or containing carbon —'**carbonate** n. salt of carbonic acid —**car'bonic** a. —**carbo'niferous** a. —'**carbonize** or -**ise** v. —**carbon black** finely divided carbon produced by incomplete combustion of natural gas or petroleum: used in pigments and ink —**carbon dating** technique for determining age of wood etc., based on its content of radioisotope ^{14}C acquired from atmosphere when it formed part of living plant —**carbon dioxide** colourless gas exhaled in respiration of animals —**carbonic acid** 1. carbon dioxide 2. compound formed by carbon dioxide and water —**carbon monoxide** colour-less, odourless poisonous gas formed when carbon compounds burn in insufficient air —**carbon paper** paper coated with a dark, waxy pigment, used for duplicating written or typed matter, producing **carbon copy** —**carbon tetrachloride** colourless volatile nonflammable liquid made from chlorine and used as solvent etc.

Carboniferous (kɑːbə'nıfərəs) a. 1. of fifth period of Palaeozoic era during which coal measures were formed —n. 2. Carboniferous period or rock system divided into **Upper Carboniferous** and **Lower Carboniferous** peri-ods

Carborundum (kɑːbə'rʌndəm) n. R artificial silicate of carbon

carboy ('kɑːbɔı) n. large glass jar protected by wicker casing

carbuncle ('kɑːbʌŋkəl) n. 1. inflamed ulcer, boil or tumour 2. fiery-red precious stone

carburettor, carburetter (kɑːbjʊ'rɛtə, 'kɑːbjʊrɛtə) or U.S. **carburetor** ('kɑːbjʊreıtə) n. device for vaporizing and mixing petrol with air in internal-combustion engine

carcass or **carcase** ('kɑːkəs) n. 1. dead animal body 2. skeleton 3. inf. person's body

carcinoma (kɑːsı'nəʊmə) n. a cancer —**car'cinogen** n. substance producing cancer

card[1] (kɑːd) n. 1. thick, stiff paper 2. piece of this giving identification etc. 3. illustrated card sending greetings etc. 4. one of the 52 playing cards making up a pack 5. inf. a character, eccentric —pl. 6. any card game 7. employee's tax and national insurance documents or information held by employer —'**cardboard** n. thin, stiff board made of paper pulp —**card index** index in which each entry is made on separate card —'**cardsharp** or '**cardsharper** n. professional card player who cheats —**card vote** UK vote by delegates, esp. at trade union conference, in which each delegate's vote counts as vote by all his constituents

card² (ka:d) *n.* **1.** instrument for combing wool *etc.* —*vt.* **2.** comb —**'carder** *n.*

cardamom *or* **cardamum** ('ka:dəməm) *n.* **1.** tropical Asian plant with large hairy leaves **2.** seeds of this plant, used *esp.* as spice or condiment

cardiac ('ka:dɪæk) *a.* **1.** pert. to the heart —*n.* **2.** person with heart disorder —**'cardiogram** *n.* tracing made by cardiograph —**'cardiograph** *n.* instrument which records movements of the heart —**'cardioid** *a.* heart-shaped —**cardi'olo-gist** *n.* —**cardi'ology** *n.* branch of medical science concerned with heart and its diseases

cardigan ('ka:dɪɡən) *n.* knitted jacket

cardinal ('ka:dɪnəl) *a.* **1.** chief, principal —*n.* **2.** highest rank, next to the Pope in R.C. Church **3.** bright red N Amer. bunting (*also* **'redbird**) —**'cardinalate** *n.* —**cardinal numbers** 1, 2, 3, *etc.* —**cardinal points** north, south, east and west

cardio- *or before vowel* **cardi-** (*comb. form*) heart, as in cardiogram

care (kɛə) *vi.* **1.** be anxious —*n.* **2.** attention **3.** pains, heed **4.** charge, protection **5.** anxiety **6.** caution —**'carefree** *a.* —**'careful** *a.* —**'careful-ly** *adv.* —**'carefulness** *n.* —**'careless** *a.* —**'carelessness** *n.* —**'caretaker** *n.* **1.** person in charge of premises *or* **2.** temporary, interim —**'careworn** *a.* showing signs of care, stress *etc.* —**care for 1.** have regard or liking for **2.** look after **3.** be disposed to

careen (kə'ri:n) *vt.* **1.** lay (ship) over on her side for cleaning and repair —*vi.* **2.** keel over **3.** sway dangerously

career (kə'rɪə) *n.* **1.** course through life **2.** profession **3.** rapid motion —*vi.* **4.** run or move at full speed —**ca'reerist** *n.* person who seeks to advance his career by any possible means

caress (kə'rɛs) *vt.* **1.** fondle, embrace, treat with affection —*n.* **2.** act or expression of affection

caret ('kærɪt) *n.* mark ($\wedge$) showing where to insert something omitted

cargo ('ka:ɡəʊ) *n.* load, freight, carried by ship, plane *etc.* (*pl.* **-es**)

Carib ('kærɪb) *n.* **1.** member of group of Amer. Indian peoples of NE South Amer. and Lesser Antilles (*pl.* **-s**, **'Carib**) **2.** family of languages spoken by these peoples

caribou ('kærɪbuː) *n.* N Amer. reindeer

caricature ('kærɪkətjʊə) *n.* **1.** likeness exaggerated or distorted to appear ridiculous —*vt.* **2.** portray in this way

carillon (kə'rɪljən) *n.* **1.** set of bells *usu.* hung in tower and played by set of keys, pedals *etc.* **2.** tune so played

cariole ('kærɪəʊl) *n.* see CARRIOLE

carl *or* **carle** (ka:l) *n. obs., Scot.* churl

Carlovingian (ka:ləʊ'vɪndʒɪən) *Hist. see* CAROLINGIAN

Carmelite ('ka:mɪlaɪt) *n. R.C.Ch.* **1.** member of order of mendicant friars **2.** member of corresponding order of nuns

carminative ('ka:mɪnətɪv) *n.* **1.** medicine to remedy flatulence —*a.* **2.** acting as this

carmine ('ka:maɪn) *n.* **1.** brilliant red colour (prepared from cochineal) —*a.* **2.** of this colour

carnage ('ka:nɪdʒ) *n.* slaughter

carnal ('ka:nəl) *a.* **1.** fleshly, sensual **2.** worldly —**'carnalism** *n.* —**car'nality** *n.* —**'carnally** *adv.* —**carnal knowledge** *chiefly law* sexual intercourse

carnation (ka:'neɪʃən) *n.* **1.** cultivated flower **2.** flesh colour

carnelian (ka:'ni:ljən) *n.* reddish-yellow translucent chalcedony, used as gemstone

carnival ('ka:nɪvəl) *n.* **1.** festive occasion **2.** travelling fair **3.** show or display for amusement

carnivorous (ka:'nɪvərəs) *a.* flesh-eating —**'carnivore** *n.*

carob ('kærəb) *n.* **1.** evergreen Mediterranean tree with edible pods **2.** long blackish sugary pod of this tree, used for fodder and sometimes human food

carol ('kærəl) *n.* **1.** song or hymn of joy or praise (*esp.* Christmas carol) —*vi.* **2.** sing carols (**-ll-**)

Caroline ('kærəlaɪn) *or* **Carolean** (kærə-'li:ən) *a.* of Charles I or Charles II (kings of England, Scotland and Ireland), society over which they ruled or their government (*also* **Caro'linian**)

Carolingian (kærə'lɪndʒɪən) *Hist. a.* **1.** of Frankish dynasty founded by Pepin the Short —*n.* **2.** member of dynasty of Carolingian Franks (*also* **Carlo'vingian, Caro'linian**)

carotid (kə'rɒtɪd) *n.* **1.** either of two principal arteries that supply blood to head and neck —*a.* **2.** of either of these arteries

carouse (kə'raʊz) *vi.* **1.** have merry drinking spree —*n.* **2.** merry drinking party (*also* **ca'rousal**) —**ca'rouser** *n.*

carousel (kærə'sɛl, -'zɛl) *n.* US merry-go-round

carp¹ (ka:p) *n.* freshwater fish

carp² (ka:p) *vi.* **1.** complain about small faults or errors **2.** nag —**'carper** *n.* —**'carping** *a.* —**'carpingly** *adv.*

carpal ('ka:pəl) *n.* any bone of wrist

carpel ('ka:pəl) *n.* female reproductive organ of flowering plants, consisting of ovary, style and stigma

carpenter ('kɑːpɪntə) n. worker in timber as in building etc. —'**carpentry** n. art of carpenter

carpet ('kɑːpɪt) n. 1. heavy fabric for covering floor —vt. 2. cover (floor) with carpet 3. inf. call up for censure —'**carpetbag** n. travelling bag —'**carpetbagger** n. political adventurer —**carpet slipper** slipper orig. made with woollen upper resembling carpeting

carpus ('kɑːpəs) n. 1. wrist 2. eight small bones of human wrist (pl. **carpi** ('kɑːpaɪ))

carrageen, carragheen or **carageen** ('kærəɡiːn) n. edible red seaweed of N Amer. and N Europe, used to make jelly etc. (also **Irish moss**)

carriage ('kærɪdʒ) n. 1. railway coach 2. bearing, conduct 3. horse-drawn vehicle 4. act, cost, of carrying —**carriage clock** portable clock, usu. in rectangular case, orig. used by travellers —**carriage forward** charge for conveying, to be paid by receiver —**carriage paid** charge for conveying, to be paid by sender —'**carriageway** n. part of road along which traffic passes in single line

carriole or **cariole** ('kærɪəʊl) n. small open carriage for one

carrion ('kærɪən) n. rotting dead flesh —**carrion crow** scavenging European crow

carrot ('kærət) n. 1. plant with orange-red edible root 2. inducement —'**carroty** a. red, reddish

carry ('kærɪ) vt. 1. convey, transport 2. capture, win 3. effect 4. conduct (oneself) in specified manner —vi. 5. (of projectile, sound) reach or penetrate to distance ('**carried**, '**carrying**) —n. 6. range —'**carrier** n. 1. one that carries goods 2. one who, himself immune, communicates a disease to others 3. aircraft carrier —**carrier bag** UK large paper or plastic bag for shopping etc. —**carrier pigeon** homing pigeon, esp. for carrying messages —**carrier wave** Rad. wave of fixed amplitude and frequency, modulated to carry signal in radio transmission etc. (also '**carrier**) —'**carrycot** n. light cot with handles, similar to but smaller than body of pram —**carry-out** n. chiefly Scot. 1. alcohol bought at off-licence etc. for consumption elsewhere 2. shop which sells hot cooked food for consumption away from premises —**carry on** 1. continue 2. inf. fuss unnecessarily 3. inf. have an affair —**carry out** 1. perform; cause to be implemented 2. accomplish

cart (kɑːt) n. 1. open (two-wheeled) vehicle, esp. pulled by horse —vt. 2. convey in cart 3. carry with effort —'**cartage** n. —'**carter** n. —'**carthorse** n. —'**cartwheel** n. 1. large, spoked wheel 2. sideways somersault —'**cartwright** n. maker of carts

carte blanche ('kɑːt 'blɑːntʃ) Fr. complete discretion or authority

cartel (kɑː'tɛl) n. 1. industrial combination for the purpose of fixing prices, output etc. 2. alliance of political parties etc. to further common aims

Cartesian (kɑː'tiːzɪən) a. 1. pert. to French philosopher René Descartes (1596–1650) or his system of coordinates —n. 2. adherent of his philosophy —**Cartesian coordinates** system of coordinates that defines location of point in terms of perpendicular distance from each of set of mutually perpendicular axes

Carthusian (kɑː'θjuːzɪən) n. R.C.Ch. member of monastic order founded by Saint Bruno

cartilage ('kɑːtɪlɪdʒ) n. 1. firm elastic tissue in the body 2. gristle —**cartilaginous** (kɑːtɪ'lædʒɪnəs) a.

cartogram ('kɑːtəɡræm) n. map showing statistical information in diagrammatic form

cartography (kɑː'tɒɡrəfɪ) n. mapmaking —car'**tographer** n. —carto'**graphic(al)** a.

carton ('kɑːtən) n. cardboard or plastic container

cartoon (kɑː'tuːn) n. 1. drawing, esp. humorous or satirical 2. sequence of drawings telling story 3. preliminary design for painting —car'**toonist** n.

cartouche or **cartouch** (kɑː'tuːʃ) n. 1. carved or cast ornamental tablet or panel in form of scroll 2. oblong figure enclosing characters expressing royal or divine names in Egyptian hieroglyphics

cartridge ('kɑːtrɪdʒ) n. 1. case containing charge for gun 2. container for film, magnetic tape etc. 3. unit in head of gramophone pick-up —**cartridge paper** strong, thick paper

carve (kɑːv) vt. 1. cut 2. hew 3. sculpture 4. engrave 5. cut (meat) in pieces or slices —'**carver** n. —'**carving** n.

carvel ('kɑːvəl) n. see CARAVEL.

caryatid (kærɪ'ætɪd) n. supporting column in shape of female figure

Casanova (kæsə'nəʊvə) n. any man noted for amorous adventures

casbah ('kæzbɑː) n. (sometimes C-) 1. citadel of various N Afr. cities 2. quarter where casbah is located (also '**kasbah**)

cascade (kæs'keɪd) n. 1. waterfall 2. anything resembling this —vi. 3. fall in cascades

cascara (kæs'kɑːrə) n. 1. dried bark of cascara buckthorn, used as laxative and stimulant (also **cascara sagrada**) 2. shrub or small tree of NW North Amer. (also **cascara buckthorn**)

case[1] (keɪs) n. 1. instance 2. event, circumstance 3. question at issue 4. state of affairs, condition 5. arguments supporting particular action etc. 6. Med. patient under treatment 7. lawsuit 8.

grounds for suit **9.** grammatical relation of words in sentence —**case history** record of person's background, medical history *etc.* —case law law established by following judicial decisions given in earlier cases

case² (keɪs) *n.* **1.** box, sheath, covering **2.** receptacle **3.** box and contents —*vt.* **4.** put in a case —'**casing** *n.* **1.** protective cover **2.** material for cover **3.** frame containing door or window (*also* **case**) —**case-harden** *vt.* **1.** harden by carbonizing the surface of (*esp.* iron) by converting into steel **2.** make hard, callous

casein ('keɪsɪɪn, -siːn) *n.* protein in milk and its products —'**caseous** *a.* like cheese

casement ('keɪsmənt) *n.* window opening on hinges

cash (kæʃ) *n.* **1.** money, banknotes and coins —*vt.* **2.** turn into or exchange for money —ca'**shier** *n.* one in charge of receiving and paying of money —**cash-and-carry** *a./adv.* sold on basis of cash payment for merchandise that is not delivered —'**cashbook** *n.* —**cash crop** crop grown for sale rather than subsistence —**cash flow** movement of money into and out of a business —**cash register** till that records amount of money put in —**cash on delivery** service entailing cash payment to carrier on delivery of merchandise

cashew ('kæʃuː, kæ'ʃuː) *n.* **1.** tropical tree bearing kidney-shaped nuts **2.** nut of this tree, edible only when roasted (*also* **cashew nut**)

cashier (kæ'ʃɪə) *vt.* dismiss from office or service

cashmere ('kæʃmɪə) *n.* **1.** fine soft fabric **2.** shawl made from goat's wool

casino (kə'siːnəʊ) *n.* building, institution for gambling (*pl.* **-s**)

cask (kɑːsk) *n.* **1.** barrel **2.** container for wine

casket ('kɑːskɪt) *n.* **1.** small case for jewels *etc.* **2.** US coffin

casque (kæsk) *n.* Zool. helmet or helmetlike structure, as on bill of most hornbills

Cassandra (kə'sændrə) *n.* **1.** Gr. myth. daughter of Priam and Hecuba, endowed with gift of prophecy but fated never to be believed **2.** anyone whose prophecies of doom are unheeded

cassata (kə'sɑːtə) *n.* ice cream, *esp.* containing fruit and nuts

cassava (kə'sɑːvə) *n.* **1.** any of various tropical plants, *esp.* Amer. species (**bitter cassava, sweet cassava**) (*also* '**manioc**) **2.** starch derived from root of this plant: source of tapioca

casserole ('kæsərəʊl) *n.* **1.** fireproof cooking and serving dish **2.** kind of stew cooked in this dish —*v.* **3.** cook or be cooked in casserole

cassette (kæ'sɛt) *n.* plastic container for film, magnetic tape *etc.*

cassia ('kæsɪə) *n.* **1.** tropical plant whose pods yield **cassia pulp**, mild laxative (*see also* SENNA) **2.** lauraceous tree of tropical Asia —**cassia bark** cinnamonlike bark of this tree, used as spice

cassis (kɑː'siːs) *n.* blackcurrant cordial

cassock ('kæsək) *n.* long tunic worn by clergymen

cassowary ('kæsəwɛərɪ) *n.* large flightless bird of NE Aust., New Guinea and adjacent islands

cast (kɑːst) *v.* **1.** throw, fling **2.** shed **3.** throw down **4.** deposit (a vote) **5.** allot, as parts in play **6.** mould, as metal (**cast** *pt./pp.*) —*n.* **7.** throw **8.** distance thrown **9.** squint **10.** mould **11.** that which is shed or ejected **12.** set of actors **13.** type, quality —'**casting** *n.* —'**castaway** *n./a.* shipwrecked (person) —**casting vote** decisive vote —**cast iron** iron containing so much carbon that it must be cast into shape —**cast-iron** *a.* **1.** made of cast iron **2.** rigid, unyielding —**cast-off** *a.* abandoned —'**castoff** *n.* **1.** person or thing discarded or abandoned **2.** Print. estimate of amount of space a piece of copy will occupy —**cast steel** steel containing varying amounts of carbon *etc.*, that is cast into shape —**cast off 1.** remove (mooring lines) that hold (vessel) to dock **2.** knot (row of stitches, *esp.* final row) in finishing off knitted or woven material **3.** Print. estimate amount of space that will be taken up by (book *etc.*)

castanets (kæstə'nɛts) *pl.n.* in Spanish dancing, two small curved pieces of wood *etc.* clicked together in hand

caste (kɑːst) *n.* **1.** section of society in India **2.** social rank

castellated ('kæstɪleɪtɪd) *a.* **1.** having turrets and battlements, like castle **2.** having indentations similar to battlements —**castel'lation** *n.*

caster ('kɑːstə) *n.* see CASTOR

caster sugar ('kɑːstə) finely powdered sugar (*also* **castor sugar**)

castigate ('kæstɪgeɪt) *vt.* **1.** punish, rebuke severely, correct **2.** chastise —**casti'gation** *n.* —'**castigator** *n.* —**casti'gatory** *a.*

castle ('kɑːsəl) *n.* **1.** fortress **2.** country mansion **3.** chess piece —**castle in the air** or **in Spain** hope or desire unlikely to be realized; daydream

castor ('kɑːstə) *n.* **1.** bottle with perforated top **2.** small swivelled wheel on table leg *etc.*

castor oil vegetable medicinal oil

castrate (kæ'streɪt) *vt.* **1.** remove testicles of, deprive of power of generation **2.** deprive of vigour, masculinity *etc.* —cas'**tration** *n.*

casual ('kæʒjʊəl) *a.* **1.** accidental **2.** unforeseen **3.** occasional **4.** unconcerned **5.** informal —'**casually** *adv.* —'**casualty** *n.* **1.** person killed or injured in accident, war *etc.* **2.** thing lost, destroyed, in accident *etc.*

casuarina (kæsjuə'raɪnə) *n.* tree of Aust. and E Indies, having jointed leafless branches

casuist ('kæzjʊɪst) *n.* **1.** one who studies and solves moral problems **2.** quibbler —**casu'istical** *a.* —**'casuistry** *n.*

cat (kæt) *n.* any of various feline animals, including small domesticated furred animal, and lions, tigers *etc.* —**'catkin** *n.* drooping flower spike —**'catty** *a.* spiteful —**cat burglar** burglar who enters buildings by climbing through upper windows *etc.* —**'catcall** *n.* derisive cry —**'catfish** *n.* mainly freshwater fish with catlike whiskers —**'catgut** *n.* strong cord made from dried intestines of sheep *etc.*, used for stringing musical instruments and sports rackets —**'catmint** *n.* scented plant —**'catnap** *vi./n.* doze —**cat-o'-nine-tails** *n.* whip consisting of nine knotted thongs, used formerly to flog prisoners (*pl.* **-tails**) (*also* **cat**) —**cat's cradle** game played by making patterns with loop of string between fingers —**Cats'eye** *n.* R glass reflector set in road to indicate traffic lanes —**cat's-paw** *n.* **1.** person used by another as tool; dupe **2.** pattern of ripples on surface of water caused by light wind —**'catwalk** *n.* narrow, raised path or plank

C.A.T. UK College of Advanced Technology

catabolism *or* **katabolism** (kə'tæbəlɪzəm) *n.* breaking down of complex molecules, destructive metabolism

cataclysm ('kætəklɪzəm) *n.* **1.** (disastrous) upheaval **2.** deluge —**cata'clysmal** *a.*

catacomb ('kætəkəʊm) *n.* **1.** underground gallery for burial —*pl.* **2.** series of underground tunnels and caves

catafalque ('kætəfælk) *n.* temporary raised platform on which body lies in state before or during funeral

Catalan ('kætəlæn) *n.* **1.** language of Catalonia, closely related to Provençal **2.** native of Catalonia —*a.* **3.** of Catalonia

catalepsy ('kætəlɛpsɪ) *n.* condition of unconsciousness with rigidity of muscles —**cata'leptic** *a.*

catalogue *or* U.S. **catalog** ('kætəlɒg) *n.* **1.** descriptive list —*vt.* **2.** make such list of **3.** enter in catalogue

catalyst ('kætəlɪst) *n.* substance causing or assisting a chemical reaction without taking part in it —**'catalyse** *or* U.S. **-lyze** *vt.* —**ca'talysis** *n.*

catamaran (kætəmə'ræn) *n.* **1.** type of sailing boat with twin hulls **2.** raft of logs

cataplexy ('kætəplɛksɪ) *n.* **1.** sudden temporary paralysis, brought on by intense emotion

etc. **2.** state assumed by animals shamming death —**cata'plectic** *a.*

catapult ('kætəpʌlt) *n.* **1.** small forked stick with elastic sling used for throwing stones **2.** *Hist.* engine of war for hurling arrows, stones *etc.* **3.** launching device —*vt.* **4.** shoot forth (as) from catapult —*v.* **5.** move precipitately

cataract ('kætərækt) *n.* **1.** waterfall **2.** downpour **3.** disease of eye

catarrh (kə'tɑː) *n.* inflammation of a mucous membrane —**ca'tarrhal** *a.*

catastrophe (kə'tæstrəfɪ) *n.* **1.** great disaster, calamity **2.** culmination of a tragedy —**cata'strophic** *a.*

catatonia (kætə'təʊnɪə) *n.* form of schizophrenia characterized by stupor, with outbreaks of excitement —**catatonic** (kætə'tɒnɪk) *a./n.*

catch (kætʃ) *vt.* **1.** take hold of, seize **2.** understand **3.** hear **4.** contract (disease) **5.** be in time for **6.** surprise, detect —*vi.* **7.** be contagious **8.** get entangled **9.** begin to burn (**caught** *pt./pp.*) —*n.* **10.** seizure **11.** thing that holds, stops *etc.* **12.** what is caught **13.** *inf.* snag, disadvantage **14.** form of musical composition **15.** thing, person worth catching —**'catcher** *n.* —**'catching** *a.* —**'catchy** *a.* **1.** pleasant, memorable **2.** tricky —**catchment area 1.** area in which rainfall collects to form the supply of river *etc.* **2.** area from which people are allocated to a particular school, hospital *etc.* —**'catchpenny** *a.* **1.** worthless **2.** made to sell quickly —**catch phrase** frequently used phrase, *esp.* associated with particular group *etc.* —**'catchword** *n.* popular phrase or idea —**catch 22** inescapable dilemma

catechize *or* **-ise** ('kætɪkaɪz) *vt.* **1.** instruct by question and answer **2.** question —**cate'chetical** *a.* —**'catechism** *n.* —**'catechist** *n.* —**cate'chumen** *n.* one under instruction in Christianity

catechu ('kætɪtʃuː), **cachou**, *or* **cutch** (kʌtʃ) *n.* astringent resinous substance obtained from certain tropical plants, and used in dyeing *etc.*

category ('kætɪgərɪ) *n.* class, order, division —**cate'gorical** *a.* **1.** positive **2.** of category —**cate'gorically** *adv.* —**'categorize** *or* **-ise** *vt.*

catenary (kə'tiːnərɪ) *n.* **1.** curve formed by heavy flexible cord hanging from two points **2.** hanging cable between pylons along railway track, from which trolley wire is suspended —*a.* **3.** of catenary or suspended chain

catenation (kætɪ'neɪʃən) *n.* chain, or series as links of chain

cater ('keɪtə) *vi.* provide what is required or desired, *esp.* food *etc.* —**'caterer** *n.*

caterpillar ('kætəpɪlə) *n.* **1.** hairy grub of moth or butterfly **2.** type of tractor fitted with caterpillar wheels —**caterpillar wheel** articulated belt revolving round two or more wheels to propel heavy vehicle over difficult ground

caterwaul ('kætəwɔːl) vi. wail, howl

catharsis or **katharsis** (kə'θɑːsɪs) n. 1. purging of emotions through evocation of pity and fear, as in tragedy 2. *Psychoanal.* bringing repressed ideas or experiences to consciousness, by means of free association etc. 3. purgation, esp. of bowels —**ca'thartic** a. 1. purgative 2. effecting catharsis —n. 3. purgative drug or agent

Cathay (kæ'θeɪ) n. Lit., obs. China

cathedral (kə'θiːdrəl) n. 1. principal church of diocese —a. 2. pert. to, containing cathedral

Catherine wheel ('kæθrɪn) 1. firework which rotates, producing sparks 2. circular window having ribs radiating from centre

catheter ('kæθɪtə) n. Med. long slender flexible tube for inserting into bodily cavity for introducing or withdrawing fluid

cathode ('kæθəʊd) n. negative electrode —**cathode rays** stream of electrons —**cathode-ray tube** vacuum tube in which beam of electrons is focused on to fluorescent screen to give visible spot of light

catholic ('kæθəlɪk, 'kæθlɪk) a. 1. universal 2. including whole body of Christians 3. (C-) relating to R.C. Church —n. 4. (C-) adherent of R.C. Church —**Ca'tholicism** n. —**catho'licity** n. —**ca'tholicize** or **-cise** v.

cation ('kætaɪən) n. positively charged ion; ion attracted to cathode during electrolysis —**cati'onic** a.

cattle ('kætəl) pl.n. beasts of pasture, esp. oxen, cows —**cattle-grid** n. heavy grid over ditch in road to prevent passage of livestock —**cattle-man** n.

Caucasoid ('kɔːkəzɔɪd) a. of, pert. to, light-complexioned racial group of mankind —**Cau'casian** a. 1. Caucasoid 2. of Caucasus in SW Soviet Union —n. 3. member of Caucasoid race; White person 4. native of Caucasus

caucus ('kɔːkəs) n. group, meeting, esp. of members of political party, with power to decide policy etc.

caudal ('kɔːdəl) a. 1. Anat. of posterior part of body 2. Zool. resembling or in position of tail —'**caudate** or '**caudated** a. having tail

caudle ('kɔːdəl) n. hot spiced wine drink made with gruel, formerly used medicinally

caught (kɔːt) pt./pp. of CATCH

caul (kɔːl) n. Anat. portion of amniotic sac sometimes covering child's head at birth

cauldron or **caldron** ('kɔːldrən) n. large pot used for boiling

cauliflower ('kɒlɪflaʊə) n. variety of cabbage with edible white flowering head —**cauliflower ear** permanent distortion of ear as result of ruptures of blood vessels: usu. caused by blows received in boxing

caulk or **calk** (kɔːk) vt. stop up (cracks) with waterproof filler —'**caulker** n. —'**caulking** n.

cause (kɔːz) n. 1. that which produces an effect 2. reason, origin 3. motive, purpose 4. charity, movement 5. lawsuit —vt. 6. bring about, make happen —'**causal** a. —**cau'sality** n. —**cau'sation** n. —'**causative** a. 1. *Gram.* relating to form or class of verbs that express causation 2. (oft. with of) producing effect —n. 3. causative form or class of verbs —'**causeless** a. groundless

cause célèbre ('kɔːz sə'lɛbrə) Fr. famous case

causerie ('kəʊzərɪ) n. 1. informal talk 2. conversational piece of writing

causeway ('kɔːzweɪ) n. 1. raised way over marsh etc. 2. paved street

caustic ('kɔːstɪk) a. 1. burning 2. bitter, severe —n. 3. corrosive substance —'**caustically** adv. —**caustic soda** see **sodium hydroxide** at SODIUM

cauterize or **-ise** ('kɔːtəraɪz) vt. burn with caustic or hot iron —**cauteri'zation** or **-i'sation** n. —'**cautery** n.

caution ('kɔːʃən) n. 1. heedfulness, care 2. warning —vt. 3. warn —'**cautionary** a. containing warning or precept —'**cautious** a. —'**cautiously** adv. —'**cautiousness** n.

cavalcade (kævəl'keɪd) n. column or procession of riders

cavalier (kævə'lɪə) a. 1. careless, disdainful —n. 2. courtly gentleman 3. obs. horseman 4. (C-) adherent of Charles I in English Civil War —**cava'lierly** adv.

cavalry ('kævəlrɪ) n. mounted troops

cave (keɪv) n. 1. hollow place in the earth 2. den —**cavern** ('kævən) n. deep cave —**cavernous** ('kævənəs) a. —**cavernously** ('kævənəslɪ) adv. —'**caving** n. sport of exploring caves —**cavity** ('kævɪtɪ) n. hollow —'**caveman** n. prehistoric cave dweller —**cave in** 1. fall in 2. submit 3. give in

caveat ('keɪvɪæt, 'kæv-) n. 1. Law formal notice requesting court not to take action without warning person lodging caveat 2. a caution

caviar or **caviare** ('kævɪɑː, kævɪ'ɑː) n. salted sturgeon roe

cavil ('kævɪl) vi. find fault without sufficient reason, make trifling objections (-ll-) —'**caviller** n. —'**cavilling** a.

cavort (kə'vɔːt) vi. prance, frisk

cavy ('keɪvɪ) n. small S Amer. rodent

caw (kɔː) n. 1. crow's cry —vi. 2. cry so

cay (keɪ, kiː) n. low island or bank composed of sand and coral fragments

cayenne pepper (keɪ'ɛn) pungent red pepper

cayman or **caiman** ('keɪmən) n. tropical American crocodilian similar to alligator (pl. -s)

Cb Chem. columbium

CB Citizens' Band

C.B. Companion of the (Order of the) Bath

CBC Canadian Broadcasting Corporation

C.B.E. Commander of the (Order of the) British Empire

C.B.I. Confederation of British Industry

cc or **c.c.** 1. carbon copy or copies 2. cubic centimetre

cc. chapters

C.C. 1. City Council 2. County Council 3. Cricket Club

cd candela

Cd *Chem.* cadmium

C.D. 1. Civil Defence (Corps) 2. Corps Diplomatique (Diplomatic Corps)

Cdr. *Mil.* Commander

Ce *Chem.* cerium

cease (siːs) *v.* bring or come to an end —'**ceaseless** *a.* —'**ceaselessly** *adv.*

cedar ('siːdə) *n.* 1. large evergreen tree 2. its wood

cede (siːd) *v.* yield, give up, transfer, *esp.* of territory

cedilla (sɪ'dɪlə) *n.* hooklike mark (‚) placed under a letter *c* to show the sound of *s*

Ceefax ('siːfæks) *n.* **R** B.B.C. teletext service

ceilidh ('keɪlɪ) *n.* informal social gathering for singing and dancing, *esp.* in Scotland

ceiling ('siːlɪŋ) *n.* 1. inner, upper surface of a room 2. maximum price, wage *etc.* 3. *Met.* lower level of clouds 4. *Aviation* limit of height to which aircraft can climb —**ceil** *vt.* line (room), *esp.* with plaster

celandine ('seləndaɪn) *n.* yellow wild flower

celebrate ('selɪbreɪt) *v.* 1. rejoice or have festivities to mark (happy day, event *etc.*) —*vt.* 2. observe (birthday *etc.*) 3. perform (religious ceremony *etc.*) 4. praise publicly —'**celebrant** *n.* —'**celebrated** *a.* famous —**cele'bration** *n.* —**ce'lebrity** *n.* famous person 2. fame

celeriac (sɪ'lɛrɪæk) *n.* variety of celery with large turniplike root, used as vegetable

celerity (sɪ'lɛrɪtɪ) *n.* swiftness

celery ('sɛlərɪ) *n.* vegetable with long juicy edible stalks

celestial (sɪ'lɛstɪəl) *a.* 1. heavenly, divine 2. of the sky —**celestial equator** great circle lying on celestial sphere, plane of which is perpendicular to line joining north and south celestial poles (*also* **equi'noctial, equinoctial circle**) —**celestial sphere** imaginary sphere of infinitely large radius enclosing universe

celibacy ('sɛlɪbəsɪ) *n.* single life, unmarried state —'**celibate** *n./a.*

cell (sɛl) *n.* 1. small room, *esp.* in prison 2. small cavity 3. minute, basic unit of living matter 4. device converting chemical energy into electrical energy 5. small local group operating as nucleus of larger political or religious organization —'**cellular** *a.* —'**cellule** *n.* small cell

cellar ('sɛlə) *n.* 1. underground room for storage 2. stock of wine —'**cellarage** *n.* —'**cellarer** *n.* monastic official responsible for food *etc.* —**cella'ret** *n.* cabinet for wine

cello ('tʃɛləʊ) *n.* stringed instrument of violin family

cellophane ('sɛləfeɪn) *n.* **R** transparent wrapping

cellulite ('sɛljʊlaɪt) *n.* subcutaneous fat alleged to resist dieting

Celluloid ('sɛljʊlɔɪd) *n.* 1. **R** synthetic plastic substance with wide range of uses 2. coating of photographic film 3. cinema film

cellulose ('sɛljʊləʊz, -ləʊs) *n.* 1. substance of vegetable cell wall 2. group of carbohydrates 3. varnish

Celsius ('sɛlsɪəs) *a./n.* (of) scale of temperature from 0° (melting point of ice) to 100° (boiling point of water)

Celtic ('kɛltɪk, 'sɛl-) *or* **Keltic** ('kɛltɪk) *n.* 1. branch of languages including Gaelic and Welsh —*a.* 2. of Celtic peoples or languages —**Celt** *or* **Kelt** *n.* 1. person who speaks a Celtic language 2. member of Indo-European people who in pre-Roman times inhabited Brit., Gaul and Spain

cement (sɪ'mɛnt) *n.* 1. fine mortar 2. adhesive, glue —*vt.* 3. unite with cement 4. join firmly

cemetery ('sɛmɪtrɪ) *n.* burial ground, *esp.* other than churchyard

cenobite ('siːnəʊbaɪt) *n. see* COENOBITE

cenotaph ('sɛnətɑːf) *n.* monument to person buried elsewhere

Cenozoic (siːnəʊ'zəʊɪk) *see* CAINOZOIC

censer ('sɛnsə) *n.* pan in which incense is burned

censor ('sɛnsə) *n.* 1. one authorized to examine films, books *etc.* and suppress all or part if considered morally or otherwise unacceptable —*vt.* 2. ban or cut portions of (film *etc.*) 3. act as censor of (behaviour *etc.*) —**cen'sorial** *a.* of censor —**cen'sorious** *a.* fault-finding —**cen'soriousness** *n.* —'**censorship** *n.*

censure ('sɛnʃə) *n.* 1. blame 2. harsh criticism —*vt.* 3. blame 4. criticize harshly

census ('sɛnsəs) *n.* official counting of people, things *etc.*

cent (sɛnt) *n.* hundredth part of dollar *etc.*

cent. 1. centigrade 2. central 3. century

centaur ('sɛntɔː) *n.* mythical creature, half man, half horse

centenary (sɛn'tiːnərɪ) *n.* 1. 100 years 2. celebration of hundredth anniversary —*a.* 3. pert. to a hundred —**cente'narian** *n.* one a hundred years old —**centennial** (sɛn'tɛnɪəl) *a.* lasting, happening every hundred years

centi- *or before vowel* **cent-** (*comb. form*) **1.** one hundredth, as in *centimetre* **2.** *rare* hundred, as in *centipede*

centigrade ('sɛntɪgreɪd) *a.* **1.** Celsius **2.** having one hundred degrees

centigram *or* **centigramme** ('sɛntɪgræm) *n.* hundredth part of gram

centilitre *or U.S.* **centiliter** ('sɛntɪliːtə) *n.* hundredth part of litre

centime ('sɒntiːm; *Fr.* sã'tim) *n.* monetary unit of France *etc.*, worth one hundredth of standard unit of currency

centimetre *or U.S.* **centimeter** ('sɛntɪmiːtə) *n.* hundredth part of metre —**centimetre-gram-second** *n. see* CGS UNITS

centipede ('sɛntɪpiːd) *n.* small segmented animal with many legs

CENTO ('sɛntəʊ) Central Treaty Organization

centre *or U.S.* **center** ('sɛntə) *n.* **1.** midpoint **2.** pivot, axis **3.** point to or from which things move or are drawn **4.** place for specific organization or activity —'**central** *a.* —**cen'trality** *n.* —**centrali'zation** *or* -**li'sation** *n.* —'**centralize** *or* -**lise** *vt.* **1.** bring to a centre **2.** concentrate under one control —'**centrally** *adv.* —'**centric** *a.* —**cen'trifugal** *a.* tending from centre —'**centrifuge** *n.* **1.** rotating machine that separates liquids from solids or other liquids by centrifugal force **2.** rotating device for subjecting human beings or animals to varying accelerations —*vt.* **3.** subject to action of centrifuge —**cen'tripetal** *a.* tending towards centre —'**centrist** *n.* person holding moderate political views —**central bank** national bank that does business mainly with government and other banks —**central heating** method of heating building from one central source —**central processing unit** part of computer that performs logical and arithmetical operations on data —**central reserve** *or* **reservation** UK strip that separates two sides of motorway or dual carriageway —'**centreboard** *n.* supplementary keel for sailing vessel —'**centrefold** *or U.S.* '**centerfold** *n.* large coloured illustration folded to form central spread of magazine —**centre forward** Soccer, hockey *etc.* central forward in attack —**centre half** Soccer defender in middle of defence —**centre of gravity** point through which resultant of gravitational forces on body always acts —'**centrepiece** *n.* object used as centre of something, *esp.* for decoration

centuplicate (sɛn'tjuːplɪkeɪt) *vt.* **1.** increase 100 times —*a.* (sɛn'tjuːplɪkɪt) **2.** increased hundredfold —*n.* (sɛn'tjuːplɪkɪt) **3.** one hundredfold (*also* '**centuple**)

centurion (sɛn'tjʊərɪən) *n.* Roman commander of 100 men

century ('sɛntʃərɪ) *n.* **1.** 100 years **2.** any set of 100

cephalic (sɪ'fælɪk) *a.* **1.** of head **2.** situated in, on or near head

cephalopod ('sɛfələpɒd) *n.* any of various marine molluscs characterized by well-developed head and eyes and ring of sucker-bearing tentacles, including octopus

ceramic (sɪ'ræmɪk) *n.* **1.** hard brittle material of baked clay **2.** object made of this —*pl.* **3.** (*with sing. v.*) art, techniques of making ceramic objects **4.** such objects —*a.* **5.** of ceramic or ceramics

cere (sɪə) *n.* soft waxy swelling, containing nostrils, at base of upper beak, as in parrot

cereal ('sɪərɪəl) *n.* **1.** any edible grain, *eg* wheat, rice *etc.* **2.** (breakfast) food made from grain —*a.* **3.** of cereal

cerebellum (sɛrɪ'bɛləm) *n.* one of major divisions of vertebrate brain whose function is coordination of voluntary movements (*pl.* -s, -la (-lə))

cerebrum ('sɛrɪbrəm) *n.* **1.** anterior portion of brain of vertebrates: dominant part of brain in man, associated with intellectual function *etc.* **2.** brain as whole (*pl.* -s, -bra (-brə)) —**cerebral** ('sɛrɪbrəl; *U.S. also* sə'riːbrəl) *a.* pert. to brain —'**cerebrate** *vi. usu. jocular* use the mind; think; ponder; consider —**cere'bration** *n.* —**cerebro-'spinal** *a.* of brain and spinal cord —**cerebro-'vascular** *a.* of blood vessels and blood supply of brain —**cerebral palsy** impairment of muscular function and weakness of limbs, caused by damage to brain before or during birth

cerecloth ('sɪəkləʊθ) *n.* waxed waterproof cloth formerly used for shrouds

ceremony ('sɛrɪmənɪ) *n.* **1.** formal observance **2.** sacred rite **3.** courteous act —**cere'monial** *a./n.* —**cere'monially** *adv.* —**cere'monious** *a.* —**cere'moniously** *adv.* —**cere'moniousness** *n.*

cerise (sə'riːz, -'riːs) *n./a.* clear, pinkish red

cerium ('sɪərɪəm) *n.* steel-grey element of lanthanide series of metals, used in lighter flints

CERN (sɜːn) Conseil Européen pour la Recherche Nucléaire; organization of European states with centre in Geneva, for research in high-energy particle physics

cert (sɜːt) *n. inf.* something certain (*esp. in* **a dead cert**)

cert. 1. certificate **2.** certification **3.** certified

certain ('sɜːtən) *a.* **1.** sure **2.** settled, inevitable **3.** some, one **4.** of moderate (quantity, degree *etc.*) —'**certainly** *adv.* —'**certainty** *n.* —'**certitude** *n.* confidence

certes ('sɜːtɪz) *adv. obs.* with certainty; truly

certify ('sɜːtɪfaɪ) *vt.* **1.** declare formally **2.**

endorse, guarantee **3.** declare legally insane (**-fied, -fying**) —**certificate** (sə'tıfıkıt) n. **1.** written declaration —vt. (sə'tıfıkeıt) **2.** authorize by or present with official document —**certifi'cation** n. —'**certified** a. **1.** holding or guaranteed by certificate **2.** endorsed, guaranteed **3.** (of person) declared legally insane —'**certifier** n. —**Certificate of Secondary Education** UK examination the first grade pass of which is equivalent to GCE O level

cerulean (sı'ruːlıən) a. sky-blue

cervix ('sɜːvıks) n. neck, esp. of womb —'**cervical** a. —**cervical smear** Med. smear taken from neck of uterus for detection of cancer (see also PAP TEST)

cesium ('siːzıəm) n. US caesium

cessation (sɛ'seıʃən) n. ceasing, stopping; pause

cession ('sɛʃən) n. yielding up

cesspool ('sɛspuːl) or **cesspit** ('sɛspıt) n. pit in which filthy water collects, receptacle for sewage

cestus or **caestus** ('sɛstəs) n. in classical Roman boxing, pugilist's gauntlet of bull's hide studded with metal (pl. **-tus, -es**)

cesura (sı'zjʊərə) n. Prosody see CAESURA

cetacean (sı'teıʃən) a. **1.** of order of aquatic mammals having no hind limbs and blowhole for breathing: includes toothed and whalebone whales (also **ce'taceous**) —n. **2.** whale

cetane ('siːteın) n. colourless liquid hydrocarbon used in determination of cetane number of diesel fuel (also '**hexadecane**) —**cetane number** measure of quality of diesel fuel expressed as percentage of cetane (also **cetane rating**)

Cf Chem. californium

cf. confer (Lat., compare)

c/f carried forward

CFL Canadian Football League

cg centigram

cgs units metric system of units based on centimetre, gram, second

ch. 1. chapter **2.** church

cha-cha-cha (tʃɑːtʃɑː'tʃɑː) or **cha-cha** n. **1.** modern ballroom dance from Latin Amer. **2.** music composed for this dance —vi. **3.** perform this dance

chafe (tʃeıf) vt. **1.** make sore or worn by rubbing **2.** make warm by rubbing **3.** vex, irritate —**chafing dish** vessel with heating apparatus beneath it, for cooking or keeping food warm at table

chafer ('tʃeıfə) n. any of various beetles, such as cockchafer

chaff (tʃɑːf) n. **1.** husks of corn **2.** worthless matter **3.** banter —vt. **4.** tease good-naturedly

chaffer ('tʃæfə) vi. **1.** haggle, bargain —n. **2.** bargaining

chaffinch ('tʃæfıntʃ) n. small songbird

chagrin ('ʃægrın) n. **1.** vexation, disappointment —vt. **2.** embarrass **3.** annoy **4.** disappoint

chain (tʃeın) n. **1.** series of connected links or rings **2.** thing that binds **3.** connected series of things or events **4.** surveyor's measure —vt. **5.** fasten with chain **6.** confine **7.** restrain —**chain armour** —**chain gang** US group of prisoners chained together —**chain mail** —**chain reaction** —**chain smoker** one who smokes cigarettes etc. continuously, esp. lighting one from preceding one —**chain stitch** —**chain store**

chair (tʃɛə) n. **1.** movable seat, with back, for one person **2.** seat of authority **3.** professorship **4.** iron support for rail on railway —vt. **5.** preside over **6.** carry in triumph —'**chairlift** n. series of chairs fixed to cable for conveying people (esp. skiers) up mountain —'**chairman** n. one who presides over meeting —'**chairmanship** n.

chaise (ʃeız) n. light horse-drawn carriage —**chaise longue** (lɒŋ) sofa

chalcedony (kæl'sɛdənı) n. whitish or bluish-white variety of quartz

chalet ('ʃæleı) n. Swiss wooden house

chalice ('tʃælıs) n. **1.** Poet. cup; bowl **2.** communion cup

chalk (tʃɔːk) n. **1.** white substance, carbonate of lime **2.** crayon —v. **3.** rub, draw, mark with chalk —'**chalkiness** n. —'**chalky** a.

challenge ('tʃælındʒ) vt. **1.** call to fight or account **2.** dispute **3.** stimulate **4.** object to **5.** claim —n. **6.** call to engage in fight etc. **7.** questioning of statement etc. **8.** demanding situation etc. **9.** demand by sentry etc. for identification or password —'**challenger** n. —'**challenging** a. difficult but stimulating

chamber ('tʃeımbə) n. **1.** room for assembly **2.** assembly, body of men **3.** compartment **4.** cavity **5.** obs. room —pl. **6.** office or apartments of barrister **7.** lodgings —**chamberlain** ('tʃeımbəlın) n. official at court of a monarch having charge of domestic and ceremonial affairs —'**chambermaid** n. servant with care of bedrooms —**chamber music** music for performance by a few instruments —**chamber of commerce** organization composed mainly of local businessmen to promote and protect their interests —**chamber pot** vessel for urine

chameleon (kə'miːlıən) n. **1.** small lizard famous for its power of changing colour **2.** changeable person

chamfer ('tʃæmfə) vt. **1.** groove **2.** bevel **3.** flute —n. **4.** groove

chamois ('ʃæmwɑː) n. **1.** goatlike mountain antelope **2.** ('ʃæmı) soft pliable leather

champ[1] (tʃæmp) v. 1. munch (food) noisily, as horse 2. be nervous, impatient

champ[2] (tʃæmp) n. inf. champion

champagne (ʃæmˈpeɪn) n. light, sparkling white wine of several varieties

champers (ˈʃæmpəz) n. sl. champagne

champion (ˈtʃæmpɪən) n. 1. one that excels all others 2. defender of a cause 3. one who fights for another 4. hero —vt. 5. fight for, maintain —ˈchampionship n.

chance (tʃɑːns) n. 1. unpredictable course of events 2. fortune, luck 3. opportunity 4. possibility 5. risk 6. probability —vt. 7. risk —vi. 8. happen —a. 9. casual, unexpected —ˈchancy a. risky

chancel (ˈtʃɑːnsəl) n. part of church where altar is

chancellor (ˈtʃɑːnsələ) n. 1. high officer of state 2. head of university —ˈchancellorship n. —ˈchancellery or ˈchancellory n. —Chancellor of the Exchequer UK cabinet minister responsible for finance

chancery (ˈtʃɑːnsərɪ) n. division of British High Court of Justice

chancre (ˈʃæŋkə) n. Pathol. small hard growth: first sign of syphilis —ˈchancrous a.

chandelier (ʃændɪˈlɪə) n. hanging frame with branches for holding lights

chandler (ˈtʃɑːndlə) n. dealer in ropes, ships' supplies etc.

change (tʃeɪndʒ) v. 1. alter, make or become different 2. put on (different clothes, fresh coverings) —vt. 3. put or give for another 4. exchange, interchange —n. 5. alteration, variation 6. variety 7. conversion of money 8. small money, coins 9. balance received on payment —changeaˈbility n. —ˈchangeable a. —ˈchangeably adv. —ˈchangeful a. —ˈchangeless a. —ˈchangeling n. child believed substituted for another by fairies —change of life menopause

channel (ˈtʃænəl) n. 1. bed of stream 2. strait 3. deeper part of strait, bay, harbour 4. groove 5. means of passing or conveying 6. band of radio frequencies 7. television broadcasting station —vt. 8. groove, furrow 9. guide, convey

chant (tʃɑːnt) n. 1. simple song or melody 2. rhythmic or repetitious slogan —vi. 3. sing or utter chant 4. speak monotonously or repetitiously

chanticleer (tʃæntɪˈklɪə) or **chantecler** (tʃæntɪˈkleə) n. cock

chantry (ˈtʃɑːntrɪ) n. Christianity 1. endowment for singing of Masses for soul of founder 2. chapel or altar so endowed

chanty (ˈʃæntɪ, ˈtʃæn-) n. see SHANTY[2]

chaos (ˈkeɪɒs) n. 1. disorder, confusion 2. state of universe before Creation —chaˈotic a.

chap[1] (tʃæp) v. (of skin) become dry, raw and cracked, esp. by exposure to cold and wind (-pp-) —chapped a.

chap[2] (tʃæp) n. inf. fellow, man

chapatti or **chapati** (tʃəˈpætɪ, -ˈpɑːtɪ) n. in Indian cookery, flat unleavened bread resembling pancake (pl. -ti, -s, -es)

chapel (ˈtʃæpəl) n. 1. private church 2. subordinate place of worship 3. division of church with its own altar 4. Nonconformist place of worship 5. (meeting of) members of trade union in particular newspaper office, printing house etc.

chaperon or **chaperone** (ˈʃæpərəʊn) n. 1. one who attends young unmarried lady in public as protector —vt. 2. attend in this way

chaplain (ˈtʃæplɪn) n. clergyman attached to chapel, regiment, warship, institution etc. —ˈchaplaincy n. his office

chaplet (ˈtʃæplɪt) n. 1. ornamental wreath of flowers worn on head 2. string of beads 3. R.C.Ch. string of prayer beads constituting one third of rosary; prayers counted on this string 4. narrow moulding in form of string of beads

chapman (ˈtʃæpmən) n. obs. trader, esp. itinerant pedlar

chappie (ˈtʃæpɪ) n. inf. see CHAP[2]

chaps (tʃæps, ʃæps) pl.n. cowboy's leggings of thick leather

chapter (ˈtʃæptə) n. 1. division of book 2. section, heading 3. assembly of clergy, bishop's council etc. 4. organized branch of society, fraternity —ˈchapterhouse n.

char[1] (tʃɑː) vt. scorch, burn to charcoal (-rr-) —charred a.

char[2] (tʃɑː) inf. n. 1. charwoman —vi. 2. do cleaning as job (-rr-)

char[3] or **charr** (tʃɑː) n. troutlike small fish

char[4] (tʃɑː) n. sl. tea

charabanc (ˈʃærəbæŋ) n. UK coach, esp. for sightseeing

character (ˈkærɪktə) n. 1. nature 2. total of qualities making up individuality 3. moral qualities 4. reputation, esp. good one 5. statement of qualities of person 6. an eccentric 7. personality in play or novel 8. letter, sign or any distinctive mark 9. essential feature —characterˈistic n./a. —characterˈistically adv. —characteriˈzation or -iˈsation n. —ˈcharacterize or -ise vt. 1. mark out, distinguish 2. describe by peculiar qualities —ˈcharacterless a.

charade (ʃəˈrɑːd) n. 1. absurd act 2. travesty —pl. 3. word-guessing parlour game with syllables of word acted

charcoal (ˈtʃɑːkəʊl) n. 1. black residue of wood, bones etc., produced by smothered burning 2. charred wood —charcoal-burner n.

chard (tʃɑːd) *n.* beet with large succulent leaves and thick stalks, used as vegetable (*also* **Swiss chard**)

charge (tʃɑːdʒ) *vt.* **1.** ask as price **2.** bring accusation against **3.** lay task on **4.** command **5.** attack **6.** deliver injunction against **7.** fill with electricity **8.** fill, load —*vi.* **9.** make onrush, attack —*n.* **10.** cost, price **11.** accusation **12.** attack, onrush **13.** command, exhortation **14.** accumulation of electricity —*pl.* **15.** expenses —'**chargeable** *a.* —'**charger** *n.* **1.** strong, fast battle horse **2.** that which charges, *esp.* electrically

chargé d'affaires ('ʃɑːʒeɪ dæ'feə) **1.** temporary head of diplomatic mission in absence of ambassador or minister **2.** head of diplomatic mission of lowest level (*pl.* **chargés d'affaires** ('ʃɑːʒeɪ, -ʒeɪz))

chariot ('tʃærɪət) *n.* **1.** two-wheeled car used in ancient fighting **2.** state carriage —**chario'teer** *n.*

charisma (kə'rɪzmə) *or* **charism** ('kærɪzəm) *n.* special power of individual to inspire fascination, loyalty *etc.* —**charis'matic** *a.*

charity ('tʃærɪtɪ) *n.* **1.** the giving of help, money *etc.* to those in need **2.** organization for doing this **3.** the money *etc.* given **4.** love, kindness **5.** disposition to think kindly of others —'**charitable** *a.* —'**charitably** *adv.*

charlatan ('ʃɑːlət'n) *n.* quack, impostor —'**charlatanry** *n.*

Charles's Wain ('tʃɑːlzɪz weɪn) the Plough

charleston ('tʃɑːlstən) *n.* fast, rhythmic dance of 1920s

charlie ('tʃɑːlɪ) *n. inf.* fool

charlock ('tʃɑːlɒk) *n.* weedy Eurasian plant with yellow flowers (*also* **wild mustard**)

charlotte ('ʃɑːlət) *n.* **1.** dessert made with fruit and bread or cake crumbs, sponge cake *etc.* **2.** cold dessert made with sponge fingers, cream *etc.* (*also* **charlotte russe**)

charm (tʃɑːm) *n.* **1.** attractiveness **2.** anything that fascinates **3.** amulet **4.** magic spell —*vt.* **5.** bewitch **6.** delight, attract —**charmed** *a.* —'**charmer** *n.* —'**charming** *a.*

charnel house ('tʃɑːn'l) *esp.* formerly, vault for bones of the dead

chart (tʃɑːt) *n.* **1.** map of sea **2.** diagram or tabulated statement —*vt.* **3.** map **4.** represent on chart —**the charts** *inf.* lists produced weekly of best-selling pop records

charter ('tʃɑːtə) *n.* **1.** document granting privileges *etc.* **2.** patent —*vt.* **3.** let or hire **4.** establish by charter

Chartism ('tʃɑːtɪzəm) *n. English hist.* movement to achieve certain political reforms, demand for which were embodied in charters presented to Parliament —'**Chartist** *n./a.*

chartreuse (ʃɑː'trɜːz; *Fr.* ʃar'trøːz) *n.* **1.** either of two liqueurs, green or yellow, made from herbs **2.** yellowish-green colour

charwoman ('tʃɑːwumən) *n.* woman paid to clean office, house *etc.*

chary ('tʃeərɪ) *a.* cautious, sparing —'**charily** *adv.* —'**chariness** *n.* caution

Charybdis (kə'rɪbdɪs) *n.* ship-devouring monster in classical mythology, identified with whirlpool off coast of Sicily

chase[1] (tʃeɪs) *vt.* **1.** hunt, pursue **2.** drive (from, away, into *etc.*) —*n.* **3.** pursuit, hunting **4.** the hunted **5.** hunting ground —'**chaser** *n.* drink of beer, soda *etc.* taken after spirit

chase[2] (tʃeɪs) *vt.* engrave —'**chaser** *n.* —'**chasing** *n.*

chase[3] (tʃeɪs) *n.* **1.** *Letterpress print.* rectangular steel frame into which metal type and blocks are locked for printing **2.** part of cannon enclosing bore **3.** groove or channel, *esp.* to take pipe *etc.* —*vt.* **4.** cut groove, furrow or flute in (surface *etc.*) (*also* '**chamfer**)

chasm ('kæzəm) *n.* **1.** deep cleft, fissure **2.** abyss

chassé ('ʃæseɪ) *n.* **1.** rapid gliding step used in dancing —*vi.* **2.** perform the step

chassis ('ʃæsɪ) *n.* **1.** framework, wheels and machinery of motor vehicle excluding body and coachwork **2.** underframe of aircraft (*pl.* **-sis** (-sɪz))

chaste (tʃeɪst) *a.* **1.** virginal **2.** pure **3.** modest **4.** virtuous —'**chastely** *adv.* —'**chastity** ('tʃæstɪtɪ) *n.*

chasten ('tʃeɪs'n) *vt.* **1.** correct by punishment **2.** restrain, subdue —'**chastened** *a.* —**chastise** (tʃæs'taɪz) *vt.* inflict punishment on —**chastisement** (tʃæs'taɪzmənt) *n.*

chasuble ('tʃæzjub'l) *n.* priest's long sleeveless outer vestment

chat[1] (tʃæt) *vi.* **1.** talk idly or familiarly (-**tt**-) —*n.* **2.** familiar idle talk —'**chattily** *adv.* —'**chatty** *a.*

chat[2] (tʃæt) *n.* any of various European songbirds, Amer. warblers, Aust. wrens

chateau *or* **château** ('ʃætəʊ) *n. esp.* in France, castle, country house (*pl.* **-teaux** (-təʊ, -təʊz), **-s**)

chatelaine ('ʃætəleɪn; *Fr.* ʃat'lɛn) *n.* **1.** *esp.* formerly, mistress of castle or large household **2.** chain or clasp worn at waist by women in 16th to 19th century, with handkerchief *etc.* attached

chattel ('tʃæt'l) *n.* (*usu. pl.*) any movable property

chatter ('tʃætə) *vi.* **1.** talk idly or rapidly **2.** rattle teeth —*n.* **3.** idle talk —'**chatterer** *n.* —'**chattering** *n.* —'**chatterbox** *n.* one who chatters incessantly

chauffeur ('ʃəʊfə, ʃəʊ'fɜː) *n.* paid driver of motorcar (**chauf'feuse** *fem.*)

chauvinism ('ʃəʊvɪnɪzəm) n. 1. aggressive patriotism 2. smug sense of superiority

cheap (tʃiːp) a. 1. low in price 2. inexpensive 3. easily obtained 4. of little value or estimation 5. mean, inferior —'**cheapen** vt. —'**cheaply** adv. —'**cheapness** n. —**cheap-jack** inf. n. 1. person who sells cheap and shoddy goods —a. 2. shoddy, inferior —'**cheapskate** n. inf. miserly person

cheat (tʃiːt) vt. 1. deceive, defraud, swindle, impose upon —vi. 2. practise deceit to gain advantage —n. 3. fraud

check (tʃɛk) vt. 1. stop 2. restrain 3. hinder 4. repress 5. control 6. examine for accuracy, quality etc. —n. 7. repulse 8. stoppage 9. restraint 10. brief examination for correctness or accuracy 11. pattern of squares on fabric 12. threat to king at chess —'**checkmate** n. 1. Chess final winning move 2. any overthrow, defeat —vt. 3. Chess place (opponent's king) in checkmate 4. defeat —'**checkout** n. counter in supermarket where customers pay —'**checkup** n. examination (esp. medical) to see if all is in order

checked (tʃɛkt) a. having pattern of small squares

checker ('tʃɛkə) see CHEQUER

Cheddar ('tʃɛdə) n. (sometimes c-) smooth hard orange or whitish cheese

cheek (tʃiːk) n. 1. side of face below eye 2. inf. impudence —vt. 3. inf. address impudently —'**cheeky** a.

cheep (tʃiːp) vi./n. (utter) high-pitched cry, as of young bird

cheer (tʃɪə) vt. 1. comfort 2. gladden 3. encourage by shouts —vi. 4. shout applause —n. 5. shout of approval 6. happiness, good spirits 7. mood 8. obs. rich food —'**cheerful** a. —'**cheerfully** adv. —'**cheerfulness** n. —'**cheerily** adv. —'**cheerless** a. —'**cheerlessness** n. —**cheers** interj. inf., chiefly UK 1. drinking toast 2. goodbye, cheerio 3. thanks —'**cheery** a. —**three cheers** three shouts of hurrah in unison to honour someone or celebrate something

cheerio (tʃɪərɪ'əʊ) inf. interj. 1. chiefly UK farewell greeting 2. chiefly UK drinking toast —n. 3. NZ small sausage

cheese (tʃiːz) n. 1. curd of milk coagulated, separated from whey and pressed —'**cheesiness** n. —'**cheesy** a. —'**cheeseburger** n. hamburger cooked with cheese on top —'**cheesecake** n. 1. tart filled with cheese, esp. cream cheese, cream, sugar etc. 2. sl. women displayed for their sex appeal, as in photographs or films —'**cheesecloth** n. loosely woven cotton cloth —'**cheeseparing** a. mean —**cheesed off** UK sl. bored; disgusted; angry

cheetah or **chetah** ('tʃiːtə) n. large, swift, spotted feline animal

chef (ʃɛf) n. head cook, esp. in restaurant

chef-d'œuvre (ʃɛ'dœːvr) Fr. masterpiece

chem. 1. chemical 2. chemistry

chemin de fer (ʃə'mæn də 'fɛə) gambling game, variation of baccarat

chemise (ʃə'miːz) n. loose-fitting dress hanging straight from shoulders; loose shirtlike undergarment (also **shift**)

chemistry ('kɛmɪstrɪ) n. science concerned with properties of substances and their combinations and reactions —'**chemical** n./a. —'**chemically** adv. —'**chemist** n. 1. qualified dispenser of prescribed medicines 2. shop that sells medicines etc. 3. one trained in chemistry —**chemical engineer** —**chemical engineering** engineering concerned with design and manufacture of plant used in industrial chemical processes —**chemical warfare** warfare using asphyxiating gases, poisons etc.

chemotherapy (kɛməʊ'θɛrəpɪ) n. treatment of disease by chemical means

chemurgy ('kɛmɜːdʒɪ) n. branch of applied chemistry devoted to the development of agricultural products —**che'murgic(al)** a.

chenille (ʃə'niːl) n. soft cord, fabric of silk or worsted

cheongsam ('tʃɒŋ'sæm) n. (Chinese) straight dress with slit in one side of skirt

cheque or U.S. **check** (tʃɛk) n. 1. written order to banker to pay money from one's account 2. printed slip of paper used for this —'**chequebook** or U.S. '**checkbook** n. book of cheques —**cheque card** banker's card

chequer or U.S. **checker** ('tʃɛkə) n. 1. marking as on chessboard 2. marble, peg etc. used in games, eg Chinese chequers —pl. 3. squares like those of chessboard 4. (with sing. v.) draughts —vt. 5. mark in squares 6. variegate —'**chequered** or esp. U.S. '**checkered** a. 1. marked in squares 2. uneven, varied

cherish ('tʃɛrɪʃ) vt. 1. treat with affection 2. protect 3. foster

cheroot (ʃə'ruːt) n. cigar with both ends open

cherry ('tʃɛrɪ) n. 1. small red fruit with stone 2. tree bearing it —a. 3. ruddy, bright red

cherub ('tʃɛrəb) n. 1. winged creature with human face 2. angel (pl. '**cherubim, -s**) —**che'rubic** a.

chervil ('tʃɜːvɪl) n. a herb

Ches. Cheshire

chess (tʃɛs) n. game of skill played by two with 32 pieces on chequered board of 64 squares —'**chessboard** n. —'**chessmen** pl.n. pieces used in chess

chest (tʃɛst) n. 1. upper part of trunk of body 2.

large, strong box —**chest of drawers** piece of furniture containing drawers

chesterfield ('tʃɛstəfiːld) n. padded sofa

chestnut ('tʃɛsnʌt) n. 1. large reddish-brown nut growing in prickly husk 2. tree bearing it 3. inf. old joke 4. horse of golden-brown colour —a. 5. reddish-brown

cheval glass (ʃə'væl) full-length mirror mounted to swivel within frame

chevalier (ʃɛvə'lɪə) n. 1. member of order of merit, such as French Legion of Honour 2. lowest title of rank in old French nobility 3. obs. knight 4. chivalrous man; gallant

Cheviot ('tʃɪvɪət, 'tʃɛv-) n. 1. Brit. sheep reared for its wool 2. (oft. c-) rough woollen fabric

chevron ('ʃɛvrən) n. Mil. V-shaped band of braid worn on sleeve to designate rank

chew (tʃuː) v. 1. grind with teeth —n. 2. act of chewing 3. something that is chewed —'**chewy** a. firm, sticky when chewed —**chewing gum** —**chew the fat** sl. 1. argue over a point 2. talk idly; gossip

chi (kaɪ) n. 22nd letter in Gr. alphabet (χ, Χ)

chianti (kɪ'æntɪ) n. It. wine

chiaroscuro (kɪɑːrəˈskʊərəʊ) n. 1. artistic distribution of light and dark masses in picture 2. monochrome painting using light and dark only (pl. -s)

chic (ʃiːk, ʃɪk) a. 1. stylish, elegant —n. 2. stylishness, esp. in dress

chicane (ʃɪ'keɪn) n. 1. bridge or whist hand without trumps 2. Motor racing barrier placed before dangerous corner to reduce speeds 3. rare chicanery —vt. 4. deceive or trick by chicanery —vi. 5. use chicanery —chi'**canery** n. 1. quibbling 2. trick, artifice

chick (tʃɪk) n. 1. young of birds, esp. of hen 2. sl. girl, young woman —'**chicken** n. 1. domestic fowl bred for flesh or eggs 2. its flesh as food 3. sl. cowardly person —a. 4. sl. easily scared; cowardly; timid —**chicken feed** trifling amount (of money) —**chicken-hearted** a. cowardly —'**chickenpox** n. infectious disease, esp. of children —'**chickpea** n. dwarf pea —'**chickweed** n. weed with small white flowers

chicle ('tʃɪkəl) n. substance obtained from sapodilla; main ingredient of chewing gum

chicory ('tʃɪkərɪ) n. salad plant of which the root is ground and used with, or instead of, coffee

chide (tʃaɪd) vt. scold, reprove, censure (**chid** pt., '**chidden, chid** pp., '**chiding** pr.p.)

chief (tʃiːf) n. 1. head or principal person —a. 2. principal, foremost, leading —'**chiefly** adv. —'**chieftain** ('tʃiːftən, -tɪn) n. leader, chief of clan or tribe —**chief petty officer** senior naval rank for personnel without commissioned or warrant rank —**chief technician** noncommissioned

officer in Royal Air Force, junior to flight sergeant

chiffchaff ('tʃɪftʃæf) n. common European warbler

chiffon (ʃɪ'fɒn, 'ʃɪfɒn) n. thin gauzy material —**chiffo'nier** n. ornamental cupboard

chignon ('ʃiːnjɒn) n. roll, knot of hair worn at back of head

chigoe ('tʃɪɡəʊ) n. tropical flea, female of which burrows into skin of man etc. (also '**chigger**)

Chihuahua (tʃɪ'wɑːwɑː, -wə) n. breed of tiny dog, orig. from Mexico

chilblain ('tʃɪlbleɪn) n. inflamed sore on hands, legs etc., due to cold

child (tʃaɪld) n. 1. young human being 2. offspring (pl. **children** ('tʃɪldrən)) —'**childhood** n. period between childhood and puberty —'**childish** a. 1. of or like a child 2. silly 3. trifling —'**childishly** adv. —'**childless** a. —'**childlike** a. 1. of or like a child 2. innocent 3. frank 4. docile —'**childbed** n. state of giving birth to child —**child benefit** UK regular government payment to parents of children up to a certain age —'**childbirth** n. —**child minder** person who looks after children, esp. those whose parents are working —**child's play** very easy task

chiliad ('kɪlɪæd) n. 1. group of one thousand 2. thousand years

chill (tʃɪl) n. 1. coldness 2. cold with shivering 3. anything that damps, discourages —v. 4. make, become cold (esp. food, drink) —**chilled** a. —'**chilliness** n. —'**chilly** a.

chilli ('tʃɪlɪ) n. 1. small red hot-tasting seed pod 2. plant producing it

Chiltern Hundreds ('tʃɪltən) UK Stewardship of the Chiltern Hundreds; nominal office that MP applies for to resign seat

chime (tʃaɪm) n. 1. sound of bell 2. harmonious, ringing sound —vi. 3. ring harmoniously 4. agree —vt. 5. strike (bells) —**chime in** come into conversation with agreement

chimera or **chimaera** (kaɪ'mɪərə, kɪ-) n. 1. fabled monster, made up of parts of various animals 2. wild fancy —**chimeric(al)** (kaɪ'mɛrɪk(əl), kɪ-) a. fanciful

chimney ('tʃɪmnɪ) n. 1. a passage for smoke 2. narrow vertical cleft in rock (pl. -s)

chimp (tʃɪmp) n. inf. chimpanzee

chimpanzee (tʃɪmpæn'ziː) n. gregarious, intelligent ape of Afr.

chin (tʃɪn) n. part of face below mouth —**chinless wonder** UK inf. person, esp. upperclass, lacking strength of character —'**chinwag** n. UK inf. chat

china ('tʃaɪnə) n. 1. fine earthenware, porcelain 2. cups, saucers etc. collectively —**china clay** see KAOLIN

chincherinchee (tʃɪntʃərɪn'tʃiː, -'rɪntʃɪ) n. S Afr. plant with white or yellow flower spikes

chinchilla (tʃɪn'tʃɪlə) n. S Amer. rodent with soft, grey fur

chine (tʃaɪn) n. **1.** backbone **2.** joint of meat **3.** ridge or crest of land

Chinese (tʃaɪ'niːz) a. **1.** of China, its people or their languages —n. **2.** native of China or descendant of one (pl. **-ese**) **3.** any of languages of China —**Chinese lantern** Asian plant cultivated for its orange-red inflated calyx

chink[1] (tʃɪŋk) n. cleft, crack

chink[2] (tʃɪŋk) n. **1.** light metallic sound —v. **2.** (cause to) make this sound

chinoiserie (ʃiːnwɑːzə'riː, -'wɑːzərɪ) n. **1.** style of decorative art based on imitations of Chinese motifs **2.** object or objects in this style

chinook (tʃɪ'nuːk, -'nʊk) n. **1.** warm dry wind blowing down eastern slopes of Rocky Mountains **2.** warm moist wind blowing on to Washington and Oregon coasts

chintz (tʃɪnts) n. cotton cloth printed in coloured designs

chip (tʃɪp) n. **1.** splinter **2.** place where piece has been broken off **3.** thin strip of potato, fried **4.** tiny wafer of silicon forming integrated circuit in computer etc. —vt. **5.** chop into small pieces **6.** break small pieces from **7.** shape by cutting off pieces —vi. **8.** break off (**-pp-**) —**chip-based** a. using microchips in electronic equipment —'**chipboard** n. thin rigid sheet made of compressed wood particles —**chip in 1.** interrupt **2.** contribute

chipmunk ('tʃɪpmʌŋk) n. small, striped N Amer. squirrel

chipolata (tʃɪpə'lɑːtə) n. small sausage

Chippendale ('tʃɪpəndeɪl) a. (of furniture) in style of Thomas Chippendale, characterized by use of Chinese and Gothic motifs etc.

chirography (kaɪ'rɒgrəfɪ) n. calligraphy

chiromancy ('kaɪrəmænsɪ) n. palmistry —'**chiromancer** n.

chiropodist (kɪ'rɒpədɪst) n. one who treats disorders of feet —**chi'ropody** n.

chiropractor ('kaɪrəpræktə) n. one skilled in treating bodily disorders by manipulation, massage etc. —**chiro'practic** n.

chirp (tʃɜːp) n. **1.** short, sharp cry of bird —vi. **2.** make this sound —'**chirpy** a. inf. happy

chisel ('tʃɪzl) n. **1.** cutting tool, usu. bar of steel with edge across main axis —vt. **2.** cut, carve with chisel **3.** sl. cheat (**-ll-**)

chit[1] (tʃɪt) n. informal note, memorandum

chit[2] (tʃɪt) n. child, young girl

chitchat ('tʃɪttʃæt) n. **1.** gossip —vi. **2.** gossip

chitin ('kaɪtɪn) n. polysaccharide that is principal component of outer coverings of arthropods etc. —'**chitinous** a.

chivalry ('ʃɪvəlrɪ) n. **1.** bravery and courtesy **2.** medieval system of knighthood —'**chivalrous** a. —'**chivalrously** adv.

chive (tʃaɪv) n. herb with mild onion flavour

chivy, chivvy ('tʃɪvɪ) or **chevy** ('tʃɛvɪ) UK vt. **1.** harass; nag **2.** hunt —vi. **3.** run about ('chivied, 'chivying, 'chivvied, 'chivvying or 'chevied, 'chevying) —n. **4.** hunt **5.** obs. hunting cry

chloral hydrate ('klɔːrəl) colourless crystalline soluble solid produced by reaction of chloral with water and used as sedative

chlorine ('klɔːriːn) or **chlorin** ('klɔːrɪn) n. nonmetallic element, yellowish-green poison gas —'**chlorate** n. salt of chloric acid —'**chloric** a. —'**chloride** n. **1.** compound of chlorine **2.** bleaching agent —'**chlorinate** vt. **1.** disinfect **2.** purify with chlorine

chloroform ('klɔːrəfɔːm) n. **1.** volatile liquid formerly used as anaesthetic —vt. **2.** render insensible with it

chlorophyll or U.S. **chlorophyl** ('klɔːrəfɪl) n. green colouring matter in plants

chock (tʃɒk) n. block or wedge to prevent heavy object rolling or sliding —**chock-full** or **chock-a-block** a. packed full

chocolate ('tʃɒkəlɪt, 'tʃɒklɪt, -lət) n. **1.** paste from ground cacao seeds **2.** confectionery, drink made from this —a. **3.** dark brown —**choc-ice** n. chocolate-covered slice of ice cream —**chocolate-box** a. inf. sentimentally pretty or appealing

choice (tʃɔɪs) n. **1.** act or power of choosing **2.** alternative **3.** thing or person chosen —a. **4.** select, fine, worthy of being chosen —'**choicely** adv.

choir (kwaɪə) n. **1.** band of singers, esp. in church **2.** part of church set aside for them

choke (tʃəʊk) vt. **1.** hinder, stop the breathing of **2.** smother, stifle **3.** obstruct —vi. **4.** suffer choking —n. **5.** act, noise of choking **6.** device in carburettor to increase richness of petrol-air mixture —**choked** a. —'**choker** n. **1.** woman's high collar **2.** neckband or necklace worn tightly around throat **3.** high clerical collar; stock **4.** person or thing that chokes —'**chokebore** n. gun with bore narrowed towards muzzle —'**choke-damp** n. carbon dioxide gas in coal mines

choler ('kɒlə) n. bile, anger —'**choleric** a. bad-tempered

cholera ('kɒlərə) n. deadly infectious disease marked by vomiting and diarrhoea

cholesterol (kə'lɛstərɒl) or **cholesterin** (kə'lɛstərɪn) n. substance found in animal tissue and fat

chomp (tʃɒmp) or **chump** (tʃʌmp) v. chew noisily

choose (tʃuːz) vt. **1.** pick out, select **2.** take by preference —vi. **3.** decide, think fit (**chose, 'chosen, 'choosing**) —**'chooser** n. —**'choosy** a. fussy

chop[1] (tʃop) vt. **1.** cut with blow **2.** hack (**-pp-**) —n. **3.** hewing blow **4.** slice of meat containing rib or other bone —**'chopper** n. **1.** short axe **2.** inf. helicopter **3.** inf. large motorbike —**'choppy** a. (of sea) having short, broken waves

chop[2] (tʃop) vt. exchange, bandy (esp. in **chop logic, chop and change**) (**-pp-**)

chops (tʃops) pl.n. inf. jaws, cheeks

chopsticks ('tʃopstiks) pl.n. implements used by Chinese for eating food

chop suey ('suːɪ) a kind of rich Chinese stew with rice

choral ('kɔːrəl) a. of, for, sung by, a choir

chorale or **choral** (kɒ'rɑːl) n. slow, stately hymn tune

chord (kɔːd) n. **1.** emotional response, esp. of sympathy **2.** simultaneous sounding of musical notes **3.** straight line joining ends of arc

chore (tʃɔː) n. **1.** (unpleasant) task **2.** odd job

chorea (kɒ'rɪə) n. disorder of central nervous system characterized by uncontrollable jerky movements (also **Saint Vitus's dance**)

choreography (kɒrɪ'ɒɡrəfɪ) or **choreography** (kɒ'rɛɡrəfɪ) n. **1.** art of arranging dances, esp. ballet **2.** art, notation of ballet dancing —**chore'ographer** or **cho'regrapher** n. —**choreo'graphic** or **chore'graphic** a.

chorography n. art of describing and making maps of particular regions —**choro'graphic** a.

choroid ('kɔːrɔɪd) or **chorioid** ('kɔːrɪɔɪd) n. vascular membrane of eyeball between sclera and retina

chorology (kɒ'rɒlədʒɪ) n. science of geographical distribution of plants and animals —**cho'rologist** n.

chortle ('tʃɔːt[ə]l) vi. **1.** chuckle happily —n. **2.** gleeful chuckle

chorus ('kɔːrəs) n. **1.** band of singers **2.** combination of voices singing together **3.** refrain —vt. **4.** sing or say together —**choric** ('kɒrɪk) a. —**chorister** ('kɒrɪstə) n.

chose (tʃəʊz) pt. of CHOOSE —**'chosen** pp. of CHOOSE

chough (tʃʌf) n. black passerine bird of Europe, Asia and Afr., with red bill

choux pastry (ʃuː) very light pastry made with eggs

chow (tʃaʊ) n. inf. food

chow-chow n. thick-coated dog with curled tail, orig. from China (also **chow**)

chowder ('tʃaʊdə) n. chiefly US thick soup or stew containing clams or fish

chow mein (meɪn) Chinese-American dish, consisting of mushrooms, meat, shrimps etc.

chrism or **chrisom** ('krɪzəm) n. mixture of

olive oil and balsam used for sacramental anointing

Christ (kraɪst) n. **1.** Jesus of Nazareth, regarded by Christians as fulfilling Old Testament prophecies of Messiah **2.** Messiah as subject of Old Testament prophecies **3.** image of Christ —interj. **4.** offens. sl. oath expressing annoyance etc. (see also JESUS)

Christian ('krɪstʃən) n. **1.** follower of Christ —a. **2.** following Christ **3.** relating to Christ or his religion **4.** exhibiting kindness or goodness —**christen** ('krɪsən) vt. baptise, give name to —**Christendom** ('krɪsəndəm) n. all the Christian world —**Christi'anity** n. religion of Christ —**'christianize** or **-ise** vt. —**Christian name** name given at baptism —**Christian Science** religious system founded by Mrs. Eddy in U.S.A.

Christmas ('krɪsməs) n. festival of birth of Christ —**'Christmassy** a. —**Christmas box** tip, present given at Christmas —**Christmas card** —**Christmas rose** evergreen plant of S Europe and W Asia, with white or pinkish winter-blooming flowers (also **'hellebore, winter rose**) —**Christmas tree**

Christy or **Christie** ('krɪstɪ) n. Skiing turn in which body is swung sharply round with skis parallel

chromatic (krə'mætɪk) a. **1.** of colour **2.** Mus. of scale proceeding by semitones

chromatin ('krəʊmətɪn) n. part of protoplasmic substance in nucleus of cells which takes colour in staining tests

chromatography (krəʊmə'tɒɡrəfɪ) n. technique of separating and analysing components of mixture by selective adsorption in column of powder or on strip of paper

chrome (krəʊm) n. metal used in alloys and for plating

chromosome ('krəʊməsəʊm) n. microscopic gene-carrying body in tissue of a cell

chromosphere ('krəʊməsfɪə) n. layer of incandescent gas surrounding the sun

Chron. Chronicles

chronic ('krɒnɪk) a. **1.** lasting a long time **2.** habitual **3.** inf. serious **4.** inf. of bad quality

chronicle ('krɒnɪk[ə]l) n. **1.** record of events in order of time **2.** account —vt. **3.** record —**'chronicler** n.

chronology (krə'nɒlədʒɪ) n. **1.** determination of sequence of past events **2.** arrangement in order of occurrence —**chrono'logical** a. arranged in order of time —**chrono'logically** adv. —**chro'nologist** n.

chronometer (krə'nɒmɪtə) n. **1.** instrument for measuring time exactly **2.** watch —**chrono-'metrical** a. —**chro'nometry** n.

chrysalis ('krɪsəlɪs) n. **1.** resting state of insect

between grub and butterfly *etc.* **2.** case enclosing it (*pl.* **-es, chrysalides** (krɪˈsælɪdiːz))

chrysanthemum (krɪˈsænθəməm) *n.* garden flower of various colours

chub (tʃʌb) *n.* **1.** European freshwater fish **2.** any of various N Amer. fishes, *esp.* whitefishes and minnows

chubby (ˈtʃʌbɪ) *a.* plump

chuck[1] (tʃʌk) *vt.* **1.** *inf.* throw **2.** pat affectionately (under chin) **3.** *inf.* give up, reject

chuck[2] (tʃʌk) *n.* **1.** cut of beef **2.** device for gripping, adjusting bit in power drill *etc.*

chuckle (ˈtʃʌkəl) *vi.* **1.** laugh softly —*n.* **2.** such laugh —**ˈchucklehead** *n.* *inf.* stupid person; blockhead; dolt

chuff[1] (tʃʌf) *n.* **1.** puffing sound as of steam engine —*vi.* **2.** move while emitting such sounds

chuff[2] (tʃʌf) *vt.* (*usu.* as *pp./a.* **chuffed**) *UK sl.* please, delight

chug (tʃʌg) *n.* **1.** short dull sound, such as that made by engine —*vi.* **2.** (of engine *etc.*) operate while making such sounds (**-gg-**)

chukker *or* **chukka** (ˈtʃʌkə) *n.* period of play in game of polo

chum (tʃʌm) *n.* *inf.* close friend —**ˈchummy** *a.*

chump (tʃʌmp) *n.* **1.** *inf.* stupid person **2.** heavy block of wood **3.** thick blunt end of anything, *esp.* meat **4.** *UK sl.* head (*esp.* in **off one's chump**)

chunk (tʃʌŋk) *n.* thick, solid piece —**ˈchunky** *a.*

church (tʃɜːtʃ) *n.* **1.** building for Christian worship **2.** (**C-**) whole body or sect of Christians **3.** clergy —**ˈchurchman** *n.* —**Church of England** reformed state Church in England, with Sovereign as temporal head —**ˈchurchwarden** *n.* **1.** officer who represents interests of parish **2.** long clay pipe —**ˈchurchyard** *n.*

churl (tʃɜːl) *n.* **1.** rustic **2.** ill-bred fellow —**ˈchurlish** *a.* —**ˈchurlishly** *adv.* —**ˈchurlishness** *n.*

churn (tʃɜːn) *n.* **1.** large container for milk **2.** vessel for making butter —*v.* **3.** shake up, stir (liquid) violently

chute (ʃuːt) *n.* **1.** slide for sending down parcels, coal *etc.* **2.** channel **3.** slide into swimming pool **4.** narrow passageway, *eg* for spraying, counting cattle, sheep *etc.* **5.** *inf.* parachute

chutney (ˈtʃʌtnɪ) *n.* pickle of fruit, spices *etc.*

chyle (kaɪl) *n.* milky fluid composed of lymph and emulsified fat globules, formed in small intestine during digestion

chyme (kaɪm) *n.* thick fluid mass of partially digested food that leaves stomach

C.I.A. *US* Central Intelligence Agency

cicada (sɪˈkɑːdə) *or* **cicala** *n.* cricketlike insect

cicatrix (ˈsɪkətrɪks) *n.* scar of healed wound —**cicatriˈzation** *or* **-iˈsation** *n.* —**ˈcicatrize** *or* **-ise** *v.* heal

cicely (ˈsɪsəlɪ) *n.* perennial plant similar to chervil, used as herb (*also* **sweet cicely**)

cicerone (sɪsəˈrəʊnɪ, tʃɪtʃ-) *n.* person who conducts and informs sightseers (*pl.* **-s, -ni** (-nɪ))

C.I.D. Criminal Investigation Department

-cide (*n. comb. form*) **1.** person or thing that kills, as in *insecticide* **2.** killing; murder, as in *homicide* —**-cidal** (*a. comb. form*)

cider *or* **cyder** (ˈsaɪdə) *n.* fermented drink made from apples

c.i.f. *or* **C.I.F.** cost, insurance and freight (included in price quoted)

cigar (sɪˈɡɑː) *n.* roll of tobacco leaves for smoking —**cigaˈrette** *n.* finely-cut tobacco rolled in paper for smoking —**cigarette card** small picture card, formerly given away with cigarettes, now collected as hobby

cilium (ˈsɪlɪəm) *n.* **1.** short thread projecting from surface of cell *etc.*, whose rhythmic beating causes movement **2.** eyelash (*pl.* **cilia** (ˈsɪlɪə)) —**ˈciliary** *a.* of cilia —**ˈciliate** *or* **ˈciliated** *a.* —**ciliary body** part of eye that joins choroid to iris

C in C *or* **C.-in-C.** Commander-in-Chief

cinch (sɪntʃ) *n.* *inf.* easy task, certainty

cinchona (sɪŋˈkəʊnə) *n.* **1.** tree or shrub of S Amer. having medicinal bark **2.** dried bark of this tree, which yields quinine **3.** any of drugs derived from cinchona bark

cincture (ˈsɪŋktʃə) *n.* something that encircles, *esp.* belt or girdle

cinder (ˈsɪndə) *n.* remains of burned coal

Cinderella (sɪndəˈrelə) *n.* **1.** girl who achieves fame after being obscure **2.** poor, neglected or unsuccessful person or thing

cine camera (ˈsɪnɪ) camera for taking moving pictures —**cine film**

cinema (ˈsɪnɪmə) *n.* **1.** building used for showing of films **2.** films generally or collectively —**cineˈmatograph** *n.* combined camera, printer and projector —**cinemaˈtography** *n.*

cineraria (sɪnəˈrɛərɪə) *n.* garden plant with daisylike flowers

cinerarium (sɪnəˈrɛərɪəm) *n.* place for keeping ashes of dead after cremation (*pl.* **-ria** (-rɪə))

cinerary (ˈsɪnərərɪ) *a.* pert. to ashes

cinnabar (ˈsɪnəbɑː) *n.* **1.** heavy red mineral consisting of mercuric sulphide: chief ore of mercury **2.** red form of mercuric sulphide, *esp.* when used as pigment **3.** bright red; vermilion **4.** large red-and-black European moth

cinnamon (ˈsɪnəmən) *n.* **1.** spice got from bark of Asian tree **2.** the tree —*a.* **3.** light-brown colour

cinque (sɪŋk) *n.* number five in cards, dice *etc.* —**ˈcinquefoil** *n.* plant with five-lobed leaves

cipher or **cypher** ('saɪfə) n. 1. secret writing 2. arithmetical symbol 3. person of no importance 4. monogram —vt. 5. write in cipher

circa ('sɜːkə) Lat. about, approximately

circadian (sɜː'keɪdɪən) a. of biological processes that occur at 24-hour intervals

circle ('sɜːkəl) n. 1. perfectly round figure 2. ring 3. Theat. section of seats above main level of auditorium 4. group, society with common interest 5. spiritualist seance 6. class of society —vt. 7. surround —vi. 8. move round —'circular a. 1. round 2. moving round —n. 3. letter sent to several persons —circulari'zation or -i'sation n. —'circularize or -ise vt. 1. distribute circulars to 2. canvass or petition, as for votes etc. by distributing letters etc. 3. make circular —'circulate vi. 1. move round 2. pass from hand to hand or place to place —vt. 3. send round —circu'lation n. 1. flow of blood from, and back to, heart 2. act of moving round 3. extent of sale of newspaper etc. —'circulatory a. —circular saw saw in which circular disc with toothed edge is rotated at high speed —circulating library 1. esp. US lending library 2. small library circulated in turn to group of institutions

circuit ('sɜːkɪt) n. 1. complete round or course 2. area 3. path of electric current 4. round of visitation, esp. of judges 5. series of sporting events 6. district —circuitous (sə'kjuːɪtəs) a. round about, indirect —circuitously (sə'kjuːɪtəslɪ) adv. —'circuitry n. electrical circuit(s) —circuit breaker device that when abnormal conditions stops flow of current in electrical circuit

circum- (comb. form) around; surrounding; on all sides, as in circumlocution, circumpolar. Such compounds are not given here where the meaning may easily be found from the simple word

circumambient (sɜːkəm'æmbɪənt) a. surrounding

circumcise ('sɜːkəmsaɪz) vt. cut off foreskin of —circum'cision n.

circumference (sə'kʌmfərəns) n. boundary line, esp. of circle

circumflex ('sɜːkəmflɛks) n. 1. mark (ˆ) placed over vowel to show it is pronounced with rising and falling pitch or as long vowel —a. 2. (of nerves etc.) bending or curving around

circumlocution (sɜːkəmlə'kjuːʃən) n. round-about speech

circumnavigate (sɜːkəm'nævɪgeɪt) vt. sail or fly right round —circumnavi'gation n. —cir-cum'navigator n.

circumscribe (sɜːkəm'skraɪb, 'sɜːkəm-skraɪb) vt. confine, bound, limit, hamper

circumspect ('sɜːkəmspɛkt) a. watchful, cautious, prudent —circum'spection n. —'cir-cumspectly adv.

circumstance ('sɜːkəmstəns) n. 1. detail 2. event 3. matter of fact —pl. 4. state of affairs 5. condition in life, esp. financial 6. surroundings or things accompanying an action —circum'stantial a. 1. depending on detail or circumstances 2. detailed, minute 3. incidental —circumstanti'ality n. —circum'stantially adv. —circum'stantiate vt. 1. prove by details 2. describe exactly —circumstantial evidence indirect evidence that tends to establish conclusion by inference

circumvent (sɜːkəm'vɛnt) vt. outwit, evade, get round —circum'vention n.

circus ('sɜːkəs) n. 1. (performance of) travelling group of acrobats, clowns, performing animals etc. 2. circular structure for public shows 3. circular space in town where roads converge

cirque (sɜːk) n. steep-sided semicircular depression found in mountainous regions

cirrhosis (sɪ'rəʊsɪs) n. any of various chronic progressive diseases of liver —cirrhotic (sɪ'rɒtɪk) a.

cirrus ('sɪrəs) n. high wispy cloud (pl. cirri ('sɪraɪ)) —cirro'cumulus n. high cloud of ice crystals grouped into small separate globular masses (pl. -li (-laɪ)) —cirro'stratus n. uniform layer of cloud above about 6000 metres (pl. -tai (-taɪ))

cisalpine (sɪs'ælpaɪn) a. on this (southern) side of Alps, as viewed from Rome

cisco ('sɪskəʊ) n. N Amer. whitefish (pl. -s, -es)

cist (sɪst) or **kist** (kɪst) n. box-shaped burial chamber made from stone slabs or hollowed tree-trunk

Cistercian (sɪ'stɜːʃən) n. member of Christian order of monks and nuns, which follows strict form of Benedictine rule (also White Monk)

cistern ('sɪstən) n. water tank

cistus ('sɪstəs) n. any of various shrubs or herbaceous plants cultivated for yellow-white or reddish roselike flowers (also 'rockrose)

citadel ('sɪtədəl, -del) n. fortress in, near or commanding a city

cite (saɪt) vt. 1. quote 2. bring forward as proof 3. commend (soldier etc.) for outstanding bravery etc. 4. summon to appear before court of law —ci'tation n. 1. quoting 2. commendation for bravery etc.

cithara ('sɪθərə) or **kithara** ('kɪθərə) n. stringed musical instrument of ancient Greece, similar to lyre

citizen ('sɪtɪzən) n. 1. native, naturalized member of state, nation etc. 2. inhabitant of city —'citizenry n. citizens collectively —'citizenship n. —Citizens' Band range of radio frequencies assigned officially for use by public for private communication

citron ('sıtrən) *n.* **1.** fruit like a lemon **2.** the tree —'**citric** *a.* of the acid of lemon or citron —**citrus fruit** citrons, lemons, limes, oranges *etc.*

citronella (sıtrə'nɛlə) *n.* **1.** tropical Asian grass with bluish-green lemon-scented leaves **2.** aromatic oil obtained from this grass, used in perfumes *etc.* (*also* **citronella oil**)

cittern ('sıt3ən), **cither** ('sı$ə), *or* **cithern** ('sı$ən) *n.* medieval stringed instrument resembling lute but having wire strings and flat back

city ('sıtı) *n.* large town —**city editor** (on newspaper) **1.** UK editor in charge of financial and commercial news **2.** US editor in charge of local news —**city father** person who is prominent in public affairs of city —**the City 1.** area in central London where United Kingdom's major financial business is transacted **2.** financial institutions located in this area

civet ('sıvıt) *n.* strong, musky perfume —**civet-cat** *n.* catlike animal producing it

civic ('sıvık) *a.* pert. to city or citizen —'**civics** *pl.n.* (*with sing. v.*) study of the rights and responsibilities of citizenship —**civic centre** UK public buildings of town, including recreational facilities and offices of local administration

civil ('sıvəl) *a.* **1.** relating to citizens of state **2.** not military **3.** refined, polite **4.** *Law* not criminal —**ci'vilian** *n.* nonmilitary person —**ci'vility** *n.* —**'civilly** *adv.* —**civil defence** organizing of civilians to deal with enemy attacks —**civil disobedience** refusal to obey laws, pay taxes *etc.*: nonviolent means of protesting —**civil engineer** person qualified to design and construct roads, bridges *etc.* —**civil engineering** —**civil law 1.** law of state relating to private affairs **2.** body of law in ancient Rome, *esp.* as applicable to private citizens **3.** law based on Roman system —**civil liberty** right of individual to freedom of speech and action —**civil marriage** *Law* marriage performed by official other than clergyman —**civil rights** *pl.n.* **1.** personal rights of individual citizen —*a.* **2.** of equality in social, economic and political rights —**civil service** service responsible for public administration of government of a country —**civil war** war between factions within same nation

civilize *or* **-ise** ('sıvılaız) *vt.* **1.** bring out of barbarism **2.** refine —**civili'zation** *or* **-i'sation** *n.* —'**civilized** *or* **-ised** *a.*

civvy ('sıvı) *sl. n.* **1.** civilian —*pl.* **2.** civilian clothing —**civvy street** civilian life

cl centilitre

Cl *Chem.* chlorine

clack (klæk) *n.* **1.** sound, as of two pieces of wood striking together —*v.* **2.** make such sound **3.** jabber

clad (klæd) *pt./pp.* of **clothe** (*see* CLOTHE)

cladding ('klædıŋ) *n.* material used for outside facing of building *etc.*

claim (kleım) *vt.* **1.** demand as right **2.** assert **3.** call for —*n.* **4.** demand for thing supposed due **5.** right **6.** thing claimed **7.** plot of mining land marked out by stakes as required by law —'**claimant** *n.*

clairvoyance (klɛə'vɔıəns) *n.* power of seeing things not present to senses, second sight —**clair'voyant** *n./a.*

clam (klæm) *n.* edible mollusc

clamber ('klæmbə) *vi.* climb with difficulty or awkwardly

clammy ('klæmı) *a.* moist and sticky —'**clamminess** *n.*

clamour *or* U.S. **clamor** ('klæmə) *n.* **1.** loud shouting, outcry, noise —*vi.* **2.** shout, call noisily —'**clamorous** *a.* —'**clamorously** *adv.*

clamp[1] (klæmp) *n.* **1.** tool for holding or compressing —*vt.* **2.** fasten, strengthen with or as with clamp

clamp[2] (klæmp) *n.* **1.** mound of harvested root crop, covered with straw and earth to protect it from winter weather —*vt.* **2.** enclose in mound

clan (klæn) *n.* **1.** tribe or collection of families under chief and of common ancestry **2.** faction, group —'**clannish** *a.* —'**clannishly** *adv.* —'**clannishness** *n.*

clandestine (klæn'dɛstın) *a.* **1.** secret **2.** sly

clang (klæŋ) *v.* **1.** (cause to) make loud ringing sound —*n.* **2.** loud ringing sound —'**clanger** *n.* **1.** *inf.* conspicuous mistake **2.** that which clangs

clangor *or* **clangour** ('klæŋgə, 'klæŋə) *n.* **1.** loud resonant noise **2.** uproar —*vi.* **3.** make loud resonant noise —'**clangorous** *or* '**clangourous** *a.*

clank (klæŋk) *n.* **1.** short sound as of pieces of metal struck together —*v.* **2.** cause, move with, such sound

clap[1] (klæp) *v.* **1.** (cause to) strike with noise **2.** strike (hands) together **3.** applaud —*vt.* **4.** pat **5.** place or put quickly (**-pp-**) —*n.* **6.** hard, explosive sound **7.** slap —'**clapper** *n.* —'**clapping** *n.* —'**claptrap** *n. inf.* empty words

clap[2] (klæp) *n. sl.* gonorrhoea

claque (klæk) *n.* **1.** group of people hired to applaud **2.** group of fawning admirers

claret ('klærət) *n.* a dry dark red wine of Bordeaux

clarify ('klærıfaı) *v.* make or become clear, pure or more easily understood (**-fied, -fying**) —**clarifi'cation** *n.* —'**clarity** *n.* clearness

clarinet (klærı'nɛt) *n.* woodwind musical instrument

clarion ('klærɪən) n. 1. clear-sounding trumpet 2. rousing sound

clary ('klɛərɪ) n. herb

clash (klæʃ) n. 1. loud noise, as of weapons striking 2. conflict, collision —vi. 3. make clash 4. come into conflict 5. (of events) coincide 6. (of colours) look ugly together —vt. 7. strike together to make clash

clasp (klɑːsp) n. 1. hook or other means of fastening 2. embrace —vt. 3. fasten 4. embrace, grasp —**clasp knife**

class (klɑːs) n. 1. any division, order, kind, sort 2. rank 3. group of school pupils etc. taught together 4. division by merit 5. quality 6. inf. excellence; elegance —vt. 7. assign to proper division —**classifi'cation** n. —**'classified** a. 1. arranged in classes 2. secret 3. (of advertisements) arranged under headings in newspapers —**'classify** vt. arrange methodically in classes (**-fied, -fying**) —**'classy** a. inf. stylish, elegant —**class-conscious** a. aware of belonging to particular social rank —**class-consciousness** n.

classic ('klæsɪk) a. 1. of first rank 2. of highest rank generally, but esp. of art 3. refined 4. typical 5. famous —n. 6. (literary) work of recognized excellence —pl. 7. ancient Latin and Greek literature —**'classical** a. 1. of Greek and Roman literature, art, culture 2. of classic quality 3. Mus. of established standards of form, complexity etc. —**'classically** adv. —**'classicism** n. —**'classicist** n.

clatter ('klætə) n. 1. rattling noise 2. noisy conversation —v. 3. (cause to) make clatter

clause (klɔːz) n. 1. part of sentence, containing verb 2. article in formal document as treaty, contract etc.

claustrophobia (ˌklɔːstrə'fəʊbɪə, ˌklɒs-) n. abnormal fear of confined spaces

clavichord ('klævɪkɔːd) n. musical instrument with keyboard, forerunner of piano

clavicle ('klævɪkl) n. collarbone —**cla'vicular** a. pert. to this

clavier (klə'vɪə, 'klævɪə) n. keyboard instrument; keyboard

claw (klɔː) n. 1. sharp hooked nail of bird or beast 2. foot of bird of prey 3. clawlike article —vt. 4. tear with claws 5. grip

clay (kleɪ) n. 1. fine-grained earth, plastic when wet, hardening when baked 2. earth —**'clayey** a. —**clay pigeon** disc of baked clay hurled into air as target to be shot at

claymore ('kleɪmɔː) n. ancient Highland two-edged sword

CLC Canadian Labour Congress

clean (kliːn) a. 1. free from dirt, stain or defilement 2. pure 3. guiltless 4. trim, shapely —adv. 5. so as to leave no dirt 6. entirely —vt. 7. free from dirt —**'cleaner** n. —**cleanliness**

('klɛnlɪnɪs) n. —**cleanly** ('klɛnlɪ) adv. 1. in a clean manner —a. ('klɛnlɪ) 2. clean —**'cleanness** n. —**cleanse** (klɛnz) vt. make clean —**clean-cut** a. 1. clearly outlined; neat 2. definite —**come clean** inf. confess

clear (klɪə) a. 1. pure, undimmed, bright 2. free from cloud 3. transparent 4. plain, distinct 5. without defect or drawback 6. unimpeded —adv. 7. brightly 8. wholly, quite —vt. 9. make clear 10. acquit 11. pass over or through 12. make as profit 13. free from obstruction, difficulty 14. free by payment of dues —vi. 15. become clear, bright, free, transparent —**'clearance** n. 1. making clear 2. removal of obstructions, surplus stock etc. 3. certificate that ship has been cleared at custom house 4. space for moving part, vehicle, to pass within, through or past something —**'clearing** n. land cleared of trees —**'clearly** adv. —**'clearness** n. —**clear-cut** a. 1. definite; not vague 2. clearly outlined —**clearing bank** UK bank that makes use of central clearing house in London —**clearing house** 1. Banking institution where cheques etc. drawn on member banks are cancelled against each other 2. central agency for collection and distribution of information —**clear-sighted** a. discerning —**'clearway** n. stretch of road on which motorists may stop only in an emergency

clearstory ('klɪəstɔːrɪ) n. see CLERESTORY

cleat (kliːt) n. 1. wedge 2. piece of wood or iron with two projecting ends round which ropes are made fast

cleave¹ (kliːv) vt. 1. split asunder —vi. 2. crack, part asunder (**clove, cleft** pt., **'cloven, cleft** pp., **'cleaving** pr.p.) —**'cleavage** n. —**'cleaver** n. short chopper

cleave² (kliːv) vi. 1. stick, adhere 2. be loyal (**cleaved, 'cleaving**)

clef (klɛf) n. Mus. mark to show pitch of stave

cleft (klɛft) n. 1. crack, fissure, chasm 2. opening made by cleaving —v. 3. pt./pp. of CLEAVE¹ —**cleft palate** congenital fissure in midline of hard palate, oft. associated with harelip —**cleft stick** situation involving choice between two equally unsatisfactory alternatives

cleg (klɛg) n. horsefly

clematis ('klɛmətɪs) n. flowering climbing perennial plant

clement ('klɛmənt) a. 1. merciful 2. gentle 3. mild —**'clemency** n. —**'clemently** adv.

clench (klɛntʃ) vt. 1. set firmly together 2. grasp, close (fist)

clerestory or **clearstory** ('klɪəstɔːrɪ) n. 1. row of windows in upper part of wall of church that divides nave from aisle 2. part of wall in which these windows are set —**'clerestoried** or **'clearstoried** a.

clergy ('klɜːdʒɪ) *n.* body of appointed ministers of Christian Church —'**clergyman** *n.*

clerical ('klerɪkᵊl) *a.* 1. of clergy 2. of, connected with, office work —'**cleric** *n.* clergyman —'**clericalism** *n.*

clerk (klɑːk; *U.S.* klɜːk) *n.* 1. subordinate who keeps files *etc.* in an office 2. officer in charge of records, correspondence *etc.*, of department or corporation 3. *US* shop assistant —'**clerkly** *a.* —'**clerkship** *n.* —**clerk of the works** employee who supervises building work

clever ('klevə) *a.* 1. intelligent 2. able, skilful, adroit —'**cleverly** *adv.* —'**cleverness** *n.*

clew (kluː) *n.* 1. ball of thread or yarn 2. *Naut.* lower corner of sail —*vt.* 3. coil into ball

cliché ('kliːʃeɪ) *n.* stereotyped hackneyed phrase

click' (klɪk) *n.* 1. short, sharp sound, as of latch in door 2. catch —*v.* 3. (cause to) make short, sharp sound

click² (klɪk) *vi.* 1. *sl.* be a success 2. *inf.* become clear 3. *inf.* strike up friendship

client ('klaɪənt) *n.* 1. customer 2. one who employs professional person —**clientele** (kliːɒn'tel) *n.* body of clients

cliff (klɪf) *n.* steep rock face —'**cliffhanger** *n.* tense situation, *esp.* in film *etc.*

climacteric (klaɪ'mæktərɪk, klaɪmæk'terɪk) *n.* 1. critical event or period 2. *see* MENOPAUSE 3. period in life of man corresponding to menopause, characterized by diminished sexual activity —*a.* (*also* **climac'teric**) 4. involving crucial event or period

climate ('klaɪmɪt) *n.* 1. condition of country with regard to weather 2. prevailing feeling, atmosphere —**cli'matic** *a.* of climate

climax ('klaɪmæks) *n.* 1. highest point, culmination 2. point of greatest excitement, tension in story *etc.* —**cli'mactic** *a.*

climb (klaɪm) *v.* 1. go up or ascend 2. progress with difficulty 3. creep up, mount 4. slope upwards —'**climber** *n.* —'**climbing** *n.*

clime (klaɪm) *n.* 1. region, country 2. climate

clinch (klɪntʃ) *vt.* 1. *see* CLENCH 2. settle, conclude (an agreement) —'**clincher** *n. inf.* something decisive

cling (klɪŋ) *vi.* 1. adhere 2. be firmly attached 3. be dependent (on) (**clung** *pt./pp.*)

Clingfilm ('klɪŋfɪlm) *n.* R thin polythene material having power to adhere closely: used for wrapping food

clinic ('klɪnɪk) *n.* place for medical examination, advice or treatment —'**clinical** *a.* 1. relating to clinic, care of sick *etc.* 2. objective, unemotional 3. bare, plain —'**clinically** *adv.* —**clinical thermometer** thermometer used for taking body temperature

clink' (klɪŋk) *n.* 1. sharp metallic sound —*v.* 2. (cause to) make this sound

clink² (klɪŋk) *n. sl.* prison

clinker ('klɪŋkə) *n.* 1. fused coal residues from fire or furnace 2. hard brick

clinker-built *or* **clincher-built** *a.* (of boat) with outer boards or plates overlapping

clip' (klɪp) *vt.* 1. cut with scissors 2. cut short (-pp-) —*n.* 3. *inf.* sharp blow —'**clipper** *n.* —'**clipping** *n.* something cut out, *esp.* article from newspaper; cutting —**clip joint** *sl.* nightclub *etc.* in which customers are overcharged

clip² (klɪp) *n.* device for gripping or holding together, *esp.* hair, clothing *etc.* —'**clipboard** *n.* portable writing board with clip at top for holding paper

clipper ('klɪpə) *n.* fast sailing ship

clippie ('klɪpɪ) *n. UK inf.* bus conductress

clique (kliːk, klɪk) *n.* 1. small exclusive set 2. faction, group of people —'**cliquish** *a.*

clitoris ('klɪtərɪs, 'klaɪ-) *n.* small erectile part of female genitals

cloak (kləʊk) *n.* 1. loose outer garment 2. disguise, pretext —*vt.* 3. cover with cloak 4. disguise, conceal —**cloak-and-dagger** *a.* concerned with intrigue and espionage —'**cloakroom** *n.* place for keeping coats, hats, luggage

clobber ('klɒbə) *inf. vt.* 1. beat, batter 2. defeat utterly —*n.* 3. belongings

cloche (klɒʃ) *n.* 1. cover to protect young plants 2. woman's close-fitting hat

clock (klɒk) *n.* 1. instrument for measuring time 2. device with dial for recording or measuring —'**clockwise** *adv./a.* in the direction that the hands of a clock rotate —'**clockwork** *n.* mechanism similar to that of a clock, as in a wind-up toy —**clock in** *or* **on, out** *or* **off** record arrival or departure on automatic time recorder

clod (klɒd) *n.* 1. lump of earth 2. blockhead —'**cloddish** *a.* —'**clodhopper** *n. inf.* 1. clumsy person; lout 2. (*usu. pl.*) large heavy shoe

clog (klɒg) *vt.* 1. hamper, impede, choke up (-gg-) —*n.* 2. obstruction, impediment 3. wooden-soled shoe —**clog dance**

cloisonné (klwɑː'zɒneɪ) *n.* 1. enamel decoration in compartments formed by small fillets of metal —*a.* 2. of cloisonné

cloister ('klɔɪstə) *n.* 1. covered pillared arcade 2. monastery or convent —'**cloistered** *a.* confined, secluded, sheltered

clomp (klɒmp) *see* CLUMP²

clone (kləʊn) *n.* 1. group of organisms, cells of same genetic constitution as another, derived by asexual reproduction, as graft of plant *etc.* —*v.* 2. (cause to) produce clone

clop (klɒp) *vi.* move, sound, as horse's hooves (-pp-)

close¹ (kləʊs) a. 1. adjacent, near 2. compact 3. crowded 4. affectionate, intimate 5. almost equal 6. careful, searching 7. confined 8. secret 9. unventilated, stifling 10. reticent 11. niggardly 12. strict, restricted —adv. 13. nearly 14. tightly —n. 15. shut-in place 16. precinct of cathedral —'**closely** adv. —'**closeness** n. —**close-fisted** a. 1. mean 2. avaricious —**close harmony** singing in which all parts except bass lie close together —**close quarters** cramped space or position —**close season** time when it is illegal to kill certain kinds of game and fish —**close shave** inf. narrow escape —'**closeup** n. close view, esp. portion of cinema film —**at close quarters** engaged in hand-to-hand combat; in close proximity; very near together

close² (kləʊz) vt. 1. shut 2. stop up 3. prevent access to 4. finish —vi. 5. come together 6. grapple —n. 7. end —**closed circuit** complete electrical circuit through which current can flow —**closed shop** place of work in which all workers must belong to a trade union

closet ('klɒzɪt) n. 1. US cupboard 2. small private room 3. water closet, lavatory —a. 4. US private, secret —vt. 5. shut up in private room, esp. for conference 6. conceal

closure ('kləʊʒə) n. 1. act of closing 2. ending of debate by majority vote or other authority

clot (klɒt) n. 1. mass or lump 2. inf. fool 3. Med. coagulated mass of blood —vt. 4. form into lumps —vi. 5. coagulate (-tt-)

cloth (klɒθ) n. woven fabric —**clothe** (kləʊð) vt. put clothes on (**clothed** or **clad** pt./pp.) —**clothes** (kləʊðz) pl.n. 1. dress 2. bed coverings —**clothier** ('kləʊðɪə) n. —**clothing** ('kləʊðɪŋ) n. —**clotheshorse** ('kləʊðhɔːs) n. 1. frame on which to hang laundry for drying or airing 2. inf. excessively fashionable person

cloud (klaʊd) n. 1. condensed water vapour floating in air 2. state of gloom 3. multitude —vt. 4. overshadow, dim, darken —vi. 5. become cloudy —'**cloudless** a. —'**cloudy** a. —'**cloudburst** n. heavy downpour

clout (klaʊt) n. 1. inf. blow 2. short, flat-headed nail 3. influence, power —vt. 4. inf. strike

clove¹ (kləʊv) n. 1. dried flower bud of tropical tree, used as spice 2. one of small bulbs making up compound bulb

clove² (kləʊv) pt. of CLEAVE¹ —'**cloven** pp. of CLEAVE¹ —**cloven hoof** or **foot** 1. divided hoof of cow, deer etc. 2. symbol of Satan

clove hitch knot for securing rope to spar, post or larger rope

clover ('kləʊvə) n. low-growing forage plant, trefoil —'**cloverleaf** n. 1. arrangement of connecting roads, resembling four-leaf clover, that joins two intersecting main roads —a. 2. in

shape of leaf of clover —**be in clover** be in luxury

clown (klaʊn) n. 1. comic entertainer in circus 2. jester, fool —vi. 3. play jokes or tricks 4. act foolishly —'**clownish** a.

cloy (klɔɪ) vt. weary by sweetness, sameness etc.

club (klʌb) n. 1. thick stick 2. bat, stick used in some games 3. association for pursuance of common interest 4. building used by such association 5. one of the suits at cards —vt. 6. strike with club —vi. 7. join for a common object (-bb-) —**club foot** deformed foot —**club root** fungal disease of cabbages etc., in which roots become thickened and distorted

cluck (klʌk) vi./n. (make) noise of hen

clue (kluː) n. 1. indication, esp. of solution of mystery or puzzle —vt. 2. (usu. with up) provide with helpful information —'**clueless** a. sl. helpless; stupid —**not have a clue** be ignorant or incompetent

clump¹ (klʌmp) n. 1. cluster of trees or plants 2. compact mass

clump² (klʌmp) vi. 1. walk, tread heavily —n. 2. dull, heavy tread or similar sound

clumsy ('klʌmzɪ) a. 1. awkward, unwieldy, ungainly 2. badly made or arranged —'**clumsily** adv. —'**clumsiness** n.

clung (klʌŋ) pt./pp. of CLING

clunk (klʌŋk) n. (sound of) blow or something falling

cluster ('klʌstə) n. 1. group, bunch —v. 2. gather, grow in cluster

clutch¹ (klʌtʃ) v. 1. grasp eagerly 2. snatch (at) —n. 3. grasp, tight grip 4. device enabling two revolving shafts to be connected and disconnected at will

clutch² (klʌtʃ) n. 1. set of eggs hatched at one time 2. brood of chickens

clutter ('klʌtə) v. 1. strew 2. crowd together in disorder —n. 3. disordered, obstructive mass of objects

Clydesdale ('klaɪdzdeɪl) n. heavy powerful carthorse, orig. from Scotland

cm or **cm.** centimetre

Cm Chem. curium

Cmdr. Mil. Commander

C.N.D. UK Campaign for Nuclear Disarmament

Co Chem. cobalt

CO Colorado

Co. or **co.** Company

Co. County

C.O. Commanding Officer

co- (comb. form) 1. together, as in coproduction 2. partnership or equality, as in costar, copilot 3. to similar degree, as in coextend 4. Maths., astron. of complement of angle, as in cosecant

c/o 1. care of 2. carried over

coach (kəʊtʃ) n. **1.** long-distance or touring bus **2.** large four-wheeled carriage **3.** railway carriage **4.** tutor, instructor —vt. **5.** instruct —**coach-builder** n. —'**coachman** n. —'**coachwork** n. **1.** design and manufacture of car bodies **2.** body of car

coadjutor (kəʊ'ædʒʊtə) n. **1.** bishop appointed as assistant to diocesan bishop **2.** rare assistant

coagulate (kəʊ'ægjʊleɪt) v. **1.** curdle, clot, form into a mass **2.** congeal, solidify —**coagu'lation** n.

coal (kəʊl) n. **1.** mineral consisting of carbonized vegetable matter, used as fuel **2.** glowing ember —v. **3.** supply with or take in coal —'**coalface** n. exposed seam of coal in mine —'**coalfield** n. district in which coal is found —**coal gas** mixture of gases produced by distillation of bituminous coal and used for heating and lighting —**coal tar** black tar, produced by distillation of bituminous coal, that can be further distilled to yield benzene etc. —**coal tit** small songbird having black head with white patch on nape

coalesce (kəʊə'lɛs) vi. unite, merge —**coa'lescence** n.

coalfish ('kəʊlfɪʃ) n. food fish with dark-coloured skin

coalition (kəʊə'lɪʃən) n. alliance, esp. of political parties

coaming ('kəʊmɪŋ) n. raised frame round ship's hatchway for keeping out water

coarse (kɔːs) a. **1.** rough, harsh **2.** unrefined **3.** indecent —'**coarsely** adv. —'**coarsen** v. make or become coarse —'**coarseness** n. —**coarse fish** freshwater fish not of salmon family —**coarse fishing**

coast (kəʊst) n. **1.** sea shore —v. **2.** move under momentum **3.** sail along (coast) —vi. **4.** proceed without making much effort —'**coaster** n. **1.** small ship **2.** that which, one who, coasts **3.** small table mat for glasses etc. —'**coastguard** n. **1.** maritime force which aids shipping, prevents smuggling etc. **2.** member of such force (also '**coastguardsman**)

coat (kəʊt) n. **1.** sleeved outer garment **2.** animal's fur or feathers **3.** covering layer —vt. **4.** cover with layer **5.** clothe —**coat of arms** armorial bearings

coax (kəʊks) vt. wheedle, cajole, persuade, force gently

coaxial (kəʊ'æksɪəl) or **coaxal** (kəʊ'æksəl) a. having the same axis —**coaxial cable** high-frequency cable with outer conductor tube surrounding insulated central conductor

cob (kɒb) n. **1.** short-legged stout horse **2.** male swan **3.** head of corn **4.** round loaf of bread

cobalt ('kəʊbɔːlt) n. **1.** metallic element **2.** blue pigment from it —**cobalt bomb 1.** cobalt-60

device used in radiotherapy **2.** nuclear weapon consisting of hydrogen bomb encased in cobalt

cobber ('kɒbə) n. **A** obs., NZ friend; mate: used as term of address to males

cobble ('kɒbəl) vt. **1.** patch roughly **2.** mend (shoes) —n. **3.** round stone —'**cobbler** n. shoe mender —'**cobblestone** n. rounded stone used for paving (also '**cobble**)

cobbler ('kɒblə) n. **1.** sweetened iced drink, usu. made from fruit and wine **2.** chiefly US hot dessert of fruit covered with cakelike crust

cobblers ('kɒbləz) pl.n. UK vulg. sl. testicles —**(a load of old) cobblers** rubbish; nonsense

COBOL ('kəʊbɒl) computer programming language for general commercial use

cobra ('kəʊbrə) n. venomous, hooded snake of Asia and Afr.

cobweb ('kɒbwɛb) n. spider's web

coca ('kəʊkə) n. either of two shrubs, native to Andes, whose dried leaves contain cocaine

Coca-Cola (kəʊkə'kəʊlə) n. R carbonated soft drink

cocaine or **cocain** (kə'keɪn) n. addictive narcotic drug used medicinally as anaesthetic

coccus ('kɒkəs) n. spherical or nearly spherical bacterium, such as staphylococcus (pl. -ci (-saɪ))

coccyx ('kɒksɪks) n. small triangular bone at end of spinal column (pl. **coccyges** (kɒk'saɪdʒiːz))

cochineal (kɒtʃɪ'niːl, 'kɒtʃɪniːl) n. scarlet dye from Mexican insect

cochlea ('kɒklɪə) n. spiral tube that forms part of internal ear, converting sound vibrations into nerve impulses (pl. -leae (-liː))

cock (kɒk) n. **1.** male bird, esp. of domestic fowl **2.** tap for liquids **3.** hammer of gun **4.** its position drawn back —vt. **5.** draw back (gun hammer) to firing position **6.** raise, turn in alert or jaunty manner —'**cockerel** n. young cock —**cock-a-hoop** a. **1.** in very high spirits **2.** boastful **3.** askew; confused —**cock-a-leekie** or **cocky-leeky** n. soup made from fowl boiled with leeks etc. —**cock-and-bull story** inf. obviously improbable story, esp. one used as excuse —'**cockcrow** or '**cockcrowing** n. daybreak —**cocked hat** hat with brims turned up and caught together to give two or three points —'**cockeyed** a. **1.** crosseyed **2.** with a squint **3.** askew —**cockfight** n. staged fight between roosters —'**cockscomb** or '**coxcomb** n. **1.** comb of domestic cock **2.** garden plant with flowers in broad spike resembling comb of cock **3.** inf. conceited dandy —'**cockshy** n. UK **1.** target in throwing games **2.** throw itself (also **shy**) —**cock'sure** a. overconfident; arrogant —**knock into a cocked hat** sl. outdo, defeat

cockade (kɒ'keɪd) n. rosette, badge for hat

cockatoo (kɒkə'tuː, 'kɒkətuː) n. Aust., New Guinea, crested parrot

cockatrice ('kɒkətrɪs, -traɪs) n. fabulous animal similar to basilisk

cockchafer ('kɒktʃeɪfə) n. large, flying beetle

cocker spaniel ('kɒkə) small compact spaniel

cockle[1] ('kɒkəl) n. shellfish —**cockleshell** n. 1. shell of cockle 2. shell of certain other molluscs 3. small light boat

cockle[2] ('kɒkəl) v. 1. wrinkle 2. pucker

cockney ('kɒknɪ) n. (oft. C-) native of London, esp. of East End (pl. -s)

cockpit ('kɒkpɪt) n. 1. pilot's seat, compartment in small aircraft 2. driver's seat in racing car 3. orig. enclosure for cockfighting

cockroach ('kɒkrəʊtʃ) n. kind of insect, household pest

cocktail ('kɒkteɪl) n. 1. short drink of spirits with flavourings etc. 2. appetizer

cocky ('kɒkɪ) a. conceited, pert

cocoa ('kəʊkəʊ) or **cacao** n. 1. powder made from seed of cacao (tropical) tree 2. drink made from the powder

coconut or **cocoanut** ('kəʊkənʌt) n. 1. tropical palm 2. very large, hard nut from this palm —**coconut matting** coarse matting made from fibrous husk of coconut

cocoon (kə'kuːn) n. 1. sheath of insect in chrysalis stage 2. any protective covering

cocopan ('kəʊkəʊpæn) n. SA small truck on rails used esp. in mines

cocotte (kəʊ'kɒt, kə-) n. 1. small fireproof dish in which individual portions of food are cooked and served 2. prostitute; promiscuous woman

cod (kɒd) n. large sea fish of northern hemisphere —**cod-liver oil** oil extracted from livers of cod and related fish, rich in vitamins A and D

C.O.D. cash on delivery

coda ('kəʊdə) n. Mus. final part of musical composition

coddle ('kɒdəl) vt. overprotect, pamper

code (kəʊd) n. 1. system of letters, symbols and rules for their association to transmit messages secretly or briefly 2. scheme of conduct 3. collection of laws —**codifi'cation** n. —'**codify** vt.

codeine ('kəʊdiːn) n. alkaline sedative, analgesic drug

codex ('kəʊdeks) n. ancient manuscript volume, esp. of Bible etc. (pl. **codices** ('kəʊdɪsiːz, 'kɒdɪ-))

codger ('kɒdʒə) n. inf. old man

codicil ('kɒdɪsɪl) n. addition to will —**codi'cillary** a.

codpiece ('kɒdpiːs) n. bag covering male genitals, attached to breeches: worn in 15th and 16th centuries

coeducation (kəʊɛdjʊ'keɪʃən) n. instruction in schools etc. attended by both sexes —**co-ed** n. 1. coeducational school etc. —a. 2. coeducational —**coedu'cational** a. of education of boys and girls together in mixed classes

coefficient (kəʊɪ'fɪʃənt) n. Maths. numerical or constant factor

coelenterate (sɪ'lɛntəreɪt, -rɪt) n. any of various invertebrates having saclike body with single opening (mouth), such as jellyfishes

coeliac or US. **celiac** ('siːlɪæk) a. pert. to belly —**coeliac disease** intestinal disorder caused by inadequate absorption of gluten

coenobite or **cenobite** ('siːnəʊbaɪt) n. member of religious order following communal rule of life —**coenobitic(al)** or **cenobitic(al)** (siːnəʊ'bɪtɪk(əl)) a.

coequal (kəʊ'iːkwəl) a. 1. of same size, rank etc. —n. 2. person or thing equal with another —**coe'quality** n.

coerce (kəʊ'ɜːs) vt. compel, force —**co'ercion** n. forcible compulsion or restraint —**co'ercive** or **co'ercible** a.

coeval (kəʊ'iːvəl) a. of same age or generation

coexist (kəʊɪg'zɪst) vi. exist together —**coex'istence** n. —**coex'istent** a.

coextend (kəʊɪk'stɛnd) v. extend or cause to extend equally in space or time —**coex'tension** n. —**coex'tensive** a.

C. of E. Church of England

coffee ('kɒfɪ) n. 1. seeds of tropical shrub 2. drink made from roasting and grinding these —**coffee bar** café; snack bar —**coffee mill** machine for grinding roasted coffee beans —**coffee table** low table on which coffee may be served

coffer ('kɒfə) n. 1. chest for valuables 2. treasury, funds

cofferdam ('kɒfədæm) n. watertight structure enabling construction work to be done under water

coffin ('kɒfɪn) n. box in which corpse is buried or cremated

C. of S. Church of Scotland

cog (kɒg) n. 1. one of series of teeth on rim of wheel 2. person, thing forming small part of big process, organization etc. —'**cogwheel** n.

cogent ('kəʊdʒənt) a. convincing, compelling, persuasive —'**cogency** n. —'**cogently** adv.

cogitate ('kɒdʒɪteɪt) vi. think, reflect, ponder —**cogi'tation** n. —'**cogitative** a.

Cognac ('kɒnjæk) n. French brandy

cognate ('kɒgneɪt) a. of same stock, related, kindred —**cog'nation** n.

cognition (kɒg'nɪʃən) n. act or faculty of knowing —**cog'nitional** a.

cognizance or **cognisance** ('kɒgnızəns, 'kɒnı-) n. knowledge, perception —'**cognizable** or '**cognisable** a. —'**cognizant** or '**cognisant** a.

cognomen (kɒg'nəʊmɛn) n. surname, nickname (pl. -s, -**nomina** (-'nɒmɪnə, -'nəʊ-))

cognoscenti (kɒnjəʊ'ʃɛntı, kɒgnə-) or **conoscenti** (kɒnəʊ'ʃɛntı) pl.n. people with knowledge in particular field, art (sing. -te (-tiː))

cohabit (kəʊ'hæbɪt) vi. live together as husband and wife

coheir (kəʊ'ɛə) n. a joint heir (**co'heiress** fem.)

cohere (kəʊ'hɪə) vi. stick together, be consistent —**co'herence** n. —**co'herent** a. 1. capable of logical speech, thought 2. connected, making sense 3. sticking together —**co'herently** adv. —**co'hesion** n. cohering —**co'hesive** a.

cohort ('kəʊhɔːt) n. 1. troop 2. associate

COHSE ('kəʊzı) Confederation of Health Service Employees

C.O.I. UK Central Office of Information

coif (kɔɪf) n. 1. close-fitting cap worn under veil in Middle Ages 2. leather cap worn under chainmail hood 3. (kwɑːf) rare coiffure —vt. 4. cover with or as if with coif 5. (kwɑːf) arrange (hair) (-**ff**-)

coiffure (kwɑː'fjʊə) n. hairstyle —**coiffeur** (kwɑː'fɜː) n. hairdresser

coign of vantage (kɔɪn) advantageous position for observation or action

coil (kɔɪl) vt. 1. lay in rings 2. twist into winding shape —vi. 3. twist, take up a winding shape or spiral —n. 4. series of rings 5. device in vehicle etc. to transform low-tension current to higher voltage for ignition purposes 6. contraceptive device inserted in womb

coin (kɔɪn) n. 1. piece of money 2. money —vt. 3. make into money, stamp 4. invent —'**coinage** n. 1. coining 2. coins collectively —'**coiner** n. maker of counterfeit money

coincide (kəʊɪn'saɪd) vi. 1. happen together 2. agree exactly —**co'incidence** n. —**co'incident** a. coinciding —**coinci'dental** a.

Cointreau (kwɒːntrəʊ) n. R colourless liqueur with orange flavouring

coir ('kɔɪə) n. fibre of coconut husk

coitus ('kɔʊɪtəs) or **coition** (kəʊ'ɪʃən) n. sexual intercourse

coke[1] (kəʊk) n. residue left from distillation of coal, used as fuel

coke[2] (kəʊk) n. sl. cocaine

Coke (kəʊk) n. R short for COCA-COLA

col (kɒl) n. high mountain pass

Col. 1. Colonel 2. Colossians

cola or **kola** ('kəʊlə) n. 1. tropical tree 2. its nut, used to flavour drink

colander ('kɒləndə, 'kʌl-) or **cullender** n. culinary strainer perforated with small holes

cold (kəʊld) a. 1. lacking heat 2. indifferent,

unmoved, apathetic 3. dispiriting 4. reserved or unfriendly 5. (of colours) giving an impression of coldness —n. 6. lack of heat 7. illness, marked by runny nose etc. —'**coldly** adv. —'**coldness** n. —**cold-blooded** a. 1. lacking pity, mercy 2. having body temperature that varies with that of the surroundings —**cold chisel** toughened steel chisel —**cold cream** emulsion of water and fat for softening and cleansing skin —**cold feet** sl. loss of confidence —**cold frame** unheated wooden frame with glass top, used to protect young plants —**cold front** Met. boundary line between warm air mass and cold air pushing it —**cold-hearted** a. lacking in feeling or warmth; unkind —**cold-heartedness** n. —**cold shoulder** inf. show of indifference; slight —**cold-shoulder** vt. inf. treat with indifference —**cold sore** cluster of blisters at margin of lips, caused by viral infection (also **herpes labialis**) —**cold storage** 1. method of preserving perishable foods etc. by keeping them at artificially reduced temperature 2. inf. state of temporary suspension —**cold sweat** inf. bodily reaction to fear or nervousness, characterized by chill and moist skin —**cold war** economic, diplomatic but nonmilitary hostility —(**out**) **in the cold** inf. neglected; ignored

cole (kəʊl) n. any of various plants such as cabbage and kale (also '**colewort**)

coleopteran (kɒlɪ'ɒptərən) n. 1. any of order of insects, including beetles, in which forewings form shell-like protective elytra (also **cole'opteron**) —a. 2. of this order (also **cole'opterous**)

coleslaw ('kəʊlslɔː) n. salad dish based on shredded cabbage

coletit ('kəʊltɪt) n. see **coal tit** at COAL

coleus ('kəʊlɪəs) n. plant cultivated for its variegated leaves

coley ('kəʊlɪ, 'kɒlɪ) n. UK any of various edible fishes, esp. coalfish

colic ('kɒlɪk) n. severe pains in the intestines —**co'litis** n. inflammation of the colon

coliseum (kɒlɪ'sɪəm) or **colosseum** (kɒlə'sɪəm) n. large building, such as stadium, used for entertainments etc.

collaborate (kə'læbəreɪt) vi. work with another on a project —**collabo'ration** n. —**col'laborator** n. one who works with another, esp. one who aids an enemy in occupation of his own country

collage (kə'lɑːʒ, kɒ-) n. (artistic) composition of bits and pieces stuck together on background

collagen ('kɒlədʒən) n. fibrous protein of connective tissue and bones that yields gelatin on boiling

collapse (kə'læps) vi. 1. fall 2. give way 3. lose strength, fail —n. 4. act of collapsing 5. breakdown —**col'lapsible** or **col'lapsable** a.

collar ('kɒlə) n. 1. band, part of garment, worn round neck —vt. 2. seize by collar 3. inf. capture, seize —'**collarbone** n. bone from shoulder to breastbone

collate (kɒ'leɪt, kə-) vt. 1. compare carefully 2. place in order (as printed sheets for binding) —col'**lation** n. 1. collating 2. light meal

collateral (kɒ'lætərəl, kə-) n. 1. security pledged for repayment of loan —a. 2. accompanying 3. side by side 4. of same stock but different line 5. subordinate

colleague ('kɒliːg) n. associate, companion in office or employment, fellow worker

collect[1] (kə'lɛkt) vt. 1. gather, bring together —vi. 2. come together 3. inf. receive money —adv./a. 4. US (of telephone calls etc.) on transferred-charge basis —col'**lected** a. 1. calm 2. gathered —col'**lection** n. —col'**lective** n. 1. factory, farm etc., run on principles of collectivism —a. 2. formed or assembled by collection 3. forming whole or aggregate 4. of individuals acting in cooperation —col'**lectively** adv. —col'**lectivism** n. theory that the state should own all means of production —col'**lector** n. —**collective bargaining** negotiation between trade union and employer or employers' organization on incomes and working conditions of employees —**collector's item** any rare or beautiful object thought worthy of collection

collect[2] ('kɒlɛkt) n. short prayer

colleen ('kɒliːn, kɒ'liːn) n. Irish name for girl

college ('kɒlɪdʒ) n. 1. place of higher education 2. society of scholars 3. association —col'**legian** n. student —col'**legiate** a.

collide (kə'laɪd) vi. 1. strike or dash together 2. come into conflict —**collision** (kə'lɪʒən) n. colliding

collie ('kɒlɪ) n. any of several breeds of dog orig. bred to herd sheep

collier ('kɒlɪə) n. 1. coal miner 2. coal ship —'**colliery** n. coal mine

collimate ('kɒlɪmeɪt) vt. 1. adjust line of sight of (optical instrument) 2. make parallel or bring into line —colli'**mation** n.

collocate ('kɒləkeɪt) vt. group, place together —collo'**cation** n.

collodion (kə'ləʊdɪən) or **collodium** (kə-'ləʊdɪəm) n. chemical solution used in photography and medicine

colloid ('kɒlɔɪd) n. suspension of particles in a solution

collop ('kɒləp) n. dial. 1. slice of meat 2. small piece of anything

colloquial (kə'ləʊkwɪəl) a. pert. to, or used in, informal conversation —col'**loquialism** n. —'**colloquy** n. 1. conversation 2. dialogue

colloquium (kə'ləʊkwɪəm) n. 1. gathering for discussion 2. academic seminar (pl. -s, -quia (-kwɪə))

collusion (kə'luːʒən) n. secret agreement for a fraudulent purpose, esp. in legal proceedings —col'**lusive** a.

collywobbles ('kɒlɪwɒbəlz) pl.n. sl. 1. upset stomach 2. intense feeling of nervousness

cologne (kə'ləʊn) n. perfumed liquid (also **eau de cologne**)

colon[1] ('kəʊlən) n. mark (:) indicating break in sentence

colon[2] ('kəʊlən) n. part of large intestine from caecum to rectum

colonel ('kɜːnəl) n. commander of regiment or battalion —'**colonelcy** n.

colonnade (kɒlə'neɪd) n. row of columns

colony ('kɒlənɪ) n. 1. body of people who settle in new country but remain subject to parent state 2. country so settled 3. distinctive group living together —co'**lonial** a. of colony —co'**lonialism** n. policy and practice of extending control over weaker peoples or areas (also **im'perialism**) —co'**lonialist** n./a. —'**colonist** n. —**coloni'zation** or -i'**sation** n. —'**colonize** or -**ise** v.

colophon ('kɒləfən, -fɒn) n. publisher's imprint or device

Colorado beetle (kɒlə'rɑːdəʊ) black-and-yellow beetle that is serious pest of potatoes

coloratura (kɒlərə'tʊərə) n. Mus. 1. florid virtuoso passage 2. soprano who specializes in such music (also **coloratura soprano**)

colossus (kə'lɒsəs) n. 1. huge statue 2. something, somebody very large (pl. **colossi** (kə'lɒsaɪ), -es) —co'**lossal** a. huge, gigantic

colostomy (kə'lɒstəmɪ) n. surgical formation of opening from colon on to surface of body, which functions as anus

colostrum (kə'lɒstrəm) n. thin milky secretion from nipples that precedes and follows true lactation

colour or U.S. **color** ('kʌlə) n. 1. hue, tint 2. complexion 3. paint 4. pigment 5. fig. semblance, pretext 6. fig. timbre, quality 7. fig. mood —pl. 8. flag 9. Sport distinguishing badge, symbol —vt. 10. stain, dye, paint, give colour to 11. fig. disguise 12. fig. influence or distort —vi. 13. become coloured 14. blush —colo'**ration** n. —'**colourable** a. 1. capable of being coloured 2. appearing to be true; plausible 3. pretended; feigned —'**coloured** a. 1. possessing colour 2. having strong element of fiction or fantasy; distorted (esp. in **highly coloured**) —**Coloured** a. 1. non-White 2. in S Afr. of mixed descent —'**colourful** a. 1. with bright or varied colours 2. distinctive —'**colouring** n. 1. process or art of applying colour 2. anything used to give colour, such as paint 3. appearance with regard to shade and colour **4.** arrangements of colours, as in markings of birds **5.** colour of complexion **6.** false appearance —'**colourless** a. **1.** without colour **2.** lacking interest **3.** grey; pallid **4.** without prejudice; neutral —**colour bar** discrimination against people of different race, esp. as practised by Whites against Blacks —**colour sergeant** sergeant who carries regimental, battalion or national colours

colt (kəolt) n. young male horse —'**coltish** a. **1.** inexperienced; unruly **2.** playful and lively

coltsfoot ('kəoltsfot) n. wild plant with heart-shaped leaves and yellow flowers (pl. **-s**)

columbine ('kɒləmbaɪn) n. flower with five spurred petals

column ('kɒləm) n. **1.** long vertical cylinder, pillar **2.** support **3.** division of page **4.** Journalism regular feature in paper **5.** body of troops —**columnar** (kə'lʌmnə) a. —'**columnist** n. journalist writing regular feature for newspaper

com- or **con-** (comb. form) together; with; jointly, as in commingle

coma ('kəomə) n. state of unconsciousness —'**comatose** a.

comb (kəom) n. **1.** toothed instrument for tidying, arranging, ornamenting hair **2.** cock's crest **3.** mass of honey cells —vt. **4.** use comb on **5.** search with great care —'**comber** n. **1.** person, tool or machine that combs wool, flax etc. **2.** long curling wave; roller

combat ('kɒmbæt, -bət, 'kʌm-) vt./n. fight, contest —'**combatant** n. —'**combative** a. —**combat fatigue** see battle fatigue at BATTLE

combe or **comb** (ku:m) n. see COOMB

combine (kəm'baɪn) v. **1.** join together **2.** ally —n. ('kɒmbaɪn) **3.** trust, syndicate, esp. of businesses, trade organizations etc. —**combination** (kɒmbɪ'neɪʃən) n. —**combinative** ('kɒmbɪneɪtɪv) a. —**combination lock** lock that can only be opened when set of dials is turned to show specific sequence of numbers —**combine harvester** machine to harvest and thresh grain in one operation —**combining form** linguistic element that occurs only as part of compound word, such as anthropo- in anthropology

combo ('kɒmbəo) n. **1.** small group of jazz musicians **2.** inf. any combination (pl. **-s**)

combustion (kəm'bʌstʃən) n. process of burning —**combusti'bility** n. —**com'bustible** a.

come (kʌm) vi. **1.** approach, arrive, move towards something or someone nearer **2.** reach **3.** happen as a result **4.** occur **5.** be available **6.** originate **7.** become, turn out to be (**came**, **come**, '**coming**) —'**coming** a. **1.** (of time etc.) approaching; next **2.** promising (esp. in up and coming) —n. **3.** arrival; approach —'**comeback** n. inf. **1.** return to active life after retirement **2.** retort —'**comedown** n. **1.** setback **2.** descent in

social status —**come-hither** a. inf. alluring; seductive —**come-on** n. inf. anything that serves as lure —**come'uppance** n. sl. just retribution —**come on 1.** (of power etc.) start functioning **2.** progress **3.** advance, esp. in battle **4.** begin **5.** make entrance on stage —**come on strong** make forceful or exaggerated impression —**have it coming to one** inf. deserve what one is about to suffer

Comecon ('kɒmɪkɒn) n. association of Soviet-oriented Communist nations, founded in 1949 to coordinate economic development etc.

comedy ('kɒmɪdɪ) n. **1.** dramatic or other work of light, amusing character **2.** humour **3.** Class. lit. play in which main characters triumph over adversity —co'**median** n. **1.** entertainer who tells jokes etc. **2.** actor in comedy (**comedi'enne** fem.)

comely ('kʌmlɪ) a. fair, pretty, good-looking —'**comeliness** n.

comestible (kə'mɛstɪbəl) n. (usu. pl.) food

comet ('kɒmɪt) n. luminous heavenly body consisting of diffuse head, nucleus and long tail —'**cometary** a.

comfit ('kʌmfɪt, 'kɒm-) n. sweet

comfort ('kʌmfət) n. **1.** wellbeing **2.** ease **3.** consolation **4.** means of consolation or satisfaction —vt. **5.** soothe **6.** cheer, gladden, console —'**comfortable** ('kʌmftəbəl) a. **1.** free from pain etc. **2.** inf. well-off financially —'**comfortably** ('kʌmftəblɪ) adv. —'**comforter** n. **1.** one who comforts **2.** baby's dummy **3.** woollen scarf —'**comfy** a. inf. comfortable

comfrey ('kʌmfrɪ) n. wild plant with hairy leaves

comic ('kɒmɪk) a. **1.** relating to comedy **2.** funny, laughable —n. **3.** comedian **4.** magazine consisting of strip cartoons —'**comical** a. —'**comically** adv. —**comic strip** sequence of drawings in newspaper etc., relating comic or adventurous situation

comity ('kɒmɪtɪ) n. **1.** mutual civility; courtesy **2.** friendly recognition accorded by nation to laws and usages of another (also **comity of nations**)

comm. 1. commonwealth **2.** communist

comma ('kɒmə) n. punctuation mark (,) separating parts of sentence

command (kə'mɑːnd) vt. **1.** order **2.** rule **3.** compel **4.** have in one's power **5.** overlook, dominate **6.** receive as due —vi. **7.** exercise rule —n. **8.** order **9.** power of controlling, ruling, dominating, overlooking **10.** knowledge, mastery **11.** post of one commanding **12.** district commanded, jurisdiction —'**commandant** n. —**comman'deer** vt. seize for military use, appropriate —**com'mander** n. —**com'manding**

a. **1.** in command **2.** with air of authority —**com'mandment** *n.*

commando (kə'mɑːndəʊ) *n.* (member of) special military unit trained for airborne, amphibious attack (*pl.* **-s**)

commedia dell'arte (kɒm'mɛdjə del'lɑːte) *It.* form of improvised comedy in Italy in 16th to 18th cent., with stock characters such as Punchinello, Harlequin *etc.*

commemorate (kə'mɛməreɪt) *vt.* **1.** celebrate, keep in memory by ceremony **2.** be a memorial of —**commemo'ration** *n.* —**com-'memorative** *a.*

commence (kə'mɛns) *v.* begin —**com'mencement** *n.*

commend (kə'mɛnd) *vt.* **1.** praise **2.** commit, entrust —**com'mendable** *a.* —**com'mendably** *adv.* —**commen'dation** *n.* —**com'mendatory** *a.*

commensurate (kə'mɛnsərɪt, -ʃə-) *a.* **1.** equal in size or length of time **2.** in proportion, adequate —**com'mensurable** *a.* **1.** *Maths.* having common factor; having units of same dimensions and being related by whole numbers **2.** proportionate

comment ('kɒmɛnt) *n.* **1.** remark, criticism **2.** gossip **3.** note, explanation —*vi.* **4.** remark, note **5.** write notes explaining or criticizing a text —'**commentary** *n.* **1.** explanatory notes or comments **2.** spoken accompaniment to film *etc.* —'**commentate** *vi.* —'**commentator** *n.* author, speaker of commentary

commerce ('kɒmɜːs) *n.* **1.** buying and selling **2.** dealings **3.** trade —**com'mercial** *a.* **1.** of, concerning, business, trade, profit *etc.* —*n.* **2.** advertisement, *esp.* on radio or television —**com'mercialize** *or* **-lise** *vt.* **1.** make commercial **2.** exploit for profit, *esp.* at expense of quality —**commercial traveller** travelling salesman

commie *or* **commy** ('kɒmɪ) *n./a. inf., offens.* communist

commination (kɒmɪ'neɪʃən) *n.* act of threatening punishment or vengeance —**comminatory** ('kɒmɪnətərɪ) *a.*

commingle (kɒ'mɪŋgəl) *v.* mix or be mixed

comminute ('kɒmɪnjuːt) *vt.* **1.** break (bone) into small fragments **2.** divide (property) into small lots —**commi'nution** *n.*

commis ('kɒmɪs, 'kɒmɪ) *n.* **1.** agent or deputy **2.** apprentice waiter or chef (*pl.* **-mis**)

commiserate (kə'mɪzəreɪt) *vi.* (*usu. with* with) pity, condole, sympathize —**commiser'a-tion** *n.*

commissar ('kɒmɪsɑː, kɒmɪ'sɑː) *n.* official of Communist Party responsible for political education

commissariat (kɒmɪ'sɛərɪət) *n.* military department of food supplies and transport

commissary ('kɒmɪsərɪ) *n.* **1.** US shop supplying food or equipment, as in military camp **2.** US army officer responsible for supplies **3.** US restaurant in film studio **4.** representative or deputy, *esp.* of bishop

commission (kə'mɪʃən) *n.* **1.** something entrusted to be done **2.** delegated authority **3.** body entrusted with some special duty **4.** payment by percentage for doing something **5.** warrant, *esp.* royal warrant, giving authority **6.** document appointing soldier, sailor or airman to officer's rank **7.** doing, committing —*vt.* **8.** charge with duty or task **9.** *Mil.* confer a rank on **10.** give order for —**com'missioner** *n.* one empowered to act by commission or warrant **2.** member of commission or government board —**commissioned officer** military officer holding commission, such as Second Lieutenant in British Army, Acting Sub-Lieutenant in Royal Navy, Pilot Officer in Royal Air Force, and officers of all ranks senior to these —**commissioner for oaths** solicitor authorized to authenticate oaths on sworn statements

commissionaire (kəmɪʃə'nɛə) *n.* messenger, porter, doorkeeper (*usu.* uniformed)

commit (kə'mɪt) *vt.* **1.** entrust, give in charge **2.** perpetrate, be guilty of **3.** pledge, promise **4.** compromise, entangle **5.** send for trial (*-tt-*) —**com'mitment** *n.* —**com'mittal** *n.*

committee (kə'mɪtɪ) *n.* body appointed, elected for special business usu. from larger body

commode (kə'məʊd) *n.* **1.** chest of drawers **2.** stool containing chamber pot

commodious (kə'məʊdɪəs) *a.* roomy

commodity (kə'mɒdɪtɪ) *n.* **1.** article of trade **2.** anything useful

commodore ('kɒmədɔː) *n.* **1.** naval officer, senior to captain **2.** president of yacht club **3.** senior captain in convoy of merchant ships

common ('kɒmən) *a.* **1.** shared by or belonging to all, or to several **2.** public, general **3.** ordinary, usual, frequent **4.** inferior **5.** vulgar —*n.* **6.** land belonging to community —*pl.* **7.** ordinary people **8.** (C-) lower House of British Parliament, House of Commons —**commo'nality** *n.* **1.** fact of being common **2.** commonalty —'**commonalty** *n.* general body of people —'**commoner** *n.* one of the common people, *ie* not of the nobility —'**commonly** *adv.* —**common fraction** *see* simple fraction *at* SIMPLE —**common law** body of law based on judicial decisions and custom —**common-law marriage** state of marriage deemed to exist between man and woman after years of cohabitation —**Common Market** European Economic Community —'**common-place** *a.* **1.** ordinary, everyday —*n.* **2.** trite remark **3.** anything occurring frequently

—**common room** *chiefly* **UK** sitting room in schools *etc.* —**common sense** sound, practical understanding —**common time** *Mus.* time signature indicating four crotchet beats to bar; four-four time —'**commonwealth** *n.* 1. republic 2. (**C-**) federation of self-governing states

commotion (kə'məʊʃən) *n.* stir, disturbance, tumult

commune[1] (kə'mjuːn) *vi.* converse together intimately —**com'munion** *n.* 1. sharing of thoughts, feelings *etc.* 2. fellowship 3. body with common faith 4. (**C-**) participation in sacrament of the Lord's Supper 5. (**C-**) that sacrament, Eucharist

commune[2] ('kɒmjuːn) *n.* group of families, individuals living together and sharing property, responsibility *etc.* —'**communal** *a.* for common use

communicate (kə'mjuːnɪkeɪt) *vt.* 1. impart, convey 2. reveal —*vi.* 3. give or exchange information 4. have connecting passage, door 5. receive Communion —**com'municable** *a.* —**com'municant** *n.* one who receives Communion —**communi'cation** *n.* 1. act of giving, *esp.* information 2. information, message 3. (*usu. pl.*) passage (road, railway *etc.*) or means of exchanging messages (radio, post *etc.*) between places —*pl.* 4. connections between military base and front —**com'municative** *a.* free with information —**communication cord** UK cord or chain which may be pulled by passenger to stop train in emergency

communiqué (kə'mjuːnɪkeɪ) *n.* official announcement

communism ('kɒmjunɪzəm) *n.* doctrine that all goods, means of production *etc.* should be property of community —'**communist** *n./a.* —**commu'nistic** *a.*

community (kə'mjuːnɪtɪ) *n.* 1. body of people with something in common, *eg* district of residence, religion *etc.* 2. society, the public 3. joint ownership 4. similarity, agreement —**community centre** building for communal activities

commute (kə'mjuːt) *vi.* 1. travel daily some distance to work —*vt.* 2. exchange 3. change (punishment *etc.*) into something less severe 4. change (duty *etc.*) for money payment —**commu'tation** *n.* —**com'mutative** *a.* relating to or involving substitution —'**commutator** *n.*

compact[1] (kəm'pækt) *a.* 1. neatly arranged or packed 2. solid, concentrated 3. terse —*v.* 4. make, become compact —*vt.* 5. compress —**com'pactly** *adv.* —**com'pactness** *n.*

compact[2] ('kɒmpækt) *n.* small case to hold face powder, powder puff and mirror

compact[3] ('kɒmpækt) *n.* agreement, covenant, treaty, contract

companion[1] (kəm'pænjən) *n.* 1. mate, fellow, comrade, associate 2. person employed to live with another —**com'panionable** *a.* —**com'panionship** *n.*

companion[2] (kəm'pænjən) *n.* 1. raised cover over staircase from deck to cabin of ship 2. deck skylight —**com'panionway** *n.* staircase from deck to cabin

company ('kʌmpənɪ) *n.* 1. gathering of persons 2. companionship, fellowship 3. guests 4. business firm 5. division of regiment under captain 6. crew of ship 7. actors in play —**company sergeant-major** *Mil.* senior noncommissioned officer in company

compare (kəm'pɛə) *vt.* 1. notice or point out likenesses and differences of 2. liken 3. make comparative and superlative of (adjective or adverb) —*vi.* 4. compete —**comparability** (kɒmpərə'bɪlɪtɪ) *n.* —**comparable** ('kɒmpərəb'l) *a.* —**comparative** (kəm'pærətɪv) *a.* 1. that may be compared 2. not absolute 3. relative, partial 4. *Gram.* denoting form of adjective, adverb, indicating 'more' —*n.* 5. comparative form of adjective or adverb —**comparatively** (kəm'pærətɪvlɪ) *adv.* —**comparison** (kəm'pærɪsən) *n.* act of comparing —**compare with** be like

compartment (kəm'pɑːtmənt) *n.* 1. division or part divided off, *eg* in railway carriage 2. section —**compart'mentalize** *or* **-lise** *vt.* put into categories *etc.*, *esp.* to excessive degree

compass ('kʌmpəs) *n.* 1. instrument for showing the north 2. (*usu. pl.*) instrument for drawing circles 3. circumference, measurement round 4. space, area 5. scope, reach —*vt.* 6. surround 7. comprehend 8. attain, accomplish

compassion (kəm'pæʃən) *n.* pity, sympathy —**com'passionate** *a.* —**com'passionately** *adv.*

compatible (kəm'pætəb'l) *a.* 1. capable of harmonious existence 2. consistent, agreeing —**compati'bility** *n.* —**com'patibly** *adv.*

compatriot (kəm'pætrɪət) *n.* fellow countryman

compeer ('kɒmpɪə) *n.* equal, associate, companion

compel (kəm'pɛl) *vt.* 1. force, oblige 2. bring about by force (**-ll-**)

compendium (kəm'pɛndɪəm) *n.* 1. collection of different games 2. abridgment, summary (*pl.* **-s, -ia** (**-ɪə**)) —**com'pendious** *a.* brief but inclusive —**com'pendiously** *adv.*

compensate ('kɒmpɛnseɪt) *vt.* 1. make up for 2. recompense suitably 3. reward —*vi.* 4. (*with* for) supply an equivalent —**compen'sation** *n.*

compere ('kɒmpɛə) *n.* 1. one who presents artists in cabaret, television shows *etc.* —*v.* 2. act as compere (for)

compete (kəm'piːt) *vi.* (*oft. with* with) strive in rivalry, contend, vie —**competition** (kɒmpɪ-

'tɪʃən) n. —**competitive** (kəm'pɛtɪtɪv) a.
—**competitor** (kəm'pɛtɪtə) n.

competent ('kɒmpɪtənt) a. 1. able, skilful 2. properly qualified 3. proper, due, legitimate 4. suitable, sufficient —'**competence** n. efficiency —'**competently** adv.

compile (kəm'paɪl) vt. 1. make up (eg book) from various sources or materials 2. gather, put together —**compilation** (kɒmpɪ'leɪʃən) n. —com'**piler** n.

complacent (kəm'pleɪsənt) a. 1. self-satisfied 2. pleased, gratified —com'**placence** or com'**placency** n. —com'**placently** adv.

complain (kəm'pleɪn) vi. 1. grumble 2. bring charge, make known a grievance 3. (with of) make known that one is suffering from —com'**plainant** n. —com'**plaint** n. 1. statement of a wrong, grievance 2. ailment, illness

complaisant (kəm'pleɪzənt) a. obliging, willing to please, compliant —com'**plaisance** n. 1. act of pleasing 2. affability

complement ('kɒmplɪmənt) n. 1. person or thing that completes something 2. full allowance, equipment etc. —vt. ('kɒmplɪmɛnt) 3. add to, make complete —comple'**mentary** a.

complete (kəm'pliːt) a. 1. full, perfect 2. finished, ended 3. entire 4. thorough —vt. 5. make whole, perfect 6. finish —com'**pletely** adv. —com'**pleteness** n. —com'**pletion** n.

complex ('kɒmplɛks) a. 1. intricate, compound, involved —n. 2. complicated whole 3. group of related buildings 4. psychological abnormality, obsession —com'**plexity** n. —**complex fraction** Maths. fraction in which numerator or denominator or both contain fractions (also **compound fraction**) —**complex number** number of form a + bi, where a and b are real numbers and i = √ −1

complexion (kəm'plɛkʃən) n. 1. look, colour, of skin, esp. of face, appearance 2. aspect, character 3. disposition

compliant (kəm'plaɪənt) a. see COMPLY

complicate ('kɒmplɪkeɪt) vt. make intricate, involved, difficult, mix up —compli'**cation** n.

complicity (kəm'plɪsɪtɪ) n. partnership in wrongdoing

compliment ('kɒmplɪmənt) n. 1. expression of regard, praise 2. flattering speech —pl. 3. expression of courtesy, formal greetings —vt. ('kɒmplɪmɛnt) 4. praise, congratulate —compli'**mentary** a. 1. expressing praise 2. free of charge

compline ('kɒmplɪn, -plaɪn) or **complin** ('kɒmplɪn) n. last service of day in R.C. Church

comply (kəm'plaɪ) vi. consent, yield, do as asked (com'**plied**, com'**plying**) —com'**pliance** n. —com'**pliant** a.

component (kəm'pəʊnənt) n. 1. part, element, constituent of whole —a. 2. composing, making up

comport (kəm'pɔːt) vi. 1. agree —vt. 2. behave

compose (kəm'pəʊz) vt. 1. arrange, put in order 2. write, invent 3. make up 4. calm 5. settle, adjust —com'**posed** a. calm —com'**poser** n. one who composes, esp. music —**composite** a. made up of distinct parts —compo'**sition** n. —**compositor** (kəm'pɒzɪtə) n. typesetter, one who arranges type for printing —com'**posure** n. calmness —**composite school** C one offering both academic and nonacademic courses

compos mentis ('kɒmpəs 'mɛntɪs) Lat. of sound mind

compost ('kɒmpɒst) n. fertilizing mixture of decayed vegetable matter for soil

compote ('kɒmpəʊt) n. fruit stewed or preserved in syrup

compound¹ ('kɒmpaʊnd) n. 1. mixture, joining 2. substance, word, made up of parts —a. 3. not simple 4. composite, mixed —vt. (kəm'paʊnd) 5. mix, make up, put together 6. intensify, make worse 7. Law agree not to prosecute in return for a consideration —v. 8. compromise, settle (debt) by partial payment —**compound eye** convex eye of insects and some crustaceans, consisting of numerous separate units —**compound fracture** fracture in which broken bone pierces skin —**compound interest** interest calculated on both principal and its accrued interest —**compound sentence** sentence containing at least two coordinate clauses —**compound time** Mus. time in which number of beats per bar is multiple of three

compound² ('kɒmpaʊnd) n. (fenced or walled) enclosure containing houses etc.

comprehend (kɒmprɪ'hɛnd) vt. 1. understand, take in 2. include, comprise —compre'**hensible** a. —compre'**hension** n. —compre'**hensive** a. 1. wide, full 2. taking in much —compre'**hensively** adv. —compre'**hensiveness** n. —**comprehensive school** secondary school for children of all abilities

compress (kəm'prɛs) vt. 1. squeeze together 2. make smaller in size, bulk —n. ('kɒmprɛs) 3. pad of lint applied to wound, inflamed part etc. —com'**pressible** a. —com'**pression** n. in internal combustion engine, squeezing of explosive charge before ignition, to give additional force —com'**pressor** n. esp. machine to compress air, gas

comprise (kəm'praɪz) vt. include, contain —com'**prisable** a.

compromise ('kɒmprəmaɪz) n. 1. meeting halfway, coming to terms by giving up part of claim 2. middle course —v. 3. settle (dispute) by making concessions —vt. 4. expose to risk or suspicion

Comptometer (kɒmp'tɒmɪtə) n. R calculating machine

comptroller (kən'trəʊlə) n. controller (in some titles)

compulsion (kəm'pʌlʃən) n. 1. act of compelling 2. irresistible impulse —**com'pulsive** a. —**com'pulsorily** adv. —**com'pulsory** a. not optional

compunction (kəm'pʌŋkʃən) n. regret for wrongdoing

compute (kəm'pjuːt) v. reckon, calculate, esp. using computer —**compu'tation** n. reckoning, estimate —**com'puter** n. electronic machine for storing, retrieving information and performing calculations —**com'puterize** or **-ise** v. equip with, perform by computer

comrade ('kɒmreɪd, -rɪd) n. mate, companion, friend —'**comradeship** n.

con[1] (kɒn) inf. n. 1. confidence trick —vt. 2. swindle, defraud

con[2] (kɒn) n. contra, against —**pros and cons** (arguments) for and against

con[3] or (esp. U.S.) **conn** (kɒn) vt. direct steering of (ship) —'**conner** n.

concatenate (kɒn'kætɪneɪt) vt. link together —**concate'nation** n. connected chain (as of circumstances)

concave ('kɒnkeɪv, kɒn'keɪv) a. hollow, rounded inwards —**concavity** (kɒn'kævɪtɪ) n.

conceal (kən'siːl) vt. hide, keep secret —**con'cealment** n.

concede (kən'siːd) vt. 1. admit, admit truth of 2. grant, allow —vi. 3. yield

conceit (kən'siːt) n. 1. vanity, overweening opinion of oneself 2. far-fetched comparison —**con'ceited** a.

conceive (kən'siːv) vt. 1. believe 2. form conception of 3. become pregnant with —vi. 4. become pregnant —**con'ceivable** a. —**con'ceivably** adv. —**conceive of** have an idea of; imagine; think of

concentrate ('kɒnsəntreɪt) vt. 1. focus (one's efforts etc.) 2. increase in strength 3. reduce to small space —vi. 4. devote all attention 5. come together —n. 6. concentrated material or solution —**concen'tration** n. —**concentration camp** prison camp, esp. one in Nazi Germany

concentric (kən'sentrɪk) a. having the same centre

concept ('kɒnsɛpt) n. 1. abstract idea 2. mental expression —**con'ceptual** a. —**con'ceptualize** or **-ise** v.

conception (kən'sɛpʃən) n. 1. idea, notion 2. act of conceiving

concern (kən'sɜːn) vt. 1. relate or apply to 2. interest, affect, trouble 3. (with in or with) involve (oneself) —n. 4. affair 5. regard, worry 6. importance 7. business enterprise —**con'cerned**

a. 1. connected 2. interested 3. worried 4. involved —**con'cerning** prep. respecting, about

concert ('kɒnsət) n. 1. musical entertainment 2. harmony, agreement —v. (kən'sɜːt) 3. arrange, plan together —**con'certed** a. 1. mutually arranged, planned 2. determined —**concer'tina** n. 1. musical instrument with bellows and keys —vi. 2. fold, collapse, as bellows —**concerto** (kən'tʃɛətəʊ) n. musical composition for solo instrument and orchestra (pl. **-s**) —**concert pitch** 1. frequency of 440 hertz assigned to A above middle C 2. inf. state of extreme readiness

concession (kən'sɛʃən) n. 1. act of conceding 2. thing conceded 3. grant 4. special privilege 5. C land division in township survey —**conces-sio'naire**, **con'cessioner** or **con'cessionary** n. someone who holds or operates concession —**con'cessive** a.

conch (kɒŋk, kɒntʃ) n. seashell —**conchology** (kɒŋ'kɒlədʒɪ) n. study, collection of shells and shellfish

concierge (kɒnsɪ'ɛəʒ) n. in France, caretaker, doorkeeper

conciliate (kən'sɪlɪeɪt) vt. pacify, win over from hostility —**concili'ation** n. —**con'ciliator** n. —**con'ciliatory** a.

concise (kən'saɪs) a. brief, terse —**con'cisely** adv. —**con'ciseness** n. —**concision** (kən'sɪʒən) n.

conclave ('kɒnkleɪv) n. 1. private meeting 2. assembly for election of Pope

conclude (kən'kluːd) vt. 1. end, finish 2. deduce 3. settle 4. decide —vi. 5. come to an end —**con'clusion** n. —**con'clusive** a. decisive, convincing —**con'clusively** adv.

concoct (kən'kɒkt) vt. 1. make (mixture), with various ingredients 2. make up 3. contrive, plan —**con'coction** n.

concomitant (kən'kɒmɪtənt) a. accompanying —**con'comitance** n. existence

concord ('kɒŋkɔːd) n. 1. agreement 2. harmony —**con'cordance** n. 1. agreement 2. index to words of book (esp. Bible) —**con'cordant** a. —**con'cordat** n. pact or treaty, esp. between Vatican and another state concerning interests of religion in that state

concourse ('kɒŋkɔːs) n. 1. crowd 2. large, open place in public area

concrete ('kɒŋkriːt) n. 1. mixture of sand, cement etc., used in building —a. 2. made of concrete 3. particular, specific 4. perceptible, actual 5. solid —'**concretely** adv. —**con'cretion** n. 1. mass of compressed particles 2. stonelike growth in body

concubine ('kɒŋkjʊbaɪn, 'kɒn-) n. 1. woman living with man as his wife, but not married to him **2.** 'secondary' wife of inferior legal status —**concubinage** (kɒn'kjuːbɪnɪdʒ) n.

concupiscence (kɒn'kjuːpɪsəns) n. lust

concur (kən'kɜː) vi. **1.** agree, express agreement **2.** happen together **3.** coincide (-**rr**-) —**con'currence** n. —**con'current** a. —**con'currently** adv. at the same time

concuss (kən'kʌs) vt. injure (brain) by blow, fall etc. —**con'cussion** n. **1.** brain injury **2.** physical shock

condemn (kən'dɛm) vt. **1.** blame **2.** find guilty **3.** doom **4.** find, declare unfit for use —**condemnation** (kɒndɛm'neɪʃən) n. —**condemnatory** (kɒndɛm'neɪtərɪ) a.

condense (kən'dɛns) vt. **1.** concentrate, make more solid **2.** turn from gas into liquid **3.** pack into few words —vi. **4.** turn from gas to liquid —**conden'sation** n. —**con'denser** n. **1.** Elec. apparatus for storing electrical energy, a capacitor **2.** apparatus for reducing vapours to liquid form **3.** a lens or mirror for focusing light —**condensed milk** milk reduced by evaporation to thick concentration, with sugar added

condescend (kɒndɪ'sɛnd) vi. **1.** treat graciously one regarded as inferior **2.** do something below one's dignity —**conde'scending** a. —**conde'scension** n.

condign (kən'daɪn) a. (esp. of punishment) fitting; deserved

condiment ('kɒndɪmənt) n. relish, seasoning for food

condition (kən'dɪʃən) n. **1.** state or circumstances of anything **2.** thing on which statement or happening or existing depends **3.** stipulation, prerequisite **4.** health, physical fitness **5.** rank —vt. **6.** accustom **7.** regulate **8.** make fit, healthy **9.** be essential to happening or existence of —**con'ditional** a. **1.** dependent on circumstances or events —n. **2.** Gram. conditional verb form, clause etc. —**conditioned reflex** in psychology and physiology, automatic response induced by stimulus repeatedly applied

condole (kən'dəʊl) vi. **1.** grieve (with), offer sympathy **2.** commiserate (with) —**con'dolence** n.

condom ('kɒndəm) n. sheathlike rubber contraceptive device worn by man

condominium (kɒndə'mɪnɪəm) n. joint rule by two or more states

condone (kən'dəʊn) vt. overlook, forgive, treat as not existing

condor ('kɒndɔː) n. large vulture found in the Andes

conduce (kən'djuːs) vi. (with to) **1.** help, promote **2.** tend (towards) —**con'ducive** a.

conduct ('kɒndʌkt) n. **1.** behaviour **2.** management —vt. (kən'dʌkt) **3.** escort, guide **4.** lead, direct **5.** manage **6.** transmit (heat,

electricity) —**con'ductance** n. ability of system to conduct electricity —**con'duction** n. —**con'ductive** a. —**conduc'tivity** n. —**con'ductor** n. **1.** person in charge of bus etc., who collects fares **2.** director of orchestra **3.** one who leads, guides **4.** substance capable of transmitting heat, electricity etc. **5.** US official in charge of passenger train

conduit ('kɒndɪt, -djʊt) n. channel or pipe for conveying water, electric cables etc.

cone (kəʊn) n. **1.** solid figure with circular base, tapering to a point **2.** fruit of pine, fir etc. —'**conic(al)** a. of or like cone —**conic section** one of group of curves formed by intersection of plane and right circular cone

confabulate (kən'fæbjʊleɪt) vi. chat —'**confab** n. inf. shortened form of confabu'lation n. confidential conversation

confection (kən'fɛkʃən) n. prepared delicacy, esp. something sweet —**con'fectioner** n. dealer in fancy cakes, pastries, sweets etc. —**con'fectionery** n. sweets, cakes etc.

confederate (kən'fɛdərɪt) n. **1.** ally **2.** accomplice —v. (kən'fɛdəreɪt) **3.** unite —**con'federacy** n. —**confede'ration** n. alliance of political units

confer (kən'fɜː) vt. **1.** grant, give **2.** bestow **3.** award —vi. **4.** consult together (-**rr**-) —'**conference** n. meeting for consultation or deliberation —**con'ferment** n.

confess (kən'fɛs) vt. **1.** admit, own **2.** (of priest) hear sins of —vi. **3.** acknowledge **4.** declare one's sins orally to priest —**con'fession** n. —**con'fessional** n. confessor's stall or box —**con'fessor** n. priest who hears confessions

confetti (kən'fɛtɪ) n. small bits of coloured paper for throwing at weddings

confide (kən'faɪd) vi. **1.** (with in) tell secrets, trust —vt. **2.** entrust —**confidant** (kɒnfɪ'dænt, 'kɒnfɪdænt) n. one entrusted with secrets (-**e** fem.) —**confidence** (kɒnfɪdəns) n. **1.** trust **2.** boldness, assurance **3.** intimacy **4.** something confided, secret —**confident** ('kɒnfɪdənt) a. **1.** having or showing certainty; sure **2.** sure of oneself **3.** presumptuous —**confidential** (kɒnfɪ'dɛnʃəl) a. **1.** private **2.** secret **3.** entrusted with another's confidences —**confidentially** (kɒnfɪ'dɛnʃəlɪ) adv. —**confidently** (kɒnfɪdəntlɪ) adv. —**con'fiding** a. unsuspicious; trustful —**confidence trick** swindle in which victim entrusts money etc., to thief, believing him honest

configuration (kənfɪgjʊ'reɪʃən) n. shape, aspect, conformation, arrangement

confine (kən'faɪn) vt. **1.** keep within bounds **2.** keep in house, bed etc. **3.** shut up, imprison —**con'finement** n. **1.** act of confining or state of

being confined **2.** period of birth of child
—'**confines** pl.n. boundaries, limits

confirm (kən'fɜːm) vt. **1.** make certain of,
verify **2.** strengthen, settle **3.** make valid, ratify
4. administer confirmation to —**confir'mation**
n. **1.** making strong, certain **2.** rite administered
by bishop to confirm vows made at baptism
—**con'firmative** or **con'firmatory** a. **1.** tending
to confirm or establish **2.** corroborative
—**con'firmed** a. (of habit etc.) long-established

confiscate ('konfiskeit) vt. seize by authority
—**confis'cation** n. —**con'fiscatory** a.

conflagration (konflə'greiʃən) n. great destructive fire

conflate (kən'fleit) vt. combine, blend to form
whole

conflict ('konflikt) n. **1.** struggle, trial of
strength **2.** disagreement —vi. (kən'flikt) **1.** be
at odds (with), be inconsistent (with) **4.** clash

confluence ('konfluəns) or **conflux**
('konflʌks) n. **1.** union of streams **2.** meeting
place —'**confluent** a.

conform (kən'fɔːm) vi. **1.** comply with
accepted standards, conventions etc. —v. **2.**
adapt to rule, pattern, custom etc. —**con'form-
able** a. —**con'formably** adv. —**confor'mation** n.
structure, adaptation —**con'formist** n. one who
conforms, esp. excessively —**con'formity** n.
compliance

confound (kən'faund) vt. **1.** baffle, perplex **2.**
confuse **3.** defeat —**con'founded** a. esp. inf.
damned

confrère ('konfreə) n. fellow member of
profession etc.

confront (kən'frʌnt) vt. **1.** face **2.** bring face to
face (with) —**confron'tation** n.

Confucianism (kən'fjuːʃənizəm) n. ethical
system of Confucius, Chinese philosopher,
emphasizing devotion to family, peace and
justice

confuse (kən'fjuːz) vt. **1.** bewilder **2.** jumble **3.**
make unclear **4.** mistake (one thing) for another
5. disconcert —**con'fusion** n.

confute (kən'fjuːt) vt. prove wrong **2.**
disprove —**confu'tation** n.

conga ('kongə) n. Latin American dance
performed by number of people in single file

congé ('konʒei) n. **1.** permission to depart or
dismissal, esp. when formal **2.** farewell

congeal (kən'dʒiːl) v. solidify by cooling or
freezing —**conge'lation** n.

congener (kən'dʒiːnə, 'kondʒinə) n. member
of class, group etc. esp. any animal of specified
genus

congenial (kən'dʒiːnjəl) a. **1.** pleasant, to one's
liking **2.** of similar disposition, tastes etc.
—**congeni'ality** n. —**con'genially** adv.

congenital (kən'dʒenitəl) a. **1.** existing at birth
2. dating from birth

conger ('kongə) n. variety of large, voracious,
sea eel

congeries (kən'dʒiəriːz) n. sing. and pl.
collection or mass of small bodies, conglomera-
tion

congest (kən'dʒest) v. overcrowd or clog
—**con'gested** a. —**con'gestion** n. abnormal
accumulation, overcrowding

conglomerate (kən'glomərit) n. **1.** thing,
substance (esp. rock) composed of mixture of
other, smaller elements or pieces **2.** business
organization comprising many companies —v.
(kən'gloməreit) **3.** gather together —a. **4.** made
up of heterogeneous elements **5.** (of sedimentary rocks) consisting of rounded fragments
within finer matrix —**conglomer'ation** n.

congratulate (kən'grætjuleit) vt. express
pleasure at good fortune, success etc.
—**congratu'lation** n. —**con'gratulatory** a.

congregate ('kongrigeit) v. **1.** assemble **2.**
collect, flock together —**congre'gation** n.
assembly, esp. for worship —**congre'gational** a.
—**Congre'gationalism** n. system in which each
separate church is self-governing —**Congre'ga-
tionalist** n.

congress ('kongres) n. **1.** meeting **2.** formal
assembly for discussion **3.** legislative body
—**con'gressional** a. —'**congressman** n. member of the U.S. Congress

congruent ('kongruənt) a. **1.** suitable, accordant **2.** fitting together, esp. triangles —'**congru-
ence** n. —**con'gruity** n. —'**congruous** a.

conic(al) ('konik(əl)) a. see CONE

conifer ('kəunifə, 'kon-) n. cone-bearing tree,
as fir, pine etc. —**co'niferous** a.

conjecture (kən'dʒektʃə) n. **1.** guess, guesswork —v. **2.** guess, surmise —**con'jectural** a.

conjoin (kən'dʒɔin) vt. **1.** combine —vi. **2.**
come, or act, together —**con'joint** a. concerted,
united —**con'jointly** adv.

conjugal ('kondʒugəl) a. **1.** relating to
marriage **2.** between married persons —**conju-
'gality** n.

conjugate ('kondʒugeit) vt. inflect verb in its
various forms (past, present etc.) —**conju'gation** n.

conjunction (kən'dʒʌŋkʃən) n. **1.** union **2.**
simultaneous happening **3.** part of speech
joining words, phrases etc. —**con'junctive** a.
—**con'juncture** n.

conjunctiva (kondʒʌŋk'taivə) n. mucous
membrane lining eyelid —**conjuncti'vitis** n.
inflammation of this

conjure ('kʌndʒə) vi. **1.** produce magic effects
2. perform tricks by jugglery etc. **3.** invoke
devils —vt. (kən'dʒuə) **4.** implore earnestly

—**conju'ration** n. —**'conjurer** or **'conjuror** n. —**conjure up** 1. present to the mind 2. call up (spirit or devil) by incantation

conk (koŋk) inf. vt. 1. strike (esp. on head) —n. 2. nose —**conk out** inf. 1. break down 2. tire suddenly; collapse

conker ('koŋkə) n. inf. horse chestnut

connect (kə'nɛkt) v. 1. join together, unite —vt. 2. associate in the mind —**con'nection** or **con'nexion** n. 1. association 2. train etc. timed to enable passengers to transfer from another 3. family relation —**con'nective** a. —**connecting rod** that part of engine which transfers motion from piston to crankshaft

conning tower ('koniŋ) armoured control position in submarine, battleship etc. (see also CONⁿ)

connive (kə'naɪv) vi. 1. plot, conspire 2. assent, refrain from preventing or forbidding —**con'nivance** n.

connoisseur (koni'sɜː) n. 1. critical expert in matters of taste, esp. fine arts 2. competent judge

connote (kə'nəʊt) vt. imply, mean in addition to primary meaning —**conno'tation** n.

connubial (kə'njuːbɪəl) a. of marriage

conquer ('koŋkə) vt. 1. win by force of arms, overcome 2. defeat —vi. 3. be victorious —'**conqueror** n. —'**conquest** n.

conquistador (kon'kwɪstədɔː) n. adventurer or conqueror, esp. one of Sp. conquerors of New World in 16th cent. (pl. **-s, -dores** (-dɔːrɛs))

Cons. Conservative

consanguinity (konsæŋ'gwɪnɪtɪ) n. kinship —**consan'guineous** a.

conscience ('konʃəns) n. sense of right or wrong governing person's words and actions —**consci'entious** a. 1. scrupulous 2. obedient to the dictates of conscience —**consci'entiously** adv. —**conscience money** money paid voluntarily to compensate for dishonesty, esp. for taxes formerly evaded —**conscience-stricken** a. feeling anxious or guilty (also **conscience-smitten**) —**conscientious objector** one who refuses military service on moral or religious grounds

conscious ('konʃəs) a. 1. aware 2. awake to one's surroundings and identity 3. deliberate, intentional —'**consciously** adv. —'**consciousness** n. being conscious

conscript ('konskrɪpt) n. 1. one compulsorily enlisted for military service —vt. (kon'skrɪpt) 2. enrol for compulsory military service —**con'scription** n.

consecrate ('konsɪkreɪt) vt. make sacred —**conse'cration** n.

consecutive (kən'sɛkjʊtɪv) a. in unbroken succession —**con'secutively** adv.

consensus (kən'sɛnsəs) n. widespread agreement, unanimity

consent (kən'sɛnt) vi. 1. agree, comply —n. 2. acquiescence 3. permission 4. agreement —**con'sentient** a.

consequence ('konsɪkwəns) n. 1. result, effect, outcome 2. that which naturally follows 3. significance, importance —'**consequent** a. —**conse'quential** a. important —'**consequently** adv. therefore, as a result

conservatoire (kən'sɜːvətwɑː) n. school for teaching music

conserve (kən'sɜːv) vt. 1. keep from change or decay 2. preserve 3. maintain —n. ('konsɜːv, kən'sɜːv) 4. jam, preserved fruit etc. —**con'servancy** n. 1. UK court or commission with jurisdiction over river, port etc. 2. conservation —**conser'vation** n. protection, careful management of natural resources and environment —**conser'vationist** n./a. —**con'servatism** n. —**con'servative** a. 1. tending, or wishing to conserve 2. moderate —n. 3. Pol. one who desires to preserve institutions of his country against change and innovation 4. one opposed to hasty changes or innovations —**con'servatory** n. greenhouse —**conservation of energy** principle that total energy of isolated system is constant and independent of changes occurring within system —**conservation of mass** principle that total mass of isolated system is constant and independent of chemical and physical changes taking place within system

consider (kən'sɪdə) vt. 1. think over 2. examine 3. make allowance for 4. have as opinion 5. discuss —**con'siderable** a. 1. important 2. somewhat large —**con'siderably** adv. —**con'siderate** a. thoughtful for others' feelings, careful —**con'siderately** adv. —**conside'ration** n. 1. deliberation 2. point of importance 3. thoughtfulness 4. bribe, recompense —**con'sidered** a. 1. presented or thought out with care 2. esteemed —**con'sidering** prep. 1. in view of —adv. 2. inf. all in all; taking circumstances into account —conj. 3. in view of the fact (that)

consign (kən'saɪn) vt. 1. commit, hand over 2. entrust to carrier —**consign'ee** n. —**con'signment** n. goods consigned —**con'signor** n.

consist (kən'sɪst) vi. 1. be composed (of) 2. (with in) have as basis 3. agree (with), be compatible (with) —**con'sistency** or **con'sistence** n. 1. agreement 2. harmony 3. degree of firmness —**con'sistent** a. 1. unchanging, constant 2. agreeing (with) —**con'sistently** adv.

consistory (kən'sɪstərɪ) n. ecclesiastical court or council, esp. of Pope and Cardinals

console¹ (kən'səʊl) vt. comfort, cheer in distress —**conso'lation** n. —**consolatory** (kən'sɒlətərɪ) a.

console³ ('kɒnsəul) n. 1. bracket supporting shelf 2. keyboard, stops etc., of organ 3. cabinet for television, radio etc.

consolidate (kən'sɒlɪdeɪt) vt. 1. combine into connected whole 2. make firm, secure —**consoli'dation** n.

consols ('kɒnsɒlz, kən'sɒlz) pl.n. Brit. government securities

consommé (kən'sɒmeɪ) n. clear meat soup

consonant ('kɒnsənənt) n. 1. sound making a syllable only with vowel 2. non-vowel —a. 3. agreeing, in accord —'**consonance** n.

consort (kən'sɔːt) vi. 1. associate, keep company —n. ('kɒnsɔːt) 2. husband, wife, esp. of ruler 3. ship sailing with another —**con'sortium** n. association of banks, companies etc.

conspectus (kən'spɛktəs) n. 1. a comprehensive view or survey of subject 2. synopsis

conspicuous (kən'spɪkjʊəs) a. 1. striking, noticeable, outstanding 2. prominent 3. eminent —**con'spicuously** adv.

conspire (kən'spaɪə) vi. 1. combine for evil purpose 2. plot, devise —**conspiracy** (kən'spɪrə-sɪ) n. —**conspirator** (kən'spɪrətə) n. —**conspiratorial** (kənspɪrə'tɔːrɪəl) a.

constable ('kʌnstəbʰl, 'kɒn-) n. 1. policeman of the lowest rank 2. Hist. officer of the peace —**con'stabulary** n. police force

constant ('kɒnstənt) a. 1. fixed, unchanging 2. steadfast 3. always duly happening or continuing —n. 4. quantity that does not vary —'**constancy** n. 1. steadfastness 2. loyalty —'**constantly** adv.

constellation (kɒnstɪ'leɪʃən) n. group of stars

consternation (kɒnstə'neɪʃən) n. alarm, dismay, panic —'**consternate** vt.

constipation (kɒnstɪ'peɪʃən) n. difficulty in emptying bowels —'**constipate** vt. affect with this disorder

constituent (kən'stɪtjʊənt) a. 1. going towards making up whole 2. having power to make, alter constitution of state 3. electing representative —n. 4. component part 5. element 6. elector —**con'stituency** n. 1. body of electors 2. parliamentary division

constitute ('kɒnstɪtjuːt) vt. 1. compose, set up, establish, form 2. make into, found, give form to —**consti'tution** n. 1. structure, composition 2. health 3. character, disposition 4. principles on which state is governed —**consti'tutional** a. 1. pert. to constitution 2. in harmony with political constitution —n. 3. walk taken for health's sake —**consti'tutionally** adv. —'**constitutive** a. 1. having power to enact or establish 2. see CONSTITUENT (sense 1)

constrain (kən'streɪn) vt. force, compel —**con'straint** n. 1. compulsion 2. restraint 3. embarrassment, tension

constriction (kən'strɪkʃən) n. compression, squeezing together —**con'strict** vt. —**con'strictive** a. —**con'strictor** n. that which constricts (see also BOA (sense 1))

construct (kən'strʌkt) vt. 1. make, build, form 2. put together 3. compose —n. ('kɒnstrʌkt) 4. something formulated systematically —**con'struction** n. —**con'structive** a. 1. serving to improve 2. positive —**con'structively** adv.

construe (kən'struː) vt. 1. interpret 2. deduce 3. analyse grammatically

consul ('kɒnsʰl) n. 1. officer appointed by a government to represent it in a foreign country 2. in ancient Rome, one of the chief magistrates —**consular** ('kɒnsjʊlə) a. —**consulate** ('kɒnsjʊ-lɪt) n. —'**consulship** n.

consult (kən'sʌlt) vt. seek counsel, advice, information from —**con'sultant** n. 1. specialist, expert 2. senior hospital physician or surgeon —**consul'tation** n. 1. consulting 2. appointment to seek professional advice, esp. of doctor, lawyer —**con'sultative** a. 1. having privilege of consulting, but not of voting 2. advisory

consume (kən'sjuːm) vt. 1. eat or drink 2. engross, possess 3. use up 4. destroy —**con'sumer** n. 1. buyer or user of commodity 2. one who consumes —**con'sumerism** n. 1. protection of interests of consumers 2. advocacy of high rate of consumption as basis for sound economy —**consumption** (kən'sʌmpʃən) n. 1. using up 2. destruction 3. wasting disease, esp. tuberculosis of the lungs —**consumptive** (kən'sʌmptɪv) a./n. —**consumptiveness** (kən-'sʌmptɪvnɪs) n.

consummate ('kɒnsəmeɪt) vt. 1. perfect 2. fulfil 3. complete (esp. marriage by sexual intercourse) —a. (kən'sʌmɪt, 'kɒnsəmɪt) 4. of greatest perfection or completeness —**con'summately** adv. —**consum'mation** n.

cont. continued

contact ('kɒntækt) n. 1. touching 2. being in touch 3. junction of two or more electrical conductors 4. useful acquaintance —vt. ('kɒntækt, kən'tækt) 5. put, come or be in touch (with) —**contact lens** lens fitting over eyeball to correct defect of vision

contagion (kən'teɪdʒən) n. 1. passing on of disease by touch, contact 2. contagious disease 3. harmful physical or moral influence —**con'tagious** a. communicable by contact, catching

contain (kən'teɪn) vt. 1. hold 2. have room for 3. include, comprise 4. restrain —**con'tainer** n. 1. box etc. for holding 2. large cargo-carrying standard-sized receptacle for different modes of transport —**container'ization** or -**i'sation** n. —**con'tainerize** or -**ise** vt. 1. convey in standard-sized containers 2. adapt to use of standard-sized containers —**con'tainment** n. act of containing, *esp.* of restraining power of hostile country or operations of hostile military force

contaminate (kən'tæmɪneɪt) *vt.* **1.** stain, pollute, infect **2.** make radioactive —**contami-'nation** *n.* pollution

contemn (kən'tɛm) *vt.* regard with contempt; scorn

contemplate ('kɒntɛmpleɪt) *vt.* **1.** reflect, meditate on **2.** gaze upon **3.** intend —**contem-'plation** *n.* **1.** thoughtful consideration **2.** spiritual meditation —**'contemplative** *a./n.* (one) given to contemplation

contemporary (kən'tɛmprərɪ) *a.* **1.** existing or lasting at same time **2.** of same age **3.** present-day —*n.* **4.** one existing at same time as another —**contempo'raneous** *a.*

contempt (kən'tɛmpt) *n.* **1.** feeling that something is worthless, despicable *etc.* **2.** expression of this feeling **3.** state of being despised, disregarded **4.** wilful disrespect of authority

contend (kən'tɛnd) *vi.* **1.** strive, fight —*v.* **2.** dispute —*vt.* **3.** maintain —**con'tention** *n.* **1.** strife **2.** debate **3.** subject matter of dispute —**con'tentious** *a.* **1.** quarrelsome **2.** causing dispute —**con'tentiously** *adv.*

content[1] ('kɒntɛnt) *n.* **1.** that contained **2.** holding capacity —*pl.* **3.** that contained **4.** index of topics in book

content[2] (kən'tɛnt) *a.* **1.** satisfied **2.** willing —*vt.* **3.** satisfy —*n.* **4.** satisfaction —**con'tented** *a.* —**con'tentment** *n.*

conterminous (kən'tɜːmɪnəs) *or* **coterminous** (kəʊ'tɜːmɪnəs) *a.* **1.** of the same extent (in time *etc.*) **2.** meeting along a common boundary **3.** meeting end to end

contest ('kɒntɛst) *n.* **1.** competition **2.** conflict —*vt.* (kən'tɛst) **3.** dispute, debate **4.** fight or compete for —**con'testable** *a.* —**con'testant** *n.* —**contes'tation** *n.*

context ('kɒntɛkst) *n.* **1.** words coming before, after a word or passage **2.** conditions and circumstances of event, fact *etc.* —**con'textual** *a.*

contiguous (kən'tɪgjʊəs) *a.* touching, near —**conti'guity** *n.*

continent[1] ('kɒntɪnənt) *n.* large continuous mass of land —**conti'nental** *a.* —**continental breakfast** light breakfast of coffee and rolls —**continental drift** *Geol.* theory that earth's continents move gradually over surface of planet on substratum of magma —**continental quilt** UK quilt, stuffed with down, used as bed cover in place of top sheet and blankets (*also* **'duvet**) —**continental shelf** sea bed surrounding continent at depths of up to about 200 metres

continent[2] ('kɒntɪnənt) *a.* **1.** able to control

one's urination and defecation **2.** sexually chaste —**'continence** *n.*

contingent (kən'tɪndʒənt) *a.* **1.** depending **2.** possible **3.** accidental —*n.* **4.** group (of troops, sportsmen *etc.*) part of or representative of a larger group —**con'tingency** *n.* —**con'tingently** *adv.*

continue (kən'tɪnjuː) *v.* **1.** remain, keep in existence **2.** carry on, last, go on **3.** resume **4.** prolong —**con'tinual** *a.* recurring frequently, *esp.* at regular intervals —**con'tinually** *adv.* —**con'tinuance** *n.* **1.** act of continuing **2.** duration of action *etc.* **3.** US adjournment of legal proceeding —**continu'ation** *n.* **1.** extension, extra part **2.** resumption **3.** constant succession, prolongation —**conti'nuity** *n.* **1.** logical sequence **2.** state of being continuous —**con'tinuo** *n. Mus.* bass part underlying piece of concerted music (*also* **basso continuo, thorough bass**) **2.** thorough-bass part as played on keyboard instrument (*pl.* **-s**) —**con'tinuous** *a.* unceasing —**con'tinuously** *adv.* —**con'tinuum** *n.* continuous series or whole with no part perceptibly different from adjacent parts (*pl.* **-'tinua, -s**)

contort (kən'tɔːt) *vt.* twist out of normal shape —**con'tortion** *n.* —**con'tortionist** *n.* one who contorts his body to entertain

contour ('kɒntʊə) *n.* outline, shape, *esp.* mountains, coast *etc.* —**contour line** line on map drawn through places of same height —**contour map**

contra- (*comb. form*) against, as in *contraposition.* Such words are omitted where the meaning may easily be inferred from the simple word

contraband ('kɒntrəbænd) *n.* **1.** smuggled goods **2.** illegal traffic in such goods —*a.* **3.** prohibited by law

contraception (kɒntrə'sɛpʃən) *n.* prevention of conception usu. by artificial means, birth control —**contra'ceptive** *a./n.*

contract (kən'trækt) *v.* **1.** make or become smaller, shorter —*vi.* ('kɒntrækt) **2.** make a contract —*vt.* **3.** become affected by **4.** incur **5.** undertake by contract —*n.* ('kɒntrækt) **6.** bargain, agreement **7.** formal document recording agreement **8.** agreement enforceable by law —**con'tracted** *a.* drawn together —**con'tractile** *a.* tending to contract —**con-'traction** *n.* —**con'tractor** *n.* one making contract, *esp.* builder —**con'tractual** *a.*

contradict (kɒntrə'dɪkt) *vt.* **1.** deny **2.** be at variance or inconsistent with —**contra'diction** *n.* —**contra'dictious** *a.* —**contra'dictor** *n.* —**contra'dictory** *a.*

contradistinction (kɒntrədɪ'stɪŋkʃən) *n.* distinction made by contrasting different qualities

contralto (kən'træltəʊ) n. lowest of three female voices (pl. **-s**)

contraption (kən'træpʃən) n. 1. gadget 2. device 3. construction, device oft. overelaborate or eccentric

contrapuntal (kɒntrə'pʌntəl) a. Mus. pert. to counterpoint

contrary ('kɒntrərɪ) a. 1. opposed 2. opposite, other 3. (kən'treərɪ) perverse, obstinate —n. 4. something the exact opposite of another —adv. 5. in opposition —**contra'riety** n. —**con'trarily** adv. —'**contrariwise** adv. conversely

contrast (kən'trɑːst) vt. 1. distinguish by comparison of unlike or opposite qualities —vi. 2. show great difference —n. ('kɒntrɑːst) 3. striking difference 4. T.V. sharpness of image

contravene (kɒntrə'viːn) vt. 1. transgress, infringe 2. conflict with 3. contradict —**contra'vention** n.

contretemps ('kɒntrətɑːn) n. unexpected and embarrassing situation or mishap

contribute (kən'trɪbjuːt) v. 1. give, pay to common fund 2. write (articles etc.) for the press —vi. 3. help to occur —**contri'bution** n. —**con'tributive** a. —**con'tributor** n. 1. one who writes articles for newspapers etc. 2. one who donates —**con'tributory** a. 1. partly responsible 2. giving to pension fund etc.

contrite (kən'traɪt, 'kɒntraɪt) a. remorseful for wrongdoing, penitent —**con'tritely** adv. —**contrition** (kən'trɪʃən) n.

contrive (kən'traɪv) vt. 1. manage 2. devise, invent, design —v. 3. plot, scheme —**con'trivance** n. artifice or device —**con'trived** a. obviously planned, artificial —**con'triver** n.

control (kən'trəʊl) vt. 1. command, dominate 2. regulate 3. direct, check, test (**-ll-**) —n. 4. power to direct or determine 5. curb, check 6. standard of comparison in experiment —pl. 7. system of instruments to control car, aircraft etc. —**con'trollable** a. —**con'troller** n. 1. one who controls 2. official controlling expenditure —**control tower** tower in airfield from which take-offs and landings are directed

controversy ('kɒntrəvɜːsɪ, kən'trɒv-) n. dispute, debate, esp. over public issues —**contro'versial** a. —**contro'versialist** n. —'**controvert** vt. 1. deny 2. argue about —**contro'vertible** a.

contumacy ('kɒntjʊməsɪ) n. stubborn disobedience —**contu'macious** a.

contumely ('kɒntjʊmɪlɪ) n. insulting language or treatment —**contumelious** (kɒntjʊ'miːlɪəs) a. abusive, insolent

contusion (kən'tjuːʒən) n. bruise —**con'tuse** vt. bruise

conundrum (kə'nʌndrəm) n. riddle, esp. with punning answer

conurbation (kɒnɜː'beɪʃən) n. densely populated urban sprawl formed by spreading of towns

convalesce (kɒnvə'lɛs) vi. recover health after illness, operation etc. —**conva'lescence** n. —**conva'lescent** a./n.

convection (kən'vɛkʃən) n. transmission, esp. of heat, by currents in liquids or gases —**con'vector** n.

convene (kən'viːn) vt. call together, assemble, convoke —**convention** (kən'vɛnʃən) n. 1. assembly 2. treaty, agreement 3. rule 4. practice based on agreement 5. accepted usage —**conventional** (kən'vɛnʃənəl) a. 1. (slavishly) observing customs of society 2. customary 3. (of weapons, war etc.) not nuclear —**conventionality** (kənvɛnʃə'nælɪtɪ) n. —**conventionally** (kən'vɛnʃənəlɪ) adv.

convenient (kən'viːnɪənt) a. 1. handy 2. favourable to needs, comfort 3. well-adapted to one's purpose —**con'venience** n. 1. ease, comfort, suitability 2. (public) lavatory —a. 3. (of food) quick to prepare —**con'veniently** adv.

convent ('kɒnvənt) n. 1. religious community, esp. of nuns 2. their building 3. school in which teachers are nuns (also **convent school**) —**con'ventual** a.

conventicle (kən'vɛntɪkəl) n. 1. secret or unauthorized assembly for worship 2. small meeting house or chapel, esp. of Dissenters

converge (kən'vɜːdʒ) vi. 1. move towards same point 2. meet, join 3. Maths. (of infinite series) approach finite limit as number of terms increases —**con'vergence** or **con'vergency** n. —**con'vergent** a.

conversant (kən'vɜːsənt) a. acquainted, familiar, versed (in)

converse[1] (kən'vɜːs) vi. 1. talk —n. ('kɒnvɜːs) 2. talk —**conver'sation** n. —**conver'sational** a. —**conver'sationalist** n.

converse[2] ('kɒnvɜːs) a. 1. opposite, turned round, reversed —n. 2. the opposite, contrary

convert (kən'vɜːt) vt. 1. apply to another purpose 2. change 3. transform 4. cause to adopt (another) religion, opinion —vi. 5. Rugby make a conversion —n. ('kɒnvɜːt) 6. converted person —**con'version** n. 1. change of state 2. unauthorized appropriation 3. change of opinion, religion or party 4. Rugby score made after a try by kicking ball over crossbar —**con'verter** n. 1. one who, that which converts 2. electrical machine for changing alternating current into direct current 3. vessel in which molten metal is refined —**con'vertible** n. 1. car with folding roof —a. 2. capable of being converted 3. (of car) having folding or removable roof

convex ('kɒnvɛks, kɒn'vɛks) a. 1. curved outwards 2. of a rounded form —**con'vexity** n.

convey (kən'veı) vt. 1. carry, transport 2. impart, communicate 3. Law make over, transfer —**con'veyance** n. 1. carrying 2. vehicle 3. act by which title to property is transferred —**con'veyancer** n. one skilled in legal forms of transferring property —**con'veyancing** n. this work —**conveyor belt** continuous moving belt for transporting things, esp. in factory

convict (kən'vıkt) vt. 1. prove or declare guilty —n. ('kɒnvıkt) 2. person found guilty of crime 3. criminal serving prison sentence —**con'viction** n. 1. verdict of guilty 2. being convinced, firm belief, state of being sure

convince (kən'vıns) vt. firmly persuade, satisfy by evidence or argument —**con'vincing** a. capable of compelling belief, effective

convivial (kən'vıvıəl) a. sociable, festive, jovial —**convivi'ality** n.

convoke (kən'vəʊk) vt. call together —**convo-'cation** n. calling together, assembly, esp. of clergy, university graduates etc.

convolute ('kɒnvəlu:t) vt. twist, coil, tangle —**'convoluted** a. —**convo'lution** n.

convolvulus (kən'vɒlvjʊləs) n. genus of plants with twining stems

convoy ('kɒnvɔı) n. 1. party of ships, troops, lorries etc. travelling together for protection —vt. 2. escort for protection

convulse (kən'vʌls) vt. 1. shake violently 2. affect with violent involuntary contractions of muscles —**con'vulsion** n. 1. violent upheaval —pl. 2. spasms 3. fits of laughter or hysteria —**con'vulsive** a. —**con'vulsively** adv.

cony or **coney** ('kəʊnı) n. rabbit

coo (ku:) n. 1. cry of doves —vi. 2. make such cry (**cooed**, **'cooing**)

cooee or **cooey** ('ku:i:) interj. 1. call to attract attention —n. 2. A, NZ inf. calling distance (esp. in **within (a) cooee (of)**) —vi. 3. utter this call ('**cooeeing**, '**cooeed** or '**cooeying**, '**cooeyed**)

cook (kuk) vt. 1. prepare (food) for table, esp. by heat 2. inf. falsify (accounts etc.) —vi. 3. undergo cooking 4. act as cook —n. 5. one who prepares food for table —'**cooker** n. 1. cooking apparatus 2. cooking apple —'**cookery** n. —'**cookie** n. esp. US biscuit —**cook up** 1. inf. invent, plan 2. prepare (meal)

cool (ku:l) a. 1. moderately cold 2. unexcited, calm 3. lacking friendliness or interest 4. inf. calmly insolent 5. inf. sophisticated, elegant —v. 6. make, become cool —n. 7. cool time, place etc. 8. inf. calmness, composure —'**coolant** n. fluid used for cooling tool, machinery etc. —'**cooler** n. 1. vessel in which liquids are cooled 2. sl. prison —'**coolly** adv. —**cooling tower** structure, designed to permit free passage of air, inside which hot water trickles down, becoming cool as it does so

coolie or **cooly** ('ku:lı) n. oft. offens. cheaply hired oriental unskilled labourer

coomb, combe, coombe, or **comb** (ku:m) n. valley

coon (ku:n) n. sl. offens. coloured person

coop[1] (ku:p) n. 1. cage or pen for fowls —vt. (oft. with up) 2. shut up in a coop 3. confine

coop[2] or **co-op** ('kəʊɒp) n. cooperative society or shop run by one

cooper ('ku:pə) n. one who makes casks

cooperate or **co-operate** (kəʊ'ɒpəreıt) vi. work together —**coope'ration** or **co-operation** n. —**co'operative** or **co-operative** a. 1. willing to cooperate 2. (of an enterprise) owned collectively and managed for joint economic benefit —n. 3. cooperative organization, such as farm —**co'operator** or **co-operator** n.

coopt or **co-opt** (kəʊ'ɒpt) vt. bring on (committee etc.) as member, colleague, without election by larger body choosing fresh members

coordinate or **co-ordinate** (kəʊ'ɔ:dıneıt) vt. 1. bring into order as parts of whole 2. place in same rank 3. put into harmony —n. (kəʊ'ɔ:dınıt) 4. Maths. any of set of numbers defining location of point —pl. 5. clothes of matching or harmonious colours and design, suitable for wearing together —a. (kəʊ'ɔ:dınıt) 6. equal in degree, status etc. —**coordi'nation** or **co-ordination** n. —**co'ordinative** or **co-ordinative** a.

coot (ku:t) n. 1. small black water fowl 2. sl. silly (old) person

cop (kɒp) sl. vt. 1. catch 2. (usu. with it) be punished —n. 3. policeman 4. a capture —**cop-out** n. sl. act of copping out —**cop out** sl. fail to assume responsibility, fail to perform

copal ('kəʊpəl, -pæl) n. resin used in varnishes

copartner (kəʊ'pa:tnə) n. joint partner —**co'partnership** n.

cope[1] (kəʊp) vi. deal successfully

cope[2] (kəʊp) n. ecclesiastical vestment like long cloak

Copernican (kə'pз:nıkən) a. pert. to Copernicus, Polish astronomer (1473-1543), or to his system —**Copernican system** theory published by Copernicus, which stated that earth and planets rotated around sun

copestone ('kəʊpstəʊn) n. 1. stone used to form coping (also **coping stone**) 2. stone at top of wall etc.

copier ('kɒpıə) n. see COPY

copilot ('kəʊpaılət) n. second or relief pilot of aircraft

coping ('kəʊpıŋ) n. top course of wall, usu. sloping to throw off rain

coping saw handsaw with U-shaped frame for cutting curves in material too thick for fret saw

copious ('kɔupɪəs) a. 1. abundant 2. plentiful 3. full, ample —'**copiously** adv. —'**copiousness** n.

copper[1] ('kɔpə) n. 1. reddish-brown malleable ductile metal 2. bronze money, coin 3. large washing vessel —vt. 4. cover with copper —**copper-bottomed** a. reliable, esp. financially —'**copperplate** n. 1. plate of copper for engraving, etching 2. print from this 3. copybook writing 4. fine handwriting based upon that used on copperplate engravings —'**coppersmith** n. one who works with copper

copper[2] ('kɔpə) n. sl. policeman

coppice ('kɔpɪs) n. wood of small trees

copra ('kɔprə) n. dried coconut kernels

Copt (kɔpt) n. 1. member of Coptic Church 2. Egyptian descended from ancient Egyptians —'**Coptic** n. 1. Afro-Asiatic language, written in Greek alphabet but descended from ancient Egyptian —a. 2. of this language 3. of Copts

copula ('kɔpjulə) n. 1. word, esp. verb acting as connecting link in sentence 2. connection, tie

copulate ('kɔpjuleɪt) vi. unite sexually —**copu'lation** n. —'**copulative** a.

copy ('kɔpɪ) n. 1. imitation 2. single specimen of book 3. matter for printing 4. Journalism inf. suitable material for an article —vt. 5. make copy of, imitate 6. transcribe 7. follow example of ('**copied**, '**copying**) —'**copier** n. person or device that copies —'**copyist** n. —'**copybook** n. 1. book of specimens, esp. of penmanship, for imitation 2. chiefly US book for or containing documents —a. 3. trite, unoriginal —'**copycat** n. inf. person, esp. child, who imitates another —'**copyhold** n. Law formerly, tenure less than freehold of land in England evidenced by copy of Court roll —'**copyright** n. 1. legal exclusive right to print and publish book, article, work of art etc. —vt. 2. protect by copyright —'**copywriter** n. one who composes advertisements —**blot one's copybook** inf. sully one's reputation

coquette (kəu'kɛt, kɒ'kɛt) n. woman who flirts —**co'quetry** n. —**co'quettish** a.

coracle ('kɔrəkəl) n. boat of wicker covered with skins

coral ('kɔrəl) n. 1. hard substance made by sea polyps and forming growths, islands, reefs 2. ornament of coral —a. 3. made of coral 4. of deep pink colour —'**coralline** a.

cor anglais ('kɔːr 'ɑːngleɪ) oboe set a fifth lower than ordinary oboe

corbel ('kɔːbəl) n. stone or timber projection from wall to support something

corbie ('kɔːbɪ) n. Scot. 1. raven 2. crow

cord (kɔːd) n. 1. thin rope or thick string 2. rib on cloth 3. ribbed fabric —vt. 4. fasten with cord —'**cordage** n.

cordate ('kɔːdeɪt) a. heart-shaped

cordial ('kɔːdɪəl) a. 1. hearty, sincere, warm —n. 2. sweet, fruit-flavoured drink —**cordi'ality** n. —'**cordially** adv.

cordite ('kɔːdaɪt) n. explosive compound

cordon ('kɔːdən) n. 1. chain of troops or police 2. fruit tree grown as single stem —vt. 3. (oft. with off) form cordon around

cordon bleu (Fr. kɔrdɔ̃ 'blø) (esp. of food preparation) of highest standard

cordovan ('kɔːdəvən) n. fine leather now made principally from horsehide

corduroy ('kɔːdərɔɪ, kɔːdə'rɔɪ) n. cotton fabric with velvety, ribbed surface

cordwainer ('kɔːdweɪnə) n. obs. shoemaker or worker in leather

core (kɔː) n. 1. horny seed case of apple and other fruits 2. central or innermost part of anything —vt. 3. take out the core of

co-respondent (kəurɪ'spɒndənt) n. one cited in divorce case, alleged to have committed adultery with the respondent

corgi ('kɔːgɪ) n. a small Welsh dog

coriaceous (kɒrɪ'eɪʃəs) a. of, like leather

coriander (kɒrɪ'ændə) n. herb

Corinthian (kə'rɪnθɪən) a. 1. of Corinth 2. of Corinthian order of architecture, ornate Greek

cork (kɔːk) n. 1. bark of an evergreen Mediterranean oak tree 2. piece of it or other material, esp. used as stopper for bottle etc. —vt. 3. stop up with cork —'**corkage** n. charge for opening wine bottles in restaurant —**corked** a. tainted through having cork containing excess tannin —'**corker** n. sl. something, someone outstanding —'**corkscrew** n. tool for pulling out corks

corm (kɔːm) n. underground stem like a bulb, but more solid

cormorant ('kɔːmərənt) n. large voracious sea bird

corn[1] (kɔːn) n. 1. grain, fruit of cereals 2. grain of all kinds 3. US maize 4. oversentimental, trite quality in play, film etc. —vt. 5. preserve (meat) with salt —'**corny** a. inf. trite, oversentimental, hackneyed —'**corncrake** n. brown bird with harsh call, land rail —'**cornflakes** pl.n. breakfast cereal —'**cornflour** n. finely ground maize —'**cornflower** n. blue flower growing in cornfields

corn[2] (kɔːn) n. painful horny growth on foot or toe

cornea ('kɔːnɪə) n. transparent membrane covering front of eye

cornel ('kɔːnəl) n. any small tree with very hard wood, as the dogwood etc.

cornelian (kɔː'niːlɪən) n. precious stone, kind of chalcedony

corner ('kɔːnə) n. 1. part of room where two sides meet 2. remote or humble place 3. point where two walls, streets *etc.* meet **4.** angle, projection **5.** *Business* buying up of whole existing stock of commodity **6.** *Sport* free kick or shot from corner of field —*vt.* **7.** drive into position of difficulty, or leaving no escape **8.** acquire enough of (commodity) to attain control of the market **9.** attain control of (market) in such a manner (*also* en'gross) —*vi.* **10.** move round corner —'**cornered** *a.* —'**cornerstone** *n.* indispensable part, basis

cornet ('kɔːnɪt) *n.* **1.** trumpet with valves **2.** cone-shaped ice-cream wafer

cornice ('kɔːnɪs) *n.* **1.** projection near top of wall **2.** ornamental, carved moulding below ceiling

Cornish ('kɔːnɪʃ) *a.* **1.** of Cornwall or its inhabitants —*n.* **2.** formerly, language of Cornwall: extinct by 1800 —*pl.* **3.** natives of Cornwall —'**Cornishman** *n.* —**Cornish pasty** ('pæstɪ) *Cookery* pastry case with filling of meat and vegetables

cornucopia (kɔːnjuˈkəupɪə) *n.* symbol of plenty, consisting of goat's horn, overflowing with fruit and flowers

corolla (kəˈrɒlə) *n.* flower's inner envelope of petals

corollary (kəˈrɒlərɪ) *n.* **1.** inference from a preceding statement **2.** deduction **3.** result

corona (kəˈrəunə) *n.* **1.** halo around heavenly body **2.** flat projecting part of cornice **3.** top or crown (*pl.* **-s, -nae** (-niː)) —**co'ronal** *a.*

coronary ('kɒrənərɪ) *a.* **1.** of blood vessels surrounding heart —*n.* **2.** coronary thrombosis —**coronary thrombosis** formation of obstructing clot in coronary artery

coronation (kɒrəˈneɪʃən) *n.* ceremony of crowning a sovereign

coroner ('kɒrənə) *n.* officer who holds inquests on bodies of persons supposed killed by violence, accident *etc.* —'**coronership** *n.*

coronet ('kɒrənɪt) *n.* small crown

corporal[1] ('kɔːpərəl) *a.* **1.** of the body **2.** material, not spiritual —**corporal punishment** punishment (flogging *etc.*) of physical nature

corporal[2] ('kɔːpərəl, 'kɔːprəl) *n.* **1.** noncommissioned officer below sergeant **2.** *Navy* petty officer under a master-at-arms —**Corporal of Horse** noncommissioned rank in British army, above that of sergeant and below that of staff sergeant

corporation (kɔːpəˈreɪʃən) *n.* **1.** association, body of persons legally authorized to act as an individual **2.** authorities of town or city —'**corporate** *a.*

corporeal (kɔːˈpɔːrɪəl) *a.* **1.** of the body, material **2.** tangible

corps (kɔː) *n.* **1.** military force, body of troops **2.** any organized body of persons (*pl.* **corps** (kɔːz))

—**corps de ballet** members of ballet company who dance together in group —**corps diplomatique** (dɪpləuˈmæ'tiːk) body of diplomats accredited to state (*also* **diplomatic corps**)

corpse (kɔːps) *n.* dead body

corpulent ('kɔːpjulənt) *a.* fat —'**corpulence** *n.*

corpus ('kɔːpəs) *n.* **1.** collection or body of works, *esp.* by single author **2.** main part or body of something (*pl.* **-pora** (-pərə))

corpuscle ('kɔːpʌsəl) *n.* minute organism or particle, *esp.* red and white corpuscles of blood

corral (kɒˈrɑːl) *n.* US enclosure for cattle, or for defence

correct (kəˈrɛkt) *vt.* **1.** set right **2.** indicate errors in **3.** rebuke, punish **4.** counteract, rectify —*a.* **5.** right, exact, accurate **6.** in accordance with facts or standards —**cor'rection** *n.* —**cor'rective** *n./a.* —**cor'rectly** *adv.* —**cor'rectness** *n.*

correlate ('kɒrɪleɪt) *vt.* **1.** bring into reciprocal relation —*n.* **2.** either of two things or words necessarily implying the other —**corre'lation** *n.* —**cor'relative** *a./n.*

correspond (kɒrɪˈspɒnd) *vi.* **1.** be in agreement, be consistent (with) **2.** be similar (to) **3.** exchange letters —**corre'spondence** *n.* **1.** agreement, corresponding **2.** similarity **3.** exchange of letters **4.** letters received —**corre'spondent** *n.* **1.** writer of letters **2.** one employed by newspaper *etc.* to report on particular topic, country *etc.* —**correspondence school** educational institution that offers tuition by post

corridor ('kɒrɪdɔː) *n.* **1.** passage in building, railway train *etc.* **2.** strip of territory (or air route) not under control of state through which it passes —**corridors of power** higher echelons of government considered as location of power and influence

corrie ('kɒrɪ) *n.* **1.** *Scot.* circular hollow on hillside **2.** *Geol.* see CIRQUE

corrigendum (kɒrɪˈdʒɛndəm) *n.* thing to be corrected (*pl.* **-da** (-də))

corrigible ('kɒrɪdʒɪbl) *a.* **1.** capable of being corrected **2.** submissive

corroborate (kəˈrɒbəreɪt) *vt.* confirm, support (statement *etc.*) —**corrobo'ration** *n.* —**cor'roborative** *a.*

corroboree (kəˈrɒbərɪ) *n.* A **1.** native assembly of sacred, festive or warlike character **2.** any noisy gathering

corrode (kəˈrəud) *vt.* eat, wear away, eat into (by chemical action, disease *etc.*) —**cor'rosion** *n.* —**cor'rosive** *a.*

corrugate ('kɒrugeɪt) *v.* wrinkle, bend into wavy ridges —'**corrugated** *a.* —**corru'gation** *n.*

corrupt (kəˈrʌpt) *a.* **1.** lacking integrity **2.** open to, or involving, bribery **3.** wicked **4.** spoilt by mistakes, altered for the worse (of words, literary passages *etc.*) —*vt.* **5.** make evil, pervert **6.** bribe **7.** make rotten —**corrupti'bility** *n.* —**cor'ruptible** *a.* —**cor'ruption** *n.* —**cor'ruptly** *adv.*

corsage (kɔː'sɑː3) *n.* (flower, spray, worn on) bodice of woman's dress

corsair ('kɔːseə) *n.* pirate

corselet ('kɔːslɪt) *n.* **1.** piece of armour to cover the trunk **2.** one-piece foundation garment

corset ('kɔːsɪt) *n.* close-fitting undergarment stiffened to give support or shape to the body

cortege *or* **cortège** (kɔː'teɪ3) *n.* formal (funeral) procession

cortex ('kɔːtɛks) *n.* **1.** *Anat.* outer layer **2.** bark **3.** sheath (*pl.* **cortices** ('kɔːtɪsiːz)) —**'cortical** *a.*

cortisone ('kɔːtɪzəʊn) *n.* synthetic hormone used in the treatment of a variety of diseases

corundum (kə'rʌndəm) *n.* native crystalline aluminium oxide, used as abrasive

coruscate ('kɒrəskeɪt) *vi.* emit flashes of light; sparkle —**corus'cation** *n.*

corvette (kɔː'vɛt) *n.* lightly armed warship for escort and antisubmarine duties

corymb ('kɒrɪmb, -rɪm) *n.* inflorescence in form of flat-topped flower cluster with oldest flowers at periphery

coryza (kə'raɪzə) *n.* acute inflammation of mucous membrane of nose, with discharge of mucus; head cold

cos² *or* **cos lettuce** (kɒs) *n.* lettuce with long slender head and crisp leaves

cos² (kɒz) cosine

cosec ('kəʊsɛk) cosecant

cosecant (kəʊ'siːkənt) *n.* (of angle) trigonometric function that in right-angled triangle is ratio of length of hypotenuse to that of opposite side

cosh (kɒʃ) *n.* **1.** blunt weapon —*vt.* **2.** strike with one

cosignatory (kəʊ'sɪgnətərɪ, -trɪ) *n.* **1.** person, country *etc.* that signs document jointly with others —*a.* **2.** signing jointly

cosine ('kəʊsaɪn) *n.* in a right-angled triangle, the ratio of a side adjacent to a given angle and the hypotenuse

cosmetic (kɒz'mɛtɪk) *n.* **1.** preparation to beautify or improve skin, hair *etc.* —*a.* **2.** designed to improve appearance only

cosmic ('kɒzmɪk) *a.* **1.** relating to the universe **2.** of the vastness of the universe —**cosmic rays** high-energy electromagnetic rays from space

cosmo- *or before vowel* **cosm-** (*comb. form*) world; universe, as in *cosmology, cosmonaut*

cosmopolitan (kɒzmə'pɒlɪt²n) *n.* **1.** person who has lived and travelled in many countries —*a.* **2.** familiar with many countries **3.**

sophisticated **4.** free from national prejudice —**cosmo'politanism** *n.* —**cos'mopolite** *n.*

cosmos¹ ('kɒzmɒs) *n.* the world or universe considered as an ordered system —**cos'mogony** *n.* study of origin and development of universe or system in universe —**cos'mographer** *n.* —**cosmo'graphic** *a.* —**cos'mography** *n.* description or mapping of the universe —**cosmo'logical** *a.* —**cos'mology** *n.* the science or study of the universe —**cosmonaut** ('kɒzmənɔːt) *n.* Soviet astronaut

cosmos² ('kɒzmɒs) *n.* plant cultivated for brightly coloured flowers (*pl.* **-mos, -es**)

Cossack ('kɒsæk) *n.* member of tribe in SE Russia

cosset ('kɒsɪt) *vt.* pamper, pet

cost (kɒst) *n.* **1.** price **2.** expenditure of time, labour *etc.* —*pl.* **3.** expenses of lawsuit —*vt.* **4.** have as price **5.** entail payment, loss or sacrifice of (*cost* *pt./pp.*) —**'costing** *n.* system of calculating cost of production —**'costliness** *n.* —**'costly** *a.* valuable **2.** expensive —**cost of living** basic cost of food, clothing and shelter necessary to maintain life —**cost price** price at which article is bought by one intending to resell it

costal ('kɒst²l) *a.* pert. to side of body or ribs —**'costate** *a.* ribbed

costermonger ('kɒstəmʌŋgə) *or* **coster** *n.* UK, *rare* person who sells fruit *etc.* from barrow

costive ('kɒstɪv) *a.* **1.** constipated **2.** niggardly

costume ('kɒstjuːm) *n.* **1.** style of dress of particular place or time, or for particular activity **2.** theatrical clothes —**cos'tumier** *n.* dealer in costumes —**costume jewellery** artificial jewellery

cosy *or U.S.* **cozy** ('kəʊzɪ) *a.* **1.** snug, comfortable, sheltered —*n.* **2.** covering to keep teapot *etc.* hot —**'cosily** *or U.S.* **'cozily** *adv.*

cot¹ (kɒt) *n.* **1.** child's bed usu. with barred sides **2.** swinging bed on ship —**cot death** unexplained death of baby while asleep

cot² (kɒt) *n.* **1.** *Lit., obs.* small cottage **2.** small shelter, *esp.* for pigeons, sheep *etc.* (*also* **cote**)

cot³ (kɒt) cotangent

cotangent (kəʊ'tændʒənt) *n.* (of angle) trigonometric function that in right-angled triangle is ratio of length of adjacent side to that of opposite side

cote (kəʊt) *or* **cot** *n.* shelter, shed for animals or birds, *eg* dovecot(e)

coterie ('kəʊtərɪ) *n.* **1.** exclusive group of people with common interests **2.** social clique

cotillion *or* **cotillon** (kə'tɪljən, kəʊ-) *n. Hist.* lively dance

cotoneaster (kətəʊnɪ'æstə) *n.* garden shrub with red berries

cottage ('kɒtɪdʒ) *n.* small house —**cottage**

cheese mild, soft cheese —**cottage industry** industry in which workers work in their own homes —**cottage pie** UK *see* **shepherd's pie** at SHEPHERD

cotter ('kɒtə) *n.* pin, wedge *etc.* to prevent relative motion of two parts of machine *etc.*

cotton ('kɒtən) *n.* 1. plant 2. white downy fibrous covering of its seeds 3. thread or cloth made of this —**cotton wool** 1. *chiefly* UK bleached sterilized cotton from which impurities have been removed 2. cotton in natural state 3. UK *inf.* state of pampered comfort and protection —**cotton to** or **on to** understand (idea *etc.*)

cotyledon (kɒtɪ'liːdən) *n.* primary leaf of plant embryos

couch (kautʃ) *n.* 1. piece of furniture for reclining on by day, sofa —*vt.* 2. express in a particular style of language 3. cause to lie down —'**couchant** *a. Her.* lying down

couch grass (kautʃ, kuːtʃ) type of creeping grass

cougar ('kuːgə) *n.* puma

cough (kɒf) *vi.* 1. expel air from lungs with sudden effort and noise, oft. to remove obstruction —*n.* 2. act of coughing —**cough drop** lozenge to relieve cough —**cough mixture** medicine that relieves coughing

could (kud) *pt. of* CAN¹

coulomb ('kuːlɒm) *n.* unit of quantity of electricity

coulter ('kəultə) *n.* sharp blade or disc at front of plough

council ('kaunsəl) *n.* 1. deliberative or administrative body 2. one of its meetings 3. local governing authority of town *etc.* —'**councillor** or U.S. '**councilor** *n.* member of council

counsel ('kaunsəl) *n.* 1. advice, deliberation, debate 2. barrister; barristers 3. plan, policy —*vt.* 4. advise, recommend (-**ll**-) —'**counsellor** or U.S. '**counselor** *n.* adviser —**keep one's counsel** keep a secret

count¹ (kaunt) *vt.* 1. reckon, calculate, number 2. include 3. consider to be —*vi.* 4. depend (on) 5. be of importance —*n.* 6. reckoning 7. total number reached by counting 8. item in list of charges or indictment 9. act of counting —'**countless** *a.* too many to be counted —'**countdown** *n.* act of counting backwards to time critical operation exactly, such as launching of rocket —**counting house** room or building for book-keeping —**count down** count backwards to time critical operation exactly —**count out** 1. *inf.* leave out; exclude 2. (of boxing referee) judge (floored boxer) to have failed to recover within specified time

count² (kaunt) *n.* nobleman corresponding to

British earl —'**countess** *n.* wife or widow of count or earl

countenance ('kauntɪnəns) *n.* 1. face or its expression 2. support, approval 3. composure; self-control —*vt.* 4. give support to, approve

counter¹ ('kauntə) *n.* 1. horizontal surface in bank, shop *etc.*, over which business is transacted 2. disc, token used for counting or scoring, *esp.* in board games

counter² ('kauntə) *adv.* 1. in opposite direction 2. contrary —*vt.* 3. oppose, contradict 4. *Fencing* parry —*n.* 5. parry

counter- (*comb. form*) reversed, opposite, rival, retaliatory, as in *counterclaim, counterclockwise, counterirritant, countermarch, countermeasure, countermine, counter-revolution*. Such words are not given here where the meaning may be inferred from the simple word

counteract (kauntər'ækt) *vt.* neutralize, hinder —**counter'action** *n.*

counterattack ('kauntərətæk) *v./n.* attack after enemy's advance

counterbalance ('kauntəbæləns) *n.* weight balancing or neutralizing another

counterfeit ('kauntəfɪt) *a.* 1. sham, forged —*n.* 2. imitation, forgery —*vt.* 3. imitate with intent to deceive 4. forge —'**counterfeiter** *n.* —'**counterfeitly** *adv.*

counterfoil ('kauntəfɔɪl) *n.* part of cheque, receipt, postal order, kept as record

counterintelligence (kauntərɪn'telɪdʒəns) *n.* activities designed to frustrate enemy espionage

countermand (kauntə'maːnd) *vt.* cancel (previous order)

counterpane ('kauntəpeɪn) *n.* top cover for bed

counterpart ('kauntəpaːt) *n.* 1. thing so like another as to be mistaken for it 2. something complementary to or correlative of another

counterpoint ('kauntəpɔɪnt) *n.* 1. melody added as accompaniment to given melody 2. art of so adding melodies

counterpoise ('kauntəpɔɪz) *n.* 1. force, influence *etc.* that counterbalances another 2. state of balance; equilibrium 3. weight that balances another —*vt.* 4. oppose with something of equal effect, weight or force; offset 5. bring into equilibrium

counterproductive (kauntəprə'dʌktɪv) *a.* tending to hinder achievement of aim; having effects contrary to those intended

Counter-Reformation (kauntərefə'meɪʃən) *n.* reform movement in Catholic Church in 16th and early 17th centuries

countersign ('kauntəsaɪn, kauntə'saɪn) *vt.* 1. sign document already signed by another 2. ratify

countersink ('kauntəsɪŋk) *vt.* enlarge (upper

part of hole drilled in timber *etc.*) to take head of screw, bolt *etc.* below surface

countertenor ('kaunta'tena) *n.* **1.** adult male voice with alto range **2.** singer with such voice

countervail (kaunta'veil, 'kauntaveil) *v.* **1.** act or act against with equal power or force —*vt.* **2.** make up for; compensate; offset

counterweight ('kauntaweit) *n.* counterbalancing weight, influence or force

countess ('kauntis) *n. see* COUNT[2]

country ('kʌntri) *n.* **1.** region, district **2.** territory of nation **3.** land of birth, residence *etc.* **4.** rural districts as opposed to town **5.** nation —'**countrified** *a.* rural in manner or appearance —**country-and-western** *n.* urban 20th-century White folk music of SE Amer. —**country club** club in the country, having sporting and social facilities —**country dance** folk dance in which couples face one another in line —'**countryman** *n.* **1.** rustic **2.** compatriot —'**countryside** *n.* **1.** rural district **2.** its inhabitants

county ('kaunti) *n.* **1.** division of country **2.** shire —*a.* **3.** *UK inf.* upper-class; of or like landed gentry —**county town** town in which county's affairs are or were administered

coup (ku:) *n.* **1.** successful stroke, move or gamble **2.** (*short for* **coup d'état**) sudden, violent seizure of government

coup de grâce (ku də 'gra:s) *Fr.* **1.** mortal or finishing blow, *esp.* delivered as act of mercy to sufferer **2.** final or decisive stroke (*pl.* **coups de grâce** (ku də 'gra:s))

coupé ('ku:pei) *n.* sporty style of motor car, *usu.* with two doors

couple ('kʌp°l) *n.* **1.** two, pair **2.** indefinite small number **3.** two people who regularly associate with each other or live together **4.** any two persons —*vt.* **5.** connect, fasten together **6.** associate, connect in the mind —*vi.* **7.** join —'**coupler** *n.* —'**couplet** *n.* two lines of verse, *esp.* rhyming and of equal length —'**coupling** *n.* connection, *esp.* chain between railway wagons

coupon ('ku:pon) *n.* **1.** ticket or voucher entitling holder to discount, gift *etc.* **2.** detachable slip used as order form **3.** (in betting *etc.*) printed form on which to forecast results

courage ('kʌrɪdʒ) *n.* bravery, boldness —cou'**rageous** *a.* —cou'**rageously** *adv.*

courgette (kuə'ʒet) *n.* type of small vegetable marrow

courier ('kuəriə) *n.* **1.** express messenger **2.** person who looks after, guides travellers

course (kɔ:s) *n.* **1.** movement in space or time **2.** direction of movement **3.** successive development, sequence **4.** line of conduct or action **5.** series of lectures, exercises *etc.* **6.** any of successive parts of meal **7.** continuous line of

masonry at particular level in building **8.** area where golf is played **9.** track or ground on which a race is run —*vt.* **10.** hunt —*vi.* **11.** run swiftly, gallop about **12.** (of blood) circulate —'**courser** *n. Poet.* swift horse —'**coursing** *n.* **1.** (of hounds or dogs) hunting by sight **2.** sport in which hounds are matched against one another in pairs for hunting of hares by sight

court (kɔ:t) *n.* **1.** space enclosed by buildings, yard **2.** area marked off or enclosed for playing various games **3.** retinue and establishment of sovereign **4.** body with judicial powers, place where it meets, one of its sittings **5.** attention, homage, flattery —*vt.* **6.** woo, try to win or attract **7.** seek, invite —'**courtier** *n.* one who frequents royal court —'**courtliness** *n.* —'**courtly** *a.* ceremoniously polite **2.** characteristic of a court —'**courtship** *n.* wooing —**court card** king, queen or jack at cards —'**courthouse** *n.* public building in which courts of law are held —**court martial** court of naval or military officers for trying naval or military offences (*pl.* **court martials, courts martial**) —**court plaster** plaster, composed of isinglass on silk, formerly used to cover superficial wounds —**court shoe** low-cut shoe for women, without laces or straps —'**courtyard** *n.* paved space enclosed by buildings or walls

courtesan *or* **courtezan** (kɔ:ti'zæn) *n. obs.* **1.** court mistress **2.** high-class prostitute

courtesy ('kɜ:tisi) *n.* **1.** politeness, good manners **2.** act of civility —'**courteous** *a.* polite —'**courteously** *adv.* —**courtesy title** title accorded by usage to which one has no valid claim

cousin ('kʌz°n) *n.* **1.** son or daughter of uncle or aunt **2.** formerly, any kinsman —'**cousinly** *a.*

couture (ku:'tuə) *n.* high-fashion designing and dressmaking —**couturier** (ku:'tuəriei) *n.* person who designs, makes and sells fashion clothes for women (**couturière** (ku:tuːriˈɛə) *fem.*)

cove[1] (kəuv) *n.* small inlet of coast, sheltered bay

cove[2] (kəuv) *n. sl.* fellow, chap

coven ('kʌv°n) *n.* gathering of witches

covenant ('kʌvənənt) *n.* **1.** contract, mutual agreement **2.** compact —*v.* **3.** agree to a covenant (concerning) —'**Covenanter** *n. Scot. hist.* person upholding either of two 17th-cent. Presbyterian covenants

Coventry ('kɒvəntri) *n.* —**send to Coventry** ostracize; ignore

cover ('kʌvə) *vt.* **1.** place or spread over **2.** extend over, spread over **3.** bring upon (oneself) **4.** screen, protect **5.** travel over **6.** include **7.** be sufficient to meet **8.** *Journalism* report **9.** point a gun at —*n.* **10.** lid, wrapper, envelope, binding, screen, anything which covers —'**cov-**

erage n. amount, extent covered —'**coverlet** n. top covering of bed —**cover charge** fixed charge added to cost of food in restaurant etc. —**covering letter** accompanying letter sent as explanation, introduction or record —**cover point** Cricket fielding position in covers; fielder in this position —**cover-up** n. concealment or attempted concealment of crime etc. —**cover up 1.** cover completely **2.** attempt to conceal (mistake or crime)

covert ('kʌvət) a. **1.** secret, veiled, concealed, sly —n. **2.** thicket, place sheltering game —'**covertly** adv.

covet ('kʌvɪt) vt. long to possess, esp. what belongs to another —'**covetous** a. avaricious —'**covetousness** n.

covey ('kʌvɪ) n. brood of partridges or quail (pl. -s)

cow[1] (kau) n. **1.** the female of the bovine and of certain other animals, eg elephant, whale **2.** inf. disagreeable woman —'**cowboy** n. herdsman in charge of cattle on western plains of U.S. **2.** inf. ruthless or unscrupulous operator in business etc. —**cow parsley** Eurasian umbelliferous hedgerow plant —'**cowpox** n. disease of cows, source of vaccine

cow[2] (kau) vt. frighten into submission, overawe, subdue

coward ('kauəd) n. one who lacks courage, shrinks from danger —'**cowardice** n. —'**cowardly** a.

cower ('kauə) vi. crouch, shrink in fear

cowl (kaul) n. **1.** monk's hooded cloak **2.** its hood **3.** hooded top for chimney, ship's funnel etc.

cowling ('kaulɪŋ) n. covering for aircraft engine

co-worker n. fellow worker; associate

cowry or **cowrie** ('kaurɪ) n. brightly-marked sea shell

cowslip ('kauslɪp) n. wild species of primrose

coxcomb ('kɒkskəum) n. obs. one given to showing off

coxswain ('kɒksən, -sweɪn) n. steersman of boat —**cox** n. **1.** coxswain —v. **2.** command or steer

coy (kɔɪ) a. (pretending to be) shy, modest —'**coyly** adv. —'**coyness** n.

coyote ('kɔɪəʊt, kɔɪ'əʊtɪ; esp. U.S. 'kaɪəʊt, kaɪ'əʊtɪ) n. N Amer. prairie wolf

coypu ('kɔɪpuː) n. aquatic rodent, orig. from S Amer., yielding nutria fur

cozen ('kʌzᵊn) vt. flatter in order to cheat, beguile

cp. compare

C.P. 1. Canadian Pacific **2.** Cape Province **3.** Communist Party

cpd. compound

Cpl. Corporal

C.P.U. central processing unit

CQ symbol transmitted by amateur radio operator requesting communication with any other amateur radio operator

Cr Chem. chromium

crab[1] (kræb) n. **1.** edible crustacean with ten legs, noted for sidelong and backward walk **2.** type of louse —vi. **3.** catch crabs **4.** move sideways —'**crabbed** ('kræbɪd) a. (of handwriting) hard to read —'**crabby** a. bad-tempered —**crab louse** parasitic louse that infests pubic region in man —**catch a crab** Rowing dig oar too deeply for clean retrieval

crab[2] (kræb) inf. vi. **1.** find fault; grumble (-bb-) —n. **2.** irritable person

crab apple wild sour apple

crack (kræk) v. **1.** break, split partially **2.** break with sharp noise **3.** cause to make sharp noise, as of whip, rifle etc. **4.** yield **5.** inf. tell (joke) **6.** solve, decipher —vi. **7.** make sharp noise **8.** split, fissure **9.** (of the voice) lose clearness when changing from boy's to man's —n. **10.** sharp explosive noise **11.** split, fissure **12.** flaw **13.** inf. joke, esp. sarcastic **14.** dial. chat **a. 15.** inf. special, smart, of great reputation for skill etc. —**cracked** a. **1.** damaged by cracking **2.** sl. crazy —'**cracker** n. **1.** decorated paper tube, pulled apart with a bang, containing paper hat, motto, toy etc. **2.** explosive firework **3.** thin dry biscuit —'**crackers** a. sl. unbalanced, crazy —'**cracking 1.** inf. fast; vigorous (esp. **in a cracking pace**) —adv./a. **2.** UK inf. first-class; excellent —n. **3.** process of breaking down hydrocarbons by heat and pressure, as in producing petrol —'**crackle** n. **1.** sound of repeated small cracks —vi. **2.** make this sound —'**crackling** n. **1.** crackle **2.** crisp skin of roast pork —'**crackbrained** a. insane, idiotic, crazy —'**crackpot** inf. n. **1.** eccentric person; crank —a. **2.** eccentric; crazy —'**cracksman** n. burglar, esp. safe-breaker —**get cracking** inf. start doing something quickly or with increased speed

cradle ('kreɪdᵊl) n. **1.** infant's bed (on rockers) **2.** fig. earliest resting-place or home **3.** supporting framework —vt. **4.** hold or rock as in a cradle **5.** cherish —'**cradling** n.

craft[1] (krɑːft) n. **1.** skill, ability, power **2.** cunning **3.** skilled trade **4.** members of a trade —'**craftily** adv. —'**craftsman** n. —'**craftsmanship** n. —'**crafty** a. cunning, shrewd

craft[2] (krɑːft) n. **1.** vessel **2.** ship (pl. **craft**)

crag (kræg) n. steep rugged rock —'**craggy** a. rugged

crake (kreɪk) n. any of various birds of rail family

cram (kræm) vt. **1.** fill quite full **2.** stuff, force **3.** pack tightly **4.** feed to excess **5.** prepare quickly for examination —*vi.* **6.** study, *esp.* for examination, by hastily memorizing (**-mm-**) —*n.* **7.** act or condition of cramming **8.** crush

cramp (kræmp) *n.* **1.** painful muscular contraction —*n.* clamp for holding masonry, timber *etc.* together —*vt.* **3.** restrict, hamper **4.** hem in, keep within too narrow limits

crampon ('kræmpən) *or* **crampoon** (kræm'puːn) *n.* spike in shoe for mountain climbing, *esp.* on ice

cranberry ('krænbərɪ, -brɪ) *n.* edible red berry of dwarf evergreen shrub

crane (kreɪn) *n.* **1.** wading bird with long legs, neck, and bill **2.** machine for moving heavy weights —*v.* **3.** stretch (neck) to see

crane fly insect with long spindly legs (*also* **daddy-long-legs**)

cranesbill ('kreɪnzbɪl) *n.* plant with pink or purple flowers and beaked fruits

craniometry (kreɪnɪ'ɒmɪtrɪ) *n.* the study of the measurements of the human head

cranium ('kreɪnɪəm) *n.* skull (*pl.* **-s, -nia** (-nɪə)) —'**cranial** *a.* —**cranio'logical** *a.* —**crani'ologist** *n.* —**crani'ology** *n.* branch of science concerned with shape and size of human skull

crank (kræŋk) *n.* **1.** arm at right angles to axis, for turning main shaft, changing reciprocal into rotary motion *etc.* **2.** *inf.* eccentric person, faddist —*v.* **3.** start (engine) by turning crank —'**cranky** *a.* **1.** eccentric **2.** bad-tempered **3.** shaky —'**crankpin** *n.* short cylindrical surface fitted between two arms of crank parallel to main shaft of crankshaft —'**crankshaft** *n.* principal shaft of engine

cranny ('krænɪ) *n.* small opening, chink —'**crannied** *a.*

crap (kræp) *n.* gambling game played with two dice (*also* **craps**)

crape (kreɪp) *n.* crepe, *esp.* when used for mourning clothes

crapulent ('kræpjʊlənt) *or* **crapulous** ('kræpjʊləs) *a.* **1.** given to or resulting from intemperance **2.** suffering from intemperance; drunken —'**crapulence** *n.*

crash (kræʃ) *v.* **1.** (cause to) make loud noise **2.** (cause to) fall with crash **3.** cause (aircraft) to hit land or water or (of aircraft) land in this way **4.** (cause to) collide (with another car *etc.*) **5.** move noisily or violently —*vi.* **6.** break, smash **7.** collapse, fail, *esp.* financially —*n.* **8.** loud, violent fall or impact **9.** collision, *esp.* between vehicles **10.** sudden, uncontrolled descent of aircraft to land **11.** sudden collapse or downfall **12.** bankruptcy —*a.* **13.** requiring, using, great effort to achieve results quickly —*a. inf.* thorough (*esp. in* **crashing bore**) —**crash helmet** helmet worn by motorcyclists *etc.* to

protect head —**crash-land** *v.* land (aircraft) in emergency, *esp.* with damage to craft

crass (kræs) *a.* grossly stupid —'**crassly** *adv.* —'**crassness** *n.*

crate (kreɪt) *n.* large (*usu.* wooden) container for packing goods

crater ('kreɪtə) *n.* **1.** mouth of volcano **2.** bowl-shaped cavity, *esp.* one made by explosion of large shell, bomb, mine *etc.*

cravat (krə'væt) *n.* man's neckcloth

crave (kreɪv) *v.* **1.** have very strong desire (for), long (for) —*vt.* **2.** ask humbly **3.** beg —'**craving** *n.*

craven ('kreɪvən) *a.* **1.** cowardly, abject, spineless —*n.* **2.** coward

craw (krɔː) *n.* **1.** bird's or animal's stomach **2.** bird's crop

crawfish ('krɔːfɪʃ) *n. see* CRAYFISH

crawl (krɔːl) *vi.* **1.** move on belly or on hands and knees **2.** move very slowly **3.** ingratiate oneself, cringe **4.** swim with crawl-stroke **5.** be overrun (with) —*n.* **6.** crawling motion **7.** very slow pace or motion **8.** racing stroke at swimming —'**crawler** *n.*

crayfish ('kreɪfɪʃ) *or esp. U.S.* **crawfish** *n.* edible freshwater crustacean like lobster

crayon ('kreɪən, -ɒn) *n.* stick or pencil of coloured chalk, wax *etc.*

craze (kreɪz) *n.* **1.** short-lived current fashion **2.** strong desire or passion, mania **3.** madness —'**crazed** *a.* **1.** demented **2.** (of porcelain) having fine cracks —'**crazy** *a.* **1.** insane **2.** very foolish **3.** (*with* about *or* over) madly eager (for) —**crazy paving** paving made with flat irregularly shaped slabs of stone

creak (kriːk) *n.* **1.** harsh grating noise —*vi.* **2.** make creaking sound

cream (kriːm) *n.* **1.** fatty part of milk **2.** various foods, dishes, resembling cream **3.** cosmetic *etc.* with creamlike consistency **4.** yellowish-white colour **5.** best part of anything —*vt.* **6.** take cream from **7.** take best part from **8.** beat to creamy consistency —'**creamer** *n.* **1.** vessel or device for separating cream from milk **2.** powdered milk substitute for coffee —'**creamery** *n.* **1.** establishment where milk and cream are made into butter and cheese **2.** place where dairy products are sold —'**creamy** *a.* —**cream cheese** soft white cheese made from soured cream or milk —**cream of tartar** potassium hydrogen tartrate, *esp.* when used in baking powders

crease (kriːs) *n.* **1.** line made by folding **2.** wrinkle **3.** *Cricket* line defining bowler's and batsman's positions **4.** superficial bullet wound —*v.* **5.** make, develop creases

create (kriː'eɪt) *vt.* **1.** bring into being **2.** give rise to **3.** make —*vi.* **4.** *inf.* make a fuss —**cre'ation** *n.* —**cre'ative** *a.* —**cre'ator** *n.*

creature ('kriːtʃə) *n.* **1.** living being **2.** thing created **3.** dependant —**creature comforts** bodily comforts

crèche (krɛʃ, kreɪʃ) *n.* day nursery for very young children

credence ('kriːdəns) *n.* **1.** belief, credit **2.** side-table for elements of the Eucharist before consecration

credentials (krɪ'dɛnʃəlz) *pl.n.* **1.** testimonials **2.** letters of introduction, *esp.* those given to ambassador

credible ('krɛdɪb^əl) *a.* **1.** worthy of belief **2.** trustworthy —**credi'bility** *n.* —**'credibly** *adv.* —**credibility gap** disparity between claims or statements and facts

credit ('krɛdɪt) *n.* **1.** commendation, approval **2.** source, cause, of honour **3.** belief, trust **4.** good name **5.** influence, honour or power based on trust of others **6.** system of allowing customers to take goods for later payment **7.** money at one's disposal in bank *etc.* **8.** side of book on which such sums are entered **9.** reputation for financial reliability —*pl.* **10.** list of those responsible for production of film —*vt.* **11.** (with with) attribute **12.** believe **13.** put on credit side of account —'**creditable** *a.* bringing honour —'**creditably** *adv.* —'**creditor** *n.* one to whom debt is due —**credit card** card issued by banks *etc.* enabling holder to obtain goods and services on credit

credo ('kriːdəʊ, 'kreɪ-) *n.* formal statement of beliefs, principles or opinions (*pl.* -s)

credulous ('krɛdjʊləs) *a.* too easy of belief, easily deceived or imposed on, gullible —**cre'dulity** *n.* —'**credulousness** *n.*

creed (kriːd) *n.* **1.** formal statement of Christian beliefs **2.** statement, system of beliefs or principles

creek (kriːk) *n.* narrow inlet on seacoast

creel (kriːl) *n.* angler's fishing basket

creep (kriːp) *vi.* **1.** make way along ground, as snake **2.** move with stealthy, slow movements **3.** crawl **4.** act in servile way **5.** (of skin or flesh) feel shrinking, shivering sensation, due to fear or repugnance (**crept** *pt./pp.*) —*n.* **6.** creeping **7.** *sl.* repulsive person —*pl.* **8.** *sl.* feeling of fear or repugnance —'**creeper** *n.* creeping or climbing plant, *eg* ivy —'**creepy** *a.* *inf.* **1.** uncanny, unpleasant **2.** causing flesh to creep —**creepy-crawly** UK *inf.* *n.* **1.** small crawling creature (*pl.* -**crawlies**) —*a.* **2.** feeling or causing sensation as of creatures crawling on skin

cremation (krɪ'meɪʃən) *n.* burning as means of disposing of corpses —**cre'mate** *vt.* —**crema'torium** *n.* place for cremation

crème de la crème (krɛm də la 'krɛm) *n.* *Fr.* the very best

crème de menthe ('krɛm də 'mɛnθ, 'mɪnt, 'kriːm, 'kreɪm) liqueur flavoured with pepper-mint

crenate ('kriːneɪt) *or* **crenated** *a.* having scalloped margin, as certain leaves —**crena'tion** *n.*

crenellated *or* U.S. **crenelated** ('krɛnɪleɪtɪd) *a.* having battlements

creole ('kriːəʊl) *n.* **1.** hybrid language **2.** (C-) native-born W Indian, Latin American, of European descent

creosote ('kriːəsəʊt) *n.* oily antiseptic liquid distilled from coal or wood tar, used for preserving wood —*vt.* **2.** coat or impregnate with creosote

crepe *or* **crape** (kreɪp) *n.* **1.** fabric with crimped surface **2.** very thin pancake, oft. folded round filling —**crepe de Chine** (də 'ʃiːn) very thin crepe of silk or similar light fabric —**crepe paper** thin crinkled paper resembling crepe —**crepe rubber** rough-surfaced rubber used for soles of shoes

crepitate ('krɛpɪteɪt) *vi.* make rattling or crackling sound

crepitus ('krɛpɪtəs) *n.* **1.** crackling chest sound heard in pneumonia *etc.* **2.** grating sound of two ends of broken bone rubbing together

crept (krɛpt) *pt./pp. of* CREEP

crepuscular (krɪ'pʌskjʊlə) *a.* **1.** of or like twilight; dim **2.** (of creatures) active at twilight

Cres. Crescent

crescendo (krɪ'ʃɛndəʊ) *n.* **1.** gradual increase of loudness, *esp.* in music —*adv.* **2.** with a crescendo

crescent ('krɛs^ənt, -z^ənt) *n.* **1.** (shape of) moon as seen in first or last quarter **2.** any figure of this shape **3.** row of houses built on curve

cress (krɛs) *n.* any of various plants with edible pungent leaves

crest (krɛst) *n.* **1.** comb or tuft on bird's or animal's head **2.** plume on top of helmet **3.** top of mountain, ridge, wave *etc.* **4.** badge above shield of coat of arms, also used separately on seal, plate *etc.* —*vt.* **5.** crown **6.** reach top of —'**crestfallen** *a.* cast down by failure, dejected

cretaceous (krɪ'teɪʃəs) *a.* chalky

Cretaceous (krɪ'teɪʃəs) *a.* **1.** of last period of Mesozoic era, during which chalk deposits were formed —*n.* **2.** Cretaceous period or rock system

cretin ('krɛtɪn) *n.* **1.** person afflicted with cretinism **2.** *inf.* stupid person —'**cretinism** *n.* deficiency in thyroid gland causing physical and mental retardation

cretonne (krɛ'tɒn, 'krɛtɒn) *n.* unglazed cotton cloth printed in coloured patterns

crevasse (krɪ'væs) *n.* deep open chasm, *esp.* in glacier

crevice ('krɛvɪs) *n.* cleft, fissure, chink

crew (kruː) *n.* 1. ship's, boat's or aircraft's company, excluding passengers 2. *inf.* gang, set —*v.* 3. serve as crew (on) —**crew cut** man's closely cropped haircut

crewel ('kruːɪl) *n.* fine worsted yarn, used in fancy work and embroidery

crib (krɪb) *n.* 1. child's cot 2. barred rack used for fodder 3. plagiarism 4. translation used by students, sometimes illicitly —*vt.* 5. confine in small space 6. copy unfairly (**-bb-**)

cribbage ('krɪbɪdʒ) *n.* card game for two, three or four players

crick (krɪk) *n.* spasm or cramp in muscles, *esp.* in neck

cricket[1] ('krɪkɪt) *n.* chirping insect

cricket[2] ('krɪkɪt) *n.* outdoor game played with bats, ball and wickets by teams of eleven a side —'**cricketer** *n.*

cri de coeur (kri də 'kœːr) *Fr.* heartfelt or impassioned appeal (*pl.* **cris de coeur** (kri də 'kœːr))

cried (kraɪd) *pt./pp.* of CRY

crier ('kraɪə) *n.* 1. person or animal that cries 2. formerly, official who made public announcements, *esp.* in town or court

crime (kraɪm) *n.* 1. violation of law (usu. a serious offence) 2. wicked or forbidden act 3. *inf.* something to be regretted —**criminal** ('krɪmɪnəl) *a./n.* —**criminality** (krɪmɪ'nælɪtɪ) *n.* —**criminally** ('krɪmɪnəlɪ) *adv.* —**criminology** (krɪmɪ'nɒlədʒɪ) *n.* study of crime and criminals

crimp (krɪmp) *vt.* 1. pinch into tiny parallel pleats 2. wrinkle

Crimplene ('krɪmpliːn) *n.* R crease-resistant synthetic material, similar to Terylene

crimson ('krɪmzən) *a./n.* 1. (of) rich deep red —*v.* 2. turn crimson

cringe (krɪndʒ) *vi.* 1. shrink, cower 2. behave obsequiously

crinkle ('krɪŋk'l) *v./n.* wrinkle

crinoline ('krɪnəlɪn) *n.* hooped petticoat or skirt

cripple ('krɪp'l) *n.* 1. one not having normal use of limbs, disabled or deformed person —*vt.* 2. maim, disable, impair 3. weaken, lessen efficiency of

crisis ('kraɪsɪs) *n.* 1. turning point or decisive moment, *esp.* in illness 2. time of acute danger or difficulty (*pl.* **crises** ('kraɪsiːz))

crisp (krɪsp) *a.* 1. brittle but firm 2. brisk, decided 3. clear-cut 4. fresh, invigorating 5. (of hair) curly —*n.* 6. very thin, fried slice of potato, eaten cold —*v.* 7. make or become crisp —'**crisper** *n.* refrigerator compartment for storing salads *etc.* —'**crispy** *a.* —'**crispbread** *n.* thin, dry biscuit

crisscross ('krɪskrɒs) *v.* 1. (cause to) move in crosswise pattern 2. mark with or consist of pattern of crossing lines —*a.* 3. (*esp.* of lines) crossing one another in different directions —*n.* 4. pattern made of crossing lines —*adv.* 5. in crosswise manner or pattern

criterion (kraɪ'tɪərɪən) *n.* standard of judgment (*pl.* **-ria** (-rɪə))

critical ('krɪtɪk'l) *a.* 1. fault-finding 2. discerning 3. skilled in or given to judging 4. of great importance, crucial, decisive —'**critic** *n.* 1. one who passes judgment 2. writer expert in judging works of literature, art *etc.* —'**critically** *adv.* —'**criticism** *n.* —'**criticize** *or* **-ise** *v.* —**critique** (krɪ'tiːk) *n.* critical essay, carefully written criticism —**critical path analysis** technique for planning projects with reference to critical path, which is sequence of stages requiring longest time

croak (krəʊk) *vi.* 1. utter deep hoarse cry, as raven, frog 2. talk dismally 3. *sl.* die —*n.* 4. deep hoarse cry —'**croaker** *n.* —'**croaky** *a.* hoarse

Croatian (krəʊ'eɪʃən) *a.* 1. of Croatia, its people or their dialect of Serbo-Croatian —*n.* 2. dialect of Croatia 3. native or inhabitant of Croatia

crochet ('krəʊʃeɪ, -ʃɪ) *n.* 1. kind of handicraft like knitting, done with small hooked needle —*vi.* 2. do such work —*vt.* 3. make (garment *etc.*) by such work

crock (krɒk) *n.* 1. earthenware jar or pot 2. broken piece of earthenware 3. *inf.* old broken-down person or person 4. *inf.* cripple —'**crockery** *n.* earthenware dishes, utensils *etc.*

crocodile ('krɒkədaɪl) *n.* 1. large amphibious reptile 2. line of children walking two by two —**crocodilian** (krɒkə'dɪlɪən) *n.* 1. large predatory reptile, such as crocodile, alligator *etc.* —*a.* 2. of crocodiles or crocodilians —**crocodile tears** insincere grief

crocus ('krəʊkəs) *n.* small bulbous plant with yellow, white or purple flowers

Croesus ('kriːsəs) *n.* very rich man

croft (krɒft) *n. Scot.* small piece of arable land, smallholding —'**crofter** *n.* one who works croft

croissant ('krwʌsɒŋ) *n.* crescent-shaped roll of yeast dough like pastry

Cro-Magnon man ('krəʊ'mænjɒn) early type of modern man who lived in Europe during late Palaeolithic times

cromlech ('krɒmlɛx) *n.* prehistoric structure, monument of flat stone resting on two upright ones

crone (krəʊn) *n.* witchlike old woman

crony ('krəʊnɪ) *n.* intimate friend

crook (krʊk) *n.* 1. hooked staff 2. any hook, bend, sharp turn 3. *inf.* swindler, criminal —**crooked** ('krʊkɪd) *a.* 1. bent, twisted 2. deformed 3. *inf.* dishonest

croon (kruːn) v. hum, sing in soft, low tone —**'crooner** n.

crop (krɒp) n. 1. produce of cultivation of any plant or plants 2. harvest (lit. or fig.) 3. pouch in bird's gullet 4. stock of whip 5. hunting whip 6. short haircut —vt. 7. cut short 8. poll, clip 9. (of animals) bite, eat down —vi. 10. raise, produce or occupy land with crop (-**pp**-) —**'cropper** n. inf. 1. heavy fall 2. disastrous failure —**crop-dusting** n. spreading fungicide etc. on crops from aircraft —**crop up** inf. happen unexpectedly

croquet ('krəʊkeɪ, -kɪ) n. lawn game played with balls, wooden mallets and hoops

croquette (krəʊ'kɛt, krɒ-) n. fried ball of minced meat, fish etc. in breadcrumbs

crosier or **crozier** ('krəʊʒə) n. bishop's or abbot's staff

cross (krɒs) n. 1. structure or symbol of two intersecting lines or pieces (at right angles) 2. such a structure of wood as means of execution by tying or nailing victim to it 3. symbol of Christian faith 4. any thing or mark in the shape of cross 5. misfortune, annoyance, affliction 6. intermixture of breeds, hybrid —v. 7. move or go across (something) 8. intersect —vi. 9. meet and pass —vt. 10. mark with lines across 11. (with out) delete 12. place or put in form of cross 13. make sign of cross on or over 14. modify breed of animals or plants by intermixture 15. thwart 16. oppose —a. 17. out of temper, angry 18. peevish, perverse 19. transverse 20. intersecting 21. contrary 22. adverse —**'crossing** n. 1. intersection of roads, rails etc. 2. part of street where pedestrians are expected to cross —**'crossly** adv. —**'crosswise** adv./a. —**'crossbar** n. 1. horizontal bar, line, stripe etc. 2. horizontal beam across pair of goal posts 3. horizontal bar on man's bicycle —**cross-bench** n. (usu. pl.) UK seat in Parliament occupied by neutral or independent member —**cross-bencher** n. —**'crossbill** n. bird whose mandibles cross when closed —**'crossbow** n. bow fixed across wooden shoulder stock —**'crossbreed** n. breed produced from parents of different breeds —**cross'check** v. 1. verify (report etc.) by consulting other sources —n. 2. act of crosschecking —**cross-country** n. long race held over open ground —**cross-examination** n. —**cross-examine** vt. examine (witness already examined by other side) —**cross-eyed** a. having eye(s) turning inward —**cross-fertilization** n. fertilization of one plant by pollen of another —**'crossfire** n. 1. Mil. converging fire from one or more positions 2. lively exchange of ideas, opinions etc. —**cross-grained** a. perverse —**'crosspatch** n. inf. bad-tempered person —**cross-ply** a. (of tyre) having fabric cords in outer casing running diagonally

—**cross-purpose** n. contrary aim or purpose —**cross-question** vt. 1. cross-examine —n. 2. question asked in cross-examination —**cross-refer** v. refer from one part to another —**cross-reference** n. reference within text to another part of text —**'crossroads** n. —**cross section** 1. transverse section 2. group of people fully representative of a nation, community etc. —**cross-stitch** n. 1. embroidery stitch made by two stitches forming cross —v. 2. embroider (piece of needlework) with cross-stitch —**cross-talk** n. 1. Rad., telephony unwanted sounds picked up on receiving channel 2. UK rapid or witty talk —**crossword (puzzle)** puzzle built up of intersecting words, of which some letters are common, the words being indicated by clues —**at cross-purposes** conflicting; opposed; disagreeing —**the Cross** 1. cross on which Jesus Christ was executed 2. model or picture of this

crosse (krɒs) n. light staff with triangular frame to which network is attached, used in playing lacrosse

crotch (krɒtʃ) n. 1. angle between legs, genital area 2. fork

crotchet ('krɒtʃɪt) n. musical note, equal to half the length of a minim

crotchety ('krɒtʃɪtɪ) a. 1. peevish 2. irritable

croton ('krəʊtən) n. any chiefly tropical shrub or tree, seeds of which yield croton oil, formerly used as purgative

crouch (kraʊtʃ) vi. 1. bend low 2. huddle down close to ground 3. stoop servilely, cringe —n. 4. act of stooping or bending

croup[1] (kruːp) n. throat disease of children, with cough

croup[2] (kruːp) n. 1. hindquarters of horse 2. place behind saddle

croupier ('kruːpɪə) n. person dealing cards, collecting money etc. at gambling table

crouton ('kruːtɒn) n. small piece of fried or toasted bread, usu. served in soup

crow[1] (krəʊ) n. large black carrion-eating bird —**'crowfoot** n. any of several plants that have yellow or white flowers and leaves resembling foot of crow (pl. -**s**) —**crow's-foot** n. wrinkle at corner of eye —**crow's-nest** n. lookout platform high on ship's mast

crow[2] (krəʊ) vi. 1. utter cock's cry 2. boast one's happiness or superiority —n. 3. cock's cry

crowbar ('krəʊbɑː) n. iron bar, usu. beaked, for levering

crowd (kraʊd) n. 1. throng, mass —vi. 2. flock together —vt. 3. cram, force, thrust, pack 4. fill with people —**crowd out** exclude by excess already in

crown (kraʊn) n. 1. monarch's headdress 2. wreath for head 3. monarch 4. monarchy 5. royal power 6. formerly, British coin of five shillings **7.** various foreign coins **8.** top of head **9.** summit, top **10.** completion or perfection of thing —*vt.* **11.** put crown on **12.** confer title upon **13.** occur as culmination of series of events **14.** *inf.* hit on head —**crown court** *English law* court of criminal jurisdiction holding sessions throughout England and Wales —**crown green** bowling green in which sides are lower than middle —**crown jewels** jewellery, including regalia, used by sovereign on state occasion —**crown land** public land —**crown prince** heir to throne

crozier ('krəʊʒə) *n. see* CROSIER

CRT cathode-ray tube

crucial ('kruːʃəl) *a.* **1.** decisive, critical **2.** *inf.* very important

cruciate ('kruːʃut, -eɪt) *a.* cross-shaped

crucible ('kruːsɪbᵊl) *n.* small melting pot

crucify ('kruːsɪfaɪ) *vt.* **1.** put to death on cross **2.** treat cruelly **3.** *inf.* ridicule (**'crucified, 'crucifying**) —**'crucifix** *n.* **1.** cross **2.** image of (Christ on the) Cross —**cruci'fixion** *n.* —**'cruciform** *a.*

crude (kruːd) *a.* **1.** lacking taste, vulgar **2.** in natural or raw state, unrefined **3.** rough, unfinished —**'crudely** *adv.* —**'crudity** *n.*

cruel ('kruːəl) *a.* **1.** delighting in others' pain **2.** causing pain or suffering —**'cruelly** *adv.* —**'cruelty** *n.*

cruet ('kruːɪt) *n.* **1.** small container for salt, pepper, vinegar, oil *etc.* **2.** stand holding such containers

cruise (kruːz) *vi.* **1.** travel about in a ship for pleasure *etc.* **2.** (of vehicle, aircraft) travel at safe, average speed *—n.* **3.** cruising voyage, *esp.* organized for holiday purposes —**'cruiser** *n.* **1.** ship that cruises **2.** warship lighter and faster than battleship —**'cruiserweight** *n. Boxing* light-heavyweight

crumb (krʌm) *n.* **1.** small particle, fragment, *esp.* of bread —*vt.* **2.** reduce to, break into, cover with crumbs —**'crumby** *a.*

crumble ('krʌmbᵊl) *v.* **1.** break into small fragments, disintegrate, crush **2.** perish, decay *—vi.* **3.** fall apart or away *—n.* **4.** pudding covered with crumbly mixture —**'crumbly** *a.*

crummy ('krʌmɪ) *a. sl.* inferior, contemptible

crump (krʌmp) *vi.* **1.** thud, explode with dull sound *—n.* **2.** crunching sound **3.** *inf.* shell, bomb

crumpet ('krʌmpɪt) *n.* **1.** flat, soft cake eaten with butter **2.** *sl.* sexually desirable woman or women

crumple ('krʌmpᵊl) *v.* **1.** (cause to) collapse **2.** make or become crushed, wrinkled, creased —**'crumpled** *a.*

crunch (krʌntʃ) *n.* **1.** sound made by chewing crisp food, treading on gravel, hard snow *etc.* **2.** *inf.* critical moment or situation *—v.* **3.** (cause to) make crunching sound

crupper ('krʌpə) *n.* **1.** strap holding back saddle in place by passing round horse's tail **2.** horse's hindquarters

crusade (kruː'seɪd) *n.* **1.** medieval Christian war to recover Holy Land **2.** campaign against something believed to be evil **3.** concerted action to further a cause —*vi.* **4.** campaign vigorously for something **5.** go on crusade —**cru'sader** *n.*

cruse (kruːz) *n.* small earthenware jug or pot

crush¹ (krʌʃ) *vt.* **1.** compress so as to break, bruise, crumple **2.** break to small pieces **3.** defeat utterly, overthrow *—n.* **4.** act of crushing **5.** crowd of people *etc.* **6.** drink prepared by or as if by crushing fruit

crush² (krʌʃ) *n. inf.* infatuation

crust (krʌst) *n.* **1.** hard outer part of bread **2.** similar hard outer casing on anything —*v.* **3.** cover with, form, crust —**'crustily** *adv.* —**'crusty** *a.* **1.** having, or like, crust **2.** short-tempered

crustacean (krʌ'steɪʃən) *n.* hard-shelled animal, *eg* crab, lobster —**crus'taceous** *a.*

crutch (krʌtʃ) *n.* **1.** staff with crosspiece to go under armpit of lame person **2.** support **3.** groin, crotch

crux (krʌks) *n.* **1.** that on which a decision turns **2.** anything that puzzles very much (*pl.* **-es, cruces** ('kruːsiːz))

cry (kraɪ) *vi.* **1.** weep **2.** wail **3.** utter call **4.** shout **5.** clamour or beg (for) —*vt.* **6.** utter loudly, proclaim (**cried, 'crying**) *—n.* **7.** loud utterance **8.** scream, wail, shout **9.** call of animal **10.** fit of weeping **11.** watchword —**'crying** *a.* notorious; lamentable (*esp. in* **crying shame**)

cryogenics (kraɪə'dʒɛnɪks) *n.* branch of physics concerned with phenomena at very low temperatures —**cryo'genic** *a.*

crypt (krɪpt) *n.* vault, *esp.* under church —**'cryptic** *a.* secret, mysterious —**'cryptically** *adv.* —**'cryptogram** *n.* piece of writing in code —**cryp'tography** *n.* art of writing, decoding ciphers

cryptogam ('krɪptəʊgæm) *n.* nonflowering plant, *eg* fern, moss *etc.*

crystal ('krɪstᵊl) *n.* **1.** clear transparent mineral **2.** very clear glass **3.** cut-glass ware **4.** characteristic form assumed by many substances, with definite internal structure and external shape of symmetrically arranged plane surfaces —**'crystalline** *or* **'crystalloid** *a.* —**crystalli'zation** *or* **-i'sation** *n.* —**'crystallize** *or* **-ise** *v.* **1.** (cause to) form into crystals **2.** (cause to) become definite —**crystal'lographer** *n.* —**crystal'lography** *n.* science of the structure, forms and properties of crystals

—**crystal gazer** —**crystal gazing** 1. act of staring into crystal ball supposedly to arouse visual perceptions of future *etc.* 2. act of trying to foresee or predict

Cs *Chem.* caesium

CSE Certificate of Secondary Education

CS gas gas causing tears, salivation and painful breathing, used in chemical warfare and civil disturbances

CST US, **C** Central Standard Time

CT Connecticut

ct. 1. cent 2. carat 3. court

ctenophore ('tɛnəfɔː, 'tiːnə-) *n.* marine invertebrate whose body bears eight rows of fused cilia for locomotion

CTV Canadian Television (Network Ltd.)

cu *or* **cu.** cubic

Cu *Chem.* copper

cub (kʌb) *n.* 1. young of fox and other animals 2. (C-) Cub Scout —*v.* 3. give birth to (cubs) (**-bb-**) —**Cub Scout** member of junior branch of the Scout Association

cubbyhole ('kʌbɪhəʊl) *n.* small, enclosed space or room

cube (kjuːb) *n.* 1. regular solid figure contained by six equal square sides 2. cube-shaped block 3. product obtained by multiplying number by itself twice —*vt.* 4. multiply thus —'**cubic**(al) *a.* —'**cubism** *n.* style of art in which objects are presented as assemblage of geometrical shapes —'**cubist** *n./a.* —**cube root** number or quantity whose cube is a given number or quantity —**cubic measure** system of units for measurement of volumes

cubicle ('kjuːbɪkᵊl) *n.* partially or totally enclosed section of room, as in dormitory

cubit ('kjuːbɪt) *n.* old measure of length, about 18 inches

cuckold ('kʌkəld) *n.* 1. man whose wife has committed adultery —*vt.* 2. make cuckold of

cuckoo ('kukuː) *n.* 1. migratory bird which deposits its eggs in nests of other birds 2. its call —*a.* 3. *sl.* crazy —'**cuckoopint** *n.* European plant with arrow-shaped leaves, pale purple spadix and scarlet berries (*also* **lords-and-ladies**) —**cuckoo spit** white frothy mass on plants, produced by froghopper larvae

cucumber ('kjuːkʌmbə) *n.* 1. plant with long fleshy green fruit 2. the fruit, used in salad

cud (kʌd) *n.* food which ruminant animal brings back into mouth to chew again —**chew the cud** reflect, meditate

cuddle ('kʌdᵊl) *vt.* 1. hug —*vi.* 2. lie close and snug, nestle —*n.* 3. close embrace, *esp.* when prolonged

cuddy ('kʌdɪ) *n.* small cabin in boat

cudgel ('kʌdʒᵊl) *n.* 1. short thick stick —*vt.* 2. beat with cudgel (**-ll-**)

cue¹ (kjuː) *n.* 1. last words of actor's speech *etc.* as signal to another to act or speak 2. signal, hint, example for action

cue² (kjuː) *n.* 1. long tapering rod used in billiards 2. pigtail

cuff¹ (kʌf) *n.* 1. ending of sleeve 2. wristband —**cuff link** one pair of linked buttons to join buttonholes on shirt cuffs —**off the cuff** *inf.* without preparation

cuff² (kʌf) *vt.* 1. strike with open hand —*n.* 2. blow of this kind

cuirass (kwɪ'ræs) *n.* metal or leather armour of breastplate and backplate

Cuisenaire rod (kwizə'nɛə) **R** one of set of rods of various colours and lengths representing different numbers, used to teach arithmetic to young children

cuisine (kwɪ'ziːn) *n.* 1. style of cooking 2. menu, food offered by restaurant *etc.*

cul-de-sac ('kʌldəsæk, 'kʊl-) *n.* 1. street, lane open only at one end 2. blind alley (*pl.* **culs-de-sac**)

culinary ('kʌlɪnərɪ) *a.* of, for, suitable for, cooking or kitchen

cull (kʌl) *vt.* 1. gather, select 2. take out (selected animals) from herd —*n.* 3. act of culling

culminate ('kʌlmɪneɪt) *vi.* 1. reach highest point 2. come to climax, to a head —culmi'nation *n.*

culottes (kjuː'lɒts) *pl.n.* flared trousers (*esp.* for women) cut to look like skirt

culpable ('kʌlpəbᵊl) *a.* blameworthy —**culpa'bility** *n.* —'**culpably** *adv.*

culprit ('kʌlprɪt) *n.* one guilty of usu. minor offence

cult (kʌlt) *n.* 1. system of religious worship 2. pursuit of, devotion to, some person, thing, or activity

cultivate ('kʌltɪveɪt) *vt.* 1. till and prepare (ground) to raise crops 2. develop, improve, refine 3. devote attention to, cherish 4. practise 5. foster —'**cultivable** *or* '**cultivatable** *a.* (of land) capable of being cultivated —culti'vation *n.* —'**cultivator** *n.*

culture ('kʌltʃə) *n.* 1. state of manners, taste and intellectual development at a time or place 2. cultivating 3. artificial rearing 4. set of bacteria so reared —'**cultural** *a.* —'**cultured** *a.* refined, showing culture —**cultured pearl** pearl artificially induced to grow in oyster shell

culvert ('kʌlvət) *n.* tunnelled drain for passage of water under road, railway *etc.*

cum (kʌm) *Lat.* with

cumbersome ('kʌmbəsəm) *or* **cumbrous** ('kʌmbrəs) *a.* awkward, unwieldy —'**cumber** *vt.* 1. obstruct; hinder 2. *obs.* inconvenience

—'**cumbrance** n. 1. burden; obstacle; hindrance 2. trouble; bother

Cumbrian ('kʌmbrɪən) a./n. (native or inhabitant) of Cumbria, county of NW England

cumin or **cummin** ('kʌmɪn) n. herb

cummerbund or **kummerbund** ('kʌmə-bʌnd) n. broad sash worn round waist

cumquat ('kʌmkwɒt) n. see KUMQUAT

cumulative ('kjuːmjʊlətɪv) a. 1. becoming greater by successive additions 2. representing the sum of many items

cumulus ('kjuːmjʊləs) n. cloud shaped in rounded white woolly masses (pl. **cumuli** ('kjuːmjʊlaɪ))

cuneiform ('kjuːnɪfɔːm) a. wedge-shaped, esp. of ancient Babylonian writing

cunning ('kʌnɪŋ) a. 1. crafty, sly 2. ingenious —n. 3. skill in deceit or evasion 4. skill, ingenuity —'**cunningly** adv.

cup (kʌp) n. 1. small drinking vessel with handle at one side 2. any small drinking vessel 3. contents of cup 4. various cup-shaped formations, cavities, sockets etc. 5. cup-shaped trophy as prize 6. portion, lot 7. iced drink of wine and other ingredients 8. either of two cup-shaped parts of brassiere etc. —vt. 9. shape as cup (hands etc.) —'**cupful** n. (pl. '**cupfuls**) —'**cupping** n. Med. formerly, use of evacuated glass cup to draw blood to surface of skin for bloodletting —**cupboard** ('kʌbəd) n. piece of furniture, recess in room, with door, for storage —**cupboard love** show of love inspired by selfish or greedy motive —**Cup Final** 1. annual final of F.A. Cup soccer competition 2. final of any cup competition —**cup tie** Sport eliminating match between two teams in cup competition

cupel ('kjuːpəl, kjuːˈpɛl) n. small vessel used in refining metals

Cupid ('kjuːpɪd) n. god of love

cupidity (kjuːˈpɪdɪtɪ) n. 1. greed for possessions 2. covetousness

cupola ('kjuːpələ) n. dome

cupreous ('kjuːprɪəs) a. of, containing, copper

cupronickel (kjuːprəʊˈnɪkəl) n. copper alloy containing up to 40 per cent nickel

cur (kɜː) n. 1. dog of mixed breed 2. surly, contemptible or mean person

curaçao (kjʊərəˈsəʊ) n. liqueur flavoured with bitter orange peel

curare or **curari** (kjʊˈrɑːrɪ) n. poisonous resin of S Amer. tree, now used as muscle relaxant in medicine

curate ('kjuːrɪt) n. parish priest's appointed assistant —'**curacy** n. his office

curative ('kjuːrətɪv) a. 1. tending to cure disease —n. 2. anything able to heal or cure

curator (kjuːˈreɪtə) n. custodian, esp. of

museum, library etc. —cura'**torial** a. —cu'ra**torship** n.

curb (kɜːb) n. 1. check, restraint 2. chain or strap passing under horse's lower jaw and giving powerful control with reins —vt. 3. restrain 4. apply curb to

curd (kɜːd) n. coagulated milk —'**curdle** v. turn into curd, coagulate —'**curdy** a.

cure (kjʊə) vt. 1. heal, restore to health 2. remedy 3. preserve (fish, skins etc.) —n. 4. remedy 5. course of medical treatment 6. successful treatment, restoration to health —cura'**bility** n. —'**curable** a. —**cure of souls** care of parish or congregation

curet or **curette** (kjʊəˈrɛt) n. surgical instrument for removing dead tissue etc. from some body cavities —**curettage** (kjʊərɪˈtɑːʒ, kjʊəˈrɛtɪdʒ) n.

curfew ('kɜːfjuː) n. 1. official regulation restricting or prohibiting movement of people, esp. at night 2. time set as deadline by such regulation

curia ('kjʊərɪə) n. 1. papal court and government of Roman Catholic Church 2. (in Middle Ages) court held in king's name (pl. **curiae** ('kjʊəriːiː))

curie ('kjʊərɪ, -riː) n. standard unit of radium emanation

curio ('kjʊərɪəʊ) n. rare or curious thing of the kind sought for collections (pl. -s)

curious ('kjʊərɪəs) a. 1. eager to know, inquisitive 2. prying 3. puzzling, strange, odd —curi'**osity** n. 1. eagerness to know 2. inquisitiveness 3. strange or rare thing —'**curiously** adv.

curium ('kjʊərɪəm) n. element produced from plutonium

curl (kɜːl) vi. 1. take spiral or curved shape or path —vt. 2. bend into spiral or curved shape —n. 3. spiral lock of hair 4. spiral, curved state, form or motion —'**curler** n. 1. pin, clasp or roller for curling hair 2. person or thing that curls 3. person who plays curling —'**curling** n. game like bowls, played with large rounded stones on ice —'**curly** a. —**curling tongs** heated, metal, scissor-like device for curling hair

curlew ('kɜːljuː) n. large long-billed wading bird

curlicue or **curlycue** ('kɜːlɪkjuː) n. intricate ornamental curl or twist

curmudgeon (kɜːˈmʌdʒən) n. surly or miserly person

currach or **curragh** ('kʌrəx, 'kʌrə) n. Scot., Irish coracle

currant ('kʌrənt) n. 1. dried type of grape 2. fruit of various plants allied to gooseberry 3. any of these plants

current ('kʌrənt) a. 1. of immediate present, going on 2. up-to-date, not yet superseded 3. in circulation or general use —n. 4. body of water or air in motion 5. tendency, drift 6. transmission of electricity through conductor —'**currency** n. 1. money in use 2. state of being in use 3. time during which thing is current —'**currently** adv. —**current account** bank account against which cheques are drawn at any time

curricle ('kʌrɪkəl) n. two-wheeled open carriage drawn by two horses side by side

curriculum (kə'rɪkjuləm) n. specified course of study (pl. **-s**, **-la** (-lə)) —**curriculum vitae** ('viːtaɪ, 'vaɪtiː) outline of person's educational and professional history, usu. for job applications (pl. **curricula vitae**)

curry[1] ('kʌrɪ) n. 1. highly-flavoured, pungent condiment, preparation of turmeric 2. dish flavoured with it —vt. 3. prepare, flavour dish with curry ('**curried**, '**currying**)

curry[2] ('kʌrɪ) vt. 1. groom (horse) with comb 2. dress (leather) ('**curried**, '**currying**) —**curry comb** metal comb for grooming horse —**curry favour** try to win favour unworthily, ingratiate oneself

curse (kɜːs) n. 1. profane or obscene expression of anger etc. 2. utterance expressing extreme ill will towards some person or thing 3. affliction, misfortune, scourge —v. 4. utter curse, swear (at) —vt. 5. afflict —**cursed** ('kɜːsɪd, kɜːst) a. 1. hateful 2. wicked 3. deserving of, or under, a curse —**cursedly** ('kɜːsɪdlɪ) adv. —**cursedness** ('kɜːsɪdnɪs) n.

cursive ('kɜːsɪv) a. written in running script, with letters joined

cursor ('kɜːsə) n. 1. sliding part of measuring instrument, esp. on slide rule 2. movable point of light etc. that identifies specific position on visual display unit

cursory ('kɜːsərɪ) a. rapid, hasty, not detailed, superficial —'**cursorily** adv.

curt (kɜːt) a. short, rudely brief, abrupt —'**curtly** adv. —'**curtness** n.

curtail (kɜː'teɪl) vt. cut short, diminish —**cur'tailment** n.

curtain ('kɜːtən) n. 1. hanging drapery at window etc. 2. cloth hung as screen 3. screen separating audience and stage in theatre 4. end to act or scene etc. —pl. 5. inf. death or ruin: the end —vt. 6. provide, cover with curtain —**curtain call** return to stage by performers to acknowledge applause —**curtain-raiser** n. 1. short play coming before main one 2. any preliminary event

curtsy or **curtsey** ('kɜːtsɪ) n. 1. woman's bow or respectful gesture made by bending knees and lowering body —vi. 2. make a curtsy

curve (kɜːv) n. 1. line of which no part is straight 2. bent line or part —v. 3. bend into curve —**cur'vaceous** a. inf. shapely —'**curvature** n. 1. a bending 2. bent shape —**curvi'linear** a. of bent lines

curvet (kɜː'vɛt) n. 1. Dressage low leap with all four feet off the ground —vi. 2. prance or frisk about

cushion ('kuʃən) n. 1. bag filled with soft stuffing or air, to support or ease body 2. any soft pad or support 3. resilient rim of billiard table —vt. 4. provide, protect with cushion 5. lessen effects of

cushy ('kuʃɪ) a. inf. soft, comfortable, pleasant, light, well-paid

cusp (kʌsp) n. pointed end, esp. of tooth —'**cuspid** n. pointed tooth —'**cuspidal** a. 1. ending in point 2. of, or like, cusp

cuspidor ('kʌspɪdɔː) n. spittoon

cuss (kʌs) inf. n. 1. curse; oath 2. person or animal, esp. annoying one —v. 3. see CURSE (sense 4) —**cussed** ('kʌsɪd) a. inf. 1. see cursed at CURSE 2. obstinate 3. annoying —'**cussedness** n.

custard ('kʌstəd) n. 1. dish made of eggs and milk 2. sweet sauce of milk and cornflour

custody ('kʌstədɪ) n. safekeeping, guardianship, imprisonment —**cus'todian** n. keeper, caretaker, curator

custom ('kʌstəm) n. 1. habit 2. practice 3. fashion, usage 4. business patronage 5. toll, tax —pl. 6. duties levied on imports 7. government department which collects these 8. area in airport etc. where customs officials examine baggage for dutiable goods —'**customarily** adv. —'**customary** a. usual, habitual —'**customer** n. 1. one who enters shop to buy, esp. regularly 2. purchaser —**custom-built** a. chiefly US (of cars, houses etc.) made to specifications of buyer —**custom-made** a. chiefly US (of suits etc.) made to specifications of buyer —**customs duties** taxes laid on imported or exported goods —**customs house** building where customs are collected

cut (kʌt) vt. 1. sever, penetrate, wound, divide, or separate with pressure of edge or edged instrument 2. pare, detach, trim, or shape by cutting 3. divide 4. intersect 5. reduce, decrease 6. abridge 7. inf. ignore (person) 8. strike (with whip etc.) 9. hit (cricket ball) to point's left 10. inf. stay deliberately away from —vi. Cine. 11. call a halt to shooting sequence 12. (with to) move quickly to another scene (**cut**, '**cutting**) —n. 13. act of cutting 14. stroke 15. blow, wound (of knife, whip etc.) 16. reduction, decrease 17. fashion, shape 18. incision 19. engraving 20. piece cut off 21. division 22. inf. share, esp. of profits —'**cutter** n. 1. one who, that which, cuts

2. warship's rowing and sailing boat **3.** small sloop-rigged vessel with straight running bowsprit —'**cutting** n. **1.** act of cutting, thing cut off or out, *esp.* excavation (for road, canal *etc.*) through high ground **2.** shoot, twig of plant **3.** piece cut from newspaper *etc.* —a. **4.** sarcastic, unkind —'**cutaway** n. **1.** man's coat cut diagonally from front waist to back of knees **2.** drawing or model of machine *etc.* in which part of casing is omitted to reveal workings —'**cutback** n. decrease; reduction —**cut glass** glass, *esp.* vases *etc.*, decorated by facet-cutting or grinding —**cut-price** *or esp.* *U.S.* **cut-rate** a. **1.** available at prices or rates below standard price or rate **2.** offering goods or services at prices below standard price —'**cutthroat** a. **1.** merciless —n. **2.** murderer **3.** *UK* razor with long blade that usu. folds into handle (*also* **cutthroat razor**) —**cut back 1.** shorten by cutting off end; prune **2.** reduce or make reduction (in) —**cut dead** refuse to recognize an acquaintance —**cut in 1.** drive in front of another's vehicle so as to affect his driving **2.** interrupt (in conversation) **3.** intrude

cutaneous (kju:'teɪnɪəs) a. of skin

cute (kju:t) a. appealing, attractive, pretty

cuticle ('kju:tɪkəl) n. dead skin, *esp.* at base of fingernail

cutis ('kju:tɪs) n. *Anat.* skin (*pl.* -**tes** (-ti:z), -**es**)

cutlass ('kʌtləs) n. short broad-bladed sword

cutlery ('kʌtlərɪ) n. knives, forks, spoons *etc.* —'**cutler** n. one who makes, repairs, deals in knives and cutting implements

cutlet ('kʌtlɪt) n. small piece of meat grilled or fried

cuttlefish ('kʌtəlfɪʃ) n. sea mollusc like squid (*also* '**cuttle**) —'**cuttlebone** n. internal shell of cuttlefish, used as mineral supplement to diet of cagebirds and as polishing agent

Cwlth. Commonwealth

cwm (ku:m) n. **1.** in Wales, valley **2.** *Geol.* see CIRQUE

c.w.o. *or* **C.W.O.** cash with order

cwt. hundredweight

-**cy** (*comb. form*) **1.** state, quality, condition, as in *plutocracy, lunacy* **2.** rank, office, as in *captaincy*

cyan ('saɪən, 'saɪən) n. **1.** green-blue colour —a. **2.** of this colour

cyanide ('saɪənaɪd) *or* **cyanid** ('saɪənɪd) n. extremely poisonous chemical compound —**cy'anogen** n. poisonous gas composed of nitrogen and carbon

cyanosis (saɪə'nəʊsɪs) n. blueness of the skin

cybernetics (saɪbə'nɛtɪks) *pl.n.* (*with sing. v.*) comparative study of control mechanisms of electronic and biological systems

cyclamate ('saɪkləmeɪt, 'sɪkləmeɪt) n. com-

pound formerly used as food additive and sugar substitute

cyclamen ('sɪkləmən, -mɛn) n. plant with flowers having turned-back petals

cycle ('saɪkəl) n. **1.** recurrent series or period **2.** rotation of events **3.** complete series or period **4.** development following course of stages **5.** series of poems *etc.* **6.** bicycle —vi. **7.** move in cycles **8.** ride bicycle —'**cyclic(al)** a. —'**cyclist** n. bicycle rider —**cy'clometer** n. instrument for measuring circles or recording distance travelled by wheel, *esp.* of bicycle

cyclo- *or before vowel* **cycl-** (*comb. form*) **1.** indicating circle or ring, as in *cyclotron* **2.** denoting cyclic compound, as in *cyclopropane*

cyclone ('saɪkləʊn) n. **1.** system of winds moving round centre of low pressure **2.** circular storm —**cy'clonic** (saɪ'klɒnɪk) a.

cyclopedia *or* **cyclopaedia** (saɪkləʊ'pi:dɪə) n. see ENCYCLOPEDIA

cyclopropane (saɪkləʊ'prəʊpeɪn) n. colourless gaseous hydrocarbon, used as anaesthetic

Cyclops ('saɪklɒps) n. *Class. myth.* one of race of giants having single eye in middle of forehead (*pl.* **Cyclopes** (saɪ'kləʊpi:z), -**es**)

cyclorama (saɪkləʊ'ra:mə) n. **1.** picture on interior wall of cylindrical room, designed to appear in natural perspective to spectator **2.** *Theat.* curtain or wall curving along back of stage —**cyclo'ramic** (saɪkləʊ'ræmɪk) a.

cyclostyle ('saɪkləstaɪl) vt. **1.** produce (pamphlets *etc.*) in large numbers for distribution —a./n. **2.** (of) machine, method for doing this

cyclotron ('saɪklətrɒn) n. powerful apparatus which accelerates the circular movement of subatomic particles in a magnetic field, used for work in nuclear disintegration *etc.*

cygnet ('sɪgnɪt) n. young swan

cylinder ('sɪlɪndə) n. **1.** roller-shaped solid or hollow body, of uniform diameter **2.** piston chamber of engine —**cy'lindrical** a. —'**cylindroid** a.

cymbal ('sɪmbəl) n. one of pair of two brass plates struck together to produce ringing or clashing sound in music

cyme (saɪm) n. inflorescence in which first flower is terminal bud of main stem and subsequent flowers develop as terminal buds of lateral stems —**cy'miferous** a.

Cymric *or* **Kymric** ('kɪmrɪk) a. Welsh

cynic ('sɪnɪk) n. one who expects, believes, the worst about people, their motives, or outcome of events —'**cynical** a. —'**cynicism** n. being cynical

cynosure ('sɪnəzjʊə, -ʃʊə) n. centre of attraction

cypher ('saɪfə) see CIPHER

cypress ('saiprəs) *n.* coniferous tree with very dark foliage

Cypriot ('sipriət) *or* **Cypriote** ('sipriəʊt) *n.* 1. native of Cyprus 2. dialect of Greek spoken in Cyprus —*a.* 3. relating to Cyprus

Cyrillic (si'rilik) *a.* 1. relating to alphabet devised supposedly by Saint Cyril, for Slavonic languages —*n.* 2. this alphabet

cyst (sist) *n.* sac containing liquid secretion or pus —**'cystic** *a.* 1. of cysts 2. of the bladder —**cys'titis** *n.* inflammation of bladder —**cystic fibrosis** congenital disease, usu. affecting children, characterized by chronic infection of respiratory tract and pancreatic insufficiency

cytology (sai'tolədʒi) *n.* study of plant and animal cells

cytoplasm ('saitəʊplæzəm) *n.* protoplasm of cell excluding nucleus

czar (zɑː) *n.* emperor, king, *esp.* of Russia 1547-1917 —**Cza'rina**, **Cza'ritsa**, **Tsa'ritsa** *or* **Tza'ritsa** *n.* wife of Czar

czardas ('tʃɑːdæʃ) *n.* 1. Hungarian national dance of alternating slow and fast sections 2. music for this dance

Czech (tʃek) *n.* member of western branch of Slavs —**Czechoslovak** (tʃekəʊ'sləʊvæk) *or* **Czechoslovakian** (tʃekəʊsləʊ'vækiən) *a.* 1. of Czechoslovakia, its peoples or languages —*n.* 2. (loosely) either of two languages of Czechoslovakia: Czech or Slovak

---

D,d

d *or* **D** (diː) *n.* 1. fourth letter of English alphabet 2. speech sound represented by this letter (*pl.* **d's**, **D's** *or* **Ds**)

d *Phys.* density

D 1. *Mus.* second note of scale of C major; major or minor key having this note as its tonic 2. *Chem.* deuterium 3. Roman numeral, 500

d. 1. day 2. denarius (*Lat.*, penny) 3. departs 4. diameter 5. died

D. Democratic

dab[1] (dæb) *vt.* 1. apply with momentary pressure (*esp.* anything wet and soft) 2. strike feebly (-**bb-**) —*n.* 3. smear 4. slight blow or tap 5. small mass —**'dabchick** *n.* small grebe —**dab hand** *inf.* someone good at something

dab[2] (dæb) *n.* small flatfish

dabble ('dæbəl) *vi.* 1. splash about 2. be desultory student or amateur —**'dabbler** *n.*

da capo (dɑː 'kɑːpəʊ) *Mus.* repeat from beginning

dace (deis) *n.* small freshwater fish (*pl.* **dace**, **-s**)

dachshund ('dækshʊnd) *n.* short-legged long-bodied dog

Dacron ('deikron, 'dæk-) *n.* US R Terylene

dactyl ('dæktil) *n.* metrical foot of one long followed by two short syllables

dad (dæd) *or* **daddy** ('dædi) *n. inf.* father —**daddy-longlegs** *n. inf.* crane fly

Dada ('dɑːdɑː) *or* **Dadaism** ('dɑːdɑːizəm) *n.* artistic movement of early 20th century, founded on principles of incongruity and irreverence towards accepted aesthetic criteria —**'Dadaist** *n./a.*

dado ('deidəʊ) *n.* lower part of room wall when lined or painted separately (*pl.* **-es**, **-s**)

daemon ('diːmən) *or* **daimon** ('daimɒn) *n.* 1. demigod 2. guardian spirit of place or person

daff (dæf) *inf.* daffodil

daffodil ('dæfədil) *n.* spring flower, yellow narcissus (*also* **Lent lily**)

daft (dɑːft) *a.* foolish, crazy

dag (dæg) *n.* 1. daglock 2. A, NZ *sl.* eccentric character —**'daglock** *n.* dung-caked locks of wool around hindquarters of sheep

dagga ('dæxə, 'dɑːgə) *n.* SA hemp, smoked as narcotic

dagger ('dægə) *n.* short, edged stabbing weapon

dago ('deigəʊ) *n. offens.* Spaniard or other Latin (*pl.* **-s**, **-es**)

daguerreotype (də'gerəʊtaip) *n.* 1. early photographic process 2. photograph formed by this process

dahlia ('deiljə) *n.* garden plant of various colours

Dáil Éireann ('dɔil 'ɛərən) *or* **Dáil** *n.* lower chamber of parliament in the Irish Republic

daily ('deili) *a.* 1. done, occurring, published every day —*adv.* 2. every day —*n.* 3. daily newspaper 4. charwoman

dainty ('deinti) *a.* 1. delicate 2. elegant, choice 3. pretty and neat 4. fastidious —*n.* 5. delicacy —**'daintily** *adv.* —**'daintiness** *n.*

daiquiri ('daikiri, 'dæk-) *n.* iced drink containing rum, lime juice and sugar (*pl.* **-s**)

dairy ('dɛəri) *n.* place for processing milk and its products —**'dairying** *n.* —**dairy cattle** cows raised mainly for milk —**dairy farm** farm specializing in producing milk—**'dairymaid** *n.* —**'dairyman** *n.* —**dairy products** milk, cheese, butter *etc.*

dais ('deiis, deis) *n.* raised platform, usu. at end of hall

daisy ('deizi) *n.* flower with yellow centre and white petals —**daisy-wheel** *n.* flat, wheel-shaped device with printing characters at end of spokes

Dalai Lama ('dælai 'lɑːmə) head of Buddhist hierarchy in Tibet

dale (deɪl) *n.* valley —**'dalesman** *n.* native of dale, *esp.* of N England

dalles (dælz) *pl.n.* C river rapids flowing between high rock walls

dally ('dælɪ) *vi.* 1. trifle, spend time in idleness or amusement 2. loiter ('dallied, 'dallying) —'**dalliance** *n.*

Dalmatian (dæl'meɪʃən) *n.* large dog, white with black spots

dal segno ('dæl 'sɛnjəʊ) *Mus.* repeat from point marked with sign to word *fine*

dam[1] (dæm) *n.* 1. barrier to hold back flow of waters 2. water so collected —*vt.* 3. hold with or as with dam (-**mm**-)

dam[2] (dæm) *n.* female parent (used of animals)

damage ('dæmɪdʒ) *n.* 1. injury, harm, loss —*pl.* 2. sum claimed or adjudged in compensation for injury —*vt.* 3. harm

damask ('dæməsk) *n.* 1. figured woven material of silk or linen, *esp.* white table linen with design shown up by light 2. colour of damask rose, velvety red —**damascene** ('dæməsiːn) *vt.* decorate (steel *etc.*) with inlaid gold or silver —**damask rose** fragrant rose used to make the perfume attar

dame (deɪm) *n.* 1. *obs.* lady 2. (**D-**) title of lady in Order of the British Empire 3. *sl. chiefly US* woman

damn (dæm) *vt.* 1. condemn to hell 2. be the ruin of 3. give hostile reception to —*vi.* 4. curse (**damned, 'damning**) —*interj.* 5. expression of annoyance, impatience *etc.* —**damnable** ('dæmnəbəl) *a.* 1. deserving damnation 2. hateful, annoying —**dam'nation** *n.* —**damnatory** ('dæmnətərɪ) *a.*

damp (dæmp) *a.* 1. moist 2. slightly moist —*n.* 3. diffused moisture 4. in coal mines, dangerous gas —*vt.* 5. make damp 6. (*oft. with* down) deaden, discourage —'**dampen** *v.* 1. make, become damp —*vt.* 2. stifle, deaden —'**damper** *n.* 1. anything that discourages or depresses 2. plate in flue to control draught —'**dampcourse** *n.* layer of impervious material in wall, to stop moisture rising (*also* **damp-proof course**)

damsel ('dæmzəl) *n. obs.* girl

damson ('dæmzən) *n.* 1. small dark purple plum 2. tree bearing it 3. its colour

dan (dæn) *n. Judo* 1. any one of 12 black-belt grades of proficiency 2. competitor entitled to dan grading

Dan. *Bible* Daniel

dance (dɑːns) *vi.* 1. move with measured rhythmic steps, usu. to music 2. be in lively movement 3. bob up and down —*vt.* 4. perform (dance) 5. cause to dance —*n.* 6. lively, rhythmical movement 7. arrangement of such movements 8. tune for them 9. social gathering for the purpose of dancing —'**dancer** *n.*

D and C dilation and curettage (of womb)

dandelion ('dændɪlaɪən) *n.* yellow-flowered wild plant

dander ('dændə) *n. inf.* temper, fighting spirit

dandle ('dændəl) *vt.* 1. move (young child) up and down (on knee or in arms) 2. pet; fondle

dandruff ('dændrəf) *or* **dandriff** ('dændrɪf) *n.* dead skin in small scales among the hair

dandy ('dændɪ) *n.* 1. man excessively concerned with smartness of dress —*a.* 2. *inf.* excellent —'**dandify** *vt.* dress like or cause to resemble a dandy —'**dandyism** *n.*

Dane (deɪn) *n.* 1. native of Denmark 2. Viking who invaded England from late 8th to 11th cent. A.D. —'**Danish** *a.* 1. of Denmark —*n.* 2. official language of Denmark 3. people of Denmark collectively

danger ('deɪndʒə) *n.* 1. liability or exposure to harm 2. risk, peril —'**dangerous** *a.* —'**dangerously** *adv.* —**danger money** extra money paid to compensate for risks involved in certain dangerous jobs

dangle ('dæŋgəl) *vi.* 1. hang loosely and swaying —*vt.* 2. hold suspended 3. tempt with

dank (dæŋk) *a.* unpleasantly damp and chilly —'**dankness** *n.*

danseuse (dɑ̃'sɜːz) *n.* female dancer

daphne ('dæfnɪ) *n.* ornamental shrub with bell-shaped flowers

dapper ('dæpə) *a.* neat and precise, *esp.* in dress, spruce

dapple ('dæpəl) *v.* mark or become marked with spots —'**dappled** *a.* 1. spotted 2. mottled 3. variegated —**dapple-grey** *a.* (of horse) grey marked with darker spots

Darby and Joan ('dɑːbɪ, dʒəʊn) elderly married couple living in domestic harmony —**Darby and Joan club** for elderly people

dare (dɛə) *v.* 1. venture, have courage (to) —*vt.* 2. challenge —*n.* 3. challenge —'**daring** *a.* 1. bold —*n.* 2. adventurous courage —'**daredevil** *a./n.* reckless (person)

dark (dɑːk) *a.* 1. without light 2. gloomy 3. deep in tint 4. secret 5. unenlightened 6. wicked —*n.* 7. absence of light, colour or knowledge —'**darken** *v.* —'**darkly** *adv.* —'**darkness** *n.* —**Dark Ages** *Hist.* period from about 5th cent. A.D. to about 1000 A.D. —**Dark Continent** Africa when relatively unexplored —**dark horse** somebody, *esp.* competitor in race, about whom little is known —'**darkroom** *n.* darkened room for processing film

darling ('dɑːlɪŋ) *a./n.* much loved or very lovable (person)

darn[1] (dɑːn) *vt.* 1. mend by filling (hole) with interwoven yarn —*n.* 2. place so mended —'**darning** *n.*

darn[2] (dɑːn) *interj.* mild expletive

darnel ('dɑːnəl) n. grass that grows as weed in grain fields

dart (dɑːt) n. **1.** small light pointed missile **2.** darting motion **3.** small seam or intake in garment —pl. **4.** indoor game played with numbered target and miniature darts —vt. **5.** cast, throw rapidly (glance etc.) —vi. **6.** go rapidly or abruptly —'**dartboard** n. circular piece of wood etc. used as target in darts

Darwinian (dɑː'wɪnɪən) a. pert. to Charles Darwin or his theory of evolution

dash (dæʃ) vt. **1.** smash, throw, thrust, send with violence **2.** cast down **3.** tinge, flavour, mix —vi. **4.** move, go with great speed or violence —n. **5.** rush **6.** vigour **7.** smartness **8.** small quantity, tinge **9.** stroke (-) between words —'**dashboard** n. C ledge along top of boards at ice-hockey rink —'**dashing** a. spirited, showy —'**dashboard** n. in car etc., instrument panel in front of driver

dassie ('dæsɪ) n. SA hyrax

dastard ('dæstəd) n. obs. contemptible, sneaking coward —'**dastardly** a.

dasyure ('dæsjʊə) n. **1.** small carnivorous marsupial of Aust., New Guinea and adjacent islands **2.** ursine dasyure (see TASMANIAN DEVIL)

data ('deɪtə, 'dɑːtə) pl.n. (oft. with sing. v.) **1.** series of observations, measurements or facts **2.** information —**data bank** or **base** store of information, esp. in form that can be handled by computer —**data processing** sequence of operations performed on data, esp. by computer, to extract information etc.

date¹ (deɪt) n. **1.** day of the month **2.** statement on document of its time of writing **3.** time of occurrence **4.** period of work of art etc. **5.** engagement, appointment —vt. **6.** mark with date **7.** refer to date of **8.** reveal age of **9.** inf. accompany on social outing —vi. **10.** exist (from) **11.** betray time or period of origin, become old-fashioned —'**dateless** a. **1.** without date **2.** immemorial —**date line** (oft. D- L-) line (approx. 180° meridian) E of which is one day earlier than W of it —'**dateline** n. Journalism date and location of story, placed at top of article —**date stamp 1.** adjustable rubber stamp for recording date **2.** inked impression made by this

date² (deɪt) n. **1.** sweet, single-stone fruit of palm **2.** the palm

dative ('deɪtɪv) n. noun case indicating indirect object etc.

datum ('deɪtəm, 'dɑːtəm) n. thing given, known, or assumed as basis for reckoning, reasoning etc. (pl. '**data**)

daub (dɔːb) vt. **1.** coat, plaster, paint coarsely or roughly —n. **2.** rough picture **3.** smear —'**dauber** n.

daughter ('dɔːtə) n. one's female child

—'**daughterly** a. —**daughter-in-law** n. son's wife

daunt (dɔːnt) vt. frighten, esp. into giving up purpose —'**dauntless** a. intrepid, fearless

dauphin ('dɔːfɪn; Fr. do'fɛ̃) n. formerly, eldest son of French king

davenport ('dævənpɔːt) n. **1.** small writing table with drawers **2.** US large couch or settee

davit ('dævɪt, 'deɪ-) n. crane, usu. one of pair, at ship's side for lowering and hoisting boats

Davy Jones's locker ('deɪvɪ 'dʒəʊnɪz) sea, considered as sailors' grave

Davy lamp miner's safety lamp

daw (dɔː) n. obs. jackdaw

dawdle ('dɔːdəl) vi. idle, waste time, loiter —'**dawdler** n.

dawn (dɔːn) n. **1.** first light, daybreak **2.** first gleam or beginning of anything —vi. **3.** begin to grow light **4.** appear, begin **5.** (begin to) be understood —'**dawning** n. —**dawn chorus** singing of birds at dawn

day (deɪ) n. **1.** period of 24 hours **2.** time when sun is above horizon **3.** point or unit of time **4.** daylight **5.** part of day occupied by certain activity, time period **6.** special or designated day —**day bed** couch intended for use as seat and as bed —'**daybook** n. Book-keeping book in which day's sales etc. are entered for later transfer to ledger —'**dayboy** n. UK boy who attends boarding school daily, but returns home each evening ('**daygirl** fem.) —'**daybreak** n. dawn —**day centre** place providing meals etc. where the elderly, handicapped etc. may spend the day —'**daydream** n. **1.** idle fancy —vi. **2.** indulge in idle fantasy —'**daylight** n. **1.** natural light **2.** dawn —pl. **3.** consciousness, wits —**daylight robbery** inf. blatant overcharging —**daylight saving** in summer, time set one hour ahead of local standard time, giving extra daylight in evenings —**day release** UK system of releasing employees for part-time education —**day room** communal living room in residential institution —'**dayspring** n. dawn —'**daystar** n. morning star —'**daytime** n. time between sunrise and sunset —**day-to-day** a. routine; everyday

Dayak ('daɪæk) n. see DYAK

daze (deɪz) vt. **1.** stupefy, stun, bewilder —n. **2.** stupefied or bewildered state —**dazed** a.

dazzle ('dæzəl) vt. **1.** blind, confuse or overpower with brightness, light, brilliant display or prospects —n. **2.** brightness that dazzles the vision —'**dazzlement** n.

dB or **db** decibel(s)

D.B.E. Dame Commander of the British Empire

DBS Direct Broadcasting by Satellite

DC direct current

D.C. District of Columbia

D.C.B. Dame Commander of the Order of the Bath

D.C.M. Distinguished Conduct Medal

~~**DD** Doctor of Divinity~~

D-day n. day selected for start of something, esp. Allied invasion of Europe in 1944

DDT dichlorodiphenyltrichloroethane, hydrocarbon compound used as an insecticide

DE Delaware

de- (comb. form) removal of, from, reversal of, as in delouse, desegregate. Such words are not given here where the meaning may be inferred from the simple word

deacon ('diːkən) n. 1. one in lowest degree of holy orders 2. one who superintends secular affairs of presbyterian church ('**deaconess** fem.)

deactivate (diːˈæktɪveɪt) vt. 1. make (bomb etc.) harmless or inoperative 2. make less radioactive

dead (dɛd) a. 1. no longer alive 2. obsolete 3. numb, without sensation 4. no longer functioning, extinguished 5. lacking lustre, movement or vigour 6. sure, complete —n. 7. dead person or persons (oft. in pl., **the dead**) —adv. 8. utterly —'**deaden** vt. —'**deadly** a. 1. fatal 2. deathlike —adv. 3. as if dead —**dead-and-alive** a. dull —'**deadbeat** a./n. inf. lazy, useless (person) —**dead duck** sl. person or thing doomed to death, failure etc., esp. because of mistake —**dead end** 1. cul-de-sac 2. situation in which further progress is impossible —'**deadhead** n. US, C log sticking out of water as hindrance to navigation —**dead heat** race in which competitors finish exactly even —**dead letter** 1. law no longer observed 2. letter which post office cannot deliver —'**deadline** n. limit of time allowed —'**deadlock** n. standstill —**dead loss** 1. complete loss for which no compensation is paid 2. inf. useless person or thing —**deadly nightshade** plant with poisonous black berries —**dead man's handle** or **pedal** safety switch on piece of machinery that allows operation only while depressed by operator —**dead march** solemn funeral music to accompany procession —'**deadpan** a. expressionless —**dead reckoning** calculation of ship's position from log and compass, when observations cannot be taken —**dead set** adv. 1. absolutely —n. 2. resolute attack —**dead weight** 1. heavy weight or load 2. oppressive burden 3. difference between loaded and unloaded weights of ship 4. intrinsic invariable weight of structure —'**deadwood** n. 1. dead trees or branches 2. inf. useless person; encumbrance —**dead of night** time of greatest stillness and darkness

deaf (dɛf) a. 1. wholly or partly without hearing 2. unwilling to listen —'**deafen** vt. make deaf —'**deafness** n. —**deaf aid** hearing aid —**deaf-and-dumb** a. 1. unable to hear or speak 2. for use of deaf-mutes —**deaf-mute** n. 1. person unable to hear or speak —a. 2. unable to hear or speak

deal¹ (diːl) vt. 1. distribute, give out 2. inflict —vi. 3. act 4. treat 5. do business (with, in) (**dealt** pt./pp.) —n. 6. agreement 7. treatment 8. share 9. business transaction —'**dealer** n. 1. one who deals (esp. cards) 2. trader —'**dealings** pl.n. transactions or relations with others —**deal with** handle, act towards

deal² (diːl) n. (plank of) fir or pine wood

dealt (dɛlt) pt./pp. of DEAL¹

dean¹ (diːn) n. 1. university or college official 2. head of cathedral chapter —'**deanery** n. cathedral dean's house or appointment

dean² (diːn) n. see DENE

dear (dɪə) a. 1. beloved 2. precious 3. costly, expensive —n. 4. beloved one —adv. 5. at a high price —'**dearly** adv. —'**dearness** n.

dearth (dɜːθ) n. scarcity

death (dɛθ) n. 1. dying 2. end of life 3. end, extinction 4. annihilation 5. (**D-**) personification of death, as skeleton —'**deathless** a. immortal —'**deathly** a./adv. like death —'**deathbed** n. bed in which person is about to die —'**deathblow** n. thing or event that destroys life or hope, esp. suddenly —**death certificate** legal document issued by doctor, certifying death of person and stating cause if known —**death duty** tax on property left at death —**death mask** cast of person's face taken after death —**death penalty** capital punishment —**death rate** ratio of deaths in specified area etc. to population of that area etc. (also **mortality rate**) —**death's-head** n. human skull or representation of one —'**deathtrap** n. building etc. considered unsafe —**death warrant** official authorization for carrying out sentence of death —**deathwatch beetle** beetle that bores into wood —**sign one's (own) death warrant** cause one's own destruction

debacle (deɪˈbɑːkᵊl, dɪ-) n. utter collapse, rout, disaster

debar (dɪˈbɑː) vt. 1. shut out 2. stop 3. prohibit 4. preclude (**-rr-**)

debark (dɪˈbɑːk) v. disembark

debase (dɪˈbeɪs) vt. 1. lower in value, quality or character 2. adulterate —de'**basement** n.

debate (dɪˈbeɪt) v. 1. argue, discuss, esp. in a formal assembly 2. consider (something) —n. 3. discussion 4. controversy —de'**batable** a. —de'**bater** n.

debauch (dɪˈbɔːtʃ) vt. 1. lead into a life of depraved self-indulgence —n. 2. bout of sensual indulgence —**debau'chee** n. dissipated person —de'**bauchery** n.

debenture (dɪ'bɛntʃə) *n.* bond of company or corporation —**debenture stock** shares issued by company, which guarantee fixed return at regular intervals

debility (dɪ'bɪlɪtɪ) *n.* 1. feebleness, *esp.* of health 2. languor —**de'bilitate** *vt.* weaken, enervate

debit ('dɛbɪt) *Accounting n.* 1. entry in account of sum owed 2. side of book in which such sums are entered —*vt.* 3. charge, enter as due

debonair *or* **debonnaire** (dɛbə'nɛə) *a.* 1. suave 2. genial 3. affable

debouch (dɪ'bautʃ) *vi.* move out from narrow place to wider one —**de'bouchment** *n.*

debrief (diː'briːf) *v.* (of soldier *etc.*) report to superior on result of mission

debris *or* **débris** ('deɪbrɪ, 'dɛbrɪ) *n.* fragments, rubbish

debt (dɛt) *n.* 1. what is owed 2. state of owing —'**debtor** *n.* —**debt of honour** debt that is morally but not legally binding

debug (diː'bʌg) *vt. inf.* 1. remove concealed microphones from (room *etc.*) 2. remove defects in (device *etc.*) 3. remove insects from ('**gg**-)

debunk (diː'bʌŋk) *vt.* expose falseness, pretentiousness of, *esp.* by ridicule

debut ('deɪbjuː, 'dɛbjuː) *n.* first appearance in public —**debutante** ('dɛbjutɑːnt, -tænt) *n.* girl making official debut into society

Dec. December

deca-, **deka-** *or before vowel* **dec-**, **dek-** (*comb. form*) ten, as in *decalitre*

decade ('dɛkeɪd, dɪ'keɪd) *n.* 1. period of ten years 2. set of ten

decadent ('dɛkədənt) *a.* 1. declining, deteriorating 2. morally corrupt —'**decadence** *or* '**decadency** *n.*

decaffeinated (dɪ'kæfɪneɪtɪd) *a.* (of coffee) with caffeine removed

decagon ('dɛkəgɒn) *n.* figure of 10 angles —**de'cagonal** *a.*

decagram *or* **decagramme** ('dɛkəgræm) *n.* measure of weight equal to 10 litres

decahedron (dɛkə'hiːdrən) *n.* solid of 10 faces —**deca'hedral** *a.*

decalcify (diː'kælsɪfaɪ) *vt.* deprive of lime, as bones or teeth of their calcareous matter (**-fied**, **-fying**)

decalitre *or U.S.* **decaliter** ('dɛkəliːtə) *n.* 10 litres

Decalogue ('dɛkəlɒg) *n.* the Ten Commandments

decametre *or U.S.* **decameter** ('dɛkəmiːtə) *n.* 10 metres

decamp (dɪ'kæmp) *vi.* 1. make off 2. break camp 3. abscond

decanal (dɪ'keɪnəl) *a.* of dean, deanery

decant (dɪ'kænt) *vt.* pour off (liquid, as wine) without disturbing sediment —**de'canter** *n.* stoppered bottle for wine or spirits

decapitate (dɪ'kæpɪteɪt) *vt.* behead —**decapi'tation** *n.* —**de'capitator** *n.*

decapod ('dɛkəpɒd) *n.* 1. crustacean having five pairs of walking limbs, as crab *etc.* 2. cephalopod mollusc having eight short tentacles and two longer ones, as squid *etc.*

decarbonize *or* **-ise** (diː'kɑːbənaɪz) *vt.* remove deposit of carbon, as from motor cylinder —**decarboni'zation** *or* **-i'sation** *n.*

decasyllable ('dɛkəsɪləbəl) *n.* ten-syllabled line —**decasyl'labic** *a.*

decathlon (dɪ'kæθlɒn) *n.* athletic contest with ten events

decay (dɪ'keɪ) *v.* 1. rot, decompose 2. (cause to) fall off, decline —*n.* 3. rotting 4. a falling away, break up

decease (dɪ'siːs) *n.* 1. death —*vi.* 2. die —**de'ceased** *n./a.*

deceive (dɪ'siːv) *vt.* 1. mislead 2. delude 3. cheat —**de'ceit** *n.* 1. fraud 2. duplicity —**de'ceitful** *a.* —**de'ceiver** *n.*

decelerate (diː'sɛləreɪt) *vi.* slow down

December (dɪ'sɛmbə) *n.* twelfth and last month of year

decennial (dɪ'sɛnɪəl) *a.* of period of ten years —**de'cennially** *adv.*

decent ('diːsənt) *a.* 1. respectable 2. fitting, seemly 3. not obscene 4. adequate 5. *inf.* kind —'**decency** *n.* —'**decently** *adv.*

decentralize *or* **-ise** (diː'sɛntrəlaɪz) *vt.* divide (government, organization) among local centres

deception (dɪ'sɛpʃən) *n.* 1. deceiving 2. illusion 3. fraud 4. trick —**de'ceptive** *a.* 1. misleading 2. apt to mislead

deci- (*comb. form*) one tenth, as in *decimetre*

decibel ('dɛsɪbɛl) *n.* unit for measuring intensity of a sound

decide (dɪ'saɪd) *vt.* 1. settle, determine, bring to resolution 2. give judgment on —*vi.* 3. come to a decision, conclusion —**de'cided** *a.* 1. unmistakable 2. settled 3. resolute —**de'cidedly** *adv.* certainly, undoubtedly —**decision** (dɪ'sɪʒən) *n.* —**de'cisive** *a.* —**de'cisively** *adv.*

deciduous (dɪ'sɪdjuəs) *a.* 1. (of trees) losing leaves annually 2. (of antlers, teeth *etc.*) being shed at the end of a period of growth

decigram ('dɛsɪgræm) *n.* tenth of gram

decilitre *or U.S.* **deciliter** ('dɛsɪliːtə) *n.* tenth of litre

decimal ('dɛsɪməl) *a.* 1. relating to tenths 2. proceeding by tens —*n.* 3. decimal fraction —**decimali'zation** *or* **-i'sation** *n.* —'**decimalize** *or* **-ise** *vt.* convert into decimal fractions or system —**decimal system** system of weights and measures or coinage, in which value of each denomination is ten times the one below it

decimate ('dɛsɪmeɪt) vt. kill a tenth or large proportion of —**deci'mation** n. —'**decimator** n.

decimetre or U.S. **decimeter** ('dɛsɪmiːtə) n. tenth of metre

decipher (dɪ'saɪfə) vt. 1. make out meaning of 2. decode —**de'cipherable** a.

deck (dɛk) n. 1. platform or floor, esp. one covering whole or part of ship's hull 2. turntable of record-player 3. part of tape recorder supporting tapes —vt. 4. array, decorate —**deck chair** folding chair made of canvas suspended in wooden frame —**deck hand** 1. seaman assigned duties on deck of ship 2. UK seaman who has seen sea duty for at least one year 3. helper aboard yacht

deckle edge ('dɛkªl) 1. rough edge of paper oft. left as ornamentation 2. imitation of this

declaim (dɪ'kleɪm) vi. 1. speak dramatically, rhetorically or passionately 2. protest loudly —**declamation** (dɛklə'meɪʃən) n. —**declamatory** (dɪ'klæmətərɪ) a.

declare (dɪ'klɛə) vt. 1. announce formally 2. state emphatically 3. show 4. name (as liable to customs duty) —vi. 5. take sides (for) 6. Cricket bring innings to an end before last wicket has fallen —**declaration** (dɛklə'reɪʃən) n. —**declarative** (dɪ'klærətɪv) or **declaratory** (dɪ'klærətərɪ) a. —**de'clarer** n. Bridge person who names trumps or calls 'No trumps'

declassify (diː'klæsɪfaɪ) vt. release (document etc.) from security list (-**fying, -fied**) —**declassifi'cation** n.

decline (dɪ'klaɪn) v. 1. refuse 2. list case endings of (nouns) —vi. 3. slope, bend or sink downwards 4. deteriorate gradually 5. grow smaller, diminish —n. 6. gradual deterioration 7. movement downwards 8. diminution 9. downward slope —**declension** (dɪ'klɛnʃən) n. 1. group of nouns 2. falling off 3. declining —**de'clinable** a. —**decli'nation** (dɛklɪ'neɪʃən) n. 1. sloping away, deviation 2. angle

declivity (dɪ'klɪvɪtɪ) n. downward slope

declutch (dɪ'klʌtʃ) vi. disengage clutch of car etc.

decoction (dɪ'kɒkʃən) n. 1. extraction of essence by boiling down 2. such essence —**de'coct** vt. boil down

decode (diː'kəʊd) vt. convert from code into intelligible language

decoke (diː'kəʊk) vt. see DECARBONIZE

décolleté (deɪ'kɒlteɪ) a. (of women's garment) having a low-cut neckline —**décolletage** (deɪkɒl'tɑːʒ) n. low-cut dress or neckline

decommission (diːkə'mɪʃən) vt. dismantle (industrial plant or nuclear reactor) to an extent such that it can be safely abandoned

decompose (diːkəm'pəʊz) v. 1. separate into elements 2. rot —**decompo'sition** n. decay

decompress (diːkəm'prɛs) vt. 1. free from pressure 2. return to condition of normal atmospheric pressure —**decom'pression** n. —**decompression sickness** or **illness** disorder characterized by severe pain etc., caused by sudden change in atmospheric pressure

decongestant (diːkən'dʒɛstənt) a./n. (drug) relieving (esp. nasal) congestion

decontaminate (diːkən'tæmɪneɪt) vt. free from contamination, eg from poisons, radioactive substances etc. —**decontami'nation** n.

decontrol (diːkən'trəʊl) vt. release from state control (-**ll**-)

décor or **decor** ('deɪkɔː) n. 1. decorative scheme of room etc. 2. stage decoration, scenery

decorate ('dɛkəreɪt) vt. 1. beautify by additions 2. paint or wallpaper room etc. 3. invest (with an order, medal etc.) —**deco'ration** n. —'**decorative** a. —'**decorator** n. —**Decorated style** 14th-century style of English architecture characterized by geometrical tracery etc.

decorum (dɪ'kɔːrəm) n. seemly behaviour, propriety, decency —'**decorous** a. —'**decorously** adv.

decoy ('diːkɔɪ, dɪ'kɔɪ) n. 1. something used to entrap others or to distract their attention 2. bait, lure —v. (dɪ'kɔɪ) 3. lure, be lured as with decoy

decrease (dɪ'kriːs) v. 1. diminish, lessen —n. ('diːkriːs, dɪ'kriːs) 2. lessening

decree (dɪ'kriː) n. 1. order having the force of law 2. edict —vt. 3. determine judicially 4. order —**decree absolute** final decree in divorce proceedings, which leaves parties free to remarry —**decree nisi** decree coming into effect within a certain time, unless cause is shown for rescinding it (esp. in divorce cases)

decrement ('dɛkrɪmənt) n. 1. act or state of decreasing 2. quantity lost by decrease

decrepit (dɪ'krɛpɪt) a. 1. old and feeble 2. broken down, worn out —**de'crepitude** n.

decrescendo (diːkrɪ'ʃɛndəʊ) a. diminuendo

decretal (dɪ'kriːtªl) n. 1. R.C.Ch. papal decree; edict on doctrine or church law —a. 2. of decree

decry (dɪ'kraɪ) vt. disparage (**de'cried, de'crying**)

dedicate ('dɛdɪkeɪt) vt. 1. commit wholly to special purpose or cause 2. inscribe or address (book etc.) 3. devote to God's service —'**dedicated** a. 1. devoted to particular purpose or cause 2. Comp. designed to fulfil one function 3. manufactured for specific purpose —**dedi'cation** n. —'**dedicator** n. —'**dedicatory** a.

deduce (dɪ'djuːs) vt. draw as conclusion from facts —**de'duct** vt. take away, subtract

—de'ductible a. **1.** capable of being deducted **2.** US tax-deductible **—de'duction** n. **1.** deducting **2.** amount subtracted **3.** conclusion deduced **4.** inference from general to particular **—de'ductive** a. **—de'ductively** adv.

deed (diːd) n. **1.** action **2.** exploit **3.** legal document **—deed box** strong box in which deeds and other documents are kept **—deed poll** Law deed made by one party only, esp. one by which person changes his name

deejay ('diːdʒei) inf. disc jockey

deem (diːm) vt. judge, consider, regard **—'deemster** n. title of either of two justices in Isle of Man (also **'dempster**)

deep (diːp) a. **1.** extending far down, in or back **2.** at, of given depth **3.** profound **4.** heartfelt **5.** hard to fathom **6.** cunning **7.** engrossed, immersed **8.** (of colour) dark and rich **9.** (of sound) low and full —n. **10.** deep place **11.** the sea —adv. **12.** far down etc. **—'deepen** v. **—'deeply** adv. **—deep field** Cricket position behind bowler, near boundary **—deep'freeze** n. refrigerator storing frozen food **—deep-laid** a. (of plot or plan) carefully worked out and kept secret **—deep-rooted** or **deep-seated** a. (of ideas etc.) firmly fixed or held; ingrained

deer (diə) n. family of ruminant animals typically with antlers in male (pl. **deer, -s**) **—'deerhound** n. large rough-coated dog **—'deerskin** n. hide of deer **—'deerstalker** n. **1.** one who stalks deer **2.** kind of cloth hat with peaks

deface (dɪ'feis) vt. **1.** spoil or mar surface of **2.** disfigure **—de'facement** n.

de facto (dei 'fæktəʊ) Lat. existing in fact, whether legally recognized or not

defalcate ('diːfælkeit) vi. Law misuse or misappropriate property or funds entrusted to one

defame (dɪ'feim) vt. speak ill of, dishonour by slander or rumour **—defamation** (dɛfə'meiʃən) n. **—defamatory** (dɪ'fæmətəri) a.

default (dɪ'fɔːlt) n. **1.** failure to act, appear or pay —vi. **2.** fail (to pay) **—de'faulter** n. esp. soldier guilty of military offence **—in default of** in the absence of

defeat (dɪ'fiːt) vt. **1.** overcome, vanquish **2.** thwart —n. **3.** overthrow **4.** lost battle or encounter **5.** frustration **—de'featism** n. attitude tending to accept defeat **—de'featist** n./a.

defecate ('dɛfikeit) vi. **1.** empty the bowels —vt. **2.** clear of impurities **—defe'cation** n.

defect (dɪ'fɛkt, 'diːfɛkt) n. **1.** lack **2.** blemish, failing —vi. (dɪ'fɛkt) **3.** desert one's country, cause etc., esp. to join opponents **—de'fection** n. abandonment of duty or allegiance **—de'fective** a. **1.** incomplete **2.** faulty

defend (dɪ'fɛnd) vt. **1.** protect **2.** support by

argument, evidence **3.** (try to) maintain (title etc.) against challenger **—de'fence** or U.S. **de'fense** n. **—de'fendant** n. person accused in court **—de'fender** n. **—defensi'bility** n. **—de'fensible** a. **—de'fensive** a. **1.** serving for defence —n. **2.** position or attitude of defence

defer[1] (dɪ'fɜː) vt. put off, postpone (**-rr-**) **—de'ferment** n.

defer[2] (dɪ'fɜː) vi. submit to opinion or judgment of another (**-rr-**) **—deference** ('dɛfərəns) n. respect for another inclining one to accept his views etc. **—deferential** (dɛfə'rɛnʃəl) a. **—deferentially** (dɛfə'rɛnʃəli) adv.

defiance (dɪ'faiəns) n. see DEFY

deficient (dɪ'fiʃənt) a. lacking or falling short in something, insufficient **—de'ficiency** n. **—deficit** ('dɛfisit, dɪ'fisit) n. amount by which sum of money is too small **—deficiency disease** any condition, such as pellagra, produced by lack of vitamins etc.

defile[1] (dɪ'fail) vt. **1.** make dirty, pollute, soil **2.** sully **3.** desecrate **—de'filement** n.

defile[2] ('diːfail, dɪ'fail) n. **1.** narrow pass or valley —vi. **2.** march in file

define (dɪ'fain) vt. **1.** state contents or meaning of **2.** show clearly the form or outline of **3.** lay down clearly, fix **4.** mark out **—de'finable** a. **—definite** ('dɛfinit) a. **1.** exact, defined **2.** clear, specific **3.** certain, sure **—definitely** (dɛfinitli) adv. **—definition** (dɛfi'niʃən) n. **—definitive** (dɪ'finitiv) a. conclusive, to be looked on as final **—de'finitively** (dɪ'finitivli) adv.

deflate (diː'fleit) v. **1.** (cause to) collapse by release of gas **2.** Econ. cause deflation of (an economy etc.) —vt. **3.** take away self-esteem from **—de'flation** n. **1.** deflating **2.** Econ. reduction of economic and industrial activity **—de'flationary** a.

deflect (dɪ'flɛkt) v. (cause to) turn from straight course **—de'flection** or **de'flexion** n.

deflower (diː'flaʊə) vt. deprive of virginity, innocence etc. **—deflo'ration** (diːflɔː'reiʃən) n.

defoliate (diː'fəʊlieit) v. (cause to) lose leaves, esp. by action of chemicals **—de'foliant** n. **—defoli'ation** n.

deforest (diː'fɒrist) vt. clear of trees **—defores'tation** n.

deform (dɪ'fɔːm) vt. **1.** spoil shape of **2.** make ugly **3.** disfigure **—defor'mation** n. **—de'formed** a. **—de'formity** n.

defraud (dɪ'frɔːd) vt. cheat, swindle

defray (dɪ'frei) vt. provide money for (expenses etc.)

defrock (diː'frɒk) vt. deprive (priest, minister) of ecclesiastical status

defrost (diː'frɒst) v. **1.** make, become free of frost, ice **2.** thaw

deft (dɛft) a. skilful, adroit —**'deftly** adv. —**'deftness** n.

defunct (dɪ'fʌŋkt) a. 1. dead 2. obsolete

defuse or U.S. (sometimes) **defuze** (diː'fjuːz) vt. 1. remove fuse of (bomb etc.) 2. remove tension from (situation etc.)

defy (dɪ'faɪ) vt. 1. challenge, resist successfully 2. disregard (**de'fied, de'fying**) —**de'fiance** n. resistance —**de'fiant** a. 1. openly and aggressively hostile 2. insolent —**de'fiantly** adv.

degauss (diː'gaʊs) vt. equip (ship) with apparatus which prevents it detonating magnetic mines

degenerate (dɪ'dʒɛnəreɪt) vi. deteriorate to lower mental, moral or physical level —a. (dɪ'dʒɛnərɪt) 2. fallen away in quality —n. (dɪ'dʒɛnərɪt) 3. degenerate person —**de'generacy** n. —**degene'ration** n. —**de'generative** a.

degrade (dɪ'greɪd) vt. 1. dishonour 2. debase 3. reduce to lower rank —vi. 4. decompose chemically —**de'gradable** a. capable of chemical, biological decomposition —**degradation** (degrə'deɪʃən) n. —**de'graded** a. shamed, humiliated

degree (dɪ'griː) n. 1. step, stage in process, scale, relative rank, order, condition, manner, way 2. university rank 3. unit of measurement of temperature or angle —**third degree** severe, lengthy examination, esp. of accused person by police, to extract information, confession

dehisce (dɪ'hɪsənt) a. opening, as capsule of plant —**de'hisce** vi. burst open —**de'hiscence** n.

dehumanize or -**ise** (diː'hjuːmənaɪz) vt. 1. deprive of human qualities 2. render mechanical, artificial or routine

dehumidify (diːhjuː'mɪdɪfaɪ) vt. extract moisture from

dehydrate (diː'haɪdreɪt) vt. remove moisture from —**dehy'dration** n.

de-ice (diː'aɪs) vt. dislodge ice from (eg windscreen) or prevent its forming

deify (diːɪfaɪ, 'deɪ-) vt. make god of, treat, worship as god (**'deified, 'deifying**) —**deifi'cation** n. —**'deiform** a. godlike in form

deign (deɪn) vi. 1. condescend, stoop 2. think fit

deism ('diːɪzəm, 'deɪ-) n. belief in god but not in revelation —**'deist** n. —**'deistic** a. —**'deity** n. 1. divine status or attributes 2. a god

déjà vu ('deɪʒæ 'vuː) Fr. experience of perceiving new situation as if it had occurred before

deject (dɪ'dʒɛkt) vt. dishearten, cast down, depress —**de'jected** a. —**de'jection** n.

de jure (deɪ 'dʒʊəreɪ) Lat. in law, by right

dekko ('dɛkəʊ) n. sl. look

delay (dɪ'leɪ) vt. 1. postpone, hold back —vi. 2. be tardy, linger (**de'layed, de'laying**) —n. 3. act

or instance of delaying 4. interval of time between events

delectable (dɪ'lɛktəbᵊl) a. delightful —**delec'tation** n. pleasure

delegate ('dɛlɪgeɪt, -gɪt) n. 1. person chosen to represent another —vt. ('dɛlɪgeɪt) 2. send as deputy 3. commit (authority, business etc.) to a deputy —**'delegacy** n. —**dele'gation** n.

delete (dɪ'liːt) vt. remove, cancel, erase —**de'letion** n.

deleterious (dɛlɪ'tɪərɪəs) a. harmful, injurious

Delft (dɛlft) n. 1. town in Netherlands 2. tinglazed earthenware orig. from Delft, usu. with blue decoration on white ground (also 'delftware)

deliberate (dɪ'lɪbərɪt) a. 1. intentional 2. wellconsidered 3. without haste, slow —vt. (dɪ'lɪbəreɪt) 4. consider, debate —**de'liberately** adv. —**delibe'ration** n. —**de'liberative** a.

delicate ('dɛlɪkɪt) a. 1. exquisite 2. not robust, fragile 3. sensitive 4. requiring tact 5. deft —**'delicacy** n. —**'delicately** adv.

delicatessen (dɛlɪkə'tɛsᵊn) n. shop selling esp. imported or unusual foods

delicious (dɪ'lɪʃəs) a. delightful, pleasing to senses, esp. taste —**de'liciously** adv.

delight (dɪ'laɪt) vt. 1. please greatly —vi. 2. take great pleasure (in) —n. 3. great pleasure —**de'lightful** a. charming

delimitation (dɪlɪmɪ'teɪʃən) n. assigning of boundaries —**de'limit** vt.

delineate (dɪ'lɪnɪeɪt) vt. portray by drawing or description —**deline'ation** n. —**de'lineator** n.

delinquent (dɪ'lɪŋkwənt) n. someone, esp. young person, guilty of delinquency —**de'linquency** n. (minor) offence or misdeed

deliquesce (dɛlɪ'kwɛs) vi. become liquid —**deli'quescence** n. —**deli'quescent** a.

delirium (dɪ'lɪrɪəm) n. 1. disorder of the mind, esp. in feverish illness 2. violent excitement (pl. -s, -liria (-'lɪrɪə)) —**de'lirious** a. 1. raving 2. light-headed, wildly excited —**delirium tremens** ('trɛmɛnz, 'triː-) disordered mental state produced by advanced alcoholism (also **D.T.s**)

deliver (dɪ'lɪvə) vt. 1. carry (goods etc.) to destination 2. hand over 3. release 4. give birth (to) or assist in birth (of) 5. utter or present (speech etc.) —**de'liverance** n. rescue —**de'liverer** n. —**de'livery** n.

dell (dɛl) n. wooded hollow

Delphic ('dɛlfɪk) or **Delphian** a. pert. to Delphi or to the oracle of Apollo

delphinium (dɛl'fɪnɪəm) n. garden plant with tall spikes of usu. blue flowers (pl. -s, -ia (-ɪə))

delta ('dɛltə) n. 1. alluvial tract where river at mouth breaks into several streams 2. fourth letter in Gr. alphabet (Δ or δ) 3. shape of this letter **—delta wing** triangular swept-back aircraft wing

delude (dɪˈluːd) vt. 1. deceive 2. mislead **—deˈlusion** n. **—deˈlusive** a.

deluge (ˈdɛljuːdʒ) n. 1. flood, great flow 2. rush 3. downpour, cloudburst —vt. 4. flood 5. overwhelm

de luxe (də ˈlʌks, ˈluks) 1. rich, sumptuous 2. superior in quality

delve (dɛlv) v. 1. (with into) search intensively 2. dig

demagnetize or **-ise** (diːˈmæɡnətaɪz) vt. deprive of magnetic polarity

demagogue or U.S. (sometimes) **demagog** (ˈdɛməɡɒɡ) n. mob leader or agitator **—demagogic** (dɛməˈɡɒɡɪk) a. **—demagogy** (ˈdɛməɡɒɡɪ) n.

deman (diːˈmæn) vt. UK reduce the manpower of (plant, industry etc.)

demand (dɪˈmɑːnd) vt. 1. ask as giving an order 2. ask as by right 3. call for as due, right or necessary —n. 4. urgent request, claim, requirement 5. call (for specific commodity) **—deˈmanding** a. requiring great skill, patience etc.

demarcate (ˈdiːmɑːkeɪt) vt. mark boundaries or limits of **—demarˈcation** or **demarˈkation** n.

demean (dɪˈmiːn) vt. degrade, lower, humiliate

demeanour or U.S. **demeanor** (dɪˈmiːnə) n. 1. conduct, behaviour 2. bearing

demented (dɪˈmɛntɪd) a. 1. mad, crazy 2. beside oneself **—dementia** (dɪˈmɛnʃə, -ʃɪə) n. form of insanity

demerara (dɛməˈrɛərə, -ˈrɑːrə) n. kind of brown cane sugar

demerge (dɪˈmɜːdʒ) v. 1. split (business concern) into two or more independent companies —vi. 2. (of companies) be so split 3. undo previous merger **—deˈmerger** n.

demerit (dɪˈmɛrɪt) n. 1. bad point 2. undesirable quality

demesne (dɪˈmeɪn, -ˈmiːn) n. 1. estate, territory 2. sphere of action **—hold in demesne** have unrestricted possession of

demi- (comb. form) half, as in demigod. Such words are not given here where the meaning may be inferred from the simple word

demijohn (ˈdɛmɪdʒɒn) n. large wicker-cased bottle

demilitarize or **-ise** (diːˈmɪlɪtəraɪz) vt. prohibit military presence or function in (an area) **—demilitariˈzation** or **-iˈsation** n.

demimonde (dɛmɪˈmɒnd) n. class of women of doubtful reputation

demise (dɪˈmaɪz) n. 1. death 2. conveyance by will or lease 3. transfer of sovereignty on death or abdication —vt. 4. convey to another by will 5. lease

demisemiquaver (ˈdɛmɪsɛmɪkweɪvə) n. Mus. note having time value of one thirty-second of semibreve

demist (diːˈmɪst) v. free or become free of condensation **—deˈmister** n.

demiurge (ˈdɛmɪɜːdʒ) n. name given in some philosophies (esp. Platonic) to the creator of the world and man

demo (ˈdɛməʊ) inf. demonstration

demob (diːˈmɒb) vt. inf. demobilize (-bb-)

demobilize or **-ise** (diːˈməʊbɪlaɪz) vt. 1. disband (troops) 2. discharge (soldier) **—demobiliˈzation** or **-iˈsation** n.

democracy (dɪˈmɒkrəsɪ) n. 1. government by the people or their elected representatives 2. state so governed **—ˈdemocrat** n. advocate of democracy **—demoˈcratic** a. 1. connected with democracy 2. favouring popular rights **—demoˈcratically** adv. **—democratiˈzation** or **-iˈsation** n. **—deˈmocratize** or **-ise** vt.

demodulation (diːˌmɒdjʊˈleɪʃən) n. Electron. process by which output wave or signal is obtained having characteristics of original modulating wave or signal

demography (dɪˈmɒɡrəfɪ) n. study of population statistics, as births, deaths, diseases **—deˈmographer** n. **—demoˈgraphic** a.

demolish (dɪˈmɒlɪʃ) vt. 1. knock down (buildings etc.) 2. destroy utterly 3. overthrow **—demoˈlition** n.

demon (ˈdiːmən) n. 1. devil, evil spirit 2. very cruel or malignant person 3. person very good at or devoted to a given activity **—demoniac** (dɪˈməʊnɪæk) n. one possessed with a devil **—demoˈniacal** a. **—deˈmonic** a. of the nature of a devil **—demoˈnology** n. study of demons

demonetize or **-ise** (diːˈmʌnɪtaɪz) vt. 1. deprive (metal) of its capacity as monetary standard 2. withdraw from use as currency **—demonetiˈzation** or **-iˈsation** n.

demonstrate (ˈdɛmənstreɪt) vt. 1. show by reasoning, prove 2. describe, explain by specimens or experiments —vi. 3. make exhibition of support, protest etc. by public parade, rally 4. make show of armed force **—deˈmonstrable** a. **—deˈmonstrably** adv. **—demonˈstration** n. 1. making clear, proving by evidence 2. exhibition and description 3. organized expression of public opinion 4. display of armed force **—deˈmonstrative** a. 1. expressing feelings, emotions easily and unreservedly 2. pointing out 3. conclusive **—ˈdemonstrator** n. 1. one who demonstrates equipment, products etc. 2. one who takes part in a public demonstration 3. professor's assistant in laboratory etc.

demoralize or **-ise** (dɪˈmɒrəlaɪz) vt. 1.

deprive of courage and discipline **2.** undermine morally —**demorali'zation** or **-i'sation** n.

demote (dɪ'məut) vt. reduce in status or rank —**de'motion** n.

demotic (dɪ'mɒtɪk) a. **1.** of common people; popular **2.** of simplified form of hieroglyphics used in ancient Egypt —n. **3.** demotic script of ancient Egypt

demur (dɪ'mɜː) vi. **1.** make difficulties, object (**-rr-**) —n. **2.** raising of objection **3.** objection raised —**de'murrer** n. Law exception taken to opponent's point

demure (dɪ'mjuə) a. reserved, quiet —**de-'murely** adv.

demurrage (dɪ'mʌrɪdʒ) n. charge for keeping ship etc. beyond time agreed for unloading

demystify (diː'mɪstɪfaɪ) vt. remove mystery from; make clear —**demystifi'cation** n.

den (dɛn) n. **1.** cave or hole of wild beast **2.** lair **3.** small room, esp. study **4.** site, haunt

denarius (dɪ'nɛərɪəs) n. **1.** ancient Roman silver coin, oft. called penny in translation **2.** gold coin worth 25 silver denarii (pl. **-narii** (-'nɛərɪaɪ))

denary ('diːnərɪ) a. **1.** calculated by tens; decimal **2.** containing ten parts; tenfold

denationalize or **-ise** (diː'næʃənəlaɪz) vt. return (an industry) from public to private ownership —**denationali'zation** or **-i'sation** n.

denature (diː'neɪtʃə) or **denaturize, -ise** (diː'neɪtʃəraɪz) vt. deprive of essential qualities, adulterate —**denatured alcohol** spirit made undrinkable

dendrology (dɛn'drɒlədʒɪ) n. natural history of trees

dene or **dean** (diːn) n. valley

dengue ('dɛŋgɪ) or **dandy** n. infectious tropical fever

denial (dɪ'naɪəl) n. see DENY

denier ('dɛnɪə, 'dɛnjə) n. unit of weight of silk, rayon and nylon yarn

denigrate ('dɛnɪgreɪt) vt. belittle or disparage character of

denim ('dɛnɪm) n. strong cotton drill for trousers, overalls etc.

denizen ('dɛnɪzən) n. inhabitant

denominate (dɪ'nɒmɪneɪt) vt. give name to —**denomi'nation** n. **1.** distinctly named church or sect **2.** name, esp. of class or group —**denomi'national** a. —**de'nominator** n. divisor in vulgar fraction

denote (dɪ'nəut) vt. **1.** stand for, be the name of **2.** mark, indicate, show —**deno'tation** n.

denouement (deɪ'nuːmɒn) or **dénouement** (Fr. denu'mã) n. **1.** unravelling of dramatic plot **2.** final solution of mystery

denounce (dɪ'naʊns) vt. **1.** speak violently against **2.** accuse **3.** terminate (treaty)

—**denunci'ation** n. denouncing —**denunciatory** (dɪ'nʌnsɪətərɪ) a.

dense (dɛns) a. **1.** thick, compact **2.** stupid —**'densely** adv. —**'density** n. mass per unit of volume

dent (dɛnt) n. **1.** hollow or mark left by blow or pressure —vt. **2.** make dent in **3.** mark with dent

dental ('dɛntəl) a. **1.** of, pert. to teeth or dentistry **2.** pronounced by applying tongue to teeth —**'dentate** a. toothed —**dentifrice** ('dɛntɪfrɪs) n. powder, paste or wash for cleaning teeth —**'dentist** n. surgeon who attends to teeth —**'dentistry** n. art of dentist —**den'tition** n. **1.** teething **2.** arrangement of teeth —**'denture** n. (usu. pl.) set of false teeth —**dental floss** soft thread for cleaning between teeth —**dental surgeon** dentist

dentine ('dɛntiːn) or **dentin** ('dɛntɪn) n. the hard bonelike part of a tooth

denude (dɪ'njuːd) vt. **1.** strip, make bare **2.** expose (rock) by erosion of plants, soil etc. —**denudation** (dɛnju'deɪʃən) n.

denumerable (dɪ'njuːmərəbəl) a. Maths. capable of being counted by correspondence with positive integers; countable

denunciation (dɪnʌnsɪ'eɪʃən) n. see DE-NOUNCE

deny (dɪ'naɪ) vt. **1.** declare untrue **2.** contradict **3.** reject, disown **4.** refuse to give **5.** refuse **6.** (refl.) abstain from (**de'nied, de'nying**) —**de'niable** a. —**de'nial** n.

deodar ('diːəʊdɑː) n. **1.** Himalayan cedar with drooping branches **2.** fragrant wood of this tree

deodorize or **-ise** (diː'əʊdəraɪz) vt. rid of smell or mask smell of —**de'odorant** n. —**deodori'zation** or **-i'sation** n. —**de'odorizer** or **-iser** n.

deontology (diːɒn'tɒlədʒɪ) n. science of ethics and moral obligations —**deon'tologist** n.

Deo volente ('deɪəʊ vɒ'lɛntɪ) Lat. God willing

deoxidize or **-ise** (diː'ɒksɪdaɪz) vt. deprive of oxygen —**deoxidi'zation** or **-i'sation** n.

dep. 1. depart(s) **2.** departure **3.** deposed **4.** deposit **5.** deputy

depart (dɪ'pɑːt) vi. **1.** go away **2.** start out, set forth **3.** deviate, vary **4.** die —**de'parture** n.

department (dɪ'pɑːtmənt) n. **1.** division **2.** branch **3.** province —**depart'mental** a. —**depart'mentally** adv. —**department store** large shop selling all kinds of goods

depend (dɪ'pɛnd) vi. **1.** (usu. with on) rely entirely **2.** be contingent, await settlement or decision —**de'pendable** a. reliable —**de'pend-ant** n. one for whose maintenance another is responsible —**de'pendence** n. —**de'pendency** n. subject territory —**de'pendent** a. depending

depict (dɪ'pɪkt) vt. **1.** give picture of **2.** describe in words —**de'piction** n. —**de'pictor** n.

depilatory (dɪ'pɪlətərɪ, -trɪ) n. 1. substance that removes hair —a. 2. serving to remove hair

deplete (dɪ'pliːt) vt. 1. empty 2. reduce 3. exhaust —de'pletion n.

deplore (dɪ'plɔː) vt. 1. lament, regret 2. deprecate, complain of —de'plorable a. 1. lamentable 2. disgraceful

deploy (dɪ'plɔɪ) v. 1. (of troops, ships) (cause to) adopt battle formation —vt. 2. arrange —de'ployment n.

depolarize or **-ise** (diː'pəʊləraɪz) vt. deprive of polarity —depolari'zation or -i'sation n.

deponent (dɪ'pəʊnənt) a. 1. (of verb) having passive form but active meaning —n. 2. deponent verb 3. one who makes statement on oath 4. deposition

depopulate (dɪ'pɒpjʊleɪt) v. (cause to) be reduced in population —depopu'lation n.

deport (dɪ'pɔːt) vt. expel from a country, banish —depor'tation n.

deportment (dɪ'pɔːtmənt) n. behaviour, conduct, bearing —de'port vt. behave, carry (oneself)

depose (dɪ'pəʊz) vt. 1. remove from office, esp. of sovereign —vi. 2. make statement on oath, give evidence —de'posable a. —de'posal n. 1. removal from office 2. statement made on oath

deposit (dɪ'pɒzɪt) vt. 1. set down, esp. carefully 2. give into safekeeping, esp. in bank 3. let fall (as sediment) —n. 4. thing deposited 5. money given in part payment or as security 6. sediment —de'positary n. person with whom thing is deposited —deposition (dɛpə'zɪʃən) n. 1. statement written and attested 2. act of deposing or depositing —de'positor n. —de'pository n. place for safekeeping —deposit account UK bank account that earns interest and usu. requires notice of withdrawal

depot ('dɛpəʊ) n. 1. storehouse 2. building for storage and servicing of buses, railway engines etc. 3. US railway station

deprave (dɪ'preɪv) vt. make bad, corrupt, pervert —depravity (dɪ'prævɪtɪ) n. wickedness, viciousness

deprecate ('dɛprɪkeɪt) vt. 1. express disapproval of 2. advise against —depre'cation n. —depre'catory a.

depreciate (dɪ'priːʃɪeɪt) vt. 1. lower price, value or purchasing power of 2. belittle —vi. 3. fall in value —depreci'ation n. —de'preciator n. —de'preciatory a.

depredation (dɛprɪ'deɪʃən) n. plundering, pillage —'depredate vt. plunder, despoil —'depredator n.

depress (dɪ'prɛs) vt. 1. affect with low spirits 2. lower in level or activity —de'pressant n. —de'pressed a. 1. low in spirits; downcast 2. lower than surrounding surface 3. pressed down;

flattened 4. characterized by economic hardship (also dis'tressed) 5. lowered in force etc. 6. Bot., zool. flattened —de'pression n. 1. hollow 2. low spirits, dejection, despondency 3. low state of trade, slump —de'pressive a.

deprive (dɪ'praɪv) vt. strip, dispossess —depri'vation (dɛprɪ'veɪʃən) n. —de'prived a. lacking adequate food, care, amenities etc.

dept. department

depth (dɛpθ) n. 1. (degree of) deepness 2. deep place, abyss 3. intensity (of colour, feeling) 4. profundity (of mind) —depth charge or bomb bomb for use against submarines

depute (dɪ'pjuːt) vt. 1. allot 2. appoint as agent or substitute —a./n. ('dɛpjuːt) 3. in Scotland, assistant —depu'tation n. persons sent to speak for others —'deputize or -ise vi. 1. act for another —vt. 2. depute —'deputy n. 1. assistant 2. substitute, delegate

derail (dɪ'reɪl) v. (cause to) go off the rails, as train etc. —de'railment n.

derailleur (də'reɪljə) a./n. (of) gear-change mechanism for bicycles

derange (dɪ'reɪndʒ) vt. 1. put out of place, out of order 2. upset 3. make insane —de'rangement n.

derby ('dɑːbɪ) n. US bowler hat

Derby ('dɑːbɪ, U.S. 'dɜːbɪ) n. 1. horserace, esp. famous one at Epsom, England 2. contest between local teams

deregulate (dɪ'rɛgjʊleɪt) v. 1. cancel regulations (concerning an activity or process) —vt. 2. exempt (an activity) from regulations —deregu'lation n.

derelict ('dɛrɪlɪkt) a. 1. abandoned, forsaken 2. falling into ruins, dilapidated —n. 3. social outcast, vagrant 4. abandoned property, ship etc. —dere'liction n. 1. neglect (of duty) 2. abandoning

derestrict (diːrɪ'strɪkt) vt. render or leave free from restriction, esp. road from speed limits

deride (dɪ'raɪd) vt. speak of or treat with contempt, ridicule —derision (dɪ'rɪʒən) n. ridicule —de'risive a. —de'risory a. mocking, ridiculing

de rigueur (də rɪ'gɜː) Fr. required by etiquette or fashion

derive (dɪ'raɪv) vt. 1. deduce, get (from) 2. show origin of —vi. 3. issue, be descended (from) —derivation (dɛrɪ'veɪʃən) n. —derivative (dɪ'rɪvətɪv) a./n.

derma ('dɜːmə) or **dermis** ('dɜːmɪs) n. the fine skin, below the epidermis, containing blood vessels

dermatitis (dɜːmə'taɪtɪs) n. inflammation of skin

dermato-, derma- or before vowel

dermat-, derm- (*comb. form*) skin, as in *dermatitis*

dermatology (dɜːmə'tɒlədʒɪ) *n.* science of skin —**derma'tologist** *n.* physician specializing in skin diseases

derogate ('dɛrəgeɪt) *vi.* 1. (*with* from) cause to seem inferior; detract 2. (*with* from) deviate in standard or quality —*vt.* 3. cause to seem inferior *etc.*; disparage —**dero'gation** *n.*

derogatory (dɪ'rɒgətərɪ) *a.* disparaging, belittling, intentionally offensive

derrick ('dɛrɪk) *n.* 1. hoisting machine 2. framework over oil well *etc.*

derring-do ('dɛrɪŋ'duː) *n.* (act of) spirited bravery, boldness

derringer or **deringer** ('dɛrɪndʒə) *n.* small pistol with large bore

derv (dɜːv) *n.* diesel oil for road vehicles (*d*iesel *e*ngine *r*oad *v*ehicle)

dervish ('dɜːvɪʃ) *n.* member of Muslim ascetic order, noted for frenzied, whirling dance

desalination (diːsælɪ'neɪʃən) or **desalinization, -isation** *n.* process of removing salt, *esp.* from sea water

descant ('dɛskænt) *n.* 1. *Mus.* decorative variation sung as accompaniment to basic melody —*vi.* (with *on* or *upon*) 2. talk in detail (about) 3. dwell (on) at length

descend (dɪ'sɛnd) *vi.* 1. come or go down 2. slope down 3. stoop, condescend 4. spring (from ancestor *etc.*) 5. pass to heir, be transmitted 6. swoop on, attack —*vt.* 7. go or come down —**des'cendant** *n.* person descended from an ancestor —**des'cendent** *a.* 1. descending —*n.* 2. descendant —**des'cent** *n.*

describe (dɪ'skraɪb) *vt.* 1. give detailed account of 2. pronounce, label 3. trace out (geometrical figure *etc.*) —**description** (dɪ'skrɪpʃən) *n.* 1. detailed account 2. marking out 3. kind, sort, species —**descriptive** (dɪ'skrɪptɪv) *a.*

descry (dɪ'skraɪ) *vt.* make out, catch sight of, *esp.* at a distance, espy (**de'scried, de'scrying**)

desecrate ('dɛsɪkreɪt) *vt.* 1. violate sanctity of 2. profane 3. convert to evil use —**dese'cration** *n.*

desert[1] ('dɛzət) *n.* 1. uninhabited and barren region —*a.* 2. barren, uninhabited, desolate —**desert boots** ankle-high boots with soft soles

desert[2] (dɪ'zɜːt) *vt.* 1. abandon, forsake, leave —*vi.* 2. (*esp.* of soldiers *etc.*) run away from service —**de'serter** *n.* —**de'sertion** *n.*

desert[3] (dɪ'zɜːt) *n.* 1. (*usu. pl.*) what is due as reward or punishment 2. merit, virtue

deserve (dɪ'zɜːv) *vt.* 1. show oneself worthy of 2. have by conduct a claim to —**de'served** *a.* rightfully earned; justified; warranted —**deservedly** (dɪ'zɜːvɪdlɪ) *adv.* —**deservedness**

deshabille (deɪzæ'biːl) *n.* see DISHABILLE

desiccate ('dɛsɪkeɪt) *vt.* 1. dry 2. dry up —**desic'cation** *n.*

desideratum (dɪzɪdə'rɑːtəm) *n.* something lacked and wanted (*pl.* **-ta** (-tə))

design (dɪ'zaɪn) *vt.* 1. make working drawings for 2. sketch 3. plan out 4. intend, select for —*n.* 5. outline sketch 6. working plan 7. art of making decorative patterns *etc.* 8. project, purpose, mental plan —**designedly** (dɪ'zaɪnɪdlɪ) *adv.* on purpose —**de'signer** *n. esp.* one who draws designs for manufacturers —**de'signing** *a.* crafty, scheming

designate ('dɛzɪgneɪt) *vt.* 1. name 2. pick out 3. appoint to office —*a.* ('dɛzɪgnɪt, -neɪt) 4. appointed but not yet installed —**desig'nation** *n.* name, appellation

desire (dɪ'zaɪə) *vt.* 1. wish, long for 2. ask for, entreat —*n.* 3. longing, craving 4. expressed wish, request 5. sexual appetite 6. something wished for or requested —**desira'bility** *n.* —**de'sirable** *a.* worth desiring —**de'sirous** *a.* filled with desire

desist (dɪ'zɪst) *vi.* cease, stop

desk (dɛsk) *n.* 1. table or other piece of furniture designed for reading or writing at 2. counter 3. editorial section of newspaper *etc.* covering specific subject

desolate ('dɛsəlɪt) *a.* 1. uninhabited 2. neglected, barren, ruinous 3. solitary 4. dreary, dismal, forlorn —*vt.* ('dɛsəleɪt) 5. depopulate, lay waste 6. overwhelm with grief —**deso'lation** *n.*

despair (dɪ'spɛə) *vi.* 1. (*oft. with* of) lose hope —*n.* 2. loss of all hope 3. cause of this 4. despondency

despatch (dɪ'spætʃ) *see* DISPATCH

desperate ('dɛspərɪt, -prɪt) *a.* 1. reckless from despair 2. difficult; dangerous 3. frantic 4. hopelessly bad 5. leaving no room for hope —**desperado** (dɛspə'rɑːdəʊ) *n.* reckless, lawless person (*pl.* **-es, -s**) —'**desperately** *adv.* —**despe'ration** *n.*

despise (dɪ'spaɪz) *vt.* look down on as contemptible, inferior —**despicable** ('dɛspɪkəbəl, dɪ'spɪk-) *a.* base, contemptible, vile —**despicably** (dɪ'spɪkəblɪ) *adv.*

despite (dɪ'spaɪt) *prep.* in spite of

despoil (dɪ'spɔɪl) *vt.* plunder, rob, strip —**despoliation** (dɪspəʊlɪ'eɪʃən) *n.*

despondent (dɪ'spɒndənt) *a.* dejected, depressed —**de'spond** *vi.* —**de'spondency** *n.* —**de'spondently** *adv.*

despot ('dɛspɒt) *n.* tyrant, oppressor —**des'potic** *a.* —**des'potically** *adv.* —'**despotism** *n.* autocratic government, tyranny

despumate (dɪ'spjuːmeɪt, 'dɛspjʊmeɪt) vi. 1. throw off impurities 2. form scum

desquamate ('dɛskwəmeɪt) vi. (of skin) come off in scales —**desqua'mation** n.

dessert (dɪ'zɜːt) n. sweet course, or fruit, served at end of meal —**des'sertspoon** n. spoon intermediate in size between tablespoon and teaspoon

destination (dɛstɪ'neɪʃən) n. 1. place a person or thing is bound for 2. goal 3. purpose

destine ('dɛstɪn) vt. 1. ordain or fix beforehand 2. set apart, devote

destiny ('dɛstɪnɪ) n. 1. course of events; person's fate 2. the power which foreordains

destitute ('dɛstɪtjuːt) a. 1. in absolute want 2. in great need, devoid (of) 3. penniless —**desti'tution** n.

destroy (dɪ'strɔɪ) vt. 1. ruin 2. pull to pieces 3. undo 4. put an end to 5. demolish 6. annihilate —**de'stroyer** n. 1. one who destroys 2. small, swift, heavily armed warship —**de'struct** vt. destroy (one's own missile etc.) for safety —**de'structible** a. —**de'struction** n. 1. ruin, overthrow 2. death —**de'structive** a. 1. destroying 2. negative, not constructive —**de'structively** adv. —**de'structor** n. that which destroys, esp. incinerator

desuetude (dɪ'sjuːɪtjuːd, 'dɛswɪtjuːd) n. disuse, discontinuance

desultory ('dɛsəltərɪ, -trɪ) a. 1. passing, changing fitfully from one thing to another 2. aimless 3. unmethodical

detach (dɪ'tætʃ) vt. unfasten, disconnect, separate —**de'tachable** a. —**de'tached** a. 1. standing apart, isolated 2. impersonal, disinterested —**de'tachment** n. 1. aloofness 2. detaching 3. a body of troops detached for special duty

detail ('diːteɪl) n. 1. particular 2. small or unimportant part 3. treatment of anything item by item 4. party or man assigned for duty in army —vt. 5. relate in full 6. appoint for duty

detain (dɪ'teɪn) vt. 1. keep under restraint 2. hinder 3. keep waiting —**de'tention** n. confinement 2. arrest 3. detaining

detect (dɪ'tɛkt) vt. find out or discover existence, presence, nature or identity of —**de'tection** n. —**de'tective** n. 1. policeman or private agent employed in detecting crime —a. 2. employed in detection —**de'tector** n. esp. mechanical sensing device or device for detecting radio signals

détente (deɪ'tɑːnt; Fr. de'tãt) n. lessening of tension in political or international affairs

detention (dɪ'tɛnʃən) n. see DETAIN

deter (dɪ'tɜː) vt. 1. discourage, frighten 2. hinder, prevent (-**rr**-) —**de'terrent** a./n.

detergent (dɪ'tɜːdʒənt) n. 1. cleansing,

purifying substance —a. 2. having cleansing power —**de'terge** vt.

deteriorate (dɪ'tɪərɪəreɪt) v. become or make worse —**deterio'ration** n.

determine (dɪ'tɜːmɪn) vt. 1. make up one's mind on, decide 2. fix as known 3. bring to a decision 4. be deciding factor in 5. Law —vi. 6. come to an end 7. come to decision —**de'terminable** a./n. —**de'terminant** a./n. —**de'terminate** a. fixed in scope or nature —**determi'nation** n. 1. determining 2. firm or resolute conduct or purpose 3. resolve —**de'termined** a. resolute —**de'terminism** n. theory that human action is settled by forces independent of will —**de'terminist** n./a.

detest (dɪ'tɛst) vt. hate, loathe —**de'testable** a. —**de'testably** adv. —**detes'tation** n.

dethrone (dɪ'θrəʊn) vt. remove from throne, depose —**de'thronement** n.

detonate ('dɛtəneɪt) v. 1. cause (bomb, mine etc.) to explode —vi. 2. (of bomb, mine etc.) explode —**deto'nation** n. —**detonator** n. mechanical, electrical device, or small amount of explosive, used to set off main explosive charge

detour ('diːtʊə) n. 1. course which leaves main route to rejoin it later 2. roundabout way —vi. 3. make detour

detoxify (diː'tɒksɪfaɪ) vt. remove poison from (-**fying, -fied**) —**detoxifi'cation** n.

detract (dɪ'trækt) v. take away (a part) from, diminish —**de'traction** n. —**de'tractive** a. —**de'tractor** n.

detriment ('dɛtrɪmənt) n. harm done, loss, damage —**detri'mental** a. damaging, injurious —**detri'mentally** adv.

detritus (dɪ'traɪtəs) n. worn-down matter, such as gravel or rock debris —**de'trital** a. —**detrition** (dɪ'trɪʃən) n. wearing away from solid bodies by friction

de trop (də 'tro) Fr. not wanted, superfluous

detrude (dɪ'truːd) vt. thrust down —**de'trusion** n.

detumescence (diːtjʊ'mɛsəns) n. subsidence of swelling

deuce (djuːs) n. 1. two 2. card with two spots 3. Tennis forty all 4. in exclamatory phrases, the devil —**deuced** ('djuːsɪd, djuːst) a. inf. excessive

Deut. Deuteronomy

deuterium (djuː'tɪərɪəm) n. form of hydrogen twice as heavy as normal gas —**deuteron** n. nucleus of this gas

Deutsche Mark ('dɔɪtʃə) or **Deutschmark** n. monetary unit of W Germany

deutzia ('djuːtsɪə, 'dɔɪtsɪə) n. shrub with white or pink flower clusters

devalue (diː'væljuː) or **devaluate** (diː'væljʊeɪt) v. 1. (of currency) reduce or be reduced in value —*vt.* **2.** reduce the value or worth of —**devalu'ation** *n.*

devastate ('dɛvəsteɪt) *vt.* **1.** lay waste **2.** ravage **3.** *inf.* overwhelm —**devas'tation** *n.*

develop (dɪ'vɛləp) *vt.* **1.** bring to maturity **2.** elaborate **3.** bring forth, bring out **4.** evolve **5.** treat (photographic plate or film) to bring out image **6.** improve value or change use of (land) by building *etc.* —*vi.* **7.** grow to maturer state (**de'veloped, de'veloping**) —**de'veloper** *n.* **1.** one who develops land **2.** chemical for developing film —**de'velopment** *n.* —**developing country** poor country seeking to develop its resources by industrialization —**development area** *UK* depressed area which is given government assistance to establish new industry

deviate ('diːvɪeɪt) *vi.* leave the way, turn aside, diverge —**'deviant** *n./a.* (person) deviating from normal, *esp.* in sexual practices —**devi'ation** *n.* —**'deviator** *n.* —**'devious** *a.* **1.** deceitful, underhand **2.** roundabout, rambling **3.** erring

device (dɪ'vaɪs) *n.* **1.** contrivance, invention **2.** apparatus **3.** stratagem **4.** scheme, plot **5.** heraldic or emblematic figure or design

devil ('dɛvəl) *n.* **1.** personified spirit of evil **2.** superhuman evil being **3.** person of great wickedness, cruelty *etc.* **4.** *inf.* fellow **5.** *inf.* something difficult or annoying **6.** energy, dash, unconquerable spirit **7.** *inf.* rogue, rascal **8.** *English law* junior barrister working without payment to gain experience —*vi.* **9.** do work that passes for employer's, as for lawyer or author —*vt.* **10.** grill with hot condiments (-**ll-**) —**'devilish** *a.* **1.** like, of the devil **2.** evil —*adv.* **3.** *inf.* very, extremely —**'devilment** *n.* **1.** wickedness **2.** wild and reckless mischief, revelry, high spirits —**'devilry** *n.* —**devil-may-care** *a.* happy-go-lucky —**devil's advocate 1.** one who advocates opposing, unpopular view, *usu.* for sake of argument **2.** *R.C.Ch.* one appointed to state disqualifications of person whom it is proposed to make a saint

devious (dɪ'viːəs) *a.* **see** DEVIATE.

devise (dɪ'vaɪz) *vt.* **1.** plan, contrive **2.** invent **3.** plot **4.** leave by will —**devi'see** *n.* —**de'visor** *n.*

devitrification (diːvɪtrɪfɪ'keɪʃən) *n.* loss of glassy or vitreous condition —**de'vitrify** *vt.* deprive of character or appearance of glass (-**fied, -fying**)

devoid (dɪ'vɔɪd) *a.* (*usu. with* of) empty, lacking, free (from)

devolve (dɪ'vɒlv) *vi.* **1.** pass or fall (to, upon) —*vt.* **2.** throw (duty *etc.*) on to another —**devo'lution** *n.* devolving, *esp.* transfer of authority from central to regional government

Devonian (də'vəʊnɪən) *a.* **1.** of fourth period of

Palaeozoic era, between Silurian and Carboniferous periods **2.** of Devon —*n.* **3.** Devonian period or rock system

devote (dɪ'vəʊt) *vt.* set apart, give up exclusively (to person, purpose *etc.*) —**de'voted** *a.* loving, attached —**devotee** (dɛvəʊ'tiː) *n.* **1.** ardent enthusiast **2.** zealous worshipper —**de'votion** *n.* **1.** deep affection, loyalty **2.** dedication **3.** religious earnestness —*pl.* **4.** prayers, religious exercises —**de'votional** *a.*

devour (dɪ'vaʊə) *vt.* **1.** eat greedily **2.** consume, destroy **3.** read, gaze at eagerly —**de'vourer** *n.*

devout (dɪ'vaʊt) *a.* **1.** earnestly religious, pious **2.** sincere, heartfelt —**de'voutly** *adv.*

dew (djuː) *n.* **1.** moisture from air deposited as small drops on cool surface between nightfall and morning **2.** any beaded moisture —*vt.* **3.** wet with or as with dew —**'dewiness** *n.* —**'dewy** *a.* —'**dewclaw** *n.* partly developed inner toe of dogs —'**dewlap** *n.* fold of loose skin hanging from neck —**dew point** temperature at which dew begins to form —**dew pond** small natural pond —**dew-worm** *n.* **C** large earthworm used as bait —**dewy-eyed** *a.* naive, innocent

dewberry ('djuːbərɪ, -brɪ) *n.* bramble with blue-black fruits

Dewey Decimal System ('djuːɪ) system of library book classification with ten main subject classes (*also* **decimal classification**)

DEW line (djuː) distant early warning line, network of sensors situated in Arctic regions of N Amer.

dexterity (dɛk'stɛrɪtɪ) *n.* **1.** manual skill **2.** neatness **3.** deftness **4.** adroitness —'**dexter** *a. Her.* on the bearer's right-hand side of a shield —'**dexterous** *a.* showing dexterity, skilful

dextrin ('dɛkstrɪn) *or* **dextrine** ('dɛkstrɪn, -triːn) *n.* sticky substance obtained from starch, used as thickening agent in foods and as gum

dextrose ('dɛkstrəʊz, -trəʊs) *n.* white, soluble, sweet-tasting crystalline solid, occurring naturally in fruit, honey, animal tissue

D.F. Defender of the Faith

D.F.C. Distinguished Flying Cross

D.F.M. Distinguished Flying Medal

dg *or* **dg.** decigram

dharma ('dɑːmə) *n.* **1.** *Hinduism* social custom regarded as religious and moral duty **2.** *Hinduism* essential principle of cosmos; natural law; conduct that conforms with this **3.** *Buddhism* ideal truth

dhow (daʊ) *n.* lateen-rigged Arab sailing vessel

DHSS Department of Health and Social Security

di-¹ (*comb. form*) **1.** twice; two; double, as in *dicotyledon* **2.** containing two specified atoms or groups of atoms, as in *carbon dioxide*

di-² (*comb. form*) *see* DIA-

dia- *or before vowel* **di-** (*comb. form*) through

diabetes (daɪə'biːtɪs, -tiːz) n. any of various disorders characterized by excretion of abnormal amount of urine, *esp.* diabetes mellitus, in which body fails to store and utilize glucose —**diabetic** (daɪə'bɛtɪk) n./a.

diabolic (daɪə'bɒlɪk) a. devilish —**dia'bolical** a. *inf.* very bad —**dia'bolically** adv. —**di'abolism** n. devil-worship

diabolo ('dɪæbələʊ) n. game in which top is spun into air from string attached to two sticks

diaconal (daɪ'ækənəl) a. pert. to deacon —**di'aconate** n. 1. office, rank of deacon 2. body of deacons

diacritic (daɪə'krɪtɪk) n. sign above letter or character indicating special phonetic value *etc.* —a. 2. diacritical —**dia'critical** a. 1. of a diacritic 2. showing a distinction (*also* **dia'critic**)

diadem ('daɪədɛm) n. a crown

diaeresis or (*esp. U.S.*) **dieresis** (daɪ'ɛrɪsɪs) n. mark (¨) placed over vowel to show that it is sounded separately from preceding one, as in Noël (*pl.* **-ses** (-siːz))

diagnosis (daɪəg'nəʊsɪs) n. identification of disease from symptoms (*pl.* **-ses** (-siːz)) —'**diagnose** v. —**diag'nostic** a.

diagonal (daɪ'ægənəl) a. 1. from corner to corner 2. oblique —n. 3. line from corner to corner —**di'agonally** adv.

diagram ('daɪəgræm) n. drawing, figure in lines, to illustrate something being expounded —**diagram'matic** a. —**diagram'matically** adv.

dial ('daɪəl) n. 1. face of clock *etc.* 2. plate marked with graduations on which pointer moves (as on meter, weighing machine *etc.*) 3. numbered disc on front of telephone 4. *sl.* face —vt. 5. operate (telephone) 6. indicate on dial (-ll-) —**'dialling tone** or U.S. **dial tone** continuous purring heard over telephone indicating that number can be dialled

dialect ('daɪəlɛkt) n. 1. characteristic speech of district 2. local variety of a language —**dia'lectal** a.

dialectic (daɪə'lɛktɪk) n. art of arguing —**dia'lectical** a. —**dia'lectically** adv. —**dialec'tician** n. 1. logician 2. reasoner

dialogue or U.S. (*oft.*) **dialog** ('daɪəlɒg) n. 1. conversation between two or more (persons) 2. representation of such conversation in drama, novel *etc.* 3. discussion between representatives of two states, countries *etc.*

dialysis (daɪ'ælɪsɪs) n. *Med.* filtering of blood through membrane to remove waste products

diamagnetism (daɪə'mægnɪtɪzəm) n. phenomenon exhibited by substances that are repelled by both poles of magnet

diamanté (daɪə'mæntɪ) n. (fabric covered

with) glittering particles —**dia'mantine** a. like diamond

diameter (daɪ'æmɪtə) n. 1. (length of) straight line from side to side of figure or body (*esp.* circle) through centre 2. thickness —**dia'metrical** a. opposite —**dia'metrically** adv.

diamond ('daɪəmənd) n. 1. very hard and brilliant precious stone, also used in industry as an abrasive 2. rhomboid figure 3. suit at cards 4. playing field in baseball —**diamond jubilee** or **wedding** 60th (sometimes 75th) anniversary

dianthus (daɪ'ænθəs) n. genus of herbaceous flowers, *eg* pinks and carnations

diapason (daɪə'peɪzən) n. 1. fundamental organ stop 2. compass of voice or instrument

diaper ('daɪəpə) n. 1. US baby's napkin 2. fabric with small diamond pattern 3. pattern of that kind —'**diapered** a.

diaphanous (daɪ'æfənəs) a. transparent

diaphoretic (daɪəfə'rɛtɪk) n. 1. diaphoretic drug —a. 2. relating to or causing perspiration

diaphragm ('daɪəfræm) n. 1. muscular partition dividing two cavities of body, midriff 2. plate or disc wholly or partly closing tube or opening 3. any thin dividing or covering membrane —**diaphragmatic** (daɪəfræg'mætɪk) a.

diapositive (daɪə'pɒzɪtɪv) n. positive transparency; slide

diarrhoea or *esp.* U.S. **diarrhea** (daɪə'rɪə) n. excessive looseness of the bowels —**diar'rhoeal** or *esp.* U.S. **diar'rheal** a.

diary ('daɪərɪ) n. 1. daily record of events, engagements, thoughts *etc.* 2. book for this —'**diarist** n. writer of diary

Diaspora (daɪ'æspərə) n. 1. dispersion of Jews from Palestine after Babylonian captivity; Jewish communities that arose after this 2. (*oft.* **d-**) dispersion, as of people orig. of one nation

diastase ('daɪəsteɪs, -steɪz) n. enzyme that converts starch into sugar

diastole (daɪ'æstəlɪ) n. dilation of chambers of heart

diathermy ('daɪəθɜːmɪ) or **diathermia** (daɪə'θɜːmɪə) n. heating of body tissues with electric current for medical or surgical purposes

diatom ('daɪətəm) n. one of order of microscopic algae —**dia'tomic** a. of two atoms

diatonic (daɪə'tɒnɪk) a. *Mus.* 1.pert. to regular major and minor scales 2. (of melody). composed in such a scale

diatribe ('daɪətraɪb) n. violently bitter verbal attack, invective, denunciation

dibble ('dɪbəl) n. 1. small tool used to make holes in ground for bulbs *etc.* (*also* '**dibber**) —v. 2. make hole in (ground) with dibble 3. plant (seeds *etc.*) with dibble

dice (daɪs) *pl.n.* **1.** (*also functions as sing., orig. sing.* **die**) cubes each with six sides marked one to six for games of chance —*vi.* **2.** gamble with dice —*vt.* **3.** cut into small cubes —'**dicer** *n.* —'**dicey** *a. inf.* dangerous, risky

dicephalous (daɪ'sɛfələs) *a.* two-headed

dichotomy (daɪ'kɒtəmɪ) *n.* division into two parts

dichroism ('daɪkrəʊɪzəm) *n.* property possessed by some crystals of exhibiting different colours when viewed from different directions —di'**chroic** *a.*

dichromatic (daɪkrəʊ'mætɪk) *a.* **1.** having two colours (*also* di'**chroic**) **2.** (of animal species) having two different colour varieties **3.** able to perceive only two colours

dick (dɪk) *n. sl.* **1.** fellow, person **2.** detective

Dickensian (dɪ'kɛnzɪən) *a.* **1.** of Charles Dickens or his novels **2.** denoting poverty, distress and exploitation as depicted in Dickens's novels **3.** grotesquely comic, as some Dickens characters

dicker ('dɪkə) *chiefly US v.* **1.** trade (goods) by bargaining; barter —*n.* **2.** petty bargain or barter

dicky[1] *or* **dickey** ('dɪkɪ) *n.* detachable false shirt front (*pl.* '**dickies, 'dickeys**) —'**dickybird** *n. inf.* child's word for small bird

dicky[2] *or* **dickey** ('dɪkɪ) *a. sl.* shaky, unsound

dicotyledon (daɪkɒtɪ'liːdən) *n.* flowering plant having two embryonic seed leaves

Dictaphone ('dɪktəfəʊn) *n.* R tape recorder, used *esp.* for dictation

dictate (dɪk'teɪt) *v.* **1.** say or read for another to transcribe —*vt.* **2.** prescribe, lay down —*vi.* **3.** seek to impose one's will on others —*n.* ('dɪkteɪt) **4.** bidding —dic'**tation** *n.* —dic'**tator** *n.* absolute ruler —dicta'**torial** *a.* **1.** despotic **2.** overbearing —dicta'**torially** *adv.* —dic'**tator-ship** *n.*

diction ('dɪkʃən) *n.* **1.** choice and use of words **2.** enunciation

dictionary ('dɪkʃənərɪ) *n.* **1.** book setting forth, alphabetically, words of language with meanings *etc.* **2.** reference book with items in alphabetical order

dictum ('dɪktəm) *n.* **1.** pronouncement **2.** saying, maxim (*pl.* **-s, -ta** (-tə))

did (dɪd) *pt. of* DO[1]

didactic (dɪ'dæktɪk) *a.* **1.** designed to instruct **2.** (of people) opinionated, dictatorial —di'**dacti-cism** *n.*

diddle ('dɪdəl) *vt. inf.* cheat

didgeridoo (dɪdʒərɪ'duː) *n. Mus.* native Aust. wind instrument

die[1] (daɪ) *vi.* **1.** cease to live **2.** come to an end **3.** stop functioning **4.** *inf.* be nearly overcome (with laughter *etc.*) (**died, 'dying**) —'**diehard** *n.* one

who resists (reform *etc.*) to the end —**be dying for** be looking eagerly forward to

die[2] (daɪ) *n. see* DICE

die[3] (daɪ) *n.* **1.** shaped block of hard material to form metal in forge, press *etc.* **2.** tool for cutting thread on pipe *etc.* —**die-cast** *vt.* shape or form (object) by introducing molten metal or plastic into reusable mould —**die-casting** *n.*

dieldrin ('diːldrɪn) *n.* highly toxic crystalline insecticide

dielectric (daɪɪ'lɛktrɪk) *n.* **1.** substance through or across which electric induction takes place **2.** nonconductor **3.** insulator

dieresis (daɪ'ɛrɪsɪs) *n. see* DIAERESIS

diesel ('diːzəl) *a.* **1.** pert. to internal-combustion engine using oil as fuel —*n.* **2.** this engine **3.** diesel oil or fuel —**diesel-electric** *n.* **1.** locomotive fitted with diesel engine driving electric generator —*a.* **2.** of such locomotive or system —**diesel oil** *or* **fuel** fuel, distilled from petroleum, used in diesel engines

diet[1] ('daɪət) *n.* **1.** restricted or regulated course of feeding **2.** kind of food lived on **3.** food —*vi.* **4.** follow a dietary regimen, as to lose weight —'**dietary** *a.* **1.** relating to diet —*n.* **2.** a regulated diet **3.** system of dieting —die'**tetic** *a.* —die'**tetics** *pl.n.* (*with sing. v.*) science of diet —die'**titian** *or* die'**tician** *n.* one skilled in dietetics

diet[2] ('daɪət) *n.* **1.** parliament of some countries **2.** formal assembly

differ ('dɪfə) *vi.* **1.** be unlike **2.** disagree —'**difference** *n.* **1.** unlikeness **2.** degree or point of unlikeness **3.** disagreement **4.** remainder left after subtraction —'**different** *a.* unlike —'**dif-ferently** *adv.*

differentia (dɪfə'rɛnʃɪə) *n. Logic* feature by which subclasses of same class of named objects can be distinguished (*pl.* **-tiae** (-ʃiː))

differential (dɪfə'rɛnʃəl) *a.* **1.** varying with circumstances **2.** special **3.** *Maths.* pert. to an infinitesimal change in variable quantity **4.** *Phys. etc.* relating to difference between sets of motions acting in the same direction or between pressures *etc.* —*n.* **5.** *Maths.* infinitesimal difference between two consecutive states of variable quantity **6.** differential gear **7.** difference between rates of pay for different types of labour —differ'**entially** *adv.* —differ-'**entiate** *vt.* **1.** serve to distinguish between, make different —*vi.* **2.** discriminate —**differen-ti'ation** *n.* —**differential calculus** method of calculating relative rate of change for continuously varying quantities —**differential gear** epicyclic gear mounted in driving axle of vehicle, that permits one driving wheel to rotate faster than the other, as when cornering

difficult ('dɪfɪkəlt) *a.* **1.** requiring effort, skill *etc.* to do or understand, not easy **2.** obscure —'**difficulty** *n.* **1.** being difficult **2.** difficult task, problem **3.** embarrassment **4.** hindrance **5.** obscurity **6.** trouble

diffident ('dıfıdənt) *a.* lacking confidence, timid, shy —'**diffidence** *n.* shyness —'**diffidently** *adv.*

diffract (dı'frækt) *vt.* break up, *esp.* of rays of light, sound-waves —**dif'fraction** *n.* deflection of ray of light, electromagnetic wave caused by obstacle

diffuse (dı'fju:z) *vt.* **1.** spread abroad —*a.* (dı'fju:s) **2.** widely spread **3.** loose, verbose, wordy —**diffusely** (dı'fju:slı) *adv.* **1.** loosely **2.** wordily —**dif'fusible** *a.* —**dif'fusion** *n.* —**diffusive** (dı'fju:sıv) *a.* —**diffusively** (dı'fju:sıvlı) *adv.*

dig (dıg) *vi.* **1.** work with spade **2.** search, investigate —*vt.* **3.** turn up with spade **4.** hollow out, make hole in **5.** excavate **6.** thrust **7.** (*oft. with out or up*) discover by searching (**dug**, '**digging**) —*n.* **8.** piece of digging **9.** archaeological excavation **10.** thrust **11.** jibe, taunt —*pl.* **12.** *inf.* lodgings —'**digger** *n.* **1.** one who digs **2.** goldminer **3.** Aust. or N.Z. soldier

digest (dı'dʒɛst, daı-) *vt.* **1.** prepare (food) in stomach *etc.* for assimilation **2.** bring into handy form by sorting, tabulating, summarizing **3.** reflect on **4.** absorb —*vi.* **5.** (of food) undergo digestion —*n.* ('daıdʒɛst) **6.** methodical summary, *esp.* of laws **7.** magazine containing condensed version of articles *etc.* already published elsewhere —**di'gestible** *a.* —**di'gestion** *n.* digesting —**di'gestive** *a.* relating to digestion —*n.* **2.** substance that aids digestion —**digestive biscuit** round semisweet biscuit made from wholemeal flour

digit ('dıdʒıt) *n.* **1.** finger or toe **2.** any of the numbers 0 to 9 —'**digital** *a.* **1.** of, resembling digits **2.** performed with fingers **3.** displaying information (time *etc.*) by numbers rather than by pointer on dial —'**digitate** *or* '**digitated** *a.* having separate fingers, toes —**digital clock** *or* **watch** clock or watch in which time is indicated by digits rather than by hands on dial —**digital computer** electronic computer consisting of numbers, letters *etc.* that are represented internally in binary notation

digitalis (dıdʒı'teılıs) *n.* drug made from foxglove

dignity ('dıgnıtı) *n.* **1.** stateliness, gravity **2.** worthiness, excellence, repute **3.** honourable office or title —'**dignified** *a.* stately, majestic —'**dignify** *vt.* give dignity to (-**fied, -fying**) —'**dignitary** *n.* holder of high office

digraph ('daıgra:f) *n.* combination of two letters used to represent single sound such as *gh* in *tough*

digress (daı'grɛs) *vi.* turn from main course, *esp.* to deviate from subject in speaking or writing —**di'gression** *n.* —**di'gressive** *a.*

dihedral (daı'hi:drəl) *a.* having two plane faces or sides

dik-dik ('dıkdık) *n.* small Afr. antelope

dike (daık) *n. see* DYKE

diktat ('dıkta:t) *n.* arbitrary decree

dilapidate (dı'læpıdeıt) *v.* (cause to) fall into ruin —**di'lapidated** *a.* **1.** in ruins **2.** decayed —dilapi'dation *n.*

dilate (daı'leıt, dı-) *vt.* **1.** widen, expand —*vi.* **2.** expand **3.** talk or write at length (on) —**di'lation** *or* **dilatation** (daılə'teıʃən) *n.*

dilatory ('dılətərı) *a.* tardy, slow, belated —'**dilatorily** *adv.* —'**dilatoriness** *n.* delay

dilemma (dı'lɛmə, daı-) *n.* **1.** position in fact or argument offering choice only between unwelcome alternatives **2.** predicament

dilettante (dılı'tæntı) *n.* **1.** person with taste and knowledge of fine arts as pastime **2.** dabbler (*pl.* **dilettanti** (dılı'tæntı)) —*a.* **3.** amateur, desultory —**dilet'tantism** *n.*

diligent ('dılıdʒənt) *a.* unremitting in effort, industrious, hard-working —'**diligence** *n.*

dill (dıl) *n.* yellow-flowered herb with medicinal seeds

dilly ('dılı) *n. sl., chiefly US* remarkable person or thing

dilly-dally ('dılıdælı) *vi. inf.* **1.** loiter **2.** vacillate

dilute (daı'lu:t) *vt.* **1.** reduce (liquid) in strength, *esp.* by adding water **2.** thin **3.** reduce in force, effect *etc.* —*a.* **4.** weakened thus —**diluent** ('dıljuənt) *a./n.* —**di'lution** *n.*

diluvial (daı'lu:vıəl, dı-) *or* **diluvian** *a.* of, connected with, a deluge or flood, *esp.* the Flood of the Book of Genesis

dim (dım) *a.* **1.** indistinct, faint, not bright **2.** mentally dull **3.** unfavourable ('**dimmer** *comp.*, '**dimmest** *sup.*) —*v.* **4.** make, grow dim (-**mm**-) —'**dimly** *adv.* —'**dimmer** *n.* device for dimming electric lights —'**dimness** *n.* —'**dimwit** *n. inf.* stupid or silly person —**dim-witted** *a.*

dime (daım) *n.* 10-cent piece, coin of U.S. and Canad.

dimension (dı'mɛnʃən) *n.* **1.** measurement, size **2.** aspect —**di'mensional** *a.* —**fourth dimension** *Phys.* **1.** time **2.** supranatural, fictional dimension additional to those of length, breadth, thickness

diminish (dı'mınıʃ) *v.* lessen —**dimi'nution** *n.* —**di'minutive** *a.* **1.** very small —*n.* **2.** derivative word, affix implying smallness —**diminished responsibility** *Law* plea under which mental derangement is submitted as demonstrating lack of criminal responsibility

diminuendo (dɪmɪnjuˈɛndəʊ) *a. Mus.* (of sound) dying away

dimity (ˈdɪmɪtɪ) *n.* strong cotton fabric

dimple (ˈdɪmpəl) *n.* 1. small hollow in surface of skin, *esp.* of cheek 2. any small hollow —*v.* 1. mark with, show dimples

din (dɪn) *n.* continuous roar of confused noises —**din into** instil into by constant repetition

dinar (ˈdiːnɑː) *n.* 1. standard monetary unit of Iraq, Jordan, Libya, Yugoslavia *etc.* 2. an Iranian monetary unit

dine (daɪn) *vi.* 1. eat dinner —*vt.* 2. give dinner to —'**diner** *n.* 1. one who dines 2. *chiefly* US small cheap restaurant 3. railway restaurant car —**dining car** railway coach in which meals are served (*also* **restaurant car**) —**dining room** room where meals are eaten

ding (dɪŋ) *v.* 1. ring (*esp.* with tedious repetition) —*vi.* 2. make (imitation of) sound of bell —*n.* 1. this sound —**ding-dong** *n.* 1. sound of bell 2. imitation of sound of bell 3. violent exchange of blows or words —*a.* 3. sounding or ringing repeatedly

dinghy, dingy, *or* **dingey** (ˈdɪŋɪ) *n.* 1. small open boat 2. collapsible rubber boat

dingle (ˈdɪŋgəl) *n.* dell

dingo (ˈdɪŋgəʊ) *n. Aust.* wild dog

dingy (ˈdɪndʒɪ) *a.* dirty-looking, dull —'**dinginess** *n.*

dinkum (ˈdɪŋkəm) *a.* **A, NZ** *inf.* genuine; right —**dinkum oil** truth

dinky (ˈdɪŋkɪ) *a. inf.* 1. **UK** small and neat; dainty 2. **US** inconsequential; insignificant

dinner (ˈdɪnə) *n.* 1. chief meal of the day 2. official banquet —**dinner jacket** man's semiformal evening jacket without tails, usu. black

dinosaur (ˈdaɪnəsɔː) *n.* extinct reptile, oft. of gigantic size —**dino'saurian** *a.*

dint (dɪnt) *n.* dent, mark —**by dint of** by means of

diocese (ˈdaɪəsɪs) *n.* district, jurisdiction of bishop —**diocesan** (daɪˈɒsɪsən) *a.* 1. of diocese —*n.* 2. bishop, clergyman, people of diocese

diode (ˈdaɪəʊd) *n.* 1. semiconductor device for converting alternating current to direct current 2. electronic valve having two electrodes between which current can flow in only one direction

dioecious (daɪˈiːʃəs) *a.* (of plants) having male and female reproductive organs on separate plants

Dionysian (daɪəˈnɪzɪən) *a.* 1. of Dionysus, Gr. god of wine and revelry 2. (*oft.* **d-**) wild; orgiastic

dioptre *or* **U.S. diopter** (daɪˈɒptə) *n.* unit for measuring refractive power of lens —**di'optrics**

pl.n. (*with sing. v.*) that part of the science of optics which deals with refraction of light

diorama (daɪəˈrɑːmə) *n.* miniature three-dimensional scene, *esp.* as museum exhibit

dioxide (daɪˈɒksaɪd) *n.* oxide with two parts of oxygen to one of the other constituents

dioxin (daɪˈɒksɪn) *n.* any of various by-products of manufacture of certain herbicides and bacdericides

dip (dɪp) *vt.* 1. put partly or briefly into liquid, *esp.* to coat 2. immerse 3. lower and raise again 4. take up in ladle, bucket *etc.* 5. direct (headlights of vehicle) downwards —*vi.* 6. plunge partially or temporarily 7. go down, sink 8. slope downwards (**-pp-**) —*n.* 9. act of dipping 10. bathe 11. liquid chemical in which livestock are immersed to treat insect pests *etc.* 12. downward slope 13. hollow 14. creamy (savoury) mixture in which crisps *etc.* are dipped before being eaten 15. lottery —'**dipstick** *n.* graduated rod dipped into container to indicate fluid level —**dip switch** device for dipping car headlights —**dip into** 1. glance at 2. make inroads into for funds

Dip. A. D. Diploma in Art and Design

Dip. Ed. UK Diploma in Education

diphtheria (dɪpˈθɪərɪə) *n.* infectious disease of throat with membranous growth —**diphtheritic** (dɪpθəˈrɪtɪk) *a.*

diphthong (ˈdɪfθɒŋ) *n.* union of two vowel sounds in single compound sound

diploma (dɪˈpləʊmə) *n.* 1. document vouching for person's proficiency 2. title to degree, honour *etc.*

diplomacy (dɪˈpləʊməsɪ) *n.* 1. management of international relations 2. skill in negotiation 3. tactful, adroit dealing —'**diplomat** *n.* one engaged in official diplomacy —**diplo'matic** *a.* —**diplo'matically** *adv.* —**di'plomatist** *n.* 1. diplomat 2. tactful person —**diplomatic immunity** immunity from local jurisdiction *etc.* afforded to diplomatic staff abroad

diplopia (dɪˈpləʊpɪə) *n.* double vision

dipolar (daɪˈpəʊlə) *a.* having two poles

dipole (ˈdaɪpəʊl) *n.* type of radio and television aerial

dipper (ˈdɪpə) *n.* 1. ladle, bucket, scoop 2. diving bird (*also* **water ouzel**)

dipsomania (dɪpsəʊˈmeɪnɪə) *n.* uncontrollable craving for alcohol —**dipso'maniac** *n.* victim of this

dipterous (ˈdɪptərəs) *a.* 1. of order of insects having single pair of wings and sucking or piercing mouthparts (*also* '**dipteran**) 2. *Bot.* having two winglike parts

diptych (ˈdɪptɪk) *n.* 1. ancient tablet hinged in centre, folding together like a book 2. painting, carving on two hinged panels

dire (daɪə) a. 1. terrible 2. urgent

direct (dɪˈrɛkt, daɪ-) vt. 1. control, manage, order 2. tell or show the way 3. aim, point, turn 4. address (letter etc.) 5. supervise (actors etc.) in play or film —a. 6. frank, straightforward 7. straight 8. going straight to the point 9. immediate 10. lineal —di'rection n. 1. directing 2. aim, course of movement 3. address, instruction —di'rectional a. 1. of or relating to spatial direction 2. Electron. having or relating to increased sensitivity to radio waves etc. coming from particular direction; (of aerial) transmitting or receiving radio waves more effectively in some directions than in others 3. Phys., electron. concentrated in, following or producing motion in particular direction —di'rective a./n. —di'rectly adv. —di'rectness n. —di'rector n. 1. one who directs, esp. a film 2. member of board managing company (di'rectress fem.) —di'rectorate n. 1. body of directors 2. office of director —di'rectorship n. —di'rectory n. 1. alphabetical book of names, addresses, streets etc. 2. (D-) French revolutionary government 1795-9 —direct current continuous electric current that flows in one direction —direct-grant school UK formerly, school financed by endowment, fees and state grant conditional upon admittance of percentage of nonpaying pupils —direction finder radio receiver that determines the direction of incoming waves —direct object Gram. noun, pronoun or noun phrase whose referent receives direct action of verb —direct speech or esp. U.S. direct discourse reporting of what someone has said or written by quoting exact words —direct tax tax paid by person or organization on which it is levied

dirge (dɜːdʒ) n. song of mourning

dirigible (dɪˈrɪdʒɪbəl) a. 1. steerable —n. 2. balloon; airship

dirk (dɜːk) n. short dagger orig. carried by Scottish clansmen

dirndl (ˈdɜːndəl) n. full, gathered skirt

dirt (dɜːt) n. 1. filth 2. soil, earth 3. obscene or pornographic material 4. contamination —'dirtiness n. —'dirty a. 1. unclean, filthy 2. obscene 3. unfair 4. dishonest —dirt-cheap a./adv. inf. at extremely low price —dirt track loose-surfaced track, eg for motorcycle racing

dis- (comb. form) negation, opposition, deprivation; in many verbs indicates undoing of the action of simple verb. In the following list, the meaning may be inferred from the word to which dis- is prefixed

disable (dɪsˈeɪbəl) vt. 1. make unable 2. cripple, maim —disa'bility n. 1. incapacity 2. drawback

disabuse (dɪsəˈbjuːz) vt. 1. undeceive, disillusion 2. free from error

disadvantage (dɪsədˈvɑːntɪdʒ) n. 1. drawback 2. hindrance 3. detriment —vt. 4. handicap —disad'vantaged a. deprived, discriminated against, underprivileged —disadvan'tageous a.

disaffected (dɪsəˈfɛktɪd) a. ill-disposed, alienated, estranged —disaf'fection n.

disagree (dɪsəˈɡriː) vi. 1. (oft. with with) 1. be at variance 2. conflict 3. (of food etc.) have bad effect (on) —disa'greeable a. unpleasant —disa'greement n. 1. difference of opinion 2. discord 3. discrepancy

disallow (dɪsəˈlaʊ) vt. reject as untrue or invalid —disal'lowance n.

disappear (dɪsəˈpɪə) vi. 1. vanish 2. cease to exist 3. be lost —disap'pearance n.

disappoint (dɪsəˈpɔɪnt) vt. fail to fulfil (hope), frustrate —disap'pointment n.

disarm (dɪsˈɑːm) vt. 1. deprive of arms or weapons 2. reduce war weapons of (a country) 3. win over —dis'armament n. —dis'arming a. removing hostility, suspicion

disarray (dɪsəˈreɪ) vt. 1. throw into disorder, derange —n. 2. disorderliness, esp. of clothing

disassociate (dɪsəˈsəʊʃɪeɪt) v. see DISSOCIATE

disaster (dɪˈzɑːstə) n. calamity, sudden or great misfortune —dis'astrous a. calamitous

disappro'bation	discon'tinue
disap'proval	discon'tinuous
disap'prove	dis'courteous
disar'range	dis'courtesy
disa'vow	disem'bark
dis'band	disen'chant
disbe'lief	disen'cumber
disbe'lieve	disen'tangle
discom'pose	disen'tanglement
discom'posure	disequi'librium
discon'nect	dises'tablish
discon'tent	dises'tablishment
discon'tented	dis'franchise
discon'tentment	dis'harmony

dis'hearten	dispro'portionate
dis'heartenment	disre'gard
dis'honest	dis'reputable
dis'honesty	disre'pute
disin'ter	disre'spect
disin'terment	disre'spectful
dis'join	dissatis'faction
dis'loyal	dis'satisfy
dis'loyalty	dis'similar
dis'mast	dissimi'larity
dis'mount	dis'symmetry
disorgani'zation	dis'trust
dis'organize	dis'trustful
dispro'portion	disu'nite

disbar (dɪs'bɑː) vt. Law expel from the bar

disbud (dɪs'bʌd) vt. remove superfluous buds, shoots from

disburse (dɪs'bɜːs) vt. pay out —**dis'bursement** n.

disc (dɪsk) n. 1. thin, flat, circular object like a coin 2. gramophone record —**disc brake** brake in which two pads rub against flat disc attached to wheel hub when brake is applied —**disc harrow** or **plough** harrow or plough which cuts soil with inclined discs —**disc jockey** announcer playing records, oft. on radio

discard (dɪs'kɑːd) vt. 1. reject 2. give up 3. cast off, dismiss

discern (dɪ'sɜːn) vt. 1. make out 2. distinguish —**dis'cernible** a. —**dis'cerning** a. 1. discriminating 2. penetrating —**dis'cernment** n. insight

discharge (dɪs'tʃɑːdʒ) vt. 1. release 2. dismiss 3. emit 4. perform (duties), fulfil (obligations) 5. let go 6. fire off 7. unload 8. pay —n. ('dɪstʃɑːdʒ, dɪs'tʃɑːdʒ) 9. discharging 10. being discharged 11. release 12. matter emitted 13. document certifying release, payment etc.

disciple (dɪ'saɪpəl) n. follower, one who takes another as teacher and model —**dis'cipleship** n.

discipline ('dɪsɪplɪn) n. 1. training that produces orderliness, obedience, self-control 2. result of such training in order, conduct etc. 3. system of rules etc. —vt. 4. train 5. punish —**discipli'narian** n. one who enforces rigid discipline —'**disciplinary** a.

disclaim (dɪs'kleɪm) vt. deny, renounce —**dis'claimer** n. repudiation, denial

disclose (dɪs'kləʊz) vt. 1. allow to be seen 2. make known —**dis'closure** n. revelation

disco ('dɪskəʊ) discotheque

discobolus (dɪs'kɒbələs) n. discus thrower (pl. -li (-laɪ))

discolour or U.S. **discolor** (dɪs'kʌlə) vt. alter colour of, stain —**discolor'ation** n.

discomfit (dɪs'kʌmfɪt) vt. embarrass, disconcert, baffle —**dis'comfiture** n.

discomfort (dɪs'kʌmfət) n. 1. inconvenience, distress or mild pain 2. something that disturbs or deprives of ease —vt. 3. make uncomfortable or uneasy

discommode (dɪskə'məʊd) vt. 1. put to inconvenience 2. disturb —**discom'modious** a.

disconcert (dɪskən'sɜːt) vt. 1. ruffle, confuse 2. upset, embarrass

disconsolate (dɪs'kɒnsəlɪt) a. unhappy, downcast, forlorn

discord ('dɪskɔːd) n. 1. strife 2. difference, dissension 3. disagreement of sounds —**dis'cordance** n. —**dis'cordant** a. —**dis'cordantly** adv.

discotheque ('dɪskətɛk) n. 1. club etc. for

dancing to recorded music 2. mobile equipment for providing music for dancing

discount (dɪs'kaʊnt, 'dɪskaʊnt) vt. 1. consider as possibility but reject as unsuitable, inappropriate etc. 2. deduct (amount, percentage) from usual price 3. sell at reduced price —n. ('dɪskaʊnt) 4. amount deducted from cost, expressed as cash amount or percentage

discountenance (dɪs'kaʊntɪnəns) vt. 1. abash 2. discourage 3. frown upon

discourage (dɪs'kʌrɪdʒ) vt. 1. reduce confidence of 2. deter 3. show disapproval of —**dis'couragement** n.

discourse ('dɪskɔːs, dɪs'kɔːs) n. 1. conversation 2. speech, treatise, sermon —vi. (dɪs'kɔːs) 3. speak, converse, lecture

discover (dɪ'skʌvə) vt. 1. (be the first to) find out, light upon 2. make known —**dis'coverable** a. —**dis'coverer** n. —**dis'covery** n.

discredit (dɪs'krɛdɪt) vt. 1. damage reputation of 2. cast doubt on 3. reject as untrue —n. 4. disgrace 5. doubt —**dis'creditable** a.

discreet (dɪ'skriːt) a. prudent, circumspect —**dis'creetly** adv. —**dis'creetness** n.

discrepancy (dɪ'skrɛpənsɪ) n. conflict, variation, as between figures —**dis'crepant** a.

discrete (dɪs'kriːt) a. separate, disunited, discontinuous

discretion (dɪ'skrɛʃən) n. 1. quality of being discreet 2. prudence 3. freedom to act as one chooses —**dis'cretionary** or **dis'cretional** a.

discriminate (dɪ'skrɪmɪneɪt) vi. 1. single out particular person, group etc. for special favour or disfavour 2. distinguish (between) 3. be discerning —**discrimi'nation** n. —**dis'criminatory** or **dis'criminative** a. 1. based on prejudice; biased 2. capable of making fine distinctions

discursive (dɪ'skɜːsɪv) a. passing from subject to subject, rambling

discus ('dɪskəs) n. disc-shaped object thrown in athletic competition (pl. **-es, disci** ('dɪskaɪ))

discuss (dɪs'kʌs) vt. 1. exchange opinions about 2. debate —**dis'cussion** n.

disdain (dɪs'deɪn) n. 1. scorn, contempt —vt. 2. scorn —**dis'dainful** a. —**dis'dainfully** adv.

disease (dɪ'ziːz) n. 1. illness 2. disorder of health —**dis'eased** a.

disembodied (dɪsɪm'bɒdɪd) a. (of spirit) released from bodily form

disembowel (dɪsɪm'baʊəl) vt. take out entrails of (-**ll-**)

disenchanted (dɪsɪn'tʃɑːntɪd) a. disillusioned

disengage (dɪsɪn'geɪdʒ) v. 1. release or become released from connection etc. 2. Mil. withdraw (forces) from close action 3. Fencing move (one's blade) from one side of opponent's blade to another in circular motion —**disen'gaged** a. —**disen'gagement** n.

disfavour or U.S. **disfavor** (dɪsˈfeɪvə) n. 1. disapproval; dislike 2. state of being disapproved of or disliked 3. unkind act —vt. 4. treat with disapproval or dislike

disfigure (dɪsˈfɪgə) vt. mar appearance of —**disfiguˈration** n. —**disˈfigurement** n. blemish, defect

disgorge (dɪsˈgɔːdʒ) vt. 1. vomit 2. give up —**disˈgorgement** n.

disgrace (dɪsˈgreɪs) n. 1. shame, loss of reputation, dishonour —vt. 2. bring shame or discredit upon —**disˈgraceful** a. shameful —**disˈgracefully** adv.

disgruntled (dɪsˈgrʌntᵊld) a. 1. vexed 2. put out

disguise (dɪsˈgaɪz) vt. 1. change appearance of, make unrecognizable 2. conceal, cloak 3. misrepresent —n. 4. false appearance 5. costume, mask etc. to conceal identity

disgust (dɪsˈgʌst) n. 1. violent distaste, loathing, repugnance —vt. 2. affect with loathing

dish (dɪʃ) n. 1. shallow vessel for food 2. portion or variety of food 3. contents of dish 4. sl. attractive person —vt. 5. put in dish —ˈ**dishy** a. sl., chiefly UK good-looking, attractive —ˈ**dishcloth** n. cloth or rag for washing or drying dishes —**dish up** 1. serve (meal etc.) 2. inf. prepare or present, esp. attractively

dishabille (dɪsæˈbiːl) or **deshabille** n. state of being partly or carelessly dressed

dishevelled (dɪˈʃɛvᵊld) a. 1. with disordered hair 2. ruffled, untidy, unkempt

dishonour or U.S. **dishonor** (dɪsˈɒnə) vt. 1. treat with disrespect 2. fail or refuse to pay 3. cause disgrace of (woman) by seduction or rape —n. 4. lack of honour or respect 5. state of shame or disgrace 6. person or thing that causes loss of honour 7. insult; affront 8. refusal or failure to accept or pay a commercial paper —**disˈhonourable** or U.S. **disˈhonorable** a. characterized by or causing dishonour or discredit 2. having little or no integrity; unprincipled

disillusion (dɪsɪˈluːʒən) vt. 1. destroy ideals, illusions, or false ideas of —n. 2. act of disillusioning or being disillusioned (also **disilˈlusionment**)

disincentive (dɪsɪnˈsɛntɪv) n. 1. something that acts as deterrent —a. 2. acting as deterrent

disincline (dɪsɪnˈklaɪn) v. make or be unwilling, reluctant or averse —**disinclination** (dɪsɪnklɪˈneɪʃən) n.

disinfectant (dɪsɪnˈfɛktənt) n. substance that prevents or removes infection —**disinˈfect** vt.

disinformation (dɪsɪnfəˈmeɪʃən) n. deliberately leaked false information intended to mislead foreign agents

disingenuous (dɪsɪnˈdʒɛnjʊəs) a. not sincere or frank

disinherit (dɪsɪnˈhɛrɪt) vt. deprive of inheritance

disintegrate (dɪsˈɪntɪgreɪt) vi. break up, fall to pieces —**disinteˈgration** n.

disinterest (dɪsˈɪntrɪst) n. freedom from bias or involvement —**disˈinterested** a.

disjoint (dɪsˈdʒɔɪnt) vt. 1. put out of joint 2. break the natural order or logical arrangement of —**disˈjointed** a. 1. (of discourse) incoherent 2. disconnected

disjunctive (dɪsˈdʒʌŋktɪv) a. 1. serving to disconnect or separate 2. Gram. denoting word, esp. conjunction, that serves to express opposition or contrast 3. Logic characterizing, containing or included in disjunction —n. 4. Gram. disjunctive word, esp. conjunction 5. Logic disjunctive proposition

disk (dɪsk) n. see DISC

dislike (dɪsˈlaɪk) vt. 1. consider unpleasant or disagreeable —n. 2. aversion; antipathy —**disˈlikable** or **disˈlikeable** a.

dislocate (ˈdɪsləkeɪt) vt. 1. put out of joint 2. disrupt, displace —**disloˈcation** n.

dislodge (dɪsˈlɒdʒ) vt. drive out or remove from hiding place or previous position —**disˈlodgement** or **disˈlodgment** n.

dismal (ˈdɪzməl) a. 1. depressing 2. depressed 3. cheerless, dreary, gloomy —**disˈmally** adv.

dismantle (dɪsˈmæntᵊl) vt. take apart —**disˈmantlement** n.

dismay (dɪsˈmeɪ) vt. 1. dishearten, daunt —n. 2. consternation, horrified amazement 3. apprehension

dismember (dɪsˈmɛmbə) vt. 1. remove limbs or members of 2. divide, partition —**disˈmemberment** n.

dismiss (dɪsˈmɪs) vt. 1. remove, discharge from employment 2. send away 3. reject —**disˈmissal** n.

disobey (dɪsəˈbeɪ) v. refuse or fail to obey —**disobedience** (dɪsəˈbiːdɪəns) n. —**disobedient** (dɪsəˈbiːdɪənt) a.

disoblige (dɪsəˈblaɪdʒ) vt. disregard the wishes, preferences of

disorder (dɪsˈɔːdə) n. 1. disarray, confusion, disturbance 2. upset of health, ailment —vt. 3. upset order of 4. disturb health of —**disˈorderly** a. 1. untidy 2. unruly

disorientate (dɪsˈɔːrɪənteɪt) or **disorient** vt. cause (someone) to lose his bearings, confuse

disown (dɪsˈəʊn) vt. refuse to acknowledge

disparage (dɪˈspærɪdʒ) vt. 1. speak slightingly of 2. belittle —**disˈparagement** n.

disparate (ˈdɪspərɪt) a. essentially different, unrelated —**disˈparity** n. 1. inequality 2. incongruity

dispassionate (dɪs'pæʃənɪt) a. 1. unswayed by passion 2. calm, impartial

dispatch or **despatch** (dɪ'spætʃ) vt. 1. send off to destination or on an errand 2. send off 3. finish off, get done with speed 4. inf. eat up 5. kill —n. 6. sending off 7. efficient speed 8. official message, report —**dispatch rider** horseman or motorcyclist who carries dispatches

dispel (dɪ'spel) vt. clear, drive away, scatter (-ll-)

dispense (dɪ'spens) vt. 1. deal out 2. make up (medicine) 3. administer (justice) 4. grant exemption from —**dis'pensable** a. —**dis'pensary** n. place where medicine is made up —**dispen'sation** n. 1. act of dispensing 2. licence; exemption 3. provision of nature or providence —**dis'penser** n. —**dispense with** 1. do away with 2. manage without

disperse (dɪ'spɜːs) v. scatter —**dis'persal** or **dis'persion** n. —**dis'persed** a. 1. scattered 2. placed here and there

dispirited (dɪ'spɪrɪtɪd) a. dejected, disheartened —**dis'piritedly** adv. —**dis'piriting** a.

displace (dɪs'pleɪs) vt. 1. move from the usual place 2. remove from office 3. take place of —**dis'placement** n. displacing 2. weight of liquid displaced by a solid in a fluid —**displaced person** person forced from his home country, esp. by war etc.

display (dɪ'spleɪ) vt. 1. spread out for show 2. show, expose to view 3. (of visual display unit etc.) represent (data) visually, as on cathode-ray tube screen —n. 4. displaying 5. parade 6. show, exhibition 7. ostentation 8. Electron. device capable of representing data visually, as on cathode-ray tube screen

displease (dɪs'pliːz) v. 1. offend 2. annoy —**displeasure** (dɪs'pleʒə) n. anger, vexation

disport (dɪ'spɔːt) v.refl. 1. amuse oneself 2. frolic, gambol

dispose (dɪ'spəʊz) vt. 1. arrange 2. distribute 3. incline 4. adjust —vi. 5. determine —**dis'posable** a. designed to be thrown away after use —**dis'posal** n. —**dis'posed** a. having inclination as specified (towards something) —**dispo'sition** n. 1. inclination 2. temperament 3. arrangement 4. plan —**dispose of** 1. sell, get rid of 2. have authority over 3. deal with

dispossess (dɪspə'zes) vt. cause to give up possession (of)

disprove (dɪs'pruːv) vt. to show (assertion, claim etc.) to be incorrect

dispute (dɪ'spjuːt) v. 1. debate, discuss —vt. 2. call in question 3. debate, argue 4. oppose, contest —**dis'putable** a. —**dis'putant** n. —**dispu'tation** n. —**dispu'tatious** a. 1. argumentative 2. quarrelsome

disqualify (dɪs'kwɒlɪfaɪ) vt. make ineligible, unfit for some special purpose

disquiet (dɪs'kwaɪət) n. 1. anxiety, uneasiness —vt. 2. cause (someone) to feel this —**dis'quietude** n. feeling of anxiety

disquisition (dɪskwɪ'zɪʃən) n. learned or elaborate treatise, discourse or essay

disrepair (dɪsrɪ'pɛə) n. state of bad repair, neglect

disrobe (dɪs'rəʊb) v. 1. undress —vt. 2. divest of robes

disrupt (dɪs'rʌpt) vt. 1. interrupt 2. throw into turmoil or disorder —**dis'ruption** n. —**dis'ruptive** a.

dissect (dɪ'sekt, daɪ-) vt. 1. cut up (body, organism) for detailed examination 2. examine or criticize in detail —**dis'section** n. —**dis'sector** n. anatomist

dissemble (dɪ'sembəl) v. 1. conceal, disguise (feelings etc.) —vt. 2. simulate —**dis'sembler** n.

disseminate (dɪ'semɪneɪt) vt. spread abroad, scatter —**dissemi'nation** n. —**dis'seminator** n.

dissent (dɪ'sent) vi. 1. differ in opinion 2. express such difference 3. disagree with doctrine etc. of established church —n. 4. such disagreement —**dis'sension** n. —**dis'senter** n. —**dis'sentient** a./n.

dissertation (dɪsə'teɪʃən) n. 1. written thesis 2. formal discourse —**'dissertate** vi. hold forth

disservice (dɪs'sɜːvɪs) n. ill turn, wrong, injury

dissident ('dɪsɪdənt) n./a. (one) not in agreement, esp. with government —**'dissidence** n. 1. dissent 2. disagreement

dissimulate (dɪ'sɪmjʊleɪt) v. dissemble, practise deceit —**dissimu'lation** n. —**dis'simulator** n.

dissipate ('dɪsɪpeɪt) vt. 1. scatter 2. waste, squander —**'dissipated** a. 1. indulging in pleasure without restraint, dissolute 2. scattered, wasted —**dissi'pation** n. 1. scattering 2. frivolous, dissolute way of life

dissociate (dɪ'səʊʃɪeɪt, -sɪ-) v. 1. separate —vt. 2. disconnect, sever —**dissoci'ation** n.

dissolute ('dɪsəluːt) a. lax in morals

dissolution (dɪsə'luːʃən) n. 1. break-up 2. termination of parliament, meeting or legal relationship 3. destruction 4. death

dissolve (dɪ'zɒlv) vt. 1. absorb or melt in fluid 2. break up, put an end to, annul —vi. 3. melt in fluid 4. disappear, vanish 5. break up, scatter —**dis'solvable** or **dissoluble** (dɪ'sɒljubəl) a. capable of being dissolved —**dis'solvent** n. thing with power to dissolve

dissonant ('dɪsənənt) a. jarring, discordant —**'dissonance** n.

dissuade (dɪ'sweɪd) vt. advise to refrain, persuade not to do something —**dis'suasion** n. —**dis'suasive** a.

dissyllable (dɪ'sɪləbᵊl) *or* **disyllable** ('daɪsɪləbᵊl) *n.* word or metrical foot having two syllables —**dissyl'labic** *or* **disyl'labic** *a.*

distaff ('dɪstɑːf) *n.* cleft stick to hold wool *etc.* for spinning —**distaff side 1.** maternal side **2.** female line of family

distance ('dɪstəns) *n.* **1.** amount of space between two things **2.** remoteness **3.** aloofness, reserve —*vt.* **4.** hold or place at distance —'**distant** *a.* **1.** far off, remote **2.** haughty, cold —'**distantly** *adv.*

distaste (dɪs'teɪst) *n.* **1.** dislike of food or drink **2.** aversion, disgust —**dis'tasteful** *a.* unpleasant, displeasing to feelings —**dis'tastefully** *adv.* —**dis'tastefulness** *n.*

distemper (dɪs'tɛmpə) *n.* **1.** disease of dogs **2.** method of painting on plaster without oil **3.** paint used for this —*vt.* **4.** paint with distemper

distend (dɪ'stɛnd) *v.* swell out by pressure from within, inflate —**dis'tensible** *a.* —**dis'tension** *n.*

distich ('dɪstɪk) *n.* couplet

distil *or U.S.* **distill** (dɪs'tɪl) *vt.* **1.** vaporize and recondense (a liquid) **2.** purify, separate, concentrate (liquids) by this method **3.** *fig.* extract quality of —*vi.* **4.** trickle down (-**ll**-) —'**distillate** *n.* distilled liquid, *esp.* as fuel for some engines —**distil'lation** *n.* **1.** distilling **2.** process of evaporating or boiling liquid and condensing its vapour **3.** purification or separation of mixture by using different evaporation rates or boiling points of their components **4.** process of obtaining essence or extract of substance, usu. by heating in solvent **5.** distillate **6.** concentrated essence —**dis'tiller** *n.* one who distils, *esp.* manufacturer of alcoholic spirits —**dis'tillery** *n.*

distinct (dɪs'tɪŋkt) *a.* **1.** clear, easily seen **2.** definite **3.** separate, different —**dis'tinction** *n.* **1.** point of difference **2.** act of distinguishing **3.** eminence, repute, high honour, high quality —**dis'tinctive** *a.* characteristic —**dis'tinctly** *adv.* —**dis'tinctness** *n.*

distingué (dɪsˈtæ̃geɪ) *Fr.* distinguished; noble

distinguish (dɪs'tɪŋgwɪʃ) *vt.* **1.** make difference in **2.** recognize, make out **3.** honour **4.** make prominent or honoured (*usu. refl.*) **5.** class —*vi.* **6.** (*usu.* with between *or* among) draw distinction, grasp difference —**dis'tinguishable** *a.* —**dis'tinguished** *a.* **1.** noble, dignified **2.** famous, eminent

distort (dɪs'tɔːt) *vt.* **1.** put out of shape, deform **2.** misrepresent **3.** garble, falsify —**dis'tortion** *n.*

distract (dɪs'trækt) *vt.* **1.** draw attention of (someone) away from work *etc.* **2.** divert **3.** perplex, bewilder **4.** drive mad —**dis'traction** *n.*

distraint (dɪs'treɪnt) *n.* legal seizure of goods to enforce payment —**dis'train** *vt.* —**dis'trainment** *n.*

distrait (dɪs'treɪ; *Fr.* di'stre) *a.* **1.** absent-minded **2.** abstracted

distraught (dɪs'trɔːt) *a.* **1.** bewildered, crazed with grief **2.** frantic, distracted

distress (dɪs'trɛs) *n.* **1.** severe trouble, mental pain **2.** severe pressure of hunger, fatigue or want **3.** *Law* distraint —*vt.* **4.** afflict, give mental pain —**dis'tressed** *a.* **1.** much troubled; upset; afflicted **2.** in financial straits; poor **3.** *Econ.* see **depressed** (sense 4) *at* DEPRESS —**dis'tressful** *a.*

distribute (dɪs'trɪbjuːt) *vt.* **1.** deal out, dispense **2.** spread, dispose at intervals **3.** classify —**distri'bution** *n.* —**dis'tributive** *a.* —**dis'tributor** *n.* rotary switch distributing electricity in car engine

district ('dɪstrɪkt) *n.* **1.** region, locality **2.** portion of territory —**district nurse** UK nurse appointed to attend patients within particular district, usu. in patients' homes

disturb (dɪs'tɜːb) *vt.* trouble, agitate, unsettle, derange —**dis'turbance** *n.* —**dis'turbed** *a.* *Psych.* emotionally or mentally unstable —**dis'turber** *n.*

disuse (dɪs'juːs) *n.* state of being no longer used —**disused** (dɪs'juːzd) *a.*

disyllable ('daɪsɪləbᵊl) *n.* see DISSYLLABLE

ditch (dɪtʃ) *n.* **1.** long narrow hollow dug in ground for drainage *etc.* —*v.* **2.** make ditch in **3.** run (car *etc.*) into ditch —*vt.* **4.** *sl.* abandon, discard

dither ('dɪðə) *vi.* **1.** be uncertain or indecisive —*n.* **2.** this state

dithyramb ('dɪθɪræm, -ræmb) *n.* ancient Gr. hymn sung in honour of Dionysus —**dithy'rambic** *a.*

dittany ('dɪtənɪ) *n.* aromatic plant native to Greece

ditto ('dɪtəʊ) *n.* **1.** the aforementioned; the above; the same: used in lists *etc.* to avoid repetition, and symbolized by two small marks (,,) placed under thing to be repeated **2.** *inf.* duplicate (*pl.* **-s**) —*adv.* **3.** in same way —*interj.* **4.** *inf.* used to avoid repeating or confirm agreement with preceding sentence —*vt.* **5.** copy; repeat (**-toing, -toed**)

ditty ('dɪtɪ) *n.* simple song

diuretic (daɪjʊ'rɛtɪk) *a.* **1.** increasing the discharge of urine —*n.* **2.** substance with this property

diurnal (daɪ'ɜːnᵊl) *a.* **1.** daily **2.** in or of daytime **3.** taking a day

divalent (daɪ'veɪlənt, 'daɪveɪ-) *a.* capable of combining with two atoms of hydrogen or their equivalent —**di'valency** *n.*

divan (dɪ'væn) *n.* **1.** bed, couch without back or head **2.** backless low cushioned seat

dive (daɪv) *vi.* **1.** plunge under surface of water **2.** descend suddenly **3.** disappear **4.** go deep down 5. rush or go quickly (**dived** or *U.S.* **dove,** **dived,** '**diving**) —*n.* 6. act of diving 7. *sl.* disreputable bar or club —'**diver** *n.* 1. one who descends into deep water 2. any of various kinds of diving bird —**dive bomber** aircraft which attacks after diving steeply —**diving bell** early diving submersible having open bottom and being supplied with compressed air —**diving board** platform or springboard from which swimmers may dive —**diving suit** or **dress** waterproof suit used by divers, having heavy detachable helmet and air supply

diverge (daɪ'vɜːdʒ) *vi.* 1. get farther apart 2. separate —**di'vergence** or **di'vergency** *n.* —**di'vergent** *a.*

divers ('daɪvəz) *a. obs.* some, various

diverse (daɪ'vɜːs, 'daɪvɜːs) *a.* different, varied —**di'versely** *adv.* —**diversifi'cation** *n.* —**di'versify** *vt.* 1. make diverse or varied 2. give variety to (-**ified,** -**ifying**) —**di'versity** *n.*

divert (daɪ'vɜːt) *vt.* 1. turn aside, ward off 2. amuse, entertain —**di'version** *n.* 1. a diverting 2. official detour for traffic when main route is closed 3. amusement —**di'verting** *a.*

divertissement (dɪ'vɜːtɪsmənt) *n.* brief entertainment or diversion, usu. between acts of play

divest (daɪ'vɛst) *vt.* 1. unclothe, strip 2. dispossess, deprive

divide (dɪ'vaɪd) *vt.* 1. make into two or more parts, split up, separate 2. distribute, share 3. classify —*v.* 4. diverge in opinion —*vi.* 5. become separated 6. part into two groups for voting —*n.* 7. watershed —**dividend** ('dɪvɪdɛnd) *n.* 1. share of profits, of money divided among creditors *etc.* 2. number to be divided by another —**di'viders** *pl.n.* measuring compasses

divine (dɪ'vaɪn) *a.* 1. of, pert. to, proceeding from, God 2. sacred 3. heavenly —*n.* 4. theologian 5. clergyman —*vt.* 6. guess 7. predict, foresee, tell by inspiration or magic —**divina'tion** (dɪvɪ'neɪʃən) *n.* divining —**di'vinely** *adv.* —**di'viner** *n.* —**divinity** (dɪ'vɪnɪtɪ) *n.* 1. quality of being divine 2. god 3. theology —**divining rod** (forked) stick said to move when held over ground where water is present (*also* **dowsing rod**)

division (dɪ'vɪʒən) *n.* 1. act of dividing 2. part of whole 3. barrier 4. section 5. political constituency 6. difference in opinion *etc.* 7. *Maths.* method of finding how many times one number is contained in another 8. army unit 9. separation, disunion —**di'visible** *a.* capable of division —**di'visional** —**divisive** (dɪ'vaɪsɪv) *a.* causing disagreement —**divisor** (dɪ'vaɪzə) *n. Maths.* number which divides dividend —**division sign** symbol ÷, placed between dividend and divisor to indicate division, as in 12 ÷ 6 = 2

divorce (dɪ'vɔːs) *n.* 1. legal dissolution of marriage 2. complete separation, disunion —*v.* 3. separate or be separated by divorce —*vt.* 4. separate 5. sunder —**divorcée** (dɪvɔː'siː) or (*masc.*) **divorcé** (dɪ'vɔːseɪ) *n.*

divot ('dɪvət) *n.* piece of turf

divulge (daɪ'vʌldʒ) *vt.* reveal, let out (secret) —**di'vulgence** *n.*

divvy ('dɪvɪ) *inf. vt.* 1. esp. US (*esp. with up*) divide and share —*n.* 2. dividend

dixie ('dɪksɪ) *n.* 1. *inf.* (military) cooking utensil or mess tin 2. (**D-**) southern states of U.S.A. (*also* '**Dixieland**) —'**Dixieland** *n.* 1. jazz derived from New Orleans tradition of playing, but with more emphasis on melody, regular rhythms *etc.* 2. Dixie

D.I.Y. or **d.i.y.** do-it-yourself

dizzy ('dɪzɪ) *a.* 1. feeling dazed, unsteady, as if about to fall 2. causing or fit to cause dizziness, as speed *etc.* 3. *inf.* silly —*vt.* 4. make dizzy ('**dizzied,** '**dizzying**) —'**dizzily** *adv.* —'**dizziness** *n.*

D.J. or **d.j.** 1. dinner jacket 2. disc jockey

djellaba ('dʒɛləbə) *n. see* JELLABA

djinni or **djinny** (dʒɪ'niː, 'dʒɪnɪ) *n. see* JINNI (*pl.* **djinn** (dʒɪn))

dl decilitre

D.Litt. or **D.Lit.** 1. Doctor of Letters 2. Doctor of Literature

dm decimetre

D.Mus. or **DMus** Doctor of Music

DNA deoxyribonucleic acid, main constituent of the chromosomes of all organisms

D-notice *n. UK* official notice sent to newspapers *etc.* prohibiting publication of certain security information

do[1] (duː; *unstressed* də, dʊ) *vt.* 1. perform, effect, transact, bring about, finish 2. work at 3. work out, solve 4. suit 5. cover (distance) 6. provide, prepare 7. *sl.* cheat, swindle 8. frustrate —*vi.* 9. (*oft. with* for) look after 10. act 11. manage 12. work 13. fare 14. serve, suffice 15. happen —*v. aux.* 16. makes negative and interrogative sentences and expresses emphasis (**did, done,** '**doing**) —*n.* 17. *inf.* celebration, festivity —'**doer** *n.* active or energetic person —**do-gooder** *n. inf.* well-intentioned person, *esp.* naive or impractical one —**do-it-yourself** *n.* hobby of constructing and repairing things oneself —**do away with** destroy —**do up** 1. fasten 2. renovate —**do with** 1. need 2. make use of —**do without** deny oneself

do[2] (dəʊ) *n. see* DOH (*pl.* **-s**)

do. ditto (*It.,* the same)

dobbin ('dɒbɪn) *n.* name for horse, *esp.* workhorse

Doberman pinscher ('dəʊbəmən 'pɪnʃə)

breed of large dog with glossy black-and-tan coat

doc (dɒk) *n. inf.* doctor

docile ('dəusaıl) *a.* willing to obey, submissive —**docility** (dəu'sılıtı) *n.*

dock[1] (dɒk) *n.* **1.** artificial enclosure near harbour for loading or repairing ships —*v.* **2.** (of vessel) put or go into dock **3.** (of spacecraft) link or be linked together in space —'**docker** *n.* one who works at docks, *esp.* loading *etc.* cargoes —'**dockyard** *n.* enclosure with docks, for building or repairing ships

dock[2] (dɒk) *n.* **1.** solid part of tail **2.** cut end, stump —*vt.* **3.** cut short, *esp.* tail **4.** curtail, deduct (an amount) from

dock[3] (dɒk) *n.* enclosure in criminal court for prisoner

dock[4] (dɒk) *n.* coarse weed

docket ('dɒkıt) *n.* **1.** piece of paper sent with package *etc.* with details of contents, delivery instructions *etc.* —*vt.* **2.** fix docket to

doctor ('dɒktə) *n.* **1.** medical practitioner **2.** one holding university's highest degree in any faculty —*vt.* **3.** treat medically **4.** repair, mend **5.** falsify (accounts *etc.*) **6.** *inf.* castrate, spay —'**doctoral** *a.* —'**doctorate** *n.*

doctrine ('dɒktrın) *n.* **1.** what is taught **2.** teaching of church, school or person **3.** belief, opinion, dogma —**doctri'naire** *n.* **1.** person who stubbornly applies theory without regard for circumstances —*a.* **2.** adhering to a doctrine in a stubborn, dogmatic way —**doctrinal** (dɒk'traın²l) *a.*

document ('dɒkjumənt) *n.* **1.** piece of paper *etc.* providing information or evidence —*vt.* ('dɒkjument) **2.** furnish with proofs, illustrations, certificates —**docu'mentary** *a./n. esp.* (of) type of film dealing with real life, not fiction —**documen'tation** *n.*

dodder ('dɒdə) *vi.* totter or tremble, as with age —'**dodderer** *n.* feeble or inefficient person

doddle ('dɒd²l) *n. UK sl.* something easily accomplished

dodecagon (dəu'dɛkəgon) *n.* polygon having twelve sides

dodecahedron (dəudɛkə'hi:drən) *n.* solid figure having twelve plane faces

dodge (dɒdʒ) *v.* **1.** avoid or attempt to avoid (blow, discovery *etc.*) as by moving quickly **2.** evade (questions) by cleverness —*n.* **3.** trick, artifice **4.** ingenious method **5.** act of dodging —'**dodger** *n.* shifty person —'**dodgy** *a. inf.* **1.** dangerous **2.** unreliable **3.** tricky

Dodgem ('dɒdʒəm) *n.* **R** car used for bumping other cars in rink at funfair

dodo ('dəudəu) *n.* large extinct bird (*pl.* -s, -es)

doe (dəu) *n.* female of deer, hare, rabbit —'**doeskin** *n.* **1.** skin of deer, lamb or sheep **2.** very supple leather made from this **3.** heavy smooth cloth

Doe (dəu) *n. Law* formerly, name of fictitious plaintiff in action of ejectment

D.O.E. UK Department of the Environment

doek (dʊk) *n. SA inf.* head cloth worn *esp.* by Afr. women

doer ('du:ə) *n. see* DO[1]

does (dʌz) third pers. sing., pres. ind. active of DO[1]

doff (dɒf) *vt.* **1.** take off (hat, clothing) **2.** discard, lay aside

dog (dɒg) *n.* **1.** domesticated carnivorous four-legged mammal **2.** male of wolf, fox and other animals **3.** person (in contempt, abuse or playfully) **4.** name given to various mechanical contrivances acting as holdfasts **5.** device with tooth which penetrates or grips object and detains it **6.** firedog —*vt.* **7.** follow steadily or closely (-**gg**-) —**dogged** ('dɒgıd) *a.* persistent, resolute, tenacious —'**doggy** *a.* —'**doglike** *a.* —'**dogcart** *n.* open vehicle with crosswise back-to-back seats —**dog collar 1.** collar for dog **2.** *inf.* clerical collar **3.** *inf.* tight-fitting necklace —**dog days** *inf.* hot season of the rising of Dog Star **2.** period of inactivity —**dog-ear** *n.* **1.** turned-down corner of page in book —*vt.* **2.** turn down corners of (pages) —**dog-end** *n. inf.* **1.** cigarette end **2.** rejected piece of anything —'**dogfight** *n.* **1.** skirmish between fighter planes **2.** savage contest characterized by disregard of rules —'**dogfish** *n.* very small species of shark —'**doghouse** *n.* **1.** US kennel **2.** *inf.* disfavour (*esp.* **in** in the doghouse) —'**dogleg** *n.* sharp bend or angle —**dog paddle** swimming stroke in which swimmer paddles his hands in imitation of swimming dog —**dog-paddle** *vi.* swim using dog paddle —**dog rose** wild rose —'**dogsbody** *n. inf.* drudge —**Dog Star** star Sirius —**dog-tired** *a. inf.* exhausted —**dog train** C sleigh drawn by dog team —'**dogwatch** *n.* in ships, short half-watch, 4-6, 6-8 p.m. —'**dogwood** *n.* any of various shrubs and trees —**go to the dogs** degenerate —**the dogs** greyhound race meeting

doge (dəudʒ) *n.* formerly, chief magistrate in Venice

doggerel ('dɒgərəl) *or* **dogrel** ('dɒgrəl) *n.* slipshod, unpoetic or trivial verse

doggo ('dɒgəu) *adv.* —**lie doggo** *inf.* keep quiet, still, hidden

dogie, dogy, *or* **dogey** ('dəugı) *n.* US, C motherless calf (*pl.* -**gies** *or* -**geys**)

dogma ('dɒgmə) *n.* **1.** article of belief, *esp.* one laid down authoritatively by church **2.** body of beliefs (*pl.* -**s**, -**ata** (-ətə)) —**dog'matic(al)** *a.* **1.** asserting opinions with arrogance **2.** relating to dogma —**dog'matically** *adv.* —'**dogmatism** *n.*

arrogant assertion of opinion —'**dogmatist** *n.*
—'**dogmatize** *or* -**ise** *v.*

doh (dəʊ) *n. Mus.* in tonic sol-fa, first degree of
any major scale (*pl.* -**s**)

doily *or* **doyley** ('dɔɪlɪ) *n.* small cloth, paper,
piece of lace to place under cake, dish *etc.*

Dolby ('dɒlbɪ) *n.* **R** system used in tape
recorders which reduces noise level on
recorded or broadcast sound

dolce ('dɒltʃɪ) *a. Mus.* sweet

doldrums ('dɒldrəmz) *pl.n.* **1.** state of
depression, dumps **2.** region of light winds and
calms near the equator

dole (dəʊl) *n.* **1.** charitable gift **2.** (*usu. with* the)
inf. payment under unemployment insurance
—*vt.* **3.** (*usu. with* out) deal out sparingly

doleful ('dəʊlful) *a.* dreary, mournful —'**dole-
fully** *adv.*

doll (dɒl) *n.* **1.** child's toy image of human being
2. *sl.* attractive girl or woman —**doll up** dress up
in latest fashion or smartly

dollar ('dɒlə) *n.* standard monetary unit of
many countries, *esp.* U.S.A. and (since 1966)
Aust.

dollop ('dɒləp) *n. inf.* semisolid lump

dolly ('dɒlɪ) *n.* **1.** child's word for doll **2.** wheeled
support for film, TV camera **3.** any of various
metal devices used as aids in hammering,
riveting —**dolly bird** *sl., chiefly UK* attractive,
fashionable girl

dolman sleeve ('dɒlmən) sleeve that is wide
at armhole and tapers to tight wrist

dolmen ('dɒlmɛn) *n.* kind of cromlech **2.**
stone table

dolomite ('dɒləmaɪt) *n.* type of limestone

dolour *or U.S.* **dolor** ('dɒlə) *n.* grief, sadness,
distress —'**dolorous** *a.* —'**dolorously** *adv.*

dolphin ('dɒlfɪn) *n.* sea mammal, smaller than
whale, with beaklike snout —**dolphi'narium** *n.*
pool or aquarium for dolphins

dolt (dəʊlt) *n.* stupid fellow —'**doltish** *a.*

-**dom** (*comb. form*) **1.** state, condition, as in
freedom **2.** rank, office or domain as in
earldom **3.** collection of persons, as in
officialdom

domain (də'meɪn) *n.* **1.** lands held or ruled over
2. sphere, field of influence **3.** province

dome (dəʊm) *n.* **1.** rounded vault forming a roof
2. something of this shape

Domesday Book *or* **Doomsday Book**
('du:mzdeɪ) record of survey of England in 1086

domestic (də'mɛstɪk) *a.* **1.** of, in the home **2.**
home-loving **3.** (of animals) tamed, kept by man
4. of, in one's own country, not foreign —*n.* **5.**
house servant —**do'mesticate** *vt.* **1.** tame
(animals) **2.** accustom to home life **3.** adapt to an
environment —**domesti'cation** *n.* —**domes'ti-**

city *n.* —**domestic science** study of cooking and
other subjects concerned with household skills

domicile ('dɒmɪsaɪl) *or* **domicil** ('dɒmɪsɪl) *n.*
person's regular place of abode —'**domiciled** *a.*
living —**domi'ciliary** (dɒmɪ'sɪlɪərɪ) *a.* of a
dwelling place

dominate ('dɒmɪneɪt) *vt.* **1.** rule, control, sway
2. (of heights) overlook —*vi.* **3.** control, be the
most powerful or influential member or part of
something —'**dominant** *a./n.* —**domi'nation** *n.*
—**domi'neer** *vi.* act imperiously, tyrannize

dominee ('du:mɪnɪ, 'dʊə-) *n.* **SA** minister of
Dutch Reformed Church

Dominican (də'mɪnɪkən) *n.* **1.** friar or nun of
the order of St. Dominic —*a.* **2.** pert. to this
order

dominion (də'mɪnjən) *n.* **1.** sovereignty, rule **2.**
territory of government

Dominion Day *see* **Canada Day** *at* CANADIAN

dominoes ('dɒmɪnəʊz) *pl.n.* **1.** game played
with 28 oblong flat pieces marked on one side
with 0 to 6 spots on each half of the face —*sing.*
2. one of these pieces **3.** cloak with eye mask for
masquerading —**domino theory** theory that
event in one place, *esp.* political takeover, will
influence occurrence of similar events elsewhere

don[1] (dɒn) *vt.* put on (clothes) (-**nn**-)

don[2] (dɒn) *n.* **1.** fellow or tutor of college **2.** Sp.
title, Sir —'**donnish** *a.* of or resembling
university don, *esp.* denoting pedantry or
fussiness

Doña ('dɒnjə) *n.* Sp. title of address equivalent
to *Mrs.* or *Madam*

donate (dəʊ'neɪt) *v.* give —**do'nation** *n.* gift to
fund —'**donor** *n.*

done (dʌn) *pp. of* DO[1]

dong (dɒŋ) *n.* **1.** imitation of sound of bell —*vi.* **2.**
make such sound

donga ('dɒŋɡə) *n.* **SA, A** deep gully

donjon ('dʌndʒɒn, 'dɒn-) *n. see* DUNGEON

Don Juan ('dɒn 'dʒuːən) **1.** legendary Sp.
nobleman and philanderer **2.** successful seducer
of women

donkey ('dɒŋkɪ) *n.* ass (*pl.* -**s**) —**donkey engine**
auxiliary engine —**donkey jacket** short, thick
jacket, oft. worn by workmen —**donkey's years**
inf. a long time —**donkey-work** *n.* drudgery

Donna ('dɒnə) *n.* It. title of address equivalent
to *Madam*

Don Quixote ('dɒn kiː'həʊtɪ, 'kwɪksət)
impractical idealist

doodle ('duːd³l) *v.* **1.** scribble absent-mindedly
—*n.* **2.** picture *etc.* drawn aimlessly —'**doodlebug** *n.* **1.** *see* V-1 **2.** diviner's rod

doom (duːm) *n.* **1.** fate, destiny **2.** ruin **3.** judicial
sentence, condemnation **4.** the Last Judgment
—*vt.* **5.** sentence, condemn **6.** destine to

destruction or suffering —'**doomsday** or '**domesday** n. the day of the Last Judgment

door (dɔː) n. hinged or sliding barrier to close any entrance —'**doorjamb** n. one of two vertical members forming sides of doorframe (also '**doorpost**) —'**doorman** n. man employed to attend doors of certain buildings —'**doormat** n. 1. mat at entrance for wiping shoes on 2. sl. person who offers little resistance to ill-treatment —'**doorstop** n. any device which prevents open door from moving —'**doorway** n. entrance with or without door —**door to door** 1. (of selling etc.) from one house to next 2. (of journeys etc.) direct

dope (dəup) n. 1. kind of varnish 2. drug, esp. illegal, narcotic drug 3. inf. information 4. inf. stupid person —vt. 5. drug (esp. of racehorses) —'**dopey** or '**dopy** a. inf. 1. foolish 2. drugged 3. half asleep

Doppelgänger ('dɒpºlgɛŋə) n. Legend ghostly duplicate of living person

Doppler effect ('dɒplə) change in apparent frequency of sound or light wave etc. as result of relative motion between observer and source (also **Doppler shift**)

Doric ('dɒrɪk) a. 1. of the inhabitants of Doris, in ancient Greece, or their dialect —n. 2. dialect of Dorians 3. style of Gr. architecture 4. rustic dialect —**Dorian** ('dɔːrɪən) a./n. (member) of early Gr. race

dormant ('dɔːmənt) a. 1. not active, in state of suspension 2. sleeping —'**dormancy** n.

dormer ('dɔːmə) n. upright window set in sloping roof

dormitory ('dɔːmɪtərɪ, -trɪ) n. sleeping room with many beds —**dormitory town** town whose inhabitants travel elsewhere to work

Dormobile ('dɔːməʊbiːl) n. R vanlike vehicle specially equipped for living in while travelling

dormouse ('dɔːmaʊs) n. small hibernating mouselike rodent

dorp (dɔːp) n. SA small town

dorsal ('dɔːsºl) a. Anat., zool. of, on back

dory ('dɔːrɪ) n. deep-bodied type of fish, esp. John Dory

dose (dəus) n. 1. amount (of drug etc.) administered at one time 2. inf. instance or period of something unpleasant, esp. disease —vt. 3. give doses to —'**dosage** n.

doss (dɒs) inf. n. 1. temporary bed —vi. 2. sleep in dosshouse 3. sleep —'**dosshouse** n. cheap lodging house

dossier ('dɒsɪeɪ) n. set of papers on some particular subject or event

dot¹ (dɒt) n. 1. small spot, mark —vt. 2. mark with dots 3. sprinkle 4. sl. hit —'**dotty** a. 1. sl. crazy 2. sl. (with about) extremely fond (of) 3. marked with dots

dot² (dɒt) n. dowry

dote (dəut) vi. 1. (with on or upon) be passionately fond (of) 2. be silly or weak-minded —'**dotage** n. senility —'**dotard** n. —'**doting** a. blindly affectionate

dotterel or **dottrel** ('dɒtrəl) n. kind of plover

dottle ('dɒtºl) n. plug of tobacco left in pipe after smoking

double ('dʌbºl) a. 1. of two parts, layers etc., folded 2. twice as much or as many 3. of two kinds 4. designed for two users 5. ambiguous 6. deceitful —adv. 7. twice 8. to twice the amount or extent 9. in a pair —n. 10. person or thing exactly like, or mistakable for, another 11. quantity twice as much as another 12. sharp turn 13. running pace —pl. 14. game between 2 pairs of players —v. 15. make, become double 16. increase twofold 17. fold in two 18. get round, sail round (headland etc.) —vi. 19. turn sharply —'**doubly** adv. —**double agent** spy employed simultaneously by two opposing sides —**double-barrelled** or U.S. -**barreled** a. 1. (of gun) having two barrels 2. extremely forceful 3. UK (of surnames) having two hyphenated parts 4. serving two purposes; ambiguous —**double bass** largest and lowest-toned instrument in violin form —**double-breasted** a. (of garment) having overlapping fronts —**double-check** v. check again; verify —**double check** 1. second examination or verification 2. Chess simultaneous check from two pieces —**double chin** fold of fat under chin —**double cream** thick cream with high fat content —**double-cross** vt. cheat; betray —**double-crosser** n. —**double dagger** character (‡) used in printing to indicate cross-reference —**double-dealing** n. artifice, duplicity —**double-decker** n. 1. chiefly UK bus with two passenger decks 2. inf., chiefly US thing or structure having two decks, layers etc. —**double Dutch** inf. incomprehensible talk, gibberish —**double-edged** a. 1. acting in two ways 2. (of remark etc.) having two possible interpretations 3. (of knife etc.) having cutting edge on either side of blade —**double entry** book-keeping system in which transaction is entered as debit in one account and as credit in another —**double glazing** two panes of glass in window to insulate against cold, sound etc. —**double-jointed** a. having unusually flexible joints permitting abnormal degree of motion —**double pneumonia** pneumonia affecting both lungs —**double-quick** a./adv. very fast —**double standard** set of principles that allows greater freedom to one person or group than another —**double take** delayed reaction to a remark, situation etc. —**double talk** 1. rapid speech with mixture of nonsense syllables and real words; gibberish 2. empty, deceptive or ambiguous talk —**double time** 1. doubled wage rate for working on public holidays *etc.* **2.** *Mus.* two beats per bar **3.** *U.S. Army* fast march; slow running pace, keeping in step

double entendre (ɑːnˈtɑːndrə) word or phrase with two meanings, one usu. indelicate

doublet ('dʌblɪt) *n.* **1.** close-fitting body garment formerly worn by men **2.** one of two words from same root but differing in form and usu. in meaning, as *warden* and *guardian* **3.** false gem of thin layer of gemstone fused on to base of glass *etc.*

doubloon (dʌˈbluːn) *n.* ancient Sp. gold coin

doubt (daʊt) *vt.* **1.** hesitate to believe **2.** call into question **3.** suspect —*vi.* **4.** be wavering or uncertain in belief or opinion —*n.* **5.** uncertainty, wavering in belief **6.** state of affairs giving cause for uncertainty —'**doubter** *n.* —'**doubtful** *a.* —'**doubtfully** *adv.* —'**doubtless** *adv./a.*

douche (duːʃ) *n.* **1.** jet or spray of water applied to (part of) body —*vt.* **2.** give douche to

dough (dəʊ) *n.* **1.** flour or meal kneaded with water **2.** *sl.* money —'**doughy** *a.* —'**doughnut** *n.* sweetened and fried ball or ring-shaped piece of dough

doughty ('daʊtɪ) *a.* valiant —'**doughtily** *adv.* —'**doughtiness** *n.* boldness

dour (dʊə) *a.* grim, stubborn, severe

douse *or* **dowse** (daʊs) *vt.* **1.** thrust into water **2.** extinguish (light)

dove (dʌv) *n.* bird of pigeon family —**dovecot** ('dʌvkɒt) *or* **dovecote** ('dʌvkəʊt) *n.* house for doves —'**dovetail** *n.* **1.** joint made with fan-shaped tenon —*v.* **2.** fit closely, neatly, firmly together

dowager ('daʊədʒə) *n.* widow with title or property derived from deceased husband

dowdy ('daʊdɪ) *a.* **1.** unattractively or shabbily dressed —*n.* **2.** woman so dressed

dowel ('daʊəl) *n.* wooden, metal peg, *esp.* joining two adjacent parts

dower ('daʊə) *n.* **1.** widow's share for life of husband's estate —*vt.* **2.** endow —'**dowry** *n.* **1.** property wife brings to husband at marriage **2.** any endowment —**dower house** house for use of widow, *oft.* on her deceased husband's estate

down[1] (daʊn) *adv.* **1.** to, in, or towards, lower position **2.** below the horizon **3.** (of payment) on the spot, immediate —*prep.* **4.** from higher to lower part of **5.** at lower part of **6.** along —*a.* **7.** depressed, miserable —*vt.* **8.** knock, pull, push down **9.** *inf.* drink, *esp.* quickly —'**downward** *a./adv.* —'**downwards** *adv.* —'**downcast** *a.* **1.** dejected **2.** looking down —'**downfall** *n.* **1.** sudden loss of health, reputation *etc.* **2.** fall of rain, snow *etc.*, *esp.* sudden heavy one —'**downgrade** *vt.* **1.** reduce in importance or value, *esp.* to demote (person) to poorer job **2.**

speak of disparagingly —*n.* **3.** *chiefly US* downward slope —**down'hearted** *a.* discouraged; dejected —**down'hill** *a.* **1.** going or sloping down —*adv.* **2.** towards bottom of hill; downwards —*n.* **3.** downward slope of hill; descent **4.** skiing race downhill —**down payment** deposit paid on item purchased on hire-purchase *etc.* —'**downpour** *n.* heavy fall of rain —'**downright** *a.* **1.** plain, straightforward —*adv.* **2.** quite, thoroughly —'**down'stage** *a./adv.* at, to front of stage —'**down'stairs** *adv.* **1.** down the stairs; to or on lower floor —*n.* **2.** lower or ground floor **3.** *UK inf.* servants of household collectively —'**down'stream** *adv./a.* in or towards lower part of stream; with current —**down-to-earth** *a.* sensible; practical; realistic —'**downtrodden** *a.* **1.** subjugated; oppressed **2.** trodden down —'**down'wind** *a.* in same direction towards which wind is blowing; with wind from behind —**down and out** finished, defeated —**down under** *inf.* Australia and New Zealand —**go downhill** *inf.* decline; deteriorate —**have a down on** *inf.* have grudge against —**on the downgrade** waning in importance *etc.*

down[2] (daʊn) *n.* **1.** soft underfeathers, hair or fibre **2.** fluff —'**downy** *a.*

down[3] (daʊn) *n.* *obs.* hill, *esp.* sand dune (*also* **downs**) —'**downland** *n.* open high land (*also* **downs**)

Downing Street ('daʊnɪŋ) **1.** street in London: official residences of prime minister of Great Britain and chancellor of the exchequer **2.** *inf.* prime minister; British Government

Down's syndrome (daʊnz) *Pathol.* chromosomal abnormality resulting in flat face and nose, short stubby fingers, vertical fold of skin at inner edge of eye and mental retardation

dowry ('daʊərɪ) *n. see* DOWER

dowse (daʊz) *vi.* use divining rod —'**dowser** *n.* water diviner

doxology (dɒkˈsɒlədʒɪ) *n.* short hymn of praise to God

doyen ('dɔɪən) *n.* senior member of a body or profession (**doyenne** (dɔɪˈɛn) *fem.*)

doyley ('dɔɪlɪ) *n. see* DOILY

doz. dozen

doze (dəʊz) *vi.* **1.** sleep drowsily, be half-asleep —*n.* **2.** nap —'**dozy** *a.* **1.** drowsy **2.** *inf.* stupid

dozen ('dʌz²n) *n.* (set of) twelve

D.Phil., D.Ph., *or* **DPh** Doctor of Philosophy (*also* **Ph.D., PhD**)

DPP *or* **D.P.P.** Director of Public Prosecutions

Dr. 1. Doctor **2.** Drive

drab[1] (dræb) *a.* **1.** dull, monotonous **2.** of a dingy brown colour —*n.* **3.** mud colour

drab[2] (dræb) *obs. n.* **1.** slatternly woman **2.** whore —*vi.* **3.** consort with prostitutes (**-bb-**)

drachm (dræm) *n.* unit of weight, 1/8 of fluid ounce, 1/16 of avoirdupois ounce (*also* **fluid dram**)

drachma ('drækmə) *n.* monetary unit of Greece (*pl.* **-s, -mae** (-miː))

Draconian (dreɪ'kəʊnɪən) *or* **Draconic** (dreɪ'kɒnɪk) *a.* (*oft.* d-) 1. like the laws of Draco 2. very harsh, cruel

draft[1] (drɑːft) *n.* 1. design, sketch 2. rough copy of document 3. order for money 4. detachment of men, *esp.* troops, reinforcements —*vt.* 5. make sketch, plan or rough design of 6. make rough copy of (writing *etc.*) —*v.* 7. detach (military personnel) from one unit to another

draft[2] (drɑːft) *vt.* **US** select for compulsory military service

drag (dræg) *vt.* 1. pull along with difficulty or friction 2. trail on ground 3. sweep with net or grapnels 4. protract —*vi.* 5. lag, trail 6. (*oft. with* on *or* out) be tediously protracted (**-gg-**) —*n.* 7. check on progress 8. checked motion 9. iron shoe to check wheel 10. type of carriage 11. lure for hounds to hunt 12. kind of harrow 13. sledge, net, grapnel, rake 14. *inf.* tedious person or thing 15. *sl.* women's clothes worn by man (*esp.* **in in drag**) —**'dragnet** *n.* 1. fishing net to be dragged along sea floor 2. comprehensive search, *esp.* by police for criminal *etc.* —**'dragster** *n.* car designed, modified for drag racing —**drag race** motor car race where cars are timed over measured distance

dragée (dræ'ʒeɪ) *n.* sugar-coated sweet, nut or pill

draggle ('drægəl) *v.* 1. make or become wet or dirty by trailing on ground —*vi.* 2. lag; dawdle

dragoman ('drægəʊmən) *n.* in some Middle Eastern countries, *esp.* formerly, professional interpreter or guide (*pl.* **-s, -men**)

dragon ('drægən) *n.* 1. mythical fire-breathing monster, like winged crocodile 2. type of large lizard —**'dragonfly** *n.* long-bodied insect with gauzy wings

dragoon (drə'guːn) *n.* cavalryman of certain regiments —*vt.* 2. oppress 3. coerce

drain (dreɪn) *vt.* 1. draw off (liquid) by pipes, ditches *etc.* 2. dry 3. drink to dregs 4. empty, exhaust —*vi.* 5. flow off or away 6. become rid of liquid —*n.* 7. channel for removing liquid 8. sewer 9. depletion, strain —**'drainage** *n.* —**draining board** sloping grooved surface at side of sink for draining washed dishes *etc.* (*also* **'drainer**) —**'drainpipe** *n.* pipe for carrying off rainwater *etc.* —**drainpipe trousers** *or* **'drain- pipes** *pl.n.* trousers with narrow legs

drake (dreɪk) *n.* male duck

dram (dræm) *n.* 1. small draught of strong drink 2. drachm

drama ('drɑːmə) *n.* 1. stage play 2. art or literature of plays 3. playlike series of events —**dra'matic** *a.* 1. pert. to drama 2. suitable for stage representation 3. with force and vividness of drama 4. striking 5. tense 6. exciting —**'dramatist** *n.* writer of plays —**dramati'za- tion** *or* **-i'sation** *n.* —**'dramatize** *or* **-ise** *vt.* adapt novel for acting

dramatis personae ('drɑːmətɪs pəˈsəʊnaɪ) characters in play

dramaturgy ('dræmətɜːdʒɪ) *n.* technique of writing and producing plays —**drama'turgic(al)** *a.* —**'dramaturgist** *or* **'dramaturge** *n.* play- wright

drank (dræŋk) *pt. of* DRINK

drape (dreɪp) *vt.* 1. cover, adorn with cloth 2. arrange in graceful folds —**'draper** *n.* dealer in cloth, linen *etc.* —**'drapery** *n.*

drastic ('dræstɪk) *a.* 1. extreme, forceful 2. severe

draught *or* *U.S.* **draft** (drɑːft) *n.* 1. current of air between apertures in room *etc.* 2. act or action of drawing 3. dose of medicine 4. act of drinking 5. quantity drunk at once 6. inhaling 7. depth of ship in water 8. the drawing in of, or fish taken in, net 9. (*now usu.* **draft**) preliminary plan or layout for work to be executed —*pl.* 10. game played on chessboard with flat round 'men' —*a.* 11. for drawing 12. drawn —*vt.* 13. *see* DRAFT[2] —**'draughty** *or* *U.S.* **'drafty** *a.* full of air currents —**'draughtboard** *n.* board with 64 squares of alternating colours, for playing draughts or chess on —**draught horse** horse for pulling or carrying heavy loads —**'draughtsman** *or* *U.S.* **'draftsman** *n.* one who makes drawings, plans *etc.* —**'draughtsmanship** *or* *U.S.* **'drafts- manship** *n.*

draw (drɔː) *vt.* 1. pull, pull along, haul 2. inhale 3. entice, attract 4. delineate, portray with pencil *etc.* 5. frame, compose, draft, write 6. bring (upon, out *etc.*) 7. get by lot 8. (of ship) require (depth of water) 9. take from (well, barrel *etc.*) 10. receive (money) 11. bend (bow) —*vi.* 12. pull, shrink 13. make, admit current of air 14. make pictures with pencil *etc.* 15. finish game with equal points, goals *etc.*, tie 16. write orders for money 17. come, approach (near) (**drew** *pt.*, **drawn** *pp.*) —*n.* 18. act of drawing 19. casting of lots 20. game or contest ending in a tie —**'drawable** *a.* —**'drawer** ('drɔːə) *n.* 1. one or that which draws 2. (drɔː) sliding box in table or chest —*pl.* (drɔːz) 3. two-legged undergarment —**'drawing** *n.* 1. art of depicting in line 2. sketch so done 3. action of verb —**'drawback** *n.* 1. anything that takes away from satisfaction 2. snag —**'drawbridge** *n.* hinged bridge that can be raised or lowered —**drawing pin** *UK* short tack with broad head, for fastening papers to drawing board *etc.* —**drawing room** living room, sitting room —**'drawstring** *n.* cord *etc.*

run through hem around opening, so that when it is pulled tighter, the opening closes —**draw near** approach —**draw out** lengthen —**draw up** 1. arrange 2. stop

drawl (drɔːl) v. 1. speak or utter (words) slowly —n. 2. such speech —'**drawlingly** adv.

drawn (drɔːn) v. 1. pp. of DRAW —a. 2. haggard, tired or tense in appearance

dray (dreɪ) n. low cart without sides for heavy loads

dread (drɛd) vt. 1. fear greatly —n. 2. awe, terror —a. 3. feared, awful —'**dreadful** a. disagreeable, shocking, bad —'**dreadnought** n. large battleship mounting heavy guns

dream (driːm) n. 1. vision during sleep 2. fancy 3. reverie 4. aspiration 5. very pleasant idea, person, thing —vi. 6. have dreams —vt. 7. see, imagine in dreams 8. think of as possible (**dreamt** (drɛmt) or **dreamed** pt./pp.) —'**dreamer** n. —'**dreamless** a. —'**dreamy** a. 1. given to daydreams, unpractical, vague 2. inf. wonderful

dreary ('drɪərɪ) a. dismal, dull —**drear** a. Lit. dreary —'**drearily** adv. —'**dreariness** n. gloom

dredge[1] (drɛdʒ) v. 1. bring up (mud etc.) from sea bottom 2. deepen (channel) by dredge —vt. 3. search for, produce (obscure, remote, unlikely material) —n. 4. form of scoop or grab —'**dredger** n. ship for dredging

dredge[2] (drɛdʒ) vt. sprinkle with flour etc. —'**dredger** n.

dregs (drɛgz) pl.n. 1. sediment, grounds 2. worthless part

drench (drɛntʃ) vt. 1. wet thoroughly, soak 2. make (animal) take dose of medicine —n. 3. soaking 4. dose for animal

Dresden ('drɛzdən) n. 1. city in East Germany 2. delicate and decorative porcelain ware made near Dresden (also **Dresden china**) —a. 3. of Dresden china

dress (drɛs) vt. 1. clothe 2. array for show 3. trim, smooth, prepare surface of 4. prepare (food) for table 5. put dressing on (wound) 6. align (troops) —vi. 7. put on one's clothes 8. form in proper line —n. 9. one-piece garment for woman 10. clothing 11. clothing for ceremonial evening wear —'**dresser** n. 1. one who dresses, esp. actors or actresses 2. surgeon's assistant 3. kitchen sideboard —'**dressing** n. 1. something applied to something else, as sauce to food, ointment to wound, manure to land etc. 2. inf. scolding, as in *dressing down* —'**dressy** a. 1. stylish 2. fond of dress —**dress circle** first gallery in theatre —**dress coat** cutaway coat worn by men as evening dress —**dressing gown** loose robe worn while one is resting or before dressing —**dressing room** room, esp. one in theatre for changing costumes and make-up —**dressing**

station Mil. first-aid post close to combat area —**dressing table** —'**dressmaker** n. —**dress rehearsal** 1. last rehearsal of play etc. using costumes etc. as for first night 2. any full-scale practice —**dress suit** man's evening suit, esp. tails

dressage ('drɛsɑːʒ) n. method of training horse in special manoeuvres to show obedience

drew (druː) pt. of DRAW

drey or **dray** (dreɪ) n. squirrel's nest

dribble ('drɪb°l) v. 1. (allow to) flow in drops, trickle 2. Football work (ball) forward with short kicks —vi. 3. run at the mouth —n. 4. trickle, drop —'**driblet** n. small portion or instalment

dried (draɪd) pt./pp. of DRY

drier ('draɪə) comp. of DRY

driest ('draɪɪst) sup. of DRY

drift (drɪft) vi. 1. be carried as by current of air, water 2. move aimlessly or passively —n. 3. process of being driven by current 4. slow current or course 5. deviation from course 6. tendency 7. meaning 8. wind-heaped mass of snow, sand etc. 9. material driven or carried by water —'**drifter** n. 1. one who, that which drifts 2. inf. aimless person with no fixed job etc. —'**driftwood** n. wood washed ashore by sea

drill[1] (drɪl) n. 1. boring tool or machine 2. exercise of soldiers or others in handling of arms and manoeuvres 3. routine teaching —v. 4. bore, pierce (hole) in (material) (as if) with drill 5. exercise in military and other routine —vi. 6. practise routine

drill[2] (drɪl) n. 1. machine for sowing seed 2. small furrow for seed 3. row of plants —v. 4. sow (seed) in drills or furrows

drill[3] (drɪl) n. coarsely woven twilled fabric

drill[4] (drɪl) n. W Afr. monkey

drink (drɪŋk) v. 1. swallow (liquid) 2. take (intoxicating liquor), esp. to excess —vt. 3. absorb (**drank** pt., **drunk** pp.) —n. 4. liquid for drinking 5. portion of this 6. act of drinking 7. intoxicating liquor or excessive consumption of it —'**drinkable** a. —'**drinker** n. —**drink to** or **drink the health of** express good wishes etc. by drinking a toast to

drip (drɪp) v. 1. fall or let fall in drops (**-pp-**) —n. 2. act of dripping 3. drop 4. Med. intravenous administration of solution 5. inf. dull, insipid person —'**dripping** n. 1. melted fat that drips from roasting meat —a. 2. very wet —**drip-dry** a. (of fabric) drying free of creases if hung up while wet —'**dripstone** n. projection over window or door to stop dripping of water

drive (draɪv) vt. 1. urge in some direction 2. make move and steer (vehicle, animal etc.) 3. urge, impel 4. fix by blows, as nail 5. chase 6. convey in vehicle 7. hit ball with force as in golf, tennis —*vi.* **8.** keep machine, animal going, steer it **9.** be conveyed in vehicle **10.** rush, dash, drift fast (**drove, driven** ('drɪvən), '**driving**) —*n.* **11.** act, action of driving **12.** journey in vehicle **13.** private road leading to house **14.** capacity for getting things done **15.** united effort, campaign **16.** energy **17.** forceful stroke in cricket, golf, tennis —'**driver** *n.* **1.** one that drives **2.** *Golf* club used for tee shots —**drive-in** *a.* **1.** denoting public facility or service designed for use by patrons in cars —*n.* **2.** *chiefly US* cinema designed to be used in such a manner —'**driveway** *n.* path for vehicles, oft. connecting house with public road —'**driving belt** belt that communicates motion to machinery —'**driving licence** official document authorizing person to drive motor vehicle

drivel ('drɪvəl) *vi.* **1.** run at mouth or nose **2.** talk nonsense (**-ll-**) —*n.* **3.** silly or senseless talk —'**driveller** *n.*

drizzle ('drɪzəl) *vi.* **1.** rain in fine drops —*n.* **2.** fine, light rain

drogue (drəʊg) *n.* **1.** any funnel-like device, *esp.* of canvas, used as sea anchor **2.** small parachute **3.** wind indicator **4.** windsock towed behind target aircraft **5.** funnel-shaped device on end of refuelling hose of tanker aircraft to receive probe of aircraft being refuelled

droll (drəʊl) *a.* funny, odd, comical —'**drollery** *n.* —'**drolly** *adv.*

dromedary ('drʌmədərɪ) *n.* one-humped camel bred *esp.* for racing

drone (drəʊn) *n.* **1.** male of honey bee **2.** lazy idler **3.** deep humming **4.** bass pipe of bagpipe **5.** its note —*vi.* **6.** hum **7.** talk in monotonous tone

drongo ('drɒŋgəʊ) *n.* black tropical bird

drool (druːl) *vi.* slaver, drivel

droop (druːp) *vi.* **1.** hang down **2.** wilt, flag —*vt.* **3.** let hang down —*n.* **4.** drooping condition —'**droopy** *a.*

drop (drɒp) *n.* **1.** globule of liquid **2.** very small quantity **3.** fall, descent **4.** distance through which thing falls **5.** thing that falls, as gallows platform —*vt.* **6.** let fall **7.** let fall in drops **8.** utter casually **9.** set down, unload **10.** discontinue —*vi.* **11.** fall **12.** fall in drops **13.** lapse **14.** come or go casually (**-pp-**) —'**droplet** *n.* —'**dropper** *n.* **1.** small tube having rubber bulb at one end for dispensing drops of liquid **2.** person or thing that drops —'**droppings** *pl.n.* dung of rabbits, sheep, birds *etc.* —'**dropout** *n.* person who fails to complete course of study or one who rejects conventional society —**drop scone** scone made by dropping spoonful of batter on hot griddle

dropsy ('drɒpsɪ) *n.* disease causing watery fluid to collect in the body —'**dropsical** *a.*

droshky ('drɒʃkɪ) *or* **drosky** ('drɒskɪ) *n.* open four-wheeled carriage, formerly used in Russia

dross (drɒs) *n.* **1.** scum of molten metal **2.** impurity, refuse **3.** anything of little or no value

drought (draʊt) *n.* long spell of dry weather

drove[1] (drəʊv) *pt. of* DRIVE

drove[2] (drəʊv) *n.* **1.** herd, flock, crowd, *esp.* in motion —*v.* **2.** drive (cattle *etc.*) *esp.* a long distance —'**drover** *n.* driver of cattle

drown (draʊn) *v.* **1.** die or kill by immersion in liquid —*vt.* **2.** get rid of as by submerging in liquid **3.** (*sometimes with* out) make (sound) inaudible by louder sound

drowsy ('draʊzɪ) *a.* **1.** half asleep **2.** lulling **3.** dull —**drowse** *v.* —'**drowsily** *adv.* —'**drowsiness** *n.*

drub (drʌb) *vt.* thrash, beat (**-bb-**) —'**drubbing** *n.* beating

drudge (drʌdʒ) *vi.* **1.** work at menial or distasteful tasks, slave —*n.* **2.** one who drudges hack —'**drudgery** *n.*

drug (drʌg) *n.* **1.** medical substance **2.** narcotic **3.** commodity which is unsaleable because of overproduction —*vt.* **4.** mix drugs with **5.** administer drug to, *esp.* one inducing unconsciousness (**-gg-**) —**drug addict** person abnormally dependent on narcotic drugs —'**drugstore** *n.* *US* pharmacy where wide variety of goods is available

drugget ('drʌgɪt) *n.* coarse woollen fabric, *esp.* used for carpeting

druid ('druːɪd) *n.* (*sometimes* D-) **1.** member of ancient order of Celtic priests **2.** Eisteddfod official —**dru'idic(al)** *a.* —'**druidism** *n.*

drum (drʌm) *n.* **1.** percussion instrument of skin stretched over round hollow frame, played by beating with sticks **2.** various things shaped like drum **3.** *see* **eardrum** *at* EAR —*vi.* **4.** play drum —*v.* **5.** tap, thump continuously (**-mm-**) —'**drummer** *n.* one who plays drum —'**drum-fire** *n.* heavy continuous rapid artillery fire —**drumhead court-martial** summary court-martial held at war front —**drum major** leader of military band —'**drumstick** *n.* **1.** stick for beating drum **2.** lower joint of cooked fowl's leg —**drum out** expel (from club *etc.*) —**drum up** obtain (support *etc.*) by solicitation or canvassing

drunk (drʌŋk) *a.* **1.** overcome by strong drink **2.** *fig.* overwhelmed by strong emotion —*v.* **3.** *pp. of* DRINK —'**drunkard** *n.* one given to excessive drinking —'**drunken** *a.* **1.** intoxicated **2.** habitually drunk **3.** caused by, showing intoxication —'**drunkenness** *n.*

drupe (druːp) *n.* fruit that has fleshy or fibrous part around stone that encloses seed, as peach *etc.*

dry (draɪ) *a.* **1.** without moisture **2.** rainless **3.** not yielding milk or other liquid **4.** cold, unfriendly **5.** caustically witty **6.** having prohibition of alcoholic drink **7.** uninteresting **8.** needing effort to study **9.** lacking sweetness (as wines) —vt. **10.** remove water, moisture —vi. **11.** become dry **12.** evaporate (**dried, 'drying**) —'**dryer** or '**drier** n. **1.** person or thing that dries **2.** apparatus for removing moisture —'**dryly** or '**drily** adv. —'**dryness** n. —**dry battery** electric battery without liquid —**dry cell** primary cell in which electrolyte is in form of paste or is treated in some way to prevent spilling —**dry-clean** vt. clean (clothes) with solvent other than water —**dry-cleaner** n. —**dry dock** dock that can be pumped dry for work on ship's bottom —**dry farming** methods of producing crops in areas of low rainfall —**dry fly** Angling artificial fly designed to be floated on surface of water —**dry ice** solid carbon dioxide —**dry measure** unit or system of units for measuring dry goods, such as grains etc. —**dry point 1.** needle for engraving without acid **2.** engraving so made —**dry rot** fungoid decay in wood —**dry run** practice, rehearsal in simulated conditions —**dry-stone** a. (of wall) made without mortar —**dry out 1.** make or become dry **2.** inf. (cause) to undergo treatment for alcoholism or drug addiction

dryad ('draɪəd, -æd) n. wood nymph

dryly ('draɪlɪ) adv. see DRY

D.Sc. Doctor of Science

D.S.C. Distinguished Service Cross

D.S.M. Mil. Distinguished Service Medal

D.S.O. Distinguished Service Order

D.T.'s inf. delirium tremens

dual ('djuːəl) a. **1.** twofold **2.** of two, double, forming pair —'**dualism** n. recognition of two independent powers or principles, eg good and evil, mind and matter —**du'ality** n. —**dual carriageway** UK road on which traffic travelling in opposite directions is separated by central strip of turf etc.

dub (dʌb) vt. **1.** confer knighthood on **2.** give title to **3.** provide (film) with soundtrack not in original language **4.** smear with grease, dubbin (**-bb-**) —'**dubbin** or '**dubbing** n. grease for making leather supple

dubious ('djuːbɪəs) a. **1.** causing doubt, not clear or decided **2.** of suspect character —**du'biety** n. uncertainty, doubt

ducal ('djuːkˀl) a. of duke or duchy

ducat ('dʌkət) n. former gold coin of Italy etc.

duchess ('dʌtʃɪs) n. duke's wife or widow

duchy ('dʌtʃɪ) n. territory of duke, dukedom

duck¹ (dʌk) n. **1.** common swimming bird (**drake** masc.) **2.** Cricket batsman's score of nothing **3.** UK inf. dear, darling (as term of address) (also **ducks**) —v. **4.** plunge (someone) under water **5.** bob down —'**duckling** n. —'**ducky** or '**duckie** inf. UK **1.** darling, dear —a. **2.** delightful; fine —**duck-billed platypus**

see PLATYPUS —'**duckweed** n. plant that floats on ponds etc.

duck² (dʌk)- n. **1.** strong linen or cotton fabric —pl. **2.** trousers made of this fabric

duck³ (dʌk) n. amphibious vehicle used in World War II

duct (dʌkt) n. channel, tube —'**ductile** a. **1.** capable of being drawn into wire **2.** flexible and tough **3.** docile —**ductility** (dʌk'tɪlɪtɪ) n. —'**ductless** a. (of glands) secreting directly certain substances essential to health

dud (dʌd) n. **1.** futile, worthless person or thing **2.** shell that fails to explode —a. **3.** worthless

dude (djuːd) n. **1.** tourist, esp. in ranch district —**dude ranch** ranch serving as guesthouse and showplace

dudgeon ('dʌdʒən) n. anger, indignation, resentment

duds (dʌdz) pl.n. inf. clothes

due (djuː) a. **1.** owing **2.** proper to be given, inflicted etc. **3.** adequate, fitting **4.** under engagement to arrive, be present **5.** timed (for) —adv. **6.** (with points of compass) exactly —n. **7.** person's right **8.** (usu. pl.) charge, fee etc. —'**duly** adv. **1.** properly **2.** fitly **3.** rightly **4.** punctually —**due to 1.** attributable to **2.** caused by

duel ('djuːəl) n. **1.** arranged fight with deadly weapons, between two persons **2.** keen two-sided contest —vi. **3.** fight in duel (**-ll-**) —'**duellist** n.

duenna (djuː'ɛnə) n. **1.** Sp. lady-in-waiting **2.** elderly governess, guardian, chaperon

duet (djuː'ɛt) n. piece of music for two performers —**du'ettist** n.

duff¹ (dʌf) n. kind of boiled pudding

duff² (dʌf) vt. **1.** manipulate, alter (article) so as to make it look like new **2.** mishit, esp. at golf —a. **3.** sl. bad, useless

duffel or **duffle** ('dʌfˀl) n. **1.** coarse woollen cloth **2.** coat made of this —**duffel bag** large cylindrical cloth bag for clothing etc.

duffer ('dʌfə) n. stupid inefficient person

dug¹ (dʌg) pt./pp. of DIG

dug² (dʌg) n. udder, teat of animal

dugong ('duːgɒŋ) n. whalelike mammal of tropical seas

dugout ('dʌgaut) n. **1.** covered excavation to provide shelter for troops etc. **2.** canoe of hollowed-out tree **3.** Sport covered enclosure where players wait when not on the field

duiker or **duyker** ('daɪkə) n. small Afr. antelope (also '**duikerbok**)

duke (djuːk) n. **1.** peer of rank next below prince **2.** sovereign of small state called duchy ('**duchess** fem.) —'**dukedom** n.

dukes (djuːks) pl.n. sl. fists

dulcet ('dʌlsɪt) a. (of sounds) sweet, melodious

dulcimer ('dʌlsɪmə) n. percussion instrument consisting of set of strings stretched over sounding board, played with two hammers

dull (dʌl) a. 1. stupid 2. insensible 3. sluggish 4. tedious 5. lacking liveliness or variety 6. gloomy, overcast —v. 7. make or become dull —'**dullard** n. —'**dully** adv.

duly ('dju:lɪ) adv. see DUE

dumb (dʌm) a. 1. incapable of speech 2. silent 3. inf. stupid —'**dumbly** adv. —'**dumbness** n. —'**dumbbell** n. weight for exercises —dumb'**found** vt. confound into silence —**dumb show** acting without words —'**dumbwaiter** n. 1. UK stand placed near dining table to hold food; revolving circular tray placed on table to hold food 2. lift for carrying rubbish etc. between floors

dumdum ('dʌmdʌm) n. soft-nosed expanding bullet

dummy ('dʌmɪ) n. 1. tailor's or dressmaker's model 2. imitation object 3. Cards hand exposed on table and played by partner 4. Sports feigned move or pass 5. baby's dummy teat 6. prototype of book, indicating appearance of finished product; designer's layout of page —a. 7. sham, bogus —**dummy run** experimental run; practice; rehearsal

dump (dʌmp) vt. 1. throw down in mass 2. deposit 3. unload 4. send (low-priced goods) for sale abroad —n. 5. rubbish heap 6. inf. dirty, unpleasant place 7. temporary depot of stores or munitions —pl. 8. low spirits, dejection

dumpling ('dʌmplɪŋ) n. small round pudding of dough, oft. fruity —'**dumpy** a. short, stout —**dumpy level** surveyor's levelling instrument

dun[1] (dʌn) vt. 1. persistently press (debtor) for payment of debts (-nn-) —n. 2. one who duns

dun[2] (dʌn) a. 1. of dull greyish-brown —n. 2. this colour 3. horse of this colour

dunce (dʌns) n. slow learner, stupid pupil

dunderhead ('dʌndəhɛd) n. blockhead —'**dunderheaded** a.

dune (dju:n) n. sandhill on coast or desert

dung (dʌŋ) n. 1. excrement of animals 2. manure —vt. 3. manure (ground) —'**dunghill** n. 1. heap of dung 2. foul place, condition or person

dungaree (dʌŋgə'ri:) n. 1. coarse cotton fabric —pl. 2. overalls made of this material

dungeon ('dʌndʒən) n. 1. underground cell or vault for prisoners, donjon 2. formerly, tower or keep of castle

dunk (dʌŋk) vt. 1. dip (bread etc.) in liquid before eating it 2. submerge

dunlin ('dʌnlɪn) n. small sandpiper

dunnage ('dʌnɪdʒ) n. material for packing cargo

dunnock ('dʌnək) n. hedge sparrow

duo ('dju:əʊ) n. pair of performers (pl. -s, dui ('dju:i:))

duodecimo (dju:əʊ'dɛsɪməʊ) n. 1. size of book in which each sheet is folded into 12 leaves 2. book of this size (pl. -s) —a. 3. of this size —**duo'decimal** a. 1. computed by twelves 2. twelfth

duodenum (dju:əʊ'di:nəm) n. upper part of small intestine —**duo'denal** a.

duologue or U.S. (sometimes) **duolog** ('dju:əlɒg) n. 1. part or all of play in which speaking roles are limited to two actors 2. rare dialogue

dupe (dju:p) n. 1. victim of delusion or sharp practice —vt. 2. deceive for advantage, impose upon

duple ('dju:p^əl) a. 1. rare double 2. Mus. (of time or music) having two beats in bar

duplex ('dju:plɛks) a. twofold

duplicate ('dju:plɪkeɪt) vt. 1. make exact copy of 2. double —a. ('dju:plɪkɪt) 3. double 4. exactly the same as something else —n. ('dju:plɪkɪt) 5. exact copy —dupli'**cation** n. —'**duplicator** n. machine for making copies —du'**plicity** n. deceitfulness, double-dealing, bad faith

Dur. Durham

durable ('djʊərəb^əl) a. lasting, resisting wear —dura'**bility** n. —'**durably** adv. —**durable goods** goods that require infrequent replacement (also '**durables**)

dura mater ('djʊərə 'meɪtə) outermost and toughest of three membranes covering brain and spinal cord (also '**dura**)

durance ('djʊərəns) n. obs. imprisonment

duration (dju'reɪʃən) n. length of time something lasts

durbar ('dɜːbɑː, dɜː'bɑː) n. formerly, court of native ruler or governor in India or levée at such court

duress (dju'rɛs, djʊə-) n. compulsion by use of force or threats

during ('djʊərɪŋ) prep. throughout, in the time of, in the course of

durst (dɜːst) obs. pt. of DARE

dusk (dʌsk) n. 1. darker stage of twilight 2. partial darkness —'**duskily** adv. —'**dusky** a. 1. dark 2. dark-coloured

dust (dʌst) n. 1. fine particles, powder of earth or other matter, lying on surface or blown along by wind 2. ashes of the dead —vt. 3. sprinkle with powder 4. rid of dust —'**duster** n. cloth for removing dust —'**dusty** a. covered with dust —'**dustbin** n. large, usu. cylindrical container for household rubbish —'**dustbowl** n. area in which dust storms have carried away the top soil —'**dustcart** n. road vehicle for collecting refuse —**dust cover 1.** large cloth used to protect furniture from dust (also '**dustsheet**) 2.

removable paper cover to protect bound book (also **dust jacket**) **3.** Perspex cover for gramophone turntable —'**dustman** n. UK man whose job is to collect domestic refuse —'**dustpan** n. short-handled hooded shovel into which dust is swept —**dust-up** n. inf. fight; argument —**dust up** attack

Dutch (dʌtʃ) a. pert. to the Netherlands, its inhabitants or its language —**Dutch barn** UK farm building consisting of steel frame and curved roof —**Dutch cap** contraceptive diaphragm (also **cap**) —**Dutch courage** drunken bravado —**Dutch elm disease** fungal disease of elm trees characterized by withering of foliage and stems —**Dutch oven 1.** iron or earthenware container with cover, used for stews etc. **2.** metal box, open in front, for cooking in front of open fire —**Dutch treat** meal etc. where each person pays his own share —**Dutch uncle** inf. person who criticizes or reproves frankly and severely

duty ('djuːtɪ) n. **1.** moral or legal obligation **2.** that which is due **3.** tax on goods **4.** military service **5.** one's proper employment —'**duteous** a. —'**dutiable** a. liable to customs duty —'**dutiful** a. —**duty-bound** a. morally obliged —**duty-free** a./adv. with exemption from customs or excise duties

duvet ('duːveɪ) n. quilt filled with down or artificial fibre (also **continental quilt**)

dux (dʌks) n. head pupil of school or class, leader

D.V. Deo volente

dwarf (dwɔːf) n. **1.** very undersized person **2.** mythological, small, manlike creature (pl. **-s**, **dwarves**) —a. **3.** unusually small, stunted —vt. **4.** make seem small by contrast **5.** make stunted —'**dwarfish** a.

dwell (dwɛl) vi. **1.** live, make one's abode (in) **2.** fix one's attention, write or speak at length (on) (**dwelt** pt./pp.) —'**dweller** n. —'**dwelling** n. house

dwindle ('dwɪndᵊl) vi. grow less, waste away, decline

Dy Chem. dysprosium

Dyak or **Dayak** ('daɪæk) n. member of Malaysian people of Borneo (pl. **-s, -ak**)

dye (daɪ) vt. **1.** impregnate (cloth etc.) with colouring matter **2.** colour thus (**dyed**, '**dyeing**) —n. **3.** colouring matter in solution or which may be dissolved for dyeing **4.** tinge, colour —'**dyeing** n. process or industry of colouring yarns etc. —'**dyer** n. —**dyed-in-the-wool** a. **1.** extreme or unchanging in opinion etc. **2.** (of fabric) made of dyed yarn

dying ('daɪɪŋ) v. **1.** pr.p. of DIE¹ —a. **2.** relating to or occurring at moment of death

dyke or esp. U.S. **dike** (daɪk) n. **1.** embankment to prevent flooding **2.** ditch

dynamics (daɪ'næmɪks) pl.n. **1.** (with sing. v.) branch of physics dealing with force as producing or affecting motion **2.** physical forces —dy'**namic** a. **1.** of, relating to motive force, force in operation **2.** energetic and forceful —dy'**namical** a. —dy'**namically** adv. —'**dynamism** n. **1.** Philos. theory that attempts to explain phenomena in terms of immanent force or energy **2.** forcefulness of energetic personality

dynamite ('daɪnəmaɪt) n. **1.** high explosive mixture —vt. **2.** blow up with this —'**dynamiter** n.

dynamo ('daɪnəməʊ) n. **1.** machine to convert mechanical into electrical energy, generator of electricity (pl. **-s**) **2.** inf. energetic, hard-working person —dyna'**mometer** n. instrument to measure energy expended

dynasty ('dɪnəstɪ) n. line, family, succession of hereditary rulers —'**dynast** n. —dy'**nastic** a. of dynasty

dyne (daɪn) n. cgs unit of force

dys- (comb. form) **1.** diseased; abnormal **2.** difficult; painful **3.** bad

dysentery ('dɪsᵊntrɪ) n. infection of intestine causing severe diarrhoea

dysfunction (dɪs'fʌŋkʃən) n. abnormal, impaired functioning, esp. of bodily organ

dyslexia (dɪs'lɛksɪə) n. impaired ability to read, caused by brain disorder —dys'**lexic** a.

dysmenorrhoea or esp. U.S. **dysmenorrhea** (dɪsmɛnə'rɪə) n. abnormally difficult or painful menstruation

dyspepsia (dɪs'pɛpsɪə) n. indigestion —dys-'**peptic** a./n.

dysprosium (dɪs'prəʊsɪəm) n. metallic element of lanthanide series

dystrophy ('dɪstrəfɪ) n. wasting of body tissues, esp. muscles

dz. dozen

E,e

e or **E** (iː) n. **1.** fifth letter of English alphabet **2.** any of several speech sounds represented by this letter, as in he, bet (pl. **e's, E's** or **Es**)

e 1. Maths. transcendental number used as base of natural logarithms **2.** electron

E 1. Mus. third note of scale of C major; major or minor key having this note as its tonic **2.** Phys. energy; electromotive force **3.** East **4.** Eastern **5.** English **6.** Egypt(ian)

e. engineer(ing)

E. Earl

ea. each

each (iːtʃ) *a./pron.* every (one) taken separately

eager ('iːgə) *a.* 1. having a strong wish (for something) 2. keen, impatient —'**eagerly** *adv.* —'**eagerness** *n.* —**eager beaver** *inf.* person who displays conspicuous diligence

eagle ('iːgl) *n.* 1. large bird with keen sight which preys on small birds and animals 2. *Golf* score of two strokes under par for a hole —'**eaglet** *n.* young eagle —**eagle-eyed** *a.* having keen eyesight

ear[1] (iə) *n.* 1. organ of hearing, *esp.* external part of it 2. sense of hearing 3. sensitiveness to sounds 4. attention —'**earache** *n.* acute pain in ear —'**eardrum** *n. see* **tympanic membrane** at TYMPANUM —'**earmark** *vt.* 1. assign, reserve for definite purpose 2. make identification mark on ear (of sheep *etc.*) —*n.* 3. this mark —'**earmuffs** *pl.n.* pads of fur *etc.* for keeping ears warm —'**earphone** *n.* receiver for radio *etc.* held to or put in ear —**ear-piercing** *a.* deafening —'**earring** *n.* ornament for lobe of ear —'**earshot** *n.* hearing distance —**ear trumpet** trumpet-shaped instrument formerly used as hearing aid —'**earwig** *n.* small insect with pincerlike tail

ear[2] (iə) *n.* spike, head of corn

earl (ɜːl) *n.* Brit. nobleman ranking next below marquis —'**earldom** *n.* his domain, title

early ('ɜːlɪ) *a./adv.* 1. before expected or usual time 2. in first part, near or nearer beginning of some portion of time —**early bird** *inf.* one who arrives or rises early

earn (ɜːn) *vt.* 1. obtain by work or merit 2. gain —'**earnings** *pl.n.*

earnest[1] ('ɜːnɪst) *a.* 1. serious, ardent 2. sincere —'**earnestly** *adv.* —**in earnest** serious, determined

earnest[2] ('ɜːnɪst) *n.* 1. money paid over in token to bind bargain, pledge 2. foretaste

earth (ɜːθ) *n.* 1. planet or world we live on 2. ground, dry land 3. mould, soil, mineral 4. fox's hole 5. wire connecting electrical apparatus to earth —*vt.* 6. cover with earth 7. connect electrically with earth —'**earthen** *a.* made of clay or earth —'**earthly** *a.* possible, feasible —'**earthy** *a.* 1. of earth 2. uninhibited 3. vulgar —**earth closet** lavatory in which earth is used to cover excreta —'**earthenware** *n.* (vessels of) baked clay —'**earthnut** *n.* 1. plant of Europe and Asia, having edible dark brown tubers 2. any of various plants having edible root, tuber or underground pod, such as peanut —'**earthquake** *n.* convulsion of earth's surface —**earth science** any of various sciences, such as geology, concerned with structure *etc.* of the earth —'**earthwork** *n.* bank of earth in

fortification —'**earthworm** *n.* —**come back or down to earth** return to reality from fantasy

ease (iːz) *n.* 1. comfort 2. freedom from constraint, annoyance, awkwardness, pain or trouble 3. idleness —*v.* 4. make or become less burdensome 5. give bodily or mental ease to 6. (cause to) move carefully or gradually —*vt.* 7. slacken 8. relieve of pain —'**easement** *n. Law* right of way *etc.* over another's land —'**easily** *adv.* —'**easiness** *n.* 1. quality or condition of being easy to accomplish *etc.* 2. ease or relaxation of manner —'**easy** *a.* 1. not difficult 2. free from pain, care, constraint or anxiety 3. compliant 4. characterized by low demand 5. fitting loosely 6. *inf.* having no preference for any particular course of action —**easy chair** comfortable upholstered armchair —**easygoing** *a.* 1. not hasty 2. indolent

easel ('iːzl) *n.* frame to support artist's canvas *etc.*

east (iːst) *n.* 1. part of horizon where sun rises 2. eastern lands, orient —*a.* 3. on, in or near east 4. coming from east —*adv.* 5. from or to east —'**easterly** *a./adv.* from or to east —'**eastern** *a.* of, dwelling in, east —'**easterner** *n.* —'**easting** *n.* distance eastwards of a point from a given meridian —'**eastward** *a./n.* —'**eastwards** or 'eastward *adv.* —**Eastern Church** 1. any of Christian Churches of former Byzantine Empire 2. any Church owing allegiance to Orthodox Church —**eastern hemisphere** (*oft.* E- H-) 1. that half of the globe containing Europe, Asia, Afr. and Aust. 2. lands in this, *esp.* Asia

Easter ('iːstə) *n.* movable festival of the Resurrection of Christ —**Easter egg** chocolate egg or hen's egg with its shell painted, given as gift at Easter —'**Eastertide** *n.* Easter season

easy ('iːzɪ) *a. see* EASE

eat (iːt) *v.* 1. chew and swallow 2. gnaw —*vt.* 3. consume, destroy 4. wear away (ate *pt.*, 'eaten *pp.*) —'**eatable** *a.* —'**eating** *n.* 1. food, *esp.* in relation to quality or taste —*a.* 2. suitable for eating —**eats** *pl.n. sl.* articles of food —**eat one's words** take back something said

eau de Cologne (əʊ də kə'ləʊn) *Fr.* light perfume

eau de vie (əʊ də 'viː) brandy

eaves (iːvz) *pl.n.* overhanging edges of roof —'**eavesdrop** *vi.* listen secretly —'**eavesdropper** *n.* —'**eavesdropping** *n.*

ebb (ɛb) *vi.* 1. flow back 2. decay —*n.* 3. flowing back of tide 4. decline, decay —**ebb tide**

ebony ('ɛbənɪ) *n.* 1. hard black wood —*a.* 2. made of, black as ebony —'**ebonite** *n.* vulcanite —'**ebonize** or -**ise** *vt.* make colour of ebony

ebullient (ɪ'bʌljənt, ɪ'bʊl-) *a.* 1. exuberant 2. boiling —e'**bullience** *n.* —**ebullition** (ɛbə'lɪʃən) *n.* 1. boiling 2. effervescence 3. outburst

EC East Central

eccentric (ık'sɛntrık) a. 1. odd, unconventional 2. irregular 3. not placed, or not having axis placed, centrally 4. not circular (in orbit) —n. 5. odd, unconventional person 6. mechanical contrivance to change circular into to-and-fro movement —ec'centrically adv. —eccen'tricity n.

Eccles. or **Eccl.** Bible Ecclesiastes

ecclesiastic (ıklizı'æstık) n. 1. clergyman —a. 2. of, relating to the Christian Church —ecclesi'astical a. —ecclesi'ology n. science of church building and decoration

eccrinology (ɛkrı'nɒlədʒı) n. branch of physiology that relates to bodily secretions

E.C.G. 1. electrocardiogram 2. electrocardiograph

echelon ('ɛʃəlɒn) n. 1. level, grade, of responsibility or command 2. formation of troops, planes etc. in parallel divisions, each slightly to left or right of the one in front

echidna (ı'kıdnə) n. spine-covered mammal of Aust. and New Guinea (pl. -s, -nae (-niː)) (also **spiny anteater**)

echinoderm (ı'kaınəʊdɜːm) n. marine invertebrate characterized by tube feet, calcite body-covering, and five-part symmetrical body

echo ('ɛkəʊ) n. 1. repetition of sounds by reflection 2. close imitation (pl. -es) —vt. 3. repeat as echo, send back the sound of 4. imitate closely —vi. 5. resound 6. be repeated ('echoed, 'echoing) —echoic (ɛ'kəʊık) a. 1. characteristic of or resembling echo 2. onomatopoeic —echo chamber room with walls that reflect sound, used to make acoustic measurements and in recording (also **reverberation chamber**) —echolo'cation n. determination of position of object by measuring reflected sound —echo sounder —echo sounding system of ascertaining depth of water by measuring time required to receive echo from sea bottom or submerged object

éclair (eı'klɛə, ı'klɛə) n. finger-shaped, iced cake filled with cream

éclat (eı'klɑː) n. 1. splendour 2. renown 3. acclamation

eclectic (ı'klɛktık, ɛ'klɛk-) a. 1. selecting 2. borrowing one's philosophy from various sources 3. catholic in views or taste —n. 4. person who favours eclectic approach —e'clecticism n.

eclipse (ı'klıps) n. 1. blotting out of sun, moon etc. by another heavenly body 2. obscurity —vt. 3. obscure, hide 4. surpass —e'cliptic a. 1. of eclipse —n. 2. apparent path of sun

eclogue ('ɛklɒg) n. short poem, esp. pastoral dialogue

eco- (comb. form) ecology; ecological, as in ecosphere

ecology (ı'kɒlədʒı) n. science of plants and animals in relation to their environment —eco'logical a. —e'cologist n. specialist in or advocate of ecological studies

econ. 1. economical 2. economics 3. economy

economy (ı'kɒnəmı) n. 1. careful management of resources to avoid unnecessary expenditure or waste 2. sparing, restrained or efficient use 3. system of interrelationship of money, industry and employment in a country —eco'nomic a. 1. of economics 2. profitable 3. economical —eco'nomical a. not wasteful of money, time, effort etc. 2. frugal —eco'nomically adv. —eco'nomics pl.n. 1. (with sing. v.) study of economies of nations 2. (with pl. v.) financial aspects —e'conomist n. specialist in economics —e'conomize or -ise v. limit or reduce (expense, waste etc.)

ecosystem ('iːkəʊsıstəm, 'ɛkəʊ-) n. Ecol. system involving interactions between community and its non-living environment

ecru ('ɛkruː, 'eıkruː) n./a. (of) colour of unbleached linen

ecstasy ('ɛkstəsı) n. 1. exalted state of feeling, mystic trance 2. frenzy —ec'static a. —ec'statically adv.

E.C.T. electroconvulsive therapy

ecto- (comb. form) outer, outside, as in ectoplasm

-ectomy (comb. form) surgical excision of part, as in appendectomy

ectoplasm ('ɛktəʊplæzəm) n. in spiritualism, supposedly a semiluminous plastic substance which exudes from medium's body

ecumenical, oecumenical (iːkjuː'mɛnıkəl, ɛk-) or **ecumenic, oecumenic** a. of the Christian Church throughout the world, esp. with regard to its unity —ecu'menicalism, ecu'menicism or ecu'menism n.

eczema ('ɛksımə) n. skin disease

ed. 1. edited 2. edition (pl. eds.) 3. editor (pl. eds.) 4. education

-ed[1] (comb. form) forming past tense of most English verbs

-ed[2] (comb. form) forming past participle of most English verbs

-ed[3] (comb. form) possessing or having characteristics of, as in salaried, red-blooded

Edam ('iːdæm) n. round yellow cheese with red outside covering

E.D.C. European Defence Community

Edda ('ɛdə) n. collection of old Icelandic myths

eddy ('ɛdı) n. 1. small whirl in water, smoke etc. —vi. 2. move in whirls ('eddied, 'eddying)

edelweiss ('eıdəlvaıs) n. white-flowered alpine plant

Eden ('iːdən) n. 1. garden in which Adam and Eve were placed at the Creation 2. any delightful, happy place or state

edentate (iː'denteɪt) n. 1. any mammal of the order *Edentata*, which have few or no teeth, such as anteater —a. 2. of the order *Edentata*

edge (edʒ) n. 1. border, boundary 2. cutting side of blade 3. sharpness 4. advantage 5. acrimony, bitterness —vt. 6. give edge or border to 7. move gradually —vi. 8. advance sideways or gradually —'**edgeways** or '**edgewise** adv. —'**edging** n. —'**edgy** a. irritable, sharp or keen in temper —**on edge** 1. nervy, irritable 2. excited

edible ('edɪbᵊl) a. eatable, fit for eating —**edi'bility** n.

edict ('iːdɪkt) n. order proclaimed by authority, decree

edifice ('edɪfɪs) n. building, esp. big one

edify ('edɪfaɪ) vt. improve morally, instruct (-**fied, -fying**) —**edifi'cation** n. improvement of mind or morals

edit ('edɪt) vt. prepare (book, film, tape etc.) for publication or broadcast —e'**dition** n. 1. form in which something is published 2. number of copies of new publication printed at one time —'**editor** n. —**edi'torial** a. 1. of editor —n. 2. article stating opinion of newspaper etc.

edit. 1. edited 2. edition 3. editor

E.D.P. electronic data processing

educate ('edjukeɪt) vt. 1. provide schooling for 2. teach 3. train mentally and morally 4. train 5. improve, develop —**educa'bility** or **educat-a'bility** n. —'**educable** or '**educatable** a. capable of being trained or educated —'**educat-ed** a. 1. having education, esp. a good one 2. cultivated —**edu'cation** n. —**edu'cational** a. —**edu'cationalist** or **edu'cationist** n. one versed in theory and practice of education —**edu'cationally** adv. —'**educative** a. —'**educator** n. —**educated guess** guess based on experience or information

educe (ɪ'djuːs) vt. 1. bring out, elicit, develop 2. infer, deduce —e'**ducible** a. —**eduction** (ɪ'dʌkʃən) n.

Edwardian (ed'wɔːdɪən) a. of reign of Edward VII, king of Great Britain and Ireland —**Ed'wardianism** n.

-ee (comb. form) 1. recipient of action, as in *assignee* 2. person in specified state or condition, as in *absentee*

EEC European Economic Community

EEG electroencephalogram

eel (iːl) n. snakelike fish

e'en (iːn) adv./n. Poet., obs. even, evening

-eer or **-ier** (comb. form) 1. person who is concerned with something specified, as in *auctioneer, engineer, profiteer* 2. be concerned with something specified, as in *electioneer*

e'er (εə) adv. Poet., obs. ever

eerie ('ɪərɪ) a. 1. weird, uncanny 2. causing superstitious fear

efface (ɪ'feɪs) vt. wipe or rub out —**ef'faceable** a. —**ef'facement** n.

effect (ɪ'fekt) n. 1. result, consequence 2. efficacy 3. impression 4. condition of being operative —pl. 5. property 6. lighting, sounds etc. to accompany film, broadcast etc. —vt. 7. bring about, accomplish —**ef'fective** a. 1. having power to produce effects 2. in effect, operative 3. serviceable 4. powerful 5. striking —**ef'fectively** adv. —**ef'fectual** a. 1. successful in producing desired effect 2. satisfactory 3. efficacious —**ef'fectually** adv. —**ef'fectuate** vt.

effeminate (ɪ'femɪnɪt) a. (of man or boy) womanish, unmanly —**ef'feminacy** n.

efferent ('efərənt) a. conveying outward or away

effervesce (efə'ves) vi. 1. give off bubbles 2. be in high spirits —**effer'vescence** n. —**effer'vescent** a.

effete (ɪ'fiːt) a. worn-out, feeble

efficacious (efɪ'keɪʃəs) a. 1. producing or sure to produce desired effect 2. effective 3. powerful 4. adequate —'**efficacy** n. 1. potency 2. force 3. efficiency

efficient (ɪ'fɪʃənt) a. capable, competent, producing effect —**ef'ficiency** n. —**ef'ficiently** adv.

effigy ('efɪdʒɪ) n. image, likeness

effloresce (eflɔː'res) vi. burst into flower —**efflo'rescence** n. —**efflo'rescent** a.

effluent ('efluənt) n. 1. liquid discharged as waste 2. stream flowing from larger stream, lake etc. —a. 3. flowing out —'**effluence** or '**effluent** n. —'**effluvium** n. something flowing out invisibly, esp. affecting lungs or sense of smell (pl. -**ia** (-ɪə))

effort ('efət) n. 1. exertion 2. endeavour, attempt 3. something achieved —'**effortless** a.

effrontery (ɪ'frʌntərɪ) n. brazen impudence

effulgent (ɪ'fʌldʒənt) a. radiant, shining brightly —**ef'fulgence** n.

effusion (ɪ'fjuːʒən) n. (unrestrained) outpour-ing —**ef'fuse** v. pour out, shed —**ef'fusive** a. gushing, demonstrative —**ef'fusively** adv. —**ef'fusiveness** n.

eft (eft) n. dial., obs. newt

EFT electronic funds transfer

EFTA ('eftə) European Free Trade Association

e.g. exempli gratia (*Lat.*, for example)

egalitarian (ɪgælɪ'teərɪən) a. 1. believing that all people should be equal 2. promoting this ideal —n. 3. adherent of egalitarian principles —**egali'tarianism** n.

egg¹ (eg) n. oval or round object produced by female of bird etc., from which young emerge,

esp. egg of domestic hen, used as food —**egg cup**
n. —'**egghead** *n. inf.* intellectual —**egg'nog** *n.*
egg-noggin *n.* drink made of eggs, milk, sugar,
spice, and brandy, rum *etc.* (*also* **egg flip**)
—'**eggplant** *n. esp.* US aubergine —'**eggshell** *n.*
1. outer layer of bird's egg —*a.* 2. (of paint)
having matt finish

egg² (εg) *vt.* —**egg on** 1. encourage, urge 2.
incite

eglantine ('εglǝntaɪn) *n.* sweet brier

ego ('iːgǝʊ, 'εgǝʊ) *n.* 1. the self 2. the conscious
thinking subject 3. one's image of oneself 4.
morale —'**egoism** *n.* 1. systematic selfishness 2.
theory that bases morality on self-interest
—'**egoist** *n.* —**ego'istic(al)** *a.* —'**egotism** *n.* 1.
selfishness 2. self-conceit —'**egotist** *n.* —**ego-
'tistic(al)** *a.* —**ego'centric** *a.* 1. self-centred 2.
egoistic 3. centred in the ego —**ego trip** *inf.*
something undertaken to boost person's own
image or appraisal of himself

egregious (ɪ'griːdʒǝs, -dʒɪǝs) *a.* 1. outstandingly bad, blatant 2. (*esp.* of mistake *etc.*) absurdly
obvious

egress ('iːgrεs) *n.* 1. way out 2. departure

egret ('iːgrɪt) *n.* 1. lesser white heron 2. down of
dandelion

Egyptian (ɪ'dʒɪpʃǝn) *a.* 1. of Egypt —*n.* 2.
native or inhabitant of Egypt —**Egyp'tologist** *n.*
—**Egyp'tology** *n.* study of archaeology and
language of ancient Egypt

eh (eɪ) *interj.* exclamation expressing surprise
or inquiry, or to seek confirmation of statement
or question

EHF extremely high frequency

eider *or* **eider duck** ('aɪdǝ) *n.* Arctic duck
—'**eiderdown** *n.* 1. its breast feathers 2. quilt
(stuffed with feathers)

eight (eɪt) *n.* 1. cardinal number one above
seven 2. eight-oared boat 3. its crew —*a.* 4.
amounting to eight —'**eigh'teen** *a./n.* eight
more than ten —'**eigh'teenth** *a./n.*
—'**eigh'teenthly** *adv.* —**eighth** *a./n.* ordinal
number of eight —'**eighthly** *adv.* —'**eightieth**
a./n. —'**eighty** *a./n.* ten times eight
—**eightsome reel** Scottish dance for eight
people —**figure of eight** 1. a skating figure 2.
any figure shaped as 8

einsteinium (aɪn'staɪnɪǝm) *n.* radioactive
element artificially produced from plutonium

Eire ('εǝrǝ) *n.* the Republic of Ireland

E.I.S. Educational Institute of Scotland

eisteddfod (aɪ'stεdfǝd) *n.* 1. annual congress of
Welsh bards 2. local gathering for competition
in music and other performing arts

either ('aɪðǝ, 'iːðǝ) *a./pron.* 1. one or the other
2. one of two 3. each —*adv./conj.* 4. bringing in
first of alternatives or strengthening an added
negation

ejaculate (ɪ'dʒækjʊleɪt) *v.* 1. eject (semen) 2.
exclaim, utter suddenly —**ejacu'lation** *n.*
—e'**jaculatory** *a.*

eject (ɪ'dʒεkt) *vt.* 1. throw out 2. expel, drive out
—e'**jection** *n.* —e'**jectment** *n.* —e'**jector** *n.*
—**ejection seat** *or* **ejector seat** seat, *esp.* in
military aircraft, that ejects occupant in
emergency

eke out (iːk) 1. make (supply) last, *esp.* by
frugal use 2. supply deficiencies of 3. make with
difficulty (a living *etc.*)

elaborate (ɪ'læbǝrɪt) *a.* 1. carefully worked out,
detailed 2. complicated —*vi.* (ɪ'læbǝreɪt) 3.
expand —*vt.* (ɪ'læbǝreɪt) 4. work out in detail 5.
take pains with —**elabo'ration** *n.*

élan (eɪ'lɑːn) *n.* 1. dash 2. ardour 3. impetuosity

eland ('iːlǝnd) *n.* largest S Afr. antelope,
resembling elk

elapse (ɪ'læps) *vi.* (of time) pass

elastic (ɪ'læstɪk) *a.* 1. resuming normal shape
after distortion, springy 2. flexible —*n.* 3. tape,
fabric, containing interwoven strands of flexible
rubber —e'**lasticated** *a.* —**elas'ticity** *n.*
—**elastic band** *see* **rubber band** *at* RUBBER¹

elation (ɪ'leɪʃǝn) *n.* 1. high spirits 2. pride
—e'**late** *vt.* (*usu. passive*) 1. raise the spirits of 2.
make happy 3. exhilarate

elbow ('εlbǝʊ) *n.* 1. joint between fore and
upper parts of arm (*esp.* outer part of it) 2. part
of sleeve covering this —*vt.* 3. shove, strike with
elbow —**elbow grease** hard work —'**elbowroom**
n. sufficient room

elder¹ ('εldǝ) *a. comp. of* OLD 1. older, senior
—*n.* 2. person of greater age 3. old person 4.
official of certain churches —'**elderly** *a.*
growing old —'**eldest** *a. sup. of* OLD oldest

elder² ('εldǝ) *n.* white-flowered tree —'**elder-
berry** *n.* 1. fruit of elder 2. elder (tree)

El Dorado (εl dɒ'rɑːdǝʊ) fictitious country
rich in gold

eldritch *or* **eldrich** ('εldrɪtʃ) *a.* 1. hideous 2.
weird 3. uncanny 4. haggish

elect (ɪ'lεkt) *vt.* 1. choose by vote 2. choose —*a.*
3. appointed but not yet in office 4. chosen,
select, choice —e'**lection** *n.* choosing, *esp.* by
voting —**election'eer** *vi.* busy oneself in
political elections —e'**lective** *a.* appointed,
filled or chosen by election —e'**lector** *n.* one
who elects —e'**lectoral** *a.* —e'**lectorate** *n.* body
of electors —e'**lectorship** *n.*

elect. *or* **elec.** 1. electric(al) 2. electricity

electricity (ɪlεk'trɪsɪtɪ, iːlεk-) *n.* 1. form of
energy associated with stationary or moving
electrons or other charged particles 2. electric
current or charge 3. science dealing with
electricity —e'**lectric** *a.* 1. derived from,
produced by, producing, transmitting or
powered by electricity 2. excited, emotionally

charged —e'**lectrical** a. —**elec'trician** n. one trained in installation etc. of electrical devices —**electrifi'cation** n. —e'**lectrify** vt. —**electric blanket** blanket containing electric heating element —**electric chair** US chair in which criminals sentenced to death are electrocuted —**electric eel** eel-like freshwater fish of N South Amer., having electric organs in body —**electric eye** see PHOTOCELL —**electric fire** appliance that supplies heat by means of electrically operated metal coil —**electric organ** Mus. organ in which sound is produced by electric devices instead of wind —**electric shock** effect of an electric current passing through body

electro- or sometimes before vowel **electr-** (comb. form) by, caused by electricity, as in electrotherapy. Such words are not given here where the meaning may easily be inferred from the simple word

electrocardiograph (ɪlɛktrəʊ'kɑːdɪəʊɡrɑːf, -ɡræf) n. instrument for recording electrical activity of heart —**electro'cardiogram** n. tracing produced by this

electroconvulsive therapy (ɪlɛktrəʊkən-'vʌlsɪv) see **shock therapy** at SHOCK[1]

electrocute (ɪ'lɛktrəkjuːt) vt. execute, kill by electricity —**electro'cution** n.

electrode (ɪ'lɛktrəʊd) n. conductor by which electric current enters or leaves battery, vacuum tube etc.

electrodynamics (ɪlɛktrəʊdaɪ'næmɪks) pl.n. (with sing. v.) dynamics of electricity

electroencephalograph (ɪlɛktrəʊɛn'sɛfələ-ɡrɑːf, -ɡræf) n. instrument for recording electrical activity of brain —**electroen'cephalo-gram** n. tracing produced by this

electrolyse or U.S. -**yze** (ɪ'lɛktrəʊlaɪz) vt. decompose by electricity —**elec'trolysis** n.

electrolyte (ɪ'lɛktrəʊlaɪt) n. solution, molten substance that conducts electricity

electromagnet (ɪlɛktrəʊ'mæɡnɪt) n. magnet containing coil of wire through which electric current is passed —**electromag'netic** a. —**electro'magnetism** n. 1. magnetism produced by electric current 2. branch of physics concerned with interaction of electric and magnetic fields

electromotive (ɪlɛktrəʊ'məʊtɪv) a. of, concerned with or producing electric current —**electromotive force** Phys. 1. source of energy that can cause current to flow in electrical circuit 2. rate at which energy is drawn from this source

electron (ɪ'lɛktrɒn) n. one of fundamental particles of matter identified with unit of charge of negative electricity and essential component of the atom —**elec'tronic** a. 1. of electrons or electronics 2. using devices, such as semicon-

ductors, transistors or valves, dependent on action of electrons —**elec'tronics** pl.n. 1. (with sing. v.) technology concerned with development of electronic devices and circuits 2. science of behaviour and control of electrons —**electronic brain** inf. electronic computer —**electronic data processing** data processing largely performed by electronic equipment —**electronic music** music consisting of sounds produced by electric currents prerecorded on magnetic tape —**electronic organ** Mus. keyboard instrument in which sounds are produced by electronic or electrical means —**electron microscope** microscope that uses electrons and electron lenses to produce magnified image —**electron tube** electrical device, such as valve, in which flow of electrons between electrodes takes place —**electron volt** unit of energy used in nuclear physics

electroplate (ɪ'lɛktrəʊpleɪt) vt. 1. coat with silver etc. by electrolysis —n. 2. articles electroplated

electroscope (ɪ'lɛktrəʊskəʊp) n. instrument to show presence or kind of electricity

electroshock therapy (ɪ'lɛktrəʊʃɒk) see **shock therapy** at SHOCK[1]

electrostatics (ɪlɛktrəʊ'stætɪks) n. branch of physics concerned with static electricity —**electro'static** a.

electrotype (ɪ'lɛktrəʊtaɪp) n. 1. art of producing copies of type etc. by electric deposition of copper upon mould 2. copy so produced

electrum (ɪ'lɛktrəm) n. alloy of gold and silver used in jewellery etc.

eleemosynary (ɛliː'mɒsɪnərɪ) a. 1. charitable 2. dependent on charity

elegant ('ɛlɪɡənt) a. 1. graceful, tasteful 2. refined —'**elegance** n.

elegy ('ɛlɪdʒɪ) n. lament for the dead in poem or song —**elegiac** (ɛlɪ'dʒaɪək) a. 1. suited to elegies 2. plaintive —**elegiacs** (ɛlɪ'dʒaɪəks) pl.n. elegiac verses

element ('ɛlɪmənt) n. 1. substance which cannot be separated into other substances by ordinary chemical techniques 2. component part 3. small amount, trace 4. heating wire in electric kettle, stove etc. 5. proper abode or sphere 6. situation in which person is happiest or most effective (esp. in **in** or **out of one's element**) —pl. 7. powers of atmosphere 8. rudiments, first principles —**ele'mental** a. 1. fundamental 2. of powers of nature —**ele'men-tary** a. rudimentary, simple —**elementary particle** any of several entities, such as electrons etc., that are less complex than atoms —**elementary school** UK former name for primary school

elephant ('ɛlɪfənt) *n.* huge four-footed, thick-skinned animal with ivory tusks and long trunk —**elephan'tiasis** *n.* disease with hardening of skin and enlargement of legs *etc.* —**ele'phantine** *a.* unwieldy, clumsy, heavily big

elevate ('ɛlɪveɪt) *vt.* raise, lift up, exalt —**ele'vation** *n.* 1. raising 2. height, *esp.* above sea level 3. angle above horizon, as of gun 4. drawing of one side of building *etc.* —'**elevator** *n.* US lift

eleven (ɪ'lɛvən) *n.* 1. number next above 10 2. team of 11 persons —*a.* 3. amounting to eleven —**e'levenfold** *a./adv.* —**e'levenses** *pl.n.* *inf.* light mid-morning snack —**e'leventh** *a.* ordinal number of eleven —**eleven-plus** *n.* *esp.* formerly, examination taken by children aged 11 or 12, that selects suitable candidates for grammar schools —**eleventh hour** latest possible time

elf (ɛlf) *n.* 1. fairy 2. woodland sprite (*pl.* **elves**) —'**elfin**, '**elfish**, '**elvish** *or* '**elflike** *a.* roguish, mischievous

elicit (ɪ'lɪsɪt) *vt.* 1. draw out, evoke 2. bring to light

elide (ɪ'laɪd) *v.* omit (a vowel or syllable) at beginning or end of word—**e'lision** *n.*

eligible ('ɛlɪdʒəbl) *a.* 1. fit or qualified to be chosen 2. suitable, desirable —**eligi'bility** *n.*

eliminate (ɪ'lɪmɪneɪt) *vt.* remove, get rid of, set aside —**elimi'nation** *n.* —**e'liminator** *n.* one who, that which, eliminates

elision (ɪ'lɪʒən) *n. see* ELIDE

elite *or* **élite** (ɪ'liːt, eɪ-) *n.* 1. choice or select body 2. the pick or best part of society 3. typewriter typesize (12 letters to inch) —*a.* 4. of or suitable for an elite —**e'litism** *n.* 1. belief that society should be governed by an elite 2. pride in being one of an elite group

elixir (ɪ'lɪksə) *n.* 1. preparation sought by alchemists to change base metals into gold, or to prolong life 2. sovereign remedy

Elizabethan (ɪlɪzə'biːθən) *a.* 1. of reigns of Elizabeth I (queen of England, 1558-1603) or Elizabeth II (queen of Great Britain and N Ireland since 1952) 2. of style of architecture used in England during reign of Elizabeth I —*n.* 3. person who lived in England during reign of Elizabeth I

elk (ɛlk) *n.* large deer

ell (ɛl) *n.* obsolete unit of length, approximately 45 inches

ellipse (ɪ'lɪps) *n.* oval —**el'lipsoid** *n.* 1. geometric surface whose plane sections are ellipses or circles 2. solid having this shape —**ellip'soidal** *a.* —**el'liptical** *a.* 1. relating to or having the shape of an ellipse 2. relating to or resulting from ellipsis 3. (of speech *etc.*) very concise, obscure; circumlocutory (*also* **el'liptic**) —**el'liptically** *adv.*

ellipsis (ɪ'lɪpsɪs) *n. Gram.* omission of parts of word or sentence (*pl.* **ellipses** (ɪ'lɪpsiːz))

elm (ɛlm) *n.* 1. tree with serrated leaves 2. its wood

elocution (ɛlə'kjuːʃən) *n.* art of public speaking, voice management —**elo'cutionist** *n.* 1. teacher of this 2. specialist in verse speaking

elongate ('iːlɒŋɡeɪt) *vt.* lengthen, extend, prolong —**elon'gation** *n.*

elope (ɪ'ləʊp) *vi.* run away from home with lover —**e'lopement** *n.*

eloquence ('ɛləkwəns) *n.* fluent, powerful use of language —'**eloquent** *a.* —'**eloquently** *adv.*

Elsan ('ɛlsæn) *n.* **R** type of portable chemical lavatory

else (ɛls) *adv.* 1. besides, instead 2. otherwise —**else'where** *adv.* in or to some other place

elucidate (ɪ'luːsɪdeɪt) *vt.* throw light upon, explain —**eluci'dation** *n.* —**e'lucidatory** *a.*

elude (ɪ'luːd) *vt.* 1. escape, slip away from, dodge 2. baffle —**e'lusion** *n.* 1. act of eluding 2. evasion —**e'lusive** *a.* difficult to catch hold of, deceptive —**e'lusively** *adv.* —**e'lusory** *a.*

elver ('ɛlvə) *n.* young eel

elves (ɛlvz) *n.,* *pl.* of ELF

Elysium (ɪ'lɪzɪəm) *n.* 1. *Gr. myth.* dwelling place of blessed after death (*also* **Elysian fields**) 2. state or place of perfect bliss

em (ɛm) *n. Print.* the square of any size of type

em- (*comb. form*) *see* EN-

'em (əm) *pron. inf.* them

emaciate (ɪ'meɪsɪeɪt) *v.* make or become abnormally thin —**emaci'ation** *n.*

emanate ('ɛmɒneɪt) *vi.* issue, proceed, originate —**ema'nation** *n.* —**emanative** ('ɛmənətɪv) *a.*

emancipate (ɪ'mænsɪpeɪt) *vt.* set free —**emanci'pation** *n.* act of setting free, *esp.* from social, legal restraint 2. state of being set free —**emanci'pationist** *n.* advocate of emancipation of slaves, women *etc.* —**e'mancipator** *n.* —**emancipatory** (ɪ'mænsɪpətərɪ, -trɪ) *a.*

emasculate (ɪ'mæskjʊleɪt) *vt.* 1. castrate 2. enfeeble, weaken —**emascu'lation** *n.* —**e'masculative** *a.*

embalm (ɪm'bɑːm) *vt.* preserve (corpse) from decay by use of chemicals, herbs *etc.* —**em'balmment** *n.*

embankment (ɪm'bæŋkmənt) *n.* artificial mound carrying road, railway, or serving to dam water

embargo (ɛm'bɑːɡəʊ) *n.* 1. order stopping movement of ships 2. suspension of commerce 3. ban (*pl.* **-es**) —*vt.* 4. put under embargo 5. requisition

embark (ɛm'bɑːk) *v.* 1. put, go, on board ship,

aircraft *etc.* **2.** (*with on* or *upon*) commence (new project, venture *etc.*) —**embar'kation** *n.*

embarrass (ɪm'bærəs) *vt.* **1.** perplex, disconcert **2.** abash **3.** confuse **4.** encumber **5.** involve in financial difficulties —**em'barrassment** *n.*

embassy ('ɛmbəsɪ) *n.* **1.** office, work or official residence of ambassador **2.** deputation

embattle (ɪm'bæt³l) *vt.* **1.** deploy (troops) for battle **2.** fortify (position *etc.*)

embed or **imbed** (ɪm'bɛd) *vt.* fix fast in something solid

embellish (ɪm'bɛlɪʃ) *vt.* adorn, enrich —**em'bellishment** *n.*

ember ('ɛmbə) *n.* **1.** glowing cinder —*pl.* **2.** redhot ashes

Ember days days appointed by Church for fasting in each quarter

embezzle (ɪm'bɛz³l) *vt.* divert fraudulently, misappropriate (money in trust *etc.*) —**em'bezzlement** *n.* —**em'bezzler** *n.*

embitter (ɪm'bɪtə) *vt.* make bitter —**em'bitterment** *n.*

emblazon (ɪm'bleɪz³n) *vt.* adorn richly, *esp.* heraldically

emblem ('ɛmbləm) *n.* **1.** symbol **2.** badge, device —**emblem'atic** *a.* —**emblem'atically** *adv.*

embody (ɪm'bɒdɪ) *vt.* **1.** give body, concrete expression to **2.** represent, include, be expression of (**em'bodied, em'bodying**) —**em'bodiment** *n.*

embolden (ɪm'bəʊld³n) *vt.* make bold

embolism ('ɛmbəlɪzəm) *n. Med.* obstruction of artery by blood clot or air bubble

embolus ('ɛmbələs) *n.* material, such as blood clot, that impedes circulation (*pl.* **-li** (-laɪ))

emboss (ɪm'bɒs) *vt.* mould, stamp or carve in relief

embrace (ɪm'breɪs) *vt.* **1.** clasp in arms, hug **2.** seize, avail oneself of, accept **3.** comprise —*n.* **4.** act of embracing

embrasure (ɪm'breɪʒə) *n.* **1.** opening in wall for cannon **2.** bevelling of wall at sides of window

embrocation (ɛmbrəʊ'keɪʃən) *n.* lotion for rubbing limbs *etc.* to relieve pain —**'embrocate** *vt.*

embroider (ɪm'brɔɪdə) *vt.* **1.** ornament with needlework **2.** embellish, exaggerate (story) —**em'broidery** *n.*

embroil (ɪm'brɔɪl) *vt.* **1.** bring into confusion **2.** involve in hostility —**em'broilment** *n.*

embryo ('ɛmbrɪəʊ) *n.* **1.** unborn or undeveloped offspring, germ **2.** undeveloped thing (*pl.* **-s**) —**embry'ologist** *n.* —**embry'ology** *n.* —**embry'onic** *a.*

embus (ɪm'bʌs) *v.* (*esp.* of troops) put into, mount bus (**-ss-**)

emend (ɪ'mɛnd) *vt.* remove errors from, correct —**emen'dation** *n.* —**'emendator** *n.* —**e'mendatory** *a.*

emerald ('ɛmərəld, 'ɛmrəld) *n.* **1.** bright green precious stone —*a.* **2.** of the colour of emerald —**Emerald Isle** *Poet.* Ireland

emerge (ɪ'mɜːdʒ) *vi.* **1.** come up, out **2.** rise to notice **3.** come into view **4.** come out on inquiry —**e'mergence** *n.* —**e'mergent** *a.* —**e'mersion** *n.* **1.** act or instance of emerging **2.** *Astron.* reappearance of celestial body after eclipse or occultation

emergency (ɪ'mɜːdʒənsɪ) *n.* **1.** sudden unforeseen thing or event needing prompt action **2.** difficult situation **3.** exigency, crisis

emeritus (ɪ'mɛrɪtəs) *a.* retired, honourably discharged but retaining one's title (*eg* professor) on honorary basis

emery ('ɛmərɪ) *n.* hard mineral used for polishing —**emery board** nailfile of cardboard or wood coated with crushed emery —**emery paper** stiff paper coated with finely powdered emery

emetic (ɪ'mɛtɪk) *n./a.* (medicine) causing vomiting

emf or **EMF** electromotive force

emigrate ('ɛmɪgreɪt) *vi.* go and settle in another country —**'emigrant** *n.* —**emi'gration** *n.* —**'emigratory** *a.*

émigré ('ɛmɪgreɪ) *n.* emigrant, *esp.* one forced to leave his country for political reasons

éminence grise (eminãs 'griz) *Fr.* person who wields power and influence unofficially (*pl. éminences grises* (eminãs 'griz))

eminent ('ɛmɪnənt) *a.* distinguished, notable —**'eminence** *n.* **1.** distinction **2.** height **3.** rank **4.** fame **5.** rising ground **6.** (E-) title of cardinal —**'eminently** *adv.*

emir (ɛ'mɪə) *n.* (in Islamic world) **1.** independent ruler or chieftain **2.** military commander or governor **3.** male descendant of Mohammed —**e'mirate** *n.*

emissary ('ɛmɪsərɪ, -ɪsrɪ) *n.* agent, representative (*esp.* of government) sent on mission

emit (ɪ'mɪt) *vt.* give out, put forth (**-tt-**) —**e'mission** *n.* —**e'mitter** *n.*

Emmenthal ('ɛməntɑːl) or **Emmenthaler** *n.* hard Swiss cheese with many holes

emollient (ɪ'mɒljənt) *a.* **1.** softening, soothing —*n.* **2.** ointment or other softening application

emolument (ɪ'mɒljʊmənt) *n.* salary, pay, profit from work

emotion (ɪ'məʊʃən) *n.* mental agitation, excited state of feeling, as joy, fear *etc.* —**e'mote** *vi. inf.* display exaggerated emotion, as in acting —**e'motional** *a.* **1.** given to emotion **2.** appealing to the emotions —**e'motive** *a.* tending to arouse emotion

Emp. 1. Emperor **2.** Empire **3.** Empress

empanel or **impanel** (ɪmˈpænl) vt. Law **1.** enter on list (names of persons to be summoned for jury service) **2.** select (jury) from such list (-ll-) —em'**panelment** or im'**panelment** n.

empathy ('ɛmpəθɪ) n. power of understanding, imaginatively entering into, another's feelings —em'**pathic** or empa'**thetic** a.

emperor ('ɛmpərə) n. ruler of an empire ('**empress** fem.) —**emperor penguin** Antarctic penguin, the largest known, reaching a height of 1.3 m (4 ft.)

emphasis ('ɛmfəsɪs) n. **1.** importance attached **2.** stress on words **3.** vigour of speech, expression (pl. -ses (-sɪːz)) —'**emphasize** or -ise vt. —em'**phatic** a. **1.** forceful, decided **2.** stressed —em'**phatically** adv.

empire ('ɛmpaɪə) n. large territory, esp. aggregate of states under supreme ruler, supreme control —**empire-builder** n. inf. person who seeks extra power, esp. by increasing his staff —**empire-building** n./a.

empirical (ɛmˈpɪrɪkəl) a. relying on experiment or experience, not on theory —em'**piric** a. **1.** empirical —n. **2.** one who relies solely on experience and observation —em'**pirically** adv. —**empiricism** (ɛmˈpɪrɪsɪzəm) n.

emplacement (ɪmˈpleɪsmənt) n. **1.** putting in position **2.** gun platform

emplane (ɪmˈpleɪn) v. board or put on board aeroplane

employ (ɪmˈplɔɪ) vt. **1.** provide work for (a person) in return for money, hire **2.** keep busy **3.** use (em'**ployed**, em'**ploying**) —em'**ployee** n. —em'**ployer** n. —em'**ployment** n. **1.** an employing, being employed **2.** work, trade **3.** occupation

emporium (ɛmˈpɔːrɪəm) n. **1.** large general shop **2.** centre of commerce (pl. -s, -ria (-rɪə))

empower (ɪmˈpaʊə) vt. **1.** enable **2.** authorize

empress (ɛmˈprɪs) n. see EMPEROR

empty ('ɛmptɪ) a. **1.** containing nothing **2.** unoccupied **3.** senseless **4.** vain, foolish —v. **5.** make, become devoid of content **6.** discharge (contents) (into) ('**emptied**, '**emptying**) —'**empties** pl.n. empty boxes, bottles etc. —'**emptiness** n. —**empty-handed** a. **1.** carrying nothing in hands **2.** having gained nothing —**empty-headed** a. lacking sense

empyrean (ɛmpaɪˈriːən) n. **1.** obs. in ancient cosmology, highest part of the heavens **2.** Poet. heavens; sky —a., also empy'**real 3.** of sky **4.** heavenly, sublime

EMS European Monetary System

emu ('iːmjuː) n. large Aust. flightless bird like ostrich

emulate ('ɛmjʊleɪt) vt. **1.** strive to equal or excel **2.** imitate —emu'**lation** n. **1.** rivalry **2.** competition —'**emulative** a. —'**emulator** n. —'**emulous** a. eager to equal or surpass another or his deeds

emulsion (ɪˈmʌlʃən) n. **1.** light-sensitive coating of film **2.** milky liquid with oily or resinous particles in suspension **3.** paint etc. in this form —e'**mulsify** v. (e'**mulsified**, e'**mulsifying**) —e'**mulsive** a.

en (ɛn) n. Print. unit of measurement, half an em

en- or **em-** (comb. form) put in, into, on, as in enrage. Such words are not given here where the meaning may easily be inferred from the simple word

-en (comb. form) cause to be; become; cause to have, as in blacken, heighten

-en (comb. form) of; made of; resembling, as in ashen, wooden

enable (ɪnˈeɪbəl) vt. make able, authorize, empower, supply with means (to do something) —**enabling act** legislative act conferring certain powers on person or organization

enact (ɪnˈækt) vt. **1.** make law **2.** represent or perform as in a play —en'**actment** n.

enamel (ɪˈnæməl) n. **1.** glasslike coating applied to metal etc. to preserve surface **2.** coating of teeth **3.** any hard outer coating —vt. **4.** decorate with enamel **5.** ornament with glossy variegated colours, as if with enamel **6.** portray in enamel (-ll-)

enamour or U.S. **enamor** (ɪnˈæmə) vt. **1.** inspire with love **2.** charm **3.** bewitch

en bloc (ã ˈblɔk) Fr. **1.** in a lump or block **2.** all together

enc. 1. enclosed **2.** enclosure

encamp (ɪnˈkæmp) v. set up (in) camp —en'**campment** n. camp

encapsulate or **incapsulate** (ɪnˈkæpsjʊleɪt) vt. **1.** enclose in capsule **2.** put in concise or abridged form

encase or **incase** (ɪnˈkeɪs) vt. place or enclose as in case —en'**casement** or in'**casement** n.

encaustic (ɪnˈkɔstɪk) a. **1.** with colours burnt in —n. **2.** art of ornament by burnt-in colours

-ence or **-ency** (comb. form) action, state, condition, quality, as in benevolence, residence, patience, fluency, permanency

enceinte (ɒnˈsænt) a. pregnant

encephalitis (ɛnsɛfəˈlaɪtɪs) n. inflammation of brain —**encephalitic** (ɛnsɛfəˈlɪtɪk) a.

encephalo- or before vowel **encephal-** (comb. form) brain, as in encephalogram, encephalitis

encephalogram (ɛnˈsɛfələgræm) n. x-ray photograph of brain

enchain (ɪnˈtʃeɪn) vt. **1.** bind with chains **2.** hold

fast or captivate (attention *etc.*) —en'chain-
ment *n.*

enchant (ɪn'tʃɑːnt) *vt.* **1.** bewitch **2.** delight
—en'chanter *n.* (-tress *fem.*) —en'chantment
n.

enchilada (entʃɪ'lɑːdə) *n.* Mexican dish of
tortilla filled with meat, served with chilli sauce

encircle (ɪn'sɜːkəl) *vt.* **1.** surround **2.** enfold **3.**
go round so as to encompass —en'circlement *n.*

enclave ('ɛnkleɪv) *n.* portion of territory
entirely surrounded by foreign land

enclitic (ɪn'klɪtɪk) *a.* **1.** pronounced as part of
another word —*n.* **2.** enclitic word or form

enclose or **inclose** (ɪn'kləʊz) *vt.* **1.** shut in **2.**
surround **3.** envelop **4.** place in with something
else (in letter *etc.*) —en'closure or in'closure
n. —enclosed order Christian religious order
whose members do not go into the outside world

encomium (ɛn'kəʊmɪəm) *n.* **1.** formal praise **2.**
eulogy —en'comiast *n.* one who composes
encomiums —encomi'astic *a.* —encomi'astically *adv.*

encompass (ɪn'kʌmpəs) *vt.* **1.** surround,
encircle **2.** contain

encore ('ɒŋkɔː) *interj.* **1.** again, once more —*n.*
2. call for repetition of song *etc.* **3.** the repetition
—*vt.* **4.** ask to repeat

encounter (ɪn'kauntə) *vt.* **1.** meet unexpectedly **2.** meet in conflict **3.** be faced with (difficulty)
—*n.* **4.** casual or unexpected meeting **5.** hostile
meeting; contest —encounter group group of
people who meet to develop self-awareness and
mutual understanding by openly expressing
feelings *etc.*

encourage (ɪn'kʌrɪdʒ) *vt.* **1.** hearten, animate,
inspire with hope **2.** embolden —en'couragement *n.*

encroach (ɪn'krəʊtʃ) *vi.* **1.** intrude (on) as
usurper **2.** trespass —en'croachment *n.*

encrust or **incrust** (ɪn'krʌst) *v.* cover with or
form a crust or hard covering

encumber or **incumber** (ɪn'kʌmbə) *vt.* **1.**
hamper **2.** burden —en'cumbrance or in'cumbrance *n.* impediment, burden

-ency (*comb. form*) see -ENCE

encyclical (ɛn'sɪklɪkəl) *a.* **1.** sent to many
persons or places —*n.* **2.** circular letter, *esp.*
from Pope

encyclopedia or **encyclopaedia** (ɛnsaɪ-
kləʊ'piːdɪə) *n.* book, set of books of information
on all subjects, or on every branch of subject,
usu. arranged alphabetically —encyclo'pedic
or encyclo'paedic *a.* —encyclo'pedist or
encyclo'paedist *n.*

end (ɛnd) *n.* **1.** limit **2.** extremity **3.** conclusion,
finishing **4.** fragment **5.** latter part **6.** death **7.**
event, issue **8.** purpose, aim **9.** *Sport* either of the
defended areas of a playing field *etc.* —*vt.* **10.**

put an end to —*vi.* **11.** come to an end, finish
—'ending *n.* —'endless *a.* —'endmost *a.*
nearest end; most distant —'endways *adv.*
—'endpapers *pl.n.* blank pages at beginning
and end of book —end product final result of
process *etc., esp.* in manufacturing —end of
steel C (town at) point to which railway tracks
have been laid —end it all *inf.* commit suicide

endanger (ɪn'deɪndʒə) *vt.* put in danger or
peril —en'dangerment *n.*

endear (ɪn'dɪə) *vt.* make dear or beloved
—en'dearing *a.* —en'dearingly *adv.* —en'dear-
ment *n.* **1.** loving word **2.** tender affection

endeavour or *U.S.* **endeavor** (ɪn'dɛvə) *vi.* **1.**
try, strive —*n.* **2.** attempt, effort

endemic (ɛn'dɛmɪk) *a.* **1.** regularly occurring
in a country or district —*n.* **2.** endemic disease

endive ('ɛndaɪv) *n.* curly-leaved chicory used
as salad

endo- or before vowel **end-** (*comb. form*)
within, as in *endocardium, endocrine.* Such
words are not given here where the meaning
may easily be inferred from the simple word

endocardium (ɛndəʊ'kɑːdɪəm) *n.* lining
membrane of the heart

endocrine ('ɛndəʊkraɪn, -krɪn) *a.* of those
glands (thyroid, pituitary *etc.*) which secrete
hormones directly into bloodstream

endogenous (ɛn'dɒdʒɪnəs) *a. Biol.* developing
or originating within an organism —en'dogeny
n.

endorphin (ɛn'dɔːfɪn) *n.* chemical occurring
in brain, which has similar effect to morphine

endorse or **indorse** (ɪn'dɔːs) *vt.* **1.** sanction **2.**
confirm **3.** write (*esp.* sign name) on back of **4.**
record (conviction) on (driving licence)
—endor'sation *n.* C approval, support —en-
'dorsement or in'dorsement *n.*

endow (ɪn'dau) *vt.* **1.** provide permanent
income for **2.** furnish (with) —en'dowment *n.*
—endowment assurance or insurance life
insurance that provides for payment of
specified sum to policyholder at designated date
or to his beneficiary should he die before this
date

endue or **indue** (ɪn'djuː) *vt.* invest, furnish
(with quality *etc.*)

endure (ɪn'djuə) *vt.* **1.** undergo **2.** tolerate, bear
—*vi.* **3.** last —en'durable *a.* —en'durance *n.* act
or power of enduring —en'during *a.* **1.**
permanent **2.** having forbearance —en'during-
ness *n.*

enema ('ɛnɪmə) *n.* medicine, liquid injected
into rectum

enemy ('ɛnəmɪ) *n.* **1.** hostile person **2.** opponent
3. armed foe **4.** hostile force

energy ('ɛnədʒɪ) *n.* **1.** vigour, force, activity **2.**
source(s) of power, as oil, coal *etc.* **3.** capacity of

machine, battery *etc.* for work or output of power —**ener'getic** *a.* —**ener'getically** *adv.* —'**energize** *or* -**ise** *vt.* give vigour to

enervate ('ɛnəveɪt) *vt.* weaken, deprive of vigour —**ener'vation** *n.* lassitude, weakness

enfant terrible (ãfã tɛ'ribl) *Fr.* person given to unconventional conduct or indiscreet remarks (*pl.* **enfants terribles** (ãfã tɛ'ribl))

enfeeble (ɪn'fiːbəl) *vt.* weaken, debilitate —**en'feeblement** *n.*

enfilade (ɛnfɪ'leɪd) *n.* fire from artillery, sweeping line from end to end

enfold *or* **infold** (ɪn'fəʊld) *vt.* 1. cover by enclosing 2. embrace —**en'folder** *or* **in'folder** *n.*

enforce (ɪn'fɔːs) *vt.* 1. compel obedience to 2. impose (action) upon 3. drive home —**en'forceable** *a.* —**en'forcement** *n.*

enfranchise (ɪn'fræntʃaɪz) *vt.* 1. give right of voting to 2. give parliamentary representation to 3. set free —**en'franchisement** *n.*

Eng. 1. England 2. English

eng. 1. engine 2. engineer 3. engineering 4. engraved 5. engraver 6. engraving

engage (ɪn'geɪdʒ) *vt.* 1. employ 2. reserve, hire 3. bind by contract or promise 4. order 5. pledge oneself 6. betroth 7. undertake 8. attract 9. occupy 10. bring into conflict 11. interlock —*vi.* 12. employ oneself (in) 13. promise 14. begin to fight —**en'gaged** *a.* 1. betrothed 2. in use 3. occupied, busy —**en'gagement** *n.* —**en'gaging** *a.* charming

engender (ɪn'dʒɛndə) *vt.* 1. give rise to 2. beget 3. rouse

engine ('ɛndʒɪn) *n.* 1. any machine to convert energy into mechanical work, as steam or petrol engine 2. railway locomotive 3. fire engine —**engi'neer** *n.* 1. one who is in charge of engines, machinery *etc.* or construction work (*eg* roads, bridges) or installation of plant 2. one who originates, organizes something 3. US driver of railway locomotive —*vt.* 4. construct as engineer 5. contrive —**engi'neering** *n.*

English ('ɪŋglɪʃ) *n.* 1. the language of Britain, the U.S.A., most parts of the Commonwealth and certain other countries 2. the people of England —*a.* 3. relating to England

engorge (ɪn'gɔːdʒ) *vt.* 1. *Pathol.* congest with blood 2. eat (food) greedily 3. gorge (oneself) —**en'gorgement** *n.*

engraft *or* **ingraft** (ɪn'grɑːft) *vt.* 1. graft on 2. plant deeply 3. incorporate

engrain (ɪn'greɪn) *vt. see* INGRAIN

engrave (ɪn'greɪv) *vt.* 1. cut in lines on metal for printing 2. carve, incise 3. impress deeply —**en'graver** *n.* —**en'graving** *n.* copy of picture printed from engraved plate

engross (ɪn'grəʊs) *vt.* 1. absorb (attention) 2.

occupy wholly 3. write out in large letters or in legal form 4. corner —**en'grossment** *n.*

engulf *or* **ingulf** (ɪn'gʌlf) *vt.* swallow up

enhance (ɪn'hɑːns) *vt.* heighten, intensify, increase value or attractiveness of —**en'hancement** *n.*

enigma (ɪ'nɪgmə) *n.* 1. puzzling thing or person 2. riddle —**enig'matic(al)** *a.* —**enig'matically** *adv.*

enjambment *or* **enjambement** (ɪn'dʒæmmənt) *n.* in verse, continuation of sentence beyond end of line

enjoin (ɪn'dʒɔɪn) *vt.* 1. command 2. impose, prescribe

enjoy (ɪn'dʒɔɪ) *vt.* 1. delight in 2. take pleasure in 3. have use or benefit of —*v. refl.* 4. be happy —**en'joyable** *a.* —**en'joyment** *n.*

enkindle (ɪn'kɪndəl) *vt.* 1. set on fire; kindle 2. excite to activity or ardour; arouse

enlarge (ɪn'lɑːdʒ) *vt.* 1. make bigger 2. reproduce on larger scale, as photograph —*vi.* 3. grow bigger 4. talk, write in greater detail 5. be capable of reproduction on larger scale —**en'largeable** *a.* —**en'largement** *n.* —**en'larger** *n.* optical instrument for enlarging photographs

enlighten (ɪn'laɪtn) *vt.* 1. give information to 2. instruct, inform 3. *Poet.* shed light on —**en'lightenment** *n.*

enlist (ɪn'lɪst) *v.* (persuade to) enter armed forces —**en'listment** *n.*

enliven (ɪn'laɪvən) *vt.* brighten, make more lively, animate

en masse (*Fr.* ã 'mas) 1. in a group, body 2. all together

enmesh, inmesh (ɪn'mɛʃ) *or* **immesh** (ɪ'mɛʃ) *vt.* entangle

enmity ('ɛnmɪtɪ) *n.* ill will, hostility

ennoble (ɪ'nəʊbəl) *vt.* make noble, elevate —**en'noblement** *n.*

ennui ('ɒnwiː) *n.* boredom —'**ennuied** *or* **ennuyé** ('ɒnwiːjeɪ) *a.*

enormous (ɪ'nɔːməs) *a.* very big, vast —**e'normity** *n.* 1. a gross offence 2. great wickedness 3. *inf.* great size

enough (ɪ'nʌf) *a.* 1. as much or as many as need be 2. sufficient —*n.* 3. sufficient quantity —*adv.* 4. (just) sufficiently

enounce (ɪ'naʊns) *vt.* 1. state 2. enunciate, proclaim —**e'nouncement** *n.*

en passant (ɒn pæ'sɑːnt) *Fr.* in passing, by the way

enplane (ɛn'pleɪn) *vi.* board aircraft

enquire (ɪn'kwaɪə) *vi. see* INQUIRE

enrapture (ɪn'ræptʃə) *vt.* 1. delight excessively 2. charm —**en'rapt** *or* **en'raptured** *a.* entranced

enrich (ɪn'rɪtʃ) *vt.* 1. make rich 2. add to —**en'richment** *n.*

enrol *or U.S.* **enroll** (ɪnˈrəʊl) *vt.* 1. write name of on roll or list 2. engage, enlist, take in as member 3. enter, record —*vi.* 4. become member (-ll-) —**en'rolment** *or U.S.* **en'rollment** *n.*

en route (ɒn ˈruːt) *Fr.* on the way

ensconce (ɪnˈskɒns) *vt.* 1. place snugly 2. establish in safety

ensemble (ɒnˈsɒmbəl) *n.* 1. whole 2. all parts taken together 3. woman's complete outfit 4. company of actors, dancers *etc.* 5. *Mus.* group of soloists performing together 6. *Mus.* concerted passage 7. general effect —*adv.* 8. all together or at once

enshrine *or* **inshrine** (ɪnˈʃraɪn) *vt.* 1. set in shrine 2. preserve with great care and sacred affection

enshroud (ɪnˈʃraʊd) *vt.* cover or hide as with shroud

ensign (ˈensaɪn) *n.* 1. (*also* ˈensən) naval or military flag 2. badge 3. (in U.S. Navy) commissioned officer of lowest rank

ensilage (ˈensɪlɪdʒ) *n. see* SILAGE

enslave (ɪnˈsleɪv) *vt.* make into slave —**en'slavement** *n.* bondage —**en'slaver** *n.*

ensnare *or* **insnare** (ɪnˈsnɛə) *vt.* 1. capture in snare or trap 2. trick into false position 3. entangle

ensue (ɪnˈsjuː) *vi.* follow, happen after

en suite (ã ˈsɥɪt) forming a set or single unit

ensure (ɛnˈʃʊə, -ˈʃɔː) *or* (*esp. U.S.*) **insure** (ɪnˈ) *vt.* 1. make safe or sure 2. make certain to happen 3. secure

E.N.T. *Med.* ear, nose and throat

-ent (*comb. form*) causing or performing action or existing in certain condition; agent that performs action, as in *astringent, dependent*

entablature (ɛnˈtæblətʃə) *n. Archit.* part of classical temple above columns, having architrave, frieze and cornice

entail (ɪnˈteɪl) *vt.* 1. involve as result, necessitate 2. *Law* restrict (ownership of property) to designated line of heirs

entangle (ɪnˈtæŋɡəl) *vt.* 1. ensnare 2. perplex —**en'tanglement** *n.*

entente (*Fr.* ãˈtãt) *n.* friendly understanding between nations —**entente cordiale** (kɔrˈdjal) 1. friendly understanding between political powers 2. (*oft.* E- C-) understanding reached between France and Britain in April 1904 over colonial disputes

enter (ˈentə) *vt.* 1. go, come into 2. penetrate 3. join 4. write in, register —*vi.* 5. go, come in 6. join a party *etc.* 7. begin —**'entrance** *n.* 1. going, coming in 2. door, passage to enter 3. right to enter 4. fee paid for this —**'entrant** *n.* one who enters, *esp.* contest —**'entry** *n.* 1. entrance 2. entering 3. item entered, *eg* in account, list

enteric (ɛnˈtɛrɪk) *or* **enteral** (ˈentərəl) *a.* of intestines —**ente'ritis** *n.* bowel inflammation

enterprise (ˈentəpraɪz) *n.* 1. bold or difficult undertaking 2. bold spirit 3. force of character in launching out 4. business, company —**'enterprising** *a.*

entertain (entəˈteɪn) *vt.* 1. amuse, divert 2. receive as guest 3. maintain 4. consider favourable 5. take into consideration —**enter'tainer** *n.* —**enter'taining** *a.* serving to entertain; amusing —**enter'tainment** *n.*

enthral *or U.S.* **enthrall** (ɪnˈθrɔːl) *vt.* captivate, thrill, hold spellbound (-ll-) —**en'thralment** *or U.S.* **en'thrallment** *n.*

enthrone (ɛnˈθrəʊn) *vt.* 1. place on throne 2. honour; exalt 3. assign authority to —**en'thronement** *n.*

enthusiasm (ɪnˈθjuːzɪæzəm) *n.* ardent eagerness, zeal —**en'thuse** *v.* (cause to) show enthusiasm —**en'thusiast** *n.* ardent supporter —**enthusi'astic** *a.* —**enthusi'astically** *adv.*

entice (ɪnˈtaɪs) *vt.* allure, attract, inveigle, tempt —**en'ticement** *n.* —**en'ticing** *a.* alluring

entire (ɪnˈtaɪə) *a.* 1. whole, complete 2. unbroken —**en'tirely** *adv.* —**entirety** (ɪnˈtaɪərɪtɪ) *n.*

entitle (ɪnˈtaɪtəl) *vt.* 1. give claim to 2. qualify 3. give title to 4. style

entity (ˈentɪtɪ) *n.* 1. thing's being or existence 2. reality 3. thing having real existence

entomb (ɪnˈtuːm) *vt.* 1. place in or as if in tomb; bury 2. serve as tomb for —**en'tombment** *n.*

entomology (entəˈmɒlədʒɪ) *n.* study of insects —**entomo'logical** *a.* —**ento'mologist** *n.* —**ento'mologize** *or* **-ise** *vi.*

entourage (ɒntʊˈrɑːʒ) *n.* 1. associates, retinue 2. surroundings

entozoon (entəʊˈzəʊɒn) *n.* internal parasite (*pl.* **-zoa** (-ˈzəʊə)) —**entozoic** (entəʊˈzəʊɪk) *a.*

entr'acte (ɒnˈtrækt) *n.* 1. interval between acts of play *etc.* 2. *esp.* formerly, entertainment during such interval

entrails (ˈentreɪlz) *pl.n.* 1. bowels, intestines 2. inner parts

entrain (ɪnˈtreɪn) *v.* board or put aboard train —**en'trainment** *n.*

entrance[1] (ˈentrəns) *n. see* ENTER

entrance[2] (ɪnˈtrɑːns) *vt.* 1. delight 2. throw into a trance

entrap (ɪnˈtræp) *vt.* catch or snare as in trap 2. trick into difficulty *etc.* (-pp-) —**en'trapment** *n.*

entreat *or* **intreat** (ɪnˈtriːt) *vt.* 1. ask earnestly 2. beg, implore —**en'treaty** *n.* earnest request

entrecôte (*Fr.* ãtrəˈkoːt) *n.* beefsteak cut from between ribs

entrée ('ɒntreɪ) *n.* 1. (dish served before) main course of meal 2. right of access, admission

entrench *or* **intrench** (ɪn'trɛntʃ) *vt.* 1. establish in fortified position with trenches 2. establish firmly —**en'trenchment** *or* **in'trenchment** *n.*

entrepreneur (ɒntrəprə'nɜː) *n.* person who attempts to profit by risk and initiative

entropy ('ɛntrəpɪ) *n.* 1. unavailability of the heat energy of a system for mechanical work 2. measurement of this

entrust *or* **intrust** (ɪn'trʌst) *vt.* 1. commit, charge (with) 2. (*oft. with* to) put into care or protection of

entwine *or* **intwine** (ɪn'twaɪn) *vt.* 1. plait, interweave 2. wreathe 3. embrace

enumerate (ɪ'njuːməreɪt) *vt.* 1. mention one by one 2. count —**enumer'ation** *n.* —**e'numerative** *a.* —**e'numerator** *n.*

enunciate (ɪ'nʌnsɪeɪt) *vt.* 1. state clearly 2. proclaim 3. pronounce —**enunci'ation** *n.* —**e'nunciative** *a.* —**e'nunciator** *n.*

enuresis (ɛnjʊ'riːsɪs) *n.* involuntary discharge of urine, *esp.* during sleep —**enuretic** (ɛnjʊ'rɛtɪk) *a.*

envelop (ɪn'vɛləp) *vt.* 1. wrap up, enclose 2. surround 3. encircle —**en'velopment** *n.*

envelope ('ɛnvələʊp, 'ɒn-) *n.* 1. folded, gummed cover of letter 2. covering, wrapper

envenom (ɪn'vɛnəm) *vt.* 1. put poison, venom in 2. embitter

environ (ɪn'vaɪrən) *vt.* surround —**en'vironment** *n.* 1. surroundings 2. conditions of life or growth —**environ'mental** *a.* —**environ'mentalist** *n.* ecologist —**en'virons** *pl.n.* districts round town *etc.*, outskirts

envisage (ɪn'vɪzɪdʒ) *vt.* 1. conceive of as possibility 2. visualize

envoy[1] ('ɛnvɔɪ) *n.* 1. messenger 2. diplomatic minister of rank below ambassador

envoy[2] *or* **envoi** ('ɛnvɔɪ) *n.* 1. concluding stanza, notably in ballades 2. postscript in other forms of verse or prose

envy ('ɛnvɪ) *vt.* 1. grudge (another's good fortune, success or qualities) 2. feel jealous of ('envied, 'envying) —*n.* 3. bitter contemplation of another's good fortune 4. jealousy 5. object of this feeling —**'enviable** *a.* arousing envy —**'envious** *a.* full of envy

enzyme ('ɛnzaɪm) *n.* any of group of complex proteins produced by living cells and acting as catalysts in biochemical reactions

Eocene ('iːəʊsiːn) *a.* 1. of second epoch of Tertiary period, during which hooved mammals appeared —*n.* 2. Eocene epoch or rock series

eolith ('iːəʊlɪθ) *n.* early flint implement —**Eo'lithic** *a.* of the period before Stone Age

-eous (*comb. form*) relating to or having nature of, as in *gaseous*

EP 1. extended-play 2. electroplate

epaulet *or* **epaulette** ('ɛpəlɛt, -lɪt) *n.* shoulder ornament on uniform

épée ('ɛpeɪ) *n.* sword similar to foil but with heavier blade —**'épéeist** *n.*

epergne (ɪ'pɜːn) *n.* ornamental centrepiece for table, holding flowers *etc.*

Eph. *or* **Ephes.** *Bible* Ephesians

ephedrine *or* **ephedrin** (ɪ'fɛdrɪn, 'ɛfɪdriːn, -drɪn) *n.* alkaloid used for treatment of asthma and hay fever

ephemeral (ɪ'fɛmərəl) *a.* short-lived, transient —**e'phemeron** *n.* ephemeral thing (*pl.* **-s, -ra** (-rə)) (*also* **e'phemera** (*pl.* **-s, -rae, -raɪ**))) —**e'phemerous** *a.*

epi-, eph-, *or before vowel* **ep-** (*comb. form*) 1. upon; above, as in *epidermis* 2. in addition to, as in *epiphenomenon* 3. after, as in *epilogue* 4. near, as in *epicalyx*

epic ('ɛpɪk) *n.* 1. long poem or story telling of achievements of hero or heroes 2. film *etc.* about heroic deeds —*a.* 3. of, like, an epic 4. impressive, grand

epicene ('ɛpɪsiːn) *a.* common to both sexes

epicentre *or U.S.* **epicenter** ('ɛpɪsɛntə) *n.* focus of earthquake —**epi'central** *a.*

epicure ('ɛpɪkjʊə) *n.* one delighting in eating and drinking —**epicu'rean** *a.* 1. of Epicurus, who taught that pleasure, in the shape of practice of virtue, was highest good 2. given to refined sensuous enjoyment —*n.* 3. such person or philosopher —**epicu'reanism** *n.* —**'epicurism** *n.*

epicycle ('ɛpɪsaɪkəl) *n.* circle whose centre moves on circumference of greater circle

epidemic (ɛpɪ'dɛmɪk) *a.* 1. (*esp.* of disease) prevalent and spreading rapidly 2. widespread —*n.* 3. widespread occurrence of a disease 4. rapid development, spread or growth of something —**epi'demical** *a.* —**epidemiological** (ɛpɪdiːmɪə'lɒdʒɪkəl) *a.* —**epidemiologist** (ɛpɪdiːmɪ'ɒlədʒɪst) *n.* —**epidemiology** (ɛpɪdiːmɪ'ɒlədʒɪ) *n.* branch of medical science concerned with epidemic diseases

epidermis (ɛpɪ'dɜːmɪs) *n.* outer skin

epidiascope (ɛpɪ'daɪəskəʊp) *n.* optical device for projecting magnified image on to screen

epidural (ɛpɪ'djʊərəl) *n./a.* (of) spinal anaesthetic used for relief of pain during childbirth

epiglottis (ɛpɪ'glɒtɪs) *n.* cartilage that covers opening of larynx in swallowing —**epi'glottic** *a.*

epigram ('ɛpɪɡræm) *n.* concise, witty poem or saying —**epigram'matic(al)** *a.* —**epigram-'matically** *adv.* —**epi'grammatist** *n.*

epigraph ('ɛpɪɡrɑːf, -ɡræf) *n.* inscription

epilepsy ('ɛpɪlɛpsɪ) *n.* disorder of nervous

system causing fits and convulsions —**epi'leptic** n. 1. sufferer from this —a. 2. of, subject to, this

epilogue ('ɛpɪlɒg) n. short speech or poem at end, esp. of play

Epiphany (ɪ'pɪfənɪ) n. festival of the announcement of Christ to the Magi, celebrated Jan. 6th

Epis. 1. Episcopal; Episcopalian (also **Episc.**) 2. Epistle

episcopal (ɪ'pɪskəpəl) a. 1. of bishop 2. ruled by bishops —e'**piscopacy** n. government by body of bishops —**Episco'palian** a. 1. of branch of Anglican church —n. 2. member, adherent of Episcopalian church —e'**piscopate** n. 1. bishop's office, see, or duration of office 2. body of bishops

episode ('ɛpɪsəʊd) n. 1. incident 2. section of (serialized) book, television programme etc. —**episodic(al)** (ɛpɪ'sɒdɪk(əl)) a.

epistemology (ɪpɪstɪ'mɒlədʒɪ) n. study of source, nature and limitations of knowledge —**episte'mological** a. —**episte'mologist** n.

epistle (ɪ'pɪs²l) n. 1. letter, esp. of apostle 2. poem in letter form —**epistolary** (ɪ'pɪstələrɪ) a. —**epistoler** (ɪ'pɪstələ) n.

epitaph ('ɛpɪtɑːf, -tæf) n. memorial inscription on tomb

epithelium (ɛpɪ'θiːlɪəm) n. tissue covering external and internal surfaces of body (pl. -s, -lia (-lɪə)) —**epi'thelial** or **epi'thelioid** a.

epithet ('ɛpɪθɛt) n. additional, descriptive word or name —**epi'thetic(al)** a.

epitome (ɪ'pɪtəmɪ) n. 1. typical example 2. summary —e'**pitomist** n. —e'**pitomize** or **-ise** vt. typify

E.P.N.S. electroplated nickel silver

epoch ('iːpɒk) n. 1. beginning of period 2. period, era, esp. one of notable events —**epochal** ('ɛpɒk²l) a.

epode ('ɛpəʊd) n. third, or last, part of lyric ode

eponym ('ɛpənɪm) n. 1. name, esp. place name, derived from name of real or mythical person 2. name of person from which such name is derived —e'**ponymous** a. —e'**ponymously** adv. —e'**ponymy** n.

epoxy (ɪ'pɒksɪ) a. Chem. of, consisting of, or containing oxygen atom joined to two different groups that are themselves joined to other groups —**epoxy** or **epoxide resin** any of various thermosetting synthetic resins containing epoxy groups: used in surface coatings, adhesives etc.

epsilon ('ɛpsɪlɒn) n. fifth letter of Gr. alphabet (Ε, ε)

Epsom salts ('ɛpsəm) medicinal preparation of hydrated magnesium sulphate, used as purgative etc.

equable ('ɛkwəb²l) a. 1. even-tempered, placid 2. uniform —**equa'bility** n. —'**equably** adv.

equal ('iːkwəl) a. 1. the same in number, size, merit etc. 2. identical 3. fit or qualified 4. evenly balanced —n. 5. one equal to another —vt. 6. be equal to (-ll-) —**equality** (ɪ'kwɒlɪtɪ) n. 1. state of being equal 2. uniformity —**equali'zation** or **-i'sation** n. —'**equalize** or **-ise** v. make, become, equal —'**equally** adv.

equanimity (iːkwə'nɪmɪtɪ, ɛkwə-) n. calmness, composure, steadiness

equate (ɪ'kweɪt) vt. 1. make equal 2. bring to a common standard —**equation** (ɪ'kweɪʒən, -ʃən) n. 1. equating of two mathematical expressions 2. balancing

equator (ɪ'kweɪtə) n. imaginary circle round earth equidistant from the poles —**equa'torial** a.

equerry (ɪ'kwɛrɪ) n. 1. officer in attendance on sovereign 2. officer in royal household in charge of horses

equestrian (ɪ'kwɛstrɪən) a. 1. of, skilled in, horse-riding 2. mounted on horse —n. 3. rider

equi- (comb. form) equal, at equal, as in equidistant. Such words are not given here where the meaning can easily be inferred from the simple word

equiangular (iːkwɪ'æŋgjʊlə) a. having equal angles

equilateral (iːkwɪ'lætərəl) a. having equal sides

equilibrium (iːkwɪ'lɪbrɪəm) n. state of steadiness, equipoise or stability (pl. -s, -ria (-rɪə))

equine ('ɛkwaɪn) a. of, like a horse

equinox ('iːkwɪnɒks) n. 1. time when sun crosses equator and day and night are equal —pl. 2. points at which sun crosses equator —**equinoctial** (iːkwɪ'nɒkʃəl) a.

equip (ɪ'kwɪp) vt. supply, fit out, array (-pp-) —**equipage** ('ɛkwɪpɪdʒ) n. 1. carriage, horses and attendants 2. obs. outfit, requisites —e'**quipment** n.

equipoise ('ɛkwɪpɔɪz) n. 1. perfect balance 2. counterpoise 3. equanimity —vt. 4. counterbalance

equitation (ɛkwɪ'teɪʃən) n. study and practice of riding and horsemanship

equity ('ɛkwɪtɪ) n. 1. fairness 2. use of principles of justice to supplement law 3. system of law so made —'**equitable** a. fair, reasonable, just —'**equitably** adv.

equiv. equivalent

equivalent (ɪ'kwɪvələnt) a. 1. equal in value 2. having the same meaning or result 3. tantamount 4. corresponding —e'**quivalence** or e'**quivalency** n.

equivocal (ɪ'kwɪvək²l) a. 1. of double or doubtful meaning 2. questionable 3. liable to suspicion —**equivo'cality** n. —e'**quivocate** vi.

use equivocal words to mislead —**equivo'cation** *n.* —e'**quivocator** *n.*

er (ə, ɜː) *interj.* sound made when hesitating in speech

Er *Chem.* erbium

E.R. Elizabeth Regina (*Lat.,* Queen Elizabeth)

-er' (*comb. form*) **1.** person or thing that performs specified action, as in *reader* **2.** person engaged in profession *etc.,* as in *writer* **3.** native or inhabitant of, as in *Londoner* **4.** person or thing having certain characteristic, as in *newcomer*

-er² (*comb. form*) forming comparative degree of adjective or adverb, as in *deeper, faster*

era ('ɪərə) *n.* **1.** system of time in which years are numbered from particular event **2.** time of the event **3.** memorable date, period

eradicate (ɪ'rædɪkeɪt) *vt.* **1.** wipe out, exterminate **2.** root out —**e'radicable** *a.* —**eradi'cation** *n.* —**e'radicative** *a./n.* —**e'radicator** *n.*

erase (ɪ'reɪz) *vt.* **1.** rub out **2.** remove, *eg* recording from magnetic tape —**e'raser** *n.* —**e'rasure** *n.*

erbium ('ɜːbɪəm) *n.* metallic element of the lanthanide series

ere (ɛə) *prep./conj.* **1.** *Poet.* before **2.** sooner than —**ere'long** *adv. obs., poet.* before long; soon

erect (ɪ'rɛkt) *a.* **1.** upright —*vt.* **2.** set up **3.** build —**e'rectile** *a.* —**e'rection** *n. esp.* an erect penis —**e'rector** *n.*

eremite ('ɛrɪmaɪt) *n.* Christian hermit or recluse —**eremitic(al)** (ɛrɪ'mɪtɪk(ə)l) *a.* —**er'emitism** *n.*

erg (ɜːg) *n.* cgs unit of work or energy

ergo ('ɜːgəʊ) *adv.* therefore

ergonomics (ɜːgə'nɒmɪks) *pl.n.* (*with sing. v.*) study of relationship between workers and their environment

ergot ('ɜːgət, -gɒt) *n.* **1.** disease of grain **2.** diseased seed used as drug —**'ergotism** *n.* disease caused by eating ergot-infested bread

erica ('ɛrɪkə) *n.* genus of plants including heathers

Erin ('ɪərɪn, 'ɛərɪn) *n. obs., poet.* Ireland

ermine ('ɜːmɪn) *n.* **1.** stoat in northern regions, *esp.* in winter **2.** its white winter fur

erne *or* **ern** (ɜːn) *n.* fish-eating sea eagle

Ernie ('ɜːnɪ) *n. UK* computer that randomly selects winning numbers of Premium Bonds (*Electronic Random Number Indicating Equipment*)

erode (ɪ'rəʊd) *v.* **1.** wear away —*vt.* **2.** eat into —**e'rosion** *n.* —**e'rosive** *a.*

erogenous (ɪ'rɒdʒɪnəs) *or* **erogenic** (ɛrə'dʒɛnɪk) *a.* sensitive to sexual stimulation

erotic (ɪ'rɒtɪk) *a.* relating to, or treating of,

sexual pleasure —**e'rotica** *n.* sexual literature or art —**e'roticism** *n.*

err (ɜː) *vi.* **1.** make mistakes **2.** be wrong **3.** sin —**er'ratic** *a.* irregular in movement, conduct *etc.* —**er'ratically** *adv.* —**erratum** (ɪ'rɑːtəm) *n.* printing mistake noted for correction (*pl.* **-ta** (-tə)) —**er'roneous** *a.* mistaken, wrong —**'error** *n.* **1.** mistake **2.** wrong opinion **3.** sin

errand ('ɛrənd) *n.* **1.** short journey for simple business **2.** purpose of such journey **3.** the business, mission of messenger —**errand boy**

errant ('ɛrənt) *a.* **1.** wandering in search of adventure **2.** erring —**'errancy** *n.* erring state or conduct —**'errantry** *n.* state or conduct of knight errant

ersatz ('ɛəzæts, 'ɜː-) *a.* substitute, imitation

Erse (ɜːs) *n.* **1.** see Gaelic *at* GAEL —*a.* **2.** of or relating to Gaelic language

erst (ɜːst) *adv.* of old, formerly

eruct (ɪ'rʌkt) *or* **eructate** *v.* **1.** belch **2.** (of volcano) pour out (fumes or volcanic matter) —**eruc'tation** *n.*

erudite ('ɛrʊdaɪt) *a.* learned —**erudition** (ɛrʊ'dɪʃən) *n.* learning

erupt (ɪ'rʌpt) *vi.* burst out —**e'ruption** *n.* **1.** bursting out, *esp.* volcanic outbreak **2.** rash on the skin —**e'ruptive** *a.*

-ery *or* **-ry** (*comb. form*) **1.** place of business or activity, as in *bakery, refinery* **2.** class or collection of things, as in *cutlery* **3.** qualities, actions, as in *snobbery, trickery* **4.** practice, occupation, as in *husbandry* **5.** state, condition, as in *slavery*

erysipelas (ɛrɪ'sɪpɪləs) *n.* acute skin infection

erythema (ɛrɪ'θiːmə) *n.* patchy inflammation of skin —**erythematic** (ɛrɪθɪ'mætɪk) *or* **ery'thematous** *a.*

erythrocyte (ɪ'rɪθrəʊsaɪt) *n.* red blood cell of vertebrates that transports oxygen and carbon dioxide —**erythrocytic** (ɪrɪθrəʊ'sɪtɪk) *a.*

Es *Chem.* einsteinium

escalate ('ɛskəleɪt) *v.* increase, be increased, in extent, intensity *etc.*

escalator ('ɛskəleɪtə) *n.* moving staircase —**escalator clause** clause in contract stipulating adjustment in wages *etc.* in event of large rise in cost of living *etc.*

escallop (ɛ'skɒləp, ɛ'skæl-) *see* SCALLOP

escalope ('ɛskəlɒp) *n.* thin slice of meat, usu. veal

escape (ɪ'skeɪp) *vi.* **1.** get free **2.** get off safely **3.** go unpunished **4.** find way out —*vt.* **5.** elude **6.** be forgotten by —*n.* **7.** escaping —**escapade** ('ɛskəpeɪd, ɛskə'peɪd) *n.* wild (mischievous) adventure —**es'capement** *n.* **1.** mechanism consisting of toothed wheel and anchor, used in timepieces to provide periodic impulses to pendulum or balance **2.** any similar mechanism that regulates movement —**es'capism** n. taking refuge in fantasy to avoid facing disagreeable facts —**escapologist** (ɛskə'pɒlədʒist) n. entertainer specializing in freeing himself from confinement —**escape road** road provided on hill for driver to drive into if his brakes fail —**escape velocity** minimum velocity necessary for a body to escape from the gravitational field of the earth *etc.*

escarp (ɪ'skɑːp) n. steep bank under rampart —**es'carpment** n. **1.** steep hillside **2.** escarp

-escent (*a. comb. form*) beginning to be, do, show *etc.*, as in *convalescent, luminescent* —**-escence** (*n. comb. form*)

eschatology (ɛskə'tɒlədʒi) n. study of death, judgment and last things —**eschato'logical** a.

escheat (ɪs'tʃiːt) *Law* n. **1.** before 1926, reversion of property to Crown in absence of legal heirs **2.** property so reverting —v. **3.** take (land) by escheat or (of land) revert by escheat —**es'cheatable** a. —**es'cheatage** n.

eschew (ɪs'tʃuː) vt. avoid, abstain from, shun

eschscholtzia (ɪs'kɒlʃə) n. garden plant with bright flowers, California poppy

escort ('ɛskɔːt) n. **1.** armed guard for traveller *etc.* **2.** person or persons accompanying another —vt. (ɪs'kɔːt) **3.** accompany or attend as escort

escritoire (ɛskrɪ'twɑː) n. type of writing desk

esculent ('ɛskjʊlənt) a. edible

escutcheon (ɪs'kʌtʃən) n. **1.** shield with coat of arms **2.** ornamental plate round keyhole *etc.* —**blot on one's escutcheon** stain on one's honour

-ese (*comb. form*) place of origin, language, style, as in *Cantonese, Japanese, journalese*

Eskimo ('ɛskɪməʊ) n. **1.** one of aboriginal race inhabiting N Amer., Greenland *etc.* (*pl.* **-s**) **2.** their language

E.S.N. educationally subnormal

esoteric (ɛsəʊ'tɛrɪk) a. abstruse, obscure **2.** secret **3.** restricted to initiates

E.S.P. extrasensory perception

esp. especially

espadrille (ɛspə'drɪl) n. canvas shoe, *esp.* with braided cord sole

espalier (ɪ'spæljə) n. **1.** shrub, (fruit) tree trained to grow flat, as against wall *etc.* **2.** trellis for this

esparto *or* **esparto grass** (ɛ'spɑːtəʊ) n. kind of grass yielding fibre used for making rope *etc.*

especial (ɪ'spɛʃəl) a. **1.** pre-eminent, more than ordinary **2.** particular —**es'pecially** adv.

Esperanto (ɛspə'ræntəʊ) n. artificial language designed for universal use —**Espe'rantist** n. one who uses Esperanto

espionage ('ɛspɪənɑːʒ) n. **1.** spying **2.** use of secret agents

esplanade (ɛsplə'neɪd) n. level space, *esp.* used as public promenade

espouse (ɪ'spaʊz) vt. **1.** support, embrace (cause *etc.*) **2.** *obs.* marry —**es'pousal** n.

espresso (ɛ'sprɛsəʊ) n. strong coffee made by forcing steam through ground coffee beans

esprit (ɛ'spriː) n. **1.** spirit **2.** animation —**esprit de corps** (də 'kɔː) attachment, loyalty to the society *etc.* one belongs to

espy (ɪ'spaɪ) vt. catch sight of (**es'pied, es'pying**) —**es'pial** n. observation

Esq. Esquire

-esque (*comb. form*) specified character, manner, style or resemblance, as in *picturesque, Romanesque, statuesque*

esquire (ɪ'skwaɪə) n. **1.** gentleman's courtesy title used on letters **2.** formerly, squire

ESRO ('ɛzrəʊ) European Space Research Organization

-ess (*comb. form*) female, as in *actress*

essay ('ɛseɪ; *def. 3 also* ɛ'seɪ) n. **1.** prose composition **2.** short treatise **3.** attempt —vt. (ɛ'seɪ) **4.** try, attempt **5.** test (**es'sayed, es'saying**) —'**essayist** n.

essence ('ɛsns) n. **1.** all that makes thing what it is **2.** existence, being **3.** entity, reality **4.** extract got by distillation —**es'sential** a. **1.** necessary, indispensable **2.** inherent **3.** of, constituting essence of thing —n. **4.** indispensable element **5.** chief point —**essenti'ality** n. —**essential oil** any of various volatile oils in plants, having odour *etc.* of plant from which they are extracted

E.S.T. C, US Eastern Standard Time

est. 1. established **2.** estimate(d)

-est (*comb. form*) forming superlative degree of adjective or adverb, as in *fastest*

establish (ɪ'stæblɪʃ) vt. **1.** make secure **2.** set up **3.** settle **4.** prove —**es'tablishment** n. **1.** permanent organized body, full number of regiment *etc.* **2.** household **3.** business **4.** public institution —**Established Church** church officially recognized as national institution —**the Establishment** group, class of people holding authority within a society

estate (ɪ'steɪt) n. **1.** landed property **2.** person's property **3.** area of property development, *esp.* of houses or factories **4.** class as part of nation **5.** rank, state, condition of life —**estate agent** one who sells houses *etc.* for others —**estate car** car with rear door and luggage space behind rear seats —**estate duty** *see* **death duty** *at* DEATH

esteem (ɪ'stiːm) vt. **1.** think highly of **2.** consider —n. **3.** favourable opinion, regard, respect

ester ('ɛstə) n. *Chem.* organic compound produced by reaction between acid and alcohol

estimate ('ɛstɪmeɪt) vt. **1.** form approximate

idea of (amounts, measurements *etc.*) **2.** form opinion of **3.** quote probable price for —*n.* ('estimit) **4.** approximate judgment of amounts *etc.* **5.** amount *etc.* arrived at **6.** opinion **7.** price quoted by contractor —**'estimable** *a.* worthy of regard —**esti'mation** *n.* **1.** opinion, judgment **2.** esteem

estrange (ı'streındʒ) *vt.* **1.** lose affection of **2.** alienate —**es'trangement** *n.*

estuary ('estjʊərı) *n.* tidal mouth of river, inlet —**'estuarine** *a.*

-et (*comb. form*) small, lesser, as in *islet*, *baronet*

eta ('iːtə) *n.* seventh letter in Gr. alphabet (H, η)

E.T.A. estimated time of arrival

et al. 1. et alibi (*Lat.*, and elsewhere) **2.** et alii (*Lat.*, and others)

etc. et cetera

et cetera (ıt 'setrə) *Lat.* and the rest, and others, and so on —**et'ceteras** *pl.n.* miscellaneous extras

etch (etʃ) *v.* **1.** make (engraving) by eating away surface of metal plate with acids *etc.* —*vt.* **2.** imprint vividly —**'etcher** *n.* —**'etching** *n.*

eternal (ı'tɜːnəl) *a.* **1.** without beginning or end **2.** everlasting **3.** changeless —**e'ternally** *adv.* —**e'ternity** *n.* —**eternal triangle** emotional relationship in which there are conflicts involving a man and two women or a woman and two men —**eternity ring** ring, *esp.* one set all around with stones to symbolize continuity

ethane ('iːθeın, 'eθ-) *n.* odourless flammable gaseous alkane obtained from natural gas and petroleum

ether ('iːθə) *n.* **1.** colourless volatile liquid used as anaesthetic **2.** intangible fluid formerly supposed to fill all space **3.** the clear sky, region above clouds —**ethereal** (ı'θıərıəl) *a.* **1.** light, airy **2.** heavenly, spiritlike —**ethereality** (ıθıərı'ælıtı) *n.* —**ethereali'zation** *or* **-i'sation** *n.* —**etherealize** *or* **-ise** (ı'θıərıəlaız) *vt.* **1.** make or regard as being ethereal **2.** add ether to or make into ether

ethic ('eθık) *or* **ethical** *a.* relating to morals —**'ethically** *adv.* —**'ethics** *pl.n.* **1.** (*with sing. v.*) science of morals **2.** moral principles, rules of conduct

Ethiopian (iːθı'əʊpıən) *a.* **1.** of Ethiopia (state in NE Afr.) —*n.* **2.** native of Ethiopia **3.** any of languages of Ethiopia, *esp.* Amharic —*n./a.* **4.** *obs.* Negro

ethnic ('eθnık) *or* **ethnical** *a.* of race or relating to classification of humans into social, cultural *etc.*, groups —**ethno'graphic** —**eth'nography** *n.* description of races of men —**ethno'logical** *a.* —**eth'nology** *n.* the study of human races

ethos ('iːθɒs) *n.* distinctive character, spirit *etc.* of people, culture *etc.*

ethyl ('iːθaıl, 'eθıl) *n.* (C_2H_5) radical of ordinary alcohol and ether —**ethylene** ('eθıliːn) *n.* poisonous gas used as anaesthetic and fuel —**ethyl alcohol** *see* ALCOHOL (sense 1)

etiolate ('iːtıəʊleıt) *v.* **1.** *Bot.* whiten (green plant) through lack of sunlight **2.** (cause to) become pale and weak —**etio'lation** *n.*

etiquette ('etıket, etı'ket) *n.* conventional code of conduct or behaviour

Eton collar ('iːtən) broad stiff white collar worn outside Eton jacket

Eton crop short mannish hair style worn by women in 1920s

Eton jacket waist-length jacket, open in front, formerly worn by pupils of Eton College, public school for boys in S England

Etruscan (ı'trʌskən) *or* **Etrurian** (ı'trʊərıən) *n.* **1.** member of ancient people of Etruria in central Italy **2.** language of ancient Etruscans —*a.* **3.** of Etruria, Etruscans, their culture or their language

et seq. 1. et sequens (*Lat.*, and the following) **2.** (*also* **et seqq.**) et sequentia (*Lat.*, and those that follow)

-ette (*comb. form*) **1.** small, as in *cigarette* **2.** female, as in *majorette* **3.** imitation, as in *Leatherette*

étude ('eıtjuːd) *n.* short musical composition, study, intended often as technical exercise

ety., etym., *or* **etymol. 1.** etymological **2.** etymology

etymology (etı'mɒlədʒı) *n.* **1.** tracing, account of, formation of word's origin, development **2.** science of this —**etymo'logical** *a.* —**etymo'logically** *adv.* —**ety'mologist** *n.*

Eu *Chem.* europium

eu- (*comb. form*) well, as in *eugenic, euphony*

eucalyptus (juːkə'lıptəs) *or* **eucalypt** ('juːkəlıpt) *n.* mostly Aust. genus of tree, the gum tree, yielding timber and oil, used medicinally from leaves

Eucharist ('juːkərıst) *n.* **1.** Christian sacrament of the Lord's Supper **2.** the consecrated elements —**Eucha'ristic** *a.*

Euclidean *or* **Euclidian** (juː'klıdıən) *a.* denoting system of geometry based on axioms of Gr. mathematician Euclid

eugenic (juː'dʒenık) *a.* relating to, or tending towards, production of fine offspring —**eu'genicist** *n.* —**eu'genics** *pl.n.* (*with sing. v.*) this science

eulogy ('juːlədʒı) *n.* **1.** speech or writing in praise of person **2.** praise —**'eulogist** *n.* —**eulo'gistic** *a.* —**eulo'gistically** *adv.* —**'eulogize** *or* **-ise** *v.*

eunuch ('juːnək) *n.* castrated man, *esp.* formerly one employed in harem

euphemism ('juːfɪmɪzəm) *n.* 1. substitution of mild term for offensive or hurtful one 2. instance of this —'**euphemist** *n.* —**euphe'mistic** *a.* —**euphe'mistically** *adv.* —'**euphemize** *or* -**ise** *v.*

euphony ('juːfənɪ) *n.* pleasantness of sound —**euphonic** (juː'fɒnɪk) *or* **euphonious** (juː'fəʊnɪəs) *a.* pleasing to ear —**euphonium** (juː'fəʊnɪəm) *n.* brass musical instrument, basstenor tuba

euphoria (juː'fɔːrɪə) *n.* sense of wellbeing or elation —**euphoric** (juː'fɒrɪk) *a.*

euphuism ('juːfjuːɪzəm) *n.* affected high-flown manner of writing, *esp.* in imitation of Lyly's *Euphues* (1580) —**euphu'istic** *a.*

Eur. Europe(an)

Eurasian (jʊə'reɪʃən, -ʒən) *a.* 1. of mixed European and Asiatic descent 2. of Europe and Asia —*n.* 3. one of this descent

Euratom (jʊə'rætɒm) *n.* European Atomic Energy Commission

eureka (jʊ'riːkə) *interj.* exclamation of triumph at finding something

eurhythmics *or esp. U.S.* **eurythmics** (juː'rɪðmɪks) *pl.n.* (*with sing. v.*) system of training through physical movement to music —**eu'rhythmy** *or* **eu'rythmy** *n.*

Euro- ('jʊərəʊ-) *or before vowel* **Eur-** (*comb. form*) Europe; European

Eurodollar ('jʊərəʊdɒlə) *n.* U.S. dollar as part of European holding

European (jʊərə'pɪən) *n./a.* (native) of Europe —**European Atomic Energy Commission** authority established by Common Market to develop peaceful uses of nuclear energy —**European Economic Community** association of a number of European nations for trade

europium (jʊ'rəʊpɪəm) *n.* silvery-white element of the lanthanide series

eurythmics (juː'rɪðmɪks) *n. esp. US see* EURHYTHMICS

Eustachian tube (juː'steɪʃən) passage leading from pharynx to middle ear

euthanasia (juːθə'neɪzɪə) *n.* 1. gentle, painless death 2. putting to death in this way, *esp.* to relieve suffering

euthenics (juː'θɛnɪks) *pl.n.* (*with sing. v.*) science of the relation of environment to human beings

eV electronvolt

evacuate (ɪ'vækjʊeɪt) *vt.* 1. empty 2. cause to withdraw 3. discharge —**evacu'ation** *n.* —**evacu'ee** *n.* person moved from danger area, *esp.* in time of war

evade (ɪ'veɪd) *vt.* 1. avoid, escape from 2. elude —**e'vasion** *n.* 1. subterfuge 2. excuse 3.

equivocation —**e'vasive** *a.* elusive, not straightforward —**e'vasively** *adv.*

evaluate (ɪ'væljʊeɪt) *vt.* find or judge value of —**evalu'ation** *n.*

evanesce (evə'nes) *vi.* fade away —**eva'nescence** *n.* —**eva'nescent** *a.* fleeting, transient

evangelical (iːvæn'dʒelɪkəl) *a.* 1. of, or according to, gospel teaching 2. of Protestant sect which maintains salvation by faith —*n.* 3. member of evangelical sect —**evan'gelicalism** *n.* —**e'vangelism** *n.* —**e'vangelist** *n.* 1. writer of one of the four gospels 2. ardent, zealous preacher of the gospel 3. revivalist —**evangeli-'zation** *or* -**i'sation** *n.* —**e'vangelize** *or* -**ise** *vt.* 1. preach gospel to 2. convert

evaporate (ɪ'væpəreɪt) *vi.* 1. turn into, pass off in, vapour —*vt.* 2. turn into vapour —**evapo'ration** *n.* —**e'vaporative** *a.* —**e'vaporator** *n.* —**evaporated milk** thick unsweetened tinned milk from which some of the water has been evaporated

evasion (ɪ'veɪʒən) *n. see* EVADE

eve (iːv) *n.* 1. evening before (festival *etc.*) 2. time just before (event *etc.*) 3. *obs.* evening —'**even** *n. obs.* evening —'**evensong** *n.* evening prayer

even[1] ('iːvən) *a.* 1. flat, smooth 2. uniform in quality, equal in amount, balanced 3. divisible by two 4. impartial —*vt.* 5. make even 6. smooth 7. equalize —*adv.* 8. equally 9. simply 10. notwithstanding —'**evens** *as/adv.* 1. (of bet) winning identical sum if successful 2. (of runner) offered at such odds —**even-handed** *a.* fair; impartial —**even-handedly** *adv.* —**even-handedness** *n.*

even[2] ('iːvən) *n. obs.* eve; evening

evening ('iːvnɪŋ) *n.* 1. the close of day or early part of night 2. decline, end —**evening dress** attire for formal occasion during evening —**evening star** planet, usu. Venus, seen in west just after sunset

event (ɪ'vent) *n.* 1. happening 2. notable occurrence 3. issue, result 4. any one contest in series in sporting programme —**e'ventful** *a.* full of exciting events —**e'venting** *n. chiefly UK* sport of taking part in equestrian competitions, usu. involving cross-country riding, jumping and dressage —**e'ventual** *a.* 1. resulting in the end 2. ultimate 3. final —**eventu'ality** *n.* possible event —**e'ventually** *adv.* —**e'ventuate** *vi.* 1. turn out 2. happen 3. end —**in the event that** if it should happen that

ever ('evə) *adv.* 1. always 2. constantly 3. at any time —**ever'more** *adv.* —'**evergreen** *n./a.* (tree or shrub) bearing foliage throughout year —**ever'lasting** *a.* 1. eternal 2. lasting for an indefinitely long period —**ever'lastingly** *adv.*

every ('evrɪ) *a.* 1. each of all 2. all possible

—'**everybody** *pron.* —'**everyday** *a.* usual, ordinary —'**Everyman** *n.* (*oft.* e-) ordinary person; common man —'**everyone** *pron.* —'**everything** *pron.* —'**everywhere** *adv.* to or in all places

evict (ɪ'vɪkt) *vt.* expel by legal process, turn out —e'**viction** *n.* —e'**victor** *n.*

evident ('ɛvɪdənt) *a.* plain, obvious —'**evidence** *n.* 1. ground of belief 2. sign, indication 3. testimony —*vt.* 4. indicate, prove —evi'**dential** *a.* —'**evidently** *adv.* —in **evidence** conspicuous

evil ('iːvəl) *a.* 1. bad, harmful —*n.* 2. what is bad or harmful 3. sin —'**evilly** *adv.* —'**evildoer** *n.* sinner —**evil-eyed** *a.* —**the evil eye** 1. look superstitiously supposed to have power of inflicting harm *etc.* 2. power to inflict harm *etc.* by such a look

evince (ɪ'vɪns) *vt.* show, indicate

eviscerate (ɪ'vɪsəreɪt) *vt.* 1. remove internal organs of 2. deprive of meaning or significance —evisceri'**ation** *n.* —e'**viscerator** *n.*

evoke (ɪ'vəʊk) *vt.* 1. draw forth 2. call to mind —**evocation** (ɛvəʊ'keɪʃən) *n.* —**evocative** (ɪ'vɒkətɪv) *a.*

evolve (ɪ'vɒlv) *v.* 1. develop or cause to develop gradually —*vi.* 2. undergo slow changes in process of growth —**evolution** (iːvə'luːʃən) *n.* 1. evolving 2. development of species from earlier forms —**evolutional** (iːvə'luːʃənəl) *a.* —**evolutionary** (iːvə'luːʃənərɪ) *a.* —**evolutionist** (iːvə'luːʃənɪst) *n.*

ewe (juː) *n.* female sheep

ewer ('juːə) *n.* pitcher, water jug for washstand

ex¹ (ɛks) *prep.* 1. *Fin.* excluding; without 2. *Comm.* without charge to buyer until removed from —**ex cathedra** (kə'θiːdrə) 1. with authority 2. (of papal pronouncements) defined as infallibly true —**ex gratia** ('greɪʃə) given as favour, *esp.* where no legal obligation exists —**ex hypothesi** (haɪ'pɒθəsɪ) in accordance with hypothesis stated —**ex libris** ('liːbrɪs) from the library of —**ex officio** (ə'fɪʃɪəʊ, ə'fɪsɪəʊ) by right of position or office —**ex post facto** ('fæktəʊ) having retrospective effect

ex² (ɛks) *n. inf.* ex-wife, ex-husband *etc.*

ex-, e-, or ef- (*comb. form*) out from, from, out of, formerly, as in *exclaim, evade, effusive, exodus.* Such words are not given here where the meaning may easily be inferred from the simple word

Ex. Exodus

ex. 1. example 2. except(ed) 3. extra

exacerbate (ɪg'zæsəbeɪt, ɪk'sæs-) *vt.* 1. aggravate, make worse 2. embitter —exacer'**bation** *n.*

exact (ɪg'zækt) *a.* 1. precise, accurate, strictly correct —*vt.* 2. demand, extort 3. insist upon 4. enforce —ex'**acting** *a.* making rigorous or

excessive demands —ex'**action** *n.* 1. act of exacting 2. that which is exacted, as excessive work *etc.* 3. oppressive demand —ex'**actitude** *n.* —ex'**actly** *adv.* —ex'**actness** *n.* 1. accuracy 2. precision —ex'**actor** *n.*

exaggerate (ɪg'zædʒəreɪt) *vt.* 1. magnify beyond truth, overstate 2. enlarge 3. overestimate —**exagger'ation** *n.* —ex'**aggerative** *a.* —ex'**aggerator** *n.*

exalt (ɪg'zɔːlt) *vt.* 1. raise up 2. praise 3. make noble, dignify —**exal'tation** *n.* 1. an exalting 2. elevation in rank, dignity or position 3. rapture

exam (ɪg'zæm) examination

examine (ɪg'zæmɪn) *vt.* 1. investigate 2. look at closely 3. ask questions of 4. test knowledge or proficiency of 5. inquire into —**exami'nation** *n.* —**exami'nee** *n.* —ex'**aminer** *n.*

example (ɪg'zɑːmpl) *n.* 1. thing illustrating general rule 2. specimen 3. model 4. warning 5. precedent 6. instance

exasperate (ɪg'zɑːspəreɪt) *vt.* 1. irritate, enrage 2. intensify, make worse —**exasper'ation** *n.*

excavate ('ɛkskəveɪt) *vt.* 1. hollow out 2. unearth 3. make (hole) by digging —**exca'vation** *n.* —'**excavator** *n.*

exceed (ɪk'siːd) *vt.* 1. be greater than 2. go beyond 3. surpass —ex'**ceeding** *a.* 1. very great; exceptional; excessive —*adv.* 2. *obs.* to a great or unusual degree —ex'**ceedingly** *adv.* 1. very 2. greatly

excel (ɪk'sɛl) *vt.* 1. surpass, be better than —*vi.* 2. be very good, pre-eminent (**-ll-**) —'**excellence** *n.* —'**Excellency** *n.* title borne by viceroys, ambassadors —'**excellant** *a.* very good

except (ɪk'sɛpt) *prep.* 1. not including 2. but —*conj.* 3. *obs.* unless —*vt.* 4. leave or take out 5. exclude —ex'**cepting** *prep.* not including —ex'**ception** *n.* 1. thing excepted, not included in a rule 2. objection —ex'**ceptionable** *a.* open to objection —ex'**ceptional** *a.* not ordinary, *esp.* much above average —ex'**ceptionally** *adv.*

excerpt ('ɛksɜːpt) *n.* 1. quoted or extracted passage from book *etc.* —*vt.* (ɛk'sɜːpt) 2. extract, quote (passage from book *etc.*) —ex'**cerption** *n.*

excess (ɪk'sɛs, 'ɛksɛs) *n.* 1. an exceeding 2. amount by which thing exceeds 3. too great amount 4. intemperance, immoderate conduct —ex'**cessive** *a.* —ex'**cessively** *adv.* —**excess luggage** *or* **baggage** luggage that is more in weight or number of items than airline *etc.* will carry free

exchange (ɪks'tʃeɪndʒ) *vt.* 1. give (something) in return for something else 2. barter —*n.* 3. giving one thing and receiving another 4. thing given for another 5. building where merchants meet for business 6. central telephone office where connections are made *etc.* —**exchange-ability** *n.* —**ex'changeable** *a.* —**exchange rate** rate at which currency unit of one country may be exchanged for that of another

exchequer (ıks'tʃɛkə) *n.* government department in charge of revenue

excise[1] ('ɛksaız, ɛk'saız) *n.* duty charged on home goods during manufacture or before sale

excise[2] (ık'saız) *vt.* cut out, cut away —**excision** (ɛk'sıʒən) *n.*

excite (ık'saıt) *vt.* 1. arouse to strong emotion, stimulate 2. rouse up, set in motion 3. *Elec.* magnetize poles of —**excita'bility** *n.* —**ex'citable** *a.* —**ex'citably** *adv.* —**exci'tation** *n.* —**ex'cited** *a.* emotionally or sexually aroused —**ex'citedness** *n.* —**ex'citement** *n.* —**ex'citing** *a.* 1. thrilling 2. rousing to action

exclaim (ık'skleım) *vi.* 1. speak suddenly —*v.* 2. cry out —**exclamation** (ɛkskləˈmeıʃən) *n.* —**exclamatory** (ıks'klæmətərı) *a.* —**exclamation mark** *or U.S.* **point** punctuation mark ! used after exclamations and vehement commands

exclude (ık'sklu:d) *vt.* 1. shut out 2. debar 3. reject, not consider —**ex'clusion** *n.* —**ex'clusive** *a.* 1. excluding 2. inclined to keep out (from society *etc.*) 3. sole, only 4. select —*n.* 5. something exclusive, *esp.* story appearing only in one newspaper —**ex'clusively** *adv.*

excommunicate (ɛkskə'mju:nıkeıt) *vt.* cut off from the sacraments of the Church —**excommuni'cation** *n.*

excoriate (ık'skɔːrıeıt) *vt.* 1. strip (skin) from (person or animal) 2. denounce vehemently —**excori'ation** *n.*

excrement ('ɛkskrımənt) *n.* waste matter from body, *esp.* from bowels 2. dung —**excreta** (ık'skri:tə) *pl.n.* excrement —**excrete** (ık'skri:t) *vt.* discharge from the system —**excretion** (ık'skri:ʃən) *n.* —**excretory** (ık'skri:tərı) *a.*

excrescent (ık'skrɛsənt) *a.* 1. growing out of something 2. redundant —**ex'crescence** *n.* unnatural outgrowth

excruciate (ık'skru:ʃıeıt) *vt.* torment acutely, torture in body or mind —**ex'cruciating** *a.* —**excruci'ation** *n.*

exculpate ('ɛkskʌlpeıt, ık'skʌlpeıt) *vt.* free from blame, acquit —**excul'pation** *n.* —**ex'culpatory** *a.*

excursion (ık'skɜːʃən, -ʒən) *n.* 1. journey, ramble, trip for pleasure 2. digression —**ex'cursive** *a.* 1. tending to digress 2. involving detours —**ex'cursiveness** *n.* —**ex'cursus** *n.* digression (*pl.* **-es, -sus** (*rare*))

excuse (ık'skju:z) *vt.* 1. forgive, overlook 2. try to clear from blame 3. seek exemption for 4. set free, remit —*n.* (ık'skju:s) 5. that which serves to excuse 6. apology —**ex'cusable** *a.*

exeat ('ɛksıət) *n. UK* 1. leave of absence from school 2. bishop's permission for priest to leave diocese to take up appointment elsewhere

exec. 1. executive 2. executor

execrate ('ɛksıkreıt) *vt.* 1. loathe, detest 2. denounce, deplore 3. curse —**'execrable** *a.* abominable, hatefully bad —**exe'cration** *n.* —**'execrative** *or* **'execratory** *a.*

execute ('ɛksıkju:t) *vt.* 1. inflict capital punishment on, kill 2. carry out, perform 3. make, produce 4. sign (document) —**ex'ecutant** *n.* performer, *esp.* of music —**exe'cution** *n.* —**exe'cutioner** *n.* one employed to execute criminals —**ex'ecutive** *n.* 1. person in administrative position 2. executive body 3. committee carrying on business of society *etc.* —*a.* 4. carrying into effect, *esp.* of branch of government enforcing laws —**ex'ecutor** *n.* person appointed to carry out provisions of a will (**ex'ecutrix** *fem.*)

exegesis (ɛksı'dʒiːsıs) *n.* explanation, *esp.* of Scripture (*pl.* **-geses** (-'dʒiːsiːz)) —**exegetic(al)** (ɛksı'dʒɛtık(ə)l) *a.*

exemplar (ıg'zɛmplə, -plɑː) *n.* model type —**ex'emplarily** *adv.* —**ex'emplary** *a.* 1. fit to be imitated, serving as example 2. commendable 3. typical —**exemplifi'cation** *n.* —**ex'emplify** *vt.* 1. serve as example of 2. illustrate 3. exhibit 4. make attested copy of (**-fied, -fying**)

exempt (ıg'zɛmpt) *vt.* 1. free 2. excuse —*a.* 3. freed (from), not liable (for) 4. not affected (by) —**ex'emption** *n.*

exequies ('ɛksıkwız) *pl.n.* funeral rites or procession

exercise ('ɛksəsaız) *vt.* 1. use, employ 2. give exercise to 3. carry out, discharge 4. trouble, harass —*vi.* 5. take exercise —*n.* 6. use of limbs for health 7. practice for training 8. task for training 9. lesson 10. employment 11. use (of limbs, faculty *etc.*)

exert (ıg'zɜːt) *vt.* 1. apply (oneself) diligently, make effort 2. bring to bear —**ex'ertion** *n.* effort, physical activity

exeunt ('ɛksıʌnt) *Lat. Theat.* they leave the stage: stage direction —**exeunt omnes** ('ɒmneız) they all go out

exfoliate (ɛks'fəʊlıeıt) *v.* peel in scales, layers

exhale (ɛks'heıl, ıg'zeıl) *v.* 1. breathe out 2. give, pass off as vapour

exhaust (ıg'zɔːst) *vt.* 1. tire out 2. use up 3. empty 4. draw off 5. treat, discuss thoroughly —*n.* 6. used steam or fluid from engine 7. waste gases from internal-combustion engine 8. passage for, or coming out of this —**exhaust-i'bility** *n.* —**ex'haustible** *a.* —**ex'haustion** *n.* 1. state of extreme fatigue 2. limit of endurance —**ex'haustive** *a.* comprehensive

exhibit (ıg'zıbıt) *vt.* 1. show, display 2. manifest

3. show publicly (oft. in competition) —*n.* **4.** thing shown, *esp.* in competition or as evidence in court —**exhi'bition** *n.* **1.** display, act of displaying **2.** public show (of works of art *etc.*) —**exhi'bitionism** *n.* —**exhi'bitionist** *n.* one with compulsive desire to draw attention to himself or to expose genitals publicly —**exhibition'istic** *a.* —**ex'hibitor** *n.* one who exhibits, *esp.* in show —**ex'hibitory** *a.*

exhilarate (ɪgˈzɪləreɪt) *vt.* enliven, gladden —**exhila'ration** *n.* high spirits, enlivenment

exhort (ɪgˈzɔːt) *vt.* urge, admonish earnestly —**exhor'tation** *n.* —**ex'horter** *n.*

exhume (ɛksˈhjuːm) *vt.* unearth (what has been buried), disinter —**exhu'mation** *n.*

exigent (ˈɛksɪdʒənt) *a.* **1.** exacting **2.** urgent, pressing —**'exigence** *or* **'exigency** *n.* **1.** pressing need **2.** emergency —**'exigible** *a.* liable to be exacted or demanded

exiguous (ɪgˈzɪgjʊəs, ɪkˈsɪg-) *a.* scanty, meagre

exile (ˈɛgzaɪl, ˈɛksaɪl) *n.* **1.** banishment, expulsion from one's own country **2.** long absence abroad **3.** one banished or permanently living away from his home or country —*vt.* **4.** banish, expel

exist (ɪgˈzɪst) *vi.* be, have being, live —**ex'istence** *n.* —**ex'istent** *a.*

existential (ɛgzɪˈstɛnʃəl) *a.* **1.** of existence **2.** *Philos.* based on personal experience **3.** of existentialism —**exis'tentialism** *n.* theory which holds that man is free and responsible for his own acts

exit (ˈɛgzɪt, ˈɛksɪt) *n.* **1.** way out **2.** going out **3.** death **4.** actor's departure from stage —*vi.* **5.** go out

exo- (*comb. form*) external, outside, or beyond, as in *exothermal*

exocrine (ˈɛksəʊkraɪn) *a.* of gland (*eg* salivary, sweat) secreting its products through ducts

Exod. *Bible* Exodus

exodus (ˈɛksədəs) *n.* **1.** departure, *esp.* of crowd **2.** (E-) second book of Old Testament

exonerate (ɪgˈzɒnəreɪt) *vt.* **1.** free, declare free, from blame **2.** exculpate **3.** acquit —**exoner'ation** *n.* —**ex'onerative** *a.*

exorbitant (ɪgˈzɔːbɪtənt) *a.* very excessive, inordinate, immoderate —**ex'orbitance** *n.* —**ex'orbitantly** *adv.*

exorcise *or* **-ize** (ˈɛksɔːsaɪz) *vt.* cast out (evil spirits) by invocation **2.** free (person) of evil spirits —**exorcism** (ˈɛksɔːsɪzəm) *n.* —**exorcist** (ˈɛksɔːsɪst) *n.*

exordium (ɛkˈsɔːdɪəm) *n.* introductory part of a speech or treatise (*pl.* **-s**, **-ia** (-ɪə)) —**ex'ordial** *a.*

exoteric (ɛksəʊˈtɛrɪk) *a.* **1.** understandable by the many **2.** ordinary, popular

exotic (ɪgˈzɒtɪk) *a.* **1.** brought in from abroad, foreign **2.** rare, unusual, having strange or bizarre allure —*n.* **3.** exotic plant *etc.* —**ex'otica** *pl.n.* (collection of) exotic objects —**ex'oticism** *n.* —**exotic dancer** striptease or belly dancer

expand (ɪkˈspænd) *v.* **1.** increase **2.** spread out **3.** dilate **4.** develop —**ex'pandable** or **ex'pandible** *a.* —**ex'panse** *n.* **1.** wide space **2.** open stretch of land —**expansi'bility** *n.* —**ex'pansible** *a.* —**ex'pansion** *n.* —**ex'pansionism** *n.* practice of expanding economy or territory of country —**ex'pansionist** *n./a.* —**expansion'istic** *a.* —**ex'pansive** *a.* **1.** wide **2.** extensive **3.** friendly, talkative

expatiate (ɪkˈspeɪʃɪeɪt) *vi.* **1.** speak or write at great length **2.** enlarge —**expati'ation** *n.*

expatriate (ɛksˈpætrɪeɪt) *vt.* **1.** banish, exile **2.** withdraw (oneself) from one's native land —*a./n.* (ɛksˈpætrɪɪt, -eɪt) **3.** (person) exiled or banished from his native country —**expatri'ation** *n.*

expect (ɪkˈspɛkt) *vt.* **1.** regard as probable **2.** look forward to **3.** await **4.** hope for —**ex'pectancy** *n.* **1.** state or act of expecting **2.** that which is expected **3.** hope —**ex'pectant** *a.* looking or waiting for, *esp.* for birth of child —**ex'pectantly** *adv.* —**expec'tation** *n.* **1.** act or state of expecting **2.** prospect of future good **3.** what is expected **4.** promise **5.** value of something expected —*pl.* **6.** prospect of fortune or profit by will

expectorate (ɪkˈspɛktəreɪt) *v.* spit out (phlegm *etc.*) —**ex'pectorant** *Med. a.* **1.** promoting secretion, liquefaction or expulsion of sputum from respiratory passages —*n.* **2.** expectorant drug or agent —**expecto'ration** *n.*

expedient (ɪkˈspiːdɪənt) *a.* **1.** fitting, advisable, politic, suitable, convenient —*n.* **2.** something suitable, useful, *esp.* in emergency —**ex'pediency** *n.* —**ex'pediently** *adv.*

expedite (ˈɛkspɪdaɪt) *vt.* **1.** help on, hasten **2.** dispatch —**expedition** (ɛkspɪˈdɪʃən) *n.* **1.** journey for definite (oft. scientific or military) purpose **2.** people, equipment comprising expedition **3.** excursion **4.** promptness —**expeditionary** (ɛkspɪˈdɪʃənərɪ) *a.* —**expeditious** (ɛkspɪˈdɪʃəs) *a.* prompt, speedy

expel (ɪkˈspɛl) *vt.* **1.** drive, cast out **2.** exclude **3.** discharge (**-ll-**) —**expulsion** (ɪkˈspʌlʃən) *n.* —**expulsive** (ɪkˈspʌlsɪv) *a.*

expend (ɪkˈspɛnd) *vt.* **1.** spend, pay out **2.** use up —**ex'pendable** *a.* likely, or meant, to be used up or destroyed —**ex'penditure** *n.* —**ex'pense** *n.* **1.** cost **2.** (cause of) spending —*pl.* **3.** charges, outlay incurred —**ex'pensive** *a.* high-priced, costly, dear —**expense account 1.** arrangement by which expenses are refunded to employee by employer **2.** record of such expenses

experience (ɪkˈspɪərɪəns) *n.* **1.** observation of

facts as source of knowledge **2.** being affected consciously by event **3.** the event **4.** knowledge, skill, gained from life, by contact with facts and events —*vt.* **5.** undergo, suffer, meet with —**ex'perienced** *a.* skilled, expert, capable —**experi'ential** *a.*

experiment (ɪk'spɛrɪmənt) *n.* **1.** test, trial, something done in the hope that it may succeed, or to test theory —*vi.* (ɪk'spɛrɪmɛnt) **2.** make experiment —**experi'mental** *a.* —**experi'mentalist** *n.* —**experi'mentally** *adv.*

expert ('ɛkspɜːt) *n.* **1.** one skilful, knowledgeable, in something **2.** authority —*a.* **3.** practised, skilful —**expertise** (ɛkspɜː'tiːz) *n.*

expiate ('ɛkspɪeɪt) *vt.* **1.** pay penalty for **2.** make amends for —**expi'ation** *n.* —**'expiator** *n.* —**'expiatory** *a.*

expire (ɪk'spaɪə) *vi.* **1.** come to an end **2.** give out breath **3.** die —*vt.* **4.** breathe out —**expiration** (ɛkspɪ'reɪʃən) *n.* —**ex'piratory** *a.* —**ex'piry** *n.* end

explain (ɪk'spleɪn) *vt.* **1.** make clear, intelligible **2.** interpret **3.** elucidate **4.** give details of **5.** account for —**explanation** (ɛksplə'neɪʃən) *n.* —**explanatory** (ɪks'plænətərɪ, -trɪ) *or* **explanative** (ɪks'plænətɪv) *a.*

expletive (ɪk'spliːtɪv) *n.* **1.** exclamation **2.** oath —*a.* **3.** serving only to fill out sentence *etc.*

explicable ('ɛksplɪkəbəl, ɪk'splɪk-) *a.* explainable —**'explicate** *vt.* develop, explain —**ex'plicative** *or* **ex'plicatory** *a.*

explicit (ɪk'splɪsɪt) *a.* **1.** stated in detail **2.** stated, not merely implied **3.** outspoken **4.** clear, plain **5.** unequivocal

explode (ɪk'spləʊd) *vi.* **1.** go off with bang **2.** burst violently **3.** (of population) increase rapidly —*vt.* **4.** make explode **5.** discredit, expose (a theory *etc.*) —**ex'plosion** *n.* —**ex'plosive** *a./n.*

exploit ('ɛksplɔɪt) *n.* **1.** brilliant feat, deed —*vt.* (ɪk'splɔɪt) **2.** turn to advantage **3.** make use of for one's own ends —**exploi'tation** *n.* —**ex'ploiter** *n.*

explore (ɪk'splɔː) *vt.* **1.** investigate **2.** examine **3.** scrutinize **4.** examine (country *etc.*) by going through it —**explo'ration** *n.* —**exploratory** (ɪk'splɔrətərɪ, -trɪ) *a.* —**ex'plorer** *n.*

explosion (ɪk'spləʊʒən) *n. see* EXPLODE

expo ('ɛkspəʊ) *n. inf.* exposition, large international exhibition

exponent (ɪk'spəʊnənt) *n. see* EXPOUND

export (ɪk'spɔːt, 'ɛkspɔːt) *vt.* **1.** send (goods) out of the country —*n./a.* ('ɛkspɔːt) **2.** (of) goods or services sold to foreign country or countries —**expor'tation** *n.* —**ex'porter** *n.*

expose (ɪk'spəʊz) *vt.* **1.** exhibit **2.** disclose, reveal **3.** lay open **4.** leave unprotected **5.** subject (photographic plate or film) to light —**ex'posed** *a.* **1.** not concealed **2.** without shelter from the elements **3.** vulnerable —**exposedness** (ɪk-'spəʊzɪdnɪs) *n.* —**ex'posure** *n.* **1.** act of exposing or condition of being exposed **2.** position or outlook of building **3.** lack of shelter from weather, *esp.* cold **4.** exposed surface **5.** *Photog.* act of exposing film or plate to light *etc.*; area on film or plate that has been exposed **6.** *Photog.* intensity of light falling on film or plate multiplied by time of exposure; combination of lens aperture and shutter speed used in taking photograph **7.** appearance before public, as on TV

exposé (ɛks'pəʊzeɪ) *n.* newspaper article *etc.* disclosing scandal, crime *etc.*

exposition (ɛkspə'zɪʃən) *n. see* EXPOUND

expostulate (ɪk'spɒstjʊleɪt) *vi.* **1.** remonstrate **2.** reason (in a kindly manner) —**expostu'lation** *n.* —**ex'postulatory** *a.*

expound (ɪk'spaʊnd) *vt.* explain, interpret —**exponent** (ɪk'spəʊnənt) *n.* **1.** one who expounds or promotes (idea, cause *etc.*) **2.** performer, executant **3.** *Maths.* small, raised number showing the power of a factor —**expo'nential** *n.* —**expo'sition** *n.* **1.** explanation, description **2.** exhibition of goods *etc.* —**expositor** (ɪk'spɒzɪtə) *n.* one who explains, interpreter —**expository** (ɪks'spɒzɪtərɪ, -trɪ) *a.* explanatory

express (ɪk'sprɛs) *vt.* **1.** put into words **2.** make known or understood by words, behaviour *etc.* **3.** squeeze out —*a.* **4.** definitely stated **5.** specially designed **6.** clear **7.** positive **8.** speedy **9.** (of messenger) specially sent **10.** (of train) fast and making few stops —*adv.* **11.** specially **12.** on purpose **13.** with speed —*n.* **14.** express train or messenger **15.** rapid parcel delivery service —**ex'pressible** *a.* —**ex'pression** *n.* **1.** expressing **2.** word, phrase **3.** look, aspect **4.** feeling **5.** utterance —**ex'pressionism** *n.* theory that art depends on expression of artist's creative self, not on mere reproduction —**ex'pressive** *a.* —**ex'pressly** *adv.* —**ex'pressway** *n. esp.* US urban motorway

expresso (ɪk'sprɛsəʊ) *n. see* ESPRESSO

expropriate (ɛks'prəʊprɪeɪt) *vt.* **1.** dispossess **2.** take out of owner's hands —**expropri'ation** *n.* —**ex'propriator** *n.*

expulsion (ɪk'spʌlʃən) *n. see* EXPEL

expunge (ɪk'spʌndʒ) *vt.* strike out, erase —**ex'punction** *n.*

expurgate ('ɛkspəgeɪt) *vt.* remove objectionable parts from (book *etc.*), purge —**expur'gation** *n.* —**'expurgator** *n.* —**ex'purgatory** *a.*

exquisite (ɪk'skwɪzɪt, 'ɛkskwɪzɪt) *a.* **1.** of extreme beauty or delicacy **2.** keen, acute **3.** keenly sensitive —**ex'quisitely** *adv.*

ex-serviceman n. man who has served in the armed forces

extant (ɛk'stænt, 'ɛkstənt) a. still existing

extempore (ɪk'stɛmpərɪ) a./adv. without previous thought or preparation —**extempo'raneous** a. —**ex'temporary** a. —**extempori'zation** or **-i'sation** n. —**ex'temporize** or **-ise** vi. 1. speak without preparation —vt. 2. devise for the occasion

extend (ɪk'stɛnd) vt. 1. stretch out, lengthen 2. prolong in duration 3. widen in area, scope 4. accord, grant —vi. 5. reach 6. cover a certain area 7. have a certain range or scope 8. become larger or wider —**ex'tendible**, **ex'tendable**, **ex'tensible** or **ex'tensile** a. that can be extended —**ex'tension** n. 1. stretching out, prolongation, enlargement 2. expansion 3. continuation, additional part, as of telephone etc. —**ex'tensive** a. wide, large, comprehensive —**ex'tensor** n. straightening muscle —**ex'tent** n. 1. space or degree to which thing is extended 2. size 3. compass 4. volume —**extended family** nuclear family together with blood relatives, oft. spanning three or more generations —**extended-play** a. denoting gramophone record same size as a single but with longer playing time

extenuate (ɪk'stɛnjʊeɪt) vt. make less blameworthy, mitigate —**extenu'ation** n. —**ex'tenuatory** a.

exterior (ɪk'stɪərɪə) n. 1. the outside 2. outward appearance —a. 3. outer, outward, external —**exterior angle** 1. angle of polygon contained between one side extended and adjacent side 2. any of four angles made by transversal that are outside region between two intersected lines

exterminate (ɪk'stɜːmɪneɪt) vt. destroy utterly, annihilate, root out, eliminate —**extermi'nation** n. —**ex'terminator** n. destroyer

external (ɪk'stɜːnəl) a. outside, outward —**externali'zation**, **exteriorization** or **-isation** (ɪkstɪərɪəraɪ'zeɪʃən) n. —**ex'ternalize**, **ex'teriorize** or **-ise** vt. 1. make external 2. Psychol. attribute (one's feelings) to one's surroundings —**ex'ternally** adv.

extinct (ɪk'stɪŋkt) a. 1. having died out or come to an end 2. no longer existing 3. quenched, no longer burning —**ex'tinction** n.

extinguish (ɪk'stɪŋgwɪʃ) vt. 1. put out, quench 2. wipe out —**ex'tinguishable** a. —**ex'tinguisher** n. device, esp. spraying liquid or foam, used to put out fires

extirpate ('ɛkstɜːpeɪt) vt. 1. root out 2. destroy utterly —**extir'pation** n. —**'extirpator** n.

extol or U.S. **extoll** (ɪk'stəʊl) vt. praise highly (**-ll-**)

extort (ɪk'stɔːt) vt. 1. get by force or threats 2. wring out 3. exact —**ex'tortion** n. —**ex'tortion-**

ate a. (of prices etc.) excessive, exorbitant —**ex'tortioner** n.

extra ('ɛkstrə) a. 1. additional 2. larger, better, than usual —adv. 3. additionally 4. more than usually —n. 5. extra thing 6. something charged as additional 7. Cricket run not scored off bat 8. Cine. actor hired for crowd scenes

extra- (comb. form) beyond, as in extradition, extramural, extraterritorial. Such words are not given here where the meaning may easily be inferred from the simple word

extract (ɪk'strækt) vt. 1. take out, esp. by force 2. obtain against person's will 3. get by pressure, distillation etc. 4. deduce 5. derive 6. copy out, quote —n. ('ɛkstrækt) 7. passage from book, film etc. 8. matter got by distillation 9. concentrated solution —**ex'traction** n. 1. extracting, esp. of tooth 2. ancestry —**ex'tractor** n. —**extractor fan** device for extracting stale air, fumes etc.

extracurricular (ɛkstrəkə'rɪkjʊlə) a. 1. taking place outside normal school timetable 2. beyond regular duties etc.

extradition (ɛkstrə'dɪʃən) n. delivery, under treaty, of foreign fugitive from justice to authorities concerned —**extraditable** ('ɛkstrədaɪtəbəl) a. —**extradite** ('ɛkstrədaɪt) vt. 1. surrender (alleged offender) for trial to foreign state 2. procure extradition of

extramural (ɛkstrə'mjʊərəl) a. 1. connected with but outside normal courses etc. of university or college 2. situated outside walls or boundaries of a place

extraneous (ɪk'streɪnɪəs) a. 1. not essential 2. irrelevant 3. added from without, not belonging

extraordinary (ɪk'strɔːdnrɪ) a. 1. out of the usual course 2. additional 3. unusual, surprising, exceptional —**ex'traordinarily** adv.

extrapolate (ɪk'stræpəleɪt) v. 1. infer (something not known) from known facts 2. Maths. estimate (a value) beyond known values

extrasensory (ɛkstrə'sɛnsərɪ) a. of perception apparently gained without use of known senses

extraterrestrial (ɛkstrətɪ'rɛstrɪəl) a. of, or from outside the earth's atmosphere

extravagant (ɪk'strævɪgənt) a. 1. wasteful 2. exorbitant 3. wild, absurd —**ex'travagance** n. —**ex'travagantly** adv. —**extrava'ganza** n. elaborate, lavish, entertainment, display etc.

extravert ('ɛkstrəvɜːt) n. see EXTROVERT

extreme (ɪk'striːm) a. 1. of high or highest degree 2. severe 3. going beyond moderation 4. at the end 5. outermost —n. 6. utmost degree 7. thing at one end or the other, first and last of series —**ex'tremely** adv. —**ex'tremism** n. —**ex'tremist** n. 1. advocate of extreme measures —a. 2. of immoderate or excessive

actions, opinions *etc.* —**extremity** (ık'strɛmıtı) *n.* 1. end —*pl.* 2. hands and feet 3. utmost distress 4. extreme measures —**extreme unction** sacrament in which dying person is anointed by priest

extricate ('ɛkstrıkeıt) *vt.* disentangle, unravel, set free —**extricable** *a.* —**extri'cation** *n.*

extrinsic (ɛk'strınsık) *a.* accessory, not belonging, not intrinsic —**ex'trinsically** *adv.*

extrovert *or* **extravert** ('ɛkstrəvɜːt) *n.* one who is interested in other people and things rather than his own feelings —**extro'version** *or* **extra'version** *n.*

extrude (ık'struːd) *vt.* 1. squeeze, force out 2. (*esp.* of molten metal or plastic *etc.*) shape by squeezing through suitable nozzle or die

exuberant (ıg'zjuːbərənt) *a.* 1. high-spirited, vivacious 2. prolific, abundant, luxurious —**ex'uberance** *n.* —**ex'uberantly** *adv.*

exude (ıg'zjuːd) *vi.* 1. ooze out —*vt.* 2. give off (moisture) —**exu'dation** *n.* —**ex'udative** *a.*

exult (ıg'zʌlt) *vi.* 1. rejoice 2. triumph —**ex'ultancy** *n.* —**ex'ultant** *a.* triumphant —**exul'tation** *n.*

-ey (*comb. form*) *see* -Y¹, -Y²

eye (aı) *n.* 1. organ of sight 2. look, glance 3. attention 4. aperture 5. view 6. judgment 7. watch, vigilance 8. thing, mark resembling eye 9. slit in needle for thread —*vt.* 10. look at 11. observe —**'eyeless** *a.* —**'eyelet** *n.* small hole for rope *etc.* to pass through —**'eyeball** *n.* ball of eye —**'eyebrow** *n.* fringe of hair above eye —**eye-catcher** *n.* —**eye-catching** *a.* striking —**'eyeful** *n. inf.* 1. view, glance *etc.* 2. beautiful sight, *esp.* a woman —**'eyeglass** *n.* 1. glass to assist sight —**monocle** —*pl.* 3. *chiefly US* spectacles —**'eyehole** *n.* 1. hole through which rope *etc.* is passed 2. *inf.* cavity containing eyeball 3. peephole —**'eyelash** *n.* hair fringing eyelid —**'eyelid** *n.* either of two muscular folds of skin that can be moved to cover exposed portion of eyeball —**'eyeliner** *n.* cosmetic used to outline eyes —**eye-opener** *n. inf.* 1. surprising news 2. revealing statement —**'eyepiece** *n.* lens or lenses in optical instrument nearest eye of observer —**eye shadow** coloured cosmetic put on around the eyes —**'eyeshot** *n.* range of vision —**'eyesight** *n.* ability to see —**'eyesore** *n.* 1. ugly object 2. thing that annoys one to see —**'eyestrain** *n.* fatigue of eyes, resulting from excessive use or uncorrected defects of vision —**'eyetooth** *n.* canine tooth —**'eyewash** *n. inf.* deceptive talk *etc.*, nonsense —**'eyewitness** *n.* one who saw something for himself —**an eye for an eye** retributive justice; retaliation

eyrie ('ıərı, 'ɛərı, 'aıərı) *or* **aerie** *n.* 1. nest of bird of prey, *esp.* eagle 2. high dwelling place

F,f

f *or* **F** (ɛf) *n.* 1. sixth letter of English alphabet 2. speech sound represented by this letter, as in *fat* (*pl.* **f's, F's** *or* **Fs**)

f, f/, *or* **f:** f number

f. *Mus.* forte

f. *or* **F.** 1. female 2. *Gram.* feminine 3. folio (*pl.* **ff.** *or* **FF.**) 4. following (page) (*pl.* **ff.**) 5. franc 6. furlong

F 1. *Mus.* fourth note of scale of C major; major or minor key having this note as tonic 2. Fahrenheit 3. *Chem.* fluorine 4. *Phys.* force 5. farad 6. *Genetics* generation of filial offspring, F_1 being first generation 7. Fellow

fa (faː) *n. see* FAH

FA Football Association

Fabian ('feıbıən) *a.* 1. of or resembling delaying tactics of Q. Fabius Maximus, Roman general; cautious —*n.* 2. member of Fabian Society, socialist organization advocating gradual reforms

fable ('feıb³l) *n.* 1. short story with moral, *esp.* one with animals as characters 2. tale 3. legend 4. fiction; lie —*v.* 5. tell (fables) —*vi.* 6. tell lies —*vt.* 7. talk of in manner of fable —**fabulist** ('fæbjʊlıst) *n.* writer of fables —**fabulous** ('fæbjʊləs) *a.* 1. amazing 2. *inf.* extremely good 3. told of in fables

fabric ('fæbrık) *n.* 1. cloth 2. texture 3. frame, structure —**'fabricate** *vt.* 1. build 2. frame 3. construct 4. invent (lie *etc.*) 5. forge (document) —**fabri'cation** *n.* —**'fabricator** *n.*

façade *or* **facade** (fə'sɑːd, fæ-) *n.* 1. front of building 2. *fig.* outward appearance

face (feıs) *n.* 1. front of head 2. distorted expression 3. outward appearance 4. front, upper surface or chief side of anything 5. dial of a clock *etc.* 6. dignity 7. *inf.* make-up (*esp.* in **put one's face on**) 8. *Print.* printing surface of type character; style or design of character on type (*also* **'typeface**) —*vt.* 9. look or front towards 10. meet (boldly) 11. give a covering surface to —*vi.* 12. turn —**'faceless** *a.* 1. without a face 2. anonymous —**'facer** *n.* 1. person or thing that faces 2. *UK inf.* difficulty, problem —**facet** ('fæsıt) *n.* 1. one side of many-sided body, *esp.* cut gem 2. one aspect —**facial** ('feıʃəl) *a.* 1. pert. to face —*n.* 2. cosmetic treatment for face —**'facing** *n.* 1. piece of material used *esp.* to conceal seam and prevent fraying 2. (*usu. pl.*) collar, cuffs *etc.* of military uniform jacket 3. outer layer or coat of material applied to surface of wall —**face card** court card —**face-lift** *n.* 1. operation to tighten skin of face to remove wrinkles 2. improvement, renovation

—**face-saving** a. maintaining dignity —**face value** 1. value on face of commercial paper or coin 2. apparent value —**face up to** accept (unpleasant fact etc.) —**on the face of it** to all appearances

facetious (fə'siːʃəs) a. 1. (sarcastically) witty 2. humorous, given to jesting, esp. at inappropriate time

facia ('feɪʃɪə) n. see FASCIA

-**facient** (comb. form) state; quality, as in absorbefacient

facile ('fæsaɪl) a. 1. easy 2. working easily 3. easy-going 4. superficial, silly —**facilitate** (fə'sɪlɪteɪt) vt. make easy, help progress of —**facilitation** (fəsɪlɪ'teɪʃən) n. —**facility** (fə'sɪlɪtɪ) n. 1. easiness 2. dexterity —pl. 3. opportunities, good conditions 4. means, equipment for doing something

facsimile (fæk'sɪmɪlɪ) n. exact copy

fact (fækt) n. 1. thing known to be true 2. deed 3. reality —**factual** a. —**as a matter of fact, in (point of) fact** in reality or actuality —**fact of life** (esp. unpleasant) inescapable truth

faction[1] ('fækʃən) n. 1. (dissenting) minority group within larger body 2. dissension —'**factious** a. of or producing factions

faction[2] ('fækʃən) n. dramatization of factual event

factitious (fæk'tɪʃəs) a. 1. artificial 2. specially made up 3. unreal

factor ('fæktə) n. 1. something contributing to a result 2. one of numbers which multiplied together give a given number 3. agent, dealer —**fac'torial** Maths. n. 1. product of all positive integers from one up to and including given integer —a. 2. of factorials or factors —**fac'totum** n. man-of-all-work

factory ('fæktərɪ) n. building where things are manufactured —**factory farm** farm where animals are intensively reared using modern industrial methods —**factory ship** vessel that processes fish supplied by fleet

faculty ('fækəltɪ) n. 1. inherent power 2. power of the mind 3. ability, aptitude 4. department of university 5. members of profession 6. authorization —**facultative** a. 1. optional 2. contingent

fad (fæd) n. 1. short-lived fashion 2. whim —'**faddish** or '**faddy** a.

fade (feɪd) vi. 1. lose colour, strength 2. wither 3. grow dim 4. disappear gradually —vt. 5. cause to fade —'**fadeless** a. —**fade-in, fade-out** n. 1. Rad. variation in strength of signals 2. T.V., cine. gradual appearance and disappearance of picture

faeces or esp. U.S. **feces** ('fiːsiːz) pl.n. excrement, waste matter —**faecal** or esp. U.S. **fecal** ('fiːkəl) a.

faerie or **faery** ('feɪərɪ, 'feərɪ) obs., poet. n. 1. fairyland —a./n. 2. see FAIRY

Faeroese or **Faroese** (fɛərəʊ'iːz) a. 1. of Faeroes, islands in N Atlantic —n. 2. language of Faeroes 3. native of Faeroes (pl. **-ese**)

faff (fæf) vi. (oft. with about) UK inf. dither; fuss

fag (fæg) n. 1. inf. boring task 2. sl. cigarette 3. US sl. male homosexual 4. UK esp. formerly, young public school boy who performs menial chores for older boy or prefect —v. 5. inf. (esp. with out) tire —vi. 6. do menial tasks for a senior boy in school (**-gg-**) —**fag end** 1. last part, inferior remnant 2. UK inf. stub of cigarette

faggot[1] or esp. U.S. **fagot** ('fægət) n. 1. bundle of sticks for fuel etc. 2. ball of chopped liver etc.

faggot[2] ('fægət) n. US sl. male homosexual

fah or **fa** (fɑː) n. Mus. 1. in fixed system of solmization, note F 2. in tonic sol-fa, fourth degree of major scale

Fah. or **Fahr.** Fahrenheit

Fahrenheit ('færənhaɪt) a. measured by thermometric scale with freezing point of water 32°, boiling point 212°

faïence (faɪ'ɑːns, feɪ-) n. glazed earthenware or china

fail (feɪl) vi. 1. be unsuccessful 2. stop operating or working 3. be below the required standard 4. be insufficient 5. run short 6. be wanting when in need 7. lose power 8. die away 9. become bankrupt —vt. 10. disappoint, give no help to 11. neglect 12. judge (candidate) to be below required standard —'**failing** n. 1. deficiency 2. fault —prep. 3. in default of —'**failure** n. —**fail-safe** a. (of device) ensuring safety or remedy of malfunction in machine, weapon etc. —**without fail** certainly

fain (feɪn) obs. a. 1. glad, willing; constrained —adv. 2. gladly

faint (feɪnt) a. 1. feeble, dim, pale 2. weak 3. dizzy, about to lose consciousness —vi. 4. lose consciousness temporarily —**faint-hearted** a. timid

fair[1] (feə) a. 1. just, impartial 2. according to rules, legitimate 3. blond 4. beautiful 5. ample 6. of moderate quality or amount 7. unblemished 8. plausible 9. middling 10. (of weather) favourable —adv. 11. honestly 12. absolutely; quite —'**fairing** n. Aviation streamlined casing, or any part so shaped that it provides streamline form —'**fairish** a. —'**fairly** adv. 1. moderately 2. as deserved; justly 3. positively —'**fairness** n. —**Fair Isle** intricate multicoloured pattern knitted with Shetland wool —**fair play** (abidance by) established standard of decency —'**fairway** n. 1. navigable channel 2. Golf trimmed turf between rough —**fair-weather** a. 1. suitable for use in fair weather only 2.

unreliable in difficult situations —**the fair sex** women collectively

fair² (feə) n. 1. travelling entertainment with sideshows, amusements etc. 2. large exhibition of commercial or industrial products 3. periodical market often with amusements —'**fairground** n.

fairy ('fɛərɪ) n. 1. imaginary small creature with powers of magic 2. sl. male homosexual —a. 3. of fairies 4. like fairy, beautiful and delicate —**fairy godmother** benefactress, esp. unknown —**fairy lamp** small coloured lamp for decorations —'**fairyland** n. —**fairy lights** small, coloured, decorative lights, esp. on Christmas tree —**fairy ring** circle of darker colour in grass —**fairy tale** 1. story of imaginary beings and happenings, esp. as told to children 2. highly improbable account

fait accompli (fɛ takɔ̃'pli) Fr. something already done that cannot be altered

faith (feɪθ) n. 1. trust 2. belief (without proof) 3. religion 4. promise 5. loyalty, constancy —'**faithful** a. constant, true —'**faithfully** adv. —'**faithless** a. —**faith healing** method of treating illness by religious faith

fake (feɪk) vt. 1. conceal defects of by artifice 2. touch up 3. counterfeit 4. sham —n. 5. fraudulent object, person, act —a. 6. not genuine —'**faker** n. 1. one who deals in fakes 2. swindler

fakir (fə'kɪə, 'feɪkə) n. 1. member of Islamic religious order 2. Hindu ascetic

Falange ('fælændʒ) n. Fascist movement in Spain —Fa'**langist** n./a.

falchion ('fɔːltʃən, 'fɔːlʃən) n. broad curved medieval sword

falcon ('fɔːlkən, 'fɔːkən) n. small bird of prey, esp. trained in hawking for sport —'**falconer** n. one who keeps, trains or hunts with falcons —'**falconry** n. hawking

falderal ('fældɪræl) or **folderol** n. 1. showy but worthless trifle 2. nonsense 3. nonsensical refrain in old songs

fall (fɔːl) vi. 1. drop, come down freely 2. become lower 3. decrease 4. hang down 5. come to the ground, cease to stand 6. perish 7. collapse 8. be captured 9. revert 10. lapse 11. be uttered 12. become 13. happen (**fell** pt., '**fallen** pp.) —n. 14. falling 15. amount that falls 16. amount of descent 17. decrease 18. collapse, ruin 19. drop 20. (oft. pl.) cascade 21. cadence 22. yielding to temptation 23. US autumn 24. rope of hoisting tackle —**fall guy** inf., chiefly US victim of confidence trick —**falling sickness** or evil former name for epilepsy —**falling star** inf. meteor —'**fallout** n. radioactive particles spread as result of nuclear explosion —**fall for** inf. 1. fall in love with 2. be taken in by —**fall out** disagree

fallacy ('fæləsɪ) n. 1. incorrect, misleading opinion or argument 2. flaw in logic 3. illusion —**fallacious** (fə'leɪʃəs) a. —**falli'bility** n. —'**fallible** a. liable to error —'**fallibly** adv.

fallen ('fɔːlən) v. 1. pp. of FALL —a. 2. having sunk in reputation or honour 3. killed in battle with glory —**fallen arch** collapse of arch formed by instep of foot, resulting in flat feet

Fallopian tube (fə'ləʊpɪən) either of pair of tubes through which egg cells pass from ovary to womb

fallow¹ ('fæləʊ) a. 1. ploughed and harrowed but left without crop 2. uncultivated 3. neglected

fallow² ('fæləʊ) a. brown or reddish-yellow —**fallow deer** deer of this colour

false (fɔːls) a. 1. wrong, erroneous 2. deceptive 3. faithless 4. sham, artificial —'**falsehood** n. —'**falsely** adv. —'**falseness** n. faithlessness —**falsifi'cation** n. —'**falsify** vt. 1. alter fraudulently 2. misrepresent 3. disappoint (hopes etc.) ('falsified, 'falsifying) —'**falsity** n. —**false pretences** misrepresentation of facts to gain advantage (esp. **in under false pretences**)

falsetto (fɔːl'sɛtəʊ) n. forced voice above natural range (pl. **-s**)

Falstaffian (fɔːl'stɑːfɪən) a. like Shakespeare's Falstaff, fat, convivial and boasting

falter ('fɔːltə) vi. 1. hesitate 2. waver 3. stumble —'**falteringly** adv.

fame (feɪm) n. 1. reputation 2. renown —**famed** a. —'**famous** a. 1. widely known 2. inf. excellent

familiar (fə'mɪljə) a. 1. well-known 2. frequent, customary 3. intimate 4. closely acquainted 5. unceremonious 6. impertinent, too friendly —n. 7. familiar friend 8. familiar demon —**famili'ar-ity** n. —**familiari'zation** or **-ri'sation** n. —fa'**miliarize** or **-rise** vt. —fa'**miliarly** adv.

family ('fæmɪlɪ, 'fæmlɪ) n. 1. group of parents and children, or near relatives 2. person's children 3. all descendants of common ancestor 4. household 5. group of allied objects —fa'**milial** a. —**family man** married man who has children, esp. one who is devoted to his family —**family name** surname, esp. representing family honour —**family planning** control of number of children in family, esp. by contraception —**family tree** chart showing relationships and lines of descent of family (also **genealogical tree**)

famine ('fæmɪn) n. 1. extreme scarcity of food 2. starvation 3. acute shortage of anything —'**famished** a. very hungry

famous ('feɪməs) a. see FAME

fan¹ (fæn) n. 1. instrument for producing current of air, esp. for ventilating or cooling 2. folding object of paper etc. used, esp. formerly, for cooling the face 3. outspread feathers of a bird's tail —*vt.* **4.** blow or cool with fan —*v.* **5.** spread out like fan (*-nn-*) —**fan belt** belt that drives cooling fan in car engine —'**fanjet** *n. see* TURBOFAN —'**fanlight** *n.* (fan-shaped) window over door —'**fantail** *n.* kind of bird (*esp.* pigeon) with fan-shaped tail —**fan vaulting** *Archit.* vaulting having ribs that radiate, like those of fan, from top of capital (*also* **palm vaulting**)

fan² (fæn) *n. inf.* **1.** devoted admirer **2.** enthusiast, particularly for sport *etc.*

Fanagalo ('fænɔgɔlɔʊ) *or* **Fanakalo** *n.* SA pidgin language of Zulu, English and Afrikaans

fanatic (fɔ'nætɪk) *a.* **1.** filled with abnormal enthusiasm, *esp.* in religion —*n.* **2.** fanatic person —**fa'natical** *a.* —**fa'natically** *adv.* —**fa'naticism** *n.*

fancy ('fænsɪ) *a.* **1.** ornamental, not plain **2.** of whimsical or arbitrary kind —*n.* **3.** whim, caprice **4.** liking, inclination **5.** imagination **6.** mental image —*vt.* **7.** imagine **8.** be inclined to believe **9.** *inf.* have a liking for ('**fancied,** '**fancying**) —*interj.* **10.** exclamation of surprise (*also* **fancy that**) —'**fancier** *n.* one with liking and expert knowledge (respecting some specific thing) —'**fanciful** *a.* —'**fancifully** *adv.* —**fancy dress** costume worn at masquerades *etc.* representing historical figure *etc.* —**fancy-free** *a.* having no commitments —**fancy goods** small decorative gifts —**fancy man** *sl.* **1.** woman's lover **2.** pimp —**fancy woman** *sl.* **1.** mistress **2.** prostitute

fandango (fæn'dæŋgɔʊ) *n.* **1.** lively Sp. dance with castanets **2.** music for this dance (*pl.* **-s**)

fanfare ('fænfɛɔ) *n.* **1.** a flourish of trumpets or bugles **2.** ostentatious display

fang (fæŋ) *n.* **1.** snake's poison tooth **2.** long, pointed tooth

fantasy *or* **phantasy** ('fæntɔsɪ) *n.* **1.** power of imagination, *esp.* extravagant **2.** mental image **3.** fanciful invention or design —**fantasia** (fæn'teɪzɪɔ) *n.* fanciful musical composition —'**fantasize** *or* **-sise** *v.* —**fan'tastic** *a.* **1.** quaint **2.** grotesque **3.** extremely fanciful, wild **4.** *inf.* very good **5.** *inf.* very large —**fan'tastically** *adv.*

FAO Food and Agriculture Organization (of the United Nations)

far (fɑː) *adv.* **1.** at or to a great distance or advanced point **2.** at or to a remote time **3.** by very much —*a.* **4.** distant **5.** more distant ('**farther,** '**further** *comp.,* '**farthest,** '**furthest** *sup.*) —'**faraway** *a.* **1.** distant **2.** absent-minded —**Far East** countries of E Asia, including China, Japan *etc.* —**Far Eastern** —**far-fetched** *a.* incredible —**far-flung** *a.* **1.** widely distributed **2.** far distant; remote —**Far North** Arctic and sub-Arctic regions —**far-off** *a.* remote; distant —**far-out** *a. sl.* **1.** bizarre, avant-garde **2.** wonderful —**far-sighted** *a.* **1.** possessing prudence and

foresight **2.** *Med.* of or suffering from hyperopia **3.** long-sighted —**far and away** by a very great margin —**far out** *sl.* expression of amazement or delight

farad ('færɔd) *n.* unit of electrical capacity —**faradaic** (færɔ'deɪɪk) *a.*

farce (fɑːs) *n.* **1.** comedy of boisterous humour **2.** absurd and futile proceeding —'**farcical** *a.* ludicrous —'**farcically** *adv.*

fare (fɛɔ) *n.* **1.** charge for passenger's transport **2.** passenger **3.** food —*vi.* **4.** get on **5.** happen **6.** travel, progress —**fare stage 1.** section of bus journey for which set charge is made **2.** bus stop marking end of such section —**fare'well** *interj.* **1.** goodbye —*n.* **2.** leave-taking

farina (fɔ'riːnɔ) *n.* **1.** flour or meal made from cereal grain **2.** *chiefly UK* starch —**farinaceous** (færɪ'neɪʃɔs) *a.* **1.** mealy **2.** starchy

farm (fɑːm) *n.* **1.** tract of land for cultivation or rearing livestock **2.** unit of land, water, for growing or rearing a particular crop, animal *etc.* —*v.* **3.** cultivate (land) **4.** rear (livestock) on farm —'**farmer** *n.* —**farm hand** person hired to work on farm —'**farmhouse** *n.* —'**farmstead** *n.* farm or part of farm consisting of main buildings together with adjacent grounds —'**farmyard** *n.* —**farm out 1.** send (work) to be done by others **2.** put into care of others

faro ('fɛɔrɔʊ) *n.* card game

farrago (fɔ'rɑːgɔʊ) *n.* medley, hotchpotch (*pl.* **-s**)

farrier ('færɪɔ) *n.* one who shoes, cares for horses —'**farriery** *n.* his art

farrow ('færɔʊ) *n.* **1.** litter of pigs —*v.* **2.** give birth to (litter)

fart (fɑːt) *vulg. n.* **1.** (audible) emission of gas from anus —*vi.* **2.** break wind

farther ('fɑːðɔ) *adv./a. comp. of* FAR further —'**farthermost** *a.* most distant —'**farthest** *adv./a. sup. of* FAR furthest

farthing ('fɑːðɪŋ) *n.* formerly, coin worth quarter of penny

farthingale ('fɑːðɪŋgeɪl) *n. Hist.* hoop worn under skirts

fasces ('fæsiːz) *pl.n.* **1.** bundle of rods bound together round axe, forming Roman badge of authority **2.** emblem of It. fascists

fascia *or* **facia** ('feɪʃɔ) *n.* **1.** flat surface above shop window **2.** *Archit.* long flat surface between mouldings under eaves **3.** face of wood or stone in a building **4.** dashboard (*pl.* **-ciae** (-ʃiiː))

fascinate ('fæsɪneɪt) *vt.* **1.** attract and delight by rousing interest and curiosity **2.** render motionless, as with a fixed stare —**fasci'nation** *n.*

Fascism ('fæʃɪzɔm) *n.* **1.** authoritarian political system opposed to democracy and liberalism **2.** (*oft.* **f-**) behaviour (*esp.* by those in authority) *n.*

supposedly typical of this system —'**Fascist** *a./n.*

fashion ('fæʃən) *n.* **1.** (latest) style, *esp.* of dress *etc.* **2.** manner, mode **3.** form, type —*vt.* **4.** shape, make —'**fashionable** *a.* —'**fashionably** *adv.*

fast[1] (fɑːst) *a.* **1.** (capable of) moving quickly **2.** permitting, providing, rapid progress **3.** ahead of true time **4.** *obs.* dissipated **5.** firm, steady **6.** permanent —*adv.* **7.** rapidly **8.** tightly —'**fastness** *n.* **1.** fast state **2.** fortress, stronghold —'**fastback** *n.* car with back forming continuous slope from roof to rear —**fast-breeder reactor** nuclear reactor that uses little or no moderator and produces more fissionable material than it consumes —**fast food** food, *esp.* hamburgers *etc.*, prepared and served very quickly

fast[2] (fɑːst) *vi.* **1.** go without food, or some kinds of food —*n.* **2.** act or period of fasting —'**fasting** *n.*

fasten ('fɑːsən) *vt.* **1.** attach, fix, secure —*vi.* **2.** become joined **3.** (*usu. with* on) seize (upon) —'**fastening** *n.* something that fastens, such as clasp

fastidious (fæ'stɪdɪəs) *a.* **1.** hard to please **2.** discriminating, particular

fat (fæt) *n.* **1.** oily animal substance **2.** fat part —*a.* **3.** having too much fat **4.** containing fat, greasy **5.** profitable **6.** fertile ('**fatter** *comp.*, '**fattest** *sup.*) —*vt.* **7.** feed (animals) for slaughter (**-tt-**) —'**fatness** *n.* —'**fatten** *v.* —'**fatty** *a./n.* —'**fathead** *n. inf.* dolt, idiot —**fat stock** livestock fattened and ready for market —**fatty acid** any of class of aliphatic carboxylic acids, such as palmitic acid

fate (feɪt) *n.* **1.** power supposed to predetermine events **2.** goddess of destiny **3.** destiny **4.** person's appointed lot or condition **5.** death; destruction —*vt.* **6.** preordain —'**fatal** *a.* **1.** deadly, ending in death **2.** destructive **3.** disastrous **4.** inevitable —'**fatalism** *n.* **1.** belief that everything is predetermined **2.** submission to fate —'**fatalist** *n.* —fatal'**istic** *a.* —fatal'**istically** *adv.* —**fatality** (fə'tælɪtɪ) *n.* **1.** accident resulting in death **2.** person killed in war, accident —'**fatally** *adv.* —'**fateful** *a.* **1.** fraught with destiny **2.** prophetic

father ('fɑːðə) *n.* **1.** male parent **2.** forefather, ancestor **3.** (**F-**) God **4.** originator, early leader **5.** priest, confessor **6.** oldest member of a society —*vt.* **7.** beget **8.** originate **9.** pass as father or author of **10.** act as father to —'**fatherhood** *n.* —'**fatherless** *a.* —'**fatherly** *a.* —**father-in-law** *n.* husband's or wife's father —'**fatherland** *n.* **1.** person's native country **2.** country of person's ancestors

fathom ('fæðəm) *n.* **1.** measure of six feet of water —*vt.* **2.** sound (water) **3.** get to bottom of,

understand —'**fathomable** *a.* —'**fathomless** *a.* too deep to fathom

fatigue (fə'tiːg) *n.* **1.** weariness **2.** toil **3.** weakness of metals *etc.* subjected to stress **4.** soldier's nonmilitary duty —*pl.* **5.** special clothing worn by military personnel to carry out such duties —*vt.* **6.** weary

fatuous ('fætjuəs) *a.* very silly, idiotic —fa'**tuity** *n.*

faucet ('fɔːsɪt) *n.* US tap

fault (fɔːlt) *n.* **1.** defect **2.** flaw **3.** misdeed **4.** blame, culpability **5.** blunder, mistake **6.** *Tennis* ball wrongly served **7.** *Geol.* break in strata —*vt.* **8.** find fault in —*v.* **9.** (cause to) undergo fault —*vi.* **10.** commit a fault —'**faultily** *adv.* —'**faultless** *a.* —'**faultlessly** *adv.* —'**faulty** *a.* —**to a fault** excessively

faun (fɔːn) *n.* mythological woodland being with tail and horns

fauna ('fɔːnə) *n.* animals of region or period collectively (*pl.* **-s, -ae** (-iː))

faux pas (fəʊ 'pɑː) social blunder or indiscretion (*pl.* **faux pas** (fəʊ 'pɑːz))

favour *or U.S.* **favor** ('feɪvə) *n.* **1.** goodwill **2.** approval **3.** especial kindness **4.** partiality **5.** small gift or toy given to guest at party *etc.* **6.** *Hist.* badge or knot of ribbons —*vt.* **7.** regard or treat with favour **8.** oblige **9.** treat with partiality **10.** aid **11.** support **12.** resemble —'**favourable** *or U.S.* '**favorable** *a.* **1.** advantageous, encouraging, promising **2.** giving consent —'**favourably** *or U.S.* '**favorably** *adv.* —'**favoured** *or U.S.* '**favored** *a.* **1.** treated with favour **2.** having appearance (as specified), as in *ill-favoured* —'**favourite** *or U.S.* **favorite** ('feɪvərɪt) *n.* **1.** favoured person or thing **2.** horse *etc.* expected to win race —*a.* **3.** chosen, preferred —'**favouritism** *or U.S.* '**favoritism** ('feɪvərɪtɪzəm) *n.* practice of showing undue preference

fawn[1] (fɔːn) *n.* **1.** young deer —*a.* **2.** light yellowish-brown

fawn[2] (fɔːn) *vi.* **1.** (of person) cringe, court favour servilely **2.** (*esp.* of dog) show affection by wagging tail and grovelling

fay (feɪ) *n.* fairy, sprite

F.B.I. US Federal Bureau of Investigation

F.C. Football Club

F.D. Fidei Defensor

Fe *Chem.* iron

fealty ('fiːəltɪ) *n.* **1.** fidelity of vassal to his lord **2.** loyalty

fear (fɪə) *n.* **1.** dread, alarm, anxiety, unpleasant emotion caused by coming evil or danger —*vi.* **2.** have this feeling, be afraid —*vt.* **3.** regard with fear **4.** shrink from **5.** revere —'**fearful** *a.* **1.** afraid **2.** causing fear **3.** *inf.* very unpleasant —'**fearfully** *adv.* —'**fearless** *a.* intrepid —'**fearlessly** *adv.* —'**fearsome** *a.*

feasible ('fiːzəbᵊl) a. 1. able to be done 2. likely —**feasi'bility** n. —**feasibly** adv.

feast (fiːst) n. 1. banquet, lavish meal 2. religious anniversary 3. something very pleasant, sumptuous —vi. 4. partake of banquet; fare sumptuously —vt. 5. regale with feast 6. provide delight for —**feaster** n.

feat (fiːt) n. 1. notable deed 2. surprising or striking trick

feather ('feðə) n. 1. one of the barbed shafts which form covering of birds 2. anything resembling this —vt. 3. provide, line with feathers —vi. 4. grow feathers —v. 5. turn (oar) edgeways —**feathery** a. —**feather bed** mattress filled with feathers —**feather'bed** vt. pamper, spoil —**featherbrain** or **featherhead** n. frivolous or forgetful person —**featherbrained** or **featherheaded** a. —**featherweight** n. very light person or thing —**feather one's nest** enrich oneself —**the white feather** cowardice

feature ('fiːtʃə) n. 1. (usu. pl.) part of face 2. characteristic or notable part of anything 3. main or special item —vt. 4. portray 5. Cine. present in leading role in a film 6. give prominence to —vi. 7. be prominent —**featureless** a. without striking features

Feb. February

febrile ('fiːbraɪl) a. of fever

February ('fɛbruərɪ) n. second month of year (normally containing 28 days; in leap year, 29)

feckless ('fɛklɪs) a. spiritless; weak; irresponsible

feculent ('fɛkjʊlənt) a. full of sediment, turbid —**feculence** n.

fecund ('fiːkənd, 'fɛk-) a. fertile, fruitful, fertilizing —**fecundate** vt. fertilize, impregnate —**fecun'dation** n. —**fecundity** (fɪ'kʌndɪtɪ) n.

Fed. or **fed.** 1. Federal 2. Federation 3. Federated

fed (fɛd) pt./pp. of FEED —**fed up** bored, dissatisfied

federal ('fɛdərəl) a. of or like the government of states which are united but retain internal independence —**federalism** n. —**federalist** n./a. —**federate** v. form into, become, a federation —**fede'ration** n. 1. league 2. federal union

fee (fiː) n. payment for professional and other services

feeble ('fiːbᵊl) a. 1. weak 2. lacking strength or effectiveness, insipid —**feebly** adv. —**feebleminded** a. 1. lacking in intelligence 2. mentally defective

feed (fiːd) vt. 1. give food to 2. supply, support —vi. 3. take food (**fed** pt./pp.) —n. 4. feeding 5. fodder, pasturage 6. allowance of fodder 7. material supplied to machine 8. part of machine taking in material —**feeder** n. 1. one who or that which feeds 2. child's bib 3. tributary channel —**feedback** n. 1. return of part of output of electrical circuit or loudspeakers. In **negative feedback** rise in output energy reduces input energy; in **positive feedback** increase in output energy reinforces input energy 2. information received in response to enquiry etc. —**feedlot** n. area, building where cattle are fattened for market

feel (fiːl) vt. 1. perceive, examine by touch 2. experience 3. find (one's way) cautiously 4. be sensitive to 5. believe, consider —vi. 6. have physical or emotional sensation of (something) (**felt** pt./pp.) —n. 7. act or instance of feeling 8. quality or impression of something perceived by feeling 9. sense of touch —**feeler** n. 1. special organ of touch in some animals 2. proposal put forward to test others' opinion 3. that which feels —**feeling** n. 1. sense of touch 2. ability to feel 3. physical sensation 4. emotion 5. sympathy, tenderness 6. conviction or opinion not solely based on reason 7. susceptibilities —a. 8. sensitive, sympathetic, heartfelt —**feel for** show sympathy or compassion towards —**feel like** have an inclination for

feet (fiːt) n., pl. of FOOT

feign (feɪn) v. pretend, sham

feint¹ (feɪnt) n. 1. sham attack or blow meant to deceive opponent 2. semblance, pretence —vi. 3. make feint

feint² (feɪnt) n. Print. narrowest rule used in production of ruled paper

feldspar ('fɛldspɑː, 'fɛlspɑː) or **felspar** n. crystalline mineral found in granite etc. —**feldspathic** (fɛld'spæθɪk, fɛl'spæθ-) or **fel'spathic** a.

felicity (fɪ'lɪsɪtɪ) n. 1. great happiness, bliss 2. appropriate expression or style —**fe'licitate** vt. congratulate —**felici'tation** n. (usu. in pl.) —**fe'licitous** a. 1. apt, well-chosen 2. happy

feline ('fiːlaɪn) a. 1. of cats 2. catlike —**felinity** (fɪ'lɪnɪtɪ) n.

fell¹ (fɛl) pt. of FALL

fell² (fɛl) vt. 1. knock down 2. cut down (tree) —**feller** n.

fell³ (fɛl) a. obs. fierce, terrible —**one fell swoop** a single hasty action or occurrence

fell⁴ (fɛl) n. skin or hide with hair

fell⁵ (fɛl) n. mountain, stretch of moorland, esp. in N of England

fellatio (fɪ'leɪʃɪəʊ) n. sexual activity in which penis is stimulated by partner's mouth

felloe ('fɛləʊ) or **felly** n. outer part (or section) of wheel

fellow ('fɛləʊ) n. 1. man, boy 2. person 3. comrade, associate 4. counterpart, like thing 5. member (of society, college etc.) —a. 6. of the same class, associated —'**fellowship** n. 1. fraternity 2. friendship 3. in university etc., research post; special scholarship —'**fellow traveller** 1. companion on journey 2. non-Communist who sympathizes with Communism

felon ('fɛlən) n. one guilty of felony —fe'**lonious** a. —'**felony** n. serious crime

felspar ('fɛlspɑː) n. see FELSPAR

felt[1] (fɛlt) pt./pp. of FEEL

felt[2] (fɛlt) n. 1. soft, matted fabric made by bonding fibres chemically and by pressure 2. thing made of this —vt. 3. make into, or cover with, felt —vi. 4. become matted like felt —**felt-tip pen** pen whose writing point is made from pressed fibres (also **fibre-tip pen**)

fem. feminine

female ('fiːmeɪl) a. 1. of sex which bears offspring 2. relating to this sex —n. 3. one of this sex

feminine ('fɛmɪnɪn) a. 1. of women 2. womanly 3. denoting class or type of grammatical inflection in some languages —femi'**ninity** n. —'**feminism** n. advocacy of equal rights for women —'**feminist** n./a.

femur ('fiːmə) n. thigh-bone —'**femoral** a. of the thigh

fen (fɛn) n. tract of marshy land, swamp —'**fenny** a.

fence (fɛns) n. 1. structure of wire, wood etc. enclosing an area 2. Machinery guard, guide 3. sl. dealer in stolen property —vt. 4. erect fence on or around 5. (with in) enclose —vi. 6. fight (as sport) with swords 7. avoid question etc. 8. sl. deal in stolen property —'**fencing** n. art of swordplay

fend (fɛnd) vt. 1. (usu. with off) ward off, repel —vi. 2. provide (for oneself etc.) —'**fender** n. 1. low metal frame in front of fireplace 2. name for various protective devices 3. frame 4. edge 5. buffer 6. US mudguard of car

fenestration (fɛnɪ'streɪʃən) n. arrangement of windows in a building

Fenian ('fiːnɪən, 'fiːnjən) n. 1. formerly, member of Irish revolutionary organization founded in U.S.A. in 19th century to fight for independent Ireland —a. 2. of Fenians

fennel ('fɛnl) n. yellow-flowered fragrant herb

fenugreek ('fɛnjuɡriːk) n. heavily scented leguminous plant

feoff (fiːf) Hist. n. 1. see FIEF —vt. 2. invest with benefice or fief

-fer (n. comb. form) person or thing that bears something specified, as in crucifer, conifer —**-ferous** (a. comb. form) bearing, producing, as in coniferous

feral[1] ('fɪərəl) a. wild, uncultivated

feral[2] ('fɪərəl) a. obs. funereal, gloomy

feria ('fɪərɪə) n. Eccles. ordinary weekday, not festival or fast day

fermata (fə'mɑːtə) n. Mus. pause (pl. **-s**, **-te** (-tɪ))

ferment ('fɜːmɛnt) n. 1. leaven, substance causing thing to ferment 2. excitement, tumult —v. (fə'mɛnt) 3. (cause to) undergo chemical change with effervescence, liberation of heat and alteration of properties, eg process set up in dough by yeast 4. (cause to) become excited —**fermen'tation** n.

fermium ('fɜːmɪəm) n. transuranic element artificially produced by neutron bombardment of plutonium

fern (fɜːn) n. plant with feathery fronds —'**fernery** n. place for growing ferns —'**ferny** a. full of ferns

ferocious (fə'rəʊʃəs) a. fierce, savage, cruel —**ferocity** (fə'rɒsɪtɪ) n.

ferret ('fɛrɪt) n. 1. tamed animal like weasel, used to catch rabbits, rats etc. —vt. (usu. with out) 2. drive out with ferrets 3. search out —vi. 4. search about, rummage

ferric ('fɛrɪk) a. pert. to, containing, iron —fer'**riferous** a. yielding iron —'**ferrous** a. of or containing iron in divalent state —**ferruginous** (fɛ'ruːdʒɪnəs) a. 1. containing iron 2. reddish-brown —ferro'**concrete** n. concrete strengthened by framework of metal

Ferris wheel ('fɛrɪs) in fairground, large, vertical wheel with seats for riding

ferro- (comb. form) 1. property or presence of iron, as in ferromagnetism 2. presence of iron in divalent state, as in ferrocyanide

ferrule ('fɛruːl) n. metal cap to strengthen end of stick etc.

ferry ('fɛrɪ) n. 1. boat etc. for transporting people, vehicles, across body of water, esp. as repeated or regular service 2. place for ferrying —v. 3. carry, travel, by ferry —vt. 4. convey (passengers etc.) ('**ferried, ferrying**) —'**ferryman** n.

fertile ('fɜːtaɪl) a. 1. (capable of) producing offspring, bearing crops etc. 2. fruitful, producing abundantly 3. inventive —**fertility** (fɜː'tɪlɪtɪ) n. —**fertilization** or **-lisation** (fɜːtɪlaɪ'zeɪʃən) n. —**fertilize** or **-lise** ('fɜːtɪlaɪz) vt. make fertile —**fertilizer** or **-liser** ('fɜːtɪlaɪzə) n.

ferule ('fɛruːl) n. 1. flat piece of wood, such as ruler, formerly used in some schools to cane children on hand —vt. 2. punish with ferule

fervent ('fɜːvənt) or **fervid** ('fɜːvɪd) a. ardent, vehement, intense —'**fervency** n. —'**fervently** or '**fervidly** adv. —'**fervour** or U.S. '**fervor** n.

fescue ('fɛskjuː) or **fescue grass** n. grass used as pasture, with stiff narrow leaves

fesse *or* **fess** (fɛs) *n. Her.* horizontal band across shield

festal ('fɛstəl) *a.* 1. of feast or holiday 2. merry, gay —'**festally** *adv.*

fester ('fɛstə) *v.* 1. (cause to) form pus —*vi.* 2. rankle 3. become embittered

festival ('fɛstɪvəl) *n.* 1. day, period set aside for celebration, *esp.* of religious feast 2. organized series of events, performances *etc.*, usu. in one place —'**festive** *a.* 1. joyous, merry 2. of feast —**fes'tivity** *n.* 1. gaiety, mirth 2. rejoicing —*pl.* 3. festive proceedings

festoon (fɛ'stuːn) *n.* 1. chain of flowers, ribbons *etc.* hung in curve between two points —*vt.* 2. form into, adorn with festoons

fetch[1] (fɛtʃ) *vt.* 1. go and bring 2. draw forth 3. be sold for —*n.* 4. trick —'**fetching** *a.* attractive —**fetch up** 1. *inf.* arrive 2. *sl.* vomit (food *etc.*)

fetch[2] (fɛtʃ) *n.* ghost or apparition of living person

fête *or* **fete** (feɪt) *n.* 1. gala, bazaar *etc.*, *esp.* one held out of doors 2. festival, holiday, celebration —*vt.* 3. feast 4. honour with festive entertainment

fetid *or* **foetid** ('fɛtɪd, 'fiː-) *a.* stinking

fetish *or* **fetich** ('fɛtɪʃ, 'fiːtɪʃ) *n.* 1. (inanimate) object believed to have magical powers 2. excessive attention to something 3. object, activity, to which excessive devotion is paid

fetlock ('fɛtlɒk) *n.* projection behind and above horse's hoof, or tuft of hair on this

fetter ('fɛtə) *n.* 1. chain or shackle for feet 2. check, restraint —*pl.* 3. captivity —*vt.* 4. chain up 5. restrain, hamper

fettle ('fɛtəl) *n.* condition, state of health

fetus ('fiːtəs) *n. see* FOETUS

feu (fjuː) *n.* in Scotland, tenure of land in return for fixed annual payment

feud (fjuːd) *n.* 1. bitter, lasting, mutual hostility, *esp.* between two families or tribes 2. vendetta —*vi.* 3. carry on feud

feudal ('fjuːdəl) *a.* 1. of, like, medieval social and economic system based on holding land from superior in return for service 2. *inf.* very old-fashioned —'**feudalism** *n.*

fever ('fiːvə) *n.* 1. condition of illness with high body temperature 2. intense nervous excitement —'**fevered** *a.* —'**feverish** *a.* 1. having fever 2. accompanied by, caused by, fever 3. in a state of restless excitement —'**feverishly** *adv.* —'**feverfew** *n.* bushy plant with white flower heads —**fever pitch** 1. very fast pace 2. intense excitement

few (fjuː) *a.* 1. not many —*n.* 2. small number —**a good few, quite a few** several

fey (feɪ) *a.* 1. clairvoyant, visionary 2. *esp. Scot.* fated to die

fez (fɛz) *n.* red, brimless, orig. Turkish tasselled cap (*pl.* '**fezzes**)

ff *Mus.* fortissimo

ff. 1. folios 2. and the following (pages *etc.*)

fiancé (fɪ'ɒnseɪ) *n.* person engaged to be married (**fi'ancée** *fem.*)

fiasco (fɪ'æskəʊ) *n.* breakdown, total failure (*pl.* **-s, -es**)

fiat ('faɪət) *n.* 1. decree 2. official permission

fib (fɪb) *n.* 1. trivial lie, falsehood —*vi.* 2. tell fib (**-bb-**) —'**fibber** *n.*

fibre *or U.S.* **fiber** ('faɪbə) *n.* 1. filament forming part of animal or plant tissue 2. substance that can be spun (*eg* wool, cotton) —'**fibril** *or* **fi'brilla** *n.* small fibre or part of fibre 2. *Biol.* root hair (*pl.* **-s** *or* **-brillae** (-'brɪliː)) —'**fibroid** *a. Anat.* (of structures or tissues) containing or resembling fibres —*n.* 2. benign tumour derived from fibrous connective tissue (*also* **fi'broma**) —**fi'brosis** *n.* formation of abnormal amount of fibrous tissue in organ *etc.* —**fibro'sitis** *n.* inflammation of tissues of muscle sheaths —'**fibrous** *a.* made of fibre —'**fibreboard** *n.* building material of compressed plant fibres —'**fibreglass** *n.* material made of fine glass fibres —**fibre optics** use of bundles of long transparent glass fibres in transmitting light

fibrin ('fɪbrɪn) *n.* insoluble protein in blood, causing coagulation

fibula ('fɪbjʊlə) *n.* slender outer bone of lower leg (*pl.* **-lae** (-liː), **-s**) —'**fibular** *a.*

fickle ('fɪkəl) *a.* changeable, inconstant —'**fickleness** *n.*

fiction ('fɪkʃən) *n.* 1. prose, literary works of the imagination 2. invented statement or story —'**fictional** *a.* —'**fictionalize** *or* **-lise** *vt.* make into fiction —**fic'titious** *a.* 1. not genuine, false 2. imaginary 3. assumed

fiddle ('fɪdəl) *n.* 1. violin 2. triviality 3. *inf.* illegal, fraudulent arrangement —*vi.* 4. play fiddle 5. make idle movements, fidget, trifle —*v.* 6. *sl.* cheat, contrive —'**fiddling** *a.* trivial —'**fiddly** *a.* small, awkward to handle —**fiddler crab** burrowing crab of Amer. coastal regions, male of which has one pincerlike claw enlarged —'**fiddlesticks** *interj.* nonsense

Fidei Defensor ('faɪdiaɪ dɪ'fɛnsɔː) *Lat.* Defender of the Faith

fidelity (fɪ'dɛlɪtɪ) *n.* 1. faithfulness 2. quality of sound reproduction

fidget ('fɪdʒɪt) *v.* 1. move restlessly 2. be uneasy —*n.* 3. (*oft. pl.*) nervous restlessness, restless mood 4. one who fidgets —'**fidgety** *a.*

fiduciary (fɪ'duːʃɪərɪ) *a.* 1. held, given in trust 2. relating to trustee —*n.* 3. trustee

fie (faɪ) *interj. obs., jocular* exclamation of distaste or mock dismay

fief or **feoff** (fiːf) n. Hist. land held of a superior in return for service

field (fiːld) n. 1. area of (farming) land 2. enclosed piece of land 3. tract of land rich in specified product (eg goldfield) 4. players in a game or sport collectively 5. all competitors but the favourite 6. battlefield 7. area over which electric, gravitational, magnetic force can be exerted 8. surface of shield, coin etc. 9. sphere of knowledge 10. range, area of operation —vt. 11. Sport stop or return (ball) 12. send (player, team) on to sportsfield —vi. 13. Sport (of player or team) act or take turn as fielder(s) —'**fielder** n. —**field day** 1. day of manoeuvres, outdoor activities 2. important occasion —**field events** throwing and jumping events in athletics —'**fieldfare** n. type of thrush with pale grey head and rump —**field glasses** binoculars —**field hockey** US, C hockey played on field, as distinct from ice hockey —**field marshal** army officer of highest rank —**field officer** officer holding rank of major, lieutenant colonel or colonel —'**fieldsman** n. Cricket player in field; member of fielding side (also '**fielder**) —**field sports** outdoor sports, such as hunting or fishing —'**fieldwork** n. research, practical work, conducted away from classroom, laboratory etc. —**field of view** area covered in telescope, camera etc.

fiend (fiːnd) n. 1. demon, devil 2. wicked person 3. person very fond of or addicted to something, eg fresh-air fiend, drug fiend —'**fiendish** a. 1. wicked 2. inf. difficult; unpleasant

fierce (fɪəs) a. 1. savage, wild, violent 2. rough 3. severe 4. intense —'**fiercely** adv. —'**fierceness** n.

fiery ('faɪərɪ) a. 1. consisting of fire 2. blazing, glowing, flashing 3. irritable 4. spirited ('**fierier** comp., '**fieriest** sup.) —'**fierily** adv.

fiesta (fɪ'estə) n. (esp. in Spain and Latin America) 1. (religious) celebration 2. carnival

FIFA ('fiːfə) Fédération Internationale de Football Association

fife (faɪf) n. 1. high-pitched flute —v. 2. play (music) on fife —'**fifer** n.

fifteen ('fɪf'tiːn) see FIVE

fig (fɪg) n. 1. soft, pear-shaped fruit 2. tree bearing it 3. something of negligible value

fig. 1. figurative(ly) 2. figure

fight (faɪt) v. 1. contend (with) in battle or in single combat 2. maintain (cause etc.) against opponent —vt. 3. resolve by combat (**fought** pt./pp.) —n. 4. battle, struggle or physical combat 5. quarrel, dispute, contest 6. resistance 7. boxing match —'**fighter** n. 1. one who fights 2. Mil. aircraft designed for destroying other aircraft —**fighting chance** chance of success dependent on struggle

figment ('fɪgmənt) n. invention, purely imaginary thing

figure ('fɪgə) n. 1. numerical symbol 2. amount, number 3. form, shape 4. bodily shape 5. appearance, esp. conspicuous appearance 6. character, personage 7. space enclosed by lines, or surfaces 8. diagram, illustration 9. likeness, image 10. pattern, movement in dancing, skating, etc. 11. abnormal form of expression for effect in speech, eg metaphor —vt. 12. calculate, estimate 13. inf., US, NZ consider 14. represent by picture or diagram 15. ornament —vi. 16. (oft. with in) show, appear, be conspicuous, be included —**figu'ration** n. 1. Mus. florid ornamentation of musical passage 2. instance of representing figuratively, as by allegory 3. figurative representation 4. decorating with design —'**figurative** a. 1. metaphorical 2. full of figures of speech —'**figuratively** adv. —**figurine** (fɪgə'riːn) n. statuette —'**figurehead** n. 1. nominal leader 2. ornamental figure under bowsprit of ship —**figure of speech** expression of language by which literal meaning of word is not employed

figwort ('fɪgwɜːt) n. plant related to foxglove, having small greenish flowers

filament ('fɪləmənt) n. 1. fine wire in electric light bulb and radio valve which is heated by electric current 2. threadlike body

filbert ('fɪlbət) n. 1. N temperate shrub with edible nuts 2. this nut (also '**hazelnut**, '**cobnut**)

filch (fɪltʃ) vt. steal, pilfer

file[1] (faɪl) n. 1. box, folder, clip etc. holding papers for reference 2. papers so kept 3. information about specific person, subject 4. orderly line, as of soldiers, one behind the other —vt. 5. arrange (papers etc.) and put them away for reference 6. Law place on records of a court 7. bring (suit) in lawcourt —vi. 8. march in file —'**filing** n. —**single** (or **Indian**) **file** single line of people one behind the other

file[2] (faɪl) n. 1. roughened tool for smoothing or shaping —vt. 2. apply file to, smooth, polish —'**filing** n. 1. action of using file 2. scrap of metal removed by file

filial ('fɪljəl) a. of, befitting, son or daughter —'**filially** adv.

filibuster ('fɪlɪbʌstə) US n. 1. process of obstructing legislation by using delaying tactics —v. 2. obstruct (legislation) with delaying tactics —vi. 3. engage in unlawful military action

filigree ('fɪlɪgriː) or **filagree** ('fɪləgriː) n. fine tracery or openwork of metal, usu. gold or silver wire

Filipino (fɪlɪ'piːnəʊ) n. 1. native of the Philippines —a. 2. of the Philippines

fill (fɪl) vt. 1. make full 2. occupy completely 3.

hold, discharge duties of **4.** stop up **5.** satisfy, fulfil —*vi.* **6.** become full —*n.* **7.** full supply **8.** as much as desired **9.** soil *etc.* to bring area of ground up to required level —'**filler** *n.* **1.** person or thing that fills **2.** object or substance used to add weight *etc.* or to fill in gap **3.** paste used for filling in cracks *etc.* before painting **4.** inner portion of cigar **5.** *Journalism* space-filling item in newspaper *etc.* —'**filling** *n.* —**filling station** garage selling oil, petrol *etc.* —**fill the bill** *inf.* supply all that is wanted

fillet ('filit) *n.* **1.** boneless slice of meat, fish **2.** narrow strip —*vt.* **3.** cut into fillets, bone —'**filleted** *a.*

fillip ('filip) *n.* **1.** stimulus **2.** sudden release of finger bent against thumb **3.** snap so produced —*vt.* **4.** stimulate **5.** give fillip to

filly ('fili) *n.* female horse under four years old

film (film) *n.* **1.** sequence of images projected on screen, creating illusion of movement **2.** story *etc.* presented thus, and shown in cinema or on television **3.** sensitized celluloid roll used in photography, cinematography **4.** thin skin or layer **5.** dimness on eyes **6.** slight haze —*a.* **7.** connected with cinema —*vt.* **8.** photograph with cine camera **9.** make cine film of (scene, story *etc.*) —*vi.* **10.** cover, become covered, with film —'**filmy** *a.* **1.** membranous **2.** gauzy —**film star** popular cinema actor or actress —**film strip** strip of film composed of images projected separately as slides

filter ('filtə) *n.* **1.** cloth or other material, or a device, permitting fluid to pass but retaining solid particles **2.** anything performing similar function —*v.* **3.** (*oft. with* out) remove or separate (suspended particles *etc.*) from (liquid, gas *etc.*) by action of filter —*vi.* **4.** pass slowly (as if) through filter —'**filtrate** *n.* filtered gas or liquid —**filter paper** porous paper for filtering liquids —**filter tip 1.** attachment to mouth end of cigarette for trapping impurities **2.** cigarette having such attachment —**filter-tipped** *a.*

filth (filθ) *n.* **1.** disgusting dirt **2.** pollution **3.** obscenity —'**filthily** *adv.* —'**filthiness** *n.* —'**filthy** *a.* **1.** unclean **2.** foul

fin (fin) *n.* **1.** propelling or steering organ of fish **2.** anything like this, *eg* stabilizing plane of aeroplane

fin. **1.** finance **2.** financial

finagle (fi'neig²l) *inf.* *vt.* **1.** get or achieve by craftiness —*v.* **2.** use trickery on (person) —**fi'nagler** *n.*

final ('fain³l) *a.* **1.** at the end **2.** conclusive —*n.* **3.** game, heat, examination *etc.* coming at end of series —**finale** (fi'nɑːli) *n.* **1.** closing part of musical composition, opera *etc.* **2.** termination —'**finalist** *n.* contestant who has reached last stage of competition —**fi'nality** *n.* —'**finalize** *or* **-lise** *v.* —'**finally** *adv.*

finance (fi'næns, 'fainæns) *n.* **1.** management of money **2.** (*also pl.*) money resources —*vt.* **3.** find capital for —**fi'nancial** *a.* of finance —**fi'nancially** *adv.* —**fi'nancier** *n.* —**financial year** UK **1.** annual period at end of which firm's accounts are made up **2.** annual period ending Apr. 5th, over which Budget estimates are made by British Government

finch (fintʃ) *n.* one of family of small singing birds

find (faind) *vt.* **1.** come across, light upon **2.** obtain **3.** realize **4.** experience, discover **5.** discover by searching **6.** supply (as funds) **7.** *Law* give a verdict (upon) (**found** *pt./pp.*) —*n.* **8.** finding **9.** (valuable) thing found —'**finder** *n.* —'**finding** *n.* judicial verdict —**find out 1.** gain knowledge of (something); learn **2.** detect crime, deception *etc.* of (someone)

fine¹ (fain) *a.* **1.** choice, of high quality, excellent **2.** delicate **3.** subtle **4.** pure **5.** in small particles **6.** slender **7.** handsome **8.** showy **9.** *inf.* healthy, at ease, comfortable **10.** free from rain —*vt.* **11.** make clear or pure **12.** refine **13.** thin —'**finely** *adv.* —'**fineness** *n.* —'**finery** *n.* showy dress —**finesse** (fi'nɛs) *n.* elegant, skilful management —**fine art** art produced for its aesthetic value —**fine-drawn** *a.* **1.** (of distinctions *etc.*) precise; subtle **2.** (of wire *etc.*) drawn out until very fine —'**fine'spun** *a.* **1.** spun out to fine thread **2.** excessively subtle or refined —**fine-tooth comb** *or* **fine-toothed comb** comb with fine, closely set teeth —**go over** *or* **through with a fine-tooth(ed) comb** examine very thoroughly

fine² (fain) *n.* **1.** sum fixed as penalty —*vt.* **2.** punish by fine —**in fine 1.** in conclusion **2.** in brief

fines herbes (*Fr.* fin 'zɛrb) mixture of finely chopped herbs, used to flavour omelettes *etc.*

finger ('fiŋgə) *n.* **1.** one of the jointed branches of the hand **2.** any of various things like this —*vt.* **3.** touch or handle with fingers —'**fingering** *n.* **1.** *Mus.* technique of using one's fingers **2.** *Mus.* numerals in musical part indicating this **3.** fine wool yarn for manufacture of stockings *etc.* —'**fingerboard** *n.* part of musical instrument on which fingers are placed —**finger bowl** small bowl filled with water for rinsing fingers at table after meal —**finger plate** ornamental plate above door handle to prevent finger marks —'**fingerprint** *n.* impression of tip of finger, *esp.* as used for identifying criminals —'**finger-stall** *n.* cover to protect finger

finial ('fainiəl) *n.* *Archit.* ornament at apex of pinnacles, gables, spires *etc.*

finicky ('finiki) *or* **finicking** *a.* **1.** fastidious, fussy **2.** too fine

finis ('finis) *Lat.* end, *esp.* of book

finish ('finiʃ) *v.* 1. bring, come to an end, conclude —*vt.* 2. complete 3. perfect 4. kill —*n.* 5. end 6. way in which thing is finished, as an oak finish of furniture 7. final appearance —'**finisher** *n.* —'**finishing school** private school for girls, that teaches social graces

finite ('faınaıt) *a.* bounded, limited

Finn (fın) *n.* native of Finland —'**Finnish** *a.* 1. of Finland —*n.* 2. official language of Finland

finnan haddock ('fınən) *or* **haddie** ('hædı) smoked haddock

fiord (fjɔːd) *n. see* FJORD

fipple ('fıpˀl) *n.* wooden plug forming flue in end of pipe —**fipple flute** end-blown flute with fipple, such as recorder

fir (fɜː) *n.* 1. kind of coniferous resinous tree 2. its wood

fire (faıə) *n.* 1. state of burning, combustion, flame, glow 2. mass of burning fuel 3. destructive burning, conflagration 4. device for heating a room *etc.* 5. ardour, keenness, spirit 6. shooting of firearms —*vt.* 7. discharge (firearm) 8. propel from firearm 9. *inf.* dismiss from employment 10. bake 11. make burn 12. supply with fuel 13. inspire 14. explode —*vi.* 15. discharge firearm 16. begin to burn —'**firing** *n.* 1. process of baking ceramics *etc.* in kiln 2. act of stoking fire or furnace 3. discharge of firearm 4. something used as fuel —**fire alarm** device to give warning of fire —'**firearm** *n.* gun, rifle, pistol *etc.* —'**fireball** *n.* 1. ball-shaped discharge of lightning 2. region of hot ionized gas at centre of nuclear explosion 3. *Astron.* large bright meteor 4. *sl.* energetic person —'**firebomb** *n. see* INCENDIARY (sense 6) —'**firebrand** *n.* 1. burning piece of wood 2. energetic (troublesome) person —'**firebreak** *n.* strip of cleared land to arrest progress of bush or grass fire —'**firebrick** *n.* refractory brick made of fire clay, for lining furnaces *etc.* —**fire brigade** organized body of men and appliances to put out fires and rescue those in danger —'**firebug** *n. inf.* person who intentionally sets fire to buildings *etc.* —**fire clay** heat-resistant clay used in making of firebricks *etc.* —'**firecracker** *n.* small cardboard container filled with explosive powder —'**firecrest** *n.* small European warbler —'**firedamp** *n.* explosive hydrocarbon gas forming in mines —'**firedog** *n.* either of pair of metal stands used to support logs in open fire —**fire drill** rehearsal of procedures for escape from fire —**fire-eater** *n.* 1. performer who simulates swallowing of fire 2. belligerent person —**fire engine** vehicle with apparatus for extinguishing fires —**fire escape** means, *esp.* stairs, for escaping from burning buildings —'**firefly** *n.* insect giving off

phosphorescent glow —'**fireguard** *or* **fire screen** *n.* protective grating in front of fire —**fire hall** C fire station —**fire irons** tongs, poker and shovel —'**firelighter** *n.* composition of highly combustible material for kindling domestic fire —'**fireman** *n.* 1. member of fire brigade 2. stoker 3. assistant to locomotive driver —'**fireplace** *n.* recess in room for fire —**fire raiser** person who deliberately sets fire to property *etc.* —**fire ship** burning vessel sent drifting against enemy ships —**fire station** building housing fire brigade —'**firetrap** *n.* building unsafe in case of fire —'**firework** *n.* 1. (*oft. pl.*) device to give spectacular effects by explosions and coloured sparks —*pl.* 2. outburst of temper, anger —**firing line** 1. *Mil.* positions from which fire is delivered 2. leading position in an activity —**firing party** *or* **squad** detachment sent to fire volleys at military funeral, or to shoot criminal

firkin ('fɜːkın) *n.* 1. small cask 2. UK measure of 9 gallons

firm[1] (fɜːm) *a.* 1. solid 2. fixed, stable 3. steadfast 4. resolute 5. settled —*v.* 6. make, become firm

firm[2] (fɜːm) *n.* 1. commercial enterprise 2. partnership

firmament ('fɜːməmənt) *n.* expanse of sky, heavens

first (fɜːst) *a.* 1. earliest in time or order 2. foremost in rank or position 3. most excellent 4. highest, chief —*n.* 5. beginning 6. first occurrence of something 7. first-class honours degree at university —*adv.* 8. before others in time, order *etc.* —'**firstly** *adv.* —**first aid** help given to injured person before arrival of doctor —**first class** *n.* 1. class of highest value, quality *etc.* —*a.* 2. of highest class 3. excellent 4. of most comfortable class of accommodation in hotel, train *etc.* 5. UK of letters handled faster than second-class letters —**first-class** *adv.* by first-class mail, means of transportation *etc.* —**first cousin** son or daughter of one's aunt or uncle —**first-day cover** *Philately* envelope postmarked on first day of issue of its stamps —**first finger** finger next to thumb —**first-foot** *chiefly Scot. n.* 1. first person to enter household in New Year (*also* **first-footer**) —*v.* 2. enter the house of (someone) as first-foot —**first-footing** *n.* —**first fruits** 1. first results or profits of undertaking 2. fruit that ripens first —**first-hand** *a.* obtained directly from the first source —**first lady** (*oft.* F- L-) US wife or official hostess of state governor or president —**first mate** *or* **officer** officer of merchant vessel immediately below captain —**first offender** person convicted of criminal offence for first time —**first person** grammatical category of pronouns and verbs used by speaker to refer to himself —**first-rate**

a. of highest class or quality —**first water** 1. finest quality of precious stone 2. best quality

firth (fɜːθ) *or* **frith** *n.* *esp.* in Scotland, arm of the sea, river estuary

fiscal ('fɪskəl) *a.* of government finances —**fiscal year** US financial year

fish (fɪʃ) *n.* 1. vertebrate cold-blooded animal with gills, living in water 2. its flesh as food (*pl.* **fish, -es**) —*vi.* 3. (attempt to) catch fish 4. search (for something) 5. (*with* for) try to get information indirectly —'**fisher** *n.* —'**fishery** *n.* 1. business of fishing 2. fishing ground —'**fishy** *a.* 1. of, like, or full of fish 2. dubious, open to suspicion —**fish cake** fried flattened ball of flaked fish mixed with mashed potatoes —'**fisherman** *n.* one who catches fish for a living or for pleasure —**fish-eye lens** *Photog.* lens of short focal length, that covers almost 180° —'**fish'finger** *n.* small piece of fish covered in breadcrumbs —**fish-kettle** *n.* oval pot for cooking fish —**fish meal** ground dried fish used as fertilizer *etc.* —'**fishmonger** *n.* seller of fish —**fish slice** 1. fish carver 2. flat-bladed utensil for turning or lifting food in frying —'**fishwife** *n.* coarse, scolding woman —**fish out** find, extract

fishplate ('fɪʃpleɪt) *n.* piece of metal holding rails together

fissure ('fɪʃə) *n.* cleft, split, cleavage —**fissile** ('fɪsaɪl) *a.* 1. capable of splitting 2. tending to split —'**fission** *n.* 1. splitting 2. reproduction by division of living cells with two parts, each of which becomes complete organism 3. splitting of atomic nucleus with release of large amount of energy —'**fissionable** *a.* capable of undergoing nuclear fission —**fissiparous** (fɪ'sɪpərəs) *a.* reproducing by fission

fist (fɪst) *n.* clenched hand —'**fisticuffs** *pl.n.* fighting

fistula ('fɪstjʊlə) *n.* pipelike ulcer (*pl.* **-s, -lae** (-liː))

fit¹ (fɪt) *vt.* 1. be suited to 2. be properly adjusted to 3. arrange, adjust, apply, insert 4. supply, furnish —*vi.* 5. be correctly adjusted or adapted 6. be of right size (**-tt-**) —*a.* 7. well-suited, worthy 8. qualified 9. proper, becoming 10. ready 11. in good condition or health ('**fitter** *comp.,* '**fittest** *sup.*) —*n.* 12. way anything fits, its style 13. adjustment —'**fitly** *adv.* —'**fitment** *n.* piece of furniture —'**fitness** *n.* —'**fitted** *a.* 1. designed for excellent fit 2. (of carpet) cut to cover floor completely 3. (of furniture) built to fit particular space —'**fitter** *n.* 1. one who, that which, makes fit 2. one who supervises making and fitting of garments 3. mechanic skilled in fitting up metalwork —'**fitting** *a.* 1. appropriate, suitable, proper —*n.* 2. fixture 3. apparatus 4. action of

fitting —**fit in** 1. give place or time to 2. belong or conform, *esp.* after adjustment

fit² (fɪt) *n.* 1. seizure with convulsions, spasms, loss of consciousness *etc.,* of epilepsy, hysteria *etc.* 2. sudden passing attack of illness 3. passing state, mood —'**fitful** *a.* spasmodic, capricious —'**fitfully** *adv.* —**have** *or* **throw a fit** *inf.* become very angry

five (faɪv) *a./n.* cardinal number after four —'**fif'teen** *a./n.* ten plus five —'**fif'teenth** *a./n.* —**fifth** (fɪfθ) *a./n.* ordinal number of five —**fifthly** ('fɪfθlɪ) *adv.* —**fiftieth** ('fɪftɪɪθ) *a./n.* —**fifty** ('fɪftɪ) *a./n.* five tens —'**fiver** *n.* UK *inf.* five-pound note —**fives** *pl.n.* (*with sing. v.*) ball game played with hand or bat in a court —**fifth column** organization spying for enemy within country at war —**fifty-fifty** *a./adv. inf.* in equal parts —**five-a-side** *n.* football with teams of five —**five-o'clock shadow** beard growth visible late in day on man's shaven face —'**fivepins** *pl.n.* bowling game played *esp.* in Canada —**Five-Year Plan** in socialist economies, government plan for economic development over five-year period

fix (fɪks) *vt.* 1. fasten, make firm or stable 2. set, establish 3. appoint, assign, determine 4. make fast 5. repair 6. *inf.* influence the outcome of unfairly or by deception 7. *inf.* bribe 8. *inf.* give (someone) his just deserts —*vi.* 9. become firm or solidified 10. determine —*n.* 11. difficult situation 12. position of ship, aircraft ascertained by radar, observation *etc.* 13. *sl.* dose of narcotic drug —**fix'ation** *n.* 1. act of fixing 2. preoccupation, obsession 3. situation of being set in some way of acting or thinking —'**fixative** *a.* 1. capable of, or tending to fix —*n.* 2. fluid sprayed over drawings to prevent smudging *etc.* 3. substance added to liquid to make it less volatile —**fixed** *a.* 1. attached so as to be immovable 2. stable 3. steadily directed 4. established as to relative position 5. always at same time 6. (of ideas *etc.*) firmly maintained 7. (of element) held in chemical combination 8. (of substance) nonvolatile 9. arranged 10. *inf.* equipped; provided for 11. *inf.* illegally arranged —'**fixedly** ('fɪksɪdlɪ) *adv.* intently —'**fixity** *n.* —'**fixture** *n.* 1. thing fixed in position 2. thing attached to house 3. date for sporting event 4. the event —**fixed star** star whose position appears to be stationary over long period of time —**fix** (**someone**) **up** attend to (someone's) needs —**fix up** arrange

fizz (fɪz) *vi.* 1. hiss, splutter —*n.* 2. hissing noise 3. effervescent liquid, such as soda water, champagne —'**fizzle** *vi.* 1. splutter weakly —*n.* 2. fizzling noise 3. fiasco —'**fizzy** *a.* effervescent —**fizzle out** *inf.* come to nothing, fail

fjord *or* **fiord** (fjɔːd) *n. esp.* in Norway, long, narrow inlet of sea

FL Florida

fl. 1. floor 2. *floruit* (*Lat.*, (he or she) flourished) 3. fluid

flabbergast ('flæbəgɑːst) *vt.* overwhelm with astonishment

flabby ('flæbɪ) *a.* 1. hanging loose, limp 2. out of condition, too fat 3. feeble 4. yielding —**flab** *n. inf.* unsightly fat on the body —'**flabbiness** *n.*

flaccid ('flæksɪd) *a.* flabby, lacking firmness —**flac'cidity** *n.*

flag[1] (flæg) *n.* 1. banner, piece of bunting attached to staff or halyard as standard or signal 2. small paper emblem sold on flag days —*vt.* 3. decorate or mark with flag(s) 4. send or communicate (messages *etc.*) by flag signals (**-gg-**) —**flag day** day on which small flags or emblems are sold in streets for charity —'**flagpole** *or* '**flagstaff** *n.* pole on which flag is hoisted and displayed (*pl.* **-poles** *or* **-staffs, -staves** (-steɪvz)) —'**flagship** *n.* 1. admiral's ship 2. most important ship of fleet —**flag down** warn or signal (vehicle) to stop —**flag of convenience** national flag flown by ship registered in that country to gain financial or legal advantage —**flag of truce** white flag indicating invitation to enemy to negotiate

flag[2] (flæg) *n.* water plant with sword-shaped leaves, *esp.* the iris —'**flaggy** *a.*

flag[3] (flæg) *n.* 1. flat slab of stone —*pl.* 2. pavement of flags —*vt.* 3. furnish (floor *etc.*) with flagstones (**-gg-**) —'**flagstone** *n.*

flag[4] (flæg) *vi.* 1. droop, fade 2. lose vigour (**-gg-**)

flagellate ('flædʒɪleɪt) *vt.* scourge, flog —'**flagellant** *n.* one who scourges himself, *esp.* in religious penance —flagel'lation *n.* —'**flagellator** *n.*

flagellum (fləˈdʒɛləm) *n. Biol.* whiplike outgrowth from cell that acts as organ of locomotion 2. *Bot.* long thin shoot (*pl.* **-la** (-lə), **-s**)

flageolet (flædʒəˈlɛt) *n.* small flutelike instrument

flagon ('flægən) *n.* large bottle of wine *etc.*

flagrant ('fleɪgrənt) *a.* glaring, scandalous, blatant —'**flagrancy** *n.* —'**flagrantly** *adv.*

flail (fleɪl) *n.* 1. instrument for threshing corn by hand —*v.* 2. beat with, move as, flail

flair (flɛə) *n.* 1. natural ability 2. elegance

flak *or* **flack** (flæk) *n.* 1. anti-aircraft fire 2. *inf.* adverse criticism

flake (fleɪk) *n.* 1. small, thin piece, *esp.* particle of snow 2. piece chipped off —*v.* 3. (cause to) peel off in flakes —'**flaky** *a.* —**flake out** *inf.* collapse, sleep from exhaustion

flambé ('flɒmbeɪ) *a.* (of food) served in flaming brandy *etc.*

flamboyant (flæmˈbɔɪənt) *a.* 1. florid, gorgeous, showy 2. exuberant, ostentatious

flame (fleɪm) *n.* 1. burning gas, *esp.* above fire 2. visible burning 3. passion, *esp.* love 4. *inf.* sweetheart —*vi.* 5. give out flames, blaze 6. shine 7. burst out —'**flaming** *a.* 1. burning with flames 2. glowing brightly 3. ardent 4. *inf.* a common intensifier —**flame-thrower** *n.* weapon that ejects stream of burning fluid

flamenco (fləˈmɛŋkəʊ) *n.* Sp. dance to guitar

flamingo (fləˈmɪŋgəʊ) *n.* large pink bird with long neck and legs (*pl.* **-s, -es**)

flammable ('flæməbᵊl) *a.* liable to catch fire

flan (flæn) *n.* open sweet or savoury tart

flange (flændʒ) *n.* 1. projecting flat rim, collar or rib —*v.* 2. provide with or take form of flange

flank (flæŋk) *n.* 1. part of side between hips and ribs 2. side of anything, *esp.* body of troops —*vt.* 3. guard or strengthen on flank 4. attack flank of 5. be at, move along either side of

flannel ('flænᵊl) *n.* 1. soft woollen fabric for clothing, *esp.* trousers 2. small piece of cloth for washing face and hands 3. *inf.* insincere talk —*pl.* 4. trousers *etc.* made of flannel —*vt.* 5. *UK inf.* flatter (**-ll-**) —**flanne'lette** *n.* cotton fabric imitating flannel —'**flannelly** *a.*

flap (flæp) *v.* 1. move (wings, arms *etc.*) as bird flying 2. (cause to) sway —*vt.* 3. strike with flat object —*vi.* 4. *inf.* be agitated, flustered (**-pp-**) —*n.* 5. act of flapping 6. broad piece of anything hanging from hinge or loosely from one side 7. movable part of aircraft wing 8. *inf.* state of excitement or panic —'**flapper** *n.* in 1920s, young woman, *esp.* one flaunting unconventional behaviour —'**flapjack** *n.* 1. chewy biscuit made with rolled oats 2. *chiefly US* pancake

flare (flɛə) *vi.* 1. blaze with unsteady flame 2. *inf.* (with up) suddenly burst into anger 3. spread outwards, as bottom of skirt —*n.* 4. instance of flaring 5. signal light —**flare-path** *n.* area lit up to facilitate landing or takeoff of aircraft —**flare-up** *n.* 1. sudden burst of fire 2. *inf.* sudden burst of emotion —**flare up** 1. burst suddenly into fire 2. *inf.* burst into anger

flash (flæʃ) *n.* 1. sudden burst of light or flame 2. sudden short blaze 3. very short time 4. brief news item 5. ribbon; badge 6. display —*vi.* 7. break into sudden flame 8. gleam 9. burst into view 10. move very fast 11. appear suddenly 12. *sl.* expose oneself indecently —*vt.* 13. cause to gleam 14. emit (light *etc.*) suddenly —*a.* 15. showy 16. sham (*also* '**flashy**) —'**flasher** *n.* 1. something which flashes 2. *sl.* someone who indecently exposes himself —'**flashing** *n.* weatherproof material used to cover valleys between slopes of roof *etc.* —'**flashback** *n.* break in continuity of book, play or film, to introduce what has taken place previously —'**flashbulb** *n. Photog.* small light bulb triggered, *usu.* electrically, to produce bright flash of light —'**flashcube** n. boxlike camera attachment, holding four flashbulbs, that turns so that each flashbulb can be used —'**flashlight** n. 1. esp. US torch 2. Photog. brief bright light emitted by electronic flash (also **flash**) —**flash point** temperature at which a vapour ignites —**flash in the pan** person etc. that enjoys only short-lived success

flask (flɑːsk) n. 1. long-necked bottle for scientific use 2. pocket bottle 3. vacuum flask

flat[1] (flæt) a. 1. level 2. spread out 3. at full length 4. smooth 5. downright 6. dull, lifeless 7. Mus. below true pitch 8. (of tyre) deflated, punctured 9. (of battery) fully discharged, dead ('**flatter** comp., '**flattest** sup.) —adv. 10. completely, utterly; absolutely —n. 11. flat object, surface or part 12. Mus. note half tone below natural pitch —'**flatly** adv. —'**flatness** n. —'**flatten** v. —'**flatfish** n. type of fish which swims along sea floor on one side of body with both eyes on uppermost side —'**flatfoot** n. 1. condition in which instep arch of foot is flattened 2. sl. policeman (pl. **-s**, **-feet**) —'**flatiron** n. formerly, iron for pressing clothes —**flat race** race over level ground with no jumps —**flat rate** the same rate in all cases —**flat spin** 1. aircraft spin in which longitudinal axis is more nearly horizontal than vertical 2. inf. state of confusion —'**flatworm** n. parasitic or free-living invertebrate, such as fluke or tapeworm, having flattened body —**flat out** at, with maximum speed or effort

flat[2] (flæt) n. suite of rooms comprising a residence entirely on one floor of building —'**flatlet** n. small flat

flatter ('flætə) vt. 1. fawn on 2. praise insincerely 3. gratify vanity of 4. represent too favourably —'**flatterer** n. —'**flattery** n.

flatulent ('flætjʊlənt) a. 1. suffering from, generating (excess) gases in intestines 2. pretentious —'**flatulence** n. 1. flatulent condition 2. verbosity, emptiness

flaunt (flɔːnt) v. 1. show off 2. wave proudly

flautist ('flɔːtɪst) or U.S. **flutist** ('fluːtɪst) n. flute player

flavescent (fləˈvesənt) a. yellowish; turning yellow

flavour or U.S. **flavor** ('fleɪvə) n. 1. mixed sensation of smell and taste 2. distinctive taste, savour 3. undefinable characteristic, quality of anything —vt. 4. give flavour to 5. season —'**flavouring** or U.S. '**flavoring** n.

flaw[1] (flɔː) n. 1. crack 2. defect, blemish —vt. 3. make flaw in —'**flawless** a. perfect

flaw[2] (flɔː) n. sudden gust of wind; squall

flax (flæks) n. 1. plant grown for its textile fibre and seeds 2. its fibres, spun into linen thread

—'**flaxen** a. 1. of flax 2. light yellow, straw-coloured

flay (fleɪ) vt. 1. strip skin off 2. criticize severely

flea (fliː) n. small, wingless, jumping, blood-sucking insect —'**fleabag** n. unkempt person, horse etc. —'**fleabite** n. 1. insect's bite 2. trifling injury 3. trifle —**flea-bitten** a. 1. bitten by flea 2. mean, worthless 3. scruffy —**flea market** market for cheap goods —'**fleapit** n. inf. shabby cinema or theatre

fleck (flek) n. 1. small mark, streak or particle —vt. 2. mark with flecks

fled (fled) pt./pp. of FLEE

fledged (fledʒd) a. 1. (of birds) able to fly 2. experienced, trained —'**fledgling** or '**fledgeling** n. 1. young bird 2. inexperienced person

flee (fliː) v. run away (from) (**fled**, '**fleeing**)

fleece (fliːs) n. 1. sheep's wool —vt. 2. rob —'**fleecy** a.

fleet[1] (fliːt) n. 1. number of warships organized as unit 2. number of ships, cars etc. operating together —**fleet chief petty officer** noncommissioned officer in Royal Navy comparable in rank to warrant officer in army or Royal Air Force

fleet[2] (fliːt) a. swift, nimble —'**fleeting** a. passing, transient —'**fleetingly** adv.

Fleet Street (fliːt) 1. street in London where many newspaper offices are situated 2. Brit. journalism or journalists collectively

Flemish ('flemɪʃ) n. 1. one of two official languages of Belgium —a. 2. of Flanders —'**Fleming** n. native of Flanders, medieval principality in the Low Countries, or of Flemish-speaking Belgium —**the Flemish** Flemings collectively

flense (flens), **flench** (flentʃ), or **flinch** (flintʃ) vt. strip (esp. whale) of flesh

flesh (fleʃ) n. 1. soft part, muscular substance, between skin and bone 2. in plants, pulp 3. fat 4. sensual appetites —'**fleshily** adv. —'**fleshly** a. 1. carnal 2. material —'**fleshy** a. 1. plump 2. pulpy —'**fleshpots** pl.n. (places catering for) self-indulgent living —**flesh wound** wound affecting superficial tissues —**in the flesh** in person; actually present

fleur-de-lis or **fleur-de-lys** (flɜːdəˈliː) n. 1. heraldic lily with three petals 2. iris (pl. **fleurs-de-lis** or **fleurs-de-lys** (flɜːdəˈliːz))

flew (fluː) pt. of FLY[1]

flews (fluːz) pl.n. fleshy hanging lip of bloodhound or similar dog

flex (fleks) n. 1. flexible insulated electric cable —v. 2. bend, be bent —**flexi**'**bility** n. —'**flexible** a. 1. easily bent 2. manageable 3. adaptable —'**flexibly** adv. —'**flexion** or '**flection** n. 1. bending 2. bent state —'**flexitime** n. system permitting variation in starting and finishing times of work, providing an agreed number of hours is worked over a specified period

flibbertigibbet ('flɪbətɪdʒɪbɪt) n. flighty, gossiping person

flick (flɪk) vt. 1. strike lightly, jerk —n. 2. light blow 3. jerk —pl. 4. sl. cinema —**flick knife** knife with retractable blade that springs out when button is pressed

flicker ('flɪkə) vi. 1. burn, shine, unsteadily 2. waver, quiver —n. 3. unsteady light or movement

flight (flaɪt) n. 1. act or manner of flying through air 2. number flying together, as birds 3. journey in aircraft 4. Air Force unit of command 5. power of flying 6. swift movement or passage 7. sally 8. distance flown 9. feather etc. fitted to arrow or dart to give it stability in flight 10. stairs between two landings 11. running away —**flight deck** 1. crew compartment in airliner 2. upper deck of aircraft carrier where aircraft take off —**flight lieutenant** officer holding commissioned rank senior to flying officer and junior to squadron leader in Royal Air Force —**flight recorder** electronic device in aircraft storing information about its flight —**flight sergeant** noncommissioned officer in Royal Air Force, junior in rank to master aircrew

flighty ('flaɪtɪ) a. 1. frivolous 2. erratic

flimsy ('flɪmzɪ) a. 1. frail, weak 2. thin 3. easily destroyed —'**flimsily** adv.

flinch (flɪntʃ) vi. shrink, draw back, wince

fling (flɪŋ) v. 1. throw, send, move, with force (**flung** pt./pp.) —n. 2. throw 3. hasty attempt 4. spell of indulgence 5. vigorous dance

flint (flɪnt) n. 1. hard steel-grey stone 2. piece of this 3. hard substance used (as flint) for striking fire —'**flintily** adv. —'**flinty** a. 1. like or consisting of flint 2. hard, cruel —'**flintlock** n. 1. gunlock in which charge is ignited by spark produced by flint in hammer 2. firearm having such lock

flip (flɪp) vt. 1. throw or flick lightly 2. turn over —vi. 3. sl., chiefly US fly into rage or emotional outburst (also **flip one's lid** or **top**) (-pp-) —n. 4. instance, act, of flipping 5. drink with beaten egg —a. 6. US inf. flippant; pert —'**flippancy** n. —'**flippant** a. treating serious things lightly —'**flippantly** adv. —'**flipper** n. 1. limb, fin for swimming —pl. 2. fin-shaped rubber devices worn on feet to help in swimming —**flip side** less important side of pop record

flirt (flɜːt) vi. 1. toy, play with another's affections 2. trifle, toy (with) —n. 3. person who flirts —flir'**tation** n. —flir'**tatious** a.

flit (flɪt) vi. 1. pass lightly and rapidly 2. dart 3. dial. move house 4. inf. go away hastily, secretly (-tt-)

flitch (flɪtʃ) n. side of bacon

flittermouse ('flɪtəmaʊs) n. dial. bat (the animal)

float (fləʊt) vi. 1. rest, drift on surface of liquid 2. be suspended freely 3. move aimlessly —vt. 4. (of liquid) support, bear alone 5. in commerce, get (company) started 6. Fin. allow (currency) to fluctuate against other currencies in accordance with market forces —n. 7. anything small that floats (esp. to support something else, eg fishing net) 8. small delivery vehicle, esp. powered by batteries 9. motor vehicle carrying tableau etc. in parade 10. sum of money used to provide change —'**floating** a. 1. having little or no attachment 2. (of organ etc.) displaced and abnormally movable 3. uncommitted, unfixed 4. Fin. (of capital) available for current use; (of debt) short-term and unfunded; (of currency) free to fluctuate against other currencies in accordance with market forces —flo'**tation** or floa'**tation** n. act of floating, esp. floating of company —**floating rib** any rib of lower two pairs of ribs, which are not attached to breastbone —**floating voter** voter of no fixed political allegiance

flocculent ('flɒkjʊlənt) a. like tufts of wool

flock[1] (flɒk) n. 1. number of animals of one kind together 2. body of people 3. religious congregation —vi. 4. gather in a crowd

flock[2] (flɒk) n. 1. lock, tuft of wool etc. 2. wool refuse for stuffing cushions etc. —'**flocky** a.

floe (fləʊ) n. sheet of floating ice

flog (flɒg) vt. 1. beat with whip, stick etc. 2. sl. sell (-gg-) —**flog a dead horse** pursue line of attack or argument from which no results can come

flood (flʌd) n. 1. inundation, overflow of water 2. rising of tide 3. outpouring 4. flowing water —vt. 5. inundate 6. cover, fill with water —vi. 7. arrive, move etc. in great numbers —'**floodgate** n. gate, sluice for letting water in or out —'**floodlight** n. broad, intense beam of artificial light —'**floodlit** a. —**flood tide** 1. the rising tide 2. fig. peak of prosperity

floor (flɔː) n. 1. lower surface of room 2. set of rooms on one level, storey 3. flat space 4. (right to speak in) legislative hall —vt. 5. supply with floor 6. knock down 7. confound —'**flooring** n. material for floors —**floor plan** drawing to scale of arrangement of rooms on one floor of building —**floor show** entertainment in night-club etc.

floozy, floozie, or **floosie** ('fluːzɪ) n. sl. disreputable woman

flop (flɒp) vi. 1. bend, fall, collapse loosely, carelessly 2. fall flat on floor, on water etc. 3. inf. go to sleep 4. inf. fail (-pp-) —n. 5. flopping movement or sound 6. inf. failure —'**floppily** adv. —'**floppiness** n. —'**floppy** a. limp, unsteady

—**floppy disk** flexible magnetic disk that stores information and can be used to store data in memory of digital computer

flora ('flɔːrə) *n.* **1.** plants of a region **2.** list of them (*pl.* **-s, -rae** (-riː)) —'**floral** *a.* of flowers —**flo'rescence** *n.* state or time of flowering —'**floret** *n.* small flower forming part of composite flower —**flori'bunda** *n.* type of rose whose flowers grow in large clusters —**flori'cultural** *a.* —'**floriculture** *n.* cultivation of flowers —**flori'culturist** *n.* —**florist** ('flɒrɪst) *n.* dealer in flowers

Florentine ('flɒrəntaɪn) *a.* **1.** of Florence in Italy —*n.* **2.** native of Florence

florid ('flɒrɪd) *a.* **1.** with red, flushed complexion **2.** ornate

florin ('flɒrɪn) *n.* formerly, Brit. silver two-shilling piece

floss (flɒs) *n.* **1.** mass of fine, silky fibres, *eg* of cotton, silk **2.** fluff —'**flossy** *a.* light and downy

flotation or **floatation** (fləʊ'teɪʃən) *n.* see FLOAT

flotilla (flə'tɪlə) *n.* **1.** fleet of small vessels **2.** group of destroyers

flotsam ('flɒtsəm) *n.* **1.** floating wreckage **2.** discarded waste objects

flounce[1] (flaʊns) *vi.* **1.** go, move abruptly and impatiently —*n.* **2.** fling, jerk of body or limb

flounce[2] (flaʊns) *n.* ornamental gathered strip on woman's garment

flounder[1] ('flaʊndə) *vi.* **1.** plunge and struggle, *esp.* in water or mud **2.** proceed in bungling, hesitating manner —*n.* **3.** act of floundering

flounder[2] ('flaʊndə) *n.* flatfish

flour (flaʊə) *n.* **1.** powder prepared by sifting and grinding wheat *etc.* **2.** fine soft powder —*vt.* **3.** sprinkle with flour —'**flouriness** *n.* —'**floury** *a.*

flourish ('flʌrɪʃ) *vi.* **1.** thrive **2.** be in the prime —*vt.* **3.** brandish, wave about **4.** display —*n.* **5.** ornamental curve **6.** showy gesture in speech *etc.* **7.** waving of hand, weapon *etc.* **8.** fanfare (of trumpets)

flout (flaʊt) *vt.* **1.** show contempt for, mock **2.** defy

flow (fləʊ) *vi.* **1.** glide along as stream **2.** circulate, as the blood **3.** move easily **4.** move in waves **5.** hang loose **6.** be present in abundance —*n.* **7.** act, instance of flowing **8.** quantity that flows **9.** rise of tide **10.** ample supply —**flow chart** diagram showing sequence of operations in industrial *etc.* process

flower ('flaʊə) *n.* **1.** coloured (not green) part of plant from which fruit is developed **2.** bloom, blossom **3.** ornamentation **4.** choicest part, pick —*pl.* **5.** chemical sublimate —*vi.* **6.** produce flowers **7.** bloom **8.** come to prime condition —*vt.* **9.** ornament with flowers —'**flowered** *a.* **1.**

having flowers **2.** decorated with floral design —'**floweret** *n.* small flower —'**flowery** *a.* **1.** abounding in flowers **2.** full of fine words, ornamented with figures of speech —**flower girl** girl selling flowers

flown (fləʊn) *pp.* of FLY[1]

fl. oz. fluid ounce(s)

flu (fluː) influenza

fluctuate ('flʌktjʊeɪt) *v.* **1.** vary —*vi.* **2.** rise and fall, undulate —**fluctu'ation** *n.*

flue (fluː) *n.* passage or pipe for smoke or hot air, chimney

fluent ('fluːənt) *a.* **1.** speaking, writing a given language easily and well **2.** easy, graceful

fluff (flʌf) *n.* **1.** soft, feathery stuff **2.** down **3.** *inf.* mistake —*v.* **4.** make or become soft, light **5.** *inf.* make mistake (in) —'**fluffy** *a.*

fluid ('fluːɪd) *a.* **1.** flowing easily **2.** not solid —*n.* **3.** gas or liquid —**flu'idity** *n.* —**fluid ounce** unit of capacity 1/20 of pint

fluke[1] (fluːk) *n.* **1.** flat triangular point of anchor —*pl.* **2.** whale's tail

fluke[2] (fluːk) *n.* **1.** stroke of luck, accident —*vt.* **2.** gain, make, hit by accident or by luck —'**fluky** *a.* **1.** uncertain **2.** got by luck

fluke[3] (fluːk) *n.* **1.** flatfish **2.** parasitic worm

flume (fluːm) *n.* narrow (artificial) channel for water

flummery ('flʌmərɪ) *n.* **1.** nonsense, idle talk, humbug **2.** dish of milk, flour, eggs *etc.*

flummox ('flʌməks) *vt.* bewilder, perplex

flung (flʌŋ) *pt./pp.* of FLING

flunk (flʌŋk) US, NZ *inf.* **1.** (cause to) fail to reach required standard (in) —*vi.* **2.** (*with* out) be dismissed from school

flunky or **flunkey** ('flʌŋkɪ) *n.* **1.** servant, *esp.* liveried manservant **2.** servile person

fluorescence (flʊə'rɛsəns) *n.* emission of light or other radiation from substance when bombarded by particles (electrons *etc.*) or other radiation, as in fluorescent lamp —**fluo'resce** *vi.* —**fluo'rescent** *a.* —**fluorescent lamp** lamp in which ultraviolet radiation from electrical gas discharge causes layer of phosphor on tube's inside surface to fluoresce —'**fluoroscope** *n.* device consisting of fluorescent screen and x-ray source that enables x-ray image of person *etc.* to be observed directly —**fluo'roscopy** *n.* examination of person *etc.* by means of fluoroscope

fluorspar ('flʊəspɑː), **fluor** ('fluːɔ), or *U.S.* **fluorite** ('flʊəraɪt) *n.* mineral containing fluorine —'**fluoridate** *vt.* —**fluori'dation** *n.* —'**fluoride** *n.* salt containing fluorine, *esp.* as added to domestic water supply as protection against tooth decay —'**fluorinate** *vt.* treat or cause to combine with fluorine —'**fluorine** *n.* nonmetallic element, yellowish gas

flurry ('flʌrɪ) *n.* **1.** squall, gust **2.** bustle, commotion **3.** death struggle of whale **4.** fluttering (as of snowflakes) —*vt.* **5.** agitate, bewilder, fluster ('**flurried,** '**flurrying**)

flush¹ (flʌʃ) *vi.* **1.** blush **2.** (of skin) redden **3.** flow suddenly or violently —*vt.* **4.** cleanse (*eg* toilet) by rush of water **5.** excite —*n.* **6.** reddening, blush **7.** rush of water **8.** excitement **9.** elation **10.** glow of colour **11.** freshness, vigour —*a.* **12.** full **13.** *inf.* having plenty of money **14.** *inf.* well supplied **15.** level with surrounding surface

flush² (flʌʃ) *vt.* cause to leave cover and take flight

flush³ (flʌʃ) *n.* set of cards all of one suit

fluster ('flʌstə) *v.* **1.** make or become nervous, agitated —*n.* **2.** state of confusion or agitation

flute (fluːt) *n.* **1.** wind instrument of tube with holes stopped by fingers or keys and blowhole in side **2.** groove, channel —*vi.* **3.** play on flute —*vt.* **4.** make grooves in —'**fluted** *a.* —'**fluting** *n.*

flutter ('flʌtə) *v.* **1.** flap (as wings) rapidly without flight or in short flights **2.** be or make excited, agitated —*vi.* **3.** quiver —*n.* **4.** flapping movement **5.** nervous agitation **6.** *inf.* modest wager

fluvial ('fluːvɪəl) *a.* of rivers

flux (flʌks) *n.* **1.** discharge **2.** constant succession of changes **3.** substance mixed with metal to clean, aid adhesion in soldering *etc.* **4.** measure of strength in magnetic field

fly¹ (flaɪ) *vi.* **1.** move through air on wings or in aircraft **2.** pass quickly **3.** rush **4.** flee, run away —*vt.* **5.** operate (aircraft) **6.** cause to fly **7.** set flying —*v.* **8.** float loosely (**flew** *pt.,* **flown** *pp.*) —*n.* **9.** (zip or buttons fastening) opening in trousers **10.** flap in garment or tent **11.** flying —'**flier** *or* '**flyer** *n.* **1.** person or thing that flies **2.** aviator, pilot **3.** *inf.* long, flying leap **4.** rectangular step in straight flight of stairs **5.** *Athletics inf.* flying start —'**flying** *a.* hurried, brief —'**flyaway** *a.* **1.** (of hair *etc.*) loose and fluttering **2.** frivolous, flighty; giddy —**fly-by-night** *inf. a.* **1.** untrustworthy, *esp.* in finance —*n.* **2.** untrustworthy person —**fly-fish** *vi.* fish with artificial fly as lure —**flying boat** aeroplane fitted with floats instead of landing wheels —**flying buttress** *Archit.* arched or slanting structure attached at only one point to a mass of masonry —**flying colours** conspicuous success —**flying doctor** (*esp.* Aust.) doctor visiting patients in outback areas by aircraft —**flying fish** fish with winglike fins used for gliding above the sea —**flying fox** large fruit-eating bat —**flying officer** officer holding commissioned rank senior to pilot officer but junior to flight lieutenant in Brit. and certain other air forces —**flying saucer** unidentified (disc-shaped) flying object, supposedly from outer space —**flying**

squad special detachment of police, soldiers *etc.,* ready to act quickly —**flying start 1.** in sprinting, start by competitor anticipating starting signal **2.** start to race in which competitor is already travelling at speed as he passes starting line **3.** any promising beginning **4.** initial advantage —'**flyleaf** *n.* blank leaf at beginning or end of book —'**flyover** *n.* road passing over another by bridge —'**flypaper** *n.* paper with sticky and poisonous coating, *usu.* hung from ceiling to trap flies —**fly sheet 1.** fly (in tent) **2.** short handbill —**fly spray** liquid sprayed from aerosol to destroy flies —'**flytrap** *n.* **1.** insectivorous plant **2.** device for catching flies —'**flyweight** *n.* **1.** professional boxer weighing not more than 112 lbs. (51 kg); amateur boxer weighing 106-112 lbs. (48-51 kg) **2.** in Olympic wrestling, wrestler weighing not more than 115 lbs. (52 kg) —'**flywheel** *n.* heavy wheel regulating speed of machine

fly² (flaɪ) *n.* two-winged insect, *esp.* common housefly —'**flyblown** *a.* infested with larvae of blowfly —'**flycatcher** *n.* small insect-eating songbird

fly³ (flaɪ) *a. sl.* sharp and knowing

Fm *Chem.* fermium

FM frequency modulation

fm. **1.** fathom (*also* **fm**) **2.** from

F.M. Field Marshal

f-number *or* **f number** *n. Photog.* numerical value of relative aperture

fo. folio

F.O. Flying Officer

foal (fəʊl) *n.* **1.** young of horse, ass *etc.* —*v.* **2.** bear (foal)

foam (fəʊm) *n.* **1.** collection of small bubbles on liquid **2.** froth of saliva or sweat **3.** light cellular solid used for insulation, packing *etc.* —*v.* **4.** (cause to) produce foam —*vi.* **5.** be very angry (*esp. in* **foam at the mouth**) —'**foamy** *a.* —**foam rubber** rubber treated to form firm, spongy foam

fob¹ (fɒb) *n.* **1.** short watch chain **2.** small pocket in waistband of trousers or waistcoat

f.o.b. *or* **F.O.B.** *Comm.* free on board

fob off 1. ignore, dismiss (someone or something) in offhand (insulting) manner **2.** dispose of (-**bb**-)

fo'c's'le *or* **fo'c'sle** ('fəʊksəl) *n. see* FORECASTLE

focus ('fəʊkəs) *n.* **1.** point at which rays meet after being reflected or refracted (*also* **focal point**) **2.** state of optical image when it is clearly defined **3.** state of instrument producing such image **4.** point of convergence **5.** point on which interest, activity is centred (*pl.* **-es, foci** ('fəʊsaɪ)) —*vt.* **6.** bring to focus, adjust **7.** concentrate —*vi.* **8.** come to focus **9.** converge ('focused, 'focusing) —'focal a. of, at focus —**focal length** or **distance** distance from focal point of lens to reflecting surface

fodder ('fɒdə) n. bulk food for livestock

foe (fəu) n. enemy

foetid ('fetid, 'fiː-) a. see FETID

foetus or **fetus** ('fiːtəs) n. fully-developed young in womb or egg —'**foetal** or '**fetal** a.

fog (fɒg) n. 1. thick mist 2. dense watery vapour in lower atmosphere 3. cloud of anything reducing visibility —vt. 4. cover in fog 5. puzzle (-gg-) —'**foggy** a. —'**fogbound** a. prevented from operation by fog —'**foghorn** n. instrument to warn ships in fog

fogy or **fogey** ('fəugɪ) n. old-fashioned person

foible ('fɔɪbəl) n. minor weakness; idiosyncrasy

foil[1] (fɔɪl) vt. baffle, defeat, frustrate —'**foilable** a.

foil[2] (fɔɪl) n. 1. metal in thin sheet 2. anything which sets off another thing to advantage 3. Archit. small arc between cusps

foil[3] (fɔɪl) n. light, slender, flexible sword tipped by button

foist (fɔɪst) vt. (usu. with off or on) sell, pass off (inferior or unwanted thing) as valuable

fold[1] (fəuld) vt. 1. double up, bend part of 2. interlace (arms) 3. wrap up 4. clasp (in arms) 5. Cooking mix gently —vi. 6. become folded 7. admit of being folded 8. inf. fail —n. 9. folding 10. coil 11. winding 12. line made by folding 13. crease 14. foldlike geological formation —'**folder** n. binder, file for loose papers —'**foldaway** a. (of bed etc.) able to be folded away when not in use —**folding door** door in form of hinged leaves that can be folded one against another

fold[2] (fəuld) n. 1. enclosure for sheep 2. body of believers, church

-**fold** (comb. form) having so many parts; being so many times as much or as many, as in hundredfold

folderol ('fɒldərɒl) n. see FALDERAL

foliage ('fəulɪɪdʒ) n. leaves collectively, leafage —**foli'aceous** a. of or like leaf —'**foliate** a. leaflike, having leaves —**foli'ation** n. 1. Bot. process of producing leaves; state of being in leaf; arrangement of leaves in leaf bud 2. Archit. ornamentation consisting of cusps and foils 3. consecutive numbering of leaves of book 4. Geol. arrangement of constituents of rock in leaflike layers

folio ('fəulɪəu) n. 1. sheet of paper folded in half to make two leaves of book 2. book of largest common size made up of such sheets 3. page numbered on one side only 4. page number (pl. -s)

folk (fəuk) n. 1. (with pl. v.) people in general 2. family, relatives 3. race of people —'**folksy** a.

inf., chiefly US 1. of or like ordinary people 2. friendly; affable 3. affectedly simple —**folk dance** —**folk etymology** gradual change in form of word through influence of more familiar word with which it becomes associated —'**folklore** n. traditions, customs, beliefs popularly held —**folk music** 1. music passed on from generation to generation 2. any music composed in this idiom —**folk song** 1. song handed down among common people 2. modern song in folk idiom

follicle ('fɒlɪkəl) n. 1. small sac 2. seed vessel —**fol'licular** a.

follow ('fɒləu) v. 1. go or come after —vt. 2. accompany, attend on 3. keep to (path etc.) 4. take as guide, conform to 5. engage in 6. have a keen interest in 7. be consequent on 8. grasp meaning of —vi. 9. come next 10. result —'**follower** n. 1. disciple 2. supporter —'**following** a. 1. about to be mentioned —n. 2. body of supporters —**follow-on** n. Cricket immediate second innings forced on team scoring prescribed number of runs fewer than its opponents in first innings —**follow-through** n. in ball games, continuation of stroke after impact with ball —**follow-up** n. something done to reinforce initial action —**follow on** (of team) play follow-on

folly ('fɒlɪ) n. 1. foolishness 2. foolish action, idea etc. 3. useless, extravagant structure

foment (fə'ment) vt. 1. foster, stir up 2. bathe with hot lotions —**fomen'tation** n.

fond (fɒnd) a. 1. tender, loving 2. obs. credulous 3. obs. foolish —'**fondly** adv. —'**fondness** n. —**fond of** having liking for

fondant ('fɒndənt) n. 1. soft sugar mixture for sweets 2. sweet made of this

fondle ('fɒndəl) vt. caress

fondue ('fɒndjuː; Fr. fɔ̃'dy) n. Swiss dish of sauce (esp. cheese) into which pieces of bread etc. are dipped

font (fɒnt) n. bowl for baptismal water, usu. on pedestal

fontanelle or **fontanel** (fɒntə'nel) n. soft, membranous gap between bones of baby's skull

food (fuːd) n. 1. solid nourishment 2. what one eats 3. mental or spiritual nourishment —**food poisoning** acute illness caused by food that is naturally poisonous or contaminated by bacteria —'**foodstuff** n. food

fool (fuːl) n. 1. silly, empty-headed person 2. dupe 3. simpleton 4. Hist. jester, clown 5. dessert of puréed fruit mixed with cream etc. —vt. 6. delude, dupe —vi. 7. act as fool —'**foolery** n. 1. habitual folly 2. act of playing the fool 3. absurdity —'**foolish** a. 1. ill-considered, silly 2. stupid —'**foolishly** adv. —'**foolhardiness** n. —'**foolhardy** a. foolishly adventurous —'**fool-**

proof a. proof against failure —**fool's cap** 1. jester's or dunce's cap 2. this as watermark —'**foolscap** n. size of paper which formerly had this mark —**fool's errand** fruitless undertaking —**fool's paradise** illusory happiness

foot (fut) n. 1. lowest part of leg, from ankle down 2. lowest part of anything, base, stand 3. end of bed etc. 4. infantry 5. measure of twelve inches 6. division of verse (pl. **feet**) —v. 7. dance (also **foot it**) —vt. 8. walk over (esp. in **foot it**) 9. pay cost of (esp. in **foot the bill**) —'**footage** n. 1. length in feet 2. length, of film used —'**footie** or '**footy** n. sl. football —'**footing** n. 1. basis, foundation 2. firm standing, relations, conditions —pl. 3. (concrete) foundations for walls of buildings —**foot-and-mouth disease** infectious viral disease in sheep, cattle etc. —'**football** n. 1. game played with large blown-up ball 2. the ball —'**footballer** n. —**football pools** form of gambling on results of football matches —'**footboard** n. 1. treadle or foot-operated lever on machine 2. vertical board at foot of bed —**foot brake** brake operated by pressure on foot pedal —'**footbridge** n. narrow bridge for pedestrians —'**footfall** n. sound of footstep —**foot fault** Tennis fault of overstepping baseline while serving —'**foothill** n. (oft. pl.) low hill at foot of mountain —'**foothold** n. 1. place affording secure grip for the foot 2. secure position from which progress may be made —'**footlights** pl.n. lights across front of stage —'**footloose** a. free from any ties —'**footman** n. liveried servant —'**footnote** n. note of reference or explanation printed at foot of page —'**footpad** n. obs. robber, highwayman —'**footpath** n. narrow path for pedestrians —'**footplate** n. platform for driver and fireman of locomotive —**foot-pound** n. unit of measurement of work in f.p.s. system —'**footprint** n. mark left by foot —'**footrest** n. something that provides support for feet —'**footslog** vi. walk, go on foot —'**footslogger** n. —'**footsore** a. having sore feet, esp. from walking —'**footwear** n. anything worn to cover feet —'**footwork** n. skilful use of feet, as in sports etc.

footle ('fuːt^əl) vi. inf. (oft. with around or about) loiter aimlessly

fop (fɒp) n. man excessively concerned with fashion —'**foppery** n. —'**foppish** a. —'**foppishly** adv.

for (fɔː; unstressed fə) prep. 1. intended to reach 2. directed or belonging to 3. because of 4. instead of 5. towards 6. on account of 7. in favour of 8. respecting 9. during 10. in search of 11. in payment of 12. in the character of 13. in spite of —conj. 14. because —**for it** inf. liable for punishment or blame

for- (comb. form) from, away, against, as in forswear, forbid. Such words are not given here where the meaning may easily be inferred from the simple word

forage ('fɒrɪdʒ) n. 1. food for cattle and horses —vi. 2. collect forage 3. make roving search —**forage cap** soldier's undress cap

foramen (fɒ'reɪmɛn) n. natural hole, esp. in bone (pl. **-ramina** (-'ræmɪnə), **-s**)

forasmuch as (fərəz'mʌtʃ) conj. seeing that

foray ('fɒreɪ) n. 1. raid, inroad —vi. 2. make one —'**forayer** n.

forbear[1] ('fɔːbɛə) n. see FOREBEAR

forbear[2] (fɔː'bɛə) v. 1. (esp. with from) cease; refrain (from) —vi. 2. be patient (**for'bore** pt., **for'borne** pp.) —for'**bearance** n. self-control; patience —for'**bearing** a.

forbid (fə'bɪd) vt. prohibit, refuse to allow (**for'bade** (fə'bæd, -'beɪd) pt., **for'bidden** pp., **for'bidding** pr.p.) —for'**bidding** a. 1. uninviting 2. threatening

force (fɔːs) n. 1. strength, power 2. compulsion 3. that which tends to produce a change in a physical system 4. mental or moral strength 5. body of troops, police etc. 6. group of people organized for particular task or duty 7. effectiveness, operative state 8. violence —vt. 9. constrain, compel 10. produce by effort, strength 11. break open 12. urge, strain 13. drive 14. hasten maturity of —**forced** a. 1. accomplished by great effort 2. compulsory 3. unnatural 4. strained —'**forceful** a. 1. powerful 2. persuasive —'**forcible** a. 1. done by force 2. efficacious, compelling, impressive 3. strong —'**forcibly** adv. —**force-feed** vt. force (person or animal) to eat or swallow (food)

forcemeat ('fɔːsmiːt) n. mixture of chopped ingredients used for stuffing (also **farce**)

forceps ('fɔːsɪps) pl.n. surgical pincers

ford (fɔːd) n. 1. shallow place where river may be crossed —vt. 2. cross (river etc.) over shallow area —'**fordable** a.

fore[1] (fɔː) a. 1. in front ('**former**, '**further** comp., '**foremost, first**, '**furthest** sup.) —n. 2. front part

fore[2] (fɔː) interj. golfer's warning

fore- (comb. form) previous, before, front

fore-and-aft a. placed in line from bow to stern of ship

forearm ('fɔːrɑːm) n. 1. arm between wrist and elbow —vt. (fɔːr'ɑːm) 2. arm beforehand

forebear or **forbear** ('fɔːbɛə) n. ancestor

forebode (fɔː'bəʊd) vt. indicate in advance —**fore'boding** n. anticipation of evil

forecast ('fɔːkɑːst) vt. 1. estimate beforehand (esp. weather); prophesy —n. 2. prediction

forecastle, **fo'c's'le**, or **fo'c'sle** ('fəʊks^əl) n. 1. forward raised part of ship 2. sailors' quarters

foreclose (fɔː'kləʊz) vt. 1. take away power of

redeeming (mortgage) **2.** prevent **3.** shut out, bar —**fore'closure** n.

forecourt ('fɔːkɔːt) n. courtyard, open space, in front of building

forefather ('fɔːfɑːðə) n. ancestor

forefinger ('fɔːfɪŋɡə) n. finger next to thumb

forefoot ('fɔːfut) n. either of front feet of quadruped

forefront ('fɔːfrʌnt) n. **1.** extreme front **2.** position of most prominence or action

foregather (fɔːˈɡæðə) vi. see FORGATHER

forego¹ (fɔːˈɡəu) vt. precede in time, place (-'went pt., -'gone pp., -'going pr.p.) —**fore'going** a. going before, preceding —**fore'gone** a. **1.** determined beforehand **2.** preceding —**foregone conclusion** result that might have been foreseen

forego² (fɔːˈɡəu) vt. see FORGO

foreground ('fɔːɡraund) n. part of view, esp. in picture, nearest observer

forehand ('fɔːhænd) a. (of stroke in racket games) made with inner side of wrist leading

forehead ('forid) n. part of face above eyebrows and between temples

foreign ('forin) a. **1.** not of, or in, one's own country **2.** relating to, or connected with other countries **3.** irrelevant **4.** coming from outside **5.** unfamiliar, strange —**'foreigner** n. —**foreign minister** or **secretary** (oft. F- M- or S-) cabinet minister responsible for country's dealings with other countries —**foreign office** ministry of country or state that is concerned with dealings with other states

foreknow (fɔːˈnəu) vt. know in advance —**foreknowledge** (fɔːˈnɒlɪdʒ) n.

foreland ('fɔːlənd) n. **1.** headland, promontory **2.** land lying in front of something, such as water

foreleg ('fɔːlɛɡ) n. either of front legs of horse or other quadruped

forelimb ('fɔːlɪm) n. either of front limbs of four-limbed vertebrate

forelock ('fɔːlɒk) n. lock of hair above forehead

foreman ('fɔːmən) n. **1.** one in charge of work **2.** leader of jury

foremast ('fɔːmɑːst; Naut. 'fɔːməst) n. mast nearest bow

foremost ('fɔːməust) a./adv. first in time, place, importance etc.

forenoon ('fɔːnuːn) n. morning

forensic (fəˈrɛnsɪk) a. of courts of law —**forensic medicine** application of medical knowledge in legal matters

foreordain (fɔːrɔːˈdeɪn) vt. determine (events etc.) in future —**foreordination** (fɔːrɔːdɪˈneɪʃən) n.

forepaw ('fɔːpɔː) n. either of front feet of most land mammals that do not have hooves

foreplay ('fɔːpleɪ) n. sexual stimulation before intercourse

forerunner ('fɔːrʌnə) n. one who goes before, precursor

foresail ('fɔːseɪl; Naut. 'fɔːsəl) n. Naut. **1.** aftermost headsail of fore-and-aft rigged vessel **2.** lowest sail set on foremast of square-rigged vessel

foresee (fɔːˈsiː) vt. see beforehand (-'saw pt., -'seen pp.)

foreshadow (fɔːˈʃædəu) vt. show, suggest beforehand

foreshore ('fɔːʃɔː) n. part of shore between high and low tide marks

foreshorten (fɔːˈʃɔːtən) vt. **1.** draw (object) so that it appears shortened **2.** make shorter

foresight ('fɔːsaɪt) n. **1.** foreseeing **2.** care for future

foreskin ('fɔːskɪn) n. skin that covers the glans penis

forest ('forist) n. **1.** area with heavy growth of trees and plants **2.** these trees **3.** fig. something resembling forest —vt. **4.** plant, create forest in (an area) —**fores'tation** n. planting of trees over wide area —**'forester** n. one skilled in forestry —**'forestry** n. study, management of forest planting and maintenance

forestall (fɔːˈstɔːl) vt. **1.** anticipate **2.** prevent, guard against in advance

foretaste ('fɔːteɪst) n. **1.** anticipation **2.** taste beforehand

foretell (fɔːˈtɛl) vt. prophesy (**fore'told** pt./pp.)

forethought ('fɔːθɔːt) n. thoughtful consideration of future events

foretoken ('fɔːtəukən) n. **1.** sign of future event —vt. (fɔːˈtəukən) **2.** foreshadow

foretop ('fɔːtɒp; Naut. 'fɔːtəp) n. platform at top of foremast

for ever or **forever** (fɔːˈrɛvə, fə-) adv. **1.** always **2.** eternally **3.** inf. for a long time

forewarn (fɔːˈwɔːn) vt. warn, caution in advance

forewent (fɔːˈwɛnt) pt. of FOREGO¹, FOREGO²

foreword ('fɔːwɜːd) n. preface

forfeit ('fɔːfɪt) n. **1.** thing lost by crime or fault **2.** penalty, fine —a. **3.** lost by crime or fault —vt. **4.** lose by penalty —**'forfeiture** n.

forgather or **foregather** (fɔːˈɡæðə) vi. **1.** meet together, assemble **2.** associate

forgave (fəˈɡeɪv) pt. of FORGIVE

forge¹ (fɔːdʒ) n. **1.** place where metal is worked, smithy **2.** furnace, workshop for melting or refining metal —vt. **3.** shape (metal) by heating in fire and hammering **4.** make, shape **5.** invent **6.** make a fraudulent imitation of, counterfeit —**'forger** n. —**'forgery** n. **1.** forged document, banknote etc. **2.** the making of it

forge² (fɔːdʒ) vi. advance steadily

forget (fə'gɛt) *vt.* 1. lose memory of 2. neglect, overlook (**for'got** *pt.*, **for'gotten** *or* (US, *obs.*) **for'got** *pp.*, **for'getting** *pr.p.*) —**for'getful** *a.* liable to forget —**for'getfully** *adv.* —**forget-me-not** *n.* plant with small blue flower

forgive (fə'gɪv) *v.* 1. cease to blame or hold resentment (against) —*vt.* 2. pardon —**for'giveness** *n.* —**for'giving** *a.* willing to forgive

forgo *or* **forego** (fɔː'gəʊ) *vt.* go without, give up (-'**went** *pt.*, -'**gone** *pp.*, -'**going** *pr.p.*)

forgot (fə'gɒt) *pt./*(US, *obs.*) *pp. of* FORGET

fork (fɔːk) *n.* 1. pronged instrument for eating food 2. pronged tool for digging or lifting 3. division into branches 4. point of this division 5. one of the branches —*vi.* 6. branch —*vt.* 7. dig, lift, throw with fork 8. make fork-shaped —**forked** *a.* 1. having fork or forklike parts 2. zigzag —**fork-lift truck** vehicle having two power-operated horizontal prongs that can be raised and lowered —**fork out** *inf.* pay (reluctantly)

forlorn (fə'lɔːn) *a.* 1. forsaken 2. desperate —**forlorn hope** anything undertaken with little hope of success

form (fɔːm) *n.* 1. shape 2. visible appearance 3. visible person or animal 4. structure 5. nature 6. species, kind 7. regularly drawn up document, *esp.* printed one with blanks for particulars 8. condition, *esp.* good condition 9. class in school 10. customary way of doing things 11. set order of words 12. long seat without back, bench 13. hare's nest 14. *esp.* US *see* FORME —*vt.* 15. shape, mould 16. arrange, organize 17. train 18. shape in the mind, conceive 19. go to make up, make part of —*vi.* 20. come into existence or shape —**for'mation** *n.* 1. forming 2. thing formed 3. structure, shape, arrangement 4. military order —**formative** *a.* 1. of, relating to, development 2. serving or tending to form 3. used in forming —**formless** *a.*

-form (*comb. form*) having shape or form of; resembling, as in *cruciform, vermiform*

formal ('fɔːml) *a.* 1. ceremonial 2. according to rule 3. of outward form or routine 4. of, for, formal occasions 5. according to rule that does not matter 6. precise; stiff —**formalism** *n.* 1. quality of being formal 2. exclusive concern for form, structure, technique in an activity, *eg* art —**formalist** *n.* —**for'mality** *n.* 1. observance required by custom or etiquette 2. condition or quality of being formal 3. conformity to custom, conventionality, mere form 4. in art, precision, stiffness, as opposed to originality —**formali'zation** *or* **-li'sation** *n.* —**formalize** *or* **-lise** *vt.* 1. make formal 2. make official or valid 3. give definite form to —**formally** *adv.*

formaldehyde (fɔː'mældɪhaɪd) *n.* colourless, poisonous, pungent gas, used in making antiseptics and in chemistry —**formalin** *n.* solution of formaldehyde in water, used as disinfectant, preservative *etc.*

format ('fɔːmæt) *n.* 1. size and shape of book 2. organization of television show *etc.*

forme *or* U.S. **form** (fɔːm) *n.* Print. frame for type

former ('fɔːmə) *a.* 1. earlier in time 2. of past times 3. first named —*n.* 4. first named thing, person or fact —**formerly** *adv.* previously

Formica (fɔː'maɪkə) *n.* R type of laminated sheet used to make heat-resistant surfaces

formic acid ('fɔːmɪk) acid found in insects (*esp.* ants) and some plants

formidable ('fɔːmɪdəbl) *a.* 1. to be feared 2. overwhelming, terrible, redoubtable 3. likely to be difficult, serious —**formidably** *adv.*

formula ('fɔːmjʊlə) *n.* 1. set form of words setting forth principle, method or rule for doing, producing something 2. substance so prepared 3. specific category of car in motor racing 4. recipe 5. *Science, maths.* rule, fact expressed in symbols and figures (*pl.* **-ulae** (-juliː), **-s**) —**formulary** *n.* collection of formulas —**formulate** *vt.* 1. reduce to, express in formula, or in definite form 2. devise —**formu'lation** *n.* —**formulator** *n.*

fornication (fɔːnɪ'keɪʃən) *n.* sexual intercourse outside marriage —**fornicate** *vi.*

forsake (fə'seɪk) *vt.* 1. abandon, desert 2. give up (**for'sook, for'saken, for'saking**)

forsooth (fə'suːθ) *adv. obs.* in truth

forswear (fɔː'swɛə) *vt.* 1. renounce 2. deny —*v. refl.* 3. perjure (-'**swore** *pt.*, -'**sworn** *pp.*)

forsythia (fɔː'saɪθɪə) *n.* widely cultivated shrub with yellow flowers

fort (fɔːt) *n.* fortified place, stronghold —**hold the fort** *inf.* guard something temporarily

forte¹ (fɔːt, 'fɔːteɪ) *n.* one's strong point, that in which one excels

forte² ('fɔːtɪ) *adv. Mus.* loudly (**for'tissimo** *sup.*)

forth (fɔːθ) *adv.* 1. onwards 2. into view —**forth'coming** *a.* 1. about to come 2. ready when wanted 3. willing to talk, communicative —**forth'with** *adv.* at once, immediately

forthright ('fɔːθraɪt) *a.* direct, outspoken

fortieth ('fɔːtɪɪθ) *see* FOUR

fortify ('fɔːtɪfaɪ) *vt.* 1. strengthen 2. provide with defensive works (**fortified, fortifying**) —**fortifi'cation** *n.*

fortitude ('fɔːtɪtjuːd) *n.* courage in adversity or pain, endurance

fortnight ('fɔːtnaɪt) *n.* two weeks —**fortnightly** *a./adv.*

FORTRAN ('fɔːtræn) high-level computer programming language for mathematical and scientific purposes

fortress ('fɔːtrɪs) *n*. fortified place, *eg* castle, stronghold

fortuitous (fɔː'tjuːɪtəs) *a*. accidental, by chance —**for'tuitously** *adv*. —**for'tuity** *n*.

fortune ('fɔːtʃən) *n*. 1. good luck 2. prosperity, wealth 3. chance, luck —**'fortunate** *a*. —**'fortunately** *adv*. —**fortune-hunter** *n*. person seeking fortune, *esp*. by marriage —**fortune-teller** *n*. one who predicts a person's future

forty ('fɔːtɪ) *see* FOUR —**forty winks** short sleep, nap

forum ('fɔːrəm) *n*. (place or medium for) meeting, assembly for open discussion or debate

forward ('fɔːwəd) *a*. 1. lying in front of something 2. onward 3. presumptuous, impudent 4. advanced, progressive 5. relating to the future —*n*. 6. player placed in forward position in various team games, *eg* football —*adv*. 7. towards the future 8. towards the front, to the front 9. into view 10. ('fɔːwəd; *Naut*. 'fɒrəd) at, in fore part of ship 11. onwards, so as to make progress —*vt*. 12. help forward 13. send, dispatch —**'forwardly** *adv*. pertly —**'forwardness** *n*. —**'forwards** *adv*.

forwent (fɔː'wɛnt) *pt. of* FORGO

fosse *or* **foss** (fɒs) *n*. ditch; moat

fossil ('fɒsəl) *n*. 1. remnant or impression of animal or plant, *esp*. prehistoric one, preserved in earth 2. *inf*. person, idea *etc*. that is outdated and incapable of change —*a*. 3. of, like or forming fossil 4. dug from earth 5. *inf*. antiquated —**'fossilize** *or* **-ise** *v*. 1. turn into fossil —*vt*. 2. petrify

foster ('fɒstə) *vt*. 1. promote growth or development of 2. bring up (child) *esp*. not one's own —**foster brother, sister, father, mother, parent, child** one related by upbringing, not blood

fought (fɔːt) *pt./pp. of* FIGHT

foul (faʊl) *a*. 1. loathsome, offensive 2. stinking 3. dirty 4. unfair 5. (of weather) wet, rough 6. obscene, disgustingly abusive 7. charged with harmful matter, clogged, choked —*n*. 8. act of unfair play 9. the breaking of a rule —*adv*. 10. unfairly —*v*. 11. make, become foul 12. jam —*vt*. 13. collide with —**'foully** *adv*. —**foul play** 1. unfair conduct, *esp*. with violence 2. violation of rules in game —**fall foul of** 1. get into trouble with 2. (of ships) collide with

foulard (fuː'lɑːd) *n*. soft light fabric of silk or rayon

found¹ (faʊnd) *pt./pp. of* FIND

found² (faʊnd) *vt*. 1. establish, institute 2. lay base of 3. base, ground —**foun'dation** *n*. 1. basis 2. base, lowest part of building 3. founding 4. endowed institution *etc*. 5. cosmetic used as base for make-up —**'founder** *n*. ('**foundress** *fem*.) —**foundation garment** woman's undergar-

ment worn to shape and support figure (*also* **foun'dation**) —**foundation stone** one of stones forming foundation of building, *esp*. stone laid with public ceremony

found³ (faʊnd) *vt*. 1. melt and run into mould 2. cast —**'founder** *n*. —**'foundry** *n*. 1. place for casting 2. art of this

founder ('faʊndə) *vi*. 1. collapse 2. sink 3. become stuck as in mud *etc*.

foundling ('faʊndlɪŋ) *n*. deserted infant

fount (faʊnt) *n*. 1. fountain 2. assortment of printing type of one size

fountain ('faʊntɪn) *n*. 1. jet of water, *esp*. ornamental one 2. spring 3. source —**'fountain-head** *n*. source —**fountain pen** pen with ink reservoir

four (fɔː) *n./a*. cardinal number next after three —**'fortieth** *a./n*. —**'forty** *n./a*. four tens —**'four'teen** *n./a*. four plus ten —**'four'teenth** *a*. —**fourth** *a*. ordinal number of four —**'fourthly** *adv*. —**four-in-hand** *n*. 1. road vehicle drawn by four horses and driven by one driver 2. four-horse team 3. US long narrow tie tied in flat slipknot with ends dangling —**four-leaf clover** *or* **four-leaved clover** clover with four leaves rather than three, supposed to bring good luck —**four-letter word** any of several short English words referring to sex or excrement: regarded generally as offensive —**four-poster** *n*. bed with four posts for curtains *etc*. —**four'score** *a./n. obs*. eighty —**foursome** *n*. 1. group of four people 2. game or dance for four people —**four'square** *a*. firm, steady —**four-stroke** *n*. internal-combustion engine firing once every four strokes of piston —**fourth estate** (*sometimes* F- E-) journalists; journalism —**on all fours** on hands and knees

fowl (faʊl) *n*. 1. domestic cock or hen 2. bird, its flesh —*vi*. 3. hunt wild birds —**'fowler** *n*. —**fowling piece** light gun

fox (fɒks) *n*. 1. red bushy-tailed animal 2. its fur 3. cunning person —*vt*. 4. perplex 5. discolour (paper) with brown spots 6. mislead —*vi*. 7. act craftily —**'foxy** *a*. 1. of or resembling fox, *esp*. in craftiness 2. of reddish-brown colour 3. (of paper *etc*.) spotted, *esp*. by mildew 4. US physically attractive —**'foxglove** *n*. tall flowering plant —**'foxhole** *n. sl*. in war, small trench giving protection —**'foxhound** *n*. dog bred for hunting foxes —**fox hunt** 1. hunting of foxes with hounds 2. instance of this 3. organization for fox-hunting within area —**fox-hunting** *n*. —**fox terrier** small dog now mainly kept as pet —**'foxtrot** *n*. 1. (music for) ballroom dance —*vi*. 2. perform this dance

foyer ('fɔɪeɪ, 'fɔɪə) *n*. entrance hall in theatres, hotels *etc*.

F.P. or **f.p. 1.** freezing point (*also* **fp**) **2.** fully paid

F.P.A. Family Planning Association

f.p.s. 1. feet per second **2.** foot-pound-second

Fr *Chem.* francium

fr. 1. fragment **2.** franc **3.** from

Fr. 1. Father **2.** Frater (*Lat.* brother) **3.** French **4.** Friday

fracas ('frækɑ:) *n.* noisy quarrel; uproar; brawl

fraction ('frækʃən) *n.* **1.** numerical quantity not an integer **2.** fragment, piece —**'fractional** *a.* **1.** constituting a fraction **2.** forming but a small part **3.** insignificant

fractious ('frækʃəs) *a.* **1.** unruly **2.** irritable

fracture ('fræktʃə) *n.* **1.** breakage, part broken **2.** breaking of bone **3.** breach, rupture —*v.* **4.** break

fragile ('frædʒaɪl) *a.* **1.** breakable **2.** frail, delicate —**fragility** (frə'dʒɪlɪtɪ) *n.*

fragment ('frægmənt) *n.* **1.** piece broken off **2.** small portion **3.** incomplete part —*v.* (fræg'mɛnt) **4.** (cause to) break into fragments —**'fragmentary** *a.*

fragrant ('freɪɡrənt) *a.* sweet-smelling —**'fragrance** *n.* scent —**'fragrantly** *adv.*

frail (freɪl) *a.* **1.** fragile, delicate **2.** infirm, in weak health **3.** morally weak —**'frailly** *adv.* —**'frailty** *n.*

frame (freɪm) *n.* **1.** that in which thing is set, as square of wood round picture *etc.* **2.** structure **3.** build of body **4.** constitution **5.** mood **6.** individual exposure on strip of film **7.** *Snooker etc.* wooden triangle used to set up balls, balls when set up or single game finished when all balls have been potted —*vt.* **8.** put together, make **9.** adapt **10.** put into words **11.** put into frame **12.** *sl.* conspire to incriminate on false charge —**frame-up** *n. sl.* **1.** plot **2.** manufactured evidence —**'framework** *n.* **1.** structure into which completing parts can be fitted **2.** supporting work

franc (fræŋk; *Fr.* frɑ̃) *n.* monetary unit of France, Switzerland and other countries

franchise ('fræntʃaɪz) *n.* **1.** right of voting **2.** citizenship **3.** privilege or right, *esp.* right to sell certain goods

Franciscan (fræn'sɪskən) *n.* monk or nun of the order founded by St. Francis of Assisi

francium ('frænsɪəm) *n.* radioactive element of alkali-metal group

Franco- ('fræŋkəʊ-) (*comb. form*) France; French, as in *Franco-Prussian*

francolin ('fræŋkəʊlɪn) *n.* Afr. or Asian partridge

frangipani (frændʒɪ'pɑːnɪ) *n.* tropical Amer. shrub (*pl.* **-s**, **-'pani**)

frank (fræŋk) *a.* **1.** candid, outspoken **2.** sincere —*n.* **3.** official mark on letter either cancelling stamp or ensuring delivery without stamp —*vt.*

4. mark letter thus —**'frankly** *adv.* candidly —**'frankness** *n.* —**franking machine** machine that prints marks on letters *etc.* indicating that postage has been paid

Frank (fræŋk) *n.* member of group of W Germanic peoples who gradually conquered most of Gaul and Germany in late 4th century A.D. —**'Frankish** *n.* **1.** ancient W Germanic language of Franks —*a.* **2.** of Franks or their language

Frankenstein's monster ('fræŋkɪnstaɪnz) creation or monster that brings disaster and is beyond the control of its creator

frankfurter ('fræŋkfɜːtə) *n.* smoked sausage

frankincense ('fræŋkɪnsɛns) *n.* aromatic gum resin burned as incense

frantic ('fræntɪk) *a.* **1.** distracted with rage, grief, joy *etc.* **2.** frenzied —**'frantically** *adv.*

frappé ('fræpeɪ) *n.* **1.** drink consisting of liqueur *etc.* poured over crushed ice —*a.* **2.** (*esp.* of drinks) chilled

fraternal (frə'tɜːnəl) *a.* of brother; brotherly —fra'ternally *adv.* —fra'ternity *n.* **1.** brotherliness **2.** brotherhood **3.** US college society —fraterni'zation or **-ni'sation** *n.* —'fraternize or **-nise** *vi.* associate, make friends —fratri'cidal *a.* —'fratricide *n.* killing, killer of brother or sister

Frau (frau) *n.* married German woman: usu. used as title equivalent to *Mrs.* (*pl.* **Frauen** ('frauən), **-s**)

fraud (frɔːd) *n.* **1.** criminal deception **2.** swindle, imposture **3.** *inf.* person who acts in false or deceitful way —**'fraudulence** *n.* —**'fraudulent** *a.*

fraught (frɔːt) *a.* —**fraught with** filled with, involving

Fräulein (*Ger.* 'frɔɪlaɪn) *n.* unmarried German woman: oft. used as title equivalent to *Miss* (*pl.* **-lein** or *English* **-s**)

fray¹ (freɪ) *n.* **1.** fight **2.** noisy quarrel

fray² (freɪ) *v.* **1.** wear through by rubbing **2.** make, become ragged at edge

frazil ('freɪzɪl) *n.* **C** broken spikes of ice formed in turbulent water

frazzle ('fræzəl) *inf. v.* **1.** make or become exhausted **2.** make or become irritated —*n.* **3.** exhausted state

freak (friːk) *n.* **1.** abnormal person, animal, thing —*a.* **2.** oddly different from what is normal —**'freakish** or (*inf.*) **'freaky** *a.* —**freak out** *inf.* (cause to) hallucinate, be wildly excited *etc.*

freckle ('frɛkəl) *n.* **1.** light brown spot on skin, *esp.* caused by sun **2.** any small spot —*v.* **3.** mark or become marked in freckles —**'freckled** *a.*

free (friː) *a.* **1.** able to act at will, not under compulsion or restraint **2.** (*with* from) not restricted or affected by **3.** not subject to cost or tax **4.** independent **5.** not exact or literal **6.** generous **7.** not in use **8.** (of person) not occupied, having no engagement **9.** loose, not fixed —*vt.* **10.** set at liberty **11.** (*with of* or from) remove (obstacles, pain *etc.*), rid (of) —**free, 'freeing**) —**'freedom** *n.* —**'freely** *adv.* —**'freeboard** *n.* space between deck of vessel and waterline —**Free Church** *chiefly* UK any Protestant Church, *esp.* Presbyterian, other than Established Church —**free enterprise** economic system in which commercial organizations compete for profit with little state control —**free flight** flight of rocket *etc.* when engine has ceased to produce thrust —**free-for-all** *n.* brawl —**'freehand** *a.* drawn without guiding instruments —**'freehold** *n.* **1.** tenure of land without obligation of service or rent **2.** land so held —**free house** public house not bound to sell only one brewer's products —**free kick** *Soccer* place kick awarded for foul or infringement —**'freelance** *a./n.* **1.** self-employed, unattached person —*vi.* **2.** work as freelance —*adv.* **3.** as freelance —**free-living** *a.* **1.** given to indulgence of appetites **2.** (of animals *etc.*) not parasitic —**free love** practice of sexual relationships without fidelity to single partner —**'Freemason** *n.* member of secret fraternity for mutual help —**free-range** *a.* kept, produced in natural, nonintensive conditions —**free speech** right to express opinions publicly —**free'standing** *a.* not attached to or supported by another object —**'freestyle** *n.* **1.** race, as in swimming, in which each participant may use style of his or her choice **2.** style of professional wrestling with no internationally agreed set of rules (*also* **all-in wrestling**) —**free'thinker** *n.* sceptic who forms his own opinions, *esp.* in religion —**free trade** international trade free of protective tariffs —**free verse** unrhymed verse without metrical pattern —**'freeway** *n.* US major road —**free'wheel** *n.* **1.** device in rear hub of bicycle wheel that permits wheel to rotate while pedals are stationary —*vi.* **2.** coast —**free will 1.** apparent human ability to make choices not externally determined **2.** doctrine that human beings have such freedom of choice **3.** ability to make choice without coercion —**free-will** *a.* voluntary; spontaneous —**the Free World** non-Communist countries collectively —**free on board** (of shipment of goods) delivered on board ship *etc.* without charge to buyer —**International freestyle** amateur style of wrestling with agreed set of rules —**the Free World** non-Communist countries collectively

freesia ('friːzɪə) *n.* plant with fragrant, tubular flowers

freeze (friːz) *v.* **1.** change (by reduction of temperature) from liquid to solid, as water to ice —*vt.* **2.** preserve (food *etc.*) by extreme cold,

as in freezer **3.** fix (prices *etc.*) —*vi.* **4.** feel very cold **5.** become rigid as with fear **6.** stop (**froze, 'frozen, 'freezing**) —**'freezer** *n.* insulated cabinet for long-term storage of perishable foodstuffs —**frozen** ('frəʊz⁽ə⁾n) *a.* (of credits *etc.*) unrealizable —**freeze-dry** *vt.* preserve (substance) by rapid freezing and subsequently drying in vacuum —**freezing point** temperature at which liquid becomes solid

freight (freɪt) *n.* **1.** commercial transport (*esp.* by railway, ship) **2.** cost of this **3.** goods so carried —*vt.* **4.** send as or by freight —**'freightage** *n.* money paid for freight —**'freighter** *n.* —**'freightliner** *n.* goods train, lorry carrying containers

French (frɛntʃ) *n.* **1.** language spoken by people of France —*a.* **2.** of France —**French bread** crisp white bread in long slender loaf —**French Canadian** Canadian citizen whose native language is French —**French-Canadian** *a.* of French Canadians —**French chalk** variety of talc used to mark cloth or remove grease stains —**French dressing** salad dressing —**French fried potatoes** chips (*also* (US) **French fries**) —**French horn** musical wind instrument —**French knickers** women's underpants with wide legs —**French leave** unauthorized leave —**French letter** UK *sl.* condom —**French polish** varnish for wood made from shellac dissolved in alcohol —**French window** window extended to floor level and used as door

frenetic (frɪ'nɛtɪk) *a.* frenzied

frenzy ('frɛnzɪ) *n.* **1.** violent mental derangement **2.** wild excitement —**'frenzied** *a.*

frequent ('friːkwənt) *a.* **1.** happening often **2.** common **3.** numerous —*vt.* (frɪ'kwɛnt) **4.** go often to —**'frequency** *n.* **1.** rate of occurrence **2.** in radio *etc.*, cycles per second of alternating current —**fre'quentative** *a.* expressing repetition —**'frequently** *adv.* —**frequency modulation** *Rad.* method of transmitting information in which frequency of carrier wave is varied

fresco ('frɛskəʊ) *n.* **1.** method of painting in watercolour on plaster of wall before it dries **2.** painting done thus (*pl.* **-es, -s**)

fresh (frɛʃ) *a.* **1.** not stale **2.** new **3.** additional **4.** different **5.** recent **6.** inexperienced **7.** pure **8.** not pickled, frozen *etc.* **9.** not faded or dimmed **10.** not tired **11.** (of wind) strong **12.** *inf.* impudent **13.** *inf.* arrogant —**'freshen** *v.* —**'freshet** *n.* **1.** rush of water at river mouth **2.** flood of river water —**'freshly** *adv.* —**'freshman** or **'fresher** *n.* first-year student —**'freshness** *n.* —**'freshwater** *a.* **1.** of or living in fresh water **2.** (*esp.* of sailor who has not sailed on sea) inexperienced **3.** US little known

fret[1] (frɛt) *v.* **1.** irritate or be irritated **2.** worry

(-tt-) —*n.* **3.** irritation —'**fretful** *a.* irritable, (easily) upset

fret² (frɛt) *n.* **1.** repetitive geometrical pattern **2.** small bar on fingerboard of guitar *etc.* —*vt.* **3.** ornament with carved pattern (-tt-) —**fret saw** saw with narrow blade and fine teeth, used for fretwork —'**fretwork** *n.* carved or open woodwork in ornamental patterns and devices

Freudian ('frɔɪdɪən) *a.* pert. to Austrian psychologist Sigmund Freud, or his theories —**Freudian slip** any action, such as slip of tongue, that may reveal unconscious thought

Fri. Friday

friable ('fraɪəb'l) *a.* easily crumbled —fria'**bili**ty *or* '**friableness** *n.*

friar ('fraɪə) *n.* member of mendicant religious order —'**friary** *n.* house of friars —**friar's balsam** compound containing benzoin, used as inhalant

fricassee (frɪkə'siː, 'frɪkəsɪ) *n.* **1.** dish of pieces of chicken or meat, fried or stewed and served with rich sauce —*vt.* **2.** cook thus

fricative ('frɪkətɪv) *n.* **1.** consonant produced by partial occlusion of air stream, such as (f) or (z) —*a.* **2.** relating to fricative

friction ('frɪkʃən) *n.* **1.** rubbing **2.** resistance met with by body moving over another **3.** clash of wills *etc.*, disagreement —'**frictional** *a.*

Friday ('fraɪdɪ) *n.* sixth day of week —**Good Friday** the Friday before Easter

fridge (frɪdʒ) *inf.* refrigerator

fried (fraɪd) *pt./pp. of* FRY¹

friend (frɛnd) *n.* **1.** one well known to another and regarded with affection and loyalty **2.** intimate associate **3.** supporter **4.** (F-) Quaker —'**friendless** *a.* —'**friendliness** *n.* —'**friendly** *a.* **1.** having disposition of a friend, kind **2.** favourable —'**friendship** *n.* —**friendly society** UK association of people who pay regular dues in return for sickness benefits *etc.* —**Friends of the Earth** organization of environmentalists and conservationists

frier ('fraɪə) *n. see* **fryer** *at* FRY¹

frieze (friːz) *n.* ornamental band, strip (on wall)

frieze² (friːz) *n.* kind of coarse woollen cloth

frigate ('frɪgɪt) *n.* **1.** old (sailing) warship corresponding to modern cruiser **2.** fast destroyer-like warship equipped for escort and antisubmarine duties —**frigate bird** bird of tropical and antarctic seas, with wide wingspan

fright (fraɪt) *n.* **1.** sudden fear **2.** shock **3.** alarm **4.** grotesque or ludicrous person or thing —*vt.* **5.** *obs.* frighten —'**frighten** *vt.* cause fear, fright in —'**frightful** *a.* **1.** terrible, calamitous **2.** shocking **3.** *inf.* very great, very large —'**frightfully** *adv. inf.* **1.** terribly **2.** very —'**frightfulness** *n.*

frigid ('frɪdʒɪd) *a.* **1.** formal, dull **2.** (sexually) unfeeling **3.** cold —fri'**gidity** *n.* —'**frigidly** *adv.* —**Frigid Zone** cold region inside Arctic or Antarctic Circle where sun's rays are very oblique

frill (frɪl) *n.* **1.** fluted strip of fabric gathered at one edge **2.** ruff of hair, feathers around neck of dog, bird *etc.* **3.** fringe **4.** (*oft. pl.*) unnecessary words, politeness; superfluous thing; adornment —*vt.* **5.** make into, decorate with frill

fringe (frɪndʒ) *n.* **1.** ornamental edge of hanging threads, tassels *etc.* **2.** anything like this **3.** hair cut in front and falling over brow **4.** edge, limit —*vt.* **5.** adorn with fringe **6.** be fringe for —*a.* **7.** (of theatre *etc.*) unofficial, unconventional, extra —**fringe benefit** benefit provided by employer to supplement employee's regular pay

frippery ('frɪpərɪ) *n.* **1.** finery **2.** trivia

Frisbee ('frɪzbɪ) *n.* **R** plastic disc thrown with spinning motion for recreation

Frisian ('frɪʒən) *or* **Friesian** ('friːʒən) *n.* **1.** language spoken in NW Netherlands and adjacent islands **2.** speaker of this language —*a.* **3.** of this language or its speakers

frisk (frɪsk) *vi.* **1.** move, leap playfully —*vt.* **2.** wave briskly **3.** *inf.* search (person) for concealed weapons *etc.* —*n.* **4.** playful antic or movement **5.** *inf.* instance of frisking a person —'**friskily** *adv.* —'**frisky** *a.*

fritillary (frɪ'tɪlərɪ) *n.* plant with purple or white bell-shaped flowers

fritter¹ ('frɪtə) *vt.* (*usu. with* away) waste

fritter² ('frɪtə) *n.* piece of food fried in batter

frivolous ('frɪvələs) *a.* **1.** not serious, flippant **2.** unimportant —fri'**volity** *n.*

frizz (frɪz) *vt.* **1.** crisp, curl into small curls —*n.* **2.** frizzed hair —'**frizzy** *a.* crimped

frizzle ('frɪz'l) *v.* fry, toast or grill with sizzling sound

fro (frəʊ) *adv.* away, from (*only in* **to and fro**)

frock (frɒk) *n.* **1.** woman's dress **2.** various similar garments —*vt.* **3.** invest with office of priest —**frock coat** man's double-breasted skirted coat, as worn in 19th century

frog¹ (frɒg) *n.* tailless amphibious animal developed from tadpole —'**frogman** *n.* swimmer equipped for swimming, working underwater —'**frogmarch** *n.* any method of moving person against his will

frog² (frɒg) *n.* **1.** military-style coat fastening of button and loop **2.** attachment to belt to carry sword

frolic ('frɒlɪk) *n.* **1.** merrymaking —*vi.* **2.** behave playfully ('**frolicked,** '**frolicking**) —'**frolicsome** *a.*

from (frɒm; *unstressed* frəm) *prep.* expressing point of departure, source, distance, cause, change of state *etc.*

frond (frɒnd) n. plant organ consisting of stem and foliage, usually with fruit forms, esp. in ferns

front (frʌnt) n. **1.** fore part **2.** position directly before or ahead **3.** seaside promenade **4.** battle line or area **5.** Met. dividing line between two air masses of different characteristics **6.** outward aspect, bearing **7.** inf. something serving as a respectable cover for another, usu. criminal activity **8.** field of activity **9.** group with common goal —v. **10.** look, face (on to) —vt. **11.** inf. be a cover for —a. **12.** of, at the front —'**frontage** n. **1.** façade of building **2.** extent of front —'**frontal** a. —'**frontier** n. part of country which borders on another —**front bench 1.** UK foremost bench of either Government or Opposition in House of Commons **2.** leadership (**frontbenchers**) of either group, who occupy this bench **3.** leadership of government or opposition in various legislative assemblies —'**frontispiece** n. illustration facing title page of book —'**frontrunner** n. inf. leader in race etc.

frost (frɒst) n. **1.** frozen dew or mist **2.** act or state of freezing **3.** weather in which temperature falls below point at which water turns to ice —v. **4.** cover, be covered with frost or something similar in appearance —vt. **5.** give slightly roughened surface to —'**frostily** adv. —'**frosting** n. **1.** esp. US icing **2.** rough or matt finish on glass etc. —'**frosty** a. **1.** accompanied by frost **2.** chilly, cold **3.** unfriendly —'**frostbite** n. destruction by cold of tissue, esp. of fingers, ears etc.

froth (frɒθ) n. **1.** collection of small bubbles, foam **2.** scum **3.** idle talk —v. **4.** (cause to) foam —'**frothily** adv. —'**frothy** a.

froward ('frəʊəd) a. obstinate; contrary

frown (fraʊn) vi. **1.** wrinkle brows —n. **2.** act of frowning **3.** show of dislike or displeasure

frowsty ('fraʊstɪ) a. stale, musty

frowzy or **frowsy** ('fraʊzɪ) a. **1.** dirty **2.** unkempt

froze (frəʊz) pt. of FREEZE —'**frozen** pp. of FREEZE

F.R.S. Fellow of the Royal Society

fructify ('frʌktɪfaɪ) v. (cause to) bear fruit ('**fructified**, '**fructifying**) —fructifi'cation n.

fructose ('frʌktəʊs) n. crystalline sugar occurring in many fruits

frugal ('fruːɡəl) a. **1.** sparing, thrifty, economical **2.** meagre —fru'gality n. —'**frugally** adv.

fruit (fruːt) n. **1.** seed and its envelope, esp. edible one **2.** vegetable products **3.** (usu. in pl.) result, benefit —vi. **4.** bear fruit —'**fruiterer** n. dealer in fruit —'**fruitful** a. **1.** bearing fruit in abundance **2.** productive, prolific **3.** producing results or profits —**fruition** (fruː'ɪʃən) n. **1.**

enjoyment **2.** realization of hopes —'**fruitless** a. **1.** unproductive **2.** without fruit —'**fruity** a. **1.** of or resembling fruit **2.** (of voice) mellow, rich **3.** inf., chiefly UK erotically stimulating; salacious —**fruit machine** gambling machine operated by coins

frump (frʌmp) n. dowdy woman —'**frumpish** or '**frumpy** a.

frustrate (frʌ'streɪt) vt. **1.** thwart, balk **2.** disappoint —frus'tration n.

frustum ('frʌstəm) n. Geom. **1.** part of cone or pyramid contained between base and plane parallel to base that intersects solid **2.** part of such solid contained between two parallel planes intersecting solid (pl. -s, -ta (-tə))

fry[1] (fraɪ) vt. **1.** cook with fat —vi. **2.** be cooked thus (**fried**, '**frying**) —n. **3.** fried meat **4.** dish of anything fried —'**fryer** or '**frier** n. **1.** one that fries **2.** utensil for deep-frying foods —**frying pan** shallow pan for frying —**fry-up** n. UK inf. **1.** act of preparing mixed fried dish **2.** dish itself —**out of the frying pan into the fire** from bad situation to worse one

fry[2] (fraɪ) n. young fishes —**small fry** young or insignificant beings

f-stop n. any of settings for f-number of camera

ft. 1. feet **2.** foot **3.** fort

fth. or **fthm.** fathom

fuchsia ('fjuːʃə) n. ornamental shrub with purple-red flowers

fuddle ('fʌdəl) v. **1.** (cause to) be intoxicated, confused —n. **2.** this state

fuddy-duddy ('fʌdɪdʌdɪ) n. inf. (elderly) dull person

fudge[1] (fʌdʒ) n. soft, variously flavoured sweet

fudge[2] (fʌdʒ) vt. **1.** make, do carelessly or dishonestly **2.** fake

fuel (fjʊəl) n. **1.** material for burning as source of heat or power **2.** something which nourishes —vt. **3.** provide with fuel —**fuel cell** cell in which chemical energy is converted directly into electrical energy —**fuel injection** system for introducing fuel directly into combustion chambers of internal-combustion engine without use of carburettor

fug (fʌɡ) n. stuffy indoor atmosphere —'**fuggy** a.

fugitive ('fjuːdʒɪtɪv) n. **1.** one who flees, esp. from arrest or pursuit —a. **2.** fleeing, elusive

fugue (fjuːɡ) n. musical composition in which themes are repeated in different parts

Führer or **Fuehrer** ('fyːrər) n. leader, title of Ger. dictator, esp. Hitler

-ful (comb. form) **1.** full of; characterized by, as in painful, restful **2.** able or tending to, as in useful **3.** as much as will fill thing specified, as in mouthful

fulcrum ('fʊlkrəm, 'fʌl-) *n.* point on which lever is placed for support (*pl.* **-cra** (-krə))

fulfil *or U.S.* **fulfill** (fʊl'fɪl) *vt.* 1. satisfy 2. carry out 3. obey (**-ll-**) —**ful'filment** *or U.S.* **ful'fillment** *n.*

full[1] (fʊl) *a.* 1. containing as much as possible 2. abundant 3. complete 4. ample 5. plump 6. (of garment) of ample cut —*adv.* 7. very 8. quite 9. exactly —**'fully** *adv.* —**'fullness** *or esp. U.S.* **'fulness** *n.* —**'fulsome** *a.* excessive —**'fullback** *n. Soccer etc.* defensive player or position held by this player —**full-blooded** *a.* 1. (*esp.* of horses) of unmixed ancestry 2. having great vigour —**full-blown** *a.* 1. characterized by fullest or best development 2. in full bloom —**full-bodied** *a.* having full rich flavour or quality —**full house 1.** *Poker* hand with three cards of same value and another pair 2. theatre *etc.* filled to capacity 3. in bingo *etc.*, set of numbers needed to win —**full-scale** *a.* 1. (of plan *etc.*) of actual size 2. using all resources —**full stop** punctuation mark (.) at end of sentence —**full-time** *a.* for entire time appropriate to activity —**full time** *adv.* 1. on full-time basis —*n.* 2. end of match —**fully fashioned** *a.* (of stockings *etc.*) shaped so as to fit closely —**fully fledged** *or* **full-fledged** *a.* 1. (of bird) having acquired adult feathers and being able to fly 2. completely developed 3. of full rank or status

full[2] (fʊl) *v.* become or make (cloth *etc.*) more compact during manufacture through shrinking and pressing —**fuller's earth** absorbent clay used for clarifying oils and fats, fulling cloth *etc.*

fulmar ('fʊlmə) *n.* Arctic sea bird

fulminate ('fʌlmɪneɪt) *vi.* 1. (*esp. with* against) criticize harshly —*n.* 2. chemical compound exploding readily —**fulmi'nation** *n.*

fulsome ('fʊlsəm) *a. see* FULL[1]

fumble ('fʌmb³l) *vi.* 1. grope about —*vt.* 2. handle awkwardly —*n.* 3. awkward attempt

fume (fjuːm) *vi.* 1. be angry 2. emit smoke or vapour —*n.* 3. smoke 4. vapour —**'fumigate** *vt.* apply fumes or smoke to, *esp.* for disinfection —**fumi'gation** *n.* —**'fumigator** *n.*

fumitory ('fjuːmɪtərɪ) *n.* plant with spurred flowers

fun (fʌn) *n.* anything enjoyable, amusing *etc.* —**'funnily** *adv.* —**'funny** *a.* 1. comical 2. odd 3. difficult to explain —**'funfair** *n. UK* amusement park, fairground

function ('fʌŋkʃən) *n.* 1. work a thing is designed to do 2. (large) social event 3. duty 4. profession 5. *Maths.* quantity whose value depends on varying value of another —*vi.* 6. operate, work —**'functional** *a.* 1. having a special purpose 2. practical, necessary 3. capable of operating —**'functionary** *n.* official

fund (fʌnd) *n.* 1. stock or sum of money 2. supply, store —*pl.* 3. money resources —*vt.* 4. in financial, business dealings, furnish money to in form of fund

fundamental (fʌndə'mɛnt³l) *a.* 1. of, affecting, or serving as the base 2. essential, primary —*n.* 3. basic rule or fact —**'fundament** *n.* 1. buttocks 2. foundation —**funda'mentalism** *n.* —**funda'mentalist** *n.* one laying stress on belief in literal and verbal inspiration of Bible and other traditional creeds —**fundamental particle** *see* **elementary particle** *at* ELEMENT

funeral ('fjuːnərəl) *n.* (ceremony associated with) burial or cremation of dead —**funereal** (fjuː'nɪərɪəl) *a.* 1. like a funeral 2. dark 3. gloomy —**funeral director** undertaker —**funeral parlour** place where dead are prepared for burial or cremation

fungus ('fʌŋgəs) *n.* plant without leaves, flowers or roots, as mushroom, mould (*pl.* **fungi** ('fʌndʒaɪ, 'fʌŋgaɪ), **-es**) —**'fungal** *or* **'fungous** *a.* —**'fungicide** ('fʌndʒɪsaɪd) *n.* fungus destroyer —**'fungoid** *a.* resembling fungus

funicular (fjuː'nɪkjʊlə) *n.* cable railway on mountainside with two counterbalanced cars

funk (fʌŋk) *n.* panic (*esp. in* blue funk)

funky ('fʌŋkɪ) *a. inf.* (of jazz, pop *etc.*) passionate and soulful, reminiscent of early blues

funnel ('fʌn³l) *n.* 1. cone-shaped vessel or tube 2. chimney of locomotive or ship 3. ventilating shaft —*v.* 4. (cause to) move as through funnel —*vt.* 5. concentrate, focus (**-ll-**)

funny ('fʌnɪ) *a. see* FUN —**funny bone** area near elbow where sharp tingling sensation is experienced when struck

fur (fɜː) *n.* 1. soft hair of animal 2. garment *etc.* of dressed skins with such hair 3. furlike coating —*vt.* 4. cover with fur (**-rr-**) —**'furrier** *n.* dealer in furs —**'furry** *a.* of, like fur

fur. furlong

furbelow ('fɜːbɪləʊ) *n.* 1. flounce, ruffle 2. (*oft. pl.*) showy ornamentation —*vt.* 3. put furbelow on (garment *etc.*)

furbish ('fɜːbɪʃ) *vt.* clean up

furcate ('fɜːkeɪt) *a.* forked, branching

furious ('fjʊərɪəs) *a.* 1. extremely angry 2. violent —**'furiously** *adv.* —**'furiousness** *n.*

furl (fɜːl) *vt.* roll up and bind (sail, umbrella *etc.*)

furlong ('fɜːlɒŋ) *n.* eighth of mile

furlough ('fɜːləʊ) *n. US* leave of absence, *esp.* to soldier

furnace ('fɜːnɪs) *n.* 1. apparatus for applying great heat to metals 2. closed fireplace for heating boiler *etc.* 3. hot place

furnish ('fɜːnɪʃ) *vt.* 1. fit up (house) with furniture 2. equip 3. supply, yield —**'furnishings** *pl.n.* furniture, carpets *etc.* with which room is furnished —'**furniture** *n.* movable contents of a house or room

furore (fjʊ'rɔːrɪ) *or esp. U.S.* **furor** ('fjʊərɔː) *n.* 1. public outburst, *esp.* of protest 2. sudden enthusiasm

furrow ('fʌrəʊ) *n.* 1. trench as made by plough 2. groove —*vt.* 3. make furrows in

further ('fɜːðə) *adv. comp. of* FAR *and* FORE¹ 1. more 2. in addition 3. at or to a greater distance or extent —*a. comp. of* FAR *and* FORE¹ 4. more distant 5. additional —*vt.* 6. help forward, promote —'**furtherance** *n.* —'**furtherer** *n.* —'**furthermore** *adv.* besides —'**furthermost** *a.* —'**furthest** *a./adv. sup. of* FAR, FORE¹ —**further education** UK formal education beyond school other than at university or polytechnic

furtive ('fɜːtɪv) *a.* stealthy, sly, secretive —'**furtively** *adv.*

fury ('fjʊərɪ) *n.* 1. wild rage, violent anger 2. violence of storm *etc.* 3. (*usu. pl.*) snake-haired avenging deity

furze (fɜːz) *n.* prickly shrub, gorse

fuscous ('fʌskəs) *a.* dark-coloured

fuse (fjuːz) *v.* 1. blend by melting 2. melt with heat 3. amalgamate 4. (cause to) fail as a result of blown fuse —*n.* 5. soft wire, with low melting point, used as safety device in electrical systems 6. device (*orig.* combustible cord) for igniting bomb *etc.* —'**fusible** *a.* —'**fusion** *n.* 1. melting 2. state of being melted 3. union of things, as atomic nuclei, as if melted together

fuselage ('fjuːzɪlɑːʒ) *n.* body of aircraft

fusil ('fjuːzɪl) *n.* light flintlock musket —**fusi'lier** *n.* soldier of certain regiments —**fusil'lade** *n.* continuous discharge of firearms

fuss (fʌs) *n.* 1. needless bustle or concern 2. complaint, objection —*vi.* 3. make fuss —'**fussily** *adv.* —'**fussiness** *n.* —'**fussy** *a.* 1. particular 2. faddy 3. overmeticulous 4. overelaborate —'**fusspot** *n.* UK *inf.* person who fusses unnecessarily

fustian ('fʌstɪən) *n.* 1. thick cotton cloth 2. inflated language

fusty ('fʌstɪ) *a.* 1. mouldy 2. smelling of damp 3. old-fashioned —'**fustily** *adv.* —'**fustiness** *n.*

futile ('fjuːtaɪl) *a.* useless, ineffectual 2. trifling —**futility** (fjuː'tɪlɪtɪ) *n.*

future ('fjuːtʃə) *n.* 1. time to come 2. what will happen 3. tense of verb indicating this 4. likelihood of development —*a.* 5. that will be 6. of, relating to, time to come —'**futurism** *n.* movement in art marked by revolt against tradition —'**futurist** *n./a.* —**futur'istic** *a.* ultramodern —**fu'turity** *n.* —**future perfect** *Gram. a.* 1. denoting tense of verbs describing action that will have been performed by certain time —*n.* 2. future perfect tense; verb in this tense

fuze (fjuːz) *n.* US *see* FUSE (sense 6)

fuzz (fʌz) *n.* 1. fluff 2. fluffy or frizzed hair 3. blur 4. *sl.* police(man) —'**fuzzy** *a.* 1. fluffy 2. frizzy 3. blurred, indistinct

fwd. forward

-fy (*comb. form*) make; become, as in *beautify*

G, g

g *or* **G** (dʒiː) *n.* 1. seventh letter of English alphabet 2. speech sound represented by this letter, usu. as in *grass*, or as in *page* (*pl.* **g's, G's** *or* **Gs**)

g 1. gram(s) 2. (acceleration due to) gravity

G 1. *Mus.* fifth note of scale of C major; major or minor key having this note as its tonic 2. gravitational constant 3. *Phys.* conductance 4. German 5. giga 6. good 7. *sl., chiefly US* grand (thousand dollars or pounds)

Ga *Chem.* gallium

GA Georgia

gabble ('gæbəl) *v.* 1. talk, utter inarticulately or too fast ('**gabbled, 'gabbling**) —*n.* 2. such talk —**gab** *vi.* 1. talk excessively; chatter (**-bb-**) —*n.* 2. idle or trivial talk —'**gabby** *a. inf.* talkative —**gift of the gab** eloquence, loquacity

gaberdine ('gæbədiːn, gæbə'diːn) *n.* 1. fine twill cloth like serge used *esp.* for raincoats 2. *Hist.* loose upper garment worn by Jews

gable ('geɪbəl) *n.* triangular upper part of wall at end of ridged roof (*also* **gable end**)

gad (gæd) *vi.* (*esp. with* about) go around in search of pleasure (**-dd-**) —'**gadabout** *n.* pleasure-seeker

gadfly ('gædflaɪ) *n.* 1. cattle-biting fly 2. worrying person

gadget ('gædʒɪt) *n.* 1. small mechanical device 2. object valued for its novelty or ingenuity —'**gadgetry** *n.*

gadoid ('geɪdɔɪd) *a.* 1. of order of marine fishes typically having pectoral and pelvic fins close together and small cycloid scales —*n.* 2. gadoid fish

gadolinium (gædə'lɪnɪəm) *n.* malleable ferromagnetic element of lanthanide series of metals

gadwall ('gædwɔːl) *n.* duck related to mallard

Gael (geɪl) *n.* one who speaks Gaelic —**Gaelic** ('geɪlɪk, 'gæ-) *n.* 1. language of Ireland and Scottish Highlands —*a.* 2. of Gaels, their language or customs

gaff¹ (gæf) *n.* 1. stick with iron hook for landing fish 2. spar for top of fore-and-aft sail —*vt.* 3. seize (fish) with gaff

gaff² (gæf) *n. sl.* nonsense —**blow the gaff** UK *sl.* divulge a secret

gaffe (gæf) *n.* social blunder, *esp.* tactless remark

gaffer ('gæfə) *n.* **1.** old man **2.** *inf.* foreman, boss

gag[1] (gæg) *vt.* **1.** stop up (person's mouth) with cloth *etc.* —*vi.* **2.** *sl.* retch, choke (**-gg-**) —*n.* **3.** cloth *etc.* put into, tied across mouth

gag[2] (gæg) *n.* joke, funny story, gimmick

gaga ('gɑːgɑː) *a. sl.* **1.** senile **2.** crazy

gage[1] (geɪdʒ) *n.* **1.** pledge, thing given as security **2.** challenge, or something symbolizing one

gage[2] (geɪdʒ) *see* GAUGE

gaggle ('gægəl) *n.* **1.** flock of geese **2.** *inf.* disorderly crowd

gaiety ('geɪɪtɪ) *n. see* GAY

gain (geɪn) *vt.* **1.** obtain, secure **2.** obtain as profit **3.** win **4.** earn **5.** reach —*v.* **6.** increase, improve —*vi.* **7.** (*usu. with* on *or* upon) get nearer **8.** (of watch, machine *etc.*) operate too fast —*n.* **9.** profit **10.** increase, improvement —'**gainful** *a.* profitable; lucrative —'**gainfully** *adv.*

gainsay (geɪn'seɪ) *vt.* deny; contradict (**gain'said, gain'saying**)

gait (geɪt) *n.* **1.** manner of walking **2.** pace

gaiter ('geɪtə) *n.* covering of leather, cloth *etc.* for lower leg

gal *or* **gal.** gallon

Gal. *Bible* Galatians

gala ('gɑːlə, 'geɪlə) *n.* **1.** festive occasion **2.** show **3.** competitive sporting event

galah (gə'lɑː) *n.* Aust. grey cockatoo with reddish breast

galantine ('gæləntiːn) *n.* cold dish of meat or poultry, boned, cooked, then pressed and glazed

galaxy ('gæləksɪ) *n.* **1.** system of stars bound by gravitational forces **2.** splendid gathering, *esp.* of famous people —**ga'lactic** *a.*

gale (geɪl) *n.* **1.** strong wind **2.** *inf.* loud outburst, *esp.* of laughter

galena (gə'liːnə) *or* **galenite** (gə'liːnaɪt) *n.* bluish-grey or black mineral consisting of lead sulphide: principal ore of lead

gall[1] (gɔːl) *n.* **1.** impudence **2.** bitterness —**gall bladder** sac attached to liver, reservoir for bile —'**gallstone** *n.* hard secretion in gall bladder or ducts leading from it

gall[2] (gɔːl) *n.* **1.** painful swelling, *esp.* on horse **2.** sore caused by chafing —*vt.* **3.** make sore by rubbing **4.** vex, irritate —'**galling** *a.* irritating, exasperating, humiliating

gall[3] (gɔːl) *n.* abnormal outgrowth on trees *etc.*

gallant ('gælənt) *a.* **1.** fine, stately, brave **2.** (gə'lænt, 'gælənt) (of man) very attentive to women; chivalrous —*n.* **3.** ('gælənt, gə'lænt) **3.** lover, suitor **4.** fashionable young man —'**gallantly** *adv.* —'**gallantry** *n.*

galleon ('gælɪən) *n.* large, high-built sailing ship of war

gallery ('gælərɪ) *n.* **1.** covered walk with side openings, colonnade **2.** platform or projecting upper floor in church, theatre *etc.* **3.** group of spectators **4.** long, narrow platform on outside of building **5.** room or rooms for special purposes, *eg* showing works of art **6.** passage in wall, open to interior of building **7.** horizontal passage, as in mine *etc.*

galley ('gælɪ) *n.* **1.** one-decked vessel with sails and oars, usu. rowed by slaves or criminals **2.** kitchen of ship or aircraft **3.** large rowing boat **4.** *Print.* tray for holding composed type —**galley proof** printer's proof in long slip form —**galley slave 1.** one condemned to row in galley **2.** drudge

galliard ('gæljəd) *n.* **1.** dance in triple time for two persons **2.** music for this dance

Gallic ('gælɪk) *a.* **1.** of ancient Gaul **2.** French —'**Gallicism** *n.* French word or idiom

gallinaceous (gælɪ'neɪʃəs) *a.* of order of birds, including domestic fowl, pheasants *etc.*, having heavy rounded body and strong legs

gallium ('gælɪəm) *n.* soft, grey metal of great fusibility

gallivant ('gælɪvænt) *vi.* gad about

Gallo- ('gæləʊ-) (*comb. form*) Gaul; France, as in *Gallo-Roman*

gallon ('gælən) *n.* liquid measure of eight pints (4.55 litres)

gallop ('gæləp) *v.* **1.** go, ride at gallop —*vi.* **2.** move fast —*n.* **3.** horse's fastest pace with all four feet off the ground at once in each stride **4.** ride at this pace —'**galloper** *n.* —'**galloping** *a.* **1.** at a gallop **2.** speedy, swift

gallows ('gæləʊz) *n.* structure, usu. of two upright beams and crossbar, *esp.* for hanging criminals

Gallup Poll ('gæləp) method of finding out public opinion by questioning a cross section of the population

galoot *or* **galloot** (gə'luːt) *n. inf.* silly, clumsy person

galore (gə'lɔː) *adv.* in plenty

galoshes *or* **goloshes** (gə'lɒʃɪz) *pl.n.* waterproof overshoes

galumph (gə'lʌmpf, -'lʌmf) *vi. inf.* leap or move about clumsily or joyfully

galvanic (gæl'vænɪk) *a.* **1.** of, producing, concerning electric current, *esp.* when produced chemically **2.** *inf.* resembling effect of electric shock; startling —'**galvanize** *or* **-ise** *vt.* **1.** stimulate to action; excite; startle **2.** cover (iron *etc.*) with protective zinc coating —**galva'nometer** *n.* instrument for detecting or measuring small electric currents

gambit ('gæmbɪt) *n.* **1.** *Chess* opening involving

offer of a pawn **2.** any opening manoeuvre, comment *etc.* intended to secure an advantage

gamble ('gæmbᵊl) *vi.* **1.** play games of chance to win money **2.** act on expectation of something —*n.* **3.** risky undertaking **4.** bet, wager —'**gambler** *n.*

gamboge (gæm'bəʊdʒ, -'buːʒ) *n.* gum resin used as yellow pigment

gambol ('gæmbᵊl) *vi.* **1.** skip, jump playfully (-**ll**-) —*n.* **2.** playful antic

game (geɪm) *n.* **1.** diversion, pastime **2.** jest **3.** contest for amusement **4.** scheme, strategy **5.** animals or birds hunted **6.** their flesh —*a.* **7.** brave **8.** willing —*vi.* **9.** gamble —'**gamester** *n.* gambler —'**gaming** *n.* gambling —'**gamy** *or* '**gamey** *a.* **1.** having smell or flavour of game **2.** *inf.* spirited; plucky; brave —'**gamecock** *n.* fowl bred for fighting —'**gamekeeper** *n.* man employed to breed and take care of game —**game laws** laws governing hunting and preservation of game —'**gamesmanship** *n. inf.* art of winning games or defeating opponents by cunning practices without actually cheating

game² (geɪm) *a.* lame, crippled

gamete ('gæmiːt, gə'miːt) *n. Biol.* sexual cell that unites with another for reproduction or the formation of a new individual

gamin ('gæmin) *n.* street urchin

gamine ('gæmiːn) *n.* slim, boyish girl; elfish tomboy

gamma ('gæmə) *n.* third letter of Gr. alphabet (Γ, γ) —**gamma ray** very penetrative electromagnetic ray

gammon¹ ('gæmən) *n.* **1.** cured or smoked ham **2.** bottom piece of flitch of bacon

gammon² ('gæmən) *n.* **1.** double victory in backgammon in which player throws off all his pieces before his opponent throws any —*vt.* **2.** score such a victory over

gammy ('gæmɪ) *a. UK sl. see* GAME²

gamp (gæmp) *n. inf.* large umbrella, usu. clumsy or very worn

gamut ('gæmət) *n.* whole range or scale (*orig.* of musical notes)

gander ('gændə) *n.* **1.** male goose **2.** *inf.* a quick look (*esp.* in **take** (*or* **have**) **a gander**)

gang¹ (gæŋ) *n.* **1.** (criminal) group **2.** organized group of workmen —*vi.* **3.** (*esp.* with together) form gang —'**ganger** *n.* foreman of a gang of labourers —**gang up on** *inf.* combine against

gang² (gæŋ) *n. see* GANGUE

gangling ('gæŋglɪŋ) *or* **gangly** *a.* lanky, awkward in movement

ganglion ('gæŋglɪən) *n.* nerve nucleus (*pl.* -**glia** (-glɪə), -**s**)

gangplank ('gæŋplæŋk) *or* **gangway** *n.* portable bridge for boarding or leaving vessel

gangrene ('gæŋgriːn) *n.* death or decay of

body tissue as result of disease or injury —**gangrenous** ('gæŋgrɪnəs) *a.*

gangster ('gæŋstə) *n.* **1.** member of criminal gang **2.** notorious or hardened criminal

gangue *or* **gang** (gæŋ) *n.* valueless and undesirable material in ore

gangway ('gæŋweɪ) *n.* **1.** *see* GANGPLANK **2.** passage between row of seats —*interj.* **3.** clear a path

gannet ('gænɪt) *n.* predatory sea bird

ganoid ('gænɔɪd) *a./n.* (fish) with smooth, hard, enamelled, bony scales, *eg* sturgeon

gantry ('gæntrɪ) *or* **gauntry** *n.* **1.** structure to support crane, railway signals *etc.* **2.** framework beside rocket on launching pad (*also* **gantry scaffold**)

gaol (dʒeɪl) *see* JAIL

gap (gæp) *n.* **1.** breach, opening, interval **2.** cleft **3.** empty space

gape (geɪp) *vi.* **1.** stare in wonder **2.** open mouth wide, as in yawning **3.** be, become wide open —*n.* **4.** act of gaping

garage ('gærɑːʒ, -rɪdʒ) *n.* **1.** (part of) building to house cars **2.** refuelling and repair centre for cars —*vt.* **3.** leave (car) in garage

garb (gɑːb) *n.* **1.** dress **2.** fashion of dress —*vt.* **3.** dress, clothe

garbage ('gɑːbɪdʒ) *n.* rubbish

garble ('gɑːbᵊl) *vt.* jumble or distort (story, account *etc.*)

garçon (*Fr.* gar'sɔ̃) *n.* waiter, *esp.* French

garden ('gɑːdᵊn) *n.* **1.** ground for growing flowers, fruit, or vegetables —*vi.* **2.** cultivate garden —'**gardener** *n.* —'**gardening** *n.* —**garden centre** place selling gardening tools, plants *etc.* —**garden city** *UK* planned town of limited size surrounded by rural belt

gardenia (gɑː'diːnɪə) *n.* (sub)tropical shrub with fragrant white or yellow flowers

garfish ('gɑːfɪʃ) *n.* elongated bony fish

garganey ('gɑːgənɪ) *n.* small Eurasian duck related to mallard

gargantuan (gɑː'gæntjʊən) *a.* (*sometimes* G-) immense, enormous, huge

gargle ('gɑːgᵊl) *vi.* **1.** wash throat with liquid kept moving by the breath —*vt.* **2.** wash (throat) thus —*n.* **3.** gargling **4.** preparation for this purpose

gargoyle ('gɑːgɔɪl) *n.* carved (grotesque) face on waterspout, *esp.* on Gothic church

garish ('gɛərɪʃ) *a.* **1.** showy **2.** gaudy

garland ('gɑːlənd) *n.* **1.** wreath of flowers worn or hung as decoration —*vt.* **2.** decorate with garlands

garlic ('gɑːlɪk) *n.* (bulb of) plant with strong smell and taste, used in cooking and seasoning

garment ('gɑːmənt) *n.* **1.** article of clothing —*pl.* **2.** clothes

garner ('gɑːnə) vt. store up, collect, as if in granary

garnet ('gɑːnɪt) n. red semiprecious stone

garnish ('gɑːnɪʃ) vt. 1. adorn, decorate (esp. food) —n. 2. material for this

garret ('gærɪt) n. room on top floor, attic

garrison ('gærɪsən) n. 1. troops stationed in town, fort etc. 2. fortified place —vt. 3. station (troops) in (fort etc.)

garrotte or **garotte** (gə'rɒt) n. 1. Spanish capital punishment by strangling 2. apparatus for this —vt. 3. execute, kill thus —**gar'rotter** or **ga'rotter** n.

garrulous ('gærʊləs) a. (frivolously) talkative —**gar'rulity** n. loquacity

garter ('gɑːtə) n. band worn round leg to hold up sock or stocking —**garter stitch** knitting with all rows in plain stitch

gas (gæs) n. 1. air-like substance, esp. one that does not liquefy or solidify at ordinary temperatures 2. fossil fuel in form of gas, used for heating or lighting 3. gaseous anaesthetic 4. poisonous or irritant substance dispersed through atmosphere in warfare etc. 5. inf., esp. US petrol 6. inf. idle, boastful talk (pl. -es, 'gasses) —vt. 7. project gas over 8. poison with gas —vi. 9. inf. talk idly, boastfully (-ss-) —'gaseous a. of, like gas —'gassy a. —'gasbag n. sl. person who talks idly —**gas chamber** or **oven** airtight room into which poison gas is introduced to kill people —**gas gangrene** gangrene resulting from infection of wound by anaerobic bacteria —'gasholder n. gasometer; vessel for storing or measuring gas —'gasman n. man employed to read household gas meters, supervise gas fittings etc. —**gas mask** mask with chemical filter to guard against poisoning by gas —**gas meter** apparatus for measuring amount of gas passed through it —ga'someter n. tank for storing coal gas etc. (also 'gasholder) —**gas ring** circular assembly of gas jets used for cooking —'gasworks pl.n. (with sing. v.) plant where gas, esp. coal gas, is made

gash (gæʃ) n. 1. gaping wound, slash —vt. 2. cut deeply

gasket ('gæskɪt) n. rubber, asbestos etc. used as seal between metal faces, esp. in engines

gasoline or **gasolene** ('gæsəliːn) n. US petrol

gasp (gɑːsp) vi. 1. catch breath with open mouth, as in exhaustion or surprise —n. 2. convulsive catching of breath

gasteropod ('gæstərəpɒd) n. see GASTROPOD

gastric ('gæstrɪk) a. of stomach —**gastroente'ritis** n. inflammation of stomach and intestines —'gastronome, gas'tronomer or gas'tronomist n. gourmet —gastro'nomical a. —ga'stronomy n. art of good eating —**gastric juice** digestive fluid secreted by stomach,

containing hydrochloric acid etc. —**gastric ulcer** ulcer of stomach lining

gastro- or oft. before vowel **gastr-** (comb. form) stomach, as in gastroenteritis, gastritis

gastropod ('gæstrəpɒd) or **gasteropod** n. mollusc, eg snail, with disclike organ of locomotion on ventral surface

gate (geɪt) n. 1. opening in wall, fence etc. 2. barrier for closing it 3. sluice 4. any entrance or way out 5. (entrance money paid by) those attending sporting event —**gate-crash** v. enter (meeting, social function etc.) uninvited —'gatehouse n. house built at or over gateway —**gate-leg table** or **gate-legged table** table with leaves supported by hinged leg swung out from frame

gâteau ('gætəʊ) n. elaborate, rich cake (pl. -teaux (-təʊz))

gather ('gæðə) v. 1. (cause to) assemble 2. increase gradually 3. draw together —vt. 4. collect 5. learn, understand 6. draw (material) into small tucks or folds —'gathering n. assembly

GATT (gæt) General Agreement on Tariffs and Trade

gauche (gəʊʃ) a. tactless, blundering —**gaucherie** (gəʊʃə'riː, 'gəʊʃərɪ) n. awkwardness, clumsiness

gaucho ('gaʊtʃəʊ) n. S Amer. cowboy (pl. -s)

gaud (gɔːd) n. showy ornament —'gaudily adv. —'gaudiness n. —'gaudy a. showy in tasteless way

gauge or **gage** (geɪdʒ) n. 1. standard measure, as of diameter of wire, thickness of sheet metal etc. 2. distance between rails of railway 3. capacity, extent 4. instrument for measuring such things as wire, rainfall, height of water in boiler etc. —vt. 5. measure 6. estimate

Gaul (gɔːl) n. 1. native of Gaul, region in Roman times stretching from N Italy to S Netherlands 2. Frenchman

gaunt (gɔːnt) a. lean, haggard

gauntlet ('gɔːntlɪt) n. 1. armoured glove 2. glove covering part of arm —**run the gauntlet** 1. formerly, run as punishment between two lines of men striking at runner with sticks etc. 2. be exposed to criticism or unpleasant treatment 3. undergo ordeal —**throw down the gauntlet** offer challenge

gauntry ('gɔːntrɪ) n. see GANTRY

gauss (gaʊs) n. unit of density of magnetic field (pl. gauss)

gauze (gɔːz) n. thin transparent fabric of silk, wire etc. —'gauzy a.

gave (geɪv) pt. of GIVE

gavel ('gævəl) n. mallet of presiding officer or auctioneer

gavotte or **gavot** (gə'vɒt) n. 1. lively dance 2. music for it

gawk (gɔːk) vi. stare stupidly —'**gawky** a. clumsy, awkward

gawp or **gaup** (gɔːp) vi. sl. 1. stare stupidly 2. gape

gay (geɪ) a. 1. merry 2. lively 3. cheerful 4. bright 5. light-hearted 6. showy 7. given to pleasure 8. inf. homosexual —'**gaiety** n. 1. state or condition of being gay 2. festivity; merrymaking —'**gaily** adv.

gaze (geɪz) vi. 1. look fixedly —n. 2. fixed look

gazebo (gə'ziːbəʊ) n. summer-house, turret on roof, with extensive view (pl. **-s, -es**)

gazelle (gə'zɛl) n. small graceful antelope

gazette (gə'zɛt) n. 1. official newspaper for announcements of government appointments etc. 2. newspaper title —vt. 3. publish in gazette —**gazetteer** (gæzɪ'tɪə) n. geographical dictionary

gazump (gə'zʌmp) v. raise (price of something, esp. house) after agreeing it with prospective buyer

G.B. Great Britain

G.B.E. (Knight or Dame) Grand Cross of the British Empire

g.b.h. grievous bodily harm

G.C. George Cross

G.C.B. (Knight) Grand Cross of the Bath (Brit. title)

G.C.E. or **GCE** General Certificate of Education

G clef see **treble clef** at TREBLE

G.C.M.G. (Knight or Dame) Grand Cross of the Order of St. Michael and St. George

G.C.V.O. or **GCVO** (Knight or Dame) Grand Cross of the Royal Victorian Order

Gd Chem. gadolinium

Gdns. Gardens

G.D.P. gross domestic product

GDR German Democratic Republic

Ge Chem. germanium

gean (giːn) n. 1. white-flowered tree with round, edible red fruit 2. its fruit

gear (gɪə) n. 1. set of wheels working together, esp. by engaging cogs 2. connection by which engine, motor etc. is brought into work 3. arrangement by which driving wheel of cycle, car etc. performs more or fewer revolutions relative to pedals, pistons etc. 4. equipment 5. clothing 6. goods, utensils 7. apparatus, tackle, tools 8. rigging 9. harness —vt. 10. adapt (one thing) so as to conform with another 11. provide with gear 12. put in gear —'**gearing** n. 1. assembly of gears for transmitting motion 2. act or technique of providing gears to transmit motion 3. Acc., UK ratio of company's debt capital to its equity capital —'**gearbox** n. case

protecting gearing of bicycle, car etc. —**gear lever** or U.S. '**gearshift** n. lever used to move gear wheels relative to each other in motor vehicle etc. —'**gearwheel** n. toothed wheel in system of gears (also **gear**) —**in gear** connected up and ready for work —**out of gear** 1. disconnected, out of working order 2. upset

gecko ('gɛkəʊ) n. insectivorous lizard of warm regions (pl. **-s, -es**)

gee (dʒiː) interj. 1. exclamation to horse etc. to encourage it to turn to right, go on or go faster (also **gee up**) —vt. 2. (usu. with up) move (horse etc.) ahead; urge on

geelbek ('xɪːlbɛk) n. edible S Afr. marine fish

geese (giːs) n., pl. of GOOSE

geezer ('giːzə) n. inf. old (eccentric) man

Geiger counter ('gaɪgə) or **Geiger-Müller counter** ('mʊlə) instrument for detecting radioactivity, cosmic radiation and charged atomic particles

geisha ('geɪʃə) n. in Japan, professional female companion for men

gel (dʒɛl) n. 1. jellylike substance —vi. 2. form a gel (**-ll-**) (also **jell**)

gelatin ('dʒɛlətɪn) or **gelatine** ('dʒɛlətiːn) n. 1. substance prepared from animal bones etc., producing edible jelly 2. anything resembling this —**ge'latinous** a. like gelatin or jelly

geld (gɛld) vt. castrate —'**gelding** n. castrated horse

gelid ('dʒɛlɪd) a. very cold

gelignite ('dʒɛlɪgnaɪt) n. powerful explosive consisting of dynamite in gelatin form

gem (dʒɛm) n. 1. precious stone, esp. when cut and polished 2. treasure —vt. 3. adorn with gems (**-mm-**)

geminate ('dʒɛmɪneɪt) v. double, pair, repeat —**gemi'nation** n.

Gemini ('dʒɛmɪnaɪ, -niː) n. (twins) 3rd sign of zodiac, operative May 21st-June 20th

gemma ('dʒɛmə) n. asexual reproductive structure in mosses etc. that becomes detached from parent and develops into new individual (pl. **-mae** (-miː))

gemsbok or **gemsbuck** ('gɛmzbʌk) n. S Afr. oryx

gen (dʒɛn) n. inf. information —**gen someone up** UK inf. brief someone in detail

gen. 1. gender 2. general 3. genitive 4. genus

Gen. 1. General 2. Bible Genesis

-gen (comb. form) 1. producing; that which produces, as in hydrogen 2. something produced, as in antigen

gendarme ('ʒɒndɑːm) n. policeman in France

gender ('dʒɛndə) n. 1. sex, male or female 2. grammatical classification of nouns, according to sex (actual or attributed)

gene (dʒiːn) *n.* biological factor determining inherited characteristics

genealogy (dʒiːnɪ'ælədʒɪ) *n.* **1.** account of descent from ancestors **2.** pedigree **3.** study of pedigrees —**genea'logical** *a.* —**gene'alogist** *n.*

genera ('dʒɛnərə) *n., pl. of* GENUS

general ('dʒɛnərəl, 'dʒɛnrəl) *a.* **1.** common, widespread **2.** not particular or specific **3.** applicable to all or most **4.** not restricted to one department **5.** usual, prevalent **6.** miscellaneous **7.** dealing with main element only **8.** vague, indefinite —*n.* **9.** army officer of rank above colonel —**gene'rality** *n.* **1.** general principle **2.** vague statement **3.** indefiniteness —**generali-'zation** *or* **-i'sation** *n.* **1.** general conclusion from particular instance **2.** inference —**general-ize** *or* **-ise** *vt.* **1.** reduce to general laws —*vi.* **2.** draw general conclusions —**'generally** *adv.* —**General Certificate of Education** public examination for which certificates are awarded at ordinary, advanced or scholarship level —**general election 1.** election in which representatives are chosen in all constituencies of a state **2.** US final election from which successful candidates are sent to legislative body **3.** US, C national, state or provincial election —**general practitioner** nonspecialist doctor with practice serving particular local area —**general-purpose** *a.* having a variety of uses —**general strike** strike by all or most of workers of country *etc.*

generalissimo (dʒɛnərə'lɪsɪməʊ, dʒɛnrə-) *n.* supreme commander of combined military, naval and air forces (*pl.* **-s**)

generate ('dʒɛnəreɪt) *vt.* **1.** bring into being **2.** produce —**gene'ration** *n.* **1.** bringing into being **2.** all persons born about same time **3.** average time between two such generations (about 30 years) —**'generative** *a.* —**'generator** *n.* **1.** apparatus for producing steam, electricity *etc.* **2.** begetter —**generation gap** years separating one generation from next, *esp.* regarded as representing difference in outlook and lack of understanding between them

generic (dʒɪ'nɛrɪk) *a.* belonging to, characteristic of class or genus —**ge'nerically** *adv.*

generous ('dʒɛnərəs, 'dʒɛnrəs) *a.* **1.** liberal, free in giving **2.** abundant —**gene'rosity** *n.* —**'generously** *adv.*

genesis ('dʒɛnɪsɪs) *n.* **1.** origin **2.** mode of formation **3.** (**G-**) first book of Bible (*pl.* **-eses** (-ɪsiːz))

-genesis (*comb. form*) genesis, development, generation, as in *biogenesis, parthenogenesis*

genet ('dʒɛnɪt) *or* **genette** (dʒɪ'nɛt) *n.* catlike mammal of Afr. and S Europe

genetics (dʒɪ'nɛtɪks) *pl.n.* (*with sing. v.*) scientific study of heredity and variation in organisms —**ge'netic** *a.* —**genetic code** *Biochem.* order in which four nitrogenous bases of DNA are arranged in molecule, which determines type and amount of protein synthesized in cell —**genetic engineering** alteration of structure of chromosomes in living organisms to produce effects beneficial to man in medicine, agriculture *etc.*

Geneva Convention (dʒɪ'niːvə) international agreement, formulated in 1864, establishing code for wartime treatment of sick or wounded: revised to cover maritime warfare and prisoners of war

genial ('dʒiːnjəl, -nɪəl) *a.* **1.** cheerful, warm in behaviour **2.** mild, conducive to growth —**geni'ality** *n.* —**'genially** *adv.*

genie ('dʒiːnɪ) *n.* in fairy tales, servant appearing by, and working, magic

genital ('dʒɛnɪtəl) *a.* relating to sexual organs or reproduction —**'genitals** *pl.n.* the sexual organs

genitive ('dʒɛnɪtɪv) *a./n.* possessive (case) —**genitival** (dʒɛnɪ'taɪvəl) *a.*

genius ('dʒiːnɪəs, -njəs) *n.* **1.** (person with) exceptional power or ability, *esp.* of mind **2.** distinctive spirit or nature (of nation *etc.*)

genocide ('dʒɛnəʊsaɪd) *n.* murder of a nationality or ethnic group

-genous (*comb. form*) **1.** yielding; generating, as in *erogenous* **2.** generated by; issuing from, as in *endogenous*

genre ('ʒɑːnrə) *n.* **1.** kind **2.** sort **3.** style **4.** painting of homely scene

gent (dʒɛnt) *inf. n.* **1.** gentleman —*pl.* **2.** men's public lavatory

genteel (dʒɛn'tiːl) *a.* **1.** well-bred **2.** stylish **3.** affectedly proper —**gen'teelly** *adv.*

gentian ('dʒɛnʃən) *n.* plant, usu. with blue flowers —**gentian violet** violet dye used as antiseptic *etc.*

Gentile ('dʒɛntaɪl) *a.* **1.** of race other than Jewish **2.** heathen —*n.* **3.** person, *esp.* Christian, who is not a Jew

gentle ('dʒɛntəl) *a.* **1.** mild, quiet, not rough or severe **2.** soft and soothing **3.** courteous **4.** moderate **5.** gradual **6.** noble **7.** well-born —**gen'tility** *n.* **1.** noble birth **2.** respectability, politeness —**'gentleness** *n.* **1.** quality of being gentle **2.** tenderness —**'gently** *adv.* —**'gentry** *n.* people of social standing next below nobility —**'gentlefolk** *or* **'gentlefolks** *pl.n.* persons regarded as being of good breeding —**'gentle-man** *n.* **1.** chivalrous well-bred man **2.** man of good social position **3.** man (used as a mark of politeness) —**'gentlemanly** *or* **'gentlemanlike** *a.* —**gentlemen's agreement** agreement binding by honour but not valid in law —**'gentlewoman** *n.*

genuflect ('dʒɛnjuflɛkt) vi. bend knee, esp. in worship —**genu'flection** or **genu'flexion** n.

genuine ('dʒɛnjʊɪn) a. 1. real, true, not fake; authentic 2. sincere 3. pure

genus ('dʒiːnəs) n. class, order, group (esp. of insects, animals etc.) with common characteristics, usu. comprising several species (pl. -es, 'genera)

geo- (comb. form) earth, as in geomorphology

geocentric (dʒiːəʊ'sɛntrɪk) a. Astron. 1. measured, seen from the earth 2. having the earth as centre —**geo'centrically** adv.

geode ('dʒiːəʊd) n. 1. cavity lined with crystals 2. stone containing this

geodesic (dʒiːə'dɛsɪk, -'diː-) a. of geometry of curved surfaces (also **geo'detic**) —**geodesic dome** light but strong hemispherical construction formed from set of polygons

geodesy (dʒiː'ɒdɪsɪ) n. science of measuring the earth's surface

geog. 1. geographer 2. geographic(al) 3. geography

geography (dʒiː'ɒgrəfɪ) n. science of earth's form, physical features, climate, population etc. —**ge'ographer** n. —**geo'graphic(al)** a. —**geo'graphically** adv. —**geographical mile** see nautical mile at NAUTICAL

geoid ('dʒiːɔɪd) n. 1. hypothetical surface that corresponds to mean sea level, extending under continents 2. shape of the earth

geol. 1. geologic(al) 2. geologist 3. geology

geology (dʒɪ'ɒlədʒɪ) n. science of earth's crust, rocks, strata etc. —**geo'logical** a. —**geo'logically** adv. —**ge'ologist** n.

geometry (dʒɪ'ɒmɪtrɪ) n. science of properties and relations of lines, surfaces etc. —**geo'metric(al)** a. —**geo'metrically** adv. —**geome'trician** n. —**geometric progression** sequence of numbers, each of which differs from succeeding one by constant ratio, as 1, 2, 4, 8 —**geometric series** such numbers written as sum

geophysics (dʒiːəʊ'fɪzɪks) pl.n. (with sing. v.) science dealing with the physics of the earth —**geo'physical** a. —**geo'physicist** n.

Geordie ('dʒɔːdɪ) n. native of Tyneside

George Cross (dʒɔːdʒ) British award for bravery

georgette or **georgette crepe** (dʒɔː'dʒɛt) n. fine, silky, semitransparent fabric

Georgian ('dʒɔːdʒjən) a. of the times of the four Georges (1714-1830) or of George V (1910-36)

georgic ('dʒɔːdʒɪk) n. poem on rural life, esp. one by Virgil

geostationary (dʒiːəʊ'steɪʃənərɪ) a. (of satellite) in orbit around earth so it remains over same point on surface

geotropism (dʒɪ'ɒtrəpɪzəm) n. response of plant part to stimulus of gravity

Ger. 1. German 2. Germany

geranium (dʒɪ'reɪnɪəm) n. 1. common cultivated plant with red, pink or white flowers, pelargonium 2. strong pink colour

gerbil or **gerbille** ('dʒɜːbɪl) n. burrowing desert rodent of Asia and Afr.

gerent ('dʒɛrənt) n. ruler, governor, director

gerfalcon ('dʒɜːfɔːlkən, -fɔːkən) n. see GYRFALCON

geriatrics (dʒɛrɪ'ætrɪks) pl.n. (with sing. v.) branch of science dealing with old age and its diseases —**geri'atric** a./n. old (person)

germ (dʒɜːm) n. 1. microbe, esp. causing disease 2. elementary thing 3. rudiment of new organism, of animal or plant —**germi'cidal** a. —**'germicide** n. substance for destroying disease germs —**germ cell** sexual reproductive cell —**germ warfare** use of bacteria against enemy

german ('dʒɜːmən) a. 1. of the same parents 2. closely akin (only in brother-, sister-, cousin-german)

German ('dʒɜːmən) n./a. (language or native) of Germany —**Ger'manic** n. 1. branch of Indo-European family of languages including Dutch, German etc. 2. unrecorded language from which these languages developed (also Proto-Germanic) —a. 3. of this group of languages 4. of Germany, German language or any people that speaks Germanic language —**German measles** see RUBELLA

germander (dʒɜː'mændə) n. European plant having two-lipped flowers with very small upper lip

germane (dʒɜː'meɪn) a. relevant, pertinent

germanium (dʒɜː'meɪnɪəm) n. grey element that is semiconducting metalloid

germinate ('dʒɜːmɪneɪt) v. (cause to) sprout or begin to grow —**germi'nation** n. —**'germinative** a.

gerontology (dʒɛrɒn'tɒlədʒɪ) n. scientific study of ageing and problems of elderly people —**geron'tologist** n.

gerrymander ('dʒɛrɪmændə) vt. 1. divide constituencies of (voting area) so as to give one party unfair advantage 2. manipulate or adapt to one's advantage —n. 3. act or result of gerrymandering

gerund ('dʒɛrənd) n. noun formed from verb, eg living

gerundive (dʒɪ'rʌndɪv) n. 1. in Latin grammar, adjective formed from verb, expressing desirability etc. of activity denoted by verb —a. 2. of gerund or gerundive

gesso ('dʒɛsəʊ) n. 1. white ground of plaster and size, used to prepare panels etc. for painting *etc.* **2.** any white substance, *esp.* plaster of Paris, that forms ground when mixed with water

Gestapo (gɛ'stɑːpəu) *n.* secret state police in Nazi Germany

gestate ('dʒɛsteɪt) *v.* carry (developing young) in uterus during pregnancy —**ges'tation** *n.*

gesticulate (dʒɛ'stɪkjuleɪt) *vi.* use expressive movements of hands and arms when speaking —**gesticu'lation** *n.*

gesture ('dʒɛstʃə) *n.* **1.** movement to convey meaning **2.** indication of state of mind —*vi.* **3.** make such a movement

get (gɛt) *vt.* **1.** obtain, procure **2.** contract **3.** catch **4.** earn **5.** cause to go or come **6.** bring into position or state **7.** induce **8.** engender **9.** *inf.* understand —*vi.* **10.** succeed in coming or going **11.** (*oft.* with to) reach, attain **12.** become (**got,** '**getting**) —'**getaway** *n.* escape —**get-together** *n. inf.* small informal social gathering —**get-up** *n. inf.* **1.** costume, outfit **2.** arrangement of book *etc.* —**get-up-and-go** *n. inf.* energy, drive —**get across** (cause to) be understood —**get at 1.** gain access to **2.** mean, intend **3.** annoy **4.** criticize **5.** influence —**get by** *inf.* manage, *esp.* in spite of difficulties —**get on 1.** grow late **2.** (of person) grow old **3.** make progress, manage, fare **4.** (*oft.* with) establish friendly relationship **5.** (*with* with) continue to do —**get (one's) goat** *sl.* make (one) angry, annoyed —**get one's own back** *inf.* obtain one's revenge —**have got** possess —**have got to** must, have to

geum ('dʒiːəm) *n.* garden plant with orange, yellow or white flowers

geyser ('giːzə, *U.S.* 'gaɪzər) *n.* **1.** hot spring throwing up spout of water from time to time **2.** apparatus for heating water and delivering it from a tap

ghastly ('gɑːstlɪ) *a.* **1.** *inf.* unpleasant **2.** deathlike, pallid **3.** *inf.* unwell **4.** horrible —*adv.* **5.** sickly

ghat (gɔːt) *n.* (in India) **1.** stairs leading down to river **2.** mountain pass

ghee (giː) *n.* clarified butter used in Indian cookery

gherkin ('gɜːkɪn) *n.* small cucumber used in pickling

ghetto ('gɛtəu) *n.* densely populated (*esp.* by one racial group) slum area (*pl.* **-s, -es**)

ghost (gəust) *n.* **1.** spirit, dead person appearing again **2.** spectre **3.** semblance **4.** faint trace **5.** one who writes work to appear under another's name —*v.* **6.** ghostwrite —*vt.* **7.** haunt —'**ghostly** *a.* —**ghost town** deserted town, *esp.* one in western U.S.A. that was formerly a boom town —'**ghostwrite** *v.* write (article *etc.*) on behalf of person who is then credited as author (*also* **ghost**) —'**ghostwriter** *n.*

ghoul (guːl) *n.* **1.** malevolent spirit **2.** person

with morbid interests **3.** fiend —'**ghoulish** *a.* **1.** of or like ghoul **2.** horrible

G.H.Q. *Mil.* General Headquarters

ghyll (gɪl) *n. see* GILL³

GI (*short for* **Government Issue,** stamped on U.S. military equipment) *inf.* U.S. soldier

giant ('dʒaɪənt) *n.* **1.** mythical being of superhuman size **2.** very tall person, plant *etc.* —*a.* **3.** huge —**gi'gantic** *a.* enormous, huge

giaour ('dʒauə) *n.* derogatory non-Muslim, *esp.* Christian

gib (gɪb) *n.* **1.** metal wedge, pad or thrust bearing let into steam engine crosshead —*vt.* **2.** fasten or supply with gib (**-bb-**)

Gib (dʒɪb) *n. inf.* Gibraltar

gibber ('dʒɪbə) *vi.* **1.** make meaningless sounds with mouth **2.** jabber, chatter —'**gibberish** *n.* meaningless speech or words

gibbet ('dʒɪbɪt) *n.* **1.** gallows **2.** post with arm on which executed criminals were formerly hung **3.** death by hanging —*vt.* **4.** hang on gibbet **5.** hold up to scorn

gibbon ('gɪbən) *n.* type of ape

gibbous ('gɪbəs) *or* **gibbose** ('gɪbəus) *a.* **1.** (of moon *etc.*) more than half illuminated **2.** hunchbacked **3.** bulging —'**gibbousness** *or* **gibbosity** (gɪ'bɒsɪtɪ) *n.*

gibe *or* **jibe** (dʒaɪb) *v.* **1.** utter taunts (at) **2.** mock **3.** jeer —*n.* **4.** taunt **5.** provoking remark

giblets ('dʒɪblɪts) *pl.n.* internal edible parts of fowl, as liver, gizzard *etc.*

giddy ('gɪdɪ) *a.* **1.** dizzy, feeling as if about to fall **2.** liable to cause this feeling **3.** flighty, frivolous —'**giddily** *adv.* —'**giddiness** *n.*

gift (gɪft) *n.* **1.** thing given, present **2.** faculty, power —*vt.* **3.** present, endow, bestow —'**gifted** *a.* talented —**gift token** voucher given as present which recipient can exchange for gift

gig (gɪg) *n.* **1.** light, two-wheeled carriage **2.** *inf.* single booking of musicians to play at concert *etc.* **3.** cluster of fish-hooks

giga- ('gɪgə, 'gaɪgə) (*comb. form*) 10⁹, as in *gigavolt*

gigantic (dʒaɪ'gæntɪk) *a. see* GIANT

giggle ('gɪgəl) *vi.* **1.** laugh nervously, foolishly —*n.* **2.** such a laugh **3.** joke

gigolo ('ʒɪgələu) *n.* **1.** man kept by (older) woman **2.** man paid to escort women

gigot ('dʒɪgət) *n.* **1.** leg of lamb or mutton **2.** leg-of-mutton sleeve

gild¹ (gɪld) *vt.* **1.** put thin layer of gold on **2.** make falsely attractive (**gilded** *pt.,* **gilt** *or* '**gilded** *pp.*) —**gilt** *a.* **1.** gilded —*n.* **2.** thin layer of gold applied in gilding **3.** superficial appearance —**gilt-edged** *a.* **1.** (of securities) dated over short, medium, or long term, and characterized by minimum risk and usu. issued by Government **2.** (of books *etc.*) having gilded edges

gild² (gild) *n.* see GUILD

gill¹ (gil) *n.* (*usu. pl.*) breathing organ in fish

gill² (dʒil) *n.* liquid measure, quarter of pint (0.142 litres)

gill³ *or* **ghyll** (gil) *n.* UK *dial.* **1.** narrow stream; rivulet **2.** wooded ravine

gillie, ghillie, *or* **gilly** ('gili) *n.* in Scotland, attendant for hunting or fishing

gillyflower *or* **gilliflower** ('dʒiliflauə) *n.* fragrant flower

gilt (gilt) *n.* young female pig

gimbals ('dʒimbəlz, 'gim-) *pl.n.* pivoted rings, for keeping things, *eg* compass, horizontal at sea

gimcrack ('dʒimkræk) *a.* **1.** cheap; shoddy —*n.* **2.** cheap showy trifle

gimlet ('gimlit) *n.* boring tool, usu. with screw point —**gimlet-eyed** *a.* having a piercing glance

gimmick ('gimik) *n.* clever device, stratagem *etc.*, *esp.* designed to attract attention or publicity

gimp *or* **guimpe** (gimp) *n.* narrow fabric or braid used as edging or trimming

gin¹ (dʒin) *n.* spirit flavoured with juniper berries —**gin rummy** version of rummy in which player may go out if odd cards outside his sequences total less than ten points

gin² (dʒin) *n.* **1.** primitive engine in which vertical shaft is turned to drive horizontal beam in a circle **2.** machine for separating cotton from seeds **3.** snare, trap

ginger ('dʒindʒə) *n.* **1.** plant with hot-tasting spicy root used in cooking *etc.* **2.** the root **3.** *inf.* spirit, mettle **4.** light reddish-yellow colour —**gingery** *a.* **1.** of, like ginger **2.** hot **3.** high-spirited **4.** reddish —**ginger ale** ginger-flavoured soft drink —**ginger beer** effervescing beverage made by fermenting ginger —**gingerbread** *n.* cake flavoured with ginger —**ginger group** group within a party, association *etc.* that enlivens or radicalizes its parent body —**ginger snap** *or* **nut** crisp biscuit flavoured with ginger —**ginger up** stimulate

gingerly ('dʒindʒəli) *adv.* **1.** cautiously, warily, reluctantly —*a.* **2.** cautious, reluctant or timid

gingham ('giŋəm) *n.* cotton cloth, usu. checked, woven from dyed yarn

gingivitis (dʒindʒi'vaitis) *n.* inflammation of gums

ginkgo ('giŋkgəu) *or* **gingko** ('giŋkəu) *n.* ornamental Chinese tree (*pl.* -**es**)

ginseng ('dʒinsɛŋ) *n.* **1.** plant of China or of N Amer., whose roots are used medicinally in China **2.** root of this plant or substance obtained from root

gip (dʒip) *vt./n.* **1.** see GYP¹ —**2.** see GYP²

Gipsy ('dʒipsi) *n.* see GYPSY

giraffe (dʒi'rɑːf, -'ræf) *n.* Afr. ruminant animal, with spotted coat and very long neck and legs

gird¹ (gɜːd) *vt.* **1.** put belt round **2.** fasten (clothes) thus **3.** equip with sword **4.** prepare (oneself) **5.** encircle (**girt, 'girded** *pt./pp.*) —**'girder** *n.* large beam, *esp.* of steel

gird² (gɜːd) *dial. v.* **1.** jeer (at); mock —*n.* **2.** taunt; gibe

girdle¹ ('gɜːdəl) *n.* **1.** corset **2.** waistband **3.** anything that surrounds, encircles —*vt.* **4.** surround, encircle

girdle² ('gɜːdəl) *n.* griddle

girl (gɜːl) *n.* **1.** female child **2.** young (unmarried) woman —**'girlhood** *n.* —**'girlie** *a.* *inf.* (of magazine) featuring nude or scantily dressed women —**'girlish** *a.* —**girl Friday** female employee with wide range of secretarial and clerical duties —**'girlfriend** *n.* **1.** female friend with whom male is romantically or sexually involved **2.** any female friend —**Girl Guide** see GUIDE (sense 5)

giro ('dʒairəu) *n.* system operated by banks and post offices which provides for the transfer of money between accounts or by giro cheque (*pl.* -**s**)

girt¹ (gɜːt) *pt./pp.* of GIRD¹

girt² (gɜːt) *vt.* **1.** bind; encircle; gird **2.** measure girth of

girth (gɜːθ) *n.* **1.** measurement around something **2.** leather or cloth band put around horse's belly to hold saddle *etc.* —*vt.* **3.** surround, secure with girth

gist (dʒist) *n.* substance, main point (of remarks *etc.*)

give (giv) *vt.* **1.** bestow, confer ownership of, make present of **2.** deliver **3.** impart **4.** assign **5.** yield, supply **6.** utter, emit **7.** be host of (party *etc.*) **8.** make over **9.** cause to have —*vi.* **10.** yield, give way, move (**gave, 'given, 'giving**) —*n.* **11.** yielding, elasticity —**give-and-take** *n.* **1.** mutual concessions, shared benefits and cooperation **2.** smoothly flowing exchange of ideas and talk —**'giveaway** *n.* **1.** betrayal or disclosure, *esp.* when unintentional —*a.* **2.** very cheap (*esp.* in **giveaway prices**) —**give and take** make mutual concessions —**give away 1.** donate or bestow as gift *etc.* **2.** sell very cheaply **3.** reveal, betray **4.** fail to use (opportunity) through neglect **5.** present (bride) formally to her husband in marriage ceremony —**give or take** plus or minus —**give up 1.** acknowledge defeat **2.** abandon

gizzard ('gizəd) *n.* part of bird's stomach

glabrous ('gleibrəs) *a. Biol.* without hairs or any unevenness; smooth

glacé ('glæsi) *a.* **1.** crystallized, candied, iced **2.** glossy

glacier ('glæsɪə, 'gleɪs-) n. river of ice, slow-moving mass of ice formed by accumulated snow in mountain valleys —**glacial** ('gleɪsɪəl, -ʃəl) a. 1. of ice, or of glaciers 2. very cold —**glaciated** ('gleɪsɪeɪtɪd) a. —**glaciation** (gleɪsɪ'eɪʃən) n. —**glacial period** time when large part of earth's surface was covered by ice

glad (glæd) a. 1. pleased 2. happy, joyous 3. giving joy —'**gladden** vt. make glad —'**gladly** adv. —'**gladness** n. —**glad eye** inf. inviting or seductive glance (esp. in **give** (someone) **the glad eye**) —'**gladrags** pl.n. sl. clothes for special occasions

glade (gleɪd) n. clear, grassy space in wood or forest

gladiator ('glædɪeɪtə) n. trained fighter in Roman arena

gladiolus (glædɪ'əʊləs) n. kind of iris, with sword-shaped leaves (pl. **-lus, -li** (-laɪ))

Gladstone bag ('glædstən) travelling bag

glair (glɛə) n. 1. white of egg 2. sticky substance —vt. 3. smear with white of egg —'**glairy** a.

Glam. (glæm) Glamorgan

glamour or U.S. (sometimes) **glamor** ('glæmə) n. alluring charm, fascination —'**glamorize, -ise,** or U.S. (sometimes) '**glamorize** vt. make appear glamorous —'**glamorous** a.

glance (glɑːns) vi. 1. look rapidly or briefly 2. allude briefly to or touch on subject 3. (usu. with off) glide off (something struck) —n. 4. brief look 5. flash 6. gleam 7. sudden (deflected) blow

gland (glænd) n. one of various small organs controlling different bodily functions by chemical means —'**glanders** n. contagious horse disease —'**glandular** a. —**glandular fever** acute disease characterized by fever, swollen lymph nodes etc. (also **infectious mononucleosis**)

glare (glɛə) vi. 1. look fiercely 2. shine brightly, intensely 3. be conspicuous —n. 4. angry stare —'**glaring** a.

glass (glɑːs) n. 1. hard transparent substance made by fusing sand, soda, potash etc. 2. things made of it 3. tumbler 4. its contents 5. mirror 6. telescope 7. barometer 8. microscope —pl. 10. spectacles —'**glassily** adv. —'**glassiness** n. —'**glassy** a. 1. like glass 2. expressionless —**glass-blower** n. —**glassblowing** n. process of shaping molten glass by blowing air into it through tube —'**glasshouse** n. 1. greenhouse 2. inf. army prison —**glass-paper** n. paper coated with pulverized glass for coating —**glass wool** insulating fabric

Glaswegian (glæz'wiːdʒən) a. 1. of Glasgow, city in Scotland —n. 2. native or inhabitant of Glasgow

glaucoma (glɔː'kəʊmə) n. eye disease —**glau'comatous** a.

glaucous ('glɔːkəs) a. 1. Bot. covered with waxy or powdery bloom 2. bluish-green

glaze (gleɪz) vt. 1. furnish with glass 2. cover with glassy substance —vi. 3. become glassy —vt. 4. transparent coating 5. substance used for this 6. glossy surface —'**glazier** n. person who glazes windows

G.L.C. Greater London Council

gleam (gliːm) n. 1. slight or passing beam of light 2. faint or momentary show —vi. 3. give out gleams

glean (gliːn) v. 1. pick up (facts etc.) 2. gather (useful remnants of crop) in cornfields after harvesting —'**gleaner** n. —'**gleanings** pl.n.

glebe (gliːb) n. land belonging to parish church or benefice

glee (gliː) n. 1. mirth, merriment 2. musical composition for three or more voices —'**gleeful** a. —'**gleefully** adv.

glen (glɛn) n. narrow valley, usu. wooded and with a stream, esp. in Scotland

glengarry (glɛn'gærɪ) n. Scottish woollen boat-shaped cap with ribbons hanging down back

glib (glɪb) a. 1. fluent but insincere or superficial 2. plausible —'**glibly** adv. —'**glibness** n.

glide (glaɪd) vi. 1. pass smoothly and continuously 2. (of aeroplane) move without use of engines —n. 3. smooth, silent movement 4. Mus. sounds made in passing from tone to tone —'**glider** n. aircraft without engine which moves in air currents —'**gliding** n. sport of flying gliders

glimmer ('glɪmə) vi. 1. shine faintly, flicker —n. 2. glow or twinkle of light —'**glimmering** n. 1. faint gleam of light 2. faint idea, notion

glimpse (glɪmps) n. 1. brief or incomplete view —vt. 2. catch glimpse of

glint (glɪnt) v. 1. flash —vi. 2. glance, glitter 3. reflect —n. 4. bright gleam; flash

glissade (glɪ'sɑːd, -'seɪd) n. 1. gliding dance step 2. slide, usu. on feet down slope of ice —vi. 3. perform glissade

glisten ('glɪsən) vi. gleam by reflecting light

glister ('glɪstə) vi./n. obs. glitter

glitter ('glɪtə) vi. 1. shine with bright quivering light, sparkle 2. be showy —n. 3. lustre 4. sparkle —**glitter ice** C ice formed from freezing rain

gloaming ('gləʊmɪŋ) n. Scot., poet. evening twilight

gloat (gləʊt) vi. regard, dwell (on) with smugness or malicious satisfaction

glob (glɒb) n. inf. soft lump or mass

globe (gləʊb) n. 1. sphere with map of earth or stars 2. heavenly sphere, esp. the earth 3. ball, sphere —'**global** a. —**globular** ('glɒbjʊlə) a. globe-shaped —**globule** ('glɒbjuːl) n. 1. small round particle **2.** drop —'**globetrotter** n. (habitual) worldwide traveller —**the globe** the world; the earth

globulin ('globjulin) n. kind of simple protein

glockenspiel ('glokənspiːl, -ʃpiːl) n. percussion instrument of metal bars which are struck with hammers

glomerate ('glomərɪt) a. **1.** gathered into rounded mass **2.** Anat. (esp. of glands) conglomerate in structure

gloom (gluːm) n. **1.** darkness **2.** melancholy, depression —'**gloomily** adv. —'**gloomy** a.

glory ('glɔːrɪ) n. **1.** renown, honourable fame **2.** splendour **3.** exalted or prosperous state **4.** heavenly bliss —vi. **5.** take pride ('**gloried**, '**glorying**) —glorifi'**cation** n. —'**glorify** vt. **1.** make glorious **2.** invest with glory (**-ified**, **-ifying**) —'**glorious** a. **1.** illustrious **2.** splendid **3.** excellent **4.** delightful —'**gloriously** adv. —**glory hole** inf. untidy cupboard, room or receptacle for storage

Glos. (glos) Gloucestershire

gloss[1] (glos) n. **1.** surface shine, lustre —vt. **2.** put gloss on **3.** (esp. with over) (try to) cover up, pass over (fault, error) —'**glossiness** n. —'**glossy** a. **1.** smooth, shiny —n. **2.** magazine printed on shiny paper

gloss[2] (glos) n. **1.** marginal interpretation of word **2.** comment, explanation —vt. **3.** interpret **4.** comment **5.** (oft. with over) explain away —'**glossary** n. list of items peculiar to a field of knowledge with explanations

glottis ('glotɪs) n. human vocal apparatus, larynx (pl. **-es**, **-tides** (-tɪdiːz)) —'**glottal** or '**glottic** a.

glove (glʌv) n. **1.** (oft. pl.) covering for the hand —vt. **2.** cover with, or as with glove —**glove box** or **compartment** small storage area in dashboard of car —**the gloves 1.** boxing gloves **2.** boxing

glow (gləʊ) vi. **1.** give out light and heat without flames **2.** shine **3.** experience feeling of wellbeing or satisfaction **4.** be or look hot **5.** burn with emotion —n. **6.** shining heat **7.** warmth of colour **8.** feeling of wellbeing **9.** ardour —'**glowworm** n. female insect giving out green light

glower ('glaʊə) vi. **1.** scowl —n. **2.** sullen or angry stare

gloxinia (glok'sɪnɪə) n. tropical plant with large bell-shaped flowers

glucose ('gluːkəʊz, -kəʊs) n. type of sugar found in fruit etc.

glue (gluː) n. **1.** any natural or synthetic adhesive **2.** any sticky substance —vt. **3.** fasten with glue —'**gluey** a.

glum (glʌm) a. sullen, moody, gloomy

glut (glʌt) n. **1.** surfeit, excessive amount —vt. **2.**

feed, gratify to the full or to excess **3.** overstock (market etc.) with commodity (**-tt-**)

gluten ('gluːtən) n. protein present in cereal grain —'**glutinous** a. sticky, gluey

glutton[1] ('glʌtən) n. **1.** greedy person **2.** one with great liking or capacity for something —'**gluttonous** a. like glutton, greedy —'**gluttony** n.

glutton[2] ('glʌtən) n. wolverine

glycerin ('glɪsərɪn), **glycerine** ('glɪsərɪn, glɪsə'riːn), or **glycerol** ('glɪsərɒl) n. colourless sweet liquid with wide application in chemistry and industry

glycogen ('glaɪkəʊdʒən) n. polysaccharide consisting of glucose units: form in which carbohydrate is stored in animals —**glyco'genesis** n. —**glyco'genic** a.

glyptic ('glɪptɪk) a. pert. to carving, esp. on precious stones

gm. gram

G.M. George Medal

G-man n. **1.** US sl. FBI agent **2.** Irish political detective

GMT Greenwich Mean Time

gnarled (nɑːld) or **gnarly** a. **1.** knobby, rugged **2.** (esp. of hands) twisted

gnash (næʃ) vt. grind (teeth) together as in anger or pain

gnat (næt) n. small, biting, two-winged fly

gnaw (nɔː) v. **1.** bite or chew steadily **2.** (esp. with at) cause distress (to)

gneiss (naɪs) n. coarse-grained metamorphic rock

gnome (nəʊm) n. **1.** legendary creature like small old man **2.** Facetious, derogatory international financier

gnomic ('nəʊmɪk, 'nom-) a. of or like an aphorism

gnomon ('nəʊmon) n. **1.** stationary arm that projects shadow on sundial **2.** geometric figure remaining after parallelogram has been removed from corner of larger parallelogram

gnostic ('nostɪk) a. **1.** of, relating to knowledge, esp. spiritual knowledge —n. **2.** (G-) adherent of Gnosticism —'**Gnosticism** n. religious movement characterized by belief in intuitive spiritual knowledge: regarded as heresy by Christian Church

GNP Gross National Product

gnu (nuː) n. S Afr. antelope somewhat like ox (pl. **-s**, **gnu**)

go (gəʊ) vi. **1.** move along, make way **2.** be moving **3.** depart **4.** function **5.** make specified sound **6.** fail, give way, break down **7.** elapse **8.** be kept, put **9.** be able to be put **10.** result **11.** (with towards) contribute to (result) **12.** (with towards) tend to **13.** be accepted, have force **14.** become (**went** pt., **gone** pp.) —n. **15.** going **16.**

energy, vigour **17.** attempt **18.** turn —'**goer** n. **1.** person who attends something regularly, as in *filmgoer* **2.** person or thing that goes, *esp.* very fast **3.** **A** *inf.* acceptable idea *etc.* **4.** **A, NZ** energetic person —'**going** n. **1.** departure; farewell **2.** condition of road surface with regard to walking *etc.* **3.** *inf.* speed, progress *etc.* —a. **4.** thriving (*esp. in* a **going concern**) **5.** current; accepted **6.** available —**goner** ('gɒnə) n. person beyond help or recovery, *esp.* person about to die —**go-ahead** n. **1.** *inf.* permission to proceed —a. **2.** enterprising, ambitious —**go-between** n. person who acts as intermediary for two people or groups —**go-by** n. *sl.* deliberate snub or slight (*esp. in* **give** (a person) the **go-by**) —**go-getter** n. *inf.* ambitious person —**go-go dancer** dancer, usu. scantily dressed, who performs rhythmic and oft. erotic modern dance routines in nightclubs *etc.* —**going-over** n. *inf.* **1.** check; examination; investigation **2.** castigation; thrashing (*pl.* **goings-over**) —**goings-on** *pl.n. inf.* **1.** actions or conduct, *esp.* regarded with disapproval **2.** happenings or events, *esp.* mysterious or suspicious —**go-kart** or **go-cart** n. see KART —**go-slow** n. deliberate slackening of the rate of production as form of industrial protest —**go down 1.** move to lower place or level; sink, decline, decrease *etc.* **2.** be defeated; lose **3.** be remembered or recorded (*esp. in* **go down in history**) **4.** (*usu. with* with) UK fall ill; be infected

goad (gəʊd) n. **1.** spiked stick for driving cattle **2.** anything that urges to action **3.** incentive —vt. **4.** urge on **5.** torment

goal (gəʊl) n. **1.** end of race **2.** object of effort **3.** posts through which ball is to be driven in football *etc.* **4.** the score so made —'**goalkeeper** n. *Sport* player in goal whose duty is to prevent ball from entering it

goat (gəʊt) n. four-footed animal with long hair, horns and beard —**goa'tee** n. pointed tuftlike beard growing on chin —**goat-herd** n. —'**goatsucker** n. US nightjar —**get (someone's) goat** *sl.* annoy (someone)

gob (gɒb) n. **1.** lump **2.** *sl.* mouth —'**gobbet** n. lump (of food) —'**gobble** v. eat hastily, noisily or greedily

gobble ('gɒb³l) n. **1.** throaty, gurgling cry of the turkey-cock —vi. **2.** make this sound —'**gobbler** n. male turkey

gobbledegook or **gobbledygook** ('gɒb³ldɪguːk) n. pretentious language, *esp.* as used by officials

goblet ('gɒblɪt) n. drinking cup

goblin ('gɒblɪn) n. *Folklore* small, usu. malevolent being

goby ('gəʊbɪ) n. small spiny-finned fish having ventral fins modified as sucker

god (gɒd) n. **1.** superhuman being worshipped as having supernatural power **2.** object of worship, idol **3.** (**G-**) in monotheistic religions, the Supreme Being, creator and ruler of the universe ('**goddess** *fem.*) —'**godlike** a. —'**godliness** n. —'**godly** a. devout, pious —'**godchild** n. person sponsored by adults at baptism ('**godson** or '**goddaughter**) —**god-fearing** a. religious, good —'**godforsaken** a. hopeless, dismal —'**godhead** n. divine nature or deity —'**godparent** n. sponsor at baptism ('**godfather** or '**godmother**) —'**godsend** n. something unexpected but welcome —'**God**'**speed** *interj./n.* expression of good wishes for person's success and safety

godetia (gə'diːʃə) n. annual garden plant

godwit ('gɒdwɪt) n. large shore bird of N regions

goffer ('gəʊfə) vt. **1.** press pleats into (frill) **2.** decorate (edges of book) —n. **3.** ornamental frill made by pressing pleats **4.** decoration formed by goffering books

gogga ('xɒxə) n. SA *inf.* insect, creepy-crawly

goggle ('gɒg³l) vi. **1.** (of eyes) bulge **2.** stare —*pl.n.* **3.** protective spectacles —'**gogglebox** n. UK *sl.* television set

Goidelic (gɔɪ'dɛlɪk) n. **1.** N group of Celtic languages, consisting of Irish Gaelic, Scottish Gaelic and Manx —a. **2.** of or characteristic of this group of languages

goitre or **U.S. goiter** ('gɔɪtə) n. enlargement of thyroid gland, in some cases nearly doubling size of neck

gold (gəʊld) n. **1.** yellow precious metal **2.** coins made of this **3.** wealth **4.** beautiful or precious thing **5.** colour of gold —a. **6.** of, like gold —'**golden** a. —'**goldcrest** n. small bird with yellow crown —**gold-digger** n. woman skilful in extracting money from men —**golden age 1.** *Class. myth.* first and best age of mankind, when existence was happy, prosperous and innocent **2.** most flourishing period, *esp.* in history of art or nation —**golden eagle** large eagle of mountainous regions of N hemisphere —**Golden Fleece** *Gr. myth.* fleece of winged ram stolen by Jason and Argonauts —**golden handshake** *inf.* money given to employee on retirement or for loss of employment —**golden mean** middle course between extremes —**golden**'**rod** n. tall plant with golden flower spikes —**golden rule** important principle —**golden wedding** fiftieth wedding anniversary —'**goldfield** n. place where gold deposits are known to exist —'**goldfinch** n. bird with yellow feathers —'**goldfish** n. any of various ornamental pond or aquarium fish —**gold plate 1.** thin coating of gold, usu. produced by electroplating **2.** vessels or utensils made of gold —**gold-plate** vt. —**gold**

rush large-scale migration of people to territory where gold has been found —'**goldsmith** *n.* 1. dealer in articles made of gold 2. artisan who makes such articles —**gold standard** financial arrangement whereby currencies of countries accepting it are expressed in fixed terms of gold

golf (golf) *n.* 1. outdoor game in which small hard ball is struck with clubs into a succession of holes —*vi.* 2. play this game —'**golfer** *n.* —**golf club** 1. long-shafted club with wood or metal head used to strike golf ball 2. (premises of) association of golf players, usu. having its own course and facilities —**golf course** or **links** area of open land on which golf is played

Goliath (gə'laɪəθ) *n. Bible* Philistine giant killed by David with stone from sling

golliwog ('gɒlɪwɒg) *n.* black-faced doll

golly ('gɒlɪ) *interj.* exclamation of mild surprise

goloshes (gə'lɒʃɪz) *pl.n. see* GALOSHES

-gon (*comb. form*) figure having specified number of angles, as in *pentagon*

gonad ('gɒnæd) *n.* gland producing gametes

gondola ('gɒndələ) *n.* Venetian canal boat —**gondo'lier** *n.* rower of gondola

gone (gɒn) *pp. of* GO

gonfalon ('gɒnfələn) *n.* 1. banner hanging from crossbar, used *esp.* by certain medieval Italian republics 2. battle flag suspended crosswise on staff, usu. having serrated edge

gong (gɒŋ) *n.* 1. metal plate with turned rim which resounds as bell when struck with soft mallet 2. anything used thus

gonorrhoea or *esp. U.S.* **gonorrhea** (gɒnə'rɪə) *n.* a venereal disease

good (gud) *a.* 1. commendable 2. right 3. proper 4. excellent 5. beneficial 6. well-behaved 7. virtuous 8. kind 9. financially safe or secure 10. adequate 11. sound 12. valid ('**better** *comp.*, **best** *sup.*) —*n.* 13. benefit 14. wellbeing 15. profit —*pl.* 16. property 17. wares —'**goodly** *a.* large, considerable —'**goodness** *n.* —**Good Book** the Bible —**good-hearted** *a.* kind and generous —**Good Samaritan** 1. *N.T.* figure in one of Christ's parables who is example of compassion towards those in distress 2. kindly person who helps another in difficulty —**good sort** *inf.* agreeable person —**good turn** helpful, friendly act; good deed; favour —**good will** 1. kindly feeling, heartiness 2. value of a business in reputation *etc.* over and above its tangible assets —**goody-goody** 1. *inf.* smugly virtuous or sanctimonious person —*a.* 2. smug and sanctimonious

goodbye (gud'baɪ) *interj./n.* form of address on parting

gooey ('guːɪ) *a. inf.* sticky, soft —**goo** *n. inf.* 1. sticky substance 2. coy or sentimental language or ideas

goof (guːf) *inf. n.* 1. mistake 2. stupid person —*vi.* 3. make mistake —'**goofy** *a.* silly, sloppy

googly ('guːglɪ) *n. Cricket* ball which changes direction unexpectedly on the bounce

goon (guːn) *n. inf.* stupid fellow

goosander (guː'sændə) *n.* type of duck

goose (guːs) *n.* 1. web-footed bird 2. its flesh 3. simpleton (*pl.* **geese**) —**goose flesh** bristling of skin due to cold, fright —**goose step** formal parade step

gooseberry ('guzbərɪ, -brɪ) *n.* 1. thorny shrub 2. its hairy fruit 3. *inf.* unwelcome third party (*oft. in* play **gooseberry**)

gopher ('gəʊfə) *n.* various species of Amer. burrowing rodents

Gordian knot ('gɔːdɪən) 1. in Greek legend, complicated knot, tied by King Gordius, that Alexander the Great cut with sword 2. intricate problem (*esp. in* cut the Gordian knot)

gore[1] (gɔː) *n.* (dried) blood from wound —'**gorily** *adv.* —'**gory** *a.* 1. horrific; bloodthirsty 2. involving bloodshed and killing 3. covered in gore

gore[2] (gɔː) *vt.* pierce with horns

gore[3] (gɔː) *n.* 1. triangular piece inserted to shape garment —*vt.* 2. shape thus

gorge (gɔːdʒ) *n.* 1. ravine 2. disgust, resentment —*vi.* 3. eat greedily —'**gorget** *n.* armour, ornamentation or clothing for throat —**gorge oneself** stuff oneself with food

gorgeous ('gɔːdʒəs) *a.* 1. splendid, showy, dazzling 2. *inf.* extremely pleasing

Gorgon ('gɔːgən) *n.* terrifying or repulsive woman

Gorgonzola (gɔːgən'zəʊlə) *n.* blue-veined Italian cheese

gorilla (gə'rɪlə) *n.* largest anthropoid ape, found in Afr.

gormandize or **-dise** ('gɔːməndaɪz) *v.* eat (food) hurriedly or like a glutton

gormless ('gɔːmlɪs) *a. inf.* stupid

gorse (gɔːs) *n.* prickly shrub

gory ('gɔːrɪ) *a. see* GORE[1]

gosh (gɒʃ) *interj.* exclamation of mild surprise or wonder

goshawk ('gɒshɔːk) *n.* large hawk

gosling ('gɒzlɪŋ) *n.* young goose

gospel ('gɒspəl) *n.* 1. unquestionable truth 2. (G-) any of first four books of New Testament

gossamer ('gɒsəmə) *n.* 1. filmy substance like spider's web 2. thin gauze or silk fabric

gossip ('gɒsɪp) *n.* 1. idle (malicious) talk about other persons, *esp.* regardless of facts 2. one who talks thus (*also* '**gossipmonger**) —*vi.* 3. engage in gossip 4. chatter —**gossip column** part of newspaper devoted to gossip about well-known people

got (gɒt) *pt./pp. of* GET

Goth (gɒθ) *n.* **1.** member of East Germanic people who invaded Roman Empire from 3rd to 5th cent. **2.** rude or barbaric person —'**Gothic** *a.* **1.** *Archit.* of the pointed arch style common in Europe from 12th-16th centuries **2.** of Goths **3.** (*sometimes* g-) barbarous **4.** (*sometimes* g-) of literary style characterized by gloom, the grotesque, and the supernatural —*n.* **5.** (of type) German black letter

gotten ('gɒtⁿn) *US pp. of* GET

gouache (gu'ɑ:ʃ) *n.* **1.** painting technique using opaque watercolour in which pigments are bound with glue (*also* **body colour**) **2.** paint used in this technique **3.** painting done by this method

Gouda ('gaʊdə) *n.* large, flat, round Dutch cheese with mild flavour

gouge (gaʊdʒ) *vt.* (*usu. with* out) **1.** scoop out, force out —*n.* **3.** chisel with curved cutting edge

goulash ('gu:læʃ) *n.* stew of meat and vegetables seasoned with paprika (*also* **Hungarian goulash**)

gourd (gʊəd) *n.* **1.** trailing or climbing plant **2.** its large fleshy fruit **3.** its rind as vessel

gourmand ('gʊəmənd) *or* **gormand** ('gɔ:mənd) *n.* glutton

gourmet ('gʊəmeɪ) *n.* connoisseur of wine, food **2.** epicure

gout (gaʊt) *n.* disease characterized by inflammation, *esp.* of joints —'**gouty** *a.*

Gov. *or* **gov.** **1.** government **2.** governor

govern ('gʌvⁿn) *vt.* **1.** rule, direct, guide, control **2.** decide, determine **3.** be followed by (grammatical case *etc.*) —'**governable** *a.* —'**governance** *n.* act of governing —'**governess** *n.* woman teacher, *esp.* in private household —'**government** *n.* **1.** exercise of political authority in directing a people, state *etc.* **2.** system by which community is ruled **3.** body of people in charge of government of state **4.** ministry **5.** executive power **6.** control **7.** direction **8.** exercise of authority —**govern'mental** *a.* —'**governor** *n.* **1.** one who governs, *esp.* one invested with supreme authority in state *etc.* **2.** chief administrator of an institution **3.** member of committee responsible for an organization or institution **4.** regulator for speed of engine —**governor general 1.** representative of Crown in dominion of commonwealth **2.** *UK* governor with jurisdiction over other governors (*pl.* **governors general, governor generals**)

Govt. *or* **govt.** government

gown (gaʊn) *n.* **1.** loose flowing outer garment **2.** woman's (long) dress **3.** official robe, as in university *etc.*

goy (gɔɪ) *n. sl.* derogatory word used by Jews for non-Jew (*pl.* **goyim** ('gɔɪɪm), **-s**)

G.P. General Practitioner

G.P.O. General Post Office

Gr. 1. Grecian **2.** Greece **3.** Greek

gr. 1. grain(s) **2.** gram(me)(s) **3.** gross

grab (græb) *vt.* **1.** grasp suddenly **2.** snatch (**-bb-**) —*n.* **3.** sudden clutch **4.** quick attempt to seize **5.** device or implement for clutching

grace (greɪs) *n.* **1.** charm, elegance **2.** accomplishment **3.** good will, favour **4.** sense of propriety **5.** postponement granted **6.** short thanksgiving before or after meal **7.** title of duke or archbishop —*pl.* **8.** affectation of manner (*esp. in* **airs and graces**) —*vt.* **9.** add grace to, honour —'**graceful** *a.* —'**gracefully** *adv.* —'**graceless** *a.* shameless, depraved —'**gracious** *a.* **1.** favourable **2.** kind **3.** pleasing **4.** indulgent, beneficent, condescending —'**graciously** *adv.* —**grace note** *Mus.* melodic ornament

Graces ('greɪsɪz) *pl.n. Gr. myth.* three sister goddesses, givers of charm and beauty

grade (greɪd) *n.* **1.** step, stage **2.** degree of rank *etc.* **3.** class **4.** mark, rating **5.** slope —*vt.* **6.** arrange in classes **7.** assign grade to **8.** level (ground), move (earth) with grader —**gradation** (grə'deɪʃən) *n.* **1.** series of degrees or steps **2.** each of them **3.** arrangement in steps **4.** in painting, gradual passing from one shade *etc.* to another —'**grader** *n.* **1.** person or thing that grades **2.** machine with wide blade used in road making —**make the grade** succeed

gradient ('greɪdɪənt) *n.* (degree of) slope

gradual ('grædjʊəl) *a.* **1.** taking place by degrees **2.** slow and steady **3.** not steep —'**gradually** *adv.*

graduate ('grædjʊeɪt) *vi.* **1.** take university degree —*vt.* **2.** divide into degrees **3.** mark, arrange according to scale —*n.* ('grædjʊɪt) **4.** holder of university degree —**gradu'ation** *n.* —**graduated pension** *UK* national pension scheme in which employees' contributions are scaled in accordance with their wage rate

Graeco- *or esp. U.S.* **Greco-** ('gri:kəʊ-, 'grɛkəʊ-) (*comb. form*) Greek, as in *Graeco-Roman*

graffiti (græ'fi:ti:) *pl.n.* (*oft.* obscene) writing, drawing on walls (*sing.* **graf'fito**)

graft[1] (grɑ:ft) *n.* **1.** shoot of plant set in stalk of another **2.** the process **3.** surgical transplant of skin to an area of body in need of tissue —*vt.* **4.** insert (shoot) in another stalk **5.** transplant (living tissue in surgery)

graft[2] (grɑ:ft) *n. inf.* **1.** hard work **2.** self-advancement, profit by unfair means, *esp.* through official or political privilege **3.** bribe **4.** swindle —'**grafter** *n.*

Grail (greɪl) *n. see* **Holy Grail** *at* HOLY

grain (greɪn) *n.* **1.** seed, fruit of cereal plant **2.** wheat and allied plants **3.** small hard particle **4.** unit of weight, 1/7000th of pound avoirdupois

(0.0648 gram) **5.** texture **6.** arrangement of fibres **7.** any very small amount —'**grainy** a.

gram or **gramme** (græm) n. unit of weight in metric system, one thousandth of a kilogram

-gram (comb. form) drawing; something written or recorded, as in hexagram, telegram

gramineous (grə'mɪnɪəs) a. **1.** of or belonging to grass family **2.** resembling grass; grasslike (also **graminaceous** (græmɪ'neɪjəs))

graminivorous (græmɪ'nɪvərəs) a. (of animals) feeding on grass

grammar ('græmə) n. **1.** science of structure and usages of language **2.** book on this **3.** correct use of words —**grammarian** (grə'meərɪən) n. —**gram'matical** a. according to grammar —**gram'matically** adv. —**grammar school** esp. formerly, state-maintained secondary school providing education with strong academic bias

gramophone ('græməfəʊn) n. instrument for reproducing sounds on discs, record-player

grampus ('græmpəs) n. **1.** type of dolphin **2.** person who huffs, breathes heavily

gran (græn) or **granny** ('grænɪ) n. inf. grandmother —**granny flat** flat in or added to house (for elderly parent) —**granny knot** or **granny's knot** reef knot with ends crossed wrong way

granary ('grænərɪ; U.S. 'greɪnərɪ) n. **1.** storehouse for grain **2.** rich grain growing region

grand (grænd) a. **1.** imposing **2.** magnificent **3.** majestic **4.** noble **5.** splendid **6.** eminent **7.** lofty **8.** chief, of chief importance **9.** final (total) —**grandeur** ('grændʒə) n. **1.** nobility **2.** magnificence **3.** dignity —**gran'diloquence** n. —**gran'diloquent** a. pompous in speech —**gran'diloquently** adv. —'**grandiose** a. **1.** imposing **2.** affectedly grand **3.** striking —**grandchild** ('græntʃaɪld) n. child of one's child (**grandson** ('grænsʌn, 'grænd-) or **granddaughter** ('grændɔːtə)) —**grand duke 1.** prince or nobleman who rules territory, state or principality **2.** son or male descendant in male line of Russian tsar —**grandfather clock** long-pendulum clock in tall standing wooden case —**grand jury** Law esp. in U.S.A., jury summoned to inquire into accusations of crime and ascertain whether evidence is adequate to found indictment —**Grand National** annual steeple-chase run at Aintree, Liverpool —**grand opera** opera with serious plot and fully composed text —**grandparent** ('grænpeərənt, 'grænd-) n. parent of parent (**grandfather** ('grænfɑːðə, 'grænd-) or **grandmother** ('grænmʌðə, 'grænd-)) —**grand piano** large harp-shaped piano with horizontal strings —**grandstand**

('grænstænd, 'grænd-) n. structure with tiered seats for spectators

grande dame (grãd 'dam) Fr. woman regarded as most experienced or prominent member of her profession etc.

grandee (græn'diː) n. Spanish nobleman of highest rank

grand mal ('grɒn 'mæl) form of epilepsy characterized by convulsions and loss of consciousness

Grand Prix (Fr. grã 'priː) any of series of international motor races

grange (greɪndʒ) n. country house with farm buildings

granite ('grænɪt) n. hard crystalline igneous rock —**gra'nitic** a.

granivorous (græ'nɪvərəs) a. feeding on grain or seeds

grant (grɑːnt) vt. **1.** consent to fulfil (request) **2.** permit **3.** bestow **4.** admit —n. **5.** sum of money provided by government for specific purpose, as education **6.** gift **7.** allowance, concession —**gran'tee** n. —'**granter** or (Law) '**grantor** n. —**grant-in-aid** n. money granted by central to local government for programme etc. (pl. **grants-in-aid**)

granule ('grænjuːl) n. small grain —'**granular** a. of or like grains —'**granulate** vt. **1.** form into grains —vi. **2.** take form of grains —**granu'lation** n.

grape (greɪp) n. fruit of vine —**grape hyacinth** plant with clusters of small, rounded blue flowers —'**grapeshot** n. bullets scattering when fired —'**grapevine** n. **1.** grape-bearing vine **2.** inf. unofficial means of conveying information

grapefruit ('greɪpfruːt) n. subtropical citrus fruit

graph (grɑːf, græf) n. drawing depicting relation of different numbers, quantities etc. (also **chart**)

-graph (n. comb. form) **1.** instrument that writes or records, as in telegraph **2.** writing, record; drawing, as in autograph, lithograph —'**grapher** (n. comb. form) **1.** person skilled in subject, as in geographer, photographer **2.** person who writes or draws in specified way, as in stenographer, lithographer —**graphic(al)** (a. comb. form) —'**graphy** (n. comb. form) **1.** form of writing, representing etc., as in calligraphy, photography **2.** art; descriptive science, as in choreography, oceanography

graphic ('græfɪk) or **graphical** a. **1.** vividly descriptive **2.** of, in, relating to, writing, drawing, painting etc. —'**graphically** adv. —'**graphics** pl.n. **1.** (with sing. v.) art of drawing in accordance with mathematical principles **2.** (with sing. v.) study of writing systems **3.** (with pl. v.) drawings etc. in layout of magazine or book —'**graphite** *n.* form of carbon (used in pencils) —**gra**'**phology** *n.* study of handwriting —**graphic arts** fine or applied visual arts based on drawing or use of line, *esp.* illustration and print-making —**graph paper** paper with intersecting lines for drawing graphs *etc.*

grapnel ('græpnəl) *n.* 1. hooked iron instrument for seizing anything 2. small anchor with several flukes

grapple ('græpəl) *v.* 1. come to grips, wrestle 2. cope, contend —*n.* 3. grappling 4. grapnel —**grappling iron** or **hook** grapnel, *esp.* for securing ships

grasp (grɑːsp) *v.* 1. (try, struggle to) seize hold (of) —*vt.* 2. understand —*n.* 3. act of grasping 4. grip 5. comprehension —'**grasping** *a.* greedy, avaricious

grass (grɑːs) *n.* 1. common type of plant with jointed stems and long narrow leaves (including cereals, bamboo *etc.*) 2. such plants grown as lawn 3. pasture 4. *sl.* marijuana 5. *sl.* informer, *esp.* criminal who betrays others to police —*vt.* 6. cover with grass —*vi.* 7. *sl.* (*with* on) inform —**grass hockey** C hockey played on field —'**grasshopper** *n.* jumping, chirping insect —**grass roots** fundamentals —'**grassroots** *a.* coming from ordinary people, the rank and file —**grass widow** wife whose husband is absent

grate[1] (greɪt) *vt.* 1. rub into small bits on rough surface —*vi.* 2. rub with harsh noise 3. have irritating effect —'**grater** *n.* utensil with rough surface for reducing substance to small particles

grate[2] (greɪt) *n.* framework of metal bars for holding fuel in fireplace —'**grating** *n.* framework of parallel or latticed bars covering opening

grateful ('greɪtful) *a.* 1. thankful 2. appreciative 3. pleasing —**gratefully** *adv.* —'**gratefulness** *n.* —**gratitude** ('grætɪtjuːd) *n.* sense of being thankful for favour

gratify ('grætɪfaɪ) *vt.* 1. satisfy 2. please 3. indulge —**gratifi**'**cation** *n.*

gratin (*Fr.* gra'tɛ̃) *n.* method of cooking to form light crust 2. dish so cooked

gratis ('greɪtɪs, 'grætɪs, 'grɑːtɪs) *adv./a.* free, for nothing

gratuitous (grə'tjuːɪtəs) *a.* 1. given free 2. uncalled for —**gra**'**tuitously** *adv.* —**gra**'**tuity** *n.* 1. gift of money for services rendered 2. donation

gravamen (grə'veɪmɛn) *n.* 1. *Law* part of accusation weighing most heavily against accused 2. *Law* substance of complaint 3. *rare* grievance (*pl.* **-vamina** (-'væmɪnə))

grave[1] (greɪv) *n.* 1. hole dug to bury corpse 2. *Poet.* death —'**gravestone** *n.* monument on grave —'**graveyard** *n.*

grave[2] (greɪv) *a.* 1. serious, weighty 2. dignified, solemn 3. plain, dark in colour 4. deep in note —'**gravely** *adv.*

grave[3] (greɪv) *vt.* clean (ship's bottom) by scraping —**graving dock** dry dock

grave[4] (grɑːv) *n. Phonet.* accent (`) used to indicate quality of vowel, full pronunciation of syllable *etc.*

gravel ('grævəl) *n.* 1. small stones 2. coarse sand —*vt.* 3. cover with gravel (-ll-) —'**gravelly** *a.*

graven ('greɪvən) *a.* carved, engraved

Graves (grɑːv) *n.* 1. (*sometimes* g-) white or red wine from district around Bordeaux, France 2. dry or medium sweet white wine from any country

gravid ('grævɪd) *a.* pregnant

gravimetric (grævɪ'mɛtrɪk) *a.* 1. of measurement by weight 2. *Chem.* of analysis of quantities by weight

gravitate ('grævɪteɪt) *vi.* 1. move by gravity 2. tend (towards centre of attraction) 3. sink, settle down —**gravi**'**tation** *n.*

gravity ('grævɪtɪ) *n.* 1. force of attraction of one body for another, *esp.* of objects to the earth 2. heaviness 3. importance 4. seriousness 5. staidness

gravy ('greɪvɪ) *n.* 1. juices from meat in cooking 2. sauce for food made from these —**gravy boat** small boat-shaped vessel for serving gravy

gray (greɪ) *see* GREY —'**grayling** *n.* fish of salmon family

graze[1] (greɪz) *v.* feed on (grass, pasture) —'**grazier** *n.* one who raises cattle for market —'**grazing** *n.* 1. vegetation on ranges or pastures that is available for livestock to feed upon 2. land on which this is growing

graze[2] (greɪz) *vt.* 1. touch lightly in passing, scratch, scrape —*n.* 2. grazing 3. abrasion

grease (griːs) *n.* 1. soft melted fat of animals 2. thick oil as lubricant —*vt.* (griːs, griːz) 3. apply grease to —'**greaser** *n.* 1. one who greases 2. *inf.* mechanic 3. *sl.* unpleasant, dirty person —'**greasily** *adv.* —'**greasiness** *n.* —'**greasy** *a.* —**grease gun** appliance for injecting oil or grease into machinery —**grease monkey** *inf.* mechanic —'**greasepaint** *n.* theatrical make-up —**grease the palm** (or **hand**) of bribe

great (greɪt) *a.* 1. large, big 2. important 3. preeminent, distinguished 4. *inf.* excellent —'**greatly** *adv.* —'**greatness** *n.* —**Great Bear** *see* URSA MAJOR —**great circle** circular section of sphere with radius equal to that of sphere —'**greatcoat** *n.* overcoat, *esp.* military —**Great Dane** breed of very large dog —**Great Russian** *n.* 1. *Linguis.* Russian 2. member of chief East Slavonic people of Russia —*a.* 3. of this people or their language —**great seal** (*oft.* G- S-) principal seal of nation *etc.* used to authenticate documents of highest importance —**Great War** World War I

great- (*comb. form*) indicates a degree further removed in relationship, as in *great-grandfather*

greave (griːv) *n.* (*oft. pl.*) armour for leg below knee

grebe (griːb) *n.* aquatic bird

Grecian ('griːʃən) *a.* of (ancient) Greece —**Grecian profile** profile in which nose and forehead form almost straight line

Greco- (*comb. form*) *esp.* US *see* GRAECO-

greed (griːd) *n.* excessive consumption of, desire for, food, wealth —**'greedily** *adv.* —**'greediness** *n.* voracity of appetite —**'greedy** *a.* 1. gluttonous 2. eagerly desirous 3. voracious 4. covetous

Greek (griːk) *n.* 1. native language of Greece —*a.* 2. of Greece, the Greeks or the Greek language —**Greek cross** cross with four arms of same length —**Greek Orthodox Church** 1. established Church of Greece, in which Metropolitan of Athens has primacy of honour (*also* **Greek Church**) 2. *see* Orthodox Church *at* ORTHODOX

green (griːn) *a.* 1. of colour between blue and yellow 2. grass-coloured 3. emerald 4. unripe 5. (of bacon) unsmoked 6. inexperienced 7. gullible 8. envious 9. (*oft.* G-) concerned with preserving the environment —*n.* 10. colour 11. area of grass, *esp.* for playing bowls *etc.* 12. area of green 13. (G-) member of political movement whose main concern is preserving the environment —*pl.* 13. green vegetables —**'greenery** *n.* vegetation —**green bean** any bean plant, such as French bean, having narrow green edible pods —**green belt** area of farms, open country around a town —**Green Cross Code** UK code for children giving rules for road safety —**green-eyed** *a.* jealous, envious —**green-eyed monster** jealousy, envy —**'greenfinch** *n.* European finch with dull green plumage in male —**green fingers** talent for gardening —**'greenfly** *n.* aphid, small green garden pest —**'greengage** *n.* kind of plum —**'greengrocer** *n.* dealer in vegetables and fruit —**'greengrocery** *n.* —**'greenhorn** *n.* inexperienced person, newcomer —**'greenhouse** *n.* glasshouse for rearing plants —**'greenkeeper** *n.* person responsible for maintaining golf course *etc.* —**green light** 1. signal to go, *esp.* green traffic light 2. permission to proceed with project *etc.* —**green paper** (*oft.* G- P-) UK government document containing policy proposals to be discussed, *esp.* by Parliament —**green pepper** green unripe fruit of sweet pepper, eaten raw or cooked —**green pound** unit of account used in calculating Britain's contributions to and payments from Community

Agricultural Fund of EEC —**'greenroom** *n.* room for actors when offstage —**'greenshank** *n.* large European sandpiper —**greenstick fracture** fracture in children in which bone is partly bent and splinters only on convex side of bend —**'greenstone** *n.* New Zealand jade —**'greensward** *n.* turf

Greenwich Mean Time *or* **Greenwich Time** ('grɪnɪdʒ) local time of 0° meridian passing through Greenwich, England: standard time for Britain and basis for calculating times throughout world

greet (griːt) *vt.* 1. meet with expressions of welcome 2. accost, salute 3. receive —**'greeting** *n.*

gregarious (grɪ'gɛərɪəs) *a.* 1. fond of company, sociable 2. living in flocks —**gre'gariousness** *n.*

Gregorian calendar (grɪ'gɔːrɪən) calendar introduced by Pope Gregory XIII, whereby ordinary year is made to consist of 365 days

Gregorian chant *see* PLAINSONG

gremlin ('grɛmlɪn) *n.* imaginary being blamed for mechanical and other troubles

grenade (grɪ'neɪd) *n.* explosive shell or bomb, thrown by hand or shot from rifle —**grenadier** (grɛnə'dɪə) *n.* 1. soldier of Grenadier Guards 2. formerly, grenade thrower

grenadine (grɛnə'diːn, 'grɛnədiːn) *n.* syrup made from pomegranate juice, for sweetening and colouring drinks

grew (gruː) *pt. of* GROW

grey *or* U.S. **gray** (greɪ) *a.* 1. between black and white, as ashes or lead 2. clouded 3. dismal 4. turning white 5. aged 6. intermediate, indeterminate —*n.* 7. grey colour 8. grey or whitish horse —**Grey Friar** Franciscan friar —**'greyhen** *n.* female of black grouse —**'greyhound** *n.* swift slender dog used in coursing and racing —**greylag** *or* **greylag goose** *n.* large grey Eurasian goose —**grey matter** 1. greyish tissue of brain and spinal cord, containing nerve cell bodies and fibres 2. *inf.* brains; intellect

grid (grɪd) *n.* 1. network of horizontal and vertical lines, bars *etc.* 2. any interconnecting system of links 3. national network of electricity supply

griddle ('grɪdəl) *n.* flat iron plate for cooking (*also* **'girdle**)

gridiron ('grɪdaɪən) *n.* 1. frame of metal bars for grilling 2. (field of play for) American football

grief (griːf) *n.* deep sorrow —**'grievance** *n.* real or imaginary grounds for complaint —**grieve** *vi.* 1. feel grief —*vt.* 2. cause grief to —**'grievous** *a.* 1. painful, oppressive 2. very serious —**grief-stricken** *a.* stricken with grief; sorrowful

griffin ('grɪfɪn), **griffon,** *or* **gryphon** *n.*

fabulous monster with eagle's head and wings and lion's body

grill (gril) *n.* 1. device on cooker to radiate heat downwards 2. food cooked under grill 3. gridiron —*v.* 4. cook (food) under grill —*vt.* 5. subject to severe questioning —'**grilling** *a.* 1. very hot —*n.* 2. severe cross-examination —'**grillroom** *n.* restaurant where grilled food is served

grille *or* **grill** (gril) *n.* grating, crosswork of bars over opening

grilse (grils) *n.* salmon at stage when it returns for first time from sea (*pl.* **-s, grilse**)

grim (grim) *a.* 1. stern 2. of stern or forbidding aspect, relentless 3. joyless —'**grimly** *adv.*

grimace (grɪ'meɪs) *n.* 1. wry face —*vi.* 2. pull wry face

grimalkin (grɪ'mælkɪn, -'mɔːl-) *n.* 1. old cat, *esp.* female cat 2. crotchety or shrewish old woman

grime (graɪm) *n.* 1. ingrained dirt, soot —*vt.* 2. soil, dirty, blacken —'**grimy** *a.*

grin (grɪn) *vi.* 1. show teeth, as in laughter (**-nn-**) —*n.* 2. grinning smile

grind (graɪnd) *vt.* 1. crush to powder 2. oppress 3. make sharp, smooth 4. grate —*vi.* 5. perform action of grinding 6. rub together 7. *inf.* study hard 7. grate (**ground** *pt./pp.*) —*n.* 8. *inf.* hard work 9. act of grinding —'**grinder** *n.* —'**grindstone** *n.* stone used for grinding

gringo ('grɪŋgəʊ) *n.* in Mexico, contemptuous name for foreigner, *esp.* Englishman or American (*pl.* **-s**)

grip (grɪp) *n.* 1. firm hold, grasp 2. grasping power 3. mastery 4. handle 5. suitcase or travelling bag (*also* '**handgrip**) —*vt.* 6. grasp or hold tightly 7. hold interest or attention of (**-pp-**)

gripe (graɪp) *vi.* 1. *inf.* complain (persistently) —*n.* 2. intestinal pain (*esp.* in infants) 3. *inf.* complaint

grippe *or* **grip** (grɪp) *n.* influenza

grisly ('grɪzlɪ) *a.* grim, causing terror, ghastly

grist (grɪst) *n.* corn to be ground —**grist to** (*or* **for**) **the** (*or* **one's**) **mill** something which can be turned to advantage

gristle ('grɪsəl) *n.* cartilage, tough flexible tissue

grit (grɪt) *n.* 1. rough particles of sand 2. coarse sandstone —*n./a.* 4. (G-) C *inf.* Liberal —*pl.* 5. wheat *etc.* coarsely ground —*vt.* 6. clench, grind (teeth) (**-tt-**) —'**grittiness** *n.* —'**gritty** *a.*

grizzle[1] ('grɪzəl) *v.* make, become grey —'**grizzled** *a.* —'**grizzly** *a.* —**grizzly bear** large Amer. bear

grizzle[2] ('grɪzəl) *vi. inf.* grumble, whine, complain

groan (grəʊn) *vi.* 1. make low, deep sound of

grief or pain 2. be in pain or overburdened —*n.* 3. groaning sound

groat (grəʊt) *n.* formerly, silver coin worth four pennies

groats (grəʊts) *pl.n.* hulled and crushed grain of oats, wheat or certain other cereals

grocer ('grəʊsə) *n.* dealer in foodstuffs —'**groceries** *pl.n.* commodities sold by grocer —'**grocery** *n.* trade, premises of grocer

grog (grɒg) *n.* spirit (*esp.* rum) and water —'**groggy** *a. inf.* unsteady, shaky, weak

grogram ('grɒgrəm) *n.* coarse fabric of silk, wool, or silk mixed with wool or mohair, formerly used for clothing

groin (grɔɪn) *n.* 1. fold where legs meet abdomen 2. euphemism for genitals 3. *Archit.* edge made by intersection of two vaults —*vt.* 4. build with groins

groom (gruːm, grʊm) *n.* 1. person caring for horses 2. *see* **bridegroom** *at* BRIDE 3. officer in royal household —*vt.* 4. tend or look after 5. brush or clean (*esp.* horse) 6. train (someone for something) —'**groomsman** *n.* friend attending bridegroom —**well-groomed** *a.* neat, smart

groove (gruːv) *n.* 1. narrow channel, hollow, *esp.* cut by tool 2. rut, routine —*vt.* 3. cut groove in —'**groovy** *a. sl.* fashionable, exciting

grope (grəʊp) *vi.* feel about, search blindly

groper ('grəʊpə) *or* **grouper** *n.* large marine fish of warm and tropical seas

grosbeak ('grəʊsbiːk, 'grɒs-) *n.* finch with large powerful bill

grosgrain ('grəʊgreɪn) *n.* heavy ribbed silk or rayon fabric used for trimming clothes *etc.*

gros point (grəʊ) *n.* 1. needlepoint stitch covering two horizontal and two vertical threads 2. work done in this stitch

gross (grəʊs) *a.* 1. very fat 2. total, not net 3. coarse 4. indecent 5. flagrant 6. thick, rank —*n.* 7. twelve dozen —'**grossly** *adv.* —**gross national product** total value of final goods and services produced annually by nation

grotesque (grəʊ'tɛsk) *a.* 1. (horribly) distorted 2. absurd —*n.* 3. 16th-cent. decorative style using distorted human, animal and plant forms 4. grotesque person, thing —**gro'tesquely** *adv.*

grotto ('grɒtəʊ) *n.* cave

grotty ('grɒtɪ) *a. inf.* dirty, untidy, unpleasant

grouch (graʊtʃ) *inf. n.* 1. persistent grumbler 2. discontented mood —*vi.* 3. grumble, be peevish

ground[1] (graʊnd) *n.* 1. surface of earth 2. soil, earth 3. (*oft. pl.*) reason, motive 4. coating to work on with paint 5. background, main surface worked on in painting, embroidery *etc.* 6. special area 7. bottom of sea —*pl.* 8. dregs, *esp.* from coffee 9. enclosed land round house —*vt.* 10. establish 11. instruct (in elements) 12. place on ground —*vi.* 13. run ashore —'**grounded** *a.*

(of aircraft) unable or not permitted to fly —'**grounding** n. basic general knowledge of a subject —'**groundless** a. without reason —**ground crew** group of people in charge of maintenance and repair of aircraft —**ground floor** floor of building level or almost level with ground —'**groundnut** n. 1. earthnut 2. peanut —'**groundsheet** n. waterproof sheet on ground under tent etc. —'**groundsman** n. person employed to maintain sports ground etc. —'**groundspeed** n. aircraft's speed in relation to ground —**ground swell** n. considerable swell of sea, oft. caused by distant storm 2. rapidly developing general opinion —'**groundwork** n. 1. preliminary work as foundation or basis 2. ground or background of painting etc. —**get in on the ground floor** inf. be in project etc. from its inception

ground² (graund) pt./pp. of GRIND

groundsel ('graunsal) n. yellow flowered plant

group (gru:p) n. 1. number of persons or things considered as collective unit 2. number of persons bound together by common interests etc. 3. small musical band of players or singers 4. class 5. two or more figures forming one artistic design —v. 6. place, fall into group —**group captain** officer holding commissioned rank senior to squadron leader but junior to air commodore in British R.A.F. and certain other air forces —**group therapy** Psych. simultaneous treatment of number of individuals brought together to share their problems in group discussion

grouper ('gru:pa) n. see GROPER

grouse¹ (graus) n. 1. game bird 2. its flesh (pl. **grouse**)

grouse² (graus) vi. 1. grumble, complain —n. 2. complaint —'**grouser** n. grumbler

grout (graut) n. 1. thin fluid mortar —vt. 2. fill up with grout

grove (grəuv) n. 1. small group of trees 2. road lined with trees

grovel ('grɒvəl) vi. 1. abase oneself 2. lie face down (**-ll-**)

grow (grəu) vi. 1. develop naturally 2. increase in size, height etc. 3. be produced 4. become by degrees —vt. 5. produce by cultivation (**grew** pt., **grown** pp.) —'**growth** n. 1. growing 2. increase 3. what has grown or is growing —**growing pains** 1. pains in joints sometimes experienced by growing children 2. difficulties besetting new enterprise in early stages —**grown-up** a./n. adult

growl (graul) v. 1. make low guttural sound of anger 2. rumble 3. murmur, complain —n. 4. act or sound of growling

groyne or esp. U.S. **groin** (grɔin) n. wall or

jetty built out from riverbank or shore to control erosion

grub (grʌb) vt. 1. (oft. with up or out) dig superficially 2. root up —vi. 3. dig, rummage 4. plod (**-bb-**) —n. 5. larva of insect 6. sl. food —'**grubby** a. dirty

grudge (grʌdʒ) vt. 1. be unwilling to give, allow —n. 2. ill will

gruel ('gru:əl) n. food of oatmeal etc., boiled in milk or water —'**gruelling** or U.S. '**grueling** a./n. exhausting, severe (experience)

gruesome ('gru:səm) a. fearful, horrible, grisly —'**gruesomeness** n.

gruff (grʌf) a. rough in manner or voice, surly —'**gruffly** adv.

grumble ('grʌmbəl) vi. 1. complain 2. rumble, murmur 3. make growling sounds —n. 4. complaint 5. low growl —'**grumbler** n.

grumpy ('grʌmpi) or **grumpish** a. ill-tempered, surly —'**grumpily** or '**grumpishly** adv.

grunt (grʌnt) vi. 1. make sound characteristic of pig —n. 2. deep, hoarse sound of pig 3. gruff noise

Gruyère or **Gruyère cheese** ('gru:jɛə) n. pale yellow whole milk cheese with holes

gryphon ('grifən) n. see GRIFFIN

grysbok ('graisbok) n. small Afr. antelope

G.S. 1. General Secretary 2. General Staff

G-string n. 1. very small covering for genitals 2. Mus. string tuned to G

G-suit n. close-fitting garment worn by crew of high-speed aircraft, pressurized to prevent blackout during manoeuvres

GT gran turismo (touring car, used of (sports) car capable of high speed)

guanaco (gwɑ:'nɑ:kəu) n. cud-chewing S Amer. mammal closely related to domesticated llama (pl. **-s**)

guano ('gwɑ:nəu) n. sea bird manure (pl. **-s**)

guarantee (gærən'ti:) n. 1. formal assurance, esp. in writing, that product etc. will meet certain standards, last for given time etc. —vt. 2. give guarantee of, for something 3. secure (against risk etc.) (**guaran'teed, guaran'tee-ing**) —**guaran'tor** n. one who undertakes fulfilment of another's promises —'**guaranty** n. 1. pledge of responsibility for fulfilling another person's obligations in case of default 2. thing given or taken as security for guaranty 3. act of providing security 4. guarantor —v. 5. guarantee

guard (gɑ:d) vt. 1. protect, defend —vi. 2. be careful, take precautions —n. 3. person, group that protects, supervises, keeps watch 4. sentry 5. soldiers protecting anything 6. official in charge of train 7. protection 8. screen for enclosing anything dangerous 9. protector 10. posture of defence —pl. 11. (**G-**) any of certain

British regiments —'**guarded** a. 1. kept under surveillance 2. prudent, restrained or noncommittal —'**guardedly** adv. —'**guardian** n. 1. keeper, protector 2. person having custody of infant etc. —'**guardianship** n. care —'**guardhouse** or '**guardroom** n. place for stationing those on guard or for prisoners —'**guardsman** n. soldier in Guards

guava ('gwɑːvə) n. tropical tree with fruit used to make jelly

gubernatorial (gjuːbənə'tɔːrɪəl, guː-) a. chiefly US of or relating to governor

gudgeon¹ ('gʌdʒən) n. small freshwater fish

gudgeon² ('gʌdʒən) n. 1. pivot bearing 2. socket for rudder 3. kind of connecting pin

guelder-rose ('gɛldərəʊz) n. shrub with clusters of white flowers

guerdon ('gɜːdən) n. reward

Guernsey ('gɜːnzɪ) n. 1. breed of cattle 2. close-fitting knitted jumper

guerrilla or **guerilla** (gə'rɪlə) n. member of irregular armed force, esp. fighting established force, government etc.

guess (gɛs) vt. 1. estimate without calculation 2. conjecture, suppose 3. US consider, think —vi. 4. form conjectures —n. 5. estimate —'**guesswork** n. 1. set of conclusions etc. arrived at by guessing 2. process of making guesses

guest (gɛst) n. 1. one entertained at another's house 2. one living in hotel —'**guesthouse** n. boarding house, usu. without alcoholic licence

guff (gʌf) n. sl. silly talk

guffaw (gʌ'fɔː) n. 1. burst of boisterous laughter —vi. 2. laugh in this way

guide (gaɪd) n. 1. one who shows the way 2. adviser 3. book of instruction or information 4. contrivance for directing motion 5. (usu. G-) member of organization for girls equivalent to Scouts —vt. 6. lead, act as guide to 7. arrange —'**guidance** n. —'**guider** n. adult leader of company of Guides —**guided missile** missile whose flight path is controlled by radio or preprogrammed homing mechanism —**guide dog** dog trained to lead blind person —'**guideline** n. principle put forward to determine course of action

guidon ('gaɪdən) n. 1. pennant, used as marker, esp. by cavalry regiments 2. man or vehicle that carries this

guild or **gild** (gɪld) n. 1. organization, club 2. society for mutual help, or with common object 3. Hist. society of merchants or tradesmen —'**guildhall** n. meeting place of guild or corporation

guilder ('gɪldə) or **gulden** ('gʊldən) n. 1. standard monetary unit of Netherlands (also '**gilder**) 2. former gold or silver coin of

Germany, Austria or Netherlands (pl. -s, -der or -s, -den)

guile (gaɪl) n. cunning, deceit —'**guileful** a. —'**guilefully** adv. —'**guileless** a.

guillemot ('gɪlɪmɒt) n. species of sea bird

guillotine ('gɪlətiːn) n. 1. device for beheading 2. machine for cutting paper 3. in parliament etc., method of restricting length of debate by fixing time for taking vote —vt. (gɪlə'tiːn) 4. behead 5. use guillotine on 6. limit (debate) by guillotine

guilt (gɪlt) n. 1. fact, state of having done wrong 2. responsibility for criminal or moral offence —'**guiltily** adv. —'**guiltiness** n. —'**guiltless** a. innocent —'**guilty** a. having committed an offence

guinea ('gɪnɪ) n. formerly, gold coin worth 21 shillings —**guinea fowl** bird allied to pheasant —**guinea pig** 1. rodent originating in S Amer. 2. inf. person or animal used in experiments

guipure (gɪ'pjʊə) n. 1. any of many types of lace that have their pattern connected by threads, rather than supported on net mesh (also **guipure lace**) 2. heavy corded trimming; gimp

guise (gaɪz) n. external appearance, esp. one assumed —'**guiser** or '**guising** n. in Scotland and N England, custom of disguising oneself in fancy dress and visiting people's houses at Hallowe'en

guitar (gɪ'tɑː) n. usu. 6-stringed instrument played by plucking or strumming —**gui'tarist** n. player of guitar

Gulag ('guːlæg) n. central administrative department of Soviet security service, responsible for prisons, labour camps etc.

gulch (gʌltʃ) n. 1. ravine 2. gully

gulf (gʌlf) n. 1. large inlet of the sea 2. chasm 3. large gap —**Gulf Stream** warm ocean current flowing from Gulf of Mexico towards NW Europe (also **North Atlantic Drift**) —'**gulfweed** n. seaweed forming dense floating masses in tropical Atlantic waters, esp. Gulf Stream (also **sar'gasso**, **sargasso weed**)

gull¹ (gʌl) n. long-winged web-footed sea bird

gull² (gʌl) n. 1. dupe, fool —vt. 2. dupe, cheat —**gulli'bility** n. —'**gullible** a. easily imposed on, credulous

gullet ('gʌlɪt) n. food passage from mouth to stomach

gully ('gʌlɪ) n. channel or ravine worn by water

gulp (gʌlp) vt. 1. swallow eagerly —vi. 2. gasp, choke —n. 3. act of gulping

gum¹ (gʌm) n. firm flesh in which teeth are set —'**gummy** a. toothless —'**gumboil** n. abscess on gum

gum² (gʌm) n. 1. sticky substance issuing from certain trees 2. an adhesive 3. chewing gum

—*vt.* **4.** stick with gum (-**mm**-) —'**gummy** *a.* —'**gumboots** *pl.n.* boots of rubber —**gum resin** mixture of resin and gum obtained from various plants and trees —'**gumtree** *n.* any species of eucalypt —**gum up the works** *inf.* impede progress —**up a gum tree** *sl.* in a difficult position

gumption ('gʌmpʃən) *n.* **1.** resourcefulness **2.** shrewdness, sense

gun (gʌn) *n.* **1.** weapon with metal tube from which missiles are discharged by explosion **2.** cannon, pistol *etc.* —*vt.* **3.** (*oft. with* down) shoot **4.** race (engine of car) —*vi.* **5.** hunt with gun (-**nn**-) —'**gunner** *n.* '**gunnery** *n.* use or science of large guns —'**gunboat** *n.* small warship —**gunboat diplomacy** diplomacy conducted by threats of military intervention —'**guncotton** *n.* cellulose nitrate containing large amount of nitrogen: used as explosive —**gun dog** (breed of) dog used to find or retrieve game —'**gunman** *n.* armed criminal —'**gunmetal** *n.* alloy of copper and tin or zinc, formerly used for guns —'**gunpoint** *n.* muzzle of gun —'**gunpowder** *n.* explosive mixture of saltpetre, sulphur and charcoal —'**gunroom** *n.* in warship, mess room of junior officers —'**gunrunner** *n.* '**gunrunning** *n.* smuggling of guns and ammunition into country —'**gunshot** *n.* **1.** shot or range of gun —*a.* **2.** caused by missile from gun —'**gunstock** *n.* wooden handle or support to which is attached barrel of rifle —**gunwale** *or* **gunnel** ('gʌnəl) *n.* upper edge of ship's side —**at gunpoint** under threat of being shot

gunge (gʌndʒ) *n. inf.* any sticky, unpleasant substance

gunk (gʌŋk) *n. inf.* any dirty, oily matter

gunny ('gʌnɪ) *n.* strong, coarse sacking made from jute

guppy ('gʌpɪ) *n.* small colourful aquarium fish

gurgle ('gɜːgəl) *n.* **1.** bubbling noise —*vi.* **2.** utter, flow with gurgle

Gurkha ('gɜːkə) *n.* **1.** any of a warlike people in Nepal **2.** member of this people serving as soldier in British army

gurnard ('gɜːnəd) *or* **gurnet** ('gɜːnɪt) *n.* spiny armour-headed sea fish

guru ('guruː, 'gʊruː) *n.* spiritual teacher, *esp.* in India

gush (gʌʃ) *vi.* **1.** flow out suddenly and copiously, spurt —*n.* **2.** sudden and copious flow **3.** effusiveness —'**gusher** *n.* **1.** gushing person **2.** something, such as spurting oil well, that gushes

gusset ('gʌsɪt) *n.* triangle or diamond-shaped piece of material let into garment —'**gusseted** *a.*

gust (gʌst) *n.* **1.** sudden blast of wind **2.** burst of rain, anger, passion *etc.* —'**gusty** *a.*

gustation (gʌ'steɪʃən) *n.* act of tasting or faculty of taste —'**gustatory** *a.*

gusto ('gʌstəʊ) *n.* enjoyment, zest

gut (gʌt) *n.* **1.** (*oft. pl.*) entrails, intestines **2.** material made from guts of animals, *eg* for violin strings *etc.* —*pl.* **3.** *inf.* essential, fundamental part **4.** courage —*vt.* **5.** remove guts from (fish *etc.*) **6.** remove, destroy contents of (house) (-**tt**-) —'**gutless** *a.* lacking courage —'**gutsy** *a. inf.* **1.** greedy **2.** courageous

gutta-percha ('gʌtə'pɜːtʃə) *n.* (tropical tree producing) whitish rubber substance

gutter ('gʌtə) *n.* **1.** shallow trough for carrying off water from roof or side of street —*vt.* **2.** make channels in —*vi.* **3.** flow in streams **4.** (of candle) melt away by wax forming channels and running down —**gutter press** journalism that relies on sensationalism —'**guttersnipe** *n.* **1.** neglected slum child **2.** mean vindictive person

guttural ('gʌtərəl) *a.* **1.** of, relating to, or produced in, the throat —*n.* **2.** guttural sound or letter

guy[1] (gaɪ) *n.* **1.** effigy of Guy Fawkes burnt on Nov. 5th **2.** *inf.* person (*usu.* male) —*vt.* **3.** make fun of, ridicule —**wise guy** *inf., usu. disparaging* clever person

guy[2] (gaɪ) *n.* **1.** rope, chain to steady, secure something (*eg* tent) —*vt.* **2.** keep in position by guy —'**guyrope** *n.*

guzzle ('gʌzəl) *v.* eat or drink greedily

gybe *or* **jibe** (dʒaɪb) *vi.* **1.** (of boom of fore-and-aft sail) swing over to other side with following wind **2.** alter course thus

gym (dʒɪm) *n.* **1.** gymnasium **2.** gymnastics —**gym shoe** *see* PLIMSOLL —'**gymslip** *n.* tunic or pinafore dress worn by schoolgirls, oft. part of school uniform

gymkhana (dʒɪm'kɑːnə) *n.* competition or display of horse riding

gymnasium (dʒɪm'neɪzɪəm) *n.* place equipped for muscular exercises, athletic training (*pl.* -**s**, -**nasia** (-'neɪzɪə)) —'**gymnast** *n.* expert in gymnastics —**gym'nastics** *pl.n.* muscular exercises, with or without apparatus, *eg* parallel bars

gymnosperm ('dʒɪmnəʊspɜːm, 'gɪm-) *n.* seed-bearing plant in which ovules are borne naked on open scales, oft. in cones; any conifer or related plant

gynaecology *or U.S.* **gynecology** (gaɪnɪ'kɒlədʒɪ) *n.* branch of medicine dealing with diseases in women —**gynaeco'logical** *or U.S.* **gyneco'logical**, **gynaeco'logic** *or U.S.* **gyneco'logic** *a.* —**gynae'cologist** *or U.S.* **gyne'cologist** *n.*

gyp[1] (dʒɪp) *sl. vt.* **1.** swindle, cheat, defraud —*n.* **2.** act of cheating **3.** person who gyps

gyp[2] (dʒɪp) *n. UK, NZ sl.* severe pain

gypsophila (dʒɪpˈsɒfɪlə) *n.* garden plant with small white or pink flowers

gypsum ('dʒɪpsəm) *n.* crystalline sulphate of lime: source of plaster

Gypsy *or* **Gipsy** ('dʒɪpsɪ) *n.* one of wandering race originally from NW India, Romany

gyrate (dʒaɪˈreɪt) *vi.* move in circle, spirally, revolve —**gy'ration** *n.* —**gy'rational** *a.* —**gyratory** ('dʒaɪrətɔrɪ) *a.* revolving, spinning

gyrfalcon *or* **gerfalcon** ('dʒɜːfɔːlkən, -fɔːkən) *n.* large, rare falcon

gyro ('dʒaɪrəʊ) *n.* 1. *see* GYROCOMPASS 2. *see* GYROSCOPE (*pl.* **-s**)

gyro- *or before vowel* **gyr-** (*comb. form*) 1. rotating or gyrating motion, as in *gyroscope* 2. gyroscope, as in *gyrocompass*

gyrocompass ('dʒaɪrəʊkʌmpəs) *n.* compass using gyroscope to indicate true north

gyroscope ('dʒaɪrəskəʊp) *n.* disc or wheel so mounted as to be able to rotate about any axis, *esp.* to keep disc (with compass *etc.*) level despite movement of ship *etc.* —**gyroscopic** (dʒaɪrə'skɒpɪk) *a.*

gyrostabilizer *or* **-liser** (dʒaɪrəʊ'steɪbɪlaɪzə) *n.* gyroscopic device to prevent rolling of ship or aeroplane

gyve (dʒaɪv) *obs. vt.* 1. shackle, fetter —*n.* 2. (*usu. pl.*) fetter

H,h

h *or* **H** (eɪtʃ) 1. eighth letter of English alphabet 2. speech sound represented by this letter 3. something shaped like an H

H 1. (of pencils) hard 2. *Chem.* hydrogen

ha hectare

habeas corpus ('heɪbɪəs 'kɔːpəs) writ issued to produce prisoner in court

haberdasher ('hæbədæʃə) *n.* dealer in articles of dress, ribbons, pins, needles *etc.* —**'haberdashery** *n.*

habiliments (hə'bɪlɪmənts) *pl.n.* dress

habit ('hæbɪt) *n.* 1. settled tendency or practice 2. constitution 3. customary apparel, *esp.* of nun or monk 4. woman's riding dress —**ha'bitual** *a.* 1. formed or acquired by habit 2. usual, customary —**ha'bitually** *adv.* —**ha'bituate** *vt.* accustom —**habitu'ation** *n.* —**habitué** (hə'bɪtjʊeɪ) *n.* constant visitor

habitable ('hæbɪtəbl) *a.* fit to live in —**'habitant** *n.* **C** (descendant of) original French settler —**'habitat** *n.* natural home (of animal *etc.*) —**habi'tation** *n.* dwelling place

hachure (hæ'fjʊə) *n.* shading of short lines drawn on relief map to indicate gradients

hacienda (hæsɪ'ɛndə) *n.* ranch or large estate in Spanish Amer.

hack[1] (hæk) *vt.* 1. cut, chop (at) violently 2. *Sport* foul by kicking the shins —*vi.* 3. *inf.* utter harsh, dry cough —*n.* 4. cut or gash 5. any tool used for shallow digging

hack[2] (hæk) *n.* 1. horse for ordinary riding 2. drudge, *esp.* writer of inferior literary works —**hack work** dull, repetitive work

hackle ('hækl) *n.* 1. neck feathers of turkey *etc.* —*pl.* 2. hairs on back of neck of dog and other animals, which are raised in anger

hackney ('hæknɪ) *n.* carriage or coach kept for hire

hackneyed ('hæknɪd) *a.* (of words *etc.*) stale, trite because of overuse

hacksaw ('hæksɔː) *n.* handsaw for cutting metal

had (hæd) *pt./pp.* of HAVE

haddock ('hædək) *n.* large, edible seafish

hadedah ('hɑːdɪdɑː) *n.* S Afr. ibis

Hades ('heɪdiːz) *n.* 1. abode of the dead 2. underworld 3. hell

hadj (hædʒ) *n. see* HAJJ

haematite *or U.S.* **hematite** ('hiːmətaɪt, 'hɛm-) *n.* ore of iron

haematology *or U.S.* **hematology** (hiːmə'tɒlədʒɪ) *n.* branch of medicine concerned with diseases of blood

haemo-, haema-, *or before vowel* **haem-** (*comb. form*) blood

haemoglobin *or U.S.* **hemoglobin** (hiːməʊ'gləʊbɪn) *n.* colouring and oxygen-bearing matter of red blood corpuscles

haemophilia *or U.S.* **hemophilia** (hiːməʊ'fɪlɪə) *n.* hereditary tendency to intensive bleeding as blood fails to clot —**haemo'philiac** *or U.S.* **hemo'philiac** *n.*

haemorrhage *or U.S.* **hemorrhage** ('hɛmərɪdʒ) *n.* profuse bleeding

haemorrhoids *or U.S.* **hemorrhoids** ('hɛmərɔɪdz) *pl.n.* swollen veins in rectum (*also* **piles**)

hafnium ('hæfnɪəm) *n.* metallic element found in zirconium ores

haft (hɑːft) *n.* 1. handle (of knife *etc.*) —*vt.* 2. provide with haft

hag (hæg) *n.* 1. ugly old woman 2. witch —**hag-ridden** *a.* troubled, careworn

haggard ('hægəd) *a.* 1. wild-looking 2. anxious, careworn —*n.* 3. *Falconry* untamed hawk

haggis ('hægɪs) *n.* Scottish dish made from sheep's heart, lungs, liver, chopped with oatmeal, suet, onion *etc.* and boiled in stomach-bag

haggle ('hægl) *vi.* (*oft. with* over) bargain, wrangle (over price, terms *etc.*)

hagiology (hægɪ'ɒlədʒɪ) *n.* literature of the

lives and legends of saints —**hagi'ographer** n.
—**hagi'ography** n. writing of this

ha-ha¹ ('hɑ:'hɑ:) or **haw-haw** ('hɔ:'hɔ:)
interj. 1. representation of the sound of laughter
2. exclamation expressing derision, mockery
etc.

ha-ha² ('hɑ:hɑ:) or **haw-haw** ('hɔ:hɔ:) n.
sunken fence bordering garden etc., that allows
uninterrupted views from within

haiku ('haɪku:) or **hokku** ('hoku:) n.
epigrammatic Japanese verse form in 17
syllables (pl. **-ku**)

hail¹ (heɪl) n. 1. (shower of) pellets of ice 2.
intense shower, barrage —v. 3. pour down as
shower of hail —**'hailstone** n.

hail² (heɪl) vt. 1. greet, esp. enthusiastically 2.
acclaim, acknowledge 3. call —**hail from** come
from —**Hail Mary** see AVE MARIA

hair (hɛə) n. 1. filament growing from skin of
animal, as covering of man's head 2. such
filaments collectively —**'hairiness** n. —**'hairy**
a. —**'hairdo** n. way of dressing hair
—**'hairdresser** n. one who attends to and cuts
hair, esp. women's hair —**'hairgrip** n. chiefly
UK tightly bent metal hair clip (also (esp. US)
bobby pin) —**'hairline** a./n. very fine (line)
—**'hairpiece** n. 1. wig or toupee 2. false hair
attached to one's real hair to give it greater bulk
or length —**'hairpin** n. pin for keeping hair in
place —**hairpin bend** U-shaped turn of road
—**hair-raising** a. terrifying —**hair's-breadth** n.
very short margin or distance —**hair shirt**
rough shirt worn as penance by religious
ascetics —**hair slide** ornamental hinged clip for
the hair —**'hairsplitting** n. making of overfine
distinctions —**'hairspring** n. very fine, delicate
spring in timepiece —**hair trigger** trigger
operated by light touch

hajj or **hadj** (hædʒ) n. pilgrimage to Mecca
that every Muslim is required to make (pl.
'hajjes or **'hadjes**) —**'hajji, 'hadji,** or **'haji** n.
Muslim who has made pilgrimage to Mecca (pl.
'hajjis, 'hadjis, or **'hajis**)

hake (heɪk) n. edible fish of the cod family

halberd ('hælbəd) or **halbert** n. combined
spear and battleaxe

halcyon ('hælsɪən) n. bird fabled to calm the
sea and to breed on floating nest, kingfisher
—**halcyon days** time of peace and happiness

hale¹ (heɪl) a. robust, healthy (esp. in **hale and
hearty**)

hale² (heɪl) vt. pull; drag —**'haler** n.

half (hɑ:f) n. 1. either of two equal parts of
something (pl. **halves**) —a. 2. forming half
—adv. 3. to the extent of half —**half-and-half** n.
mixture of half one thing and half another thing
—**'halfback** n. Football man behind forwards
—**half-baked** a. 1. underdone 2. inf. immature,

silly —**half-blood** n. 1. relationship between
individuals having only one parent in common;
individual having such relationship 2. half-breed
—**half-breed** or **half-caste** n. person with
parents of different races —**half-brother,
-sister** n. brother (sister) by one parent only
—**half-cock** n. halfway position of firearm's
hammer when trigger is locked —**half-cocked**
a. ill-prepared —**half-crown** n. formerly, British
coin worth 12½ (new) pence —**half-hearted** a.
unenthusiastic —**half-hitch** n. knot made by
passing end of piece of rope around itself and
through loop thus made —**half-life** n. time taken
for half the atoms in radioactive material to
decay —**half-mast** n. (of flag) halfway position
to which flag is lowered on mast to mourn dead
—**half measures** inadequate measures or
actions —**half-nelson** n. hold in wrestling
—**halfpenny** ('heɪpnɪ) n. 1. British coin worth
half a new penny (also (inf.) **half**) 2. formerly,
coin worth half an old penny —**half-size** n. any
size, esp. in clothing, halfway between two sizes
—**half term** UK short holiday midway through
academic term —**half-timbered** or **half-timber**
a. (of building) having exposed timber
framework filled with brick —**half-time** n. Sport
rest period between two halves of game —**half-
title** n. 1. title of book as printed on right-hand
page preceding title page 2. title on separate
page preceding section of book —**'halftone** n.
illustration printed from relief plate, showing
light and shadow by means of minute dots
—**half-track** n. vehicle with caterpillar tracks
on wheels that supply motive power only —**half-
true** a. —**half-truth** n. partially true statement
intended to mislead —**half' way** adv./a. at or
to half distance —**halfway house** 1. place to rest
midway on journey 2. halfway point in any
progression 3. centre or hostel to facilitate
readjustment to private life of released
prisoners etc. —**'halfwit** n. 1. mentally-retarded
person 2. stupid person —**by halves** imperfectly
—**go halves** share expenses etc. equally —**half
seas over** inf. drunk —**meet halfway** compromise with

halibut ('hælɪbət) n. large edible flatfish

halitosis (hælɪ'təʊsɪs) n. bad-smelling breath

hall (hɔ:l) n. 1. (entrance) passage 2. large room
or building belonging to particular group or
used for particular purpose, esp. public
assembly —**'hallway** n. hall or corridor

hallelujah, halleluiah (hælɪ'lu:jə), or **alleluia** (ælɪ'lu:jə) n./interj. exclamation of praise
to God

hallmark ('hɔ:lmɑ:k) n. 1. mark used to
indicate standard of tested gold and silver 2.
mark of excellence 3. distinguishing feature

hallo (hə'ləʊ) interj. see HELLO

halloo (hə'luː), **hallo,** or **halloa** (hə'ləʊ) n. 1. call to spur on hunting dogs —vi. 2. shout loudly

hallow ('hæləʊ) vt. make or honour as holy —**Hallowe'en** or **Halloween** (hæləʊ'iːn) n. the evening of Oct. 31st, the day before Allhallows or All Saints' Day

hallucinate (hə'luːsɪneɪt) vi. suffer illusions —**halluci'nation** n. illusion —**hal'lucinatory** a. —**hal'lucinogen** n. drug inducing hallucinations

halm (hɑːm) n. see HAULM

halo ('heɪləʊ) n. 1. circle of light round moon, sun etc. 2. disc of light round saint's head in picture 3. aura surrounding admired person, thing etc. (pl. **-es, -s**) —vt. 4. surround with halo

halogen ('hælədʒen) n. any of the chemical elements fluorine, chlorine, bromine, iodine, and astatine —**halogenous** (hə'lɒdʒɪnəs) a.

halt¹ (hɔːlt) n. 1. interruption or end to progress etc., esp. as command to stop marching 2. minor railway station without station buildings —v. 3. (cause to) stop

halt² (hɔːlt) vi. falter, fail —**'halting** a. hesitant, lame

halter ('hɔːltə) n. 1. rope or strap with headgear to fasten horses or cattle 2. low-cut dress style with strap passing behind neck 3. noose for hanging a person —vt. 4. put halter on

halve (hɑːv) vt. 1. cut in half 2. reduce to half 3. share

halyard or **halliard** ('hæljəd) n. rope for raising sail, signal flags etc.

ham (hæm) n. 1. meat, esp. salted or smoked, from thigh of pig 2. actor adopting exaggerated, unconvincing style 3. amateur radio enthusiast —v. 4. overact (**-mm-**) —**'hammy** a. inf. 1. (of actor) tending to overact 2. (of play, performance etc.) overacted —**ham-fisted** or **ham-handed** a. clumsy —**'hamstring** n. 1. tendon at back of knee —vt. 2. cripple by cutting this

hamadryad (hæmə'draɪəd) n. Class. myth. nymph which inhabits tree and dies with it

hamburger ('hæmbɜːgə) n. fried cake of minced beef, esp. served in bread roll

Hamitic (hæ'mɪtɪk, hə-) n. 1. group of N Afr. languages related to Semitic —a. 2. denoting this group of languages 3. denoting Hamites, group of peoples of N Afr., including ancient Egyptians, supposedly descended from Noah's son Ham

hamlet ('hæmlɪt) n. small village

hammer ('hæmə) n. 1. tool usu. with heavy head at end of handle, for beating, driving nails etc. 2. machine with similar function 3. contrivance for exploding charge of gun 4. auctioneer's mallet 5. metal ball on wire thrown in sports —v. 6. strike (blows) with, or as with, hammer —**'hammerhead** n. shark with wide,

flattened head —**'hammertoe** n. deformed toe —**hammer and sickle** emblem on flag of Soviet Union, representing industrial workers and peasants respectively —**hammer out** solve problem by full investigation of difficulties

hammock ('hæmək) n. bed of canvas etc., hung on cords

hamper¹ ('hæmpə) n. 1. large covered basket 2. large parcel, box etc. of food, wines etc., esp. one sent as Christmas gift

hamper² ('hæmpə) vt. impede, obstruct movements of

hamster ('hæmstə) n. type of rodent, sometimes kept as pet

hamstrung ('hæmstrʌŋ) a. 1. crippled 2. thwarted

hand (hænd) n. 1. extremity of arm beyond wrist 2. side, quarter, direction 3. style of writing 4. cards dealt to player 5. measure of four inches 6. manual worker 7. sailor 8. help, aid 9. pointer on dial 10. applause —vt. 11. pass 12. deliver 13. hold out —**'handful** n. 1. small quantity or number 2. inf. person or thing causing problems (pl. **-s**) —**'handily** adv. —**'handiness** n. 1. dexterity 2. state of being near, available —**'handy** a. 1. convenient 2. clever with the hands —**'handbag** n. 1. woman's bag for personal articles 2. bag for carrying in hand —**'handbill** n. small printed notice —**'handbook** n. small reference or instruction book —**'handcuff** n. 1. fetter for wrist, usu. joined in pair —vt. 2. secure thus —**handi:craft** n. 1. manual occupation or skill —**'handiwork** n. 1. thing done by particular person —**handkerchief** ('hæŋkətʃɪf, -tʃiːf) n. 1. small square of fabric carried in pocket for wiping nose etc. 2. neckerchief —**hand-me-down** n. inf. 1. something, esp. outgrown garment, passed down from one person to another 2. anything already used by another —**hand-out** n. 1. money, food etc. given free 2. pamphlet giving news, information etc. —**hand-pick** vt. select with great care —**hand-picked** a. —**'handset** n. telephone mouthpiece and earpiece mounted as single unit —**hands-on** a. involving active participation and operating experience —**'handspring** n. gymnastic feat in which person leaps forwards or backwards into handstand and then on to his feet —**'handstand** n. act of supporting body in upside-down position by hands alone —**hand-to-hand** a./adv. at close quarters —**hand-to-mouth** a./adv. with barely enough money or food to satisfy immediate needs —**'handwriting** n. way person writes —**'handyman** n. 1. man employed to do various tasks 2. man skilled in odd jobs —**hand in glove** very intimate

h & c hot and cold (water)

handicap ('hændɪkæp) n. 1. something that hampers or hinders 2. race, contest in which chances are equalized by starts, weights carried etc. 3. condition so imposed 4. any physical disability —vt. 5. hamper 6. impose handicaps on (-pp-) —'**handicapped** a. physically or mentally disabled

handle ('hænd³l) n. 1. part of utensil etc. which is to be held —vt. 2. touch, feel with hands 3. manage 4. deal with 5. trade —'**handler** n. 1. person who trains and controls animals 2. trainer or second of boxer —'**handlebars** pl.n. curved metal bar used to steer bicycle, motorbike etc.

handsome ('hændsəm) a. 1. of fine appearance 2. generous 3. ample —'**handsomely** adv.

hanepoot ('hɑːnəpɔːt) n. SA type of grape

hang (hæŋ) vt. 1. suspend 2. kill by suspension by neck (hanged pt./pp.) 3. attach, set up (wallpaper, doors etc.) —vi. 4. be suspended (hung pt./pp.) —'**hanger** n. frame on which clothes etc. can be hung —'**hangdog** a. sullen, dejected —**hanger-on** n. sycophantic follower or dependant (pl. hangers-on) —**hang-glider** n. glider like large kite, with pilot hanging in frame below —**hang-gliding** n. —'**hangman** n. executioner —'**hangnail** n. piece of skin hanging loose at base or side of fingernail —'**hangover** n. after-effects of too much drinking —**hang-up** n. inf. persistent emotional problem —**hang out** inf. reside, frequent

hangar ('hæŋə) n. large shed for aircraft

hank (hæŋk) n. coil, skein, length, esp. as measure of yarn

hanker ('hæŋkə) vi. (with for or after) have a yearning

hanky or **hankie** ('hæŋkɪ) n. inf. handkerchief

hanky-panky ('hæŋkɪ'pæŋkɪ) n. inf. 1. trickery 2. illicit sexual relations

Hansard ('hænsɑːd) n. official printed record of speeches, debates etc. in Brit., Aust. and other parliaments

Hanseatic League (hænsɪ'ætɪk) commercial organization of towns in N Germany formed to protect and control trade

hansom ('hænsəm) n. (sometimes H-) two-wheeled horse-drawn cab for two to ride inside with driver mounted up behind

Hants. (hænts) Hampshire

haphazard (hæp'hæzəd) a. 1. random 2. careless

hapless ('hæplɪs) a. unlucky

happen ('hæpən) vi. 1. come about, occur 2. chance (to do) —'**happening** n. occurrence, event

happy ('hæpɪ) a. 1. glad 2. content 3. lucky, fortunate 4. apt —'**happily** adv. —'**happiness** n. —**happy-go-lucky** a. casual, light-hearted

harakiri (hærə'kırı) or **harikari** n. formerly, in Japan, ritual suicide by disembowelling

harangue (hə'ræŋ) n. 1. vehement speech 2. tirade —v. 3. address (person or crowd) in angry, forceful or persuasive way

harass ('hærəs) vt. worry, trouble, torment —'**harassment** n.

harbinger ('hɑːbɪndʒə) n. 1. one who announces another's approach 2. forerunner, herald

harbour or U.S. **harbor** ('hɑːbə) n. 1. shelter for ships 2. shelter —vt. 3. give shelter or protection to 4. maintain (secretly) (esp. grudge etc.)

hard (hɑːd) a. 1. firm, resisting pressure 2. solid 3. difficult to understand 4. harsh, unfeeling 5. difficult to bear 6. practical, shrewd 7. heavy 8. strenuous 9. (of water) not making lather well with soap 10. (of drugs) highly addictive —adv. 11. vigorously 12. with difficulty 13. close —'**harden** v. —'**hardly** adv. 1. unkindly, harshly 2. scarcely, not quite 3. only just —'**hardness** n. —'**hardship** n. 1. ill luck 2. severe toil, suffering 3. instance of this —'**hardback** n. 1. book bound in stiff covers —a. 2. of or denoting hardback or publication of hardbacks (also '**casebound**, '**hardbound**, '**hardcover**) —**hard-bitten** a. inf. tough and realistic —'**hardboard** n. thin stiff sheet made of compressed sawdust and woodchips —**hard-boiled** a. 1. boiled so long as to be hard 2. inf. (of person) experienced, unemotional, unsympathetic —**hard copy** Comp. output that can be read by eye —**hard core** 1. members of group who form intransigent nucleus resisting change 2. material, such as broken stones, used to form foundation for road etc. —**hard-core** a. 1. (of pornography) depicting sexual acts in explicit detail 2. completely established in belief etc. —**hard court** tennis court made of asphalt, concrete etc. —**hard-headed** a. shrewd —**hard'hearted** a. unkind or intolerant —**hard'heartedness** n. —**hard labour** formerly, penalty of compulsory labour in addition to imprisonment —**hard line** uncompromising course or policy —**hard'liner** n. —**hard palate** anterior bony portion of roof of mouth —**hard-pressed** a. 1. in difficulties 2. closely pursued —**hard sell** aggressive technique of selling or advertising —**hard shoulder** surfaced verge at motorway edge for emergency stops —'**hardware** n. 1. tools, implements 2. necessary (parts of) machinery 3. Comp. mechanical and electronic parts —'**hardwood** n. wood from deciduous trees —**hard of hearing** rather deaf —**hard up** very short of money

hardy ('hɑːdɪ) a. 1. robust, vigorous 2. bold 3. (of plants) able to grow in the open all year round —'**hardihood** n. extreme boldness, audacity —'**hardily** adv. —'**hardiness** n.

hare (heə) n. animal like large rabbit, with longer legs and ears, noted for speed —'**harebell** n. round-leaved bell-flower —'**hare-brained** a. rash, wild —'**harelip** n. fissure of upper lip —**hare and hounds** paper chase

harem ('heərəm, hɑː'riːm) or **hareem** (hɑː'riːm) n. **1.** women's part of Mohammedan dwelling **2.** one man's wives collectively

haricot ('hærɪkəʊ) n. type of French bean that can be dried and stored

harikari (hærɪ'kɑːrɪ) n. see HARAKIRI

hark (hɑːk) vi. listen —**hark back** return to previous subject of discussion)

harlequin ('hɑːlɪkwɪn) n. stock comic character, esp. masked clown in diamond-patterned costume —**harlequi'nade** n. **1.** scene in pantomime **2.** buffoonery

Harley Street ('hɑːlɪ) street in central London famous for its large number of medical specialists' consulting rooms

harlot ('hɑːlət) n. whore, prostitute —'**harlotry** n.

harm (hɑːm) n. **1.** damage, injury —vt. **2.** cause harm to —'**harmful** a. —'**harmfully** adv. —'**harmless** a. unable or unlikely to hurt —'**harmlessly** adv.

harmony ('hɑːmənɪ) n. **1.** agreement **2.** concord **3.** peace **4.** Mus. combination of notes to make chords **5.** melodious sound —**harmonic** (hɑː'mɒnɪk) a. **1.** of harmony —n. **2.** tone or note whose frequency is a multiple of its pitch —**harmonica** (hɑː'mɒnɪkə) n. any of various musical instruments, esp. mouth organ —**harmonics** (hɑː'mɒnɪks) pl.n. **1.** science of musical sounds **2.** harmonious sounds —**har'monious** a. —**har'moniously** adv. —**'harmonist** n. —**har'monium** n. small organ —**harmoni'zation** or **-ni'sation** n. —**'harmonize** or **-nise** vt. **1.** bring into harmony **2.** cause to agree **3.** reconcile —vi. **4.** be in harmony **5.** sing in harmony, as with other singers

harness ('hɑːnɪs) n. **1.** equipment for attaching horse to cart, plough etc. **2.** any such equipment —vt. **3.** put on, in harness **4.** utilize energy or power of (waterfall etc.) —**in harness** in or at one's routine work

harp (hɑːp) n. **1.** musical instrument of strings played by hand —vi. **2.** play on harp **3.** (with on or upon) dwell (on) continuously —'**harper** or '**harpist** n. —'**harpsichord** n. stringed instrument like piano

harpoon (hɑː'puːn) n. **1.** barbed spear with rope attached for catching whales —vt. **2.** catch, kill with or as if with a harpoon —**har'pooner** n. —**harpoon gun** gun for firing harpoon in whaling

harpy ('hɑːpɪ) n. **1.** monster with body of woman and wings and claws of bird **2.** cruel, grasping person

harridan ('hærɪdⁿn) n. shrewish old woman, hag

harrier ('hærɪə) n. **1.** hound used in hunting hares **2.** falcon **3.** cross-country runner

harrow ('hærəʊ) n. **1.** implement for smoothing, levelling, or stirring up soil —vt. **2.** draw harrow over **3.** distress greatly —'**harrowing** a. **1.** heart-rending **2.** distressful

harry ('hærɪ) vt. **1.** harass **2.** ravage (-**ried**, -**rying**)

harsh (hɑːʃ) a. **1.** rough, discordant **2.** severe **3.** unfeeling —'**harshly** adv.

hart (hɑːt) n. male deer —**hartshorn** ('hɑːtshɔːn) n. material made from harts' horns, formerly chief source of ammonia

hartal (hɑː'tɑːl) n. in India, act of suspending work, esp. in political protest

hartebeest ('hɑːtɪbiːst) or **hartbeest** ('hɑːtbiːst) n. Afr. antelope

harum-scarum ('heərəm'skeərəm) a. **1.** reckless, wild **2.** giddy

harvest ('hɑːvɪst) n. **1.** (season for) gathering in grain **2.** gathering **3.** crop **4.** product of action —v. **5.** reap and gather in (crop) —'**harvester** n.

has (hæz) third person sing. pres. indicative of HAVE —**has-been** n. inf. person or thing that is no longer popular, successful etc.

hash (hæʃ) n. **1.** dish of hashed meat etc. **2.** inf. hashish —vt. **3.** cut up small, chop **4.** mix up

hashish ('hæʃɪʃ, -iːʃ) or **hasheesh** n. resinous extract of Indian hemp, esp. used as hallucinogen

haslet ('hæzlɪt) or **harslet** ('hɑːzlɪt, 'hæs-) n. loaf of cooked minced pig's offal, eaten cold

hasp (hɑːsp) n. **1.** clasp passing over staple for fastening door etc. —vt. **2.** fasten, secure with hasp

hassle ('hæsəl) inf. n. **1.** quarrel **2.** great deal of bother or trouble —vi. **3.** quarrel, fight —vt. **4.** harass (persistently)

hassock ('hæsək) n. **1.** kneeling-cushion **2.** tuft of grass

hast (hæst) obs. second person sing. pres. indicative of HAVE

haste (heɪst) n. **1.** speed, quickness, hurry —vi. **2.** Poet. hasten —**hasten** ('heɪsⁿn) v. (cause to) hurry, increase speed —'**hastily** adv. —'**hasty** a.

hat (hæt) n. head-covering, usu. with brim —'**hatter** n. dealer in, maker of hats —**hat trick** any three successive achievements, esp. in sport

hatch[1] (hætʃ) v. **1.** (of young, esp. of birds) (cause to) emerge from egg —vt. **2.** contrive, devise —'**hatchery** n.

hatch² ('hætʃ) n. **1.** hatchway **2.** trapdoor over it **3.** opening in wall or door, as service hatch, to facilitate service of meals *etc.* between two rooms **4.** lower half of divided door —'**hatchback** n. car with single lifting door in rear —'**hatchway** n. opening in deck of ship *etc.*

hatch³ ('hætʃ) vt. **1.** engrave or draw lines on for shading **2.** shade with parallel lines

hatchet ('hætʃit) n. small axe —**hatchet job** *inf.* malicious verbal or written attack —**hatchet man** *inf.* person carrying out unpleasant assignments for another —**bury the hatchet** make peace

hate (heit) vt. **1.** dislike strongly, bear malice towards —n. **2.** intense dislike **3.** that which is hated —'**hateful** a. detestable —'**hatefully** adv. —**hatred** ('heitrid) n. extreme dislike, active ill-will

hauberk ('hɔːbɜːk) n. long coat of mail

haughty ('hɔːti) a. proud, arrogant —'**haughtily** adv. —'**haughtiness** n.

haul (hɔːl) vt. **1.** pull, drag with effort —vi. **2.** (of wind) shift —n. **3.** hauling **4.** something that is hauled **5.** catch of fish **6.** acquisition **7.** distance (to be) covered —'**haulage** n. **1.** carrying of loads **2.** charge for this —'**haulier** n. firm, person that transports goods by road

haulm or **halm** (hɔːm) n. **1.** stalks of beans, potatoes, grasses *etc.* collectively **2.** single stem of such plant

haunch (hɔːntʃ) n. **1.** human hip or fleshy hindquarter of animal **2.** leg and loin of venison

haunt (hɔːnt) vt. **1.** visit regularly **2.** visit in form of ghost **3.** recur to —n. **4.** place frequently visited —'**haunted** a. **1.** frequented by ghosts **2.** worried —'**haunting** a. **1.** (of memories) poignant or persistent **2.** poignantly sentimental —'**hauntingly** adv.

hautboy ('əʊbɔɪ) n. **1.** strawberry with large fruit **2.** *obs.* oboe

haute couture (ot kuˈtyːr) *Fr.* high fashion

hauteur (əʊˈtɜː) n. haughty spirit

Havana cigar (həˈvænə) fine quality of cigar (*also* Haˈvana)

have (hæv) vt. **1.** hold, possess **2.** be possessed, affected with **3.** cheat, outwit **4.** engage in **5.** obtain **6.** contain **7.** allow **8.** cause to be (done) **9.** give birth to **10.** as auxiliary, forms perfect and other tenses (*pres. tense:* I *have*, thou *hast*, he *has*, we, you, they *have*) (*had*, '*having*) —**have to** be obliged to

haven ('heivən) n. place of safety

haver ('heivə) vi. UK **1.** *dial.* babble; talk nonsense **2.** dither —n. **3.** (*usu. pl.*) *Scot.* nonsense

haversack ('hævəsæk) n. canvas bag for provisions *etc.*, carried on back or shoulder when hiking

havoc ('hævək) n. **1.** devastation, ruin **2.** *inf.* confusion, chaos

haw (hɔː) n. **1.** fruit of hawthorn **2.** hawthorn

hawfinch ('hɔːfintʃ) n. uncommon European finch

hawk¹ (hɔːk) n. **1.** bird of prey smaller than eagle **2.** supporter, advocate of warlike policies —vi. **3.** hunt with hawks **4.** soar and swoop like hawk —**hawk-eyed** a. **1.** having extremely keen sight **2.** vigilant or observant

hawk² (hɔːk) vt. offer (goods) for sale, as in street —'**hawker** n.

hawk³ (hɔːk) vi. clear throat noisily

hawse (hɔːz) n. part of ship's bows with holes for cables

hawser ('hɔːzə) n. large rope or cable

hawthorn ('hɔːθɔːn) n. thorny shrub or tree having pink or white flowers and reddish fruits (*also* (*UK*) **may, may tree, 'mayflower**)

hay (hei) n. grass mown and dried —'**haybox** n. box filled with hay in which heated food is left to finish cooking —**hay fever** allergic reaction to pollen, dust *etc.* —'**haymaker** n. **1.** person who cuts or turns hay **2.** either of two machines, one designed to crush stems of hay, the other to break and bend them, in order to cause more rapid and even drying **3.** *Boxing sl.* wild swinging punch —'**haymaking** a./n. —'**haystack** n. large pile of hay —'**haywire** a. **1.** crazy **2.** disorganized

hazard ('hæzəd) n. **1.** chance **2.** risk, danger —vt. **3.** expose to risk **4.** run risk of —'**hazardous** a. risky

haze (heiz) n. **1.** mist, oft. due to heat **2.** obscurity —'**hazy** a. **1.** misty **2.** obscured **3.** vague

hazel ('heizəl) n. **1.** bush bearing nuts **2.** yellowish-brown colour of the nuts —a. **3.** light yellowish brown

Hb haemoglobin

HB UK (on pencils) hard-black

H.B.C. Hudson's Bay Company

H-bomb hydrogen bomb

H.C.F. or **h.c.f.** highest common factor

he (hiː; *unstressed* i) pron. **1.** (*third person masculine pronoun*) person, animal already referred to **2.** (*comb. form*) male, as in *he*-goat —**he-man** n. *inf.* strongly built muscular man

He *Chem.* helium

HE or **H.E. 1.** high explosive **2.** His Eminence **3.** His (*or* Her) Excellency

head (hɛd) n. **1.** upper part of person's or animal's body, containing mouth, sense organs and brain **2.** upper part of anything **3.** chief of organization, school *etc.* **4.** chief part **5.** aptitude, capacity **6.** culmination or crisis (*esp. in* **bring** *or* **come to a head**) **7.** leader **8.** section of chapter **9.** title **10.** headland **11.** person, animal considered as unit **12.** white froth on beer *etc.* **13.** *inf.* headache —*a.* **14.** chief, principal **15.** (of wind) contrary —*vt.* **16.** be at the top, head of **17.** lead, direct **18.** provide with head **19.** hit (ball) with head —*vi.* **20.** (*with* for) make (for) **21.** form a head —'**header** *n.* **1.** *inf.* headlong fall or dive **2.** brick laid with end in face of wall **3.** action of striking ball with head —'**heading** *n.* title —**heads** *adv. inf.* with obverse side (of coin) uppermost —'**heady** *a.* apt to intoxicate or excite —'**headache** *n.* **1.** continuous pain in head **2.** *inf.* worrying circumstance —'**headboard** *n.* vertical board at head of bed —'**headdress** *n.* any head covering, *esp.* ornate one —'**headgear** *n.* **1.** hat, headdress *etc.* **2.** any part of horse's harness worn on head **3.** hoisting mechanism at pithead of mine —**head-hunter** *n.* —**head-hunting** *n.* **1.** practice among certain peoples of removing heads of slain enemies and preserving them as trophies **2.** (of company or corporation) recruitment of, or drive to recruit, new high-level personnel —'**headland** *n.* promontory —'**headlight** *n.* powerful lamp carried on front of locomotive, motor vehicle *etc.* —'**headline** *n.* news summary, *usu.* in large type in newspaper —'**headlong** *adv.* **1.** with head foremost **2.** with great haste —**head-on** *adv./a.* **1.** (of collision *etc.*) front foremost **2.** with directness —'**headphones** *pl.n.* electrical device consisting of two earphones held in position by strap over head (*also* (*inf.*) **cans**) —'**headquarters** *pl.n.* **1.** residence of commander-in-chief **2.** centre of operations —'**headroom** *or* '**headway** *n.* height of bridge *etc.*; clearance —'**headshrinker** *n.* **1.** *sl.* psychiatrist (*also* **shrink**) **2.** head-hunter who shrinks heads of his victims —'**headstall** *n.* part of bridle that fits round horse's head —**head start** initial advantage in competitive situation —'**headstone** *n.* gravestone —'**headstrong** *a.* self-willed —'**headwaters** *pl.n.* tributary streams of river —'**headway** *n.* advance, progress —'**headwind** *n.* wind blowing directly against course of aircraft or ship —'**headword** *n.* key word placed at beginning of line *etc.* as in dictionary entry

heal (hiːl) *v.* make or become well —**health** (hɛlθ) *n.* **1.** soundness of body **2.** condition of body **3.** toast drunk in person's honour —**healthily** ('hɛlθɪlɪ) *adv.* —**healthiness** ('hɛlθɪnɪs) *n.* —**healthy** ('hɛlθɪ) *a.* **1.** of strong constitution **2.** of or producing good health, wellbeing *etc.* **3.** vigorous —**health centre** surgery and offices of group medical practice —**health visitor UK** nurse who visits and gives advice to old and sick in their homes

heap (hiːp) *n.* **1.** pile of things lying one on another **2.** great quantity —*vt.* **3.** pile **4.** load (with)

hear (hɪə) *vt.* **1.** perceive by ear **2.** listen to **3.**

Law try (case) **4.** heed —*vi.* **5.** perceive sound **6.** (*with* of *or* about) learn (**heard** (hɜːd) *pt./pp.*) —'**hearer** *n.* —'**hearing** *n.* **1.** ability to hear **2.** earshot **3.** judicial examination —'**hearsay** *n.* **1.** rumour —*a.* **2.** based on hearsay —**hear! hear!** exclamation of approval, agreement

hearken *or* U.S. (*sometimes*) **harken** ('hɑːkən) *vi.* listen

hearse (hɜːs) *n.* funeral carriage for carrying coffin to grave

heart (hɑːt) *n.* **1.** organ which makes blood circulate **2.** seat of emotions and affections **3.** mind, soul, courage **4.** central part **5.** playing card marked with symbol of heart **6.** one of these marks —'**hearten** *v.* make, become cheerful —'**heartily** *adv.* —'**heartless** *a.* unfeeling —'**hearty** *a.* **1.** friendly **2.** vigorous **3.** in good health **4.** satisfying the appetite —'**heartache** *n.* intense anguish or mental suffering —**heart attack** sudden severe malfunction of heart —'**heartbreak** *n.* intense and overwhelming grief or disappointment —'**heartbreaking** *a.* —'**heartburn** *n.* pain in higher intestine —**heart failure 1.** inability of heart to pump adequate amount of blood to tissues **2.** sudden cessation of heartbeat, resulting in death —'**heartfelt** *a.* sincerely and strongly felt —'**heartfree** *a.* with the affections free or disengaged —**heart-rending** *a.* **1.** overwhelming with grief **2.** agonizing —**heart-searching** *n.* examination of one's feelings or conscience —'**heartsease** *n.* wild pansy —**heart-throb** *n. sl.* object of infatuation —**heart-to-heart** *a.* **1.** (*esp.* of conversation) concerned with personal problems —*n.* **2.** intimate conversation —**heart-warming** *a.* **1.** pleasing; gratifying **2.** emotionally moving —'**heartwood** *n.* central core of dark hard wood in tree trunks —**by heart** by memory

hearth (hɑːθ) *n.* **1.** part of room where fire is made **2.** home

heat (hiːt) *n.* **1.** hotness **2.** sensation of this **3.** hot weather or climate **4.** warmth of feeling, anger *etc.* **5.** sexual excitement caused by readiness to mate in female animals **6.** one of many races *etc.* to decide persons to compete in finals —*v.* **7.** make, become hot —'**heated** *a.* angry —'**heatedly** *adv.* —'**heater** *n.* any device for supplying heat, such as a convector —**heat pump** device for extracting heat from substance that is at slightly higher temperature than its surroundings and delivering it to factory *etc.* at much higher temperature —'**heatstroke** *n.* condition resulting from prolonged exposure to intense heat, characterized by fever —**heat wave** continuous spell of abnormally hot weather

heath (hiːθ) *n.* **1.** tract of wasteland **2.** low-growing evergreen shrub

heathen ('hiːðən) a. 1. not adhering to a religious system 2. pagan 3. barbarous 4. unenlightened —n. 5. heathen person (pl. -s, 'heathen) —'heathendom n. —'heathenish a. 1. of or like heathen 2. rough 3. barbarous —'heathenism n.

heather ('hɛðə) n. shrub growing on heaths and mountains —'heathery a.

Heath Robinson (hiːθ 'rɒbɪnsən) (of mechanical device) absurdly complicated in design

heave (hiːv) vt. 1. lift with effort 2. throw (something heavy) 3. utter (sigh) —vi. 4. swell, rise 5. feel nausea —n. 6. act or effort of heaving

heaven ('hɛvən) n. 1. abode of God 2. place of bliss 3. (also pl.) sky —'heavenly a. 1. lovely, delightful, divine 2. beautiful 3. of or like heaven

heavy ('hɛvɪ) a. 1. weighty, striking, falling with force 2. dense 3. sluggish 4. difficult, severe 5. sorrowful 6. serious 7. dull —'heavily adv. —'heaviness n. —heavy-duty a. made to withstand hard wear, bad weather etc. —heavy-handed a. 1. clumsy 2. harsh or oppressive —heavy-hearted a. sad; melancholy —heavy industry basic, large-scale industry producing metal, machinery etc. —heavy-metal a. of type of rock music characterized by strong beat and amplified instrumental effects —heavy water deuterium oxide, water in which normal hydrogen content has been replaced by deuterium

Heb. or **Hebr.** 1. Hebrew 2. Bible Hebrews

hebdomadal (hɛb'dɒmədəl) a. weekly

Hebrew ('hiːbruː) n. 1. member of an ancient Semitic people 2. their language 3. its modern form, used in Israel —He'braic(al) a. of or characteristic of Hebrews, their language or culture

heckle ('hɛkəl) v. interrupt or try to annoy (speaker) by questions, taunts etc.

hectare ('hɛktɑː) n. one hundred ares or 10 000 square metres (2.471 acres)

hectic ('hɛktɪk) a. rushed, busy

hecto- or before vowel **hect-** (comb. form) one hundred, esp. in metric system, as in hectolitre, hectometre

hector ('hɛktə) vt. 1. bully —vi. 2. bluster —n. 3. blusterer

heddle ('hɛdəl) n. Weaving one of set of frames of vertical wires

hedge (hɛdʒ) n. 1. fence of bushes —vt. 2. surround with hedge 3. obstruct 4. hem in 5. guard against risk of loss in (bet etc.), esp. by laying bets with other bookmakers —vi. 6. make or trim hedges 7. be evasive 8. secure against loss —'hedgehog n. small animal covered with spines —'hedgerow n. bushes forming hedge —hedge sparrow small brownish songbird

hedonism ('hiːdənɪzəm, 'hɛd-) n. 1. doctrine

that pleasure is the chief good 2. indulgence in sensual pleasure —he'donics pl.n. (with sing. v.) 1. branch of psychology concerned with the study of pleasant and unpleasant sensations 2. in philosophy, study of pleasures —'hedonist n. —hedo'nistic a.

heed (hiːd) vt. take notice of —'heedful a. —'heedless a. careless

heehaw (hiː'hɔː) interj. imitation or representation of braying sound of donkey

heel (hiːl) n. 1. hinder part of foot 2. part of shoe supporting this 3. sl. undesirable person —vt. 4. supply with heel 5. touch (ground, ball) with heel —'heelball n. mixture of beeswax and lampblack used by shoemakers and in taking rubbings, esp. brass rubbings

heel (hiːl) v. 1. (of ship) (cause to) lean to one side —n. 2. heeling, list

hefty ('hɛftɪ) a. 1. bulky 2. weighty 3. strong

hegemony (hɪ'gɛmənɪ) n. leadership, political domination —hegemonic (hɛgə'mɒnɪk) a.

Hegira or **Hejira** ('hɛdʒɪrə) n. 1. flight of Mohammed from Mecca to Medina in 622 A.D. 2. (oft. h-) escape or flight

heifer ('hɛfə) n. young cow

height (haɪt) n. 1. measure from base to top 2. quality of being high 3. elevation 4. highest degree 5. (oft. pl.) hilltop —'heighten vt. 1. make higher 2. intensify —height of land US, C watershed

heinous ('heɪnəs, 'hiː-) a. atrocious, extremely wicked, detestable

heir (ɛə) n. person entitled to inherit property or rank ('heiress fem.) —'heirloom n. thing that has been in family for generations

held (hɛld) pt./pp. of HOLD

helical ('hɛlɪkəl) a. spiral

helicopter ('hɛlɪkɒptə) n. aircraft made to rise vertically by pull of airscrew revolving horizontally —'heliport n. airport for helicopters

helio- or before vowel **heli-** (comb. form) sun, as in heliocentric

heliocentric (hiːlɪəʊ'sɛntrɪk) a. 1. having sun at its centre 2. measured in relation to sun —helio'centrically adv.

heliograph ('hiːlɪəʊɡrɑːf) n. signalling apparatus employing mirror to reflect sun's rays

heliostat ('hiːlɪəʊstæt) n. astronomical instrument used to reflect light of sun in constant direction

heliotherapy (hiːlɪəʊ'θɛrəpɪ) n. therapeutic use of sunlight

heliotrope ('hiːlɪətrəʊp, 'hɛljə-) n. 1. plant with purple flowers 2. bluish-violet to purple colour —**heliotropic** (hiːlɪəʊ'trɒpɪk) a. growing, turning towards source of light

helium ('hiːlɪəm) n. very light nonflammable gaseous element

helix ('hiːlɪks) n. 1. spiral 2. incurving fold that forms margin of external ear (pl. **helices** ('hɛlɪsiːz), **-es**)

hell (hɛl) n. 1. abode of the damned 2. abode of the dead generally 3. place or state of wickedness, misery or torture —'**hellish** a./adv. —**hell'bent** a. (with on) inf. strongly or rashly intent —'**hellfire** n. 1. torment of hell, envisaged as eternal fire —a. 2. characterizing sermons that emphasize this —**Hell's Angel** member of motorcycle gang who typically dress in leather clothing, noted for their lawless behaviour

hellebore ('hɛlɪbɔː) n. plant with white flowers that bloom in winter, Christmas rose

Hellenic (hɛ'lɛnɪk, -'liː-) a. pert. to inhabitants of Greece —'**Hellenist** n.

hello, hallo, or hullo (hɛ'ləʊ, hə-; 'hɛləʊ) interj. expression of greeting or surprise

helm (hɛlm) n. tiller, wheel for turning ship's rudder

helmet ('hɛlmɪt) n. defensive or protective covering for head (also **helm**)

helminth ('hɛlmɪnθ) n. parasitic worm, esp. nematode or fluke —**hel'minthic or helmin-thoid** ('hɛlmɪnθɔɪd, hɛl'mɪnθɔɪd) a.

Helot ('hɛlət, 'hiː-) n. 1. in ancient Sparta, member of class of serfs owned by state 2. (usu. **h-**) serf or slave —'**Helotism** n. —'**Helotry** n.

help (hɛlp) vt. 1. aid, assist 2. support 3. succour 4. remedy, prevent —n. 5. act of helping or being helped 6. person or thing that helps —'**helper** n. —'**helpful** a. —'**helping** n. single portion of food taken at meal —'**helpless** a. 1. useless, incompetent 2. unaided 3. unable to help —'**helplessly** adv. —'**helpmate or 'helpmeet** n. 1. helpful companion 2. husband or wife

helter-skelter ('hɛltə'skɛltə) adv./a./n. 1. (in) hurry and confusion —n. 2. high spiral slide at fairground

helve (hɛlv) n. handle of hand tool such as axe or pick

hem[1] (hɛm) n. 1. border of cloth, esp. one made by turning over edge and sewing it down —vt. 2. sew thus 3. (usu. with in) confine, shut in (**-mm-**) —'**hemstitch** n. 1. ornamental stitch —v. 2. decorate (hem etc.) with hemstitches

hem[2] (hɛm) n./interj. 1. representation of sound of clearing throat, used to gain attention etc. —vi. 2. utter this sound (**-mm-**) —**hem (or hum) and haw** hesitate in speaking

hemi- (comb. form) half, as in hemisphere

hemisphere ('hɛmɪsfɪə) n. 1. half sphere 2. half of celestial sphere 3. half of the earth —**hemispheric(al)** (hɛmɪ'sfɛrɪk(ə)l) a.

hemistich ('hɛmɪstɪk) n. half line of verse

hemlock ('hɛmlɒk) n. 1. poisonous plant 2. poison extracted from it 3. US evergreen of pine family

hemo- (comb. form) US see HAEMO-

hemp (hɛmp) n. 1. Indian plant 2. its fibre used for rope etc. 3. any of several narcotic drugs made from varieties of hemp —'**hempen** a. made of hemp or rope

hen (hɛn) n. female of domestic fowl and others —'**henpeck** vt. (of woman) harass (a man, esp. husband) by nagging

henbane ('hɛnbeɪn) n. poisonous plant with sticky hairy leaves

hence (hɛns) adv. 1. from this point 2. for this reason —'**hence'forward or 'hence'forth** adv. from now onwards

henchman ('hɛntʃmən) n. trusty follower

henge (hɛndʒ) n. circular monument, oft. containing circle of stones

henna ('hɛnə) n. 1. flowering shrub 2. reddish dye made from it

henotheism ('hɛnəʊθiːɪzəm) n. belief in one god (of several) as special god of one's family, tribe etc.

henry ('hɛnrɪ) n. SI unit of electrical inductance

hepatic (hɪ'pætɪk) a. pert. to the liver —**hepa'titis** n. inflammation of the liver

hepta- or before vowel hept- (comb. form) seven, as in heptameter

heptagon ('hɛptəgən) n. figure with seven angles —**hep'tagonal** a.

heptarchy ('hɛptɑːkɪ) n. rule by seven

her (hɜː; unstressed hə, ə) a. objective and possessive case of SHE —**hers** pron. of her —**her'self** pron.

herald ('hɛrəld) n. 1. messenger, envoy 2. officer who makes royal proclamations, arranges ceremonies, regulates armorial bearings etc. —vt. 3. announce 4. proclaim approach of —**he'raldic** a. —'**heraldry** n. study of (right to have) heraldic bearings

herb (hɜːb; U.S. ɜːrb) n. 1. plant with soft stem which dies down after flowering 2. plant, such as rosemary, used in cookery or medicine —**her'baceous** a. 1. of, like herbs 2. flowering perennially —'**herbage** n. 1. herbs 2. grass 3. pasture —'**herbal** a. 1. of herbs —n. 2. book on herbs —'**herbalist** n. 1. writer on herbs 2. dealer in medicinal herbs —**her'barium** n. collection of dried plants (pl. **-s, -ia** (-ɪə)) —'**herbicide** n. chemical which destroys plants —**her'bivorous** a. feeding on plants

Hercules ('hɜːkjʊliːz) n. mythical hero noted for strength —**herculean** (hɜːkjʊ'liːən) a. requiring great strength, courage etc.

herd (hɜːd) n. 1. company of animals, usu. of same species, feeding or travelling together 2. herdsman —v. 3. collect or be collected together

—*vt.* **4.** tend (livestock) —**herd instinct** *Psychol.* inborn tendency to associate with others and follow group's behaviour —'**herdsman** *n.*

here (hiə) *adv.* **1.** in this place **2.** at or to this point —here'**after** *adv.* **1.** in time to come —*n.* **2.** future existence —here'**by** *adv.* by means of or as result of this —here·to'fore *adv.* before —here'**with** *adv.* together with this

heredity (hi'rɛdɪtɪ) *n.* tendency of organism to transmit its nature to its descendants —here'**ditament** *n. Law* property that can be inherited —he'reditarily *adv.* —he'reditary *a.* **1.** descending by inheritance **2.** holding office by inheritance **3.** that can be transmitted from one generation to another

heresy ('hɛrəsɪ) *n.* opinion contrary to orthodox opinion or belief —'**heretic** *n.* one holding opinions contrary to orthodox faith —he'retical *a.* —he'retically *adv.*

heritage ('hɛrɪtɪdʒ) *n.* **1.** what may be or is inherited **2.** anything from past, *esp.* owned or handed down by tradition —'**heritable** *a.* that can be inherited

hermaphrodite (hɜː'mæfrədaɪt) *n.* **1.** animal or flower that has both male and female reproductive organs **2.** person having both male and female characteristics

hermetic (hɜː'mɛtɪk) *or* **hermetical** *a.* sealed so as to be airtight —her'metically *adv.*

hermit ('hɜːmɪt) *n.* one living in solitude, *esp.* from religious motives —'**hermitage** *n.* his abode —**hermit crab** soft-bodied crustacean living in and carrying about empty shells of molluscs

hernia ('hɜːnɪə) *n.* projection of (part of) organ through lining encasing it (*pl.* -**s**, -**iae** (-iː)) —'**hernial** *a.*

hero ('hɪərəʊ) *n.* **1.** one greatly regarded for achievements or qualities **2.** principal character in play *etc.* **3.** illustrious warrior **4.** demigod (*pl.* -**es**) (**heroine** ('hɛrəʊɪn) *fem.*) —**heroic** (hɪ'rəʊɪk) *a.* **1.** of, like hero **2.** courageous, daring —**heroically** (hɪ'rəʊɪkəlɪ) *adv.* —**heroics** (hɪ'rəʊɪks) *pl.n.* extravagant behaviour —**heroism** ('hɛrəʊɪzəm) *n.* **1.** qualities of hero **2.** courage, boldness —**heroic verse** type of verse suitable for epic or heroic subjects —**hero worship 1.** admiration of heroes or of great men **2.** excessive admiration of others —**hero-worship** *vt.* feel admiration or adulation for

heroin ('hɛrəʊɪn) *n.* white crystalline derivative of morphine, a highly addictive narcotic

heron ('hɛrən) *n.* long-legged wading bird —'**heronry** *n.* place where herons breed

herpes ('hɜːpiːz) *n.* any of several skin diseases, including shingles (**herpes zoster**) and cold sores (**herpes simplex**)

Herr (*German* hɛr) *n.* German man: used before name as title equivalent to *Mr* (*pl.* **Herren** ('hɛrən))

herring ('hɛrɪŋ) *n.* important food fish of northern hemisphere —'**herringbone** *n.* stitch or pattern of zigzag lines —**herring gull** common gull that has white plumage with black-tipped wings

Herts. (hɑːts) Hertfordshire

hertz (hɜːts) *n.* SI unit of frequency (*pl.* **hertz**)

hesitate ('hɛzɪteɪt) *vi.* **1.** hold back **2.** feel or show indecision **3.** be reluctant —'**hesitancy** *or* **hesi'tation** *n.* **1.** wavering **2.** doubt **3.** stammering —'**hesitant** *a.* undecided, pausing —'**hesitantly** *adv.*

Hesperus ('hɛspərəs) *n.* evening star, *esp.* Venus

hessian ('hɛsɪən) *n.* coarse jute cloth

hest (hɛst) *n.* behest, command

hetaera (hɪ'tɪərə) *or* **hetaira** (hɪ'taɪrə) *n. esp.* in ancient Greece, prostitute, *esp.* educated courtesan (*pl.* -**taerae** (-'tɪəriː) *or* -**tairai** (-'taɪraɪ))

hetero- (*comb. form*) other; different, as in *heterosexual*

heterodox ('hɛtərəʊdɒks) *a.* not orthodox —'**heterodoxy** *n.*

heterodyne ('hɛtərəʊdaɪn) *v.* **1.** *Electron.* mix (two alternating signals) to produce two signals having frequencies corresponding to sum and difference of original frequencies —*a.* **2.** produced by, operating by, or involved in heterodyning two signals

heterogeneous (hɛtərəʊ'dʒiːnɪəs) *a.* composed of diverse elements —hetero'ge'neity *n.*

heteromorphic (hɛtərəʊ'mɔːfɪk) *or* **heteromorphous** *a. Biol.* **1.** differing from normal form **2.** (*esp.* of insects) having different forms at different stages of life cycle —hetero'morphism *n.*

heterosexual (hɛtərəʊ'sɛksjuəl) *n.* person sexually attracted to members of the opposite sex —**heterosexu'ality** *n.*

het up (hɛt) *inf.* angry; excited

heuchera ('hɔɪkərə) *n.* plant with ornamental foliage

heuristic (hjʊə'rɪstɪk) *a.* serving to find out or to stimulate investigation

hew (hjuː) *v.* chop, cut with axe (**hewn, hewed** *pp.*) —'**hewer** *n.*

hexa- *or before vowel* **hex-** (*comb. form*) six, as in *hexachord*

hexagon ('hɛksəgən) *n.* figure with six angles —hex'agonal *a.*

hexagram ('hɛksəgræm) *n.* star-shaped figure formed by extending sides of regular hexagon to meet at six points

hexameter (hɛk'sæmɪtə) *n.* line of verse of six feet

hexapod ('hɛksəpɒd) *n.* insect

hey (heɪ) *interj.* expression indicating surprise, dismay, discovery *etc.* —'**heyday** *n.* bloom, prime —**hey presto** exclamation used by conjurors to herald climax of trick

Hf *Chem.* hafnium

HF, H.F., hf, *or* **h.f.** high frequency

hf. half

Hg *Chem.* mercury

HGV *UK* heavy goods vehicle

H.H. 1. His (*or* Her) Highness **2.** His Holiness (title of Pope)

HI Hawaii

hiatus (haɪ'eɪtəs) *n.* break or gap where something is missing (*pl.* **-es, hi'atus**)

hibernate ('haɪbəneɪt) *vi.* pass the winter, *esp.* in a torpid state —**hiber'nation** *n.* —**hibernator** *n.*

Hibernian (haɪ'bɜːnɪən) *a./n.* Irish (person)

hibiscus (hɪ'bɪskəs) *n.* flowering (sub)tropical shrub

hiccup ('hɪkʌp) *n.* **1.** spasm of the breathing organs with an abrupt cough-like sound —*vi.* **2.** make a hiccup or hiccups (*also* '**hiccough**)

hick (hɪk) *inf. a.* **1.** rustic **2.** unsophisticated —*n.* **3.** person like this

hickory ('hɪkərɪ) *n.* **1.** N Amer. nut-bearing tree **2.** its tough wood

hide[1] (haɪd) *vt.* **1.** put, keep out of sight **2.** conceal, keep secret —*vi.* **3.** conceal oneself (**hid** *pt.*, **hidden** ('hɪdən) *or* **hid** *pp.*, '**hiding** *pr.p.*) —*n.* **4.** place of concealment, *eg* for birdwatcher —'**hideaway** *n.* hiding place or secluded spot —'**hide-out** *n.* hiding place

hide[2] (haɪd) *n.* skin of animal —'**hiding** *n. sl.* thrashing —'**hidebound** *a.* **1.** restricted, *esp.* by petty rules *etc.* **2.** narrow-minded **3.** (of tree) having bark so close that it impedes growth

hideous ('hɪdɪəs) *a.* repulsive, revolting —'**hideously** *adv.*

hie (haɪ) *v. obs.* hasten (**hied** *pt./pp.*, '**hying** *or* '**hieing** *pr.p.*)

hierarchy ('haɪərɑːkɪ) *n.* system of persons or things arranged in graded order —**hier'archic(al)** *a.*

hieratic (haɪə'rætɪk) *a.* **1.** of priests **2.** of cursive form of hieroglyphics used by priests in ancient Egypt —*n.* **3.** hieratic script of ancient Egypt —**hier'atically** *adv.*

hieroglyphic (haɪərə'glɪfɪk) *a.* **1.** of a system of picture writing, *esp.* as used in ancient Egypt —*n.* **2.** symbol representing object, concept, or sound **3.** symbol, picture, difficult to decipher —'**hieroglyph** *n.*

hi-fi ('haɪ'faɪ) *inf. a.* **1.** *see* **high-fidelity** *at* **HIGH** —*n.* **2.** high-fidelity equipment

higgledy-piggledy ('hɪgəldɪ'pɪgəldɪ) *adv./a. inf.* in confusion

high (haɪ) *a.* **1.** tall, lofty **2.** far up **3.** (of roads) main **4.** (of meat) tainted **5.** (of season) well advanced **6.** (of sound) acute in pitch **7.** expensive **8.** of great importance, quality, or rank **9.** *inf.* in state of euphoria, *esp.* induced by drugs **10.** *inf.* bad-smelling —*adv.* **11.** far up **12.** strongly, to a great extent **13.** at, to a high pitch **14.** at a high rate —'**highly** *adv.* —'**highness** *n.* **1.** quality of being high **2.** (**H-**) title of prince or princess —'**highball** *n. US* long iced drink consisting of spirit base with soda water *etc.* —'**highbrow** *sl. n.* **1.** intellectual, *esp.* intellectual snob —*a.* **2.** intellectual **3.** difficult **4.** serious —'**highchair** *n.* long-legged chair for child, *esp.* one with table-like tray —**High Church** party within Church of England emphasizing authority of sacraments, rituals and ceremonies —**high commissioner** senior diplomatic representative sent by one Commonwealth country to another —**higher education** education and training at colleges, universities *etc.* —**high explosive** extremely powerful chemical explosive —**highfa'lutin** *or* **highfa'luting** *a. inf.* pompous or pretentious —**high-fidelity** *a.* of high-quality sound-reproducing equipment —**high-flier** *or* **high-flyer** *n.* **1.** person extreme in aims, ambition *etc.* **2.** person of great ability, *esp.* in career —**high-flown** *a.* extravagant, bombastic —**high frequency** radio frequency lying between 30 and 3 megahertz —**High German** standard German language, historically developed from the form of W Germanic spoken in S Germany —**high-handed** *a.* domineering, dogmatic —**high jump** athletic event in which competitor has to jump over high bar —**Highland** ('haɪlənd) *a.* of, from the Highlands of Scotland —**highland(s)** ('haɪlənd(z)) (*pl.*)*n.* relatively high ground —**high-level language** *Comp.* programming language closer to human language or mathematical notation than to machine language —'**highlight** *n.* **1.** lightest or brightest area in painting, photograph *etc.* **2.** outstanding feature —*vt.* **3.** bring into prominence —**highly strung** excitable, nervous —**High Mass** solemn and elaborate sung Mass —**high-minded** *a.* having or characterized by high moral principles —**high-mindedness** *n.* —**high-powered** *a.* **1.** (of optical instrument or lens) having high magnification **2.** dynamic and energetic —**high-pressure** *a.* **1.** having, using, or designed to withstand pressure above normal **2.** *inf.* (of selling) persuasive in aggressive and persistent manner —**high priest 1.** *Judaism* priest of highest rank **2.** head of cult —**high-rise** *a.* of building that has many storeys —**high school 1.** *UK see* **grammar school** *at* **GRAMMAR 2.** *US, NZ* secondary school —**high seas** open seas, outside jurisdiction of any one nation —**high-sounding** a. pompous, imposing —**high-spirited** a. vivacious, bold or lively —**high tea** early evening meal usu. with cooked course followed by cakes *etc.*, accompanied by tea —**high-tension** a. carrying or operating at relatively high voltage —**high tide 1.** tide at its highest level **2.** culminating point —**high time** latest possible time —**high treason** act of treason directly affecting sovereign or state —**high water 1.** high tide **2.** state of any stretch of water at its highest level —'**highway 1.** main road **2.** ordinary route —**Highway Code** UK regulations and recommendations applying to all road users —'**highwayman** n. formerly, robber on road, *esp.* mounted —**the high jump** UK *inf.* severe reprimand or punishment

hijack *or* **highjack** ('haɪdʒæk) vt. **1.** divert or wrongfully take command of (vehicle or its contents) while in transit **2.** rob —'**hijacker** *or* '**highjacker** n.

hike (haɪk) vi. **1.** walk a long way (for pleasure) in country —vt. **2.** pull (up), hitch —n. **3.** long walk —'**hiker** n.

hilarity (hɪ'lærɪtɪ) n. cheerfulness, gaiety —**hilarious** (hɪ'lɛərɪəs) a.

hill (hɪl) n. **1.** natural elevation, small mountain **2.** mound —'**hillock** n. little hill —'**hilly** a. —'**hillbilly** n. unsophisticated (country) person

hilt (hɪlt) n. handle of sword *etc.* —**to the hilt** to the full

hilum ('haɪləm) n. *Bot.* scar on seed marking its point of attachment to seed stalk (pl. **-la** (-lə))

him (hɪm; *unstressed* ɪm) pron. objective case of HE —**him'self** pron. emphatic form of HE

hind[1] (haɪnd) *or* **hinder** ('haɪndə) a. at the back, posterior —'**hindquarter** n. **1.** one of two back quarters of carcass of beef *etc.* —pl. **2.** rear, *esp.* of four-legged animal —'**hindsight** n. **1.** ability to understand, after something has happened, what should have been done **2.** firearm's rear sight

hind[2] (haɪnd) n. female of deer

hinder ('hɪndə) vt. obstruct, impede, delay —'**hindrance** n.

Hindi ('hɪndɪ) n. language of N central India —'**Hindu** *or* '**Hindoo** n. person who adheres to **Hinduism**, the dominant religion of India —**Hindustani, Hindoostani** (hɪndu'stɑːnɪ), *or* **Hindo'stani** n. **1.** dialect of Hindi spoken in Delhi **2.** all spoken forms of Hindi and Urdu considered together —a. **3.** of or relating to these languages or Hindustan

hinge (hɪndʒ) n. **1.** movable joint, as that on which door hangs —vt. **2.** attach with, or as with, hinge —vi. **3.** turn, depend (on)

hinny ('hɪnɪ) n. sterile hybrid offspring of male horse and female donkey

hint (hɪnt) n. **1.** slight indication or suggestion —v. **2.** (*sometimes with* at) suggest indirectly

hinterland ('hɪntəlænd) n. district lying behind coast, or near city, port *etc.*

hip[1] (hɪp) n. **1.** (*oft. pl.*) either side of body below waist and above thigh **2.** angle formed where sloping sides of roof meet **3.** fruit of rose, *esp.* wild

hip[2] (hɪp) a. sl. **1.** aware of or following latest trends **2.** informed

hippie *or* **hippy** ('hɪpɪ) n. (young) person whose behaviour, dress *etc.* implies rejection of conventional values

hippo ('hɪpəʊ) n. *inf.* hippopotamus (pl. **-s**)

Hippocratic oath (hɪpəʊ'krætɪk) oath taken by doctor to observe code of medical ethics

hippodrome ('hɪpədrəʊm) n. **1.** music hall **2.** variety theatre **3.** circus

hippogriff *or* **hippogryph** ('hɪpəʊgrɪf) n. griffinlike creature with horse's body

hippopotamus (hɪpə'pɒtəməs) n. large Afr. animal living in rivers (pl. **-es**, **-mi** (-maɪ))

hire (haɪə) vt. **1.** obtain temporary use of by payment **2.** engage for wage —n. **3.** hiring or being hired **4.** payment for use of something —'**hireling** n. one who serves for wages —**hire-purchase** n. system by which something becomes hirer's after stipulated number of payments

hirsute ('hɜːsjuːt) a. hairy

his (hɪz; *unstressed* ɪz) pron./a. belonging to him

Hispanic (hɪ'spænɪk) a. of or derived from Spain or the Spanish —**His'panicism** n.

hispid ('hɪspɪd) a. **1.** rough with bristles or minute spines **2.** bristly, shaggy —**his'pidity** n.

hiss (hɪs) vi. **1.** make sharp sound of letter s, *esp.* in disapproval —vt. **2.** express disapproval of, deride thus —n. **3.** sound like that of prolonged s —'**hissing** n.

hist. 1. historian **2.** historical **3.** history

histamine ('hɪstəmiːn) n. substance released by body tissues, sometimes creating allergic reactions

histogeny (hɪ'stɒdʒənɪ) n. formation and development of organic tissues

histogram ('hɪstəgræm) n. graph using vertical columns to illustrate frequency distribution

histology (hɪ'stɒlədʒɪ) n. branch of biology concerned with the structure of organic tissues —**his'tologist** n.

history ('hɪstərɪ) n. **1.** record of past events **2.** study of these **3.** past events **4.** train of events, public or private **5.** course of life or existence **6.** systematic account of phenomena —**historian** n. writer of history —**historic** (hɪ'stɒrɪk) a. noted in history —**historical** (hɪ'stɒrɪkəl) a. **1.** of, based on, history **2.** belonging to the past

—**historically** (hɪˈstɒrɪkəlɪ) *adv.* —**histoˈricity** *n.* historical authenticity —**historiˈographer** *n.* 1. official historian 2. one who studies historical method

histrionic (hɪstrɪˈɒnɪk) *a.* excessively theatrical, insincere, artificial in manner —**histriˈonics** *pl.n.* behaviour like this

hit (hɪt) *vt.* 1. strike with blow or missile 2. affect injuriously 3. reach —*vi.* 4. strike a blow 5. (*with* upon) light (upon) (**hit, ˈhitting**) —*n.* 6. blow 7. *inf.* success —**ˈhitter** *n.* —**hit-and-run** *a.* 1. denoting motor-vehicle accident in which driver leaves scene without stopping 2. (of attack *etc.*) relying on surprise allied to rapid departure from scene of operations —**hit man** *US* hired assassin —**hit parade** list of currently most popular songs, ranked in order of sales per record —**hit it off** get along (with person) —**hit or miss** casual; haphazard —**hit the hay** *sl.* go to bed —**hit the trail** *or* **road** *inf.* 1. proceed on journey 2. leave

hitch (hɪtʃ) *vt.* 1. fasten with loop *etc.* 2. raise, move with jerk —*vi.* 3. be caught or fastened —*n.* 4. difficulty 5. knot, fastening 6. jerk —**ˈhitchhike** *or* **hitch** *vi.* travel by begging free rides

hither (ˈhɪðə) *adv.* 1. to or towards this place (*esp.* in **come hither**) —*a.* 2. *obs.* situated on this side —**ˈhither'to** *adv.* up to now or to this time

hive (haɪv) *n.* 1. structure in which bees live or are housed 2. *fig.* place swarming with busy occupants —*v.* 3. gather, place bees, in hive —**hive away** store, keep —**hive off** 1. transfer 2. dispose of

hives (haɪvz) *pl.n.* eruptive skin disease

H.M. His (*or* Her) Majesty

H.M.C.S. His (*or* Her) Majesty's Canadian Ship

H.M.I. *UK* His (*or* Her) Majesty's Inspector (of schools)

H.M.S. His (*or* Her) Majesty's Service *or* Ship

H.M.S.O. *UK* His (*or* Her) Majesty's Stationery Office

H.N.C. *UK* Higher National Certificate

H.N.D. *UK* Higher National Diploma

ho (həʊ) *interj.* 1. imitation or representation of sound of deep laugh (*also* **ho-ho**) 2. exclamation used to attract attention *etc.*

Ho *Chem.* holmium

hoard (hɔːd) *n.* 1. stock, store, *esp.* hidden away —*vt.* 2. amass and hide away 3. store

hoarding (ˈhɔːdɪŋ) *n.* 1. large board for displaying advertisements 2. temporary wooden fence round building or piece of ground

hoarse (hɔːs) *a.* rough, harsh-sounding, husky —**ˈhoarsely** *adv.* —**ˈhoarseness** *n.*

hoary (ˈhɔːrɪ) *a.* 1. grey with age 2. greyish-white 3. of great antiquity 4. venerable —**ˈhoarfrost** *n.* frozen dew

hoax (həʊks) *n.* 1. practical joke 2. deceptive trick —*vt.* 3. play trick upon 4. deceive —**ˈhoaxer** *n.*

hob (hɒb) *n.* 1. flat-topped casing of fireplace 2. top area of cooking stove —**ˈhobnail** *n.* large-headed nail for boot soles

hobble (ˈhɒbəl) *vi.* 1. walk lamely —*vt.* 2. tie legs of (horse *etc.*) together —*n.* 3. straps or ropes put on an animal's legs to prevent it straying 4. limping gait

hobbledehoy (hɒbəldɪˈhɔɪ) *n.* *obs.* rough, ill-mannered clumsy youth

hobby (ˈhɒbɪ) *n.* 1. favourite occupation as pastime 2. small falcon —**ˈhobbyhorse** *n.* 1. toy horse 2. favourite topic, preoccupation

hobgoblin (hɒbˈɡɒblɪn) *n.* mischievous fairy

hobnob (ˈhɒbnɒb) *vi.* (*oft.* *with* with) 1. be familiar 2. *obs.* drink (**-bb-**)

hobo (ˈhəʊbəʊ) *n.* shiftless, wandering person (*pl.* **-s, -es**)

Hobson's choice (ˈhɒbsənz) choice of taking what is offered or nothing at all

hock[1] (hɒk) *n.* 1. backward-pointing joint on leg of horse *etc.*, corresponding to human ankle —*vt.* 2. disable by cutting tendons of hock

hock[2] (hɒk) *n.* dry white wine

hock[3] (hɒk) *inf.*, *chiefly US vt.* 1. pawn, pledge —*n.* 2. state of being in pawn —**ˈhocker** *n.* —**in hock** 1. in prison 2. in debt 3. in pawn

hockey (ˈhɒkɪ) *n.* 1. team game played on field with ball and curved sticks 2. *US,* *C* ice hockey

hocus-pocus (ˈhəʊkəsˈpəʊkəs) *n.* 1. trickery 2. mystifying jargon

hod (hɒd) *n.* 1. small trough on a staff for carrying mortar, bricks *etc.* 2. tall, narrow coal scuttle

hoe (həʊ) *n.* 1. tool for weeding, breaking ground *etc.* —*v.* 2. dig, weed or till (surface soil) with hoe (**hoed, ˈhoeing**)

hog (hɒɡ) *n.* 1. pig, *esp.* castrated male for fattening 2. greedy, dirty person —*vt.* 3. *inf.* eat, use selfishly (**-gg-**) —**ˈhogback** *n.* 1. narrow ridge with steep sides (*also* **hog's back**) 2. *Archaeol.* tomb with sloping sides —**ˈhogshead** *n.* 1. large cask 2. liquid measure, having several values, used *esp.* for alcoholic beverages —**ˈhogwash** *n.* 1. nonsense 2. pig food

Hogmanay (hɒɡməˈneɪ) *n.* in Scotland, last day of year

hoick (hɔɪk) *vt.* raise abruptly and sharply

hoi polloi (ˈhɔɪ pəˈlɔɪ) 1. the common mass of people 2. the masses

hoist (hɔɪst) *vt.* raise aloft, raise with tackle *etc.*

hoity-toity (hɔɪtɪˈtɔɪtɪ) *a.* *inf.* arrogant, haughty

hokum (ˈhəʊkəm) *n.* *US sl.* 1. claptrap; bunk 2. obvious or hackneyed material of a sentimental nature in film *etc.*

hold¹ (həʊld) *vt.* **1.** keep fast, grasp **2.** support in or with hands *etc.* **3.** maintain in position **4.** have capacity for **5.** own, occupy **6.** carry on **7.** detain **8.** celebrate **9.** keep back **10.** believe —*vi.* **11.** cling **12.** remain fast or unbroken **13.** (*with* to) abide (by) **14.** keep **15.** remain relevant, valid or true (**held** *pt./pp.*) —*n.* **16.** grasp **17.** influence —'**holder** *n.* —'**holding** *n.* (*oft. pl.*) property, such as land or stocks and shares —'**holdall** *n.* valise or case for carrying clothes *etc.* —'**holdfast** *n.* clamp —**holding company** company with controlling shareholdings in other companies —'**holdup** *n.* **1.** armed robbery **2.** delay

hold² (həʊld) *n.* space in ship or aircraft for cargo

hole (həʊl) *n.* **1.** hollow place, cavity **2.** perforation **3.** opening **4.** *inf.* unattractive place **5.** *inf.* difficult situation —*vt.* **6.** make holes in **7.** drive into a hole —*vi.* **8.** go into a hole —'**holey** *a.* —**hole-and-corner** *a. inf.* furtive or secretive

holiday ('hɒlɪdeɪ) *n.* day or other period of rest from work *etc.*, *esp.* spent away from home

holland ('hɒlənd) *n.* linen fabric —'**Hollands** *n.* spirit, gin

holler ('hɒlə) *inf. v.* **1.** shout or yell (something) —*n.* **2.** shout; call

hollo ('hɒləʊ) *or* **holla** ('hɒlə) *n./interj.* **1.** cry for attention, or of encouragement (*pl.* **-s**) —*vi.* **2.** shout

hollow ('hɒləʊ) *a.* **1.** having a cavity, not solid **2.** empty **3.** false **4.** insincere **5.** not full-toned —*n.* **6.** cavity, hole, valley —*vt.* **7.** make hollow, make hole in **8.** excavate

holly ('hɒlɪ) *n.* evergreen shrub with prickly leaves and red berries

hollyhock ('hɒlɪhɒk) *n.* tall plant bearing many large flowers

holmium ('hɒlmɪəm) *n.* silver-white metallic element of lanthanide series

holm oak (həʊm) evergreen Mediterranean oak tree

holocaust ('hɒləkɔːst) *n.* great destruction of life, *esp.* by fire

holograph ('hɒləgræf, -grɑːf) *n.* document wholly written by the signer

holography (hɒ'lɒgrəfɪ) *n.* science of using lasers to produce photographic record (**holo-gram**) which can reproduce a three-dimensional image

holster ('həʊlstə) *n.* leather case for pistol, hung from belt *etc.*

holt (həʊlt) *n. Poet.* wood, wooded hill

holy ('həʊlɪ) *a.* **1.** belonging, devoted to God **2.** free from sin **3.** divine **4.** consecrated —'**holily** *adv.* —'**holiness** *n.* sanctity **2.** (**H-**) Pope's title —**holier-than-thou** *a.* offensively sanctimonious or self-righteous —**Holy Communion** service of the Eucharist —**holy day** day of religious festival —**Holy Ghost** *or* **Spirit** third person of Trinity —**Holy Grail** cup or dish used by Christ at the Last Supper —**holy orders 1.** sacrament whereby person is admitted to Christian ministry **2.** grades of Christian ministry **3.** status of ordained Christian minister —**Holy See** *R.C.Ch.* **1.** the see of the pope as bishop of Rome **2.** Roman curia —**Holy Week** week before Easter —**the Holy Land** Palestine

homage ('hɒmɪdʒ) *n.* **1.** tribute, respect, reverence **2.** formal acknowledgment of allegiance

homburg ('hɒmbɜːg) *n.* man's hat of soft felt with dented crown and stiff upturned brim

home (həʊm) *n.* **1.** dwelling-place **2.** residence **3.** native place **4.** institution for the elderly, infirm *etc.* —*a.* **5.** of one's home, country *etc.* —*adv.* **6.** to, at one's home **7.** to the point —*v.* **8.** direct or be directed on to a point or target —'**homeless** *a.* —'**homely** *a.* plain —'**homeward** *a./adv.* —'**homewards** *adv.* —**home-brew** *n.* alcoholic drink made at home —**Home Counties** counties surrounding London —**home economics** study of diet, budgeting and other subjects concerned with running a home —**home help** *UK* woman employed, *esp.* by local authority, to do housework in person's home —**Home Office** *UK* government department responsible for inter-nal affairs —**home rule 1.** self-government **2.** partial autonomy sometimes granted to national minority or colony —**Home Secretary** *UK* head of Home Office —'**homesick** *a.* depressed by absence from home —'**homesickness** *n.* —'**homespun** *a.* **1.** domestic **2.** simple —*n.* **3.** cloth made of homespun yarn —'**homestead** *n.* **1.** house with outbuildings, *esp.* on farm **2.** *US, C* house and land occupied by owner and exempt from seizure and forced sale for debt —'**homesteader** *n.* —'**homework** *n.* school work to be done at home —'**homing** *a. Zool.* of ability to return home after travelling great distances —**homing pigeon** domestic pigeon developed for its homing instinct, used for racing (*also* '**homer**) —**bring home to** impress deeply upon —**home and dry** safe or successful

homeo-, homoeo-, *or* **homoio-** (*comb. form*) like, similar, as in *homeomorphism*

homeopathy *or* **homoeopathy** (həʊmɪ'ɒpə-θɪ) *n.* treatment of disease by small doses of drug that produces, in healthy person, symptoms similar to those of disease being treated —'**homeopath** *or* '**homoeopath** *n.* one who believes in or practises homeopathy —**homeo**'**pathic** *or* **homoeo**'**pathic** *a.* —**homeo-**'**pathically** *or* **homoeo**'**pathically** *adv.*

homicide ('hɒmɪsaɪd) *n.* **1.** killing of human being **2.** killer —**homi**'**cidal** *a.*

homily ('hɒmɪlɪ) *n.* **1.** sermon **2.** religious

discourse —**homi'letic** a. —**homi'letics** pl.n. (with sing. v.) art of preaching

hominid ('hɒmɪnɪd) n. **1.** member of mammal family, extinct or living —a. **2.** of or belonging to mammal family

hominoid ('hɒmɪnɔɪd) a. **1.** manlike **2.** of or belonging to primate family, which includes anthropoid apes and man —n. **3.** hominoid animal

Homo ('həʊməʊ) n. genus to which modern man belongs —**Homo sapiens** ('sæpɪɛnz) specific name of modern man

homo- (comb. form) same, as in homosexual. Such words are not given here where the meaning may easily be inferred from the simple word

homogeneous (ˌhəʊməʊ'dʒiːnɪəs, hɒm-) a. **1.** formed of uniform parts **2.** similar, uniform **3.** of the same nature —**homoge'neity** n. —**homogenize** or -**nise** (hɒ'mɒdʒɪnaɪz) vt. break up fat globules in (milk and cream) to distribute them evenly

homograph ('hɒməʊɡrɑːf) n. one of group of words spelt in the same way but having different meanings —**homo'graphic** a.

homologous (hɒʊ'mɒləɡəs, hɒ-), **homological** (ˌhɒʊmə'lɒdʒɪkəl, hɒm-), or **homologic** a. having the same relation, relative position etc. —**'homologue** n. homologous thing

homonym ('hɒmənɪm) n. word of same form as another, but having different meaning —**homo'nymic** or **ho'monymous** a.

homosexual (ˌhɒʊməʊ'sɛksjʊəl, hɒm-) n. **1.** person sexually attracted to members of the same sex —a. **2.** of or relating to homosexuals or homosexuality —**homosexu'ality** n.

Hon or **Hon. 1.** Honourable **2.** (also **h-**) honorary

hone (həʊn) n. **1.** whetstone —vt. **2.** sharpen with hone

honest ('ɒnɪst) a. **1.** not cheating, lying, stealing etc. **2.** genuine **3.** without pretension —**'honestly** adv. —**'honesty** n. **1.** quality of being honest **2.** plant with silvery seed pods

honey ('hʌnɪ) n. sweet fluid made by bees —**'honeyed** or **'honied** a. Poet. **1.** flattering or soothing **2.** made sweet or agreeable **3.** full of honey —**'honeybee** n. any of various social bees widely domesticated as source of honey and beeswax (also **hive bee**) —**'honeycomb** n. **1.** wax structure in hexagonal cells in which bees place honey, eggs etc. —vt. **2.** fill with cells or perforations —**'honeydew** n. **1.** sweet sticky substance found on plants **2.** type of sweet melon —**'honeymoon** n. holiday taken by newlywedded pair —**'honeysuckle** n. climbing plant

honk (hɒŋk) n. **1.** call of wild goose **2.** any sound like this, esp. sound of motor horn —vi. **3.** make this sound

honky-tonk ('hɒŋkɪtɒŋk) n. **1.** US sl. cheap disreputable nightclub etc. **2.** style of ragtime piano-playing

honour or U.S. **honor** ('ɒnə) n. **1.** personal integrity **2.** renown **3.** reputation **4.** sense of what is right or due **5.** chastity **6.** high rank or position **7.** source, cause of honour **8.** pleasure, privilege —pl. **9.** mark of respect **10.** distinction in examination —vt. **11.** respect highly **12.** confer honour on **13.** accept or pay (bill etc.) when due —**hono'rarium** n. a fee (pl. **-s**, **-ia** (-ɪə)) —**'honorary** a. **1.** conferred for the sake of honour only **2.** holding position without pay or usual requirements **3.** giving services without pay —**hono'rific** a. conferring honour —**'honourable** or U.S. **'honorable** a. —**'honourably** or U.S. **'honorably** adv.

hooch or **hootch** (huːtʃ) n. US sl. alcoholic drink, esp. illicitly distilled spirits

hood (hʊd) n. **1.** covering for head and neck, oft. part of cloak or gown **2.** hoodlike thing as (adjustable) top of motorcar, perambulator etc. **3.** esp. US car bonnet —**'hooded** a. covered with or shaped like hood —**hooded crow** crow that has grey body and black head, wings, and tail (also (Scot.) **'hoodie, hoodie crow**) —**'hoodwink** vt. deceive

hoodlum ('huːdləm) n. gangster, bully —**hood** n. US sl. hoodlum

hoodoo ('huːduː) n. cause of bad luck

hooey ('huːɪ) n./interj. sl. nonsense

hoof (huːf) n. horny casing of foot of horse etc. (pl. **-s**, **hooves**) —**on the hoof** (of livestock) alive

hoo-ha ('huːhɑː) n. needless fuss, bother etc.

hook (hʊk) n. **1.** bent piece of metal used to suspend, hold, or pull something **2.** something resembling hook in shape or function **3.** curved cutting tool **4.** Boxing blow delivered with bent elbow —vt. **5.** grasp, catch, hold, as with hook **6.** fasten with hook **7.** Golf drive (ball) widely to the left **8.** Cricket hit off (ball) to leg —**hooked** a. **1.** shaped like hook **2.** caught **3.** sl. addicted —**'hooker** n. **1.** US sl. prostitute **2.** Rugby player who uses feet to get ball in scrum —**hook-up** n. linking of radio, television stations —**'hookworm** n. parasitic worm infesting humans and animals

hookah or **hooka** ('hʊkə) n. oriental pipe in which smoke is drawn through water and long tube

hooligan ('huːlɪɡən) n. violent, irresponsible (young) person —**'hooliganism** n.

hoop (huːp) n. **1.** rigid circular band of metal, wood etc. **2.** such a band used for binding barrel etc., for use as toy, or for jumping through as in circus acts —vt. **3.** bind with hoops **4.** encircle

—go through the hoop(s) *inf.* go through an ordeal or test

hoopla ('huːplɑː) *n.* game played at fairgrounds *etc.*, by throwing rings at objects for prizes

hoopoe ('huːpuː) *n.* bird with large crest

hooray (huːˈreɪ) *or* **hoorah** (huːˈrɑː) *interj.* **1.** *see* HURRAH **2.** (huːˈruː) **A, NZ** cheerio (*also* **hoo'roo**)

hoot (huːt) *n.* **1.** owl's cry or similar sound **2.** cry of disapproval or derision **3.** *inf.* funny person or thing —*vi.* **4.** utter hoot, *esp.* in derision **5.** sound motor horn **6.** *inf.* laugh —**'hooter** *n.* **1.** device (*eg* horn) to emit hooting sound **2.** *sl.* nose

Hoover ('huːvə) *n.* **1. R** vacuum cleaner —*v.* **2.** (h-) vacuum

hooves (huːvz) *n., pl. of* HOOF

hop¹ (hop) *vi.* **1.** spring on one foot **2.** *inf.* move quickly (-pp-) —*n.* **3.** leap, skip **4.** one stage of journey —**'hopscotch** *n.* children's game of hopping in pattern drawn on ground

hop² (hop) *n.* **1.** climbing plant with bitter cones used to flavour beer *etc.* —*pl.* **2.** the cones

hope (həʊp) *n.* **1.** expectation of something desired **2.** thing that gives, or object of, this feeling —*v.* **3.** feel hope —**'hopeful** *a.* —**'hopefully** *adv. inf.* it is hoped —**'hopeless** *a.* —**young hopeful** promising boy or girl

hopper ('hopə) *n.* **1.** one who hops **2.** device for feeding material into mill or machine, or grain into railway truck *etc.* **3.** mechanical hop-picker **4. SA** *see* COOCPAN

horal ('hɔːrəl) *or* **horary** ('hɔːrərɪ) *a. obs.* **1.** pert. to an hour **2.** hourly

horde (hɔːd) *n.* large crowd, *esp.* moving together

horehound *or* **hoarhound** ('hɔːhaʊnd) *n.* plant with bitter juice formerly used medicinally

horizon (həˈraɪzᵊn) *n.* **1.** boundary of part of the earth seen from any given point **2.** line where earth and sky seem to meet **3.** boundary of mental outlook —**horizontal** (horɪˈzontᵊl) *a.* parallel with horizon, level —**horizontally** (horɪˈzontəlɪ) *adv.*

hormone ('hɔːməʊn) *n.* **1.** substance secreted by certain glands which stimulates organs of the body **2.** synthetic substance with same effect

horn (hɔːn) *n.* **1.** hard projection on heads of certain animals, *eg* cows **2.** substance of horns **3.** various things made of, or resembling it **4.** wind instrument *orig.* made of horn **5.** device, *esp.* in car, emitting sound as warning *etc.* —**horned** *a.* having horns —**'horny** *a.* **1.** of, like or hard as horn **2.** having horn(s) **3.** *sl.* sexually aroused —**'hornbeam** *n.* tree with smooth grey bark —**'hornbill** *n.* type of bird with horny growth on large bill —**'hornbook** *n.* page bearing religious text or alphabet, held in frame with thin window

of horn over it —**horn of plenty** *see* CORNUCOPIA —**'hornpipe** *n.* lively dance, *esp.* associated with sailors

hornblende ('hɔːnblend) *n.* mineral consisting of silica, with magnesia, lime, or iron

hornet ('hɔːnɪt) *n.* large insect of wasp family

horologe ('horələdʒ) *n. rare* any timepiece —**ho'rology** *n.* art or science of clock-making and measuring time

horoscope ('horəskəʊp) *n.* **1.** observation of, or scheme showing disposition of planets *etc.*, at given moment, *esp.* birth, by which character and abilities of individual are predicted **2.** telling of person's fortune by this method

horror ('horə) *n.* **1.** terror **2.** loathing, fear **3.** its cause —**hor'rendous** *a.* horrific —**horrible** *a.* exciting horror, hideous, shocking —**'horribly** *adv.* —**'horrid** *a.* **1.** unpleasant, repulsive **2.** *inf.* unkind —**hor'rific** *a.* particularly horrible —**'horrify** *vt.* move to horror (-ified, -ifying)

hors d'oeuvre (ɔː ˈdɜːvr) small dish served before main meal

horse (hɔːs) *n.* **1.** four-footed animal used for riding and draught **2.** cavalry **3.** vaulting-block **4.** frame for support *etc.*, *esp.* for drying clothes —*vt.* **5.** provide with horse or horses —**'horsy** *or* **'horsey** *a.* **1.** having to do with horses **2.** devoted to horses or horse racing —**horse brass** decorative brass ornament, *orig.* attached to horse's harness —**horse chestnut** tree with conical clusters of white or pink flowers and large nuts —**'horseflesh** *n.* **1.** horses collectively **2.** flesh of horse, *esp.* edible horse meat —**'horsefly** *n.* large, bloodsucking fly —**horse laugh** harsh boisterous laugh —**'horseman** *n.* rider on horse ('horsewoman *fem.*) —**'horseplay** *n.* rough or rowdy play —**'horsepower** *n.* unit of power of engine *etc.* 550 foot-pounds per second —**'horseradish** *n.* plant with pungent root —**horse sense** *see* **common sense** at COMMON —**'horseshoe** *n.* **1.** protective U-shaped piece of iron nailed to horse's hoof **2.** thing so shaped —**'horsetail** *n.* green flowerless plant with erect, jointed stem —**horse about** *or* **around** *inf.* play roughly, boisterously

hortatory ('hɔːtətərɪ) *or* **hortative** ('hɔːtətɪv) *a.* tending to exhort; encouraging —**hor'tation** *n.*

horticulture ('hɔːtɪkʌltʃə) *n.* art or science of gardening —**horti'cultural** *a.* —**horti'culturist** *n.*

Hos. *Bible* Hosea

hosanna (həʊˈzænə) *n./interj.* cry of praise, adoration

hose (həʊz) *n.* **1.** flexible tube for conveying liquid or gas **2.** stockings —*vt.* **3.** water with hose —**'hosier** *n.* dealer in stockings *etc.* —**'hosiery** *n.* stockings *etc.*

hospice ('hɒspɪs) *n. obs.* traveller's house of rest kept by religious order

hospital ('hɒspɪtəl) *n.* institution for care of sick —**hospitali'zation** *or* **-li'sation** *n.* —'**hospitalize** *or* **-lise** *vt.* place for care in hospital

hospitality (hɒspɪ'tælɪtɪ) *n.* friendly and liberal reception of strangers or guests —'**hospitable** *a.* welcoming, kindly —'**hospitably** *adv.*

host[1] (həʊst) *n.* **1.** one who entertains another ('**hostess** *fem.*) **2.** innkeeper **3.** compere of show **4.** animal, plant on which parasite lives —*v.* **5.** be host of (party, programme *etc.*)

host[2] (həʊst) *n.* large number

Host (həʊst) *n.* consecrated bread of the Eucharist

hosta ('hɒstə) *n.* garden plant with large ornamental leaves

hostage ('hɒstɪdʒ) *n.* person taken or given as pledge or security

hostel ('hɒstəl) *n.* building providing accommodation at low cost for particular category of people, as students or the homeless —'**hostelry** *n. obs.* inn

hostile ('hɒstaɪl) *a.* **1.** opposed, antagonistic **2.** warlike **3.** of or relating to an enemy **4.** unfriendly —**hostility** (hɒ'stɪlɪtɪ) *n.* enmity —*pl.* **2.** acts of warfare

hot (hɒt) *a.* **1.** of high temperature, very warm, giving out heat **2.** angry **3.** severe **4.** recent, new **5.** much favoured **6.** spicy **7.** *sl.* good, quick, smart **8.** *sl.* stolen (**'hotter** *comp.*, '**hottest** *sup.*) —'**hotly** *adv.* —'**hotness** *n.* —**hot air** *inf.* boastful, empty talk —'**hotbed** *n.* **1.** bed of earth heated by manure and grass for young plants **2.** any place encouraging growth —**hot-blooded** *a.* passionate, excitable —**hot dog** hot sausage, *esp.* frankfurter, in split bread roll —'**hotfoot** *vi./adv.* (go) quickly —'**hothead** *n.* hasty, intemperate person —**hot-headed** *a.* impetuous, rash or hot-tempered —**hot-headedness** *n.* —'**hothouse** *n.* **1.** forcing house for plants **2.** heated building for cultivating tropical plants in cold or temperate climates —**hot line** direct communication link between heads of government *etc.* —**hot money** capital that is transferred from one commercial centre to another seeking best opportunity for short-term gain —'**hotplate** *n.* **1.** heated plate on electric cooker **2.** portable device for keeping food warm —'**hotpot** *n. UK* casserole covered with layer of potatoes —**hot rod** car with engine that has been modified to produce increased power —**hot seat 1.** *inf.* difficult or dangerous position **2.** *US sl.* electric chair —**hot-foot** it go quickly —**in hot water** *inf.* in trouble

hotchpotch ('hɒtʃpɒtʃ) *or esp. U.S.* **hodge-** **podge** ('hɒdʒpɒdʒ) *n.* **1.** medley **2.** dish of many ingredients

hotel (həʊ'tɛl) *n.* commercial establishment providing lodging and meals —**hotel keeper** *or* **ho'telier** *n.*

Hottentot ('hɒtəntɒt) *n.* member of a native S Afr. race, now nearly extinct (*pl.* **-tot, -s**)

hough (hɒx) *see* HOCK[1]

hound (haʊnd) *n.* **1.** hunting dog —*vt.* **2.** chase, pursue **3.** urge on

hour (aʊə) *n.* **1.** twenty-fourth part of day **2.** sixty minutes **3.** time of day **4.** appointed time —*pl.* **5.** fixed periods for work, prayers *etc.* **6.** book of prayers —'**hourly** *adv.* **1.** every hour **2.** frequently —*a.* **3.** frequent **4.** happening every hour —'**hourglass** *n.* **1.** device consisting of two transparent chambers linked by narrow channel, containing quantity of sand that takes specified time to trickle from one chamber to the other —*a.* **2.** well-proportioned with small waist

houri ('hʊərɪ) *n.* beautiful nymph of the Muslim paradise (*pl.* **-s**)

house (haʊs) *n.* **1.** building for human habitation **2.** building for other specified purpose **3.** legislative or other assembly **4.** family **5.** business firm **6.** theatre audience —*v.* (haʊz) **7.** give or receive shelter, lodging or storage —*vt.* **8.** cover; contain —**housing** ('haʊzɪŋ) *n.* **1.** (providing of) houses **2.** part or structure designed to cover, protect, contain —**house arrest** confinement to one's own home rather than in prison —'**houseboat** *n.* boat for living in on river *etc.* —'**housebound** *a.* unable to leave one's house because of illness *etc.* —'**housebreaker** *n.* burglar —'**housecoat** *n.* woman's long loose garment for casual wear at home —'**household** *n.* inmates of house collectively —'**householder** *n.* **1.** occupier of house as his dwelling **2.** head of household —**household name** *or* **word** person or thing that is very well known —'**housekeeper** *n.* person managing affairs of household —'**housekeeping** *n.* (money for) running household —'**housemaid** *n.* maidservant who cleans rooms *etc.* —**housemaid's knee** inflammation and swelling of bursa in front of kneecap —'**houseman** *n.* junior doctor who is member of medical staff of hospital —**House of Commons** *UK, C* lower chamber of Parliament —**House of Lords** *UK* upper chamber of Parliament, composed of the peers of the realm —**house-proud** *a.* preoccupied with appearance of one's house —'**housetop** *n.* roof of house —**house-train** *vt. UK* train (pets) to urinate and defecate outdoors —**house-warming** *n.* party to celebrate entry into new house —'**housewife** *n.* woman who runs a household —'**housework** *n.* work of running home, such as cleaning *etc.* —**housey-**

housey n. gambling game, bingo —**proclaim from the housetops** announce publicly

hove (həʊv) chiefly Naut. pt./pp. of HEAVE

hovel ('hɒvəl) n. mean dwelling

hover ('hɒvə) vi. 1. (of bird etc.) hang in the air 2. loiter 3. be in state of indecision —'**hovercraft** n. type of craft which can travel over both land and sea on a cushion of air

how (haʊ) adv. 1. in what way 2. by what means 3. in what condition 4. to what degree —**howbeit** (haʊ'biːɪt) adv. obs. nevertheless —**how'ever** adv. 1. nevertheless 2. in whatever way, degree 3. all the same

howdah ('haʊdə) n. (canopied) seat on elephant's back

howitzer ('haʊɪtsə) n. short gun firing shells at high elevation

howl (haʊl) vi. 1. utter long loud cry —n. 2. such cry —'**howler** n. 1. one that howls 2. inf. stupid mistake —'**howling** a. inf. great

hoyden or **hoiden** ('hɔɪdən) n. wild, boisterous girl, tomboy —'**hoydenish** or '**hoidenish** a.

H.P. 1. high pressure 2. horsepower (also hp) 3. UK hire purchase (also h.p.)

H.Q. or **h.q.** headquarters

hr. or **hr** hour

H.R.H. His (or Her) Royal Highness

HT Phys. high tension

hub (hʌb) n. 1. middle part of wheel, from which spokes radiate 2. central point of activity

hubble-bubble ('hʌbəl'bʌbəl) n. 1. see HOOKAH 2. turmoil 3. gargling sound

hubbub ('hʌbʌb) n. 1. confused noise of many voices 2. uproar

hubris ('hjuːbrɪs) or **hybris** ('haɪbrɪs) n. 1. pride or arrogance —hu'**bristic** or hy'**bristic** a.

huckaback ('hʌkəbæk) n. coarse absorbent linen or cotton fabric used for towels etc. (also **huck**)

huckster ('hʌkstə) n. 1. person using aggressive or questionable methods of selling —vt. 2. sell (goods) thus

huddle ('hʌdəl) n. 1. crowded mass 2. inf. impromptu conference —v. 3. heap, crowd together 4. hunch (oneself)

hue (hjuː) n. colour, complexion

hue and cry 1. public uproar, outcry 2. formerly, loud outcry usu. in pursuit of wrongdoer

huff (hʌf) n. 1. passing mood of anger —v. 2. make or become angry, resentful —vi. 3. blow, puff heavily —'**huffily** adv. —'**huffy** a.

hug (hʌg) vt. 1. clasp tightly in the arms 2. cling to 3. keep close to (-**gg**-) —n. 4. fond embrace

huge (hjuːdʒ) a. very big —'**hugely** adv. very much

huggermugger ('hʌgəmʌgə) n. 1. confusion 2. rare secrecy —a./adv. obs. 3. with secrecy 4. in

confusion —vt. 5. obs. keep secret —vi. 6. obs. act secretly

Huguenot ('hjuːgənəʊ, -nɒt) n. 1. French Calvinist, esp. of 16th or 17th century —a. 2. designating French Protestant Church

huh (spelling pron. hʌ) interj. exclamation of derision, bewilderment, inquiry etc.

hula ('huːlə) or **hula-hula** n. native dance of Hawaii

Hula-Hoop n. R hoop of plastic etc. swung round body by wriggling hips

hulk (hʌlk) n. 1. body of abandoned vessel 2. offens. large, unwieldy person or thing —'**hulking** a. unwieldy, bulky

hull (hʌl) n. 1. frame, body of ship 2. calyx of strawberry, raspberry, or similar fruit 3. shell, husk —vt. 4. remove shell, hull from 5. pierce hull of (vessel etc.)

hullabaloo or **hullaballoo** (hʌləbə'luː) n. 1. uproar, clamour, row

hullo (hʌ'ləʊ) interj. see HELLO

hum (hʌm) vi. 1. make low continuous sound as bee 2. sl. smell unpleasantly 3. sl. be very active —vt. 4. sing with closed lips (-**mm**-) —n. 5. humming sound 6. sl. smell 7. sl. great activity 8. in radio, disturbance affecting reception —'**hummingbird** n. very small bird whose wings make humming noise

human ('hjuːmən) a. of, relating to, or characteristic of mankind —**humane** (hjuː'meɪn) a. 1. benevolent, kind 2. merciful —'**humanism** n. 1. belief in human effort rather than religion 2. interest in human welfare and affairs 3. classical literary culture —'**humanist** n. —humani'**tarian** n. 1. philanthropist 2. having the welfare of mankind at heart —hu'**manity** n. 1. human nature 2. human race 3. kindliness —pl. 4. study of literature, philosophy, the arts —'**humanize** or **-ise** vt. 1. make human 2. civilize —'**humanly** adv. —'**humanoid** a. 1. like human being in appearance —n. 2. being with human being rather than anthropoid characteristics 3. in science fiction, robot or creature resembling human being —**human'kind** n. whole race of man

humble ('hʌmbəl) a. 1. lowly, modest —vt. 2. bring low, abase, humiliate —'**humbly** adv. —**humble pie** formerly, pie made from heart, entrails etc. of deer —**eat humble pie** be forced to behave humbly

humbug ('hʌmbʌg) n. 1. impostor 2. sham, nonsense, deception 3. sweet of boiled sugar —vt. 4. deceive; defraud (-**gg**-)

humdinger ('hʌmdɪŋə) n. sl. excellent person or thing

humdrum ('hʌmdrʌm) a. commonplace, dull, monotonous

humeral ('hjuːmərəl) a. of shoulder —'**humer-**

us *n.* long bone of upper arm (*pl.* **-meri** (-mərai))

humid ('hju:mɪd) *a.* moist, damp —**hu'midifier** *n.* device for increasing amount of water vapour in air in room *etc.* —**hu'midify** *vt.* —**hu'midity** *n.*

humiliate (hju:'mɪlɪeɪt) *vt.* lower dignity of, abase, mortify —**humili'ation** *n.*

humility (hju:'mɪlɪtɪ) *n.* **1.** state of being humble **2.** meekness

hummock ('hʌmək) *n.* **1.** low knoll, hillock **2.** ridge of ice

humour *or U.S.* **humor** ('hju:mə) *n.* **1.** faculty of saying or perceiving what excites amusement **2.** state of mind, mood **3.** temperament **4.** *obs.* any of various fluids of body —*vt.* **5.** gratify, indulge —**'humorist** *n.* person who acts, speaks, writes humorously —**'humorous** *a.* funny **2.** amusing —**'humorously** *adv.*

hump (hʌmp) *n.* **1.** normal or deforming lump, *esp.* on back **2.** hillock **3.** *inf.* dejection —*vt.* **4.** make hump-shaped **5.** *sl.* carry, heave —**'humpback** *n.* person with hump —**'humpbacked** *a.* having a hump

humph (*spelling pron.* hʌmf) *interj.* exclamation of annoyance, indecision *etc.*

humus ('hju:məs) *n.* decayed vegetable and animal mould

Hun (hʌn) *n.* **1.** member of Asiatic nomadic peoples who invaded Europe in 4th and 5th centuries A.D. **2.** *inf. derog.* German **3.** *inf.* vandal —**'Hunlike** *a.* —**'Hunnish** *a.*

hunch (hʌntʃ) *n.* **1.** intuition or premonition **2.** hump —*vt.* **3.** thrust, bend into hump —**'hunchback** *n.* humpback

hundred ('hʌndrəd) *n./a.* cardinal number, ten times ten —**'hundredfold** *a./adv.* —**'hundredth** *a./n.* ordinal number of a hundred —**hundreds and thousands** tiny beads of coloured sugar, used in decorating cakes *etc.* —**'hundredweight** *n.* weight of 112 lbs. (50.8 kg), 20th part of ton

hung (hʌŋ) *v.* **1.** *pt./pp.* of HANG —*a.* **2.** (of jury *etc.*) unable to decide **3.** not having majority —**hung-over** *a. inf.* suffering from aftereffects of excessive drinking —**hung parliament** parliament in which no party has absolute majority —**hung up** *inf.* **1.** delayed **2.** emotionally disturbed

hunger ('hʌŋgə) *n.* **1.** discomfort, exhaustion from lack of food **2.** strong desire —*vi.* **3.** (*usu.* with **for** *or* **after**) have great desire (for) —**'hungrily** *adv.* —**'hungry** *a.* having keen appetite —**hunger strike** refusal of all food, as protest

hunk (hʌŋk) *n.* **1.** thick piece **2.** *sl., chiefly US* sexually attractive man

hunkers ('hʌŋkəz) *pl.n. dial.* haunches

hunt (hʌnt) *v.* **1.** (seek out to) kill or capture for sport or food **2.** search (for) —*n.* **3.** chase, search **4.** track of country hunted over **5.** (party organized for) hunting **6.** pack of hounds **7.** hunting district or society —**'hunter** *n.* **1.** one who hunts (**'huntress** *fem.*) **2.** horse, dog bred for hunting —**'huntsman** *n.* man in charge of pack of hounds

hurdle ('hɜːd³l) *n.* **1.** portable frame of bars for temporary fences or for jumping over **2.** obstacle —*pl.* **3.** race over hurdles —*vi.* **4.** race over hurdles —**'hurdler** *n.* one who races over hurdles

hurdy-gurdy ('hɜːdɪ'gɜːdɪ) *n.* mechanical (musical) instrument (*eg* barrel organ)

hurl (hɜːl) *vt.* throw violently —**hurly-burly** *n.* loud confusion

hurling ('hɜːlɪŋ) *or* **hurley** *n.* Irish game like hockey

hurrah (hu'rɑː), **hooray** (hu:'reɪ), *or* **hoorah** (hu:'rɑː) *interj.* exclamation of joy or applause

hurricane ('hʌrɪk²n) *n.* very strong, potentially destructive wind or storm —**hurricane lamp** lamp with glass covering round flame

hurry ('hʌrɪ) *v.* **1.** (cause to) move or act in great haste (**'hurried, 'hurrying**) —*n.* **2.** undue haste **3.** eagerness —**'hurriedly** *adv.*

hurst (hɜːst) *n. obs.* **1.** wood **2.** sandbank

hurt (hɜːt) *vt.* **1.** injure, damage, give pain to **2.** wound feelings of, distress —*vi.* **3.** feel pain (**hurt** *pt./pp.*) —*n.* **4.** wound, injury, harm —**'hurtful** *a.*

hurtle ('hɜːt²l) *vi.* **1.** move rapidly **2.** rush violently **3.** whirl

husband ('hʌzbənd) *n.* **1.** married man —*v.* **2.** economize, manage or use to best advantage —**'husbandry** *n.* **1.** farming **2.** economy

hush (hʌʃ) *v.* **1.** make or be silent —*n.* **2.** stillness **3.** quietness —**hush-hush** *a. inf.* secret —**hush up** suppress (rumours, information), make secret

husk (hʌsk) *n.* **1.** dry covering of certain seeds and fruits **2.** worthless outside part —*vt.* **3.** remove husk from —**'husky** *a.* **1.** rough in tone **2.** hoarse **3.** dry as husk, dry in the throat **4.** of, full of, husks **5.** *inf.* big and strong

husky ('hʌskɪ) *n.* **1.** Arctic sledgedog **2. C** *sl.* Inuit

hussar (hu'zɑː) *n.* lightly armed cavalry soldier

hussy ('hʌsɪ, -zɪ) *n.* cheeky girl or young woman

hustings ('hʌstɪŋz) *pl.n.* **1.** platform from which parliamentary candidates were nominated **2.** political campaigning

hustle ('hʌs²l) *v.* **1.** push about, jostle, hurry —*vi.* **2.** *sl.* solicit —*n.* **3.** instance of hustling —**'hustler** *n.*

hut (hʌt) *n.* any small house or shelter, usu. of wood or metal

hutch (hʌtʃ) *n.* box-like pen for rabbits *etc.*

hyacinth ('haɪəsɪnθ) *n.* 1. bulbous plant with bell-shaped flowers, *esp.* purple-blue 2. this blue 3. orange gem jacinth

hyaena (haɪ'iːnə) *n. see* HYENA

hyaline ('haɪəlɪn) *a.* clear, translucent

hybrid ('haɪbrɪd) *n.* 1. offspring of two plants or animals of different species 2. mongrel —*a.* 3. crossbred —'**hybridism** *n.* —'**hybridize** *or* -**ise** *v.* (cause to) produce hybrids; cross-breed

hydatid ('haɪdətɪd) *a./n.* (of) watery cyst, resulting from development of tapeworm larva causing serious disease (in man)

hydra ('haɪdrə) *n.* 1. fabulous many-headed water serpent 2. any persistent problem 3. freshwater polyp (*pl.* -**s**, -**drae** (-driː)) —**hydra-headed** *a.* hard to root out

hydrangea (haɪ'dreɪndʒə) *n.* ornamental shrub with pink, blue, or white flowers

hydrant ('haɪdrənt) *n.* water-pipe with nozzle for hose

hydrate ('haɪdreɪt) *n.* 1. chemical compound containing water that is chemically combined with substance —*v.* 2. (cause to) undergo treatment or impregnation with water —**hy-'dration** *n.* —'**hydrator** *n.*

hydraulic (haɪ'drɔlɪk) *a.* concerned with, operated by, pressure transmitted through liquid in pipe —**hy'draulics** *pl.n.* (*with sing. v.*) science of mechanical properties of liquid in motion

hydro ('haɪdrəu) *n.* UK hotel or resort offering facilities for hydropathic treatment (*pl.* -**s**)

Hydro ('haɪdrəu) *n.* C hydroelectric power company

hydro- *or before vowel* **hydr-** (*comb. form*) 1. water, as in *hydroelectric* 2. presence of hydrogen, as in *hydrocarbon*

hydrocarbon (haɪdrəu'kɑːbən) *n.* compound of hydrogen and carbon

hydrocephalus (haɪdrəu'sɛfələs) *or* **hydrocephaly** (haɪdrəu'sɛfəlɪ) *n.* accumulation of cerebrospinal fluid within ventricles of brain —**hydrocephalic** (haɪdrəusɛ'fælɪk) *or* **hydro-'cephalous** *a.*

hydrochloric acid (haɪdrə'klɒrɪk) strong colourless acid used in many industrial and laboratory processes

hydrocyanic acid (haɪdrəusaɪ'ænɪk) *see* **hydrogen cyanide** *at* HYDROGEN

hydrodynamics (haɪdrəudaɪ'næmɪks, -dɪ-) *pl.n.* (*with sing. v.*) science of the motions of system wholly or partly fluid

hydroelectric (haɪdrəuɪ'lɛktrɪk) *a.* pert. to generation of electricity by use of water

hydrofoil ('haɪdrəfɔɪl) *n.* fast, light vessel with hull raised out of water at speed by vanes in water

hydrogen ('haɪdrɪdʒən) *n.* colourless gas which combines with oxygen to form water —'**hydrogenate** *v.* (cause to) undergo reaction with hydrogen —**hydrogen'ation** *n.* —**hydrogen bomb** atom bomb of enormous power in which hydrogen nuclei are converted into helium nuclei —**hydrogen cyanide** colourless poisonous liquid with faint odour of bitter almonds, used for making plastics and as war gas —**hydrogen peroxide** colourless liquid used as antiseptic and bleach

hydrography (haɪ'drɒgrəfɪ) *n.* description of waters of the earth —**hy'drographer** *n.* —**hydro'graphic** *a.*

hydrology (haɪ'drɒlədʒɪ) *n.* study of distribution, use *etc.* of the water of the earth and its atmosphere —**hydrologic** (haɪdrə'lɒdʒɪk) *a.* —**hy'drologist** *n.*

hydrolysis (haɪ'drɒlɪsɪs) *n.* decomposition of chemical compound reacting with water

hydrometer (haɪ'drɒmɪtə) *n.* device for measuring relative density of liquid

hydrophilic (haɪdrəu'fɪlɪk) *a. Chem.* tending to dissolve in, mix with, or be wetted by water —'**hydrophile** *n.*

hydrophobia (haɪdrə'fəubɪə) *n.* aversion to water, esp. as symptom of rabies

hydrophone ('haɪdrəfəun) *n.* instrument for detecting sound through water

hydroplane ('haɪdrəupleɪn) *n.* 1. light skimming motorboat 2. seaplane 3. vane controlling motion of submarine *etc.*

hydroponics (haɪdrəu'pɒnɪks) *pl.n.* (*with sing. v.*) science of cultivating plants in water without using soil

hydrosphere ('haɪdrəsfɪə) *n.* watery part of earth's surface, including oceans, lakes, water vapour in atmosphere *etc.*

hydrostatics (haɪdrəu'stætɪks) *pl.n.* (*with sing. v.*) branch of science concerned with mechanical properties and behaviour of fluids that are not in motion —**hydro'static** *a.*

hydrotherapy (haɪdrəu'θɛrəpɪ) *n. Med.* treatment of disease by external application of water

hydrotropism (haɪ'drɒtrəpɪzəm) *n.* directional growth of plants in response to water

hydrous ('haɪdrəs) *a.* containing water

hydroxide (haɪ'drɒksaɪd) *n.* 1. base or alkali containing ion OH⁻ 2. any compound containing -OH group

hydrozoan (haɪdrəu'zəuən) *n.* 1. any coelenterate of the class *Hydrozoa*, which includes hydra and Portuguese man-of-war —*a.* 2. of *Hydrozoa*

hyena *or* **hyaena** (haɪ'iːnə) *n.* wild animal related to dog

hygiene ('haɪdʒiːn) *n.* 1. principles and

practice of health and cleanliness **2.** study of these principles —**hy'gienic** a. —**hy'gienically** adv. —**'hygienist** n.

hygrometer (hai'gromitə) n. instrument for measuring humidity of air

hygroscopic (haigrə'skopik) a. readily absorbing moisture from the atmosphere

hymen ('haimen) n. **1.** membrane partly covering vagina of virgin **2.** (**H-**) Greek god of marriage

hymenopterous (haimi'noptərəs) a. of large order of insects having two pairs of membranous wings —**hyme'nopteran** or **hyme'nopteron** n. any hymenopterous insect (pl. **-terans, -tera** (-tərə) or **-terons**)

hymn (him) n. **1.** song of praise, esp. to God —vt. **2.** praise in song —**hymnal** ('himnəl) n. **1.** of hymns —n. **2.** book of hymns (also **hymn book**) —**hymnodist** ('himnədist) n. —**hymnody** ('himnədi) n. singing or composition of hymns

hyoscyamine (haiə'saiəmiːn) n. poisonous alkaloid occurring in henbane and related plants and used in medicine

hype[1] (haip) n. **1.** hypodermic syringe **2.** drug addict —vi. **3.** (with up) inject oneself with drug

hype[2] (haip) sl. n. **1.** deception; racket **2.** intensive or exaggerated publicity or sales promotion —vt. **3.** market or promote, using exaggerated or intensive publicity

hyper- (comb. form) over, above, excessively, as in hyperactive. Such words are not given here where the meaning may easily be inferred from the simple word

hyperbola (hai'pɜːbələ) n. curve produced when cone is cut by plane making larger angle with the base than the side makes (pl. **-s, -le** (-liː))

hyperbole (hai'pɜːbəli) n. rhetorical exaggeration —**hyperbolic(al)** (haipə'bolik(ə)l) a.

Hyperborean (haipə'bɔːriən) a./n. (inhabitant) of extreme north

hypercritical (haipə'kritikəl) a. too critical —**hyper'criticism** n.

hyperglycaemia or U.S. **hyperglycemia** (haipəglai'siːmiə) n. Pathol. abnormally large amount of sugar in blood —**hypergly'caemic** or U.S. **hypergly'cemic** a.

hypermarket ('haipəmaːkit) n. UK huge self-service store

hyperon ('haipəron) n. Phys. any baryon that is not a nucleon

hyperopia (haipə'rəupiə) n. inability to see near objects clearly because images received by eye are focused behind retina —**hyperopic** (haipə'ropik) a.

hypersensitive (haipə'sensitiv) a. unduly vulnerable emotionally or physically

hypersonic (haipə'sonik) a. concerned with

or having velocity of at least five times that of sound in same medium under the same conditions —**hyper'sonics** n.

hypertension (haipə'tenʃən) n. abnormally high blood pressure

hypertrophy (hai'pɜːtrəfi) n. **1.** enlargement of organ or part resulting from increase in size of cells —v. **2.** (cause to) undergo this condition

hyperventilation (haipəventi'leiʃən) n. increase in rate of breathing, sometimes resulting in cramp and dizziness

hyphen ('haifən) n. short line (-) indicating that two words or syllables are to be connected —'**hyphenate** vt. —'**hyphenated** a. joined by hyphen

hypno- or before vowel **hypn-** (comb. form) **1.** sleep, as in hypnopaedia **2.** hypnosis, as in hypnotherapy

hypnosis (hip'nəusis) n. induced state like deep sleep in which subject acts on external suggestion (pl. **-ses** (-siːz)) —**hypnotic** (hip'notik) a. of hypnosis or of the person or thing producing it —'**hypnotism** n. —'**hypnotist** n. —'**hypnotize** or **-tise** vt. affect with hypnosis —**hypno'therapy** n. use of hypnosis in treatment of physical or mental disorders

hypo ('haipəu) n. sodium thiosulphate, used as fixer in developing photographs

hypo- or before vowel **hyp-** (comb. form) under, below, less, as in hypocrite, hyphen. Such words are not given here where meaning may easily be inferred from simple word

hypocaust ('haipəkɔːst) n. ancient Roman underfloor heating system

hypochondria (haipə'kondriə) n. morbid depression, without cause, about one's own health —**hypo'chondriac** a./n. —**hypochondriacal** (haipəukon'draiəkəl) a.

hypocrisy (hi'pokrəsi) n. **1.** assuming of false appearance of virtue **2.** insincerity —'**hypocrite** n. —**hypo'critical** a. —**hypo'critically** adv.

hypodermic (haipə'dɜːmik) a. **1.** introduced, injected beneath the skin —n. **2.** hypodermic syringe or needle

hypogastric (haipə'gæstrik) a. relating to, situated in, lower part of abdomen

hypostasis (hai'postəsis) n. **1.** Metaphys. essential nature of anything **2.** Christianity any of the three persons of the Godhead **3.** accumulation of blood in organ or part as result of poor circulation (pl. **-ses** (-siːz)) —**hypostatic** (haipə'stætik) or **hypo'statical** a.

hypotension (haipəu'tenʃən) n. Pathol. abnormally low blood pressure —**hypo'tensive** a.

hypotenuse (hai'potinjuːz) n. side of a right-angled triangle opposite the right angle

hypothecate (hai'poθikeit) vt. Law pledge

(personal property) as security for debt without transferring possession —**hypothe'cation** n. —**hy'pothecator** n.

hypothermia (haɪpəʊ'θɜːmɪə) n. condition of having body temperature reduced to dangerously low level

hypothesis (haɪ'pɒθɪsɪs) n. 1. suggested explanation of something 2. assumption as basis of reasoning (pl. -**eses** (-ɪsiːz)) —**hy'pothesize** or -**ise** v. —**hypo'thetical** a. —**hypo'thetically** adv.

hypso- or before vowel **hyps-** (comb. form) height, as in hypsometry

hypsography (hɪp'sɒɡrəfɪ) n. branch of geography dealing with altitudes

hypsometer (hɪp'sɒmɪtə) n. instrument for measuring altitudes —**hyp'sometry** n. science of measuring altitudes

hyrax ('haɪræks) n. genus of hoofed but rodent-like animals (pl. -**es, hyraces** ('haɪrəsiːz))

hyssop ('hɪsəp) n. small aromatic herb

hysterectomy (hɪstə'rɛktəmɪ) n. surgical operation for removing the uterus

hysteresis (hɪstə'riːsɪs) n. Phys. lag or delay in changes in variable property of a system

hysteria (hɪ'stɪərɪə) n. 1. mental disorder with emotional outbursts 2. any frenzied emotional state 3. fit of crying or laughing —**hysterical** (hɪ'stɛrɪkᵊl) a. —**hysterically** (hɪ'stɛrɪkəlɪ) adv. —**hysterics** (hɪ'stɛrɪks) pl.n. fits of hysteria

Hz hertz

I,i

i or **I** (aɪ) n. 1. ninth letter of English alphabet 2. any of several speech sounds represented by this letter 3. something shaped like I (pl. **i's, I's** or **Is**) —**dot one's i's and cross one's t's** pay attention to detail

I (aɪ) pron. the pronoun of the first person singular

I 1. Chem. iodine 2. Phys. current 3. Phys. isospin 4. Roman numeral, one

IA Iowa

-ia (comb. form) 1. in place names, as in Columbia 2. in names of diseases, as in pneumonia 3. in words denoting condition or quality, as in utopia 4. in names of botanical genera and zoological classes, as in Reptilia 5. in collective nouns borrowed from Latin, as in regalia

IAEA International Atomic Energy Agency

-ial (comb. form) of or relating to, as in managerial

iamb ('aɪæm, 'aɪæmb) or **iambus** (aɪ'æmbəs)

n. metrical foot of short and long syllable (pl. '**iambs** or -**buses, -bi** (-baɪ)) —**i'ambic** a.

IATA (aɪ'ɑːtə, iː'ɑːtə) International Air Transport Association

iatric (aɪ'ætrɪk) or **iatrical** a. of medicine or physicians, esp. as suffix -**iatrics, -iatry**, as in paediatrics, psychiatry

I.B.A. Independent Broadcasting Authority

Iberian (aɪ'bɪərɪən) a. of Iberia, ie Spain and Portugal

ibex ('aɪbɛks) n. wild goat with large horns (pl. -**es, ibices** ('ɪbɪsiːz, 'aɪ-), '**ibex**)

ibid. or **ib.** ibidem (Lat., in the same place)

ibis ('aɪbɪs) n. storklike bird

-ible (a. comb. form) see -**ABLE** —**ibility** (n. comb. form) —**ibly** (adv. comb. form)

IBM International Business Machines Corporation

i/c 1. in charge (of) 2. internal combustion

-ic (comb. form) 1. of, relating to or resembling, as in periodic (also -**ical**) 2. Chem. indicating that element is chemically combined in higher of two possible valence states, as in ferric

I.C.A. 1. UK Institute of Contemporary Arts 2. Institute of Chartered Accountants

-ical (a. comb. form) see -**IC** (sense 1) —**ically** (adv. comb. form)

ICBM intercontinental ballistic missile

ice (aɪs) n. 1. frozen water 2. frozen confection, ice cream —v. 3. (oft. with up, over etc.) cover, become covered with ice —vt. 4. cool with ice 5. cover with icing —'**icicle** n. tapering spike of ice hanging where water has dripped —'**icily** adv. —'**iciness** n. —'**icing** n. mixture of sugar and water etc. used to decorate cakes —'**icy** a. 1. covered with ice 2. cold 3. chilling —**ice age** see **glacial period** at GLACIER —'**iceberg** n. large floating mass of ice —'**icebox** n. 1. compartment in refrigerator for storing or making ice 2. insulated cabinet packed with ice for storing food —'**icebreaker** n. 1. vessel for breaking up ice in bodies of water (also '**iceboat**) 2. device for breaking ice into smaller pieces —'**icecap** n. mass of glacial ice that permanently covers polar regions etc. —**ice cream** sweetened frozen dessert made from cream, eggs etc. —**ice floe** sheet of floating ice —**ice hockey** team game played on ice with puck —**ice lolly** ice cream, flavoured ice on stick —**ice pack** 1. bag etc. containing ice, applied to part of body to reduce swelling etc. 2. see **pack ice** at PACK —**ice skate** boot having steel blade fitted to sole to enable wearer to glide over ice —**ice-skate** vi. glide over ice on ice skates —**ice-skater** n. —**on thin ice** unsafe; vulnerable

I.C.E. UK Institution of Civil Engineers

Icelandic (aɪsˈlændɪk) a. 1. of Iceland —n. 2. official language of Iceland

I.Chem.E. Institution of Chemical Engineers

ichneumon (ɪkˈnjuːmən) n. greyish-brown mongoose

ichor (ˈaɪkɔː) n. 1. Gr. myth. fluid said to flow in veins of gods 2. Pathol. foul-smelling watery discharge from wound or ulcer —**ichorous** a.

ichthyology (ɪkθɪˈɒlədʒɪ) n. scientific study of fish —**ichthyosaurus** (ɪkθɪəˈsɔːrəs) n. prehistoric marine animal (pl. -i (-aɪ))

I.C.I. Imperial Chemical Industries

icicle (ˈaɪsɪkəl) n. see ICE

icon or **ikon** (ˈaɪkɒn) n. image, representation, esp. of religious figure —**iʹconoclasm** n. —iʹconoclast n. 1. one who attacks established principles etc. 2. breaker of icons —iconoʹclastic a. —icoʹnography n. 1. icons collectively 2. study of icons

icono- or before vowel **icon-** (comb. form) image; likeness, as in iconology

ictus (ˈɪktəs) n. 1. Prosody metrical or rhythmical stress in verse feet, as contrasted with stress accent on words 2. Med. sudden attack or stroke (pl. -es, -tus) —ʹictal a.

id (ɪd) n. Psychoanal. the mind's instinctive energies

ID 1. identification 2. Idaho

-id (comb. form) member of zoological family, as in cyprinid

-idae (comb. form) name of zoological family, as in Felidae

idea (aɪˈdɪə) n. 1. notion in the mind 2. conception 3. vague belief 4. plan, aim —iʹdeal n. 1. conception of something that is perfect 2. perfect person or thing —a. 3. perfect 4. visionary 5. existing only in idea —iʹdeaism n. 1. tendency to seek perfection in everything 2. philosophy that mind is the only reality —iʹdealist n. 1. one who holds doctrine of idealism 2. one who strives after the ideal 3. impractical person —idealʹistic a. —idealiʹzation or -iʹsation n. —iʹdealize or -ise vt. portray as ideal —iʹdeally adv.

idée fixe (ide ˈfiks) Fr. fixed idea; obsession (pl. idées fixes (ide ˈfiks))

idem (ˈaɪdɛm, ˈɪdɛm) Lat., the same

identity (aɪˈdɛntɪtɪ) n. 1. individuality 2. being the same, exactly alike —iʹdentical a. very same —iʹdentically adv. —iʹdentifiable a. —identifiʹcation n. —iʹdentify vt. 1. establish identity of 2. treat as identical —v. 3. associate (oneself) (iʹdentified, iʹdentifying) —identification parade group of persons assembled for purpose of discovering whether witness can identify suspect —iʹdentikit n. R set of pictures of parts of faces that can be built up to form likeness of person sought by police etc.

ideo- (comb. form) idea; ideas, as in ideology

ideogram (ˈɪdɪəʊgræm) or **ideograph** (ˈɪdɪəʊɡrɑːf) n. picture, symbol, figure etc. suggesting an object without naming it —ideʹography n. representation of things by ideographs

ideology (aɪdɪˈɒlədʒɪ) n. body of ideas, beliefs of group, nation etc. —ideoʹlogical a.

ides (aɪdz) n. the 15th of March, May, July and Oct. and the 13th of other months of the Ancient Roman calendar

id est (ɪd ɛst) Lat., that is

idiocy (ˈɪdɪəsɪ) n. see IDIOT

idiom (ˈɪdɪəm) n. 1. way of expression natural or peculiar to a language or group 2. characteristic style of expression —idioʹmatic a. 1. using idioms 2. colloquial

idiosyncrasy (ɪdɪəˈsɪŋkrəsɪ) n. peculiarity of mind, temper or disposition in a person

idiot (ˈɪdɪət) n. 1. mentally deficient person 2. foolish, senseless person —ʹidiocy n. 1. state of being an idiot 2. foolish act or remark —idiʹotic a. utterly senseless or stupid —idiʹotically adv. —idiot board sl. autocue

idle (ˈaɪdəl) a. 1. unemployed 2. lazy 3. useless; vain 4. groundless —vi. 5. be idle 6. (of engine) run slowly with gears disengaged —vt. 7. (esp. with away) waste —ʹidleness n. —ʹidler n. —ʹidly adv.

idol (ˈaɪdəl) n. 1. image of deity as object of worship 2. object of excessive devotion —iʹdolater n. worshipper of idols (iʹdolatress fem.) —iʹdolatrous a. —iʹdolatry n. —ʹidolize or -ise vt. 1. love or venerate to excess 2. make an idol of

idyll or U.S. (sometimes) **idyl** (ˈɪdɪl) n. 1. short descriptive poem of picturesque or charming scene or episode, esp. of rustic life 2. charming or picturesque scene or event —iʹdyllic a. 1. of, like, idyll 2. delightful —iʹdyllically adv.

i.e. id est

I.E.E. Institution of Electrical Engineers

if (ɪf) conj. 1. on condition or supposition that 2. whether 3. although —n. 4. uncertainty, doubt (esp. in ifs and buts)

-iferous (comb. form) containing, yielding, as in carboniferous

igloo or **iglu** (ˈɪgluː) n. dome-shaped Eskimo house of snow and ice

igneous (ˈɪgnɪəs) a. (esp. of rocks) formed as molten rock cools and hardens

ignis fatuus (ˈɪgnɪs ˈfætjʊəs) will-o'-the-wisp (pl. ignes fatui (ˈɪgniːz ˈfætjʊaɪ))

ignite (ɪgˈnaɪt) v. (cause to) burn —**ignition** (ɪgˈnɪʃən) n. 1. act of kindling or setting on fire 2. in internal-combustion engine, means of firing explosive mixture, usu. electric spark

ignoble (ɪgˈnəʊbəl) a. 1. mean, base 2. of low birth —**ig'nobly** adv.

ignominy (ˈɪgnəmɪnɪ) n. 1. dishonour, disgrace 2. shameful act —**igno'minious** a.

ignore (ɪgˈnɔː) vt. disregard; leave out of account —**ignoramus** (ɪgnəˈreɪməs) n. ignorant person (pl. **-es**) —**'ignorance** n. lack of knowledge —**'ignorant** a. 1. lacking knowledge 2. uneducated 3. unaware —**'ignorantly** adv.

iguana (ɪˈgwɑːnə) n. large tropical American lizard

ikebana (iːkəˈbɑːnə) n. Japanese decorative art of flower arrangement

ikon (ˈaɪkɒn) n. see ICON

IL Illinois

il- (comb. form) see IN-

ileum (ˈɪlɪəm) n. lower part of small intestine —**'ileac** a.

ilex (ˈaɪlɛks) n. any of genus of trees or shrubs such as holly and inkberry

ilium (ˈɪlɪəm) n. uppermost and widest of three sections of hipbone (pl. **-ia** (-ɪə)) —**'iliac** a.

ilk (ɪlk) a. same —**of that ilk** 1. of the same type or class 2. Scot. of the place of the same name

ill (ɪl) a. 1. not in good health 2. bad, evil 3. faulty 4. unfavourable —n. 5. evil, harm 6. mild disease —adv. 7. badly 8. hardly, with difficulty —**'illness** n. —**ill-advised** a. imprudent, injudicious —**ill-bred** a. badly brought up; lacking good manners —**ill-considered** a. done without due consideration; not thought out —**ill-disposed** a. (oft. with towards) not kindly disposed —**ill fame** bad reputation —**ill-fated** a. unfortunate —**ill-favoured** a. ugly, deformed —**ill-founded** a. not founded on true or reliable premises; unsubstantiated —**ill-gotten** a. obtained dishonestly —**ill-mannered** a. boorish, uncivil —**ill-natured** a. naturally unpleasant and mean —**ill-omened** a. unlucky, inauspicious —**ill-starred** a. unlucky, ill-fated —**ill-timed** a. inopportune —**ill-treat** vt. treat cruelly —**ill-use** (ˈɪlˈjuːz) vt. 1. use badly or cruelly; abuse —n. (ˈɪlˈjuːs), also **ill-usage** 2. harsh or cruel treatment; abuse —**ill will** unkind feeling, hostility —**house of ill fame** brothel

illegal (ɪˈliːgəl) a. 1. forbidden by law; unlawful; illicit 2. unauthorized or prohibited by code of official or accepted rules —**ille'gality** n. —**il'legally** adv.

illegible (ɪˈlɛdʒɪbəl) a. unable to be read or deciphered —**illegi'bility** or **il'legibleness** n.

illegitimate (ɪlɪˈdʒɪtɪmɪt) a. 1. born out of wedlock 2. unlawful 3. not regular —**ille'gitimacy** n.

illiberal (ɪˈlɪbərəl) a. 1. narrow-minded; prejudiced; intolerant 2. not generous; mean 3. lacking in culture or refinement —**illiber'ality** n.

illicit (ɪˈlɪsɪt) a. 1. illegal 2. prohibited, forbidden

illimitable (ɪˈlɪmɪtəbəl) a. that cannot be limited, boundless, unrestricted, infinite —**il-'limitableness** n.

illiterate (ɪˈlɪtərɪt) a. 1. not literate, unable to read or write 2. violating accepted standards in reading and writing 3. uneducated, ignorant, uncultured —n. 4. illiterate person —**il'literacy** n.

illogical (ɪˈlɒdʒɪkəl) a. 1. characterized by lack of logic; senseless; unreasonable 2. disregarding logical principles —**illogi'cality** or **il'logicalness** n. —**il'logically** adv.

illuminate (ɪˈluːmɪneɪt) vt. 1. light up 2. clarify 3. decorate with lights 4. decorate with gold and colours —**il'luminant** n. agent of lighting —**illumi'nation** n. —**il'luminative** a.

illusion (ɪˈluːʒən) n. deceptive appearance or belief —**il'lusionist** n. conjuror —**il'lusory** or **il'lusive** a. false

illust. or **illus.** 1. illustrated 2. illustration

illustrate (ˈɪləstreɪt) vt. 1. provide with pictures or examples 2. exemplify —**illus'tra-tion** n. 1. picture, diagram 2. example 3. act of illustrating —**'illustrative** a. providing explana-tion —**'illustrator** n.

illustrious (ɪˈlʌstrɪəs) a. famous, distinguished, exalted

I.L.O. International Labour Organization

I.L.P. Independent Labour Party

im- (comb. form) see IN-

image (ˈɪmɪdʒ) n. 1. representation or likeness of person or thing 2. optical counterpart, as in mirror 3. double, copy 4. general impression 5. mental picture created by words, esp. in literature 6. personality presented to the public by a person —vt. rare 7. make image of 8. reflect —**'imagery** n. images collectively, esp. in literature

imagine (ɪˈmædʒɪn) vt. 1. picture to oneself 2. think 3. conjecture —**i'maginable** a. —**i'magi-nary** a. existing only in fancy —**imagi'nation** n. 1. faculty of making mental images of things not present 2. fancy —**im'aginative** a. —**im'agina-tively** adv.

imago (ɪˈmeɪgəʊ) n. last, perfected state of insect life 2. image (pl. **-s**, **imagines** (ɪˈmædʒɪniːz))

imam (ɪˈmɑːm) n. Islamic minister or priest

imbalance (ɪmˈbæləns) n. lack of balance, proportion

imbecile (ˈɪmbɪsiːl, -saɪl) n. 1. idiot —a. 2. idiotic —**imbecility** (ɪmbɪˈsɪlɪtɪ) n.

imbed (ɪmˈbɛd) vt. see EMBED

imbibe (ɪmˈbaɪb) vt. 1. drink in 2. absorb —vi. 3. drink

imbricate (ˈɪmbrɪkɪt, -keɪt) a. lying over each

other in regular order, like tiles or shingles on roof (*also* **imbricated**) —**imbri'cation** *n.*

imbroglio (ım'brəuliəʊ) *n.* complicated situation, plot (*pl.* **-s**)

imbue (ım'bjuː) *vt.* inspire

I. Mech. E. Institution of Mechanical Engineers

IMF International Monetary Fund

imitate ('ımıteıt) *vt.* 1. take as model 2. mimic, copy —**imitable** *a.* —**imi'tation** *n.* 1. act of imitating 2. copy of original 3. likeness 4. counterfeit —**imitative** *a.* —**imitator** *n.*

immaculate (ı'mækjulıt) *a.* 1. spotless 2. pure 3. unsullied

immanent ('ımənənt) *a.* existing within, inherent —**immanence** *n.*

immaterial (ımə'tıərıəl) *a.* 1. unimportant, trifling 2. not consisting of matter 3. spiritual

immeasurable (ı'mεʒərəbəl) *a.* incapable of being measured, *esp.* by virtue of great size; limitless —**immeasura'bility** *or* **im'measurableness** *n.* —**im'measurably** *adv.*

immediate (ı'miːdɪət) *a.* 1. occurring at once 2. direct, not separated by others —**im'mediacy** *n.* —**im'mediately** *adv.*

immemorial (ımı'mɔːrɪəl) *a.* beyond memory

immense (ı'mεns) *a.* huge, vast —**im'mensely** *adv.* —**im'mensity** *n.* vastness

immerse (ı'mɜːs) *vt.* 1. dip, plunge into liquid 2. involve, engross —**im'mersion** *n.* immersing —**immersion heater** *or* **im'merser** *n.* electric appliance for heating liquid in which it is immersed

immigrate ('ımıgreıt) *vi.* come into country as settler —**'immigrant** *n./a.* —**immi'gration** *n.*

imminent ('ımınənt) *a.* 1. liable to happen soon 2. close at hand —**'imminence** *n.* —**'imminently** *adv.*

immobilize *or* **-ise** (ı'məʊbılaız) *vt.* 1. make immobile 2. *Fin.* convert (circulating capital) into fixed capital —**immobili'zation** *or* **-i'sation** *n.* —**im'mobilizer** *or* **-iser** *n.*

immolate ('ıməʊleıt) *vt.* kill, sacrifice —**immo'lation** *n.*

immoral (ı'mɒrəl) *a.* 1. corrupt 2. promiscuous 3. indecent 4. unethical —**immo'rality** *n.*

immortal (ı'mɔːtəl) *a.* 1. deathless 2. famed for all time —*n.* 3. immortal being 4. god 5. one whose fame will last —**immor'tality** *n.* —**im'mortalize** *or* **-ise** *vt.*

immune (ı'mjuːn) *a.* 1. proof (against a disease *etc.*) 2. secure 3. exempt —**im'munity** *n.* 1. state of being immune 2. freedom from prosecution, tax *etc.* —**immuni'zation** *or* **-ni'sation** *n.* process of making immune to disease —**'immunize** *or* **-nise** *vt.* make immune —**immu'nology** *n.* branch of biology concerned with study of immunity

immure (ı'mjʊə) *vt.* imprison, wall up

immutable (ı'mjuːtəbəl) *a.* unchangeable

imp (ımp) *n.* 1. little devil 2. mischievous child —**'impish** *a.* of or like an imp; mischievous

imp. 1. imperative 2. imperfect

impact ('ımpækt) *n.* 1. collision 2. profound effect —*vt.* (ım'pækt) 3. drive, press —**im'pacted** *a.* 1. (of tooth) wedged against another tooth below gum 2. (of fracture) having jagged broken ends wedged into each other

impair (ım'pεə) *vt.* weaken, damage —**im'pairment** *n.*

impala (ım'pɑːlə) *n.* antelope of S Afr.

impale *or* **empale** (ım'peıl) *vt.* 1. pierce with sharp instrument 2. combine (two coats of arms) by placing them side by side with line between —**im'palement** *or* **em'palement** *n.*

impanel (ım'pænl) *vt. esp.* US *see* EMPANEL

impart (ım'pɑːt) *vt.* 1. communicate (information *etc.*) 2. give

impartial (ım'pɑːʃəl) *a.* 1. not biased or prejudiced 2. fair —**imparti'ality** *n.*

impassable (ım'pɑːsəbəl) *a.* 1. not capable of being passed 2. blocked, as mountain pass

impasse (ım'pɑːs, æm'pɑːs) *n.* 1. deadlock 2. place, situation, from which there is no outlet

impassible (ım'pæsəbəl) *a. rare* 1. not susceptible to pain or injury 2. impassive; unmoved —**impassi'bility** *or* **im'passibleness** *n.*

impassioned (ım'pæʃənd) *a.* deeply moved, ardent

impassive (ım'pæsıv) *a.* 1. showing no emotion 2. calm —**impas'sivity** *n.*

impasto (ım'pæstəʊ) *n.* 1. paint applied thickly, so that brush marks are evident 2. technique of painting in this way

impeach (ım'piːtʃ) *vt.* 1. charge with crime 2. call to account 3. denounce —**im'peachable** *a.* —**im'peachment** *n.*

impeccable (ım'pεkəbəl) *a.* without flaw or error —**impecca'bility** *n.*

impecunious (ımpı'kjuːnıəs) *a.* poor —**impecuni'osity** *n.*

impede (ım'piːd) *vt.* hinder —**im'pedance** *n.* *Elec.* measure of opposition offered to flow of alternating current —**impediment** (ım'pεdımənt) *n.* 1. obstruction 2. defect —**impedimenta** (ımpεdı'mεntə) *pl.n.* 1. any objects that impede progress, *esp.* baggage and equipment carried by army 2. *Law* obstructions to making of contract, *esp.* of marriage

impel (ım'pεl) *vt.* 1. induce, incite 2. drive, force (**-ll-**) —**im'peller** *n.*

impend (ım'pεnd) *vi.* 1. threaten, be imminent 2. (*with* over) *rare* hang —**im'pending** *a.*

impenitent (ım'pεnıtənt) *a.* not sorry or penitent; unrepentant —**im'penitence** *n.*

imperative (ɪmˈpɛrətɪv) a. 1. necessary 2. peremptory 3. expressing command —n. 4. imperative mood —im'**peratively** adv.

imperceptible (ɪmpəˈsɛptɪbəl) a. too slight, subtle, gradual etc. to be perceived —impercep'ti'bility n. —imper'ceptibly adv.

imperfect (ɪmˈpɜːfɪkt) a. 1. exhibiting or characterized by faults, mistakes etc., defective 2. not complete or finished; deficient 3. Gram. denoting tense of verbs usu. used to describe continuous or repeated past actions or events 4. Law legally unenforceable 5. Mus. proceeding to dominant from tonic, subdominant or any chord other than dominant 6. Mus. of or relating to all intervals other than fourth, fifth and octave —n. 7. Gram. (verb in) imperfect tense —imper'fection n. 1. condition or quality of being imperfect 2. fault, defect

imperial (ɪmˈpɪərɪəl) a. 1. of empire or emperor 2. majestic 3. denoting weights and measures established by law in Brit. —im'perialism n. 1. extension of empire 2. belief in colonial empire —im'perialist a./n. —imperial'istic a.

imperil (ɪmˈpɛrɪl) vt. bring into peril, endanger (-ll-)

imperious (ɪmˈpɪərɪəs) a. domineering; haughty; dictatorial

impermeable (ɪmˈpɜːmɪəbəl) a. (of substance) not allowing passage of fluid through interstices —impermea'bility n.

impersonal (ɪmˈpɜːsənəl) a. 1. objective, having no personal significance 2. devoid of human warmth, personality etc. 3. (of verb) without personal subject —imperson'ality n.

impersonate (ɪmˈpɜːsəneɪt) vt. 1. pretend to be (another person) 2. imitate 3. play the part of —imperson'ation n. —im'personator n.

impertinent (ɪmˈpɜːtɪnənt) a. insolent, rude —im'pertinence n. —im'pertinently adv.

imperturbable (ɪmpəˈtɜːbəbəl) a. calm, not excitable —imper'turbably adv.

impervious (ɪmˈpɜːvɪəs) or **imperviable** a. 1. not affording passage 2. (oft. with to) not receptive (to feeling, argument etc.) —im'perviously adv. —im'perviousness n.

impetigo (ɪmpɪˈtaɪgəʊ) n. contagious skin disease

impetuous (ɪmˈpɛtjʊəs) a. likely to act without consideration, rash —impetu'osity n. —im'petuously adv.

impetus (ˈɪmpɪtəs) n. 1. force with which body moves 2. impulse

impinge (ɪmˈpɪndʒ) vi. 1. (usu. with on or upon) encroach 2. (usu. with on, against or upon) collide (with) —im'pingement n.

impious (ˈɪmpɪəs) a. irreverent, profane, wicked —impiety (ɪmˈpaɪɪtɪ) n. 1. lack of

reverence or proper respect for a god 2. any lack of proper respect 3. impious act

implacable (ɪmˈplækəbəl) a. 1. not to be appeased 2. unyielding —implaca'bility n.

implant (ɪmˈplɑːnt) vt. 1. insert, fix —n. (ˈɪmplɑːnt) 2. anything implanted, esp. surgically, such as tissue graft

implement (ˈɪmplɪmənt) n. 1. tool, instrument, utensil —vt. 2. carry out (instructions etc.); put into effect

implicate (ˈɪmplɪkeɪt) vt. 1. involve, include 2. imply 3. rare entangle —impli'cation n. something implied —im'plicit a. 1. implied but not expressed 2. absolute and unreserved

implode (ɪmˈpləʊd) v. collapse inwards

implore (ɪmˈplɔː) vt. entreat earnestly

imply (ɪmˈplaɪ) vt. 1. indicate by hint, suggest 2. mean (im'plied, im'plying)

impolitic (ɪmˈpɒlɪtɪk) a. not politic or expedient —im'politicly adv.

imponderable (ɪmˈpɒndərəbəl, -drəbəl) a. 1. unable to be weighed or assessed —n. 2. something difficult or impossible to assess —impondera'bility n. —im'ponderably adv.

import (ɪmˈpɔːt, ˈɪmpɔːt) vt. 1. bring in, introduce (esp. goods from foreign country) 2. imply —n. (ˈɪmpɔːt) 3. thing imported 4. meaning 5. importance 6. C sl. sportsman not native to area where he plays —im'portable a. —impor'tation n. —im'porter n.

important (ɪmˈpɔːtənt) a. 1. of great consequence 2. momentous 3. pompous —im'portance n. —im'portantly adv.

importune (ɪmˈpɔːtjuːn) vt. request, demand of (someone) persistently —im'portunate a. persistent —im'portunately adv. —impor'tunity n.

impose (ɪmˈpəʊz) vt. 1. levy (tax, duty etc.) —vi. 2. (usu. with on or upon) take advantage (of), practise deceit (on) —im'posing a. impressive —impo'sition n. 1. that which is imposed 2. tax 3. burden 4. deception —'impost n. duty, tax on imports

impossible (ɪmˈpɒsəbəl) a. 1. incapable of being done or experienced 2. absurd 3. unreasonable —impossi'bility n. —im'possibly adv.

impost (ˈɪmpəʊst) n. Archit. member at top of column that supports arch

impostor or **imposter** (ɪmˈpɒstə) n. deceiver, one who assumes false identity —im'posture n.

impotent (ˈɪmpətənt) a. 1. powerless 2. (of males) incapable of sexual intercourse —'impotence n. —'impotently adv.

impound (ɪmˈpaʊnd) vt. 1. take legal possession of and, oft., place in a pound (cars, animals etc.) 2. confiscate

impoverish or **empoverish** (ɪmˈpɒvərɪʃ) vt. make poor or weak —im'poverishment or em'poverishment n.

impracticable (ɪmˈpræktɪkəbˀl) a. 1. incapable of being put into practice or accomplished 2. unsuitable for desired use —impractica'bility n. —im'practicably adv.

impractical (ɪmˈpræktɪkˀl) a. 1. not practical or workable 2. not gifted with practical skills —impracti'cality n. —im'practically adv.

imprecation (ɪmprɪˈkeɪʃən) n. 1. invoking of evil 2. curse —'imprecate v.

impregnable (ɪmˈprɛgnəbˀl) a. 1. proof against attack 2. unassailable 3. unable to be broken into —impregna'bility n. —im'pregnably adv.

impregnate ('ɪmprɛgneɪt) vt. 1. saturate, infuse 2. make pregnant —impreg'nation n.

impresario (ɪmprɪˈsɑːrɪəʊ) n. organizer of public entertainment; manager of opera, ballet etc. (pl. -s)

impress[1] (ɪmˈprɛs) vt. 1. affect deeply, usu. favourably 2. imprint, stamp 3. fix —n. ('ɪmprɛs) 4. act of impressing 5. mark impressed —impressi'bility a. —im'pressible a. —im'pression n. 1. effect produced, esp. on mind 2. notion, belief 3. imprint 4. a printing 5. total of copies printed at once 6. printed copy —impressiona'bility n. —im'pressionable a. susceptible to external influences —im'pressionism n. art style that renders general effect without detail —im'pressionist n. —impres'sion'istic a. —im'pressive a. making deep impression

impress[2] (ɪmˈprɛs) vt. press into service

imprest (ɪmˈprɛst) vt. 1. advance on loan by government —n. 2. money advanced by government

imprimatur (ɪmprɪˈmeɪtə, -ˈmɑː-) n. licence to print book etc.

imprint ('ɪmprɪnt) n. 1. mark made by pressure 2. characteristic mark 3. publisher's or printer's name and address in book etc. —vt. (ɪmˈprɪnt) 4. produce (mark) on (surface) by pressure, printing or stamping 5. fix in mind

imprison (ɪmˈprɪzən) vt. put in prison —im'prisonment n.

improbity (ɪmˈprəʊbɪtɪ) n. dishonesty, wickedness, unscrupulousness

impromptu (ɪmˈprɒmptjuː) adv./a. 1. extempore; unrehearsed —n. 2. improvisation

improper (ɪmˈprɒpə) a. 1. lacking propriety; not seemly or fitting 2. unsuitable for certain use or occasion; inappropriate 3. irregular; abnormal —impropriety (ɪmprəˈpraɪɪtɪ) n. 1. lack of propriety; indecency 2. improper act or use 3. state of being improper —improper fraction

fraction in which numerator is greater than denominator, as 7/6

improve (ɪmˈpruːv) v. make or become better in quality, standard, value etc. —im'provable a. —im'provement n. —im'prover n.

improvident (ɪmˈprɒvɪdənt) a. 1. thriftless; imprudent 2. negligent —im'providence n.

improvise ('ɪmprəvaɪz) v. 1. perform or make quickly from materials at hand 2. perform (poem, piece of music etc.), composing as one goes along —improvi'sation n.

impudent ('ɪmpjʊdənt) a. disrespectful, impertinent —'impudence n. —'impudently adv.

impugn (ɪmˈpjuːn) vt. call in question, challenge

impulse ('ɪmpʌls) n. 1. sudden inclination to act 2. sudden application of force 3. motion caused by it 4. stimulation of nerve moving muscle —im'pulsion n. impulse —im'pulsive a. given to acting without reflection, rash

impunity (ɪmˈpjuːnɪtɪ) n. freedom, exemption from injurious consequences or punishment

impurity (ɪmˈpjʊərɪtɪ) n. 1. quality of being impure 2. impure thing or element 3. Electron. small quantity of element added to pure semiconductor crystal to control its electrical conductivity

impute (ɪmˈpjuːt) vt. ascribe, attribute —imputa'bility n. —impu'tation n. 1. that which is imputed as a charge or fault 2. reproach, censure

in (ɪn) prep. 1. expresses inclusion within limits of space, time, circumstance, sphere etc. —adv. 2. in or into some state, place etc. 3. inf. in vogue etc. —a. 4. inf. fashionable —in for about to be affected by —ins and outs intricacies, complications; details

In Chem. indium

IN Indiana

in. inch(es)

in-[1], **il-**, **im-**, or **ir-** (comb. form) 1. not; non-, as in incredible, illegal, imperfect, irregular 2. lack of, as in inexperience. See the list on page 256

in-[2], **il-**, **im-**, or **ir-** (comb. form) 1. in; into; towards; within; on, as in infiltrate, immigrate 2. having intensive or causative function, as in inflame, imperil

in absentia (ɪn æbˈsɛntɪə) Lat. in absence of (someone indicated)

inadvertent (ɪnədˈvɜːtənt) a. 1. not attentive 2. negligent 3. unintentional —inad'vertence or inad'vertency n. —inad'vertently adv.

inalienable (ɪnˈeɪljənəbˀl) a. not able to be transferred to another —inaliena'bility n.

inamorata (ɪnæməˈrɑːtə) or (masc.) **inamorato** (ɪnæməˈrɑːtəʊ) n. person with whom one is in love; lover (pl. -s)

inane (ɪ'neɪn) *a.* foolish, silly, vacant —**inanition** (ɪnə'nɪʃən) *n.* **1.** exhaustion **2.** silliness —**inanity** (ɪ'nænɪtɪ) *n.*

inanimate (ɪn'ænɪmɪt) *a.* **1.** lacking qualities of living beings **2.** appearing dead **3.** lacking vitality

inapposite (ɪn'æpəzɪt) *a.* not appropriate or pertinent

inapt (ɪn'æpt) *a.* **1.** not apt or fitting **2.** lacking skill; inept —**in'aptitude** *or* **in'aptness** *n.*

inasmuch as (ɪnəz'mʌtʃ) seeing that

inaugurate (ɪn'ɔːɡjʊreɪt) *vt.* **1.** begin, initiate the use of, *esp.* with ceremony **2.** admit to office —**in'augural** *a.* —**in'augurally** *adv.* —**inaugu-'ration** *n.* **1.** act of inaugurating **2.** ceremony to celebrate the initiation or admittance of

inauspicious (ɪnɔː'spɪʃəs) *a.* not auspicious; unlucky; unfavourable —**inaus'piciously** *adv.*

inboard ('ɪnbɔːd) *a.* inside hull or bulwarks

inborn ('ɪn'bɔːn) *a.* existing from birth; inherent

inbreed (ɪn'briːd) *v.* breed from union of closely related individuals ('**in'bred** *pt./pp.*) —'**in'bred** *a.* **1.** produced as result of inbreeding **2.** inborn, ingrained —'**in'breeding** *n.*

inc. 1. inclusive **2.** incorporated **3.** increase

incalculable (ɪn'kælkjʊləbəl) *a.* beyond calculation; very great

in camera in secret or private session

incandescent (ɪnkæn'dɛsənt) *a.* **1.** glowing with heat, shining **2.** (of artificial light) produced by glowing filament —**incan'desce** *vi.* glow —**incan'descence** *n.*

incantation (ɪnkæn'teɪʃən) *n.* magic spell or formula, charm

incapacitate (ɪnkə'pæsɪteɪt) *vt.* **1.** disable; make unfit **2.** disqualify —**inca'pacity** *n.*

incarcerate (ɪn'kɑːsəreɪt) *vt.* imprison —**in-carce'ration** *n.* —**in'carcerator** *n.*

incarnate (ɪn'kɑːneɪt) *vt.* **1.** embody in flesh, *esp.* in human form —*a.* (ɪn'kɑːnɪt, -neɪt) **2.** embodied in flesh, in human form **3.** typified —**incar'nation** *n.*

incendiary (ɪn'sɛndɪərɪ) *a.* **1.** of malicious setting on fire of property **2.** creating strife, violence *etc.* **3.** designed to cause fires —*n.* **4.** fire raiser **5.** agitator **6.** bomb filled with inflammatory substance —**in'cendiarism** *n.*

incense[1] ('ɪnsɛns) *n.* **1.** gum, spice giving perfume when burned **2.** its smoke —*vt.* **3.** burn incense to **4.** perfume with it

incense[2] (ɪn'sɛns) *vt.* enrage

incentive (ɪn'sɛntɪv) *n.* **1.** something that arouses to effort or action **2.** stimulus

inception (ɪn'sɛpʃən) *n.* beginning

incessant (ɪn'sɛsənt) *a.* unceasing

incest ('ɪnsɛst) *n.* sexual intercourse between two people too closely related to marry —**in'cestuous** *a.*

inch[1] (ɪntʃ) *n.* **1.** one twelfth of foot, or 0.0254 metre —*v.* **2.** move very slowly

inch[2] (ɪntʃ) *n.* Scot., Irish small island

imma·ture	in·applicable
im·miscible	inap·propriate
im·mobile	inar·ticulate
im·moderate	inar·tistic
im·modest	inat·tentive
im·mov(e)able	in·audible
im·palpable	in·capable
im·patience	in·comparable
im·patient	incom·patible
im·penetrable	incom·plete
im·permanent	incompre·hensible
imper·missible	incon·clusive
im·plausible	incon·siderable
impo·lite	incon·siderate
impre·cise	incon·sistent
im·probable	incon·solable
im·prudent	incon·spicuous
im·pure	incon·stant
ina·bility	incon·testable
inac·cessible	in·continent
in·accurate	incon·venience
in·adequate	incon·venient
inad·missible	incor·rect
inad·visable	incor·ruptible
in·curable	inex·tinguishable
inde·cipherable	in·fertile
inde·cision	infer·tility
inde·cisive	in·formal
inde·finable	in·frequent
in·definite	in·gratitude
inde·structible	in·hospitable
indis·cernible	inju·dicious
indis·putable	inof·fensive
indis·tinct	in·sanitary
indis·tinguishable	in·sensitive
inef·ficient	in·separable
ine·lastic	insig·nificant
in·elegant	insin·cere
in·equable	in·soluble
in·equitable	in·solvent
ines·sential	insta·bility
inex·act	insub·stantial
inex·cusable	insuf·ficient
inex·pedient	insur·mountable
inex·pensive	in·tangible
inex·perience	in·tolerable
inex·perienced	in·tolerant
in·expert	in·variable

inchoate (ɪnˈkəʊeɪt, -ˈkəʊɪt) a. 1. just begun 2. undeveloped

incident (ˈɪnsɪdənt) n. 1. event, occurrence —a. (usu. with to) 2. naturally attaching (to) 3. striking, falling (upon) —ˈincidence n. 1. degree, extent or frequency of occurrence 2. a falling on, or affecting —inciˈdental a. occurring as a minor part or an inevitable accompaniment or by chance —inciˈdentally adv. 1. by chance 2. by the way —inciˈdentals pl.n. accompanying items —incidental music background music for film etc.

incinerate (ɪnˈsɪnəreɪt) vt. burn up completely; reduce to ashes —incinerˈation n. —inˈcinerator n. furnace or apparatus for incinerating something, esp. refuse

incipient (ɪnˈsɪpɪənt) a. beginning

incise (ɪnˈsaɪz) vt. produce (lines etc.) by cutting into surface of (something) with sharp tool —incision (ɪnˈsɪʒən) n. 1. act of incising 2. cut, gash, notch 3. cut made with knife during surgical operation —inˈcisive a. 1. (of remark etc.) keen, biting 2. sharp —inˈcisor n. cutting tooth

incite (ɪnˈsaɪt) vt. stir up or provoke to action —inciˈtation or inˈcitement n.

incl. 1. including 2. inclusive

inclement (ɪnˈklemənt) a. (of weather) stormy, severe, cold —inˈclemency n.

incline (ɪnˈklaɪn) v. 1. lean, slope 2. (cause to) be disposed —vt. 3. bend or lower (head etc.) —n. (ˈɪnklaɪn, ɪnˈklaɪn) 4. slope —inclination (ɪnklɪˈneɪʃən) n. 1. liking, tendency, preference 2. sloping surface 3. degree of deviation —inclined plane plane whose angle to horizontal is less than right angle

inclose (ɪnˈkləʊz) vt. see ENCLOSE

include (ɪnˈkluːd) vt. 1. have as (part of) contents 2. comprise 3. add in 4. take in —inˈclusion n. —inˈclusive a. including (everything) —inˈclusively adv.

incognito (ɪnkɒgˈniːtəʊ) or (fem.) **incognita** adv./a. 1. under assumed identity —n. 2. assumed identity (pl. -s)

incognizant (ɪnˈkɒgnɪzənt) a. unaware —inˈcognizance n.

incoherent (ɪnkəʊˈhɪərənt) a. 1. lacking clarity, disorganized 2. inarticulate —incoˈherence n. —incoˈherently adv.

income (ˈɪnkʌm, ˈɪnkəm) n. 1. amount of money, esp. annual, from salary, investments etc. 2. receipts —income tax personal tax levied on annual income

incoming (ˈɪnkʌmɪŋ) a. 1. coming in 2. about to come into office; next 3. (of interest etc.) being received; accruing

incommensurable (ɪnkəˈmenʃərəbəl) a. 1. incapable of being measured comparatively 2.

incommensurate 3. Maths. having no common factor other than 1 —n. 4. something incommensurable —incommensuraˈbility n.

incommensurate (ɪnkəˈmenʃərɪt) a. 1. disproportionate 2. incommensurable

incommode (ɪnkəˈməʊd) vt. trouble, inconvenience, disturb —incomˈmodious a. 1. cramped 2. inconvenient

incommunicado (ɪnkəmjuːnɪˈkɑːdəʊ) a./adv. deprived (by force or by choice) of communication with others

incomparable (ɪnˈkɒmpərəbəl, -prəbəl) a. 1. beyond or above comparison; matchless; unequalled 2. lacking basis for comparison; not having qualities or features that can be compared —incomparaˈbility or inˈcomparableness n. —inˈcomparably adv.

incompetent (ɪnˈkɒmpɪtənt) a. 1. not possessing necessary ability, skill etc. to do or carry out task; incapable 2. marked by lack of ability, skill etc. 3. Law not legally qualified —n. 4. incompetent person —inˈcompetence or inˈcompetency n.

incongruous (ɪnˈkɒŋgrʊəs) or **incongruent** a. 1. not appropriate 2. inconsistent, absurd —inˈcongruity n. —inˈcongruously adv.

inconsequential (ɪnkɒnsɪˈkwenʃəl) or **inconsequent** (ɪnˈkɒnsɪkwənt) a. 1. illogical 2. irrelevant; trivial

incontrovertible (ɪnkɒntrəˈvɜːtəbəl) a. undeniable; indisputable

incorporate (ɪnˈkɔːpəreɪt) v. 1. include 2. unite into one body 3. form into corporation —incorpoˈration n.

incorporeal (ɪnkɔːˈpɔːrɪəl) a. 1. without material form, body or substance 2. spiritual, metaphysical 3. Law having no material existence —incorpoˈreity or incorporeˈality n.

incorrigible (ɪnˈkɒrɪdʒəbəl) a. 1. beyond correction or reform 2. firmly rooted —incorrigiˈbility n.

increase (ɪnˈkriːs) v. 1. make or become greater in size, number etc. —n. (ˈɪnkriːs) 2. growth, enlargement —inˈcreasingly adv. more and more

incredible (ɪnˈkredəbəl) a. 1. unbelievable 2. inf. marvellous; amazing

incredulous (ɪnˈkredjʊləs) a. unbelieving —inˈcredulity n.

increment (ˈɪnkrɪmənt) n. increase, esp. one of a series

incriminate (ɪnˈkrɪmɪneɪt) vt. 1. imply guilt of 2. charge with crime —inˈcriminatory a.

incrust (ɪnˈkrʌst) v. see ENCRUST

incubate (ˈɪnkjubeɪt) vt. 1. provide (eggs, embryos, bacteria etc.) with heat or other favourable condition for development —vi. 2. develop in this way —incuˈbation n. —ˈincuba-

tor *n.* apparatus for artificially hatching eggs, for rearing premature babies

incubus (ˈɪŋkjubəs) *n.* **1.** nightmare; obsession **2.** (*orig.*) demon believed to afflict sleeping person (*pl.* **-bi** (-baɪ), **-es**)

inculcate (ˈɪnkʌlkeɪt, ɪnˈkʌlkeɪt) *vt.* impress on the mind —**incul'cation** *n.* —'**inculcator** *n.*

inculpate (ˈɪnkʌlpeɪt, ɪnˈkʌlpeɪt) *vt.* incriminate; cause blame to be imputed to —**incul'pation** *n.* —**in'culpative** *or* **in'culpatory** *a.*

incumbent (ɪnˈkʌmbənt) *a.* **1.** lying, resting —*n.* **2.** holder of office, *esp.* church benefice —**in'cumbency** *n.* **1.** obligation **2.** office or tenure of incumbent —**it is incumbent on** it is the duty of

incur (ɪnˈkɜː) *vt.* **1.** fall into **2.** bring upon oneself (**-rr-**) —**in'cursion** *n.* **1.** invasion **2.** penetration

incuse (ɪnˈkjuːz) *vt.* **1.** impress by striking or stamping —*a.* **2.** hammered —*n.* **3.** impression made by stamping

ind. 1. independent **2.** index **3.** indicative

Ind. 1. Independent **2.** India **3.** Indian **4.** Indies

indaba (ɪnˈdɑːbə) *n.* **SA 1.** meeting, discussion **2.** problem

indebted (ɪnˈdɛtɪd) *a.* **1.** owing gratitude (for help, favours *etc.*) **2.** owing money —**in'debtedness** *n.*

indecent (ɪnˈdiːsənt) *a.* **1.** offensive to standards of decency, *esp.* in sexual matters **2.** unseemly, improper (*esp. in* **indecent haste**) —**in'decency** *n.* **1.** state or quality of being indecent **2.** indecent act *etc.* —**indecent exposure** offence of indecently exposing one's body, *esp.* genitals, in public

indeed (ɪnˈdiːd) *adv.* **1.** in truth, really, in fact, certainly —*interj.* **2.** denoting surprise, doubt *etc.*

indefatigable (ɪndɪˈfætɪɡəbəl) *a.* untiring —**inde'fatigably** *adv.*

indefeasible (ɪndɪˈfiːzəbəl) *a.* that cannot be lost or annulled —**indefeasi'bility** *n.*

indefensible (ɪndɪˈfɛnsəbəl) *a.* not justifiable or defensible —**inde'fensibly** *adv.*

indelible (ɪnˈdɛlɪbəl) *a.* **1.** that cannot be blotted out, effaced or erased **2.** producing such a mark —**indeli'bility** *n.* —**in'delibly** *adv.*

indelicate (ɪnˈdɛlɪkɪt) *a.* **1.** coarse **2.** embarrassing, tasteless

indemnity (ɪnˈdɛmnɪtɪ) *n.* **1.** compensation for loss **2.** security against loss —**indemnifi'cation** *n.* —**in'demnify** *vt.* **1.** give indemnity to **2.** compensate (**in'demnified, in'demnifying**)

indent (ɪnˈdɛnt) *v.* **1.** set (written matter *etc.*) in from margin *etc.* **2.** notch (edge, border *etc.*); make (something) jagged **3.** cut (document in duplicate) so that irregular lines may be

matched **4.** make an order upon (someone) or for (something) —*n.* (ˈɪndɛnt) **5.** notch **6.** order, requisition —**inden'tation** *n.* **1.** hollowed, notched or cut place, as an edge or coastline **2.** series of hollows, notches or cuts **3.** act of indenting; condition of being indented **4.** leaving of space or amount of space left between margin and start of indented line (*also* **in'dention, 'indent**) —**in'dention** *n.* indentation (on page) —**in'denture** *n.* **1.** indented document **2.** contract, *esp.* one binding apprentice to master —*vt.* **3.** bind thus

independent (ɪndɪˈpɛndənt) *a.* **1.** not subject to others **2.** self-reliant **3.** free **4.** valid in itself **5.** politically of no party —**inde'pendence** *or* **inde'pendency** *n.* **1.** being independent **2.** self-reliance **3.** self-support —**inde'pendently** *adv.* —**independent clause** *Gram.* main or coordinate clause —**independent school** *UK* school that is neither financed nor controlled by government or local authorities

in-depth *a.* carefully worked out, detailed, thorough

indescribable (ɪndɪˈskraɪbəbəl) *a.* **1.** beyond description **2.** too intense *etc.* for words —**inde'scribably** *adv.*

indeterminate (ɪndɪˈtɜːmɪnɪt) *a.* **1.** uncertain **2.** inconclusive **3.** incalculable **4.** *Maths.* having no numerical meaning; (of an equation) having more than one variable and an unlimited number of solutions

index (ˈɪndɛks) *n.* **1.** alphabetical list of references, usu. at end of book **2.** pointer, indicator **3.** *Maths.* exponent (*pl.* **-es, 'indices**) —*vt.* **4.** provide (book) with index **5.** insert in index —**index finger** finger next to thumb (*also* **'forefinger**) —**index-linked** *a.* (of wages, interest rates *etc.*) directly related to cost-of-living index and rising accordingly

Indian (ˈɪndɪən) *n.* **1.** native of India **2.** aboriginal American —*a.* **3.** of India **4.** of Amer. Indians or any of their languages —'**Indic** *a.* **1.** denoting, belonging to or relating to Indian branch of Indo-European languages —*n.* **2.** this group of languages (*also* **Indo-Aryan**) —'**Indiaman** *n.* formerly, merchant ship engaged in trade with India —**Indian club** bottle-shaped club, usu. used by gymnasts *etc.* —**Indian corn** *see* MAIZE —**Indian file** single file —**Indian hemp** cannabis —**Indian ink** very dark black (drawing) ink —**Indian list** C *inf.* list of people to whom spirits may not be sold —**Indian summer** period of unusually warm weather, *esp.* in autumn —**India paper** thin soft opaque printing paper —**India rubber** rubber, eraser

indicate (ˈɪndɪkeɪt) *vt.* **1.** point out **2.** state briefly **3.** signify —**indi'cation** *n.* **1.** sign **2.** token **3.** explanation —**in'dicative** *a.* **1.** (*with of*) pointing (to) **2.** *Gram.* stating fact —*n.* **3.** *Gram.*

(verb in) indicative mood —**'indicator** *n*. **1.** one who, that which, indicates **2.** on vehicle, flashing light showing driver's intention to turn

indices ('ındısiːz) *n., pl. of* INDEX

indict (ın'daıt) *vt.* accuse, *esp.* by legal process —**in'dictable** *a.* —**in'dictment** *n.*

indifferent (ın'dıfrənt, -fərənt) *a.* **1.** uninterested **2.** unimportant **3.** neither good nor bad **4.** inferior **5.** neutral —**in'difference** *n.*

indigenous (ın'dıdʒınəs) *a.* born in or natural to a country —**indigene** ('ındıdʒiːn) *n.* **1.** aborigine **2.** native

indigent ('ındıdʒənt) *a.* poor; needy —**'indigence** *n.* poverty

indigestion (ındı'dʒestʃən) *n.* (discomfort, pain caused by) difficulty in digesting food —**indi'gestible** *a.*

indignant (ın'dıgnənt) *a.* **1.** moved by anger and scorn **2.** angered by sense of injury or injustice —**in'dignantly** *adv.* —**indig'nation** *n.* —**in'dignity** *n.* humiliation; insult, slight

indigo ('ındıgəʊ) *n.* **1.** blue dye obtained from plant **2.** the plant (*pl.* **-s, -es**) —*a.* **3.** deep blue

indirect (ındı'rɛkt) *a.* **1.** deviating from direct course or line **2.** not coming as direct effect or consequence **3.** not straightforward, open or fair —**indi'rectly** *adv.* —**indi'rectness** *n.* —**indirect object** *Gram.* noun, pronoun or noun phrase indicating recipient or beneficiary of action of verb and its direct object —**indirect speech** *or esp. U.S.* **indirect discourse** reporting of something said by conveying what was meant rather than repeating exact words (*also* **reported speech**) —**indirect tax** tax levied on goods or services rather than on individuals or companies

indiscreet (ındı'skriːt) *a.* not discreet; imprudent; tactless —**indiscretion** (ındı'skreʃən) *n.* **1.** characteristic or state of being indiscreet **2.** indiscreet act, remark *etc.*

indiscrete (ındı'skriːt) *a.* not divisible or divided into parts

indiscriminate (ındı'skrımınıt) *a.* **1.** lacking discrimination **2.** jumbled

indispensable (ındı'spɛnsəbəl) *a.* necessary; essential

indisposition (ındıspə'zıʃən) *n.* **1.** sickness **2.** disinclination —**indis'pose** *vt.* —**indis'posed** *a.* **1.** unwell, not fit **2.** disinclined

indissoluble (ındı'sɒljʊbəl) *a.* permanent

indium ('ındıəm) *n.* soft silver-white metallic element

individual (ındı'vıdjʊəl) *a.* **1.** single **2.** characteristic of single person or thing **3.** distinctive —*n.* **4.** single person or thing, *esp.* when regarded as distinct from others —**indi'vidualism** *n.* principle of asserting one's independence —**indi'vidualist** *n.* —**individual-**

-istic *a.* —**individu'ality** *n.* **1.** distinctive character **2.** personality —**indi'vidualize** *or* **-lise** *vt.* make (or treat as) individual —**indi'vidually** *adv.* singly

Indo- ('ındəʊ-) (*comb. form*) India; Indian, as in *Indo-European*

indoctrinate (ın'dɒktrıneıt) *vt.* implant beliefs in the mind of

Indo-European *a.* **1.** denoting or belonging to family of languages that includes English **2.** denoting or belonging to any of the peoples speaking these languages —*n.* **3.** Indo-European family of languages

indolent ('ındələnt) *a.* lazy —**indolence** *n.*

indomitable (ın'dɒmıtəbəl) *a.* unyielding

indoor ('ındɔː) *a.* **1.** within doors **2.** under cover —**in'doors** *adv.* inside or into house or other building

indorse (ın'dɔːs) *vt. see* ENDORSE

indubitable (ın'djuːbıtəbəl) *a.* beyond doubt; certain —**in'dubitably** *adv.*

induce (ın'djuːs) *vt.* **1.** persuade **2.** bring on **3.** cause **4.** produce by induction —**in'ducement** *n.* incentive, attraction

induct (ın'dʌkt) *vt.* install in office —**in'ductance** *n.* —**in'duction** *n.* **1.** an inducting **2.** general inference from particular instances **3.** production of electric or magnetic state in body by its being near (not touching) electrified or magnetized body **4.** in internal combustion engine, part of the piston's action which draws gas from carburettor —**in'ductive** *a.* —**in'ductively** *adv.* —**in'ductor** *n.* —**induction coil** transformer for producing high voltage from low voltage

indue (ın'djuː) *vt. see* ENDUE

indulge (ın'dʌldʒ) *vt.* **1.** gratify **2.** give free course to **3.** pamper **4.** spoil —**in'dulgence** *n.* **1.** an indulging **2.** extravagance **3.** something granted as a favour or privilege **4.** *R.C.Ch.* remission of temporal punishment due after absolution —**in'dulgent** *a.* —**in'dulgently** *adv.*

induna (ın'duːnə) *n.* **SA** headman, overseer

indurate ('ındjʊreıt) *v.* **1.** make or become hard or callous **2.** make or become hardy —*a.* ('ındjʊrıt) **3.** hardened, callous, or unfeeling —**'indurative** *a.*

industry ('ındəstrı) *n.* **1.** manufacture, processing *etc.* of goods **2.** branch of this **3.** diligence, habitual hard work —**in'dustrial** *a.* of industries, trades —**in'dustrialist** *n.* person engaged in control of industrial enterprise —**in'dustrialize** *or* **-lise** *v.* —**in'dustrious** *a.* diligent —**industrial estate** *UK* area of land set aside for industry and business —**Industrial Revolution** transformation in 18th and 19th centuries of Brit. and other countries into industrial nations

-ine (*comb. form*) 1. of, relating to or belonging to, as in *saturnine* 2. consisting of; resembling, as in *crystalline* 3. indicating any of various classes of chemical compounds, as in *chlorine, nicotine, glycerine* (*also* **-in**) 4. indicating feminine form, as in *heroine*

inebriate (ɪn'iːbrɪeɪt) *vt.* 1. make drunk; intoxicate —*a.* (ɪn'iːbrɪɪt) 2. drunken —*n.* (ɪn'iːbrɪɪt) 3. habitual drunkard —**inebri'ation** *or* **inebriety** (ɪnɪ'braɪɪtɪ) *n.* drunkenness

inedible (ɪn'ɛdɪbəl) *a.* 1. not eatable 2. unfit for food —**inedi'bility** *n.*

ineducable (ɪn'ɛdjʊkəbəl) *a.* incapable of being educated, *esp.* through mental retardation

ineffable (ɪn'ɛfəbəl) *a.* 1. too great or sacred for words 2. unutterable —**ineffa'bility** *n.* —**in'effably** *adv.*

ineligible (ɪn'ɛlɪdʒəbəl) *a.* not fit or qualified (for something) —**ineligi'bility** *n.*

ineluctable (ɪnɪ'lʌktəbəl) *a.* (*esp.* of fate) incapable of being avoided; inescapable

inept (ɪn'ɛpt) *a.* 1. absurd 2. out of place 3. clumsy —**in'eptitude** *n.*

inequality (ɪnɪ'kwɒlɪtɪ) *n.* 1. state or quality of being unequal 2. lack of smoothness or regularity 3. *Maths.* statement indicating that value of one quantity or expression is not equal to another; relation of being unequal

inert (ɪn'ɜːt) *a.* 1. without power of action or resistance 2. slow, sluggish 3. chemically unreactive —**inertia** (ɪn'ɜːʃə, -ʃɪə) *n.* 1. inactivity 2. property by which matter continues in its existing state of rest or motion in straight line, unless that state is changed by external force —**in'ertly** *adv.* —**in'ertness** *n.* —**inertia-reel seat-belt** car seat-belt in which belt is free to unwind from metal drum except when rapid deceleration occurs —**inertia selling** practice of sending unrequested goods to householders, followed by bill if goods are not returned

inescapable (ɪnɪ'skeɪpəbəl) *a.* incapable of being escaped or avoided

inestimable (ɪn'ɛstɪməbəl) *a.* too good, too great to be estimated

inevitable (ɪn'ɛvɪtəbəl) *a.* 1. unavoidable 2. sure to happen —**inevita'bility** *n.* —**in'evitably** *adv.*

inexorable (ɪn'ɛksərəbəl) *a.* relentless —**in'exorably** *adv.*

inexpiable (ɪn'ɛkspɪəbəl) *a.* 1. incapable of being expiated 2. *obs.* implacable

inexplicable (ɪnɪk'splɪkəbəl) *a.* impossible to explain

in extenso (ɪn ɪk'stɛnsəʊ) *Lat.* at full length

in extremis (ɪn ɪk'striːmɪs) *Lat.* at the point of death

inextricable (ɪnɛks'trɪkəbəl) *a.* 1. not able to be escaped from 2. not able to be disentangled

etc. 3. extremely involved or intricate —**inextrica'bility** *or* **inex'tricableness** *n.* —**inex'tricably** *adv.*

inf. 1. infinitive 2. informal 3. information

infallible (ɪn'fæləbəl) *a.* 1. unerring 2. not liable to fail 3. certain, sure —**infalli'bility** *n.* —**in'fallibly** *adv.*

infamous ('ɪnfəməs) *a.* 1. notorious 2. shocking —**'infamously** *adv.* —**'infamy** *n.*

infant ('ɪnfənt) *n.* very young child —**'infancy** *n.* —**in'fanticide** *n.* 1. murder of newborn child 2. person guilty of this —**'infantile** *a.* childish —**infantile paralysis** *see* POLIOMYELITIS —**infant school** UK school for children aged between 5 and 7

infante (ɪn'fæntɪ) *n.* formerly, son of king of Spain or Portugal, *esp.* one not heir to throne —**infanta** (ɪn'fæntə) *n.* 1. formerly, daughter of king of Spain or Portugal 2. wife of infante

infantry ('ɪnfəntrɪ) *n.* foot soldiers

infatuate (ɪn'fætjʊeɪt) *vt.* inspire with folly or foolish passion —**in'fatuated** *a.* foolishly enamoured —**infatu'ation** *n.*

infect (ɪn'fɛkt) *vt.* 1. affect (with disease) 2. contaminate —**in'fection** *n.* —**in'fectious** *a.* catching, spreading, pestilential —**infectious hepatitis** acute infectious viral disease characterized by inflammation of liver, fever and jaundice —**infectious mononucleosis** acute infectious disease characterized by fever, sore throat, swollen lymph nodes *etc.* (*also* **glandular fever**)

infelicitous (ɪnfɪ'lɪsɪtəs) *a.* unfortunate; unsuitable —**infe'licity** *n.* 1. being infelicitous 2. unsuitable or inapt remark *etc.*

infer (ɪn'fɜː) *vt.* deduce, conclude (**-rr-**) —**'inference** *n.* —**infer'ential** *a.* deduced

inferior (ɪn'fɪərɪə) *a.* 1. of poor quality 2. lower —*n.* 3. one lower (in rank *etc.*) —**infer'iority** *n.* —**inferiority complex** *Psychoanal.* repressed sense of inferiority

infernal (ɪn'fɜːnəl) *a.* 1. devilish 2. hellish 3. *inf.* irritating, confounded —**in'fernally** *adv.*

inferno (ɪn'fɜːnəʊ) *n.* 1. region of hell 2. conflagration (*pl.* **-s**)

infest (ɪn'fɛst) *vt.* inhabit or overrun in dangerously or unpleasantly large numbers —**infes'tation** *n.*

infidelity (ɪnfɪ'dɛlɪtɪ) *n.* 1. unfaithfulness 2. religious disbelief 3. disloyalty 4. treachery —**'infidel** *n.* 1. unbeliever —*a.* 2. rejecting a specific religion, *esp.* Christianity or Islam 3. of unbelievers or unbelief

infield ('ɪnfiːld) *n.* 1. *Cricket* area of field near pitch 2. *Baseball* area of playing field enclosed by base lines —**'infielder** *n.*

infighting ('ɪnfaɪtɪŋ) *n.* 1. *Boxing* combat at

close quarters **2.** intense conflict, as between members of same organization —**'infighter** n.

infiltrate ('ınfıltreıt) v. **1.** trickle through —vt. **2.** (cause to) gain access surreptitiously **3.** cause to pass through pores —**infil'tration** n.

infin. infinitive

infinite ('ınfınıt) a. boundless —**'infinitely** adv. exceedingly —**infini'tesimal** a. extremely, infinitely small —**in'finitude** n. state or quality of being infinite —**in'finity** n. unlimited and endless extent

infinitive (ın'fınıtıv) a. **1.** Gram. in mood expressing notion of verb without limitation of tense, person or number —n. **2.** verb in this mood **3.** the mood

infirm (ın'fɜːm) a. **1.** physically weak **2.** mentally weak **3.** irresolute —**in'firmary** n. hospital; sick quarters —**in'firmity** n.

infix (ın'fıks, 'ınfıks) vt. **1.** fix firmly in **2.** instil, inculcate **3.** Gram. insert (affix) into middle of word —n. ('ınfıks) **4.** Gram. affix inserted into middle of word

in flagrante delicto (ın flə' græntı dı'lıktəʊ) see FLAGRANTE DELICTO

inflame (ın'fleım) vt. **1.** rouse to anger, excitement **2.** cause inflammation in —vi **3.** become inflamed —**inflammability** (ınflæmə'bılıtı) n. —**inflammable** (ın'flæməbəl) a. **1.** easily set on fire **2.** excitable —**inflammation** (ınflə'meıʃən) n. infection of part of the body, with pain, heat, swelling and redness —**inflammatory** (ın'flæmətərı, -trı) a.

inflate (ın'fleıt) v. **1.** blow up with air, gas **2.** swell —vt. **3.** cause economic inflation of (prices etc.) —vi. **4.** undergo economic inflation —**in'flatable** a. —**in'flation** n. increase in prices and fall in value of money —**in'flationary** a.

inflect (ın'flɛkt) vt. **1.** modify (words) to show grammatical relationships **2.** bend inwards —**in'flection** or **in'flexion** n. **1.** modification of word **2.** modulation of voice

inflexible (ın'flɛksəbəl) a. **1.** incapable of being bent **2.** stern —**inflexi'bility** n.

inflict (ın'flıkt) vt. **1.** impose **2.** deliver forcibly —**in'fliction** n. **1.** inflicting **2.** punishment

in-flight a. provided during flight in aircraft

inflorescence (ınflɔː'rɛsəns) n. **1.** the unfolding of blossoms **2.** Bot. arrangement of flowers on stem

inflow ('ınfləʊ) n. **1.** something, such as liquid or gas, that flows in **2.** act of flowing in; influx

influence ('ınfluəns) n. **1.** effect of one person or thing on another **2.** power of person or thing having an effect **3.** thing, person exercising this —vt. **4.** sway **5.** induce **6.** affect —**influ'ential** a.

influenza (ınflu'ɛnzə) n. contagious feverish catarrhal virus disease

influx ('ınflʌks) n. **1.** a flowing in **2.** inflow

info ('ınfəʊ) inf. information

infold (ın'fəʊld) vt. see ENFOLD

inform (ın'fɔːm) vt. **1.** tell **2.** animate —vi. **3.** (oft. with on or against) give information (about) —**in'formant** n. one who tells —**infor'mation** n. **1.** knowledge acquired through experience or study **2.** knowledge of specific and timely events or situations; news **3.** act of informing; condition of being informed **4.** office, agency etc. providing information **5.** charge or complaint made before justices of peace, usu. on oath, to institute summary criminal proceedings **6.** Comp. results derived from processing of data according to programmed instructions **7.** Comp. information operated on by computer program (also 'data) —**infor'mational** a. —**in'formative** a. —**in'formed** a. having much knowledge or education; learned, cultured —**in'former** n. **1.** person who informs against someone, esp. criminal **2.** person who provides information —**information technology** technology concerned with collecting and storing information, esp. by computer or electronically —**information theory** collection of mathematical theories concerned with coding, transmitting, storing, retrieving and decoding information

infra ('ınfrə) adv. **1.** below **2.** under **3.** after —**infra dig** inf. beneath one's dignity —**infra'red** a. denoting rays below red end of visible spectrum —**infra'sonic** a. having frequency below that of sound

infraction (ın'frækʃən) n. see INFRINGE

infrangible (ın'frændʒıbəl) a. **1.** incapable of being broken **2.** not capable of being violated or infringed —**infrangi'bility** or **in'frangibleness** n.

infrastructure ('ınfrəstrʌktʃə) n. basic structure or fixed capital items of an organization or economic system

infringe (ın'frındʒ) vt. transgress, break —**in'fraction** n. breach, violation —**in'fringement** n.

infuriate (ın'fjʊərıeıt) vt. enrage

infuse (ın'fjuːz) v. **1.** soak to extract flavour etc. —vt. **2.** instil, charge —**in'fusible** a. capable of being infused —**in'fusion** n. **1.** an infusing **2.** liquid extract obtained

infusible (ın'fjuːzəbəl) a. not easily; not easily melted; having high melting point —**infusi'bility** or **in'fusibleness** n.

-ing¹ (comb. form) **1.** action of, process of, result of or something connected with verb, as in meeting, wedding, winnings **2.** something used in, consisting of, involving etc., as in tubing, soldiering

-ing² (comb. form) **1.** forming present participle

of verbs, as in *walking, believing* **2.** forming participial adjectives, as in *growing boy, sinking ship* **3.** forming adjectives not derived from verbs, as in *swashbuckling*

ingenious (in'dʒiːnjəs, -niəs) *a.* **1.** clever at contriving **2.** cleverly contrived —**in'geniously** *adv.* —**inge'nuity** *n.*

ingénue (ænʒei'njuː) *n.* **1.** artless girl or young woman **2.** actress playing such a part

ingenuous (in'dʒɛnjʊəs) *a.* **1.** frank **2.** naive, innocent —**in'genuously** *adv.*

ingest (in'dʒɛst) *vt.* take (food or liquid) into the body —**in'gestible** *a.* —**in'gestion** *n.*

inglenook ('iŋgəlnʊk) *n.* corner by a fireplace

inglorious (in'glɔːriəs) *a.* dishonourable, shameful, disgraceful

ingot ('iŋgət) *n.* brick of cast metal, *esp.* gold

ingrain *or* **engrain** (in'grein) *vt.* **1.** implant deeply **2.** *obs.* dye, infuse deeply —**in'grained** *or* **en'grained** *a.* **1.** deep-rooted **2.** inveterate **3.** (*esp.* of dirt) worked into or through fibre, grain, pores *etc.*

ingratiate (in'greiʃieit) *v. refl.* get (oneself) into favour —**in'gratiatingly** *adv.*

ingredient (in'griːdiənt) *n.* component part of a mixture

ingress ('iŋgrɛs) *n.* **1.** entry **2.** means or right of entrance

ingrown ('iŋgrəʊn, in'grəʊn) *a.* (*esp.* of toenail) grown abnormally into flesh **2.** grown within; native; innate

inhabit (in'hæbit) *vt.* dwell in —**in'habitable** *a.* —**in'habitant** *n.* —**inhabi'tation** *n.*

inhale (in'heil) *v.* breathe in (air *etc.*) —**in'halant** *a.* **1.** (*esp.* of medicinal preparation) inhaled for its therapeutic effect **2.** inhaling —*n.* **3.** inhalant medicinal preparation —**inha'lation** *n.* —**in'haler** *n.* device producing and assisting inhalation of therapeutic vapours

inhere (in'hiə) *vi.* **1.** (of qualities) exist **2.** (of rights) be vested —**in'herence** *or* **in'herency** *n.* —**in'herent** *a.* existing as an inseparable part

inherit (in'hɛrit) *vt.* **1.** receive as heir **2.** derive from parents —*vi.* **3.** succeed as heir —**inherita'bility** *or* **in'heritableness** *n.* —**in'heritable** *a.* **1.** capable of being transmitted by heredity **2.** capable of being inherited —**in'heritance** *n.*

inhesion (in'hiːʒən) *n.* inherence

inhibit (in'hibit) *vt.* **1.** restrain (impulse, desire *etc.*) **2.** hinder (action) **3.** forbid —**inhibition** (ini'biʃən, inhi-) *n.* **1.** repression of emotion, instinct **2.** a stopping or retarding —**in'hibitory** *a.*

inhuman (in'hjuːmən) *a.* **1.** cruel, brutal **2.** not human —**inhu'manity** *n.*

inhume (in'hjuːm) *vt.* bury, inter —**inhu'mation** *n.*

inimical (i'nimikəl) *a.* **1.** unfavourable **2.** unfriendly; hostile

inimitable (i'nimitəbəl) *a.* defying imitation

iniquity (i'nikwiti) *n.* **1.** gross injustice **2.** wickedness, sin —**in'iquitous** *a.* **1.** unfair, unjust **2.** sinful **3.** *inf.* outrageous

initial (i'niʃəl) *a.* **1.** of, occurring at the beginning —*n.* **2.** initial letter, *esp.* of person's name —*vt.* **3.** mark, sign with one's initials (-ll-) —**in'itially** *adv.* —**initial teaching alphabet** alphabet of 44 characters for teaching beginners to read English

initiate (i'niʃieit) *vt.* **1.** originate, begin **2.** admit into closed society **3.** instruct in elements of something —*n.* (i'niʃiit, -eit) **4.** initiated person —**initi'ation** *n.* —**in'itiative** *n.* **1.** first step, lead **2.** ability to act independently —*a.* **3.** originating —**in'itiatory** *a.*

inject (in'dʒɛkt) *vt.* **1.** introduce (*esp.* fluid, medicine *etc.* with syringe) —**in'jection** *n.*

injunction (in'dʒʌŋkʃən) *n.* **1.** judicial order to restrain **2.** authoritative order

injury ('indʒəri) *n.* **1.** physical damage or harm **2.** wrong —'**injurable** *a.* —'**injure** *vt.* **1.** do harm or damage to **2.** offend, *esp.* by injustice —'**injured** *a.* —**in'jurious** *a.* —**in'juriously** *adv.* —**injury time** *Soccer* extra time added on to compensate for time spent attending to injured players during match

injustice (in'dʒʌstis) *n.* **1.** want of justice **2.** wrong **3.** injury **4.** unjust act

ink (iŋk) *n.* **1.** fluid used for writing or printing —*vt.* **2.** mark with ink **3.** cover, smear with ink —'**inker** *n.* —'**inky** *a.* **1.** resembling ink, *esp.* in colour; dark; black **2.** of, containing or stained with ink —'**inkstand** *n.* —'**inkwell** *n.* vessel for holding ink

inkling ('iŋkliŋ) *n.* hint, slight knowledge or suspicion

inkosi (iŋ'kɔːsi) *n.* SA chief, leader

inlaid ('inleid, in'leid) *pt./pp. of* INLAY

inland ('inlænd, -lənd) *n.* **1.** interior of country —*a.* ('inlənd) **2.** in interior of country **3.** away from the sea **4.** within a country —*adv.* **5.** in or towards the inland

in-law *n.* relative by marriage

inlay (in'lei) *vt.* **1.** embed **2.** decorate with inset pattern ('**inlaid** *pt./pp.*) —*n.* ('inlei) **3.** inlaid piece or pattern

inlet ('inlet) *n.* **1.** entrance **2.** mouth of creek **3.** piece inserted

in loco parentis (in 'ləʊkəʊ pə'rɛntis) *Lat.* in place of a parent

inmate ('inmeit) *n.* occupant, *esp.* of prison, hospital *etc.*

inmost ('inməʊst) *a. sup. of* IN most inward, deepest

inn (in) *n.* **1.** public house providing food and

accommodation **2.** hotel —**'innkeeper** n. —**Inns of Court 1.** four societies admitting to English Bar **2.** their buildings

innards ('inədz) *pl.n. inf.* internal organs or working parts (*orig.* **'inwards**)

innate (i'neit, 'ineit) *a.* **1.** inborn **2.** inherent

inner ('inə) *a.* **1.** lying within —*n.* **2.** ring next to bull's-eye on target —**'innermost** *a.* —**inner city** sections of a large city in or near its centre —**inner man 1.** mind; soul **2.** *jocular* stomach; appetite (**inner woman** *fem.*) —**inner tube** rubber air tube of pneumatic tyre

innings ('iniŋz) *n.* **1.** (*with sing. v.*) *Sport* player's or side's turn of batting **2.** (*sometimes with sing. v.*) spell, turn

innocent ('inəsənt) *a.* **1.** pure **2.** guiltless **3.** harmless —*n.* **4.** innocent person, *esp.* young child —**'innocence** *n.* —**'innocently** *adv.*

innocuous (i'nɒkjuəs) *a.* harmless

innovate ('inəveit) *vt.* introduce (changes, new things) —**inno'vation** *n.* —**'innovator** *n.*

innuendo (inju'endəu) *n.* **1.** allusive remark, hint **2.** indirect accusation (*pl.* **-es**)

innumerable (i'nju:mərəbəl, i'nju:mrəbəl) *or* **innumerous** *a.* countless; very numerous

innumerate (i'nju:mərit) *a.* **1.** having neither knowledge nor understanding of mathematics or science —*n.* **2.** innumerate person —in'numeracy *n.*

inoculate (i'nɒkjuleit) *vt.* immunize by injecting vaccine —**inocu'lation** *n.*

inoperable (in'ɒpərəbəl, -'ɒprə-) *a.* **1.** unworkable **2.** *Med.* that cannot be operated on —in'operative *a.* **1.** not operative **2.** ineffective

inopportune (in'ɒpətju:n) *a.* badly timed

inordinate (in'ɔ:dinit) *a.* excessive

inorganic (inɔ:'gænik) *a.* **1.** not having structure or characteristics of living organisms **2.** of substances without carbon

inpatient ('inpeiʃənt) *n.* patient that stays in hospital

in perpetuum (in pɜ:'petjuəm) *Lat.* for ever

input ('input) *n.* **1.** act of putting in **2.** that which is put in, as resource needed for industrial production *etc.* **3.** data *etc.* fed into a computer

inquest ('inkwest) *n.* **1.** legal or judicial inquiry presided over by a coroner **2.** detailed inquiry or discussion

inquietude (in'kwaiitju:d) *n.* restlessness, uneasiness, anxiety —in'quiet *a.*

inquire (in'kwaiə) *vi.* seek information —in'quirer *n.* —in'quiry *n.* **1.** question **2.** investigation

inquisition (inkwi'ziʃən) *n.* **1.** searching investigation, official inquiry **2.** *Hist.* (**I-**) tribunal for suppression of heresy —in'quisitor *n.* —inquisi'torial *a.*

inquisitive (in'kwizitiv) *a.* **1.** curious **2.** prying

in re (in 'rei) in the matter of: used *esp.* in bankruptcy proceedings

inroad ('inrəud) *n.* incursion

inrush ('inrʌʃ) *n.* sudden, usu. overwhelming, inward flow or rush; influx

ins. 1. inches **2.** insurance

insane (in'sein) *a.* **1.** mentally deranged; crazy **2.** senseless —in'sanely *adv.* **1.** like a lunatic, madly **2.** excessively —**insanity** (in'sæniti) *n.*

insatiable (in'seiʃəbəl, -ʃiə-) *or* **insatiate** (in'seiʃiit) *a.* incapable of being satisfied

inscribe (in'skraib) *vt.* **1.** write, engrave (in or on something) **2.** mark **3.** dedicate **4.** trace (figure) within another —**inscription** (in'skripʃən) *n.* **1.** inscribing **2.** words inscribed on monument *etc.*

inscrutable (in'skru:təbəl) *a.* **1.** mysterious, impenetrable **2.** affording no explanation —inscruta'bility *n.* —in'scrutably *adv.*

insect ('insekt) *n.* small invertebrate animal with six legs, usu. segmented body and two or four wings —in'secticide *n.* preparation for killing insects —**insec'tivorous** *a.* insect-eating

insecure (insi'kjuə) *a.* **1.** not safe or firm **2.** anxious, not confident

inseminate (in'semineit) *vt.* implant semen into —**artificial insemination** impregnation of the female by artificial means

insensate (in'senseit, -sit) *a.* **1.** without sensation, unconscious **2.** unfeeling

insensible (in'sensəbəl) *a.* **1.** unconscious **2.** without feeling **3.** not aware **4.** not perceptible —insensi'bility *n.* —in'sensibly *adv.* imperceptibly

insert (in'sɜ:t) *vt.* **1.** introduce **2.** place or put in, into or between —*n.* ('insɜ:t) **3.** something inserted —in'sertion *n.*

in-service *a.* denoting training that is given to employees during the course of employment

inset ('inset) *n.* **1.** something extra inserted, *esp.* as decoration —*vt.* (in'set) **2.** set or place in or within; insert

inshore ('in'ʃɔ:) *adv./a.* near shore

inside ('in'said) *n.* **1.** inner side, surface or part —*a.* ('insaid) **2.** of, in, or on inside —*adv.* (in'said) **3.** in or into the inside **4.** *sl.* in prison —*prep.* (in'said) **5.** within, on inner side of

insidious (in'sidiəs) *a.* **1.** stealthy, treacherous **2.** unseen but deadly —in'sidiously *adv.*

insight ('insait) *n.* mental penetration, discernment

insignia (in'signiə) *pl.n.* badges, emblems of honour or office (*sing.* in'signia)

insinuate (in'sinjueit) *vt.* **1.** hint **2.** work (oneself) into favour **3.** introduce gradually or subtly —insinu'ation *n.*

insipid (in'sipid) *a.* **1.** dull, spiritless **2.** tasteless —insi'pidity *n.*

insist (ɪnˈsɪst) vi. (oft. with on or upon) 1. demand persistently 2. maintain 3. emphasize —inˈsistence n. —inˈsistent a.

in situ (ɪn ˈsɪtjuː) Lat. in its original position

in so far or U.S. **insofar** adv. (usu. with as or that) to the degree or extent (that)

insole (ˈɪnsəʊl) n. 1. inner sole of shoe or boot 2. loose additional inner sole to give extra warmth or make shoe fit

insolent (ˈɪnsələnt) a. arrogantly impudent —ˈinsolence n. —ˈinsolently adv.

insomnia (ɪnˈsɒmnɪə) n. sleeplessness —inˈsomniac a./n.

insomuch (ɪnsəʊˈmʌtʃ) adv. to such an extent

insouciant (ɪnˈsuːsɪənt) a. indifferent, careless, unconcerned —inˈsouciance n.

inspan (ɪnˈspæn) vt. SA harness, yoke (-nn-)

inspect (ɪnˈspɛkt) vt. examine closely or officially —inˈspection n. —inˈspector n. 1. one who inspects 2. high-ranking police officer —inˈspectorate n. 1. office, rank or duties of inspector 2. body of inspectors 3. district under inspector —inspecˈtorial a.

inspire (ɪnˈspaɪə) vt. 1. animate, invigorate 2. arouse, create feeling, thought in 3. give rise to —vi. 4. breathe in, inhale —inspiration (ɪnspɪˈreɪʃən) n. 1. good idea 2. creative influence or stimulus

inspirit (ɪnˈspɪrɪt) vt. animate, put spirit into, encourage

inst. (instant) of the current month

install or **instal** (ɪnˈstɔːl) vt. 1. have (apparatus) put in 2. establish 3. place (person in office etc.) with ceremony —installation (ɪnstəˈleɪʃən) n. 1. act of installing 2. that which is installed

instalment or U.S. **installment** (ɪnˈstɔːlmənt) n. 1. payment of part of debt 2. any of parts of a whole delivered in succession —**installment plan** US hire-purchase

instance (ˈɪnstəns) n. 1. example, particular case 2. request 3. stage in proceedings —vt. 4. cite —**for instance** for or as an example

instant (ˈɪnstənt) n. 1. moment, point of time —a. 2. immediate 3. urgent 4. (of foods) requiring little preparation —instanˈtaneous a. happening in an instant —instanˈtaneously adv. —inˈstanter adv. Law at once —ˈinstantly adv. at once

instead (ɪnˈstɛd) adv. 1. in place of 2. as a substitute

instep (ˈɪnstɛp) n. top of foot between toes and ankle

instigate (ˈɪnstɪgeɪt) vt. 1. incite, urge 2. bring about —instiˈgation n. —ˈinstigator n.

instil or (esp. U.S.) **instill** (ɪnˈstɪl) vt. implant; inculcate —instilˈlation n. —inˈstilment n.

instinct (ˈɪnstɪŋkt) n. 1. inborn impulse or propensity 2. unconscious skill 3. intuition —inˈstinctive a. —inˈstinctively adv.

institute (ˈɪnstɪtjuːt) vt. 1. establish, found 2. appoint 3. set going —n. 4. society for promoting some public object, esp. scientific 5. its building —instiˈtution n. 1. an instituting 2. establishment for care or education, hospital, college etc. 3. an established custom or law or (inf.) figure —instiˈtutional a. 1. of institutions 2. routine —instiˈtutionalize or -ise vt. 1. subject to (adverse) effects of confinement in institution 2. place in an institution —v. 3. make or become an institution —ˈinstitutor or ˈinstituter n.

instruct (ɪnˈstrʌkt) vt. 1. teach 2. inform 3. order 4. brief (solicitor, barrister) —inˈstruction n. 1. teaching 2. order —pl. 3. directions —inˈstructive a. 1. informative 2. useful —inˈstructively adv. —inˈstructor n. (inˈstructress fem.)

instrument (ˈɪnstrəmənt) n. 1. tool, implement, means, person, thing used to make, do, measure etc. 2. mechanism for producing musical sound 3. legal document —instruˈmental a. 1. acting as instrument or means 2. helpful 3. belonging to, produced by musical instruments —instruˈmentalist n. player of musical instrument —instrumenˈtality n. agency, means —instruˈmentally adv. —instrumenˈtation n. arrangement of music for instruments

insubordinate (ɪnsəˈbɔːdɪnət) a. 1. not submissive 2. mutinous, rebellious —insubordiˈnation n.

insufferable (ɪnˈsʌfərəbəl) a. intolerable; unendurable —inˈsufferably adv.

insular (ˈɪnsjʊlə) a. 1. of an island 2. remote, detached 3. narrow-minded; prejudiced —insuˈlarity n.

insulate (ˈɪnsjʊleɪt) vt. 1. prevent or reduce transfer of electricity, heat, sound etc. to or from (body or device) by surrounding with nonconducting material 2. isolate, detach —insuˈlation n. —ˈinsulator n.

insulin (ˈɪnsjʊlɪn) n. pancreatic hormone used in treating diabetes

insult (ɪnˈsʌlt) vt. 1. behave rudely to 2. offend —n. (ˈɪnsʌlt) 3. offensive remark 4. affront —inˈsulting a. —inˈsultingly adv.

insuperable (ɪnˈsuːpərəbəl, -prəbəl, -ˈsjuː-) a. 1. that cannot be got over or surmounted 2. unconquerable —insuperaˈbility n. —inˈsuperably adv.

insupportable (ɪnsəˈpɔːtəbəl) a. 1. incapable of being endured; intolerable; insufferable 2. incapable of being supported or justified; indefensible

insure (ɪnˈʃʊə, -ˈʃɔː) vi. 1. contract for payment in event of loss, death etc. by payment of premiums —vt. 2. make such contract about 3.

(*with* against) make safe (against) —**in'surable** *a.* —**in'surance** *n.* —**in'surer** *n.* —**insurance policy** contract of insurance

insurgent (in'sɜːdʒənt) *a.* 1. in revolt —*n.* 2. rebel —**in'surgence** *or* **insur'rection** *n.* revolt

int. 1. interest 2. interior 3. internal 4. international

intact (in'tækt) *a.* 1. untouched 2. uninjured

intaglio (in'tɑːliəʊ) *n.* 1. engraved design 2. gem so cut (*pl.* **-s, -gli** (-ljiː)) —**in'tagliated** *a.*

intake ('inteik) *n.* 1. what is taken in 2. quantity taken in 3. opening for taking in 4. in car, air passage into carburettor

integer ('intidʒə) *n.* 1. whole number 2. whole of anything

integral ('intigrəl) *a.* constituting an essential part of a whole —**'integrate** *v.* 1. combine into one whole 2. unify diverse elements (of community *etc.*) —**inte'gration** *n.* —**integral calculus** branch of mathematics of changing quantities, which calculates total effects of the change —**integrated circuit** tiny electronic circuit, usu. on silicon chip

integrity (in'tegriti) *n.* 1. honesty 2. original perfect state

integument (in'tegjumənt) *n.* natural covering, skin, rind, husk

intellect ('intilɛkt) *n.* power of thinking and reasoning —**intel'lectual** *a.* 1. of, appealing to intellect 2. having good intellect —*n.* 3. one endowed with intellect and attracted to intellectual things —**intellectu'ality** *n.*

intelligent (in'telidʒənt) *a.* 1. having, showing good intellect 2. quick at understanding 3. informed —**in'telligence** *n.* 1. quickness of understanding 2. mental power or ability 3. intellect 4. information, news, *esp.* military information —**in'telligently** *adv.* —**intelli'gentsia** *n.* intellectual or cultured classes —**intelligi'bility** *n.* —**in'telligible** *a.* understandable —**in'telligibly** *adv.* —**intelligence quotient** measure of intelligence of individual, derived by dividing individual's mental age by his actual age and multiplying result by 100

intemperate (in'tempərit, -prit) *a.* 1. drinking alcohol to excess 2. immoderate 3. unrestrained —**in'temperance** *n.*

intend (in'tend) *v.* propose, mean (to do, say *etc.*) —**in'tended** *a.* 1. planned, future —*n.* 2. *inf.* proposed spouse

intense (in'tens) *a.* 1. very strong or acute 2. emotional —**intensifi'cation** *n.* —**in'tensify** *v.* 1. make or become stronger 2. increase (**in'tensified, in'tensifying**) —**in'tensity** *n.* 1. intense quality 2. strength —**in'tensive** *a.* characterized by intensity or emphasis on specified factor —**in'tensively** *adv.*

intent (in'tent) *n.* 1. purpose —*a.* 2.

concentrating 3. resolved, bent 4. preoccupied, absorbed —**in'tention** *n.* purpose, aim —**in'tentional** *a.* —**in'tently** *adv.* —**in'tentness** *n.*

inter (in'tɜː) *vt.* bury (**-rr-**) —**in'terment** *n.*

inter- (*comb. form*) between, among, mutually as in *interglacial, interrelation.* Such words are not given here where the meaning may easily be inferred from the simple word

intercol'legiate	interga'lactic
intercom'municate	intergovern'mental
inter'company	inter'knit
intercon'nect	inter'mesh
intercon'nection	inter'mingle
interdenomi'national	inter'mix
interdepart'mental	inter'racial
interde'pend	interuni'versity
interde'pendence	inter'war
inter'flow	inter'weave

interact (intər'ækt) *vi.* act on each other —**inter'action** *n.*

inter alia ('intər 'eiliə) *Lat.* among other things

interbreed (intə'briːd) *v.* breed within a related group

intercede (intə'siːd) *vi.* plead (in favour of), mediate —**intercession** (intə'sɛʃən) *n.* —**intercessor** (intə'sɛsə) *n.*

intercept (intə'sɛpt) *vt.* 1. cut off 2. seize, stop in transit —**inter'ception** *n.* —**inter'ceptor** *or* **inter'cepter** *n.* 1. one who, that which intercepts 2. fast fighter plane, missile *etc.*

interchange (intə'tʃeindʒ) *v.* 1. (cause to) exchange places —*n.* ('intətʃeindʒ) 2. motorway junction —**inter'changeable** *a.* able to be exchanged in position or use

intercity (intə'siti) *a.* linking cities directly

intercom ('intəkɒm) *n.* internal telephonic system

intercommunion (intəkə'mjuːnjən) *n.* association between Churches, involving *esp.* mutual reception of Holy Communion

intercontinental (intəkɒnti'nɛntəl) *a.* 1. connecting continents 2. (of missile) able to reach one continent from another

intercourse ('intəkɔːs) *n.* 1. mutual dealings; communication 2. sexual joining of two people; copulation

interdict ('intədikt) *n.* 1. decree of Pope restraining clergy from performing divine service 2. formal prohibition —*vt.* (intə'dikt) 3. prohibit, forbid 4. restrain —**inter'diction** *n.*

interdisciplinary (intə'disiplinəri) *a.* involving two or more academic disciplines

interest ('intrist, -tərist) *n.* 1. concern, curiosity 2. thing exciting this 3. sum paid for use of borrowed money 4. (*oft. pl.*) benefit,

advantage 5. (*oft. pl.*) right, share —*vt.* **6.** excite curiosity or concern of **7.** cause to become involved in something; concern —'**interested** *a.* **1.** showing or having interest **2.** personally involved or implicated —'**interesting** *a.* —'**interestingly** *adv.*

interface ('ɪntəfeɪs) *n.* area, surface, boundary linking two systems

interfere (ɪntə'fɪə) *vi.* **1.** meddle, intervene **2.** clash **3.** (*with* with) *euphemistic* assault sexually —**inter**'**ference** *n.* **1.** act of interfering **2.** *Rad.* interruption of reception by atmospherics or by unwanted signals

interferon (ɪntə'fɪərɒn) *n.* a cellular protein that stops the development of an invading virus

interim ('ɪntərɪm) *n.* **1.** meantime —*a.* **2.** temporary, intervening

interior (ɪn'tɪərɪə) *a.* **1.** inner **2.** inland **3.** indoors —*n.* **4.** inside **5.** inland region —**interior angle** angle of polygon contained between two adjacent sides —**interior decoration** colours, furniture *etc.* of interior of house *etc.*

interject (ɪntə'dʒɛkt) *vt.* interpose (remark *etc.*) —**inter**'**jection** *n.* **1.** exclamation **2.** interjected remark

interlace (ɪntə'leɪs) *vt.* unite, as by lacing together —**inter**'**lacement** *n.*

interlard (ɪntə'lɑːd) *vt.* intersperse

interleave (ɪntə'liːv) *vt.* insert, as blank leaves in book, between other leaves —'**interleaf** *n.* extra leaf

interlining ('ɪntəlaɪnɪŋ) *n.* material used to interline parts of garments

interlock (ɪntə'lɒk) *v.* **1.** lock together firmly —*a.* ('ɪntəlɒk) **2.** knitted with close, small stitches

interlocutor (ɪntə'lɒkjʊtə) *n.* one who takes part in conversation —**interlo**'**cution** *n.* dialogue —**inter**'**locutory** *a.*

interloper ('ɪntələʊpə) *n.* one intruding in another's affairs

interlude ('ɪntəluːd) *n.* **1.** interval (in play *etc.*) **2.** something filling an interval

intermarry (ɪntə'mærɪ) *vi.* **1.** (of families, races, religions) become linked by marriage **2.** marry within one's family —**inter**'**marriage** *n.*

intermediate (ɪntə'miːdɪɪt) *a.* coming between; interposed —**inter**'**mediary** *n./a.*

intermezzo (ɪntə'mɛtsəʊ) *n.* short performance between acts of play or opera (*pl.* **-s**, **-mezzi** (-'mɛtsiː))

interminable (ɪn'tɜːmɪnəbᵊl) *a.* endless

intermit (ɪntə'mɪt) *v.* stop for a time (**-tt-**) —**inter**'**mission** *n.* **1.** interval, as between parts of film *etc.* **2.** period between events or activities; pause **3.** act of intermitting; state of being intermitted —**inter**'**mittent** *a.* occurring at intervals

intern (ɪn'tɜːn) *vt.* **1.** confine to special area or camp —*n.* ('ɪntɜːn) **2.** internee **3.** US houseman (*also* '**interne**) —**inter**'**nee** *n.* person who is interned, *esp.* enemy citizen in wartime or terrorism suspect —**in**'**ternment** *n.*

internal (ɪn'tɜːnᵊl) *a.* **1.** inward **2.** interior **3.** of a nation's domestic as opposed to foreign affairs —*n.* **4.** *euphemistic* medical examination of vagina or uterus —**in**'**ternally** *adv.* —**internal combustion** process of exploding mixture of air and fuel in piston-fitted cylinder

international (ɪntə'næʃənᵊl) *a.* **1.** of relations between nations —*n.* **2.** game or match between teams of different countries —**inter**'**nationalism** *n.* ideal or practice of cooperation and understanding between nations —**inter**'**nationalist** *n.* —**inter**'**nationally** *adv.* —**International Phonetic Alphabet** series of signs and letters for representation of human speech sounds

Internationale (ɛtɛːnasjɔ'nal) *Fr.* socialistic hymn

internecine (ɪntə'niːsaɪn) *a.* **1.** mutually destructive **2.** deadly

interpellate (ɪn'tɜːpɛleɪt) *vt.* interrupt business of the day to demand explanation from (minister) —**interpel**'**lation** *n.*

interplanetary (ɪntə'plænɪtərɪ, -trɪ) *a.* of, linking planets

interplay ('ɪntəpleɪ) *n.* **1.** action and reaction of two things, sides *etc.* upon each other **2.** interaction **3.** reciprocation

Interpol ('ɪntəpɒl) International Criminal Police Organization

interpolate (ɪn'tɜːpəleɪt) *vt.* **1.** insert (new, *esp.* misleading matter) in (book *etc.*) **2.** interject (remark) **3.** *Maths.* estimate (a value) between known values —**interpo**'**lation** *n.*

interpose (ɪntə'pəʊz) *vt.* **1.** insert **2.** say as interruption **3.** put in the way —*vi.* **1.** intervene —**interpo**'**sition** *n.*

interpret (ɪn'tɜːprɪt) *vt.* **1.** explain **2.** *Art* render, represent —*vi.* **3.** translate, *esp.* orally —**interpre**'**tation** *n.* —**in**'**terpreter** *n.*

interregnum (ɪntə'rɛgnəm) *n.* **1.** interval between reigns **2.** gap in continuity (*pl.* **-na** (-nə), **-s**)

interrelate (ɪntərɪ'leɪt) *v.* place in or come into mutual or reciprocal relationship —**interre**'**lation** *n.*

interrogate (ɪn'tɛrəgeɪt) *vt.* question, *esp.* closely or officially —**interro**'**gation** *n.* —**inter**'**rogative** *a.* **1.** questioning —*n.* **2.** word used in asking question —**in**'**terrogator** *n.* —**inter**'**rogatory** *a.* **1.** of inquiry —*n.* **2.** question, set of questions —**interrogation mark** *see* **question mark** *at* QUESTION

interrupt (ɪntə'rʌpt) *v.* **1.** break in (upon) —*vt.* **2.** stop the course of **3.** block —**inter**'**ruption** *n.*

interscholastic (intəskə'læstık) *a.* **1.** (of sports events, competitions *etc.*) occurring between two or more schools **2.** representative of various schools

intersect (intə'sekt) *vt.* **1.** divide by passing across or through —*vi.* **2.** meet and cross —**inter'section** *n.* point where lines, roads cross

interspace (intə'speıs) *vt.* **1.** make or occupy space between —*n.* ('intəspeıs) **2.** space between or among things —**interspatial** (intə'speıʃəl) *a.*

intersperse (intə'spɜːs) *vt.* sprinkle (something) with or (something) among or in —**inter'spersion** *n.*

interstate ('intəsteıt) *a.* US between, involving two or more states

interstellar (intə'stelə) *a.* (of the space) between stars

interstice (ın'tɜːstıs) *n.* chink, gap, crevice —**inter'stitial** *a.*

intertwine (intə'twaın) *v.* twist together, entwine

interval ('intəvəl) *n.* **1.** intervening time or space **2.** pause, break **3.** short period between parts of play, concert *etc.* **4.** difference (of pitch)

intervene (intə'viːn) *vi.* **1.** come into a situation in order to change it **2.** (*with* on *or* between) be, come (between or among) **3.** occur in meantime **4.** interpose —**intervention** (intə'venʃən) *n.*

interview ('intəvjuː) *n.* **1.** meeting, *esp.* formally arranged and involving questioning of a person —*vt.* **2.** have interview with —**interview'ee** *n.* —**'interviewer** *n.*

intestate (ın'testeıt, -tıt) *a.* **1.** not having made a will —*n.* **2.** person dying intestate —**in'testacy** *n.*

intestine (ın'testın) *n.* (*usu. pl.*) lower part of alimentary canal between stomach and anus —**in'testinal** *a.* of bowels

intimate[1] ('intımıt) *a.* **1.** closely acquainted, familiar **2.** private **3.** extensive **4.** having sexual relations —*n.* **5.** intimate friend —**'intimacy** *n.*

intimate[2] ('intımeıt) *vt.* **1.** announce **2.** imply —**inti'mation** *n.* notice

intimidate (ın'tımıdeıt) *vt.* **1.** frighten into submission **2.** deter by threats —**intimi'dation** *n.* —**in'timidator** *n.*

into ('intuː; *unstressed* 'intə) *prep.* **1.** expresses motion to a point within **2.** indicates change of state **3.** indicates coming up against, encountering **4.** indicates arithmetical division

intone (ın'təun) *or* **intonate** *vt.* **1.** chant **2.** recite in monotone —**into'nation** *n.* **1.** modulation of voice **2.** intoning **3.** accent

in toto (ın 'təutəu) *Lat.* totally, entirely, completely

intoxicate (ın'toksıkeıt) *vt.* **1.** make drunk **2.** excite to excess —**in'toxicant** *a./n.* (anything) causing intoxication —**intoxi'cation** *n.*

intr. intransitive

intra- (*comb. form*) within, as in *intrastate*

intractable (ın'træktəb°l) *a.* **1.** difficult to influence **2.** hard to control

intramural (intrə'mjuərəl) *a. chiefly US Education* operating within or involving those in single establishment

intransigent (ın'trænsıdʒənt) *a.* uncompromising, obstinate

intransitive (ın'trænsıtıv) *a.* denoting a verb that does not require direct object —**intransi'tivity** *or* **in'transitiveness** *n.*

intrauterine (intrə'juːtəraın) *a.* within the womb (*see also* IUD)

intravenous (intrə'viːnəs) *a.* into a vein

in-tray *n.* tray for incoming papers *etc.* requiring attention

intrepid (ın'trepıd) *a.* fearless, undaunted —**intre'pidity** *n.*

intricate ('intrıkıt) *a.* involved, puzzlingly entangled —**'intricacy** *n.* —**'intricately** *adv.*

intrigue (ın'triːg, 'intriːg) *n.* **1.** underhand plot **2.** secret love affair —*vi.* (ın'triːg) **3.** carry on intrigue —*vt.* (ın'triːg) **4.** interest, puzzle

intrinsic (ın'trınsık) *or* **intrinsical** *a.* inherent; essential —**in'trinsically** *adv.*

intro. *or* **introd.** **1.** introduction **2.** introductory

intro- (*comb. form*) into, within, as in *introduce, introvert*

introduce (intrə'djuːs) *vt.* **1.** make acquainted **2.** present **3.** bring in **4.** bring forward **5.** bring into practice **6.** insert —**intro'duction** *n.* **1.** introducing **2.** presentation of one person to another **3.** preliminary section or treatment **4.** *Mus.* opening passage in movement or composition, that precedes main material —**intro'ductory** *a.* preliminary

introit ('introıt) *n. Eccles.* anthem sung as priest approaches altar

introspection (intrə'spekʃən) *n.* examination of one's own thoughts —**intro'spective** *a.*

introvert ('intrəvɜːt) *n. Psychoanal.* one who looks inwards rather than at the external world —**intro'versible** *a.* —**intro'version** *n.* —**intro-'versive** *a.* —**'introverted** *a.*

intrude (ın'truːd) *v.* thrust (oneself) in uninvited —**in'truder** *n.* —**in'trusion** *n.* —**in'trusive** *a.*

intrust (ın'trʌst) *vt. see* ENTRUST

intuition (intju'ıʃən) *n.* **1.** immediate mental apprehension without reasoning **2.** immediate insight —**in'tuit** *vt.* —**in'tuitive** *a.*

Inuit ('ınjuːıt) *n.* C Eskimo of N Amer. or Greenland

inundate ('ınʌndeıt) *vt.* **1.** flood **2.** overwhelm —**inun'dation** *n.*

inure *or* **enure** (ɪ'njuə) *vt.* accustom, *esp.* to hardship, danger *etc.*

in vacuo (ɪn 'vækjuəu) *Lat.* in vacuum

invade (ɪn'veɪd) *v.* **1.** enter (a country *etc.*) by force with hostile intent *—vt.* **2.** overrun **3.** pervade *—in'vader* *n.* *—in'vasion* *n.* **1.** act of invading with armed forces **2.** any encroachment or intrusion **3.** onset of something harmful, *esp.* disease

invalid¹ ('ɪnvəlɪd, -lɪd) *n.* **1.** one suffering from chronic ill health *—a.* **2.** ill, suffering from sickness or injury *—vt.* **3.** cause to become an invalid **4.** (*usu. with* out) *chiefly* UK require (member of armed forces) to retire from active service because of illness *etc.*

invalid² (ɪn'vælɪd) *a.* **1.** not valid; having no cogency or legal force **2.** *Logic* having conclusion that does not necessarily follow from its premises; not valid *—in'validate* *vt.* **1.** render weak or ineffective, as argument **2.** take away legal force or effectiveness of; annul *—invali'dation* *n.* *—in'validator* *n.*

invaluable (ɪn'væljuəbəl) *a.* priceless

Invar (ɪn'vɑː) *n.* **R** steel containing 30 per cent nickel, with low coefficient of expansion

invasion (ɪn'veɪʒən) *n. see* INVADE

inveigh (ɪn'veɪ) *vi.* speak violently *—invective* (ɪn'vektɪv) *n.* abusive speech or writing, vituperation

inveigle (ɪn'viːgəl, -'veɪ-) *vt.* entice, seduce, wheedle *—in'veiglement* *n.*

invent (ɪn'vent) *vt.* **1.** devise, originate **2.** fabricate (falsehoods *etc.*) *—in'vention* *n.* **1.** that which is invented **2.** ability to invent **3.** contrivance **4.** deceit; lie *—in'ventive* *a.* resourceful; creative *—in'ventively* *adv.* *—in'ventor* *n.*

inventory ('ɪnvəntərɪ, -trɪ) *n.* **1.** detailed list of goods *etc.* *—vt.* **2.** make list of

invert (ɪn'vɜːt) *vt.* **1.** turn upside down **2.** reverse position, relations of *—inverse* (ɪn'vɜːs, 'ɪnvɜːs) *a.* **1.** inverted **2.** opposite *—in'versely* *adv.* *—in'version* *n.* *—inverted comma* *or* **turned comma** *see* quotation mark *at* QUOTE

invertebrate (ɪn'vɜːtɪbrɪt, -breɪt) *n.* **1.** animal having no vertebral column *—a.* **2.** spineless

invest (ɪn'vest) *vt.* **1.** lay out (money, time, effort *etc.*) for profit or advantage **2.** install **3.** endow **4.** *obs.* clothe **5.** *Poet.* cover, as with garment *—in'vestiture* *n.* formal installation of person in office or rank *—in'vestment* *n.* **1.** investing **2.** money invested **3.** stocks and shares bought *—in'vestor* *n.* *—investment trust* financial enterprise that invests its subscribed capital in securities for its investors' benefit

investigate (ɪn'vestɪgeɪt) *vt.* inquire into; examine *—investi'gation* *n.* *—in'vestigator* *n.*

inveterate (ɪn'vetərɪt) *a.* **1.** deep-rooted; long-established **2.** confirmed *—in'veteracy* *n.*

invidious (ɪn'vɪdɪəs) *a.* likely to cause ill will or envy *—in'vidiously* *adv.*

invigilate (ɪn'vɪdʒɪleɪt) *vi.* supervise examination candidates *—in'vigilator* *n.*

invigorate (ɪn'vɪɡəreɪt) *vt.* give vigour to, strengthen

invincible (ɪn'vɪnsəbəl) *a.* unconquerable *—invinci'bility* *n.*

inviolable (ɪn'vaɪələbəl) *a.* **1.** not to be profaned; sacred **2.** unalterable *—in'violate* *a.* **1.** unhurt **2.** unprofaned **3.** unbroken

invisible (ɪn'vɪzəbəl) *a.* **1.** not visible; not able to be perceived by eye **2.** concealed from sight; hidden **3.** not easily seen or noticed **4.** kept hidden from public view; secret; clandestine **5.** *Econ.* of services, such as insurance and freight, rather than goods *—n.* **6.** *Econ.* invisible item of trade; service *—invisi'bility* *or* *in'visibleness* *n.* *—in'visibly* *adv.*

invite (ɪn'vaɪt) *vt.* **1.** request the company of **2.** ask courteously **3.** ask for **4.** attract, call forth *—n.* (ˈɪnvaɪt) **5.** *inf.* invitation *—invitation* (ɪnvɪ'teɪʃən) *n.* *—in'viting* *a.* tempting; alluring; attractive

invoice ('ɪnvɔɪs) *n.* **1.** a list of goods or services sold, with prices *—vt.* **2.** present with an invoice **3.** make an invoice of

invoke (ɪn'vəuk) *vt.* **1.** call on **2.** appeal to **3.** ask earnestly for **4.** summon *—invo'cation* *n.*

involuntary (ɪn'vɒləntərɪ, -trɪ) *a.* **1.** not done voluntarily **2.** unintentional **3.** instinctive

involute ('ɪnvəluːt) *a.* **1.** complex **2.** coiled spirally **3.** rolled inwards (*also* invo'luted) *—n.* **4.** *Maths.* a type of curve *—invo'lution* *n.*

involve (ɪn'vɒlv) *vt.* **1.** include **2.** entail **3.** implicate (person) **4.** concern **5.** entangle *—in'volved* *a.* **1.** complicated **2.** concerned *—in'volvement* *n.*

inward ('ɪnwəd) *a.* **1.** internal **2.** situated within **3.** spiritual, mental *—adv.* **4.** towards the inside **5.** into the mind (*also* 'inwards) *—pl.n.* **6.** *see* INNARDS *—'inwardly* *adv.* **1.** in the mind **2.** internally

iodine ('aɪədiːn) *n.* nonmetallic element found in seaweed and used in antiseptic tincture, photography and dyeing *—iodide* ('aɪədaɪd) *n.* **1.** salt of hydriodic acid, containing the iodide ion **2.** compound containing an iodine atom *—'iodize* *or* **-dise** *vt.* treat with iodine or iodide *—iodoform* (aɪ'ɒdəfɔːm) *n.* antiseptic

I.O.M. Isle of Man

ion ('aɪən, -ɒn) *n.* electrically charged atom or group of atoms *—i'onic* *a.* *—ioni'zation* *or* **-i'sation** *n.* *—'ionize* *or* **-ise** *v.* change or become changed into ions *—i'onosphere* *n.*

region of atmosphere 60 to 100 km above earth's surface

-ion (*comb. form*) action, process, state, as in *creation*, *objection*

Ionic (aɪ'ɒnɪk) *a.* Archit. distinguished by scroll-like decoration on columns

iota (aɪ'əʊtə) *n.* 1. ninth letter in Gr. alphabet (I, ɩ) 2. (*usu. with* not one *or* an) very small amount

IOU *n.* signed paper acknowledging debt

-ious (*comb. form*) characterized by; full of, as in *ambitious*, *suspicious*

I.O.W. Isle of Wight

IPA International Phonetic Alphabet

ipecac ('ɪpɪkæk) *or* **ipecacuanha** (ˌɪpɪkækjʊ-'ænə) *n.* S Amer. plant yielding an emetic

ipso facto ('ɪpsəʊ 'fæktəʊ) *Lat.* by that very fact

I.Q. intelligence quotient

Ir *Chem.* iridium

Ir. 1. Ireland 2. Irish

ir- (*comb. form*) see IN-

I.R.A. Irish Republican Army

Iranian (ɪ'reɪnɪən) *n.* 1. native or inhabitant of Iran —*a.* 2. of Iran

irascible (ɪ'ræsɪbᵊl) *a.* hot-tempered —**irasci'bility** *n.* —**i'rascibly** *adv.*

ire (aɪə) *n.* anger, wrath —**i'rate** *a.* angry

iridaceous (ˌɪrɪ'deɪʃəs, ˌaɪ-) *a.* belonging to iris family

iridescent (ˌɪrɪ'dɛsᵊnt) *a.* exhibiting changing colours like those of the rainbow —**iri'descence** *n.*

iridium (aɪ'rɪdɪəm, ɪ'rɪd-) *n.* very hard, corrosion-resistant metal

iris ('aɪrɪs) *n.* 1. circular membrane of eye containing pupil 2. plant with sword-shaped leaves and showy flowers (*pl.* **-es**, **irides** ('aɪrɪdiːz, 'ɪrɪ-))

Irish ('aɪrɪʃ) *a.* 1. of Ireland, its people or their language —*n.* 2. Irish Gaelic —**Irish coffee** coffee mixed with whiskey and topped with cream —**Irish Gaelic** Goidelic language of the Celts of Ireland; official language of the Republic of Ireland since 1921 —**Irish stew** stew made of mutton, potatoes, onions *etc.*

irk (ɜːk) *vt.* irritate, vex —**'irksome** *a.* tiresome

iron ('aɪən) *n.* 1. metallic element, much used for tools *etc.*, and the raw material of steel 2. tool *etc.* of this metal 3. appliance used, when heated, to smooth cloth 4. metal-headed golf club 5. splintlike support for malformed leg 6. great hardness, strength or resolve —*pl.* 7. fetters —*a.* 8. of, like iron 9. inflexible, unyielding 10. robust —*v.* 11. smooth, cover, fetter *etc.* with iron or an iron —**'irony** *a.* of, resembling, or containing iron —**Iron Age** era of iron implements —**iron'clad** *a.* protected with or as with iron —**Iron Curtain** 1. guarded

border between countries of Soviet bloc and the rest of Europe 2. (**i- c-**) any barrier that separates communities or ideologies —**iron hand** harsh or rigorous control —**ironing board** board, usu. on legs, with suitable covering on which to iron clothes —**iron lung** apparatus for administering artificial respiration —**iron maiden** medieval instrument of torture, consisting of enclosed space lined with iron spikes —**'ironmaster** *n.* UK manufacturer of iron —**'ironmonger** *n.* dealer in hardware —**'ironmongery** *n.* his wares —**iron pyrites** see PYRITES —**iron rations** emergency food supplies, *esp.* for military personnel in action —**'ironstone** *n.* 1. any rock consisting mainly of iron-bearing ore 2. tough durable earthenware —**'ironwood** *n.* various S Afr. trees —**'ironwork** *n.* work done in iron, *esp.* decorative work —**'ironworks** *pl.n.* (*sometimes with sing. v.*) building in which iron is smelted, cast or wrought

irony ('aɪrənɪ) *n.* 1. (*usu.* humorous or mildly sarcastic) use of words to mean the opposite of what is said 2. event, situation opposite of that expected —**i'ronic(al)** *a.* of, using irony

irradiate (ɪ'reɪdɪeɪt) *vt.* 1. treat by irradiation 2. shine upon, throw light upon, light up —**irradi'ation** *n.* impregnation by x-rays, light rays

irrational (ɪ'ræʃənᵊl) *a.* 1. inconsistent with reason or logic 2. incapable of reasoning 3. *Maths.* (of equation *etc.*) containing one or more variables in irreducible radical form or raised to fractional power —**irration'ality** *n.*

irreconcilable (ɪ'rɛkᵊnsaɪləbᵊl, ɪrɛkᵊn'saɪ-) *a.* 1. not able to be reconciled; incompatible —*n.* 2. person or thing that is implacably hostile 3. (*usu. pl.*) one of various principles *etc.* that are incapable of being brought into agreement —**irreconcila'bility** *n.* —**ir'reconcilably** *adv.*

irrecoverable (ɪrɪ'kʌvərəbᵊl, -'kʌvrə-) *a.* 1. not able to be recovered or regained 2. not able to be remedied or rectified

irredeemable (ɪrɪ'diːməbᵊl) *a.* 1. (of bonds *etc.*) without date of redemption of capital; incapable of being bought back directly or paid off 2. (of paper money) not convertible into specie 3. (of loss) not able to be recovered; irretrievable 4. not able to be improved or rectified; irreparable —**irre'deemably** *adv.*

irredentist (ɪrɪ'dɛntɪst) *n.* (*sometimes* I-) person, *esp.* member of 19th-century It. association, who favoured acquisition of territory that had once been part of his country —*a.* 2. of irredentism —**irre'dentism** *n.*

irreducible (ɪrɪ'djuːsɪbᵊl) *a.* 1. not able to be reduced or lessened 2. not able to be brought to simpler or reduced form 3. *Maths.* (of polynomial) unable to be factorized into polynomials of lower degree —**irreduci'bility** n.

irrefrangible (ɪrɪ'frændʒəbl) a. 1. inviolable 2. in optics, not susceptible to refraction

irrefutable (ɪ'refjutəbl, ɪrɪ'fjuːtəbl) a. that cannot be refuted, disproved

irreg. irregular(ly)

irregular (ɪ'regjulə) a. 1. lacking uniformity or symmetry; uneven in shape, arrangement etc. 2. not occurring at expected or equal intervals 3. differing from normal or accepted practice or routine 4. (of formation, inflections or derivations of word) not following usual pattern of formation in language 5. (of troops) not belonging to regular forces —n. 6. soldier not in regular army —**irregu'larity** n.

irrelevant (ɪ'reləvənt) a. not relating or pertinent to matter at hand; not important —**ir'relevance** or **ir'relevancy** n.

irremissible (ɪrɪ'mɪsəbl) a. 1. unpardonable; inexcusable 2. that must be done, as through duty or obligation —**irremissi'bility** n.

irreparable (ɪ'repərəbl, ɪ'reprəbl) a. not able to be repaired or remedied

irreplaceable (ɪrɪ'pleɪsəbl) a. not able to be replaced

irrepressible (ɪrɪ'presəbl) a. not capable of being repressed, controlled or restrained —**irrepressi'bility** n. —**irre'pressibly** adv.

irreproachable (ɪrɪ'prəutʃəbl) a. not deserving reproach; blameless

irresistible (ɪrɪ'zɪstəbl) a. 1. not able to be resisted or refused; overpowering 2. very fascinating or alluring —**irre'sistibly** adv.

irresolute (ɪ'rezəluːt) a. lacking resolution; wavering; hesitating —**ir'resolutely** adv. —**ir'resoluteness** or **irreso'lution** n.

irrespective (ɪrɪ'spektɪv) a. —**irrespective of** without taking account of

irresponsible (ɪrɪ'spɒnsəbl) a. 1. not showing or done with due care for consequences of one's actions or attitudes; reckless 2. not capable of bearing responsibility —**irresponsi'bility** or **irre'sponsibleness** n. —**irre'sponsibly** adv.

irretrievable (ɪrɪ'triːvəbl) a. not able to be retrieved, recovered or repaired —**irretriev-a'bility** n. —**irre'trievably** adv.

irreverence (ɪ'revərəns, ɪ'revrəns) n. 1. lack of due respect or veneration 2. disrespectful remark or act —**ir'reverent** a.

irreversible (ɪrɪ'vɜːsəbl) a. 1. not able to be reversed 2. not able to be revoked or repealed 3. Chem., phys. capable of changing or producing change in one direction only —**irreversi'bility** n. —**irre'versibly** adv.

irrevocable (ɪ'revəkəbl) a. not able to be changed, undone, altered

irrigate ('ɪrɪgeɪt) vt. water by artificial

channels, pipes etc. —**irri'gation** n. —**'irrigator** n.

irritate ('ɪrɪteɪt) vt. 1. annoy 2. inflame 3. stimulate —**'irritable** a. easily annoyed —**'irritably** adv. —**'irritant** a./n. (person or thing) causing irritation —**irri'tation** n.

irrupt (ɪ'rʌpt) vi. 1. enter forcibly 2. increase suddenly —**ir'ruption** n.

is (ɪz) third person singular, present indicative of BE

Is. 1. Bible Isaiah (also **Isa.**) 2. Island(s); Isle(s)

I.S.B.N. or **ISBN** International Standard Book Number

-ise (comb. form) see -IZE

-ish (comb. form) 1. of a nationality, as in Scottish 2. oft. derogatory having manner or qualities of; resembling, as in slavish, boyish 3. somewhat; approximately, as in yellowish, sevenish 4. concerned or preoccupied with, as in bookish

isinglass ('aɪzɪŋɡlɑːs) n. kind of gelatine obtained from some freshwater fish

Isl. 1. Island 2. Isle

Islam ('ɪzlɑːm) n. Mohammedan faith or world —**Is'lamic** a.

island ('aɪlənd) n. 1. piece of land surrounded by water 2. anything like this, as raised piece for pedestrians in middle of road —**'islander** n. inhabitant of island

isle (aɪl) n. island —**'islet** n. little island

ism ('ɪzəm) n. inf., oft. derogatory unspecified doctrine, system or practice

-ism (comb. form) 1. action, process, result, as in criticism 2. state; condition, as in paganism 3. doctrine, system, body of principles and practices, as in Leninism, spiritualism 4. behaviour; characteristic quality, as in heroism 5. characteristic usage, esp. of language, as in Scotticism

isobar ('aɪsəubɑː) n. line on map connecting places of equal mean barometric pressure —**iso'baric** a.

isochronal (aɪ'sɒkrənəl) or **isochronous** a. 1. having same duration; equal in time 2. occurring at equal time intervals; having uniform period of vibration —**i'sochronism** n.

isolate ('aɪsəleɪt) vt. place apart or alone —**iso'lation** n. —**iso'lationism** n. policy of not participating in international affairs —**iso'lationist** n./a.

isomer ('aɪsəmə) n. substance with same molecules as another but different atomic arrangement —**iso'meric** a. —**i'somerism** n.

isometric (aɪsəu'metrɪk) a. 1. having equal dimensions 2. relating to muscular contraction without movement —**iso'metrics** pl.n. (with sing. v.) system of isometric exercises

isomorphism (aɪsəu'mɔːfɪzəm) n. 1. Biol.

similarity of form **2.** *Chem.* existence of two or more substances of different composition in similar crystalline form **3.** *Maths.* one-to-one correspondence between elements of two or more sets —**iso'morphic** *or* **iso'morphous** *a.*

isosceles (aɪ'sɒsɪliːz) *a.* (of triangle) having two sides equal

isotherm ('aɪsəʊθɜːm) *n.* line on map connecting points of equal mean temperature

isotope ('aɪsətəʊp) *n.* atom of element having a different nuclear mass and atomic weight from other atoms in same element —**isotopic** (aɪsə'tɒpɪk) *a.*

isotropic (aɪsəʊ'trɒpɪk) *or* **isotropous** (aɪ'sɒtrəpəs) *a.* **1.** having uniform physical properties in all directions **2.** *Biol.* not having predetermined axes —**i'sotropy** *n.*

Israel ('ɪzreɪəl, -rɪəl) *n.* **1.** republic in SW Asia, established as modern state of Israel **2.** ancient kingdom of Jews in this region —'**Israelite** *n. Bible* member of ethnic group claiming descent from Jacob; Hebrew —**Children of Israel** the Jewish people or nation

issue ('ɪʃuː) *n.* **1.** sending or giving out officially or publicly **2.** number or amount so given out **3.** discharge **4.** offspring, children **5.** topic of discussion **6.** question, dispute **7.** outcome, result —*vi.* **8.** go out **9.** result (in) **10.** arise (from) —*vt.* **11.** emit, give out, send out **12.** distribute **13.** publish —**take issue** disagree

-ist (*comb. form*) **1.** person who performs certain action or is concerned with something specified, as in *motorist, soloist* **2.** person who practises in specific field, as in *physicist* **3.** person who advocates particular doctrine, system *etc.;* of doctrine advocated, as in *socialist* **4.** person characterized by specified trait, tendency *etc.;* of such a trait, as in *purist* —**-istic** (*a. comb. form*)

isthmus ('ɪsməs) *n.* neck of land between two seas

it (ɪt) *pron.* neuter pronoun of the third person —**its** belonging to it —**it'self** *pron.* emphatic form of IT

It. 1. Italian **2.** Italy

i.t.a. *or* **I.T.A.** initial teaching alphabet

ital. italic (type)

Italian (ɪ'tæljən) *n.* **1.** language of Italy **2.** native of Italy —*a.* **3.** of Italy —**I'talianate** *or* **Italia'nesque** *a.* Italian in style or character

italic (ɪ'tælɪk) *a.* (of type) sloping —**i'talicize** *or* **-ise** *vt.* put in italics —**i'talics** *pl.n.* italic type, now used for emphasis *etc.*

itch (ɪtʃ) *n.* **1.** irritation in the skin **2.** restless desire —*vi.* **3.** feel or produce irritating or tickling sensation **4.** have a restless desire (to do something) —'**itchy** *a.*

-ite (*comb. form*) **1.** native or inhabitant of, as in

Israelite **2.** follower or advocate of; supporter of group, as in *Luddite, labourite* **3.** *Biol.* division of body or organ, as in *neurite* **4.** mineral; rock, as in *nephrite, peridotite* **5.** commercial product, as in *vulcanite*

item ('aɪtəm) *n.* **1.** single thing in list, collection *etc.* **2.** piece of information **3.** entry in account *etc.* —*adv.* ('aɪtɛm) **4.** also —'**itemize** *or* **-ise** *vt.*

iterate ('ɪtəreɪt) *vt.* repeat —**iter'ation** *n.* —**iterative** ('ɪtərətɪv) *a.*

itinerant (ɪ'tɪnərənt, aɪ-) *a.* **1.** travelling from place to place **2.** working for a short time in various places **3.** travelling on circuit —**i'tineracy** *n.* —**i'tinerary** *n.* **1.** record, line of travel **2.** route **3.** guidebook

-itis (*comb. form*) inflammation of specified part, as in *tonsillitis*

ITV Independent Television

-ity (*comb. form*) state; condition, as in *technicality*

IUD intrauterine device (for contraception)

-ive (*comb. form*) tendency, inclination, character, quality, as in *divisive, festive, massive*

ivory ('aɪvərɪ, -vrɪ) *n.* **1.** hard white substance of the tusks of elephants *etc.* **2.** yellowish-white colour; cream —*a.* **3.** yellowish-white; cream —'**ivories** *pl.n. sl.* **1.** piano keys **2.** billiard balls **3.** teeth **4.** dice —**ivory tower** seclusion, remoteness

ivy ('aɪvɪ) *n.* climbing evergreen plant —'**ivied** *a.* covered with ivy

-ize *or* **-ise** (*comb. form*) **1.** cause to become, resemble or agree with, as in *legalize* **2.** become; change into, as in *crystallize* **3.** affect in specified way; subject to, as in *hypnotize* **4.** act according to some principle, policy *etc.,* as in *economize*

J, j

j *or* **J** (dʒeɪ) *n.* **1.** tenth letter of English alphabet **2.** speech sound represented by this letter (*pl.* **j's, J's** *or* **Js**)

jab (dʒæb) *vt.* **1.** poke roughly **2.** thrust, stab abruptly (**-bb-**) —*n.* **3.** poke **4.** *inf.* injection

jabber ('dʒæbə) *vi.* **1.** chatter **2.** talk rapidly, incoherently —'**jabberwocky** *n.* nonsense, *esp.* in verse

jabot ('ʒæbəʊ) *n.* frill, ruffle at throat or breast of garment

jacaranda (dʒækə'rændə) *n.* S Amer. tree with fernlike leaves and pale purple flowers

jacinth ('dʒæsɪnθ) *n.* reddish-orange precious stone

jack (dʒæk) *n.* 1. fellow, man 2. *inf.* sailor 3. male of some animals 4. device for lifting heavy weight, *esp.* motor car 5. various mechanical appliances 6. lowest court card, with picture of pageboy 7. *Bowls* ball aimed at 8. socket and plug connection in electronic equipment 9. small flag, *esp.* national, at sea —*vt.* 10. (*usu. with* up) lift (an object) with a jack —**Jack Frost** personification of frost —**jack-in-office** *n.* self-important petty official —**jack-in-the-box** *n.* toy consisting of figure on tight spring in box, which springs out when lid is opened (*pl.* **jack-in-the-boxes, jacks-in-the-box**) —**jack of all trades** person who undertakes many kinds of work (*pl.* **jacks of all trades**) —**jack-o'-lantern** *n.* 1. lantern made from hollowed pumpkin, cut to represent human face 2. will-o'-the-wisp —**Jack Tar** *chiefly lit.* sailor

jackal (ˈdʒækɔːl) *n.* wild, gregarious animal of Asia and Afr. closely allied to dog

jackanapes (ˈdʒækəneɪps) *n.* 1. conceited impertinent person 2. mischievous child 3. *obs.* monkey

jackass (ˈdʒækæs) *n.* 1. the male of the ass 2. blockhead —**laughing jackass** the Aust. kookaburra

jackboot (ˈdʒækbuːt) *n.* large riding boot coming above knee

jackdaw (ˈdʒækdɔː) *n.* small kind of crow

jacket (ˈdʒækɪt) *n.* 1. outer garment, short coat 2. outer casing, cover —**jacketed** *a.*

jackhammer (ˈdʒækhæmə) *n.* hand-held hammer drill

jackknife (ˈdʒæknaɪf) *n.* 1. clasp knife 2. dive with sharp bend at waist in midair —*vi.* 3. (of articulated lorry) go out of control in such a way that trailer forms right angle to tractor

jackpot (ˈdʒækpɒt) *n.* large prize, accumulated stake, as pool in poker —**hit the jackpot** win a jackpot; achieve great success, *esp.* through luck

jack rabbit US hare

jacks (dʒæks) *pl.n.* game in which bone or metal pieces (**jackstones**) are thrown and picked up between bounces of small ball

Jacobean (dʒækəˈbɪən) *a.* of the reign of James I

Jacobite (ˈdʒækəbaɪt) *n.* adherent of Stuarts after overthrow of James II

Jacquard (ˈdʒækɑːd, dʒəˈkɑːd) *n.* fabric in which design is incorporated into the weave

Jacuzzi (dʒəˈkuːzɪ) *n.* R 1. device which swirls water in bath 2. bath containing such a device

jade[1] (dʒeɪd) *n.* 1. ornamental semiprecious stone, usu. dark green 2. this colour

jade[2] (dʒeɪd) *n.* 1. old worn-out horse 2. *obs., offens.* woman considered to be disreputable —**jaded** *a.* 1. tired 2. off colour

Jaffa (ˈdʒæfə, ˈdʒɑː-) *n.* 1. port in W Israel 2. large orange with thick skin

jag[1] (dʒæg) *n.* sharp or ragged projection —**jagged** (ˈdʒægɪd) *a.*

jag[2] (dʒæg) *n. sl.* 1. intoxication from drugs or alcohol 2. bout of drinking or drug taking

jaguar (ˈdʒægjuə) *n.* large S Amer. spotted animal of cat family

jail *or* **gaol** (dʒeɪl) *n.* 1. building for confinement of criminals or suspects —*vt.* 2. send to, confine in prison —**jailer, jailor** *or* **gaoler** *n.* —**jailbird** *or* **goalbird** *n.* hardened criminal

jalopy *or* **jaloppy** (dʒəˈlɒpɪ) *n. inf.* old car

jalousie (ˈʒæluzɪ) *n.* 1. blind or shutter constructed from angled slats of wood *etc.* 2. window made of angled slats of glass

jam (dʒæm) *vt.* 1. pack together 2. (*oft. with* on) apply fiercely 3. squeeze 4. *Rad.* block (another station) with impulses of equal wavelength —*v.* 5. (cause to) stick together and become unworkable —*vi.* 6. *sl.* play in jam session (-**mm-**) —*n.* 7. fruit preserved by boiling with sugar 8. crush 9. hold-up of traffic 10. awkward situation —**jam-packed** *a.* filled to capacity —**jam session** (improvised) jazz or pop music session

jamb *or* **jambe** (dʒæm) *n.* side post of door, window *etc.*

jamboree (dʒæmbəˈriː) *n.* 1. large gathering or rally of Scouts 2. spree, celebration

jammy (ˈdʒæmɪ) *a.* UK *sl.* 1. pleasant; desirable 2. lucky

Jan. January

jangle (ˈdʒæŋgəl) *v.* 1. (cause to) sound harshly, as bell —*vt.* 2. produce jarring effect on —*n.* 3. harsh sound

janitor (ˈdʒænɪtə) *n.* 1. caretaker 2. doorkeeper (ˈjanitress *fem.*)

January (ˈdʒænjʊərɪ) *n.* first month

japan (dʒəˈpæn) *n.* 1. very hard, *usu.* black varnish —*vt.* 2. cover with this (-**nn-**)

Japanese (dʒæpəˈniːz) *a.* 1. of Japan —*n.* 2. native of Japan (*pl.* **-nese**) 3. official language of Japan

jape (dʒeɪp) *n./vi.* joke

japonica (dʒəˈpɒnɪkə) *n.* shrub with red flowers (*also* **Japanese quince**)

jar[1] (dʒɑː) *n.* 1. usu. round vessel of glass, earthenware *etc.* 2. *inf.* glass of beer

jar[2] (dʒɑː) *v.* 1. (cause to) vibrate suddenly, violently —*vt.* 2. have disturbing, painful effect on (-**rr-**) —*n.* 3. jarring sound 4. shock *etc.*

jardinière (ʒɑːdɪˈnjɛə) *n.* ornamental pot for growing plants

jargon (ˈdʒɑːgən) *n.* 1. specialized language concerned with particular subject 2. pretentious or nonsensical language

Jas. James

jasmine ('dʒæsmɪn, 'dʒæz-) n. flowering shrub

jasper ('dʒæspə) n. red, yellow, dark green or brown quartz

jaundice ('dʒɔːndɪs) n. 1. disease marked by yellowness of skin (also 'icterus) 2. bitterness, ill humour 3. prejudice —vt. 4. make prejudiced, bitter etc.

jaunt (dʒɔːnt) n. 1. short pleasurable excursion —vi. 2. go on such an excursion —**jaunting car** formerly, light, two-wheeled, one-horse car used in Ireland

jaunty ('dʒɔːntɪ) a. 1. sprightly 2. brisk 3. smart, trim —**jauntily** adv.

Javanese (dʒɑːvə'niːz) a. 1. of island of Java, in Indonesia —n. 2. native or inhabitant of Java (pl. -ese) 3. Malayan language of Java

javelin ('dʒævlɪn) n. spear, esp. for throwing in sporting events

jaw (dʒɔː) n. 1. one of bones in which teeth are set —pl. 2. mouth 3. gripping part of vice etc. 4. fig. narrow opening of gorge or valley —vi. 5. sl. talk lengthily

jay (dʒeɪ) n. noisy bird with brilliant plumage —'**jaywalk** vi. walk in or across street carelessly or illegally —'**jaywalker** n.

jazz (dʒæz) n. syncopated music and dance —'**jazzy** a. flashy, showy —**jazz up** 1. play as jazz 2. make more lively, appealing

jealous ('dʒeləs) a. 1. distrustful of the faithfulness (of) 2. envious 3. suspiciously watchful —'**jealously** adv. —'**jealousy** n.

jeans (dʒiːnz) pl.n. casual trousers, esp. made of denim

Jeep (dʒiːp) n. **R** light four-wheel drive motor utility vehicle

jeer (dʒɪə) v. 1. scoff —n. 2. scoff, taunt, gibe

Jehovah (dʒɪ'həʊvə) n. O.T. God —**Jehovah's Witness** member of Christian sect who believes end of world is near

jejune (dʒɪ'dʒuːn) a. 1. simple, naive 2. meagre

Jekyll and Hyde ('dʒekəl; haɪd) person with two distinct personalities, one good, the other evil

jell or **gel** (dʒel) v. 1. congeal —vi. 2. inf. assume definite form

jellaba or **jellabah** ('dʒeləbə) n. loose cloak with hood, worn esp. in N Afr.

jelly ('dʒelɪ) n. 1. semitransparent food made with gelatine, becoming softly stiff as it cools 2. anything of the consistency of this —'**jellyfish** n. jellylike small sea animal

jemmy ('dʒemɪ) or U.S. **jimmy** ('dʒɪmɪ) n. short steel crowbar, pinchbar

jenny ('dʒenɪ) n. 1. female ass 2. female wren

jeopardy ('dʒepədɪ) n. (usu. with in) danger —'**jeopardize** or **-ise** vt. endanger

Jer. Bible Jeremiah

jerboa (dʒɜː'bəʊə) n. 1. small Afr. burrowing rodent resembling a mouse 2. desert rat

jeremiad (dʒerɪ'maɪəd) n. lamentation; complaint

jerk[1] (dʒɜːk) n. 1. sharp, abruptly stopped movement 2. twitch 3. sharp pull 4. sl. stupid person —v. 5. move or throw with a jerk —'**jerkily** adv. —'**jerkiness** n. —'**jerky** a. uneven, spasmodic

jerk[2] (dʒɜːk) vt. 1. preserve (beef etc.) by cutting into strips and drying in sun —n. 2. jerked meat (also '**jerky**)

jerkin ('dʒɜːkɪn) n. sleeveless jacket, esp. of leather

Jerry ('dʒerɪ) n. **UK** sl. 1. German, esp. German soldier 2. Germans collectively

jerry-built ('dʒerɪ) a. of flimsy construction with cheap materials —'**jerry-builder** n.

jerry can flat-sided can for storing or transporting motor fuel etc.

jersey ('dʒɜːzɪ) n. 1. knitted jumper 2. machine-knitted fabric 3. (J-) breed of cow

jessamine ('dʒesəmɪn) n. see JASMINE

jest (dʒest) n./vi. joke —'**jester** n. joker, esp. employed by medieval ruler

Jesuit ('dʒezjʊɪt) n. member of Society of Jesus, order founded by Ignatius Loyola in 1534 —**Jesu'itical** a. of Jesuits

Jesus ('dʒiːzəs) n. 1. ?4 B.C.-?29 A.D., founder of Christianity, believed by Christians to be the Son of God (also **Jesus Christ, Jesus of Nazareth**) —interj. 2. used to express intense surprise, dismay etc. (also **Jesus wept**)

jet[1] (dʒet) n. 1. stream of liquid, gas etc., esp. shot from small hole 2. the small hole 3. spout, nozzle 4. aircraft driven by jet propulsion —vt. 5. throw out —vi. 6. shoot forth —v. 7. transport or be transported by jet (-tt-) —**jet lag** fatigue caused by crossing time zones in jet aircraft —**jet-propelled** a. driven by jet propulsion —**jet propulsion** propulsion by thrust provided by jet of gas or liquid —**jet set** rich, fashionable social set, members of which travel widely for pleasure —'**jetsetter** n.

jet[2] (dʒet) n. hard black mineral capable of brilliant polish —**jet-black** a. glossy black

jetsam ('dʒetsəm) n. cargo thrown overboard to lighten ship and later washed ashore —'**jettison** vt. 1. abandon 2. throw overboard

jetty ('dʒetɪ) n. small pier, wharf

Jew (dʒuː) n. 1. person of Hebrew religion or ancestry 2. inf., offens. miser (**Jewess** fem.) —'**Jewish** a. —'**Jewry** n. Jews collectively —**jew's-harp** n. small musical instrument held between teeth and played by finger

jewel ('dʒuːəl) n. 1. precious stone 2. ornament containing one 3. precious thing —'**jeweller** or

U.S. **'jeweler** n. dealer in jewels —**jewellery** or U.S. **jewelry** ('dʒuːəlrɪ) n.

jewfish ('dʒuːfɪʃ) n. large fish of tropical and temperate waters

Jezebel ('dʒɛzəbɛl) n. 1. O.T. wife of Ahab, king of Israel 2. (sometimes **j**-) shameless or scheming woman

jib (dʒɪb) n. 1. triangular sail set forward of mast 2. projecting arm of crane or derrick —vi. 3. object to proceeding 4. (of horse, person) stop and refuse to go on (-bb-) —**'jibber** n. —**jib boom** spar from end of bowsprit

jibe[1] (dʒaɪb) or **jib** (dʒɪb) see GYBE, GIBE

jibe[2] (dʒaɪb) vi. inf. agree; accord; harmonize

jiffy ('dʒɪfɪ) or **jiff** n. inf. very short period of time

Jiffy bag ('dʒɪfɪ) R large padded envelope

jig (dʒɪg) n. 1. lively dance 2. music for it 3. small mechanical device 4. mechanical device used as guide for cutting etc. 5. Angling any of various lures —vi. 6. dance jig 7. make jerky up-and-down movements (-gg-) —**'jigger** n. —**'jigsaw** n. machine fretsaw —**jigsaw (puzzle)** picture stuck on board and cut into interlocking pieces with jigsaw

jigger ('dʒɪgə) n. small glass for spirits

jiggery-pokery ('dʒɪgərɪ'pəʊkərɪ) n. inf. trickery, nonsense

jiggle ('dʒɪgəl) v. move (up and down etc.) with short jerky movements

jilt (dʒɪlt) vt. cast off (lover)

jim crow ('dʒɪm 'krəʊ) (oft. J- C-) US 1. policy or practice of segregating Negroes 2. derogatory Negro 3. implement for bending iron bars or rails

jimjams ('dʒɪmdʒæmz) pl.n. 1. sl. delirium tremens 2. state of nervous tension or anxiety

jingle ('dʒɪŋgəl) n. 1. mixed metallic noise, as of shaken chain 2. catchy, rhythmic verse, song etc. —v. 3. (cause to) make jingling sound

jingo ('dʒɪŋgəʊ) n. 1. loud, bellicose patriot 2. jingoism (pl. -es) —**'jingoism** n. chauvinism —**jingo'istic** a. —**by jingo** exclamation of surprise

jinks (dʒɪŋks) pl.n. boisterous merrymaking (esp. in **high jinks**)

jinni, jinnee or **djinni** (dʒɪ'niː) n. spirit in Muslim mythology who could assume human or animal form (pl. **jinn** or **djinn** (dʒɪn))

jinx (dʒɪŋks) n. 1. force, person, thing bringing bad luck —vt. 2. be or put a jinx on

jitters ('dʒɪtəz) pl.n. worried nervousness, anxiety —**'jittery** a. nervous —**'jitterbug** n. 1. fast jerky Amer. dance popular in 1940s 2. person who dances jitterbug —vi. 3. perform such dance

jiujitsu or **jiujutsu** (dʒuː'dʒɪtsuː) n. see JUJITSU

jive (dʒaɪv) n. 1. (dance performed to) rock and roll music, esp. of 1950s —vi. 2. dance the jive

job (dʒɒb) n. 1. piece of work, task 2. post, office 3. inf. difficult task 4. inf. crime, robbery —**'jobber** n. stockjobber —**'jobbing** a. doing single, particular jobs for payment —**'jobless** a./pl.n. unemployed (people) —**job centre** government office in town centre providing information about vacant jobs —**job lot** 1. assortment sold together 2. miscellaneous collection

Job's comforter (dʒəʊbz) person who adds to distress while purporting to give sympathy

jockey ('dʒɒkɪ) n. 1. professional rider in horse races (pl. **-s**) —v. 2. (esp. with for) manoeuvre ('jockeyed, 'jockeying)

jockstrap ('dʒɒkstræp) n. piece of elasticated material worn by men, esp. athletes, to support genitals (also **athletic support**)

jocose (dʒə'kəʊs) a. waggish, humorous —jo'cosely adv. —**jocosity** (dʒə'kɒsɪtɪ) n. —**jocular** ('dʒɒkjʊlə) a. 1. joking 2. given to joking —**jocularity** (dʒɒkjʊ'lærɪtɪ) n.

jocund ('dʒɒkənd) a. merry, cheerful —jo'cundity n.

jodhpurs ('dʒɒdpəz) pl.n. tight-legged riding breeches

jog (dʒɒg) vi. 1. run slowly or move at a trot, esp. for physical exercise —vt. 2. jar, nudge 3. remind, stimulate (-gg-) —n. 4. jogging —**'jogger** n. —**'jogging** n. —**jog trot** slow regular trot

joggle ('dʒɒgəl) v. 1. move to and fro in jerks 2. shake —n. 3. act of joggling

john (dʒɒn) n. US sl. lavatory

John Bull typical Englishman

joie de vivre (ʒwad 'vivr) Fr. enjoyment of life, ebullience

join (dʒɔɪn) vt. 1. put together, fasten, unite 2. become member of —vi. 3. become united, connected 4. (with up) enlist 5. (usu. with in) take part —n. 6. joining 7. place of joining —**'joiner** n. maker of finished woodwork 2. one who joins —**'joinery** n. joiner's work

joint (dʒɔɪnt) n. 1. arrangement by which two things fit together, rigidly or loosely 2. place of this 3. meat for roasting, oft. with bone 4. inf. house, place etc. 5. sl. disreputable bar or nightclub 6. sl. marijuana cigarette —a. 7. common 8. shared by two or more —vt. 9. connect by joints 10. divide at the joints —**'jointly** adv. —**joint-stock company** 1. UK business enterprise characterized by sharing of ownership between shareholders, whose liability is limited 2. US business enterprise whose owners are issued shares of transferable stock but do not enjoy limited liability —**out of joint** 1. dislocated 2. disorganized

jointure ('dʒɔintʃə) n. Law property settled on wife for her use after husband's death

joist (dʒɔist) n. one of the parallel beams stretched from wall to wall on which to fix floor or ceiling —'**joisted** a.

joke (dʒəʊk) n. 1. thing said or done to cause laughter 2. something said or done merely in fun 3. ridiculous or humorous circumstance —vi. 4. make jokes —'**joker** n. 1. one who jokes 2. sl. fellow 3. extra card in pack, counting as highest card in some games

jolly ('dʒɒlɪ) a. 1. jovial 2. festive, merry —vt. 3. (esp. with along) (try) to make (person, occasion etc.) happier ('**jollied**, '**jollying**) —jollifi'**cation** n. merrymaking —'**jollity** n.

Jolly Roger pirates' flag with white skull and crossbones on black field

jolt (dʒəʊlt) n. 1. sudden jerk 2. bump 3. shock —v. 4. move, shake with jolts —'**jolty** a.

Jonah ('dʒəʊnə) or **Jonas** ('dʒəʊnəs) n. 1. O.T. Hebrew prophet who was swallowed by whale 2. person believed to bring bad luck to those around him

jonquil ('dʒɒŋkwɪl) n. 1. fragrant yellow or white narcissus —a. 2. pale yellow

Josh. Bible Joshua

joss (dʒɒs) n. Chinese idol —**joss house** Chinese temple —**joss stick** stick of Chinese incense

jostle ('dʒɒs^al) or **justle** ('dʒʌs^al) v. knock or push against (someone)

jot (dʒɒt) n. 1. small amount, whit —vt. 2. write briefly; make note of (-tt-) —'**jotter** n. notebook

joule (dʒuːl) n. Elec. unit of work or energy

journal ('dʒɜːn^al) n. 1. daily newspaper or other periodical 2. daily record 3. logbook 4. part of axle or shaft resting on the bearings —**journa'lese** n. journalists' jargon 2. high-flown style, full of clichés —'**journalism** n. editing, writing in periodicals —'**journalist** n. —**journa'listic** a.

journey ('dʒɜːnɪ) n. 1. travelling from one place to another; excursion 2. distance travelled —vi. 3. travel

journeyman ('dʒɜːnɪmən) n. craftsman or artisan employed by another

joust (dʒaʊst) Hist. n. 1. encounter with lances between two mounted knights —vi. 2. engage in joust

Jove (dʒəʊv) n. see JUPITER (sense 1) —'**Jovian** a. —**by Jove** exclamation of surprise

jovial ('dʒəʊvɪəl) a. convivial, merry, gay

jowl (dʒaʊl) n. 1. cheek, jaw 2. outside of throat when prominent

joy (dʒɔɪ) n. 1. gladness, pleasure, delight 2. cause of this —'**joyful** a. —'**joyless** a. —'**joyous** a. 1. having happy nature or mood 2. joyful —'**joyously** adv. —**joy ride** trip, esp. in stolen car —'**joystick** n. inf. control column of aircraft

J.P. Justice of the Peace

Jr. or **jr.** Junior

jubilate ('dʒuːbɪleɪt) vi. rejoice —'**jubilant** a. exultant —'**jubilantly** adv. —**jubi'lation** n.

jubilee ('dʒuːbɪliː) n. time of rejoicing, esp. 25th or 50th anniversary

Jud. Bible Judges

Judaic (dʒuː'deɪɪk) a. of the Jews or Judaism —'**Judaism** n. 1. religion of the Jews 2. religious and cultural traditions of the Jews 3. the Jews collectively —'**Judaize** or **-ise** vt. 1. make Jewish —v. 2. conform or bring into conformity with Judaism

Judas ('dʒuːdəs) n. 1. N.T. apostle who betrayed Jesus to his enemies for 30 pieces of silver 2. person who betrays a friend; traitor

judder ('dʒʌdə) inf. vi. 1. shake, vibrate —n. 2. a vibrating motion

judge (dʒʌdʒ) n. 1. officer appointed to try cases in court of law 2. one who decides in dispute, contest etc. 3. one able to form reliable opinion, arbiter 4. umpire 5. in Jewish history, ruler —vi. 6. act as judge —vt. 7. act as judge of 8. try, estimate 9. decide —'**judgment** or '**judgement** n. 1. faculty of judging 2. sentence of court 3. opinion 4. misfortune regarded as sign of divine displeasure —**Judgment Day** occasion of Last Judgment by God at end of world

judicature ('dʒuːdɪkətʃə) n. 1. administration of justice 2. body of judges —ju'**dicial** a. 1. of, or by, a court or judge 2. having qualities proper to a judge 3. discriminating —ju'**dicially** adv. —ju'**dicious** a. well-judged, sensible, prudent

judo ('dʒuːdəʊ) n. modern sport derived from jujitsu

jug (dʒʌg) n. 1. vessel for liquids, with handle and small spout 2. its contents 3. sl. prison —vt. 4. stew (esp. hare) in jug (-gg-)

juggernaut ('dʒʌgənɔːt) n. 1. large heavy lorry 2. any irresistible, destructive force

juggle ('dʒʌg^al) v. 1. throw and catch (several objects) so most are in the air simultaneously 2. manage, manipulate (accounts etc.) to deceive —n. 3. act of juggling —'**juggler** n.

jugular vein ('dʒʌgjʊlə) one of three large veins of the neck returning blood from the head

juice (dʒuːs) n. 1. liquid part of vegetable, fruit or meat 2. inf. electric current 3. inf. petrol 4. vigour, vitality —'**juicy** a. succulent

jujitsu, jujutsu, or **jiujutsu** (dʒuː'dʒɪtsuː) n. the Japanese art of wrestling and self-defence

juju ('dʒuːdʒuː) n. 1. object superstitiously revered by certain W Afr. peoples and used as charm or fetish 2. power associated with juju

jujube ('dʒuːdʒuːb) n. 1. any of several spiny trees that have yellowish flowers and dark red edible fruits **2.** fruit of any of these trees **3.** lozenge of gelatine, sugar *etc.*

jukebox ('dʒuːkbɒks) *n.* automatic, coin-operated record-player

Jul. July

julep ('dʒuːlɪp) *n.* **1.** sweet drink **2.** medicated drink

Julian ('dʒuːljən) *a.* of Julius Caesar —**Julian calendar** calendar as adjusted by Julius Caesar in 46 B.C., in which the year was made to consist of 365 days, 6 hours, instead of 365 days

julienne (dʒuːlɪˈɛn) *n.* kind of clear soup

July (dʒuːˈlaɪ) *n.* seventh month

jumble ('dʒʌmbəl) *v.* **1.** mingle, mix in confusion **2.** remember in confused form —*n.* **3.** confused heap, muddle **4.** articles for jumble sale —**jumble sale** sale of miscellaneous, usu. second-hand, items

jumbo ('dʒʌmbəʊ) *n. inf.* **1.** elephant **2.** anything very large (*pl.* **-s**) —**jumbo jet** *inf.* large jet-propelled airliner

jump (dʒʌmp) *v.* **1.** (cause to) spring, leap (over) **2.** pass or skip (over) —*vi.* **3.** move hastily **4.** rise steeply **5.** parachute from aircraft **6.** start, jerk (with astonishment *etc.*) **7.** (of faulty film *etc.*) make abrupt movements —*vt.* **8.** come off (tracks, rails *etc.*) **9.** *inf.* attack without warning —*n.* **10.** act of jumping **11.** obstacle to be jumped **12.** distance, height jumped **13.** sudden shock **14.** sudden rise in prices —'**jumper** *n.* **1.** one who, that which jumps **2.** sweater, pullover —'**jumpy** *a.* nervous —**jumped-up** *inf.* suddenly risen in significance, *esp.* when appearing arrogant —**jump jet** *inf.* fixed-wing jet aircraft that can land and take off vertically —**jump leads** electric cables to connect discharged car battery to external battery to aid starting of engine —**jump suit** one-piece garment of trousers and top

Jun. 1. June **2.** junior (*also* **jun.**)

junction ('dʒʌŋkʃən) *n.* **1.** railway station *etc.* where lines, routes join **2.** place of joining **3.** joining

juncture ('dʒʌŋktʃə) *n.* state of affairs

June (dʒuːn) *n.* sixth month

jungle ('dʒʌŋgəl) *n.* **1.** tangled vegetation of equatorial forest **2.** land covered with it **3.** tangled mass **4.** condition of intense competition, struggle for survival —'**jungly** *a.*

junior ('dʒuːnjə) *a.* **1.** younger **2.** of lower standing —*n.* **3.** junior person —**junior school** UK school for children aged between 7 and 11 —**junior technician** rank in Royal Air Force comparable to that of private in army

juniper ('dʒuːnɪpə) *n.* evergreen shrub with berries yielding oil of juniper, used for medicine and gin making

junk[1] (dʒʌŋk) *n.* **1.** discarded, useless objects **2.**

inf. nonsense **3.** *sl.* narcotic drug —'**junkie** *or* '**junky** *n. sl.* drug addict —**junk food** food eaten in addition to or instead of regular meals, oft. with low nutritional value

junk[2] (dʒʌŋk) *n.* Chinese sailing vessel

junket ('dʒʌŋkɪt) *n.* **1.** curdled milk flavoured and sweetened —*vi.* **2.** feast, picnic

junta ('dʒʌntə) *n.* group of military officers holding power in a country

Jupiter ('dʒuːpɪtə) *n.* **1.** Roman chief of gods **2.** largest of the planets

Jurassic (dʒʊˈræsɪk) *a.* **1.** of second period of Mesozoic era —*n.* **2.** Jurassic period or rock system

juridical (dʒʊˈrɪdɪkəl) *a.* of law or administration of justice; legal

jurisdiction (dʒʊərɪsˈdɪkʃən) *n.* **1.** administration of justice **2.** authority **3.** territory covered by it —'**juris'prudence** *n.* science of, skill in, law —'**jurist** *n.* one skilled in law —**ju'ristic(al)** *a.*

jury ('dʒʊərɪ) *n.* **1.** body of persons sworn to render verdict in court of law **2.** body of judges of competition —'**juror** *or* '**juryman** *n.* one of jury —**jury box** enclosure in court where jury sit

jury- (*comb. form*) *chiefly naut.* makeshift, as in *jury-rigged*

just (dʒʌst) *a.* **1.** fair **2.** upright, honest **3.** proper, right, equitable —*adv.* **4.** exactly **5.** barely **6.** at this instant **7.** merely, only **8.** really —'**justice** *n.* **1.** quality of being just **2.** fairness **3.** judicial proceedings **4.** judge, magistrate —**jus'ticiary** *a.* **1.** of administration of justice —*n.* **2.** officer or administrator of justice; judge —'**justifiable** *a.* —'**justifiably** *adv.* —**justifi'cation** *n.* —'**justify** *vt.* **1.** prove right, true or innocent **2.** vindicate **3.** excuse (**-ified, -ifying**) —'**justly** *adv.* —**justice of the peace** lay magistrate whose function is to preserve peace in his area and try summarily minor cases

jut (dʒʌt) *vi.* **1.** (*oft. with* **out**) project, stick out (**-tt-**) —*n.* **2.** projection

jute (dʒuːt) *n.* fibre of certain plants, used for rope, canvas *etc.*

juvenile ('dʒuːvɪnaɪl) *a.* **1.** young **2.** of, for young children **3.** immature —*n.* **4.** young person, child —**juve'nescence** *n.* —**juve'nescent** *a.* becoming young —**juvenilia** (dʒuːvɪˈnɪlɪə) *pl.n.* works produced in author's youth —**juvenility** (dʒuːvɪˈnɪlɪtɪ) *n.* —**juvenile court** court dealing with young offenders or children in need of care —**juvenile delinquent** young person guilty of some offence, antisocial behaviour *etc.*

juxtapose (dʒʌkstəˈpəʊz) *vt.* put side by side —**juxtapo'sition** *n.* contiguity, being side by side

K,k

k *or* **K** (kei) *n.* **1.** 11th letter of English alphabet **2.** speech sound represented by this letter, as in *kitten* (*pl.* **k's, K's** *or* **Ks**)

k 1. kilo **2.** *Maths.* unit vector along *z*-axis **3.** knit

K 1. kelvin **2.** *Chess* king **3.** *Chem.* potassium **4.** *Phys.* kaon **5.** one thousand **6.** *Comp.* unit of 1024 words, bytes or bits

Kaffir *or* **Kafir** ('kæfə) *n.* SA *obs., offens.* any black African **—kaffirboom** ('kæfəbuəm) *n.* S Afr. flowering tree **—kaffir corn** S Afr. variety of sorghum

kaftan *or* **caftan** ('kæftæn) *n.* **1.** long coatlike Eastern garment **2.** imitation of it, *esp.* as woman's long, loose dress with sleeves

Kaiser ('kaizə) *n.* (*sometimes* **k-**) *Hist.* **1.** any of three German emperors **2.** any Austro-Hungarian emperor

kale *or* **kail** (keil) *n.* type of cabbage

kaleidoscope (kə'laidəskəup) *n.* **1.** optical toy for producing changing symmetrical patterns by multiple reflections of coloured glass chips *etc.*, in inclined mirrors enclosed in tube **2.** any complex, frequently changing pattern **—kaleidoscopic** (kəlaidə'skɒpik) *a.* swiftly changing

Kamasutra (kɑːmə'suːtrə) *n.* ancient Hindu text on erotic pleasure

kamikaze (kæmi'kɑːzi) *n.* (*oft.* **K-**) suicidal attack, *esp.* as in World War II, by Japanese pilots

kangaroo (kæŋgə'ruː) *n.* **1.** Aust. marsupial with very strongly developed hind legs for jumping **—vi. 2.** *inf.* (of car) move forward with sudden jerks **—kangaroo court** irregular, illegal court

kaolin ('keiəlin) *n.* fine white clay used for porcelain and medicinally

kaon ('keiɒn) *n.* meson that has rest mass of about 996 or 964 electron masses (*also* **K-meson**)

kapok ('keipɒk) *n.* **1.** tropical tree **2.** fibre from its seed pods used to stuff cushions *etc.*

kappa ('kæpə) *n.* tenth letter in Gr. alphabet (**K, κ**)

kaput (kæ'put) *a. inf.* ruined, broken, no good

karakul *or* **caracul** ('kærəkəl) *n.* **1.** breed of sheep of central Asia having coarse black, grey or brown hair: lambs have soft curled hair **2.** fur prepared from these lambs

karate (kə'rɑːti) *n.* Japanese system of unarmed combat using feet, hands, elbows *etc.* as weapons in a variety of ways

karoo *or* **karroo** (kə'ruː) *n.* SA high, arid plateau

kaross (kə'rɒs) *n.* SA cloak made of skins

kart (kɑːt) *n.* light low-framed vehicle with small wheels and engine for recreational racing (**karting**) (*also* **go-cart, go-kart**)

katabolism (kə'tæbəlizəm) *n. see* CATABOLISM

katydid ('keitidid) *n.* green long-horned grasshopper living in trees in N Amer.

kauri ('kauri) *n.* large N.Z. pine giving valuable timber (*pl.* **-s**)

kava ('kɑːvə) *n.* **1.** Polynesian shrub **2.** beverage prepared from the aromatic roots of this shrub

kayak *or* **kaiak** ('kaiæk) *n.* **1.** Eskimo canoe made of sealskins stretched over frame **2.** any canoe of this design

kazoo (kə'zuː) *n.* cigar-shaped musical instrument producing nasal sound

K.B. Knight of the Bath

kc kilocycle

K.C. King's Counsel

kcal kilocalorie

kea ('keiə) *n.* large New Zealand parrot with brownish-green plumage

kebab (kə'bæb) *n.* dish of small pieces of meat, tomatoes *etc.* grilled on skewers (*also* **shish kebab**)

kedge (kɛdʒ) *n.* **1.** small anchor **—vt. 2.** move (ship) by cable attached to kedge

kedgeree (kɛdʒə'riː) *n.* dish of fish cooked with rice, eggs *etc.*

keek (kiːk) *n./vi. Scot.* peep

keel (kiːl) *n.* lowest longitudinal support on which ship is built **—keelhaul** *vt.* **1.** formerly, punish by hauling under keel of ship **2.** rebuke severely **—keelson** ('kɛlsən, 'kiːl-) *or* **kelson** ('kɛlsən) *n.* line of timbers or plates bolted to keel **—keel over 1.** turn upside down **2.** *inf.* collapse suddenly **—on an even keel** well-balanced; steady

keen¹ (kiːn) *a.* **1.** sharp **2.** acute **3.** eager **4.** shrewd **5.** strong **6.** (of price) competitive **—'keenly** *adv.* **—'keenness** *n.*

keen² (kiːn) *n.* **1.** funeral lament **—vi. 2.** wail over the dead

keep (kiːp) *vt.* **1.** retain possession of, not lose **2.** store **3.** cause to continue **4.** take charge of **5.** maintain **6.** detain **7.** provide upkeep of **8.** reserve **—vi. 9.** remain good **10.** remain **11.** continue (**kept** *pt./pp.*) **—n. 12.** living or support **13.** charge or care **14.** central tower of castle, stronghold **—'keeper** *n.* **—'keeping** *n.* **1.** harmony, agreement **2.** care, charge, possession **—'keepsake** *n.* gift that evokes memories of person or event

keg (kɛg) *n.* **1.** small barrel **2.** metal container for beer

kelp (kɛlp) *n.* **1.** large seaweed **2.** its ashes, yielding iodine

kelt (kɛlt) *n.* salmon that has recently spawned

kelvin ('kɛlvin) *a.* **1.** of thermometric scale

starting at absolute zero (-273.15° Celsius) —*n.*
2. SI unit of temperature

ken (kɛn) *n.* **1.** range of knowledge —*v.* **2.** in
Scotland, know (**kenned** *or* **kent** *pt./pp.*)

kendo ('kɛndəʊ) *n.* Japanese form of fencing
using wooden staves

kennel ('kɛnəl) *n.* **1.** house, shelter for dog —*pl.*
2. place for breeding, boarding dogs —*vt.* **3.** put
into kennel (**-ll-**)

kentledge ('kɛntlɪdʒ) *n. Naut.* scrap metal
used as ballast

kepi ('keɪpiː) *n.* military cap with circular top
and horizontal peak (*pl.* **-s**)

kept (kɛpt) *pt./pp. of* KEEP

kerb *or U.S.* **curb** (kɜːb) *n.* stone edging to
footpath

kerchief ('kɜːtʃɪf) *n.* **1.** head-cloth **2.**
handkerchief

kerfuffle (kə'fʌfəl) *n. inf.* commotion, disorder

kermes ('kɜːmɪz) *n.* insect used for red
dyestuff

kernel ('kɜːnəl) *n.* **1.** inner seed of nut or fruit
stone **2.** central, essential part

kerosene *or* **kerosine** ('kɛrəsiːn) *n.* paraffin
oil distilled from petroleum or coal and shale

kestrel ('kɛstrəl) *n.* small falcon

ketch (kɛtʃ) *n.* two-masted sailing vessel

ketchup ('kɛtʃəp), **catchup** ('kætʃəp, 'kɛtʃ-),
or **catsup** ('kætsəp) *n.* sauce of vinegar,
tomatoes *etc.*

ketone ('kiːtəʊn) *n.* chemical compound with
general formula R'COR, where R and R' are
usu. alkyl or aryl groups —**ketonic** (kɪ'tɒnɪk) *a.*

kettle ('kɛtəl) *n.* metal vessel with spout and
handle, *esp.* for boiling water —**'kettledrum** *n.*
musical instrument made of membrane
stretched over copper hemisphere —**a fine
kettle of fish** awkward situation, mess

key¹ (kiː) *n.* **1.** instrument for operating lock,
winding clock *etc.* **2.** something providing
control, explanation, means of achieving an end
etc. **3.** *Mus.* set of related notes **4.** operating
lever of typewriter, piano, organ *etc.* **5.** spanner
6. mode of thought —*vt.* **7.** provide symbols on
(map *etc.*) to assist identification of positions on
it **8.** scratch (plaster surface) to provide bond
for plaster or paint **9.** insert (copy, information)
by keystroke —*a.* **10.** most important
—**'keyboard** *n.* set of keys on piano *etc.*
—**'keyhole** *n.* aperture in lock case into which
key is inserted —**key money** fee, payment
required from new tenant of house *etc.* before
he moves in —**'keynote** *n.* **1.** dominant idea **2.**
basic note of musical key —**key punch** device
having keyboard operated manually to transfer
data onto punched cards *etc.* (*also* **card punch**)
—**key-punch** *vt.* transfer (data) by key punch
—**key signature** *Mus.* sharps or flats at

beginning of each stave line to indicate key
—**'keystone** *n.* **1.** central stone of arch **2.**
something necessary to connect other related
things —**'keystroke** *n.* depression of single key
on keyboard of typewriter, computer *etc.*

key² (kiː) *n. see* CAY

kg *or* **kg.** kilogram

K.G. Knight of the Order of the Garter

K.G.B. Soviet secret police

khaki ('kɑːkɪ) *a.* **1.** dull yellowish-brown —*n.* **2.**
dull yellowish-brown colour **3.** hard-wearing
fabric of this colour, used *esp.* for military
uniforms (*pl.* **-s**)

khan (kɑːn) *n.* **1.** formerly, (title borne by)
medieval Chinese emperors and Mongol and
Turkic rulers **2.** title of respect borne by
important personages in Afghanistan and
central Asia

Khmer (kmɛə) *n.* member of a people of
Kampuchea

kHz kilohertz

kibble ('kɪbəl) *vt.* grind into small pieces

kibbutz (kɪ'buts) *n.* Jewish communal agricultural settlement in Israel (*pl.* **kibbutzim**
(kɪbut'siːm))

kibosh ('kaɪbɒʃ) *n. sl.* —**put the kibosh on 1.**
silence **2.** get rid of **3.** defeat

kick (kɪk) *vi.* **1.** strike out with foot **2.**
(*sometimes with* against) be recalcitrant **3.**
recoil —*vt.* **4.** strike or hit with foot **5.** score
(goal) with a kick **6.** *inf.* free oneself of (habit
etc.) —*n.* **7.** foot blow **8.** recoil **9.** excitement,
thrill —**'kickback** *n.* **1.** strong reaction **2.** money
paid illegally for favours done *etc.* —**'kickoff** *n.*
1. place kick from centre of field in football **2.**
time at which first such kick is due to take place
—**'kickstand** *n.* short metal bar which when
kicked into vertical position holds stationary
cycle upright —**kick-start** *vt.* start (motorcycle
engine) by pedal that is kicked downwards
—**kick-starter** *n.* this pedal —**kick off 1.** start
game of football **2.** *inf.* begin (discussion *etc.*)

kid (kɪd) *n.* **1.** young goat **2.** leather of its skin **3.**
inf. child —*vt.* **1.** tease; deceive —*vi.* **3.** behave,
speak in fun (**-dd-**) —**kid glove** glove made of
kidskin —**kid'glove** *a.* **1.** overdelicate **2.**
diplomatic; tactful —**handle with kid gloves**
treat with great tact or caution

kidnap ('kɪdnæp) *vt.* seize and hold to ransom
(**-pp-**) —**'kidnapper** *n.*

kidney ('kɪdnɪ) *n.* **1.** either of the pair of organs
which secrete urine **2.** animal kidney used as
food **3.** nature, kind (*pl.* **-s**) —**of the same** *or* **a
different kidney**) (*pl.* **-s**) —**kidney bean 1.**
dwarf French bean **2.** scarlet runner —**kidney
machine** machine carrying out functions of
kidney

kill (kɪl) *vt.* **1.** deprive of life **2.** destroy **3.**

neutralize **4.** pass (time) **5.** weaken; dilute **6.** *inf.* exhaust **7.** *inf.* cause to suffer pain **8.** *inf.* quash, defeat, veto —*n.* **9.** act or time of killing **10.** animals *etc.* killed in hunt —'**killer** *n.* one who, that which, kills —'**killing** *inf.* *a.* **1.** very tiring **2.** very funny —*n.* **3.** sudden success, *esp.* on stock market —**killer whale** ferocious toothed whale most common in cold seas —**kill-joy** *n.* person who spoils other people's pleasure

kiln (kıln) *n.* furnace, oven

kilo ('kiːləʊ) *n.* kilogram (*pl.* **-s**)

kilo- (*comb. form*) one thousand, as in *kilolitre, kilometre*

kilocycle ('kıləʊsaıkəl) *n.* *short for* kilocycle per second: former unit of frequency equal to 1 kilohertz

kilogram *or* **kilogramme** ('kıləʊgræm) *n.* weight of 1000 grams

kilohertz ('kıləʊhɜːts) *n.* one thousand cycles per second

kiloton ('kıləʊtʌn) *n.* **1.** one thousand tons **2.** explosive power, *esp.* of nuclear weapon, equal to power of 1000 tons of TNT

kilowatt ('kıləʊwɒt) *n.* *Elec.* one thousand watts —**kilowatt-hour** *n.* unit of energy equal to work done by power of 1000 watts in one hour

kilt (kılt) *n.* *usu.* tartan knee-length skirt, deeply pleated, worn orig. by Scottish Highlanders

kimono (kı'məʊnəʊ) *n.* **1.** loose, wide-sleeved Japanese robe, fastened with sash **2.** European garment like this (*pl.* **-s**)

kin (kın) *n.* **1.** family, relatives —*a.* **2.** related by blood —**kindred** ('kındrıd) *n.* **1.** relationship by blood **2.** relatives collectively —*a.* **3.** similar **4.** related —'**kinsfolk** *pl.n.* —'**kinship** *n.*

-kin (*comb. form*) small, as in *lambkin*

kind (kaınd) *n.* **1.** genus, sort, class —*a.* **2.** sympathetic, considerate **3.** good, benevolent **4.** gentle —'**kindliness** *a.* **1.** kind, genial —*adv.* **2.** in a considerate or humane way —'**kindness** *n.* —**kind-hearted** *a.* kindly, readily sympathetic —**in kind 1.** (of payment) in goods rather than money **2.** with something similar

kindergarten ('kındəgɑːtən) *n.* class, school for children of about four to six years old

kindle ('kındəl) *vt.* **1.** set on fire **2.** inspire, excite —*vi.* **3.** catch fire —'**kindling** *n.* wood, straw *etc.* to kindle fire

kinematic (kını'mætık) *a.* of motion without reference to mass or force —kine'**matics** *pl.n.* (*with sing. v.*) science of this —**kine'matograph** *n.* see **cinematograph** *at* CINEMA

kinetic (kı'nɛtık) *a.* of motion in relation to force —ki'**netics** *pl.n.* (*with sing. v.*) science of this —**kinetic art** art, *esp.* sculpture, that moves or has moving parts

king (kıŋ) *n.* **1.** male sovereign ruler of independent state, monarch **2.** piece in game of chess **3.** highest court card, with picture of a king **4.** *Draughts* two pieces on top of one another, allowed freedom of movement —'**kingdom** *n.* **1.** state ruled by king **2.** realm **3.** sphere —'**kingly** *a.* **1.** royal **2.** appropriate to a king —'**kingship** *n.* —**King Charles spaniel** toy breed of spaniel with very long ears —'**kingcup** *n.* UK any of several yellow-flowered plants, *esp.* marsh marigold —'**kingfisher** *n.* small bird with bright plumage, which dives for fish —'**kingpin** *n.* **1.** swivel pin **2.** central or front pin in bowling **3.** *inf.* chief person or thing —**king post** beam in roof framework rising from tie beam to the ridge —**King's Bench** (when sovereign is male) *another name for* **Queen's Bench** (*see* QUEEN) —**King's Counsel** (when sovereign is male) *another name for* **Queen's Counsel** (*see* QUEEN) —**King's English** (*esp.* when British sovereign is male) standard Southern British English —**king's evidence** (when sovereign is male) *another name for* **queen's evidence** (*see* QUEEN) —**king's highway** (in Britain, *esp.* when sovereign is male) public road or right of way —**king-size** *or* **king-sized** *a.* **1.** large **2.** larger than standard size

kingklip ('kıŋklıp) *n.* S Afr. marine fish

kink (kıŋk) *n.* **1.** tight twist in rope, wire, hair *etc.* **2.** crick, as of neck **3.** *inf.* eccentricity —*v.* **4.** make, become kinked —'**kinky** *a.* **1.** full of kinks **2.** *inf.* eccentric, *esp.* given to deviant (sexual) practices

kiosk ('kiːɒsk) *n.* **1.** small, sometimes movable booth selling drinks, cigarettes, newspapers *etc.* **2.** public telephone box

kipper ('kıpə) *vt.* **1.** cure (fish) by splitting open, rubbing with salt and drying or smoking —*n.* **2.** kippered fish

kirk (kɜːk) *n.* in Scotland, church

Kirsch (kıəʃ) *or* **Kirschwasser** ('kıəʃvɑːsə) *n.* brandy made from cherries

kismet ('kızmɛt, 'kıs-) *n.* fate, destiny

kiss (kıs) *n.* **1.** touch or caress with lips **2.** light touch —*vt.* **3.** touch with the lips as an expression of love, greeting *etc.* —*vi.* **4.** join lips with another person in act of love or desire —'**kisser** *n.* **1.** one who kisses **2.** *sl.* mouth; face —**kiss curl** UK circular curl of hair pressed flat against cheek or forehead —**kiss of life** mouth-to-mouth resuscitation

kist (kıst) *n.* large wooden chest

kit (kıt) *n.* **1.** outfit, equipment **2.** personal effects, *esp.* of traveller **3.** set of pieces of equipment sold ready to be assembled —'**kitbag** *n.* bag for holding soldier's or traveller's kit —**kit out** *or* **up** *chiefly* UK provide with kit of personal effects and necessities

kitchen ('kıtʃın) *n.* room used for preparing

and cooking food —**kitchen'ette** n. small room (or part of larger room) used for cooking —**kitchen garden** garden for raising vegetables, herbs etc. —**kitchen sink** n. 1. sink in kitchen —a. 2. sordidly domestic

kite (kaıt) n. 1. light papered frame flown in wind 2. sl. aeroplane 3. large hawk —**Kite mark** official mark on articles approved by British Standards Institution

kith (kıθ) n. acquaintance, kindred (only in **kith and kin**)

kitsch (kıtʃ) n. vulgarized, pretentious art, literature etc., usu. with popular, sentimental appeal

kitten ('kıt²n) n. young cat —**kittenish** a. 1. like kitten; lively 2. (of woman) flirtatious, esp. coyly

kittiwake ('kıtıweık) n. type of seagull

kitty ('kıtı) n. 1. kitten or cat 2. in some gambling games, pool 3. communal fund

kiwi ('kiːwı) n. 1. N.Z. flightless bird having long beak, stout legs and weakly barbed feathers 2. inf. New Zealander (pl. **-s**)

kl. kilolitre

klaxon ('klæks²n) n. formerly, powerful electric motor horn

kleptomania (klɛptəʊ'meınıə) n. compulsive tendency to steal esp. when there is no obvious motivation —**klepto'maniac** n.

klipspringer ('klıpsprıŋə) n. small agile Afr. antelope

kloof (kluːf) n. SA mountain pass

km or **km.** kilometre

knack (næk) n. 1. acquired facility or dexterity 2. trick 3. habit

knacker ('nækə) n. buyer of worn-out horses etc., for killing —**'knackered** a. sl. exhausted

knapsack ('næpsæk) n. soldier's or traveller's bag to strap to the back, rucksack

knapweed ('næpwiːd) n. plant having purplish thistlelike flowers

knave (neıv) n. 1. jack at cards 2. obs. rogue —'**knavery** n. villainy —'**knavish** a.

knead (niːd) vt. 1. work (flour) into dough 2. work, massage —'**kneader** n.

knee (niː) n. 1. joint between thigh and lower leg 2. part of garment covering knee 3. lap —vt. 4. strike, push with knee —'**kneecap** n. bone in front of knee —**knees-up** n. inf. party, oft. with dancing

kneel (niːl) vi. fall, rest on knees (**knelt** pt./pp.)

knell (nɛl) n. 1. sound of a bell, esp. at funeral or death 2. portent of doom

knelt (nɛlt) pt./pp. of KNEEL

knew (njuː) pt. of KNOW

knickerbockers ('nıkəbɒkəz) pl.n. loose-fitting breeches gathered at knees

knickers ('nıkəz) pl.n. woman's undergarment for lower half of body

knick-knack ('nıknæk) n. trifle, trinket

knife (naıf) n. 1. cutting blade, esp. one in handle, used as implement or weapon (pl. **knives**) —vt. 2. cut or stab with knife —**knife edge** critical, possibly dangerous situation

knight (naıt) n. 1. man of rank below baronet, having right to prefix Sir to his name 2. member of medieval order of chivalry 3. champion 4. piece in chess —vt. 5. confer knighthood on —'**knighthood** n. —'**knightly** a.

knit (nıt) v. 1. form (garment etc.) by putting together series of loops in wool or other yarn 2. draw together 3. unite ('**knitted, knit** pt./pp., '**knitting** pr.p.) —'**knitter** n. —'**knitting** n. 1. knitted work 2. act of knitting —'**knitwear** n. knitted clothes, esp. sweaters

knives (naıvz) n., pl. of KNIFE

knob (nɒb) n. rounded lump, esp. at end or on surface of anything —'**knobby** or '**knobbly** a.

knock (nɒk) vt. 1. strike, hit 2. inf. disparage —vi. 3. rap audibly 4. (of engine) make metallic noise, pink —n. 5. blow, rap —'**knocker** n. 1. metal appliance for knocking on door 2. person or thing that knocks —**knock-kneed** a. having incurved legs —'**knockout** n. 1. blow etc. that renders unconscious 2. inf. person or thing overwhelmingly attractive —**knock down** 1. strike to ground with blow, as in boxing 2. in auctions, declare (article) sold 3. demolish 4. dismantle for ease of transport 5. inf. reduce (price etc.) —**knocked up** inf. exhausted, tired, worn out —**knock off** inf. 1. cease work 2. make hurriedly 3. kill 4. steal —**knock out** 1. render unconscious 2. inf. overwhelm, amaze

knoll (nəʊl) n. small rounded hill, mound

knot (nɒt) n. 1. fastening of strands by looping and pulling tight 2. cockade, cluster 3. small closely knit group 4. tie, bond 5. hard lump, esp. of wood where branch joins or has joined 6. unit of speed of one nautical mile (1852m) per hour 7. difficulty —vt. 8. tie with knot, in knots (**-tt-**) —'**knotty** a. 1. full of knots 2. puzzling, difficult —'**knothole** n. hole in wood where knot has been

knot² (nɒt) n. small northern sandpiper with grey plumage

know (nəʊ) vt. 1. be aware of 2. have information about 3. be acquainted with 4. recognize 5. have experience of, understand —vi. 6. have information or understanding (**knew** pt., **known** pp.) —'**knowable** a. —'**knowing** a. cunning, shrewd —'**knowingly** adv. 1. shrewdly 2. deliberately —**knowledge** ('nɒlıdʒ) n. 1. knowing 2. what one knows 3. learning —**knowledgeable** or **knowledgable** ('nɒlıdʒəbəl) a. well-informed —**known** a.

identified —**know-how** *n. inf.* practical knowledge, experience, aptitude —**in the know** *inf.* informed

knuckle ('nʌkəl) *n.* **1.** bone at finger joint **2.** knee joint of calf or pig —*vt.* **3.** strike with knuckles —**knuckle-duster** *n.* metal appliance worn on knuckles to add force to blow —**knuckle down** *inf.* get down (to work) —**knuckle under** yield, submit —**near the knuckle** *inf.* approaching indecency

knur, knurr (nɜː), *or* **knar** (nɑː) *n.* **1.** knot in wood **2.** hard lump

knurl *or* **nurl** (nɜːl) *vt.* **1.** impress with series of fine ridges or serrations —*n.* **2.** small ridge, *esp.* one of series —**knurled** *or* **nurled** *a.* **1.** serrated **2.** gnarled

koala *or* **koala bear** (kəʊˈɑːlə) *n.* marsupial Aust. animal, native bear

kohl (kəʊl) *n.* powdered antimony used *esp.* in Eastern countries for darkening the eyelids

kohlrabi (kəʊlˈrɑːbɪ) *n.* type of cabbage with edible stem (*also* **turnip cabbage**)

kokanee (kəʊˈkænɪ) *n.* salmon of N Amer. lakes

kola (ˈkəʊlə) *n. see* COLA

kolinsky (kəˈlɪnskɪ) *n.* **1.** any of various Asian minks **2.** rich tawny fur of this animal

komatik (ˈkəʊmætɪk) *n.* C Eskimo sledge with wooden runners

kook (kuːk) *n.* US *inf.* eccentric or foolish person —**kooky** *or* **kookie** *a.*

kookaburra (ˈkʊkəbʌrə) *n.* large Aust. kingfisher with cackling cry (*also* **laughing jackass**)

kopeck *or* **copeck** (ˈkəʊpek) *n.* Soviet monetary unit, one hundredth of rouble

koppie *or* **kopje** (ˈkɒpɪ) *n.* SA small hill

Koran (kɔːˈrɑːn) *n.* sacred book of Muslims

kosher (ˈkəʊʃə) *a.* **1.** permitted, clean, good, as of food *etc.*, conforming to the Jewish dietary law **2.** *inf.* legitimate, authentic —*n.* **3.** kosher food

kowtow (ˈkaʊtaʊ) *n.* **1.** former Chinese custom of touching ground with head in respect **2.** submission —*vi.* (*esp. with to*) **3.** prostrate oneself **4.** be obsequious, fawn (on)

Kr *Chem.* krypton

kraal (krɑːl) *n.* SA **1.** hut village, *esp.* one surrounded by fence **2.** corral

kraken (ˈkrɑːkən) *n.* mythical Norwegian sea monster

krans (krɑːns) *n.* SA cliff

Kraut (kraʊt) *a./n. sl., offens.* German

Kremlin (ˈkremlɪn) *n.* central government of Soviet Union

krill (krɪl) *n.* small shrimplike marine animal

kris (krɪs) *n.* Malayan and Indonesian knife with scalloped edge (*also* **crease, creese**)

krona (ˈkrəʊnə) *n.* standard monetary unit of Sweden (*pl.* **-nor** (-nə))

krone (ˈkrəʊnə) *n.* standard monetary unit of Norway and Denmark (*pl.* **-ner** (-nə))

krypton (ˈkrɪptɒn) *n.* rare gaseous element present in atmosphere

KS Kansas

Kt *Chess* knight (*also* N)

kudos (ˈkjuːdɒs) *n.* **1.** fame **2.** credit

kudu *or* **koodoo** (ˈkuːduː) *n.* Afr. antelope with spiral horns

Ku Klux Klan (ˈkuː ˈklʌks ˈklæn) **1.** secret organization of White Southerners formed after U.S. Civil War to fight Black emancipation **2.** secret organization of White Protestant Americans, mainly in South, who use violence against Blacks, Jews *etc.*

kukri (ˈkʊkrɪ) *n.* heavy, curved Gurkha knife

kulak (ˈkuːlæk) *n.* independent well-to-do Russian peasant

kumara *or* **kumera** (ˈkuːmərə) *n.* NZ sweet potato

kümmel (ˈkʊməl) *n.* cumin-flavoured German liqueur

kumquat *or* **cumquat** (ˈkʌmkwɒt) *n.* **1.** small Chinese tree **2.** its round orange fruit

kung fu (ˈkʌŋ ˈfuː) Chinese martial art combining techniques of judo and karate

kW *or* **kw** kilowatt

kwashiorkor (kwæʃɪˈɔːkə) *n.* severe malnutrition of young children, resulting from dietary deficiency of protein

kWh, kwh, *or* **kw-h** kilowatt-hour

KWIC (kwɪk) keyword in context (*esp. in* KWIC index)

KWOC (kwɒk) key word out of context

KY Kentucky

kyle (kaɪl) *n. Scot.* narrow strait or channel

kymograph (ˈkaɪməgrɑːf) *n.* instrument for recording on graph pressure, oscillations, sound waves

L, l

l *or* **L** (el) *n.* **1.** 12th letter of English alphabet **2.** speech sound represented by this letter **3.** something shaped like L (*pl.* **l's, L's** *or* **Ls**)

L 1. lambert **2.** large **3.** Latin **4.** (on Brit. motor vehicles) learner driver **5.** *Phys.* length **6.** pound (*usually written:* £) **7.** longitude **8.** *Electron.* inductor (in circuit diagrams) **9.** *Phys.* latent heat **10.** *Phys.* self-inductance **11.** Roman numeral, 50

L. *or* **l. 1.** lake **2.** left **3.** line (*pl.* **LL.** *or* **ll.**) **4.** litre

la (lɑː) *n. Mus. see* LAH

La *Chem.* lanthanum

LA Louisiana

laager ('lɑːgə) *n.* SA encampment surrounded by wagons

lab (læb) *inf.* laboratory

Lab. 1. *Pol.* Labour **2.** Labrador

label ('leɪbəl) *n.* **1.** slip of paper, metal *etc.*, fixed to object to give information about it **2.** brief, descriptive phrase or term —*vt.* **3.** fasten label to **4.** mark with label **5.** describe or classify in a word or phrase (**-ll-**)

labiate ('leɪbɪeɪt, -ɪt) *n.* **1.** plant of family *Labiatae*, having square stems, aromatic leaves and two-lipped corolla —*a.* **2.** of family *Labiatae*

labium ('leɪbɪəm) *n.* **1.** lip; liplike structure **2.** any of four lip-shaped folds of vulva, comprising outer pair (**labia majora**) and inner pair (**labia minora**) (*pl.* **-bia** (-bɪə)) —**labial 1.** of the lips **2.** pronounced with the lips —*n.* **3.** speech sound pronounced thus

laboratory (ləˈbɒrətərɪ, -trɪ; *U.S.* ˈlæbrətɔːrɪ) *n.* place for scientific investigations or for manufacture of chemicals

labour *or U.S.* **labor** ('leɪbə) *n.* **1.** exertion of body or mind **2.** task **3.** workers collectively **4.** effort, pain of childbirth or time taken for this —*vi.* **5.** work hard **6.** strive **7.** maintain normal motion with difficulty **8.** (*esp.* of ship) be tossed heavily —*vt.* **9.** stress to excess —**laˈborious** *a.* tedious —**laˈboriously** *adv.* —**laboured** *or U.S.* **labored** *a.* uttered, done, with difficulty —**labourer** *or U.S.* **laborer** *n.* one who labours, *esp.* man doing manual work for wages —**labour exchange** UK *old name for* Employment Service Agency —**Labour Party 1.** Brit. political party, generally supporting interests of organized labour **2.** similar party in various other countries —**labour-saving** *a.* eliminating or lessening physical labour

Labrador ('læbrədɔː) *n.* breed of large, smooth-coated retriever dog (*also* **Labrador retriever**)

laburnum (ləˈbɜːnəm) *n.* tree with yellow hanging flowers

labyrinth ('læbərɪnθ) *n.* **1.** network of tortuous passages, maze **2.** inexplicable difficulty **3.** perplexity —**labyˈrinthine** *a.*

lac[1] (læk) *n.* resinous substance secreted by some insects

lac[2] (lɑːk) *n.* one hundred thousand (of rupees)

lace (leɪs) *n.* **1.** fine patterned openwork fabric **2.** cord, *esp.* one of pair, to draw edges together, *eg* to tighten shoes *etc.* **3.** ornamental braid —*vt.* **4.** fasten with laces **5.** flavour with spirit —**lacy** *a.* fine, like lace

lacerate ('læsəreɪt) *vt.* **1.** tear, mangle **2.** distress —**lacerable** *a.* —**lacerˈation** *n.*

lachrymal, lacrimal, *or* **lacrymal**

('lækrɪməl) *a.* of tears —**lachrymatory, lacrimatory,** *or* **lacrymatory** *a.* causing tears or inflammation of eyes —**lachrymose** *a.* tearful

lack (læk) *n.* **1.** deficiency, need —*vt.* **2.** need, be short of —**lacklustre** *or U.S.* **lackluster** *a.* lacking brilliance or vitality

lackadaisical (lækəˈdeɪzɪkəl) *a.* **1.** languid, listless **2.** lazy, careless

lackey ('lækɪ) *n.* **1.** servile follower **2.** footman (*pl.* **-s**) —*vi.* **3.** be or play, the lackey **4.** (*with for*) wait (upon)

laconic (ləˈkɒnɪk) *a.* **1.** using, expressed in few words **2.** brief, terse **3.** offhand, not caring —**laˈconically** *adv.* —**laˈconicism** *n.*

lacquer ('lækə) *n.* **1.** hard varnish —*vt.* **2.** coat with this

lacrimal ('lækrɪməl) *a. see* LACHRYMAL

lacrosse (ləˈkrɒs) *n.* ball game played with long-handled racket or crosse

lacrymal ('lækrɪməl) *a. see* LACHRYMAL

lactic ('læktɪk) *a.* of milk —**lactate** *vi.* secrete milk —**lacˈtation** *n.* —**lacˈtometer** *n.* instrument for measuring purity and density of milk —**lactose** *n.* white crystalline substance occurring in milk —**lactic acid** colourless syrupy acid found in sour milk *etc.*

lacuna (ləˈkjuːnə) *n.* gap, missing part, *esp.* in document or series (*pl.* **-nae** (-niː), **-s**)

lad (læd) *n.* boy, young fellow

ladder ('lædə) *n.* **1.** frame of two poles connected by rungs, used for climbing **2.** flaw in stockings, jumpers *etc.*, caused by running of torn stitch —**ladder back** type of chair in which back is constructed of horizontal slats between two uprights

lade (leɪd) *vt.* **1.** load **2.** ship **3.** burden, weigh down ('lɑdən *pp.*) —**lading** *n.* cargo, freight

la-di-da, lah-di-dah, *or* **la-de-da** (lɑːdiː-ˈdɑː) *a. inf.* affecting exaggeratedly genteel manners or speech

ladle ('leɪdəl) *n.* **1.** spoon with long handle and large bowl —*vt.* **2.** (*oft. with out*) serve out (as) with ladle

lady ('leɪdɪ) *n.* **1.** female counterpart of gentleman **2.** *polite term for* a woman **3.** title of some women of rank —**ladies** *or* **ladies' room** *n. inf.* women's public lavatory —**ladyship** *n.* title of a lady —**ladybird** *n.* small beetle, usu. red with black spots —**Lady Day** Feast of the Annunciation, 25th March —**lady-in-waiting** *n.* lady who attends queen or princess (*pl.* **ladies-in-waiting**) —**lady-killer** *n. inf.* man who believes he is irresistible to women —**ladylike** *a.* **1.** gracious **2.** well-mannered —**lady's finger** species of small banana —**lady's-slipper** *n.* orchid with reddish or purple flowers —**Our Lady** the Virgin Mary

lag¹ (læg) *vi.* **1.** (*oft. with* behind) go too slowly, fall behind (**-gg-**) —*n.* **2.** lagging, interval of time between events —'**laggard** *n.* one who lags —'**lagging** *a.* loitering, slow

lag² (læg) *vt.* wrap (boiler, pipes *etc.*) with insulating material (**-gg-**) —'**lagging** *n.* this material

lag³ (læg) *n. sl.* convict (*esp. in* old lag)

lager ('lɑːgə) *n.* light-bodied type of beer

lagoon (lə'guːn) *n.* saltwater lake, enclosed by atoll, or separated by sandbank from sea

lah *or* **la** (lɑː) *n. Mus.* in tonic solfa, sixth note of any major scale; submediant

laic ('leɪɪk) *a.* secular, lay —**laici'zation** *or* **-ci'sation** *n.* —'**laicize** *or* **-cise** *vt.* render secular or lay

laid (leɪd) *pt./pp. of* LAY² —**laid-back** *a.* relaxed in style or character; easy-going and unhurried —**laid paper** paper with regular mesh impressed upon it

lain (leɪn) *pp. of* LIE¹

lair (lɛə) *n.* resting place, den of animal

laird (lɛəd) *n.* Scottish landowner —'**lairdship** *n.* estate

laissez faire or laisser faire (lɛseɪ 'fɛə) *Fr.* **1.** principle of nonintervention, *esp.* by government in commercial affairs **2.** indifference

laity ('leɪɪtɪ) *n.* laymen, the people as opposed to clergy

lake¹ (leɪk) *n.* expanse of inland water —'**lakelet** *n.*

lake² (leɪk) *n.* red pigment

lam¹ (læm) *vt. sl.* beat, hit (**-mm-**) —'**lamming** *n.* beating, thrashing

lam² (læm) *n.* US *sl.* —**on the lam** making an escape

Lam. *Bible* Lamentations

lama ('lɑːmə) *n.* Buddhist priest in Tibet or Mongolia —'**Lamaism** *n.* form of Buddhism of Tibet and Mongolia —'**Lamaist** *n./a.* —'**lamasery** *n.* monastery of lamas

lamb (læm) *n.* **1.** young of the sheep **2.** its meat **3.** innocent or helpless creature —*vi.* **4.** (of sheep) give birth —'**lambkin** *n.* **1.** small lamb **2.** term of affection for child —'**lamblike** *a.* meek, gentle —'**lambskin** *n.* **1.** skin of lamb, *esp.* with wool still on **2.** material or garment prepared from this —**lamb's tails** pendulous catkins of hazel tree —**lamb's wool** soft, fine wool (*also* '**lambswool**)

lambaste *or* **lambast** (læm'beɪst) *vt.* **1.** beat **2.** reprimand

lambda ('læmdə) *n.* 11th letter in Gr. alphabet (Λ, λ)

lambent ('læmbənt) *a.* **1.** (of flame) flickering softly **2.** glowing

lambert ('læmbət) *n.* cgs unit of illumination

lame (leɪm) *a.* **1.** crippled in a limb, *esp.* leg **2.** limping **3.** (of excuse *etc.*) unconvincing —*vt.* **4.** cripple —**lame duck** disabled, weak person or thing

lamé ('lɑːmeɪ) *n./a.* (fabric) interwoven with gold or silver thread

lamella (lə'mɛlə) *n.* thin plate or scale (*pl.* **-lae** (-liː), **-s**) —la'**mellar** *or* **lamellate** ('læmɪleɪt, -lɪt) *a.*

lament (lə'mɛnt) *v.* **1.** feel, express sorrow (for) —*n.* **2.** passionate expression of grief **3.** song of grief —'**lamentable** *a.* deplorable —**lamen'tation** *n.*

lamina ('læmɪnə) *n.* thin plate, scale, flake (*pl.* **-nae** (-niː), **-s**) —'**laminate** ('læmɪneɪt) —*vt.* **1.** make (sheet of material) by bonding together two or more thin sheets **2.** split, beat, form into thin sheets **3.** cover with thin sheet of material —*n.* ('læmɪneɪt, -nɪt) **4.** laminated sheet —**lami'nation** *n.*

Lammas ('læməs) *n.* Aug. 1st, formerly a harvest festival

lammergeier *or* **lammergeyer** ('læməgaɪə) *n.* type of rare vulture

lamp (læmp) *n.* **1.** any of various appliances (*esp.* electrical) that produce light, heat, radiation *etc.* **2.** formerly, vessel holding oil burned by wick for lighting —'**lampblack** *n.* pigment made from soot —'**lamplight** *n.* —'**lamppost** *n.* post supporting lamp in street —'**lampshade** *n.*

lampoon (læm'puːn) *n.* **1.** satire ridiculing person, literary work *etc.* —*vt.* **2.** satirize, ridicule —**lam'pooner** *or* **lam'poonist** *n.*

lamprey ('læmprɪ) *n.* fish like an eel with a sucker mouth

lance (lɑːns) *n.* **1.** horseman's spear —*vt.* **2.** pierce with lance or lancet —**lanceolate** ('lɑːnsɪəleɪt, -lɪt) *a.* lance-shaped, tapering —'**lancer** *n.* formerly, cavalry soldier armed with lance —'**lancers** *pl.n.* (*with sing. v.*) **1.** quadrille for eight or sixteen couples **2.** music for this dance —**lancet** *n.* pointed two-edged surgical knife —**lance corporal** *or* **sergeant** noncommissioned officer in army

Lancs. (læŋks) Lancashire

land (lænd) *n.* **1.** solid part of earth's surface **2.** ground, soil **3.** country **4.** property consisting of land —*pl.* **5.** estates —*vi.* **6.** come to land, disembark **7.** bring an aircraft or (of aircraft) come from air to land or water **8.** alight, step down **9.** arrive on ground **10.** C be legally admitted as immigrant —*vt.* **11.** bring to land **12.** bring to some point or condition **13.** *inf.* obtain **14.** catch **15.** *inf.* strike —'**landed** *a.* possessing, consisting of lands —'**landing** *n.* **1.** act of landing **2.** platform between flights of stairs **3.** a landing stage —'**landward** *a./adv.* —'**land-**

wards adv. —**land agent 1.** person who administers landed estate and its tenancies **2.** person who acts as agent for sale of land —'**landfall** n. ship's approach to land at end of voyage —'**landgrave** n. German hist. **1.** (from 13th century to 1806) count who ruled over specified territory **2.** (after 1806) title of various sovereign princes —**landing gear** US undercarriage —**landing stage** platform for embarkation and disembarkation —'**landlocked** a. enclosed by land —'**landlord** or '**landlady** n. **1.** person who lets land, houses etc. **2.** master or mistress of inn, boarding house etc. —'**landlubber** n. person ignorant of the sea and ships —'**landmark** n. **1.** boundary mark, conspicuous object, as guide for direction etc. **2.** event, decision etc. considered as important stage in development of something —'**landmass** n. large continuous area of land —**land mine** Mil. explosive charge placed in ground, usu. detonated by stepping or driving on it —'**landowner** n. person who owns land —'**landscape** n. **1.** piece of inland scenery **2.** picture of it **3.** prospect —v. **4.** create, arrange, (garden, park etc.) —**landscape gardening** —**landscape painter** —'**landslide** or '**landslip** n. **1.** falling of soil, rock etc. down mountainside **2.** overwhelming electoral victory —**land of milk and honey 1.** land of natural fertility promised to Israelites by God **2.** any fertile land etc.

landau ('lændɔː) n. four-wheeled carriage with folding top

lane (leɪn) n. **1.** narrow road or street **2.** specified route followed by shipping or aircraft **3.** area of road for one stream of traffic

lang. language

language ('læŋgwɪdʒ) n. **1.** system of sounds, symbols etc. for communicating thought **2.** specialized vocabulary used by a particular group **3.** style of speech or expression —**language laboratory** room equipped with tape recorders etc. for learning foreign languages

languish ('læŋgwɪʃ) vi. **1.** be or become weak or faint **2.** be in depressing or painful conditions **3.** droop, pine —'**languid** a. **1.** lacking energy, interest **2.** spiritless, dull —'**languidly** adv. —'**languor** ('læŋgə) n. **1.** want of energy or interest **2.** faintness **3.** tender mood **4.** softness of atmosphere —'**languorous** ('læŋgərəs) a.

lank (læŋk) a. **1.** lean and tall **2.** greasy and limp —'**lanky** a. tall, thin and ungainly

lanolin ('lænəlɪn) or **lanoline** ('lænəlɪn, -liːn) n. grease from wool used in ointments etc.

lantern ('læntən) n. **1.** transparent case for lamp or candle **2.** erection on dome or roof to admit light —**lantern jaw** long hollow jaw that

gives face drawn appearance —**lantern-jawed** a. —'**lanthorn** n. obs. lantern

lanthanum ('lænθənəm) n. silvery-white ductile metallic element —**lanthanide series** class of 15 chemically related elements (**lanthanides**) with atomic numbers from 57 (lanthanum) to 71 (lutetium)

lanyard or **laniard** ('lænjəd) n. **1.** short cord for securing knife or whistle **2.** short nautical rope **3.** cord for firing cannon

lap¹ (læp) n. **1.** the part between waist and knees of a person when sitting **2.** fig. place where anything lies securely **3.** single circuit of racecourse, track **4.** stage or part of journey **5.** single turn of wound thread etc. —vt. **6.** enfold, wrap round **7.** overtake (opponent) to be one or more circuits ahead (**-pp-**) —'**lappet** n. flap, fold —'**lapdog** n. small pet dog —**lap joint** joint made by placing one member over another and fastening together (also **lapped joint**) —**lap of honour** ceremonial circuit of racing track etc. by winner of race

lap² (læp) v. **1.** (oft. with up) drink by scooping up with tongue **2.** (of waves etc.) beat softly (**-pp-**)

lapel (lə'pɛl) n. part of front of coat etc. folded back towards shoulders

lapidary ('læpɪdərɪ) a. **1.** of stones **2.** engraved on stone —n. **3.** cutter, engraver of stones

lapis lazuli ('læpɪs 'læzjʊlaɪ) bright blue stone or pigment

lapse (læps) n. **1.** fall (in standard, condition, virtue etc.) **2.** slip **3.** mistake **4.** passing (of time etc.) —vi. **5.** fall away **6.** end, esp. through disuse

lapwing ('læpwɪŋ) n. type of plover

larboard ('lɑːbəd) n./a. obs. port (side of ship)

larceny ('lɑːsɪnɪ) n. theft

larch (lɑːtʃ) n. deciduous coniferous tree

lard (lɑːd) n. **1.** prepared pig's fat —vt. **2.** insert strips of bacon in (meat) **3.** intersperse, decorate (speech) (with strange words etc.) —'**lardy** a. —**lardy cake** UK rich sweet cake made of bread dough, lard, sugar and dried fruit

larder ('lɑːdə) n. storeroom or cupboard for food

large (lɑːdʒ) a. **1.** broad in range or area **2.** great in size, number etc. **3.** liberal **4.** generous —adv. **5.** in a big way —'**largely** adv. —**lar'gess** or **lar'gesse** n. **1.** bounty **2.** gift, donation —'**largish** a. fairly large —**large-scale** a. wide-ranging, extensive **2.** (of maps and roads) constructed or drawn to big scale —**at large 1.** free, not confined **2.** in general **3.** fully

largo ('lɑːgəʊ) a./adv. Mus. to be performed moderately slowly

lariat ('lærɪət) n. lasso

lark¹ (lɑːk) n. small, brown singing bird, skylark

—**'larkspur** n. plant with spikes of blue, pink or white flowers

lark² (lɑːk) n. 1. frolic, spree —vi. 2. indulge in lark —**'larky** a.

larrigan ('lærɪɡən) n. knee-high moccasin boot worn by trappers etc.

larva ('lɑːvə) n. insect in immature but active stage (pl. -ae (-iː)) —**'larval** a. —**'larviform** a.

larynx ('lærɪŋks) n. part of throat containing vocal cords (pl. **larynges** (lə'rɪndʒiːz), -es) —**laryn'geal** or **la'ryngal** a. 1. of larynx 2. Phonet. articulated at larynx; glottal —**laryn'gi-tis** n. inflammation of larynx

lasagne or **lasagna** (lə'zænjə, -'sæn-) n. pasta formed in wide, flat sheets

lascar ('læskə) n. E Indian seaman

lascivious (lə'sɪvɪəs) a. lustful

laser ('leɪzə) n. device for concentrating electromagnetic radiation or light of mixed frequencies into an intense, narrow, concentrated beam

lash¹ (læʃ) n. 1. stroke with whip 2. flexible part of whip 3. eyelash —vt. 4. strike with whip, thong etc. 5. dash against (as waves) 6. attack verbally, ridicule 7. flick, wave sharply to and fro —**'lashing** n. 1. whipping, flogging 2. scolding —pl. 3. (usu. with of) UK inf. large amounts; lots —**lash out 1.** burst into or resort to verbal or physical attack 2. inf. be extravagant, as in spending

lash² (læʃ) vt. fasten or bind tightly with cord etc. —**'lashing** n. rope etc. used for binding or securing —**lash-up** n. temporary connection of equipment for experimental or emergency use

lass (læs) n. girl —**'lassie** n. inf. little lass; girl

Lassa fever ('læsə) serious viral disease of Central W Afr., characterized by high fever etc.

lassitude ('læsɪtjuːd) n. weariness

lasso (læ'suː, 'læsəʊ) n. 1. rope with noose for catching cattle etc. (pl. -s, -es) —vt. 2. catch (as) with lasso (as **las'soed, las'soing**)

last¹ (lɑːst) a./adv. 1. after all others, coming at the end 2. most recent(ly) —a. 3. sup. of LATE 4. only remaining —n. 5. last person or thing —**'lastly** adv. finally —**last-ditch** a. made or done as last desperate effort in face of opposition —**last name** see SURNAME —**last rites** Christianity religious rites prescribed for those close to death —**the Last Judgment** occasion, after resurrection of dead at end of world, when, according to Bible, God will decree final destinies of all men according to good and evil in earthly lives (also **the Last Day, 'Doomsday, Judgment Day**) —**the last straw** final irritation or problem that stretches one's endurance or patience beyond limit

last² (lɑːst) vi. continue, hold out, remain alive or unexhausted, endure —**'lasting** a. permanent; enduring —**'lastingly** adv.

last³ (lɑːst) n. model of foot on which shoes are made, repaired

lat. latitude

latch (lætʃ) n. 1. fastening for door, consisting of bar, catch for it, and lever to lift it 2. small lock with spring action —vt. 3. fasten with latch —**latchkey child** child who has to let himself in at home after school as his parents are out at work

late (leɪt) a. 1. coming after the appointed time 2. delayed 3. that was recently but now is not 4. recently dead 5. recent in date 6. of late stage of development (**'later** comp., **'latest**, **last** sup.) —adv. 7. after proper time 8. recently 9. at, till late hour —**'lately** adv. not long since —**'latish** a. rather late —**Late Greek** Greek language from about 3rd to 8th century A.D. —**Late Latin** form of written Latin used from 3rd to 7th century A.D.

lateen sail (lə'tiːn) triangular sail on long yard hoisted to head of mast

latent ('leɪtənt) a. 1. existing but not developed 2. hidden

lateral ('lætərəl) a. of, at, from the side —**'laterally** adv. —**lateral thinking** way of solving problems by employing unorthodox means

laterite ('lætəraɪt) n. brick-coloured rock or clay formed by weathering of rock in tropical regions

latex ('leɪtɛks) n. sap or fluid of plants, esp. of rubber tree (pl. -es, **latices** ('lætɪsiːz)) —**laticiferous** (lætɪ'sɪfərəs) a. bearing or containing latex or sap

lath (lɑːθ) n. thin strip of wood (pl. **laths** (lɑːðz, lɑːθs)) —**'lathing** n. —**'lathy** a. 1. like a lath 2. tall and thin

lathe (leɪð) n. machine for turning object while it is being shaped

lather ('lɑːðə) n. 1. froth of soap and water 2. frothy sweat —vi. 3. form lather —vt. 4. inf. beat

Latin ('lætɪn) n. 1. language of ancient Romans —a. 2. of ancient Romans 3. of, in their language 4. speaking a language descended from Latin —**'Latinism** n. word, idiom imitating Latin —**La'tinity** n. 1. manner of writing Latin 2. Latin style —**Latin America** those areas of Amer. whose official languages are Spanish and Portuguese, derived from Latin: S Amer., Central Amer., Mexico and certain islands in the Caribbean —**Latin American** n./a.

latitude ('lætɪtjuːd) n. 1. angular distance on meridian reckoned N or S from equator 2. deviation from a standard 3. freedom from restriction 4. scope —pl. 5. regions —**lati'tudi-nal** a. —**latitudi'narian** a. claiming, showing latitude of thought, *esp.* in religion **—latitudi-'narianism** *n.*

latrine (lə'triːn) *n.* in army *etc.,* lavatory

latter ('lætə) *a.* 1. second of two 2. later 3. more recent *—n.* 4. second or last-mentioned person or thing **—'latterly** *adv.*

lattice ('lætɪs) *n.* 1. structure of strips of wood, metal *etc.* crossing with spaces between 2. window so made **—'latticed** *a.*

laud (lɔːd) *Lit. n.* 1. praise, song of praise *—vt.* 2. praise, glorify **—lauda'bility** *n.* **—'laudable** *a.* praiseworthy **—'laudably** *adv.* **—lau'dation** *n.* 1. praise 2. honour paid **—'laudatory** *a.* expressing, containing praise

laudanum ('lɔːdⁿnəm) *n.* tincture of opium

laugh (lɑːf) *vi.* 1. make sounds instinctively expressing amusement, merriment or scorn *—n.* 2. such sound **—'laughable** *a.* ludicrous **—'laughably** *adv.* **—'laughter** *n.* **—laughing gas** nitrous oxide as anaesthetic **—laughing hyena** spotted hyena, so called from its cry **—laughing jackass** see KOOKABURRA **—laughing stock** object of general derision

launch¹ (lɔːntʃ) *vt.* 1. set afloat 2. set in motion 3. begin 4. propel (missile, spacecraft) into space 5. hurl, send *—vi.* 6. enter on course **—'launcher** *n.* installation, vehicle, device for launching rockets, missiles *etc.* **—launching pad** *or* **launch pad** platform from which spacecraft *etc.* is launched

launch² (lɔːntʃ) *n.* large power-driven boat

laundry ('lɔːndrɪ) *n.* 1. place for washing clothes, *esp.* as a business 2. clothes *etc.* for washing **—'launder** *vt.* wash and iron **—Launder'ette** *n.* **R** shop with coin-operated washing, drying machines

laureate ('lɔːrɪɪt) *a.* crowned with laurels **—'laureateship** *n.* post of poet laureate **—poet laureate** poet with appointment to Royal Household, nominally to compose verses on occasions of national importance

laurel ('lɒrəl) *n.* 1. glossy-leaved shrub, bay tree *—pl.* 2. its leaves, emblem of victory or merit

lava ('lɑːvə) *n.* molten matter thrown out by volcanoes, solidifying as it cools

lavatory ('lævətərɪ, -trɪ) *n.* toilet, water closet

lave (leɪv) *vt. obs.* wash, bathe

lavender ('lævəndə) *n.* 1. shrub with fragrant flowers 2. colour of the flowers, pale lilac **—lavender water** perfume or toilet water made from flowers of lavender plant

lavish ('lævɪʃ) *a.* 1. giving or spending profusely 2. very, too abundant *—vt.* 3. spend, bestow profusely

law (lɔː) *n.* 1. rule binding on community 2. system of such rules 3. legal science 4. knowledge, administration of it 5. *inf.* (member

of) police force 6. general principle deduced from facts 7. invariable sequence of events in nature **—'lawful** *a.* allowed by law **—'lawfully** *adv.* **—'lawless** *a.* 1. ignoring laws 2. violent **—'lawlessly** *adv.* **—'lawyer** *n.* professional expert in law **—law-abiding** *a.* 1. obedient to laws 2. well-behaved **—law agent** in Scotland, solicitor entitled to appear for client in any Sheriff Court **—'lawgiver** *n.* one who makes laws **—Law Lord** member of House of Lords who sits as highest court of appeal **—'lawsuit** *n.* prosecution of claim in court

lawn¹ (lɔːn) *n.* stretch of carefully tended turf in garden *etc.* **—lawn mower** hand- or power-operated machine for cutting grass **—lawn tennis** tennis played on grass court

lawn² (lɔːn) *n.* fine linen

lawrencium (lɔː'rɛnsɪəm) *n.* element artificially produced from californium

lawyer ('lɔːjə, 'lɔɪə) *n.* see LAW

lax (læks) *a.* 1. not strict 2. lacking precision 3. loose, slack **—'laxative** *a.* 1. having loosening effect on bowels *—n.* 2. agent stimulating evacuation of faeces **—'laxity** *or* **'laxness** *n.* 1. slackness 2. looseness of (moral) standards **—'laxly** *adv.*

lay¹ (leɪ) *pt. of* LIE¹ **—'layabout** *n.* lazy person

lay² (leɪ) *vt.* 1. deposit, set, cause to lie 2. *taboo sl.* have sexual intercourse with (laid, 'laying) *—n.* *taboo sl.* 3. act of sexual intercourse 4. sexual partner **—'layer** *n.* 1. single thickness of some substance, as stratum or coating on surface 2. laying hen 3. shoot of plant pegged down or partly covered with earth to encourage root growth *—vt.* 4. propagate (plants) by making layers **—lay-by** *n.* stopping place for traffic beside road **—lay-off** *n.* **—'layout** *n.* arrangement, *esp.* of matter for printing **—lay off** dismiss (staff) during slack period **—lay on** 1. provide, supply 2. apply 3. strike **—lay out** 1. display 2. expend 3. prepare for burial 4. *sl.* knock out **—lay waste** devastate

lay³ (leɪ) *n.* minstrel's song

lay⁴ (leɪ) *a.* 1. not clerical or professional 2. of or done by persons not clergymen **—Lay Lord** peer in House of Lords other than a Law Lord **—'layman** *n.* ordinary person **—lay reader** 1. *Ch. of England* person licensed by bishop to conduct religious services other than Eucharist 2. *R.C.Ch.* layman chosen to read epistle at Mass

layette (leɪ'ɛt) *n.* clothes, accessories *etc.* for newborn child

lay figure 1. jointed figure of the body used by artists 2. nonentity

lazy ('leɪzɪ) *a.* averse to work, indolent **—laze** *vi.* indulge in laziness **—'lazily** *adv.* **—'laziness** *n.*

lb *or* **lb.** pound

l.b.w. leg before wicket

l.c. 1. left centre (of stage *etc.*) **2.** loco citato **3.** *Print.* lower case

l.c.d., lcd, L.C.D., *or* **LCD** lowest common denominator

LCD liquid crystal display

L.C.J. UK Lord Chief Justice

l.c.m. *or* **L.C.M.** lowest common multiple

L/Cpl. lance corporal

L.D.S. 1. Latter-day Saints **2.** laus Deo semper (*Lat.*, praise be to God for ever) **3.** UK Licentiate in Dental Surgery (*also* **LDS**)

lea (liː) *n. Poet.* piece of meadow or open ground

leach (liːtʃ) *v.* **1.** remove or be removed from substance by percolating liquid **2.** (cause to) lose soluble substances by action of percolating liquid —*n.* **3.** act or process of leaching **4.** substance that is leached or constituents removed by leaching **5.** porous vessel for leaching

lead[1] (liːd) *vt.* **1.** guide, conduct **2.** persuade **3.** direct **4.** control —*vi.* **5.** be, go, play first **6.** (*with* to) result (in) **7.** give access (led (lɛd), 'leading) —*n.* **8.** leading **9.** that which leads or is used to lead **10.** example **11.** front or principal place, role *etc.* **12.** cable bringing current to electric instrument —'**leader** *n.* **1.** one who leads **2.** article in newspaper expressing editorial views (*also* **leading article**) —'**leadership** *n.* —**leading aircraftman** *Brit. Air Force* rank above aircraftman (**leading aircraftwoman** *fem.*) —**leading case** legal decision used as precedent —**leading light** *inf.* important or outstanding person, *esp.* in organization —**leading note** *Mus.* **1.** seventh degree of major or minor scale (*also* **sub'tonic**) **2.** *esp.* in cadences, note that tends most naturally to resolve to note lying one semitone above —**leading question** question worded to prompt answer desired —**leading rating** rank in Royal Navy comparable but junior to that of corporal in army —**lead time** time between design of product and its production

lead[2] (lɛd) *n.* **1.** soft heavy grey metal **2.** plummet, used for sounding depths of water **3.** graphite —*pl.* **4.** lead-covered piece of roof **5.** strips of lead used to widen spaces in printing *etc.* —*vt.* **6.** cover, weight or space with lead ('**leaded, 'leading**) —'**leaden** *a.* **1.** of, like lead **2.** heavy **3.** dull —**leaded windows** windows made of small panes framed in lead —**lead poisoning 1.** acute or chronic poisoning by lead, characterized by abdominal pain *etc.* **2.** US *sl.* death or injury resulting from being shot with bullets —'**leadsman** *n.* sailor who heaves the lead

leaf (liːf) *n.* **1.** organ of photosynthesis in plants, consisting of a flat, usu. green blade on stem **2.** two pages of book *etc.* **3.** thin sheet **4.** flap, movable part of table *etc.* (*pl.* **leaves** (liːvz)) —*v.* **5.** (*oft. with* through) turn through (pages *etc.*) cursorily —'**leafless** *a.* —'**leaflet** *n.* **1.** small leaf **2.** single sheet, often folded, of printed matter for distribution, handbill —'**leafy** *a.*

league[1] (liːg) *n.* **1.** agreement for mutual help **2.** parties to it **3.** federation of clubs *etc.* **4.** *inf.* class, level —*vi.* **5.** form an alliance; combine in an association —'**leaguer** *n.* member of league —**league football 1.** *chiefly* A rugby league football (*also* **league**) **2.** A Australian Rules competition conducted within league

league[2] (liːg) *n. obs.* measure of distance, about three miles

leak (liːk) *n.* **1.** hole, defect, that allows escape or entrance of liquid, gas, radiation *etc.* **2.** disclosure **3.** *sl.* act of urinating —*vi.* **4.** let fluid *etc.* in or out **5.** (of fluid *etc.*) find its way through leak —*vt.* **6.** let escape —*v.* **7.** (*oft. with* out) (allow to) become known little by little —'**leakage** *n.* **1.** leaking **2.** gradual escape or loss —'**leaky** *a.*

lean[1] (liːn) *a.* **1.** lacking fat **2.** thin **3.** meagre **4.** (of mixture of fuel and air) with too little fuel —*n.* **5.** lean part of meat, mainly muscular tissue

lean[2] (liːn) *v.* **1.** rest (against) **2.** bend, incline —*vi.* **3.** (*with* to or towards) tend (towards) **4.** (*with* on or upon) depend, rely (on) (**leaned** *or* **leant** (lɛnt) *pt./pp.*) —'**leaning** *n.* tendency —**lean-to** *n.* room, shed built against existing wall

leap (liːp) *vi.* **1.** spring, jump —*vt.* **2.** spring over (**leaped** *or* **leapt** (lɛpt) *pt./pp.*) —*n.* **3.** jump —'**leapfrog** *n.* **1.** game in which player vaults over another bending down —*v.* **2.** (cause to) advance by jumps or stages (**-gg-**) —**leap year** year with Feb. 29th as extra day, occurring every fourth year

learn (lɜːn) *vt.* **1.** gain knowledge of or acquire skill in (something) by study, practice or teaching —*vi.* **2.** gain knowledge **3.** be taught **4.** (*oft. with* of or about) find out (**learnt** *or* **learned** *pt./pp.*) —**learned** ('lɜːnɪd) *a.* **1.** erudite, deeply read **2.** showing much learning —**learnedly** ('lɜːnɪdlɪ) *adv.* —'**learner** *n.* —'**learning** *n.* knowledge got by study

lease (liːs) *n.* **1.** contract by which land or property is rented for stated time by owner to tenant —*vt.* **2.** let, rent by, take on lease —'**leasehold** *a.* held on lease

leash (liːʃ) *n.* **1.** thong for holding a dog **2.** set of three animals held in leash —*vt.* **3.** hold in, secure by leash

least (liːst) *sup. of* LITTLE *a.* **1.** smallest —*n.* **2.** smallest one —*adv.* **3.** in smallest degree

leather ('lɛðə) *n.* prepared skin of animal

—'**leathery** a. like leather, tough —'**leather- jacket** n. crane fly grub —'**leatherwood** n. N Amer. tree with tough, leathery bark

leave[1] (liːv) vt. 1. go away from 2. deposit 3. allow to remain 4. entrust 5. bequeath —vi. 6. go away, set out (**left**, '**leaving**)

leave[2] (liːv) n. 1. permission 2. permission to be absent from work, duty 3. period of such absence 4. formal parting —**leave of absence** 1. leave from work or duty, esp. for a long time 2. this period of time —**leave-taking** n. act of departing; farewell —**by** or **with your leave** with your permission

leave[3] (liːv) vi. produce or grow leaves (**leaved**, '**leaving**)

leaven ('lɛvən) n. 1. yeast 2. fig. transforming influence —vt. 3. raise with leaven 4. taint; modify

lecher ('lɛtʃə) n. man given to lewdness —**lech** vi. inf. (usu. with after) behave lecherously (towards) —'**lecherous** a. 1. lewd 2. provoking lust 3. lascivious —'**lecherously** adv. —'**lecher- ousness** n. —'**lechery** n.

lectern ('lɛktən) n. reading desk, esp. in church

lection ('lɛkʃən) n. 1. difference in copies of manuscript or book 2. reading —'**lectionary** n. book, list of scripture lessons for particular days —'**lector** n. reader

lecture ('lɛktʃə) n. 1. instructive discourse 2. speech of reproof —vi. 3. deliver discourse —vt. 4. reprove —'**lecturer** n. —'**lectureship** n. appointment as lecturer

LED light-emitting diode

ledge (lɛdʒ) n. 1. narrow shelf sticking out from wall, cliff etc. 2. ridge, rock below surface of sea

ledger ('lɛdʒə) n. 1. book of debit and credit accounts, chief account book of firm 2. flat stone —**ledger line** Mus. short line, above or below stave

lee (liː) n. 1. shelter 2. side of anything, esp. ship, away from wind —'**leeward** a./n. 1. (on) lee side —adv. 2. towards this side —**lee shore** shore towards which wind is blowing —'**leeway** n. 1. leeward drift of ship 2. room for free movement within limits 3. loss of progress

leech[1] (liːtʃ) n. 1. species of bloodsucking worm 2. Hist. physician —'**leechcraft** n.

leech[2] (liːtʃ) n. edge of a sail

leek (liːk) n. 1. plant like onion with long bulb and thick stem 2. this as Welsh emblem

leer (lɪə) vi. 1. glance with malign, sly or lascivious expression —n. 2. such glance —'**leery** a. 1. chiefly dial. knowing, sly 2. sl. (with of) suspicious, wary

lees (liːz) pl.n. 1. sediment of wine etc. 2. dregs of liquor

leet (liːt) n. in Scotland, selected list of candidates for office

left[1] (lɛft) a. 1. denotes the side that faces west when the front faces north 2. opposite to the right —n. 3. the left hand or part 4. Pol. reforming or radical party (also **left wing**) —adv. 5. on or towards the left —'**leftist** n./a. (person) of the political left —**left-handed** a. 1. using left hand with greater ease than right 2. performed with left hand 3. designed for use by left hand 4. awkward, clumsy 5. ironically ambiguous 6. turning from right to left; anticlockwise —adv. 7. with left hand —**left- hander** n.

left[2] (lɛft) pt./pp. of LEAVE[1]

leg (lɛg) n. 1. one of limbs on which person or animal walks, runs, stands 2. part of garment covering leg 3. anything which supports, as leg of table 4. stage of journey 5. Cricket part of field away from the striker's bat —'**leggings** pl.n. covering of leather or other material for legs —'**leggy** a. 1. long-legged 2. (of plants) straggling —**leg-pull** n. UK inf. practical joke, mild deception —'**legroom** n. room to move legs comfortably, as in car —**leg before wicket** Cricket manner of dismissal on grounds that batsman has been struck on leg by bowled ball that otherwise would have hit wicket

legacy ('lɛgəsɪ) n. 1. anything left by will, bequest 2. thing handed down to successor —**lega'tee** n. recipient of legacy

legal ('liːgəl) a. of, appointed or permitted by, or based on, law —**le'galese** n. conventional language in which legal documents are written —'**legalism** n. strict adherence to law, esp. letter of law rather than its spirit —**legal'istic** a. —**le'gality** n. —**legali'zation** or **-i'sation** n. —'**legalize** or **-ise** vt. make legal —'**legally** adv. —**legal aid** financial assistance available to persons unable to meet full cost of legal proceedings —**legal tender** currency that creditor must by law accept in redemption of debt

legate ('lɛgɪt) n. ambassador, esp. papal —'**legateship** n. —**le'gation** n. 1. diplomatic minister and his staff 2. his residence

legato (lɪ'gɑːtəʊ) adv. Mus. smoothly

legend ('lɛdʒənd) n. 1. traditional story or myth 2. traditional literature 3. famous, renowned, person or event 4. inscription —'**legendary** a.

legerdemain (lɛdʒədə'meɪn) n. 1. juggling, conjuring, sleight of hand 2. trickery

leger line ('lɛdʒə) see ledger line at LEDGER

leghorn ('lɛghɔːn) n. 1. kind of straw 2. hat made of it 3. (L-) inf. breed of fowls

legible ('lɛdʒəbəl) a. easily read —**legi'bility** n. —'**legibly** adv.

legion ('liːdʒən) n. 1. body of infantry in Roman

army **2.** various modern military bodies **3.** association of veterans **4.** large number —*a.* **5.** very numerous —**'legionary** *a./n.* —**legion-'naire** *n.* (*oft.* L-) member of military force or association —**Legionnaire's disease** sometimes fatal bacterial infection which has symptoms similar to those of pneumonia

legislator ('ledʒısleıtə) *n.* maker of laws —**'legislate** *vi.* make laws —**legis'lation** *n.* **1.** act of legislating **2.** laws which are made —**'legislative** *a.* —**'legislature** *n.* body that makes laws of a state —**legislative assembly** (*oft.* L- A-) single-chamber legislature in most Canad. provinces

legitimate (lı'dʒıtımıt) *a.* **1.** born in wedlock **2.** lawful, regular **3.** fairly deduced —*vt.* (lı'dʒıtımeıt) **4.** make legitimate —le'**gitimacy** *n.* —**le'gitimateness** *n.* —**legiti'mation** *n.* —**le'gitimism** *n.* —**le'gitimist** *n.* supporter of hereditary title to monarchy —**le'gitimize** *or* -**mise** *vt.* legitimate

leguan ('leguɑːn) *n.* large S Afr. lizard

legume ('legjuːm, lı'gjuːm) *n.* **1.** long dry fruit produced by leguminous plants; pod **2.** any of various table vegetables, *esp.* beans or peas **3.** any leguminous plant —**le'guminous** *a.* (of plants) pod-bearing

lei (leı) *n.* garland of flowers

Leics. ('lestəfə) Leicestershire

leisure ('leʒə) *n.* **1.** freedom from occupation **2.** spare time —**'leisured** *a.* with plenty of spare time —**'leisurely** *a.* **1.** deliberate, unhurried —*adv.* **2.** slowly

leitmotiv *or* **leitmotif** ('laıtməʊtiːf) *n.* Mus. recurring theme associated with some person, situation, thought

L.E.M. (lɛm) lunar excursion module

lemming ('lemıŋ) *n.* rodent of arctic regions

lemon ('lemən) *n.* **1.** pale yellow acid fruit **2.** tree bearing it **3.** its colour **4.** *sl.* useless or defective person or thing —**lemon'ade** *n.* drink made from lemon juice —**lemon curd** creamy spread made of lemons, butter *etc.* —**lemon sole** European flatfish highly valued as food

lemur ('liːmə) *n.* nocturnal animal like monkey

lend (lɛnd) *vt.* **1.** give temporary use of **2.** let out for hire or interest **3.** give, bestow (**lent**, **'lending**) —**'lender** *n.* —**lends itself to** is suitable for

length (lɛŋkθ, lɛŋθ) *n.* **1.** quality of being long **2.** measurement from end to end **3.** duration **4.** extent **5.** piece of a certain length —**'lengthen** *v.* **1.** make, become longer **2.** draw out —**'lengthily** *adv.* —**'lengthways** *or* U.S. **'lengthwise** *adv./a.* in direction of length —**'lengthy** *a.* (over)long —**at length 1.** in full detail **2.** at last

lenient ('liːnıənt) *a.* mild, tolerant, not strict —**'lenience** *or* **'leniency** *n.* —**'leniently** *adv.*

lenity ('lenıtı) *n.* **1.** mercy **2.** clemency

lens (lɛnz) *n.* piece of glass or similar material with one or both sides curved, used to converge or diverge light rays in cameras, spectacles, telescopes *etc.* (*pl.* **-es**)

lent (lɛnt) *pt./pp.* of LEND

Lent (lɛnt) *n.* period of fasting from Ash Wednesday to Easter Eve —**'Lenten** *a.* of, in or suitable to Lent

lentil ('lentıl) *n.* edible seed of leguminous plant —**len'ticular** *a.* like lentil

lento ('lentəʊ) *adv.* Mus. slowly

Leo ('liːəʊ) *n.* (lion) 5th sign of zodiac, operative c. Jul. 22nd–Aug. 21st

leonine ('liːənaın) *a.* like a lion

leopard ('lepəd) *n.* large, spotted, carnivorous animal of cat family, like panther (**'leopardess** *fem.*)

leotard ('lɪətɑːd) *n.* tight-fitting garment covering most of body, worn by acrobats, dancers *etc.*

leper ('lepə) *n.* **1.** one suffering from leprosy **2.** person ignored or despised —**'leprosy** *n.* disease forming silvery scales on the skin and eating away the parts affected —**'leprous** *a.*

Lepidoptera (lepı'dɒptərə) *pl.n.* order of insects with four wings covered with fine gossamer scales, as moths, butterflies —**lepi-'dopterist** *n.* person who studies or collects moths and butterflies —**lepi'dopterous** *a.*

leprechaun ('leprəkɔːn) *n.* mischievous elf of Irish folklore

lepton ('leptɒn) *n.* Phys. any of group of elementary particles and their antiparticles, that participate in weak interactions

lesbian ('lezbıən) *n.* homosexual woman —**'lesbianism** *n.*

lese-majesty ('liːz'mædʒıstı) *n.* **1.** treason **2.** taking of liberties

lesion ('liːʒən) *n.* **1.** injury **2.** injurious change in texture or action of an organ of the body

less (lɛs) *comp.* of LITTLE *a.* **1.** not so much —*n.* **2.** smaller part, quantity **3.** a lesser amount —*adv.* **4.** to a smaller extent or degree —*prep.* **5.** after deducting, minus —**'lessen** *v.* diminish, reduce —**'lesser** *a.* **1.** less **2.** smaller **3.** minor

-**less** (*comb. form*) **1.** without; lacking, as in *speechless* **2.** not able to (do something) or not able to be (done, performed *etc.*), as in *countless*

lessee (lɛ'siː) *n.* one to whom lease is granted

lesson ('lesən) *n.* **1.** instalment of course of instruction **2.** content of this **3.** experience that teaches **4.** portion of Scripture read in church

lessor ('lesɔː, lɛ'sɔː) *n.* grantor of a lease

lest (lɛst) *conj.* **1.** in order that not **2.** for fear that

let¹ (lɛt) *vt.* **1.** allow, enable, cause to **2.** allow to escape **3.** grant use of for rent, lease —*vi.* **4.** be leased —*v. aux.* **5.** used to express a proposal, command, threat, assumption (**let, 'letting**) —'**letdown** *n.* disappointment —**let-up** *n. inf.* lessening, abatement —**let down 1.** lower **2.** disappoint **3.** undo, shorten and resew (hem) **4.** untie (long hair that is bound up) and allow to fall loose **5.** deflate —**let off 1.** allow to disembark or leave **2.** explode or fire (bomb *etc.*) **3.** excuse from (work *etc*) **4.** *inf.* allow to get away without expected punishment *etc.* —**let's** let us: used to express suggestion *etc.* by speaker to himself and hearers

let² (lɛt) *n.* **1.** hindrance **2.** in some games, minor infringement or obstruction of ball requiring replaying of point

lethal ('liːθəl) *a.* deadly

lethargy ('lɛθədʒɪ) *n.* **1.** apathy, want of energy or interest **2.** unnatural drowsiness —le'**thargic** *a.* —le'**thargically** *adv.*

letter ('lɛtə) *n.* **1.** alphabetical symbol **2.** written message **3.** strict meaning, interpretation —*pl.* **4.** literature **5.** knowledge of books —*vt.* **6.** mark with, in, letters —'**lettered** *a.* learned —**letter bomb** explosive device in envelope, detonated when envelope is opened —'**letterhead** *n.* sheet of writing paper printed with one's address, name *etc.* —'**letterpress** *n.* printed matter as distinct from illustrations *etc.* —**letter of credit** letter issued by bank entitling bearer to draw funds from that bank or its agencies —**letters patent** document under seal of state, granting exclusive right, privilege

lettuce ('lɛtɪs) *n.* plant grown for use in salad

leucocyte *or esp. U.S.* **leukocyte** ('luːkəsaɪt) *n.* one of white blood corpuscles

leucoma (luːˈkəʊmə) *n.* disorder of the eye, characterized by opacity of the cornea

leukaemia *or esp. U.S.* **leukemia** (luːˈkiːmɪə) *n.* a progressive blood disease

Lev. *Bible* Leviticus

Levant (lɪˈvænt) *n. old name for* area of E Mediterranean now occupied by Lebanon, Syria and Israel —le'**vanter** *n.* (*sometimes* L-) **1.** easterly wind in W Mediterranean area **2.** inhabitant of the Levant —**Levantine** ('lɛvəntaɪn) *a./n.*

levee¹ ('lɛvɪ, 'lɛvɪ) *n.* **1.** Brit. sovereign's reception for men only **2.** *Hist.* reception held by sovereign on rising

levee² ('lɛvɪ) *n.* **1.** natural or artificial river embankment **2.** landing place

level ('lɛvəl) *a.* **1.** horizontal **2.** even in surface **3.** consistent in style, quality *etc.* —*n.* **4.** horizontal line or surface **5.** instrument for showing, testing horizontal plane **6.** position on scale **7.** standard, grade **8.** horizontal passage in mine —*vt.* **9.**

make level **10.** bring to same level **11.** knock down **12.** aim (gun or accusation *etc.*) —*vi.* **13.** *inf.* (*esp. with* with) be honest, frank (**-ll-**) —'**leveller** *or U.S.* '**leveler** *n.* advocate of social equality —**level crossing** point where railway line and road intersect —**level-headed** *a.* not apt to be carried away by emotion

lever ('liːvə) *n.* **1.** rigid bar pivoted about a fulcrum to transfer a force with mechanical advantage **2.** handle pressed, pulled *etc.* to operate something —*vt.* **3.** prise, move with lever —'**leverage** *n.* **1.** action, power of lever **2.** influence **3.** power to accomplish something **4.** advantage

leveret ('lɛvərɪt, -vrɪt) *n.* young hare

leviathan (lɪˈvaɪəθən) *n.* **1.** sea monster **2.** anything huge or formidable

levitation (lɛvɪˈteɪʃən) *n.* the power of raising a solid body into the air supernaturally —'**levitate** *v.* (cause to) do this

levity ('lɛvɪtɪ) *n.* **1.** inclination to make a joke of serious matters, frivolity **2.** facetiousness

levy ('lɛvɪ) *vt.* **1.** impose (tax) **2.** raise (troops) ('**levied, 'levying**) —*n.* **3.** imposition or collection of taxes **4.** enrolling of troops **5.** amount, number levied

lewd (luːd) *a.* **1.** lustful **2.** indecent —'**lewdly** *adv.* —'**lewdness** *n.*

lexicon ('lɛksɪkən) *n.* dictionary —'**lexical** *a.* —'**lexi'cographer** *n.* writer of dictionaries —**lexi'cography** *n.*

ley (leɪ, liː) *n.* **1.** arable land temporarily under grass **2.** line joining two prominent points in landscape, thought to be line of prehistoric track (*also* **ley line**)

Leyden jar ('laɪdən) *Phys.* early type of capacitor consisting of glass jar with lower part of inside and outside coated with tinfoil

L.F. *Rad.* low frequency

LG *or* **L.G.** Low German

Li *Chem.* lithium

liable ('laɪəbəl) *a.* **1.** answerable **2.** exposed **3.** subject **4.** likely —lia'**bility** *n.* **1.** state of being liable, obligation **2.** hindrance, disadvantage —*pl.* **3.** debts

liaison (lɪˈeɪzɒn) *n.* **1.** union **2.** connection **3.** intimacy, *esp.* secret —li'**aise** *vi.* communicate and maintain contact —**liaison officer** officer who keeps units of troops in touch

liana (lɪˈɑːnə) *or* **liane** (lɪˈɑːn) *n.* climbing plant of tropical forests

liar ('laɪə) *n.* one who tells lies

lib (lɪb) *inf.* liberation

lib. 1. liber (*Lat.*, book) **2.** librarian **3.** library

Lib. Liberal

libation (laɪˈbeɪʃən) *n.* drink poured as offering to the gods

libel ('laɪbəl) *n.* **1.** published statement falsely

damaging person's reputation —vt. **2.** defame falsely (**-ll-**) —**'libellous** or **'libelous** a. defamatory

liberal ('lɪbərəl, 'lɪbrəl) a. **1.** (*also* **L-**) of political party favouring democratic reforms or favouring individual freedom **2.** generous **3.** tolerant **4.** abundant **5.** (of education) designed to develop general cultural interests —n. **6.** one who has liberal ideas or opinions —**'liberalism** n. principles of Liberal Party —**libe'rality** n. munificence —**'liberalize** or **-ise** v. —**'liberally** adv.

liberate ('lɪbəreɪt) vt. set free —**libe'ration** n. —**'liberator** n.

libertarian (lɪbə'tɛərɪən) n. **1.** believer in freedom of thought etc., or in free will —a. **2.** of, like a libertarian —**liber'tarianism** n.

libertine ('lɪbətiːn, -taɪn) n. **1.** morally dissolute person —a. **2.** dissolute —**'libertinism** n.

liberty ('lɪbətɪ) n. **1.** freedom —pl. **2.** rights, privileges —**at liberty 1.** free **2.** having the right —**take liberties** be presumptuous

libido (lɪ'biːdəʊ) n. **1.** life force **2.** emotional craving, esp. of sexual origin (pl. **-s**) —**libidinous** (lɪ'bɪdɪnəs) a. lustful

Libra ('liːbrə) n. **1.** (balance) 7th sign of zodiac, operative c. Sept. 22nd–Oct. 22nd **2.** ('laɪbrə) (**l-**) Hist. a pound weight (pl. **-brae** (-briː))

library ('laɪbrərɪ) n. **1.** room, building where books are kept **2.** collection of books, gramophone records etc. **3.** reading, writing room in house —**li'brarian** n. keeper of library —**li'brarianship** n.

libretto (lɪ'brɛtəʊ) n. words of an opera (pl. **-s, -ti** (-tiː)) —**li'brettist** n.

lice (laɪs) n., pl. of LOUSE

licence or U.S. **license** ('laɪsəns) n. **1.** (document, certificate giving) leave, permission **2.** excessive liberty **3.** dissoluteness **4.** writer's, artist's transgression of rules of his art (oft. **poetic licence**) —**license** vt. grant licence to —**licen'see** n. holder of licence —**li'centiate** n. one licensed to practise art, profession

licentious (laɪ'sɛnʃəs) a. dissolute **2.** sexually immoral —**li'centiously** adv.

lichee (laɪ'tʃiː) n. see LITCHI

lichen ('laɪkən, 'lɪtʃən) n. small flowerless plants forming crust on rocks, trees etc. —**'lichened** a. —**liche'nology** n.

lich gate or **lych gate** (lɪtʃ) roofed gate of churchyard

licit ('lɪsɪt) a. rare lawful

lick (lɪk) vt. **1.** pass the tongue over **2.** touch lightly **3.** sl. defeat **4.** sl. flog, beat —n. **5.** act of licking **6.** small amount (esp. of paint etc.) **7.** block or natural deposit of salt or other chemical licked by cattle etc. **8.** inf. speed —**'licking** n. sl. beating

licorice ('lɪkərɪs) n. see LIQUORICE

lid (lɪd) n. **1.** movable cover **2.** cover of the eye **3.** sl. hat

lido ('liːdəʊ) n. pleasure centre with swimming and boating (pl. **-s**)

lie¹ (laɪ) vi. **1.** be horizontal, at rest **2.** be situated **3.** remain, be in certain state or position **4.** exist, be found **5.** recline (**lay, lain, 'lying**) —n. **6.** state (of affairs etc.) **7.** direction

lie² (laɪ) vi. **1.** make false statement (**lied, 'lying**) —n. **2.** deliberate falsehood —**'liar** n. person who tells lies —**white lie** untruth said without evil intent —**give the lie to** disprove

lief (liːf) adv. **1.** rare gladly, willingly —a. obs. **2.** ready; glad **3.** dear, beloved

liege (liːdʒ) a. **1.** bound to render or receive feudal service **2.** faithful —n. **3.** lord **4.** vassal, subject

lien (lɪən, 'liːən) n. right to hold another's property until claim is met

lieu (ljuː, luː) n. place —**in lieu (of)** instead (of)

lieutenant (lɛf'tɛnənt; in Navy, lə'tɛnənt; U.S. luː'tɛnənt) n. **1.** deputy **2.** Army rank below captain **3.** Navy rank below commander **4.** US police officer —**lieutenant colonel** officer holding commissioned rank immediately junior to colonel in certain armies, air forces and marine corps —**lieutenant commander** officer holding commissioned rank immediately junior to commander in certain navies —**lieutenant general** officer holding commissioned rank immediately junior to general in certain armies, air forces and marine corps —**lieutenant governor 1.** deputy governor **2.** US elected official who acts as deputy to state governor **3.** C representative of Crown in province: appointed by federal government

life (laɪf) n. **1.** active principle of existence of animals and plants, animate existence **2.** time of its lasting **3.** history of such existence **4.** way of living **5.** vigour, vivacity (pl. **lives**) —**'lifeless** a. **1.** dead **2.** inert **3.** dull —**life assurance** insurance providing for payment of specified sum to named beneficiary on death of policyholder (also **life insurance**) —**life belt** buoyant device to keep afloat person in danger of drowning —**'lifeblood** n. **1.** blood, considered as vital to life **2.** essential or animating force —**life buoy** buoyant device for keeping people afloat in emergency —**'lifeguard** n. person at beach or pool to guard people against risk of drowning —**life jacket** inflatable sleeveless jacket worn to keep person afloat when in danger of drowning —**'lifelike** a. closely resembling life —**'lifeline** n. **1.** line thrown or fired aboard vessel for hauling in hawser for breeches buoy **2.** line by which deep-sea diver is raised or lowered **3.** vital line of access or communication —'**lifelong** a. lasting a lifetime —**life preserver 1.** UK club kept for self-defence **2.** US life belt; life jacket —**life-size** or **life-sized** a. representing actual size —**life style** particular attitudes, habits etc. of person or group —'**lifetime** n. length of time person, animal or object lives or functions

lift (lɪft) vt. **1.** raise in position, status, mood, volume etc. **2.** take up and remove **3.** exalt spiritually **4.** inf. steal —vi. **5.** rise —n. **6.** raising apparatus **7.** cage raised and lowered in vertical shaft to transport people or goods **8.** act of lifting **9.** ride in car etc. as passenger **10.** air force acting at right angles on aircraft wing, so lifting it **11.** inf. feeling of cheerfulness, uplift —'**liftoff** n. **1.** initial movement of rocket from launching pad **2.** instant at which this occurs —**lift off** (of rocket) leave launching pad

ligament ('lɪgəmənt) n. band of tissue joining bones —'**ligature** n. **1.** anything which binds **2.** thread for tying up artery **3.** Print. character of two or more joined letters

light[1] (laɪt) a. **1.** of, or bearing little weight **2.** not severe **3.** gentle **4.** easy, requiring little effort **5.** trivial **6.** (of industry) producing small, usu. consumer goods, using light machinery —adv. **7.** in light manner —vi. **8.** alight (from vehicle etc.) **9.** (with on or upon) come by chance (upon) ('**lighted**, **lit** pt./pp.) —'**lighten** vt. reduce, remove (load etc.) —'**lightly** adv. —'**lightness** n. —**lights** pl.n. lungs of animals —**light-fingered** a. having nimble fingers, esp. for thieving or picking pockets —**light flyweight** amateur boxer weighing not more than 48 kg (106 lbs) —**light-headed** a. **1.** dizzy, inclined to faint **2.** delirious —**light-hearted** a. carefree —**light heavyweight 1.** professional boxer weighing 72.5-79.5 kg (160-175 lbs) **2.** amateur boxer weighing 75-81 kg (165-179 lbs) (also (UK) '**cruiserweight**) **3.** wrestler weighing usu. 87-97 kg (192-214 lbs) —**light middleweight** amateur boxer weighing 67-71 kg (148-157 lbs) —**light-minded** a. frivolous —'**lightweight** n./a. (person) of little weight or importance —**light welterweight** amateur boxer weighing 60-63.5 kg (132-140 lbs)

light[2] (laɪt) n. **1.** electromagnetic radiation by which things are visible **2.** source of this, lamp **3.** window **4.** mental vision **5.** light part of anything **6.** means or act of setting fire to something **7.** understanding —pl. **8.** traffic lights —a. **9.** bright **10.** pale, not dark —vt. **11.** set burning **12.** give light to —vi. **13.** take fire **14.** brighten ('**lighted**, **lit** pt./pp.) —'**lighten** vt. give light to —'**lighting** n. apparatus for supplying artificial light —'**lightning** n. visible discharge of electricity in atmosphere —'**lighthouse** n. tower with a light to guide ships —**light year**

Astron. distance light travels in one year, about six million million miles

lighter[1] ('laɪtə) n. **1.** device for lighting cigarettes etc. **2.** flat-bottomed boat for unloading ships

ligneous ('lɪgnɪəs) a. of, or of the nature of, wood —'**lignite** n. woody or brown coal

lignin ('lɪgnɪn) n. organic substance which forms characteristic part of all woody fibres

lignum vitae ('lɪgnəm 'vaɪtɪ) Lat. **1.** tropical tree **2.** its extremely hard wood

like[1] (laɪk) a. **1.** resembling **2.** similar to **3.** characteristic of —adv. **4.** in the manner of —pron. **5.** similar thing —'**likelihood** n. probability —'**likely** a. **1.** probable **2.** hopeful, promising —adv. **3.** probably —'**liken** vt. compare —'**likeness** n. **1.** resemblance **2.** portrait —'**likewise** adv. **1.** in addition; moreover; also **2.** in like manner

like[2] (laɪk) vt. find agreeable, enjoy, love —'**likable** or '**likeable** a. —'**liking** n. **1.** fondness **2.** inclination, taste

-like (comb. form) **1.** resembling, similar to, as in lifelike **2.** having characteristics of, as in childlike

lilac ('laɪlək) n. **1.** shrub bearing pale mauve or white flowers **2.** pale mauve colour —a. **3.** of lilac colour

Lilliputian (lɪlɪ'pjuːʃɪən) a. **1.** diminutive —n. **2.** midget, pygmy

Lilo ('laɪləʊ) n. **R** inflatable rubber mattress (pl. **-s**)

lilt (lɪlt) vi. **1.** (of melody) have a lilt **2.** move lightly —n. **3.** rhythmical effect in music, swing —'**lilting** a.

lily ('lɪlɪ) n. bulbous flowering plant —**lily-livered** a. cowardly; timid —**lily-white** a. **1.** of a pure white **2.** inf. pure; irreproachable —**lily of the valley** small garden plant with fragrant, white bell-like flowers

limb[1] (lɪm) n. **1.** arm or leg **2.** wing **3.** branch of tree —**limbed** a. **1.** having limbs **2.** having specified number or kind of limbs

limb[2] (lɪm) n. **1.** edge of sun or moon **2.** edge of sextant

limber[1] ('lɪmbə) n. detachable front of gun carriage

limber[2] ('lɪmbə) a. pliant, lithe —**limber up** loosen stiff muscles by exercises

limbo[1] ('lɪmbəʊ) n. (oft. L-) supposed region intermediate between Heaven and Hell for the unbaptised **2.** intermediate, indeterminate place or state (pl. **-s**)

limbo[2] ('lɪmbəʊ) n. W Indian dance in which dancers pass under a bar (pl. **-s**)

lime[1] (laɪm) n. **1.** any of certain calcium compounds used in making fertilizer, cement —vt. **2.** treat (land) with lime —'**limy** a. of, like or smeared with birdlime —'**limekiln** *n.* kiln in which calcium carbonate is calcined to produce quicklime —'**limelight** *n.* **1.** formerly, intense white light obtained by heating lime **2.** glare of publicity —'**limestone** *n.* sedimentary rock used in building

lime² (laɪm) *n.* small acid fruit like lemon —'**limy** *a.* —**lime juice** juice of lime prepared as drink

lime³ (laɪm) *n.* tree, the linden

limerick ('lɪmərɪk) *n.* self-contained, nonsensical, humorous verse of five lines

limey ('laɪmɪ) *n. US sl.* British person

limit ('lɪmɪt) *n.* **1.** utmost extent or duration **2.** boundary —*vt.* **3.** restrict, restrain, bound —'**limitable** *a.* —**limi'tation** *n.* —'**limited** *a.* **1.** restricted; confined **2.** without scope; narrow **3.** (of governing powers *etc.*) restricted or checked, by or as if by constitution, laws or assembly **4.** *chiefly* UK (of business enterprise) owned by shareholders whose liability for enterprise's debts is restricted —'**limitless** *a.* —**limited company** —**limited liability** principle whereby liability of shareholder is in proportion to amount of his stock

limn (lɪm) *vt.* paint; depict; draw —**limner** ('lɪmnə) *n.*

limousine ('lɪməziːn, lɪmə'ziːn) *n.* large, luxurious car

limp¹ (lɪmp) *a.* without firmness or stiffness —'**limply** *adv.*

limp² (lɪmp) *vi.* **1.** walk lamely —*n.* **2.** limping gait

limpet ('lɪmpɪt) *n.* shellfish which sticks tightly to rocks

limpid ('lɪmpɪd) *a.* **1.** clear **2.** translucent —**lim'pidity** *n.* —'**limpidly** *adv.*

linchpin ('lɪntʃpɪn) *n.* **1.** pin to hold wheel on its axle **2.** essential person or thing

Lincs. (lɪŋks) Lincolnshire

linctus ('lɪŋktəs) *n.* syrupy cough medicine

linden ('lɪndən) *n.* deciduous tree with fragrant flowers, the lime

line (laɪn) *n.* **1.** long narrow mark **2.** stroke made with pen *etc.* **3.** continuous length without breadth **4.** row **5.** series, course **6.** telephone connection **7.** progeny **8.** province of activity **9.** shipping company **10.** railway track **11.** any class of goods **12.** cord **13.** string **14.** wire **15.** advice, guidance **16.** *inf.* medical certificate —*vt.* **17.** cover inside of **18.** mark with lines **19.** bring into line **20.** be, form border, edge of —'**linage** *n.* **1.** number of lines in piece of written or printed matter **2.** payment for written material according to number of lines —**lineage** ('lɪnɪɪdʒ) *n.* descent from, descendants of an ancestor —**lineal** ('lɪnɪəl) *a.* **1.** of lines **2.** in direct line of descent —**lineament** ('lɪnɪəmənt)

n. feature —**linear** ('lɪnɪə) *a.* of, in lines —**lineation** (lɪnɪ'eɪʃən) *n.* **1.** marking with lines **2.** arrangement of or division into lines —'**liner** *n.* large ship or aircraft of passenger line —'**lining** *n.* covering for inside of garment *etc.* —**linear measure** system of units for measurement of length —**line drawing** drawing made with lines only —**line printer** electromechanical device that prints a line of characters at a time —'**linesman** *n.* in some sports, official who helps referee, umpire —**line-up** *n.* **1.** row or arrangement of people or things assembled for particular purpose **2.** members of such row or arrangement —**get a line on** obtain all relevant information about —**line of fire** flight path of missile discharged from firearm —**line up 1.** form, put into or organize line-up **2.** produce, organize and assemble **3.** align

linen ('lɪnɪn) *a.* **1.** made of flax —*n.* **2.** cloth made of flax **3.** linen articles collectively **4.** sheets, tablecloths *etc.*; shirts (orig. made of linen)

ling¹ (lɪŋ) *n.* slender food fish

ling² (lɪŋ) *n.* heather

-ling (*comb. form*) **1.** *oft.* disparaging person or thing associated with group, activity or quality specified, as in *nestling, underling* **2.** diminutive, as in *duckling*

linger ('lɪŋgə) *vi.* delay, loiter, remain long

lingerie ('læŋʒərɪ) *n.* women's underwear or nightwear

lingo ('lɪŋgəʊ) *n. inf.* language, speech, *esp.* applied to dialects (*pl.* -es)

lingua franca ('lɪŋgwə 'fræŋkə) *It.* language used for communication between people of different mother tongues (*pl.* **lingua francas, linguae francae** ('lɪŋgwiː 'frænsiː))

lingual ('lɪŋgwəl) *a.* **1.** of the tongue or language —*n.* **2.** sound made by the tongue, as *d, l, t* —'**linguist** *n.* one skilled in languages or language study —**lin'guistic** *a.* of languages or their study —**lin'guistics** *pl.n.* (*with sing. v.*) study, science of language

liniment ('lɪnɪmənt) *n.* embrocation

link (lɪŋk) *n.* **1.** ring of a chain **2.** connection **3.** measure, 1-100th part of chain —*vt.* **4.** join with, as with, link **5.** intertwine —*vi.* **6.** be so joined —'**linkage** *n.* —'**linkman** *n.* presenter of television or radio programme consisting of number of outside broadcasts from different locations

links (lɪŋks) *pl.n.* golf course

linnet ('lɪnɪt) *n.* songbird of finch family

lino ('laɪnəʊ) linoleum

linocut ('laɪnəʊkʌt) *n.* **1.** design cut in relief on block of linoleum **2.** print from this

linoleum (lɪ'nəʊlɪəm) *n.* floor covering of

hessian with smooth, hard, decorative coating of powdered cork, linseed oil *etc.*

linseed ('lɪnsiːd) *n.* seed of flax plant —**linseed oil** yellow oil extracted from it

linsey-woolsey ('lɪnzɪ'wʊlzɪ) *n.* rough fabric of linen warp and coarse wool or cotton filling

lint (lɪnt) *n.* soft material for dressing wounds

lintel ('lɪntl) *n.* top piece of door or window

lion ('laɪən) *n.* large animal of cat family (**'lioness** *fem.*) —**'lionize** *or* **-ise** *vt.* treat as celebrity —**lion-hearted** *a.* brave —**the lion's share** largest portion

lip (lɪp) *n.* 1. either edge of the mouth 2. edge or margin 3. *sl.* impudence —**lip-reading** *n.* method of understanding spoken words by interpreting movements of speaker's lips —**lip salve** ointment for the lips —**lip service** insincere tribute or respect —**'lipstick** *n.* cosmetic preparation in stick form, for colouring lips

liqueur (lɪ'kjʊə; *Fr.* li'kœːr) *n.* alcoholic liquor flavoured and sweetened

liquid ('lɪkwɪd) *a.* 1. fluid, not solid or gaseous 2. flowing smoothly 3. (of assets) in form of money or easily converted into money —*n.* 4. substance in liquid form —**lique'faction** *or* **liqui'faction** *n.* —**'liquefy** *or* **'liquify** *v.* make or become liquid —**li'quescence** *n.* —**li'quescent** *a.* tending to become liquid —**'liquidize** *or* **-dise** *v.* —**'liquidizer** *or* **-diser** *n.* kitchen appliance with blades for puréeing vegetables, blending liquids *etc.* (*also* **'blender**) —**liquid air** *or* **gas** air or gas reduced to liquid state on application of increased pressure at low temperature —**liquid crystal display** display of numbers, *esp.* in electronic calculator, using cells containing a liquid with crystalline properties, that change their reflectivity when an electric field is applied to them —**liquid fuel** petrol, paraffin oil *etc.,* carried in liquid form and vaporized for combustion —**liquid measure** system of units for measuring volumes of liquids

liquidate ('lɪkwɪdeɪt) *vt.* 1. pay (debt) 2. arrange affairs of and dissolve (company) 3. wipe out, kill —**liqui'dation** *n.* 1. process of clearing up financial affairs 2. state of being bankrupt —**'liquidator** *n.* official appointed to liquidate business —**li'quidity** *n.* state of being able to meet financial obligations

liquor ('lɪkə) *n.* liquid, *esp.* an alcoholic one

liquorice *or U.S.* **licorice** ('lɪkərɪs, -ərɪʃ) *n.* 1. black substance used in medicine and as a sweet 2. plant or its root from which liquorice is obtained

lira ('lɪərə; *It.* 'liːra) *n.* monetary unit of Italy and Turkey (*pl.* **lire** ('lɪərɪ; *It.* 'liːre), **-s**)

lisle (laɪl) *n.* fine hand-twisted cotton thread

lisp (lɪsp) *vi.* 1. speak with faulty pronunciation

of 's' and 'z' 2. speak falteringly —*n.* 3. such pronunciation or speech

lissom *or* **lissome** ('lɪsəm) *a.* 1. supple 2. agile

list (lɪst) *n.* 1. inventory, register 2. catalogue 3. edge of cloth —*pl.* 4. field for combat —*vt.* 5. place on list —**listed building** UK building officially recognized as having historical or architectural interest and therefore protected from demolition or alteration —**list price** selling price of merchandise as quoted in catalogue or advertisement

list² (lɪst) *vi.* 1. (of ship) lean to one side —*n.* 2. inclination of ship

listen ('lɪsən) *vi.* try to hear, attend (to) —**'listener** *n.*

listless ('lɪstlɪs) *a.* indifferent, languid —**'listlessly** *adv.*

lit (lɪt) *pt./pp. of* LIGHT¹, LIGHT²

litany ('lɪtənɪ) *n.* prayer with responses from congregation

litchi, lichee, *or* **lychee** (laɪ'tʃiː) *n.* 1. Chinese tree with red edible fruits 2. fruit of this tree, which has whitish juicy pulp and is usu. eaten dried or as preserve —**litchi nut** dried fruit of this tree

literal ('lɪtərəl) *a.* 1. according to sense of actual words, not figurative 2. exact in wording 3. of letters —**'literalism** *n.* 1. disposition to take words and statements in literal sense 2. literal or realistic portrayal in art or literature —**'literally** *adv.*

literate ('lɪtərɪt) *a.* 1. able to read and write 2. educated —*n.* 3. literate person —**'literacy** *n.* —**literati** (lɪtə'rɑːtiː) *pl.n.* scholarly, literary people

literature ('lɪtərɪtʃə, 'lɪtrɪ-) *n.* 1. books and writings, *esp.* of particular country, period or subject 2. *inf.* printed material —**'literarily** *adv.* —**'literary** *a.* of or learned in literature

lithe (laɪð) *a.* supple, pliant —**'lithesome** *a.* lissom, supple

lithium ('lɪθɪəm) *n.* one of the lightest alkaline metals

litho ('laɪθəʊ) *n.* 1. lithography 2. lithograph (*pl.* **-s**) —*a.* 3. lithographic —*adv.* 4. lithographically

litho- *or before vowel* **lith-** (*comb. form*) stone, as in **lithography**

lithography (lɪ'θɒɡrəfɪ) *n.* method of printing from metal or stone block using the antipathy of grease and water —**'lithograph** *n.* 1. print so produced —*vt.* 2. print thus —**li'thographer** *n.* —**litho'graphic** *a.*

litigate ('lɪtɪɡeɪt) *vt.* 1. contest in law —*vi.* 2. carry on a lawsuit —**'litigant** *n./a.* (person) conducting a lawsuit —**liti'gation** *n.* lawsuit —**litigious** (lɪ'tɪdʒəs) *a.* 1. given to engaging in lawsuits 2. disputatious

litmus ('lɪtməs) *n.* blue dye turned red by acids and restored to blue by alkali --**litmus paper**

litotes ('laɪtəʊtiːz) *n.* ironical understatement for rhetorical effect (*pl.* **-tes**)

litre *or U.S.* **liter** ('liːtə) *n.* measure of volume of fluid, one cubic decimetre, about 1.75 pints

Litt.D. *or* **Lit.D.** **1.** Doctor of Letters **2.** Doctor of Literature

litter ('lɪtə) *n.* **1.** untidy refuse **2.** odds and ends **3.** young of animal produced at one birth **4.** straw *etc.* as bedding for animals **5.** portable couch **6.** kind of stretcher for wounded —*v.* **7.** strew (with) litter **8.** give birth to (young) —**litter lout** *or U.S.* **'litterbug** *n. sl.* person who drops refuse in public places

little ('lɪt'l) *a.* **1.** small, not much (**less, least**) —*n.* **2.** small quantity —*adv.* **3.** to a small extent **4.** not much or often **5.** not at all (**less, least**) —**little people** *Folklore* small supernatural beings, such as leprechauns —**the Little Bear** Ursa Minor

littoral ('lɪtərəl) *a.* **1.** pert. to the seashore —*n.* **2.** coastal district

liturgy ('lɪtədʒɪ) *n.* prescribed form of public worship —**li'turgical** *a.*

live[1] (lɪv) *v.* **1.** have life **2.** pass one's life **3.** continue in life **4.** continue, last **5.** dwell **6.** feed —'**livable** *or* '**liveable** *a.* **1.** suitable for living in **2.** tolerable —'**liver** *n.* person who lives in specified way —'**living** *n.* **1.** action of being in life **2.** people now alive **3.** way of life **4.** means of living **5.** church benefice —**living room** room in house used for relaxation and entertainment —**living wage** wage adequate to maintain person and his family in reasonable comfort

live[2] (laɪv) *a.* **1.** living, alive **2.** active, vital **3.** flaming **4.** (of rail *etc.*) carrying electric current **5.** (of broadcast) transmitted during the actual performance —'**liveliness** *n.* —'**lively** *a.* brisk, active, vivid —'**liven** *vt.* (*esp. with* up) make (more) lively —'**livestock** *n.* domestic animals —**live wire 1.** wire carrying electric current **2.** able, very energetic person

livelihood ('laɪvlɪhʊd) *n.* **1.** means of living **2.** subsistence, support

livelong ('lɪvlɒŋ) *a.* lasting throughout the whole day

liver ('lɪvə) *n.* **1.** organ secreting bile **2.** animal liver as food —'**liverish** *a.* **1.** unwell, as from liver upset **2.** cross, touchy, irritable

liverwort ('lɪvəwɜːt) *n.* plant growing in wet places and resembling green seaweed or leafy moss

livery ('lɪvərɪ) *n.* **1.** distinctive dress of person or group, esp. servant(s) **2.** allowance of food for horses **3.** US a livery stable —'**liveried** *a.* (*esp.* of servants *etc.*) wearing livery —'**liveryman** *n.* member of a London guild —**livery stable**

stable where horses are kept at a charge or hired out

lives (laɪvz) *n., pl. of* LIFE

livid ('lɪvɪd) *a.* **1.** of a bluish pale colour **2.** discoloured, as by bruising **3.** *inf.* angry, furious

lizard ('lɪzəd) *n.* four-footed reptile

L.J. Lord Justice

L.L. **1.** Late Latin **2.** Low Latin **3.** Lord Lieutenant

llama ('lɑːmə) *n.* woolly animal used as beast of burden in S Amer.

LL.B. Bachelor of Laws

LL.D. Doctor of Laws

Lloyd's ('lɔɪdz) *n.* association of London underwriters originally concerned with marine insurance and shipping information and now subscribing a variety of insurance policies and publishing daily list (**Lloyd's List**) of shipping data and news

loach (ləʊtʃ) *n.* carplike freshwater fish

load (ləʊd) *n.* **1.** burden **2.** amount usu. carried at once **3.** actual load carried by vehicle **4.** resistance against which engine has to work **5.** amount of electrical energy drawn from a source —*vt.* **6.** put load on or into **7.** charge (gun) **8.** weigh down —'**loaded** *a.* **1.** carrying a load **2.** (of dice) dishonestly weighted **3.** biased **4.** (of question) containing hidden trap or implication **5.** *sl.* wealthy **6.** *sl.* drunk

loadstar ('ləʊdstɑː) *n. see* lodestar *at* LODE

loaf[1] (ləʊf) *n.* **1.** mass of bread as baked **2.** shaped mass of food (*pl.* **loaves**)

loaf[2] (ləʊf) *vi.* idle, loiter —'**loafer** *n.* idler

loam (ləʊm) *n.* fertile soil

loan (ləʊn) *n.* **1.** act of lending **2.** thing lent **3.** money borrowed at interest **4.** permission to use —*vt.* **5.** lend, grant loan of

loath *or* **loth** (ləʊθ) *a.* unwilling, reluctant —**loathe** (ləʊð) *vt.* hate, abhor —**loathing** ('ləʊðɪŋ) *n.* **1.** disgust **2.** repulsion —**loathsome** ('ləʊðsəm) *a.* disgusting

loaves (ləʊvz) *n., pl. of* LOAF[1]

lob (lɒb) *n.* **1.** in tennis *etc.*, shot pitched high in air —*v.* **2.** throw, pitch (shot) thus (**-bb-**)

lobby ('lɒbɪ) *n.* **1.** corridor into which rooms open **2.** passage or room in legislative building, esp. houses of parliament of Britain and Aust., to which the public has access **3.** group which tries to influence members of lawmaking assembly —'**lobbying** *n.* frequenting lobby to collect news or influence members —'**lobbyist** *n. chiefly US* person employed by particular interest to lobby —**lobby correspondent** reporter who frequents the lobby (in House of Commons) to gain parliamentary news

lobe (ləʊb) *n.* **1.** any rounded projection **2.** subdivision of body organ **3.** soft, hanging part of ear —'**lobar** *a.* of lobe —'**lobate** *a.* **1.** having or resembling lobes **2.** (of birds) having separate toes each fringed with weblike lobe —**lobed** a. —**lo'botomy** n. surgical incision into lobe of organ, esp. brain

lobelia (ləʊ'biːlɪə) n. garden plant with blue, red or white flowers

lobster ('lɒbstə) n. shellfish with long tail and claws, turning red when boiled

lobworm ('lɒbwɜːm) n. lugworm

local ('ləʊkəl) a. **1.** of, existing in particular place **2.** confined to a definite spot, district or part of the body **3.** of place —n. **4.** person belonging to a district **5.** inf. (nearby) pub —**locale** (ləʊ'kɑːl) n. scene of event —**lo'cality** n. **1.** place, situation **2.** district —**'localize** or -**ise** vt. assign, restrict to definite place —**'locally** adv. —**local anaesthetic** anaesthetic which produces insensibility in one part of body —**local authority** UK governing body of county etc. —**local colour** behaviour etc. characteristic of a certain region or time, introduced in novel etc. to supply realism

locate (ləʊ'keɪt) vt. **1.** attribute to a place **2.** find the place of **3.** situate —**lo'cation** n. **1.** placing **2.** situation **3.** site of film production away from studio **4.** SA black Afr. or coloured township —**locative** ('lɒkətɪv) a./n. (of) grammatical case denoting 'place where'

loch (lɒx) n. Scottish lake or long narrow bay

loci ('ləʊsaɪ) n., pl. of LOCUS

lock[1] (lɒk) n. **1.** appliance for fastening door, lid etc. **2.** mechanism for firing gun **3.** enclosure in river or canal for moving boats from one level to another **4.** extent to which vehicle's front wheels will turn **5.** appliance to check the revolution of a wheel **6.** interlocking **7.** block, jam —vt. **8.** fasten, make secure with lock **9.** join firmly **10.** cause to become immovable **11.** embrace closely —vi. **12.** become fixed or united **13.** become immovable —**'locker** n. small cupboard with lock —**'lockjaw** n. tetanus —**'locknut** n. second nut used on top of first on bolt to prevent it shaking loose —**'lockout** n. exclusion of workmen by employers as means of coercion —**'locksmith** n. one who makes and mends locks —**'lockup** n. **1.** prison **2.** garage, storage area away from main premises

lock[2] (lɒk) n. tress of hair

locket ('lɒkɪt) n. small hinged pendant for portrait etc.

loco[1] ('ləʊkəʊ) inf. locomotive

loco[2] ('ləʊkəʊ) a. **1.** sl., chiefly US insane —vt. **2.** US sl. make insane

locomotive (ləʊkə'məʊtɪv) n. **1.** engine for pulling carriages on railway tracks —a. **2.** having power of moving from place to place —**loco'motion** n. action, power of moving

locum tenens ('ləʊkəm 'tiːnɛnz) Lat.

substitute, esp. for doctor or clergyman during absence (pl. **locum tenentes** (təˈnɛntiːz)) (also **'locum**) —**locum tenency**

locus ('ləʊkəs) n. **1.** exact place or locality **2.** curve made by all points satisfying certain mathematical condition, or by point, line or surface moving under such condition (pl. **'loci**)

locust ('ləʊkəst) n. destructive winged insect —**locust bean** bean-shaped fruit of locust tree —**locust tree 1.** N. Amer. leguminous tree having prickly branches, white flowers and reddish-brown seed pods **2.** the carob

locution (ləʊ'kjuːʃən) n. **1.** a phrase **2.** speech **3.** mode or style of speaking

lode (ləʊd) n. a vein of ore —**'lodestar** or **'loadstar** n. Pole Star —**'lodestone** or **'loadstone** n. magnetic iron ore

lodge (lɒdʒ) a. **1.** house, cabin used seasonally or occasionally, eg for hunting, skiing **2.** gatekeeper's house **3.** meeting place of branch of Freemasons etc. **4.** the branch —vt. **5.** house **6.** deposit **7.** bring (a charge etc.) against someone —vi. **8.** live in another's house at fixed charge **9.** come to rest —**'lodger** n. —**'lodgings** pl.n. rented room(s) in another person's house —**'lodgment** or **'lodgement** n. lodging, being lodged

loft (lɒft) n. **1.** space between top storey and roof **2.** gallery in church etc. —vt. **3.** send (golf ball etc.) high —**'loftily** adv. haughtily —**'loftiness** n. —**'lofty** a. **1.** of great height **2.** elevated **3.** haughty

log[1] (lɒg) n. **1.** portion of felled tree stripped of branches **2.** detailed record of voyages, time travelled etc. of ship, aircraft etc. **3.** apparatus used formerly for measuring ship's speed —vt. **4.** keep a record of **5.** travel (specified distance, time) (-**gg**-) —**'logger** n. lumberjack —**'logging** n. US cutting and transporting logs to river —**'logbook** n.

log[2] (lɒg) n. logarithm

logan ('ləʊgən) n. C see BOGAN

loganberry ('ləʊgənbəri, -brɪ) n. **1.** trailing prickly plant, cross between raspberry and blackberry **2.** its purplish-red fruit

logarithm ('lɒgərɪðəm) n. one of series of arithmetical functions tabulated for use in calculation —**loga'rithmic** a.

loggerhead ('lɒgəhɛd) n. —**at loggerheads** quarrelling, disputing

loggia ('lɒdʒə, 'lɒdʒɪə) n. covered, arcaded gallery (pl. **-s, loggie** ('lɒdʒɛ))

logic ('lɒdʒɪk) n. **1.** art or philosophy of reasoning **2.** reasoned thought or argument **3.** coherence of various facts, events etc. —**'logical** a. **1.** of logic **2.** according to reason **3.** reasonable **4.** apt to reason correctly —**'logically** adv. —**lo'gician** n.

logistics (lə'dʒɪstɪks) *pl.n.* (*with sing. or pl. v.*) 1. the transport, housing and feeding of troops 2. organization of any project, operation —**lo'gistical** *a.*

logo ('ləʊgəʊ, 'lɒg-) *n.* company emblem or similar device (*pl.* **-s**)

Logos ('lɒgɒs) *n.* the Divine Word incarnate, Christ

-logue *or U.S.* **-log** (*comb. form*) speech or discourse of particular kind, as in *travelogue, monologue*

-logy (*n. comb. form*) 1. science or study of, as in *musicology* 2. writing, discourse or body of writings, as in *trilogy, phraseology, martyrology* —**-logical** *or* **-logic** (*a. comb. form*) —**-logist** (*n. comb. form*)

loin (lɔɪn) *n.* 1. part of body between ribs and hip 2. cut of meat from this —*pl.* 3. hips and lower abdomen —**'loincloth** *n.* garment covering loins only

loiter ('lɔɪtə) *vi.* 1. dawdle, hang about 2. idle —**'loiterer** *n.*

loll (lɒl) *vi.* 1. sit, lie lazily 2. (*esp.* of the tongue) hang out —*vt.* 3. hang out (tongue)

lollipop ('lɒlɪpɒp) *n.* boiled sweet *etc.* on small wooden stick —**lollipop man** *UK inf.* person holding circular sign on pole who stops traffic so children may cross road (**lollipop lady** *fem.*)

lollop ('lɒləp) *vi. chiefly UK* 1. walk or run with clumsy or relaxed bouncing movement 2. lounge

lolly ('lɒlɪ) *n.* 1. *inf.* lollipop; ice lolly 2. *sl.* money

London pride ('lʌndən) saxifrage with pinkish-white flowers

lone (ləʊn) *a.* solitary —**'loneliness** *n.* —**'lonely** *a.* 1. sad because alone 2. unfrequented 3. solitary, alone —**'loner** *n. inf.* one who prefers to be alone —**'lonesome** *a. chiefly US* lonely

long[1] (lɒŋ) *a.* 1. having length, *esp.* great length, in space or time 2. extensive 3. protracted —*adv.* 4. for a long time —**'longways** *or U.S.* **'longwise** *adv. see* **lengthways** *at* LENGTH —**'longbow** *n. esp.* in medieval England, large powerful hand-drawn bow —**long division** process of dividing one number by another and putting steps down in full —**long-drawn-out** *a.* overprolonged, extended —**'longhair** *a. inf.* of intellectuals or their tastes, *esp.* preferring classical music to jazz *etc.* (*also* **long-haired**) —**'longhand** *n.* writing of words, letters *etc.* in full —**long-headed** *a.* astute; shrewd; sagacious —**long johns** *inf.* underpants with long legs —**long jump** athletic contest in which competitors try to cover farthest distance possible with running jump from fixed board or mark —**long off** *Cricket* fielding position near boundary behind bowler on offside of pitch —**long on** *Cricket* fielding position near boundary behind bowler on leg side of pitch —**long-playing** *a.* (of record) lasting for 10 to 30 minutes because of its fine grooves —**long-range** *a.* 1. of the future 2. able to travel long distances without refuelling 3. (of weapons) designed to hit distant target —**long shot** competitor, undertaking, bet *etc.* with small chance of success —**long-standing** *a.* existing for a long time —**long-term** *a.* 1. lasting or extending over a long time 2. *Fin.* maturing after a long period —**long ton** the imperial ton (2240 lbs) —**long wave** radio wave with wavelength greater than 1000 metres —**long-winded** *a.* tediously loquacious

long[2] (lɒŋ) *vi.* have keen desire, yearn —**'longing** *n.* yearning

long. longitude

longeron ('lɒndʒərɒn) *n.* long spar running fore and aft in body of aircraft

longevity (lɒn'dʒɛvɪtɪ) *n.* long existence or life

longitude ('lɒndʒɪtjuːd) *n.* distance east or west from standard meridian —**longi'tudinal** *a.* 1. of length or longitude 2. lengthwise

longshoreman ('lɒŋʃɔːmən) *n.* US wharf labourer

loo (luː) *n. inf.* lavatory

loofah ('luːfə) *n.* 1. pod of plant used as sponge 2. the plant

look (lʊk) *vi.* 1. direct, use eyes 2. face 3. seem 4. (*with* for) search 5. (*with* for) hope 6. (*with* after) take care (of) —*n.* 7. looking 8. view 9. search 10. (*oft. pl.*) appearance —**looker-on** *n.* spectator —**looking glass** mirror —**'lookout** *n.* 1. guard 2. place for watching 3. prospect 4. watchman 5. *inf.* worry, concern —**good looks** beauty —**look after** tend —**look down on** despise

loom[1] (luːm) *n.* 1. machine for weaving 2. middle part of oar

loom[2] (luːm) *vi.* 1. appear dimly 2. seem ominously close 3. assume great importance

loon (luːn) *n. inf.* stupid, foolish person —**'loony** *a./n.* —**loony bin** *inf.* mental hospital

loop (luːp) *n.* 1. figure made by curved line crossing itself 2. similar rounded shape in cord, rope *etc.* crossed on itself 3. contraceptive coil 4. aerial manoeuvre in which aircraft describes complete circle 5. *Figure skating* curve crossing itself made on single edge —*vt.* 6. make loop in or of —**loop line** railway line which leaves, then rejoins, main line

loophole ('luːphəʊl) *n.* 1. means of escape, of evading rule without infringing it 2. vertical slit in wall, *esp.* for defence

loose (luːs) *a.* 1. not tight, fastened, fixed or tense 2. slack 3. vague 4. dissolute —*vt.* 5. free 6. unfasten 7. slacken —*vi.* 8. (*with* off) shoot, let fly (bullet *etc.*) —**'loosely** *adv.* —**'loosen** *v.*

make or become loose —'**looseness** n. —**loose-jointed** a. 1. supple and easy in movement 2. loosely built; with ill-fitting joints —**loose-leaf** a. (of binder etc.) capable of being opened to allow removal and addition of pages —**on the loose** 1. free 2. inf. on a spree

loot (luːt) n./v. plunder

lop[1] (lop) vt. (usu. with off) 1. cut away (twigs and branches) from tree 2. chop (off) (**-pp-**)

lop[2] (lop) vi. hang limply (**-pp-**) —**lop-eared** a. having drooping ears —**lop'sided** a. with one side lower than the other, badly balanced

lope (ləup) vi. run with long, easy strides

loquacious (lɒ'kweɪʃəs) a. talkative —**loquacity** (lɒ'kwæsɪtɪ) n.

loquat ('ləʊkwɒt, -kwət) n. 1. Japanese plum tree 2. its fruit

lor (lɔː) interj. nonstandard exclamation of surprise or dismay

loran ('lɔːrən) n. radio navigation system operating over long distances

lord (lɔːd) n. 1. British nobleman, peer of the realm 2. feudal superior 3. one ruling others 4. owner 5. God —v. 6. be domineering (esp. in **lord it over someone**) —'**lordliness** n. —'**lordly** a. 1. imperious, proud 2. fit for a lord —'**lordship** n. 1. rule, ownership 2. domain 3. title of some noblemen —**Lord Chief Justice** judge second only to Lord Chancellor; president of one division of High Court of Justice —**Lord (High) Chancellor** Brit. government cabinet minister who is head of judiciary in England and Wales, and Speaker of the House of Lords —**Lord Lieutenant** 1. UK representative of Crown in county 2. formerly, British viceroy in Ireland —**Lord Mayor** mayor in City of London and certain other boroughs —**Lord President of the Council** UK cabinet minister who presides at meetings of Privy Council —**Lord Privy Seal** UK senior cabinet minister without official duties —**the Lord's Day** Christian Sabbath; Sunday —**the Lord's Prayer** prayer taught by Jesus Christ to his disciples (also **Our Father, Pater'noster**) —**the Lord's Supper** see Holy Communion at HOLY —**the Lords Temporal** UK peers other than bishops in their capacity as members of House of Lords

lore (lɔː) n. 1. learning 2. body of facts and traditions

lorgnette (lɔː'njɛt) n. pair of spectacles mounted on long handle

lorikeet ('lɒrɪkiːt, lɒrɪ'kiːt) n. small parrot

loris ('lɔːrɪs) n. tree-dwelling, nocturnal Asian animal (pl. **-ris**)

lorn (lɔːn) a. poet. 1. abandoned 2. desolate

lorry ('lɒrɪ) n. motor vehicle for transporting loads by road, truck

lory ('lɔːrɪ), **lowry** or **lowrie** ('laʊrɪ) n.

small, brightly coloured parrot of Aust. and Indonesia

lose (luːz) vt. 1. be deprived of, fail to retain or use 2. let slip 3. fail to get 4. (of clock etc.) run slow by (specified amount) 5. be defeated in —vi. 6. suffer loss (**lost** pt./pp., '**losing** pr.p.) —'**loser** n. 1. person or thing that loses 2. inf. person or thing that seems destined to fail etc. —**loss** (lɒs) n. 1. a losing 2. what is lost 3. harm or damage resulting from losing —**lost** (lɒst) a. 1. unable to be found 2. unable to find one's way 3. bewildered 4. not won 5. not utilized

lot (lɒt) pron. 1. great number —n. 2. collection 3. large quantity 4. share 5. fate 6. destiny 7. item at auction 8. one of a set of objects used to decide something by chance (esp. **in** to **cast lots**) 9. area of land —pl. 10. inf. great numbers or quantity —adv. 11. inf. a great deal

loth (ləʊθ) a. see LOATH

lotion ('ləʊʃən) n. liquid for washing wounds, improving skin etc.

lottery ('lɒtərɪ) n. 1. method of raising funds by selling tickets and prizes by chance 2. gamble

lotto ('lɒtəʊ) n. game of chance like bingo

lotus or **lotos** ('ləʊtəs) n. 1. legendary plant whose fruits induce forgetfulness when eaten 2. Egyptian water lily —**lotus-eater** n. Gk myth. one of people encountered by Odysseus in N Afr. who lived in indolent forgetfulness, drugged by fruit of legendary lotus —**lotus position** seated cross-legged position used in yoga etc.

loud (laʊd) a. 1. strongly audible 2. noisy 3. obtrusive —'**loudly** adv. —'**loudmouth** n. inf. person who brags or talks too loudly —'**loudmouthed** a. —**loud'speaker** n. instrument for converting electrical signals into sound audible at a distance

lough (lɒx) n. in Ireland, loch

lounge (laʊndʒ) vi. 1. sit, lie, walk or stand in a relaxed manner —n. 2. living room of house 3. general waiting, relaxing area in airport, hotel etc. —'**lounger** n. loafer —**lounge suit** man's suit for daytime wear

lour (laʊə) see LOWER

lourie ('laʊrɪ) n. S Afr. bird with bright plumage

louse (laʊs) n. parasitic insect (pl. **lice**) —'**lousy** ('laʊzɪ) a. 1. sl. nasty, unpleasant 2. (with **with**) sl. (too) generously provided, thickly populated (with) 3. sl. bad, poor 4. having lice

lout (laʊt) n. crude, oafish person —'**loutish** a.

louvre or U.S. **louver** ('luːvə) n. 1. one of a set of boards or slats set parallel and slanted to admit air but not rain 2. ventilating structure of these

lovage ('lʌvɪdʒ) n. European umbelliferous plant used for flavouring food

love (lʌv) n. 1. warm affection 2. benevolence 3.

charity **4.** sexual passion **5.** sweetheart **6.** *Tennis etc.* score of nothing —*vt.* **7.** admire passionately **8.** delight in —*vi.* **9.** be in love —'**lovable** *or* '**loveable** *a.* —'**loveless** *a.* —'**loveliness** *n.* —'**lovely** *a.* beautiful, delightful —'**lover** *n.* —'**loving** *a.* **1.** affectionate **2.** tender —'**lovingly** *adv.* —'**lovebird** *n.* **1.** small parrot **2.** budgerigar **3.** *inf.* lover —**love child** *euphemistic* illegitimate child, bastard —**love-in-a-mist** *n.* plant with pale-blue flowers —**love letter** —**love-lies-bleeding** *n.* plant with long, drooping red flowers —'**lovelorn** *a.* forsaken by, pining for a lover —'**lovesick** *a.* pining or languishing because of love —'**lovesickness** *n.* —**lovey-dovey** *a.* making excessive or ostentatious display of affection —**loving cup** bowl formerly passed round at banquet —**make love (to)** have sexual intercourse (with)

low[1] (ləʊ) *a.* **1.** not tall, high or elevated **2.** humble **3.** coarse, vulgar **4.** dejected **5.** ill **6.** not loud **7.** moderate **8.** cheap —'**lower** *vt.* **1.** cause, allow to descend **2.** move down **3.** degrade —*vi.* **4.** diminish —*a.* **5.** below in position or rank **6.** at an early stage, period of development —'**lowliness** *n.* —'**lowly** *a.* modest, humble —**low**'**born** *or* **low**'**bred** *a. rare* of ignoble or common parentage —'**lowbrow** *n./a.* (one) having no intellectual or cultural interests —**Low Church** section of Anglican Church stressing evangelical beliefs and practices —'**lowdown** *n. inf.* inside information —**lowdown** *a. inf.* mean, shabby, dishonourable —**lower case** bottom half of compositor's type case, in which small letters are kept —**lower-case** *a.* of small letters —*vt.* **2.** print with lower-case letters —**lower class** social stratum having lowest position in social hierarchy —**lower-class** *a.* **1.** of lower class **2.** inferior; vulgar —**lower house** one of houses of bicameral legislature, usu. the larger and more representative (*also* **lower chamber**) —**low frequency 1.** in electricity, any frequency of alternating current from about 30 to 10,000 cycles **2.** frequency within audible range —**Low German** language of N Germany, spoken *esp.* in rural areas (*also* '**Plattdeutsch**) —**low-grade** *a.* of inferior quality —**low-key** *a.* subdued, restrained, not intense —'**lowland** (*n.*) **1.** low-lying country —'**Lowlander** ('ləʊləndə) *n.* —'**Lowlands** ('ləʊləndz) *n.* less mountainous parts of Scotland —**Low Latin** any form of Latin other than classical, such as Medieval Latin —**Low Mass** Mass that has simplified ceremonial form and is spoken rather than sung —**low-minded** *a.* having vulgar or crude mind and character —**low profile** position or attitude characterized by deliberate avoidance of prominence or publicity —**low-tension** *a.* carrying, operating at low voltage —**low tide 1.**

tide at lowest level or time at which it reaches this **2.** lowest point —**low water 1.** low tide **2.** state of any stretch of water at its lowest level

low[2] (ləʊ) *n.* **1.** cry of cattle, bellow —*vi.* **2.** (of cattle) utter their cry, bellow

lower ('laʊə) *or* **lour** *vi.* **1.** look gloomy or threatening, as sky **2.** scowl —*n.* **3.** scowl, frown

lox[1] (lɒks) *n.* kind of smoked salmon

lox[2] (lɒks) *n. short for* liquid oxygen, *esp.* when used as oxidizer for rocket fuels

loyal ('lɔɪəl) *a.* faithful, true to allegiance —'**loyalist** *n.* —'**Loyalist** *n.* C United Empire Loyalist —'**loyally** *adv.* —'**loyalty** *n.* —**loyal toast** toast drunk in pledging allegiance to sovereign, usu. after meal

lozenge ('lɒzɪndʒ) *n.* **1.** small sweet or tablet of medicine **2.** rhombus, diamond figure

LP long-playing (record)

LPG *or* **LP gas** liquefied petroleum gas

L-plate *n.* sign on car driven by learner driver

Lr *Chem.* lawrencium

LSD 1. lysergic acid diethylamide (hallucinogenic drug) **2.** librae, solidi, denarii (*Lat.*, pounds, shillings, pence)

L.S.E. London School of Economics

Lt. Lieutenant

Ltd. *or* **ltd.** Limited (Liability)

Lu *Chem.* lutetium

lubber ('lʌbə) *n.* **1.** clumsy fellow **2.** unskilled seaman

lubricate ('luːbrɪkeɪt) *vt.* **1.** oil, grease **2.** make slippery —'**lubricant** *n.* substance used for this —**lubri**'**cation** *n.* —'**lubricator** *n.* —**lu**'**bricity** *n.* **1.** slipperiness, smoothness **2.** lewdness

lucent ('luːsənt) *a.* bright, shining

lucerne (luː'sɜːn) *n.* fodder plant like clover, alfalfa

lucid ('luːsɪd) *a.* **1.** clear **2.** easily understood **3.** sane —**lu**'**cidity** *or* '**lucidness** *n.* —'**lucidly** *adv.*

luck (lʌk) *n.* **1.** fortune, good or bad **2.** good fortune **3.** chance —'**luckily** *adv.* fortunately —'**luckless** *a.* having bad luck —'**lucky** *a.* having good luck —**lucky dip** UK **1.** box containing small prizes for which children search **2.** *inf.* undertaking of uncertain outcome

lucre ('luːkə) *n. usu. facetious* money, wealth —'**lucrative** *a.* very profitable —**filthy lucre** *inf.* money

ludicrous ('luːdɪkrəs) *a.* absurd, laughable, ridiculous

ludo ('luːdəʊ) *n.* game played with dice and counters on board

luff (lʌf) *n.* **1.** the part of fore-and-aft sail nearest mast —*v.* **2.** sail (ship) into wind so that sails flap —*vi.* **3.** (of sails) flap

lug[1] (lʌg) *v.* drag (something heavy) with effort (**-gg-**)

lug² (lʌg) n. 1. projection, tag serving as handle or support 2. inf. ear

luggage ('lʌgidʒ) n. traveller's trunks and other baggage

lugger ('lʌgə) n. working boat (eg fishing, prawning lugger) orig. fitted with lugsail

lugsail ('lʌgsəl) n. oblong sail fixed on yard which hangs slanting on mast

lugubrious (luˈguːbriəs) a. mournful, doleful, gloomy —**luˈgubriously** adv.

lugworm ('lʌgwɜːm) n. large worm used as bait, lobworm

lukewarm (luːkˈwɔːm) a. 1. moderately warm, tepid 2. unenthusiastic

lull (lʌl) vt. 1. soothe, sing (to sleep) 2. make quiet —vi. 3. become quiet, subside —n. 4. brief time of quiet in storm etc. —**lullaby** ('lʌləbaɪ) n. lulling song, esp. for children

lumbar ('lʌmbə) a. relating to body between lower ribs and hips —**lumbago** (lʌmˈbeɪgəʊ) n. rheumatism in the lower part of the back

lumber ('lʌmbə) n. 1. disused articles, useless rubbish 2. sawn timber —vi. 3. move heavily —vt. 4. inf. burden with something unpleasant —'**lumberjack** n. US, C man who fells trees and prepares logs for transport to mill

lumen ('luːmɪn) n. SI unit of luminous flux (pl. -s, -mina (-mɪnə))

luminous ('luːmɪnəs) a. 1. bright 2. shedding light 3. glowing 4. lucid —'**luminary** n. 1. learned person 2. heavenly body giving light —**lumiˈnescence** n. emission of light at low temperatures by process (eg chemical) not involving burning —**lumiˈnosity** n.

lump (lʌmp) n. 1. shapeless piece or mass 2. swelling 3. large sum —vt. 4. (oft. with together) throw (together) in one mass or sum —vi. 5. move heavily —'**lumpish** a. 1. clumsy 2. stupid —'**lumpy** a. 1. full of lumps 2. uneven —**lump sum** relatively large sum of money, paid at one time —**lump it** inf. put up with something

lunar ('luːnə) a. relating to the moon —**lunar module** module used to carry astronauts from spacecraft to surface of moon and back

lunatic ('luːnətɪk) a. 1. insane —n. 2. insane person —'**lunacy** n. —**lunatic asylum** old name for institution for mentally ill —**lunatic fringe** extreme, radical section of group etc.

lunch (lʌntʃ) n. 1. meal taken in the middle of the day —v. 2. eat, entertain to lunch —**luncheon** ('lʌntʃən) n. a lunch —**luncheon voucher** voucher worth specified amount issued to employees and redeemable at restaurant for food

lung (lʌŋ) n. one of the two organs of respiration in vertebrates —'**lungfish** n. type of fish with air-breathing lung —'**lungworm** n.

parasitic worm infesting lungs of some animals —'**lungwort** n. flowering plant

lunge (lʌndʒ) vi. 1. thrust with sword etc. —n. 2. such thrust 3. sudden movement of body, plunge

lupin or U.S. **lupine** ('luːpɪn) n. leguminous plant with tall spikes of flowers

lupine ('luːpaɪn) a. like a wolf

lupus ('luːpəs) n. skin disease

lurch (lɜːtʃ) n. 1. sudden roll to one side —vi. 2. stagger —**leave in the lurch** leave in difficulties

lurcher ('lɜːtʃə) n. crossbred dog trained to hunt silently

lure (lʊə) n. 1. something which entices 2. bait 3. power to attract —vt. 4. entice 5. attract

lurid ('lʊərɪd) a. 1. vivid in shocking detail, sensational 2. pale, wan 3. lit with unnatural glare —'**luridly** adv.

lurk (lɜːk) vi. lie hidden —'**lurking** a. (of suspicion) not definite

luscious ('lʌʃəs) a. 1. sweet, juicy 2. extremely pleasurable or attractive

lush¹ (lʌʃ) a. (of grass etc.) luxuriant and juicy, fresh

lush² (lʌʃ) n. US sl. 1. heavy drinker 2. alcoholic —'**lushy** a.

lust (lʌst) n. 1. strong desire for sexual gratification 2. any strong desire —vi. 3. have passionate desire —'**lustful** a. —'**lustily** adv. —'**lusty** a. vigorous, healthy

lustration (lʌsˈtreɪʃən) n. purification by sacrifice —'**lustral** a. used in lustration —'**lustrate** vt.

lustre or U.S. **luster** ('lʌstə) n. 1. gloss, sheen 2. splendour 3. renown 4. glory 5. glossy material 6. metallic pottery glaze —'**lustrous** a. shining, luminous

lute¹ (luːt) n. old stringed musical instrument played with the fingers —'**lutenist** or 'lutist n.

lute² (luːt) n. 1. composition to make joints airtight —vt. 2. close with lute

lutetium or **lutecium** (luˈtiːʃɪəm) n. silvery-white metallic element of lanthanide series

Lutheran ('luːθərən) n. 1. follower of Luther, German leader of Protestant Reformation, or member of Lutheran Church —a. 2. of Luther or his doctrines 3. of Lutheran Church —'**Lutheranism** n.

lutz (luts) n. Ice-skating jump from one skate with complete turn in air and return to other skate

lux (lʌks) n. SI unit of illumination (pl. **lux**)

luxe (lʌks, luks; Fr. lyks) n. see DE LUXE

luxury ('lʌkʃərɪ) n. 1. possession and use of costly, choice things for enjoyment 2. enjoyable but not necessary thing 3. comfortable surroundings —**luxuriance** (lʌgˈzjʊərɪəns) n. abundance, proliferation —**luxuriant** (lʌgˈzjʊərɪənt) a. 1. growing thickly 2. abundant

—**luxuriantly** (lʌgˈzjuərɪəntlɪ) *adv.* —**luxuriate** (lʌgˈzjuərɪeɪt) *vi.* **1.** indulge in luxury **2.** flourish profusely **3.** take delight —**luxurious** (lʌgˈzjuərɪəs) *a.* **1.** fond of luxury **2.** self-indulgent **3.** sumptuous —**luxuriously** (lʌgˈzjuərɪəslɪ) *adv.*

LV luncheon voucher

lyceum (laɪˈsɪəm) *n.* public building for concerts *etc.*

lychee (laɪˈtʃiː) *n. see* LITCHI

lych gate (lɪtʃ) *see* LICH GATE

lyddite (ˈlɪdaɪt) *n.* powerful explosive used in shells

lye (laɪ) *n.* water made alkaline with wood ashes *etc.* for use as cleansing agent

lying (ˈlaɪɪŋ) *pr.p. of* LIE¹, LIE² —**lying-in** *n.* confinement in childbirth (*pl.* **lyings-in**)

lymph (lɪmf) *n.* colourless bodily fluid, mainly of white blood cells —**lymphatic** *a.* **1.** of lymph **2.** flabby, sluggish —*n.* **3.** vessel in the body conveying lymph —**lymph node** any of numerous bean-shaped masses of tissue, situated along course of lymphatic vessels

lynch (lɪntʃ) *vt.* put to death without trial —**lynch law** procedure of self-appointed court trying and executing accused

lynx (lɪŋks) *n.* animal of cat family —**lynx-eyed** *a.* having keen sight

lyre (laɪə) *n* instrument like harp —**lyric** (ˈlɪrɪk) *n.* **1.** lyric poem —*pl.* **2.** words of popular song —**lyric(al)** (ˈlɪrɪk(ə)l)) *a.* **1.** of short personal poems expressing emotion **2.** of lyre **3.** meant to be sung —**lyricist** (ˈlɪrɪsɪst) *n.* —**lyrist** (ˈlɪrɪst) *n.* **1.** lyric poet **2.** (ˈlaɪərɪst) player on lyre —**lyrebird** *n.* Aust. bird, the male of which displays tail shaped like a lyre —**wax lyrical** express great enthusiasm

-lyte (*n. comb. form*) substance that can be decomposed or broken down, as in *electrolyte* —**-lytic** (*a. comb. form*) loosening, dissolving, as in *paralytic*

M,m

m *or* **M** (ɛm) *n.* **1.** 13th letter of English alphabet **2.** speech sound represented by this letter (*pl.* **m's, M's** *or* **Ms**)

m metre(s)

M 1. Mach **2.** mega- **3.** *Currency* mark(s) **4.** million **5.** UK motorway **6.** Roman numeral, 1000

m. 1. male **2.** married **3.** masculine **4.** mile **5.** minute

M. 1. Medieval **2.** Monsieur

ma (mɑː) *n. inf.* mother

MA Massachusetts

M.A. Master of Arts

ma'am (mæm, mɑːm; *unstressed* məm) *n.* madam

mac *or* **mack** (mæk) *n.* UK *inf.* mackintosh

Mac-, Mc- *or* **M'-** (*comb. form*) in surnames of Gaelic origin, son of, as in *MacDonald*

macabre (məˈkɑːbə, -brə) *a.* gruesome, ghastly

macadam (məˈkædəm) *n.* road surface made of pressed layers of small broken stones —**ma'cadamize** *or* **-ise** *vt.* pave (road) with this

macaroni *or* **maccaroni** (mækəˈrəunɪ) *n.* pasta in long, thin tubes (*pl.* **-s, -es**)

macaroon (mækəˈruːn) *n.* small cake, biscuit containing almonds

macaw (məˈkɔː) *n.* kind of parrot

mace¹ (meɪs) *n.* **1.** staff with metal head **2.** staff of office

mace² (meɪs) *n.* spice made of the husk of the nutmeg

macerate (ˈmæsəreɪt) *v.* **1.** soften by soaking **2.** (cause to) waste away —**mace'ration** *n.*

machete (məˈʃetɪ, -ˈtʃeɪ-) *n.* broad, heavy knife used for cutting or as a weapon

Machiavellian (mækɪəˈvelɪən) *a.* politically unprincipled, crafty, perfidious, subtle, deep-laid

machination (mækɪˈneɪʃən) *n.* (*usu. pl.*) plotting, intrigue —**'machinate** *v.* lay or devise (plots)

machine (məˈʃiːn) *n.* **1.** apparatus combining action of several parts to apply mechanical force **2.** controlling organization **3.** mechanical appliance **4.** vehicle —*vt.* **5.** sew, print, shape *etc.* with machine —**ma'chinery** *n.* **1.** parts of machine collectively **2.** machines —**ma'chinist** *n.* one who makes *or* works machines —**machine gun** gun firing repeatedly and continuously with an automatic loading and firing mechanism —**machine-readable** *a.* (of data) in a form that can be directly fed into a computer —**machine shop** workshop in which machine tools are operated —**machine tool** power-driven machine, such as lathe, for cutting or shaping metals *etc.*

machismo (mæˈkɪzməʊ, -ˈtʃɪz-) *n.* strong or exaggerated masculine pride or masculinity (*oft.* **macho** (ˈmætʃəʊ))

Mach (number) (mæk) *n.* the ratio of the air speed of an aircraft to the velocity of sound under given conditions

mack (mæk) *n.* UK *inf. see* MAC

mackerel (ˈmækrəl) *n.* edible sea fish with blue and silver stripes

mackintosh *or* **macintosh** (ˈmækɪntɒʃ) *n.* **1.** waterproof raincoat of rubberized cloth **2.** any raincoat

macramé (məˈkrɑːmɪ) *n.* ornamental work of knotted cord

macro- *or before vowel* **macr-** (*comb. form*)

1. large, long, or great in size or duration, as in *macroscopic* 2. *Pathol.* abnormal enlargement, as in *macrocephaly*

macrobiotics (mækrəʊbaɪˈɒtɪks) *pl.n.* (*with sing. v.*) dietary system advocating whole grain and vegetables grown without chemical additives

macrocosm (ˈmækrəkɒzəm) *n.* 1. the universe 2. any large, complete system

macron (ˈmækrɒn) *n.* diacritical mark (−) placed over letter to represent long vowel

macroscopic (mækrəʊˈskɒpɪk) *a.* 1. visible to the naked eye 2. concerned with large units —**macro'scopically** *adv.*

mad (mæd) *a.* 1. suffering from mental disease, insane 2. wildly foolish 3. very enthusiastic 4. excited 5. *inf.* furious, angry —'**madden** *vt.* make mad —'**madly** *adv.* —'**madness** *n.* 1. insanity 2. folly —'**madhouse** *n. inf.* 1. mental hospital or asylum 2. state of uproar or confusion —'**madman** *n.*

madam (ˈmædəm) *n.* 1. polite form of address to a woman 2. *inf.* precocious or conceited girl

madame (ˈmædəm) *n.* married Frenchwoman

madcap (ˈmædkæp) *n.* 1. reckless person —*a.* 2. reckless

madder (ˈmædə) *n.* 1. climbing plant 2. its root 3. red dye made from this

made (meɪd) *pt./pp. of* MAKE —**made-up** *a.* 1. invented 2. wearing make-up 3. put together

Madeira (məˈdɪərə) *n.* rich sherry wine —**Madeira cake** rich sponge cake

mademoiselle (mædmwɑːˈzɛl) *n.* 1. young unmarried French girl or woman 2. French teacher or governess

Madonna (məˈdɒnə) *n.* 1. the Virgin Mary 2. picture or statue of her

madrepore (mædrɪˈpɔː) *n.* kind of coral

madrigal (ˈmædrɪɡəl) *n.* 1. unaccompanied part song 2. short love poem or song

maelstrom (ˈmeɪlstrəʊm) *n.* 1. great whirlpool 2. turmoil

maenad (ˈmiːnæd) *n. Class. lit.* frenzied female worshipper of Dionysus

maestoso (maɪˈstəʊsəʊ) *adv. Mus.* grandly, in majestic manner

maestro (ˈmaɪstrəʊ) *n.* 1. outstanding musician, conductor 2. man regarded as master of any art (*pl.* **-tri** (trɪ), **-s**)

mae west (meɪ) *sl.* inflatable life jacket

Mafia (ˈmæfɪə) *n.* international secret criminal organization, *orig.* Italian

magazine (mæɡəˈziːn) *n.* 1. periodical publication with stories and articles by different writers 2. appliance for supplying cartridges automatically to gun 3. storehouse for explosives or arms

magenta (məˈdʒɛntə) *a./n.* (of) deep purplish-red colour

maggot (ˈmæɡət) *n.* grub, larva —'**maggoty** *a.* infested with maggots

magi (ˈmeɪdʒaɪ) *pl.n.* 1. priests of ancient Persia 2. the wise men from the East at the Nativity (*sing.* **-gus** (-ɡəs))

magic (ˈmædʒɪk) *n.* 1. art of supposedly invoking supernatural powers to influence events *etc.* 2. any mysterious agency or power 3. witchcraft, conjuring —*a.* 4. magical, enchanting —'**magical** *a.* —'**magically** *adv.* —ma'**gician** *n.* one skilled in magic, wizard, conjurer, enchanter —**magic lantern** early form of projector using slides

magistrate (ˈmædʒɪstreɪt, -strɪt) *n.* 1. civil officer administering law 2. justice of the peace —**magis'terial** *a.* 1. of, referring to magistrate 2. dictatorial —'**magistracy** *n.* 1. office of magistrate 2. magistrates collectively

magma (ˈmæɡmə) *n.* 1. paste or suspension consisting of finely divided solid dispersed in liquid 2. molten rock inside earth's crust

magnanimous (mæɡˈnænɪməs) *a.* noble, generous, not petty —**magna'nimity** *n.*

magnate (ˈmæɡneɪt, -nɪt) *n.* influential or wealthy person

magnesium (mæɡˈniːzɪəm) *n.* metallic element —**mag'nesia** *n.* white powder compound of this, used in medicine

magnet (ˈmæɡnɪt) *n.* 1. piece of iron, steel having properties of attracting iron, steel and pointing north and south when suspended 2. lodestone —**mag'netic** *a.* 1. with properties of magnet 2. exerting powerful attraction —**mag'netically** *adv.* —'**magnetism** *n.* 1. magnetic phenomena 2. science of magnetic phenomena 3. personal charm or power of attracting others —'**magnetite** *n.* black magnetizable mineral that is important source of iron —**magneti'zation** *or* -i'**sation** *n.* —'**magnetize** *or* -ise *vt.* 1. make into a magnet 2. attract as if by magnet 3. fascinate —**magneto** (mæɡˈniːtəʊ) *n.* apparatus for ignition in internal-combustion engine (*pl.* **-s**) —**magne'tometer** *n.* instrument used to measure magnetic force —'**magnetron** *n.* two-electrode electronic valve used with applied magnetic field to generate high-power microwave oscillations —**magnetic field** field of force surrounding permanent magnet or moving charged particle —**magnetic mine** mine designed to activate when magnetic field is detected —**magnetic needle** magnetized rod used in certain instruments for indicating direction of magnetic field —**magnetic north** direction in which compass needle points, usu. at angle of true north —**magnetic pole** 1. either of two regions in magnet where magnetic induction is concentrated **2.** either of two variable points on earth's surface towards which magnetic needle points —**magnetic storm** sudden severe disturbance of earth's magnetic field —**magnetic tape** long coated plastic strip for recording sound or video signals

Magnificat (mæg'nɪfɪkæt) *n.* hymn of Virgin Mary in *Luke* 1. 46-55, used as canticle

magnificent (mæg'nɪfɪsənt) *a.* **1.** splendid **2.** stately, imposing **3.** excellent —**mag'nificence** *n.* —**mag'nificently** *adv.*

magnify ('mægnɪfaɪ) *vt.* **1.** increase apparent size of, as with lens **2.** exaggerate **3.** make greater (**-fied, -fying**) —**magnifi'cation** *n.*

magniloquent (mæg'nɪləkwənt) *a.* **1.** speaking pompously **2.** grandiose —**mag'niloquence** *n.*

magnitude ('mægnɪtjuːd) *n.* **1.** importance **2.** greatness, size

magnolia (mæg'nəʊlɪə) *n.* shrub or tree with large white, sweet-scented flowers

magnum ('mægnəm) *n.* large wine bottle (approx. 52 fluid ounces)

magnum opus great work of art or literature

magpie ('mægpaɪ) *n.* black-and-white bird

Magyar ('mægjɑː) *n.* **1.** member of prevailing race in Hungary **2.** native speech of Hungary —*a.* **3.** pert. to Magyars **4.** *Dressmaking* cut with sleeves and bodice of garment in one piece

maharajah *or* **maharaja** (mɑːhə'rɑːdʒə) *n.* former title of some Indian princes

maharani *or* **maharanee** (mɑːhə'rɑːnɪ) *n.* **1.** wife of maharajah **2.** woman holding rank of maharajah

maharishi (mɑːhɑː'riːʃɪ, mə'hɑːrɪʃɪ) *n.* Hindu religious teacher or mystic

mahatma (mə'hɑːtmə) *n.* **1.** *Hinduism* man of saintly life with supernatural powers **2.** one endowed with great wisdom and power

mahjong *or* **mah-jongg** (mɑː'dʒɒŋ) *n.* Chinese table game for four, played with pieces called tiles

mahogany (mə'hɒgənɪ) *n.* tree yielding reddish-brown wood

mahout (mə'haʊt) *n.* in India and E Indies, elephant driver or keeper

maiden ('meɪdən) *n.* **1.** *Lit.* young unmarried woman —*a.* **2.** unmarried **3.** of, suited to maiden **4.** first **5.** having blank record —**maid** *n.* **1.** *Lit.* young unmarried woman **2.** woman servant —'**maidenhood** *n.* —'**maidenly** *a.* modest —'**maidenhair** *n.* fern with delicate stalks and fronds —'**maidenhead** *n.* **1.** hymen **2.** virginity —**maiden name** woman's surname before marriage —**maid of honour 1.** UK small tart with almond-flavoured filling **2.** unmarried lady attending queen or princess **3.** US principal

unmarried attendant of bride —**maiden over** *Cricket* over in which no runs are scored

mail[1] (meɪl) *n.* **1.** letters *etc.* transported and delivered by the post office **2.** letters *etc.* conveyed at one time **3.** the postal system **4.** train, ship *etc.* carrying mail —*vt.* **5.** send by post —**mail order 1.** order for merchandise sent by post **2.** system of buying and selling merchandise through post

mail[2] (meɪl) *n.* armour of interlaced rings or overlapping plates —**mailed** *a.* covered with mail

maim (meɪm) *vt.* cripple, mutilate

main (meɪn) *a.* **1.** chief, principal, leading —*n.* **2.** principal pipe, line carrying water, electricity *etc.* **3.** chief part **4.** strength, power **5.** *obs.* open sea —'**mainly** *adv.* for the most part, chiefly —**main chance** one's own interests (*usu. in* **have an eye to the main chance**) —**main clause** *Gram.* clause that can stand alone as sentence —**main force** physical strength —**mainland** ('meɪnlənd) *n.* stretch of land which forms main part of a country —**main line 1.** *Railways* trunk route between two points **2.** *sl.* main vein into which narcotic drug can be injected —'**main-line** *vi. sl.* inject drug thus —'**mainmast** *n.* chief mast in ship —**mainsail** ('meɪnseɪl; *Naut.* 'meɪnsəl) *n.* lowest sail of mainmast —'**mainspring** *n.* **1.** chief spring of watch or clock **2.** chief cause or motive —'**mainstay** *n.* **1.** rope from mainmast **2.** chief support —'**mainstream** *n.* **1.** main current (of river, cultural trend *etc.*) —*a.* **2.** of style of jazz that lies between traditional and modern

maintain (meɪn'teɪn) *vt.* **1.** carry on **2.** preserve **3.** support **4.** sustain **5.** keep up **6.** keep supplied **7.** affirm **8.** support by argument **9.** defend —**main'tainable** *a.* —'**maintenance** *n.* **1.** maintaining **2.** means of support **3.** upkeep of buildings *etc.* **4.** provision of money for separated or divorced spouse

maisonette *or* **maisonnette** (meɪzə'nɛt) *n.* part of house, usu. on two floors, fitted as self-contained dwelling

maître d'hôtel (mɛtrə dəʊ'tɛl) *Fr.* restaurant manager

maize (meɪz) *n.* type of corn

Maj. Major

majesty ('mædʒɪstɪ) *n.* **1.** stateliness **2.** sovereignty **3.** grandeur —**ma'jestic** *a.* **1.** splendid **2.** regal —**ma'jestically** *adv.*

majolica (mə'dʒɒlɪkə, mə'jɒl-) *or* **maiolica** (mə'jɒlɪkə) *n.* type of ornamented Italian pottery

major ('meɪdʒə) *n.* **1.** army officer ranking next above captain **2.** major scale in music **3.** US, A, NZ principal field of study at university *etc.* **4.** person of legal majority —*a.* **5.** greater in number, quality, extent **6.** significant, serious —vi. **7.** (usu. with in) **US, A, NZ** do one's principal study (in particular subject) —ma'**jority** n. **1.** greater number **2.** larger party voting together **3.** excess of the vote on one side **4.** coming of age **5.** rank of major —**major-domo** ('dɔumɒu) n. house steward (pl. **-s**) —**major general** Mil. officer immediately junior to lieutenant general —**major scale** Mus. scale with semitones instead of whole tones after third and seventh notes

make (meik) vt. **1.** construct **2.** produce **3.** create **4.** establish **5.** appoint **6.** amount to **7.** cause to (do something) **8.** accomplish **9.** reach **10.** earn —vi. **11.** tend (**made, 'making**) —n. **12.** brand, type, style —'**Maker** n. title given to God (as Creator) —'**making** n. creation —pl. **2.** necessary requirements or qualities —**make-believe** n. fantasy or pretence —'**makeshift** n. temporary expedient —**make-up** n. **1.** cosmetics **2.** characteristics **3.** layout —'**makeweight** n. trifle added to make something stronger or better —(**go to**) **meet one's Maker** die —**make believe** pretend; enact fantasy —**make up 1.** compose **2.** compile **3.** complete **4.** compensate **5.** apply cosmetics **6.** invent —**on the make** sl. **1.** intent on gain **2.** in search of sexual partner

mako ('mɑːkɒu) n. type of shark (pl. **-s**)

mal- (comb. form) ill, badly, as in malformation, malfunction

malacca or **malacca cane** (mɒ'lækɒ) n. brown cane used for walking stick

malachite ('mælɒkait) n. green mineral

maladjusted (mælɒ'dʒʌstid) a. **1.** Psychol. unable to meet the demands of society **2.** badly adjusted —**malad'justment** n.

maladministration (mælɒdminis'treiʃɒn) n. inefficient or dishonest administration

maladroit (mælɒ'drɔit) a. clumsy, awkward

malady ('mælɒdi) n. disease

malaise (mæ'leiz) n. vague, unlocated feeling of discomfort

malapropism ('mælɒprɒpizɒm) or **malaprop** n. ludicrous misuse of word

malapropos (mælæprɒ'pɒu) a./adv. inappropriate(ly)

malaria (mɒ'lɛɒrɪɒ) n. infectious disease caused by bite of some mosquitoes —ma'**larial** a.

Malathion (mælɒ'θaiɒn) n. **R** insecticide consisting of organic phosphate

Malay (mɒ'lei) n. **1.** native of Malaysia or Indonesia **2.** language of this people —**Ma'layan** a./n.

malcontent ('mælkɒntɛnt) a. **1.** actively discontented —n. **2.** malcontent person

male (meil) a. **1.** of sex producing gametes

which fertilize female gametes **2.** of men or male animals —n. **3.** male person or animal

malediction (mæli'dikʃɒn) n. curse

malefactor ('mælifæktɒ) n. criminal

maleficent (mɒ'lɛfisɒnt) a. harmful, hurtful —ma'**leficence** n.

malevolent (mɒ'lɛvɒlɒnt) a. full of ill will —ma'**levolence** n.

malice ('mælis) n. **1.** ill will **2.** spite —ma'**licious** a. **1.** intending evil or unkindness **2.** spiteful **3.** moved by hatred —ma'**liciously** adv.

malign (mɒ'lain) a. **1.** evil in influence or effect —vt. **2.** slander, misrepresent —**malignancy** (mɒ'lignɒnsi) n. —**malignant** (mɒ'lignɒnt) a. **1.** feeling extreme ill will **2.** (of disease) resistant to therapy —**malignantly** (mɒ'lignɒntli) adv. —**malignity** (mɒ'ligniti) n. malignant disposition

malinger (mɒ'lingɒ) vi. feign illness to escape duty —ma'**lingerer** n.

mall (mɔːl, mæl) n. **1.** level, shaded walk **2.** street, shopping area closed to vehicles

mallard ('mælɒd) n. wild duck

malleable ('mæliɒbɒl) a. **1.** capable of being hammered into shape **2.** adaptable —**malle-a'bility** n.

mallet ('mælit) n. **1.** (wooden) hammer **2.** croquet or polo stick

mallow ('mælɒu) n. wild plant with purple flowers

malmsey ('mɑːmzi) n. strong sweet wine

malnutrition (mælnju:'triʃɒn) n. inadequate nutrition

malodorous (mæl'ɒudɒrɒs) a. evil-smelling

malpractice (mæl'præktis) n. immoral, illegal or unethical conduct

malt (mɔːlt) n. **1.** grain used for brewing —v. **2.** make into or become malt —'**maltster** n. maker of malt

Maltese (mɔːl'tiːz) a. **1.** of or relating to Malta, its inhabitants, or their language —n. **2.** native or inhabitant of Malta (pl. **-tese**) **3.** official language of Malta —**Maltese cross** with triangular arms that taper towards centre

maltreat (mæl'triːt) vt. treat badly, handle roughly —mal'**treatment** n.

mama or chiefly U.S. **mamma** (mɒ'mɑː) n. old-fashioned mother

mamba ('mæmbɒ) n. deadly S Afr. snake

mambo ('mæmbɒu) n. Latin Amer. dance like rumba (pl. **-s**)

mamilla or U.S. **mammilla** (mæ'milɒ) n. **1.** nipple or teat **2.** any nipple-shaped prominence (pl. **-lae** (-liː)) —'**mamillary** or U.S. '**mammillary** a.

mamma ('mæmɒ) n. milk-secreting organ of

female mammals: breast in women, udder in cows *etc.* (*pl.* **-mae** (-miː)) —'**mammary** *a.*

mammal ('mæməl) *n.* animal of type that suckles its young —**mammalian** (mæ'meiliən) *a.*

mammon ('mæmən) *n.* **1.** wealth regarded as source of evil **2.** (**M-**) false god of covetousness —'**mammonism** *n.* —'**mammonist** *n.*

mammoth ('mæməθ) *n.* **1.** extinct animal like an elephant —*a.* **2.** colossal

man (mæn) *n.* **1.** human being **2.** person **3.** human race **4.** adult male **5.** SA *sl.* any person **6.** manservant **7.** piece used in chess *etc.* (*pl.* **men**) —*vt.* **8.** supply (ship *etc.*) with necessary men **9.** fortify (**-nn-**) —'**manful** *a.* brave, vigorous —'**manfully** *adv.* —'**manhood** *n.* —'**manikin**, '**manakin** *or* '**mannikin** *n.* **1.** little man **2.** model of human body **3.** lay figure —'**manlike** *a.* —'**manliness** *n.* —'**manly** *a.* —'**mannish** *a.* like a man —**man Friday 1.** loyal male servant or assistant **2.** any factotum, *esp.* in office (*also* **Girl Friday, Person Friday**) —'**manhandle** *vt.* treat roughly —'**manhole** *n.* opening through which man may pass to a drain, sewer *etc.* —**man-hour** *n.* unit of work in industry, equal to work done by one man in one hour —'**manhunt** *n.* organized search for fugitive —**man'kind** *n.* human beings in general —**man-of-war** *or* **man o' war** *n.* **1.** warship **2.** *see* **Portuguese man-of-war** at **PORTUGUESE** —'**manpower** *n.* **1.** power of human effort **2.** available number of workers —'**manslaughter** *n.* culpable homicide without malice aforethought —**man in the street** typical person —**man of letters 1.** writer **2.** scholar —**man of the world** man of wide experience

manacle ('mænəkəl) *n.* **1.** fetter, handcuff —*vt.* **2.** shackle

manage ('mænidʒ) *v.* **1.** be in charge (of), administer **2.** succeed in (doing) —*vt.* **3.** control **4.** handle, cope with **5.** conduct, carry on —'**manageable** *a.* —'**management** *n.* **1.** those who manage, as board of directors *etc.* **2.** administration **3.** skilful use of means **4.** conduct —'**manager** *n.* **1.** one in charge of business, institution, actor *etc.* (**manage'ress** *fem.*) **2.** one who manages efficiently —**mana'gerial** *a.* —'**managing** *a.* having administrative control

mañana (mɑ'njɑːnɑ) *Sp.* **1.** tomorrow **2.** some other and later time

manatee (mænə'tiː) *n.* large, plant-eating aquatic mammal

Manchu (mæn'tʃuː) *n.* **1.** member of Mongoloid people of Manchuria (*pl.* **-s, -'chu**) **2.** language of this people

Mancunian (mæŋ'kjuːniən) *n.* **1.** native or inhabitant of Manchester —*a.* **2.** of Manchester

mandala ('mændələ, mæn'dɑːlə) *n.* any of various designs, usu. circular, symbolizing the universe

mandarin ('mændərin) *n.* **1.** *Hist.* Chinese high-ranking bureaucrat **2.** *fig.* any high government official **3.** Chinese variety of orange —**mandarin duck** Asian duck, the male of which has brightly coloured patterned plumage and crest

mandate ('mændeit, -dit) *n.* **1.** command of, or commission to act for, another **2.** commission from United Nations to govern a territory **3.** instruction from electorate to representative or government —'**mandated** *a.* committed to a mandate —'**mandatory** ('mændətəri, -tri) *n.* **1.** holder of a mandate —*a.*, *also* '**mandatary 2.** compulsory

mandible ('mændibəl) *n.* **1.** lower jawbone **2.** either part of bird's beak —**man'dibular** *a.* of, like mandible

mandolin *or* **mandoline** (mændə'lin) *n.* stringed musical instrument

mandrake ('mændreik) *or* **mandragora** (mæn'drægərə) *n.* narcotic plant

mandrel *or* **mandril** ('mændrəl) *n.* **1.** axis on which material is supported in a lathe **2.** rod round which metal is cast or forged

mandrill ('mændril) *n.* large blue-faced baboon

mane (mein) *n.* long hair on neck of horse, lion *etc.* —**maned** *a.*

manganese (mæŋgə'niːz) *n.* **1.** metallic element **2.** black oxide of this

mange (meindʒ) *n.* skin disease of dogs *etc.* —'**mangy** *or* '**mangey** *a.* scruffy, shabby

mangelwurzel ('mæŋgəlwɜːzəl) *or* **mangoldwurzel** ('mæŋgəldwɜːzəl) *n.* variety of beet used as cattle food

manger ('meindʒə) *n.* eating trough in stable

mangle[1] ('mæŋgəl) *n.* **1.** machine for rolling clothes *etc.* to remove water —*vt.* **2.** press in mangle

mangle[2] ('mæŋgəl) *vt.* mutilate, spoil, hack

mango ('mæŋgəʊ) *n.* **1.** tropical fruit **2.** tree bearing it (*pl.* **-s, -es**)

mangrove ('mæŋgrəʊv, 'mæn-) *n.* tropical tree which grows on muddy banks of estuaries

mania ('meiniə) *n.* **1.** madness **2.** prevailing craze —'**maniac, maniacal** (mə'naiəkəl) *or* **manic** ('mænik) *a.* affected by mania —'**maniac** *n. inf.* **1.** mad person **2.** crazy enthusiast —**manic-depressive** *a. Psych.* **1.** pert. to mental disorder characterized by alternation between extreme confidence and deep depression —*n.* **2.** person afflicted with this disorder

manicure ('mænikjʊə) *n.* **1.** treatment and care of fingernails and hands —*vt.* **2.** apply such treatment to —'**manicurist** *n.* one doing this professionally

manifest ('mænɪfɛst) a. 1. clearly revealed, visible, undoubted —vt. 2. make manifest —n. 3. list of cargo for customs —**manifes'tation** n. —'**manifestly** adv. clearly —**mani'festo** n. declaration of policy by political party, government, or movement (pl. -s, -es)

manifold ('mænɪfould) a. 1. numerous and varied —n. 2. in internal-combustion engine, pipe with several outlets —vt. 3. make copies of (document)

manikin, manakin, or **mannikin** ('mænɪkɪn) n. see MAN

Manila (mə'nɪlə) n. 1. fibre used for ropes 2. tough paper

manipulate (mə'nɪpjuleɪt) vt. 1. handle 2. deal with skilfully 3. manage 4. falsify —**manipu'la-tion** n. 1. act of manipulating, working by hand 2. skilled use of hands —**ma'nipulative** a. —**ma'nipulator** n.

manna ('mænə) n. 1. food of Israelites in the wilderness 2. any spiritual or divine nourishment

mannequin ('mænɪkɪn) n. woman who models clothes, esp. at fashion shows

manner ('mænə) n. 1. way things happens or is done 2. sort, kind 3. custom 4. style —pl. 5. social behaviour —'**mannered** a. having idiosyncrasies or mannerisms; affected —'**mannerism** n. person's distinctive habit, trait —'**mannerly** a. polite

manoeuvre or U.S. **maneuver** (mə'nuːvə) n. 1. contrived, complicated, perhaps deceptive plan or action 2. skilful management —vt. 3. contrive or accomplish with skill or cunning —vi. 4. manipulate situations etc. in order to gain some end —v. 5. (cause to) perform manoeuvres

manor ('mænə) n. 1. Hist. land belonging to a lord 2. feudal unit of land —**ma'norial** a. —**manor house** residence of lord of manor

manqué ('mɒŋkeɪ) Fr. unfulfilled; would-be

mansard roof ('mænsɑːd, -səd) roof with break in its slope, lower part being steeper than upper

manse (mæns) n. house of minister in some religious denominations

mansion ('mænʃən) n. large house

mantel or **mantle** ('mæntəl) n. structure round fireplace —**mantel shelf** or '**mantelpiece** n. shelf at top of mantel

mantilla (mæn'tɪlə) n. in Spain, (lace) scarf worn as headdress

mantis ('mæntɪs) n. genus of insects including the stick insects and leaf insects (pl. **mantes** ('mæntiːz))

mantissa (mæn'tɪsə) n. fractional part of common logarithm

mantle ('mæntəl) n. 1. loose cloak 2. covering 3.

incandescent gauze round gas jet —vt. 4. cover 5. conceal

mantra ('mæntrə, 'mʌn-) n. Hinduism any of those parts of the sacred literature which consist of metrical psalms of praise

manual ('mænjuəl) a. 1. of, or done with, the hands 2. by human labour, not automatic —n. 3. handbook 4. textbook 5. organ keyboard

manufacture (mænju'fæktʃə) vt. 1. process, make (materials) into finished articles 2. produce (articles) 3. invent, concoct —n. 4. making of articles, materials, esp. in large quantities 5. anything produced from raw materials —**manu'facturer** n. owner of factory

manumit (mænju'mɪt) vt. free from slavery (-tt-) —**manu'mission** n.

manure (mə'njuə) vt. 1. enrich (land) —n. 2. dung or chemical fertilizer used to enrich land

manuscript ('mænjuskrɪpt) n. 1. book, document, written by hand 2. copy for printing —a. 3. handwritten

Manx (mæŋks) a. 1. of Isle of Man —n. 2. Manx language —**Manx cat** tailless breed of cat —'**Manxman** n.

many ('mɛnɪ) a. 1. numerous (**more** comp., **most** sup.) —n. 2. large number

Maoism ('mauɪzəm) n. form of Marxism advanced by Mao Tse-Tung in China —'**Maoist** n./a.

Maori ('mauri, 'mɑːri) n. 1. member of New Zealand native race (pl. -s, -ri) 2. their language

map (mæp) n. 1. flat representation of the earth or some part of it, or of the heavens —vt. 2. make a map of 3. (with out) plan (-pp-)

maple ('meɪpəl) n. tree of the sycamore family, a variety of which yields sugar —**maple leaf** leaf of maple tree, national emblem of Canada —**maple syrup** chiefly US sweet syrup made from sap of sugar maple

maquis (mɑː'kiː) n. 1. scrubby undergrowth of Mediterranean countries 2. (oft. **M**-) name adopted by French underground resistance movement in WWII

mar (mɑː) vt. spoil, impair (-rr-)

Mar. March

marabou ('mærəbuː) n. 1. kind of stork 2. its soft white lower tail feathers, used to trim hats etc. 3. kind of silk

maraca (mə'rækə) n. percussion instrument of gourd containing dried seeds etc.

maraschino (mærə'skiːnəu) n. liqueur made from cherries

marathon ('mærəθən) n. 1. long-distance race 2. endurance contest

maraud (mə'rɔːd) vi. 1. make raid for plunder —v. 2. pillage —**ma'rauder** n.

marble ('mɑːbəl) n. 1. kind of limestone capable of taking polish 2. slab of, sculpture in this **3.** small ball used in children's game —**'marbled** *a.* having mottled appearance, like marble —**'marbly** *a.*

marc (mɑːk) *n.* **1.** remains of grapes *etc.* that have been pressed for wine-making **2.** brandy distilled from these

marcasite ('mɑːkəsaıt) *n.* **1.** pale yellow crystallized iron pyrites **2.** polished form of steel or white metal used for making jewellery

march' (mɑːtʃ) *vi.* **1.** walk with military step **2.** go, progress —*vt.* **3.** cause to march —*n.* **4.** action of marching **5.** distance marched in day **6.** tune to accompany marching —**marching orders 1.** *Mil.* instructions about march, its destination *etc.* **2.** *inf.* any notice of dismissal, *esp.* from employment —**march-past** *n.* review of troops as they march past a saluting point

march² (mɑːtʃ) *n.* **1.** border or frontier —*vi.* **2.** (*oft.* with upon *or* with) share a common border (with)

March (mɑːtʃ) *n.* third month —**March hare** hare during its breeding season, noted for its excitable behaviour

marchioness ('mɑːʃənıs, mɑːʃə'nɛs) *n.* wife, widow of marquis

Mardi Gras ('mɑːdı 'grɑː) **1.** festival of Shrove Tuesday **2.** revelry celebrating this

mare' (mɛə) *n.* female horse —**mare's nest** supposed discovery which proves worthless

mare² ('mɑːreɪ, -rı) *n.* (**M-** *when part of name*) huge dry plain on surface of moon (*pl.* **maria** ('mɑːrıə))

margarine (mɑːdʒə'riːn, mɑːg-) *or* **margarin** ('mɑːdʒərın, 'mɑːg-, mɑːdʒə'riːn, mɑːg-) *n.* butter substitute made from vegetable fats

marge (mɑːdʒ) *n. inf.* margarine

margin ('mɑːdʒın) *n.* **1.** border, edge **2.** space round printed page **3.** amount allowed beyond what is necessary —**'marginal** *a.* —**marginal seat** *Pol.* constituency in which political party cannot be certain of retaining majority

marguerite (mɑːgə'riːt) *n.* large daisy

marigold ('mærıgəʊld) *n.* plant with yellow flowers

marijuana (mærıjʊ'ɑːnə) *or* **marihuana** (mærı'hwɑːnə) *n.* dried flowers and leaves of hemp plant, used as narcotic

marimba (mə'rımbə) *n.* Latin Amer. percussion instrument resembling a xylophone

marina (mə'riːnə) *n.* mooring facility for yachts and pleasure boats

marinade (mærı'neɪd) *n.* seasoned, flavoured liquid used to soak fish, meat *etc.* before cooking —**'marinate** *v.*

marine (mə'riːn) *a.* **1.** of the sea or shipping **2.** used at, found in sea —*n.* **3.** shipping, fleet **4.** soldier trained for land or sea combat —**mariner** ('mærınə) *n.* sailor

marionette (mærıə'nɛt) *n.* puppet worked with strings

marital ('mærıtəl) *a.* relating to a husband or to marriage

maritime ('mærıtaım) *a.* **1.** connected with seafaring, naval **2.** bordering on the sea **3.** (of climate) having small temperature differences between summer and winter —**Maritime Provinces** certain of the Canadian provinces with coasts facing the Gulf of St. Lawrence or Atlantic (*also* **'Maritimes**)

marjoram ('mɑːdʒərəm) *n.* aromatic herb

mark' (mɑːk) *n.* **1.** line, dot, scar *etc.* **2.** sign, token **3.** inscription **4.** letter, number showing evaluation of schoolwork *etc.* **5.** indication **6.** target —*vt.* **7.** make a mark on **8.** be distinguishing mark of **9.** indicate **10.** notice **11.** watch **12.** assess, *eg* examination paper **13.** stay close to (sporting opponent) to hamper his play —**marked** *a.* **1.** obvious, evident, or noticeable **2.** singled out, *esp.* as target of attack **3.** *Linguis.* distinguished by specific feature, as in phonology —**markedly** ('mɑːkıdlı) *adv.* —**'marker** *n.* **1.** one who, that which keeps score at games **2.** counter used at card playing *etc.* —**'marksman** *n.* skilled shot

mark² (mɑːk) *n.* German coin

market ('mɑːkıt) *n.* **1.** assembly, place for buying and selling **2.** demand for goods **3.** centre for trade —*vt.* **4.** offer or produce for sale —**'marketable** *a.* —**'marketing** *n.* business of selling goods, including advertising, packaging *etc.* —**market garden** *chiefly UK* establishment where fruit and vegetables are grown for sale —**market research** analysis of data relating to demand for product

marl (mɑːl) *n.* **1.** clayey soil used as fertilizer —*vt.* **2.** fertilize with it

marline, marlin ('mɑːlın), *or* **marling** ('mɑːlıŋ) *n.* two-strand cord —**'marlinespike, 'marlinspike** *or* **'marlingspike** *n.* pointed tool, *esp.* for unravelling rope to be spliced

marmalade ('mɑːməleɪd) *n.* preserve usu. made of oranges, lemons *etc.*

marmoreal (mɑː'mɔːrıəl) *or* **marmorean** *a.* of or like marble

marmoset ('mɑːməzɛt) *n.* small bushy-tailed monkey

marmot ('mɑːmət) *n.* burrowing rodent

maroon' (mə'ruːn) *n.* **1.** brownish-crimson **2.** firework —*a.* **3.** of the colour

maroon² (mə'ruːn) *vt.* **1.** leave (person) on deserted island or coast **2.** isolate, cut off by any means

marquee (mɑː'kiː) *n.* large tent

marquetry *or* **marqueterie** ('mɑːkıtrı) *n.* inlaid work, wood mosaic

marquis ('mɑːkwɪs, mɑː'kiː) n. nobleman of rank below duke —**marquisate** ('mɑːkwɪzɪt) n.

marquise (mɑː'kiːz) n. 1. in various countries, marchioness 2. gemstone cut in pointed oval shape

marrow ('mærəʊ) n. 1. fatty substance inside bones 2. vital part 3. vegetable marrow —**marrowy** a. —**'marrowfat** n. large pea

marry ('mærɪ) v. 1. take (someone as husband or wife) in marriage 2. unite closely —vt. 3. join as husband and wife ('**married, 'marrying)** —**marriage** ('mærɪdʒ) n. 1. state of being married 2. wedding —**marriageable** ('mærɪdʒəbl) a. —**marriage bureau** business concern set up to introduce people wishing to get married —**marriage guidance** advice given to couples who have problems in their married life —**marriage lines** certificate stating that marriage has taken place

Mars (mɑːz) n. 1. Roman god of war 2. planet nearest but one to earth —**Martian** ('mɑːʃən) a. 1. supposed inhabitant of Mars —a. 2. of Mars

Marseillaise (mɑːsə'leɪz) n. the French national anthem

marsh (mɑːʃ) n. low-lying wet land —'**marshy** a. —**marsh gas** gas composed of methane produced when vegetation decomposes under water —**marsh'mallow** n. spongy sweet orig. made from root of **marsh mallow**, shrubby plant growing near marshes

marshal ('mɑːʃəl) n. 1. high officer of state 2. US law enforcement officer —vt. 3. arrange in due order 4. conduct with ceremony (**-ll-**) —**field marshal** military officer of the highest rank —**marshalling yard** railway depot for goods trains —**Marshal of the Royal Air Force** rank in Royal Air Force comparable to that of field marshal in army

marsupial (mɑː'sjuːpɪəl, -'suː-) n. 1. animal that carries its young in pouch, eg kangaroo —a. 2. of marsupials —**mar'supium** n. external pouch in most female marsupials (pl. **-pia** (-pɪə))

mart (mɑːt) n. 1. place of trade 2. market

Martello tower (mɑː'tɛləʊ) round fort, for coast defence

marten ('mɑːtɪn) n. 1. weasel-like animal 2. its fur

martial ('mɑːʃəl) a. 1. relating to war 2. warlike, brave —**court martial** see COURT —**martial law** law enforced by military authorities in times of danger or emergency

martin ('mɑːtɪn) n. species of swallow

martinet (mɑːtɪ'nɛt) n. strict disciplinarian

martingale ('mɑːtɪŋgeɪl) n. strap to prevent horse from throwing up its head

martini (mɑː'tiːnɪ) n. 1. cocktail containing esp. vermouth, gin, bitters 2. (**M-**) **R** Italian vermouth (pl. **-s**)

Martinmas ('mɑːtɪnməs) n. feast of St. Martin, Nov. 11th

martlet ('mɑːtlɪt) n. Her. bird without feet

martyr ('mɑːtə) n. 1. one put to death for his beliefs 2. one who suffers in some cause 3. one in constant suffering —vt. 4. make martyr of —'**martyrdom** n. —**martyr'ology** n. list, history of Christian martyrs

marvel ('mɑːvl) vi. 1. wonder (**-ll-**) —n. 2. wonderful thing —'**marvellous** or U.S. '**marvelous** a. 1. amazing 2. wonderful

Marxism ('mɑːksɪzəm) n. state socialism as conceived by Karl Marx —'**Marxian** a. —'**Marxist** n./a.

marzipan ('mɑːzɪpæn) n. paste of almonds, sugar etc. used in sweets, cakes etc.

Masai ('mɑːsaɪ, mɑː'saɪ) n. 1. member of Negroid pastoral people living chiefly in Kenya and Tanzania (pl. **-s, -sai**) 2. language of this people

masc. masculine

mascara (mæ'skɑːrə) n. cosmetic for darkening eyelashes

mascot ('mæskət) n. thing supposed to bring luck

masculine ('mæskjʊlɪn) a. 1. relating to males 2. manly 3. of the grammatical gender to which names of males belong

maser ('meɪzə) n. device for amplifying microwaves

mash (mæʃ) n. 1. meal mixed with warm water 2. warm food for horses etc. 3. inf. mashed potatoes —vt. 4. make into a mash 5. crush into soft mass or pulp

mashie or **mashy** ('mæʃɪ) n. Golf iron club with deep sloping blade for lob shots

mask (mɑːsk) n. 1. covering for face 2. Surg. covering for nose and mouth 3. disguise, pretence —vt. 4. cover with mask 5. hide, disguise —**masking tape** adhesive tape used to protect surfaces surrounding an area to be painted

masochism ('mæsəkɪzəm) n. abnormal condition where pleasure (esp. sexual) is derived from pain, humiliation etc. —'**masochist** n. —**maso'chistic** a.

mason ('meɪsn) n. 1. worker in stone 2. (**M-**) Freemason —**Masonic** (mə'sɒnɪk) a. of Freemasonry —'**masonry** n. 1. stonework 2. (**M-**) Freemasonry

masque or **mask** (mɑːsk) n. Hist. form of theatrical performance —**masquerade** (mæskə'reɪd) n. 1. masked ball —vi. 2. appear in disguise

mass (mæs) n. 1. quantity of matter 2. dense collection of things 3. large quantity or number —v. 4. form into a mass —'**massive** a. large and heavy —'**massy** a. solid, weighty —**mass**

market market for mass-produced goods —**mass-market** a. of mass market —**mass media** means of communication to large numbers of people, such as television, newspapers etc. —**mass-produce** vt. produce (standardized articles) in large quantities —**mass production** —**mass spectrometer** instrument in which ions are separated by electric or magnetic fields according to their ratios of charge to mass (also '**spectroscope**) —**the masses** the populace

Mass (mæs, ma:s) n. service of the Eucharist, esp. in R.C. Church

massacre ('mæsəkə) n. 1. indiscriminate, large-scale killing, esp. of unresisting people —vt. kill indiscriminately

massage ('mæsɑːʒ, -sɑːdʒ) n. 1. rubbing and kneading of muscles etc. as curative treatment —vt. 2. apply this treatment to 3. manipulate (figures etc.) in order to deceive —**masseur** (mæ'sɜː) n. one who practises massage (**masseuse** (mæ'sɜːz) fem.)

massé or **massé shot** ('mæsɪ) n. Billiards stroke with cue upright

massif ('mæsiːf) n. compact group of mountains

mast[1] (mɑːst) n. 1. pole for supporting ship's sails 2. tall upright support for aerial etc. —'**masthead** n. 1. Naut. head of mast 2. name of newspaper, its proprietors, staff etc., printed at top of front page —vt. 3. raise (sail) to masthead

mast[2] (mɑːst) n. fruit of beech, oak etc. used as pig food

mastectomy (mæ'stɛktəmɪ) n. surgical removal of a breast

master ('mɑːstə) n. 1. one in control 2. employer 3. head of household 4. owner 5. document etc. from which copies are made 6. captain of merchant ship 7. expert 8. great artist 9. teacher —vt. 10. overcome 11. acquire knowledge of or skill in —'**masterful** a. imperious, domineering —'**masterly** a. showing great competence —'**mastery** n. 1. full understanding 2. expertise 3. authority 4. victory —**master aircrew** warrant officer rank in Royal Air Force —**master key** key that opens many different locks —'**mastermind** vt. 1. plan, direct —n. 2. very intelligent person, esp. one who directs an undertaking —'**masterpiece** n. outstanding work —'**masterstroke** n. outstanding piece of strategy etc. —**Master of Arts** (or **Science** etc.) 1. degree given by university usu. to postgraduate 2. person who has this degree —**master of ceremonies** person who presides over public ceremony etc., introducing events etc.

mastic ('mæstɪk) n. 1. gum got from certain trees 2. puttylike substance

masticate ('mæstɪkeɪt) v. chew —**masti'cation** n. —'**masticatory** a.

mastiff ('mæstɪf) n. large dog

mastitis (mæ'staɪtɪs) n. inflammation of breast or udder

mastodon ('mæstədɒn) n. extinct elephantlike mammal

mastoid ('mæstɔɪd) a. 1. nipple-shaped —n. 2. prominence on bone behind human ear —**mastoi'ditis** n. inflammation of this area

masturbate ('mæstəbeɪt) v. stimulate (one's own or one's partner's) genital organs —**mastur'bation** n.

mat[1] (mæt) n. 1. small rug 2. piece of fabric to protect another surface or to wipe feet on etc. 3. thick tangled mass —v. 4. form into such mass (-tt-) —**on the mat** inf. called up for reprimand

mat[2] or **matt** (mæt) a. dull, lustreless, not shiny

matador ('mætədɔː) n. man who slays bull in bullfights

match[1] (mætʃ) n. 1. contest, game 2. equal 3. person, thing exactly corresponding to another 4. marriage 5. person regarded as eligible for marriage —vt. 6. get something corresponding to (colour, pattern etc.) 7. oppose, put in competition with 8. join (in marriage) —vi. 9. correspond —'**matchless** a. unequalled —'**matchboard** n. long, flimsy board tongued and grooved for lining work —'**matchmaker** n. one who schemes to bring about a marriage —**match play** Golf scoring according to number of holes won and lost

match[2] (mætʃ) n. 1. small stick with head which ignites when rubbed 2. fuse —'**matchbox** n. —'**matchlock** n. early musket fired by fuse —'**matchwood** n. small splinters

mate[1] (meɪt) n. 1. comrade 2. husband, wife 3. one of pair 4. officer in merchant ship 5. inf. common Brit. and Aust. term of address, esp. between males —v. 6. marry or join in marriage 7. pair —'**matey** a. inf. friendly, sociable

mate[2] (meɪt) n./vt. Chess checkmate

mater ('meɪtə) n. sl. UK mother

material (mə'tɪərɪəl) n. 1. substance from which thing is made 2. cloth, fabric —a. 3. of matter or body 4. affecting physical wellbeing 5. unspiritual 6. important, essential —ma'terial- **ism** n. 1. excessive interest in, desire for money and possessions 2. doctrine that nothing but matter exists, denying independent existence of spirit —ma'terialist a./n. —material'istic a. —ma'terialize or -ise vi. 1. come into existence or view —vt. 2. make material —ma'terially adv. appreciably

materiel or **matériel** (mətɪərɪ'ɛl) n. equipment of organization, esp. of military force

maternal (mə'tɜːnəl) a. of, related through mother —ma'ternity n. motherhood

mathematics (mæθə'mætɪks) pl.n. (with sing. v.) science of number, quantity, shape and space —**mathe'matical** a. —**mathe'matically** adv. —**mathema'tician** n.

maths (mæθs) n. inf. mathematics

matinée ('mætɪneɪ) n. afternoon performance in theatre —**matinée coat** short coat for baby

matins or **mattins** ('mætɪnz) pl.n. morning prayers

matriarch ('meɪtrɪɑːk) n. mother as head and ruler of family —'**matriarchal** a. —'**matriarchy** n. society with matriarchal government and descent reckoned in female line

matricide ('mætrɪsaɪd, 'meɪ-) n. 1. the crime of killing one's mother 2. one who does this

matriculate (mə'trɪkjuleɪt) v. enrol, be enrolled in a college or university —**matricu'lation** n.

matrimony ('mætrɪmənɪ) n. marriage —**matri'monial** a.

matrix ('meɪtrɪks, 'mæ-) n. 1. substance, situation in which something originates, takes form, or is enclosed 2. mould for casting 3. Maths. rectangular array of elements set out in rows and columns (pl. **matrices** ('meɪtrɪsiːz, 'mæ-))

matron ('meɪtrən) n. 1. married woman 2. former name for nursing officer 3. woman who superintends domestic arrangements of public institution, boarding school etc. —'**matronly** a. sedate —**matron of honour** married woman serving as chief attendant to bride

matt (mæt) a. see MAT[2]

Matt. Bible Matthew

matter ('mætə) n. 1. substance of which thing is made 2. physical or bodily substance 3. affair, business 4. cause of trouble 5. substance of book etc. 6. pus —vi. 7. be of importance, signify —**matter-of-fact** a. unimaginative or emotionless —**matter of fact** fact that is undeniably true —**as a matter of fact** actually; in fact

mattock ('mætək) n. tool like pick with ends of blades flattened for cutting, hoeing

mattress ('mætrɪs) n. 1. stuffed flat case, often with springs, or foam rubber pad, used as part of bed 2. underlay

mature (mə'tjʊə, -'tʃʊə) a. 1. ripe, completely developed 2. grown-up —v. 3. bring, come to maturity —vi. 4. (of bill) fall due —**matu'ration** n. process of maturing —**ma'turity** n. full development

matutinal (mætjʊ'taɪnəl) a. of, occurring in, or during morning

maudlin ('mɔːdlɪn) a. weakly or tearfully sentimental

maul (mɔːl) vt. 1. handle roughly 2. beat; bruise —n. 3. heavy wooden hammer 4. Rugby loose scrum

maulstick ('mɔːlstɪk) or **mahlstick** n. light stick with ball at one end, held in left hand to support right hand while painting

maunder ('mɔːndə) vi. talk, act aimlessly, dreamily

maundy ('mɔːndɪ) n. 1. foot-washing ceremony on Thursday before Easter 2. royal alms given on that day

mausoleum (mɔːsə'lɪəm) n. stately building as a tomb (pl. **-s, -lea** (-'lɪə))

mauve (məʊv) a./n. (of) pale purple colour

maverick ('mævərɪk) n. 1. US unbranded steer, stray cow 2. independent, unorthodox person

maw (mɔː) n. stomach, crop

mawkish ('mɔːkɪʃ) a. 1. weakly sentimental, maudlin 2. sickly

max. maximum

maxi ('mæksɪ) a. 1. (of garment) reaching ankle 2. large, considerable

maxilla (mæk'sɪlə) n. jawbone (pl. **-lae** (-liː)) —**max'illary** a. of the jaw

maxim ('mæksɪm) n. 1. general truth, proverb 2. rule of conduct, principle

maximum ('mæksɪməm) n. 1. greatest size or number 2. highest point (pl. **-s, -ma** (-mə)) —a. 3. greatest —'**maximize** or **-ise** vt.

maxwell ('mækswəl) n. cgs unit of magnetic flux

may (meɪ) v. aux. expresses possibility, permission, opportunity etc. (**might** pt.) —**maybe** ('meɪbiː) adv. 1. perhaps 2. possibly

May (meɪ) n. 1. fifth month 2. (**m-**) hawthorn or its flowers —'**mayfly** n. short-lived flying insect, found near water —'**maypole** n. pole set up for dancing round on May Day, first day of May —**May queen** girl chosen to preside over May-Day celebrations

Maya ('maɪə) n. 1. member of Amer. Indian people of Yucatan, Belize and N Guatemala (pl. **-ya, -s**) 2. language of this people

Mayday ('meɪdeɪ) n. international radiotelephone distress signal

mayhap ('meɪhæp) adv. obs. perhaps

mayhem or **maihem** ('meɪhɛm) n. 1. depriving person by violence of limb, member or organ, or causing mutilation of body 2. any violent destruction 3. confusion

mayonnaise (meɪə'neɪz) n. creamy sauce of egg yolks, oil etc., esp. for salads

mayor (mɛə) n. head of municipality —'**mayoral** a. —'**mayoralty** n. (time of) office of mayor —'**mayoress** n. 1. mayor's wife 2. lady mayor

maze (meɪz) n. 1. labyrinth 2. network of paths, lines 3. state of confusion

mazurka or **mazourka** (mə'zɜːkə) n. 1. lively Polish dance like polka 2. music for it

MB Manitoba

M.B. Bachelor of Medicine

M.B.E. Member of the Order of the British Empire

M.C. 1. Master of Ceremonies **2.** Military Cross

M.C.C. Marylebone Cricket Club

M.Ch. Master of Surgery

Md *Chem.* mendelevium

MD Maryland

M.D. Doctor of Medicine

me[1] (miː, *unstressed* mɪ) *pron.* objective case of pronoun I

me[2] (miː) *n. Mus. see* MI

ME Maine

ME *or* **M.E.** Middle English

M.E. 1. Marine Engineer **2.** Mechanical Engineer **3.** Methodist Episcopal **4.** Mining Engineer **5.** in titles, Most Excellent

mea culpa ('meɪə 'kʊlpə) *Lat.* my fault

mead[1] (miːd) *n.* alcoholic drink made from honey

mead[2] (miːd) *n. obs., poet.* meadow

meadow ('mɛdəʊ) *n.* piece of grassland —'**meadowsweet** *n.* plant with dense heads of small fragrant flowers

meagre *or* **U.S. meager** ('miːgə) *a.* **1.** lean, thin **2.** scanty, insufficient

meal[1] (miːl) *n.* **1.** occasion when food is served and eaten **2.** the food —**meals-on-wheels** *n.* UK service taking hot meals to elderly, infirm *etc.* —**meal ticket 1.** US luncheon voucher **2.** *sl.* person, situation *etc.* providing source of livelihood or income

meal[2] (miːl) *n.* grain ground to powder —'**mealy** *a.* —**mealy-mouthed** *a.* euphemistic, insincere in what one says

mealie ('miːlɪ) *n.* SA maize

mean[1] (miːn) *vt.* **1.** intend **2.** signify —*vi.* **3.** have the intention of behaving (**meant** *pt./pp.*, '**meaning** *pr.p.*) —'**meaning** *n.* **1.** sense, significance —*a.* **2.** expressive —'**meaningful** *a.* of great meaning or significance —'**meaningless** *a.*

mean[2] (miːn) *a.* **1.** ungenerous, petty **2.** miserly, niggardly **3.** unpleasant **4.** callous **5.** shabby **6.** ashamed —'**meanly** *adv.* —'**meanness** *n.*

mean[3] (miːn) *n.* **1.** thing which is intermediate **2.** middle point —*pl.* **3.** that by which thing is done **4.** money **5.** resources —*a.* **6.** intermediate in time, quality *etc.* **7.** average —**means test** enquiry into person's means to decide eligibility for pension, grant *etc.* —'**meantime** *or* '**meanwhile** *adv./n.* (during) time between one happening and another —**by all means** certainly —**by no means** not at all

meander (mɪ'ændə) *vi.* **1.** flow windingly **2.** wander aimlessly

meant (mɛnt) *pt./pp. of* MEAN[1]

measles ('miːzəlz) *n.* infectious disease producing rash of red spots —'**measly** *a.* **1.** *inf.* poor, wretched, stingy **2.** of measles

measure ('mɛʒə) *n.* **1.** size, quantity **2.** vessel, rod, line *etc.* for ascertaining size or quantity **3.** unit of size or quantity **4.** course, plan of action **5.** law **6.** poetical rhythm **7.** musical time **8.** *Poet.* tune **9.** *obs.* dance —*vt.* **10.** ascertain size, quantity of **11.** indicate measurement of **12.** estimate **13.** bring into competition against —*vi.* **14.** make measurement(s) **15.** be (so much) in size or quantity —'**measurable** *a.* —'**measured** *a.* **1.** determined by measure **2.** steady **3.** rhythmical **4.** carefully considered —'**measurement** *n.* **1.** measuring **2.** size —*pl.* **3.** dimensions

meat (miːt) *n.* **1.** animal flesh as food **2.** food —'**meaty** *a.* **1.** (tasting) of, like meat **2.** brawny **3.** full of import or interest

Mecca ('mɛkə) *n.* **1.** holy city of Islam **2.** place that attracts visitors

mech. 1. mechanical **2.** mechanics **3.** mechanism

mechanic (mɪ'kænɪk) *n.* **1.** one employed in working with machinery **2.** skilled workman —*pl.* **3.** scientific theory of motion —me'**chanical** *a.* **1.** concerned with machines or operation of them **2.** worked, produced (as though) by machine **3.** acting without thought —me'**chanically** *adv.* —**mecha'nician** *n.* —**mechanical drawing** *see* **technical drawing** *at* TECHNICAL

mechanism ('mɛkənɪzəm) *n.* **1.** structure of machine **2.** piece of machinery —**mechani'zation** *or* -**i'sation** *n.* —'**mechanize** *or* -**ise** *vt.* **1.** equip with machinery **2.** make mechanical, automatic **3.** *Mil.* equip with armoured vehicles —'**mechanized** *or* -**ised** *a.*

med. 1. medical **2.** medicine **3.** medieval **4.** medium

Med (mɛd) *n. inf.* Mediterranean region

M.Ed. Master of Education

medal ('mɛdəl) *n.* piece of metal with inscription *etc.* used as reward or memento —me'**dallion** *n.* **1.** large medal **2.** any of various things like this in decorative work —'**medallist** *or* U.S. '**medalist** *n.* **1.** winner of a medal **2.** maker of medals

meddle ('mɛdəl) *vi.* interfere, busy oneself unnecessarily —'**meddlesome** *a.*

media ('miːdɪə) *n., pl. of* MEDIUM, used *esp.* of the mass media, radio, television *etc.* —**media event** event staged for or exploited by the mass media

mediaeval (mɛdɪ'iːvəl) *a. see* MEDIEVAL

medial ('miːdɪəl) *a.* **1.** in the middle **2.** pert. to a mean or average —'**median** *a./n.* middle (point or line)

mediate ('miːdɪeɪt) *vi.* **1.** intervene to reconcile —*vt.* **2.** bring about by mediation —*a.*

('miːdɪɪt) **3.** depending on mediation —**medi'a- tion** n. **1.** intervention on behalf of another **2.** act of going between —**'mediator** n.

medicine ('mɛdɪsɪn, 'mɛdsɪn) n. **1.** drug or remedy for treating disease **2.** science of preventing, diagnosing, alleviating, or curing disease —**'medic** n. inf. **1.** doctor **2.** medical orderly **3.** medical student —**'medical** a. —**'medically** adv. —me'**dicament** n. remedy —**'medicate** vt. impregnate with medicinal substances —**medi'cation** n. —**'medicative** a. healing —me'**dicinal** a. curative —**'medico** n. inf. **1.** doctor **2.** medical student (pl. **-s**) —**medical certificate** doctor's certificate giving evidence of person's fitness or unfitness for work etc. —**medicine ball** heavy ball for physical training —**medicine man** witch doctor

medieval or **mediaeval** (mɛdɪ'iːvəl) a. of Middle Ages —**medi'evalism** or **medi'aevalism** n. **1.** spirit of Middle Ages **2.** cult of medieval ideals —**medi'evalist** or **medi'aevalist** n. student of the Middle Ages —**Medieval Greek** Greek language from 7th cent. A.D.-1204 —**Medieval Latin** Latin language as used throughout Europe in Middle Ages

mediocre (miːdɪ'əʊkə) a. **1.** neither bad nor good, ordinary, middling **2.** second-rate —**medi'ocrity** (miːdɪ'ɒkrɪtɪ, mɛd-) n.

meditate ('mɛdɪteɪt) vi. **1.** be occupied in thought **2.** reflect deeply on spiritual matters —**medi'tation** n. **1.** thought **2.** absorption in thought **3.** religious contemplation —**'meditative** a. **1.** thoughtful **2.** reflective —**'meditatively** adv.

Mediterranean (mɛdɪtə'reɪnɪən) n. **1.** short for **Mediterranean Sea**, sea between S Europe, N Afr., and SW Asia **2.** native or inhabitant of Mediterranean country —a. **3.** of Mediterranean Sea

medium ('miːdɪəm) a. **1.** between two qualities, degrees etc., average —n. **2.** middle quality, degree **3.** intermediate substance conveying force **4.** means, agency of communicating news etc. to public, as radio, newspapers etc. **5.** person through whom communication can supposedly be held with spirit world **6.** surroundings, environment (pl. **-s**, **'media**) —**medium waves** Rad. waves between 100 and 1000 metres

medlar ('mɛdlə) n. **1.** tree with fruit like small apple **2.** the fruit, eaten when decayed

medley ('mɛdlɪ) n. miscellaneous mixture (pl. **-s**)

medulla (mɪ'dʌlə) n. **1.** marrow **2.** pith **3.** inner tissue —me'**dullary** a.

Medusa (mɪ'djuːzə) n. **1.** Myth. Gorgon whose head turned beholders into stone **2.** (**m-**) jellyfish (pl. **-sae** (-ziː))

meek (miːk) a. submissive, humble —**'meekly** adv. —**'meekness** n.

meerkat ('mɪəkæt) n. S Afr. mongoose

meerschaum ('mɪəʃəm) n. **1.** white substance like clay **2.** tobacco pipe bowl made of this

meet¹ (miːt) vt. **1.** come face to face with, encounter **2.** satisfy **3.** pay —vi. **4.** come face to face **5.** converge at specified point **6.** assemble **7.** come into contact (**met** pt./pp.) —n. **8.** meeting, esp. for sports —**'meeting** n. **1.** assembly **2.** encounter

meet² (miːt) a. obs. fit, suitable

mega- (comb. form) **1.** denoting 10⁶, as in megawatt **2.** in computer technology, denoting 2²⁰ (1 048 576), as in megabyte **3.** large, great, as in megalith

megadeath ('mɛgədɛθ) n. death of a million people, esp. in nuclear war

megahertz ('mɛgəhɜːts) n. one million hertz (pl. **'megahertz**)

megalith ('mɛgəlɪθ) n. great stone —**mega- 'lithic** a.

megalomania (mɛgələʊ'meɪnɪə) n. desire for, delusions of grandeur, power etc. —**megalo'ma- niac** a./n.

megalopolis (mɛgə'lɒpəlɪs) n. urban complex, usu. comprising several towns —**megalopolitan** (mɛgələʊ'pɒlɪt³n) a./n.

megaphone ('mɛgəfəʊn) n. cone-shaped instrument to amplify voice

megaton ('mɛgətʌn) n. one million tons **2.** explosive power of 1 000 000 tons of TNT

megohm ('mɛgəʊm) n. Elec. one million ohms

meiosis (maɪ'əʊsɪs) n. type of cell division in which nucleus divides into four daughter nuclei, each containing half chromosome number of parent nucleus (pl. **-ses** (-siːz)) —**meiotic** (maɪ'ɒtɪk) a.

melamine ('mɛləmiːn) n. colourless crystal- line compound used in making synthetic resins —**melamine resin** resilient kind of plastic

melancholy ('mɛlənkəlɪ) n. **1.** sadness, dejection, gloom —a. **2.** gloomy, dejected —**melancholia** (mɛlən'kəʊlɪə) n. mental disease accompanied by depression —**melancholic** ('mɛlənkɒlɪk) n./a.

Melanesian (mɛlə'niːzɪən) a. **1.** of Melanesia, its people, or their languages —n. **2.** native or inhabitant of Melanesia **3.** group or branch of languages spoken in Melanesia

mélange (me'lɑːʒ) Fr. mixture

melanin ('mɛlənɪn) n. dark pigment found in hair, skin etc. of man

Melba toast ('mɛlbə) very thin crisp toast

melee or **mêlée** ('mɛleɪ) n. confused, noisy fight or crowd

meliorate ('miːlɪəreɪt) v. improve —**melio'ra- tion** n. —**'meliorism** n. doctrine that the world may be improved by human effort —'**meliorist** *n.*

mellifluous (mɪ'lɪfluəs) *or* **mellifluent** *a.* (of sound) smooth, sweet —**mel'lifluence** *n.*

mellow ('mɛləu) *a.* 1. ripe 2. softened by age, experience 3. soft, not harsh 4. genial, gay —*v.* 5. make, become mellow

melodeon *or* **melodion** (mɪ'ləudɪən) *n. Mus.* 1. small accordion 2. keyboard instrument similar to harmonium

melodrama ('mɛlədrɑːmə) *n.* 1. play full of sensational and startling situations, often highly emotional 2. overdramatic behaviour, emotion —**melodra'matic** *a.*

melody ('mɛlədɪ) *n.* 1. series of musical notes which make tune 2. sweet sound —**melodic** (mɪ'lɒdɪk) *a.* 1. of or relating to melody 2. of or relating to part in piece of music —**me'lodious** *a.* 1. pleasing to the ear 2. tuneful —**melodist** *n.* 1. singer 2. composer

melon ('mɛlən) *n.* large, fleshy, juicy fruit

melt (mɛlt) *v.* 1. (cause to) become liquid by heat 2. dissolve 3. soften 4. (cause to) waste away 5. blend —*vi.* 6. disappear ('**melted** *pt./pp.,* '**molten** *pp.*) —'**melting** *a.* 1. softening 2. languishing 3. tender —**melting point** temperature at which solid turns into liquid —'**meltwater** *n.* melted snow or ice

mem. 1. member 2. memoir 3. memorandum 4. memorial

member ('mɛmbə) *n.* 1. any of individuals making up body or society 2. limb 3. any part of complex whole —'**membership** *n.* —**Member of Parliament** member of House of Commons or similar legislative body

membrane ('mɛmbreɪn) *n.* thin flexible tissue in plant or animal body

memento (mɪ'mɛntəu) *n.* thing serving to remind, souvenir (*pl.* -**s,** -**es**) —**memento mori** ('mɔːriː) object intended to remind people of death

memo ('mɛməu, 'miːməu) memorandum

memoir ('mɛmwɑː) *n.* 1. autobiography, personal history or biography 2. record of events

memory ('mɛmərɪ) *n.* 1. faculty of recollecting, recalling to mind 2. recollection 3. thing remembered 4. length of time one can remember 5. commemoration 6. part or faculty of computer which stores information —**memorabilia** (mɛmərə'bɪlɪə) *pl.n.* memorable events or things (*sing.* -**rabile** (-'ræbɪlɪ)) —'**memorable** *a.* worthy of remembrance, noteworthy —'**memorably** *adv.* —**memo'randum** *n.* 1. note to help the memory *etc.* 2. informal letter 3. note of contract (*pl.* -**s,** -**da** (-də)) —**me'morial** *a.* 1. of, preserving memory —*n.* 2. thing, *esp.* a monument, which serves to keep in memory

—**me'morialist** *n.* —**me'morialize** *or* -**ise** *vt.* commemorate —'**memorize** *or* -**ise** *vt.* commit to memory

memsahib ('mɛmsɑːɪb, -hɪb) *n.* formerly in India, term of respect used of European married woman

men (mɛn) *n., pl. of* MAN

menace ('mɛnɪs) *n.* 1. threat —*v.* 2. threaten

ménage (meɪ'nɑːʒ) *n.* persons of a household —*ménage à trois* (menɑːʒ ɑ 'trwɑ) *Fr.* sexual arrangement involving married couple and lover of one of them (*pl. ménages à trois* (menɑːʒ ɑ 'trwɑ))

menagerie (mɪ'nædʒərɪ) *n.* exhibition, collection of wild animals

mend (mɛnd) *vt.* 1. repair, patch 2. reform, correct, put right —*vi.* 3. improve, *esp.* in health —*n.* 4. repaired breakage, hole —**on the mend** regaining health

mendacious (mɛn'deɪʃəs) *a.* untruthful —**mendacity** (mɛn'dæsɪtɪ) *n.* (tendency to) untruthfulness

mendelevium (mɛndɪ'liːvɪəm) *n.* transuranic element artificially produced by bombardment of einsteinium

mendicant ('mɛndɪkənt) *a.* 1. begging —*n.* 2. beggar —'**mendicancy** *or* **men'dicity** *n.* begging

menhir ('mɛnhɪə) *n.* single, upright monumental stone, monolith

menial ('miːnɪəl) *a.* 1. of work requiring little skill 2. of household duties or servants 3. servile —*n.* 4. servant 5. servile person

meninges (mɪ'nɪndʒiːz) *pl.n.* three membranes that envelop brain and spinal cord (*sing.* **meninx** ('miːnɪŋks)) —**me'ningeal** *a.* —**menin'gitis** *n.* inflammation of the membranes of the brain

meniscus (mɪ'nɪskəs) *n.* 1. curved surface of liquid 2. curved lens

menopause ('mɛnəupɔːz) *n.* final cessation of menstruation

menorah (mɪ'nɔːrə) *n. Judaism* seven-branched candelabrum used in ceremonies

menses ('mɛnsiːz) *n.* 1. menstruation 2. period of time during which one menstruation occurs 3. matter discharged during menstruation (*pl.* '**menses**)

menstruation (mɛnstru'eɪʃən) *n.* approximately monthly discharge of blood and cellular debris from womb of nonpregnant woman —'**menstrual** *a.* —'**menstruate** *vi.*

mensuration (mɛnʃə'reɪʃən) *n.* measuring, *esp.* of areas

-ment (*comb. form*) 1. state; condition; quality, as in *enjoyment* 2. result or product of action, as in *embankment* 3. process; action, as in *management*

mental ('mɛntəl) *a.* **1.** of, done by the mind **2.** *inf.* feeble-minded, mad —**men'tality** *n.* state or quality of mind —**'mentally** *adv.*

menthol ('mɛnθɒl) *n.* organic compound found in peppermint, used medicinally

mention ('mɛnʃən) *vt.* **1.** refer to briefly, speak of —*n.* **2.** acknowledgment **3.** reference to or remark about person or thing —**'mentionable** *a.* fit or suitable to be mentioned

mentor ('mɛntɔː) *n.* wise, trusted adviser, guide

menu ('mɛnjuː) *n.* list of dishes to be served, or from which to order

meow, miaou, miaow (mɪ'aʊ, mjaʊ), *or* **miaul** (mɪ'aʊl, mjaʊl) *vi.* **1.** (of cat) make characteristic crying sound —*interj.* **2.** imitation of this sound

M.E.P. Member of European Parliament

mercantile ('mɜːkəntaɪl) *a.* of, engaged in trade, commerce

mercenary ('mɜːsɪnərɪ, -sɪnrɪ) *a.* **1.** influenced by greed **2.** working merely for reward —*n.* **3.** hired soldier

mercer ('mɜːsə) *n. esp.* formerly, dealer in fabrics —**'mercery** *n.* his trade, goods

mercerize *or* **-ise** ('mɜːsəraɪz) *vt.* give lustre to (cotton fabrics) by treating with chemicals —**'mercerized** *or* **-ised** *a.*

merchant ('mɜːtʃənt) *n.* **1.** one engaged in trade **2.** wholesale trader —**merchandise** ('mɜːtʃəndaɪs, -daɪz) *n.* his wares —**merchant bank** *UK* financial institution engaged in accepting foreign bills and underwriting new security issues —**'merchantman** *n.* trading ship —**merchant navy** ships engaged in a nation's commerce

mercury ('mɜːkjʊrɪ) *n.* **1.** silvery metal, liquid at ordinary temperature, quicksilver **2.** (M-) *Roman myth.* messenger of the gods **3.** (M-) planet nearest to sun —**mer'curial** *a.* **1.** relating to, containing mercury **2.** lively, changeable

mercy ('mɜːsɪ) *n.* refraining from infliction of suffering by one who has right, power to inflict it, compassion —**'merciful** *a.* —**'merciless** *a.* —**mercy killing** *see* EUTHANASIA

mere[1] (mɪə) *a.* **1.** only **2.** not more than **3.** nothing but —**'merely** *adv.*

mere[2] (mɪə) *n. obs.* lake

meretricious (mɛrɪ'trɪʃəs) *a.* **1.** superficially or garishly attractive **2.** insincere

merganser (mɜː'gænsə) *n.* large, crested diving duck

merge (mɜːdʒ) *v.* (cause to) lose identity or be absorbed —**'merger** *n.* **1.** combination of business firms into one **2.** absorption into something greater

meridian (mə'rɪdɪən) *n.* **1.** circle of the earth passing through poles **2.** imaginary circle in sky

passing through celestial poles **3.** highest point reached by star *etc.* **4.** period of greatest splendour —*a.* **5.** of meridian **6.** at peak of something

meringue (mə'ræŋ) *n.* **1.** baked mixture of white of eggs and sugar **2.** cake of this

merino (mə'riːnəʊ) *n.* **1.** breed of sheep originating in Spain (*pl.* **-s**) **2.** long, fine wool of this sheep **3.** yarn or cloth made from this wool

merit ('mɛrɪt) *n.* **1.** excellence, worth **2.** quality of deserving reward —*pl.* **3.** excellence —*vt.* **4.** deserve —**meri'tocracy** *n.* **1.** rule by persons chosen for their superior talents or intellect **2.** persons constituting such group —**meri'torious** *a.* deserving praise

merlin ('mɜːlɪn) *n.* small falcon

mermaid ('mɜːmeɪd) *n.* imaginary sea creature with upper part of woman and lower part of fish

merry ('mɛrɪ) *a.* joyous, cheerful —**'merrily** *adv.* —**'merriment** *n.* —**merry-go-round** *n.* roundabout

mésalliance (me'zælɪɒns) *n.* marriage with person of lower social status

mescaline *or* **mescalin** ('mɛskəliːn, -lɪn) *n.* hallucinogenic drug derived from **mescal buttons**, button-like tubercles of the **mescal** cactus of Mexico

mesdames ('meɪdæm) *n., pl. of* MADAME

mesdemoiselles (meɪdmwɑː'zɛl) *n., pl. of* MADEMOISELLE

mesembryanthemum (mɪzɛmbrɪ'ænθɪməm) *n.* low-growing plant with daisylike flowers of various colours

mesh (mɛʃ) *n.* **1.** (one of the open spaces of, or wires *etc.* forming) network, net —*v.* **2.** entangle, become entangled **3.** (of gears) engage —*vi.* **4.** coordinate

mesmerism ('mɛzmərɪzəm) *n. former term* for HYPNOTISM —**mes'meric** *a.* —**'mesmerist** *n.* —**'mesmerize** *or* **-ise** *vt.* **1.** hypnotize **2.** fascinate, hold spellbound

meso- *or before vowel* **mes-** (*comb. form*) middle or intermediate, as in *mesomorph*

Mesolithic (mɛsəʊ'lɪθɪk) *n.* **1.** period between Palaeolithic and Neolithic —*a.* **2.** of or relating to Mesolithic

meson ('miːzɒn) *n.* elementary atomic particle

Mesozoic (mɛsəʊ'zəʊɪk) *a.* of, denoting, or relating to era of geological time that began 225 000 000 years ago and lasted about 155 000 000 years

mess (mɛs) *n.* **1.** untidy confusion **2.** trouble, difficulty **3.** group in armed services who regularly eat together **4.** place where they eat —*vi.* **5.** make mess **6.** *Mil.* eat in a mess —*vt.* **7.** muddle —**'messy** *a.* —**mess about** *or* **around** potter about

message ('mɛsɪdʒ) n. 1. communication sent 2. meaning, moral 3. errand —'**messenger** n. bearer of message

Messiah (mɪ'saɪə) n. 1. Jews' promised deliverer 2. Christ —**Messianic** (mɛsɪ'ænɪk) a.

messieurs ('mɛsəz) n., pl. of MONSIEUR

Messrs. ('mɛsəz) n., pl. of MR.

met (mɛt) pt./pp. of MEET¹

Met (mɛt) a./n. inf. Meteorological (Office in London)

met. 1. meteorological 2. meteorology 3. metropolitan

meta- or sometimes before vowel **met-** (comb. form) change, as in metamorphose, metathesis

metabolism (mɪ'tæbəlɪzəm) n. chemical process of living body —**meta'bolic** a. —**me'tabolize** or **-ise** v.

metacarpus (mɛtə'kɑːpəs) n. 1. skeleton of hand between wrist and fingers 2. corresponding bones in other vertebrates (pl. **-pi** (-paɪ)) —**meta'carpal** a./n.

metal ('mɛtl) n. 1. mineral substance, opaque, fusible and malleable, capable of conducting heat and electricity 2. broken stone for macadamized roads —**me'tallic** a. —**'metalloid** n. 1. nonmetallic element that has some of properties of metal —a. (also **metal'loidal**) 2. of or being metalloid 3. resembling metal —**metal'lurgic** or **metal'lurgical** a. —**me'tallurgist** n. —**me'tallurgy** n. scientific study of extracting, refining metals, and their structure and properties

metal. or **metall.** 1. metallurgical 2. metallurgy

metamorphosis (mɛtə'mɔːfəsɪs) n. change of shape, character etc. (pl. **-phoses** (-fəsiːz)) —**meta'morphic** a. (esp. of rocks) changed in texture, structure by heat, pressure etc. —**meta'morphose** v. transform

metaphor ('mɛtəfə, -fɔː) n. 1. figure of speech in which term is transferred to something it does not literally apply to 2. instance of this —**meta'phorical** a. figurative —**meta'phorically** adv.

metaphysics (mɛtə'fɪzɪks) pl.n. (with sing. v.) branch of philosophy concerned with being and knowing —**meta'physical** a. —**metaphy'sician** n.

metastasis (mɪ'tæstəsɪs) n. Pathol. spreading of disease, esp. cancer cells, from one part of body to another (pl. **-ses** (-siːz)) —**metastatic** (mɛtə'stætɪk) a.

metatarsus (mɛtə'tɑːsəs) n. 1. skeleton of foot between toes and ankle 2. corresponding bones in other vertebrates (pl. **-si** (-saɪ)) —**meta'tarsal** a./n.

metathesis (mɪ'tæθəsɪs) n. transposition, esp.

of letters in word, eg Old English bridd gives modern bird (pl. **-eses** (-əsiːz))

metazoan (mɛtə'zəʊən) n. 1. any animal having a body composed of many cells —a. (also **meta'zoic**) 2. of or relating to metazoans

mete (miːt) vt. measure —**mete out** 1. distribute 2. allot as punishment

metempsychosis (mɛtəmsaɪ'kəʊsɪs) n. migration of soul from one body to another (pl. **-ses** (-siːz)) —**metempsy'chosist** n.

meteor ('miːtɪə) n. small, fast-moving celestial body, visible as streak of incandescence if it enters earth's atmosphere —**mete'oric** a. 1. of, like meteor 2. brilliant but short-lived —'**meteorite** n. fallen meteor —'**meteoroid** n. any of small celestial bodies that are thought to orbit sun —**meteor'oidal** a.

meteorology (miːtɪə'rɒlədʒɪ) n. study of earth's atmosphere, esp. for weather forecasting —**meteoro'logical** a. —**meteor'ologist** n.

meter ('miːtə) n. 1. that which measures 2. instrument for recording consumption of gas, electricity etc.

Meth. Methodist

methane ('miːθeɪn) n. inflammable gas, compound of carbon and hydrogen

methanol ('mɛθənɒl) n. colourless, poisonous liquid used as solvent and fuel (also **methyl alcohol**)

methinks (mɪ'θɪŋks) v. impers. obs. it seems to me (**me'thought** pt.)

method ('mɛθəd) n. 1. way, manner 2. technique 3. orderliness, system —**me'thodical** a. orderly —'**methodize** or **-ise** vt. reduce to order —**metho'dology** n. particular method or procedure

Methodist ('mɛθədɪst) n. 1. member of any of the churches originated by John Wesley and his followers —a. 2. of or relating to Methodism or the Methodist Church —'**Methodism** n.

meths (mɛθs) n. inf. methylated spirits

methyl ('miːθaɪl, 'mɛθɪl) n. (compound containing) a saturated hydrocarbon group of atoms —'**methylate** vt. 1. combine with methyl 2. mix with methanol —**methylated spirits** alcoholic mixture denatured with methanol

meticulous (mɪ'tɪkjʊləs) a. (over)particular about details

métier ('mɛtɪeɪ) n. 1. profession, vocation 2. forte

Métis (meɪ'tiːs) n. C person of mixed parentage

metonymy (mɪ'tɒnɪmɪ) n. figure of speech in which thing is replaced by another associated with it, eg the Crown for the king —**meto'nymical** a.

metre or U.S. **meter** ('miːtə) n. 1. unit of length in decimal system 2. SI unit of length 3. rhythm of poem —**metric** ('mɛtrɪk) a. of system of weights and measures in which metre is a unit —**metrical** ('mɛtrɪkəl) a. of measurement of poetic metre —**metricate** ('mɛtrɪkeɪt) v. convert (measuring system etc.) from nonmetric to metric units —**metri'cation** n. —**metric ton** see TONNE

Metro ('metrəʊ) n. **C** metropolitan city administration

metronome ('mɛtrənəʊm) n. instrument which marks musical time by means of ticking pendulum

metropolis (mɪ'trɒpəlɪs) n. chief city of a country, region —**metro'politan** a. **1.** of metropolis —n. **2.** bishop with authority over other bishops of a province

-metry (n. comb. form) process or science of measuring, as in geometry —**-metric** (a. comb. form)

mettle ('mɛtəl) n. courage, spirit —'**mettlesome** a. high-spirited

mew[1] (mju:) n. **1.** cry of cat, gull —vi. **2.** utter this cry

mew[2] (mju:) n. any sea gull, esp. common gull

mews (mju:z) pl.n. (sing. v.) yard, street, orig. of stables, now oft. converted to houses

Mex. 1. Mexican **2.** Mexico

mezzanine ('mɛzəni:n, 'mɛtsəni:n) n. intermediate storey, balcony between two main storeys, esp. between first and second floors

mezzo ('mɛtsəʊ) adv. Mus. moderately; quite —**mezzo-soprano** n. voice, singer between soprano and contralto (pl. **-s**)

mezzotint ('mɛtsəʊtɪnt) n. **1.** method of engraving by scraping roughened surface **2.** print so made

mf Mus. mezzo forte

MF 1. Rad. medium frequency. **2.** Middle French

mfr. 1. manufacture **2.** manufacturer

mg or **mg.** milligram(s)

Mg Chem. magnesium

M. Glam. Mid Glamorgan

Mgr. 1. manager **2.** Monseigneur **3.** Monsignor

MHG Middle High German

MHz megahertz

mi or **me** (mi:) n. Mus. in tonic sol-fa, third degree of any major scale

MI 1. Military Intelligence **2.** Michigan

MI5 Military Intelligence, section five

miaou or **miaow** (mɪ'aʊ, mjaʊ) see MEOW

miasma (mɪ'æzmə) n. unwholesome or foreboding atmosphere (pl. **-mata** (-mətə), **-s**) —**miasmatic** (mɪːəz'mætɪk) a.

mica ('maɪkə) n. mineral found as glittering scales, plates

mice (maɪs) n., pl. of MOUSE

Michaelmas ('mɪkəlməs) n. feast of Archan-

gel St. Michael, 29th September —**Michaelmas daisy** common garden flower of aster family

mickey or **micky** ('mɪkɪ) n. inf. —**take the mickey** or **micky out of** tease

Mickey Finn (fɪn) sl. drink containing drug to make drinker unconscious

micro ('maɪkrəʊ) n. inf. **1.** microcomputer **2.** microprocessor (pl. **-s**)

micro- or before vowel **micr-** (comb. form) **1.** small or minute, as in microdot **2.** magnification or amplification, as in microscope, microphone **3.** involving use of microscope, as in microscopy

microbe ('maɪkrəʊb) n. **1.** minute organism **2.** disease germ —**mi'crobial** a.

microbiology (maɪkrəʊbaɪ'ɒlədʒɪ) n. branch of biology involving study of microorganisms —**microbio'logic(al)** a.

microchemistry (maɪkrəʊ'kɛmɪstrɪ) n. chemical experimentation with minute quantities of material —**micro'chemical** a.

microchip ('maɪkrəʊtʃɪp) n. small wafer of silicon etc. containing electronic circuits (also **chip**)

microcircuit ('maɪkrəʊsɜːkɪt) n. miniature electronic circuit, esp. integrated circuit —**micro'circuitry** n.

microcomputer (maɪkrəʊkəm'pjuːtə) n. computer in which central processing unit is contained in one or more silicon chips

microcopy ('maɪkrəʊkɒpɪ) n. minute photographic replica useful for storage because of its small size

microcosm ('maɪkrəʊkɒzəm) or **microcosmos** (maɪkrəʊ'kɒzmɒs) n. **1.** miniature representation, model etc. of some larger system **2.** man as epitome of universe —**micro'cosmic** a.

microdot ('maɪkrəʊdɒt) n. extremely small microcopy

microelectronics (maɪkrəʊɪlɛk'trɒnɪks) pl.n. (with sing. v.) branch of electronics concerned with microcircuits

microfiche ('maɪkrəʊfiːʃ) n. microfilm in sheet form

microfilm ('maɪkrəʊfɪlm) n. miniaturized recording of manuscript, book on roll of film

microgroove ('maɪkrəʊgruːv) n. **1.** narrow groove of long-playing gramophone record —a. **2.** (of a record) having such grooves

micrometer (maɪ'krɒmɪtə) n. instrument for measuring very small distances or angles

microminiaturization or **-isation** (maɪkrəʊmɪnɪtʃərəɪ'zeɪʃən) n. production of small components and circuits and equipment in which they are used

micron ('maɪkrɒn) n. unit of length, one millionth of a metre

microorganism (maɪkrəʊˈɔːɡənɪzəm) n. organism of microscopic size

microphone (ˈmaɪkrəfəʊn) n. instrument for amplifying, transmitting sounds

microprint (ˈmaɪkrəʊprɪnt) n. greatly reduced photographic copy of print, read by magnifying device

microprocessor (maɪkrəʊˈprəʊsɛsə) n. integrated circuit acting as central processing unit in small computer

microscope (ˈmaɪkrəskəʊp) n. instrument by which very small body is magnified and made visible —**microscopic** (maɪkrəˈskɒpɪk) a. 1. of microscope 2. very small —**microscopy** (maɪˈkrɒskəpɪ) n. use of microscope

microstructure (ˈmaɪkrəʊstrʌktʃə) n. structure on microscopic scale, esp. of alloy as observed by etching, polishing etc. under microscope

microsurgery (maɪkrəʊˈsɜːdʒərɪ) n. minute surgical dissection or manipulation of individual cells under a microscope

microwave (ˈmaɪkrəʊweɪv) n. electromagnetic wave with wavelength of a few centimetres, used in radar, cooking etc.

micturate (ˈmɪktjʊreɪt) vi. urinate —**micturi-tion** (mɪktjʊˈrɪʃən) n.

mid (mɪd) a. intermediate, in the middle of —ˈ**mid**ˈday n. noon —**midland** (ˈmɪdlənd) n. 1. middle part of country —pl. 2. central England —ˈ**midnight** n. twelve o'clock at night —**midnight sun** sun visible at midnight during summer inside Arctic and Antarctic circles —**mid-off** n. Cricket fielding position on off side closest to bowler —**mid-on** n. Cricket fielding position on on side closest to bowler —ˈ**midshipman** n. naval officer of lowest commissioned rank —ˈ**mid**ˈ**summer** n. 1. summer solstice 2. middle of summer —ˈ**midway** a./adv. halfway —**mid-wicket** n. Cricket fielding position on on side, midway between square leg and mid-on —ˈ**mid**ˈ**winter** n.

midden (ˈmɪdən) n. 1. dunghill 2. rubbish heap

middle (ˈmɪdəl) a. 1. equidistant from two extremes 2. medium, intermediate —n. 3. middle point or part —ˈ**middling** a. 1. mediocre 2. moderate —adv. 3. inf. moderately —**middle age** period of life between youth and old age, usu. considered to be between ages of 40 and 60 —**middle-aged** a. —**Middle Ages** period from end of Roman Empire to Renaissance, roughly A.D. 500–1500 —**middle C** Mus. note written on first ledger line below treble staff or first ledger line above bass staff —**middle class** social class of businessmen, professional people etc. —**middle-class** a. —**middle ear** sound-conducting part of ear —**Middle East** (loosely)

area around E Mediterranean, esp. Israel and Arab countries from Turkey to N Afr. and eastwards to Iran —**Middle Eastern** —**Middle English** English language from about 1100 to about 1450 —**Middle High German** High German from about 1200 to about 1500 —**Middle Low German** Low German from about 1200 to about 1500 —ˈ**middleman** n. trader between producer and consumer —**middle-of-the-road** a. not extreme; moderate —**middle school** UK school for children aged between 8 or 9 and 12 or 13 —ˈ**middleweight** n. 1. professional boxer weighing 154–160 lbs. (70–72.5 kg); amateur boxer weighing 157–165 lbs. (71–75 kg) 2. wrestler weighing usu. 172–192 lbs. (78–87 kg)

midge (mɪdʒ) n. gnat or similar insect

midget (ˈmɪdʒɪt) n. very small person or thing

midi (ˈmɪdɪ) a. (of skirt etc.) reaching to below knee or midcalf

midriff (ˈmɪdrɪf) n. middle part of body

midst (mɪdst) prep. 1. in the middle of —n. 2. middle —**in the midst of** surrounded by, among

midwife (ˈmɪdwaɪf) n. trained person who assists at childbirth —**midwifery** (ˈmɪdwɪfərɪ) n. art, practice of this

mien (miːn) n. person's bearing, demeanour or appearance

might[1] (maɪt) pt. of MAY

might[2] (maɪt) n. power, strength —ˈ**mightily** adv. 1. strongly 2. powerfully —ˈ**mighty** a. 1. of great power 2. strong 3. valiant 4. important —adv. 5. inf. very

mignonette (mɪnjəˈnɛt) n. grey-green plant with sweet-smelling flowers

migraine (ˈmiːɡreɪn, ˈmaɪ-) n. severe headache, often with nausea and other symptoms

migrate (maɪˈɡreɪt) vi. move from one place to another —ˈ**migrant** n./a. —**miˈgration** n. 1. act of passing from one place, condition to another 2. number migrating together —ˈ**migratory** a. 1. of, capable of migration 2. (of animals) changing from one place to another according to season

mikado (mɪˈkɑːdəʊ) n. (oft. M-) obs. Japanese emperor

mike (maɪk) n. inf. microphone

milady or **miladi** (mɪˈleɪdɪ) n. formerly, continental title used for English gentlewoman

milch (mɪltʃ) a. giving, kept for milk

mild (maɪld) a. 1. not strongly flavoured 2. gentle, merciful 3. calm or temperate —ˈ**mildly** adv. —ˈ**mildness** n. —**mild steel** any strong tough steel that contains low quantity of carbon

mildew (ˈmɪldjuː) n. 1. destructive fungus on plants or things exposed to damp —v. 2. become tainted, affect with mildew

mile (maɪl) n. measure of length, 1760 yards, 1.609 km —ˈ**mileage** or ˈ**milage** n. 1. distance in

milfoil ('mɪlfɔɪl) *n.* yarrow

miles **2.** travelling expenses per mile **3.** miles travelled (per gallon of petrol) **4.** *inf.* advantage, profit, use —**mile'ometer** *or* **mi'lometer** *n.* device that records number of miles vehicle has travelled —'**milestone** *n.* **1.** stone marker showing distance **2.** significant event, achievement

milieu ('miːljзː) *n.* environment, condition in life

military ('mɪlɪtərɪ, -trɪ) *a.* **1.** of, for, soldiers, armies or war —*n.* **2.** armed services —'**militancy** *n.* —'**militant** *a.* **1.** aggressive, vigorous in support of cause **2.** prepared, willing to fight —'**militarism** *n.* enthusiasm for military force and methods —'**militarist** *n.* —'**militarize** *or* **-ise** *vt.* convert to military use —**militia** (mɪ'lɪʃə) *n.* military force of citizens for home service

militate ('mɪlɪteɪt) *vi.* (*esp. with* against) have strong influence, effect (on)

milk (mɪlk) *n.* **1.** white fluid with which mammals feed their young **2.** fluid in some plants —*vt.* **3.** draw milk from —'**milky** *a.* **1.** containing, like milk **2.** (of liquids) opaque, clouded —**milk-and-water** *a.* weak, feeble, or insipid —**milk bar** snack bar specializing in milk drinks —**milk float** *UK* small motor vehicle used to deliver milk to houses —'**milkmaid** *n.* *esp.* formerly, woman working with cows or in dairy —**milk run** *inf.* *Aeron.* routine and uneventful flight —**milk shake** frothy drink made of milk, flavouring, and *usu.* ice cream —'**milksop** *n.* effeminate fellow —**milk teeth** first set of teeth in young mammals —**Milky Way** luminous band of stars *etc.* stretching across sky, the galaxy —**milk of magnesia** suspension of magnesium hydroxide in water, used as laxative

mill (mɪl) *n.* **1.** factory **2.** machine for grinding, pulverizing corn, paper *etc.* —*vt.* **3.** put through mill **4.** cut fine grooves across edges of (*eg* coins) —*vi.* **5.** move in confused manner, as cattle or crowds of people —'**miller** *n.* —'**millpond** *n.* pool formed by damming stream to provide water to turn mill wheel —'**millrace** *n.* current of water driving mill wheel —'**millstone** *n.* flat circular stone for grinding

millennium (mɪ'lɛnɪəm) *n.* **1.** period of a thousand years during which some claim Christ is to reign on earth **2.** period of a thousand years **3.** period of peace, happiness (*pl.* **-s, -ia** (-ɪə))

millepede ('mɪlɪpiːd) *or* **milleped** ('mɪlɪpɛd) *n.* small animal with jointed body and many pairs of legs

miller's thumb ('mɪləz) any of several small freshwater European fishes having flattened body

millet ('mɪlɪt) *n.* a cereal grass

milli- (*comb. form*) thousandth, as in *millilitre*

milliard ('mɪliɑːd, 'mɪljɑːd) *n.* *UK* thousand million

millibar ('mɪlibɑː) *n.* unit of atmospheric pressure

milligram *or* **milligramme** ('mɪlɪgræm) *n.* thousandth part of a gram

millimetre *or* **U.S. millimeter** ('mɪlɪmiːtə) *n.* thousandth part of a metre

milliner ('mɪlɪnə) *n.* maker of, dealer in women's hats, ribbons *etc.* —'**millinery** *n.* his goods or work

million ('mɪljən) *n.* 1000 thousands —**million-**'**aire** *n.* **1.** owner of a million pounds, dollars *etc.* **2.** very rich man —'**millionth** *a./n.*

milometer (maɪ'lɒmɪtə) *n.* *see* **mileometer** *at* MILE

milt (mɪlt) *n.* spawn of male fish

mime (maɪm) *n.* **1.** acting without the use of words —*v.* **2.** act in mime

mimic ('mɪmɪk) *vt.* imitate (person, manner *etc.*), *esp.* for satirical effect ('**mimicked**, '**mimicking**) —*n.* **2.** one who, or animal which does this, or is adept at it —*a.* **3.** imitative, simulated —**mi'metic** *a.* **1.** of, resembling, or relating to imitation **2.** *Biol.* of or exhibiting protective resemblance to another species —'**mimicry** *n.* mimicking

mimosa (mɪ'məʊsə, -zə) *n.* genus of plants with fluffy, yellow flowers and sensitive leaves

min. 1. minim **2.** minimum **3.** minute

Min. 1. Minister **2.** Ministry

mina ('maɪnə) *n.* *see* MYNA

minaret (mɪnə'rɛt, 'mɪnərɛt) *n.* tall slender tower of mosque

minatory ('mɪnətərɪ, -trɪ) *or* **minatorial** *a.* threatening or menacing

mince (mɪns) *vt.* **1.** cut, chop small **2.** soften or moderate (words *etc.*) —*vi.* **3.** walk, speak in affected manner —*n.* **4.** minced meat —'**mincer** *n.* —'**mincing** *a.* affected in manner —'**mince-meat** *n.* mixture of currants, spices, suet *etc.* —**mince pie** pie containing mincemeat or mince

mind (maɪnd) *n.* **1.** thinking faculties as distinguished from the body, intellectual faculties **2.** memory, attention **3.** intention **4.** opinion **5.** sanity —*vt.* **6.** take offence at **7.** care for **8.** attend to **9.** be cautious, careful about **10.** be concerned, troubled about —*vi.* **11.** be careful —'**mindful** *a.* **1.** heedful **2.** keeping in memory —'**mindless** *a.* stupid, careless —**mind-reader** *n.* person seemingly able to discern thoughts of another —**mind's eye** visual memory or imagination

mine¹ (maɪn) *pron.* belonging to me

mine² (maɪn) *n.* **1.** deep hole for digging out

coal, metals *etc.* **2.** in war, hidden deposit of explosive to blow up ship *etc.* **3.** profitable source —*vt.* **4.** dig from mine **5.** make mine in or under **6.** place explosive mines in, on —*vi.* **7.** make, work in mine —'**miner** *n.* one who works in a mine —'**minefield** *n.* area of land or sea containing mines —'**minelayer** *n.* ship for laying mines —'**minesweeper** *n.* ship for clearing away mines

mineral ('mɪnərəl, 'mɪnrəl) *n.* **1.** naturally occurring inorganic substance, *esp.* as obtained by mining —*a.* **2.** of, containing minerals —'**mineralist** *n.* —**minera'logical** *a.* —**mineralogy** *n.* science of minerals —**mineral water** water containing some mineral, *esp.* natural or artificial kinds for drinking

minestrone (mɪnɪ'strəʊnɪ) *n.* type of soup containing pasta

mingle ('mɪŋgəl) *v.* mix, blend, unite, merge

mingy ('mɪndʒɪ) *a.* UK *inf.* miserly, stingy, or niggardly

mini ('mɪnɪ) *n.* something small or miniature —'**miniskirt** *n.* very short skirt, one at least four inches above knee

mini- (*comb. form*) smaller or shorter than standard size

miniature ('mɪnɪtʃə) *n.* **1.** small painted portrait **2.** anything on small scale —*a.* **3.** small-scale, minute —'**miniaturist** *n.* —'**miniaturize** *or* **-ise** *vt.* make or construct on a very small scale

minibus ('mɪnɪbʌs) *n.* small bus for about ten passengers

minim ('mɪnɪm) *n.* **1.** unit of fluid measure, one sixtieth of a drachm **2.** *Mus.* note half the length of semibreve

minimize *or* **-ise** ('mɪnɪmaɪz) *vt.* bring to, estimate at smallest possible amount —'**minimal** *a.* —'**minimum** *n.* **1.** lowest size or quantity (*pl.* **-s, -ma** (-mə)) —*a.* **2.** least possible —**minimum lending rate** formerly, minimum rate of interest at which the Bank of England lent money —**minimum wage** lowest wage that employer is permitted to pay by law or union contract

minion ('mɪnjən) *n.* **1.** favourite **2.** servile dependant

minister ('mɪnɪstə) *n.* **1.** person in charge of department of State **2.** diplomatic representa-

tive **3.** clergyman —*vi.* **4.** (*oft. with* to) attend to needs (of), take care (of) —**minis'terial** *a.* —**minis'terialist** *n.* supporter of government —'**ministrant** *a./n.* —**minis'tration** *n.* rendering help, *esp.* to sick —'**ministry** *n.* **1.** office of clergyman **2.** body of ministers forming government **3.** act of ministering —**minister of state** UK minister, usu. below cabinet rank, appointed to assist senior minister —**Minister of the Crown** UK any Government minister of cabinet rank

miniver ('mɪnɪvə) *n.* a white fur used in ceremonial costumes

mink (mɪŋk) *n.* **1.** variety of weasel **2.** its (brown) fur

minnow ('mɪnəʊ) *n.* small freshwater fish

Minoan (mɪ'nəʊən) *a.* **1.** of Bronze Age culture of Crete from about 3000 B.C. to about 1100 B.C. —*n.* **2.** Cretan belonging to Minoan culture

minor ('maɪnə) *a.* **1.** lesser **2.** under age —*n.* **3.** person below age of legal majority **4.** minor scale in music —mi'nority *n.* **1.** lesser number **2.** smaller party voting together **3.** ethical or religious group in a minority in any state **4.** state of being a minor —**minor scale** *Mus.* scale with semitones instead of whole tones after second and seventh notes

Minotaur ('mɪnətɔː) *n.* fabled monster, half bull, half man

minster ('mɪnstə) *n.* **1.** *Hist.* monastery church **2.** cathedral, large church

minstrel ('mɪnstrəl) *n.* **1.** medieval singer, musician, poet —*pl.* **2.** performers of negro songs —'**minstrelsy** *n.* **1.** art, body of minstrels **2.** collection of songs

mint[1] (mɪnt) *n.* **1.** place where money is coined —*vt.* **2.** coin, invent

mint[2] (mɪnt) *n.* aromatic plant

minuet (mɪnju'ɛt) *n.* **1.** stately dance **2.** music for it

minus ('maɪnəs) *prep.* **1.** less, with the deduction of, deprived of —*a.* **2.** lacking **3.** negative —*n.* **4.** the sign of subtraction (-)

minuscule ('mɪnəskjuːl) *n.* **1.** lower-case letter **2.** writing using such letters —*a.* **3.** relating to, printed in, or written in small letters **4.** very small —**minuscular** (mɪ'nʌskjʊlə) *a.*

minute[1] (maɪ'njuːt) *a.* **1.** very small **2.** precise

misad'dress	mis'count	mis'hit	misre'port
misadminis'tration	mis'deed	mis'judge	mis'state
misa'lignment	misem'ploy	mis'manage	mis'statement
misap'ply	mis'fortune	mis'management	mis'time
misbe'have	mis'govern	mis'marriage	mis'treat
mis'calculate	mis'government	misper'ception	mis'type
miscon'ceive	mis'handle	mis'phrase	misunder'stand
mis'conduct	mis'hear	mis'read	mis'use

—**mi'nutely** adv. —**minutiae** (mɪ'njuːʃiː) pl.n. trifles, precise details

minute² ('mɪnɪt) n. **1.** 60th part of hour or degree **2.** moment **3.** memorandum —pl. **4.** record of proceedings of meeting etc. —vt. **5.** make minute of **6.** record in minutes —**minute steak** small steak that can be cooked quickly

minx (mɪŋks) n. bold, flirtatious woman

Miocene ('maɪəsiːn) a. **1.** of or denoting fourth epoch of Tertiary period —n. **2.** this epoch or rock system

miracle ('mɪrəkəl) n. **1.** supernatural event **2.** marvel —**mi'raculous** a. —**mi'raculously** adv. —**miracle play** drama (esp. medieval) based on sacred subject

mirage ('mɪrɑːʒ) n. deceptive image in atmosphere, eg of lake in desert

mire (maɪə) n. **1.** swampy ground, mud —vt. **2.** stick in, dirty with mud

mirror ('mɪrə) n. **1.** glass or polished surface reflecting images —vt. **2.** reflect —**mirror image 1.** image as observed in mirror **2.** object that corresponds to another in reverse as does image in mirror

mirth (mɜːθ) n. merriment, gaiety —**'mirthful** a. —**'mirthless** a.

mis- (comb. form) wrong(ly), bad(ly). See the list on page 319

misadventure (mɪsəd'vɛntʃə) n. unlucky chance

misalliance (mɪsə'laɪəns) n. unsuitable alliance or marriage —**misal'ly** v.

misanthrope ('mɪzənθrəʊp) or **misanthropist** (mɪ'zænθrəpɪst) n. hater of mankind —**misanthropic** (mɪzən'θrɒpɪk) a. —**mi'santhropy** n.

misappropriate (mɪsə'prəʊprɪeɪt) vt. **1.** put to dishonest use **2.** embezzle —**misappropri'ation** n.

misbegotten (mɪsbɪ'gɒtən) a. **1.** unlawfully obtained or conceived **2.** badly conceived or designed **3.** Lit., dial. illegitimate; bastard

miscarry (mɪs'kærɪ) vi. **1.** bring forth young prematurely **2.** go wrong, fail —**mis'carriage** n.

miscast (mɪs'kɑːst) v. **1.** distribute (acting parts) wrongly —vt. **2.** assign to unsuitable role

miscegenation (mɪsɪdʒɪ'neɪʃən) n. interbreeding of races

miscellaneous (mɪsə'leɪnɪəs) a. mixed, assorted —**mis'cellany** n. **1.** collection of assorted writings in one book **2.** medley

mischance (mɪs'tʃɑːns) n. unlucky event

mischief ('mɪstʃɪf) n. **1.** annoying behaviour **2.** inclination to tease, disturb **3.** harm **4.** source of harm or annoyance —**'mischievous** a. **1.** (of a child) full of pranks **2.** disposed to mischief **3.** having harmful effect

miscible ('mɪsɪbəl) a. capable of mixing

misconception (mɪskən'sɛpʃən) n. wrong idea, belief

miscreant ('mɪskrɪənt) n. wicked person, evildoer, villain

misdemeanour or U.S. **misdemeanor** (mɪsdɪ'miːnə) n. **1.** formerly, offence less grave than a felony **2.** minor offence

misdoubt (mɪs'daʊt) v. obs. doubt or suspect

mise en scène (miz ɑ̃ 'sɛn) Fr. **1.** arrangement of scenery etc. in play; stage setting **2.** environment of event

miser ('maɪzə) n. **1.** hoarder of money **2.** stingy person —**'miserliness** n. —**'miserly** a. **1.** avaricious **2.** niggardly

miserable ('mɪzərəbəl) a. **1.** very unhappy, wretched **2.** causing misery **3.** worthless **4.** squalid —**'misery** n. **1.** great unhappiness **2.** distress **3.** poverty **4.** UK inf. habitually depressed, discontented person

misericord or **misericorde** (mɪ'zɛrɪkɔːd) n. ledge projecting from underside of hinged seat of choir stall in church, on which occupant can support himself while standing

misfire (mɪs'faɪə) vi. fail to fire, start, function successfully

misfit ('mɪsfɪt) n. esp. person not suited to his environment or work

misgiving (mɪs'gɪvɪŋ) n. (oft. pl.) feeling of fear, doubt etc.

misguided (mɪs'gaɪdɪd) a. foolish, unreasonable

mishap ('mɪshæp) n. minor accident

mishmash ('mɪʃmæʃ) n. confused collection or mixture

mislay (mɪs'leɪ) vt. put in place which cannot later be remembered

mislead (mɪs'liːd) vt. **1.** give false information to **2.** lead astray (**mis'led** pt./pp.) —**mis'leading** a. deceptive

misnomer (mɪs'nəʊmə) n. **1.** wrong name or term **2.** use of this

misogamy (mɪ'sɒgəmɪ, maɪ-) n. hatred of marriage —**mi'sogamist** n.

misogyny (mɪ'sɒdʒɪnɪ, maɪ-) n. hatred of women —**mi'sogynist** n.

misrepresent (mɪsrɛprɪ'zɛnt) vt. portray in wrong or misleading light

misrule (mɪs'ruːl) vt. **1.** govern inefficiently or without justice —n. **2.** inefficient or unjust government **3.** disorder

miss (mɪs) vt. **1.** fail to hit, reach, find, catch, or notice **2.** not be in time for **3.** omit **4.** notice or regret absence of **5.** avoid —vi. **6.** (of engine) misfire —n. **7.** fact, instance of missing —**'missing** a. **1.** lost **2.** absent —**missing link 1.** hypothetical extinct animal intermediate between anthropoid apes and man **2.** any missing section or part in series

Miss (mɪs) *n.* **1.** title of unmarried woman **2.** (**m-**) girl

missal ('mɪsəl) *n.* book containing prayers *etc.* of the Mass

missile ('mɪsaɪl) *n.* that which may be thrown, shot, homed to damage, destroy —**guided missile** *see* GUIDE

mission ('mɪʃən) *n.* **1.** specific task or duty **2.** calling in life **3.** delegation **4.** sending or being sent on some service **5.** those sent —**missionary** *n.* **1.** one sent to a place, society to spread religion —*a.* **2.** of, like missionary or religious mission

missis *or* **missus** ('mɪsɪz, -ɪs) *n.* (*usu. with* the) *inf.* one's wife or wife of person addressed or referred to

missive ('mɪsɪv) *n.* letter

misspend (mɪs'spɛnd) *v.* spend thoughtlessly or wastefully (-'**spending,** -'**spent**)

mist (mɪst) *n.* **1.** water vapour in fine drops —'**mistily** *adv.* —'**misty** *a.* **1.** full of mist **2.** dim **3.** obscure

mistake (mɪ'steɪk) *n.* **1.** error, blunder —*vt.* **2.** fail to understand **3.** form wrong opinion about **4.** take (person or thing) for another —**mis'taken** *a.* **1.** wrong in opinion *etc.* **2.** arising from error in judgment *etc.*

mister ('mɪstə) *n.* title of courtesy to man

mistle thrush *or* **missel thrush** ('mɪsəl) European thrush with brown back and spotted breast

mistletoe ('mɪsəltəʊ) *n.* evergreen parasitic plant with white berries, which grows on trees

mistook (mɪ'stʊk) *pt. of* MISTAKE

mistral ('mɪstrəl, mɪ'strɑːl) *n.* strong, dry, N wind in France

mistress ('mɪstrɪs) *n.* **1.** object of man's illicit love **2.** woman with mastery or control **3.** woman owner **4.** woman teacher **5.** *obs.* title given to married woman

mistrial (mɪs'traɪəl) *n.* *Law* trial made void because of some error

mistrust (mɪs'trʌst) *vt.* **1.** have doubts or suspicions about —*n.* **2.** distrust —**mis'trustful** *a.*

misunderstanding (mɪsʌndə'stændɪŋ) *n.* **1.** failure to understand properly **2.** disagreement —**misunder'stood** *a.* not properly or sympathetically understood

mite (maɪt) *n.* **1.** very small insect **2.** anything very small **3.** small but well-meant contribution

mitigate ('mɪtɪgeɪt) *vt.* make less severe —**miti'gation** *n.* —**mitigating circumstances** circumstances which lessen the culpability of an offender

mitosis (maɪ'təʊsɪs, mɪ-) *n.* cell division in which nucleus divides into daughter nuclei, each containing same number of chromosomes as parent nucleus —**mitotic** (maɪ'tɒtɪk, mɪ-) *a.*

mitre *or U.S.* **miter** ('maɪtə) *n.* **1.** bishop's headdress **2.** joint between two pieces of wood *etc.* meeting at right angles —*vt.* **3.** join with, shape for a mitre joint **4.** put mitre on

mitt (mɪt) *n.* **1.** glove leaving fingers bare **2.** baseball catcher's glove **3.** *sl.* hand

mitten ('mɪtən) *n.* glove with two compartments, one for thumb and one for fingers

mix (mɪks) *vt.* **1.** put together, combine, blend, mingle —*vi.* **2.** be mixed **3.** associate —**mixed** *a.* composed of different elements, races, sexes *etc.* —'**mixer** *n.* one who, that which mixes —'**mixture** *n.* —**mixed bag** *inf.* something composed of diverse elements, people *etc.* —**mixed blessing** situation *etc.* having advantages and disadvantages —**mixed doubles** *Tennis* game with man and woman as partners on each side —**mixed grill** dish of grilled chops, sausages, bacon *etc.* —**mixed marriage** marriage between persons of different races or religions —**mixed-up** *a.* *inf.* confused —**mix-up** *n.* confused situation

mizzen *or* **mizen** ('mɪzən) *n.* lowest fore-and-aft sail on aftermost mast of ship —**mizzenmast** *or* **mizenmast** ('mɪzənmɑːst; *Naut.* 'mɪzənməst) *n.* aftermost mast on full-rigged ship

mks units metric system of units based on the metre, kilogram and second

ml millilitre(s)

M.L. Medieval Latin

M.L.A. C Member of the Legislative Assembly

M.Litt. UK Master of Letters

Mlle *or* **Mlle.** Mademoiselle (*pl.* **Mlles, Mlles.**)

MLR minimum lending rate

mm millimetre(s)

M.M. Military Medal

Mme *or* **Mme.** Madame (*pl.* **Mmes, Mmes.**)

M.Mus. Master of Music

Mn *Chem.* manganese

MN Minnesota

MNA *or* **M.N.A.** C Member of the National Assembly

mnemonic (nɪ'mɒnɪk) *a.* **1.** helping the memory —*n.* **2.** something intended to help the memory

mo (məʊ) *n.* *inf.* moment

Mo *Chem.* molybdenum

MO Missouri

M.O. Medical Officer

-mo (*comb. form*) in bookbinding, indicating book size by specifying number of leaves formed by folding one sheet of paper, as in *sixteenmo*

moa ('məʊə) *n.* any of various extinct flightless birds of New Zealand

moan (məʊn) *n.* **1.** low murmur, usually of pain

—*v.* **2.** utter (words *etc.*) with moan —*vi.* **3.** lament

moat (mɔut) *n.* **1.** deep wide ditch, *esp.* round castle —*vt.* **2.** surround with moat

mob (mɒb) *n.* **1.** disorderly crowd of people **2.** mixed assembly —*v.* **3.** attack in mob, hustle or ill-treat (**-bb-**) —'**mobster** *n. US sl.* gangster

mobcap ('mɒbkæp) *n.* formerly, woman's large cotton cap with pouched crown

mobile ('mɔubaɪl) *a.* **1.** capable of movement **2.** easily moved or changed —*n.* **3.** hanging structure of card, plastic *etc.*, designed to move in air currents —**mobility** (mɔu'bɪlɪtɪ) *n.*

mobilize *or* **-ise** ('mɔubɪlaɪz) *vi.* **1.** (of armed services) prepare for military service —*vt.* **2.** organize for a purpose —**mobili'zation** *or* **-i'sation** *n.* in war time, calling up of men and women for active service

moccasin ('mɒkəsɪn) *n.* Amer. Indian soft shoe, *usu.* of deerskin

mocha ('mɒkə) *n.* **1.** type of strong, dark coffee **2.** this flavour

mock (mɒk) *vt.* **1.** make fun of, ridicule **2.** mimic —*vi.* **3.** scoff —*n.* **4.** act of mocking **5.** laughing stock —*a.* **6.** sham, imitation —'**mocker** *n.* —'**mockery** *n.* **1.** derision **2.** travesty —**mocking bird** N Amer. bird which imitates songs of others —**mock orange** shrub with white fragrant flowers —**mock turtle soup** imitation turtle soup made from calf's head —**mock-up** *n.* scale model —**put the mockers on** *inf.* ruin chances of success of

mod[1] (mɒd) **UK** *a.* **1.** of any fashion in dress regarded as stylish, *esp.* that of early 1960s —*n.* **2.** member of group of teenagers, orig. in mid-1960s, noted for their clothes-consciousness

mod[2] (mɒd) *n.* annual Highland Gaelic meeting with musical and literary competitions

mod. 1. moderate **2.** modern

mod cons (kɒnz) *inf.* modern conveniences

mode (mɔud) *n.* **1.** method, manner **2.** prevailing fashion **3.** *Mus.* any of various scales of notes within one octave —'**modal** *a.* **1.** of or relating to mode or manner **2.** *Gram.* expressing distinction of mood **3.** *Metaphys.* of or relating to form of thing as opposed to its substance *etc.* **4.** *Mus.* of or relating to mode —**mo'dality** *n.* —'**modish** *a.* in the fashion —**modiste** (mɔu'diːst) *n.* fashionable dressmaker or milliner

model ('mɒdəl) *n.* **1.** miniature representation **2.** pattern **3.** person or thing worthy of imitation **4.** person employed by artist to pose, or by dress designer to display clothing —*vt.* **5.** make model of **6.** mould —*v.* **7.** display (clothing) for dress designer (**-ll-**)

moderate ('mɒdərɪt) *a.* **1.** not going to extremes, temperate, medium —*n.* **2.** person of

moderate views —*v.* ('mɒdəreɪt) **3.** make, become less violent or excessive **4.** preside (over) —**mode'ration** *n.* —'**moderator** *n.* **1.** mediator **2.** president of Presbyterian body **3.** arbitrator

moderato (mɒdə'rɑːtɔu) *adv. Mus.* **1.** at moderate tempo **2.** direction indicating that tempo specified be used with restraint

modern ('mɒdən) *a.* **1.** of present or recent times **2.** in, of current fashion —*n.* **3.** person living in modern times —'**modernism** *n.* (support of) modern tendencies, thoughts *etc.* —'**modernist** *n.* —mo'**dernity** *n.* —**moderni'zation** *or* **-i'sation** *n.* —'**modernize** *or* **-ise** *vt.* bring up to date —**Modern English** English language since about 1450 —**modern languages** current European languages as subject of study

modest ('mɒdɪst) *a.* **1.** not overrating one's qualities or achievements **2.** shy **3.** moderate, not excessive **4.** decorous, decent —'**modestly** *adv.* —'**modesty** *n.*

modicum ('mɒdɪkəm) *n.* small quantity

modify ('mɒdɪfaɪ) *vt.* **1.** change slightly **2.** tone down (**-fied, -fying**) —**modifi'cation** *n.* —'**modifier** *n. esp.* word qualifying another

modulate ('mɒdjuleɪt) *vt.* **1.** regulate **2.** vary in tone —*vi.* **3.** change key of music —**modu'lation** *n.* **1.** modulating **2.** *Electron.* superimposing signals on to high-frequency carrier —'**modulator** *n.*

module ('mɒdjuːl) *n.* (detachable) unit, section, component with specific function —'**modular** *a.* of, consisting of, or resembling module or modulus

modulus ('mɒdjuləs) *n.* **1.** *Phys.* coefficient expressing specified property of specified substance **2.** *Maths.* number by which logarithm to one base is multiplied to give the corresponding logarithm to another base **3.** *Maths.* integer that can be divided exactly into the difference between two other integers (*pl.* **-li** (-laɪ))

modus operandi ('mɔudəs ɒpə'rændiː) *Lat.* method of operating, tackling task (*pl.* **modi operandi** ('mɔudiː))

modus vivendi (vɪ'vɛndiː) *Lat.* working arrangement between conflicting interests (*pl.* **modi vivendi** ('mɔudiː))

mog (mɒg) *or* **moggy** *n. UK sl.* cat

mogul ('mɔugʌl, mɔu'gʌl) *n.* important or powerful person

M.O.H. Medical Officer of Health

mohair ('mɔuhɛə) *n.* **1.** fine cloth of goat's hair **2.** hair of Angora goat

Mohammed (mɔu'hæmɪd) *n.* prophet and founder of Islam —**Mo'hammedan** *a./n.* Muslim —**Mo'hammedanism** *n.* another word (not in Muslim use) for ISLAM

moiety ('mɔɪɪtɪ) n. a half

moire (mwɑː) n. fabric, usu. silk, having watered effect —**moiré** ('mwɑːreɪ) a. 1. having watered or wavelike pattern —n. 2. such pattern, impressed on fabrics by means of engraved rollers 3. any fabric having such pattern, moire

moist (mɔɪst) a. damp, slightly wet —**moisten** ('mɔɪsən) v. —**moisture** n. liquid, esp. diffused or in drops —**moisturize** or **-ise** vt. add, restore moisture to (skin etc.)

moke (məuk) n. sl. donkey

mol Chem. mole

molar ('məulə) a. 1. (of teeth) for grinding —n. 2. molar tooth

molasses (mə'læsɪz) n. syrup, by-product of process of sugar refining

mole[1] (məul) n. small dark protuberant spot on the skin

mole[2] (məul) n. 1. small burrowing animal 2. spy, informer —**molehill** n. small mound of earth thrown up by burrowing mole —**make a mountain out of a molehill** exaggerate unimportant matter out of all proportion

mole[3] (məul) n. 1. pier or breakwater 2. causeway 3. harbour within this

mole[4] (məul) n. SI unit of amount of substance

molecule ('mɒlɪkjuːl) n. 1. simplest freely existing chemical unit, composed of two or more atoms 2. very small particle —**mo'lecular** a. of, inherent in molecules —**molecular weight** sum of all atomic weights of atoms in a molecule

molest (mə'lɛst) vt. pester, interfere with so as to annoy or injure —**molestation** (məulɛ'steɪʃən) n.

moll (mɒl) n. sl. 1. gangster's female accomplice 2. prostitute

mollify ('mɒlɪfaɪ) vt. calm down, placate, soften (**-fied, -fying**) —**mollifi'cation** n.

mollusc or U.S. **mollusk** ('mɒləsk) n. soft-bodied, usu. hard-shelled animal, eg snail, oyster

mollycoddle ('mɒlɪkɒdəl) vt. pamper

Molotov cocktail ('mɒlətɒf) incendiary petrol bomb

molten ('məultən) a. 1. liquefied; melted 2. made by having been melted —v. 3. pp. of MELT

molto ('mɒltəu) adv. Mus. very

molybdenum (mə'lɪbdɪnəm) n. silver-white metallic element

moment ('məumənt) n. 1. very short space of time 2. (present) point in time —**'momentarily** adv. —**'momentary** a. lasting only a moment —**moment of truth** moment when person or thing is put to test

momentous (məu'mɛntəs) a. of great importance

momentum (məu'mɛntəm) n. 1. force of a

moving body 2. impetus gained from motion (pl. **-ta** (-tə), **-s**)

mon. monetary

Mon. Monday

monad ('mɒnæd, 'məu-) n. 1. Philos. any fundamental singular metaphysical entity (pl. **-s, -ades** (-ədɪz)) 2. single-celled organism 3. atom, ion, or radical with valency of one —**monadic** (mɒ'nædɪk) a.

monandrous (mɒ'nændrəs) a. 1. having only one male sexual partner over a period of time 2. (of plants) having flowers with only one stamen —**mo'nandry** n.

monarch ('mɒnək) n. sovereign ruler of a state —**mon'archic** a. —**'monarchist** n. supporter of monarchy —**'monarchy** n. 1. state ruled by sovereign 2. his rule

monastery ('mɒnəstərɪ) n. house occupied by a religious order —**mo'nastic** a. 1. relating to monks, nuns, or monasteries —n. 2. monk, recluse —**mo'nasticism** n.

monaural (mɒ'nɔːrəl) a. relating to, having, or hearing with only one ear

Monday ('mʌndɪ) n. second day of the week, or first of working week

money ('mʌnɪ) n. banknotes, coin etc., used as medium of exchange (pl. **-s, -ies**) —**'monetarism** n. theory that inflation is caused by increase in money supply —**'monetarist** n./a. —**'monetary** a. —**moneti'zation** or **-i'sation** n. —**'monetize** or **-ise** vt. make into, recognize as money —**'moneyed** or **'monied** a. rich —**'moneybags** n. sl. very rich person —**money-grubbing** a. inf. seeking greedily to obtain money —**'moneylender** n. person who lends money at interest as a living —**money-spinner** n. inf. enterprise, idea etc. that is source of wealth

monger ('mʌŋgə) n. trader or dealer: usu. in compounds, as in ironmonger

mongolism ('mɒŋgəlɪzəm) n. Down's syndrome —**'mongol** n./a. (one) afflicted with this —**'mongoloid** a. relating to or characterized by mongolism

Mongoloid ('mɒŋgəlɔɪd) a. of major racial group of mankind, including most of peoples of Asia, Eskimos, and N Amer. Indians

mongoose ('mɒŋguːs) n. small animal of Asia and Afr. noted for killing snakes (pl. **-s**)

mongrel ('mʌŋgrəl) n. 1. animal, esp. dog, of mixed breed, hybrid —a. 2. of mixed breed

monitor ('mɒnɪtə) n. 1. person or device which checks, controls, warns or keeps record of something 2. pupil assisting teacher with odd jobs in school 3. television set used in a studio for checking programme being transmitted 4. type of large lizard —vt. 5. watch, check on —**mo'nition** n. warning —**'monitory** a.

monk (mʌŋk) n. one of a religious community of men bound by vows of poverty etc. —'**monkish** a. —'**monkshood** n. poisonous plant with hooded flowers

monkey ('mʌŋkɪ) n. 1. long-tailed primate 2. mischievous child —vi. 3. meddle, fool —**monkey business** inf. mischievous or dishonest behaviour or acts —**monkey nut** UK peanut —**monkey puzzle** coniferous tree with sharp stiff leaves —**monkey wrench** spanner with movable jaws

mono ('mɒnəʊ) a. 1. monophonic —n. 2. monophonic sound

mono- or before vowel **mon-** (comb. form) single, as in monosyllabic

monochrome ('mɒnəkrəʊm) n. 1. representation in one colour —a. 2. of one colour —**monochro'matic** a.

monocle ('mɒnəkəl) n. single eyeglass

monocotyledon (mɒnəʊkɒtɪ'liːdən) n. any of various flowering plants having single embryonic seed leaf and leaves with parallel veins —**monocoty'ledonous** a.

monocular (mɒ'nɒkjʊlə) a. one-eyed

monogamy (mɒ'nɒgəmɪ) n. custom of being married to one person at a time

monogram ('mɒnəgræm) n. design of letters interwoven

monograph ('mɒnəgrɑːf) n. short book on single subject

monogyny (mɒ'nɒdʒɪnɪ) n. having only one female sexual partner over a period of time —mo'**nogynous** a.

monolith ('mɒnəlɪθ) n. monument consisting of single standing stone

monologue ('mɒnəlɒg) n. 1. dramatic composition with only one speaker 2. long speech by one person

monomania (mɒnəʊ'meɪnɪə) n. excessive preoccupation with one thing

monomial (mɒ'nəʊmɪəl) n. 1. Maths. expression consisting of single term —a. 2. consisting of single algebraic term

mononucleosis (mɒnəʊnjuːklɪ'əʊsɪs) n. 1. Pathol. presence of large number of monocytes in blood 2. see **infectious mononucleosis** at INFECT

monophonic (mɒnəʊ'fɒnɪk) a. 1. (of reproduction of sound) using only one channel between source and loudspeaker (also mo'**naural**) 2. Mus. of style of musical composition consisting of single melodic line

monoplane ('mɒnəʊpleɪn) n. aeroplane with one pair of wings

monopoly (mɒ'nɒpəlɪ) n. 1. exclusive possession of trade, privilege etc. 2. (M-) R board game for two to six players —mo'**nopolist** n.

—mo'**nopolize** or -**lise** vt. claim, take exclusive possession of

monorail ('mɒnəʊreɪl) n. railway with cars running on or suspended from single rail

monosodium glutamate (mɒnəʊ'səʊdɪəm 'gluːtəmeɪt) white crystalline substance used as food additive

monosyllable ('mɒnəsɪləbəl) n. word of one syllable

monotheism ('mɒnəʊθiːɪzəm) n. belief in only one God —'**monotheist** n.

monotone ('mɒnətəʊn) n. continuing on one note —mo'**notonous** a. lacking in variety, dull, wearisome —mo'**notony** n.

monovalent (mɒnəʊ'veɪlənt) a. Chem. 1. having valency of one 2. having only one valency (also uni'**valent**) —mono'**valence** or mono'**valency** n.

monoxide (mɒ'nɒksaɪd) n. oxide that contains one oxygen atom per molecule

Monseigneur (mɔ̃sɛ'njœːr) Fr. title given to French bishops, prelates, and princes (pl. **Messeigneurs** (mesɛ'njœːr))

monsieur (məs'jɜː) n. French title of address equivalent to sir when used alone or Mr. before name

Monsignor (mɒn'siːnjə) n. R.C.Ch. ecclesiastical title attached to certain offices

monsoon (mɒn'suːn) n. 1. seasonal wind of SE Asia 2. very heavy rainfall season

monster ('mɒnstə) n. 1. fantastic imaginary beast 2. misshapen animal or plant 3. very wicked person 4. huge person, animal or thing —a. 5. huge —**mon'strosity** n. 1. monstrous being 2. deformity 3. distortion —'**monstrous** a. 1. of, like monster 2. unnatural 3. enormous 4. horrible —'**monstrously** adv.

monstrance ('mɒnstrəns) n. R.C.Ch. vessel in which consecrated Host is exposed for adoration

montage (mɒn'tɑːʒ) n. 1. elements of two or more pictures imposed upon a single background to give a unified effect 2. method of editing a film

montbretia (mɒn'briːʃə) n. plant with orange flowers on long stems

month (mʌnθ) n. 1. one of twelve periods into which the year is divided 2. period of moon's revolution —'**monthly** a. 1. happening or payable once a month —adv. 1. once a month —n. 3. magazine published every month

monument ('mɒnjʊmənt) n. anything that commemorates, esp. a building or statue —monu'**mental** a. 1. vast, lasting 2. of or serving as monument —**monumental mason** maker and engraver of tombstones

moo (muː) n. 1. cry of cow —vi. 2. make this noise, low

mooch (mu:tʃ) *vi. sl.* loaf, slouch

mood[1] (mu:d) *n.* state of mind and feelings —'**moody** *a.* 1. gloomy, pensive 2. changeable in mood

mood[2] (mu:d) *n. Gram.* form indicating function of verb

Moog synthesizer (mu:g, məʊg) R electrophonic instrument operated by keyboard and pedals

moon (mu:n) *n.* 1. satellite which takes lunar month to revolve round earth 2. any secondary planet —*vi.* 3. (*oft. with* around) go about dreamily —'**moony** *a.* 1. *inf.* dreamy or listless 2. of or like moon —'**mooncalf** *n.* 1. born fool; dolt 2. person who idles time away (*pl.* **-calves**) —'**moonlight** *n.* 1. light of moon —*vi.* 2. hold two paid occupations —'**moonlight flit** hurried departure by night to escape from one's creditors —'**moonscape** *n.* general surface of moon or representation of it —'**moonshine** *n.* 1. whisky illicitly distilled 2. nonsense —'**moonshot** *n.* launching of spacecraft *etc.* to moon —'**moonstone** *n.* transparent semiprecious stone —'**moonstruck** *a.* deranged

moor[1] (mʊə, mɔ:) *n.* tract of open uncultivated land, often hilly and heather-clad —'**moorhen** *n.* water bird

moor[2] (mʊə, mɔ:) *v.* secure (ship) with chains or ropes —'**moorage** *n.* place, charge for mooring —'**moorings** *pl.n.* 1. ropes *etc.* for mooring 2. something providing stability, security

Moor (mʊə, mɔ:) *n.* member of race in Morocco and adjoining parts of N Afr.

moose (mu:s) *n.* N Amer. deer, like elk

moot (mu:t) *a.* 1. that is open to argument, debatable —*vt.* 2. bring for discussion —*n.* 3. meeting

mop (mɒp) *n.* 1. bundle of yarn, cloth *etc.* on end of stick, used for cleaning 2. tangle (of hair *etc.*) —*vt.* 3. clean, wipe with mop or other absorbent stuff (**-pp-**)

mope (məʊp) *vi.* be gloomy, apathetic

moped ('məʊped) *n.* light motorized bicycle

moquette (mɒ'ket) *n.* thick fabric used for upholstery *etc.*

moraine (mɒ'reɪn) *n.* accumulated mass of debris, earth, stones *etc.*, deposited by glacier

moral ('mɒrəl) *a.* 1. pert. to right and wrong conduct 2. of good conduct —*n.* 3. practical lesson, *eg* of fable —*pl.* 4. habits with respect to right and wrong, *esp.* in matters of sex —'**moralist** *n.* teacher of morality —mo'**rality** *n.* 1. good moral conduct 2. moral goodness or badness 3. kind of medieval drama, containing moral lesson —'**moralize** *or* **-lise** *vi.* 1. write, talk about moral aspect of things —*vt.* 2. interpret morally —'**morally** *adv.* —**moral philosophy** branch of philosophy dealing with ethics —**moral victory** triumph that is psychological rather than practical

morale (mɒ'rɑ:l) *n.* degree of confidence, hope of person or group

morass (mɒ'ræs) *n.* 1. marsh 2. mess

moratorium (mɒrə'tɔ:rɪəm) *n.* 1. act authorizing postponement of payments *etc.* 2. delay (*pl.* **-ria** (-rɪə))

moray (mɒ'reɪ) *n.* large, voracious eel

morbid ('mɔ:bɪd) *a.* 1. unduly interested in death 2. gruesome 3. diseased

mordant ('mɔ:dənt) *a.* 1. biting 2. corrosive 3. scathing —*n.* 4. substance that fixes dyes

more (mɔ:) *comp. of* MANY *and* MUCH *a.* 1. greater in quantity or number —*adv.* 2. to a greater extent 3. in addition —*pron.* 4. greater or additional amount or number —**more'over** *adv.* besides, further

morel (mɒ'rel) *n.* edible fungus in which mushroom has pitted cap

morello (mɒ'reləʊ) *n.* variety of small dark sour cherry (*pl.* **-s**)

mores ('mɔ:reɪz) *pl.n.* customs and conventions embodying fundamental values of society *etc.*

morganatic marriage (mɔ:gə'nætɪk) marriage of king or prince in which wife does not share husband's rank or possessions and children do not inherit from father

morgen ('mɔ:gən) *n.* SA land unit, approx. two acres (0.8 hectare)

morgue (mɔ:g) *n.* mortuary

moribund ('mɒrɪbʌnd) *a.* 1. dying 2. stagnant

Mormon ('mɔ:mən) *n.* member of religious sect founded in U.S.A. —'**Mormonism** *n.*

mornay ('mɔ:neɪ) *a.* denoting cheese sauce used in various dishes

morning ('mɔ:nɪŋ) *n.* early part of day until noon —**morn** *n. Poet.* morning —**morning dress** formal day dress for men, comprising cutaway frock coat, usu. with grey trousers and top hat —**morning-glory** *n.* plant with trumpet-shaped flowers which close in late afternoon —**morning sickness** *inf.* nausea occurring shortly after rising during early months of pregnancy —**morning star** planet, usu. Venus, seen just before sunrise —**the morning after** *inf.* aftereffects of excess, *esp.* hangover

morocco (mɒ'rɒkəʊ) *n.* goatskin leather

moron ('mɔ:rɒn) *n.* 1. mentally deficient person 2. *inf.* fool —**mo'ronic** *a.*

morose (mɒ'rəʊs) *a.* sullen, moody

morphine ('mɔ:fi:n) *or* **morphia** ('mɔ:fɪə) *n.* narcotic extract of opium, drug used to induce sleep and relieve pain

morphology (mɔ:'fɒlədʒɪ) *n.* 1. science of structure of organisms 2. form and structure of words of a language —**morpho'logical** *a.*

morris dance ('mɒrɪs) English folk dance

morrow ('mɒrəʊ) n. Poet. next day

Morse (mɔːs) n. system of telegraphic signalling in which letters of alphabet are represented by combinations of dots and dashes, or short and long flashes

morsel ('mɔːsəl) n. fragment, small piece

mortal ('mɔːtəl) a. 1. subject to death 2. causing death —n. 3. mortal creature —**mor'tality** n. 1. state of being mortal 2. great loss of life 3. death rate —**mortally** adv. 1. fatally 2. deeply, intensely —**mortal sin** R.C.Ch. sin meriting damnation

mortar ('mɔːtə) n. 1. mixture of lime, sand and water for holding bricks and stones together 2. small cannon firing over short range 3. vessel in which substances are pounded —**'mortarboard** n. square academic cap

mortgage ('mɔːgɪdʒ) n. 1. conveyance of property as security for debt with provision that property be reconveyed on payment within agreed time —vt. 2. convey by mortgage 3. pledge as security —**mortga'gee** n. —**mortgag- or** (mɔːgɪ'dʒɔː) or **mortga'ger** n.

mortify ('mɔːtɪfaɪ) vt. 1. humiliate 2. subdue by self-denial —vi. 3. (of flesh) be affected with gangrene —**fied, -fying**) —**mortifi'cation** n.

mortise or **mortice** ('mɔːtɪs) n. 1. hole in piece of wood etc. to receive the tongue (tenon) and end of another piece —vt. 2. make mortise in 3. fasten by mortise and tenon —**mortise lock** lock embedded in door

mortuary ('mɔːtjʊərɪ) n. building where corpses are kept before burial —a. 2. of, for burial

mosaic (mə'zeɪɪk) n. 1. picture or pattern of small bits of coloured stone, glass etc. 2. this process of decoration

Mosaic (mə'zeɪɪk) a. of Moses

Moselle (məʊ'zɛl) n. light white wine

Moslem ('mɒzləm) n. see MUSLIM

mosque (mɒsk) n. Muslim temple

mosquito (mə'skiːtəʊ) n. various kinds of flying, biting insects (pl. -es)

moss (mɒs) n. 1. small plant growing in masses on moist surfaces 2. peat bog, swamp —**'mossy** a. covered with moss —**moss agate** agate with mosslike markings —**moss stitch** knitting stitch made up of alternate plain and purl stitches

mossie ('mɒsɪ) n. SA Cape sparrow

most (məʊst) sup. of MUCH and MANY a. 1. greatest in size, number, or degree —n. 2. greatest number, amount, or degree —adv. 3. in the greatest degree 4. US almost —**'mostly** adv. for the most part, generally, on the whole —**Most Reverend** courtesy title applied to archbishops

M.O.T. Ministry of Transport —**M.O.T. (test)**

compulsory annual test of the roadworthiness of vehicles over a certain age

mote (məʊt) n. tiny speck

motel (məʊ'tɛl) n. roadside hotel with accommodation for motorists and vehicles

motet (məʊ'tɛt) n. short sacred vocal composition

moth (mɒθ) n. 1. usu. nocturnal insect like butterfly 2. its grub —**'mothy** a. infested with moths —**'mothball** n. 1. small ball of camphor or naphthalene to repel moths from stored clothing etc. —vt. 2. put in mothballs 3. store, postpone etc. —**'motheaten** a. 1. eaten, damaged by grub of moth 2. decayed, scruffy

mother ('mʌðə) n. 1. female parent 2. head of religious community of women —a. 3. natural, native, inborn —vt. 4. act as mother to —**'motherhood** n. —**'motherly** a. —**Mother Carey's chicken** ('kɛərɪz) see **stormy petrel** at STORM —**mother country** 1. original country of colonists or settlers 2. person's native country —**mother earth** 1. earth as a mother, particularly in its fertility 2. soil; ground —**mother-in-law** n. mother of one's husband or wife —**mother of pearl** iridescent lining of certain shells —**mother tongue** 1. language first learned by child 2. language from which another has evolved

motif (məʊ'tiːf) n. 1. dominating theme 2. recurring design

motion ('məʊʃən) n. 1. process or action or way of moving 2. proposal in meeting 3. application to judge 4. evacuation of bowels —v. 5. signal or direct by sign —**'motionless** a. still, immobile

motive ('məʊtɪv) n. 1. that which makes person act in particular way 2. inner impulse —a. 3. causing motion —**'motivate** vt. 1. instigate 2. incite —**moti'vation** n. —**'motivative** a. —**mo- tive power** 1. any source of energy used to produce motion 2. means of supplying power to engine, vehicle etc.

mot juste (mo 'ʒyst) Fr. appropriate word or expression (pl. **mots justes** (mo 'ʒyst))

motley ('mɒtlɪ) a. 1. miscellaneous, varied 2. multicoloured —n. 3. motley colour or mixture 4. jester's particoloured dress

motocross ('məʊtəkrɒs) n. motorcycle race over rough course

motor ('məʊtə) n. 1. that which imparts movement 2. machine to supply motive power 3. motorcar —vi. 4. travel by car —**'motoring** n. —**'motorist** n. user of motorcar —**'motorize** or **-ise** vt. 1. equip with motor 2. provide with motor transport —**'motorbike**, **'motorboat**, **'motorcar**, **'motorcycle**, **motor scooter** n. vehicles driven by motor —**motorcade** ('məʊtəkeɪd) n. parade of cars —**motor nerve** nerve which controls muscular movement

—'**motorway** *n*. main road for fast-moving traffic, with limited access

mottle ('mɒt³l) *vt*. **1.** mark with blotches, variegate —*n*. **2.** arrangement of blotches **3.** blotch on surface

motto ('mɒtəʊ) *n*. **1.** saying adopted as rule of conduct **2.** short inscribed sentence **3.** word or sentence on heraldic crest (*pl*. **-s, -es**)

moue (mu) *Fr*. pouting look

moufflon ('mu:flɒn) *n*. wild mountain sheep

mould[1] *or U.S.* **mold** (məʊld) *n*. **1.** hollow object in which metal *etc*. is cast **2.** pattern for shaping **3.** character **4.** shape, form —*vt*. **5.** shape or pattern —'**moulding** *or U.S.* '**molding** *n*. **1.** moulded object **2.** ornamental edging **3.** decoration —'**mouldboard** *or U.S.* '**moldboard** *n*. curved blade of plough

mould[2] *or U.S.* **mold** (məʊld) *n*. fungoid growth caused by dampness —'**mouldy** *or U.S.* '**moldy** *a*. stale, musty

mould[3] *or U.S.* **mold** (məʊld) *n*. loose or surface earth —'**moulder** *or U.S.* '**molder** *vi*. decay into dust

moult *or U.S.* **molt** (məʊlt) *v*. **1.** cast or shed (fur, feathers *etc*.) —*n*. **2.** moulting

mound (maʊnd) *n*. **1.** heap of earth or stones **2.** small hill

mount (maʊnt) *vi*. **1.** rise **2.** increase **3.** get on horseback —*vt*. **4.** get up on **5.** frame (picture) **6.** fix, set up **7.** provide with horse —*n*. **8.** that on which thing is supported or fitted **9.** horse **10.** hill

mountain ('maʊntɪn) *n*. **1.** hill of great size **2.** surplus —**mountain'eer** *n*. one who lives among or climbs mountains —**mountain'eering** *n*. —'**mountainous** *a*. very high, rugged —**mountain lion** puma

mountebank ('maʊntɪbæŋk) *n*. charlatan, fake

Mountie *or* **Mounty** ('maʊntɪ) *n*. *inf*. member of Royal Canadian Mounted Police

mourn (mɔːn) *v*. feel, show sorrow (for) —'**mourner** *n*. —'**mournful** *a*. **1.** sad **2.** dismal —'**mournfully** *adv*. —'**mourning** *n*. **1.** grieving **2.** conventional signs of grief for death **3.** clothes of mourner —**mourning band** piece of black material, *esp*. armband, worn to indicate mourning

mouse (maʊs) *n*. **1.** small rodent (*pl*. **mice**) —*vi*. (maʊz) **2.** catch, hunt mice **3.** prowl —'**mouser** *n*. cat used for catching mice —'**mousy** *or* '**mousey** *a*. **1.** like mouse, *esp*. in colour **2.** meek, shy —'**mousetrap** *n*. **1.** any trap for catching mice **2.** *UK inf*. cheese of indifferent quality

mousse (muːs) *n*. sweet dish of flavoured cream whipped and chilled

moustache *or U.S.* **mustache** (mə'stɑːʃ) *n*. hair on the upper lip —**moustache cup** cup with partial cover to protect drinker's moustache

mouth (maʊθ) *n*. **1.** opening in head for eating, speaking *etc*. **2.** opening into anything hollow **3.** outfall of river **4.** entrance to harbour *etc*. —*vt*. (maʊð) **5.** declaim, *esp*. in public **6.** form (words) with lips without speaking **7.** take, move in mouth —'**mouthful** *n*. **1.** as much as is held in mouth at one time **2.** small quantity, as of food **3.** word *etc*. difficult to say —**mouth organ** harmonica —'**mouthpiece** *n*. **1.** end of anything placed between lips, *eg* pipe **2.** spokesman —'**mouthwash** *n*. medicated solution for cleansing mouth

move (muːv) *vt*. **1.** change position of **2.** stir emotions of **3.** incite **4.** propose for consideration —*vi*. **5.** change places **6.** change one's dwelling *etc*. **7.** take action —*n*. **8.** a moving **9.** motion towards some goal —'**movable** *or* '**moveable** *a./n*. —'**movement** *n*. **1.** process, action of moving **2.** moving parts of machine **3.** division of piece of music

movie ('muːvɪ) *US inf*. *n*. **1.** film —*pl*. **2.** cinema

mow (məʊ) *v*. cut (grass *etc*.) (**mown** *pp*.) —'**mower** *n*. man or machine that mows

mp *or* **m.p.** *Mus*. mezzo piano

M.P. 1. Member of Parliament **2.** Military Police **3.** Mounted Police

m.p.g. miles per gallon

m.p.h. miles per hour

M.Phil. *or* **M.Ph.** Master of Philosophy

Mr. ('mɪstə) mister

Mrs. ('mɪsɪz) title of married woman —**Mrs. Mopp** charwoman

MS Mississippi

Ms. (mɪz, məs) title used instead of Miss or Mrs.

MS. *or* **ms.** manuscript (*pl*. **MSS.** *or* **mss.**)

M.Sc. Master of Science

M.S.C. Manpower Services Commission

M.S.T. *US, C* Mountain Standard Time

MT Montana

Mt. *or* **mt.** Mount

M.Tech. Master of Technology

mu (mjuː) *n*. 12th letter in Gr. alphabet (M, μ)

much (mʌtʃ) *a*. **1.** existing in quantity —*n*. **2.** large amount **3.** a great deal **4.** important matter —*adv*. **5.** in a great degree **6.** nearly (**more** *comp*., **most** *sup*.)

mucilage ('mjuːsɪlɪdʒ) *n*. gum, glue

muck (mʌk) *n*. **1.** cattle dung **2.** unclean refuse —'**mucky** *a*. **1.** dirty **2.** messy **3.** unpleasant —'**muckrake** *vi*. seek out and expose scandal, *esp*. concerning public figures —'**muckraking** *n*. —'**muckraker** *n*. —'**muckraker** *n*. *UK inf*. profuse sweat or state of profuse sweating —**muck about** *UK sl*. **1.** waste time; misbehave **2.** annoy, interfere (with) —**muck up** *UK sl*. ruin, spoil

mucus ('mjuːkəs) *n*. viscid fluid secreted by mucous membrane —**mu'cosity** *n*. —'**mucous** *a*. **1.** resembling mucus **2.** secreting mucus **3.**

slimy —**mucous membrane** lining of canals and cavities of the body

mud (mʌd) *n.* **1.** wet and soft earth **2.** *inf.* slander —'**muddy** *a.* —'**mudguard** *n.* cover over wheel to prevent mud, water *etc.* being splashed —'**mudlark** *n.* **1.** formerly, one who made a living by picking up odds and ends in the mud of tidal rivers **2.** *sl., rare* street urchin —'**mudpack** *n.* cosmetic paste to improve complexion —'**mudslinger** *n.* —'**mudslinging** *n.* casting malicious slurs on an opponent, *esp.* in politics

muddle ('mʌdəl) *vt.* **1.** (*esp. with* up) confuse **2.** bewilder **3.** mismanage —*n.* **4.** confusion **5.** tangle

muesli ('mjuːzlɪ) *n.* mixture of grain, dried fruit *etc.* eaten with milk

muezzin (muː'ɛzɪn) *n.* crier who summons Muslims to prayer

muff[1] (mʌf) *n.* tube-shaped covering to keep the hands warm

muff[2] (mʌf) *vt.* miss, bungle, fail in

muffin ('mʌfɪn) *n.* round, spongy, flat scone

muffle ('mʌfəl) *vt.* wrap up, *esp.* to deaden sound —'**muffler** *n.* scarf

mufti ('mʌftɪ) *n.* plain clothes as distinguished from uniform, *eg* of soldier

mug[1] (mʌg) *n.* drinking cup

mug[2] (mʌg) *n. sl.* **1.** face **2.** fool, simpleton, one easily imposed upon —*vt.* **3.** *inf.* rob violently —'**mugger** *n.*

mug[3] (mʌg) *vt. inf.* (*esp. with* up) study hard

muggins ('mʌgɪnz) *n. inf.* fool, simpleton

muggy ('mʌgɪ) *a.* damp and stifling

mukluk ('mʌklʌk) *n.* **C** Eskimo's soft (sealskin) boot

mulatto (mjuː'lætəʊ) *n.* child of one White and one Negro parent (*pl.* **-s, -es**)

mulberry ('mʌlbərɪ, -brɪ) *n.* **1.** tree whose leaves are used to feed silkworms **2.** its purplish fruit

mulch (mʌltʃ) *n.* **1.** straw, leaves *etc.*, spread as protection for roots of plants —*vt.* **2.** protect thus

mulct (mʌlkt) *vt.* **1.** defraud **2.** fine

mule[1] (mjuːl) *n.* **1.** animal which is cross between horse and ass **2.** hybrid **3.** spinning machine —**muleteer** (mjuːlɪ'tɪə) *n.* mule driver —'**mulish** *a.* obstinate

mule[2] (mjuːl) *n.* backless shoe or slipper

mull[1] (mʌl) *vt.* heat (wine) with sugar and spices —**mull over** think over, ponder

mull[2] (mʌl) *n.* light muslin fabric of soft texture

mullah *or* **mulla** ('mʌlə, 'mʊlə) *n.* Muslim theologian

mullein ('mʌlɪn) *n.* plant with tall spikes of yellow flowers

mullet ('mʌlɪt) *n.* edible sea fish

mulligatawny (mʌlɪgə'tɔːnɪ) *n.* soup made with curry powder

mullion ('mʌlɪən) *n.* upright dividing bar in window —'**mullioned** *a.*

multangular (mʌl'tæŋgjʊlə) *or* **multiangular** *a.* having many angles

multi- (*comb. form*) many, as in *multiracial, multistorey*. Such words are omitted where the meaning may easily be found from the simple word

multifarious (mʌltɪ'fɛərɪəs) *a.* of various kinds or parts —**multi'fariously** *adv.*

multilateral (mʌltɪ'lætərəl, -'lætrəl) *a.* **1.** of or involving more than two nations or parties **2.** having many sides

multinational (mʌltɪ'næʃənəl) *a.* (of large business company) operating in several countries

multiple ('mʌltɪpəl) *a.* **1.** having many parts —*n.* **2.** quantity which contains another an exact number of times —**multipli'cand** *n. Maths.* number to be multiplied —**multipli'cation** *n.* —**multi'plicity** *n.* variety, greatness in number —'**multiplier** *n.* **1.** person or thing that multiplies **2.** number by which multiplicand is multiplied **3.** *Phys.* any instrument, as photomultiplier, for increasing effect —'**multiply** *vt.* **1.** increase in number **2.** add (a number) to itself a given number of times —*vi.* **3.** increase in number or amount (**-plied, -plying**) —**multiple-choice** *a.* having a number of possible given answers out of which the correct one must be chosen —**multiple sclerosis** chronic disease of central nervous system, resulting in speech disorder, partial paralysis *etc.* —**multiplication table** one of group of tables giving results of multiplying two numbers together

multiplex ('mʌltɪplɛks) *a. Telecomm.* capable of transmitting numerous messages over same wire or channel

multitude ('mʌltɪtjuːd) *n.* **1.** great number **2.** great crowd **3.** populace —**multi'tudinous** *a.* very numerous

mum[1] (mʌm) *n. inf.* mother

mumble ('mʌmbəl) *vi.* **1.** speak indistinctly —*v.* **2.** mutter

mumbo jumbo ('mʌmbəʊ) **1.** foolish religious reverence or incantation **2.** meaningless or unnecessarily complicated language

mummer ('mʌmə) *n.* actor in dumb show —**mum** *a.* **1.** silent —*v.* **2.** act in mime (**-mm-**) —'**mummery** *n.* dumb-show acting

mummy[1] ('mʌmɪ) *n.* embalmed body —'**mummify** *v.* (**-fied, -fying**)

mumps (mʌmps) *pl.n.* infectious disease marked by swelling in the glands of the neck

mun. municipal

munch (mʌntʃ) v. 1. chew noisily and vigorously 2. crunch

mundane ('mʌndeɪn, mʌn'deɪn) a. 1. ordinary, everyday 2. belonging to this world, earthly

municipal (mjuː'nɪsɪpəl) a. belonging to affairs of city or town —**munici'pality** n. 1. city or town with local self-government 2. its governing body

munificent (mjuː'nɪfɪsənt) a. very generous —**mu'nificence** n. bounty

muniments ('mjuːnɪmənts) pl.n. title deeds, documents verifying ownership

munition (mjuː'nɪʃən) n. (usu. pl.) military stores

muon ('mjuːɒn) n. positive or negative elementary particle with mass 207 times that of electron

mural ('mjuərəl) n. 1. painting on a wall —a. 2. of or on a wall

murder ('mɜːdə) n. 1. unlawful premeditated killing of human being —vt. 2. kill thus —'**murderer** n. ('**murderess** fem.) —'**murderous** a.

murk or **mirk** (mɜːk) n. thick darkness —'**murky** or '**mirky** a. gloomy

murmur ('mɜːmə) n. 1. low, indistinct sound —vi. 2. make such a sound 3. complain —vt. 4. utter in a low voice

murrain ('mʌrɪn) n. cattle plague

mus. 1. museum 2. music(al)

Mus.B. or **Mus.Bac.** Bachelor of Music

muscat ('mʌskət, -kæt) n. 1. musk-flavoured grape 2. raisin —**musca'tel** n. 1. muscat 2. strong wine made from it

muscle ('mʌsəl) n. 1. part of body which produces movement by contracting 2. system of muscles —**muscular** ('mʌskjʊlə) a. 1. with well-developed muscles 2. strong 3. of, like muscle —**musculature** ('mʌskjʊlətʃə) n. 1. arrangement of muscles in organ or part 2. total muscular system of organism —**muscle-bound** a. with muscles stiff through overdevelopment —'**muscleman** n. 1. man with highly developed muscles 2. henchman employed by gangster etc. to intimidate or use violence upon victims —**muscular dystrophy** disease with wasting of muscles —**muscle in** inf. force one's way in

Muscovy duck ('mʌskəvɪ) or **musk duck** large crested widely domesticated S Amer. duck

Mus.D. or **Mus.Doc.** Doctor of Music

muse (mjuːz) vi. 1. ponder 2. consider meditatively 3. be lost in thought —n. 4. state of musing or abstraction 5. reverie

Muse (mjuːz) n. one of the nine goddesses inspiring learning and the arts

museum (mjuː'zɪəm) n. (place housing) collection of natural, artistic, historical or scientific objects —**museum piece** 1. object fit

to be kept in museum 2. inf. person or thing regarded as antiquated

mush (mʌʃ) n. 1. soft pulpy mass 2. inf. cloying sentimentality —'**mushy** a.

mushroom ('mʌʃruːm, -rʊm) n. 1. fungoid growth, typically with stem and cap structure, some species edible —vi. 2. shoot up rapidly 3. expand —**mushroom cloud** mushroom-shaped cloud produced by nuclear explosion

music ('mjuːzɪk) n. 1. art form using melodious and harmonious combination of notes 2. laws of this 3. composition in this art —'**musical** a. 1. of, like music 2. interested in, or with instinct for, music 3. pleasant to ear —n. 4. show, film in which music plays essential part —'**musically** adv. —**mu'sician** n. —**musi'cologist** n. —**musi'cology** n. scientific study of music —**musical chairs** party game in which players walk around chairs to music, there being one fewer chairs than players: when music stops, player without a chair is eliminated —**musical comedy** light dramatic entertainment with songs, dances etc. —**music box** or **musical box** mechanical instrument that plays tunes by means of pins on revolving cylinder striking tuned teeth of comblike metal plate —**music centre** single hi-fi unit containing turntable, amplifier, radio and cassette player —**music hall** variety theatre

musk (mʌsk) n. 1. scent obtained from gland of **musk deer** 2. any of various plants with similar scent —'**musky** a. —'**muskmelon** n. any of several varieties of melon, such as cantaloupe, having ribbed or warty rind and musky aroma —**musk ox** ox of Arctic Amer. —'**muskrat** n. 1. N Amer. rodent found near water 2. its fur —**musk rose** rose cultivated for its white musk-scented flowers

muskeg ('mʌskɛg) n. C boggy hollow

muskellunge ('mʌskəlʌndʒ) or **maskinonge** ('mæskɒnɒndʒ) n. N Amer. freshwater game fish

musket ('mʌskɪt) n. Hist. infantryman's gun —**muske'teer** n. —'**musketry** n. (use of) small firearms

Muslim ('mʊzlɪm, 'mʌz-) or **Moslem** n. 1. follower of religion of Islam —a. 2. of religion, culture etc. of Islam

muslin ('mʌzlɪn) n. fine cotton fabric —'**muslined** a.

musquash ('mʌskwɒʃ) n. muskrat

mussel ('mʌsəl) n. bivalve shellfish

must¹ (mʌst; unstressed məst, məs) v. aux. 1. be obliged to, or certain to —n. 2. something one must do

must² (mʌst) n. 1. newly-pressed grape juice 2. unfermented wine

mustang ('mʌstæŋ) n. wild horse

mustard ('mʌstəd) n. 1. powder made from the

seeds of a plant, used in paste as a condiment **2.** the plant —**mustard gas** poisonous gas causing blistering

muster ('mʌstə) v. **1.** assemble —n. **2.** assembly, *esp.* for exercise, inspection

musty ('mʌstɪ) a. mouldy, stale —**must** *or* '**mustiness** n.

mutate (mjuː'teɪt) v. (cause to) undergo mutation —'**mutable** a. liable to change —'**mutant** a. mutated animal, plant *etc.* —**mu'tation** n. change, *esp.* genetic change causing divergence from kind or racial type

mute (mjuːt) a. **1.** dumb **2.** silent —n. **3.** dumb person **4.** *Mus.* contrivance to soften tone of instruments —'**muted** a. **1.** (of sound) muffled **2.** (of light) subdued —'**mutely** adv.

muti ('muːtɪ) n. **SA** (herbal) medicine

mutilate ('mjuːtɪleɪt) vt. **1.** deprive of a limb or other part **2.** damage, deface —**muti'lation** n. —'**mutilator** n.

mutiny ('mjuːtɪnɪ) n. **1.** rebellion against authority, esp. against officers of disciplined body —vi. **2.** commit mutiny (**mutinied**, '**mutinying**) —**muti'neer** n. —'**mutinous** a. rebellious

mutt (mʌt) n. *inf.* **1.** stupid person **2.** dog

mutter ('mʌtə) vi. **1.** speak with mouth nearly closed, indistinctly **2.** grumble —vt. **3.** utter in such tones —n. **4.** act, sound of muttering

mutton ('mʌt°n) n. flesh of sheep used as food —**mutton bird** migratory seabird —'**mutton-chops** pl.n. side whiskers trimmed in shape of chops —'**muttonhead** n. *sl.* fool

mutual ('mjuːtʃʊəl) a. **1.** done, possessed etc. by each of two with respect to the other **2.** reciprocal **3.** *inf.* common to both or all —'**mutually** adv.

Muzak ('mjuːzæk) n. **R** recorded light music played in shops *etc.*

muzzle ('mʌz°l) n. **1.** mouth and nose of animal **2.** cover for these to prevent biting **3.** open end of gun —vt. **4.** put muzzle on **5.** silence, gag

muzzy ('mʌzɪ) a. indistinct, confused, muddled

MV motor vessel

mW milliwatt(s)

MW megawatt(s)

Mx *Phys.* maxwell

my (maɪ) a. belonging to me —**my'self** pron. emphatic or reflexive form of I

myalgia (maɪ'ældʒɪə) n. pain in a muscle

mycelium (maɪ'siːlɪəm) n. vegetative body of fungi (pl. -**lia** (-lɪə)) —**my'celial** a.

Mycenaean (maɪsɪ'niːən) a. **1.** of ancient Mycenae or its inhabitants **2.** of Aegean civilization of Mycenae (1400 to 1100 B.C.)

mycology (maɪ'kɒlədʒɪ) n. science of fungi

myna, mynah, or **mina** ('maɪnə) n. Indian bird related to starling

myopia (maɪ'əʊpɪə) n. short-sightedness —**my-opic** (maɪ'ɒpɪk) a.

myosotis (maɪə'səʊtɪs) n. any of various kinds of small plant with blue, pink or white flowers, eg forget-me-not

myriad ('mɪrɪəd) a. **1.** innumerable —n. **2.** large indefinite number

myriapod ('mɪrɪəpɒd) n. **1.** any of group of terrestrial arthropods having long segmented body, such as the centipede —a. **2.** of or belonging to this group

myrmidon ('mɜːmɪdɒn, -d°n) n. follower or henchman

myrrh (mɜː) n. aromatic gum, formerly used as incense

myrtle ('mɜːt°l) n. flowering evergreen shrub

myself (maɪ'sɛlf) pron. see MY

mystery ('mɪstərɪ, -trɪ) n. **1.** obscure or secret thing **2.** anything strange or inexplicable **3.** religious rite **4.** in Middle Ages, biblical play —**mys'terious** a. —**mys'teriously** adv.

mystic ('mɪstɪk) n. **1.** one who seeks divine, spiritual knowledge, esp. by prayer, contemplation *etc.* —a. **2.** of hidden meaning, *esp.* in religious sense —'**mystical** a. —'**mysticism** n.

mystify ('mɪstɪfaɪ) vt. bewilder, puzzle (-**fied,** -**fying**) —**mystifi'cation** n.

mystique (mɪ'stiːk) n. aura of mystery, power *etc.*

myth (mɪθ) n. **1.** tale with supernatural characters or events **2.** invented story **3.** imaginary person or object —'**mythical** a. —**mytho'logical** a. —**my'thologist** n. —**my-'thology** n. **1.** myths collectively **2.** study of them

myxomatosis (mɪksəmə'təʊsɪs) n. contagious, fatal disease of rabbits caused by a virus

N,n

n *or* **N** (ɛn) n. **1.** 14th letter of English alphabet **2.** speech sound represented by this letter (pl. **n's,** **N's** *or* **Ns**)

n (ɛn) a. indefinite number (of) —**nth** (ɛnθ) a. **1.** *Maths.* of unspecified ordinal number, usu. greatest in series **2.** *inf.* being last or most extreme of long series —**to the nth degree** *inf.* to the utmost extreme

N 1. *Chess* knight **2.** *Chem.* nitrogen **3.** *Phys.* newton **4.** north(ern)

n. 1. neuter **2.** noun **3.** number

Na *Chem.* sodium

NAAFI ('næfɪ) n. organization providing canteens *etc.* for the services (*N*avy, *A*rmy and *A*ir *F*orce *I*nstitutes)

naartjie ('nɑːtʃɪ) n. **SA** tangerine

nab (næb) *vt. inf.* **1.** arrest criminal **2.** catch suddenly (**-bb-**)

nacre ('neɪkə) *n.* **1.** mother-of-pearl **2.** shellfish

nadir ('neɪdɪə, 'næ-) *n.* **1.** point opposite the zenith **2.** lowest point

nae (neɪ) *Scots word for* no (sense 1)

nag[1] (næg) *v.* **1.** scold or annoy constantly **2.** cause pain to constantly (**-gg-**) —*n.* **3.** nagging **4.** one who nags

nag[2] (næg) *n. inf.* **1.** horse **2.** small horse for riding

naiad ('naɪæd) *n.* water nymph (*pl.* **-s, -ades** (-ədi:z))

naïf (nɑː'iːf) *a. see* NAIVE

nail (neɪl) *n.* **1.** horny shield at ends of fingers, toes **2.** claw **3.** small metal spike for fixing wood *etc.* —*vt.* **4.** fix, stud with nails **5.** *inf.* catch —'**nailfile** *n.* small file used to trim nails —**nail set** punch for driving head of nail below or flush with surrounding surface

naive, naïve (nɑː'iːv, naɪ'iːv), *or* **naïf** *a.* simple, unaffected, ingenuous —**naiveté, naïveté** (nɑːiːv'teɪ) *or* **naivety** (naɪ'iːvtɪ) *n.*

naked ('neɪkɪd) *a.* **1.** without clothes **2.** exposed, bare **3.** undisguised —**nakedly** *adv.* —**nakedness** *n.* —**naked eye** the eye unassisted by any optical instrument

NALGO ('nælgəʊ) National and Local Government Officers' Association

namby-pamby (næmbɪ'pæmbɪ) *a.* **1.** weakly **2.** sentimental **3.** insipid —*n.* **4.** namby-pamby person

name (neɪm) *n.* **1.** word by which person, thing *etc.* is denoted **2.** reputation **3.** title **4.** credit **5.** family **6.** famous person —*vt.* **7.** give name to **8.** call by name **9.** entitle **10.** appoint **11.** mention **12.** specify —'**nameless** *a.* without a name **2.** indescribable **3.** too dreadful to be mentioned **4.** obscure —'**namely** *adv.* that is to say —**name day 1.** *R.C.Ch.* feast day of saint whose name one bears **2.** *St. Ex.* day before setting day, when stockbrokers are given names of purchasers (*also* **ticket day**) —**name-dropper** *n.* —**name-dropping** *n. inf.* referring frequently to famous people, *esp.* as though they were intimate friends, in order to impress others —'**name-plate** *n.* small panel on door bearing occupant's name —'**namesake** *n.* person with same name as another

nancy *or* **nancy boy** ('nænsɪ) *n.* effeminate or homosexual boy or man

nankeen (næn'kiːn) *or* **nankin** ('nænkɪn) *n.* **1.** buff-coloured cotton fabric **2.** pale greyish-yellow colour

nanny ('nænɪ) *n.* child's nurse —**nanny goat** she-goat

nano- (*comb. form*) 10^{-9}, as in *nanosecond*

nap[1] (næp) *vi.* **1.** take short sleep, *esp.* in daytime (**-pp-**) —*n.* **2.** short sleep

nap[2] (næp) *n.* downy surface on cloth made by projecting fibres

nap[3] (næp) *n.* card game similar to whist

napalm ('neɪpɑːm, 'næ-) *n.* jellied petrol, highly inflammable, used in bombs *etc.*

nape (neɪp) *n.* back of neck

naphtha ('næfθə, 'næp-) *n.* inflammable oil distilled from coal *etc.* —'**naphthalene** *n.* white crystalline product distilled from coal tar, used in disinfectants, mothballs *etc.*

napkin ('næpkɪn) *n.* **1.** cloth, paper for wiping fingers or lips at table, serviette **2.** small towel **3.** nappy

nappy ('næpɪ) *n.* towelling cloth or other material placed around waist, between legs, of baby to absorb its excrement

narcissus (nɑː'sɪsəs) *n.* genus of bulbous plants including daffodil, jonquil, *esp.* one with white flowers (*pl.* **-cissi** (-'sɪsaɪ)) —**narcissism** *n.* abnormal love and admiration of oneself —'**narcissist** *n.*

narcotic (nɑː'kɒtɪk) *n.* **1.** any of a group of drugs, including morphine and opium, producing numbness and stupor, used medicinally but addictive —*a.* **2.** of narcotics or narcosis —**narcosis** (nɑː'kəʊsɪs) *n.* effect of narcotic

nard (nɑːd) *n.* **1.** *see* spikenard *at* SPIKE **2.** plant whose aromatic roots were formerly used in medicine

nark (nɑːk) *vt. sl.* annoy, irritate

narrate (nə'reɪt) *vt.* relate, recount, tell (story) —**nar'ration** *n.* —'**narrative** *n.* **1.** account, story —*a.* **2.** relating —**nar'rator** *n.*

narrow ('nærəʊ) *a.* **1.** of little breadth, *esp.* in comparison to length **2.** limited **3.** barely adequate or successful —*v.* **4.** make, become narrow —'**narrowly** *adv.* —'**narrowness** *n.* —'**narrows** *pl.n.* narrow part of straits —**narrow boat** long narrow bargelike boat used on canals —**narrow gauge** smaller distance between lines of railway than standard gauge of 56½ inches —**narrow-gauge** *a.* of railway with narrow gauge —**narrow-minded** *a.* **1.** illiberal **2.** bigoted —**narrow-mindedness** *n.* prejudice, bigotry

narwhal, narwal ('nɑːwəl), *or* **narwhale** ('nɑːweɪl) *n.* arctic whale with tusk developed from teeth

N.A.S. National Association of Schoolmasters

NASA ('næsə) National Aeronautics and Space Administration

nasal ('neɪzəl) *a.* **1.** of nose —*n.* **2.** sound partly produced in nose —'**nasalize** *or* **-lise** *vt.* make nasal in sound —'**nasally** *adv.*

nascent ('næsənt, 'neɪ-) a. 1. just coming into existence 2. springing up

nasturtium (nə'stɜːʃəm) n. 1. genus of plants which includes the watercress 2. trailing garden plant with red or orange flowers

nasty ('nɑːstɪ) a. foul, disagreeable, unpleasant —'**nastily** adv. —'**nastiness** n.

nat. 1. national 2. native 3. natural

natal ('neɪtəl) a. of birth

natatory (nə'teɪtərɪ) or **natatorial** (næ-tə'tɔːrɪəl) a. of swimming —na'**tation** n.

nation ('neɪʃən) n. people or race organized as a state —**national** ('næʃənəl) a. 1. belonging or pert. to a nation 2. public, general —n. 3. member of a nation —**nationalism** ('næʃənəlɪzəm) n. 1. loyalty, devotion to one's country 2. movement for independence of state, people, ruled by another —**nationalist** ('næʃənəlɪst) n./a. —**nationality** (næʃə'nælɪtɪ) n. 1. national quality or feeling 2. fact of belonging to particular nation —**nationalization** or -**lisation** (næʃənəlaɪ'zeɪʃən) n. acquisition and management of industries by the State —**nationalize** or -**lise** ('næʃənəlaɪz) vt. convert (private industry, resources etc.) to state control —**nationally** ('næʃənəlɪ) adv. —**national assistance** old name for supplementary benefit —**national debt** total financial obligations incurred by nation's central government —**National Front** political organization opposing immigration and advocating extreme nationalism —**national grid** UK 1. network of high-voltage electric power lines linking major electric power stations 2. metric coordinate system used in Ordnance Survey maps —**National Health Service** system of medical services financed mainly by taxation —**national insurance** state insurance scheme providing payments to the unemployed, sick etc. —**national park** area of land controlled by the state to preserve its natural beauty etc. —**National Trust** organization concerned with preservation of historic buildings and areas of countryside of great beauty

native ('neɪtɪv) a. 1. inborn 2. born in particular place 3. found in pure state 4. that was place of one's birth —n. 5. one born in a place 6. member of indigenous race of a country 7. species of plant, animal etc. originating in a place

nativity (nə'tɪvɪtɪ) n. 1. birth 2. time, circumstances of birth 3. (N-) birth of Christ

NATO ('neɪtəʊ) North Atlantic Treaty Organization

NATSOPA (næt'səʊpə) National Society of Operative Printers and Assistants

natter ('nætə) vi. inf. talk idly

natterjack ('nætədʒæk) n. small European toad

natty ('nætɪ) a. neat and smart; spruce —'**nattily** adv.

nature ('neɪtʃə) n. 1. innate or essential qualities of person or thing 2. class, sort 3. life force 4. (oft. N-) power underlying all phenomena in material world 5. material world as a whole 6. natural unspoilt scenery or countryside, and plants and animals in it 7. disposition, temperament —**natural** ('nætʃrəl) a. 1. of, according to, occurring in, provided by, nature 2. inborn 3. normal 4. unaffected 5. illegitimate —n. 6. something, somebody well suited for something 7. Mus. character ( ) used to remove effect of sharp or flat preceding it —**naturalism** ('nætʃrəlɪzəm) n. 1. movement, esp. in art and literature, advocating realism 2. belief that all religious truth is based on study of natural causes and processes 3. Philos. rational account of world in terms of natural forces 4. action or thought caused by natural instincts —**naturalist** ('nætʃrəlɪst) n. student of natural history —**naturalistic** (nætʃrə'lɪstɪk) a. of or imitating nature in effect or characteristics —**naturalization** or -**lisation** (nætʃrəlaɪ'zeɪʃən) n. —**naturalize** or -**lise** ('nætʃrəlaɪz) vt. 1. admit to citizenship 2. accustom to new climate —**naturally** ('nætʃrəlɪ) adv. 1. of or according to nature 2. by nature 3. of course —'**naturism** n. 1. nature-worship 2. nudism —'**naturist** n. —**natural gas** gaseous mixture, consisting mainly of methane, trapped below ground; used extensively as fuel —**natural history** study of animals and plants —**natural number** any of positive integers 1, 2, 3, 4, ... —**natural philosophy** physical science, esp. physics —**natural resources** naturally occurring materials such as coal etc. —**natural science** any of sciences that are involved in study of physical world, including biology, physics etc. —**natural selection** process resulting in survival of those individuals from population of animals etc. that are best adapted to prevailing environmental conditions —**nature trail** path through countryside of particular interest to naturalists

naught (nɔːt) n. 1. obs. nothing 2. cipher 0 —**set at naught** defy, disregard

naughty ('nɔːtɪ) a. 1. disobedient, not behaving well 2. inf. mildly indecent —'**naughtily** adv.

nausea ('nɔːzɪə, -sɪə) n. feeling that precedes vomiting —**nauseate** vt. sicken —'**nauseous** a. 1. disgusting 2. causing nausea

nautical ('nɔːtɪkəl) a. 1. of seamen or ships 2. marine —**nautical mile** 1852 metres

nautilus ('nɔːtɪləs) n. univalvular shellfish (pl. -es, -tili (-tɪlaɪ))

naval ('neɪvəl) a. see NAVY

nave[1] (neɪv) n. main part of church

nave[2] (neɪv) n. hub of wheel

navel ('neɪvəl) n. small scar, depression in middle of abdomen where umbilical cord was attached (also um'bilicus)

navigate ('nævɪgeɪt) v. 1. plan, direct, plot path or position of (ship etc.) 2. travel —'**navigable** a. —navi'**gation** n. science of directing course of seagoing vessel, or of aircraft in flight 2. shipping —'**navigator** n. one who navigates

navvy ('nævɪ) n. labourer employed on roads, railways etc.

navy ('neɪvɪ) n. 1. fleet 2. warships of country with their crews and organization —a. 3. navy-blue —'**naval** a. of the navy —**navy-blue** a. very dark blue

Nazi ('nɑːtsɪ) n. 1. member of the National Socialist political party in Germany, 1919-45 2. one who thinks, acts like a Nazi (pl. -s) —a. 3. of Nazis —'**Nazism** or '**Naziism** n. Nazi doctrine

Nb Chem. niobium

NB New Brunswick

NB, N.B., or **n.b.** nota bene

NC North Carolina

N.C.B. National Coal Board

N.C.O. noncommissioned officer

Nd Chem. neodymium

ND North Dakota

N.D.P. C New Democratic Party

Ne Chem. neon

NE 1. northeast(ern) 2. Nebraska

Neanderthal (nɪ'ændətɑːl) a. of a type of primitive man

neap (niːp) a. low —**neap tide** the low tide at the first and third quarters of the moon

Neapolitan (nɪə'pɒlɪtən) n. 1. native of Naples —a. 2. of Naples

near (nɪə) prep. 1. close to —adv. 2. at or to a short distance —a. 3. close at hand 4. closely related 5. narrow, so as barely to escape 6. stingy 7. (of vehicles, horses etc.) left —v. 8. approach —'**nearly** adv. 1. closely 2. almost —'**nearness** n. —'**nearby** a. adjacent —**Near East** 1. see **Middle East** at MIDDLE 2. formerly, Balkan States and area of Ottoman Empire —**near-sighted** a. relating to or suffering from myopia

neat (niːt) a. 1. tidy, orderly 2. efficient 3. precise, deft 4. cleverly worded 5. undiluted 6. simple and elegant 7. sl., chiefly US pleasing; admirable; excellent —'**neaten** vt. make neat; tidy —'**neatly** adv. —'**neatness** n.

neath or '**neath** (niːθ) prep. obs. beneath

N.E.B. 1. New English Bible 2. National Enterprise Board

nebula ('nɛbjʊlə) n. Astron. diffuse cloud of particles, gases (pl. -s, -ulae (-juliː)) —'**nebulous** a. 1. cloudy 2. vague, indistinct

necessary ('nɛsɪsərɪ) a. 1. needful, requisite, that must be done 2. unavoidable, inevitable —'**necessarily** adv. —ne'**cessitate** vt. make necessary —ne'**cessitous** a. poor, needy, destitute —ne'**cessity** n. 1. something needed, requisite 2. constraining power or state of affairs 3. compulsion 4. poverty

neck (nɛk) n. 1. part of body joining head to shoulders 2. narrower part of a bottle etc. 3. narrow piece of anything between wider parts —vi. 4. sl. embrace, cuddle —'**neckerchief** n. kerchief for the neck —'**necklet** n. neck ornament, piece of fur etc. —'**necklace** ('nɛklɪs) n. ornament round the neck —'**necktie** n. US see TIE (sense 6)

necro- or before vowel **necr-** (comb. form) death, dead body, dead tissue, as in necrosis

necromancy ('nɛkrəʊmænsɪ) n. magic, esp. by communication with dead —'**necromancer** n. wizard

necrophilia (nɛkrəʊ'fɪlɪə) n. sexual attraction for or intercourse with dead bodies (also **necro'mania, ne'crophilism**)

necropolis (nɛ'krɒpəlɪs) n. cemetery (pl. -es, -oleis (-əleɪs))

nectar ('nɛktə) n. 1. honey of flowers 2. drink of the gods —'**nectary** n. honey gland of flower

nectarine ('nɛktərɪn) n. variety of peach

N.E.D.C. National Economic Development Council

née or **nee** (neɪ) a. indicating maiden name of married woman

need (niːd) vt. 1. want, require —n. 2. (state, instance of) want 3. requirement 4. necessity 5. poverty —'**needful** a. necessary, requisite —'**needless** a. unnecessary —**needs** adv. of necessity (esp. in **needs must** or **must needs**) —'**needy** a. poor, in want

needle ('niːdəl) n. 1. pointed pin with an eye and no head, for sewing 2. long, pointed pin for knitting 3. pointer of gauge, dial 4. magnetized bar of compass 5. stylus for record player 6. leaf of fir or pine 7. obelisk 8. inf. hypodermic syringe —vt. 9. inf. goad, provoke —'**needlecord** n. corduroy fabric with narrow ribs —'**needlepoint** n. 1. embroidery done on canvas with various stitches so as to resemble tapestry 2. point lace —**needle time** chiefly UK time allocated by radio channel to broadcasting of recorded music —'**needlework** n. embroidery, sewing

ne'er (nɛə) adv. Lit. never —**ne'er-do-well** n. worthless person

nefarious (nɪ'fɛərɪəs) a. wicked

neg. negative(ly)

negate (nɪ'geɪt) vt. deny, nullify —ne'**gation** n. contradiction, denial

negative ('nɛgətɪv) a. 1. expressing denial or refusal 2. lacking enthusiasm, energy, interest 3. not positive 4. (of electrical charge) having the same polarity as the charge of an electron —n. 5. negative word or statement 6. *Photog.* picture made by action of light on chemicals in which lights and shades are reversed —vt. 7. disprove, reject —**negative feedback** *see* **feedback** *at* FEED

neglect (nı'glɛkt) vt. 1. disregard, take no care of 2. omit through carelessness —vi. 3. fail (to do) —n. 4. fact of neglecting or being neglected —ne'glectful a.

negligee, negligée, *or* **negligé** ('nɛglıʒeı) n. woman's light, gauzy nightdress or dressing gown

negligence ('nɛglıdʒəns) n. 1. neglect 2. carelessness —'**negligent** a. —'**negligible** a. 1. able to be disregarded 2. very small or unimportant

negotiate (nı'gəʊʃıeıt) vi. 1. discuss with view to mutual settlement —vt. 2. arrange by conference 3. transfer (bill, cheque *etc.*) 4. get over, past, around (obstacle) —ne'gotiable a. —negoti'ation n. 1. treating with another on business 2. discussion 3. transference of (bill, cheque *etc.*) —ne'gotiator n.

Negro ('niːgrəʊ) n. member of Black orig. Afr. race (pl. -es) ('Negress fem.) —'negritude n. 1. fact of being a Negro 2. awareness and cultivation of Negro culture *etc.* —'Negroid a. of or like a Negro

negus ('niːgəs) n. hot drink of port and lemon juice

neigh (neı) n. 1. cry of horse —vi. 2. utter this cry

neighbour *or U.S.* **neighbor** ('neıbə) n. one who lives near another —'**neighbourhood** *or U.S.* '**neighborhood** n. 1. district 2. people of a district 3. region round about —'**neighbouring** *or U.S.* '**neighboring** a. situated nearby —'**neighbourly** *or U.S.* '**neighborly** a. as or befitting a good or friendly neighbour 2. friendly 3. sociable 4. helpful

neither ('naıðə, 'niːðə) a./pron. 1. not the one or the other —adv. 2. on the one hand 3. not either —conj. 4. not

nelson ('nɛlsən) n. wrestling hold in which wrestler places his arm(s) under his opponent's arm(s) from behind and exerts pressure with his palms on back of opponent's neck

nematode ('nɛmətəʊd) n. any of class of unsegmented worms having tough outer cuticle, including hookworm and filaria (also **nematode worm,** '**roundworm**)

nem. con. nemine contradicente (*Lat.,* unanimously)

nemesia (nı'miːʒə) n. garden plant with flowers of various colours

Nemesis ('nɛmısıs) n. 1. retribution 2. the goddess of vengeance (pl. -ses (-siːz))

neo- *or sometimes before vowel* **ne-** (*comb. form*) new, later, revived in modified form, based upon

neodymium (niːəʊ'dımıəm) n. silvery-white metallic element of lanthanide series

Neolithic (niːəʊ'lıθık) a. of the later Stone Age

neologism (nı'ɒlədʒızəm) *or* **neology** n. new-coined word or phrase —ne'**ologize** *or* **-gise** vi.

neon ('niːɒn) n. one of the inert constituent gases of the atmosphere, used in illuminated signs and lights —**neon lamp** tube containing neon, that gives red glow when voltage is applied

neophyte ('niːəʊfaıt) n. 1. new convert 2. beginner, novice

nephew ('nɛvjuː, 'nɛf-) n. brother's or sister's son

nephritis (nı'fraıtıs) n. inflammation of a kidney

nepotism ('nɛpətızəm) n. undue favouritism towards one's relations

Neptune ('nɛptjuːn) n. 1. god of the sea 2. planet second farthest from sun

neptunium (nɛp'tjuːnıəm) n. synthetic metallic element

nerve (nɜːv) n. 1. sinew, tendon 2. fibre or bundle of fibres conveying feeling, impulses to motion *etc.* to and from brain and other parts of body 3. assurance 4. coolness in danger 5. audacity —pl. 6. irritability, unusual sensitiveness to fear, annoyance *etc.* —vt. 7. give courage or strength to —'**nerveless** a. 1. without nerves 2. useless 3. weak 4. paralysed —'**nervous** a. 1. excitable, timid 2. apprehensive, worried 3. of the nerves —'**nervously** adv. —'**nervousness** n. —'**nervy** a. 1. nervous 2. jumpy 3. irritable 4. on edge —**nerve cell** *see* NEURON —**nerve centre** 1. group of nerve cells associated with specific function 2. principal source of control over any complex activity —**nerve gas** poisonous gas that has paralysing effect on central nervous system that can be fatal —**nerve-racking** *or* **nerve-wracking** a. very distressing, exhausting or harrowing —**nervous breakdown** condition of mental, emotional disturbance, disability —**nervous system** sensory and control apparatus of animals, consisting of network of nerve cells (*see also* NEURON)

ness (nɛs) n. headland, cape

-ness (*comb. form*) state, condition, quality, as in *greatness, selfishness*

nest (nɛst) n. 1. place in which bird lays and hatches its eggs 2. animal's breeding place 3. snug retreat —vi. 4. make, have a nest —**nest egg** (fund of) money in reserve

nestle ('nɛsəl) vi. settle comfortably, usu. pressing in or close to something

nestling ('nɛstlɪŋ, 'nɛslɪŋ) n. bird too young to leave nest

net[1] (nɛt) n. **1.** openwork fabric of meshes of cord etc. **2.** piece of it used to catch fish etc. —vt. **3.** cover with, or catch in, net (-tt-) —'**netting** n. string or wire net —'**netball** n. game in which ball has to be thrown through elevated horizontal ring, from which hangs short piece of netting

net[2] or **nett** (nɛt) a. **1.** left after all deductions **2.** free from deduction —vt. **3.** gain, yield as clear profit —**net profit** gross profit minus all operating costs not included in calculation of gross profit

nether ('nɛðə) a. lower —'**nethermost** a. farthest down; lowest —**nether world 1.** underworld **2.** hell (also **nether regions**)

netsuke ('nɛtsʊkɪ) n. carved wooden or ivory toggle or button worn in Japan

nettle ('nɛtl) n. **1.** plant with stinging hairs on the leaves —vt. **2.** irritate, provoke —**nettle rash** urticaria

network ('nɛtwɜːk) n. **1.** system of intersecting lines, roads etc. **2.** interconnecting group of people or things **3.** in broadcasting, group of stations connected to transmit same programmes simultaneously

neural ('njʊərəl) a. of the nerves

neuralgia (njʊ'rældʒə) n. pain in, along nerves, esp. of face and head —**neu'ralgic** a.

neuritis (njʊ'raɪtɪs) n. inflammation of nerves

neuro- or before vowel **neur-** (comb. form) nerve; nervous system, as in neurology

neurology (njʊ'rɒlədʒɪ) n. science, study of nerves —**neu'rologist** n.

neuron ('njʊərɒn) or **neurone** ('njʊərəʊn) n. cell specialized to conduct nerve impulses (also **nerve cell**) —**neu'ronic** a.

neurosis (njʊ'rəʊsɪs) n. relatively mild mental disorder (pl. **-ses** (-siːz)) —**neurotic** (njʊ'rɒtɪk) a. **1.** suffering from nervous disorder **2.** abnormally sensitive —n. **3.** neurotic person

neurosurgery (njʊərəʊ'sɜːdʒərɪ) n. branch of surgery concerned with nervous system —**neuro'surgical** a.

neuter ('njuːtə) a. **1.** neither masculine nor feminine —n. **2.** neuter word **3.** neuter gender —vt. **4.** castrate, spay (domestic animal)

neutral ('njuːtrəl) a. **1.** taking neither side in war, dispute etc. **2.** without marked qualities **3.** belonging to neither of two classes —n. **4.** neutral nation or a subject of one **5.** neutral gear —**neu'trality** n. —'**neutralize** or **-ise** vt. **1.** make ineffective **2.** counterbalance —**neutral gear** in vehicle, position of gears that leaves transmission disengaged

neutrino (njuː'triːnəʊ) n. Phys. stable elementary particle with zero rest mass (pl. **-s**)

neutron ('njuːtrɒn) n. electrically neutral particle of the nucleus of an atom —**neutron bomb** nuclear bomb designed to destroy people but not buildings

never ('nɛvə) adv. at no time —**never'more** adv. Lit. never again —**never-never** n. inf. hire-purchase system of buying —**neverthe'less** adv. for all that, notwithstanding

new (njuː) a. **1.** not existing before, fresh **2.** that has lately come into some state or existence **3.** unfamiliar, strange —adv. **4.** recently, fresh (usu. '**newly**) —'**newly** adv. —'**newness** n. —'**newcomer** n. recent arrival —**new'fangled** a. of new fashion —**new maths** approach to mathematics in which basic principles of set theory are introduced at elementary level —**new moon** moon when it appears as narrow waxing crescent —'**newspeak** n. language of bureaucrats and politicians, regarded as deliberately ambiguous and misleading —**New Testament** collection of writings composed soon after Christ's death and added to Jewish writings of Old Testament to make up Christian Bible —**new town** UK town planned as complete unit and built with government sponsorship, esp. to accommodate overspill population —**New Year** first day or days of year —**the New World** the Americas; western hemisphere

newel ('njuːəl) n. **1.** central pillar of winding staircase **2.** post at top or bottom of staircase rail

news (njuːz) n. **1.** report of recent happenings, tidings **2.** interesting fact not previously known —'**newsy** a. full of news —**news agency** organization that collects news reports for newspapers etc. (also **press agency**) —'**news-agent** n. shopkeeper who sells and distributes newspapers —**news bulletin** the latest news, esp. as broadcast by radio and television —'**newscast** n. news broadcast —'**newscaster** n. —**news flash** brief item of important news, oft. interrupting radio or television programme —'**newsletter** n. **1.** printed periodical bulletin circulated to members of group (also **newssheet**) **2.** Hist. written or printed account of news —'**newspaper** n. periodical publication containing news —'**newsprint** n. paper of the kind used for newspapers etc. —'**newsreel** n. cinema or television film giving news —'**newsstand** n. stand from which newspapers are sold —'**newsworthy** a. sufficiently interesting or important to be reported as news

newt (njuːt) n. small, tailed amphibious creature

newton ('njuːtən) n. SI unit of force

next (nɛkst) a./adv. **1.** nearest **2.** immediately

following —**next door** at or to adjacent house, flat *etc.* —**next-of-kin** *n.* nearest relative

nexus ('nɛksəs) *n.* tie, connection, link (*pl.* '**nexus**)

NF Newfoundland

N.F.U. National Farmers' Union

N.G.A. National Graphical Association

NH New Hampshire

N.H.S. National Health Service

Ni *Chem.* nickel

N.I. 1. UK National Insurance **2.** Northern Ireland

nib (nɪb) *n.* **1.** (split) pen point **2.** bird's beak —*pl.* **3.** crushed cocoa beans

nibble ('nɪbᵊl) *v.* **1.** take little bites (of) —*n.* **2.** little bite

nibs (nɪbz) *n.* mock title of respect, as in *his nibs*

nice (naɪs) *a.* **1.** pleasant **2.** friendly, kind **3.** attractive **4.** subtle, fine **5.** careful, exact **6.** difficult to decide —'**nicely** *adv.* —**nicety** ('naɪsɪtɪ) *n.* **1.** minute distinction or detail **2.** subtlety **3.** precision

niche (nɪtʃ, niːʃ) *n.* **1.** recess in wall **2.** suitable place in life, public estimation *etc.*

nick (nɪk) *vt.* **1.** make notch in, indent **2.** *sl.* steal —*n.* **3.** notch **4.** exact point of time **5.** *sl.* prison —**in good nick** *inf.* in good condition

nickel ('nɪkᵊl) *n.* **1.** silver-white metal much used in alloys and plating **2.** US, C five-cent piece —**nickel silver** white alloy containing copper, zinc and nickel (*also* **German silver**)

nicker[1] ('nɪkə) *vi.* **1.** (of horse) neigh softly **2.** snigger

nicker[2] ('nɪkə) *n.* UK *sl.* pound sterling (*pl.* '**nicker**)

nicknack ('nɪk,næk) *n. see* KNICK-KNACK

nickname ('nɪkneɪm) *n.* familiar name added to or replacing an ordinary name

nicotine ('nɪkətiːn) *n.* poisonous oily liquid in tobacco —'**nicotinism** *n.* tobacco poisoning

nictitate ('nɪktɪteɪt) *or* **nictate** ('nɪkteɪt) *v.* blink —**nicti'tation** *or* **nic'tation** *n.*

niece (niːs) *n.* brother's or sister's daughter

nifty ('nɪftɪ) *a. inf.* **1.** neat, smart **2.** quick

niggard ('nɪgəd) *n.* mean, stingy person —'**niggardly** *a./adv.*

nigger ('nɪgə) *n. offens.* Negro

niggle ('nɪgᵊl) *vi.* **1.** find fault continually —*vt.* **2.** annoy —'**niggling** *a.* **1.** petty **2.** irritating and persistent

nigh (naɪ) *a./adv./prep. obs., poet.* near

night (naɪt) *n.* **1.** time of darkness between sunset and sunrise **2.** end of daylight **3.** dark —'**nightie** *or* '**nighty** *n.* woman's nightdress —'**nightly** *a.* **1.** happening, done every night **2.** of the night —*adv.* **3.** every night **4.** by night —**nights** *adv. inf.* at night, *esp.* regularly —**night**

blindness *Pathol.* inability to see normally in dim light (*also* **nycta'lopia**) —'**nightcap** *n.* **1.** cap worn in bed **2.** late-night (alcoholic) drink —'**nightclub** *n.* establishment for dancing, music *etc.* opening late at night —'**nightdress** *n.* woman's loose robe worn in bed —'**nightfall** *n.* approach of darkness; dusk —'**nightingale** *n.* small bird which sings *usu.* at night —'**nightjar** *n.* nocturnal bird with harsh cry —'**nightmare** *n.* **1.** very bad dream **2.** terrifying experience —**night safe** safe built into outside wall of bank, in which customers deposit money when bank is closed —**night school** educational institution that holds classes in evening —'**nightshade** *n.* any of various plants of potato family, some of them with very poisonous berries —'**nightspot** *n. inf.* nightclub —**night-time** *n.* —**night watch 1.** guard kept at night, *esp.* for security **2.** period of time watch is kept **3.** night watchman

nihilism ('naɪɪlɪzəm) *n.* **1.** rejection of all religious and moral principles **2.** opposition to all constituted authority or government —'**nihilist** *n.* —**nihil'istic** *a.*

nil (nɪl) *n.* nothing, zero

nimble ('nɪmbᵊl) *a.* agile, active, quick, dexterous —'**nimbly** *adv.*

nimbus ('nɪmbəs) *n.* **1.** rain or storm cloud **2.** cloud of glory, halo (*pl.* **-bi** (-baɪ), **-es**)

nincompoop ('nɪnkəmpuːp, 'nɪŋ-) *n.* fool, simpleton

nine (naɪn) *a./n.* cardinal number next above eight —**nine'teen** *a./n.* nine more than ten —**nine'teenth** *a.* —**ninetieth** *a.* —'**ninety** *a./n.* nine tens —**ninth** (naɪnθ) *a.* —**ninthly** ('naɪnθlɪ) *adv.* —**nine-days wonder** something that arouses great interest but only for short period —'**ninepins** *pl.n.* (*with sing. v.*) game where wooden pins are set up to be knocked down by rolling ball, skittles —**nineteenth hole** *Golf sl.* bar in golf clubhouse

niobium (naɪ'əʊbɪəm) *n.* white superconductive metallic element that occurs principally in black mineral columbite and tantalite

nip (nɪp) *vt.* **1.** pinch sharply **2.** detach by pinching, bite **3.** check growth of (plants) thus **4.** *sl.* steal —*vi.* **5.** *inf.* hurry (**-pp-**) —*n.* **6.** pinch **7.** check to growth **8.** sharp coldness of weather **9.** short drink —'**nipper** *n.* **1.** thing (*eg* crab's claw) that nips **2.** *inf.* small child —*pl.* **3.** pincers —'**nippy** *a. inf.* **1.** cold **2.** quick

nipple ('nɪpᵊl) *n.* **1.** point of a breast, teat **2.** anything like this

Nippon ('nɪpɒn) *n.* Japan

nisi ('naɪsaɪ) *a. see* **decree nisi** *at* DECREE

Nissen hut ('nɪsᵊn) temporary military building of corrugated sheet steel

nit (nɪt) *n.* **1.** egg of louse or other parasite **2.** *inf.* nitwit —**nit-picking** *a. inf.* overconcerned with detail, *esp.* to find fault —**nitty-gritty** *n. inf.* basic facts, details —**nitwit** *n. inf.* fool

nitre *or U.S.* **niter** ('naɪtə) *n.* 1. potassium nitrate 2. sodium nitrate

nitrogen ('naɪtrədʒən) *n.* one of the gases making up the air —**nitrate** *n.* compound of nitric acid and an alkali —**nitric** *or* **nitrous** *a.* —**nitrify** *vt.* 1. treat or cause to react with nitrogen 2. treat (soil) with nitrates 3. (of nitrobacteria) convert (ammonium compounds) into nitrates by oxidation —**ni'trogenous** *a.* of, containing nitrogen —**nitric acid** colourless corrosive liquid —**nitrobac'teria** *pl.n.* soil bacteria involved in nitrification —**nitrogen cycle** natural circulation of nitrogen by living organisms —**nitroglycerin** (naɪtrəʊ'glɪsərɪn) *or* **nitroglycerine** (naɪtrəʊ'glɪsəriːn) *n.* explosive liquid —**nitrous oxide** colourless gas with sweet smell, used as anaesthetic in dentistry (*also* **laughing gas**)

nix (nɪks) *n. sl.* nothing

NJ New Jersey

NM New Mexico

NNE north-northeast

NNW north-northwest

no (nəʊ) *a.* 1. not any, not a 2. not at all —*adv.* 3. expresses negative reply to question or request —*n.* 4. refusal 5. denial 6. negative vote or voter (*pl.* **-es**) —**no-ball** *n.* 1. Cricket illegal ball for which batting side scores run 2. *Rounders* illegal ball, *esp.* one bowled too high or too low —*interj.* 3. *Cricket, rounders* call by umpire indicating no-ball —**no-claim bonus** reduction on insurance premium, *esp.* one covering motor vehicle, if no claims have been made within specified period (*also* **no-claims bonus**) —**no-go** *a. sl.* 1. not functioning properly 2. hopeless —**no-go area** district barricaded off, which police, army can only enter by force —**no-man's-land** *n.* 1. waste or unclaimed land 2. contested land between two opposing forces —**no-one** *or* **no one** nobody —**no-trump** *Cards n.* 1. bid or contract to play without trumps (*also* **no-trumps**) —*a.* 2. (of hand) of balanced distribution suitable for playing without trumps (*also* **no-trumper**) —**'noway** *adv. sl.* not at all

No *Chem.* nobelium

No. number (*pl.* **Nos.**)

n.o. *Cricket* not out

nob (nɒb) *n. sl.* 1. member of upper classes 2. head

nobble ('nɒbəl) *vt. sl.* 1. disable (*esp.* racehorse with drugs) 2. secure dishonestly 3. catch (criminal) 4. cheat, swindle

nobelium (nəʊ'biːliəm) *n.* synthetic element produced from curium

noble ('nəʊbəl) *a.* 1. of the nobility 2. showing, having high moral qualities 3. impressive,

excellent —*n.* 4. member of the nobility —**no'bility** *n.* 1. class holding special rank, usu. hereditary, in state 2. quality of being noble —**'nobly** *adv.* —**'nobleman** *n.*

noblesse oblige (nəʊ'blɛs əʊ'bliːʒ) *oft. ironic* supposed obligation of nobility to be honourable and generous

nobody ('nəʊbədɪ) *n.* 1. no person 2. person of no importance

nock (nɒk) *n.* 1. notch on arrow that fits on bowstring 2. groove at either end of bow that holds bowstring —*vt.* 3. fit (arrow) on bowstring

nocturnal (nɒk'tɜːnəl) *a.* 1. of, in, by, night 2. active by night

nocturne ('nɒktɜːn) *n.* 1. dreamy piece of music 2. night scene

nod (nɒd) *v.* 1. bow (head) slightly and quickly in assent, command *etc.* —*vi.* 2. let head droop with sleep (**-dd-**) —*n.* 3. act of nodding —**nodding acquaintance** slight knowledge of person or subject —**nod off** *inf.* fall asleep

noddle ('nɒdəl) *n. inf.* head

node (nəʊd) *n.* 1. knot or knob 2. point at which curve crosses itself —**'nodal** *a.* —**'nodical** *a.*

nodule ('nɒdjuːl) *n.* 1. little knot 2. rounded irregular mineral mass

Noel *or* **Noël** (nəʊ'ɛl) *n.* 1. Christmas 2. Christmas carol

nog *or* **nogg** (nɒg) *n.* 1. peg or block 2. stump —**'nogging** *n.* horizontal timber member in framed construction

noggin ('nɒgɪn) *n.* 1. small amount of liquor 2. small mug 3. *inf.* head

noise (nɔɪz) *n.* 1. any sound, *esp.* disturbing one 2. clamour, din 3. loud outcry 4. talk; interest —*vt.* 5. (*usu. with* abroad *or* about) spread (gossip *etc.*) —**'noiseless** *a.* without noise, quiet, silent —**'noisily** *adv.* —**'noisy** *a.* 1. making much noise 2. clamorous

noisome ('nɔɪsəm) *a.* 1. (*esp.* of smells) offensive 2. harmful, noxious

nom. nominative

nomad ('nəʊmæd) *n.* 1. member of tribe with no fixed dwelling place 2. wanderer —**no'madic** *a.*

nom de plume ('nɒm də 'pluːm) *Fr.* writer's assumed name, pen name, pseudonym (*pl.* **noms de plume**)

nomenclature (nəʊ'mɛnklətʃə; *U.S.* 'nəʊmənkleɪtʃər) *n.* terminology of particular science *etc.*

nominal ('nɒmɪnəl) *a.* 1. in name only 2. (of fee *etc.*) small, insignificant 3. of a name or names —**'nominalism** *n.* philosophical theory that general word, such as *dog*, is merely name and does not denote real object, the general idea 'dog' —**'nominalist** *n.* —**'nominally** *adv.* 1. in name only 2. not really

nominate ('nɒmɪneɪt) vt. 1. propose as candidate 2. appoint to office —**nomi'nation** n. —**'nominative** a./n. (of) case of nouns, pronouns when subject of verb —**'nominator** n. —**nomi'nee** n. candidate

non- (comb. form) negatives the idea of the simple word. See the list below

nonage ('nəʊnɪdʒ) n. 1. Law state of being under any of various ages at which person may legally enter into certain transactions 2. any period of immaturity

nonagenarian (nəʊnədʒɪ'nɛərɪən) a. 1. aged between ninety and ninety-nine —n. 2. person of such age

nonaligned (nɒnə'laɪnd) a. (of states etc.) not part of a major alliance or power bloc

nonce (nɒns) n. —**nonce word** word coined for single occasion —**for the nonce** 1. for the occasion only 2. for the present

nonchalant ('nɒnʃələnt) a. casually unconcerned, indifferent, cool —**'nonchalance** n.

noncombatant (nɒn'kɒmbətənt) n. 1. civilian during war 2. member of army who does not fight, eg doctor, chaplain

noncommissioned officer (nɒnkə'mɪʃənd) Mil. subordinate officer, risen from the ranks

noncommittal (nɒnkə'mɪtᵊl) a. avoiding definite preference or pledge

non compos mentis ('nɒn 'kɒmpəs 'mɛntɪs) Lat. of unsound mind

nonconformist (nɒnkən'fɔːmɪst) n. dissenter, esp. from Established Church —**noncon'formity** n.

nondescript ('nɒndɪskrɪpt) a. lacking distinctive characteristics, indeterminate

none (nʌn) pron. 1. no-one, not any —a. 2. no —adv. 3. in no way —**nonesuch** or **nonsuch** ('nʌnsʌtʃ) n. obs. matchless person or thing; nonpareil —**nonethe'less** adv. despite that, however

nonentity (nɒn'ɛntɪtɪ) n. 1. insignificant person, thing 2. nonexistent thing

nonevent (nɒnɪ'vɛnt) n. disappointing or insignificant occurrence, esp. one predicted to be important

nonferrous (nɒn'fɛrəs) a. 1. denoting metal other than iron 2. not containing iron

nonflammable (nɒn'flæməbᵊl) a. 1. incapable of burning 2. not easily set on fire

nonintervention (nɒnɪntə'vɛnʃən) n. refusal to intervene, esp. abstention by state from intervening in affairs of other states

noniron (nɒn'aɪən) a. not requiring ironing

nonnuclear (nɒn'njuːklɪə) a. not operated by or using nuclear energy

nonpareil ('nɒnpərəl, nɒnpə'reɪl) a. 1. unequalled, matchless —n. 2. person or thing unequalled or unrivalled

nonpartisan or **nonpartizan** (nɒnpɑː-tɪ'zæn) a. not supporting any single political party

nonplus (nɒn'plʌs) vt. disconcert, confound or bewilder completely (**-ss-**)

nonproliferation (nɒnprəlɪfə'reɪʃən) n. limitation of production esp. of nuclear weapons

nonrepresentational (nɒnrɛprɪzɛn'teɪʃənᵊl) a. Art abstract

nonsectarian (nɒnsɛk'tɛərɪən) a. not sectarian; not confined to any specific religion

nonsense ('nɒnsəns) n. 1. lack of sense 2. absurd language 3. absurdity 4. silly conduct —**non'sensical** a. 1. ridiculous 2. meaningless 3. without sense

non sequitur ('nɒn 'sɛkwɪtə) Lat. statement with little or no relation to what preceded it

nonstarter (nɒn'stɑːtə) n. 1. horse that fails to run in race for which it has been entered 2. person or thing that has little chance of success

nonsuch ('nʌnsʌtʃ) n. see nonesuch at NONE

nonac'ceptance	noncooper'ation	nonob'servance	non'shrink(able)
nonag'gression	nonde'livery	nonoper'ational	non'slip
nonalco'holic	nondenomi'national	non'party	non'smoker
nonap'pearance	non'drinker	non'payment	non'standard
nonbe'liever	non'driver	non-playing	non'stick
nonbel'ligerent	nones'sential	non'poisonous	non'stop
non'breakable	nonex'istent	non'porous	non'swimmer
non-Catholic	non'fiction	non-profit-making	non'taxable
noncom'bustible	nonin'fectious	non'racial	non'technical
non'communist	nonin'flammable	non'reader	non'toxic
noncom'petitive	nonmag'netic	non'registered	nontrans'ferable
noncom'pliance	nonma'lignant	nonrepre'sentative	non'tropical
noncon'secutive	non'member	non'resident	non'venomous
noncon'tagious	non'metal	nonre'sistant	non'verbal
noncon'tributory	non'militant	nonre'turnable	non'violent
noncontro'versial	non-negotiable	nonse'lective	non'voter

non-U *a.* UK *inf.* (*esp.* of language) not characteristic of upper class

nonunion (non'juːnjən) *a.* **1.** not belonging to trade union **2.** not favouring or employing union labour **3.** not produced by union labour

noodle[1] ('nuːd^əl) *n.* strip of pasta served in soup *etc.*

noodle[2] ('nuːd^əl) *n.* simpleton, fool

nook (nuk) *n.* sheltered corner, retreat —'**nooky** *a.*

noon (nuːn) *n.* midday, twelve o'clock —'**noonday** *n.* noon —'**noontide** *n.* the time about noon

noose (nuːs) *n.* **1.** running loop **2.** snare —*vt.* **3.** catch, ensnare in noose, lasso

nor (nɔː, *unstressed* nə) *conj.* and not

nor' *or* **nor** (nɔː) north (*esp.* in compounds)

Nor. 1. Norman **2.** north **3.** Norway **4.** Norwegian

Nordic ('nɔːdɪk) *a.* pert. to peoples of Germanic stock

norm (nɔːm) *n.* **1.** average level of achievement **2.** rule or authoritative standard **3.** model **4.** standard type or pattern —'**normal** *a.* **1.** ordinary **2.** usual **3.** conforming to type —*n.* **4.** *Geom.* perpendicular —'**nor'mality** *n.* —**normali'zation** *or* -**i'sation** *n.* —'**normalize** *or* **-ise** *vt.* **1.** bring or make into normal state **2.** bring into conformity with standard **3.** heat (steel) above critical temperature and allow it to cool in air to relieve internal stresses; anneal —'**normally** *adv.* —'**normative** *a.* creating or prescribing norm or standard

Norman ('nɔːmən) *n.* **1.** in Middle Ages, member of people of Normandy in N France, descended from 10th-century Scandinavian conquerors of the country and native French **2.** native of Normandy **3.** medieval Norman and English dialect of Old French (*also* **Norman French**) —*a.* **4.** of Normans or their dialect of French **5.** of Normandy **6.** denoting Romanesque architecture used in Britain from Norman Conquest until 12th century, characterized by massive masonry walls *etc.*

Norse (nɔːs) *a.* **1.** of ancient and medieval Scandinavia **2.** of Norway —*n.* **3.** N group of Germanic languages, spoken in Scandinavia **4.** any of these languages, *esp.* in ancient or medieval forms —'**Norseman** *n. see* VIKING —**the Norse 1.** Norwegians **2.** Vikings

north (nɔːθ) *n.* **1.** direction to the right of person facing the sunset **2.** part of the world, of country *etc.* towards this point —*adv.* **3.** towards or in the north —*a.* **4.** to, from or in the north —'**northerly** ('nɔːðəlɪ) *a.* **1.** of or situated in north —*n.* **2.** wind from the north —'**northern** ('nɔːðən) *a.* —'**northerner** ('nɔːðənə) *n.* person from the north —'**northward** ('nɔːθwəd; *Naut.* 'nɔːðəd) *a./n./adv.* —'**northwards** ('nɔːθwədz)

adv. —**northeast** (nɔːθ'iːst; *Naut.* nɔːr'iːst) *n.* **1.** direction midway between north and east **2.** (*oft.* N-) area lying in or towards this direction —*a.* **3.** (*sometimes* N-) of northeastern part of specified country *etc.* **4.** in, towards or facing northeast **5.** (*esp.* of wind) from northeast (*also* **north-** '**eastern**) —*adv.* **6.** in, to, towards or (*esp.* of wind) from northeast —**North'east** *n.* northeastern part of England, *esp.* Northumberland and Durham —**northeaster** (nɔːθ'iːstə; *Naut.* nɔːr'iːstə) *n.* strong wind or storm from northeast —**northern hemisphere** (*oft.* N- H-) half of globe lying north of equator —**northern lights** aurora borealis —**north-northeast** *n.* **1.** direction midway between north and northeast —*a./adv.* **2.** in, from or towards this direction —**north-northwest** *n.* **1.** direction midway between northwest and north —*a./adv.* **2.** in, from or towards this direction —**North Pole 1.** northernmost point on earth's axis **2.** *Astron.* point of intersection of earth's extended axis and northern half of celestial sphere (*also* **north celestial pole**) —**North-Sea gas** UK natural gas obtained from deposits below North Sea —**northwest** (nɔːθ'west; *Naut.* nɔː'west) *n.* **1.** direction midway between north and west **2.** (*oft.* N-) area lying in or towards this direction —*a.* **3.** (*sometimes* N-) of northwestern part of specified country *etc.* (*also* **north'western**) —*a./adv.* **4.** in, to, towards or (*esp.* of wind) from northwest —**northwester** (nɔːθ'westə; *Naut.* nɔː'westə) *n.* strong wind or storm from northwest —**the North Star** *see* **the Pole Star** *at* POLE[2]

Northants. (nɔː'θænts) Northamptonshire

Northd. Northumberland

Northum. Northumbria

Norw. 1. Norway **2.** Norwegian

Norwegian (nɔː'wiːdʒən) *a.* **1.** of Norway —*n.* **2.** any of various North Germanic languages of Norway **3.** native of Norway

Nos. numbers

nose (nəʊz) *n.* **1.** organ of smell, used also in breathing **2.** any projection resembling a nose, as prow of ship, aircraft *etc.* —*v.* **3.** (cause to) move forward slowly and carefully —*vt.* **4.** touch with nose **5.** smell, sniff —*vi.* **6.** smell **7.** (*with* into, around, about *etc.*) pry —'**nosy** *or* '**nosey** *a. inf.* inquisitive —'**nosebag** *n.* bag fastened around head of horse in which feed is placed —'**noseband** *n.* detachable part of horse's bridle that goes around nose —**nose dive** downward sweep of aircraft —'**nosegay** *n.* bunch of flowers —**nosy parker** *inf., chiefly* UK prying person

nosh (nɒʃ) *sl.* **n. 1.** food —*v.* **2.** eat —**nosh-up** *n.* UK *sl.* large and satisfying meal

nostalgia (nɒ'stældʒə, -dʒɪə) *n.* **1.** longing for

return of past events **2.** homesickness —**nos'talgic** a.

nostril ('nɒstrɪl) n. one of the two external openings of the nose

nostrum ('nɒstrəm) n. **1.** quack medicine **2.** secret remedy

not (nɒt) adv. expressing negation, refusal, denial —**not proven** ('pruːvən) a third verdict available to Scottish courts, returned when there is insufficient evidence to convict

nota bene ('nəʊtə 'biːnɪ) Lat. note well

notable ('nəʊtəb³l) a. **1.** worthy of note, remarkable —n. **2.** person of distinction —**nota'bility** n. an eminent person —**'notably** adv.

notary ('nəʊtərɪ) n. person authorized to draw up deeds, contracts

notation (nəʊ'teɪʃən) n. **1.** representation of numbers, quantities, by symbols **2.** set of such symbols **3.** C footnote, memorandum

notch (nɒtʃ) n. **1.** V-shaped cut or indentation **2.** inf. step, grade —vt. **3.** make notches in

note (nəʊt) n. **1.** brief comment or record **2.** short letter **3.** banknote **4.** symbol for musical sound **5.** single tone **6.** sign **7.** indication, hint **8.** fame **9.** notice **10.** regard —pl. **11.** brief jottings written down for future reference —vt. **12.** observe, record **13.** heed —'**noted** a. well-known —'**notelet** n. folded card with printed design on front, for writing short letter —'**notebook** n. small book with blank pages for writing —'**notepaper** n. paper for writing letters; writing paper —'**noteworthy** a. **1.** worth noting **2.** remarkable

nothing ('nʌθɪŋ) n. **1.** no thing **2.** not anything, nought —adv. **3.** not at all, in no way —'**nothingness** n.

notice ('nəʊtɪs) n. **1.** observation **2.** attention, consideration, **3.** warning, intimation, announcement **4.** advance notification of intention to end a contract etc., as of employment **5.** review —vt. **6.** observe, mention **7.** give attention to —'**noticeable** a. **1.** conspicuous **2.** attracting attention **3.** appreciable

notify ('nəʊtɪfaɪ) vt. **1.** report **2.** give notice of or to (-**fied**, -**fying**) —'**notifiable** a. —**notifi'cation** n.

notion ('nəʊʃən) n. **1.** concept **2.** opinion **3.** whim —'**notional** a. speculative, imaginary, abstract

notorious (nəʊ'tɔːrɪəs) a. **1.** known for something bad **2.** well-known —**notoriety** (nəʊtə'raɪɪtɪ) n. discreditable publicity

Notts. (nɒts) Nottinghamshire

notwithstanding (nɒtwɪθ'stændɪŋ) prep. **1.** in spite of —adv. **2.** all the same —conj. **3.** although

nougat ('nuːgɑː) n. chewy sweet containing nuts, fruit etc.

nought (nɔːt) n. **1.** nothing **2.** cipher 0

noun (naʊn) n. word used as name of person, idea, or thing, substantive

nourish ('nʌrɪʃ) vt. **1.** feed **2.** nurture **3.** tend **4.** encourage —'**nourishment** n.

nous (naʊs) n. **1.** mind, intellect **2.** common sense

nouveau riche (nuvo 'riʃ) Fr. person who has acquired wealth recently and is regarded as vulgarly ostentatious (pl. **nouveaux riches** (nuvo 'riʃ))

Nov. November

nova ('nəʊvə) n. star that suddenly becomes brighter then loses brightness through months or years (pl. -**vae** (-viː), -**s**)

novel[1] ('nɒvəl) n. fictitious tale in book form —**novel'lette** n. **1.** short novel **2.** trite, oversentimental novel —'**novelist** n. writer of novels

novel[2] ('nɒvəl) a. **1.** new, recent **2.** strange —'**novelty** n. **1.** newness **2.** something new or unusual **3.** small ornament, trinket

novella (nəʊ'vɛlə) n. **1.** short narrative tale, esp. one having satirical point **2.** short novel (pl. -**s**, -**le** (-lɪ))

November (nəʊ'vɛmbə) n. eleventh month

novena (nəʊ'viːnə) n. R.C.Ch. prayers, services, lasting nine consecutive days (pl. -**nae** (-niː))

novice ('nɒvɪs) n. **1.** one new to anything **2.** beginner **3.** candidate for admission to religious order —**novitiate** or **noviciate** (nəʊ'vɪʃɪt, -eɪt) n. **1.** probationary period **2.** part of religious house for novices **3.** novice

now (naʊ) adv. **1.** at the present time **2.** immediately **3.** recently (oft. with just) —conj. **4.** seeing that, since —'**nowadays** adv. in these times, at present

Nowel or **Nowell** (nəʊ'ɛl) n. see NOEL

nowhere ('nəʊwɛə) adv. not in any place or state

nowise ('nəʊwaɪz) adv. not in any manner or degree

nowt (naʊt) n. dial. nothing

noxious ('nɒkʃəs) a. poisonous, harmful

nozzle ('nɒz³l) n. pointed spout, esp. at end of hose

Np Chem. neptunium

NS Nova Scotia

N.S.B. National Savings Bank

N.S.P.C.C. National Society for the Prevention of Cruelty to Children

N.S.T. Newfoundland Standard Time

N.S.W. New South Wales

N.T. 1. National Trust **2.** New Testament **3.** Northern Territory **4.** no trumps

nt. wt. or **nt wt** net weight

nu (njuː) n. 13th letter in Gr. alphabet (N, ν)

nuance (njuː'ɑːns, 'njuːɑːns) *n.* delicate shade of difference, in colour, tone of voice *etc.*

nub (nʌb) *n.* 1. small lump 2. main point (of story *etc.*)

nubile ('njuːbail) *a.* marriageable

nucleus ('njuːkliəs) *n.* 1. centre, kernel 2. beginning meant to receive additions 3. core of the atom (*pl.* **-lei** (-liaɪ)) —'**nuclear** *a.* of, pert. to atomic nucleus —**nucle'onics** *pl.n.* (*with sing. v.*) branch of physics dealing with applications of nuclear energy —**nuclear bomb** bomb whose force is due to uncontrolled nuclear fusion or nuclear fission —**nuclear disarmament** elimination of nuclear weapons from country's armament —**nuclear energy** energy released by nuclear fission —**nuclear family** *Sociol., anthropol.* primary social unit consisting of parents and their offspring —**nuclear fission** disintegration of the atom —**nuclear fusion** reaction in which two nuclei combine to form nucleus with release of energy (*also* '**fusion**) —**nuclear physics** branch of physics concerned with structure of nucleus and particles of which it consists —**nuclear reaction** change in structure and energy content of atomic nucleus by interaction with another nucleus, particle —**nuclear reactor** *see* **reactor** *at* REACT —**nucleic acid** (njuː'kliːɪk, -'kleɪ-) *Biochem.* any of group of complex compounds with high molecular weight that are vital constituents of all living cells

nude (njuːd) *n.* 1. state of being naked 2. (picture, statue *etc.* of) naked person —*a.* 3. naked —'**nudism** *n.* practice of nudity —'**nudist** *n.* —'**nudity** *n.*

nudge (nʌdʒ) *vt.* 1. touch slightly with elbow —*n.* 2. such touch

nugatory ('njuːgətəri, -tri) *a.* trifling, futile

nugget ('nʌgɪt) *n.* rough lump of native gold

nuisance ('njuːsəns) *n.* something or someone harmful, offensive, annoying or disagreeable

N.U.J. National Union of Journalists

null (nʌl) *a.* of no effect, void —'**nullify** *vt.* 1. cancel 2. make useless or ineffective (**-fied, -fying**) —'**nullity** *n.* state of being null and void —**null set** *Maths.* set having no members (*also* **empty set**)

num. 1. number 2. numeral

Num. Numbers

N.U.M. National Union of Mineworkers

numb (nʌm) *a.* 1. deprived of feeling, *esp.* by cold —*vt.* 2. make numb 3. deaden —'**numbskull** *see* NUMSKULL

number ('nʌmbə) *n.* 1. sum, aggregate 2. word or symbol saying how many 3. single issue of a paper *etc.* issued in regular series 4. classification as to singular or plural 5. song, piece of music 6. performance 7. company,

collection 8. identifying number, as of particular house, telephone *etc.* 9. *sl.* measure, correct estimation —*vt.* 10. count 11. class, reckon 12. give a number to 13. amount to —'**numberless** *a.* countless —**number crunching** the performing of complicated calculations involving large numbers, *esp.* at high speed by computer —**number one** *n.* 1. *inf.* oneself —*a.* 2. first in importance, urgency *etc.* —'**numberplate** *n.* plate mounted on front and back of motor vehicle bearing registration number —**Number Ten** 10 Downing Street, British prime minister's official London residence

numeral ('njuːmərəl) *n.* sign or word denoting a number —'**numerable** *a.* able to be numbered or counted —'**numeracy** *n.* —'**numerate** ('njuːmərɪt) *a.* 1. able to use numbers in calculations —*vt.* ('njuːməreɪt) 2. count —nume'ration *n.* —'**numerator** *n.* top part of fraction, figure showing how many of the fractional units are taken —**nu'merical** *a.* of, in respect of, number or numbers —nume'rology *n.* study of numbers, and of their supposed influence on human affairs —'**numerous** *a.* many

numismatic (njuːmɪz'mætɪk) *a.* of coins —**numis'matics** *pl.n.* (*with sing. v.*) the study of coins —**nu'mismatist** *n.*

numskull *or* **numbskull** ('nʌmskʌl) *n.* dolt, dunce

nun (nʌn) *n.* woman living (in convent) under religious vows —'**nunnery** *n.* convent of nuns

nuncio ('nʌnʃɪəʊ, -sɪ-) *n.* ambassador of the Pope (*pl.* **-s**)

nunny bag ('nʌnɪ) **C** small sealskin haversack

NUPE ('njuːpɪ) National Union of Public Employees

nuptial ('nʌpʃəl, -tʃəl) *a.* of, relating to marriage —'**nuptials** *pl.n.* (*sometimes with sing. v.*) 1. marriage 2. wedding ceremony

N.U.R. National Union of Railwaymen

nurse (nɜːs) *n.* 1. person trained for care of sick or injured 2. woman tending another's child —*vt.* 3. act as nurse to 4. suckle 5. pay special attention to 6. harbour (grudge *etc.*) —'**nursery** *n.* 1. room for children 2. rearing place for plants —'**nursemaid** *or* '**nurserymaid** *n.* woman employed to look after children (*also* **nurse**) —'**nurseryman** *n.* one who raises plants for sale —**nursery rhyme** short traditional verse or song for children —**nursery school** school for young children —**nursery slope** gentle slope for beginners in skiing —**nursing home** private hospital or residence for aged or infirm persons —**nursing officer** administrative head of nursing staff of hospital

nurture ('nɜːtʃə) *n.* 1. bringing up 2. education

3. rearing **4.** nourishment —*vt.* **5.** bring up **6.** educate

N.U.S. 1. National Union of Seamen **2.** National Union of Students

nut (nʌt) *n.* **1.** fruit consisting of hard shell and kernel **2.** hollow metal collar into which a screw fits **3.** *inf.* head **4.** *inf.* eccentric or crazy person (*also* **'nutter**) —*vi.* **5.** gather nuts (-tt-) —**'nutty** *a.* **1.** of, like nut **2.** pleasant to taste and bite **3.** *sl.* insane, crazy (*also* **nuts**) —**'nutcase** *n. sl.* insane or foolish person —**'nutcracker** *n.* **1.** (*oft. pl.*) device for cracking shells of nuts **2.** Old World or North American bird having speckled plumage and feeding on nuts *etc.* —**'nuthatch** *n.* small songbird —**'nutmeg** *n.* aromatic seed of Indian tree —**'nutshell** *n.* shell around kernel of nut —**in a nutshell** in essence; briefly —**nuts and bolts** *inf.* essential or practical details

N.U.T. National Union of Teachers

nutria ('njuːtrɪə) *n.* fur of coypu

nutrient ('njuːtrɪənt) *a.* **1.** nourishing —*n.* **2.** something nutritious

nutriment ('njuːtrɪmənt) *n.* nourishing food —**nu'trition** *n.* **1.** receiving foods **2.** act of nourishing —**nu'tritious** *or* **'nutritive** *a.* **1.** nourishing **2.** promoting growth

nux vomica ('nʌks 'vɒmɪkə) seed of tree which yields strychnine

nuzzle ('nʌzl) *v.* **1.** burrow, press with nose —*vi.* **2.** nestle

NV Nevada

NW northwest(ern)

N.W.T. Northwest Territories (of Canada)

NY New York

nylon ('naɪlɒn) *n.* **1.** synthetic material used for fabrics, bristles, ropes *etc.* —*pl.* **2.** stockings made of this

nymph (nɪmf) *n.* legendary semidivine maiden of sea, woods, mountains *etc.*

nymphomania (nɪmfəʊ'meɪnɪə) *n.* abnormally intense sexual desire in women —**nympho'maniac** *n.*

N.Z. *or* **N. Zeal.** New Zealand

O,o

o *or* **O** (əʊ) *n.* **1.** 15th letter of English alphabet **2.** any of several speech sounds represented by this letter, as in *code, pot, cow* or *form* **3.** see NOUGHT (*pl.* **o's, O's** *or* **Os**)

O¹ 1. *Chem.* oxygen **2.** human blood type of ABO group **3.** Old

O² (əʊ) *interj.* **1.** see OH **2.** exclamation introducing invocation, entreaty, wish *etc.*

o' (ə) *prep. inf.* of

O'- (*comb. form*) in surnames of Irish Gaelic origin, descendant of, as in *O'Corrigan*

oaf (əʊf) *n.* **1.** lout **2.** dolt

oak (əʊk) *n.* **1.** common, deciduous forest tree —*pl.* **2.** (O-) horse race for fillies held annually at Epsom —**'oaken** *a.* of oak —**oak apple** *or* **gall** round gall on oak trees

oakum ('əʊkəm) *n.* loose fibre got by unravelling old rope

O. & M. organization and method (in studies of working methods)

O.A.P. old age pensioner

oar (ɔː) *n.* **1.** wooden lever with broad blade worked by the hands to propel boat **2.** oarsman —*v.* **3.** row —**'oarsman** *n.* —**'oarsmanship** *n.* skill in rowing

OAS 1. Organization of American States **2.** *Organisation de l'Armée Secrète;* organization which opposed Algerian independence by acts of terrorism

oasis (əʊ'eɪsɪs) *n.* fertile spot in desert (*pl.* **oases** (əʊ'eɪsiːz))

oast (əʊst) *n.* kiln for drying hops

oat (əʊt) *n.* **1.** (*usu. pl.*) grain of cereal plant **2.** the plant —**'oaten** *a.* —**'oatmeal** *n.*

oath (əʊθ) *n.* **1.** confirmation of truth of statement by naming something sacred **2.** curse (*pl.* **oaths** (əʊðz))

OAU Organization of African Unity

ob. 1. (on tombstones *etc.*) obiit (*Lat.,* he or she died) **2.** obiter (*Lat.,* incidentally, in passing) **3.** oboe

ob- (*comb. form*) inverse; inversely, as in *obovate*

obbligato *or* **obligato** (ɒblɪ'ɡɑːtəʊ) *Mus. a.* **1.** not to be omitted —*n.* **2.** essential part in score (*pl.* **-s, -ti** (-tiː))

obdurate ('ɒbdjʊrɪt) *a.* stubborn, unyielding —**'obduracy** *or* **'obdurateness** *n.*

O.B.E. Officer of the Order of the British Empire

obedience (ə'biːdɪəns) *n.* submission to authority —**o'bedient** *a.* **1.** willing to obey **2.** compliant **3.** dutiful —**o'bediently** *adv.*

obeisance (əʊ'beɪsəns, əʊ'biː-) *n.* **1.** bow; curtsy **2.** homage

obelisk ('ɒbɪlɪsk) *n.* tapering rectangular stone column with pyramidal apex

obese (əʊ'biːs) *a.* very fat, corpulent —**o'besity** *n.*

obey (ə'beɪ) *vt.* **1.** do the bidding of **2.** act in accordance with —*vi.* **3.** do as ordered **4.** submit to authority

obfuscate ('ɒbfʌskeɪt) *vt.* **1.** perplex **2.** darken

obituary (ə'bɪtjʊərɪ) *n.* **1.** notice, record of death **2.** biographical sketch of deceased person, *esp.* in newspaper (*also* (*inf.*) **'obit**)

obj. 1. object **2.** objective

object¹ ('ɒbdʒɪkt) *n.* **1.** material thing **2.** that to which feeling or action is directed **3.** end, aim **4.** *Gram.* word dependent on verb or preposition —**object lesson** lesson with practical and concrete illustration —**no object** not an obstacle or hindrance

object (ɒb'dʒɛkt) *vt.* **1.** state in opposition —*vi.* **2.** feel dislike or reluctance (to something) —**ob'jection** *n.* —**ob'jectionable** *a.* **1.** disagreeable **2.** justly liable to objection —**ob'jector** *n.*

objective (ɒb'dʒɛktɪv) *a.* **1.** external to the mind **2.** impartial —*n.* **3.** thing or place aimed at —**objec'tivity** *n.*

objet d'art (ɔbʒɛ 'daːr) *Fr.* small object considered to be of artistic worth (*pl.* *objets d'art* (ɔbʒɛ 'daːr))

oblate[1] ('ɒbleɪt) *a.* (of sphere) flattened at the poles

oblate[2] ('ɒbleɪt) *n.* person dedicated to religious work

oblation (ɒ'bleɪʃən) *n.* offering —**ob'lational** *a.*

obligato (ɒblɪ'gɑːtəʊ) see OBBLIGATO

oblige (ə'blaɪdʒ) *vt.* **1.** bind morally or legally to do service to **2.** compel —**obligate** ('ɒblɪgeɪt) *vt.* **1.** bind, *esp.* by legal contract **2.** put under obligation —**obligation** (ɒblɪ'geɪʃən) *n.* **1.** binding duty, promise **2.** debt of gratitude —**obligatory** (ɒ'blɪgətərɪ, -trɪ) *a.* **1.** required **2.** binding —**o'bliging** *a.* ready to serve others, civil, helpful, courteous

oblique (ə'bliːk) *a.* **1.** slanting **2.** indirect —**o'bliquely** *adv.* —**obliquity** (ə'blɪkwɪtɪ) *n.* **1.** slant **2.** dishonesty —**oblique angle** angle not a right angle

obliterate (ə'blɪtəreɪt) *vt.* blot out, efface, destroy completely —**oblite'ration** *n.*

oblivion (ə'blɪvɪən) *n.* forgetting or being forgotten —**ob'livious** *a.* **1.** forgetful **2.** unaware

oblong ('ɒblɒŋ) *a.* **1.** rectangular, with adjacent sides unequal —*n.* **2.** oblong figure

obloquy ('ɒbləkwɪ) *n.* **1.** reproach, abuse **2.** disgrace **3.** detraction

obnoxious (əb'nɒkʃəs) *a.* offensive, disliked, odious

oboe ('əʊbəʊ) *n.* woodwind instrument, hautboy —'**oboist** *n.*

obs. 1. observation **2.** obsolete

obscene (əb'siːn) *a.* **1.** indecent, lewd **2.** repulsive —**obscenity** (əb'sɛnɪtɪ) *n.*

obscure (əb'skjʊə) *a.* **1.** unclear, indistinct **2.** unexplained **3.** dark, dim **4.** humble —*vt.* **5.** make unintelligible **6.** dim **7.** conceal —**ob'scurant** *n.* one who opposes enlightenment or reform —**obscu'rantism** *n.* —**ob'scurity** *n.* **1.** indistinctness **2.** lack of intelligibility **3.** darkness **4.** obscure, *esp.* unrecognized, place or position **5.** retirement

obsequies ('ɒbsɪkwɪz) *pl.n.* funeral rites

obsequious (əb'siːkwɪəs) *a.* servile, fawning

observe (əb'zɜːv) *vt.* **1.** notice, remark **2.** watch **3.** note systematically **4.** keep, follow —*vi.* **5.** make a remark —**ob'servable** *a.* —**ob'servably** *adv.* —**ob'servance** *n.* **1.** paying attention **2.** keeping —**ob'servant** *a.* quick to notice —**obser'vation** *n.* action, habit of observing, noticing **3.** remark —**ob'servatory** *n.* place for watching stars *etc.* —**ob'server** *n.*

obsess (əb'sɛs) *vt.* haunt, fill the mind of —**ob'session** *n.* **1.** fixed idea **2.** domination of the mind by one idea —**ob'sessive** *a.*

obsidian (ɒb'sɪdɪən) *n.* fused volcanic rock, forming hard, dark, natural glass

obsolete ('ɒbsəliːt, ɒbsə'liːt) *a.* disused, out of date —**obso'lescent** *a.* going out of use

obstacle ('ɒbstəkəl) *n.* **1.** hindrance **2.** impediment, barrier, obstruction

obstetrics (ɒb'stɛtrɪks) *pl.n.* (*with sing. v.*) branch of medicine concerned with childbirth and care of women before and after childbirth —**ob'stetric(al)** *a.* —**obste'trician** *n.*

obstinate ('ɒbstɪnɪt) *a.* **1.** stubborn **2.** self-willed **3.** unyielding **4.** hard to overcome or cure —'**obstinacy** *n.* —'**obstinately** *adv.*

obstreperous (əb'strɛpərəs) *a.* unruly, noisy, boisterous

obstruct (əb'strʌkt) *vt.* **1.** block up **2.** hinder, impede —**ob'struction** *n.* —**ob'structionist** *n.* one who deliberately opposes transaction of business —**ob'structive** *a.*

obtain (əb'teɪn) *vt.* **1.** get **2.** acquire **3.** procure by effort —*vi.* **4.** be customary —**ob'tainable** *a.* procurable

obtrude (əb'truːd) *v.* thrust forward unduly —**ob'trusion** *n.* —**ob'trusive** *a.* forward, pushing —**ob'trusively** *adv.*

obtuse (əb'tjuːs) *a.* **1.** dull of perception **2.** stupid **3.** (of angle) greater than right angle **4.** not pointed —**ob'tusely** *adv.*

obverse ('ɒbvɜːs) *n.* **1.** fact, idea *etc.* which is the complement of another **2.** side of coin, medal *etc.* that has the principal design —*a.* **3.** facing the observer **4.** complementary, opposite

obviate ('ɒbvɪeɪt) *vt.* remove, make unnecessary

obvious ('ɒbvɪəs) *a.* **1.** clear, evident **2.** wanting in subtlety

O.C. Officer Commanding

occasion (ə'keɪʒən) *n.* **1.** time when thing happens **2.** reason, need **3.** opportunity **4.** special event —*vt.* **5.** cause —**oc'casional** *a.* **1.** happening, found now and then **2.** produced for some special event, as *occasional music* —**oc'casionally** *adv.* sometimes, now and then

Occident ('ɒksɪdənt) *n.* the West —**Occi'dental** *a.*

occlude (ə'kluːd) *vt.* shut in or out —**oc'clusion** *n.* —**oc'clusive** *a.* serving to occlude **—occluded front** *Met.* line occurring where cold front of depression has overtaken warm front, raising warm sector from ground level (*also* **oc'clusion**)

occult (ɒ'kʌlt, 'ɒkʌlt) *a.* **1.** secret, mysterious **2.** supernatural *—n.* **3.** esoteric knowledge *—vt.* (ɒ'kʌlt) **4.** hide from view **—occul'tation** *n.* eclipse **—'occultism** *n.* study of supernatural **—oc'cultness** *n.* mystery

occupy ('ɒkjupaɪ) *vt.* **1.** inhabit, fill **2.** employ **3.** take possession of (**-pied, -pying**) **—'occupancy** *n.* **1.** fact of occupying **2.** residing **—'occupant** *n.* **—occu'pation** *n.* **1.** employment **2.** pursuit **3.** fact of occupying **4.** seizure **—occu'pational** *a.* **1.** pert. to occupation, *esp.* of diseases arising from a particular occupation **2.** pert. to use of occupations, *eg* craft, hobbies *etc.* as means of rehabilitation **—'occupier** *n.* tenant **—occupational therapy** *Med.* therapeutic use of crafts, hobbies *etc.*, esp. in rehabilitation of emotionally disturbed patients

occur (ɔ'kɜː) *vi.* **1.** happen **2.** come to mind (**-rr-**) **—oc'currence** *n.* happening

ocean ('əʊʃən) *n.* **1.** great body of water **2.** large division of this **3.** the sea **—oceanic** (əʊʃɪ'ænɪk) *a.* **—ocean'ographer** *n.* **—ocean'ography** *n.* study of physical and biological features of the sea **—ocean'ology** *n.* study of the sea, *esp.* of its economic geography **—ocean-going** *a.* (of ship, boat *etc.*) suited for travel on ocean

ocelot ('ɒsɪlɒt, 'əʊ-) *n.* Amer. leopard

oche ('ɒkɪ) *n.* Darts mark on floor behind which player must stand to throw

ochre *or U.S.* **ocher** ('əʊkə) *n.* various earths used as yellow or brown pigments **—ochreous** ('əʊkrɪəs, 'əʊkərəs), **ochrous** ('əʊkrəs), **ochry** ('əʊkərɪ, 'əʊkrɪ) *or U.S.* **'ocherous, 'ochery** *a.*

o'clock (ə'klɒk) *adv.* by the clock

OCR optical character reader *or* recognition

Oct. October

oct- (*comb. form*) eight

octagon ('ɒktəgən) *n.* plane figure with eight angles **—oc'tagonal** *a.*

octahedron (ɒktə'hiːdrən) *n.* solid figure with eight sides (*pl.* **-s, -dra** (-drə))

octane ('ɒkteɪn) *n.* ingredient of motor fuel **—octane rating** measure of quality or type of petrol

octave ('ɒktɪv) *n.* **1.** *Mus.* eighth note above or below given note **2.** this space **3.** eight lines of verse

octavo (ɒk'teɪvəʊ) *n.* book in which each sheet is folded three times forming eight leaves (*pl.* **-s**)

octennial (ɒk'tɛnɪəl) *a.* lasting, happening every eight years

octet (ɒk'tɛt) *n.* **1.** group of eight **2.** music for eight instruments or singers

October (ɒk'təʊbə) *n.* tenth month

octogenarian (ɒktəʊdʒɪ'nɛərɪən) *or* **octogenary** (ɒk'tɒdʒɪnərɪ) *n.* **1.** person aged between eighty and ninety *—a.* **2.** of an octogenarian

octopus ('ɒktəpəs) *n.* mollusc with eight arms covered with suckers *—n./a.* (**octopod** *n./a.* (mollusc) with eight feet

octosyllable ('ɒktəsɪləbəl) *n.* word, line of verse of eight syllables

OCTU ('ɒktuː) **UK** Officer Cadets' Training Unit

ocular ('ɒkjʊlə) *a.* of eye or sight **—'ocularly** *adv.*

oculist ('ɒkjʊlɪst) *n. Med. obs.* ophthalmologist

O.D. *Med.* overdose

odd (ɒd) *a.* **1.** strange, queer **2.** incidental, random **3.** that is one in addition when the rest have been divided into equal groups **4.** not even **5.** not part of a set **—'oddity** *n.* **1.** odd person or thing **2.** quality of being odd **—'oddment** *n.* (oft. *pl.*) **1.** remnant **2.** trifle **—odds** *pl.n.* (with on *or* against) **1.** advantage conceded in betting **2.** likelihood **—odd-jobman** *or* **odd-jobber** *n.* person who does casual work, *esp.* domestic repairs **—odds-on** *a.* **1.** (of chance, horse *etc.*) rated at even money or less to win **2.** regarded as more or most likely to win, happen *etc.* **—odds and ends** odd fragments or scraps

ode (əʊd) *n.* lyric poem on particular subject

odium ('əʊdɪəm) *n.* hatred, widespread dislike **—'odious** *a.* hateful, repulsive, obnoxious

odometer (ɒ'dɒmɪtə, əʊ-) *n.* US mileometer

odour *or U.S.* **odor** ('əʊdə) *n.* smell **—odo'riferous** *a.* spreading an odour **—'odorous** *a.* **1.** fragrant **2.** scented **—'odourless** *or U.S.* **'odorless** *a.*

Odyssey ('ɒdɪsɪ) *n.* **1.** Homer's epic describing Odysseus' return from Troy **2.** any long adventurous journey

OE, O.E., *or* **OE.** Old English (language)

O.E.C.D. Organization for Economic Cooperation and Development

oedema *or* **edema** (ɪ'diːmə) *n.* swelling in body tissues, due to accumulation of fluid (*pl.* **-mata** (-mətə))

Oedipus complex ('iːdɪpəs) *Psychoanal.* usu. unconscious desire of child to possess sexually parent of opposite sex **—'oedipal** *or* **oedi'pean** *a.*

o'er (ɔː, əʊə) *prep./adv.* Poet. over

oesophagus *or U.S.* **esophagus** (iː'sɒfəgəs) *n.* canal from mouth to stomach, gullet (*pl.* **-gi** (-gaɪ)) **—oesophageal** *or U.S.* **esophageal** (iːsɒfə'dʒiːəl) *a.*

oestrogen ('iːstrədʒən, 'ɛstrə-) *or U.S.* **estrogen** *n.* hormone in females *esp.*

controlling changes, cycles in reproductive organs

of (ɒv; *unstressed* əv) *prep.* denotes removal, separation, ownership, attribute, material, quality

off (ɒf) *adv.* 1. away —*prep.* 2. away from —*a.* 3. not operative 4. cancelled or postponed 5. bad, sour *etc.* 6. distant 7. (of horses, vehicles *etc.*) right *Cricket* to bowler's left —'**offing** *n.* part of sea visible to observer on ship or shore —'**offbeat** *n.* 1. *Mus.* any of normally unaccented beats in bar —*a.* 2. unusual, unconventional or eccentric —**off chance** slight possibility —**off colour** slightly ill —**off cut** piece of paper, wood *etc.* remaining after main pieces have been cut; remnant —**off'hand** *a.* 1. without previous thought 2. curt (*also* off'**handed**) —**off key** 1. *Mus.* not in correct key; out of tune 2. out of keeping; discordant —**off-licence** *n.* place where alcoholic drinks are sold for consumption elsewhere —**off line** 1. of or concerned with part of computer system not connected to central processing unit but controlled by computer storage device 2. disconnected from computer —**off-load** *vt.* get rid of (something unpleasant or burdensome), as by delegation to another —**off-peak** *a.* of or relating to services as used outside periods of intensive use —**off-putting** *a.* UK *inf.* disconcerting or disturbing —**offset** ('ɒfsɛt) *n.* 1. that which counterbalances, compensates 2. method of printing —*vt.* ('ɒf'sɛt) 3. counterbalance, compensate for 4. print (text *etc.*) using offset process —'**offshoot** *n.* 1. shoot or branch growing from main stem of plant 2. something that develops from principal source —'**off'side** *a./adv. Sport* illegally forward —'**offspring** *n.* children, issue —**off-the-peg** *a.* (of clothing) ready to wear; not produced especially for person buying —**in the offing** likely to happen soon —**on the off chance** with hope

off. 1. office 2. officer 3. official

offal ('ɒfəl) *n.* 1. edible entrails of animal 2. refuse

offend (ə'fɛnd) *vt.* 1. hurt feelings of, displease —*vi.* 2. do wrong —**of'fence** *or U.S.* **of'fense** *n.* 1. wrong 2. crime 3. insult —**of'fender** *n.* —**of'fensive** *a.* 1. causing displeasure 2. aggressive —*n.* 3. position or movement of attack

offer ('ɒfə) *vt.* 1. present for acceptance or refusal 2. tender 3. propose 4. attempt —*vi.* 5. present itself —*n.* 6. offering, bid —'**offerer** *or* '**offeror** *n.* —'**offering** *n.* 1. something that is offered 2. contribution 3. sacrifice, as of animal, to deity —'**offertory** *n.* 1. offering of the bread and wine at the Eucharist 2. collection in church service

office ('ɒfɪs) *n.* 1. room(s), building, in which

business, clerical work *etc.* is done 2. commercial or professional organization 3. official position 4. service 5. duty 6. form of worship —*pl.* 7. task 8. service —'**officer** *n.* 1. one in command in army, navy, ship *etc.* 2. official

official (ə'fɪʃəl) *a.* 1. with, by, authority —*n.* 2. one holding office, *esp.* in public body —**of'ficialdom** *n.* officials collectively, or their attitudes, work, usu. in contemptuous sense —**officia'lese** *n.* language characteristic of official documents, *esp.* when verbose —**Official Receiver** officer who manages estate of bankrupt

officiate (ə'fɪʃɪeɪt) *vi.* 1. perform duties of office 2. perform ceremony

officious (ə'fɪʃəs) *a.* 1. importunate in offering service 2. interfering

oft (ɒft) *adv.* often (*obs., poet.* except in combinations such as *oft-repeated*)

often ('ɒfən) *adv.* many times, frequently

ogee arch ('əudʒiː) pointed arch with S-shaped curve on both sides

ogle ('əugəl) *v.* 1. stare, look (at) amorously —*n.* 2. this look —'**ogler** *n.*

ogre ('əugə) *n.* 1. *Folklore* man-eating giant 2. monster ('**ogress** *fem.*)

oh (əu) *interj.* exclamation of surprise, pain *etc.*

OH Ohio

ohm (əum) *n.* unit of electrical resistance —'**ohmic** *a.* —'**ohmmeter** *n.*

O.H.M.S. On His (*or* Her) Majesty's Service

-oid (*comb. form*) likeness, resemblance, similarity, as in *anthropoid*

oil (ɔɪl) *n.* 1. any of a number of viscous liquids with smooth, sticky feel and wide variety of uses 2. petroleum 3. any of variety of petroleum derivatives, *esp.* as fuel or lubricant —*vt.* 4. lubricate with oil 5. apply oil to —'**oily** *a.* 1. soaked in or smeared with oil or grease 2. consisting of, containing or resembling oil 3. flatteringly servile or obsequious —**oil cake** stock feed consisting of compressed linseed —'**oilcloth** *n.* waterproof material made by treating cotton fabric with drying oil or synthetic resin —'**oilfield** *n.* area containing reserves of petroleum —'**oilfired** *a.* (of central heating *etc.*) using oil as fuel —**oil painting** 1. picture painted with oil paints 2. art of painting with oil paints 3. *inf.* person or thing regarded as good-looking (*esp.* in **she's no oil painting**) —**oil rig** *see* RIG (sense 6) —'**oilskin** *n.* cloth treated with oil to make it waterproof —**oil slick** mass of floating oil covering area of water —**oil well** boring into earth or sea bed for extraction of petroleum —**well oiled** *sl.* drunk

ointment ('ɔɪntmənt) *n.* greasy preparation for healing or beautifying the skin

OK Oklahoma

O.K. *inf. a./adv.* **1.** all right —*n.* **2.** approval —*vt.* **3.** approve (**O.K.ing** (əʊˈkeɪɪŋ), **O.K.ed** (əʊˈkeɪd))

okapi (əʊˈkɑːpɪ) *n.* Afr. animal like short-necked giraffe (*pl.* **-s, -pi**)

okra (ˈəʊkrə) *n.* **1.** annual plant with yellow-and-red flowers and edible pods **2.** pod of this plant, eaten in soups, stews *etc.*

old (əʊld) *a.* **1.** aged, having lived or existed long **2.** belonging to earlier period (ˈolder, ˈelder *comp.*, ˈoldest, ˈeldest *sup.*) —ˈolden *a.* old —ˈoldie *n. inf.* old song, film, person *etc.* —ˈoldish *a.* —**old age pension** *see* PENSION —**Old Bailey** Central Criminal Court of England —**old boy 1.** (*sometimes* O- B-) UK male ex-pupil of school **2.** *inf., chiefly* UK familiar name used to refer to man; old man —**old country** country of origin of immigrant or immigrant's ancestors —**Old English** English language from time of earliest Saxon settlements in fifth century A.D. to about 1100 (*also* **Anglo-Saxon**) —**old-fashioned** *a.* **1.** in style of earlier period, out of date **2.** fond of old ways —*n.* **3.** cocktail containing spirit, bitters, fruit *etc.* —**old guard 1.** group that works for long-established principles *etc.* **2.** conservative element in political party or other groups —**old hat** old-fashioned; trite —**old maid** elderly spinster —**old man 1.** *inf.* father; husband **2.** (*sometimes* O- M-) *inf.* man in command, such as employer, foreman *etc.* **3.** *jocular* affectionate term used in addressing man —**old master 1.** one of great European painters before 19th cent. **2.** painting by one of these —**Old Nick** *inf., jocular* Satan —**old school 1.** *chiefly* UK one's former school **2.** group of people favouring traditional ideas *etc.* —**old school tie 1.** UK distinctive tie that indicates which school wearer attended **2.** attitudes, values *etc.* associated with British public schools —**Old Testament** collection of books comprising sacred Scriptures of Hebrews; first part of Christian Bible —**old wives' tale** belief passed on as piece of traditional wisdom —**Old World** eastern hemisphere —**old-world** *a.* of former times, *esp.* quaint or traditional

oleaginous (əʊlɪˈædʒɪnəs) *a.* **1.** oily, producing oil **2.** unctuous, fawning —**ole'aginousness** *n.*

oleander (əʊlɪˈændə) *n.* poisonous evergreen flowering shrub

oleo- (*comb. form*) oil, as in *oleomargarine*

O level UK **1.** basic level of General Certificate of Education **2.** pass in subject at O level

olfactory (ɒlˈfæktərɪ, -trɪ) *a.* of smelling

oligarchy (ˈɒlɪgɑːkɪ) *n.* government by a few —ˈoligarch *n.* —oliˈgarchic(al) *a.*

Oligocene (ˈɒlɪgəʊsiːn, ɒˈlɪg-) *a.* **1.** of third

epoch of Tertiary period —*n.* **2.** Oligocene epoch or rock series

olive (ˈɒlɪv) *n.* **1.** evergreen tree **2.** its oil-yielding fruit **3.** its wood —*a.* **4.** greyish-green —**olive branch** any offering of peace or conciliation —**olive oil** pale yellow oil extracted from olives, used in medicines *etc.*

Olympian (əˈlɪmpɪən) *a.* **1.** of Mount Olympus or classical Greek gods **2.** majestic in manner or bearing **3.** of ancient Olympia or its inhabitants —*n.* **4.** god of Mount Olympus **5.** inhabitant of ancient Olympia

Olympic (əˈlɪmpɪk) *a.* **1.** of Olympic Games **2.** of ancient Olympia —**Olympic Games 1.** Panhellenic festival, held every fourth year in honour of Zeus at ancient Olympia **2.** modern revival of these games

O.M. Order of Merit

ombudsman (ˈɒmbʊdzmən) *n.* official who investigates citizens' complaints against government *etc.*

omega (ˈəʊmɪgə) *n.* **1.** last letter in Gr. alphabet (Ω, ω) **2.** end

omelette *or esp. U.S.* **omelet** (ˈɒmlɪt) *n.* dish of eggs beaten up and fried with seasoning

omen (ˈəʊmən) *n.* prophetic object or happening —**ominous** (ˈɒmɪnəs) *a.* boding evil, threatening

omicron (əʊˈmaɪkrɒn, ˈɒmɪkrɒn) *n.* 15th letter in Gr. alphabet (O, o)

omit (əʊˈmɪt) *vt.* **1.** leave out, neglect **2.** leave undone (**-tt-**) —oˈmission *n.* —oˈmissive *a.*

omni- (*comb. form*) all

omnibus (ˈɒmnɪbʌs, -bəs) *n.* **1.** large road vehicle travelling on set route and taking passengers at any stage (*also* **bus**) **2.** book containing several works —*a.* **3.** serving, containing several objects

omnidirectional (ɒmnɪdɪˈrɛkʃənəl, -daɪ-) *a.* in radio, denotes transmission, reception in all directions

omnipotent (ɒmˈnɪpətənt) *a.* all-powerful —**om'nipotence** *n.*

omnipresent (ɒmnɪˈprɛzənt) *a.* present everywhere —**omni'presence** *n.*

omniscient (ɒmˈnɪsɪənt) *a.* knowing everything —**om'niscience** *n.*

omnivorous (ɒmˈnɪvərəs) *a.* **1.** devouring all foods **2.** not fastidious

on (ɒn) *prep.* **1.** above and touching, at, near, towards *etc.* **2.** attached to **3.** concerning **4.** performed upon **5.** during **6.** taking regularly —*a.* **7.** operating **8.** taking place **9.** *Cricket* denoting part of field to left of right-handed batter, and to right of bowler —*adv.* **10.** so as to be on **11.** forwards **12.** continuously *etc.* **13.** in progress —**oncoming** *a.* **1.** coming nearer in space or time; approaching —*n.* **2.** approach;

onset —'**ongoing** a. **1.** actually in progress **2.** continually moving forward —**on line** of or concerned with peripheral device that is directly connected to and controlled by central processing unit of computer —'**onrush** n. forceful forward rush or flow —'**onset** n. **1.** violent attack **2.** assault **3.** beginning —'**onslaught** n. attack —**on stream** (of manufacturing process, equipment etc.) in or about to go into operation or production —'**onward** a. **1.** advanced or advancing —adv. **2.** in advance, ahead, forward —'**onwards** adv.

ON Ontario

on- (comb. form) on, as in onlooker

onager ('ɒnədʒə) n. wild ass (pl. **-gri** (-graɪ), **-s**)

onanism ('əʊnənɪzəm) n. masturbation

O.N.C. UK Ordinary National Certificate

once (wʌns) adv. **1.** one time **2.** formerly **3.** ever —**once-over** n. inf. quick examination —**at once** immediately; simultaneously

oncost ('ɒnkɒst) n. UK (sometimes pl.) see overheads at OVERHEAD

O.N.D. UK Ordinary National Diploma

one (wʌn) a. **1.** lowest cardinal number **2.** single **3.** united **4.** only, without others **5.** identical —n. **6.** number or figure 1 **7.** unity **8.** single specimen —pron. **9.** particular but not stated person **10.** any person —'**oneness** n. **1.** unity **2.** uniformity **3.** singleness —one'**self** pron. —**one-armed bandit** inf. fruit machine operated by pulling down lever at one side —**one-horse** a. inf. small; obscure —**one-night stand 1.** performance given only once at any one place **2.** inf. sexual encounter lasting only one night —**one-off** n. UK something that is carried out or made only once (also **one-shot**) —**one-sided** a. **1.** partial **2.** uneven —**one-track** a. **1.** inf. obsessed with one idea, subject etc. **2.** having or consisting of single track —**one-way** a. denotes system of traffic circulation in one direction only

onerous ('ɒnərəs, 'əʊ-) a. burdensome

onion ('ʌnjən) n. edible bulb of pungent flavour

only ('əʊnlɪ) a. **1.** being the one specimen —adv. **2.** solely, merely, exclusively —conj. **3.** but then, excepting that

o.n.o. or near(est) offer

onomatopoeia (ɒnəmætə'piːə) n. formation of a word by using sounds that resemble or suggest the object or action to be named —**onomato-'poeic** or **onomatopoetic** (ɒnəmætəpəʊ'etɪk) a.

onto or **on to** ('ɒntʊ; unstressed 'ɒntə) prep. **1.** on top of **2.** aware of

ontology (ɒn'tɒlədʒɪ) n. science of being or reality —**onto'logical** a. —**on'tologist** n.

onus ('əʊnəs) n. responsibility, burden

onyx ('ɒnɪks) n. variety of chalcedony

oodles ('uːdəlz) pl.n. inf. abundance

oolite ('əʊəlaɪt) n. any sedimentary rock, esp. limestone, consisting of tiny spherical grains within fine matrix —**oolitic** (əʊə'lɪtɪk) a.

ooze (uːz) vi. **1.** pass slowly out —v. **2.** exude (moisture etc.) —n. **3.** sluggish flow **4.** wet mud, slime —'**oozy** a.

op. 1. opera **2.** operation **3.** opus

o.p. or **O.P.** out of print

opal ('əʊpəl) n. glassy gemstone displaying variegated colours —**opa'lescent** a.

opaque (əʊ'peɪk) a. not allowing the passage of light, not transparent —**opacity** (əʊ'pæsɪtɪ) n.

OPEC ('əʊpek) Organization of Petroleum Exporting Countries

open ('əʊpən) a. **1.** not shut or blocked up **2.** without lid or door **3.** bare **4.** undisguised **5.** not enclosed, covered or exclusive **6.** spread out, accessible **7.** frank, sincere —vt. **8.** set open, uncover, give access to **9.** disclose, lay bare **10.** begin **11.** make a hole in —vi. **12.** become open **13.** begin —n. **14.** clear space, unenclosed country **15.** Sport competition in which all may enter —'**opening** n. **1.** hole, gap **2.** beginning **3.** opportunity —a. **4.** first **5.** initial —'**openly** adv. without concealment —**open-and-shut** a. easily decided or solved —'**opencast** a. (of coal) mined from the surface, not underground —**open-ended** a. without definite limits, as of duration or amount —**open-handed** a. generous —**open-hearted** a. frank, magnanimous —**open-heart surgery** surgical repair of heart during which blood circulation is oft. maintained mechanically —**open-minded** a. unprejudiced —**open-plan** a. having no or few dividing walls between areas —**open prison** prison without restraints to prevent absconding —**open secret** something that is supposed to be secret but is widely known —**Open University** UK university for mature students studying by television and radio lectures, correspondence courses etc. —**open verdict** coroner's verdict not stating cause (of death) —'**openwork** n. pattern with interstices

opera ('ɒpərə, 'ɒprə) n. musical drama —**oper'atic** a. of opera —**ope'retta** n. light, comic opera —**opera glasses** small binoculars used by audiences in theatres etc.

operation (ɒpə'reɪʃən) n. **1.** working, way things work **2.** scope **3.** act of surgery **4.** military action —**opera'bility** n. —'**operable** a. **1.** capable of being treated by surgical operation **2.** capable of being put into practice —'**operate** vt. **1.** cause to function **2.** control functioning of —vi. **3.** work **4.** produce an effect **5.** perform act of surgery **6.** exert power —**ope'rational** a. **1.** of operation(s) **2.** working —'**operative** a. **1.** working —n. **2.** worker, esp. with a special skill —'**operator** n. —**operating theatre** room in which surgical operations are performed —**operations research** analysis of problems in business involving quantitative techniques

operculum (ɔʊˈpɜːkjʊləm) n. lid; cover (pl. **-s, -la** (-lə))

ophidian (ɒʊˈfɪdɪən) a. 1. snakelike 2. of suborder of reptiles which comprises snakes —n. 3. any reptile of this suborder

ophthalmic (ɒfˈθælmɪk) a. of eyes —**ophˈthalmia** n. inflammation of eye —**ophthalˈmologist** n. —**ophthalˈmology** n. study of eye and its diseases —**ophˈthalmoscope** n. instrument for examining interior of eye —**ophthalmic optician** optician qualified to prescribe spectacles etc.

opiate (ˈɒʊpɪɪt) see OPIUM

opinion (əˈpɪnjən) n. 1. what one thinks about something 2. belief, judgment —**opine** (ɒʊˈpaɪn) vt. 1. think —vi. 2. utter opinion —oˈpinionated a. 1. stubborn in one's opinions 2. dogmatic

opium (ˈɒʊpɪəm) n. addictive narcotic drug made from poppy —ˈ**opiate** n. 1. drug containing opium 2. narcotic —a. 3. inducing sleep 4. soothing

opossum (əˈpɒsəm) or **possum** n. small Amer. and Aust. marsupial animal

opp. 1. opposed 2. opposite

opponent (əˈpɒʊnənt) n. adversary, antagonist

opportune (ˈɒpətjuːn) a. seasonable, well-timed —**opporˈtunism** n. policy of doing what is expedient at the time regardless of principle —**opporˈtunist** n./a. —**opporˈtunity** n. 1. favourable time or condition 2. good chance

oppose (əˈpɒʊz) vt. 1. resist, withstand 2. contrast 3. set against —**opˈposer** n. —**opposite** a. 1. contrary 2. facing 3. diametrically different 4. adverse —n. 5. the contrary —prep./adv. 6. facing 7. on the other side —**oppoˈsition** n. 1. antithesis 2. resistance 3. obstruction 4. hostility 5. group opposing another 6. party opposing that in power —**opposite number** person holding corresponding position on another side or situation

oppress (əˈprɛs) vt. 1. govern with tyranny 2. weigh down —**opˈpression** n. 1. act of oppressing 2. severity 3. misery —**opˈpressive** a. 1. tyrannical 2. hard to bear 3. heavy 4. (of weather) hot and tiring —**opˈpressively** adv. —**opˈpressor** n.

opprobrium (əˈprɒʊbrɪəm) n. disgrace —**opˈprobrious** a. 1. reproachful 2. shameful 3. abusive

oppugn (əˈpjuːn) vt. call into question, dispute

opt (ɒpt) vi. make a choice —ˈ**optative** a. 1. expressing wish or desire —n. 2. mood of verb expressing wish

opt. 1. optical 2. optional

optic (ˈɒptɪk) a. 1. of eye or sight —n. 2. eye —pl. 3. (with sing. v.) science of sight and light —ˈ**optical** a. —**opˈtician** n. maker of, dealer in spectacles, optical instruments —**optical character reader** computer device enabling characters, usu. printed on paper, to be optically scanned and input to storage device

optimism (ˈɒptɪmɪzəm) n. 1. disposition to look on the bright side 2. doctrine that good must prevail in the end 3. belief that the world is the best possible world —ˈ**optimist** n. —**optiˈmistic** a. —**optiˈmistically** adv.

optimum (ˈɒptɪməm) a./n. the best, the most favourable (pl. **-s, -ma** (-mə))

option (ˈɒpʃən) n. 1. choice 2. preference 3. thing chosen 4. in business, purchased privilege of either buying or selling things at specified price within specified time —ˈ**optional** a. leaving to choice

optometrist (ɒpˈtɒmɪtrɪst) n. person usu. not medically qualified, testing eyesight, prescribing corrective lenses etc. —opˈ**tometry** n.

opulent (ˈɒpjʊlənt) a. 1. rich 2. copious —ˈ**opulence** or ˈ**opulency** n. riches, wealth

opus (ˈɒʊpəs) n. 1. work 2. musical composition (pl. **opera** (ˈɒpərə), **-es**)

or (ɔː; unstressed ə) conj. 1. introduces alternatives 2. if not

OR Oregon

-or[1] (comb. form) person or thing that does what is expressed by verb, as in actor, sailor

-or[2] (comb. form) 1. state, condition, activity, as in terror, error 2. US see -OUR

O.R. 1. Official Receiver 2. operational research

oracle (ˈɒrəkəl) n. 1. divine utterance, prophecy, oft. ambiguous, given at shrine of god 2. the shrine 3. wise or mysterious adviser 4. (O-) R ITV teletext service —oˈracular a. 1. of oracle 2. prophetic 3. authoritative 4. ambiguous

oral (ˈɔːrəl, ˈɒrəl) a. 1. spoken 2. by mouth —n. 3. spoken examination —ˈorally adv.

orange (ˈɒrɪndʒ) n. 1. bright reddish-yellow round fruit 2. tree bearing it 3. fruit's colour —**orangeˈade** n. effervescent orange-flavoured drink —ˈ**orangery** n. building, such as greenhouse, in which orange trees are grown

Orangeman (ˈɒrɪndʒmən) n. member of society founded as secret order in Ireland to uphold Protestantism

orang-utan (ɔːˌræŋuːˈtæn, ɔːˈræŋuːtæn) or **orang-outang** (ɔːˌræŋuːˈtæŋ, ɔːˈræŋuːtæŋ) n. large Indonesian ape

orator (ˈɒrətə) n. 1. maker of speech 2. skilful speaker —oˈration n. formal speech —**oraˈtorical** a. of orator or oration —ˈ**oratory** n. 1. speeches 2. eloquence 3. small private chapel

oratorio (ɒrəˈtɔːrɪəʊ) n. semi-dramatic composition of sacred music (pl. **-s**)

orb (ɔːb) n. globe, sphere —**orˈbicular** a.

orbit ('ɔːbɪt) *n.* **1.** track of planet, satellite, comet *etc.*, around another heavenly body **2.** field of influence, sphere **3.** eye socket —*v.* **4.** move in, or put into, an orbit

Orcadian (ɔːˈkeɪdɪən) *n.* **1.** native or inhabitant of the Orkneys —*a.* **2.** of or relating to the Orkneys

orchard ('ɔːtʃəd) *n.* **1.** area for cultivation of fruit trees **2.** the trees

orchestra ('ɔːkɪstrə) *n.* **1.** band of musicians **2.** place for such a band in theatre *etc.* (*also* **orchestra pit**) —**or'chestral** *a.* —**'orchestrate** *vt.* **1.** compose or arrange (music) for orchestra **2.** organize, arrange

orchid ('ɔːkɪd) *n.* genus of various flowering plants

ordain (ɔːˈdeɪn) *vt.* **1.** admit to Christian ministry **2.** confer holy orders upon **3.** decree, enact **4.** destine —**ordi'nation** *n.*

ordeal (ɔːˈdiːl) *n.* **1.** severe, trying experience **2.** *Hist.* form of trial by which accused underwent severe physical test

order ('ɔːdə) *n.* **1.** regular or proper arrangement or condition **2.** sequence **3.** peaceful condition of society **4.** rank, class **5.** group **6.** command **7.** request for something to be supplied **8.** mode of procedure **9.** instruction **10.** monastic society —*vt.* **11.** command **12.** request (something) to be supplied or made **13.** arrange —**'orderliness** *n.* —**'orderly** *a.* **1.** tidy **2.** methodical **3.** well-behaved —*n.* **4.** hospital attendant **5.** soldier following officer to carry orders —**'ordinal** *a.* **1.** showing position in a series —*n.* **2.** ordinal number —**ordinal number** number denoting order, quality or degree in group, such as *first, second, third* —**Order of Merit** UK order conferred on civilians and servicemen for eminence in any field

ordinance ('ɔːdɪnəns) *n.* **1.** decree, rule **2.** rite, ceremony

ordinary ('ɔːdənrɪ) *a.* **1.** usual, normal **2.** common **3.** plain **4.** commonplace —*n.* **5.** bishop in his province —**'ordinarily** *adv.* —**Ordinary level** UK *formal name for* O LEVEL —**ordinary rating** rank in Royal Navy comparable to that of private in army

ordinate ('ɔːdɪnɪt) *n.* vertical or *y*-coordinate of point in two-dimensional system of Cartesian coordinates

ordnance ('ɔːdnəns) *n.* **1.** big guns, artillery **2.** military stores —**Ordnance Survey** official geographical survey of Britain

Ordovician (ɔːdəʊˈvɪʃən) *a.* **1.** of, denoting or formed in second period of Palaeozoic era —*n.* **2.** Ordovician period or rock system

ordure ('ɔːdjʊə) *n.* **1.** dung **2.** filth

ore (ɔː) *n.* naturally occurring mineral which yields metal

oregano (ɒrɪˈɡɑːnəʊ) *n.* herb, variety of marjoram

organ ('ɔːɡən) *n.* **1.** musical wind instrument of pipes and stops, played by keys **2.** member of animal or plant carrying out particular function **3.** means of action **4.** medium of information, *esp.* newspaper —**or'ganic** *a.* **1.** of, derived from, living organisms **2.** of bodily organs **3.** affecting bodily organs **4.** having vital organs **5.** *Chem.* of compounds formed from carbon **6.** grown with fertilizers derived from animal or vegetable matter **7.** organized, systematic —**or'ganically** *adv.* —**'organist** *n.* organ player —**organ loft** gallery in church *etc.* for an organ

organdie *or esp. U.S.* **organdy** ('ɔːɡəndɪ) *n.* light, transparent muslin

organize *or* **-ise** ('ɔːɡənaɪz) *vt.* **1.** give definite structure to **2.** get up, arrange **3.** put into working order **4.** unite in a society —**'organism** *n.* **1.** organized body or system **2.** plant, animal —**organi'zation** *or* **-i'sation** *n.* **1.** act of organizing **2.** body of people **3.** society —**'organizer** *or* **-iser** *n.*

orgasm ('ɔːɡæzəm) *n.* sexual climax

orgy ('ɔːdʒɪ) *n.* **1.** drunken or licentious revel, debauch **2.** act of immoderation, overindulgence

oriel ('ɔːrɪəl) *n.* **1.** projecting part of an upper room with a window **2.** the window

orient ('ɔːrɪənt) *n.* **1.** (**O-**) the East **2.** lustre of best pearls —*a.* **3.** rising **4.** (**O-**) Eastern —*vt.* ('ɔːrɪɛnt) **5.** place so as to face East **6.** adjust or align (oneself *etc.*) according to surroundings or circumstances **7.** position or set (map *etc.*) with reference to compass *etc.* —**ori'ental** *a./n.* —**ori'entalist** *n.* expert in Eastern languages and history —**'orientate** *vt.* orient —**orien'ta-tion** *n.* —**orien'teering** *n.* competitive sport involving compass and map-reading skills

orifice ('ɒrɪfɪs) *n.* opening, mouth of a cavity, eg pipe

orig. **1.** origin **2.** original(ly)

origami (ɒrɪˈɡɑːmɪ) *n.* Japanese art of paper folding

origin ('ɒrɪdʒɪn) *n.* **1.** beginning **2.** source **3.** parentage

original (əˈrɪdʒɪnəl) *a.* **1.** primitive, earliest **2.** new, not copied or derived **3.** thinking or acting for oneself **4.** eccentric —*n.* **5.** pattern, thing from which another is copied **6.** unconventional or strange person —**origi'nality** *n.* power of producing something individual to oneself —**o'riginally** *adv.* **1.** at first **2.** in the beginning —**original sin** *Theol.* state of sin held to be innate in mankind as descendants of Adam

originate (əˈrɪdʒɪneɪt) *v.* come or bring into existence, begin —**origi'nation** *n.* —**o'riginator** *n.*

oriole ('ɔːrɪəʊl) *n.* tropical thrushlike bird

orison ('ɒrɪz³n) n. prayer

Orlon ('ɔːlɒn) n. **R** crease-resistant acrylic fabric used for clothing etc.

ormolu ('ɔːməluː) n. **1.** gilded bronze **2.** gold-coloured alloy **3.** articles of these

ornament ('ɔːnəmənt) n. **1.** any object used to adorn or decorate **2.** decoration —vt. ('ɔːnəment) **3.** adorn —**orna'mental** a.

ornate (ɔː'neɪt) a. highly decorated or elaborate

ornery ('ɔːnərɪ) a. US dial., inf. **1.** stubborn; vile-tempered **2.** low; treacherous **3.** ordinary

ornithology (ɔːnɪ'θɒlədʒɪ) n. science of birds —**ornitho'logical** a. —**orni'thologist** n.

orotund ('ɒrəʊtʌnd) a. **1.** full, clear and musical **2.** pompous

orphan ('ɔːfən) n. child bereaved of one or both parents —**'orphanage** n. institution for care of orphans —**'orphanhood** n.

orrery ('ɒrərɪ) n. mechanical model of solar system to show revolutions, planets etc.

orris or **orrice** ('ɒrɪs) n. any of various kinds of iris

ortho- or before vowel **orth-** (comb. form) right, correct

orthodontics (ɔːθəʊ'dɒntɪks) or **orthodontia** (ɔːθəʊ'dɒntɪə) n. branch of dentistry concerned with correcting irregularities of teeth —**ortho'dontic** a. —**ortho'dontist** n.

orthodox ('ɔːθədɒks) a. **1.** holding accepted views **2.** conventional —**'orthodoxy** n. —**Orthodox Church 1.** collective body of Eastern Churches that were separated from western Church in 11th century and are in communion with Gr. patriarch of Constantinople **2.** any of these Churches

orthography (ɔː'θɒɡrəfɪ) n. correct spelling

orthopaedics or U.S. **orthopedics** (ɔːθə'piːdɪks) pl.n. (with sing. v.) branch of surgery concerned with disorders of spine and joints and repair of deformities of these parts —**ortho'paedic** or U.S. **ortho'pedic** a.

orthopterous (ɔː'θɒptərəs) a. of large order of insects, including crickets, locusts and grass-hoppers, having leathery forewings and membranous hind wings

ortolan ('ɔːtələn) n. a small bird, esp. as table delicacy

-ory[1] (comb. form) **1.** place for, as in observatory **2.** something having specified use, as in directory

-ory[2] (comb. form) of, relating to; characterized by; having effect of, as in contributory

oryx ('ɒrɪks) n. large Afr. antelope (pl. -es, -yx)

Os Chem. osmium

O.S. 1. Old Style **2.** Ordinary Seaman **3.** UK Ordnance Survey **4.** outsize **5.** (also **OS**) Old Saxon (language)

Oscar ('ɒskə) n. any of several small gold statuettes awarded annually in U.S.A. for outstanding achievements in films

oscillate ('ɒsɪleɪt) vi. **1.** swing to and fro **2.** waver **3.** fluctuate (regularly) —**oscil'lation** n. —**'oscillator** n. —**'oscillatory** a. —**os'cillo-scope** n. electronic instrument producing visible representation of rapidly changing quantity

osculate ('ɒskjuleɪt) v. jocular kiss —**'oscular** a. —**oscu'lation** n. —**'osculatory** a.

osier ('əʊzɪə) n. species of willow used for basketwork

-osis (comb. form) **1.** process; state, as in metamorphosis **2.** diseased condition, as in tuberculosis **3.** formation or development of something, as in fibrosis

osmium ('ɒzmɪəm) n. heaviest known of metallic elements

osmosis (ɒz'məʊsɪs, ɒs-) n. percolation of fluids through porous partitions —**osmotic** (ɒz'mɒtɪk, ɒs-) a.

osprey ('ɒsprɪ, -preɪ) n. **1.** fishing hawk **2.** plume

osseous ('ɒsɪəs) a. **1.** of, like bone **2.** bony —**ossifi'cation** n. —**'ossify** v. **1.** turn into bone —vi. **2.** grow rigid (-fied, -fying)

ostensible (ɒ'stɛnsɪb³l) a. **1.** apparent **2.** professed —**os'tensibly** adv.

ostentation (ɒstɛn'teɪʃən) n. show, pretentious display —**osten'tatious** a. **1.** given to display **2.** showing off —**osten'tatiously** adv.

osteo- or before vowel **oste-** (comb. form) bone(s)

osteomyelitis (ɒstɪəʊmaɪɪ'laɪtɪs) n. inflammation of bone marrow

osteopathy (ɒstɪ'ɒpəθɪ) n. art of treating disease by removing structural derangement by manipulation, esp. of spine —**'osteopath** n. one skilled in this art

ostler ('ɒslə) or **hostler** n. Hist. stableman at an inn

ostracize or **-ise** ('ɒstrəsaɪz) vt. exclude, banish from society, exile —**'ostracism** n. social boycotting

ostrich ('ɒstrɪtʃ) n. large swift-running flightless Afr. bird

O.T. 1. occupational therapy **2.** Old Testament **3.** overtime

O.T.C. UK Officers' Training Corps

other ('ʌðə) a. **1.** not this **2.** not the same **3.** alternative, different —pron. **4.** other person or thing —**'otherwise** adv. **1.** differently **2.** in another way —conj. **3.** or else, if not —**other'worldly** a. **1.** of or relating to spiritual or imaginative world **2.** impractical, unworldly

otiose ('əʊtɪəʊs, -əʊz) a. **1.** superfluous **2.** useless

otitis (əʊ'taɪtɪs) n. inflammation of ear

otter ('ɒtə) n. furry aquatic fish-eating animal

Ottoman (ˈɒtəmən) *or* **Othman** (ˈɒθmən) *a.* 1. Turkish —*n.* 2. Turk 3. (o-) cushioned, backless seat, storage box (*pl.* -**s**)

ou (əʊ) *n. SA sl.* man —**oubaas** (ˈəʊbɑːs) *n.* man in authority

oubliette (uːblɪˈɛt) *n.* dungeon entered by trapdoor

ouch (aʊtʃ) *interj.* exclamation of sudden pain

ought (ɔːt) *v. aux.* 1. expressing duty, obligation or advisability 2. be bound

Ouija (ˈwiːdʒə) *n.* **R** board with letters and symbols used to obtain messages at seances

ouma (ˈəʊmɑː) *n. SA* 1. grandmother 2. elderly woman

ounce (aʊns) *n.* a weight, sixteenth of avoirdupois pound (28.4 grams), twelfth of troy pound (31.1 grams)

oupa (ˈəʊpɑː) *n. SA* 1. grandfather 2. elderly man

our (aʊə) *a.* belonging to us —**ours** *pron.* —**our'self** *pron.* myself, used in regal or formal style —**our'selves** *pl. pron.* emphatic or reflexive form of WE

-our (*comb. form*) state, condition, activity, as in *behaviour, labour*

-ous (*comb. form*) 1. having; full of, as in *dangerous, spacious* 2. *Chem.* indicating that element is chemically combined in lower of two possible valency states, as in *ferrous*

ousel (ˈuːzəl) *n. see* OUZEL

oust (aʊst) *vt.* put out, expel

out (aʊt) *adv.* 1. from within, away 2. wrong 3. on strike —*a.* 4. not worth considering 5. not allowed 6. unfashionable 7. unconscious 8. not in use, operation *etc.* 9. at an end 10. not burning 11. *Sport* dismissed —**outer** *a.* away from the inside —**outermost** *or* **outmost** *a.* on extreme outside —**outing** *n.* pleasure excursion —**outward** *a./adv.* —**outwardly** *adv.* —**outwards** *adv.* —**out-and-out** *a.* thoroughly; complete —**outer space** any region of space beyond atmosphere of earth —**out-of-the-way** *a.* 1. distant from more populous areas 2. uncommon or unusual —**out of date** no longer valid, current, or fashionable —**out of pocket** 1. having lost money, as in a commercial enterprise 2. without money to spend 3. (of expenses) unbudgeted and paid for in cash

out- (*comb. form*) 1. beyond, in excess, as in

outclass, outdistance, outsize 2. so as to surpass or defeat, as in *outfox, outmanoeuvre* 3. outside, away from, as in *outpatient, outgrowth*. See the list below

outback (ˈaʊtbæk) *n.* **A** remote, sparsely populated country

outbalance (aʊtˈbæləns) *vt.* 1. outweigh 2. exceed in weight

outboard (ˈaʊtbɔːd) *a.* (of boat's engine) mounted outside stern

outbreak (ˈaʊtbreɪk) *n.* sudden occurrence, *esp.* of disease or strife

outburst (ˈaʊtbɜːst) *n.* bursting out, *esp.* of violent emotion

outcast (ˈaʊtkɑːst) *n.* 1. someone rejected —*a.* 2. rejected, cast out

outclass (aʊtˈklɑːs) *vt.* excel, surpass

outcome (ˈaʊtkʌm) *n.* result

outcrop (ˈaʊtkrɒp) *n. Geol.* 1. rock coming out of stratum to the surface —*vi.* (aʊtˈkrɒp) 2. come out to the surface (-**pp-**)

outcry (ˈaʊtkraɪ) *n.* 1. widespread or vehement protest —*vt.* (aʊtˈkraɪ) 2. cry louder or make more noise than

outdo (aʊtˈduː) *vt.* surpass or exceed in performance (-**'doing, -'did, -'done**)

outdoors (aʊtˈdɔːz) *adv.* in the open air —**'outdoor** *a.*

outfall (ˈaʊtfɔːl) *n.* mouth of river

outfit (ˈaʊtfɪt) *n.* 1. equipment 2. clothes and accessories 3. *inf.* group or association regarded as a unit —**'outfitter** *n.* one who deals in outfits

outflank (aʊtˈflæŋk) *vt.* 1. get beyond the flank of (enemy army) 2. circumvent

outgoing (ˈaʊtgəʊɪŋ) *a.* 1. departing 2. friendly, sociable

outgrow (aʊtˈgrəʊ) *vt.* 1. become too large or too old for 2. surpass in growth (-**'grew, -'grown, -'growing**)

outhouse (ˈaʊthaʊs) *n.* shed *etc.* near main building

outlandish (aʊtˈlændɪʃ) *a.* queer, extravagantly strange

outlaw (ˈaʊtlɔː) *n.* 1. one beyond protection of the law 2. exile, bandit —*vt.* 3. make (someone) an outlaw 4. ban —**'outlawry** *n.*

outlay (ˈaʊtleɪ) *n.* expenditure

outlet (ˈaʊtlɛt, -lɪt) *n.* 1. opening, vent 2. means

out'bid	'outgrowth	'outpost	out'smart
out'box	out'last	out'rank	'out'spread
out'distance	out'live	out'reach	out'stare
out'face	outma'noeuvre	'outrider	'outstation
'outfield	out'match	out'rival	out'stretch
out'fight	out'number	out'run	out'value
'outflow	'outpatient	out'shine	out'vote
out'fox	out'play	'outsize	out'weigh

of release or escape **3.** market for product or service

outline ('autlaın) n. **1.** rough sketch **2.** general plan **3.** lines enclosing visible figure —vt. **4.** sketch **5.** summarize

outlook ('autluk) n. **1.** point of view **2.** probable outcome **3.** view

outlying ('autlaıŋ) a. distant, remote

outmoded (aut'məudıd) a. no longer fashionable or accepted

output ('autput) n. **1.** quantity produced **2.** Comp. information produced

outrage ('autreıdʒ) n. **1.** violation of others' rights **2.** gross or violent offence or indignity **3.** anger arising from this —vt. **4.** offend grossly **5.** insult **6.** injure, violate —**out'rageous** a.

outré (u'tre) a. **1.** extravagantly odd **2.** bizarre

outrigger ('autrıgə) n. **1.** frame, esp. with float attached, outside boat's gunwale **2.** frame on rowing boat's side with rowlock **3.** boat equipped with such a framework

outright ('autraıt) a. **1.** undisputed **2.** downright **3.** positive —adv. **4.** completely **5.** instantly or openly

outset ('autsɛt) n. beginning

outside ('aut'saıd) n. **1.** exterior **2.** C settled parts of Canada —adv. (aut'saıd) **3.** not inside **4.** in the open air —a. ('autsaıd) **5.** on exterior **6.** remote, unlikely **7.** greatest possible, probable —**out'sider** n. **1.** person outside specific group **2.** contestant thought unlikely to win —**outside broadcast** T.V., rad. broadcast not made from studio

outskirts ('autskɜːts) pl.n. outer areas, districts, esp. of city

outspan ('autspæn) n. SA **1.** unyoking of oxen **2.** area for rest

outspoken (aut'spəukən) a. frank, candid

outstanding (aut'stændıŋ) a. **1.** excellent **2.** remarkable **3.** unsettled, unpaid

outstrip (aut'strıp) vt. outrun, surpass

outwit (aut'wıt) vt. get the better of by cunning

outwork ('autwɜːk) n. part of fortress outside main wall

ouzel or **ousel** ('uːzəl) n. **1.** type of thrush **2.** kind of diving bird

ouzo ('uːzəu) n. strong aniseed-flavoured spirit from Greece

ova ('əuvə) n., pl. of OVUM

oval ('əuvəl) a. **1.** egg-shaped, elliptical —n. **2.** something of this shape

ovary ('əuvərı) n. female egg-producing organ —o'varian a.

ovation (əu'veıʃən) n. enthusiastic burst of applause

oven ('ʌvən) n. heated chamber for baking in

over ('əuvə) adv. **1.** above, above and beyond, going beyond, in excess, too much, past, finished, in repetition, across, downwards etc. —prep. **2.** above **3.** on, upon **4.** more than, in excess of, along etc. —a. **5.** upper, outer —n. **6.** Cricket set of six balls bowled by bowler from same end of pitch

over- (comb. form) too, too much, in excess, above, to a prostrate position. See the list below

over·abundance	over·eat	over·many	over·size
over·act	over·emphasize	over·modest	over·sleep
overam·bitious	over·estimate	over·much	over·specialize
over·anxious	overex·cite	over·night	over·spend
over·awe	overex·ert	'overpass	over·spill v.
over·book	overex·pand	over·pay	'overspill n.
over·burden	overex·penditure	over·play	over·stay
overca·pacity	over·fill	overpopu·lation	over·steer v.
over·cautious	over·flow v.	over·praise	'oversteer n.
over·charge	'overflow n.	over·price	over·step
'overcoat	'overgarment	overpro·duce	over·stock v.
over·compensate	over·grow	overpro·duction	'overstock n.
over·confident	over·hang	over·rate	over·stretch
overcon·sumption	over·hasty	over·reach	over·tire
over·cook	overin·dulge	overre·act	over·top
over·crowd	overin·dulgence	over·ripe	over·trump
over·curious	overin·sistent	over·run	over·turn
overde·pendent	over·joy	over·sensitive	over·use
overde·velop	over·lay	over·shadow	over·value
over·do	over·lie	'overshoe	over·weight
'overdose	over·load v.	over·shoot	over·work v.
over·due	'overload n.	oversimplifi·cation	'overwork n.
over·eager	'overlord	over·simplify	over·zealous

overall ('ɔuvərɔːl) n. 1. (also pl.) loose garment worn as protection against dirt etc. —a. 2. total

overbalance (ɔuvə'bælɒns) v. 1. lose or cause to lose balance —n. ('ɔuvəbælɒns) 2. excess of weight, value etc.

overbearing (ɔuvə'bɛərɪŋ) a. domineering

overblown (ɔuvə'blɒun) a. excessive, bombastic

overboard ('ɔuvəbɔːd) adv. from a vessel into the water

overcast ('ɔuvəkɑːst) a. covered over, esp. by clouds

overcoat ('ɔuvəkɒut) n. warm coat worn over outer clothes

overcome (ɔuvə'kʌm) vt. 1. conquer 2. surmount 3. make incapable or powerless —vi. 4. be victorious

overdraft ('ɔuvədrɑːft) n. withdrawal of money in excess of credit balance on bank account

overdrive ('ɔuvədraɪv) n. 1. very high gear in motor vehicle used at high speeds to reduce wear —vt. (ɔuvə'draɪv) 2. drive too hard or too far; overwork (-'driving, -'drove, -'driven)

overhaul (ɔuvə'hɔːl) vt. 1. examine and set in order, repair 2. overtake —n. ('ɔuvəhɔːl) 3. thorough examination, esp. for repairs

overhead ('ɔuvəhɛd) a. 1. over one's head, above —adv. (ɔuvə'hɛd) 2. aloft, above —'overheads pl.n. expenses of running a business, over and above cost of manufacturing and of raw materials

overhear (ɔuvə'hɪə) vt. hear (person, remark etc.) without knowledge of speaker (-'hearing, -'heard)

overkill ('ɔuvəkɪl) n. capacity, advantage greater than required

overland ('ɔuvəlænd) a./adv. by land

overlap (ɔuvə'læp) v. 1. (of two things) extend or lie partly over (each other) 2. cover and extend beyond (something) —vi. 3. coincide partly in time, subject etc. (-pp-) —n. ('ɔuvəlæp) 4. part that overlaps or is overlapped 5. amount, length etc. overlapping

overleaf ('ɔuvəliːf) adv. on other side of page

overlook (ɔuvə'luk) vt. 1. fail to notice 2. disregard 3. look over

overpower (ɔuvə'pauə) vt. 1. conquer by superior force 2. have such strong effect on as to make ineffective 3. supply with more power than necessary —over'powering a.

override (ɔuvə'raɪd) vt. 1. set aside, disregard 2. cancel 3. trample down

overrule (ɔuvə'ruːl) vt. 1. disallow arguments of (person) by use of authority 2. rule or decide against (decision etc.) 3. prevail over; influence 4. exercise rule over

overseas ('ɔuvə'siːz) a. 1. foreign 2. from or to

a place over the sea (also over'sea) —adv. (ɔuvə'siːz) 3. beyond the sea; abroad

overseer ('ɔuvəsɪə) n. supervisor —over'see vt. supervise

oversight ('ɔuvəsaɪt) n. 1. failure to notice 2. mistake

overt ('ɔuvəːt) a. open, unconcealed

overtake (ɔuvə'teɪk) vt. 1. move past (vehicle, person) travelling in same direction 2. come up with in pursuit 3. catch up

overthrow (ɔuvə'θrɒu) vt. 1. upset, overturn 2. defeat (-'threw, -'thrown, -'throwing) —n. ('ɔuvəθrɒu) 3. ruin 4. defeat 5. fall

overtime ('ɔuvətaɪm) n. 1. time at work, outside normal working hours 2. payment for this time

overtone ('ɔuvətɒun) n. additional meaning, nuance

overture ('ɔuvətjuə) n. 1. Mus. orchestral introduction 2. opening of negotiations 3. formal offer

overweening (ɔuvə'wiːnɪŋ) a. thinking too much of oneself

overwhelm (ɔuvə'wɛlm) vt. 1. crush 2. submerge, engulf —over'whelming a. 1. decisive 2. irresistible —over'whelmingly adv.

overwrought (ɔuvə'rɔːt) a. 1. overexcited 2. too elaborate

ovi- or **ovo-** (comb. form) egg; ovum, as in oviform

oviduct ('ɒvɪdʌkt, 'ɒu-) n. tube through which ova are conveyed from ovary (also (in mammals) Fallopian tube) —oviducal (ɒvɪ'djuːkəl, ɒu-) or ovi'ductal a.

oviform ('ɒuvɪfɔːm) a. egg-shaped

ovine ('ɒuvaɪn) a. of, like, sheep

oviparous (ɒu'vɪpərəs) a. laying eggs

ovoid ('ɒuvɔɪd) a. egg-shaped

ovoviviparous (ɒuvɒuvaɪ'vɪpərəs) a. (of certain reptiles, fishes etc.) producing eggs that hatch within body of mother —ovovivi'parity n.

ovule ('ɒvjuːl) n. unfertilized seed —'ovulate vi. produce, discharge egg from ovary —ovu'lation n.

ovum ('ɒuvəm) n. female egg cell, in which development of foetus takes place (pl. 'ova)

owe (ɒu) vt. be bound to repay, be indebted for —'owing a. owed, due —owing to caused by, as a result of

owl (aul) n. night bird of prey —'owlet n. young owl —'owlish a. solemn and dull

own (ɒun) a. 1. emphasizes possession —vt. 2. possess 3. acknowledge —vi. 4. confess —'owner n. —'ownership n. possession

ox (ɒks) n. 1. large cloven-footed and usu. horned farm animal 2. bull or cow (pl. 'oxen) —'oxbow n. 1. U-shaped harness collar of ox 2. lake formed from deep bend of river —'oxeye n.

daisylike plant —'**oxtail** n. skinned tail of ox, used esp. in soups and stews —'**oxtongue** n. 1. any of various plants having bristly tongue-shaped leaves 2. tongue of ox, braised or boiled as food

oxalis ('ɒksəlɪs, ɒk'sælɪs) n. genus of plants —**oxalic acid** (ɒk'sælɪk) poisonous acid derived from oxalis

Oxbridge ('ɒksbrɪdʒ) n. Brit. universities of Oxford and Cambridge, esp. considered as prestigious academic institutions

oxen ('ɒksən) n., pl. of ox

Oxfam ('ɒksfæm) Oxford Committee for Famine Relief

oxide ('ɒksaɪd) n. compound of oxygen and one other element —**oxidate** ('ɒksɪdeɪt) v. —**oxidation** (ɒksɪ'deɪʃən) n. act or process of oxidizing —**oxidization** or -**isation** (ɒksɪdaɪ'zeɪʃən) n. —**oxidize** or -**ise** ('ɒksɪdaɪz) v. (cause to) combine with oxide, rust

Oxon. ('ɒksən) Oxfordshire

oxygen ('ɒksɪdʒən) n. gas in atmosphere essential to life, combustion etc. —'**oxygenate**, '**oxygenize** or -**ise** vt. combine or treat with oxygen —**oxya'cetylene** a. denoting flame used for welding produced by mixture of oxygen and acetylene —**oxygen tent** Med. transparent enclosure covering patient, into which oxygen is released to help maintain respiration

oxymoron (ɒksɪ'mɔːrɒn) n. figure of speech in which two ideas of opposite meaning are combined to form an expressive phrase or epithet, as in cruel kindness (pl. -**mora** (-'mɔːrə))

oyez or **oyes** ('əʊjes, -jez) n. call, uttered three times by public crier or court official

oyster ('ɔɪstə) n. edible bivalve mollusc or shellfish —'**oystercatcher** n. shore bird

oz or **oz.** ounce

ozone ('əʊzəʊn, əʊ'zəʊn) n. form of oxygen with pungent odour —'**ozonize** or -**ise** vt.

Association 6. private account 7. public-address system 8. publicity agent 9. Publishers Association 10. purchasing agent

p.a. per annum

PABX UK private automatic branch exchange (see also PBX)

pace[1] (peɪs) n. 1. step 2. its length 3. rate of movement 4. walk, gait —vi. 5. step —vt. 6. set speed for 7. cross, measure with steps —'**pacer** n. one who sets the pace for another —'**pacemaker** n. esp. electronic device surgically implanted in those with heart disease

pace[2] ('peɪsɪ; Lat. 'pɑːkɛ) prep. with due deference to: used to acknowledge politely someone who disagrees

pachyderm ('pækɪdɜːm) n. thick-skinned animal, eg elephant —**pachy'dermatous** a. thick-skinned, stolid

pacify ('pæsɪfaɪ) vt. 1. calm 2. restore to peace (-**ified, -ifying**) —pa'**cific** a. 1. peaceable 2. calm, tranquil —**pacifi'cation** n. —**pacifi-'catory** a. tending to make peace —'**pacifier** n. 1. person or thing that pacifies 2. US baby's dummy or teething ring —'**pacifism** n. —'**pacifist** n. 1. advocate of abolition of war 2. one who refuses to participate in war

pack (pæk) n. 1. bundle 2. band of animals 3. large set of people or things 4. set of, container for, retail commodities 5. set of playing cards 6. mass of floating ice —v. 7. put (articles) together in suitcase etc. 8. press tightly together, cram —vt. 9. make into a bundle 10. fill with things 11. fill (meeting etc.) with one's own supporters 12. (oft. with off or away) send off —'**package** n. 1. parcel 2. set of items offered together —vt. 3. wrap in or put into package —'**packet** n. 1. small parcel 2. small container (and contents) 3. sl. large sum of money —**package holiday** holiday with fixed itinerary and at price inclusive of travel and lodging —**packet (boat)** n. mail-boat —'**pack-horse** n. horse for carrying goods —**pack ice** loose ice which has been compacted together —**pack saddle** saddle for carrying goods

pact (pækt) n. covenant, agreement, compact

pad[1] (pæd) n. 1. piece of soft stuff used as a cushion, protection etc. 2. block of sheets of paper 3. foot or sole of various animals 4. place for launching rockets 5. sl. residence —vt. 6. make soft, fill in, protect etc. with pad or padding (-**dd**-) —'**padding** n. 1. material used for stuffing 2. literary matter put in simply to increase quantity —**padded cell** room, esp. in mental hospital, with padded surfaces, in which violent inmates are placed

pad[2] (pæd) vi. 1. walk with soft step 2. travel slowly (-**dd**-) —n. 3. sound of soft footstep

P,p

p or **P** (piː) n. 1. 16th letter of English alphabet 2. speech sound represented by this letter (pl. **p's, P's** or **Ps**) —**mind one's p's and q's** be careful to use polite language

p 1. page 2. pence 3. penny 4. Mus. piano (softly)

P 1. (car) park 2. Chess pawn 3. Chem. phosphorus 4. pressure

Pa Chem. protactinium

PA Pennsylvania

P.A. 1. personal assistant 2. Mil. Post Adjutant 3. power of attorney 4. press agent 5. Press

paddle[1] ('pædǝl) n. 1. short oar with broad blade at one or each end —v. 2. move by, as with, paddles 3. row gently —**paddle wheel** wheel with crosswise blades striking water successively to propel ship

paddle[2] ('pædǝl) vi. 1. walk with bare feet in shallow water —n. 2. act of paddling

paddock ('pædǝk) n. small grass field or enclosure

paddy[1] ('pædɪ) n. rice growing or in the husk —**paddy field** field where rice is grown

paddy[2] ('pædɪ) n. inf. temper

padlock ('pædlɒk) n. 1. detachable lock with hinged hoop to go through staple or ring —vt. 2. fasten thus

padre ('pɑːdrɪ) n. chaplain with the armed forces

paean or U.S. (sometimes) **pean** ('piːǝn) n. song of triumph or thanksgiving

paederast ('pɛdǝræst) n. see PEDERAST

paediatrics or U.S. **pediatrics** (piːdɪ-'ætrɪks) n. branch of medicine dealing with diseases and disorders of children —**paedia'trician** or U.S. **pedia'trician** n.

paedo-, pedo- or before vowel **paed-, ped-** (comb. form) child, children, as in paedophilia

paedophilia (piːdǝʊ'fɪlɪǝ) n. condition of being sexually attracted to children —**paedophile** ('piːdǝʊfaɪl) or **paedo'philiac** n./a.

paella (pɑɪ'ɛlǝ) n. 1. Sp. dish of rice, shellfish etc. 2. pan in which paella is cooked

pagan ('peɪɡǝn) a./n. heathen —**'paganism** n.

page[1] (peɪdʒ) n. one side of leaf of book etc.

page[2] (peɪdʒ) n. 1. boy servant or attendant —vt. 2. summon by loudspeaker announcement —**'pageboy** n. medium-length hairstyle with ends of hair curled under

pageant ('pædʒǝnt) n. 1. show of persons in costume in procession, dramatic scenes etc., usu. illustrating history 2. brilliant show —**'pageantry** n.

paginate ('pædʒɪneɪt) vt. number pages of —**pagi'nation** n.

pagoda (pǝ'ɡǝʊdǝ) n. pyramidal temple or tower of Chinese or Indian type

paid (peɪd) pt./pp. of PAY —**put paid to** inf. end, destroy

pail (peɪl) n. bucket —**'pailful** n.

paillasse ('pælɪæs, pæl'æs) n. see PALLIASSE

pain (peɪn) n. 1. bodily or mental suffering 2. penalty or punishment —pl. 3. trouble, exertion —vt. 4. inflict pain upon —**pained** a. having or expressing pain or distress, esp. mental or emotional —**'painful** a. —**'painfully** adv. —**'painless** a. —**'painlessly** adv. —**'painkiller** n. drug, as aspirin, that reduces pain —**'painstaking** a. diligent, careful

paint (peɪnt) n. 1. colouring matter spread on a surface with brushes, roller, spray gun etc. —vt. 2. portray, colour, coat, or make picture of, with paint 3. apply make-up to 4. describe —**'painter** n. —**'painting** n. picture in paint

painter ('peɪntǝ) n. line at bow of boat for tying it up

pair (pɛǝ) n. 1. set of two, esp. existing or generally used together —v. 2. (oft. with off) group or be grouped in twos

paisley ('peɪzlɪ) n. pattern of small curving shapes

pajamas (pǝ'dʒɑːmǝz) pl.n. US see PYJAMAS

Pakistani (pɑːkɪ'stɑːnɪ) a. 1. of Pakistan, country in Indian subcontinent —n. 2. native or inhabitant of Pakistan

pal (pæl) n. inf. friend —**'pally** a. inf. on friendly terms

palace ('pælɪs) n. 1. residence of king, bishop etc. 2. stately mansion —**pa'latial** a. like a palace 2. magnificent —**'palatine** a. with royal privileges

paladin ('pælǝdɪn) n. Hist. knight errant

palaeo-, paleo- before vowel **palae-** or esp. U.S. **paleo-, pale-** (comb. form) old, ancient, prehistoric, as in palaeography

Palaeocene ('pælɪǝʊsiːn) a. 1. of first epoch of Tertiary period —n. 2. Palaeocene epoch or rock series

Palaeolithic (pælɪǝʊ'lɪθɪk) a. of the old Stone Age

palaeontology (pælɪɒn'tɒlǝdʒɪ) n. study of past geological periods and fossils —**palaeonto'logical** a.

Palaeozoic (pælɪǝʊ'zǝʊɪk) a. 1. of geological time that began with Cambrian period and lasted until end of Permian period —n. 2. Palaeozoic era

palanquin or **palankeen** (pælǝn'kiːn) n. covered litter, formerly used in Orient, carried on shoulders of four men

palate ('pælɪt) n. 1. roof of mouth 2. sense of taste —**'palatable** a. agreeable to eat —**'palatal** or **'palatine** a. 1. of the palate 2. made by placing tongue against palate —n. 3. palatal sound

palatial (pǝ'leɪʃǝl) a. see PALACE

palaver (pǝ'lɑːvǝ) n. 1. fuss 2. conference, discussion

pale[1] (peɪl) a. 1. wan, dim, whitish —vi. 2. whiten 3. lose superiority or importance —**'paleface** n. derogatory term for White person, said to have been used by N Amer. Indians

pale[2] (peɪl) n. stake, boundary —**'paling** n. upright plank making up fence

paleo- or before vowel **pale-** (comb. form) esp. US see PALAEO-

Palestinian (pælɪ'stɪnɪǝn) a. 1. of Palestine, former country in Middle East —n. 2. native or inhabitant of this area **3.** descendant of inhabitant of this area, displaced when Israel became state

palette or **pallet** ('pælɪt) n. artist's flat board for mixing colours on —**palette knife** spatula with thin flexible blade, used in painting etc.

palindrome ('pælɪndrəʊm) n. word, verse or sentence that is the same when read backwards or forwards

palisade (pælɪ'seɪd) n. **1.** fence of stakes —vt. **2.** enclose or protect with one

pall[1] (pɔːl) n. **1.** cloth spread over a coffin **2.** depressing, oppressive atmosphere —**pall-bearer** n. one carrying, attending coffin at funeral

pall[2] (pɔːl) vi. **1.** become tasteless or tiresome **2.** cloy

palladium (pə'leɪdɪəm) n. silvery-white element of platinum metal group, used in jewellery etc.

pallet[1] ('pælɪt) n. **1.** straw mattress **2.** small bed

pallet[2] ('pælɪt) n. portable platform for storing and moving goods

palliasse or **paillasse** ('pælɪæs, pælɪ'æs) n. straw mattress

palliate ('pælɪeɪt) vt. **1.** relieve without curing **2.** excuse —**palli'ation** n. —**palliative** ('pælɪətɪv) a. **1.** giving temporary or partial relief —n. **2.** that which excuses, mitigates or alleviates

pallid ('pælɪd) a. pale, wan, colourless —'**pallor** n. paleness

palm (pɑːm) n. **1.** inner surface of hand **2.** tropical tree **3.** leaf of the tree as symbol of victory —vt. **4.** conceal in palm of hand **5.** pass off by trickery —**palmate** ('pælmeɪt, -mɪt) or '**palmated** a. **1.** shaped like open hand **2.** Bot. having five lobes that spread out from common point **3.** (of water birds) having three toes connected by web —'**palmist** n. —'**palmistry** n. fortune-telling from lines on palm of hand —'**palmy** a. flourishing, successful —**palm oil** oil obtained from fruit of certain palms —**Palm Sunday** Sunday before Easter —**palm off** (oft. with on) **1.** offer, sell or spend fraudulently **2.** divert in order to be rid of

palomino (pælə'miːnəʊ) n. golden horse with white mane and tail (pl. **-s**)

palpable ('pælpəbl) a. **1.** obvious **2.** certain **3.** that may be touched or felt —'**palpably** adv.

palpate ('pælpeɪt) vt. Med. examine by touch

palpitate ('pælpɪteɪt) vi. throb **2.** pulsate violently —**palpi'tation** n. **1.** throbbing **2.** violent, irregular beating of heart

palsy ('pɔːlzɪ) n. paralysis

paltry ('pɔːltrɪ) a. worthless, contemptible, trifling

pampas ('pæmpəz) n. (oft. with pl. v.) vast grassy treeless plains in S Amer.

pamper ('pæmpə) vt. overindulge, spoil by coddling

pamphlet ('pæmflɪt) n. thin unbound book usu. on some topical subject

pan[1] (pæn) n. **1.** broad, shallow vessel **2.** bowl of lavatory **3.** depression in ground, esp. where salt forms —vt. **4.** wash (gold ore) in pan **5.** inf. criticize harshly (**-nn-**) —'**pantile** n. curved roofing tile —**pan out** result

pan[2] (pæn) v. move (film camera) slowly while filming to cover scene, follow moving object etc. (**-nn-**)

pan- (comb. form) all, as in panacea, pantomime. Such words are not given here where the meaning may easily be inferred from simple word

panacea (pænə'sɪə) n. universal remedy, cure for all ills

panache (pə'næʃ, -'nɑːʃ) n. dashing style

Panama hat (pænə'mɑː) straw hat

Pan-American a. of North, South and Central Amer. collectively

pancake ('pænkeɪk) n. **1.** thin cake of batter fried in pan **2.** flat cake or stick of compressed make-up —vi. **3.** Aviation make flat landing by dropping in a level position —**Pancake Day** see **Shrove Tuesday** at SHROVETIDE

panchromatic (pænkrəʊ'mætɪk) a. Photog. sensitive to light of all colours

pancreas ('pæŋkrɪəs) n. digestive gland behind stomach —**pancre'atic** a.

panda ('pændə) n. large black and white bearlike mammal of China —**panda car** police patrol car

pandemic (pæn'dɛmɪk) a. (of disease) occurring over wide area

pandemonium (pændɪ'məʊnɪəm) n. scene of din and uproar

pander ('pændə) v. **1.** (esp. with to) give gratification (to weakness or desires) —n. **2.** pimp

pandit ('pʌndɪt; spelling pron. 'pændɪt) n. see PUNDIT (sense 2)

P. & L. profit and loss

p. & p. UK postage and packing

pane (peɪn) n. single piece of glass in window or door

panegyric (pænɪ'dʒɪrɪk) n. speech of praise —**pane'gyrical** a. laudatory —**pane'gyrist** n.

panel ('pænl) n. **1.** compartment of surface, usu. raised or sunk, eg in door **2.** any distinct section of something, eg of car body **3.** strip of material inserted in garment **4.** group of persons as team in quiz game etc. **5.** list of jurors, doctors etc. **6.** thin board with picture on it —vt. **7.** adorn with panels (**-ll-**) —'**panelling** or U.S.

'paneling n. panelled work —**'panellist** or U.S. **'panelist** n. member of panel —**panel beater** one who repairs damage to car body —**panel game** quiz etc. played by group of people, esp. on TV

pang (pæŋ) n. 1. sudden pain, sharp twinge 2. compunction

pangolin (pæŋ'gəʊlɪn) n. mammal with scaly body and long snout for feeding on ants etc. (also **scaly anteater**)

panic ('pænɪk) n. 1. sudden and infectious fear 2. extreme fright 3. unreasoning terror —a. 4. of fear etc. —v. 5. feel or cause to feel panic (-**icked**, -**icking**) —**'panicky** a. 1. inclined to panic 2. nervous —**'panicmonger** n. one who starts panic —**panic-stricken** or **panic-struck** a.

panicle ('pænɪkəl) n. compound raceme, as in oat

panjandrum (pæn'dʒændrəm) n. pompous self-important man

pannier ('pænɪə) n. basket carried by beast of burden, bicycle, or on person's shoulders

panoply ('pænəplɪ) n. complete, magnificent array —**'panoplied** a.

panorama (pænə'rɑːmə) n. 1. wide or complete view 2. picture arranged round spectator or unrolled before him —**pano'ramic** a.

panpipes ('pænpaɪps) pl.n. (oft. sing., oft. P-) number of reeds or whistles of graduated lengths bound together to form musical wind instrument (also **pipes of Pan**, **'syrinx**)

pansy ('pænzɪ) n. 1. flower, species of violet 2. inf. effeminate man

pant (pænt) vi. 1. gasp for breath 2. yearn, long 3. throb —n. 4. gasp

pantaloon (pæntə'luːn) n. 1. in pantomime, foolish old man who is the butt of clown —pl. 2. inf. baggy trousers

pantechnicon (pæn'tɛknɪkən) n. large van, esp. for carrying furniture

pantheism ('pænθɪɪzəm) n. identification of God with the universe —**'pantheist** n. —**panthe'istic** a. —**'pantheon** n. temple of all gods

panther ('pænθə) n. variety of leopard

panties ('pæntɪz) pl.n. women's undergarment

pantihose ('pæntɪhəʊz) n. tights

panto ('pæntəʊ) n. UK inf. pantomime (pl. -s)

pantograph ('pæntəɡrɑːf) n. instrument for copying shape etc. to any scale

pantomime ('pæntəmaɪm) n. 1. theatrical show, usu. produced at Christmastime, oft. founded on fairy tale 2. dramatic entertainment in dumbshow

pantry ('pæntrɪ) n. room for storing food or utensils

pants (pænts) pl.n. 1. undergarment for lower trunk 2. US trousers

panzer ('pænzə; Ger. 'pantsər) a. 1. of fast mechanized armoured units employed by German army in World War II —n. 2. vehicle belonging to panzer unit, esp. tank —pl. 3. armoured troops

pap¹ (pæp) n. 1. soft food for infants, invalids etc. 2. pulp, mash 3. SA maize porridge

pap² (pæp) n. 1. breast 2. nipple

papa (pə'pɑː) n. inf. father

papacy ('peɪpəsɪ) n. 1. office of Pope 2. papal system —**'papal** a. of, relating to, the Pope

papaw or **pawpaw** ('pɔːpɔː) n. 1. tree bearing melon-shaped fruit 2. its fruit (also **papaya** (pə'paɪə))

paper ('peɪpə) n. 1. material made by pressing pulp of rags, straw, wood etc. into thin, flat sheets 2. printed sheet of paper 3. newspaper 4. article, essay 5. set of examination questions —pl. 6. documents etc. —vt. 7. cover, decorate with paper —**'paperback** n. book with flexible covers —**'paperboy** n. boy employed to deliver newspapers ('papergirl fem.) —**paper chase** cross-country run in which runner lays trail of paper for others to follow —**'paperclip** n. clip for holding sheets of paper together, esp. one of bent wire —**'paperhanger** n. person who hangs wallpaper as occupation —**'paperknife** n. knife with comparatively blunt blade for opening sealed envelopes etc. —**paper money** paper currency issued by government or central bank as legal tender —**'paperweight** n. small heavy object to prevent loose papers from scattering —**'paperwork** n. clerical work, such as writing of reports or letters

papier-mâché (pæpjeɪ'mæʃeɪ) n. pulp from rags or paper mixed with size, shaped by moulding and dried hard

papilla (pə'pɪlə) n. 1. small projection of tissue at base of hair etc. 2. any similar protuberance (pl. -**lae** (-liː)) —**pa'pillary**, **'papillate** or **'papillose** a.

papoose (pə'puːs) n. N Amer. Indian child

paprika ('pæprɪkə, pæ'priː-) n. (powdered seasoning prepared from) type of red pepper

Pap test or **smear** (pæp) Med. examination of stained cells in smear taken of bodily secretions, esp. from uterus, for detection of cancer

papyrus (pə'paɪrəs) n. 1. species of reed 2. (manuscript written on) kind of paper made from this plant (pl. -**ri** (-raɪ), -**es**)

par (pɑː) n. 1. equality of value or standing 2. face value (of stocks and shares) 3. Golf estimated standard score —**'parity** n. 1. equality 2. analogy —**par value** value imprinted on face of share certificate or bond and used to assess dividend *etc.*

par. 1. paragraph 2. parallel 3. parenthesis

para- *or before vowel* **par-** (*comb. form*) beside, beyond, as in *paradigm, parallel, parody*

parable ('pærəbəl) *n.* allegory, story with a moral lesson —**para'bolic(al)** *a.* of parable

parabola (pə'ræbələ) *n.* section of cone cut by plane parallel to the cone's side —**para'bolic** *a.* of parabola

paracetamol (pærə'si:təmɒl, -'sɛtə-) *n.* mild drug used as alternative to aspirin

parachute ('pærəʃu:t) *n.* 1. apparatus extending like umbrella used to retard the descent of a falling body —*v.* 2. land or cause to land by parachute —**'parachutist** *n.*

parade (pə'reid) *n.* 1. display 2. muster of troops 3. parade ground 4. public walk —*vi.* 5. march —*vt.* 6. display

paradigm ('pærədaim) *n.* example, model —**paradigmatic** (pærədig'mætik) *a.*

paradise ('pærədais) *n.* 1. Heaven 2. state of bliss 3. Garden of Eden

paradox ('pærədɒks) *n.* statement that seems absurd or self-contradictory but may be true —**para'doxical** *a.*

paraffin ('pærəfin) *n.* waxlike or liquid hydrocarbon mixture used as fuel, solvent, in candles *etc.*

paragon ('pærəgən) *n.* pattern or model of excellence

paragraph ('pærəgra:f, -græf) *n.* 1. section of chapter or book 2. short notice, as in newspaper —*vt.* 3. arrange in paragraphs

parakeet *or* **parrakeet** ('pærəki:t) *n.* small kind of parrot

parallax ('pærəlæks) *n.* apparent difference in object's position or direction as viewed from different points

parallel ('pærəlɛl) *a.* 1. continuously at equal distances 2. precisely corresponding —*n.* 3. line equidistant from another at all points 4. thing exactly like another 5. comparison 6. line of latitude —*vt.* 7. represent as similar, compare —**'parallelism** *n.* —**paral'lelogram** *n.* four-sided plane figure with opposite sides parallel —**parallel bars** *Gymnastics* pair of wooden bars on uprights used for exercises

paralysis (pə'rælisis) *n.* incapacity to move or feel, due to damage to nervous system (*pl.* -yses (-isi:z)) —**'paralyse** *or U.S.* -lyze *vt.* 1. afflict with paralysis 2. cripple 3. make useless or ineffectual —**para'lytic** *a./n.* (person) afflicted with paralysis —**infantile paralysis** poliomyelitis

paramedical (pærə'mɛdikəl) *a.* of persons working in various capacities in support of medical profession

parameter (pə'ræmitə) *n.* any constant limiting factor

paramilitary (pærə'militəri, -tri) *a.* of civilian group organized on military lines or in support of the military

paramount ('pærəmaunt) *a.* supreme, eminent, pre-eminent, chief

paramour ('pærəmuə) *n. esp.* formerly, illicit lover, mistress

parang ('pa:ræŋ) *n.* heavy Malay knife

paranoia (pærə'nɔiə) *n.* mental disease with delusions of fame, grandeur, persecution —**paranoiac** (pærə'nɔiæk) *a./n.* —**'paranoid** *a.* 1. of paranoia 2. *inf.* exhibiting fear of persecution *etc.* —*n.* 3. person afflicted with paranoia

parapet ('pærəpit, -pɛt) *n.* low wall, railing along edge of balcony, bridge *etc.*

paraphernalia (pærəfə'neiliə) *pl.n.* (*sometimes with sing. v.*) 1. personal belongings 2. odds and ends of equipment

paraphrase ('pærəfreiz) *n.* 1. expression of meaning of passage in other words 2. free translation —*vt.* 3. put into other words

paraplegia (pærə'pli:dʒə) *n.* paralysis of lower half of body —**para'plegic** *n./a.*

parapsychology (pærəsai'kɒlədʒi) *n.* study of subjects pert. to extrasensory perception, *eg* telepathy

Paraquat ('pærəkwɒt) *n.* **R** very poisonous weedkiller

parasite ('pærəsait) *n.* 1. animal or plant living in or on another 2. self-interested hanger-on —**parasitic** (pærə'sitik) *a.* of the nature of, living as, parasite —**'parasitism** *n.*

parasol ('pærəsɒl) *n.* sunshade

parataxis (pærə'tæksis) *n.* arrangement of sentences which omits connecting words

parathion (pærə'θaiɒn) *n.* toxic oil used as insecticide

paratroops ('pærətru:ps) *pl.n.* troops trained to descend by parachute

paratyphoid fever (pærə'taifɔid) infectious disease similar to but distinct from typhoid fever

parboil ('pa:bɔil) *vt.* boil until partly cooked

parcel ('pa:səl) *n.* 1. packet of goods, *esp.* one enclosed in paper 2. quantity dealt with at one time 3. piece of land —*vt.* 4. wrap up 5. divide into parts (-ll-)

parch (pa:tʃ) *v.* 1. dry by heating 2. make, become hot and dry 3. scorch 4. roast slightly

parchment ('pa:tʃmənt) *n.* 1. sheep, goat, calf skin prepared for writing 2. manuscript of this

pardon ('pa:dən) *vt.* 1. forgive, excuse —*n.* 2. forgiveness 3. release from punishment —**'pardonable** *a.* —**'pardonably** *adv.*

pare (pɛə) *vt.* 1. trim, cut edge or surface of 2.

decrease bit by bit —'**paring** n. piece pared off, rind

parent ('peərənt) n. father or mother —'**parentage** n. descent, extraction —**pa'rental** a. —'**parenthood** n. —**parent teacher association** group of parents of children at school and their teachers formed in order to foster better understanding between them etc.

parenthesis (pə'rɛnθɪsɪs) n. word or sentence inserted in passage independently of grammatical sequence and usu. marked off by brackets, dashes, or commas —**pa'rentheses** pl.n. round brackets, ( ), used for this —**pa'renthesize** or **-sise** vt. 1. place in parentheses 2. insert as parenthesis 3. intersperse with parentheses —**paren'thetical** a.

par excellence (par ɛksɛ'lã:s; English par 'ɛksələns) Fr. to degree of excellence; beyond comparison

pariah (pə'raɪə, 'pærɪə) n. social outcast

parietal (pə'raɪɪtəl) a. of the walls of bodily cavities, eg skull

pari-mutuel (pærɪ'mjuːtjʊəl) n. system of betting in which those who have bet on winners of race share in total amount wagered less percentage for management (pl. **pari-mutuels,** **paris-mutuels** (pærɪ'mjuːtjʊəlz))

parish ('pærɪʃ) n. 1. district under one clergyman 2. subdivision of county —**pa'rishioner** n. inhabitant of parish —**parish clerk** person designated to assist in various church duties —**parish register** book in which births, baptisms, marriages, and deaths in parish are recorded

parity ('pærɪtɪ) n. see PAR

park (pɑːk) n. 1. large area of land in natural state preserved for recreational use 2. large enclosed piece of ground, usu. with grass or woodland, attached to country house or for public use 3. space in camp for military supplies —vt. 4. leave for a short time 5. manoeuvre (car) into a suitable space 6. arrange or leave in a park —**parking meter** timing device, usu. coin-operated, that indicates how long vehicle may be left parked —**parking ticket** summons served for parking offence —'**parkland** n. grassland with scattered trees

parka ('pɑːkə) n. warm waterproof coat, oft. with hood

parkin ('pɑːkɪn) n. UK moist spicy ginger cake

Parkinson's disease ('pɑːkɪnsənz) progressive chronic disorder of central nervous system characterized by impaired muscular coordination and tremor (also '**parkinsonism**)

Parkinson's law notion, expressed facetiously as law of economics, that work expands to fill time available

Parl. 1. Parliament 2. parliamentary (also **parl.**)

parlance ('pɑːləns) n. 1. way of speaking, conversation 2. idiom

parley ('pɑːlɪ) n. 1. meeting between leaders or representatives of opposing forces to discuss terms —vi. 2. hold discussion about terms

parliament ('pɑːləmənt) n. 1. the legislature of the United Kingdom 2. any similar legislative assembly —**parliamen'tarian** n. member of parliament —**parlia'mentary** a. —**parliamentary private secretary** UK backbencher in Parliament who assists minister

parlour or U.S. **parlor** ('pɑːlə) n. 1. sitting room, room for receiving company in small house 2. place for milking cows 3. US room or shop as business premises, esp. hairdresser etc.

Parmesan cheese (pɑːmɪ'zæn) hard dry cheese used grated, esp. on pasta dishes etc.

parochial (pə'rəʊkɪəl) a. 1. narrow, provincial 2. of a parish —**pa'rochialism** n.

parody ('pærədɪ) n. 1. composition in which author's style is made fun of by imitation 2. travesty —vt. 3. write parody of (**-odied,** **-odying**) —'**parodist** n.

parole (pə'rəʊl) n. 1. early freeing of prisoner on condition he is of good behaviour 2. word of honour —vt. 3. place on parole

parotid (pə'rɒtɪd) a. 1. relating to or situated near parotid gland —n. 2. parotid gland —**parotid gland** large salivary gland in front of and below each ear

-parous (comb. form) giving birth to, as in oviparous

paroxysm ('pærəksɪzəm) n. sudden violent attack of pain, rage, laughter

parquet ('pɑːkeɪ, -kɪ) n. 1. flooring of wooden blocks arranged in pattern —vt. 2. cover (floor) with parquet —**parquetry** ('pɑːkɪtrɪ) n.

parr (pɑː) n. salmon up to two years of age (pl. **-s, parr**)

parrakeet ('pærəkiːt) n. see PARAKEET

parricide ('pærɪsaɪd) n. murder or murderer of a parent

parrot ('pærət) n. 1. any of several related birds with short hooked beak, some varieties of which can imitate speaking 2. unintelligent imitator —**parrot fever** or **disease** see psittacosis at PSITTACINE

parry ('pærɪ) vt. 1. ward off, turn aside ('**parried,** '**parrying**) —n. 2. act of parrying, esp. in fencing

parse (pɑːz) vt. 1. describe (word) 2. analyse (sentence) in terms of grammar

parsec ('pɑːsɛk) n. unit of length used in expressing distance of stars

parsimony ('pɑːsɪmənɪ) n. 1. stinginess 2. undue economy —**parsi'monious** a. sparing

parsley ('pɑːslɪ) *n.* herb used for seasoning, garnish *etc.*

parsnip ('pɑːsnɪp) *n.* edible yellow root vegetable

parson ('pɑːsən) *n.* **1.** clergyman of parish or church **2.** clergyman —**parsonage** *n.* parson's house —**parson's nose** fatty extreme end portion of tail of fowl when cooked

part (pɑːt) *n.* **1.** portion, section, share **2.** division **3.** actor's role **4.** duty **5.** (*oft. pl.*) region **6.** interest —*v.* **7.** divide **8.** separate —**parting** *n.* **1.** division between sections of hair on head **2.** separation **3.** leave-taking —**partly** *adv.* in part —**part exchange** transaction in which used goods are taken as partial payment —**part of speech** class of words sharing important syntactic or semantic features; group of words in language that may occur in similar positions or fulfil similar functions in sentence —**part song** song for several voices singing in harmony —**part-time** *a.* **1.** for less than entire time appropriate to activity —*adv.* **2.** on part-time basis —**part-timer** *n.*

part. **1.** participle **2.** particular

partake (pɑː'teɪk) *vi.* **1.** (*with* of) take or have share (in) **2.** take food or drink (-'**took,** -'**taken,** -'**taking**)

parterre (pɑː'tɛə) *n.* **1.** ornamental arrangement of beds in a flower garden **2.** the pit of a theatre

parthenogenesis (pɑːθɪnəʊ'dʒɛnɪsɪs) *n.* type of reproduction, occurring in some insects and flowers, in which unfertilized ovum develops directly into new individual —**parthenoge'netic** *a.*

Parthian shot ('pɑːθɪən) hostile remark or gesture delivered while departing

partial ('pɑːʃəl) *a.* **1.** not general or complete **2.** prejudiced **3.** (*with* to) fond (of) —**parti'ality** *n.* **1.** favouritism **2.** fondness —**partially** *adv.* partly

participate (pɑː'tɪsɪpeɪt) *v.* (*with* in) **1.** share (in) **2.** take part (in) —**par'ticipant** *n.* —**partici'pation** *n.* —**par'ticipator** *n.*

participle ('pɑːtɪsɪpəl) *n.* adjective made by inflection from verb and keeping verb's relation to dependent words —**parti'cipial** *a.*

particle ('pɑːtɪkəl) *n.* **1.** minute portion of matter **2.** least possible amount **3.** minor part of speech in grammar, prefix, suffix

parti-coloured ('pɑːtɪkʌləd) *a.* differently coloured in different parts, variegated

particular (pə'tɪkjʊlə) *a.* **1.** relating to one, not general **2.** distinct **3.** minute **4.** very exact **5.** fastidious —*n.* **6.** detail, item —*pl.* **7.** detailed account **8.** items of information —**particu'larity** *n.* —**par'ticularize** *or* **-ise** *vt.* mention in detail —**par'ticularly** *adv.*

partisan *or* **partizan** (pɑːtɪ'zæn, 'pɑːtɪzæn) *n.* **1.** adherent of a party **2.** guerrilla, member of resistance movement —*a.* **3.** adhering to faction **4.** prejudiced

partition (pɑː'tɪʃən) *n.* **1.** division **2.** interior dividing wall —*vt.* **3.** divide, cut into sections

partitive ('pɑːtɪtɪv) *a.* **1.** *Gram.* indicating that noun involved in construction refers only to part of what it otherwise refers to **2.** serving to separate or divide into parts —*n.* **3.** *Gram.* partitive linguistic element or feature

partner ('pɑːtnə) *n.* **1.** ally or companion **2.** a member of a partnership **3.** one that dances with another **4.** a husband or wife **5.** *Golf, Tennis etc.* one who plays with another against opponents —*vt.* **6.** (cause to) be a partner (of) —'**partnership** *n.* association of persons for business *etc.*

partridge ('pɑːtrɪdʒ) *n.* any of various game birds of the grouse family

parturition (pɑːtjʊ'rɪʃən) *n.* **1.** act of bringing forth young **2.** childbirth —**par'turient** *a.* **1.** of childbirth **2.** giving birth **3.** producing new idea *etc.*

party ('pɑːtɪ) *n.* **1.** social assembly **2.** group of persons travelling or working together **3.** group of persons united in opinion **4.** side **5.** person —*a.* **6.** of, belonging to, a party or faction —**party line 1.** telephone line serving two or more subscribers **2.** policies of political party —**party wall** common wall separating adjoining premises

parvenu *or* (*fem.*) **parvenue** ('pɑːvənjuː) *n.* **1.** one newly risen into position of notice, power, wealth **2.** upstart

pas (pɑː) *n.* dance step or movement, *esp.* in ballet (*pl.* **pas**)

pascal ('pæskəl) *n.* SI unit of pressure

Paschal ('pɑːskəl, 'pæskəl) *a.* of the Passover or Easter

pasha *or* **pacha** ('pɑːʃə, 'pæʃə) *n.* formerly, high official of Ottoman Empire or modern Egyptian kingdom: placed after name when used as title

pasqueflower ('pɑːskflaʊə) *n.* **1.** small purple-flowered plant of N and Central Europe and W Asia **2.** any of several related N Amer. plants

pass (pɑːs) *vt.* **1.** go by, beyond, through *etc.* **2.** exceed **3.** be accepted by **4.** undergo successfully **5.** spend **6.** transfer **7.** exchange **8.** disregard **9.** undergo (examination) successfully **10.** bring into force, sanction (a parliamentary bill *etc.*) —*vi.* **11.** go **12.** be transferred from one state or person to another **13.** elapse —*n.* **14.** way, *esp.* a narrow and difficult way **15.** permit, licence, authorization **16.** successful result from test **17.** condition **18.** *Sport* transfer of ball —'**passable** *a.* (just) acceptable —'**passing** *a.* **1.** transitory **2.**

cursory, casual —'**passbook** n. 1. book for keeping record of withdrawals from and payments into building society 2. bankbook 3. SA official document to identify bearer, his race, residence and employment —**passer-by** n. person that is passing by, esp. on foot (pl. **passers-by**) —'**passkey** n. 1. any of various keys, esp. latchkey 2. master key 3. skeleton key —**pass up** ignore, neglect; reject

passage ('pæsɪdʒ) n. 1. channel, opening 2. way through, corridor 3. part of book etc. 4. journey, voyage, fare 5. enactment of law by parliament etc. 6. rare conversation; dispute —'**passageway** n. way, esp. one in or between buildings; passage

passé ('pɑːseɪ, 'pæseɪ) a. 1. out of date 2. past the prime

passenger ('pæsɪndʒə) n. 1. traveller, esp. by public conveyance 2. one of a team who does not pull his weight

passerine ('pæsəraɪn, -riːn) a. of the order of perching birds

passim ('pæsɪm) Lat. everywhere, throughout

passion ('pæʃən) n. 1. ardent desire, esp. sexual 2. any strongly felt emotion 3. suffering (esp. that of Christ) —'**passionate** a. (easily) moved by strong emotions —'**passionflower** n. tropical Amer. plant —**passion fruit** edible fruit of passionflower —**Passion play** play depicting Passion of Christ

passive ('pæsɪv) a. 1. unresisting 2. submissive 3. inactive 4. denoting grammatical mood of verb in which the action is suffered by the subject —'**pas'sivity** n. —**passive resistance** resistance to government etc. without violence, as by fasting, demonstrating or refusing to cooperate

Passover ('pɑːsəʊvə) n. Jewish spring festival

passport ('pɑːspɔːt) n. official document granting permission to pass, travel abroad etc.

password ('pɑːswɜːd) n. 1. word, phrase, to distinguish friend from enemy 2. countersign

past (pɑːst) a. 1. ended 2. gone by 3. elapsed —n. 4. bygone times —adv. 5. by 6. along —prep. 7. beyond 8. after —**past master** 1. person with talent for, or experience in a particular activity 2. person who has held office of master in guild etc. —**past participle** participial form of verbs used to modify noun that is logically object of verb, also used in certain compound tenses and passive forms of verb —**past perfect** Gram. a. 1. denoting tense of verbs used in relating past events where action had already occurred at time of action of main verb that is itself in past tense —n. 2. past perfect tense 3. verb in this tense

pasta ('pæstə) n. any of several variously

shaped edible preparations of dough, eg spaghetti

paste (peɪst) n. 1. soft composition, as toothpaste 2. soft plastic mixture or adhesive 3. fine glass to imitate gems —vt. 4. fasten with paste —'**pasty** a. 1. like paste 2. white 3. sickly —'**pasteboard** n. stiff thick paper

pastel ('pæstəl, pæ'stel) n. 1. coloured crayon 2. art of drawing with crayons 3. pale, delicate colour —a. 4. delicately tinted

pastern ('pæstən) n. part of horse's foot between fetlock and hoof

pasteurize or **-ise** ('pæstəraɪz, -stjə-, 'pɑː-) vt. sterilize by heat —**pasteuri'zation** or **-i'sation** n.

pastiche (pæ'stiːʃ) or **pasticcio** (pæ'stɪtʃəʊ) n. 1. literary, musical, artistic work composed of parts borrowed from other works and loosely connected together 2. work imitating another's style

pastille or **pastil** ('pæstɪl) n. 1. lozenge 2. aromatic substance burnt as fumigator

pastime ('pɑːstaɪm) n. 1. that which makes time pass agreeably 2. recreation

pastor ('pɑːstə) n. clergyman in charge of a congregation —'**pastoral** a. 1. of, or like, shepherd's or rural life 2. of office of pastor —n. 3. poem describing rural life —**pastorale** (pæstə'rɑːl) n. Mus. 1. composition evocative of rural life 2. musical play based on rustic story (pl. -s, -rali (It. -'rɑːli)) —'**pastorate** n. office, jurisdiction of pastor

pastry ('peɪstrɪ) n. article of food made chiefly of flour, fat and water

pasture ('pɑːstʃə) n. 1. grass for food of cattle 2. ground on which cattle graze —v. 3. (cause to) graze —'**pasturage** n. (right to) pasture

pasty ('pæstɪ) n. small pie of meat and crust, baked without a dish

pat[1] (pæt) vt. 1. tap (-tt-) —n. 2. light, quick blow 3. small mass, as of butter, beaten into shape

pat[2] (pæt) adv. 1. exactly 2. fluently 3. opportunely —a. 4. glib 5. exactly right

pat. patent(ed)

patch (pætʃ) n. 1. piece of cloth sewed on garment 2. spot 3. plot of ground 4. protecting pad for the eye 5. small contrasting area 6. short period —vt. 7. mend 8. repair clumsily —'**patchy** a. 1. of uneven quality 2. full of patches —'**patchwork** n. 1. work composed of pieces sewn together 2. jumble

patchouli or **patchouly** ('pætʃʊlɪ, pə'tʃuːlɪ) n. 1. Indian herb 2. perfume made from it

pate (peɪt) n. 1. head 2. top of head

pâté (peɪt) n. 1. spread of finely minced liver etc. —**pâté de foie gras** (Fr. pɑte də fwɑ 'grɑ) smooth rich paste made from liver of specially fattened goose (pl. **pâtés de foie gras** (Fr. pɑte))

patella (pə'tɛlə) *n.* kneecap (*pl.* **patellae** (pə'tɛliː)) —**pa'tellar** *a.*

paten ('pætən) *n.* plate for bread in the Eucharist

patent ('peitənt, 'pætənt) *n.* **1.** deed securing to person exclusive right to invention —*a.* **2.** open **3.** ('peitənt) evident; manifest **4.** open to public perusal, as in *letters patent* —*vt.* **5.** secure a patent for —**paten'tee** *n.* one that has a patent —**patently** ('peitəntlɪ) *adv.* obviously —**patent leather** ('peitənt) (imitation) leather processed to give hard, glossy surface —**patent medicine** ('peitənt) medicine with patent, available without prescription —**Patent Office** government department that issues patents

pater ('peitə) *n.* **UK** *sl.* father

paterfamilias (peitəfə'mɪlɪæs) *n.* father of a family (*pl.* **patresfamilias** (pɑːtreizfə'mɪlɪæs))

paternal (pə'tɜːnəl) *a.* **1.** fatherly **2.** of a father —**pa'ternalism** *n.* authority exercised in a way that limits individual responsibility —**pater'nalistic** *a.* —**pa'ternity** *n.* **1.** relation of a father to his offspring **2.** fatherhood

paternoster (pætə'nɒstə) *n.* **1.** Lord's Prayer **2.** beads of rosary **3.** type of lift

path (pɑːθ) *n.* **1.** way or track **2.** course of action —**'pathway** *n.* **1.** path **2.** *Biochem.* chain of reactions associated with particular metabolic process

-path (*comb. form*) **1.** person suffering from specified disease or disorder, as in *neuropath* **2.** practitioner of particular method of treatment, as in *osteopath*

pathetic (pə'θɛtɪk) *a.* **1.** affecting or moving tender emotions **2.** distressingly inadequate —**pa'thetically** *adv.* —**pathetic fallacy** *Lit.* presentation of nature *etc.* as possessing human feelings

pathogenic (pæθə'dʒɛnɪk) *a.* producing disease —**pa'thogeny** *n.* mode of development of disease

pathology (pə'θɒlədʒɪ) *n.* science of diseases —**patho'logical** *a.* **1.** of the science of disease **2.** due to disease **3.** *inf.* compulsively motivated

pathos ('peiθɒs) *n.* power of exciting tender emotions

-pathy (*n. comb. form*) **1.** feeling, perception, as in *telepathy* **2.** disease, as in *psychopathy* **3.** method of treating disease, as in *osteopathy* —**-pathic** (*a. comb. form*)

patient ('peiʃənt) *a.* **1.** bearing trials calmly —*n.* **2.** person under medical treatment —**'patience** *n.* **1.** quality of enduring **2.** card game for one

patina ('pætɪnə) *n.* **1.** fine layer on a surface **2.** sheen of age on woodwork

patio ('pætɪəʊ) *n.* paved area adjoining house (*pl.* **-s**)

patois ('pætwɑː; *Fr.* pa'twa) *n.* regional dialect (*pl.* **patois** ('pætwɑːz; *Fr.* pa'twa))

pat. pend. patent pending

patriarch ('peitrɪɑːk) *n.* father and ruler of family, *esp.* Biblical —**patri'archal** *a.* venerable —**'patriarchy** *n.* **1.** form of social organization in which male is head of family and descent, kinship and title are traced through male line **2.** society governed by such system

patrician (pə'trɪʃən) *n.* **1.** noble of ancient Rome **2.** one of noble birth —*a.* **3.** of noble birth

patricide ('pætrɪsaɪd) *n.* murder or murderer of father

patriot ('peitrɪət, 'pæt-) *n.* one that loves his country and maintains its interests —**patriotic** (pætrɪ'ɒtɪk) *a.* inspired by love of one's country —**'patriotism** ('pætrɪətɪzəm) *n.*

patrol (pə'trəʊl) *n.* **1.** regular circuit by guard **2.** person, small group patrolling **3.** unit of Scouts or Guides —*v.* **4.** go round on guard or reconnoitring (**-ll-**)

patron ('peitrən) *n.* **1.** one who sponsors or aids artists, charities *etc.* **2.** protector **3.** regular customer **4.** guardian saint **5.** one that has disposition of church living *etc.* —**patronage** ('pætrənɪdʒ) *n.* support given by, or position of, a patron —**patronize** *or* **-ise** ('pætrənaɪz) *vt.* **1.** assume air of superiority towards **2.** frequent as customer **3.** encourage —**'patronizing** *or* **-ising** *a.* condescending

patronymic (pætrə'nɪmɪk) *n.* name derived from that of parent or an ancestor

patter ('pætə) *vi.* **1.** make noise, as sound of quick, short steps **2.** tap in quick succession **3.** pray, talk rapidly —*n.* **4.** quick succession of taps **5.** *inf.* glib, rapid speech

pattern ('pætən) *n.* **1.** arrangement of repeated parts **2.** design **3.** shape to direct cutting of cloth *etc.* **4.** model **5.** specimen —*vt.* **6.** (*with* on, after) model **7.** decorate with pattern

paucity ('pɔːsɪtɪ) *n.* **1.** scarcity **2.** smallness of quantity **3.** fewness

paunch (pɔːntʃ) *n.* belly

pauper ('pɔːpə) *n.* poor person, *esp.,* formerly, one supported by the public —**'pauperism** *n.* **1.** destitution **2.** extreme poverty

pause (pɔːz) *vi.* **1.** cease for a time —*n.* **2.** stop or rest

pavane *or* **pavan** (pə'vɑːn, 'pævən) *n.* **1.** slow, stately dance of 16th and 17th centuries **2.** music for this dance

pave (peɪv) *vt.* **1.** form surface on with stone or brick **2.** prepare, make easier (*esp. in* **pave the way**) —**'pavement** *n.* **1.** paved floor, footpath **2.** material for paving

pavilion (pə'vɪljən) *n.* **1.** clubhouse on playing field *etc.* **2.** building for housing exhibition *etc.* **3.** large ornate tent

pavlova (pæv'ləuvə) *n.* meringue cake with whipped cream and fruit

paw (pɔ:) *n.* 1. foot of animal —*v.* 2. scrape with forefoot —*vt.* 3. handle roughly 4. stroke with the hands

pawl (pɔ:l) *n.* pivoted lever shaped to engage with ratchet wheel to prevent motion in particular direction

pawn[1] (pɔ:n) *vt.* 1. deposit (article) as security for money borrowed —*n.* 2. article deposited —'**pawnbroker** *n.* lender of money on goods pledged

pawn[2] (pɔ:n) *n.* 1. piece in chess 2. *fig.* person used as mere tool

pawpaw ('pɔ:pɔ:) *n. see* PAPAW

pax (pæks) *n. chiefly R.C.Ch.* 1. kiss of peace 2. small plate formerly used to convey kiss of peace from celebrant at Mass to those attending it —*interj.* 3. *UK school sl.* call signalling end to hostilities or claiming immunity from rules of game

P.A.X. *UK* private automatic exchange

pay (peɪ) *vt.* 1. give (money *etc.*) for goods or services rendered 2. compensate 3. give, bestow 4. be profitable to 5. (*with* out) release bit by bit, as rope 6. (*with* out) spend —*vi.* 7. be remunerative or profitable (**paid,** '**paying**) —*n.* 8. wages 9. paid employment —'**payable** *a.* 1. justly due 2. profitable —**pay'ee** *n.* person to whom money is paid or due —'**payment** *n.* discharge of debt —**pay'ola** *n. inf.* 1. bribe given to secure special treatment, *esp.* to disc jockey to promote commercial product 2. practice of paying or receiving such bribes —**pay bed** bed in hospital for which user has paid as private patient —**paying guest** boarder, lodger, *esp.* in private house —'**payload** *n.* 1. part of cargo earning revenue 2. explosive power of missile *etc.* —'**paymaster** *n.* official of government *etc.*, responsible for payment of wages and salaries —'**payoff** *n.* 1. final settlement, *esp.* in retribution 2. *inf.* climax, consequence or outcome of events *etc.* 3. final payment of debt *etc.* 4. time of such payment 5. *inf.* bribe —**pay packet** envelope containing employee's wages 2. the wages —'**payroll** *n.* 1. list of employees, specifying salary or wage of each 2. total of these amounts or actual money equivalent —**pay as you earn** *UK, NZ* system by which income tax is paid by employers directly to government —**pay off** 1. pay all that is due in wages *etc.* and discharge from employment 2. pay complete amount of (debt *etc.*) 3. turn out to be profitable 4. take revenge on (person) or for (wrong done) 5. *inf.* give bribe to

P.A.Y.E. pay as you earn

Pb *Chem.* lead

PBX *UK* private branch exchange; telephone system that handles internal and external calls of building *etc.*

P.C. 1. Police Constable 2. Privy Councillor 3. C Progressive Conservative

p.c. 1. per cent 2. postcard

Pd *Chem.* palladium

pd. paid

P.D.S.A. *UK* People's Dispensary for Sick Animals

PE Prince Edward Island

P.E. physical education

pea (pi:) *n.* 1. fruit, growing in pods, of climbing plant 2. the plant —**pea-green** *a.* of shade of green like colour of green peas —**pea jacket** or '**peacoat** *n.* sailor's short heavy woollen overcoat —**pea'souper** *n. inf.* thick fog

peace (pi:s) *n.* 1. freedom from war 2. harmony 3. quietness of mind 4. calm 5. repose —'**peaceable** *a.* disposed to peace —'**peaceably** *adv.* —'**peaceful** *a.* 1. free from war, tumult 2. mild 3. undisturbed —'**peacefully** *adv.* —'**peacemaker** *n.* person who establishes peace, *esp.* between others —**peace offering** 1. something given to adversary in hope of procuring or maintaining peace 2. *Judaism* sacrificial meal shared between offerer and Jehovah —**peace pipe** pipe smoked by N Amer. Indians, *esp.* as token of peace (*also* '**calumet**)

peach[1] (pi:tʃ) *n.* 1. stone fruit of delicate flavour 2. *inf.* anything very pleasant 3. pinkish-yellow colour —'**peachy** *a.* 1. like peach 2. *inf.* fine, excellent

peach[2] (pi:tʃ) *vi. sl.* become informer

peacock ('pi:kɒk) *n.* 1. male of bird ('**peafowl**) with fanlike tail, brilliantly coloured ('**peahen** *fem.*) —*vi.* 2. strut about or pose, like a peacock

peak (pi:k) *n.* 1. pointed end of anything, *esp.* hill's sharp top 2. point of greatest development *etc.* 3. sharp increase 4. projecting piece on front of cap —*v.* 5. (cause to) form, reach peaks —**peaked** or '**peaky** *a.* 1. like, having a peak 2. sickly, wan, drawn —**peak hour** time at which maximum occurs, either in amount of traffic or demand for gas *etc.* —**peak load** maximum load on electrical power-supply system

peal (pi:l) *n.* 1. loud sound or succession of loud sounds 2. changes rung on set of bells 3. chime —*v.* 4. sound loudly

peanut ('pi:nʌt) *n.* 1. pea-shaped nut that ripens underground —*pl.* 2. *inf.* trifling amount of money

pear (pɛə) *n.* 1. tree yielding sweet, juicy fruit 2. the fruit —**pear-shaped** *a.* shaped like a pear, heavier at the bottom than the top

pearl (pɜ:l) *n.* hard, lustrous structure found in several molluscs, *esp.* pearl oyster and used as jewel —'**pearly** *a.* like pearls —**pearl barley** barley with skin ground off —**pearl diver** or

fisher person who dives for pearl-bearing molluscs

peasant ('pɛzᵊnt) n. member of low social class, *esp.* in rural district —'**peasantry** n. peasants collectively

pease (piːz) n. *obs.*, *dial.* pea (*pl.* **pease**) —**pease pudding** *chiefly UK* dish of boiled split peas

peat (piːt) n. **1.** decomposed vegetable substance found in bogs **2.** turf of it used for fuel —**peat moss** any of various mosses, *esp.* sphagnum, that grow in wet places and decay to form peat (*see also* SPHAGNUM)

pebble ('pɛbᵊl) n. **1.** small roundish stone **2.** pale, transparent rock crystal **3.** grainy, irregular surface —*vt.* **4.** pave, cover with pebbles —**pebble dash** finish for exterior walls with small stones in plaster

pecan (pɪ'kæn, 'piːkən) n. **1.** N Amer. tree, species of hickory, allied to walnut **2.** its edible nut

peccadillo (pɛkə'dɪləʊ) n. **1.** slight offence **2.** petty crime (*pl.* -es, -s)

peccary ('pɛkərɪ) n. vicious Amer. animal allied to pig

peck¹ (pɛk) n. **1.** fourth part of bushel, 2 gallons **2.** great deal

peck¹ (pɛk) v. **1.** pick, strike with or as with beak **2.** nibble —*vt.* **3.** *inf.* kiss quickly —n. **4.** act, instance of pecking —**peckish** a. *inf.* hungry

pecker ('pɛkə) n. *UK sl.* good spirits (*esp.* in **keep one's pecker up**)

pectin ('pɛktɪn) n. gelatinizing substance obtained from ripe fruits —'**pectic** a. **1.** congealing **2.** denoting pectin

pectoral ('pɛktərəl) a. **1.** of the breast —n. **2.** chest medicine **3.** breastplate —**pectoral fin** either of pair of fins, situated just behind head in fishes

peculate ('pɛkjʊleɪt) v. **1.** embezzle **2.** steal —**pecu'lation** n. —'**peculator** n.

peculiar (pɪ'kjuːlɪə) a. **1.** strange **2.** particular **3.** (*with*) belonging (to) —**peculi'arity** n. **1.** oddity **2.** characteristic **3.** distinguishing feature

pecuniary (pɪ'kjuːnɪərɪ) a. relating to, or consisting of, money

-ped or **-pede** (*comb. form*) foot or feet, as in *quadruped, centipede*

pedagogue or *U.S.* **pedagog** ('pɛdəgɒg) n. **1.** schoolmaster **2.** pedant —**peda'gogic** a. —**pedagogy** ('pɛdəgɒgɪ, -gɒdʒɪ, -gɒʊdʒɪ) n. principles, practice or profession of teaching

pedal ('pɛdᵊl) n. **1.** something to transmit motion from foot **2.** foot lever to modify tone or swell of musical instrument **3.** *Mus.* note, usu. bass, held through successive harmonies —a.

('piːdᵊl) **4.** of a foot —v. **5.** propel (bicycle) by using pedals —*vi.* **6.** use pedals (-ll-)

pedalo ('pɛdələʊ) n. small watercraft with paddle wheel propelled by foot pedals

pedant ('pɛdᵊnt) n. one who overvalues, or insists on, petty details of book-learning, grammatical rules *etc.* —**pe'dantic** a.

peddle ('pɛdᵊl) v. go round selling (goods) —'**peddler** n. one who sells narcotic drugs

pederast or **paederast** ('pɛdəræst) n. man who has homosexual relations with boy —'**pederasty** or '**paederasty** n.

pedestal ('pɛdɪstᵊl) n. base of column, pillar

pedestrian (pɪ'dɛstrɪən) n. **1.** one who walks on foot —a. **2.** going on foot **3.** commonplace; dull, uninspiring —**pe'destrianism** n. the practice of walking —**pe'destrianize** or **-ise** *vt.* convert into area for use of pedestrians only —**pedestrian crossing** place marked where pedestrians may cross road —**pedestrian precinct** area for pedestrians only to shop *etc.*

pedi- (*comb. form*) foot, as in *pedicure*

pediatrics (piːdɪ'ætrɪks) n. *see* PAEDIATRICS

pedicure ('pɛdɪkjʊə) n. medical or cosmetic treatment of feet

pedigree ('pɛdɪgriː) n. **1.** register of ancestors **2.** genealogy

pediment ('pɛdɪmənt) n. triangular part over Greek portico *etc.* —**pedi'mental** a.

pedlar or *esp. U.S.* **peddler** ('pɛdlə) n. **1.** one who sells **2.** hawker

pedo- or before vowel **ped-** (*comb. form*) *US see* PAEDO-

peduncle (pɪ'dʌŋkᵊl) n. **1.** flower stalk **2.** stalklike structure

peek (piːk) *vi./n.* peep, glance

peel¹ (piːl) *vt.* **1.** strip off skin, rind or any form of covering from —*vi.* **2.** come off, as skin, rind —n. **3.** rind, skin —**peeled** a. *inf.* (of eyes) watchful

peel² (piːl) n. *UK* fortified tower of 16th cent. on borders of Scotland

peen (piːn) n. **1.** end of hammer head opposite striking face, oft. rounded or wedge-shaped —*vt.* **2.** strike with peen of hammer or stream of metal shot

peep¹ (piːp) *vi.* **1.** look slyly or quickly —n. **2.** such a look —'**peeper** n. **1.** person who peeps **2.** (*oft. pl.*) *sl.* eye —**Peeping Tom** man who furtively observes women undressing; voyeur —'**peepshow** n. box with peephole through which series of pictures can be seen

peep² (piːp) *vi.* **1.** cry, as chick **2.** chirp —n. **3.** such a cry

peer¹ (pɪə) n. **1.** nobleman **2.** one of the same rank ('**peeress** *fem.*) —'**peerage** n. **1.** body of peers **2.** rank of peer —'**peerless** a. without match or equal —**peer group** social group composed of individuals of approximately same age

peer[2] (pɪə) *vi.* look closely and intently

peevish ('piːvɪʃ) *a.* **1.** fretful **2.** irritable —**peeved** *a. inf.* sulky, irritated —'**peevishly** *adv.* —'**peevishness** *n.* annoyance

peewit *or* **pewit** ('piːwɪt) *n. see* LAPWING

peg (pɛg) *n.* **1.** nail or pin for joining, fastening, marking *etc.* **2.** (mark of) level, standard *etc.* —*vt.* **3.** fasten with pegs **4.** stabilize (prices) **5.** *inf.* throw —*vi.* **6.** (with *away*) persevere (-**gg**-) —'**pegboard** *n.* **1.** board having pattern of holes into which small pegs can be fitted, used for playing certain games or keeping score **2.** *see* **solitaire** (sense 1) *at* SOLITARY **3.** hardboard perforated by pattern of holes in which articles may be hung, as for display —**peg leg** *inf.* **1.** artificial leg, *esp.* one made of wood **2.** person with artificial leg —**peg out** *sl.* die

peignoir ('peɪnwɑː) *n.* lady's dressing gown, jacket, wrapper

pejorative (pɪ'dʒɒrətɪv, 'piːdʒər-) *a.* (of words *etc.*) with unpleasant, disparaging connotation

Pekingese (piːkɪ'niːz) *or* **Pekinese** (piːkə'niːz) *n.* small Chinese dog (*also* **peke**) —**Peking man** (piː'kɪŋ) early type of man, remains of which were found in cave near Peking

pelargonium (pɛlə'gəʊnɪəm) *n.* plant with red, white or pink flowers

pelf (pɛlf) *n. contemptuous* money; wealth

pelican ('pɛlɪkən) *n.* large, fish-eating waterfowl with large pouch beneath its bill —**pelican crossing** road crossing with pedestrian-operated traffic-light system

pelisse (pɛ'liːs) *n.* **1.** fur-trimmed cloak **2.** loose coat, usu. fur-trimmed, worn *esp.* by women in early 19th cent.

pellagra (pə'leɪgrə, -'læ-) *n. Pathol.* disease caused by dietary deficiency of niacin, characterized by scaling of skin *etc.*

pellet ('pɛlɪt) *n.* little ball, pill

pellicle ('pɛlɪkəl) *n.* thin skin, film

pell-mell ('pɛl'mɛl) *adv.* in utter confusion, headlong

pellucid (pɛ'luːsɪd) *a.* **1.** translucent **2.** clear —**pellu'cidity** *n.*

pelmet ('pɛlmɪt) *n.* ornamental drapery or board, concealing curtain rail

pelt[1] (pɛlt) *vt.* **1.** strike with missiles —*vi.* **2.** throw missiles **3.** rush **4.** fall persistently, as rain

pelt[2] (pɛlt) *n.* raw hide or skin

pelvis ('pɛlvɪs) *n.* bony cavity at base of human trunk (*pl.* **-es, -ves** (-viːz)) —'**pelvic** *a.* pert. to pelvis

Pemb. Pembrokeshire

pen[1] (pɛn) *n.* **1.** instrument for writing —*vt.* **2.** compose **3.** write (-**nn**-) —**pen friend** pen pal

—'**penknife** *n.* small knife with one or more blades that fold into handle; pocketknife —'**penmanship** *n.* style or technique of writing by hand —**pen name** author's pseudonym —**pen pal** person with whom one exchanges letters, oft. person in another country whom one has not met (*also* **pen friend**) —'**penpusher** *n.* clerk involved with boring paperwork

pen[2] (pɛn) *n.* **1.** small enclosure, as for sheep —*vt.* **2.** put, keep in enclosure (-**nn**-)

pen[3] (pɛn) *n.* female swan

Pen. Peninsula

penal ('piːnəl) *a.* of, incurring, inflicting, punishment —'**penalize** *or* **-ise** *vt.* **1.** impose penalty on **2.** handicap —**penalty** ('pɛnltɪ) *n.* **1.** punishment for crime or offence **2.** forfeit **3.** *Sport* handicap or disadvantage imposed for infringement of rule *etc.* —**penal code** codified body of laws that relate to crime and punishment

penance ('pɛnəns) *n.* **1.** suffering submitted to as expression of penitence **2.** repentance

pence (pɛns) *n., pl.* of PENNY

penchant ('pɛntʃənt; *Fr.* pãˈʃã) *n.* inclination, decided taste

pencil ('pɛnsəl) *n.* **1.** instrument as of graphite, for writing *etc.* **2.** *Optics* narrow beam of light —*vt.* **3.** paint or draw **4.** mark with pencil (-**ll**-)

pendant ('pɛndənt) *n.* hanging ornament —'**pendent** *a.* **1.** suspended, hanging **2.** projecting

pending ('pɛndɪŋ) *prep.* **1.** during, until —*a.* **2.** awaiting settlement **3.** undecided **4.** imminent

pendulous ('pɛndjʊləs) *a.* hanging, swinging —'**pendulum** *n.* suspended weight swinging to and fro, *esp.* as regulator for clock

penetrate ('pɛnɪtreɪt) *vt.* **1.** enter into **2.** pierce **3.** arrive at the meaning of —**penetra'bility** *n.* quality of being penetrable —'**penetrable** *a.* capable of being entered or pierced —'**penetrating** *a.* **1.** sharp **2.** easily heard **3.** subtle **4.** quick to understand —**pene'tration** *n.* insight, acuteness —'**penetrative** *a.* **1.** piercing **2.** discerning —'**penetrator** *n.*

penguin ('pɛŋgwɪn) *n.* flightless, short-legged swimming bird

penicillin (pɛnɪ'sɪlɪn) *n.* antibiotic drug effective against a wide range of diseases, infections

peninsula (pɪ'nɪnsjʊlə) *n.* portion of land nearly surrounded by water —pe'ninsular *a.*

penis ('piːnɪs) *n.* male organ of copulation (and of urination) in man and many mammals (*pl.* **-es, penes** ('piːniːz))

penitent ('pɛnɪtənt) *a.* **1.** affected by sense of guilt —*n.* **2.** one that repents of sin —'**penitence** *n.* **1.** sorrow for sin **2.** repentance —peni'tential *a.* of, or expressing, penitence —peni'tentiary *a.* **1.** relating to penance, or to the rules of penance —*n.* **2.** US prison

pennant ('pɛnənt) *n.* long narrow flag

pennon ('pɛnən) *n.* small pointed or swallow-tailed flag

penny ('pɛnɪ) *n.* Brit. bronze coin, now 100th part of pound (*pl.* **pence, 'pennies**) —**'penniless** *a.* **1.** having no money **2.** poor —**Penny Black** first postage stamp, issued in Brit. in 1840 —**penny-dreadful** *n.* UK *inf.* cheap, oft. lurid book or magazine (*pl.* **-s**) —**penny-farthing** *n.* UK early type of bicycle with large front wheel and small rear wheel —**penny-pincher** *n. inf.* person who is excessively careful with money —**penny-pinching** *n./a.* —**penny-wise** *a.* greatly concerned with saving small sums of money —'**pennyworth** *n.* **1.** amount that can be bought for a penny **2.** small amount —**penny-wise and pound-foolish** careful about trifles but wasteful in large ventures

penology (piː'nɒlədʒɪ) *n.* study of punishment and prevention of crime

pension[1] ('pɛnʃən) *n.* **1.** regular payment to old people, retired public officials, soldiers *etc.* —*vt.* **2.** grant pension to —'**pensioner** *n.*

pension[2] (pã'sjõ) *Fr.* **1.** continental boarding house **2.** (full) board

pensive ('pɛnsɪv) *a.* **1.** thoughtful with sadness **2.** wistful

penstemon (pɛn'stiːmən) *n. see* PENTSTEMON

pent (pɛnt) *a.* shut up, kept in —**pent-up** *a.* not released, repressed

penta- (*comb. form*) five, as in *pentagon, pentameter*

pentacle ('pɛntəkəl) *n.* **1.** star-shaped figure with five points **2.** such figure used by Pythagoreans, black magicians *etc.* (*also* '**pentagram,** '**pentangle**)

pentagon ('pɛntəgən) *n.* plane figure having five angles —**pen'tagonal** *a.*

Pentagon ('pɛntəgən) *n.* military head-quarters in U.S.A.

pentameter (pɛn'tæmɪtə) *n.* verse of five metrical feet

Pentateuch ('pɛntətjuːk) *n.* first five books of Old Testament

pentathlon (pɛn'tæθlən) *n.* athletic contest of five events

pentatonic scale (pɛntə'tɒnɪk) *Mus.* scale consisting of five notes

Pentecost ('pɛntɪkɒst) *n.* **1.** Whitsuntide **2.** Jewish harvest festival on 50th day after Passover —**Pente'costal** *a.* **1.** of any of various Christian groups that emphasize charismatic aspects of Christianity **2.** of Pentecost or influence of Holy Ghost —*n.* **3.** member of a Pentecostal Church —**Pente'costalist** *n./a.*

penthouse ('pɛnthaʊs) *n.* apartment, flat or other structure on top, or top floor, of building

pentode ('pɛntəʊd) *n. Electron.* five-electrode thermionic valve, having anode, cathode and three grids

pentstemon (pɛnt'stiːmən) *or* **penstemon** *n.* bright-flowered garden plant

penult ('pɛnʌlt, pɪ'nʌlt) *n.* last syllable but one of word —**pe'nultimate** *a.* next before the last

penumbra (pɪ'nʌmbrə) *n.* **1.** imperfect shadow **2.** in an eclipse, the partially shadowed region which surrounds the full shadow

penury ('pɛnjʊrɪ) *n.* **1.** extreme poverty **2.** extreme scarcity —**pe'nurious** *a.* **1.** niggardly, stingy **2.** poor, scanty

peony ('piːənɪ) *n.* any of genus of N Amer. plants with showy red, pink or white flowers

people ('piːpəl) *pl.n.* **1.** persons generally **2.** community, nation **3.** family —*n.* **4.** race —*vt.* **5.** stock with inhabitants, populate

pep (pɛp) *n.* **1.** vigour **2.** energy **3.** enthusiasm —*vt.* (*usu. with* up) **4.** impart energy to **5.** speed up (**-pp-**) —**pep pill** *inf.* tablet containing stimulant —**pep talk** *inf.* enthusiastic talk designed to increase confidence, production *etc.*

pepper ('pɛpə) *n.* **1.** fruit of climbing plant, which yields pungent aromatic spice **2.** various slightly pungent vegetables, *eg* capsicum —*vt.* **3.** season with pepper **4.** sprinkle, dot **5.** pelt with missiles —'**peppery** *a.* **1.** having the qualities of pepper **2.** irritable —**pepper-and-salt** *a.* **1.** (of cloth *etc.*) marked with fine mixture of black and white **2.** (of hair) streaked with grey —'**peppercorn** *n.* **1.** dried pepper berry **2.** something trifling —**pepper mill** hand mill used to grind peppercorns —'**peppermint** *n.* **1.** plant noted for aromatic pungent liquor distilled from it **2.** a sweet flavoured with this

pepsin ('pɛpsɪn) *n.* enzyme produced in stomach, which, when activated by acid, breaks down proteins

peptic ('pɛptɪk) *a.* relating to digestion or digestive juices

per (pɜː; *unstressed* pə) *prep.* **1.** for each **2.** by **3.** in manner of

per- (*comb. form*) through, thoroughly, as in *perfect, perspicacious*

peradventure (pərəd'vɛntʃə, pɜːr-) *obs. adv.* **1.** by chance; perhaps —*n.* **2.** chance; doubt

perambulate (pə'ræmbjʊleɪt) *vt.* **1.** walk through or over **2.** traverse —*vi.* **3.** walk about —**per'ambulator** *n.* pram

per annum ('ænəm) *Lat.* by the year

per capita ('kæpɪtə) of or for each person

perceive (pə'siːv) *vt.* **1.** obtain knowledge of through senses **2.** observe **3.** understand —**per'ceivable** *a.* —**percepti'bility** *n.* —**per'ceptible** *a.* discernible, recognizable —**per-**

'ception *n.* **1.** faculty of perceiving **2.** intuitive judgment —**per'ceptive** *a.*

percentage (pə'sɛntidʒ) *n.* proportion or rate per hundred —**per cent** in each hundred —**per'centile** *n.* one of 99 actual or notional values of a variable dividing its distribution into 100 groups with equal frequencies (*also* (US) **'centile**)

perception (pə'sɛpʃən) *n. see* PERCEIVE

perch¹ (pɜːtʃ) *n.* any of a family of freshwater fishes

perch² (pɜːtʃ) *n.* **1.** resting place, as for bird **2.** formerly, measure of 5½ yards —*vt.* **3.** place, as on perch —*vi.* **4.** alight, settle on fixed body **5.** roost **6.** balance

perchance (pə'tʃɑːns) *adv. Poet.* perhaps

percipient (pə'sɪpɪənt) *a.* **1.** having faculty of perception **2.** perceiving —*n.* **3.** one who perceives

percolate ('pɜːkəleɪt) *v.* **1.** pass through fine mesh as liquor **2.** permeate **3.** filter —**perco'lation** *n.* —**'percolator** *n.* coffeepot with filter

percussion (pə'kʌʃən) *n.* **1.** collision **2.** impact **3.** vibratory shock —**per'cussionist** *n. Mus.* person who plays percussion instrument —**percussion cap** detonator consisting of paper or thin metal cap containing material that explodes when struck —**percussion instrument** one played by being struck, *eg* drum, cymbals *etc.*

perdition (pə'dɪʃən) *n.* spiritual ruin

peregrinate ('pɛrɪgrɪneɪt) *vi.* travel about, roam —**peregri'nation** *n.*

peregrine ('pɛrɪgrɪn) *n.* type of falcon

peremptory (pə'rɛmptərɪ) *a.* **1.** authoritative, imperious **2.** forbidding debate **3.** decisive

perennial (pə'rɛnɪəl) *a.* **1.** lasting through the years **2.** perpetual, unfailing —*n.* **3.** plant lasting more than two years —**pe'rennially** *adv.*

perfect ('pɜːfɪkt) *a.* **1.** complete **2.** finished **3.** whole **4.** unspoilt **5.** faultless **6.** correct, precise **7.** excellent **8.** of highest quality —*n.* **9.** tense denoting a complete act —*vt.* (pə'fɛkt) **10.** improve **11.** finish **12.** make skilful —**per'fectable** *a.* capable of becoming perfect —**per'fection** *n.* **1.** state of being perfect **2.** faultlessness —**per'fectionism** *n.* **1.** *Philos.* doctrine that man can attain perfection in this life **2.** demand for highest standard of excellence —**per'fectionist** *n.* —**'perfectly** *adv.* —**perfect participle** past participle

perfidy ('pɜːfɪdɪ) *n.* treachery, disloyalty —**per'fidious** *a.*

perforate ('pɜːfəreɪt) *vt.* make holes in, penetrate —**perfo'ration** *n.*

perforce (pə'fɔːs) *adv.* of necessity

perform (pə'fɔːm) *vt.* **1.** bring to completion **2.** accomplish; fulfil **3.** represent on stage —*vi.* **4.** function **5.** act part **6.** play, as on musical instrument —**per'formance** *n.* —**per'former** *n.*

perfume ('pɜːfjuːm) *n.* **1.** agreeable scent **2.** fragrance —*vt.* (pə'fjuːm) **3.** imbue with an agreeable odour, scent —**per'fumer** *n.* —**per'fumery** *n.* perfumes in general

perfunctory (pə'fʌŋktərɪ) *a.* **1.** superficial **2.** hasty **3.** done indifferently

pergola ('pɜːgələ) *n.* **1.** area covered by plants growing on trellis **2.** the trellis

perhaps (pə'hæps; *inf.* præps) *adv.* possibly

peri- (*comb. form*) round, as in *perimeter, period, periphrasis*

perianth ('pɛrɪænθ) *n.* outer part of flower, consisting of calyx and corolla

pericardium (pɛrɪ'kɑːdɪəm) *n.* membrane enclosing the heart (*pl.* **-dia** (-dɪə)) —**peri'cardiac** *or* **peri'cardial** *a.* —**pericar'ditis** *n.* inflammation of this

perigee ('pɛrɪdʒiː) *n.* point in its orbit around earth when moon or satellite is nearest earth

perihelion (pɛrɪ'hiːlɪən) *n.* point in orbit of planet or comet when nearest to sun (*pl.* **-lia** (-lɪə))

peril ('pɛrɪl) *n.* **1.** danger **2.** exposure to injury —**'perilous** *a.* full of peril, hazardous

perimeter (pə'rɪmɪtə) *n.* **1.** *Maths.* outer boundary of an area; length of this **2.** medical instrument for measuring the field of vision

perineum (pɛrɪ'niːəm) *n.* **1.** region of body between anus and genital organs **2.** surface of human trunk between thighs (*pl.* **-nea** (-'niːə))

period ('pɪərɪəd) *n.* **1.** particular portion of time **2.** a series of years **3.** single occurrence of menstruation **4.** cycle **5.** conclusion **6.** full stop (.) at end of sentence **7.** complete sentence —*a.* **8.** (of furniture, dress, play *etc.*) belonging to particular time in history —**peri'odic** *a.* recurring at regular intervals —**peri'odical** *a./n.* **1.** (of) publication issued at regular intervals —*a.* **2.** of a period **3.** periodic —**perio'dicity** *n.* —**periodic law** principle that chemical properties of elements are periodic functions of their atomic weights or, more accurately, of their atomic numbers —**periodic table** table of elements, arranged in order of increasing atomic number, based on periodic law

peripatetic (pɛrɪpə'tɛtɪk) *a.* itinerant, walking, travelling about

periphery (pə'rɪfərɪ) *n.* **1.** circumference **2.** surface, outside —**pe'ripheral** *a.* **1.** minor, unimportant **2.** of periphery

periphrasis (pə'rɪfrəsɪs) *n.* **1.** roundabout speech or phrase **2.** circumlocution (*pl.* **-rases** (-rəsiːz)) —**peri'phrastic** *a.*

periscope ('pɛrɪskəʊp) *n.* instrument, used

esp. in submarines, for giving view of objects on different level —**periscopic** (perɪ'skɒpɪk) *a.*

perish ('perɪʃ) *vi.* 1. die, waste away 2. decay, rot —**perisha'bility** *n.* —**'perishable** *a.* 1. that will not last long —*pl.n.* 2. perishable food —**'perishing** *a.* 1. *inf.* (of weather *etc.*) extremely cold 2. *sl.* confounded

peristalsis (perɪ'stælsɪs) *n. Physiol.* succession of waves of involuntary muscular contraction of various bodily tubes, *esp.* of alimentary tract (*pl.* **-ses** (-siːz))

peristyle ('perɪstaɪl) *n.* 1. range of pillars surrounding building, square *etc.* 2. court within this

peritoneum (perɪtə'niːəm) *n.* membrane lining internal surface of abdomen (*pl.* **-s**, **-nea** (-'niːə)) —**perito'nitis** *n.* inflammation of peritoneum

periwig ('perɪwɪg) *n. Hist.* wig

periwinkle ('perɪwɪŋkəl) *n.* 1. flowering plant 2. small edible shellfish (*also* **'winkle**)

perjure ('pɜːdʒə) *vt.* render (oneself) guilty of perjury —**'perjury** *n.* 1. crime of false testimony on oath 2. false swearing

perk[1] (pɜːk) *n. inf.* perquisite

perk[2] (pɜːk) *vi. inf.* (of coffee) percolate

perky ('pɜːkɪ) *a.* lively, cheerful, jaunty, gay —**perk up** make, become cheerful

perm (pɜːm) *n. inf. see* **permutation** (sense 3) *at* PERMUTE

permafrost ('pɜːməfrɒst) *n.* permanently frozen ground

permanent ('pɜːmənənt) *a.* 1. continuing in same state 2. lasting —**'permanence** *or* **'permanency** *n.* fixedness —**permanent wave** (treatment of hair producing) long-lasting style (*also* **perm**) —**permanent way** *chiefly UK* track of railway, including sleepers, rails *etc.*

permanganate (pə'mæŋgəneɪt, -nɪt) *n.* salt of an acid of manganese

permeate ('pɜːmɪeɪt) *vt.* pervade, saturate 2. pass through pores of —**'permeable** *a.* admitting of passage of fluids

Permian ('pɜːmɪən) *a.* 1. of last period of Palaeozoic era, between Carboniferous and Triassic periods —*n.* 2. Permian period or rock system

permit (pə'mɪt) *vt.* 1. allow 2. give leave to (**-tt-**) —*n.* ('pɜːmɪt) 3. warrant or licence to do something 4. written permission —**per'missible** *a.* allowable —**per'mission** *n.* authorization, leave, liberty —**per'missive** *a.* (too) tolerant, lenient, *esp.* sexually

permute (pə'mjuːt) *vt.* change sequence of —**permu'tation** *n.* 1. mutual transference 2. *Maths.* arrangement of a number of quantities in every possible order 3. fixed combinations for selections of results on football pools

pernicious (pə'nɪʃəs) *a.* 1. wicked or mischievous 2. extremely hurtful 3. having quality of destroying or injuring —**pernicious anaemia** form of anaemia characterized by lesions of spinal cord, weakness, diarrhoea *etc.*

pernickety (pə'nɪkɪtɪ) *a. inf.* fussy, fastidious about trifles

peroration (perə'reɪʃən) *n.* concluding part of oration —**'perorate** *vi.*

peroxide (pə'rɒksaɪd) *n.* 1. oxide of a given base containing greatest quantity of oxygen 2. *see* **hydrogen peroxide** *at* HYDROGEN

perpendicular (pɜːpən'dɪkjʊlə) *a.* 1. at right angles to the plane of the horizon 2. at right angles to given line or surface 3. exactly upright —*n.* 4. line falling at right angles on another line or plane

perpetrate ('pɜːpɪtreɪt) *vt.* perform or be responsible for (deception, crime *etc.*) —**perpe'tration** *n.* —**'perpetrator** *n.*

perpetual (pə'petjʊəl) *a.* 1. continuous 2. lasting for ever —**per'petually** *adv.* —**per'petuate** *vt.* 1. make perpetual 2. not to allow to be forgotten —**perpetu'ation** *n.* —**perpe'tuity** *n.* —**perpetual motion** motion of hypothetical mechanism that continues indefinitely without any external source of energy

perplex (pə'pleks) *vt.* 1. puzzle, bewilder 2. make difficult to understand —**per'plexity** *n.* puzzled or tangled state

perquisite ('pɜːkwɪzɪt) *n.* 1. any incidental benefit from a certain type of employment 2. casual payment in addition to salary

perry ('perɪ) *n.* fermented drink made from pears

per se (seɪ) *Lat.* by or in itself

persecute ('pɜːsɪkjuːt) *vt.* 1. oppress because of race, religion *etc.* 2. subject to persistent ill-treatment —**perse'cution** *n.* —**'persecutor** *n.*

persevere (pɜːsɪ'vɪə) *vi.* (*oft. with* in) persist, maintain effort —**perse'verance** *n.* persistence

Persian ('pɜːʃən) *a.* 1. of ancient Persia or modern Iran —*n.* 2. native or inhabitant of modern Iran; Iranian 3. language of Iran or Persia in any of ancient or modern forms —**Persian cat** long-haired domestic cat —**Persian lamb** 1. black loosely curled fur from karakul lamb 2. karakul lamb

persimmon (pɜː'sɪmən) *n.* 1. any of several tropical trees typically having hard wood 2. its fruit

persist (pə'sɪst) *vi.* (*oft. with* in) continue in spite of obstacles or objections —**per'sistence** *or* **per'sistency** *n.* —**per'sistent** *a.* 1. persisting 2. steady 3. persevering 4. lasting

person ('pɜːsən) *n.* 1. individual (human) being 2. body of human being 3. *Gram.* classification, or one of the classes, of pronouns and verb forms according to the person speaking, spoken to, or spoken of —**per'sona** n. assumed character (*pl.* **-nae** (-niː)) —**'personable** a. good-looking —**'personage** n. notable person —**'personal** a. **1.** individual, private, or one's own **2.** of, relating to grammatical person —**perso'nality** n. **1.** distinctive character **2.** a celebrity —**'personalize** or **-ise** vt. **1.** endow with personal or individual qualities **2.** mark with person's initials, name etc. **3.** take personally **4.** personify —**'personally** adv. in person —**'personalty** n. personal property —**'personate** vt. pass oneself off as —**perso'nation** n. —**personal column** newspaper column containing personal messages etc. —**personal property** *Law* all property except land and interests in land that pass to heir —**in person** actually present

persona non grata (pɜː'səʊnɒ nɒn 'grɑːtə) *Lat.* **1.** unacceptable or unwelcome person **2.** diplomat who is not acceptable to government to whom he is accredited (*pl.* **personae non gratae** (pɜː'səʊniː nɒn 'grɑːtiː))

personify (pɜː'sɒnɪfaɪ) vt. **1.** represent as person **2.** typify (**-ified, -ifying**) —**personifi'cation** n.

personnel (pɜːsə'nɛl) n. **1.** staff employed in a service or institution **2.** department that interviews or keeps records of employees

perspective (pə'spɛktɪv) n. **1.** mental view **2.** art of drawing on flat surface to give effect of solidity and relative distances and sizes **3.** drawing in perspective

Perspex ('pɜːspɛks) n. **R** transparent acrylic substitute for glass

perspicacious (pɜːspɪ'keɪʃəs) a. having quick mental insight —**perspicacity** (pɜːspɪ'kæsɪtɪ) n.

perspicuous (pə'spɪkjʊəs) a. **1.** clearly expressed **2.** lucid **3.** plain **4.** obvious —**perspi'cuity** n.

perspire (pə'spaɪə) vi. sweat —**perspiration** (pɜːspə'reɪʃən) n. sweating

persuade (pə'sweɪd) vt. **1.** bring (one to do something) by argument, charm etc. **2.** convince —**per'suasion** n. **1.** art, act of persuading **2.** way of thinking or belief —**per'suasive** a.

pert (pɜːt) a. forward, saucy

pertain (pə'teɪn) vi. (*oft. with* to) **1.** belong, relate, have reference (to) **2.** concern

pertinacious (pɜːtɪ'neɪʃəs) a. obstinate, persistent —**pertinacity** (pɜːtɪ'næsɪtɪ) or **perti'naciousness** n. doggedness, resolution

pertinent ('pɜːtɪnənt) a. relating to the matter at hand —**'pertinence** or **'pertinency** n. relevance

perturb (pə'tɜːb) vt. **1.** disturb greatly **2.** alarm —**per'turbable** a. —**pertur'bation** n. agitation of mind

peruke (pə'ruːk) n. *Hist.* wig

peruse (pə'ruːz) vt. read, *esp.* in slow and careful, or leisurely, manner —**pe'rusal** n.

pervade (pɜː'veɪd) vt. **1.** spread through **2.** be rife among —**per'vasion** n. —**per'vasive** a.

pervert (pə'vɜːt) vt. **1.** turn to wrong use **2.** lead astray —n. ('pɜːvɜːt) **3.** one who shows unhealthy abnormality, *esp.* in sexual matters —**per'verse** a. **1.** obstinately or unreasonably wrong **2.** self-willed **3.** headstrong **4.** wayward —**per'versely** adv. —**per'version** n.

pervious ('pɜːvɪəs) a. **1.** permeable **2.** penetrable, giving passage

peseta (pə'seɪtə; *Sp.* pe'seta) n. *Sp.* monetary unit

peso ('peɪsəʊ; *Sp.* 'peso) n. standard monetary unit of Argentina, Mexico etc. (*pl.* **pesos** ('peɪsəʊz; *Sp.* 'pesos))

pessary ('pɛsərɪ) n. **1.** instrument used to support mouth and neck of uterus **2.** appliance to prevent conception **3.** medicated suppository

pessimism ('pɛsɪmɪzəm) n. **1.** tendency to see the worst side of things **2.** theory that everything turns to evil —**'pessimist** n. —**pessi'mistic** a.

pest (pɛst) n. **1.** troublesome or harmful thing, person or insect **2.** *rare* plague —**'pesticide** n. chemical for killing pests, *esp.* insects —**pes'tiferous** a. **1.** troublesome **2.** bringing plague

pester ('pɛstə) vt. trouble or vex persistently, harass

pestilence ('pɛstɪləns) n. epidemic disease, *esp.* bubonic plague —**'pestilent** a. **1.** troublesome **2.** deadly —**pesti'lential** a.

pestle ('pɛsəl) n. **1.** instrument with which things are pounded in a mortar —v. **2.** pound with pestle

pet¹ (pɛt) n. **1.** animal kept for companionship etc. **2.** person regarded with affection —vt. **3.** make pet of —v. **4.** *inf.* hug, embrace, fondle (**-tt-**)

pet² (pɛt) n. fit of sulkiness, *esp.* at what is felt to be a slight; pique —**'pettish** a. peevish, petulant

Pet. *Bible* Peter

petal ('pɛtəl) n. white or coloured leaflike part of flower —**'petalled** a.

petard (pɪ'tɑːd) n. formerly, an explosive device

peter ('piːtə) vi. —**peter out** *inf.* disappear, lose power gradually

Peter Pan youthful or immature man

petersham ('piːtəʃəm) n. thick corded ribbon used to stiffen belts etc.

pethidine ('pɛθɪdiːn) n. water-soluble drug used as analgesic (*also* **me'peridine**)

petiole ('pɛtɪəʊl) n. **1.** stalk by which leaf is attached to plant **2.** *Zool.* slender stalk or stem, as between thorax and abdomen of ants —'**petiolate** a.

petit ('pɛtɪ) a. Law small, petty —**petit bourgeois** n. **1.** section of middle class with lowest social status, as shopkeepers etc. **2.** member of this stratum (pl. **petits bourgeois** ('pɛtɪ 'buəʒwɑːz)) (also **petite bourgeoisie, petty bourgeoisie**) —a. **3.** of petit bourgeois, esp. indicating sense of self-righteousness etc. —**petit four** any of various small fancy cakes and biscuits (pl. **petits fours** ('pɛtɪ 'fɔːz)) —**petit jury** jury of 12 persons empanelled to determine facts of case and decide issue pursuant to direction of court on points of law (also **petty jury**) —**petit mal** (mæl) mild form of epilepsy characterized by periods of impairment or loss of consciousness for up to 30 seconds —**petit point** (pɔɪnt, pwɔɪ) **1.** small diagonal needlepoint stitch used for fine detail **2.** work done with such stitches

petite (pə'tiːt) a. (of women) small, dainty

petition (pɪ'tɪʃən) n. **1.** entreaty, request, esp. one presented to sovereign or parliament —vt. **2.** present petition to —pe'**titionary** a.

petrel ('pɛtrəl) n. any of a family of sea birds

petrify ('pɛtrɪfaɪ) vt. **1.** turn to stone **2.** fig. make motionless with fear **3.** make dumb with amazement (-**ified, -ifying**) —petri'**faction** or petrifi'**cation** n.

petrochemical (pɛtrəʊ'kɛmɪkəl) n. **1.** any substance, such as acetone or ethanol, obtained from petroleum —a. **2.** of petrochemicals; related to petrochemistry —petro'**chemistry** n.

petrocurrency ('pɛtrəʊ'kʌrənsɪ) n. currency oil-producing countries acquire as profit from oil sales to other countries

petrodollar ('pɛtrəʊdɒlə) n. money earned by country by exporting of petroleum

petrolatum (pɛtrə'leɪtəm) n. translucent gelatinous substance obtained from petroleum

petroleum (pə'trəʊlɪəm) n. mineral oil —'**petrol** n. refined petroleum used in motorcars etc. —**petroleum jelly** see PETROLATUM —**petrol station** UK filling station

petrology (pɛ'trɒlədʒɪ) n. study of rocks and their structure

petticoat ('pɛtɪkəʊt) n. women's undergarment worn under skirts, dresses etc.

pettifogger ('pɛtɪfɒgə) n. **1.** low-class lawyer **2.** one given to mean dealing in small matters

petty ('pɛtɪ) a. **1.** unimportant, trivial **2.** small-minded, mean **3.** on a small scale —**petty cash** cash kept by firm to pay minor incidental expenses —**petty jury** see petit jury at PETIT —**petty officer** noncommissioned officer in Navy

petulant ('pɛtjʊlənt) a. given to small fits of temper, peevish —'**petulance** or '**petulancy** n.

petunia (pɪ'tjuːnɪə) n. any plant of tropical Amer. genus with funnel-shaped purple or white flowers

pew (pjuː) n. **1.** fixed seat in church **2.** inf. chair, seat

pewit or **peewit** ('piːwɪt) n. see LAPWING

pewter ('pjuːtə) n. **1.** alloy of tin and lead **2.** ware made of this

pH potential of hydrogen; measure of acidity or alkalinity of solution

phalanx ('fælæŋks) n. body of men formed in close array (pl. -**es, phalanges** (fæ'lændʒiːz))

phalarope ('fæiərəʊp) n. any of a family of small wading birds

phallus ('fæləs) n. **1.** penis **2.** symbol of it used in primitive rites (pl. -**es, -li** (-laɪ)) —'**phallic** a. —'**phallicism** n.

phantasm ('fæntæzəm) n. **1.** vision of absent person **2.** illusion —**phantasma'goria** or **phan'tasmagory** n. **1.** crowd of dim or unreal figures **2.** exhibition of illusions —**phan'tasmal** a. —'**phantasy** n. see FANTASY

phantom ('fæntəm) n. **1.** apparition, spectre, ghost **2.** fancied vision

Pharaoh ('fɛərəʊ) n. title of ancient Egyptian kings

Pharisee ('færɪsiː) n. **1.** sanctimonious person **2.** hypocrite —phari'**saic(al)** a.

pharmaceutical (fɑːmə'sjuːtɪkəl) or **pharmaceutic** a. of pharmacy —**pharma'ceutics** pl.n. (with sing. v.) science of pharmacy —'**pharmacist** n. person qualified to dispense drugs —**pharma'cology** n. study of drugs —**pharmacopoeia** or U.S. (sometimes) **pharmacopeia** (fɑːməkə'piːə) n. official book with list and directions for use of drugs —'**pharmacy** n. **1.** preparation and dispensing of drugs **2.** dispensary

pharos ('fɛərɒs) n. marine lighthouse or beacon

pharynx ('færɪŋks) n. cavity forming back part of mouth and terminating in gullet (pl. **pharynges** (fæ'rɪndʒiːz)) —pharyn'**geal** or pha'**ryngal** a. —pharyn'**gitis** n. inflammation of pharynx

phase (feɪz) n. **1.** any distinct or characteristic period or stage in a development or chain of events —vt. **2.** arrange, execute in stages or to coincide with something else

Ph.D. Doctor of Philosophy (also **D.Phil.**)

pheasant ('fɛzənt) n. any of various game birds with bright plumage

pheno- or before vowel **phen-** (comb. form) **1.** showing, manifesting, as in phenotype **2.** indicating that molecule contains benzene rings, as in phenobarbitone

phenobarbitone (fiːnəʊˈbɑːbɪtəʊn) *or* **phenobarbital** (fiːnəʊˈbɑːbɪtəl) *n.* drug inducing sleep

phenol (ˈfiːnɒl) *n.* carbolic acid

phenomenon (fɪˈnɒmɪnən) *n.* **1.** anything appearing or observed **2.** remarkable person or thing (*pl.* **phenomena** (fɪˈnɒmɪnə)) —**pheˈnomenal** *a.* **1.** relating to phenomena **2.** remarkable **3.** recognizable or evidenced by senses —**pheˈnomenalism** *n.* **1.** theory that only phenomena are real and can be known **2.** tendency to think about things as phenomena only —**pheˈnomenalist** *n./a.*

phenyl (ˈfiːnaɪl, ˈfɛnɪl) *a.* of, containing or consisting of monovalent group C₆H₅, derived from benzene

phew (fjuː) *interj.* exclamation of relief, surprise *etc.*

phi (faɪ) *n.* 21st letter in Gr. alphabet (Φ, φ) (*pl.* **-s**)

phial (ˈfaɪəl) *n.* small bottle for medicine *etc.*

Phil. 1. *Bible* Philippians **2.** Philippines **3.** Philadelphia

philander (fɪˈlændə) *vi.* (of man) flirt with women

philanthropy (fɪˈlænθrəpɪ) *n.* **1.** practice of doing good to one's fellow men **2.** love of mankind —**philanˈthropic** *a.* loving mankind, benevolent —**phiˈlanthropist** *or* **ˈphilanthrope** *n.*

philately (fɪˈlætəlɪ) *n.* stamp collecting —**philaˈtelic** *a.* —**phiˈlatelist** *n.*

-phile *or* **-phil** (*comb. form*) person or thing having fondness for something specified, as in *bibliophile*

philharmonic (fɪlhɑːˈmɒnɪk, fɪlə-) *a.* **1.** fond of music **2.** (**P-** *when part of name*) denoting orchestra, choir *etc.* devoted to music

philhellene (fɪlˈhɛliːn) *n.* **1.** lover of Greece and Greek culture **2.** *European hist.* supporter of cause of Greek national independence —**philhelˈlenic** *a.*

philippic (fɪˈlɪpɪk) *n.* bitter or impassioned speech of denunciation; invective

Philistine (ˈfɪlɪstaɪn) *n.* **1.** ignorant, smug person **2.** member of non-Semitic people who inhabited ancient Philistia —*a.* **3.** (*sometimes* **p-**) boorishly uncultured **4.** of the ancient Philistines —**philistinism** (ˈfɪlɪstɪnɪzəm) *n.*

Phillips (ˈfɪlɪps) *n.* screwdriver that can be used on screw (**Phillips screw**) that has two slots crossing at centre of head

philo- *or before vowel* **phil-** (*comb. form*) love of, as in *philology, philanthropic*

philology (fɪˈlɒlədʒɪ) *n.* science of structure and development of languages —**philoˈlogical** *a.* —**phiˈlologist** *or* **phiˈlologer** *n.*

philos. 1. philosopher **2.** philosophical

philosophy (fɪˈlɒsəfɪ) *n.* **1.** pursuit of wisdom **2.** study of realities and general principles **3.** system of theories on nature of things or on conduct **4.** calmness of mind —**phiˈlosopher** *n.* one who studies, possesses or originates philosophy —**philoˈsophic(al)** *a.* **1.** of, like philosophy **2.** wise, learned **3.** calm, stoical —**phiˈlosophize** *or* **-phise** *vi.* **1.** reason like philosopher **2.** theorize **3.** moralize

philtre *or U.S.* **philter** (ˈfɪltə) *n.* love potion

phlebitis (flɪˈbaɪtɪs) *n.* inflammation of a vein

phlegm (flɛm) *n.* **1.** viscid substance formed by mucous membrane and ejected by coughing *etc.* **2.** calmness, sluggishness —**phlegmatic(al)** (flɛgˈmætɪk(əl)) *a.* **1.** not easily agitated **2.** composed

phloem (ˈfləʊɛm) *n.* tissue in higher plants that conducts synthesized food substances to all parts of plant

phlogiston (flɒˈdʒɪstən, -tɒn) *n. Chem.* hypothetical substance formerly thought to be present in all combustible materials

phlox (flɒks) *n.* any of chiefly N Amer. genus of flowering plants (*pl.* **phlox, -es**)

phobia (ˈfəʊbɪə) *n.* **1.** fear, aversion **2.** unreasoning dislike

-phobia (*n. comb. form*) extreme abnormal fear of or aversion to, as in *acrophobia, claustrophobia* —**phobe** (*n. comb. form*) one that fears or hates, as in *xenophobe* —**-phobic** (*a. comb. form*)

Phoenician (fəˈnɪʃən, -ˈniːʃən) *n.* **1.** member of ancient Semitic people of NW Syria **2.** extinct language of this people —*a.* **3.** of Phoenicia, Phoenicians or their language

phoenix *or U.S.* **phenix** (ˈfiːnɪks) *n.* **1.** legendary bird **2.** unique thing

phone (fəʊn) *n./v. inf.* telephone —**phone-in** *n. Rad., T.V.* programme in which listeners' or viewers' questions, comments *etc.* are telephoned to studio and broadcast live as part of discussion

-phone (*n. comb. form*) **1.** device giving off sound, as in *telephone* —(*a. comb. form*) **2.** speaking a particular language, as in *Francophone* —**-phonic** (*a. comb. form*)

phoneme (ˈfəʊniːm) *n. Linguis.* one of set of speech sounds in a language, that serve to distinguish one word from another —**phoˈnemic** *a.* —**phoˈnemics** *pl. n.* (*with sing. v.*) aspect of linguistics concerned with classification and analysis of phonemes of a language

phonetic (fəˈnɛtɪk) *a.* of vocal sounds —**phoneˈtician** *or* **ˈphonetist** *n.* —**phoˈnetics** *pl.n.* (*with sing. v.*) science of vocal sounds

phoney *or* **phony** (ˈfəʊnɪ) *a. inf.* **1.** counterfeit, sham, fraudulent **2.** suspect

phono- or before vowel **phon-** (*comb. form*) sounds, as in *phonology*

phonograph ('fəʊnəgrɑːf, -græf) n. instrument recording and reproducing sounds —**phono-'graphic** a.

phonology (fə'nɒlədʒɪ) n. **1.** study of speech sounds and their development **2.** system of sounds in a language —**phono'logic(al)** a. —**pho'nologist** n.

phosphorus ('fɒsfərəs) n. toxic, flammable, nonmetallic element which appears luminous in the dark —**'phosphate, 'phosphide, 'phosphite** n. compounds of phosphorus —**'phosphor** n. substance capable of emitting light when irradiated with particles of electromagnetic radiation —**phospho'resce** vi. exhibit phosphorescence —**phospho'rescence** n. faint glow in the dark —**phos'phoric** a. of or containing phosphorus with valence of five —**'phosphorous** a. of or containing phosphorus in trivalent state

photo ('fəʊtəʊ) n. inf. photograph (pl. **-s**) —**photo finish** photo taken at end of race to show placing of contestants

photo- (*comb. form*) light, as in *photometer, photosynthesis*

photocell ('fəʊtəʊsɛl) n. device in which photoelectric or photovoltaic effect or photoconductivity is used to produce current or voltage when exposed to light or other electromagnetic radiation (also **photoelectric cell, electric eye**)

photochemistry (fəʊtəʊ'kɛmɪstrɪ) n. study of chemical action of light

photoconductivity (fəʊtəʊkɒndʌk'tɪvɪtɪ) n. change in electrical conductivity of certain substances as a result of absorption of electromagnetic radiation

photocopy ('fəʊtəʊkɒpɪ) n. **1.** photographic reproduction —vt. **2.** make photocopy of —**'photocopier** n. instrument using light-sensitive photographic materials to reproduce written, printed or graphic work

photoelectricity (fəʊtəʊɪlɛk'trɪsɪtɪ) n. electricity produced or affected by action of light —**photoe'lectric** a. of electric or electronic effects caused by light or other electromagnetic radiation —**photoelectric cell** see PHOTOCELL

photoelectron (fəʊtəʊɪ'lɛktrɒn) n. electron liberated from metallic surface by action of beam of light

Photofit ('fəʊtəʊfɪt) n. **R** method of combining photographs of facial features, hair etc. into composite picture of face: used by police to trace suspects, criminals etc.

photoflood ('fəʊtəʊflʌd) n. highly incandescent tungsten lamp used for indoor photography, television etc.

photogenic (fəʊtə'dʒɛnɪk) a. (esp. of person) capable of being photographed attractively

photograph ('fəʊtəgrɑːf, -græf) n. **1.** picture made by chemical action of light on sensitive film —vt. **2.** take photograph of —**pho'tographer** n. —**photo'graphic** a. —**pho'tography** n.

photogravure (fəʊtəʊɡrə'vjʊə) n. **1.** process of etching, product of photography **2.** picture so reproduced

photolithography (fəʊtəʊlɪ'θɒgrəfɪ) n. art of printing from photographs transferred to stone or metal plate —**photolitho'graphic** a.

photometer (fəʊ'tɒmɪtə) n. instrument for measuring intensity of light —**pho'tometry** n.

photomontage (fəʊtəʊmɒn'tɑːʒ) n. **1.** technique of producing composite picture by combining several photographs **2.** composite picture so produced

photon ('fəʊtɒn) n. quantum of electromagnetic radiation energy, as of light etc. having both particle and wave behaviour

photosensitive (fəʊtəʊ'sɛnsɪtɪv) a. sensitive to electromagnetic radiation, esp. light —**photosensi'tivity** n. —**photo'sensitize** or **-tise** vt.

Photostat ('fəʊtəʊstæt) n. **1. R** apparatus for obtaining direct, facsimile, photographic reproductions of documents, manuscripts, drawings etc., without printing from negatives —vt. **2.** take Photostat copy of

photosynthesis (fəʊtəʊ'sɪnθɪsɪs) n. process by which green plant uses sun's energy to build up carbohydrate reserves

phototropism (fəʊtəʊ'trəʊpɪzəm) n. growth response of plant parts to stimulus of light

photovoltaic effect (fəʊtəʊvɒl'teɪɪk) effect when electromagnetic radiation falls on thin film of one solid deposited on surface of dissimilar solid producing a difference in potential between the two materials

phrase (freɪz) n. **1.** group of words **2.** pithy expression **3.** mode of expression —vt. **4.** express in words —**phraseology** (freɪzɪ'ɒlədʒɪ) n. manner of expression, choice of words —**phrasal verb** phrase consisting of verb and preposition, oft. with meaning different to the parts (eg take in)

phrenology (frɪ'nɒlədʒɪ) n. **1.** formerly, study of skull's shape **2.** theory that character and mental powers are indicated by shape of skull —**phreno'logical** a. —**phre'nologist** n.

phut (fʌt) n. inf. dull, heavy sound —**go phut** collapse

phylactery (fɪ'læktərɪ) n. leather case containing religious texts worn by Jewish men

phylum ('faɪləm) n. **1.** major taxonomic division of animals and plants that contain one or more classes **2.** group of related language families or linguistic stocks (pl. **-la** (-lə))

phys. 1. physical 2. physician 3. physics 4. physiological 5. physiology

physic ('fɪzɪk) *n.* 1. *rare* medicine, *esp.* cathartic —*pl.* 2. (*with sing. v.*) science of properties of matter and energy —'**physical** *a.* 1. bodily, as opposed to mental or moral 2. material 3. of physics of body —'**physically** *adv.* —**phy'sician** *n.* qualified medical practitioner —'**physicist** *n.* one skilled in, or student of physics —**physical chemistry** chemistry concerned with way in which physical properties of substances depend on their chemical structure, properties and reactions —**physical education** training and practice in sports, gymnastics *etc.* —**physical geography** branch of geography that deals with natural features of earth's surface —**physical jerks** *sl.* physical exercises —**physical science** any science concerned with nonliving matter, such as physics, chemistry *etc.* —**physical training** method of keeping fit by following course of bodily exercises

physiognomy (fɪzɪ'ɒnəmɪ) *n.* 1. judging character by face 2. face 3. outward appearance of something

physiography (fɪzɪ'ɒgrəfɪ) *n.* science of the earth's surface —**physi'ographer** *n.*

physiology (fɪzɪ'ɒlədʒɪ) *n.* science of normal function of living things —**physi'ologist** *n.*

physiotherapy (fɪzɪəʊ'θerəpɪ) *n.* therapeutic use of physical means, as massage *etc.* —**physio'therapist** *n.*

physique (fɪ'ziːk) *n.* bodily structure, constitution and development

pi[1] (paɪ) *n.* 1. 16th letter in Gr. alphabet (Π, π) 2. *Maths.* ratio of circumference of circle to its diameter (*pl.* **-s**)

pi[2] *or* **pie** (paɪ) *n.* 1. jumbled pile of printer's type 2. jumbled mixture (*pl.* **pies**) —*vt.* 3. spill and mix (set type) indiscriminately 4. mix up (**pied** *pt./pp.,* '**piing,** '**pieing** *pr.p.*)

pia mater ('paɪə 'meɪtə) innermost of three membranes that cover brain and spinal cord

piano (pɪ'ænəʊ) *n.* 1. (*orig.* **pianoforte** (pɪænəʊ'fɔːtɪ)) musical instrument with strings which are struck by hammers worked by keyboard (*pl.* **-s**) —*a./adv.* ('pjɑːnəʊ) 2. *Mus.* to be performed softly —**pia'nissimo** *a./adv. Mus.* to be performed very quietly —'**pianist** *n.* performer on piano —**Pia'nola** *n.* R mechanically played piano —**piano accordion** accordion in which right hand plays pianolike keyboard (*see also* ACCORDION) —**piano accordionist**

piazza (pɪ'ætsə; *It.* 'pjattsa) *n.* square, marketplace

pibroch ('piːbrɒx) *n.* form of bagpipe music

pica ('paɪkə) *n.* 1. printing type of 6 lines to the inch (*also* **em, pica em**) 2. formerly, size of type

equal to 12 point 3. typewriter type size (10 letters to inch)

picador ('pɪkədɔː) *n.* mounted bullfighter with lance

picaresque (pɪkə'resk) *a.* (of fiction) episodic and dealing with adventures of rogues

piccalilli ('pɪkəlɪlɪ) *n.* pickle of mixed vegetables in mustard sauce

piccaninny *or* **pickaninny** (pɪkə'nɪnɪ) *n. offens.* small Negro child —'**piccanin** *n.* SA male Afr. child

piccolo ('pɪkələʊ) *n.* small flute (*pl.* **-s**)

pick[1] (pɪk) *vt.* 1. choose, select carefully 2. pluck, gather 3. peck at 4. pierce with something pointed 5. find occasion for —*n.* 6. act of picking 7. choicest part —**picked** *a.* selected with care —'**pickings** *pl.n.* 1. gleanings 2. odds and ends of profit —'**picky** *a. inf.* fussy; finicky —'**picklock** *n.* instrument for opening locks —**pick-me-up** *n. inf.* 1. tonic 2. stimulating drink —'**pickpocket** *n.* one who steals from another's pocket —**pick-up** *n.* 1. device for conversion of mechanical energy into electric signals, as in record player *etc.* 2. small truck —**pick on** find fault with —**pick up** 1. raise, lift 2. collect 3. improve, get better 4. accelerate

pick[2] (pɪk) *n.* tool with curved iron crossbar and wooden shaft, used for breaking up hard ground or masonry —'**pickaxe** *n.* pick

pickaback ('pɪkəbæk) *n. see* PIGGYBACK

picket ('pɪkɪt) *n.* 1. prong, pointed stake 2. party of trade unionists posted to deter would-be workers during strike —*vt.* 3. post as picket 4. beset with pickets 5. tether to peg —**picket fence** fence of pickets —**picket line** line of people acting as pickets

pickle ('pɪkəl) *n.* 1. food preserved in brine, vinegar *etc.* 2. liquid used for preserving 3. awkward situation 4. mischievous child —*pl.* 5. pickled vegetables —*vt.* 6. preserve in pickle —'**pickled** *a. inf.* drunk

picnic ('pɪknɪk) *n.* 1. pleasure excursion during which food is consumed outdoors —*vi.* 2. take part in picnic ('**picnicked,** '**picnicking**)

picot ('piːkəʊ) *n.* any of pattern of small loops, as on lace

picric acid ('pɪkrɪk) powerful acid used in dyeing, medicine and as ingredient in certain explosives

Pict (pɪkt) *n.* member of ancient race of NE Scotland —'**Pictish** *a.*

pictograph ('pɪktəgrɑːf) *n.* 1. picture or symbol standing for word or group of words, as in written Chinese 2. chart on which symbols are used to represent values (*also* '**pictogram**)

picture ('pɪktʃə) *n.* 1. drawing or painting 2. mental image 3. beautiful or picturesque object —*pl.* 4. cinema —*vt.* 5. represent in, or as in, a picture —**pic'torial** a. 1. of, in, with, painting or pictures 2. graphic —n. 3. newspaper with pictures —**pic'torially** adv. —**picturesque** (pıktʃə'rɛsk) a. 1. such as would be effective in picture 2. striking, vivid —**picture card** see **court card** at COURT —**picture moulding** 1. edge around framed picture 2. moulding or rail near top of wall from which pictures are hung (also **picture rail**) —**picture postcard** postcard with picture on one side —**picture window** large window having single pane of glass, usu. facing view

piddling ('pıdlıŋ) a. inf. petty; trifling

pidgin ('pıdʒın) n. language made up of elements of two or more other languages

pie (paı) n. 1. baked dish of meat or fruit etc., usu. with pastry crust 2. obs. magpie —**pie chart** circular graph divided into sectors proportional to magnitudes of quantities represented —**pie in the sky** inf. illusory hope of some future good

piebald ('paıbɔːld) a. 1. irregularly marked with black and white 2. motley —n. 3. piebald horse or other animal —**pied** a. 1. piebald 2. variegated

piece (piːs) n. 1. bit, part, fragment 2. single object 3. literary or musical composition etc. 4. sl. young woman 5. small object used in draughts, chess etc. —vt. 6. (with together) mend, put together —**piece goods** goods, esp. fabrics, made in standard widths and lengths —**'piecemeal** adv. by, in, or into pieces, a bit at a time —**'piecework** n. work paid for according to quantity produced

pièce de résistance (pjɛs də rezis'tɑːs) Fr. principal item

pied-à-terre (pjeta'tɛːr) Fr. flat or other lodging for occasional use (pl. **pieds-à-terre** (pjeta'tɛːr))

pier (pıə) n. 1. structure running into sea as landing stage 2. piece of solid upright masonry, esp. supporting bridge —**pier glass** tall narrow mirror designed to hang on wall between windows

pierce (pıəs) vt. 1. make hole in 2. make a way through —**'piercing** a. keen, penetrating

Pierrot ('pıərəʊ; Fr. pjɛ'ro) n. pantomime character, clown

piety ('paıtı) n. 1. godliness 2. devoutness, goodness 3. dutifulness —**'pietism** n. exaggerated or affected piety

piezoelectric effect (paıızəʊı'lɛktrık) or **piezoelectricity** (paıːzəʊılɛk'trısıtı) n. Phys. 1. production of electricity or electric polarity by applying mechanical stress to certain crystals 2. converse effect in which stress is produced in crystal as result of applied potential difference

piffle ('pıfl) n. inf. rubbish, twaddle, nonsense

pig (pıg) n. 1. wild or domesticated mammal killed for pork, ham, bacon 2. inf. greedy, dirty person 3. sl. policeman 4. oblong mass of smelted metal —vi. 5. (of sow) produce litter (-gg-) —**'piggery** n. 1. place for keeping, breeding pigs 2. greediness —**'piggish** a. 1. dirty 2. greedy 3. stubborn —**'piggy** n. child's word for a pig —**'piglet** n. young pig —**piggy bank** child's bank shaped like pig with slot for coins —**pig-headed** a. obstinate —**pig iron** crude iron produced in blast furnace and poured into moulds —**'pigskin** n. 1. skin of domestic pig 2. leather made of this skin 3. US inf. football —a. 4. made of pigskin —**'pigsty** or US. **'pigpen** n. 1. pen for pigs; sty 2. UK untidy place —**'pigswill** n. waste food etc. fed to pigs (also **pig's wash**) —**'pigtail** n. plait of hair hanging from back or either side of head

pigeon ('pıdʒın) n. 1. bird of many wild and domesticated varieties, oft. trained to carry messages 2. inf. concern, responsibility (oft. in it's his, her etc., pigeon) —**'pigeonhole** n. 1. compartment for papers in desk etc. —vt. 2. defer 3. classify —**pigeon-toed** a. with feet, toes turned inwards

piggyback ('pıgıbæk) or **pickaback** n. ride on back of man or animal, given to child

pigment ('pıgmənt) n. colouring matter, paint or dye —**pigmen'tation** n. 1. coloration in plants, animals or man caused by presence of pigments 2. deposition of pigment in animals, plants or man

pigmy ('pıgmı) see PYGMY

pike[1] (paık) n. any of various types of large, predatory freshwater fishes

pike[2] (paık) n. spear formerly used by infantry

pilaster (pı'læstə) n. square column, usu. set in wall

pilau (pı'laʊ), **pilaf**, **pilaff** ('pılæf), or **pilaw** (pı'lɔː) n. Oriental dish of meat or fowl boiled with rice, spices etc.

pilchard ('pıltʃəd) n. small sea fish like the herring

pile[1] (paıl) n. 1. heap 2. great mass of building —vt. 3. heap (up), stack (load) —vi. 4. (with in, out, off etc.) move in a group —**pile-up** n. multiple collision of vehicles —**atomic pile** nuclear reactor —**pile up** 1. gather or be gathered in pile 2. inf. (cause to) crash

pile[2] (paıl) n. beam driven into the ground, esp. as foundation for building in water or wet ground —**'piledriver** n. machine for driving down piles

pile[3] (paıl) n. 1. nap of cloth, esp. of velvet, carpet etc. 2. down

piles (paılz) pl.n. tumours of veins of rectum, haemorrhoids

pilfer ('pılfə) v. steal in small quantities

pilgrim ('pɪlgrɪm) *n.* **1.** one who journeys to sacred place **2.** wanderer, wayfarer —'**pilgrimage** *n.* —**the Pilgrim Fathers** *or* **Pilgrims** English Puritans who founded Plymouth Colony in Massachusetts

pill (pɪl) *n.* **1.** small ball of medicine swallowed whole **2.** anything disagreeable which has to be endured —'**pillbox** *n.* **1.** small box for pills **2.** small round hat —**the pill** oral contraceptive

pillage ('pɪlɪdʒ) *v.* **1.** plunder, ravage, sack —*n.* **2.** seizure of goods, *esp.* in war **3.** plunder

pillar ('pɪlə) *n.* **1.** slender, upright structure, column **2.** prominent supporter —**pillar box** *UK* red pillar-shaped public letter box situated on pavement

pillion ('pɪljən) *n.* seat, cushion, for passenger behind rider of motorcycle or horse

pillory ('pɪlərɪ) *n.* **1.** frame with holes for head and hands in which offender was formerly confined and exposed to public abuse and ridicule —*vt.* **2.** expose to ridicule and abuse **3.** set in pillory ('**pilloried**, '**pillorying**)

pillow ('pɪləʊ) *n.* **1.** cushion for the head, *esp.* in bed —*vt.* **2.** lay on, or as on, pillow —'**pillowcase** *or* '**pillowslip** *n.* removable washable cover of cotton etc. for pillow

pilot ('paɪlət) *n.* **1.** person qualified to fly an aircraft or spacecraft **2.** one qualified to take charge of ship entering or leaving harbour **3.** steersman **4.** guide —*a.* **5.** experimental and preliminary —*vt.* **6.** act as pilot to **7.** steer —'**pilotage** *n.* **1.** act of piloting ship or aircraft **2.** pilot's fee —**pilot fish** small fish of tropical and subtropical seas which oft. accompanies sharks —**pilot house** *Naut.* enclosed structure on bridge of vessel from which it can be navigated; wheelhouse —**pilot lamp** small light in electric circuit that lights when current is on —**pilot light 1.** small auxiliary flame lighting main burner in gas appliance *etc.* **2.** small electric light as indicator —**pilot officer** most junior commissioned rank in British Royal Air Force and in certain other air forces

pilule ('pɪljuːl) *n.* small pill

pimento (pɪ'mɛntəʊ) *n.* **1.** allspice **2.** sweet red pepper (*pl.* -**s**) (*also* **pimiento** (pɪ'mjɛntəʊ, -'mɛn-))

pimp (pɪmp) *n.* **1.** one who solicits for prostitute —*vi.* **2.** act as pimp

pimpernel ('pɪmpənɛl, -nəl) *n.* any of several plants with small scarlet, blue or white flowers closing in dull weather

pimple ('pɪmpᵊl) *n.* small pus-filled spot on skin

pin (pɪn) *n.* **1.** short thin piece of stiff wire with point and head, for fastening **2.** wooden or metal peg or rivet —*vt.* **3.** fasten with pin **4.** seize and hold fast (-**nn**-) —'**pinball** *n.* electrically operated table game, where small ball is shot

through various hazards —'**pincushion** *n.* cushion in which pins are stuck ready for use —'**pinhead** *n.* **1.** head of pin **2.** something very small **3.** *sl.* stupid person —**pin money** trivial sum —'**pinpoint** *vt.* mark exactly —'**pinprick** *n.* **1.** slight puncture made (as if) by pin **2.** small irritation —*vt.* **3.** puncture (as if) with pin —'**pinstripe** *n.* in textiles, very narrow stripe in fabric or fabric itself —**pin tuck** narrow, ornamental fold, *esp.* on shirt fronts *etc.* —'**pinwheel** *n. see* CATHERINE WHEEL (sense 1) —**on pins and needles** in a state of anxious suspense —**pins and needles** *inf.* tingling sensation in fingers *etc.* caused by return of normal blood circulation after its temporary impairment

pinafore ('pɪnəfɔː) *n.* **1.** apron **2.** dress with a bib top (*also* **pinafore dress**)

pince-nez ('pænsneɪ, 'pɪns-; *Fr.* pɛ̃s'ne) *n.* eyeglasses kept on nose by spring (*pl.* **pince-nez**)

pincers ('pɪnsəz) *pl.n.* **1.** tool for gripping, composed of two limbs crossed and pivoted **2.** claws of lobster *etc.*

pinch (pɪntʃ) *vt.* **1.** nip, squeeze **2.** stint **3.** *inf.* steal **4.** *inf.* arrest —*n.* **5.** nip **6.** as much as can be taken up between finger and thumb **7.** stress **8.** emergency —'**pinchbar** *n.* jemmy

pinchbeck ('pɪntʃbɛk) *n.* **1.** zinc and copper alloy —*a.* **2.** counterfeit, flashy

pine[1] (paɪn) *n.* **1.** any of a genus of evergreen coniferous trees **2.** its wood —**pine cone** seed-producing structure of pine tree

pine[2] (paɪn) *vi.* **1.** yearn **2.** waste away with grief

pineal ('pɪnɪəl) *a.* shaped like pine cone —**pineal gland** small cone-shaped gland situated at base of brain

pineapple ('paɪnæpᵊl) *n.* **1.** tropical plant with spiny leaves bearing large edible fruit **2.** the fruit

ping (pɪŋ) *n.* **1.** short high-pitched resonant sound, as of bullet striking metal or sonar echo —*vi.* **2.** make such noise

Ping-Pong ('pɪŋpɒŋ) *n.* **R** table tennis

pinion[1] ('pɪnjən) *n.* **1.** bird's wing —*vt.* **2.** disable or confine by binding wings, arms *etc.*

pinion[2] ('pɪnjən) *n.* small cogwheel

pink (pɪŋk) *n.* **1.** pale reddish colour **2.** garden plant **3.** best condition, fitness —*a.* **4.** of colour pink —*vt.* **5.** pierce **6.** ornament with perforations or scalloped, indented edge —*vi.* **7.** (of engine) knock

pinkie *or* **pinky** ('pɪŋkɪ) *n. US, Scot.* little finger

pinnace ('pɪnɪs) *n.* ship's tender

pinnacle ('pɪnəkᵊl) *n.* **1.** highest pitch or point **2.** mountain peak **3.** pointed turret on buttress or roof

pinnate ('pɪneɪt, 'pɪnɪt) a. 1. like feather 2. (of compound leaves) having leaflets growing opposite each other in pairs on either side of stem

pinny ('pɪnɪ) n. inf. pinafore

pint (paɪnt) n. liquid measure, half a quart, 1/8 gallon (.568 litre) —**pint-size** or **pint-sized** a. inf. very small

pintle ('pɪntl) n. pivot pin

pinto ('pɪntəʊ) US a. 1. marked with patches of white; piebald —n. 2. pinto horse (pl. -s)

pin-up n. inf. picture of sexually attractive person, esp. (partly) naked

pion ('paɪon) or **pi meson** n. Phys. meson having positive or negative charge and rest mass 273 times that of electron, or no charge and rest mass 264 times that of electron

pioneer (paɪə'nɪə) n. 1. explorer 2. early settler 3. originator 4. one of advance party preparing road for troops —vi. 5. act as pioneer or leader

pious ('paɪəs) a. 1. devout 2. righteous

pip[1] (pɪp) n. seed in fruit

pip[2] (pɪp) n. 1. high-pitched sound used as time signal on radio 2. spot on playing cards, dice or dominoes 3. inf. star on junior officer's shoulder showing rank

pip[3] (pɪp) n. disease of fowl —**give someone the pip** sl. annoy someone

pip[4] (pɪp) vt. UK sl. 1. wound, esp. with gun 2. defeat (person), esp. when his success seems certain (oft. in **pip at the post**) 3. blackball, ostracize (-**pp**-)

pipe (paɪp) n. 1. tube of metal or other material 2. tube with small bowl at end for smoking tobacco 3. musical instrument, whistle 4. wine cask —pl. 5. bagpipes —v. 6. play on pipe 7. utter (something) shrilly —vt. 8. convey by pipe 9. ornament with a piping or fancy edging —'**piper** n. player of pipe or bagpipes —'**piping** n. 1. system of pipes 2. decoration of icing on cake 3. fancy edging or trimming on clothes 4. act or art of playing pipe, esp. bagpipes —'**pipeclay** n. 1. white clay used in manufacture of tobacco pipes etc. and for whitening leather etc. —vt. 2. whiten with pipeclay —**pipe cleaner** short length of thin wires twisted so as to hold tiny tufts of yarn: used to clean stem of tobacco pipe —**pipe dream** fanciful, impossible plan etc. —'**pipeline** n. 1. long pipe for transporting oil, water etc. 2. means of communication —**pipe down** sl. stop talking, making noise etc. —**pipe up** 1. commence singing or playing musical instrument 2. speak up, esp. in shrill voice —**in the pipeline** 1. yet to come 2. in process of completion etc.

pipette (pɪ'pɛt) n. slender glass tube to transfer fluids from one vessel to another

pipit ('pɪpɪt) n. any of various songbirds, esp. meadow pipit

pippin ('pɪpɪn) n. any of several kinds of apple

pipsqueak ('pɪpskwiːk) n. inf. insignificant or contemptible person or thing

piquant ('piːkənt, -kɑːnt) a. 1. pungent 2. stimulating —'**piquancy** or '**piquantness** n.

pique (piːk) n. 1. feeling of injury, baffled curiosity or resentment —vt. 2. hurt pride of 3. irritate 4. stimulate

piranha or **piraña** (pɪ'rɑːnjə) n. any of various small voracious freshwater fishes of tropical Amer.

pirate ('paɪrɪt) n. 1. sea robber 2. publisher etc. who infringes copyright —n./a. 3. (person) broadcasting illegally —vt. 4. use or reproduce (artistic work etc.) illicitly —'**piracy** n. —pi'**ratic(al)** a. —pi'**ratically** adv.

pirouette (pɪrʊ'ɛt) n. 1. spinning round on the toe —vi. 2. perform pirouette

Pisces ('paɪsiːz, 'pɪ-) pl.n. (fishes) 12th sign of zodiac, operative c. Feb. 19th-Mar. 20th —**piscatorial** (pɪskə'tɔːrɪəl) or **piscatory** ('pɪskətərɪ) a. of fishing or fishes —**piscine** ('pɪsaɪn) a. of fish

pistachio (pɪ'stɑːʃɪəʊ) n. 1. small hard-shelled, sweet-tasting nut 2. tree producing that (pl. -s)

pistil ('pɪstɪl) n. seed-bearing organ of flower —'**pistillate** a. (of plants) 1. having pistils but no anthers 2. producing pistils

pistol ('pɪstl) n. 1. small firearm for one hand —vt. 2. shoot with pistol (-ll-)

piston ('pɪstən) n. in internal-combustion engine, steam engine etc., cylindrical part propelled to and fro in hollow cylinder by pressure of gas etc. to convert reciprocating motion to rotation

pit[1] (pɪt) n. 1. deep hole in ground 2. mine or its shaft 3. depression 4. part of theatre occupied by orchestra (also **orchestra pit**) 5. enclosure where animals were set to fight 6. servicing, refuelling area on motor-racing track —vt. 7. set to fight, match 8. mark with small dents or scars (-tt-) —'**pitfall** n. 1. any hidden danger 2. covered pit for catching animals or men —'**pithead** n. top of mine shaft and buildings etc. around it

pit[2] (pɪt) chiefly US n. 1. stone of cherry etc. —vt. 2. extract stone from (fruit) (-tt-)

pitapat ('pɪtəpæt) adv. 1. with quick light taps —vi. 2. make quick light taps (-tt-) —n. 3. such taps

pitch[1] (pɪtʃ) vt. 1. cast or throw 2. set up 3. set the key of (a tune) —vi. 4. fall headlong 5. (of ship) plunge lengthwise —n. 6. act of pitching 7. degree, height, intensity 8. slope 9. distance airscrew advances during one revolution 10. distance between threads of screw, teeth of saw *etc.* **11.** acuteness of tone **12.** part of ground where wickets are set up **13.** *Sport* field of play **14.** station of street vendor *etc.* **15.** *inf.* persuasive sales talk —'**pitcher** *n.* US *Baseball* player who delivers ball to batter —**pitched battle 1.** battle ensuing from deliberate choice of time and place **2.** any fierce encounter, *esp.* one with large numbers —'**pitchfork** *n.* **1.** fork for lifting hay *etc.* —*vt.* **2.** throw with, as with, pitchfork —**pitch pipe** small pipe that sounds note or notes of standard frequency, used for establishing correct starting note for unaccompanied singing —**pitch in 1.** cooperate; contribute **2.** begin energetically —**pitch into 1.** assail physically or verbally **2.** get on with doing (something)

pitch² (pɪtʃ) *n.* **1.** dark sticky substance obtained from tar or turpentine —*vt.* **2.** coat with this —'**pitchy** *a.* **1.** covered with pitch **2.** black as pitch —**pitch-black** *or* **pitch-dark** *a.* very dark —**pitch pine** any of various kinds of resinous pine

pitchblende ('pɪtʃblɛnd) *n.* mineral composed largely of uranium oxide, yielding radium

pitcher ('pɪtʃə) *n.* large jug —**pitcher plant** insectivorous plant with leaves modified to form pitcherlike organs that attract and trap insects

pith (pɪθ) *n.* **1.** tissue in stems and branches of certain plants **2.** essential substance, most important part —'**pithily** *adv.* —'**pithless** *a.* —'**pithy** *a.* **1.** terse, cogent, concise **2.** consisting of pith —**pith helmet** lightweight hat made of pith that protects wearer from sun (*also* 'topee, 'topi)

piton ('piːtɒn) *n. Mountaineering* metal spike that may be driven into crevice and used to secure rope *etc.*

pittance ('pɪtəns) *n.* **1.** small allowance **2.** inadequate wages

pitter-patter ('pɪtəpætə) *n.* **1.** sound of light rapid taps or pats, as of raindrops —*vi.* **2.** make such sound —*adv.* **3.** with such sound

pituitary (pɪ'tjuːɪtəri) *a.* of, pert. to, endocrine gland at base of brain

pity ('pɪtɪ) *n.* **1.** sympathy, sorrow for others' suffering **2.** regrettable fact —*vt.* **3.** feel pity for —('pitied, 'pitying) —'**piteous** *a.* **1.** deserving pity **2.** sad, wretched —'**pitiable** *a.* —'**pitiably** *adv.* —'**pitiful** *a.* **1.** woeful **2.** contemptible —'**pitiless** *a.* feeling no pity, hard, merciless

più (pjuː) *adv. Mus.* more (quickly *etc.*)

pivot ('pɪvət) *n.* **1.** shaft or pin on which thing turns —*vt.* **2.** furnish with pivot —*vi.* **3.** hinge on pivot —'**pivotal** *a.* **1.** of, acting as, pivot **2.** of crucial importance

pixie *or* **pixy** ('pɪksɪ) *n.* fairy

pizza ('piːtsə) *n.* dish, *orig.* It., of baked disc of dough covered with wide variety of savoury

toppings —**pizzeria** (piːtsə'riːə) *n.* place selling pizzas

pizzicato (pɪtsɪ'kɑːtəʊ) *a./n. Mus.* (note, passage) played by plucking string of violin *etc.* with finger

pl. 1. place **2.** plate **3.** plural

plaas (plɑːs) *n.* SA farm

placard ('plækɑːd) *n.* **1.** paper or card with notice on one side for posting up or carrying; poster —*vt.* **2.** post placards on **3.** advertise, display on placards

placate (plə'keɪt) *vt.* conciliate, pacify, appease —**pla'catory** *a.*

place (pleɪs) *n.* **1.** locality, spot **2.** position **3.** stead **4.** duty **5.** town, village, residence, buildings **6.** office, employment **7.** seat, space —*vt.* **8.** put in particular place **9.** set **10.** identify **11.** make (order, bet *etc.*) —'**placement** *n.* **1.** act of placing or state of being placed **2.** arrangement, position **3.** process of finding employment —**place kick** *Football* kick in which ball is placed in position before it is kicked —**place-kick** *v.* kick (ball) in this way —**place mat** small mat serving as individual table cover for person at meal —**place setting** cutlery, crockery and glassware laid for one person at dining table

placebo (plə'siːbəʊ) *n.* sugar pill *etc.* given to unsuspecting patient as active drug (*pl.* **-s, -es**)

placenta (plə'sɛntə) *n.* **1.** organ formed in uterus during pregnancy, providing nutrients for foetus **2.** afterbirth (*pl.* **-s, -tae** (-tiː)) —**pla'cental** *a.*

placer ('plæsə) *n.* surface sediment containing particles of gold or some other valuable mineral

placid ('plæsɪd) *a.* **1.** calm **2.** equable —**pla'cidity** *n.* mildness, quiet

placket ('plækɪt) *n.* opening at top of skirt *etc.* fastened with buttons, zip *etc.*

plagiarism ('pleɪdʒərɪzəm) *n.* act of taking ideas, passages *etc.* from an author and presenting them as one's own —'**plagiarize** *or* **-ise** *v.*

plague (pleɪg) *n.* **1.** highly contagious disease, *esp.* bubonic plague **2.** *inf.* nuisance **3.** affliction —*vt.* **4.** trouble, annoy

plaice (pleɪs) *n.* European flatfish

plaid (plæd) *n.* **1.** long Highland cloak or shawl **2.** checked or tartan pattern

Plaid Cymru (plaɪd 'kʌmrɪ) Welsh nationalist party

plain (pleɪn) *a.* **1.** flat, level **2.** unobstructed, not intricate **3.** clear, obvious **4.** easily understood **5.** simple **6.** ordinary **7.** without decoration **8.** not beautiful —*n.* **9.** tract of level country —*adv.* **10.** clearly —'**plainly** *adv.* —'**plainness** *n.* —**plain chocolate** chocolate with slightly bitter flavour and dark colour —**plain clothes** civilian dress, as opposed to uniform —**plain flour** flour to which no raising agent has been added —**plain sailing** unobstructed course of action —**plain speaking** frankness, candour

plainsong ('pleɪnsɒŋ) *n.* style of unison unaccompanied vocal music used in medieval Church

plaint (pleɪnt) *n.* **1.** *Law* statement of complaint **2.** *obs.* lament —**plaintiff** *n. Law* one who sues in court —**'plaintive** *a.* sad, mournful

plait (plæt) *n.* **1.** braid of hair, straw *etc.* —*vt.* **2.** form or weave into plaits

plan (plæn) *n.* **1.** scheme **2.** way of proceeding **3.** project, design **4.** drawing of horizontal section **5.** diagram, map —*vt.* **6.** make plan of **7.** arrange beforehand (**-nn-**)

planchette (plɑːn'ʃɛt) *n.* small board used in spiritualism

plane[1] (pleɪn) *n.* **1.** smooth surface **2.** a level **3.** carpenter's tool for smoothing wood —*vt.* **4.** make smooth with plane —*a.* **5.** perfectly flat or level —**'planar** *a.* **1.** of plane **2.** lying in one plane; flat —**'planer** *n.* planing machine

plane[2] (pleɪn) *vi.* **1.** (of aeroplane) glide **2.** (of boat) rise and partly skim over water —*n.* **3.** wing of aeroplane **4.** aeroplane

plane[3] (pleɪn) *n.* tree with broad leaves

planet ('plænɪt) *n.* heavenly body revolving round the sun —**'planetary** *a.* of planets

planetarium (plænɪ'tɛərɪəm) *n.* **1.** an apparatus that shows the movement of sun, moon, stars and planets by projecting lights on the inside of a dome **2.** building in which the apparatus is housed (*pl.* **-s, -ia** (-ɪə))

plangent ('plændʒənt) *a.* resounding

plank (plæŋk) *n.* **1.** long flat piece of sawn timber —*vt.* **2.** cover with planks

plankton ('plæŋktən) *n.* minute animal and vegetable organisms floating in ocean

plant (plɑːnt) *n.* **1.** any living organism feeding on inorganic substances and without power of locomotion **2.** such an organism that is smaller than tree or shrub **3.** equipment or machinery needed for manufacture **4.** building and equipment for manufacturing purposes **5.** heavy vehicles used for road building *etc.* —*vt.* **6.** set in ground to grow **7.** support, establish **8.** stock with plants **9.** *sl.* hide, *esp.* to deceive or observe —**'planter** *n.* **1.** one who plants **2.** ornamental pot or stand for house plants

plantain[1] ('plæntɪn) *n.* any of various low-growing herbs with broad leaves

plantain[2] ('plæntɪn) *n.* **1.** tropical plant like banana **2.** its fruit

plantation (plæn'teɪʃən) *n.* **1.** estate for cultivation of tea, tobacco *etc.* **2.** wood of planted trees **3.** formerly, colony

plaque (plæk, plɑːk) *n.* **1.** ornamental plate,

tablet **2.** plate of clasp or brooch **3.** filmy deposit on surfaces of teeth, conducive to decay

-plasm (*n. comb. form*) *Biol.* material forming cells, as in *protoplasm* —**plasmic** (*a. comb. form*)

plasma ('plæzmə) *or* **plasm** ('plæzəm) *n.* clear yellowish fluid portion of blood —**'plasmic** *a.*

plaster ('plɑːstə) *n.* **1.** mixture of lime, sand *etc.* for coating walls *etc.* **2.** piece of fabric spread with medicinal or adhesive substance —*vt.* **3.** apply plaster to **4.** apply like plaster —**'plastered** *a. sl.* intoxicated; drunk —**'plasterer** *n.* —**'plasterboard** *n.* thin board in form of layer of plaster compressed between two layers of fibreboard, used to form or cover walls *etc.* —**plaster of Paris** ('pærɪs) **1.** white powder that sets to hard solid when mixed with water, used for sculptures and casts *etc.* **2.** hard plaster produced when this powder is mixed with water

plastic ('plæstɪk) *n.* **1.** any of a group of synthetic products derived from casein, cellulose *etc.*, which can be readily moulded into any form and are extremely durable —*a.* **2.** made of plastic **3.** easily moulded, pliant **4.** capable of being moulded **5.** produced by moulding **6.** *sl.* superficially attractive yet unoriginal or artificial —**plasticity** (plæ'stɪsɪtɪ) *n.* ability to be moulded —**'plasticizer** *or* **-ciser** *n.* any of number of substances added to materials to soften and improve flexibility *etc.* —**plastic bomb** bomb consisting of adhesive jellylike explosive fitted around detonator —**plastic bullet** bullet consisting of cylinder of plastic about four inches long, usu. causing less severe injuries than ordinary bullet, and used *esp.* for riot control (*also* **baton round**) —**plastic surgery** repair or reconstruction of missing or malformed parts of the body for medical or cosmetic reasons

Plasticine ('plæstɪsiːn) *n.* **R** modelling material like clay

plate (pleɪt) *n.* **1.** shallow round dish **2.** flat thin sheet of metal, glass *etc.* **3.** utensils of gold or silver **4.** device for printing **5.** illustration in book **6.** device used by dentists to straighten children's teeth **7.** *inf.* set of false teeth —*vt.* **8.** cover with thin coating of gold, silver or other metal —**'plateful** *n.* —**'plater** *n.* —**plate glass** kind of thick glass used for mirrors, windows *etc.*

plateau ('plætəʊ) *n.* **1.** tract of level high land, tableland **2.** period of stability (*pl.* **-s, -eaux** (-əʊz))

platelet ('pleɪtlɪt) *n.* minute particle occurring in blood of vertebrates and involved in clotting of blood

platen ('plætən) *n.* **1.** *Printing* plate by which

paper is pressed against type **2.** roller in typewriter

platform ('plætfɔːm) *n.* **1.** raised level surface or floor, stage **2.** raised area in station from which passengers board trains **3.** political programme —**platform ticket** ticket for admission to railway platforms but not for travel

platinum ('plætɪnəm) *n.* white heavy malleable metal —**platinum-blond** *or* **platinum-blonde** *a.* **1.** (of hair) of pale silver-blond colour **2.** having hair of this colour

platitude ('plætɪtjuːd) *n.* commonplace remark —**plati'tudinous** *a.*

Platonic (pləˈtɒnɪk) *a.* **1.** of Plato or his philosophy **2.** (*oft.* **p-**) (of love) purely spiritual, friendly —**Platonism** ('pleɪtənɪzəm) *n.* **1.** teachings of Plato, Gr. philosopher, and his followers **2.** philosophical theory that meanings of general words are real entities (forms) and describe particular objects *etc.* by virtue of some relationship of these to form —**Platonist** ('pleɪtənɪst) *n.*

platoon (pləˈtuːn) *n.* body of soldiers employed as unit

platteland ('platəlant) *n.* **SA** rural district

platter ('plætə) *n.* flat dish

platypus ('plætɪpəs) *n.* small Aust. egg-laying amphibious mammal, with dense fur, webbed feet and ducklike bill (*also* **duck-billed platypus**)

plaudit ('plɔːdɪt) *n.* act of applause, hand-clapping

plausible ('plɔːzəbl) *a.* **1.** apparently fair or reasonable **2.** fair-spoken —**plausi'bility** *n.*

play (pleɪ) *vi.* **1.** amuse oneself **2.** take part in game **3.** behave carelessly; trifle **4.** act a part on the stage **5.** perform on musical instrument **6.** move with light or irregular motion, flicker *etc.* —*vt.* **7.** contend with in game **8.** take part in (game) **9.** act the part of **10.** perform (music) **11.** perform on (instrument) **12.** use, work (instrument) —*n.* **13.** dramatic piece or performance **14.** sport **15.** amusement **16.** manner of action or conduct **17.** activity **18.** brisk or free movement **19.** gambling —**player** *n.* —**playful** *a.* lively —**playback** *n.* act or process of reproducing recording, *esp.* on magnetic tape **2.** part of tape recorder serving to or used for reproducing recorded material —**playbill** *n.* **1.** poster or bill advertising play **2.** programme of play —**playboy** *n.* man, *esp.* of private means, who devotes himself to the pleasures of nightclubs, female company *etc.* —**playground** *n.* **1.** outdoor area for children's play, *esp.* one having swings *etc.* or adjoining school **2.** place popular as sports or holiday resort —**playgroup** *n.* group of young children

playing regularly under adult supervision —**playhouse** *n.* theatre —**playing card** one of set of 52 cards used in card games —**playing fields** extensive piece of ground for open-air games —**playmate** *or* **playfellow** *n.* friend or partner in play or recreation —**play-off** *n.* **1.** *Sport* extra contest to decide winner when competitors are tied **2.** *chiefly US* contest or series of games to determine championship —**playpen** *n.* small enclosure, usu. portable, in which young child can be left to play in safety —**plaything** *n.* toy —**playtime** *n.* time for play or recreation, *esp.* school break —**playwright** *n.* author of plays —**play back** reproduce (recorded material) on (magnetic tape) by means of tape recorder —**play off 1.** (*usu. with* against) manipulate as if playing game **2.** take part in play-off —**play on** words pun

plaza ('plɑːzə) *n.* **1.** open space or square **2.** complex of shops *etc.*

PLC Public Limited Company

plea (pliː) *n.* **1.** entreaty **2.** statement of prisoner or defendant **3.** excuse —**plead** *vi.* **1.** make earnest appeal **2.** address court of law —*vt.* **3.** bring forward as excuse or plea ('**pleaded** *or* (*US, Scot.*) **pled** (plɛd), '**pleading**) —'**pleadings** *pl.n.* *Law* formal written statements presented alternately by plaintiff and defendant in lawsuit

please (pliːz) *vt.* **1.** be agreeable to **2.** gratify **3.** delight —*vi.* **4.** like, be willing —*adv.* **5.** word of request —**pleasance** ('plɛzns) *n.* secluded part of garden —**pleasant** ('plɛznt) *a.* pleasing, agreeable —**pleasantly** ('plɛzntlɪ) *adv.* —**pleasantry** ('plɛzntrɪ) *n.* joke, humour —**pleasurable** ('plɛʒərəbl) *a.* giving pleasure —**pleasure** ('plɛʒə) *n.* **1.** enjoyment, satisfaction **2.** will, choice

pleat (pliːt) *n.* **1.** any of various types of fold made by doubling material back on itself —*vt.* **2.** make, gather into pleats

plebeian (pləˈbiːən) *a.* **1.** belonging to the common people **2.** low or rough —*n.* **3.** one of the common people (*also* (*offens. sl.*) **pleb** (plɛb))

plebiscite ('plɛbɪsaɪt, -sɪt) *n.* decision by direct voting of the electorate

plectrum ('plɛktrəm) *or* **plectron** ('plɛktrən) *n.* small implement for plucking strings of guitar *etc.* (*pl.* **-tra** (-trə), **-trums** *or* **-tra, -trons**)

pledge (plɛdʒ) *n.* **1.** promise **2.** thing given over as security **3.** toast —*vt.* **4.** promise formally **5.** bind or secure by pledge **6.** give over as security

Pleiocene ('plaɪəʊsiːn) *n. see* PLIOCENE

Pleistocene ('plaɪstəsiːn) *a.* **1.** of glacial period of formation —*n.* **2.** Pleistocene epoch or rock series

plenary ('pliːnərɪ, 'plɛn-) *a.* **1.** complete,

without limitations, absolute **2.** (of meeting *etc.*) with all members present

plenipotentiary ('plenɪpə'tenʃərɪ) *a./n.* (envoy) having full powers

plenitude ('plenɪtjuːd) *n.* **1.** completeness, entirety **2.** abundance

plenty ('plentɪ) *n.* **1.** abundance **2.** quite enough —'**plenteous** *a.* **1.** ample **2.** rich **3.** copious —'**plentiful** *a.* abundant

plenum ('pliːnəm) *n.* **1.** space as considered to be full of matter (opposed to vacuum) **2.** condition of fullness (*pl.* **-s, -na** (-nə))

plethora ('pleθərə) *n.* oversupply

pleura ('pluərə) *n.* membrane lining the chest and covering the lungs (*pl.* **pleurae** ('pluərɪ)) —'**pleurisy** *n.* inflammation of the pleura

pliable ('plaɪəbəl) *a.* easily bent or influenced —plia'**bility** *n.* —'**pliancy** *n.* —'**pliant** *a.* pliable

pliers ('plaɪəz) *pl.n.* tool with hinged arms and jaws for gripping

plight[1] (plaɪt) *n.* **1.** distressing state **2.** predicament

plight[2] (plaɪt) *vt.* promise —**plight one's troth** make a promise, *esp.* of marriage

Plimsoll line ('plɪmsəl) mark on ships indicating maximum draught permitted when loaded

plimsolls *or* **plimsoles** ('plɪmsəlz) *pl.n.* rubber-soled canvas shoes

plinth (plɪnθ) *n.* slab as base of column *etc.*

Pliocene *or* **Pleiocene** ('plaɪəʊsiːn) *a.* **1.** of the most recent tertiary deposits —*n.* **2.** Pliocene epoch or rock series

plissé ('pliːseɪ, 'plɪs-) *n.* **1.** fabric with wrinkled finish, achieved by treatment involving caustic soda **2.** such finish on fabric

P.L.O. Palestine Liberation Organization

plod (plɒd) *vi.* walk or work doggedly (**-dd-**)

plonk[1] (plɒŋk) *v.* **1.** drop, fall suddenly and heavily —*n.* **2.** act or sound of this

plonk[2] (plɒŋk) *n.* *inf.* alcoholic drink, *esp.* (cheap) wine

plop (plɒp) *n.* **1.** sound of object falling into water without splash —*v.* **2.** (cause to) fall with such sound (**-pp-**)

plosion ('pləʊʒən) *n.* *Phonet.* sound of abrupt break or closure, *esp.* audible release of stop (*also* **ex'plosion**) —'**plosive** *Phonet. a.* **1.** accompanied by plosion —*n.* **2.** plosive consonant; stop

plot[1] (plɒt) *n.* **1.** secret plan, conspiracy **2.** essence of story, play *etc.* —*v.* **3.** devise secretly **4.** mark position of **5.** make map of —*vi.* **6.** conspire (**-tt-**)

plot[2] (plɒt) *n.* small piece of land

plough *or esp. U.S.* **plow** (plaʊ) *n.* **1.** implement for turning up soil *etc.* **2.** similar implement for clearing snow *etc.* —*vt.* **3.** turn up

with plough, furrow —*vi.* **4.** (*with* through) work (at) slowly —'**ploughman** *or esp. U.S.* '**plowman** *n.* —**ploughman's lunch** meal of cheese, bread and oft. beer —'**ploughshare** *or esp. U.S.* '**plowshare** *n.* blade of plough —**the Plough** group of seven brightest stars in constellation Ursa Major (*also* **Charles's Wain**)

plover ('plʌvə) *n.* any of various shore birds, typically with round head, straight bill and long pointed wings

plow (plaʊ) *US see* PLOUGH

ploy (plɔɪ) *n.* **1.** stratagem **2.** occupation **3.** prank

P.L.R. Public Lending Right

pluck (plʌk) *vt.* **1.** pull, pick off **2.** strip **3.** sound strings of (guitar *etc.*) with fingers, plectrum —*n.* **4.** courage **5.** sudden pull or tug —'**pluckily** *adv.* —'**plucky** *a.* courageous

plug (plʌg) *n.* **1.** thing fitting into and filling a hole **2.** *Elec.* device connecting appliance to electricity supply **3.** tobacco pressed hard **4.** *inf.* recommendation, advertisement —*vt.* **5.** stop with plug **6.** *inf.* advertise (product, show *etc.*) by constant repetition, as on television **7.** *sl.* punch **8.** *sl.* shoot —*vi.* **9.** *inf.* (*with* away) work hard (**-gg-**) —**plug in** connect (electrical appliance) with power source by means of plug

plum (plʌm) *n.* **1.** stone fruit **2.** tree bearing it **3.** choicest part, piece, position *etc.* —*a.* **4.** choice **5.** dark reddish-purple colour —'**plummy** *a.* **1.** of plums **2.** *UK inf.* (of speech) deep, refined and somewhat drawling **3.** *UK inf.* choice; desirable

plumage ('pluːmɪdʒ) *n. see* PLUME

plumb (plʌm) *n.* **1.** ball of lead (**plumb bob**) attached to string used for sounding, finding the perpendicular *etc.* —*a.* **2.** perpendicular —*adv.* **3.** perpendicularly **4.** exactly **5.** *US inf.* downright **6.** honestly **7.** exactly —*vt.* **8.** set exactly upright **9.** find depth of **10.** reach, undergo **11.** equip with, connect to plumbing system —'**plumber** *n.* worker who attends to water and sewage systems —'**plumbing** *n.* **1.** trade of plumber **2.** system of water and sewage pipes —'**plumbline** *n.* cord with plumb attached

plume (pluːm) *n.* **1.** feather **2.** ornament of feathers or horsehair —*vt.* **3.** furnish with plumes **4.** pride (oneself) —'**plumage** *n.* bird's feathers collectively

plummet ('plʌmɪt) *vi.* **1.** plunge headlong —*n.* **2.** plumbline

plump[1] (plʌmp) *a.* **1.** of rounded form, moderately fat, chubby —*v.* **2.** (*oft. with* up *or* out) make, become plump

plump[2] (plʌmp) *vi.* **1.** sit, fall abruptly —*vt.* **2.** drop, throw abruptly —*adv.* **3.** suddenly **4.** heavily **5.** directly —**plump for** choose, vote only for

plunder ('plʌndə) *vt.* **1.** take by force **2.** rob

systematically —*vi.* **3.** rob —*n.* **4.** pillage **5.** booty, spoils

plunge (plʌndʒ) *vt.* **1.** put forcibly —*vi.* **2.** throw oneself **3.** enter, rush with violence **4.** descend very suddenly —*n.* **5.** dive —'**plunger** *n.* **1.** rubber suction cap to unblock drains **2.** pump piston —**take the plunge** *inf.* **1.** embark on risky enterprise **2.** get married

plunk (plʌŋk) *v.* **1.** pluck (string of banjo *etc.*) **2.** drop suddenly

pluperfect (pluː'pɜːfɪkt) *a./n.* (tense) expressing action completed before past point of time

plural ('pluərəl) *a.* **1.** of, denoting more than one person or thing —*n.* **2.** word in its plural form —'**pluralism** *n.* **1.** holding of more than one appointment, vote *etc.* **2.** coexistence of different social groups *etc.* in one society —'**pluralist** *n./a.* —**plu'rality** *n.* majority of votes *etc.*

plus (plʌs) *prep.* **1.** with addition of (*usu.* indicated by the sign +) —*a.* **2.** to be added **3.** positive —**plus fours** men's baggy knickerbockers reaching below knee, now only worn for golf *etc.*

plush (plʌʃ) *n.* **1.** fabric with long nap, long-piled velvet —*a.* **2.** luxurious

Pluto¹ ('pluːtəu) *n. Gr. myth.* god of underworld; Hades —**Plu'tonian** *a.* pert. to Pluto or the infernal regions, dark —**plutonic** (pluː'tɒnɪk) *a.* (of igneous rocks) derived from magma that has cooled and solidified below surface of earth

Pluto² ('pluːtəu) *n.* second smallest planet and farthest known from sun

plutocracy (pluː'tɒkrəsɪ) *n.* **1.** government by the rich **2.** state ruled thus **3.** wealthy class —'**plutocrat** *n.* wealthy man —**pluto'cratic** *a.*

plutonium (pluː'təunɪəm) *n.* radioactive metallic element used *esp.* in nuclear reactors and weapons

pluvial ('pluːvɪəl) *a.* of, caused by the action of rain

ply¹ (plaɪ) *vt.* **1.** wield **2.** work at **3.** supply pressingly **4.** urge **5.** keep busy —*vi.* **6.** go to and fro, run regularly (**plied, 'plying**)

ply² (plaɪ) *n.* **1.** fold or thickness **2.** strand of yarn —'**plywood** *n.* board of thin layers of wood glued together with grains at right angles

Plymouth Brethren ('plɪməθ) strongly Puritanical religious sect having no organized ministry

Pm *Chem.* promethium

p.m. *or* **P.M. 1.** post meridiem (*Lat.*, after noon) **2.** post-mortem

P.M. 1. Paymaster **2.** Postmaster **3.** Prime Minister

P.M.G. 1. Paymaster General **2.** Postmaster General

PMS premenstrual syndrome

PMT premenstrual tension

pneumatic (njuː'mætɪk) *a.* of, worked by, inflated with wind or air —**pneu'matics** *pl.n.* (*with sing. v.*) branch of physics concerned with mechanical properties of gases, *esp.* air

pneumonia (njuː'məunɪə) *n.* inflammation of the lungs

po (pəu) *n. UK inf.* chamber pot (*pl.* -**s**)

Po *Chem.* polonium

P.O. 1. Petty Officer **2.** postal order (*also* **p.o.**) **3.** Post Office

poach¹ (pəutʃ) *vt.* **1.** catch (game) illegally **2.** trample, make swampy or soft —*vi.* **3.** trespass for purpose of poaching **4.** encroach

poach² (pəutʃ) *vt.* simmer (eggs, fish *etc.*) gently in water *etc.* —'**poacher** *n.*

pock (pɒk) *n.* pustule, as in smallpox *etc.*

pocket ('pɒkɪt) *n.* **1.** small bag inserted in garment **2.** cavity filled with ore *etc.* **3.** socket, cavity, pouch or hollow **4.** mass of water or air differing from that surrounding it **5.** isolated group or area **6.** SA bag of vegetables or fruit —*vt.* **7.** put into one's pocket **8.** appropriate, steal —*a.* **9.** small —'**pocketbook** *n. chiefly US* small bag or case for money, papers *etc.* —'**pocketknife** *n.* small knife with one or more blades that fold into handle; penknife —**pocket money 1.** small, regular allowance given to children by parents **2.** allowance for small, occasional expenses

poco ('pəukəu; *It.* 'pɔːkɔ) *or* **un poco** *a./adv. Mus.* little; to a small degree

pod (pɒd) *n.* **1.** long seed vessel, as of peas, beans *etc.* —*v.* **2.** form pods —*vt.* **3.** shell (-**dd-**)

-pod *or* -**pode** (*comb. form*) indicating certain type or number of feet, as in *arthropod, tripod*

podgy ('pɒdʒɪ) *a.* short and fat

podium ('pəudɪəm) *n.* small raised platform (*pl.* -**s**, -**dia** (-dɪə))

poem ('pəuɪm) *n.* imaginative composition in rhythmic lines —**poesy** ('pəuɪzɪ) *n.* poetry —'**poet** *n.* writer of poems ('**poetess** *fem.*) —**poetaster** (pəuɪ'tæstə, -'teɪ-) *n.* would-be or inferior poet —**po'etic(al)** *a.* —**po'etically** *adv.* —'**poetry** *n.* art or work of poet, verse —**poetic justice** fitting retribution —**poetic licence** justifiable departure from conventional rules of form, fact *etc.*, as in poetry

po-faced *a.* wearing disapproving stern expression

pogey *or* **pogy** ('pəugɪ) *n. C sl.* **1.** unemployment insurance **2.** dole

pogo stick ('pəugəu) stout pole with handle at top, steps for feet and spring at bottom, so that user can spring up, down and along on it

pogrom ('pɒgrəm) *n.* organized persecution and massacre, *esp.* of Jews in Russia

poignant ('pɔinjənt, -nənt) *a.* 1. moving 2. biting, stinging 3. vivid 4. pungent —'**poignancy** *or* '**poignance** *n.*

poinciana (pɔinsı'ɑːnə) *n.* tropical tree with scarlet flowers

poinsettia (pɔin'setiə) *n. orig.* Amer. shrub, widely cultivated for its clusters of scarlet leaves, resembling petals

point (pɔint) *n.* 1. dot, mark 2. punctuation mark 3. item, detail 4. unit of value 5. position, degree, stage 6. moment 7. gist of an argument 8. purpose 9. striking or effective part or quality 10. essential object or thing 11. sharp end 12. single unit in scoring 13. headland 14. one of direction marks of compass 15. movable rail changing train to other rails 16. fine kind of lace 17. act of pointing 18. power point 19. printing unit, one twelfth of a pica —*pl.* 20. electrical contacts in distributor of engine —*vi.* 21. show direction or position by extending finger 22. direct attention 23. (of dog) indicate position of game by standing facing it —*vt.* 24. aim, direct 25. sharpen 26. fill up joints of (brickwork *etc.*) with mortar 27. give value to (words *etc.*) —'**pointed** *a.* 1. sharp 2. direct, telling —'**pointedly** *adv.* —'**pointer** *n.* 1. index 2. indicating rod *etc.* used for pointing 3. indication 4. dog trained to point —'**pointless** *a.* 1. blunt 2. futile, irrelevant —**point-blank** *a.* 1. aimed horizontally 2. plain, blunt —*adv.* 3. with level aim (there being no necessity to elevate for distance) 4. at short range —**point duty** police regulation of traffic —**point-to-point** *n.* steeplechase usu. for amateur riders only —**point of no return** 1. point at which irreversible commitment must be made to action *etc.* 2. point in journey at which, if one continues, supplies will be insufficient for return to starting place —**point of order** question raised in meeting as to whether rules governing procedures are being breached (*pl.* **points of order**) —**point of view** 1. position from which someone or something is observed 2. mental viewpoint or attitude (*pl.* **points of view**)

pointillism ('pwæntɪlɪzəm) *n.* technique of painting elaborated from impressionism, in which dots of unmixed colour are juxtaposed on white ground so that from distance they fuse in viewer's eye into appropriate intermediate tones —'**pointillist** *n./a.*

poise (pɔiz) *n.* 1. composure 2. self-possession 3. balance, equilibrium, carriage (of body *etc.*) —*v.* 4. (cause to) be balanced or suspended —*vt.* 5. hold in readiness

poison ('pɔizən) *n.* 1. substance which kills or injures when introduced into living organism —*vt.* 2. give poison to 3. infect 4. pervert, spoil —'**poisoner** *n.* —'**poisonous** *a.* —**poison ivy** N Amer. shrub or climbing plant that causes

itching rash on contact —**poison-pen letter** malicious anonymous letter

poke[1] (pəuk) *vt.* 1. push, thrust with finger, stick *etc.* 2. thrust —*vi.* 3. make thrusts 4. pry —*n.* 5. act of poking —'**poker** *n.* metal rod for poking fire —'**poky** *or* '**pokey** *a.* small, confined, cramped

poke[2] (pəuk) —**pig in a poke** something bought *etc.* without previous inspection

poker ('pəukə) *n.* card game —**poker face** *inf.* face without expression, as of poker player concealing value of his cards —**poker-faced** *a.*

pol. 1. political 2. politics

Pol. 1. Poland 2. Polish

polar ('pəulə) *a. see* POLE[2]

Polaris (pə'lɑːrıs) *n.* 1. brightest star in constellation Ursa Minor, situated slightly less than 1° from north celestial pole (*also* **Pole Star, North Star**) 2. type of Amer. ballistic missile, usu. fired by submarine

Polaroid ('pəulərɔid) *n.* **R** 1. type of plastic which polarizes light 2. camera that develops print very quickly inside itself

polder ('pəuldə, 'pɒl-) *n.* land reclaimed from the sea

pole[1] (pəul) *n.* 1. long rounded piece of wood *etc.* —*vt.* 2. propel with pole —**pole-vault** *vi.* perform or compete in the pole vault —**pole-vaulter** *n.* —**the pole vault** field event in which competitors attempt to clear high bar with aid of long flexible pole —**up the pole** *inf.* 1. slightly mad 2. in error, confused

pole[2] (pəul) *n.* 1. either of the ends of axis of earth or celestial sphere 2. either of opposite ends of magnet, electric cell *etc.* —'**polar** *a.* 1. pert. to the N and S pole, or to magnetic poles 2. directly opposite in tendency, character *etc.* —po'**larity** *n.* —polari'**zation** *or* -i'**sation** *n.* —'**polarize** *or* -**ise** *vt.* give polarity to —**polar bear** white Arctic bear —**polar circle** either Arctic Circle or Antarctic Circle —**the Pole Star** star closest to N celestial pole at any particular time, at present Polaris

poleaxe *or U.S.* **poleax** ('pəulæks) *n.* 1. battle-axe —*vt.* 2. hit, fell as with poleaxe

polecat ('pəulkæt) *n.* small animal of weasel family

polemic (pə'lɛmɪk) *a.* 1. controversial (*also* po'**lemical**) —*n.* 2. war of words, argument —po'**lemics** *pl.n.* (*with sing. v.*) art or practice of dispute or argument

police (pə'liːs) *n.* 1. the civil force which maintains public order —*vt.* 2. keep in order —**police dog** dog trained to help police —**po'liceman** *n.* member of police force (po'**licewoman** *fem.*) —**police state** state or country in which repressive government maintains control through police —**police**

station office or headquarters of police force of district

policy[1] ('pɒlɪsɪ) *n.* **1.** course of action adopted, *esp.* in state affairs **2.** prudence

policy[2] ('pɒlɪsɪ) *n.* insurance contract

poliomyelitis (pəʊlɪəʊmaɪə'laɪtɪs) *n.* disease of spinal cord characterized by fever and sometimes paralysis (*also* **infantile paralysis**)

polish ('pɒlɪʃ) *vt.* **1.** make smooth and glossy **2.** refine —*n.* **3.** shine **4.** polishing **5.** substance for polishing **6.** refinement

Polish ('pəʊlɪʃ) *a.* **1.** of Poland —*n.* **2.** official language of Poland

Politburo ('pɒlɪtbjʊərəʊ) *n.* **1.** executive committee of a Communist Party **2.** supreme policy-making authority in most Communist countries

polite (pə'laɪt) *a.* **1.** showing regard for others in manners, speech *etc.* **2.** refined, cultured —**po'litely** *adv.* —**po'liteness** *n.* courtesy

politic ('pɒlɪtɪk) *a.* **1.** wise **2.** shrewd **3.** expedient **4.** cunning —**po'litical** *a.* of the state or its affairs —**poli'tician** *n.* one engaged in politics —'**politics** *pl.n.* **1.** (*with sing. v.*) art of government **2.** political affairs or life —'**polity** *n.* **1.** form of government **2.** organized state **3.** civil government —**political asylum** refuge given to someone for political reasons —**political economy** *former name for* economics —**political prisoner** someone imprisoned for holding or expressing particular political beliefs —**political science** study of state, government and politics —**political scientist**

polka ('pɒlkə) *n.* **1.** lively dance in 2/4 time **2.** music for it —**polka dot** one of pattern of bold spots on fabric *etc.*

poll (pəʊl) *n.* **1.** voting **2.** counting of votes **3.** number of votes recorded **4.** canvassing of sample of population to determine general opinion **5.** (top of) head —*vt.* **6.** receive (votes) **7.** take votes of **8.** lop, shear **9.** cut horns from (animals) —*vi.* **10.** vote —'**pollster** *n.* one who conducts polls —**polling booth** voting place at election —**polling station** place to which voters go during election to cast votes

pollard ('pɒləd) *n.* **1.** hornless animal of normally horned variety **2.** tree on which a close head of young branches has been made by polling —*vt.* **3.** make a pollard of

pollen ('pɒlən) *n.* fertilizing dust of flower —'**pollinate** *vt.* —**pollen count** measure of pollen present in air over 24-hour period

pollute (pə'luːt) *vt.* **1.** make foul **2.** corrupt **3.** desecrate —**pol'lutant** *n.* —**pol'lution** *n.*

polo ('pəʊləʊ) *n.* game like hockey played by teams of 4 players on horseback —**polo neck 1.** collar on garment, worn rolled over to fit closely round neck **2.** sweater with such collar

polonaise (pɒlə'neɪz) *n.* **1.** Polish dance **2.** music for it

polonium (pə'ləʊnɪəm) *n.* radioactive element that occurs in trace amounts in uranium ores

poltergeist ('pɒltəgaɪst) *n.* noisy mischievous spirit

poltroon (pɒl'truːn) *n.* abject coward

poly ('pɒlɪ) *n. inf.* polytechnic

poly- (*comb. form*) many, as in *polysyllabic*

polyandry ('pɒlɪændrɪ) *n.* polygamy in which woman has more than one husband

polyanthus (pɒlɪ'ænθəs) *n.* cultivated primrose

polychrome ('pɒlɪkrəʊm) *a.* **1.** having various colours —*n.* **2.** work of art in many colours —**polychro'matic** *a.*

polyester (pɒlɪ'estə) *n.* any of large class of synthetic materials used as plastics, textile fibres *etc.*

polygamy (pə'lɪgəmɪ) *n.* custom of being married to several persons at same time —**po'lygamist** *n.*

polyglot ('pɒlɪglɒt) *a.* speaking, writing in several languages

polygon ('pɒlɪgɒn) *n.* figure with many angles or sides —**po'lygonal** *a.*

polygraph ('pɒlɪgrɑːf, -græf) *n.* **1.** instrument for recording pulse rate and perspiration, used *esp.* as lie detector **2.** device for producing copies of written matter

polygyny (pə'lɪdʒɪnɪ) *n.* polygamy in which man has more than one wife

polyhedron (pɒlɪ'hiːdrən) *n.* solid figure contained by many faces (*pl.* **-s, -dra** (-drə))

polymath ('pɒlɪmæθ) *n.* person of great and varied learning

polymer ('pɒlɪmə) *n.* compound, as polystyrene, that has large molecules formed from repeated units —**poly'meric** *a.* of polymer —**polymeri'zation** *or* **-i'sation** *n.* —'**polymerize** *or* **-ise** *v.*

polymorphous (pɒlɪ'mɔːfəs) *or* **polymorphic** *a.* **1.** having, taking or passing through many different forms or stages **2.** exhibiting or undergoing polymorphism

Polynesian (pɒlɪ'niːʒən, -ʒɪən) *a.* **1.** of Polynesia, group of Pacific islands, its people or any of their languages —*n.* **2.** member of people of Polynesia, generally of Caucasoid features with light skin and wavy hair **3.** branch of Malayo-Polynesian family of languages, including Maori and Hawaiian

polynomial (pɒlɪ'nəʊmɪəl) *a.* **1.** of two or more names or terms —*n.* **2.** mathematical expression consisting of sum of terms each of which is product of constant and one or more variables raised to positive or zero integral power **3.**

mathematical expression consisting of sum of a number of terms (also **multi'nomial**)

polyp ('pɒlɪp) n. 1. sea anemone or allied animal 2. tumour with branched roots (also **'polypus**)

polyphase ('pɒlɪfeɪz) a. (of alternating current of electricity) possessing number of regular sets of alternations

polyphony (pə'lɪfənɪ) n. polyphonic style of composition or piece of music utilizing it —**poly'phonic** a. 1. Mus. composed of relatively independent parts; contrapuntal 2. many-voiced

polystyrene (pɒlɪ'staɪriːn) n. synthetic material used esp. as white rigid foam for packing etc.

polytechnic (pɒlɪ'tɛknɪk) n. 1. college dealing mainly with various arts and crafts —a. 2. of or relating to technical instruction

polytheism ('pɒlɪθiːɪzəm, pɒlɪ'θiːɪzəm) n. belief in many gods —**'polytheist** n.

polythene ('pɒlɪθiːn) n. tough thermoplastic material

polyunsaturated (pɒlɪʌn'sætʃəreɪtɪd) a. of group of fats that do not form cholesterol in blood

polyurethane (pɒlɪ'jʊərəθeɪn) n. class of synthetic materials, oft. in foam or flexible form

polyvalent (pɒlɪ'veɪlənt, pə'lɪvələnt) a. having more than one valency

pomace ('pʌmɪs) n. 1. pulpy residue of apples or similar fruit after crushing and pressing, as in cider-making 2. any pulpy substance left after crushing etc.

pomade (pə'mɑːd) n. 1. perfumed oil or ointment applied to hair, to make it smooth and shiny —vt. 2. put pomade on

pomander (pəʊ'mændə) n. (container for) mixture of sweet-smelling herbs etc.

pomegranate ('pɒmɪɡrænɪt, 'pɒmɡrænɪt) n. 1. tree cultivated for its edible fruit 2. its fruit with thick rind containing many seeds in red pulp

Pomeranian (pɒmə'reɪnɪən) n. breed of small dog

pomfret or **pomfret-cake** ('pʌmfrɪt, 'pɒm-) n. small black rounded confection of liquorice (also **Pontefract cake**)

pommel ('pʌməl, 'pɒm-) n. 1. front of saddle 2. knob of sword hilt —vt. 3. see PUMMEL

pommy ('pɒmɪ) n. (sometimes P-) A, NZ sl. British person (also **pom**)

pomp (pɒmp) n. splendid display or ceremony

pompon ('pɒmpɒn) or **pompom** ('pɒmpɒm) n. tuft of ribbon, wool, feathers etc. decorating hat, shoe etc.

pompous ('pɒmpəs) a. 1. self-important 2. ostentatious 3. (of language) inflated, stilted —**pom'posity** n.

ponce (pɒns) n. sl. 1. effeminate man 2. pimp

poncho ('pɒntʃəʊ) n. loose circular cloak with hole for head (pl. -s)

pond (pɒnd) n. small body, pool or lake of still water

ponder ('pɒndə) v. 1. muse, meditate, think over 2. consider, deliberate (on)

ponderous ('pɒndərəs) a. 1. heavy, unwieldy 2. boring

pong (pɒŋ) inf. n. 1. strong (unpleasant) smell —vi. 2. stink

pontiff ('pɒntɪf) n. 1. Pope 2. high priest 3. bishop —**pon'tifical** a. —**pontificate** (pɒn'tɪfɪkɪt) n. 1. dignity or office of pontiff —vi. (pɒn'tɪfɪkeɪt) 2. speak bombastically (also **'pontify**) 3. act as pontiff

pontoon[1] ('pɒn'tuːn) n. flat-bottomed boat or metal drum for use in supporting temporary bridge

pontoon[2] (pɒn'tuːn) n. gambling card game (also **twenty-one**)

pony ('pəʊnɪ) n. 1. horse of small breed 2. very small glass, esp. for liqueurs —**'ponytail** n. long hair tied in one bunch at back of head —**pony trekking** act of riding ponies cross-country, esp. as pastime

poodle ('puːdəl) n. pet dog with long curly hair oft. clipped fancifully

poof (puf, puːf) or **poove** (puːv) n. sl. homosexual man

pooh (puː) interj. exclamation of disdain, contempt or disgust —**pooh-pooh** vt. express disdain or scorn for; dismiss, belittle

Pooh-Bah ('puː'bɑː) n. pompous official

pool[1] (puːl) n. 1. small body of still water 2. deep place in river or stream 3. puddle 4. swimming pool

pool[2] (puːl) n. 1. common fund or resources 2. group of people, eg typists, any of whom can work for any of several employers 3. collective stakes in various games 4. cartel 5. variety of billiards —pl. 6. see **football pools** at FOOT —vt. 7. put in common fund

poop (puːp) n. ship's stern

poor (pʊə, pɔː) a. 1. having little money 2. unproductive 3. inadequate, insignificant 4. needy 5. miserable, pitiable 6. feeble 7. not fertile —**'poorly** adv. 1. badly —a. 2. inf. not in good health —**'poorness** n. —**poor box** box, esp. in church, used for collection of alms or money for poor —**'poorhouse** n. formerly, publicly maintained institution offering accommodation to the poor

poort (pʊət) n. SA narrow mountain pass

pop[1] (pɒp) vi. 1. make small explosive sound 2. inf. go or come unexpectedly or suddenly —vt. 3. cause to make small explosive sound 4. put or place suddenly (-pp-) —n. 5. small explosive sound **6.** *inf.* nonalcoholic fizzy drink —'**popper** *n.* **1.** person or thing that pops **2.** UK *inf.* press stud **3.** *chiefly* US container for cooking popcorn in —'**popcorn** *n.* any kind of maize that puffs up when roasted **2.** the roasted product —'**popgun** *n.* toy gun that fires pellet or cork by means of compressed air

pop² (pɒp) *n. inf.* **1.** father **2.** old man

pop³ (pɒp) *n.* **1.** music of general appeal, *esp.* to young people —*a. inf.* **2.** popular

pop. **1.** popular **2.** population

P.O.P. Post Office Preferred (size of envelopes *etc.*)

pope (pəʊp) *n.* (*oft.* P-) bishop of Rome and head of R.C. Church —'**popery** *n. offens.* papal system, doctrines —'**popish** *a. derogatory* belonging to or characteristic of Roman Catholicism

popeyed ('pɒpaɪd) *a.* **1.** having bulging, prominent eyes **2.** staring in astonishment

popinjay ('pɒpɪndʒeɪ) *n.* **1.** conceited or talkative person **2.** *obs.* parrot

poplar ('pɒplə) *n.* tree noted for its slender tallness

poplin ('pɒplɪn) *n.* corded fabric *usu.* of cotton

poppadom *or* **poppadum** ('pɒpədəm) *n.* thin, round, crisp Indian bread

poppet ('pɒpɪt) *n.* **1.** term of affection for small child or sweetheart **2.** mushroom-shaped valve lifted from seating by applying axial force to stem (*also* **poppet valve**) **3.** *Naut.* temporary supporting brace for vessel hauled on land

poppy ('pɒpɪ) *n.* bright-flowered plant yielding opium —**Poppy Day** *inf.* Remembrance Sunday

poppycock ('pɒpɪkɒk) *n. inf.* nonsense

popsy ('pɒpsɪ) *n. old-fashioned* UK *sl.* attractive young woman

populace ('pɒpjʊləs) *n.* (*sometimes with pl. v.*) the common people, the masses

popular ('pɒpjʊlə) *a.* **1.** finding general favour **2.** of, by the people —**popu'larity** *n.* state or quality of being generally liked —**populari'zation** *or* **-i'sation** *n.* —'**popularize** *or* **-ise** *vt.* make popular —'**popularly** *adv.* —**popular front** (*oft.* P- F-) left-wing group or party that opposes spread of fascism

populate ('pɒpjʊleɪt) *vt.* fill with inhabitants —**popu'lation** *n.* **1.** inhabitants **2.** the number of such inhabitants —'**populous** *a.* thickly populated or inhabited

porbeagle ('pɔːbiːɡ°l) *n.* any of several sharks of northern seas (*also* **mackerel shark**)

porcelain ('pɔːslɪn) *n.* fine earthenware, china —**porcelain clay** kaolin

porch (pɔːtʃ) *n.* covered approach to entrance of building

porcine ('pɔːsaɪn) *a.* of, like pigs

porcupine ('pɔːkjʊpaɪn) *n.* any of various rodents covered with long, pointed quills

pore¹ (pɔː) *vi.* **1.** fix eye or mind **2.** (*with* over) study closely

pore² (pɔː) *n.* minute opening, *esp.* in skin —**po'rosity** *n.* —'**porous** *a.* **1.** allowing liquid to soak through **2.** full of pores

pork (pɔːk) *n.* pig's flesh used as food —'**porker** *n.* pig raised for food —'**porky** *a.* fleshy, fat —**porkpie hat** hat with round flat crown and brim that can be turned up or down

porn (pɔːn) *or* **porno** *n. inf.* pornography

pornography (pɔː'nɒɡrəfɪ) *n.* indecent literature, films *etc.* —**por'nographer** *n.* —**porno'graphic** *a.* —**porno'graphically** *adv.*

porphyry ('pɔːfɪrɪ) *n.* reddish stone with embedded crystals

porpoise ('pɔːpəs) *n.* blunt-nosed sea mammal like dolphin (*pl.* **-poise, -s**)

porridge ('pɒrɪdʒ) *n.* **1.** soft food of oatmeal *etc.* boiled in water **2.** *sl.* imprisonment

porringer ('pɒrɪndʒə) *n.* small dish, oft. with handle, for soup, porridge *etc.*

port¹ (pɔːt) *n.* **1.** harbour, haven **2.** town with harbour

port² (pɔːt) *n.* **1.** left side of ship or aircraft (*also* (*formerly*) '**larboard**) —*v.* **2.** turn to left side of ship

port³ (pɔːt) *n.* strong red wine

port⁴ (pɔːt) *n.* opening in side of ship —'**porthole** *n.* small opening or window in side of ship

port⁵ (pɔːt) *Mil. vt.* **1.** carry (rifle *etc.*) diagonally across body —*n.* **2.** this position

Port. **1.** Portugal **2.** Portuguese

portable ('pɔːtəb°l) *n./a.* (something) easily carried

portage ('pɔːtɪdʒ) *n.* (cost of) transport

portal ('pɔːt°l) *n.* large doorway or imposing gate

portcullis (pɔːt'kʌlɪs) *n.* defence grating to raise or lower in front of castle gateway

portend (pɔː'tɛnd) *vt.* foretell, be an omen of —'**portent** *n.* **1.** omen, warning **2.** marvel —**por'tentous** *a.* **1.** ominous, threatening **2.** pompous

porter¹ ('pɔːtə) *n.* **1.** person employed to carry burden, *esp.* on railway **2.** doorkeeper —'**porterage** *n.* (charge for) carrying of supplies

porter² ('pɔːtə) *n.* UK dark sweet ale brewed from black malt —'**porterhouse** *n.* thick choice steak of beef cut from middle ribs or sirloin (*also* **porterhouse steak**)

portfolio (pɔːt'fəʊlɪəʊ) *n.* **1.** flat portable case for loose papers **2.** office of minister of state (*pl.* **-s**)

portico ('pɔːtɪkəʊ) *n.* **1.** colonnade **2.** covered walk (*pl.* **-es, -s**)

portière (pɔːtɪ'ɛə; *Fr.* pɔr'tjɛːr) *n.* curtain hung in doorway

portion ('pɔːʃən) *n.* 1. part 2. share 3. helping 4. destiny, lot —*vt.* 5. divide into shares —'**portionless** *a.*

portly ('pɔːtlɪ) *a.* bulky, stout

portmanteau (pɔːt'mæntəʊ) *n.* leather suitcase, *esp.* one opening into two compartments (*pl.* -s, -teaux (-təʊz)) —**portmanteau word** formed by joining together beginning and end of two other words (*also* **blend**)

portray (pɔː'treɪ) *vt.* 1. make pictures of, describe —**portrait** ('pɔːtrɪt, -treɪt) *n.* likeness of (face of) individual —**portraiture** ('pɔːtrɪtʃə) *n.* —por'**trayal** *n.* act of portraying

Portuguese (pɔːtjʊ'giːz) *a.* pert. to Portugal or its inhabitants —**Portuguese man-of-war** kind of jellyfish

pose (pəʊz) *vt.* 1. place in attitude 2. put forward —*vi.* 3. assume attitude, affect or pretend to be a certain character —*n.* 4. attitude, *esp.* one assumed for effect —'**poser** *n.* one who poses —**poseur** (pəʊ'zɜː) *n.* one who assumes affected attitude to create impression

poser ('pəʊzə) *n.* puzzling question

posh (pɒʃ) *a. inf.* 1. smart, elegant, stylish 2. upper-class or genteel

posit ('pɒzɪt) *vt.* lay down as principle

position (pə'zɪʃən) *n.* 1. place 2. situation 3. location, attitude 4. status 5. state of affairs 6. employment 7. strategic point 8. *Mus.* vertical spacing or layout of written notes in chord —*vt.* 9. place in position

positive ('pɒzɪtɪv) *a.* 1. certain, sure 2. definite, absolute, unquestionable 3. utter, downright 4. confident 5. not negative 6. greater than zero 7. *Elec.* having deficiency of electrons —*n.* 8. something positive 9. *Photog.* print in which lights and shadows are not reversed —'**positively** *adv.* —'**positivism** *n.* philosophy recognizing only matters of fact and experience —'**positivist** *a./n.* (one) believing in this —**positive discrimination** provision of special opportunities for disadvantaged group —**positive feedback** *see* **feedback** (sense 1) *at* FEED

positron ('pɒzɪtrɒn) *n.* positive electron

poss. 1. possession 2. possessive 3. possible 4. possibly

posse ('pɒsɪ) *n.* 1. US body of men, *esp.* for maintaining law and order 2. C group of trained horsemen who perform at rodeos

possess (pə'zɛs) *vt.* 1. own 2. of evil spirit *etc.*) have mastery of —**pos'session** *n.* 1. act of possessing 2. thing possessed 3. ownership —**pos'sessive** *a.* 1. of, indicating possession 2. with excessive desire to possess, control —*n.* 3. possessive case in grammar

possible ('pɒsɪbəl) *a.* 1. that can, or may, be,

exist, happen or be done 2. worthy of consideration —*n.* 3. possible candidate —**possi'bility** *n.* —'**possibly** *adv.* perhaps

possum ('pɒsəm) *n. see* OPOSSUM —**play possum** pretend to be dead, asleep *etc.* to deceive opponent

post¹ (pəʊst) *n.* 1. upright pole of timber or metal fixed firmly, usu. to support or mark something —*vt.* 2. display 3. put up (notice *etc.*) on wall *etc.* —'**poster** *n.* 1. large advertising bill 2. one who posts bills —**poster paints** *or* **colours** lustreless paints used for writing posters *etc.*

post² (pəʊst) *n.* 1. official carrying of letters or parcels 2. collection or delivery of these 3. office 4. situation 5. point, station, place of duty 6. place where soldier is stationed 7. place held by body of troops 8. fort —*vt.* 9. put into official box for carriage by post 10. supply with latest information 11. station (soldiers *etc.*) in particular spot 12. transfer (entries) to ledger —*adv.* 13. in haste —'**postage** *n.* charge for delivering letters or parcels —'**postal** *a.* —**postage stamp** 1. printed paper label with gummed back for attaching to mail as official indication that required postage has been paid 2. mark printed on envelope *etc.* serving same function —**postal order** written order, available at post office, for payment of sum of money —'**postbag** *n.* 1. *chiefly UK* mailbag 2. mail received by magazine, radio programme *etc.* —'**postbox** *n. chiefly UK* box into which mail is put for collection —'**postcard** *n.* stamped card sent by post —'**postcode** *or* **postal code** *n.* system of letters and numbers used to aid sorting of mail —**post-free** *adv./a.* 1. UK with postage prepaid; postpaid 2. free of postal charge —'**postman** *n.* man who collects or delivers post —**postman's knock** parlour game involving exchange of kisses —'**postmark** *n.* official mark with name of office *etc.* stamped on letters —'**postmaster** *or* '**postmistress** *n.* official in charge of post office —**postmaster general** executive head of postal service in certain countries (*pl.* **postmasters general**) —**post office** place where postal business is conducted —'**post'paid** *adv./a.* with postage prepaid

post- (*comb. form*) after, behind, later than, as in *postwar.* Such compounds are not given here where the meaning can easily be found from the simple word

postdate (pəʊst'deɪt) *vt.* assign date to (event *etc.*) that is later than actual date

poste restante ('pəʊst rɪ'stænt) *Fr.* department of post office where travellers' letters are kept till called for

posterior (pɒ'stɪərɪə) *a.* 1. later 2. hinder —*n.* 3. the buttocks

posterity (pɒ'stɛrɪtɪ) n. 1. later generations 2. descendants

postern ('pɒstən) n. 1. private entrance 2. small door, gate

postgraduate (pəust'grædjuɪt) a. 1. carried on after graduation —n. 2. student taking course of study after graduation

posthaste ('pəust'heɪst) adv. 1. with great haste —n. 2. obs. great haste

posthumous ('pɒstjuməs) a. 1. occurring after death 2. born after father's death 3. (of book etc.) published after author's death —**posthumously** adv.

posthypnotic suggestion (pəusthɪp'nɒtɪk) suggestion made to subject while in hypnotic trance, to be acted upon some time after emerging from trance

postilion or **postillion** (pɒ'stɪljən) n. Hist. man riding one of pair of horses drawing a carriage

postimpressionism (pəustɪm'prɛʃənɪzəm) n. movement in painting at end of 19th cent. which rejected naturalism and momentary effects of impressionism but adapted its use of pure colour to paint subjects with greater subjective emotion —**postim'pressionist** n./a.

post meridiem (mə'rɪdɪəm) see P.M.

postmortem (pəust'mɔːtəm) n. 1. analysis of recent event —a. 2. taking place after death —**postmortem examination** medical examination of dead body

postnatal (pəust'neɪtəl) a. after birth

post-obit (pəust'ɒbɪt, -'ɒbɪt) a. taking effect after death

postoperative (pəust'ɒpərətɪv) a. of period following surgical operation

postpone (pəust'pəun, pə'spəun) vt. put off to later time, defer —**post'ponement** n.

postprandial (pəust'prændɪəl) a. after-dinner

postscript ('pəusskrɪpt) n. 1. note added at end of letter, after signature 2. supplement added to book, document etc.

postulant ('pɒstjulənt) n. candidate for admission to religious order

postulate ('pɒstjuleɪt) vt. 1. take for granted 2. lay down as self-evident 3. stipulate —n. ('pɒstjulɪt) 4. proposition assumed without proof 5. prerequisite —**postu'lation** n.

posture ('pɒstʃə) n. 1. attitude, position of body —vi. 2. pose

posy ('pəuzɪ) n. bunch of flowers

pot (pɒt) n. 1. round vessel 2. cooking vessel 3. trap, esp. for crabs, lobsters 4. sl. cannabis —pl. 5. inf. a lot —vt. 6. put into, preserve in pot (-tt-) —**'potted** a. 1. preserved in a pot 2. inf. abridged —**'potbellied** a. —**'potbelly** n. 1. protruding belly 2. one having such a belly —**'potboiler** n. inf. artistic work of little merit produced quickly

to make money —**pot-bound** a. (of pot plant) having grown to fill all available root space and lacking room for continued growth —**'potherb** n. any plant having leaves, stems etc. that are used in cooking —**'pothole** n. 1. pitlike cavity in rocks, usu. limestone, produced by faulting and water action 2. hole worn in road —**'potholer** n. —**'potholing** n. UK sport in which participants explore underground caves —**'pothook** n. 1. S-shaped hook for suspending pot over fire 2. long hook for lifting hot pots etc. 3. S-shaped mark, oft. made by children when learning to write —**'pothunter** n. 1. person who hunts for profit without regard to rules of sport 2. inf. person who enters competitions for sole purpose of winning prizes —**pot'luck** n. 1. whatever food is available without special preparation 2. choice dictated by lack of alternative (esp. in take potluck) —**pot plant** plant grown in flowerpot —**pot roast** meat cooked slowly in covered pot with little water —**'potsherd** n. broken fragment of pottery —**pot shot** easy or random shot —**potter's wheel** device with horizontal rotating disc, on which clay is moulded by hand —**potting shed** building in which plants are grown in flowerpots before being planted outside —**the Potteries** region of W central England in which china industries are concentrated

potable ('pəutəbəl) a. drinkable

potage (pɒ'taːʒ; English pəu'taːʒ) Fr. thick soup

potash ('pɒtæʃ) n. 1. alkali used in soap etc. 2. crude potassium carbonate

potassium (pə'tæsɪəm) n. white metallic element —**potassium nitrate** crystalline compound used in gunpowders, fertilizers and as preservative (also salt'petre, 'nitre)

potato (pə'teɪtəu) n. plant with tubers grown for food (pl. -es) —**potato crisp** see CRISP (sense 6) —**sweet potato** 1. trailing plant 2. its edible sweetish tubers

poteen (pɒ'tiːn) n. in Ireland, illicitly distilled alcoholic liquor

potent ('pəutənt) a. 1. powerful, influential 2. (of male) capable of sexual intercourse —**'potency** n. 1. physical or moral power 2. efficacy

potentate ('pəutənteɪt) n. ruler

potential (pə'tɛnʃəl) a. 1. latent, that may or might but does not now exist or act —n. 2. possibility 3. amount of potential energy 4. Elec. level of electric pressure —**potenti'ality** n. —**potential difference** difference in electric potential between two points in electric field

pother ('pɒðə) n. 1. commotion, fuss 2. choking cloud of smoke etc.

potion ('pəuʃən) n. dose of medicine or poison

potpourri (pəu'puərɪ) n. 1. mixture of rose

petals, spices *etc.* **2.** musical, literary medley (*pl.* **-s**)

pottage ('pɔtidʒ) *n.* thick soup containing vegetables and meat

potter[1] ('pɔtə) *n.* maker of earthenware vessels —'**pottery** *n.* **1.** earthenware **2.** place where it is made **3.** art of making it

potter[2] ('pɔtə) *or esp. U.S.* **putter** ('pʌtə) *vi.* work, act in feeble, unsystematic way

potty ('pɔti) *a. inf.* **1.** (of person) mad **2.** (of thing) silly, trivial

pouch (pautʃ) *n.* **1.** small bag **2.** *Anat.* any sac, pocket or pouchlike cavity —*vt.* **3.** put into pouch

pouf *or* **pouffe** (puːf) *n.* large solid cushion

poultice ('pəultɪs) *n.* soft composition of mustard, kaolin *etc.,* applied hot to sore or inflamed parts of body

poultry ('pəultrɪ) *n.* domestic fowls collectively —'**poulterer** *n.* dealer in poultry

pounce (pauns) *vi.* **1.** spring suddenly, swoop —*n.* **2.** swoop or sudden descent

pound[1] (paund) *vt.* **1.** beat, thump **2.** crush to pieces or powder —*vi.* **3.** walk, run heavily

pound[2] (paund) *n.* **1.** unit of troy weight **2.** unit of avoirdupois weight equal to 0.454 kg **3.** monetary unit in U.K. —'**poundage** *n.* **1.** charge of so much per pound of weight **2.** charge of so much per pound sterling **3.** weight expressed in pounds —**pound note** banknote valued at one pound sterling

pound[3] (paund) *n.* **1.** enclosure for stray animals or officially removed vehicles **2.** confined space

poundal ('paundəl) *n.* unit of force in the foot-pound-second system

pour (pɔː) *vi.* **1.** come out in a stream, crowd *etc.* **2.** flow freely **3.** rain heavily —*vt.* **4.** give out thus **5.** cause to run out

pourboire (pur'bwaːr) *Fr.* tip; gratuity

pout[1] (paut) *v.* **1.** thrust out (lips) —*vi.* **2.** look sulky —*n.* **3.** act of pouting —'**pouter** *n.* pigeon with power of inflating its crop

pout[2] (paut) *n.* type of food fish (*pl.* **pout, -s**)

poverty ('pɔvəti) *n.* **1.** state of being poor **2.** poorness **3.** lack of means **4.** scarcity —**poverty-stricken** *a.* suffering from extreme poverty —**poverty trap** situation of being unable to raise one's living standard because one is dependent on state benefits which are reduced if one gains any extra income

P.O.W. prisoner of war

powder ('paudə) *n.* **1.** solid matter in fine dry particles **2.** medicine in this form **3.** gunpowder **4.** face powder *etc.* —*vt.* **5.** apply powder to **6.** reduce to powder; pulverize —'**powdery** *a.* —**powder keg 1.** small barrel to hold gunpowder **2.** potential source of violence *etc.* —**powder**

puff soft pad for applying cosmetic powder —**powder room** ladies' cloakroom

power ('pauə) *n.* **1.** ability to do or act **2.** strength **3.** authority **4.** control **5.** person or thing having authority **6.** mechanical energy **7.** electricity supply **8.** rate of doing work **9.** product from continuous multiplication of number by itself —'**powered** *a.* having or operated by mechanical or electrical power —'**powerful** *a.* —'**powerless** *a.* —'**powerhouse** *or* **power station** *n.* installation for generating and distributing electric power —**power point** socket on wall for plugging in electrical appliance —**power of attorney 1.** legal authority to act for another person in certain specified matters **2.** document conferring such authority

powwow ('pauwau) *n.* **1.** conference —*vi.* **2.** confer

pox (pɔks) *n.* **1.** one of several diseases marked by pustular eruptions of skin **2.** *inf.* syphilis

pp *or* **pp. 1.** per procurationem (*Lat.,* by proxy; for and on behalf of) **2.** pianissimo

pp. pages

p.p. 1. parcel post **2.** past participle **3.** prepaid **4.** post paid **5.** by delegation to **6.** on prescriptions, after meal

ppd. 1. postpaid **2.** prepaid

P.P.S. 1. parliamentary private secretary **2.** post postscriptum (*also* **p.p.s.**)

PQ Quebec

Pr *Chem.* praseodymium

pr. 1. pair (*pl.* **prs.**) **2.** present **3.** price **4.** pronoun

P.R. 1. proportional representation **2.** public relations

practical ('præktɪkəl) *a.* **1.** given to action rather than theory **2.** relating to action or real existence **3.** useful **4.** in effect though not in name **5.** virtual —**practica'bility** *n.* —'**practicable** *a.* that can be done, used *etc.* —'**practically** *adv.* —**prac'titioner** *n.* one engaged in a profession —**practical joke** trick usu. intended to make victim appear foolish

practice ('præktɪs) *n.* **1.** habit **2.** mastery, skill **3.** exercise of art or profession **4.** action, not theory —*v.* **5.** *US see* PRACTISE

practise *or U.S.* **practice** ('præktɪs) *vt.* **1.** do repeatedly, work at to gain skill **2.** do habitually **3.** put into action —*vi.* **4.** exercise oneself **5.** exercise profession

praetor *or* **pretor** ('priːtə, -tɔː) *n.* in ancient Rome, senior magistrate ranking just below consul

pragmatic (præg'mætɪk) *a.* **1.** concerned with practical consequence **2.** of the affairs of state —**prag'matical** *a.* —'**pragmatism** *n.*

prairie ('preərɪ) *n.* large treeless tract of grassland of Central U.S.A. and Canad. —**prairie dog** small *Amer.* rodent allied to marmot

—**prairie oyster** drink consisting of raw egg, vinegar, salt and pepper: supposed cure for hangover

praise (preiz) *n.* **1.** commendation **2.** fact, state of being praised —*vt.* **3.** express approval, admiration of **4.** speak well of **5.** glorify —'**praiseworthy** *a.*

praline ('prɑːliːn) *n.* sweet composed of nuts and sugar

pram (præm) *n.* carriage for baby

prance (prɑːns) *vi.* **1.** swagger **2.** caper **3.** walk with bounds —*n.* **4.** prancing

prandial ('prændɪəl) *a.* of dinner

prang (præŋ) *inf. v.* **1.** crash or damage (car, aircraft *etc.*) **2.** damage (town *etc.*) by bombing —*n.* **3.** crash in a car, aircraft *etc.*

prank (præŋk) *n.* mischievous trick or escapade, frolic

prase (preiz) *n.* light green translucent chalcedony

praseodymium (preiziəʊ'dimiəm) *n.* malleable element of lanthanide series of metals

prate (preit) *vi.* **1.** talk idly, chatter —*n.* **2.** idle or trivial talk

prattle ('prætəl) *vi.* **1.** talk like child —*n.* **2.** trifling, childish talk —'**prattler** *n.* babbler

prawn (prɔːn) *n.* edible sea crustacean like shrimp but larger

praxis ('præksɪs) *n.* practice, *esp.* as opposed to theory (*pl.* **-es, praxes** ('præksiːz))

pray (prei) *vt.* **1.** ask earnestly, entreat —*vi.* **2.** offer prayers, *esp.* to God —**prayer** (prɛə) *n.* **1.** action, practice of praying to God **2.** earnest entreaty —**prayer rug** small carpet on which Muslim kneels while saying prayers (*also* **prayer mat**) —**prayer wheel** *Buddhism esp.* in Tibet, wheel or cylinder inscribed with prayers, each revolution of which is counted as uttered prayer —**praying mantis** *or* **mantid** *see* MANTIS

pre- (*comb. form*) before, beforehand, as in *prenatal, prerecord, preshrunk*. Such compounds are not given here where the meaning can easily be found from the simple word

preach (priːtʃ) *vi.* **1.** deliver sermon **2.** give moral, religious advice —*vt.* **3.** set forth in religious discourse **4.** advocate —'**preacher** *n.*

preamble (priː'æmbəl) *n.* introductory part of story *etc.*

prebend ('prɛbənd) *n.* stipend of canon or member of cathedral chapter —'**prebendary** *n.* holder of this

Precambrian *or* **Pre-Cambrian** (priː-'kæmbrɪən) *a.* **1.** of earliest geological era, which lasted for about 4000 000 000 years before Cambrian period —*n.* **2.** Precambrian era

precarious (prɪ'kɛərɪəs) *a.* insecure, unstable, perilous

precaution (prɪ'kɔːʃən) *n.* **1.** previous care to

prevent evil or secure good **2.** preventative measure —**pre**'**cautionary** *a.*

precede (prɪ'siːd) *vt.* go, come before in rank, order, time *etc.* —**precedence** ('prɛsɪdəns) *n.* priority in position, rank, time *etc.* —**precedent** ('prɛsɪdənt) *n.* previous example or occurrence taken as rule

precentor (prɪ'sɛntə) *n.* leader of singing choir or congregation

precept ('priːsɛpt) *n.* rule for conduct, maxim —**pre**'**ceptor** *n.* instructor —**precep**'**torial** *a.*

precinct ('priːsɪŋkt) *n.* **1.** enclosed, limited area **2.** area in town, oft. closed to traffic, reserved for particular activity **3.** *US* administrative area of city —*pl.* **4.** environs

precious ('prɛʃəs) *a.* **1.** beloved, cherished **2.** of great value, highly valued **3.** rare —**preci**'**osity** *n.* overrefinement in art or literature —'**preciously** *adv.* —'**preciousness** *n.* —**precious metal** gold, silver or platinum —**precious stone** rare mineral, such as diamond, ruby *etc.*, highly valued as gemstone

precipice ('prɛsɪpɪs) *n.* very steep cliff or rockface —**precipitous** (prɪ'sɪpɪtəs) *a.* sheer

precipitant (prɪ'sɪpɪtənt) *a.* **1.** hasty, rash **2.** abrupt —**pre**'**cipitance** *or* **pre**'**cipitancy** *n.*

precipitate (prɪ'sɪpɪteit) *vt.* **1.** hasten happening of **2.** throw headlong **3.** *Chem.* cause to be deposited in solid form from solution —*a.* (prɪ'sɪpɪtɪt) **4.** too sudden **5.** rash, impetuous —*n.* (prɪ'sɪpɪtɪt) **6.** substance chemically precipitated —**pre**'**cipitately** *adv.* —**precipi**'**tation** *n.* rain, snow, sleet *etc.*

precis *or* **précis** ('preisiː) *n.* abstract, summary (*pl.* **precis** *or* **précis** ('preisiːz))

precise (prɪ'sais) *a.* **1.** definite **2.** particular **3.** exact, strictly worded **4.** careful in observance **5.** punctilious, formal —**pre**'**cisely** *adv.* —**precision** (prɪ'sɪʒən) *n.* accuracy

preclude (prɪ'kluːd) *vt.* **1.** prevent from happening **2.** shut out

precocious (prɪ'kəʊʃəs) *a.* developed, matured early or too soon —**precocity** (prɪ'kɒsɪtɪ) *n.* or **pre**'**cociousness** *n.*

precognition (priːkɒg'nɪʃən) *n.* *Psychol.* alleged ability to foresee future events —**pre**'**cognitive** *a.*

preconceive (priːkən'siːv) *vt.* form an idea of beforehand —**precon**'**ception** *n.*

precondition (priːkən'dɪʃən) *n.* necessary or required condition

precursor (prɪ'kɜːsə) *n.* forerunner —**pre**'**cursive** *or* **pre**'**cursory** *a.*

pred. predicate

predate (priː'deit) *vt.* **1.** affix date to (document *etc.*) that is earlier than actual date **2.** assign date to (event *etc.*) that is earlier than actual or previously assigned date of occurrence **3.** be or occur at earlier date than; precede in time

predatory ('prɛdətərı) *a.* **1.** hunting, killing other animals *etc.* for food **2.** plundering —'**predator** *n.* predatory animal

predecease (priːdɪ'siːs) *vt.* die before (some other person)

predecessor ('priːdɪsɛsə) *n.* **1.** one who precedes another in an office or position **2.** ancestor

predestine (priː'dɛstɪn) *or* **predestinate** (priː'dɛstɪneɪt) *vt.* decree beforehand, foreordain —predesti'**nation** *n.*

predetermine (priːdɪ'tɜːmɪn) *vt.* **1.** determine beforehand **2.** influence, bias —**predetermi'nation** *n.*

predicament (prɪ'dɪkəmənt) *n.* perplexing, embarrassing or difficult situation

predicant ('prɛdɪkənt) *a.* **1.** of preaching —*n.* **2.** member of religious order founded for preaching, *esp.* Dominican

predicate ('prɛdɪkeɪt) *vt.* **1.** affirm, assert **2.** (*with on or upon*) *chiefly US* base (argument *etc.*) —*n.* ('prɛdɪkɪt) **3.** that which is predicated **4.** *Gram.* statement made about a subject —'**predicable** *a.* **1.** capable of being predicated —*n.* **2.** quality that can be predicated **3.** *Logic* any of five general forms of attribution, namely genus, species, differentia, property and accident —**predi'cation** *n.* —**pre'dicative** *a.*

predict (prɪ'dɪkt) *vt.* foretell, prophesy —**pre'dictable** *a.* —**pre'diction** *n.*

predikant (prɛdɪ'kænt) *n.* in S Afr., minister in Dutch Reformed Church

predilection (priːdɪ'lɛkʃən) *n.* preference, liking, partiality

predispose (priːdɪ'spəʊz) *vt.* **1.** incline, influence **2.** make susceptible

predominate (prɪ'dɒmɪneɪt) *vi.* be main or controlling element —**pre'dominance** *n.* —**pre'dominant** *a.* chief

pre-eminent (prɪ'ɛmɪnənt) *a.* excelling all others, outstanding —**pre-eminence** *n.* —**pre-eminently** *adv.*

pre-empt (prɪ'ɛmpt) *vt.* acquire in advance of or to exclusion of others —**pre-emption** *n.* —**pre-emptive** *a.*

preen (priːn) *vt.* **1.** (of birds) trim (feathers) with beak, plume **2.** smarten (oneself)

pref. 1. preface **2.** preference **3.** prefix

prefabricate (priː'fæbrɪkeɪt) *vt.* manufacture (buildings *etc.*) in shaped sections, for rapid assembly on site —'**prefab** *n.* prefabricated building, *esp.* house

preface ('prɛfɪs) *n.* **1.** introduction to book *etc.* —*vt.* **2.** introduce —'**prefatory** *a.*

prefect ('priːfɛkt) *n.* **1.** person put in authority **2.** schoolchild in position of limited power over

others —'**prefecture** *n.* office, residence, district of a prefect

prefer (prɪ'fɜː) *vt.* **1.** like better **2.** promote (*-rr-*) —**preferable** ('prɛfərəbl) *a.* more desirable —**preferably** ('prɛfərəblɪ) *adv.* —**preference** ('prɛfərəns, 'prɛfrəns) *n.* —**preferential** (prɛfə'rɛnʃəl) *a.* giving, receiving preference —**pre'ferment** *n.* promotion, advancement

prefigure (priː'fɪgə) *vt.* exhibit, suggest by previous types, foreshadow —**pre'figurative** *a.*

prefix ('priːfɪks) *n.* **1.** preposition or particle put at beginning of word or title —*vt.* (priː'fɪks, 'priːfɪks) **2.** put as introduction **3.** put before word to make compound

pregnant ('prɛgnənt) *a.* **1.** carrying foetus in womb **2.** full of meaning, significance **3.** inventive —'**pregnancy** *n.*

prehensile (prɪ'hɛnsaɪl) *a.* capable of grasping —**prehensility** (priːhɛn'sɪlɪtɪ) *n.*

prehistoric (priːhɪ'stɒrɪk) *or* **prehistorical** *a.* before period in which written history begins —pre'**history** *n.*

prejudge (priː'dʒʌdʒ) *vt.* judge beforehand, *esp.* without sufficient evidence

prejudice ('prɛdʒʊdɪs) *n.* **1.** preconceived opinion **2.** bias, partiality **3.** injury likely to happen to person or his rights as result of others' action or judgment —*vt.* **4.** influence **5.** bias **6.** injure —**preju'dicial** *a.* **1.** injurious **2.** disadvantageous

prelate ('prɛlɪt) *n.* bishop or other church dignitary of equal or higher rank —'**prelacy** *n.* his office —**prelatical** (prɪ'lætɪkəl) *a.*

preliminary (prɪ'lɪmɪnərɪ) *a.* **1.** preparatory, introductory —*n.* **2.** introductory, preparatory statement, action **3.** eliminating contest held before main competition

prelims ('priːlɪmz, prə'lɪmz) *pl.n.* **1.** pages of book, such as title page *etc.* before main text (*also* **front matter**) **2.** first public examinations taken for bachelor's degree in some universities **3.** in Scotland, school examinations taken before public examinations

prelude ('prɛljuːd) *n.* **1.** *Mus.* introductory movement **2.** performance, event *etc.* serving as introduction —*v.* **3.** serve as prelude to (something) —*vt.* **4.** introduce

premarital (priː'mærɪtəl) *a.* occurring before marriage

premature ('prɛmətjʊə, 'prɛmətjʊə) *a.* **1.** happening, done before proper time **2.** impulsive, hasty **3.** (of infant) born before end of full period of gestation

premeditate (prɪ'mɛdɪteɪt) *vt.* consider, plan beforehand —**premedi'tation** *n.*

premenstrual (priː'mɛnstrʊəl) *a.* of period in menstrual cycle just before menstruation

premier ('prɛmjə) *n.* **1.** prime minister **2.** head of government of Aust. state —*a.* **3.** chief, foremost **4.** first —'**premiership** *n.*

premiere ('prɛmɪɛə, 'prɛmɪə) *n.* first public performance of a play, film *etc.*

premise ('prɛmɪs) *n.* **1.** *Logic* proposition from which inference is drawn (*also* '**premiss**) —*pl.* **2.** house, building with its belongings **3.** *Law* beginning of deed —*vt.* (prɪ'maɪz, 'prɛmɪs) **4.** state by way of introduction

premium ('priːmɪəm) *n.* **1.** bonus **2.** sum paid for insurance **3.** excess over nominal value **4.** great value or regard —**Premium Savings Bond** bond issued by government on which no interest is paid but cash prizes can be won

premonition (prɛmə'nɪʃən) *n.* presentiment, foreboding

preoccupy (priː'ɒkjupaɪ) *vt.* occupy to the exclusion of other things (**-pying, -pied**) —**preoccu'pation** *n.* mental concentration or absorption

preordain (priːɔː'deɪn) *vt.* ordain or decree beforehand

prep (prɛp) *n. inf.* **1.** preparation for schoolwork **2.** *chiefly* US preparatory school

prep. **1.** preparation **2.** preparatory **3.** preposition

prepare (prɪ'pɛə) *vt.* **1.** make ready **2.** make —*vi.* **3.** get ready —**preparation** (prɛpə'reɪʃən) *n.* **1.** making ready beforehand **2.** something that is prepared, as a medicine **3.** at school, (time spent) preparing work for lesson —**preparatory** (prɪ'pærətərɪ) *a.* **1.** serving to prepare **2.** introductory —**preparedness** (prɪ'pɛərɪdnɪs) *n.* state of being prepared —**preparatory school 1.** UK private school for children between ages of 6 and 13, generally preparing pupils for public school **2.** in Amer., private secondary school preparing pupils for college (*also* **prep school**)

prepay (priː'peɪ) *vt.* pay in advance

prepense (prɪ'pɛns) *a.* usu. in legal contexts, premeditated (*esp.* in **malice prepense**)

preponderate (prɪ'pɒndəreɪt) *vi.* be of greater weight or power —**pre'ponderance** *n.* superiority of power, numbers *etc.*

preposition (prɛpə'zɪʃən) *n.* word marking relation between noun or pronoun and other words —**prepo'sitional** *a.*

prepossess (priːpə'zɛs) *vt.* **1.** preoccupy or engross mentally **2.** impress, *esp.* favourably, beforehand —**prepos'sessing** *a.* inviting favourable opinion, attractive, winning —**prepos'session** *n.*

preposterous (prɪ'pɒstərəs) *a.* utterly absurd, foolish

prepuce ('priːpjuːs) *n.* **1.** retractable fold of skin covering tip of penis; foreskin **2.** similar fold of skin covering tip of clitoris

Pre-Raphaelite (priː'ræfəlaɪt) *n.* **1.** member

of **Pre-Raphaelite Brotherhood,** association of painters and writers founded in 1848 to revive qualities of It. painting before Raphael —*a.* **2.** of Pre-Raphaelite painting and painters

prerequisite (priː'rɛkwɪzɪt) *n./a.* (something) required as prior condition

prerogative (prɪ'rɒgətɪv) *n.* **1.** peculiar power or right, *esp.* as vested in sovereign —*a.* **2.** privileged

pres. 1. present (time) **2.** presidential

Pres. President

presage ('prɛsɪdʒ) *n.* **1.** omen, indication of something to come —*vt.* ('prɛsɪdʒ, prɪ'seɪdʒ) **2.** foretell

presbyopia (prɛzbɪ'əʊpɪə) *n.* progressively diminishing ability of the eye to focus, *esp.* on near objects; long-sightedness

presbyter ('prɛzbɪtə) *n.* **1.** elder in early Christian church **2.** priest **3.** member of a presbytery —**Presby'terian** *a./n.* (member) of Protestant church governed by lay elders —**Presby'terianism** *n.* —'**presbytery** *n.* **1.** church court composed of all ministers within a certain district and one ruling elder from each church **2.** *R.C.Ch.* priest's house

prescience ('prɛsɪəns) *n.* foreknowledge —'**prescient** *a.*

prescribe (prɪ'skraɪb) *v.* **1.** set out rules (for) **2.** order **3.** ordain **4.** order use of (medicine) —**prescription** (prɪ'skrɪpʃən) *n.* **1.** prescribing **2.** thing prescribed **3.** written statement of it —**prescriptive** (prɪ'skrɪptɪv) *a.*

present[1] ('prɛzənt) *a.* **1.** that is here **2.** now existing or happening —*n.* **3.** present time or tense —'**presence** *n.* **1.** being present **2.** appearance, bearing —'**presently** *adv.* **1.** soon **2.** US at present —**presence of mind** ability to remain calm and act constructively during crises —**present-day** *a.* of modern day; current —**present participle** participial form of verbs used adjectivally when action it describes is contemporaneous with that of main verb of sentence and also used in formation of certain compound tenses —**present perfect** *Gram. see* PERFECT (sense 9)

present[2] (prɪ'zɛnt) *vt.* **1.** introduce formally **2.** show **3.** give **4.** offer **5.** point, aim —*n.* ('prɛzənt) **6.** gift —**pre'sentable** *a.* fit to be seen —**presentation** (prɛzən'teɪʃən) *n.*

presentiment (prɪ'zɛntɪmənt) *n.* sense of something (*esp.* evil) about to happen

preserve (prɪ'zɜːv) *vt.* **1.** keep from harm, injury or decay **2.** maintain **3.** pickle —*n.* **4.** special area **5.** that which is preserved, as fruit *etc.* **6.** place where game is kept for private fishing, shooting —**preservation** (prɛzə'veɪʃən) *n.* —**pre'servative** *n.* **1.** chemical added to perishable foods, drinks *etc.* to prevent them from rotting —*a.* **2.** tending to preserve **3.** having quality of preserving

preside (prɪ'zaɪd) *vi.* **1.** be chairman **2.** (*with* over) superintend —**presidency** ('prɛzɪdənsɪ) *n.* —**president** ('prɛzɪdənt) *n.* head of society, company, republic *etc.* —**presidential** (prɛzɪ'dɛnʃəl) *a.*

presidium (prɪ'sɪdɪəm) *n.* **1.** (*oft.* P-) in Communist countries, permanent committee of larger body, such as legislature, that acts for it when it is in recess **2.** collective presidency

press¹ (prɛs) *vt.* **1.** subject to push or squeeze **2.** smooth by pressure or heat **3.** urge steadily, earnestly —*vi.* **4.** bring weight to bear **5.** throng **6.** hasten —*n.* **7.** a pressing **8.** machine for pressing, *esp.* printing machine **9.** printing house **10.** art or process of printing **11.** newspapers collectively **12.** crowd **13.** stress **14.** large cupboard —'**pressing** *a.* **1.** urgent **2.** persistent —**press agent** person employed to advertise and secure press publicity for any person, enterprise *etc.* —**press conference** interview for press reporters given by politician *etc.* —**press gallery** area for newspaper reporters, *esp.* in legislative assembly —'**pressman** *n.* **1.** printer who attends to the press **2.** journalist —**press stud** fastening device, one part with projecting knob that snaps into hole on another part —**press-up** *n.* exercise in which body is alternately raised and lowered by arms only, trunk being kept straight (*also* (US) **push-up**)

press² (prɛs) *vt.* force to serve in navy or army —**press gang** formerly, body of men employed to press men into naval service —**press-gang** *vt.* force (someone) to do something

pressure ('prɛʃə) *n.* **1.** act of pressing **2.** influence **3.** authority **4.** difficulties **5.** *Phys.* thrust per unit area —**pressuri'zation** *or* -i'**sation** *n.* in aircraft, maintenance of normal atmospheric pressure at high altitudes —'**pressurize** *or* -**ise** *vt.* —**pressure cooker** vessel like saucepan which cooks food rapidly by steam under pressure —**pressure group** organized group which exerts influence on policies, public opinion *etc.*

Prestel ('prɛstɛl) *n.* R Post Office viewdata service

prestidigitation (prɛstɪdɪdʒɪ'teɪʃən) *n. see* **sleight of hand** *at* SLEIGHT —**presti'digitator** *n.*

prestige (prɛ'stiːʒ) *n.* **1.** reputation based on high achievement, character, wealth *etc.* **2.** power to impress or influence —**prestigious** (prɛ'stɪdʒəs) *a.*

presto ('prɛstəʊ) *adv.* **1.** *Mus.* quickly **2.** immediately (*esp. in* **hey presto**)

prestressed (priː'strɛst) *a.* (of concrete) containing stretched steel cables for strengthening

presume (prɪ'zjuːm) *vt.* **1.** take for granted —*vi.* **2.** take liberties —**pre'sumably** *adv.* **1.** probably **2.** doubtlessly —**presumption** (prɪ'zʌmpʃən) *n.* **1.** forward, arrogant opinion or conduct **2.** strong probability —**presumptive** (prɪ'zʌmptɪv) *a.* that may be assumed as true or valid until contrary is proved —**presumptuous** (prɪ'zʌmptjʊəs) *a.* forward, impudent, taking liberties —**presumptuously** (prɪ'zʌmptjʊəslɪ) *adv.* —**heir presumptive** heir whose right may be defeated by birth of nearer relative

presuppose (priːsə'pəʊz) *vt.* assume or take for granted beforehand —**presuppo'sition** *n.*

pretend (prɪ'tɛnd) *vt.* **1.** claim or allege (something untrue) **2.** make believe, as in play —*vi.* **3.** lay claim (to) —**pre'tence** *or* U.S. **pre'tense** *n.* simulation **2.** pretext —**pre'tender** *n.* claimant (to throne) —**pre'tension** *n.* —**pre'tentious** *a.* **1.** making claim to special merit or importance **2.** given to outward show

preter- (*comb. form*) beyond, more than

preterite *or esp. U.S.* **preterit** ('prɛtərɪt) *a.* **1.** past **2.** expressing past state or action —*n.* **3.** past tense

preternatural (priːtə'nætʃrəl) *a.* **1.** out of ordinary way of nature **2.** abnormal, supernatural

pretext ('priːtɛkst) *n.* **1.** excuse **2.** pretence

pretty ('prɪtɪ) *a.* **1.** having beauty that is attractive rather than imposing **2.** charming —*adv.* **3.** fairly, moderately —'**prettify** *vt.* make pretty, *esp.* in trivial way; embellish —'**prettily** *adv.* —'**prettiness** *n.* —**pretty-pretty** *a. inf.* excessively or ostentatiously pretty

pretzel ('prɛtsəl) *n.* small, brittle, savoury biscuit

prevail (prɪ'veɪl) *vi.* **1.** gain mastery **2.** triumph **3.** be in fashion, generally established —**pre'vailing** *a.* **1.** widespread **2.** predominant —**prevalence** ('prɛvələns) *n.* —**prevalent** ('prɛvələnt) *a.* extensively existing, rife

prevaricate (prɪ'værɪkeɪt) *vi.* **1.** make evasive or misleading statements **2.** quibble —**prevari'cation** *n.* —**pre'varicator** *n.*

prevent (prɪ'vɛnt) *vt.* stop, hinder —**pre'ventable** *a.* —**pre'ventative** *a.* preventing, or serving to prevent, *esp.* disease (*also* **pre'ventive**) —**pre'vention** *n.* —**pre'ventive** *a./n.*

preview ('priːvjuː) *n.* **1.** advance showing **2.** showing of scenes from forthcoming film

previous ('priːvɪəs) *a.* **1.** earlier **2.** preceding **3.** *inf.* hasty —'**previously** *adv.* before

prey (preɪ) *n.* **1.** animal hunted and killed by another carnivorous animal **2.** victim —*vi.* (*oft. with* (up)on) **3.** seize for food **4.** treat as prey **5.** afflict, obsess

price (praɪs) *n.* **1.** that for which thing is bought or sold **2.** cost **3.** value **4.** reward **5.** odds in betting —*vt.* **6.** fix, ask price for —'**priceless** *a.* **1.** invaluable **2.** *inf.* very funny —'**pricey** *or* '**pricy** *a. inf.* expensive —**price control** establishment of maximum price levels for basic goods and services by government —**at any price** whatever the price or cost

prick (prɪk) *vt.* **1.** pierce slightly with sharp point **2.** cause to feel mental pain **3.** mark by prick —*v.* **4.** (*usu. with* up) erect (ears) —*n.* **5.** slight hole made by pricking **6.** pricking or being pricked **7.** sting **8.** remorse **9.** that which pricks **10.** sharp point —'**prickle** *n.* **1.** thorn, spike —*vi.* **2.** feel tingling or pricking sensation —'**prickly** *a.* —'**prickly heat** inflammation of skin with stinging pains —**prickly pear 1.** tropical cactus having flattened or cylindrical spiny joints and oval fruit **2.** fruit of prickly pear

pride (praɪd) *n.* **1.** too high an opinion of oneself, inordinate self-esteem **2.** worthy self-esteem **3.** feeling of elation or great satisfaction **4.** something causing this **5.** group (of lions) —*v.refl.* **6.** take pride

prie-dieu (priː'djɜː) *n.* piece of furniture consisting of low surface for kneeling upon and narrow front surmounted by rest, for use when praying

priest (priːst) *or* (*fem.*) **priestess** *n.* official minister of religion, clergyman —'**priesthood** *n.* —'**priestly** *a.*

prig (prɪg) *n.* self-righteous person who professes superior culture, morality *etc.* —'**priggery** *n.* —'**priggish** *a.*

prim (prɪm) *a.* very restrained, formally prudish

prima (¹priːmə) *a.* first —**prima ballerina** leading female ballet dancer —**prima donna** (¹dɒnə) **1.** principal female singer in opera **2.** *inf.* temperamental person (*pl.* **-s**)

primacy (¹praɪməsɪ) *n.* **1.** state of being first in rank, grade *etc.* **2.** office of archbishop

prima facie (¹praɪmə ¹feɪʃɪ) *Lat.* at first sight

primal (¹praɪml) *a.* **1.** of earliest age **2.** first, original —'**primarily** *adv.* —'**primary** *a.* **1.** chief **2.** of the first stage, decision *etc.* **3.** elementary —**primary accent** *or* **stress** *Linguis.* strongest accent in word or breath group —**primary school 1.** in England and Wales, school for children below age of 11 **2.** in Scotland, school for children below age of 12 **3.** in U.S., school equivalent to first three or four grades of elementary school

primate¹ (¹praɪmeɪt) *n.* one of order of mammals including monkeys and man

primate² (¹praɪmeɪt) *n.* archbishop

prime¹ (praɪm) *a.* **1.** fundamental **2.** original **3.** chief **4.** best —*n.* **5.** first, best part of anything **6.** youth **7.** full health and vigour —*vt.* **8.** prepare (gun, engine, pump *etc.*) for use **9.** fill up, eg with

information, liquor —'**priming** *n.* powder mixture used for priming gun —**prime meridian** the 0° meridian from which other meridians are calculated, usu. taken to pass through Greenwich —**Prime Minister** leader of government —**prime number** integer that cannot be divided into other integers but is only divisible by itself or 1

prime² (praɪm) *vt.* prepare for paint with preliminary coating of oil, size *etc.* —'**primer** *n.* paint *etc.* for priming

primer (¹praɪmə) *n.* elementary school book or manual

primeval *or* **primaeval** (praɪ'miːvºl) *a.* of the earliest age of the world

primitive (¹prɪmɪtɪv) *a.* **1.** of an early undeveloped kind, ancient **2.** crude, rough

primogeniture (praɪməʊ'dʒɛnɪtʃə) *n.* rule by which real estate passes to the first-born son —**primo'genital** *a.* —**primo'genitor** *n.* **1.** forefather; ancestor **2.** earliest parent or ancestor, as of race

primordial (praɪ'mɔːdɪəl) *a.* existing at or from the beginning

primp (prɪmp) *v.* dress (oneself), *esp.* in fine clothes; prink

primrose (¹prɪmrəʊz) *n.* **1.** any of various pale-yellow spring flowers of the genus *Primula* **2.** this colour —*a.* **3.** of this colour —**primrose path** pleasurable way of life

primula (¹prɪmjʊlə) *n.* any of a genus of plants including primrose, oxlip *etc.*

Primus (¹praɪməs) *n.* **R** portable cooking stove, used *esp.* by campers

prince (prɪns) *n.* **1.** son or in Brit. grandson of king or queen **2.** ruler, chief (**prin'cess** *fem.*) —'**princely** *a.* **1.** generous, lavish **2.** stately **3.** magnificent —**princess royal** eldest daughter of Brit. or, formerly, Prussian sovereign —**Prince of Wales** eldest son and heir apparent of Brit. sovereign

principal (¹prɪnsɪpl) *a.* **1.** chief in importance —*n.* **2.** person for whom another is agent **3.** head of institution, *esp.* school or college **4.** sum of money lent and yielding interest **5.** chief actor —**princi'pality** *n.* territory, dignity of prince —**principal boy** leading male role in pantomime, played by woman —**principal parts** *Gram.* main inflected forms of verb, from which all other inflections may be deduced

principle (¹prɪnsɪpl) *n.* **1.** moral rule **2.** settled reason of action **3.** uprightness **4.** fundamental truth or element

prink (prɪŋk) *v.* **1.** dress (oneself *etc.*) finely; deck out —*vi.* **2.** preen oneself

print (prɪnt) *vt.* **1.** reproduce (words, pictures *etc.*) by pressing inked types on blocks to paper *etc.* **2.** produce thus **3.** write in imitation of this **4.**

impress **5.** *Photog.* produce (pictures) from negatives **6.** stamp (fabric) with coloured design —*n.* **7.** printed matter **8.** printed lettering **9.** written imitation of printed type **10.** photograph **11.** impression, mark left on surface by thing that has pressed against it **12.** printed cotton fabric —'**printer** *n.* one engaged in printing —'**printing** *n.* **1.** business or art of producing printed matter **2.** printed text **3.** copies of book *etc.* printed at one time (*also* **im'pression**) **4.** form of writing in which letters resemble printed letters —**printed circuit** electronic circuit with wiring printed on an insulating base —**printer's devil** apprentice or errand boy in printing establishment —**printing press** machine for printing —**print-out** *n.* printed information from computer, teleprinter *etc.* —**out of print** no longer available from publisher

prior ('praɪə) *a.* **1.** earlier —*n.* **2.** chief of religious house or order (-**ess** *fem.*) —**pri'ority** *n.* **1.** precedence **2.** something given special attention —'**priory** *n.* monastery, nunnery under prior, prioress

prise *or* **prize** (praɪz) *vt.* **1.** force open by levering **2.** obtain (information *etc.*) with difficulty

prism ('prɪzəm) *n.* transparent solid usu. with triangular ends and rectangular sides, used to disperse light into spectrum or refract it in optical instruments *etc.* —**pris'matic** *a.* **1.** of prism shape **2.** (of colour) such as is produced by refraction through prism, rainbowlike, brilliant

prison ('prɪzᵊn) *n.* jail —'**prisoner** *n.* **1.** one kept in prison **2.** captive —**prisoner of war** person, *esp.* serviceman, captured by enemy in time of war

prissy ('prɪsɪ) *a. inf.* fussy, prim

pristine ('prɪstaɪn, -tiːn) *a.* **1.** original **2.** primitive **3.** unspoiled, good

private ('praɪvɪt) *a.* **1.** secret, not public **2.** reserved for, or belonging to, or concerning, an individual only **3.** personal **4.** secluded **5.** denoting soldier of lowest rank **6.** not part of National Health Service **7.** not controlled by State —*n.* **8.** private soldier —**privacy** ('praɪvəsɪ, 'prɪvəsɪ) *n.* —'**privately** *adv.* —**privati'zation** *or* **-i'sation** *n.* —'**privatize** *or* **-ise** *vt.* take into or return to private ownership (a company or concern previously owned by the State) —**private bill** bill presented to Parliament or Congress on behalf of individual, corporation *etc.* —**private company** limited company that does not issue shares for public subscription —**private eye** *inf.* private detective —**private member's bill** parliamentary bill sponsored by Member of Parliament who is not government minister —**private parts** *or* '**privates** *pl.n.*

genitals —**private school** school accepting mostly fee-paying pupils

privateer (praɪvə'tɪə) *n. Hist.* **1.** privately owned armed vessel authorized by government to take part in war **2.** captain of such ship

privation (praɪ'veɪʃən) *n.* **1.** loss or lack of comforts or necessities **2.** hardship **3.** act of depriving —**privative** ('prɪvətɪv) *a.*

privet ('prɪvɪt) *n.* bushy evergreen shrub used for hedges

privilege ('prɪvɪlɪdʒ) *n.* **1.** advantage or favour that only a few obtain **2.** right, advantage belonging to person or class —'**privileged** *a.* enjoying special right or immunity

privy ('prɪvɪ) *a.* **1.** admitted to knowledge of secret —*n.* **2.** lavatory, *esp.* outhouse **3.** *Law* person having interest in an action —'**privily** *adv.* —**privy council** council of state of monarch —**privy purse** (*oft.* **P- P-**) **1.** allowance voted by Parliament for private expenses of monarch **2.** official responsible for dealing with monarch's private expenses (*also* **Keeper of the Privy Purse**) —**privy seal** (*oft.* **P- S-**) UK seal affixed to documents issued by royal authority: of less importance than great seal

prize¹ (praɪz) *n.* **1.** reward given for success in competition **2.** thing striven for **3.** thing won, *eg* in lottery *etc.* —*a.* **4.** winning or likely to win a prize —*vt.* **5.** value highly —'**prizefight** *n.* boxing match for money —'**prizefighter** *n.*

prize² (praɪz) *n.* ship, property captured in (naval) warfare

pro¹ (prəʊ) *adv./prep.* in favour (of)

pro² (prəʊ) *n.* **1.** professional **2.** prostitute (*pl.* **-s**) —*a.* **3.** professional

P.R.O. 1. Public Records Office **2.** public relations officer

pro- (*comb. form*) for, instead of, before, in front, as in *proconsul*, *pronoun*, *project*. Such compounds are not given here where the meaning may easily be found from the simple word

probable ('prɒbəbᵊl) *a.* likely —**proba'bility** *n.* **1.** likelihood **2.** anything that has appearance of truth —'**probably** *adv.*

probate ('prəʊbɪt, -beɪt) *n.* **1.** proving of authenticity of will **2.** certificate of this

probation (prə'beɪʃən) *n.* **1.** system of dealing with lawbreakers, *esp.* juvenile ones, by placing them under supervision of probation officer for stated period **2.** testing of candidate before admission to full membership —**pro'bationer** *n.* person on probation —**probation officer** officer of court who supervises offenders placed on probation

probe (prəʊb) *vt.* **1.** search into, examine, question closely —*n.* **2.** that which probes, or is used to probe **3.** thorough inquiry

probity ('prəʊbɪtɪ) n. honesty, uprightness, integrity

problem ('prɒbləm) n. 1. matter etc. difficult to deal with or solve 2. question set for solution 3. puzzle —**proble'matic(al)** a. 1. questionable; uncertain 2. disputable

proboscis (prəʊ'bɒsɪs) n. trunk or long snout, eg of elephant (pl. **-es, proboscides** (prəʊ'bɒsɪdiːz))

proceed (prə'siːd) vi. 1. go forward, continue 2. be carried on 3. go to law —**pro'cedural** a. —**pro'cedure** n. 1. act, manner of proceeding 2. conduct —**pro'ceeding** n. 1. act or course of action 2. transaction —pl. 3. minutes of meeting 4. methods of prosecuting charge, claim etc. —'**proceeds** pl.n. price or profit

process ('prəʊses) n. 1. series of actions or changes 2. method of operation 3. state of going on 4. action of law 5. outgrowth —vt. 6. handle, treat, prepare by special method of manufacture etc. —**pro'cession** n. 1. regular, orderly progress 2. train of persons in formal order

proclaim (prə'kleɪm) vt. announce publicly, declare —**proclamation** (prɒklə'meɪʃən) n.

proclivity (prə'klɪvɪtɪ) n. inclination, tendency

proconsul (prəʊ'kɒnsəl) n. Hist. governor of province

procrastinate (prəʊ'kræstɪneɪt, prə-) vi. put off (an action) until later, delay —**procrasti'nation** n. —**pro'crastinator** n.

procreate ('prəʊkrɪeɪt) v. produce (offspring) —**procre'ation** n.

Procrustean (prəʊ'krʌstɪən) a. compelling uniformity by violence

proctor ('prɒktə) n. university official with disciplinary powers

procure (prə'kjʊə) vt. 1. obtain, acquire 2. provide 3. bring about —vi. 4. act as pimp —**pro'curable** a. —**procuration** (prɒkjʊ'reɪʃən) n. —**procurator** ('prɒkjʊreɪtə) n. one who manages another's affairs —**pro'curement** n. —**pro'curer** n. 1. one who procures 2. pimp —**procurator fiscal** in Scotland, legal officer who performs functions of public prosecutor and coroner

prod (prɒd) vt. 1. poke with something pointed (**-dd-**) —n. 2. prodding 3. goad 4. pointed instrument

prodigal ('prɒdɪgəl) a. 1. wasteful 2. extravagant —n. 3. spendthrift —**prodi'gality** n. reckless extravagance

prodigy ('prɒdɪdʒɪ) n. 1. person with some marvellous gift 2. thing causing wonder —**pro'digious** a. 1. very great, immense 2. extraordinary —**pro'digiously** adv.

produce (prə'djuːs) vt. 1. bring into existence 2. yield 3. make 4. bring forward 5. manufacture 6. exhibit 7. present on stage, film, television 8.

Geom. extend in length —n. ('prɒdjuːs) 9. that which is yielded or made —**pro'ducer** n. person who produces, esp. play, film etc. —**product** ('prɒdʌkt) n. 1. result of process of manufacture 2. number resulting from multiplication —**pro'duction** n. 1. producing 2. things produced —**pro'ductive** a. 1. fertile 2. creative 3. efficient —**productivity** (prɒdʌk'tɪvɪtɪ) n.

proem ('prəʊem) n. introduction or preface, such as to work of literature

Prof. Professor

profane (prə'feɪn) a. 1. irreverent, blasphemous 2. not sacred —vt. 3. pollute, desecrate —**profanation** (prɒfə'neɪʃən) n. —**profanity** (prə'fænɪtɪ) n. profane talk or behaviour, blasphemy

profess (prə'fes) vt. 1. affirm, acknowledge 2. confess publicly 3. assert 4. claim, pretend —**professedly** (prə'fesɪdlɪ) adv. avowedly —**pro'fession** n. 1. calling or occupation, esp. learned, scientific or artistic 2. a professing 3. vow of religious faith on entering religious order —**pro'fessional** a. 1. engaged in a profession 2. engaged in a game or sport for money —n. 3. paid player —**pro'fessor** n. teacher of highest rank in university —**professorial** (prɒfɪ'sɔːrɪəl) a. —**professoriate** (prɒfɪ'sɔːrɪət) n. body of university professors —**pro'fessorship** n.

proffer ('prɒfə) vt./n. offer

proficient (prə'fɪʃənt) a. skilled; expert —**pro'ficiency** n.

profile ('prəʊfaɪl) n. 1. outline, esp. of face, as seen from side 2. brief biographical sketch

profit ('prɒfɪt) n. 1. (oft. pl.) money gained 2. benefit obtained —vi. 3. benefit —**profitable** a. yielding profit —**profi'teer** n. 1. one who makes excessive profits at the expense of the public —vi. 2. make excessive profits —'**profitless** a. —**profit-sharing** n. system in which portion of net profit of business is distributed to employees, usu. in proportion to wages or length of service

profligate ('prɒflɪgɪt) a. 1. dissolute 2. reckless, wasteful —n. 3. dissolute person —'**profligacy** n.

pro forma ('prəʊ 'fɔːmə) Lat. prescribing a set form

profound (prə'faʊnd) a. 1. very learned 2. deep —**profundity** (prə'fʌndɪtɪ) n.

profuse (prə'fjuːs) a. abundant, prodigal —**pro'fusion** n.

progeny ('prɒdʒɪnɪ) n. children —**progenitor** (prəʊ'dʒenɪtə) n. ancestor

progesterone (prəʊ'dʒestərəʊn) n. hormone which prepares uterus for pregnancy and prevents further ovulation

prognathous (prɒg'neɪθəs) or **prognathic** (prɒg'næθɪk) a. with projecting lower jaw

prognosis (prog'nəʊsɪs) n. 1. art of foretelling course of disease by symptoms 2. forecast (pl. **-noses** (-'nəʊsɪz)) —**prognostic** (prog'nɒstɪk) a. 1. of, serving as prognosis —n. 2. Med. any symptom used in making prognosis 3. sign of some future occurrence —**prognosticate** (prog'nɒstɪkeɪt) vt. foretell —**prognostication** (prognɒstɪ'keɪʃən) n.

programme or U.S. **program** ('prəʊgræm) n. 1. plan, detailed notes of intended proceedings 2. broadcast on radio or television 3. syllabus or curriculum —**program** n. 1. detailed instructions for computer —vt. 2. feed program into (computer) 3. arrange detailed instructions for (computer) (-mm-) —**programmer** n.

progress ('prəʊgres) n. 1. onward movement 2. development —vi. (prə'gres) 3. go forward 4. improve —**pro'gression** n. 1. moving forward 2. advance, improvement 3. increase or decrease of numbers or magnitudes according to fixed law 4. Mus. regular succession of chords —**pro'gressive** a. 1. progressing by degrees 2. favouring political or social reform

prohibit (prə'hɪbɪt) vt. forbid —**prohibition** (prəʊɪ'bɪʃən) n. 1. act of forbidding 2. interdict 3. interdiction of supply and consumption of alcoholic drinks —**pro'hibitive** a. 1. tending to forbid or exclude 2. (of prices) very high —**pro'hibitory** a.

project ('prɒdʒɛkt) n. 1. plan, scheme 2. design —vt. (prə'dʒɛkt) 3. plan 4. throw 5. cause to appear on distant background —vi. (prə'dʒɛkt) 6. stick out, protrude —**pro'jectile** (prə'dʒɛktaɪl) n. 1. heavy missile, esp. shell or ball —a. 2. designed for throwing —**projection** (prə'dʒɛkʃən) n. —**projectionist** (prə'dʒɛkʃənɪst) n. operator of film projector —**projector** (prə'dʒɛktə) n. 1. apparatus for projecting photographic images, films, slides on screen 2. one that forms scheme or design

prolapse ('prəʊlæps, prəʊ'læps) n. falling, slipping down of part of body from normal position (also **pro'lapsus**)

prolate ('prəʊleɪt) a. having polar diameter greater than the equatorial diameter

prole (prəʊl) n. derogatory sl., chiefly UK proletarian

prolegomena (prəʊlɪ'gɒmɪnə) pl.n. introductory remarks prefixed to book; preface

proletariat (prəʊlɪ'tɛərɪət) n. 1. all wage earners collectively 2. lowest class of community, working class —**prole'tarian** a./n.

proliferate (prə'lɪfəreɪt) v. grow or reproduce rapidly —**prolifer'ation** n.

prolific (prə'lɪfɪk) a. 1. producing fruit, offspring etc. in abundance 2. producing constant or successful results 3. fruitful

prolix ('prəʊlɪks, prəʊ'lɪks) a. (of speech etc.) wordy, long-winded —**pro'lixity** n.

prologue or U.S. (oft.) **prolog** ('prəʊlog) n. preface, esp. speech before play

prolong (prə'loŋ) vt. lengthen, protract —**prolongation** (prəʊloŋ'geɪʃən) n.

prom (prɒm) n. promenade (concert)

promenade (prɒmə'nɑːd) n. 1. leisurely walk 2. place made or used for this —vi. 3. take leisurely walk 4. go up and down —**promenade concert** concert at which audience stands

promethium (prə'miːθɪəm) n. radioactive element of lanthanide series artificially produced by fission of uranium

prominent ('prɒmɪnənt) a. 1. sticking out 2. conspicuous 3. distinguished —**'prominence** n.

promiscuous (prə'mɪskjʊəs) a. 1. indiscriminate, esp. in sexual relations 2. mixed without distinction —**promiscuity** (prɒmɪ'skjuːɪtɪ) n.

promise ('prɒmɪs) v. 1. give undertaking or assurance (of) —vi. 2. be likely —n. 3. undertaking to do or not to do something 4. potential —**'promising** a. showing good signs, hopeful —**'promissory** a. containing promise —**Promised Land** 1. O.T. land of Canaan, promised by God to Abraham and his descendants as their heritage 2. Christianity heaven 3. place where one expects to find greater happiness —**promissory note** written promise to pay sum to person named, at specified time

promontory ('prɒməntərɪ, -trɪ) n. point of high land jutting out into the sea, headland

promote (prə'məʊt) vt. 1. help forward 2. move up to higher rank or position 3. work for 4. encourage sale of —**pro'moter** n. —**pro'motion** n. 1. advancement 2. preferment

prompt (prɒmpt) a. 1. done at once 2. acting with alacrity 3. punctual 4. ready —vt. 5. urge, suggest —v. 6. help out (actor or speaker) by reading or suggesting next words —**'prompter** n. —**'promptitude** or **'promptness** n. —**'promptly** adv.

promulgate ('prɒmʌlgeɪt) vt. proclaim, publish —**promul'gation** n. —**'promulgator** n.

pron. 1. pronoun 2. pronunciation

prone (prəʊn) a. 1. lying face or front downwards 2. inclined —**'proneness** n.

prong (prɒŋ) n. single spike of fork or similar instrument

pronghorn ('prɒŋhɔːn) n. Amer. antelope

pronoun ('prəʊnaʊn) n. word used to replace noun —**pro'nominal** a. pert. to, like pronoun

pronounce (prə'naʊns) vt. 1. utter formally 2. form with organs of speech 3. say distinctly 4. declare —vi. 5. give opinion or decision —**pro'nounceable** a. —**pro'nounced** a. strongly marked, decided —**pro'nouncement** n. declara-

probity ('prəʊbɪtɪ) *n.* honesty, uprightness, integrity

problem ('prɒbləm) *n.* **1.** matter *etc.* difficult to deal with or solve **2.** question set for solution **3.** puzzle —**proble'matic(al)** *a.* **1.** questionable; uncertain **2.** disputable

proboscis (prəʊ'bɒsɪs) *n.* trunk or long snout, *eg* of elephant (*pl.* **-es**, **proboscides** (prəʊ'bɒsɪdiːz))

proceed (prə'siːd) *vi.* **1.** go forward, continue **2.** be carried on **3.** go to law —**pro'cedural** *a.* —**pro'cedure** *n.* **1.** act, manner of proceeding **2.** conduct —**pro'ceeding** *n.* **1.** act or course of action **2.** transaction —*pl.* **3.** minutes of meeting **4.** methods of prosecuting charge, claim *etc.* —**'proceeds** *pl.n.* price or profit

process ('prəʊsɛs) *n.* **1.** series of actions or changes **2.** method of operation **3.** state of going on **4.** action of law **5.** outgrowth —*vt.* **6.** handle, treat, prepare by special method of manufacture *etc.* —**pro'cession** *n.* **1.** regular, orderly progress **2.** train of persons in formal order

proclaim (prə'kleɪm) *vt.* announce publicly, declare —**proclamation** (prɒklə'meɪʃən) *n.*

proclivity (prə'klɪvɪtɪ) *n.* inclination, tendency

proconsul (prəʊ'kɒnsəl) *n. Hist.* governor of province

procrastinate (prəʊ'kræstɪneɪt, prə-) *vi.* put off (an action) until later, delay —**procrasti'nation** *n.* —**pro'crastinator** *n.*

procreate ('prəʊkrɪeɪt) *v.* produce (offspring) —**procre'ation** *n.*

Procrustean (prəʊ'krʌstɪən) *a.* compelling uniformity by violence

proctor ('prɒktə) *n.* university official with disciplinary powers

procure (prə'kjʊə) *vt.* **1.** obtain, acquire **2.** provide **3.** bring about —*vi.* **4.** act as pimp —**pro'curable** *a.* —**procuration** (prɒkjʊ'reɪʃən) *n.* —**procurator** ('prɒkjʊreɪtə) *n.* one who manages another's affairs —**pro'curement** *n.* —**pro'curer** *n.* **1.** one who procures **2.** pimp —**procurator fiscal** in Scotland, legal officer who performs functions of public prosecutor and coroner

prod (prɒd) *vt.* **1.** poke with something pointed (-**dd**-) —*n.* **2.** prodding **3.** goad **4.** pointed instrument

prodigal ('prɒdɪgəl) *a.* **1.** wasteful **2.** extravagant —*n.* **3.** spendthrift —**prodi'gality** *n.* reckless extravagance

prodigy ('prɒdɪdʒɪ) *n.* **1.** person with some marvellous gift **2.** thing causing wonder —**pro'digious** *a.* **1.** very great, immense **2.** extraordinary —**pro'digiously** *adv.*

produce (prə'djuːs) *vt.* **1.** bring into existence **2.** yield **3.** make **4.** bring forward **5.** manufacture **6.** exhibit **7.** present on stage, film, television **8.**

Geom. extend in length —*n.* ('prɒdjuːs) **9.** that which is yielded or made —**pro'ducer** *n.* person who produces, *esp.* play, film *etc.* —**product** ('prɒdʌkt) *n.* **1.** result of process of manufacture **2.** number resulting from multiplication —**pro'duction** *n.* **1.** producing **2.** things produced —**pro'ductive** *a.* **1.** fertile **2.** creative **3.** efficient —**productivity** (prɒdʌk'tɪvɪtɪ) *n.*

proem ('prəʊɛm) *n.* introduction or preface, such as to work of literature

Prof. Professor

profane (prə'feɪn) *a.* **1.** irreverent, blasphemous **2.** not sacred —*vt.* **3.** pollute, desecrate —**profanation** (prɒfə'neɪʃən) *n.* —**profanity** (prə'fænɪtɪ) *n.* profane talk or behaviour, blasphemy

profess (prə'fɛs) *vt.* **1.** affirm, acknowledge **2.** confess publicly **3.** assert **4.** claim, pretend —**professedly** (prə'fɛsɪdlɪ) *adv.* avowedly —**pro'fession** *n.* **1.** calling or occupation, *esp.* learned, scientific or artistic **2.** a professing **3.** vow of religious faith on entering religious order —**pro'fessional** *a.* **1.** engaged in a profession **2.** engaged in a game or sport for money —*n.* **3.** paid player —**pro'fessor** *n.* teacher of highest rank in university —**professorial** (prɒfɪ'sɔːrɪəl) *a.* —**professoriate** (prɒfɪ'sɔːrɪɪt) *n.* body of university professors —**pro'fessorship** *n.*

proffer ('prɒfə) *vt./n.* offer

proficient (prə'fɪʃənt) *a.* skilled; expert —**pro'ficiency** *n.*

profile ('prəʊfaɪl) *n.* **1.** outline, *esp.* of face, as seen from side **2.** brief biographical sketch

profit ('prɒfɪt) *n.* **1.** (*oft. pl.*) money gained **2.** benefit obtained —*v.* **3.** benefit —**'profitable** *a.* yielding profit —**profi'teer** *n.* **1.** one who makes excessive profits at the expense of the public —*vi.* **2.** make excessive profits —**'profitless** *a.* —**profit-sharing** *n.* system in which portion of net profit of business is distributed to employees, usu. in proportion to wages or length of service

profligate ('prɒflɪgɪt) *a.* **1.** dissolute **2.** reckless, wasteful —*n.* **3.** dissolute person —**'profligacy** *n.*

pro forma ('prəʊ 'fɔːmə) *Lat.* prescribing a set form

profound (prə'faʊnd) *a.* **1.** very learned **2.** deep —**profundity** (prə'fʌndɪtɪ) *n.*

profuse (prə'fjuːs) *a.* abundant, prodigal —**pro'fusion** *n.*

progeny ('prɒdʒɪnɪ) *n.* children —**progenitor** (prəʊ'dʒɛnɪtə) *n.* ancestor

progesterone (prəʊ'dʒɛstərəʊn) *n.* hormone which prepares uterus for pregnancy and prevents further ovulation

prognathous (prɒg'neɪθəs) *or* **prognathic** (prɒg'næθɪk) *a.* with projecting lower jaw

prognosis (prog'nəusıs) n. 1. art of foretelling course of disease by symptoms 2. forecast (pl. -noses (-'nəusiːz)) —**prognostic** (prog'nostık) a. 1. of, serving as prognosis —n. 2. Med. any symptom used in making prognosis 3. sign of some future occurrence —**prognosticate** (prog'nostıkeıt) vt. foretell —**prognostication** (prognostı'keıʃən) n.

programme or U.S. **program** ('prəugræm) n. 1. plan, detailed notes of intended proceedings 2. broadcast on radio or television 3. syllabus or curriculum —'**program** n. 1. detailed instructions for computer —vt. 2. feed program into (computer) 3. arrange detailed instructions for (computer) (-mm-) —'**programmer** n.

progress ('prəugres) n. 1. onward movement 2. development —vi. (prə'gres) 3. go forward 4. improve —**pro'gression** n. 1. moving forward 2. advance, improvement 3. increase or decrease of numbers or magnitudes according to fixed law 4. Mus. regular succession of chords —**pro'gressive** a. 1. progressing by degrees 2. favouring political or social reform

prohibit (prə'hıbıt) vt. forbid —**prohibition** (prəuı'bıʃən) n. 1. act of forbidding 2. interdict 3. interdiction of supply and consumption of alcoholic drinks —**pro'hibitive** a. 1. tending to forbid or exclude 2. (of prices) very high —**pro'hibitory** a.

project ('prodʒekt) n. 1. plan, scheme 2. design —vt. (prə'dʒekt) 3. plan 4. throw 5. cause to appear on distant background —vi. (prə'dʒekt) 6. stick out, protrude —**projectile** (prə'dʒektaıl) n. 1. heavy missile, esp. shell or ball —a. 2. designed for throwing —**projection** (prə'dʒekʃən) n. —**projectionist** (prə'dʒekʃənıst) n. operator of film projector —**projector** (prə'dʒektə) n. 1. apparatus for projecting photographic images, films, slides on screen 2. one that forms scheme or design

prolapse ('prəulæps, prəu'læps) n. falling, slipping down of part of body from normal position (also **pro'lapsus**)

prolate ('prəuleıt) a. having polar diameter greater than the equatorial diameter

prole (prəul) n. derogatory sl., chiefly UK proletarian

prolegomena (prəulı'gomınə) pl.n. introductory remarks prefixed to book; preface

proletariat (prəulı'teərıət) n. 1. all wage earners collectively 2. lowest class of community, working class —**prole'tarian** a./n.

proliferate (prə'lıfəreıt) v. grow or reproduce rapidly —**prolifer'ation** n.

prolific (prə'lıfık) a. 1. producing fruit, offspring etc. in abundance 2. producing constant or successful results 3. fruitful

prolix ('prəulıks, prəu'lıks) a. (of speech etc.) wordy, long-winded —**pro'lixity** n.

prologue or U.S. (oft.) **prolog** ('prəulog) n. preface, esp. speech before play

prolong (prə'loŋ) vt. lengthen, protract —**prolongation** (prəuloŋ'geıʃən) n.

prom (prom) n. promenade (concert)

promenade (promə'nɑːd) n. 1. leisurely walk 2. place made or used for this —vi. 3. take leisurely walk 4. go up and down —**promenade concert** concert at which audience stands

promethium (prə'miːθıəm) n. radioactive element of lanthanide series artificially produced by fission of uranium

prominent ('promınənt) a. 1. sticking out 2. conspicuous 3. distinguished —'**prominence** n.

promiscuous (prə'mıskjuəs) a. 1. indiscriminate, esp. in sexual relations 2. mixed without distinction —**promiscuity** (promı'skjuːıtı) n.

promise ('promıs) v. 1. give undertaking or assurance (of) —vi. 2. be likely —n. 3. undertaking to do or not to do something 4. potential —'**promising** a. showing good signs, hopeful —'**promissory** a. containing promise —**Promised Land** 1. O.T. land of Canaan, promised by God to Abraham and his descendants as their heritage 2. Christianity heaven 3. place where one expects to find greater happiness —**promissory note** written promise to pay sum to person named, at specified time

promontory ('proməntərı, -trı) n. point of high land jutting out into the sea, headland

promote (prə'məut) vt. 1. help forward 2. move up to higher rank or position 3. work for 4. encourage sale of —**pro'moter** n. —**pro'motion** n. 1. advancement 2. preferment

prompt (prompt) a. 1. done at once 2. acting with alacrity 3. punctual 4. ready —vt. 5. urge, suggest —v. 6. help out (actor or speaker) by reading or suggesting next words —'**prompter** n. —'**promptitude** or '**promptness** n. —'**promptly** adv.

promulgate ('promʌlgeıt) vt. proclaim, publish —**promul'gation** n. —'**promulgator** n.

pron. 1. pronoun 2. pronunciation

prone (prəun) a. 1. lying face or front downwards 2. inclined —'**proneness** n.

prong (proŋ) n. single spike of fork or similar instrument

pronghorn ('proŋhɔːn) n. Amer. antelope

pronoun ('prəunaun) n. word used to replace noun —**pro'nominal** a. pert. to, like pronoun

pronounce (prə'nauns) vt. 1. utter formally 2. form with organs of speech 3. say distinctly 4. declare —vi. 5. give opinion or decision —**pro'nounceable** a. —**pro'nounced** a. strongly marked, decided —**pro'nouncement** n. declaration —**pronunci'ation** n. 1. manner in which word etc. is pronounced 2. articulation 3. phonetic transcription of a word

pronto ('prontəʊ) adv. inf. at once, immediately, quickly

proof (pruːf) n. 1. evidence 2. thing which proves 3. test, demonstration 4. trial impression from type or engraved plate 5. Photog. print from a negative 6. standard of strength of alcoholic drink —a. 7. giving impenetrable defence 8. of proved strength —'**proofread** v. read and correct (proofs) —'**proofreader** n. —'**proofreading** n. —**proof spirit** UK mixture of alcohol and water or alcoholic beverage that contains 49.28 per cent of alcohol by weight, 57.1 per cent by volume at 60°F (15.6°C): used as standard of alcoholic liquids

-**proof** (comb. form) impervious to; resisting effects of, as in waterproof

prop¹ (prop) vt. 1. support, sustain, hold up (-pp-) —n. 2. pole, beam etc. used as support

prop² (prop) n. propeller —'**propjet** n. see TURBOPROP

prop³ (prop) n. (theatrical) property

prop. 1. proper(ly) 2. property 3. proposition 4. proprietor

propaganda (propə'gændə) n. organized dissemination of information to assist or damage political cause etc. —**propa'gandist** a./n.

propagate ('propəgeɪt) vt. 1. reproduce, breed, spread by sowing, breeding etc. 2. transmit —vi. 3. breed, multiply —**propa'gation** n. —'**propagative** a.

propane ('prəʊpeɪn) n. colourless, flammable gas from petroleum

propel (prə'pɛl) vt. cause to move forward (-ll-) —pro'**pellant** or pro'**pellent** n. something causing propulsion, eg rocket fuel —pro'**peller** n. revolving shaft with blades for driving ship or aircraft —pro'**pulsion** n. act of driving forward —pro'**pulsive** or pro'**pulsory** a. 1. tending, having power to propel 2. urging on

propene ('prəʊpiːn) n. colourless gaseous alkene obtained by cracking petroleum (also '**propylene**)

propensity (prə'pɛnsɪtɪ) n. 1. inclination or bent 2. tendency 3. disposition

proper ('propə) a. 1. appropriate 2. correct 3. conforming to etiquette, decorous 4. strict 5. (of noun) denoting individual person or place —'**properly** adv. —**proper fraction** fraction in which numerator has lower absolute value than denominator

property ('propətɪ) n. 1. that which is owned 2. estate whether in lands, goods or money 3. quality, attribute of something 4. article used on stage in play etc.

prophet ('profɪt) n. 1. inspired teacher or revealer of Divine Will 2. foreteller of future (-ess fem.) —'**prophecy** ('profɪsɪ) n. 1. prediction, prophetic utterance —'**prophesy** ('profɪsaɪ) v. foretell —**prophetic** (prə'fɛtɪk) a.

prophylactic (profɪ'læktɪk) n./a. 1. (something) done or used to ward off disease —n. 2. US condom —**prophy'laxis** n.

propinquity (prə'pɪŋkwɪtɪ) n. nearness, proximity, close kinship

propitiate (prə'pɪʃɪeɪt) vt. appease, gain favour of —**propiti'ation** n. —**pro'pitiatory** a. —**pro'pitious** a. favourable, auspicious

proponent (prə'pəʊnənt) n. one who advocates something

proportion (prə'pɔːʃən) n. 1. relative size or number 2. comparison 3. due relation between connected things or parts 4. share 5. relation —pl. 6. dimensions —vt. 7. arrange proportions of —**pro'portionable** a. —**pro'portional** or **pro'portionate** a. 1. having a due proportion 2. corresponding in size, number etc. —**pro'portionally** adv. —**proportional representation** representation of parties in elective body in proportion to votes they win

propose (prə'pəʊz) vt. 1. put forward for consideration 2. nominate 3. intend —vi. 4. offer marriage —**pro'posal** n. —**pro'poser** n. —**proposition** (propə'zɪʃən) n. 1. offer 2. statement, assertion 3. theorem 4. suggestion of terms 5. inf. thing to be dealt with

propound (prə'paʊnd) vt. put forward for consideration or solution

proprietor (prə'praɪətə) n. owner (-tress, -trix fem.) —pro'**prietary** a. 1. belonging to owner 2. made by firm with exclusive rights of manufacture

propriety (prə'praɪətɪ) n. properness, correct conduct, fitness

propulsion (prə'pʌlʃən) n. see PROPEL

propylene ('prəʊpɪliːn) n. see PROPENE

pro rata ('rɑːtə) Lat. in proportion

prorogue (prə'rəʊg) vt. dismiss (parliament) at end of session without dissolution

prosaic (prəʊ'zeɪɪk) a. commonplace, unromantic

pros and cons various arguments in favour of and against motion, course of action etc.

proscenium (prə'siːnɪəm) n. arch or opening framing stage (pl. -nia (-nɪə))

proscribe (prəʊ'skraɪb) vt. outlaw, condemn —**proscription** (prəʊ'skrɪpʃən) n.

prose (prəʊz) n. 1. speech or writing without rhyme or metre —'**prosily** adv. —'**prosiness** n. —'**prosy** a. tedious, dull

prosecute ('prosɪkjuːt) vt. carry on, bring legal proceedings against —**prose'cution** n. —'**prosecutor** n. (-trix fem.)

proselyte ('prɒsɪlaɪt) n. convert —**proselytism** ('prɒsɪlɪtɪzəm) n. —**proselytize** or **-ise** ('prɒsɪlɪtaɪz) v.

prosody ('prɒsədɪ) n. system, study of versification —**prosodist** n.

prospect ('prɒspɛkt) n. 1. (sometimes pl.) expectation, chance for success 2. view, outlook 3. likely customer or subscriber 4. mental view —v. (prə'spɛkt) 5. explore, esp. for gold —**pro'spective** a. 1. anticipated 2. future —**pro'spectively** adv. —**pro'spector** n. —**pro'spectus** n. circular describing company, school etc.

prosper ('prɒspə) v. (cause to) do well —**pros'perity** n. good fortune, wellbeing —**'prosperous** a. 1. doing well, successful 2. flourishing, rich, well-off —**prosperously** adv.

prostate ('prɒsteɪt) n. gland accessory to male generative organs

prosthesis ('prɒsθɪsɪs) n. (replacement of part of body with) artificial substitute (pl. **-ses** (-siːz))

prostitute ('prɒstɪtjuːt) n. 1. one who offers sexual intercourse in return for payment —vt. 2. make a prostitute of 3. put to unworthy use —**prosti'tution** n.

prostrate ('prɒstreɪt) a. 1. lying flat 2. crushed, submissive, overcome —vt. (prɒ'streɪt) 3. throw flat on ground 4. reduce to exhaustion —**pros'tration** n.

Prot. 1. Protestant 2. Protectorate

protactinium (prəʊtæk'tɪnɪəm) n. toxic radioactive element that occurs in uranium ores and is produced by neutron irradiation of thorium

protagonist (prəʊ'tægənɪst) n. 1. leading character 2. principal actor 3. champion of a cause

protasis ('prɒtəsɪs) n. introductory clause of conditional sentence (pl. **-ses** (-siːz))

protean (prəʊ'tiːən, 'prəʊtɪən) a. 1. variable 2. versatile

protect (prə'tɛkt) vt. defend, guard, keep from harm —**pro'tection** n. —**pro'tectionist** n. one who advocates protecting industries by taxing competing imports —**pro'tective** a. —**pro'tector** n. 1. one who protects 2. regent —**pro'tectorate** n. 1. relation of state to territory it protects and controls 2. such territory 3. office, period of protector of a state

protégé or (fem.) **protégée** ('prəʊtɪʒeɪ) n. one under another's care, protection or patronage

protein ('prəʊtiːn) n. any of various kinds of organic compound which form most essential part of food of living creatures

pro tempore ('prəʊ 'tɛmpərɪ) Lat. for the time being (also **pro tem**)

protest ('prəʊtɛst) n. 1. declaration or demonstration of objection —vi. (prə'tɛst) 2. object —v. 3. make declaration (against) 4. assert formally —**protes'tation** n. strong declaration

Protestant ('prɒtɪstənt) a. 1. belonging to any branch of the Western Church outside the Roman Catholic Church —n. 2. member of such a church —'**Protestantism** n.

protium ('prəʊtɪəm) n. most common isotope of hydrogen

proto- or sometimes before vowel **prot-** (comb. form) first, as in prototype

protocol ('prəʊtəkɒl) n. 1. diplomatic etiquette 2. draft of terms signed by parties as basis of formal treaty

proton ('prəʊtɒn) n. positively charged particle in nucleus of atom

protoplasm ('prəʊtəplæzəm) n. substance that is living matter of all animal and plant cells —**proto'plasmic** a.

prototype ('prəʊtətaɪp) n. 1. original or model after which thing is copied 2. pattern

protozoan (prəʊtə'zəʊən) n. minute animal of lowest and simplest class (pl. **-zoa** (-'zəʊə))

protract (prə'trækt) vt. 1. lengthen 2. prolong 3. delay 4. draw to scale —**pro'tracted** a. 1. long-drawn-out 2. tedious —**pro'traction** n. —**pro'tractor** n. instrument for measuring angles on paper

protrude (prə'truːd) v. stick out, (cause to) project —**pro'trusile** a. Zool. capable of being thrust forward —**pro'trusion** n. —**pro'trusive** a. thrusting forward —**pro'trusively** adv.

protuberant (prə'tjuːbərənt) a. bulging out —**pro'tuberance** or **pro'tuberancy** n. bulge, swelling

proud (praud) a. 1. feeling or displaying pride 2. arrogant 3. gratified 4. noble 5. self-respecting 6. stately —'**proudly** adv. —**proud flesh** flesh growing around healing wound

Prov. 1. Provençal 2. Bible Proverbs 3. Province 4. Provost

prove (pruːv) vt. 1. establish validity of 2. demonstrate, test —vi. 3. turn out (to be etc.) 4. (of dough) rise in warm place before baking (**proved**, '**proven** pp.) —**proven** ('pruːvən, 'prəʊ-) a. proved —**proving ground** place for testing new equipment etc.

provenance ('prɒvɪnəns) n. place of origin, source

Provençal (prɒvɒn'sɑːl; Fr. prɔvɑ̃'sal) a. 1. of Provence, former province of SE France, its dialect of French or its Romance language —n. 2. language of Provence, closely related to French and Italian, belonging to Romance group of Indo-European family 3. native or inhabitant of Provence

provender ('prɒvɪndə) n. fodder

proverb ('prɒvɜːb) n. short, pithy, traditional saying in common use —**pro'verbial** a.

provide (prə'vaɪd) vi. 1. make preparation —vt. 2. supply, equip, prepare, furnish, give —**pro'vider** n. —**pro'viding** or **pro'vided** conj. (sometimes with that) on condition or understanding (that)

provident ('prɒvɪdənt) a. 1. thrifty 2. showing foresight —**providence** n. 1. kindly care of God or nature 2. foresight 3. economy —**provi'dential** a. strikingly fortunate, lucky —**provi'dentially** adv.

province ('prɒvɪns) n. 1. division of a country, district 2. sphere of action —pl. 3. any part of country outside capital —**pro'vincial** a. 1. of a province 2. unsophisticated 3. narrow in outlook —n. 4. unsophisticated person 5. inhabitant of province —**pro'vincialism** n. 1. narrowness of outlook 2. lack of refinement 3. idiom peculiar to province

provision (prə'vɪʒən) n. 1. a providing, esp. for the future 2. thing provided —pl. 3. food 4. Law articles of instrument or statute —vt. 5. supply with food —**pro'visional** a. temporary 2. conditional

proviso (prə'vaɪzəʊ) n. condition (pl. **-s, -es**)

provoke (prə'vəʊk) vt. 1. irritate 2. incense 3. arouse 4. excite 5. cause —**provocation** (prɒvə'keɪʃən) n. —**provocative** (prə'vɒkətɪv) a.

provost ('prɒvəst) n. 1. one who superintends or presides 2. head of certain colleges 3. administrative head of Scottish burgh

prow (praʊ) n. bow of vessel

prowess ('praʊɪs) n. 1. bravery, fighting capacity 2. skill

prowl (praʊl) vi. 1. roam stealthily, esp. in search of prey or booty —n. 2. act of prowling —'**prowler** n. —**on the prowl** 1. moving about stealthily 2. pursuing members of opposite sex

prox. proximo

proximate ('prɒksɪmɪt) a. nearest, next, immediate —**prox'imity** n. —'**proximo** adv. in the next month

proxy ('prɒksɪ) n. 1. authorized agent or substitute 2. writing authorizing one to act as this

prude (pruːd) n. one who affects excessive modesty or propriety —'**prudery** n. —'**prudish** a.

prudent ('pruːdənt) a. 1. careful, discreet 2. sensible —'**prudence** n. 1. habit of acting with careful deliberation 2. wisdom applied to practice —**pru'dential** a.

prune[1] (pruːn) n. dried plum

prune[2] (pruːn) vt. 1. cut out (dead parts, excessive branches etc.) from 2. shorten, reduce —**pruning hook** tool with curved blade terminating in hook, used for pruning

prurient ('prʊərɪənt) a. 1. given to, springing from lewd thoughts 2. having unhealthy curiosity or desire —'**prurience** or '**pruriency** n.

pruritus (prʊə'raɪtəs) n. Pathol. intense itching —**pruritic** (prʊə'rɪtɪk) a.

prussic acid ('prʌsɪk) extremely poisonous aqueous solution of hydrogen cyanide

pry (praɪ) vi. 1. make furtive or impertinent inquiries 2. look curiously —vt. 3. US force open (**pried, 'prying**)

P.S. postscript (also **p.s.**)

Ps. or **Psa.** Bible Psalm(s)

psalm (sɑːm) n. 1. sacred song 2. (**P-**) any of the sacred songs making up the Book of Psalms in the Bible —'**psalmist** n. writer of psalms —**psalmody** ('sɑːmədɪ, 'sæl-) n. art, act of singing sacred music —**Psalter** ('sɔːltə) n. 1. book of psalms 2. copy of the Psalms as separate book —**psaltery** ('sɔːltərɪ) n. obsolete stringed instrument like lyre

PSBR public sector borrowing requirement

psephology (sɛ'fɒlədʒɪ) n. statistical study of elections

pseud (sjuːd) inf. n. 1. false or pretentious person —a. 2. sham, fake (also '**pseudo**)

pseudo- or sometimes before vowel **pseud-** (comb. form) sham, as in pseudo-Gothic, pseudomodern. Such compounds are not given here where the meaning may easily be inferred from the simple word

pseudonym ('sjuːdənɪm) n. 1. false, fictitious name 2. pen name —**pseudonymous** (sjuː-'dɒnɪməs) a.

pshaw (pʃɔː) interj. rare exclamation of disgust, impatience, disbelief etc.

psi (psaɪ) n. 23rd letter in Gr. alphabet (Ψ, ψ), transliterated as ps

psittacine ('sɪtəsaɪn, -sɪn) a. pert. to, like parrots —**psitta'cosis** n. dangerous infectious disease, germ of which is carried by parrots

psoriasis (sə'raɪəsɪs) n. skin disease characterized by formation of reddish spots and patches covered with silvery scales

psst (pst) interj. exclamation of beckoning, esp. made surreptitiously

P.S.T. US, C Pacific Standard Time

P.S.V. public service vehicle

psyche ('saɪkɪ) n. human mind or soul

psychedelic (saɪkɪ'dɛlɪk) a. 1. of or causing hallucinations 2. like intense colours etc. experienced during hallucinations

psychic ('saɪkɪk) a. 1. sensitive to phenomena lying outside range of normal experience 2. of soul or mind 3. that appears to be outside region of physical law —**psy'chiatry** n. medical treatment of mental diseases —'**psychical** a. psychic —**psycho'analyse** or esp. U.S. **psycho-**

'analyze *vt.* treat by psychoanalysis —**psycho-a'nalysis** *n.* method of studying and treating mental disorders —**psycho'analyst** *n.* —**psychogenic** (saɪkə'dʒɛnɪk) *a. Psychol.* (*esp.* of disorders or symptoms) of mental, rather than organic origin —**psychoki'nesis** *n.* (in parapsychology) alteration of state of object supposedly by mental influence alone —**psycho'logical** *a.* 1. of psychology 2. of the mind —**psy'chologist** *n.* —**psy'chology** *n.* 1. study of mind 2. *inf.* person's mental make-up —**psy'chometry** *n.* 1. measurement, testing of psychological processes 2. supposed ability to divine unknown person's qualities by handling object used or worn by him —**'psychopath** *n.* person afflicted with severe mental disorder causing him to commit antisocial, *oft.* violent acts —**psycho'pathic** *a.* —**psy'chosis** *n.* severe mental disorder in which person's contact with reality becomes distorted (*pl.* **-choses** (-'kəusiːz)) —**psychoso'matic** *a.* of physical disorders thought to have psychological causes —**psycho'therapy** *n.* treatment of disease by psychological, rather than by physical, means —**psychological moment** most appropriate time for producing desired effect —**psychological warfare** military application of psychology, *esp.* to manipulation of morale in time of war

psycho ('saɪkəu) *sl. n.* 1. psychopath (*pl.* **-s**) —*a.* 2. psychopathic

psycho- *or sometimes before vowel* **psych-** (*comb. form*) mind, psychological or mental processes, as in *psychology, psychosomatic*

Pt *Chem.* platinum

pt. 1. part 2. pint 3. point

Pt. 1. Point 2. Port

p.t. 1. past tense 2. pro tempore

P.T. 1. physical therapy 2. physical training

P.T.A. parent teacher association

ptarmigan ('tɑːmɪɡən) *n.* bird of grouse family which turns white in winter (*pl.* **-s, -gan**)

Pte. Private (soldier)

ptero- (*comb. form*) wing, as in *pterodactyl*

pterodactyl (tɛrə'dæktɪl) *n.* extinct flying reptile with batlike wings

P.T.O. *or* **p.t.o.** please turn over

ptomaine *or* **ptomain** ('təumeɪn) *n.* any of group of poisonous alkaloids found in decaying matter

Pu *Chem.* plutonium

pub (pʌb) *n.* public house, building with bar(s) and licence to sell alcoholic drinks —**pub-crawl** *sl., chiefly* UK *n.* 1. drinking tour of number of pubs or bars —*vi.* 2. make such tour

pub. 1. public 2. publication 3. published 4. publisher 5. publishing

puberty ('pjuːbətɪ) *n.* sexual maturity —**'pubertal** *a.*

pubes ('pjuːbiːz) *n.* 1. region above external genital organs, covered with hair from time of puberty 2. pubic hair (*pl.* **'pubes**) 3. *pl. of* PUBIS

pubescent (pjuː'bɛsənt) *a.* 1. arriving or arrived at puberty 2. (of certain plants and animals or their parts) covered with fine short hairs or down —**pu'bescence** *n.*

pubic ('pjuːbɪk) *a.* of the lower abdomen

pubis ('pjuːbɪs) *n.* one of three sections of hipbone that forms part of pelvis (*pl.* **-bes** (-biːz))

public ('pʌblɪk) *a.* 1. of or concerning the public as a whole 2. not private 3. open to general observation or knowledge 4. accessible to all 5. serving the people —*n.* 6. the community or its members —**'publican** *n.* keeper of public house —**'publicly** *adv.* —**public-address system** system of microphones, amplifiers and loudspeakers for increasing sound level, used in auditoriums *etc.* (*also* **P.A. system**) —**public company** limited company whose shares may be purchased by the public —**public convenience** public lavatory —**public enemy** notorious person, such as criminal, regarded as menace to public —**public house** pub —**public lending right** right of authors to receive payment when books are borrowed from public libraries —**public relations** promotion of good relations of an organization or authority with the general public —**public school** 1. in England and Wales, private independent fee-paying school 2. in some Canad. provinces, a local elementary school —**public servant** 1. elected or appointed holder of public office 2. A, NZ civil servant —**public service** government employment —**public spirit** interest in and devotion to welfare of community —**public-spirited** *a.* having or showing active interest in good of community —**public transport** trains, buses *etc.* that have fixed routes and are available to general public —**public utility** enterprise concerned with provision to public of essentials, such as electricity *etc.*

publicist ('pʌblɪsɪst) *n.* 1. writer on public concerns 2. journalist —**pub'licity** *n.* 1. process of attracting public attention 2. attention thus gained —*a.* 3. pert. to advertisement —**'publicize** *or* **-ise** *vt.* advertise

publish ('pʌblɪʃ) *vt.* 1. prepare and issue for sale (books, music *etc.*) 2. make generally known 3. proclaim —**publi'cation** *n.* —**'publisher** *n.*

puce (pjuːs) *a./n.* purplish-brown (colour)

puck[1] (pʌk) *n.* rubber disc used instead of ball in ice hockey

puck[2] (pʌk) *n.* mischievous sprite —**'puckish** *a.*

pucker ('pʌkə) v. 1. gather into wrinkles —n. 2. crease, fold

pudding ('pudɪŋ) n. 1. sweet, usu. cooked dessert, oft. made from suet, flour etc 2. sweet course of meal 3. soft savoury dish with pastry or batter 4. kind of sausage

puddle ('pʌdəl) n. 1. small muddy pool 2. rough cement for lining ponds etc. —vt. 3. line with puddle 4. make muddy

pudendum (pju:'dɛndəm) n. (oft. pl.) human external genital organs, esp. of female (pl. **-da** (-də)) —pu'dendal or 'pudic a.

pudgy ('pʌdʒɪ) a. esp. US see PODGY

puerile ('pjuəraɪl) a. 1. childish 2. foolish 3. trivial

puerperium (pju:ə'pɪərɪəm) n. period of about six weeks after childbirth —**puerperal** (pju:'ɜːpərəl) a. —**puerperal fever** formerly, blood poisoning caused by infection during childbirth

puff (pʌf) n. 1. short blast of breath, wind etc. 2. its sound 3. type of pastry 4. laudatory notice or advertisement —vi. 5. blow abruptly 6. breathe hard —vt. 7. send out in a puff 8. blow out, inflate 9. advertise 10. smoke hard —**puffed** a. 1. breathless; winded 2. swollen; puffy —**puffy** a. 1. short-winded 2. swollen —**puff adder 1.** large venomous Afr. viper that inflates its body when alarmed 2. N Amer. nonvenomous snake that inflates its body when alarmed (also **hognose snake**) —'puffball n. ball-shaped fungus —**puff pastry** or U.S. **puff paste** dough for making a rich flaky pastry

puffin ('pʌfɪn) n. any of various sea birds with large brightly-coloured beaks

pug (pʌg) n. 1. small snub-nosed dog 2. sl. boxer —**pug nose** snub nose

pugilism ('pju:dʒɪlɪzəm) n. art, practice or profession of fighting with fists; boxing —'**pugilist** n. —**pugi'listic** a.

pugnacious (pʌg'neɪʃəs) a. given to fighting —**pugnacity** (pʌg'næsɪtɪ) n.

puissant ('pju:ɪsənt) a. Poet. powerful, mighty —**puissance** ('pju:ɪsəns, 'pwi:sa:ns) n. show-jumping competition over very high fences

puke (pju:k) sl. vi. 1. vomit —n. 2. act of vomiting

pukka or **pucka** ('pʌkə) a. Anglo-Indian properly or perfectly done, constructed etc.; good; genuine

pulchritude ('pʌlkrɪtju:d) n. Lit. beauty

pule (pju:l) vi. whine; whimper

pull (pul) vt. 1. exert force on (object) to move it towards source of force 2. strain, stretch 3. tear 4. propel by rowing —n. 5. act of pulling 6. force exerted by it 7. draught of liquor 8. inf. power, influence —**pull in 1.** (of train) arrive 2. (of car etc.) draw to side of road, stop 3. attract 4. sl. arrest —**pull off** inf. carry through to successful issue —**pull out 1.** withdraw 2. extract 3. (of train) depart 4. (of car etc.) move away from side of road; move out to overtake —**pull (someone's) leg** inf. make fun of (someone) —**pull up 1.** tear up 2. recover lost ground 3. improve 4. come to a stop 5. halt 6. reprimand

pullet ('pulɪt) n. young hen

pulley ('pulɪ) n. wheel with groove in rim for cord, used to raise weights by downward pull

Pullman ('pulmən) n. railway saloon car (pl. **-s**) (also **Pullman car**)

pullover ('pul,əuvə) n. jersey, sweater without fastening, to be pulled over head

pulmonary ('pʌlmənərɪ, 'pul-) a. 1. of lungs 2. having lungs or lunglike organs

pulp (pʌlp) n. 1. soft, moist, vegetable or animal matter 2. flesh of fruit 3. any soft soggy mass —vt. 4. reduce to pulp

pulpit ('pulpɪt) n. raised (enclosed) platform for preacher

pulsar ('pʌlsɑ:) n. small dense star emitting radio waves

pulse¹ (pʌls) n. 1. movement of blood in arteries corresponding to heartbeat, discernible to touch, eg in wrist 2. any regular beat or vibration —**pul'sate** vi. throb, quiver —**pul'sation** n.

pulse² (pʌls) n. edible seeds of pod-bearing plants, eg beans

pulverize or **-ise** ('pʌlvəraɪz) vt. 1. reduce to powder 2. smash, demolish —**pulveri'zation** or **-i'sation** n.

puma ('pju:mə) n. large Amer. feline carnivore, cougar

pumice ('pʌmɪs) n. light porous variety of volcanic rock used to scour, smooth and polish (also **pumice stone**)

pummel ('pʌməl) vt. strike repeatedly (**-ll-**)

pump¹ (pʌmp) n. 1. appliance in which piston and handle are used for raising water, or putting in or taking out air, liquid etc. —vt. 2. raise, put in, take out etc. with pump 3. empty by means of pump 4. extract information from —vi. 5. work pump 6. work like pump

pump² (pʌmp) n. light shoe

pumpernickel ('pʌmpənɪkəl) n. sour black bread made of coarse rye flour

pumpkin ('pʌmpkɪn) n. any of several varieties of gourd, eaten esp. as vegetable

pun (pʌn) n. 1. humorous use of words that have the same sound, but have different meanings —vi. 2. make pun (**-nn-**) —'**punster** n.

punch¹ (pʌntʃ) n. 1. tool for perforating or stamping 2. blow with fist 3. inf. vigour —vt. 4. stamp, perforate with punch 5. strike with fist —'**punchball** n. 1. stuffed or inflated ball or bag, either suspended or supported by flexible rod, that is punched for exercise, *esp.* boxing training **2.** US game resembling baseball —**punch-drunk** *or* (*inf.*) **'punchy** *a.* dazed, as by repeated blows —**punched card** *or esp. U.S.* **punch card** card on which data can be coded in form of punched holes —**punched tape** *or U.S.* **perforated tape** strip of paper used in computers *etc.* for recording information in form of punched holes (*also* **paper tape**) —**punch line** culminating part of joke *etc.*, that gives it its point —**punch-up** *n. UK sl.* fight, brawl

punch² (pʌntʃ) *n.* drink of spirits or wine with fruit juice, spice *etc.*

punctilious (pʌŋkˈtɪlɪəs) *a.* **1.** making much of details of etiquette **2.** very exact, particular

punctual (ˈpʌŋktjʊəl) *a.* in good time, not late, prompt —**punctu'ality** *n.* —**'punctually** *adv.*

punctuate (ˈpʌŋktjʊeɪt) *vt.* **1.** insert punctuation marks into **2.** interrupt at intervals —**punctu'ation** *n.* marks, *eg* commas, colons *etc.*, put in writing to assist in making sense clear

puncture (ˈpʌŋktʃə) *n.* **1.** small hole made by sharp object, *esp.* in tyre **2.** act of puncturing —*vt.* **3.** prick hole in, perforate

pundit *or* **pandit** (ˈpʌndɪt) *n.* **1.** self-appointed expert **2.** Brahman learned in Sanskrit and, *esp.* in Hindu religion, philosophy or law

pungent (ˈpʌndʒənt) *a.* **1.** biting **2.** irritant **3.** piercing **4.** tart **5.** caustic —**'pungency** *n.*

punish (ˈpʌnɪʃ) *vt.* **1.** cause (someone) to suffer for offence **2.** inflict penalty on **3.** use or treat roughly —**'punishable** *a.* —**'punishment** *n.* —**punitive** (ˈpjuːnɪtɪv) *a.* inflicting or intending to inflict punishment

punk¹ (pʌŋk) *a./n.* **1.** inferior, rotten, worthless (person or thing) **2.** petty (hoodlum) **3.** (of) style of rock music

punk² (pʌŋk) *n.* dried decayed wood or other substance that smoulders when ignited: used as tinder

punka *or* **punkah** (ˈpʌŋkə) *n.* **1.** fan made of palm leaf or leaves **2.** large fan made of palm leaves *etc.* worked mechanically to cool room

punnet (ˈpʌnɪt) *n.* small basket for fruit

punt¹ (pʌnt) *n.* **1.** flat-bottomed, square-ended boat, propelled by pushing with pole —*vt.* **2.** propel thus

punt² (pʌnt) *Sport vt.* **1.** kick (ball) before it touches ground, when let fall from hands —*n.* **2.** such a kick

punt³ (pʌnt) *vi.* gamble, bet —**'punter** *n.* **1.** one who punts **2.** professional gambler **3.** *inf.* customer or client, *esp.* prostitute's client

puny (ˈpjuːnɪ) *a.* small and feeble

pup (pʌp) *n.* young of certain animals, *eg* dog

pupa (ˈpjuːpə) *n.* stage between larva and adult in metamorphosis of insect, chrysalis (*pl.* **pupae** (ˈpjuːpiː)) —**'pupal** *a.*

pupil¹ (ˈpjuːpəl) *n.* **1.** person being taught **2.** opening in iris of eye

puppet (ˈpʌpɪt) *n.* small doll or figure of person *etc.* controlled by operator's hand —**puppe'teer** *n.* —**'puppetry** *n.* —**puppet show** show with puppets worked by hidden showman —**puppet state** state that appears independent but is controlled by another

puppy (ˈpʌpɪ) *n.* young dog —**puppy fat** fatty tissue in child or adolescent, *usu.* disappearing with age

purblind (ˈpɜːblaɪnd) *a.* **1.** partly or nearly blind **2.** lacking in insight or understanding

purchase (ˈpɜːtʃɪs) *vt.* **1.** buy —*n.* **2.** act of buying **3.** what is bought **4.** leverage, grip

purdah (ˈpɜːdə) *n.* **1.** Muslim, Hindu custom of keeping women in seclusion **2.** screen, veil to achieve this

pure (pjʊə) *a.* **1.** unmixed, untainted **2.** simple **3.** spotless **4.** faultless **5.** innocent **6.** concerned with theory only —**'purely** *adv.* —**purifi'cation** *n.* —**'purificatory** *a.* —**'purify** *v.* make, become pure, clear or clean (-**ified, -ifying**) —**'purism** *n.* excessive insistence on correctness of language —**'purist** *n.* —**'purity** *n.* state of being pure —**purebred** (ˈpjʊəˈbrɛd) *a.* **1.** denoting of pure strain obtained through many generations of controlled breeding —*n.* (ˈpjʊəbrɛd) **2.** purebred animal

purée (ˈpjʊəreɪ) *n.* **1.** pulp of cooked fruit or vegetables —*vt.* **2.** make (cooked foods) into purée

purgatory (ˈpɜːɡətərɪ) *n.* place or state of torment, pain or distress, *esp.* temporary —**purga'torial** *a.*

purge (pɜːdʒ) *vt.* **1.** make clean, purify **2.** remove, get rid of **3.** clear out —*n.* **4.** act, process of purging **5.** removal of undesirable members from political party, army *etc.* —**purgation** (pɜːˈgeɪʃən) *n.* —**purgative** (ˈpɜːɡətɪv) *a./n.*

Puritan (ˈpjʊərɪtən) *n.* **1.** *Hist.* member of extreme Protestant party **2.** (**p-**) person of extreme strictness in morals or religion —**puri'tanic(al)** *a.* **1.** strict in the observance of religious and moral duties **2.** overscrupulous —**'puritanism** *n.*

purl¹ (pɜːl) *n.* **1.** stitch that forms ridge in knitting —*v.* **2.** knit in purl stitch

purl² (pɜːl) *vi.* flow with burbling sound, swirl, babble

purlieus (ˈpɜːljuːz) *pl.n.* outlying parts, outskirts

purlin *or* **purline** (ˈpɜːlɪn) *n.* horizontal beam that provides support for rafters of roof

purloin (pɜːˈlɔɪn) *vt.* **1.** steal **2.** pilfer

purple (´pɜːpəl) *n./a.* (of) colour between crimson and violet —**Purple Heart** decoration awarded to members of U.S. Armed Forces for wound received in action

purport (pɜː´pɔːt) *vt.* 1. claim to be (true *etc.*) 2. signify, imply —*n.* (´pɜːpɔːt) 3. meaning 4. apparent meaning 5. significance

purpose (´pɜːpəs) *n.* 1. reason, object 2. design 3. aim, intention —*vt.* 4. intend —**purposely** *adv.* —**purpose-built** *a.* made to serve specific purpose —**on purpose** intentionally

purr (pɜː) *n.* 1. (*esp.* of cats) make low vibrant sound, usu. considered as expressing pleasure *etc.* —*vi.* 2. utter this sound

purse (pɜːs) *n.* 1. small bag for money 2. resources 3. money as prize —*vt.* 4. pucker (mouth, lips *etc.*) in wrinkles —*vi.* 5. become wrinkled and drawn in —**purser** *n.* ship's officer who keeps accounts —**purse strings** control of expenditure (*esp.* in **hold** or **control the purse strings**)

purslane (´pɜːslɪn) *n.* plant used (*esp.* formerly) in salads and as potherb

pursue (pə´sjuː) *vt.* 1. run after 2. chase 3. aim at 4. engage in 5. continue 6. follow —*vi.* 7. go in pursuit 8. continue —**pur´suance** *n.* carrying out —**pur´suant** *adj. chiefly law* in agreement or conformity —**pur´suer** *n.* —**pur´suit** *n.* 1. running after, attempt to catch 2. occupation

pursuivant (´pɜːsɪvənt) *n.* officer of College of Arms below herald

purulent (´pjuərulənt) *a. see* PUS

purvey (pə´veɪ) *vt.* supply (provisions) —**pur´veyance** *n.* —**pur´veyor** *n.*

purview (´pɜːvjuː) *n.* scope, range

pus (pʌs) *n.* yellowish matter produced by suppuration —**purulence** (´pjuəruləns) *n.* —**´purulent** *a.* forming, discharging pus 2. septic

push (pʊʃ) *vt.* 1. move, try to move away by pressure 2. drive, impel 3. *inf.* sell (*esp.* narcotic drugs) illegally —*vi.* 4. make thrust 5. advance with steady effort —*n.* 6. thrust 7. persevering self-assertion 8. big military advance 9. *sl.* dismissal —**´pusher** *n.* —**´pushing** or *inf.* **´pushy** *a.* given to pushing oneself —**push-bike** *n. UK inf.* bicycle —**push button** electrical switch operated by pressing button, which closes or opens circuit —**push-button** *a.* 1. operated by push button 2. initiated as simply as by pressing button —**´pushchair** *n.* (collapsible) chair-shaped carriage for baby —**´pushover** *n. sl.* 1. something easily achieved 2. person *etc.* easily taken advantage of or defeated —**push-start** *vt.* 1. start (motor vehicle) by pushing while in gear, thus turning engine —*n.* 2. this process

pusillanimous (pjuːsɪ´lænɪməs) *a.* cowardly —**pusilla´nimity** *n.*

puss (pʊs) *n.* cat (*also* **´pussy**) —**pussy willow** willow tree with silvery silky catkins

pussyfoot (´pʊsɪfʊt) *vi. inf.* 1. move stealthily 2. act indecisively, procrastinate

pustule (´pʌstjuːl) *n.* pimple containing pus —**´pustular** *a.* —**pustulate** (´pʌstjulet) *v.* 1. (cause to) form into pustules —*a.* (´pʌstjulit) 2. covered with pustules

put (pʊt) *vt.* 1. place 2. set 3. express 4. throw (*esp.* shot) (**put, ´putting**) —*n.* 5. throw —**put across** express successfully —**put-down** *n.* cruelly critical remark —**put-up** *a.* dishonestly or craftily prearranged (*esp.* in **put-up job**) —**put down** 1. make written record of 2. repress 3. consider 4. attribute 5. put (animal) to death because of old age or illness 6. table on agenda 7. *sl.* reject, humiliate —**put off** 1. postpone 2. disconcert 3. repel —**put up** 1. erect 2. accommodate 3. nominate

putative (´pjuːtətɪv) *a.* reputed, supposed —**´putatively** *adv.*

putrid (´pjuːtrɪd) *a.* 1. decomposed 2. rotten —**´putrefy** *v.* make or become rotten (**-efied, -efying**) —**putre´faction** *n.* —**pu´trescence** *n.* —**pu´trescent** *a.* becoming rotten —**pu´tridity** *n.*

Putsch (pʊtʃ) *n.* surprise attempt to overthrow the existing power, political revolt

putt (pʌt) *vt.* strike (golf ball) along ground in direction of hole —**´putter** *n.* golf club for putting —**putting green** 1. on golf course, area of closely mown grass at end of fairway where hole is 2. area of smooth grass with several holes for putting games

puttee or **putty** (´pʌtɪ) *n.* strip of cloth wound round leg like bandage, serving as gaiter

putty (´pʌtɪ) *n.* 1. paste of whiting and oil as used by glaziers 2. jeweller's polishing powder —*vt.* 3. fix, fill with putty (**-ied, -ying**)

puzzle (´pʌzəl) *v.* 1. perplex or be perplexed —*n.* 2. bewildering, perplexing question, problem or toy —**´puzzlement** *n.*

PVC polyvinyl chloride (synthetic thermoplastic material used in insulation, shoes *etc.*)

pyaemia or **pyemia** (paɪ´iːmɪə) *n.* form of blood poisoning —**py´aemic** or **py´emic** *a.*

pye-dog or **pie-dog** (´paɪdɒg) *n.* ownerless half-wild Asian dog

pygmy or **pigmy** (´pɪgmɪ) *n.* 1. abnormally undersized person 2. (**P-**) member of one of dwarf peoples of Equatorial Afr. —*a.* 3. undersized

pyjamas or U.S. **pajamas** (pə´dʒɑːməz) *pl.n.* sleeping suit of trousers and jacket

pylon (´paɪlən) *n.* towerlike erection, *esp.* to carry electric cables

pyo- or before vowel **py-** (*comb. form*) pus, as in *pyosis*

pyorrhoea or esp. U.S. **pyorrhea** (paıə'rıə) n. inflammation of the gums with discharge of pus and loosening of teeth

pyramid ('pırəmıd) n. **1.** solid figure with sloping sides meeting at apex **2.** structure of this shape, esp. ancient Egyptian **3.** group of persons or things highest in the middle —**py'ramidal** a. —**pyramid selling** practice adopted by some manufacturers of advertising for distributors and selling them batches of goods. The first distributors then advertise for more distributors who are sold subdivisions of original batches at increased price. This process continues until final distributors are left with stock that is unsaleable except at loss

pyre (paıə) n. pile of wood for burning a dead body

pyrethrum (paı'riːθrəm) n. **1.** any of several types of cultivated chrysanthemums **2.** insecticide made from it

pyretic (paı'rɛtık) a. Pathol. of fever

Pyrex ('paırɛks) n. **R** glassware resistant to heat

pyrite ('paıraıt) n. yellow mineral consisting of iron sulphide in cubic crystalline form

pyrites (paı'raıtiːz) n. **1.** see PYRITE **2.** any of a number of other disulphides of metals, esp. of copper and tin (pl. **py'rites**)

pyro- or before vowel **pyr-** (comb. form) **1.** fire or heat, as in pyromania, pyrometer **2.** Chem. new substance obtained by heating another, as in pyroboric acid **3.** Min. having property that changes upon application of heat; having flame-coloured appearance, as in pyroxylin

pyrogenic (paırəʊ'dʒɛnık) or **pyrogenous** (paı'rodʒınəs) a. **1.** produced by or producing heat **2.** causing or resulting from fever

pyrography (paı'rogrəfı) n. **1.** art of burning designs on wood or leather with heated tools **2.** design made by this process

pyromania (paırəʊ'meınıə) n. Psych. uncontrollable impulse and practice of setting things on fire —**pyro'maniac** n.

pyrometer (paı'romıtə) n. instrument for measuring very high temperature —**py'rometry** n.

pyrotechnics (paırəʊ'tɛknıks) pl.n. **1.** (with sing. v.) manufacture of fireworks **2.** (with sing. or pl. v.) firework display —**pyro'technist** n.

Pyrrhic victory ('pırık) victory won at high cost

Pythagoras' theorem (paı'θægərəs) theorem that in right-angled triangle square of length of hypotenuse equals sum of squares of other two sides

python ('paıθən) n. large nonpoisonous snake that crushes its prey —**'pythoness** n. woman, such as Apollo's priestess at Delphi, believed to

be possessed by oracular spirit —**pythonic** (paı'θonık) a.

pyx or **pix** (pıks) n. **1.** box in Brit. Royal Mint holding specimen coins kept to be tested for weight (also **pyx chest**) **2.** vessel in which consecrated Host is preserved

---

Q,q

q or **Q** (kjuː) n. **1.** 17th letter of English alphabet **2.** speech sound represented by this letter (pl. **q's, Q's** or **Qs**)

Q 1. Chess Queen **2.** Question

q. 1. quart **2.** quarter **3.** quarto (pl. **qq., Qq.**) (also **Q.**) **4.** question

Q.C. Queen's Counsel

Q.E.D. quod erat demonstrandum (Lat., which was to be proved)

Qld. Queensland

Q.M. Quartermaster

qr. 1. quarter **2.** quire (pl. **qrs.**)

qt. 1. quart (pl. **qt., qts.**) **2.** quantity

q.t. inf. quiet —**on the q.t.** secretly

qua (kweı, kwaː) prep. in the capacity of

quack (kwæk) n. **1.** harsh cry of duck **2.** pretender to medical or other skill —vi. **3.** (of duck) utter cry

quad (kwɒd) n. **1.** quadrangle **2.** quadrant **3.** quadraphonic **4.** quadruplet

quadrangle ('kwɒdræŋgəl) n. **1.** four-sided figure **2.** four-sided courtyard in a building —**quad'rangular** a.

quadrant ('kwɒdrənt) n. **1.** quarter of circle **2.** instrument for taking angular measurements —**quad'rate** vt. make square —**quadratic** (kwɒ'drætık) a. (of equation) involving square of unknown quantity

quadraphonic or **quadrophonic** (kwɒdrə'fonık) a. (of a sound system) using four independent speakers

quadrennial (kwɒ'drɛnıəl) a. **1.** occurring every four years **2.** lasting four years —n. **3.** period of four years

quadri- or before vowel **quadr-** (comb. form) four

quadrilateral (kwɒdrı'lætərəl) a. **1.** four-sided —n. **2.** four-sided figure

quadrille (kwɒ'drıl, kwə-) n. **1.** square dance **2.** music played for it **3.** old card game

quadrillion (kwɒ'drıljən) n. **1.** in Brit. and Germany, number represented as one followed by 24 zeros (10^{24}) **2.** in Amer. and France, number represented as one followed by 15 zeros (10^{15}) (pl. **-s, quad'rillion**) —**quad'rillionth** a.

quadriplegia (kwɒdrı'pliːdʒıə) n. paralysis of

all four limbs (*also* tetra'plegia) —**quadri-**
'**plegic** *a.*

quadrivalent (kwɒdrɪ'veɪlənt) *a. Chem.*
having four valencies (*also* tetra'valent)
—**quadri'valency** *or* **quadri'valence** *n.*

quadruped ('kwɒdrʊped) *n.* four-footed animal —**quad'rupedal** *a.*

quadruple ('kwɒdrʊpəl, kwɒ'druːpəl) *a.* 1.
fourfold —*v.* 2. make, become four times as
much —**quad'ruplicate** *a.* fourfold

quadruplet ('kwɒdrʊplɪt, kwɒ'druːplɪt) *n.* one
of four offspring born at one birth

quaff (kwɒf) *v.* drink heartily or in one draught

quag (kwæg) *n.* bog, swamp

quagga ('kwægə) *n.* recently extinct member
of horse family

quail[1] (kweɪl) *n.* small bird of partridge family

quail[2] (kweɪl) *vi.* flinch; cower

quaint (kweɪnt) *a.* 1. interestingly old-fashioned
or odd 2. curious 3. whimsical —'**quaintly** *adv.*
—'**quaintness** *n.*

quake (kweɪk) *vi.* shake, tremble

Quaker ('kweɪkə) *n.* member of Christian sect,
the **Society of Friends** ('**Quakeress** *fem.*)

qualify ('kwɒlɪfaɪ) *vi.* 1. make oneself
competent —*vt.* 2. moderate 3. limit 4. make
competent 5. ascribe quality to 6. describe
(-**fied, -fying**) —**qualifi'cation** *n.* 1. thing that
qualifies, attribute 2. restriction 3. qualifying

quality ('kwɒlɪtɪ) *n.* 1. attribute, characteristic,
property 2. degree of excellence 3. rank
—'**qualitative** *a.* depending on quality —**qualitative analysis** *Chem.* decomposition of
substance to determine kinds of constituents
present; result obtained by such determination
—**quality control** control of relative quality of
manufactured product, usu. by statistical
sampling techniques

qualm (kwɑːm) *n.* 1. misgiving 2. sudden feeling
of sickness —'**qualmish** *a.*

quandary ('kwɒndərɪ) *n.* state of perplexity;
puzzling situation; dilemma

quango ('kwæŋgəʊ) *n.* quasi-autonomous
national government (*or* nongovernmental)
organization (*pl.* -**s**)

quantity ('kwɒntɪtɪ) *n.* 1. size, number, amount
2. specified or considerable amount —'**quantify**
vt. discover, express quantity of —'**quantitative**
a. involving considerations of amount or size
2. capable of being measured 3. *Prosody* of
metrical system based on length of syllables
—'**quantum** *n.* desired or required amount (*pl.*
-**ta**) —**quantitative analysis** *Chem.* decomposition of substance to determine amount of each
constituent; result obtained by such determination —**quantity surveyor** one who estimates
cost of materials, labour for building job
—**quantum theory** theory that in radiation,

energy of electrons is discharged not
continuously but in discrete units or quanta

quarantine ('kwɒrəntiːn) *n.* 1. isolation to
prevent spreading of infection —*vt.* 2. put, keep
in quarantine

quark (kwɑːk) *n. Phys.* any of several
hypothetical particles thought to be fundamental units of matter

quarrel[1] ('kwɒrəl) *n.* 1. angry dispute 2.
argument —*vi.* 3. argue 4. find fault (-**ll**-)
—'**quarrelsome** *a.*

quarrel[2] ('kwɒrəl) *n.* 1. crossbow arrow 2.
diamond-shaped pane

quarry[1] ('kwɒrɪ) *n.* 1. object of hunt or pursuit
2. prey

quarry[2] ('kwɒrɪ) *n.* 1. excavation where stone
etc. is got from ground for building *etc.* —*v.* 2.
get (stone *etc.*) from quarry ('**quarried,
'quarrying**)

quart (kwɔːt) *n.* liquid measure equal to quarter
of gallon or 2 pints (1.1 litres)

quarter ('kwɔːtə) *n.* 1. fourth part 2. US, C 25
cents 3. unit of weight, 28 lbs. 4. region, district 5.
mercy —*pl.* 6. lodgings —*vt.* 7. divide into
quarters —*v.* 8. billet or be billeted in lodgings
—'**quarterly** *a.* 1. happening, due *etc.* each
quarter of year —*n.* 2. quarterly periodical
—**quar'tet** *or* **quar'tette** *n.* 1. group of four
musicians 2. music for four performers
—'**quarto** *n.* 1. size of book in which sheets are
folded into four leaves (*pl.* -**s**) —*a.* 2. of this size
—**quarter day** any of four days in the year when
certain payments become due —'**quarterdeck**
n. after part of upper deck used *esp.* for official,
ceremonial purposes —**quarter'final** *n.* round
before semifinal in competition —**quarter horse**
small, powerful breed of horse —'**quarterlight**
n. **UK** small pivoted window in door of car
—'**quartermaster** *n.* 1. officer responsible for
stores 2. rating in navy, usu. petty officer, with
particular responsibility for navigational duties
—'**quarterstaff** *n.* long staff for fighting (*pl.*
-**staves**)

quartz (kwɔːts) *n.* stone of pure crystalline
silica —'**quartzite** *n.* quartz rock

quasar ('kweɪzɑː, -sɑː) *n.* extremely distant
starlike object emitting powerful radio waves

quash (kwɒʃ) *vt.* 1. annul 2. reject 3. subdue
forcibly

quasi- (*comb. form*) seemingly, resembling but
not actually being, as in *quasi-scientific*

quassia ('kwɒʃə) *n.* tropical Amer. tree

quaternary (kwə'tɜːnərɪ) *a.* 1. of the number
four 2. having four parts 3. (**Q-**) *Geol.* of most
recent period, after Tertiary —*n.* 4. (**Q-**)
Quaternary period or rock system

quatrain ('kwɒtreɪn) *n.* four-line stanza, *esp.*
rhymed alternately

quatrefoil ('kætrəfɔil) n. 1. leaf composed of four leaflets 2. *Archit.* carved ornament having four arcs arranged about common centre

quaver ('kweivə) vt. 1. say or sing in quavering tones —vi. 2. tremble, shake, vibrate —n. 3. musical note half length of crotchet 4. quavering trill

quay (kiː) n. 1. solid, fixed landing stage 2. wharf

queasy ('kwiːzi) a. inclined to, or causing, sickness

queen (kwiːn) n. 1. king's wife 2. female sovereign 3. piece in chess 4. fertile female bee, wasp *etc.* 5. court card with picture of a queen, ranking between king and jack 6. *inf.* male homosexual —'**queenly** a./adv. —**Queen-Anne** (æn) n. 1. style of furniture popular in early 18th century, characterized by use of curves, cabriole leg *etc.* —a. 2. in or of this style 3. of style of architecture popular in early 18th-century England, characterized by red-brick construction with classical ornamentation —**queen consort** wife of reigning king —**queen dowager** widow of king —**queen mother** widow of former king who is also mother of reigning sovereign —**Queen's Bench** one of the divisions of the High Court in England —**Queen's Counsel** 1. in England when sovereign is female, barrister appointed Counsel to Crown on recommendation of Lord Chancellor 2. in Canad., honorary title which may be bestowed by government on lawyers with long experience —**Queen's English** when Brit. sovereign is female, standard S Brit. English —**queen's evidence** evidence given by criminal against his accomplice(s) —**queen's highway** 1. in Brit. when sovereign is female, any public road or right of way 2. in Canad., main road maintained by provincial government

Queensberry rules ('kwiːnzbəri) 1. code of rules followed in modern boxing 2. *inf.* gentlemanly conduct, *esp.* in dispute

queer (kwiə) a. 1. odd, strange 2. *inf.* homosexual —n. 3. *inf.* homosexual —vt. *inf.* 4. spoil 5. interfere with

quell (kwɛl) vt. 1. crush, put down 2. allay 3. pacify

quench (kwɛntʃ) vt. 1. slake 2. extinguish, put out 3. suppress

quern (kwɜːn) n. stone hand mill

querulous ('kwɛrʊləs, 'kwɛrjʊ-) a. 1. fretful 2. peevish, whining

query ('kwiəri) n. 1. question 2. mark of interrogation —vt. 3. question ('**queried**, '**querying**)

quest (kwɛst) n./vi. search

question ('kwɛstʃən) n. 1. sentence seeking for answer 2. that which is asked 3. interrogation 4.

inquiry 5. problem 6. point for debate 7. debate, strife —vt. 8. ask questions of, interrogate 9. dispute 10. doubt —'**questionable** a. doubtful, *esp.* not clearly true or honest —**questionnaire** (kwɛstʃə'nɛə, kɛs-) n. list of questions drawn up for formal answer —**question mark** 1. punctuation mark **?**, used at end of questions *etc.* where doubt or ignorance is implied 2. this mark used for any other purpose, as to draw attention to possible mistake (*also* **interrogation mark**) —**question time** in parliamentary bodies of British type, time set aside each day for questions to government ministers

queue (kjuː) n. 1. line of waiting persons, vehicles —vi. 2. (*with* up) wait in queue

quibble ('kwibl) n. 1. trivial objection —vi. 2. make this

quiche (kiːʃ) n. open savoury tart

quick (kwik) a. 1. rapid, swift 2. keen 3. brisk 4. hasty —n. 5. sensitive flesh 6. innermost feelings (*esp.* in **cut to the quick**) —adv. 7. *inf.* rapidly —'**quicken** v. make, become faster or more lively —'**quickie** n. *inf.* a quick one —'**quickly** adv. —'**quicklime** n. calcium oxide —'**quicksand** n. loose wet sand easily yielding to pressure and engulfing persons, animals *etc.* —'**quickset** *chiefly UK* n. 1. plant or cutting, *esp.* of hawthorn, set so as to form hedge; such plants or cuttings collectively 2. hedge composed of such plants —a. 3. composed of such plants —'**quicksilver** n. mercury —'**quickstep** n. 1. ballroom dance —vi. 2. perform this dance —**quick-tempered** a. irascible —**quick-witted** a. having keenly alert mind —**quick-wittedness** n. —**the quick** *obs.* living people

quid[1] (kwid) n. piece of tobacco suitable for chewing

quid[2] (kwid) n. *inf.* pound (sterling) (*pl.* **quid**)

quiddity ('kwiditi) n. 1. essential nature 2. petty or trifling distinction; quibble

quid pro quo ('kwid prəʊ 'kwəʊ) *Lat.* something given in exchange (*pl.* **quid pro quos**)

quiescent (kwi'ɛsənt) a. 1. at rest, inactive, inert 2. silent —**qui'escence** *or* **qui'escency** n.

quiet ('kwaiət) a. 1. with little or no motion or noise 2. undisturbed 3. not showy or obtrusive —n. 4. state of peacefulness, absence of noise or disturbance —v. 5. make, become quiet —'**quieten** v. make, become quiet —'**quietly** adv. —'**quietness** *or* '**quietude** n.

quietism ('kwaiətizəm) n. passive attitude to life, *esp.* as form of religion —'**quietist** n.

quietus (kwai'iːtəs, -'eitəs) n. 1. anything that serves to quash, eliminate or kill 2. release from life; death 3. discharge or settlement of debts, duties *etc.*

quiff (kwɪf) *n.* UK tuft of hair brushed up above forehead

quill (kwɪl) *n.* **1.** large feather **2.** hollow stem of this **3.** pen, plectrum made from feather **4.** spine of porcupine

quilt (kwɪlt) *n.* **1.** padded coverlet —*vt.* **2.** stitch (two pieces of cloth) with pad between

quin (kwɪn) quintuplet

quince (kwɪns) *n.* **1.** acid pear-shaped fruit **2.** tree bearing it

quincunx ('kwɪŋkʌŋks) *n.* group of five objects arranged in shape of rectangle with one at each corner and fifth in centre

quinine (kwɪ'niːn; *U.S.* 'kwaɪnaɪn) *n.* bitter drug made from bark of tree, used to treat fever, and as tonic

Quinquagesima (kwɪŋkwə'dʒɛsɪmə) *n.* Sunday 50 days before Easter

quinquennial (kwɪŋ'kwɛnɪəl) *a.* occurring once in, or lasting, five years

quinquereme ('kwɪŋkwɪriːm) *n.* ancient Roman galley with five banks of oars

quinsy ('kwɪnzɪ) *n.* inflammation of throat or tonsils

quintessence (kwɪn'tɛsəns) *n.* **1.** purest form, essential feature **2.** embodiment —**quintes'sential** *a.*

quintet *or* **quintette** (kwɪn'tɛt) *n.* **1.** set of five singers or players **2.** composition for five voices or instruments

quintillion (kwɪn'tɪljən) *n.* **1.** in Brit. and Germany, number represented as one followed by 30 zeros (10^{30}) **2.** in Amer. and France, number represented as one followed by 18 zeros (10^{18}) (*pl.* **-s, quin'tillion**) —**quin'tillionth** *a.*

quintuple ('kwɪntjupəl, kwɪn'tjuːpəl) *vt.* **1.** multiply by five —*a.* **2.** five times as much or as many; fivefold **3.** consisting of five parts —*n.* **4.** quantity or number five times as great as another

quintuplet ('kwɪntjuplɪt, kwɪn'tjuːplɪt) *n.* one of five offspring born at one birth

quip (kwɪp) *n.* **1.** witty saying —*vi.* **2.** make quip (-**pp-**)

quire (kwaɪə) *n.* 24 sheets of writing paper

quirk (kwɜːk) *n.* **1.** individual peculiarity of character **2.** unexpected twist or turn

quisling ('kwɪzlɪŋ) *n.* traitor who aids occupying enemy force

quit (kwɪt) *vi.* **1.** stop doing a thing **2.** depart —*vt.* **3.** leave, go away from **4.** cease from (**quit** *or* **'quitted** *pt./pp.*) —*a.* **5.** free, rid —**quits** *a.* on equal or even terms by repayment *etc.* —**'quittance** *n.* **1.** discharge **2.** receipt —**'quitter** *n.* one lacking perseverance

quitch grass (kwɪtʃ) *see* COUCH GRASS

quite (kwaɪt) *adv.* **1.** wholly, completely **2.** very

considerably **3.** somewhat, rather —*interj.* **4.** exactly, just so

quiver[1] ('kwɪvə) *vi.* **1.** shake, tremble —*n.* **2.** quivering **3.** vibration

quiver[2] ('kwɪvə) *n.* carrying case for arrows

quixotic (kwɪk'sɒtɪk) *a.* unrealistically and impractically optimistic, idealistic, chivalrous

quiz (kwɪz) *n.* **1.** entertainment in which general or specific knowledge of players is tested by questions **2.** examination, interrogation —*vt.* **3.** question, interrogate (-**zz**-) —'**quizzical** *a.* **1.** questioning **2.** mocking

quod (kwɒd) *n. sl.* prison

quoin (kɔɪn, kwɔɪn) *n.* **1.** external corner of building **2.** small wedge for locking printing type into forme

quoit (kɔɪt) *n.* **1.** ring for throwing at peg as a game —*pl.* **2.** (*with sing. v.*) the game

quondam ('kwɒndæm) *a.* of an earlier time; former

quorum ('kwɔːrəm) *n.* least number that must be present in meeting to make its transactions valid

quota ('kwəʊtə) *n.* **1.** share to be contributed or received **2.** specified number, quantity, which may be imported or admitted

quote (kwəʊt) *vt.* **1.** copy or repeat passages from **2.** refer to, *esp.* to confirm view **3.** state price for —'**quotable** *a.* —**quo'tation** *n.* —**quotation mark** either of punctuation marks used to begin or end quotation, respectively " and " or ' and '

quoth (kwəʊθ) *v. obs.* said

quotidian (kwəʊ'tɪdɪən) *a.* **1.** daily **2.** everyday, commonplace

quotient ('kwəʊʃənt) *n.* number resulting from dividing one number by another

q.v. quod vide (*Lat.*, which see)

qwerty *or* **QWERTY** ('kwɜːtɪ) *n. inf.* standard typewriter keyboard

R,r

r *or* **R** (ɑː) *n.* **1.** 18th letter of English alphabet **2.** speech sound represented by this letter (*pl.* **r's, R's** *or* **Rs**) —**the three Rs** three skills regarded as fundamentals of education: reading, writing and arithmetic

R 1. *Chem.* radical **2.** rand **3.** rupee **4.** Réaumur (scale) **5.** *Phys., electron.* resistance **6.** roentgen *or* röntgen **7.** *Chess* rook **8.** Royal **9.** *Chem.* gas constant **10.** radius

R. 1. Regina (*Lat.*, Queen) **2.** Rex (*Lat.*, King) **3.** River

Ra *Chem.* radium

R.A. 1. Rear Admiral **2.** Royal Academy **3.** Royal Artillery

R.A.A.F. Royal Australian Air Force

rabbet ('ræbɪt) see REBATE²

rabbi ('ræbaɪ) *n.* Jewish learned man, spiritual leader (*pl.* **-s**) —**rabbinical** (rə'bɪnɪkəl) *or* **rab'binic** *a.*

rabbit ('ræbɪt) *n.* **1.** small burrowing rodent like hare —*vi.* **2.** hunt rabbits —**rabbit punch** sharp blow to back of neck

rabble ('ræbəl) *n.* **1.** crowd of vulgar, noisy people **2.** mob —**rabble-rouser** *n.* person who manipulates passions of mob; demagogue

Rabelaisian (ræbə'leɪzɪən, -ʒən) *a.* **1.** of or resembling work of François Rabelais, Fr. writer, characterized by broad, oft. bawdy humour and sharp satire —*n.* **2.** student or admirer of Rabelais

rabid ('ræbɪd, 'reɪ-) *a.* **1.** relating to or having rabies **2.** furious **3.** mad **4.** fanatical —'**rabidly** *adv.* —'**rabidness** *n.*

rabies ('reɪbiːz) *n. Pathol.* acute infectious viral disease transmitted by dogs *etc.*

R.A.C. 1. Royal Automobile Club **2.** Royal Armoured Corps

raccoon *or* **racoon** (rə'kuːn) *n.* small N Amer. mammal

race¹ (reɪs) *n.* **1.** contest of speed, as in running, swimming *etc.* **2.** contest, rivalry **3.** strong current of water, *esp.* leading to water wheel —*pl.* **4.** meeting for horse racing —*vt.* **5.** cause to run rapidly —*vi.* **6.** run swiftly **7.** (of engine, pedal *etc.*) move rapidly and erratically, *esp.* on removal of resistance —'**racer** *n.* person, vehicle, animal that races —'**racecourse** *n.* long broad track, over which horses are raced (*also* (*esp.* **US**) '**racetrack**) —**race meeting** prearranged fixture for racing horses *etc.* over set course —'**racetrack** *n.* **1.** circuit for motor racing *etc.* **2.** *esp.* **US** racecourse

race² (reɪs) *n.* **1.** group of people of common ancestry with distinguishing physical features, skin colour *etc.* **2.** species **3.** type —'**racial** *a.* —'**racialism** *or* '**racism** *n.* **1.** belief in innate superiority of particular race **2.** antagonism towards members of different race based on this belief —'**racialist** *or* '**racist** *a./n.* —**race relations 1.** (*with pl. v.*) relations between members of two or more human races, *esp.* within single community **2.** (*with sing. v.*) branch of sociology concerned with such relations —**race riot** riot among members of different races in same community

raceme (rə'siːm) *n.* cluster of flowers along a central stem, as in foxglove

rack¹ (ræk) *n.* **1.** framework for displaying or holding baggage, books, hats, bottles *etc.* **2.** *Mech.* straight bar with teeth on its edge, to work with pinion **3.** instrument of torture by stretching —*vt.* **4.** stretch on rack or wheel **5.** torture **6.** stretch, strain —'**racking** *a.* agonizing —**rack-and-pinion** *n.* **1.** device for converting rotary into linear motion and vice versa, in which gearwheel (pinion) engages with flat toothed bar (rack) —*a.* **2.** (of type of steering gear in motor vehicles) having track rod with rack along part of its length that engages with pinion attached to steering column —**rack railway** mountain railway having middle rail fitted with rack that engages pinion on locomotive (*also* **cog railway**) —**rack-rent** *n.* **1.** high rent that annually equals value of property upon which it is charged **2.** any extortionate rent —*vt.* **3.** charge extortionate rent for

rack² (ræk) *n.* destruction (*esp. in* **rack and ruin**)

rack³ *or* **wrack** (ræk) *n.* broken mass of clouds blown by wind

rack⁴ (ræk) *vt.* clear (wine, beer *etc.*) by drawing it off from dregs

rack⁵ (ræk) *n.* neck or rib section of mutton, lamb or pork

racket¹ ('rækɪt) *n.* **1.** loud noise, uproar **2.** occupation by which money is made illegally —**racket'eer** *n.* one making illegal profits —**racket'eering** *n.* —'**rackety** *a.* noisy

racket² *or* **racquet** ('rækɪt) *n.* **1.** bat used in tennis *etc.* —*pl.n.* **2.** (*with sing. v.*) ball game played in paved, walled court

raconteur (rækən'tɜː) *n.* skilled storyteller

racy ('reɪsɪ) *a.* **1.** spirited **2.** lively **3.** having strong flavour **4.** spicy **5.** piquant —'**racily** *adv.* —'**raciness** *n.*

RADA ('rɑːdə) **UK** Royal Academy of Dramatic Art

radar ('reɪdɑː) *n.* device for finding range and direction by ultrahigh-frequency point-to-point radio waves, which reflect back to their source and reveal position and nature of objects sought —**radar trap** device using radar to detect motorists exceeding speed limit

raddled ('rædəld) *a.* (*esp.* of person) unkempt or run-down in appearance

radial ('reɪdɪəl) *a. see* RADIUS

radiate ('reɪdɪeɪt) *v.* **1.** emit, be emitted in rays —*vi.* **2.** spread out from centre —'**radiance** *n.* **1.** brightness **2.** splendour —'**radiant** *a.* **1.** beaming **2.** shining **3.** emitting rays —*n.* **4.** point or object that emits radiation, *esp.* part of heater that gives out heat **5.** *Astron.* the point in space from which a meteor shower appears to emanate —**radi'ation** *n.* **1.** transmission of heat, light *etc.* from one body to another **2.** particles, rays, emitted in nuclear decay **3.** act of radiating —'**radiator** *n.* **1.** that which radiates, *esp.* heating apparatus for rooms **2.** cooling apparatus of car engine —**radiant energy** energy emitted or propagated in form of particles or electromagnetic radiation —**radiation sickness** *Pathol.* illness caused by overexposure of body to ionizing radiations from radioactive material *etc.*

radical ('rædɪkᵊl) *a.* **1.** fundamental, thorough **2.** extreme **3.** *Maths.* of roots of numbers or quantities —*n.* **4.** person of extreme (political) views **5.** radicle **6.** *Maths.* number expressed as root of another **7.** group of atoms of several elements which remain unchanged in a series of chemical compounds —**radicalism** *n.* —**radical sign** symbol √ placed before number or quantity to indicate extraction of root, *esp.* square root

radicle ('rædɪkᵊl) *n. Bot.* root

radio ('reɪdɪəʊ) *n.* **1.** use of electromagnetic waves for broadcasting, communication *etc.* **2.** device for receiving, amplifying radio signals **3.** broadcasting, content of radio programmes —*vt.* **4.** transmit (message *etc.*) by radio —**radio'active** *a.* emitting invisible rays that penetrate matter —**radioac'tivity** *n.* —**radio astronomy** astronomy in which radio telescope is used to detect and analyse radio signals received on earth from radio sources in space —**radiocarbon dating** technique for determining age of organic materials based on their content of radioisotope ¹⁴C acquired from atmosphere when they formed part of living plant (*see also* **carbon dating** *at* CARBON) —**radio'chemical** *a.* —**radio'chemist** *n.* —**radio'chemistry** *n.* chemistry of radioactive elements and their compounds —**radio frequency 1.** any frequency that lies in range 10 kilohertz to 300 000 megahertz and can be used for broadcasting **2.** frequency transmitted by particular radio station —**radiogram** *n.* **1.** UK unit comprising radio and gramophone **2.** message transmitted by radiotelegraphy **3.** radiograph —**radiograph** *n.* image produced on sensitized film or plate by radiation —**radi'ographer** *n.* —**radi'ography** *n.* production of image on film or plate by radiation —**radio'isotope** *n.* radioactive isotope —**radi'ologist** *n.* —**radi'ology** *n.* science of use of rays in medicine —**radioscopic** (reɪdɪəʊ'skɒpɪk) *a.* —**radi'oscopy** *n. see* **fluoroscopy** *at* FLUORESCENCE —**radiosonde** ('reɪdɪəʊsɒnd) *n.* airborne instrument to send meteorological information back to earth by radio —**radio'telegraph** *v./n.* —**radiote'legraphy** *n.* telegraphy in which messages (usu. in Morse code) are transmitted by radio waves —**radio'telephone** *n.* **1.** device for communications by means of radio waves —*v.* **2.** telephone (person) by radiotelephone —**radiote'lephony** *n.* —**radio telescope** instrument used in radio astronomy to pick up and analyse radio waves from space and to transmit radio waves —**radio'therapy** *n.* diagnosis and treatment of disease by x-rays

radio- (*comb. form*) **1.** denoting radio, broadcasting or radio frequency, as in *radiogram* **2.** indicating radioactivity or radiation, as in *radiochemistry*

radish ('rædɪʃ) *n.* pungent root vegetable

radium ('reɪdɪəm) *n.* radioactive metallic element

radius ('reɪdɪəs) *n.* **1.** straight line from centre to circumference of circle **2.** outer of two bones in forearm (*pl.* **radii** ('reɪdɪaɪ), **-es**) —**radial** *a.* **1.** arranged like radii of circle **2.** of ray or rays **3.** of radius —'**radian** *n.* SI unit of plane angle; angle between two radii of circle that cut off on circumference arc equal in length to radius —**radial-ply** *a.* (of motor tyre) having fabric cords in outer casing running radially, enabling sidewalls to be flexible

radon ('reɪdɒn) *n.* radioactive gaseous element

RAF (*nonstandard* ræf) *or* **R.A.F.** Royal Air Force

raffia *or* **raphia** ('ræfɪə) *n.* prepared palm fibre for making mats *etc.*

raffish ('ræfɪʃ) *a.* disreputable

raffle ('ræfᵊl) *n.* **1.** lottery in which an article is assigned by lot to one of those buying tickets —*vt.* **2.** dispose of by raffle

raft (rɑːft) *n.* floating structure of logs, planks *etc.*

rafter ('rɑːftə) *n.* one of main beams of roof

rag¹ (ræg) *n.* **1.** fragment of cloth **2.** torn piece **3.** *inf.* newspaper *etc.*, *esp.* one considered worthless **4.** piece of ragtime music —*pl.* **5.** tattered clothing —**ragged** ('rægɪd) *a.* **1.** shaggy **2.** torn **3.** clothed in torn clothes **4.** lacking smoothness —**rag-and-bone man** UK man who buys and sells discarded clothing *etc.* —**ragbag** *n.* confused assortment —'**ragtag** *n. derogatory* common people; rabble (*esp. in* **ragtag and bobtail**) —'**ragtime** *n.* style of jazz piano music —**rag trade** *inf.* clothing industry, trade —'**ragwort** *n.* European plant with yellow daisylike flowers (*see also* GROUNDSEL)

rag² (ræg) *vt.* **1.** tease **2.** torment **3.** play practical jokes on (**-gg-**) —*n.* **4.** period of carnival with procession *etc.* organized by students to raise money for charities

rag³ (ræg) *Jazz n.* **1.** piece of ragtime music —*vt.* **2.** compose or perform in ragtime (**-gg-**)

ragamuffin ('rægəmʌfɪn) *n.* ragged, dirty person

rage (reɪdʒ) *n.* **1.** violent anger or passion **2.** fury —*vi.* **3.** speak, act with fury **4.** proceed violently and without check (as storm, battle *etc.*) **5.** be widely and violently prevalent —**all the rage** very popular

raglan ('ræglən) a. of sleeves that continue to the neck so that there are no shoulder seams

ragout (ræ'gu:) n. highly seasoned stew of meat and vegetables

raid (reid) n. 1. rush, attack 2. foray —vt. 3. make raid on —'**raider** n.

rail[1] (reil) n. horizontal bar, esp. as part of fence, track etc. —'**railing** n. fence, barrier made of rails supported by posts —'**railhead** n. farthest point to which railway line extends —'**railway** or U.S. '**railroad** n. 1. track of iron rails on which trains run 2. company operating railway —**off the rails** inf. 1. astray 2. on wrong track 3. in error 4. leading reckless, dissipated life

rail[2] (reil) vi. (with at or against) 1. utter abuse 2. scoff 3. scold 4. reproach —'**raillery** n. banter

rail[3] (reil) n. any of various kinds of marsh bird

raiment ('reimənt) n. obs. clothing

rain (rein) n. 1. moisture falling in drops from clouds 2. fall of such drops —vi. 3. fall as rain —vt. 4. pour down like rain —'**rainy** a. —'**rainbow** n. arch of prismatic colours in sky —'**raincoat** n. light water-resistant overcoat —'**rainfall** n. 1. precipitation in form of raindrops 2. Met. amount of precipitation in specified place and time —'**rainforest** n. dense forest found in tropical areas of heavy rainfall —**rain gauge** instrument for measuring rainfall —**rain shadow** relatively dry area on leeward side of high ground in path of rain-bearing winds —**rainy day** future time of need, esp. financial

raise (reiz) vt. 1. lift up 2. set up 3. build 4. increase 5. elevate 6. promote 7. heighten, as pitch of voice 8. breed into existence 9. levy, collect 10. end (siege)

raisin ('reizən) n. dried grape

raison d'être (rɛzɔ̃ 'dɛtr) Fr. reason or justification for existence (pl. **raisons d'être** (rɛzɔ̃ 'dɛtr))

raj (rɑːdʒ) n. rule, sway, esp. in India —'**rajah** or '**raja** n. Indian prince or ruler

rake[1] (reik) n. 1. tool with long handle and crosspiece with teeth for gathering hay, leaves etc. —vt. 2. gather, smooth with rake 3. sweep, search over 4. sweep with shot —**rake-off** n. inf. monetary commission, esp. illegal

rake[2] (reik) n. dissolute or dissipated man —'**rakish** a. dissolute; profligate

rake[3] (reik) n. 1. slope, esp. backwards, of ship's funnel etc. —v. 2. incline from perpendicular —'**rakish** a. appearing dashing or speedy

rally[1] ('ræli) vt. 1. bring together, esp. what has been scattered, as routed army or dispersed troops —vi. 2. come together 3. regain health or strength, revive ('**rallied**, '**rallying**) —n. 4. act of rallying 5. assembly, esp. outdoor, of any organization 6. Tennis lively exchange of strokes

rally[2] ('ræli) v. mock or ridicule (someone) in good-natured way; chaff; tease

ram (ræm) n. 1. male sheep 2. hydraulic machine 3. battering engine —vt. 4. force, drive 5. strike against with force 6. stuff 7. strike with ram (**-mm-**) —'**ramrod** n. 1. rod for cleaning barrel of rifle etc. 2. rod for ramming in charge of muzzle-loading firearm

RAM (ræm) Comp. random access memory

R.A.M. Royal Academy of Music

Ramadan, Rhamadhan (ræmə'dɑːn) or **Ramazan** (ræmə'zɑːn) n. 1. 9th Mohammedan month 2. strict fasting observed during this time

ramble ('ræmbəl) vi. 1. walk without definite route 2. wander 3. talk incoherently 4. spread in random fashion —n. 5. rambling walk —'**rambler** n. 1. climbing rose 2. one who rambles

rambutan (ræm'buːtən) n. 1. SE Asian tree 2. its bright red edible fruit

R.A.M.C. Royal Army Medical Corps

ramekin or **ramequin** ('ræmikin) n. 1. small fireproof dish 2. savoury food baked in it

ramify ('ræmifai) v. 1. spread in branches, subdivide —vi. 2. become complex (**-ified, -ifying**) —**ramifi'cation** n. 1. branch, subdivision 2. process of branching out 3. consequence

ramp (ræmp) n. gradual slope joining two level surfaces

rampage (ræm'peidʒ) vi. 1. dash about violently —n. ('ræmpeidʒ, ræm'peidʒ) 2. angry or destructive behaviour —**ram'pageous** a. —**on the rampage** behaving violently or destructively

rampant ('ræmpənt) a. 1. violent 2. rife 3. rearing

rampart ('ræmpɑːt) n. 1. mound, wall for defence —vt. 2. defend with rampart

rampike ('ræmpaik) n. C tall tree, burnt or bare of branches

ramshackle ('ræmʃækəl) a. tumbledown, rickety, makeshift

ran (ræn) pt. of RUN

ranch (rɑːntʃ) n. 1. Amer. cattle farm —vi. 2. manage a ranch —'**rancher** n.

rancherie ('rɑːntʃəri) n. C Indian reservation

rancid ('rænsid) a. (of food) having unpleasant smell or taste —**ran'cidity** n.

rancour or U.S. **rancor** ('ræŋkə) n. bitter, inveterate hate —'**rancorous** a. 1. malignant 2. virulent

rand (rænd, ront) n. monetary unit of S Afr.

R & B rhythm and blues

R & D research and development

random ('rændəm) *a.* made or done by chance, without plan —**at random** haphazard(ly)

randy ('rændɪ) *a. sl.* sexually aroused

rang (ræŋ) *pt. of* RING[2]

range (reɪndʒ) *n.* 1. limits 2. row 3. scope, sphere 4. distance missile can travel 5. distance of mark shot at 6. place for shooting practice or rocket testing 7. rank 8. kitchen stove —*vt.* 9. set in row 10. classify 11. roam —*vi.* 12. extend 13. roam 14. pass from one point to another 15. fluctuate (as prices) —**ranger** *n.* 1. official in charge of or patrolling park *etc.* 2. (R-) member of senior branch of Guides —**rangy** *a.* 1. with long, slender limbs 2. spacious —**rangefinder** *n.* instrument for finding distance away of given object

rani *or* **ranee** ('rɑːnɪ) *n.* queen or princess; wife of rajah

rank[1] (ræŋk) *n.* 1. row, line 2. place where taxis wait 3. order 4. social class 5. status 6. relative place or position —*pl.* 7. common soldiers 8. great mass or majority of people (*also* **rank and file**) —*vt.* 9. draw up in rank, classify —*vi.* 10. have rank, place 11. have certain distinctions

rank[2] (ræŋk) *a.* 1. growing too thickly, coarse 2. offensively strong 3. rancid 4. vile 5. flagrant —**rankly** *adv.*

rankle ('ræŋkəl) *vi.* fester, continue to cause anger, resentment or bitterness

ransack ('rænsæk) *vt.* search thoroughly 2. pillage, plunder

ransom ('rænsəm) *n.* 1. release from captivity by payment 2. amount paid —*vt.* 3. pay ransom for —**ransomer** *n.*

rant (rænt) *vi.* 1. rave in violent, high-sounding language —*n.* 2. noisy, boisterous speech 3. wild gaiety —**ranter** *n.*

ranunculus (rə'nʌŋkjʊləs) *n.* any of a genus of plants that includes buttercup, crowfoot and spearwort

rap[1] (ræp) *n.* 1. smart slight blow —*vt.* 2. give rap to (**-pp-**) —**take the rap** *sl.* suffer punishment, whether guilty or not

rap[2] (ræp) *n.* the least amount (*esp. in* **not to care a rap**)

rapacious (rə'peɪʃəs) *a.* 1. greedy 2. grasping —**rapacity** (rə'pæsɪtɪ) *n.*

rape[1] (reɪp) *vt.* 1. force (woman) to submit unwillingly to sexual intercourse —*n.* 2. act of raping 3. any violation or abuse

rape[2] (reɪp) *n.* plant with oil-yielding seeds, also used as fodder (*also* **colza, cole**)

rapid ('ræpɪd) *a.* 1. quick, swift —*pl.n.* 2. part of river with fast, turbulent current —**rapidity** *or* **rapidness** *n.* —**rapidly** *adv.* —**rapid eye movement** movement of eyeballs during sleep, while sleeper is dreaming

rapier ('reɪpɪə) *n.* fine-bladed sword used as thrusting weapon

rapine ('ræpaɪn) *n.* plunder

rapport (ræ'pɔː) *n.* harmony, agreement

rapprochement (rapro'ʃmɑ̃) *Fr.* re-establishment of friendly relations between nations

rapscallion (ræp'skæljən) *n.* rascal, rogue

rapt (ræpt) *a.* engrossed, spellbound —**rapture** *n.* ecstasy —**rapturous** *a.*

raptorial (ræp'tɔːrɪəl) *a.* 1. predatory 2. of the order of birds of prey

rare[1] (reə) *a.* 1. uncommon 2. infrequent 3. of uncommon quality 4. (of atmosphere) having low density, thin —**rarely** *adv.* seldom —**rarity** *n.* 1. anything rare 2. rareness —**rare earth** 1. any oxide of lanthanide 2. any element of lanthanide series (*also* **rare-earth element**)

rare[2] (reə) *a.* (of meat) lightly cooked

rarebit ('reəbɪt) *n.* savoury cheese dish (*also* **Welsh rabbit**)

rarefy ('reərɪfaɪ) *v.* 1. make, become thin, rare or less dense —*vt.* 2. refine (**-fied, -fying**) —**rarefaction** *or* **rarefication** *n.*

raring ('reərɪŋ) *a.* enthusiastically willing, ready

rascal ('rɑːskəl) *n.* 1. rogue 2. naughty (young) person —**rascality** *n.* roguery, baseness —**rascally** *a./adv.*

rase (reɪz) *vt.* see RAZE

rash[1] (ræʃ) *a.* hasty, reckless, incautious —**rashly** *adv.*

rash[2] (ræʃ) *n.* 1. skin eruption 2. outbreak, series of (unpleasant) occurrences

rasher ('ræʃə) *n.* thin slice of bacon or ham

rasp (rɑːsp) *n.* 1. harsh, grating noise 2. coarse file —*vt.* 3. scrape with rasp —*vi.* 4. grate upon 5. irritate 6. make scraping noise 7. speak in grating voice

raspberry ('rɑːzbərɪ, -brɪ) *n.* 1. red, juicy, edible berry 2. plant which bears it 3. *inf.* spluttering noise with tongue and lips to show contempt

Rastafarian (ræstə'feərɪən) *n.* 1. member of Jamaican cult that regards Ras Tafari, former emperor of Ethiopia, Haile Selassie, as God —*a.* 2. of Rastafarians —**Rasta** *n.* —**Rasta** *a./n.*

rat (ræt) *n.* 1. small rodent 2. *inf.* contemptible person, *esp.* deserter, informer *etc.* —*vi.* 3. inform 4. (with on) betray 5. (with on) desert, abandon 6. hunt rats (**-tt-**) —**ratter** *n.* 1. dog or cat that catches and kills rats 2. *inf.* worker who works during strike; blackleg; scab (*also* **rat**) —**ratty** *a. sl.* 1. mean, ill-tempered, irritable 2. (of hair) straggly, unkempt, greasy —**rat-catcher** *n.* one whose job is to drive away or destroy vermin, *esp.* rats —**rat race** continual hectic competitive activity —**ratsbane** *n.* rat poison, *esp.* arsenic oxide —**smell a rat** have suspicions of some treacherous practice

ratchet ('rætʃɪt) *n.* set of teeth on bar or wheel allowing motion in one direction only

rate¹ (reɪt) *n.* **1.** proportion between two things **2.** charge **3.** degree of speed *etc.* —*pl.* **4.** local tax on property —*vt.* **5.** value **6.** estimate value of **7.** assess for local taxation —**ratable** *or* **rateable** *a.* **1.** that can be rated **2.** liable to pay rates —'**ratepayer** *n.* —**ratable value** *or* **rateable value** UK fixed value assigned to property by local authority, on basis of which variable annual rates are charged

rate² (reɪt) *vt.* scold, chide

rather ('rɑːðə) *adv.* **1.** to some extent **2.** preferably **3.** more willingly

ratify ('rætɪfaɪ) *vt.* confirm (**-ified, -ifying**) —**ratifi'cation** *n.*

rating ('reɪtɪŋ) *n.* **1.** valuing or assessing **2.** fixing a rate **3.** classification, *esp.* of ship **4.** rank or grade as of naval personnel **5.** angry rebuke

ratio ('reɪʃɪəʊ) *n.* **1.** proportion **2.** quantitative relation

ratiocinate (rætɪ'ɒsɪneɪt) *vi.* reason —**ratioci-'nation** *n.*

ration ('ræʃən) *n.* **1.** fixed allowance of food *etc.* —*vt.* **2.** supply with, limit to certain amount

rational ('ræʃənl) *a.* **1.** reasonable, sensible **2.** capable of thinking, reasoning —**rationale** (ræʃə'nɑːl) *n.* reasons given for actions *etc.* —'**rationalism** *n.* philosophy which regards reason as only guide or authority —'**rationalist** *n.* —**ratio'nality** *n.* —**rationali'zation** *or* **-i'sation** *n.* —'**rationalize** *or* **-ise** *vt.* **1.** justify by plausible reasoning **2.** reorganize to improve efficiency *etc.* —'**rationally** *adv.*

ratline *or* **ratlin** ('rætlɪn) *n. Naut.* any of light lines tied across shrouds of sailing vessel for climbing aloft

rattan *or* **ratan** (ræ'tæn) *n.* **1.** climbing palm with jointed stems **2.** cane made of this

rattle ('rætl) *vi.* **1.** give out succession of short sharp sounds **2.** clatter —*vt.* **3.** shake briskly causing a sharp clatter of sounds **4.** *inf.* confuse, fluster —*n.* **5.** succession of short sharp sounds **6.** baby's toy filled with small pellets for making this sound **7.** set of horny rings in rattlesnake's tail —'**rattling** *adv. inf.* very —'**rattlesnake** *n.* poisonous snake —'**rattletrap** *n. inf.* broken-down old vehicle, *esp.* car

raucous ('rɔːkəs) *a.* **1.** hoarse **2.** harsh

raunchy ('rɔːntʃɪ) *a.* US *sl.* **1.** lecherous, smutty **2.** slovenly; dirty

ravage ('rævɪdʒ) *vt.* **1.** lay waste, plunder —*n.* **2.** destruction

rave (reɪv) *vi.* **1.** talk wildly, as in delirium **2.** write or speak (about) enthusiastically —*n.* **3.** enthusiastic or extravagant praise —'**raving** *a.*

1. delirious; frenzied **2.** *inf.* exciting admiration —*adv.* **3.** so as to cause raving —**rave-up** *n. sl.* party

ravel ('rævl) *vt.* **1.** entangle **2.** fray out **3.** disentangle (**-ll-**)

raven¹ ('reɪvən) *n.* black bird like crow —*a.* **2.** jet-black

raven² ('rævən) *v.* seek (prey, plunder) —'**ravening** *a.* (of animals) voracious; predatory —'**ravenous** *a.* very hungry

ravine (rə'viːn) *n.* narrow steep-sided valley worn by stream, gorge

ravioli (rævɪ'əʊlɪ) *n.* small, thin pieces of dough filled with highly seasoned, chopped meat and cooked

ravish ('rævɪʃ) *vt.* **1.** enrapture **2.** commit rape upon —'**ravishing** *a.* lovely, entrancing

raw (rɔː) *a.* **1.** uncooked **2.** not manufactured or refined **3.** skinned **4.** inexperienced, unpractised, as recruits **5.** sensitive **6.** chilly —'**raw'boned** *a.* having lean bony physique —**raw deal** unfair or dishonest treatment —'**rawhide** *n.* **1.** untanned hide **2.** whip made of this —**in the raw 1.** *inf.* without clothes; naked **2.** in natural or unmodified state

ray¹ (reɪ) *n.* **1.** single line or narrow beam of light, heat *etc.* **2.** any of set of radiating lines —*vi.* **3.** come out in rays **4.** radiate

ray² (reɪ) *n.* marine fish, oft. very large, with winglike pectoral fins and whiplike tail

ray³ (reɪ) *n. Mus.* in tonic solfa, second degree of any major scale; supertonic

rayon ('reɪɒn) *n.* (fabric made of) synthetic fibre

raze *or* **rase** (reɪz) *vt.* **1.** destroy completely **2.** wipe out, delete **3.** level

razor ('reɪzə) *n.* sharp instrument for shaving or for cutting hair —'**razorbill** *n.* N Atlantic auk

razzle-dazzle ('ræzl'dæzl) *or* **razzmatazz** ('ræzmə'tæz) *n. sl.* **1.** noisy or showy fuss or activity **2.** spree; frolic

Rb *Chem.* rubidium

R.C. **1.** Red Cross **2.** Roman Catholic

R.C.A. **1.** Radio Corporation of America **2.** Royal College of Art

R.C.A.F. Royal Canadian Air Force

R.C.M. Royal College of Music

R.C.M.P. Royal Canadian Mounted Police

R.C.N. Royal Canadian Navy

Rd. Road

re¹ (reɪ, riː) *n. Mus. see* RAY³

re² (riː) *prep.* with reference to, concerning

Re *Chem.* rhenium

R.E. **1.** Royal Engineers **2.** religious education

re- (*comb. form*) again. See the list on pages 413, 414 where the meaning may be inferred from the word to which *re-* is prefixed

reach (riːtʃ) vt. 1. arrive at 2. extend as far as 3. succeed in touching 4. attain to —vi. 5. stretch out hand 6. extend —n. 7. act of reaching 8. power of touching 9. grasp, scope 10. range 11. stretch of river between two bends —'**reachable** a. —**reach-me-down** n. 1. see **hand-me-down** at HAND 2. ready-made garment

react (rɪˈækt) vi. act in return, opposition or towards former state —re'**actance** n. Elec. resistance in coil, apart from ohmic resistance, due to current reacting on itself —re'**action** n. 1. any action resisting another 2. counter or backward tendency 3. mental depression following overexertion 4. inf. response 5. chemical or nuclear change, combination or decomposition —re'**actionary** n./a. (person) opposed to change, esp. in politics etc. —re'**active** a. chemically active —**nuclear reactor** apparatus in which nuclear reaction is maintained and controlled to produce nuclear energy

read (riːd) vt. 1. look at and understand (written or printed matter) 2. learn by reading 3. interpret mentally 4. read and utter 5. interpret 6. study 7. understand (any indicating instrument) 8. (of instrument) register —vi. 9. be occupied in reading 10. find mentioned in reading (**read** (red) pt./pp.) —reada'**bility** n. —'**readable** a. that can be read, or read with pleasure —'**reader** n. 1. one who reads 2. university lecturer 3. school textbook 4. one who reads manuscripts submitted to publisher 5. one who reads printer's proofs —'**readership** n. all readers of particular publication or author —'**reading** n. —**read-out** n. 1. retrieving of information from computer memory or storage device 2. information retrieved —**read between the lines** inf. deduce a meaning that is implied —**read out** 1. read aloud 2. US expel from political party etc. 3. retrieve information from computer memory or storage device

ready ('redɪ) a. 1. prepared for use or action 2. willing, prompt —'**readily** adv. 1. promptly 2. willingly —'**readiness** n. —**ready-made** a. 1. made for purchase and immediate use by customer 2. extremely convenient; ideally suited 3. unoriginal, conventional —n. 4. ready-made article, esp. garment —**ready reckoner** table of numbers used to facilitate simple calculations, esp. for working out interest etc.

reagent (riːˈeɪdʒənt) n. chemical substance that reacts with another and is used to detect presence of the other —re'**agency** n.

real (rɪəl) a. 1. existing in fact 2. happening 3. actual 4. genuine 5. (of property) consisting of land and houses —'**realism** n. 1. regarding things as they are 2. artistic treatment with this outlook —'**realist** n. —rea'**listic** a. —**reality** (rɪˈælɪtɪ) n. real existence —'**really** adv. —'**realty** n. real estate —**real estate** landed property —**real tennis** ancient form of tennis played in four-walled indoor court

realize or **-ise** ('rɪəlaɪz) vt. 1. apprehend, grasp significance of 2. make real 3. convert into money —reali'**zation** or **-i'sation** n.

realm (relm) n. 1. kingdom, domain 2. province, sphere

ream¹ (riːm) n. 1. twenty quires of paper, generally 480 sheets —pl. 2. inf. large quantity of written matter

ream² (riːm) vt. enlarge, bevel out, as hole in metal —'**reamer** n. tool for this

reap (riːp) v. 1. cut and gather (harvest) —vt. 2. receive as fruit of previous activity —'**reaper** n.

rear¹ (rɪə) n. 1. back part 2. part of army, procession etc. behind others —'**rearmost** a. —**rear admiral** lowest flag rank in certain navies —'**rearguard** n. troops protecting rear of army —**rear light** or **lamp** red light attached to rear of motor vehicle —**rear-view mirror** mirror on motor vehicle enabling driver to see traffic behind —'**rearward** a. 1. towards or in

re'**activate**	reas'**semble**
read'**dress**	reas'**sert**
read'**just**	reas'**sertion**
read'**mission**	reas'**sess**
read'**mit**	reas'**sessment**
reaf'**firm**	rea'**waken**
reaffir'**mation**	re'**bid** v.
rea'**lign**	'**rebid** n.
rea'**lignment**	re'**born**
re'**allocate**	re'**build**
reap'**pear**	re'**calculate**
reap'**pearance**	re'**capture**
reap'**praisal**	re'**cast**
reap'**praise**	re'**charge**
rear'**range**	recom'**mence**
rear'**rangement**	recon'**nect**

recon'**nection**	redistri'**bution**
recon'**sider**	re'**do**
recon'**struct**	re'**draft**
recon'**struction**	re'**draw**
recon'**vene**	re'**echo**
re-'**cover**	re-'**educate**
re-'**create**	re-'**elect**
re-'**decorate**	re-'**election**
rede'**ploy**	re-'**emerge**
rede'**sign**	re-'**emergence**
rede'**velop**	re'**emphasize**
rede'**velopment**	re-'**employ**
redi'**rect**	re-'**enact**
redi'**rection**	re-'**enactment**
redis'**cover**	re-'**enforce**
redis'**tribute**	re-'**enforcement**

rear —*adv.* **2.** towards or in rear (*also* '**rearwards**) —*n.* **3.** position in rear, *esp.* rear division of military formation

rear[2] (rɪə) *vt.* **1.** care for and educate (children) **2.** breed **3.** erect —*vi.* **4.** rise, *esp.* on hind feet

reason ('riːzən) *n.* **1.** ground, motive **2.** faculty of thinking **3.** sanity **4.** sensible or logical thought or view —*vi.* **5.** think logically in forming conclusions **6.** (*usu. with* with) persuade by logical argument into doing *etc.* —'**reasonable** *a.* **1.** sensible, not excessive **2.** suitable **3.** logical —'**reasoning** *n.* **1.** drawing of conclusions from facts *etc.* **2.** arguments, proofs *etc.* so adduced

reassure (riːə'ʃuə) *vt.* restore confidence to

rebate[1] ('riːbeɪt) *n.* **1.** discount, refund —*vt.* (rɪ'beɪt) **2.** deduct

rebate[2] ('riːbeɪt, 'ræbɪt) *or* **rabbet** *n.* **1.** recess, groove cut into piece of timber to join with matching piece —*vt.* **2.** cut rebate in

rebel (rɪ'bɛl) *vi.* **1.** revolt, resist lawful authority, take arms against ruling power (**-ll-**) —*n.* ('rɛbəl) **2.** one who rebels **3.** insurgent —*a.* ('rɛbəl) **4.** in rebellion —**re'bellion** *n.* organized open resistance to authority, revolt —**re'bellious** *a.* —**re'belliously** *adv.*

rebirth (riː'bɜːθ) *n.* **1.** revival, renaissance **2.** second or new birth

rebore ('riːbɔː) *n.* boring of cylinder to regain true shape

rebound (rɪ'baʊnd) *vi.* **1.** spring back **2.** misfire, *esp.* so as to hurt perpetrator (of plan, deed *etc.*) —*n.* ('riːbaʊnd) **3.** act of springing back or recoiling **4.** return

rebuff (rɪ'bʌf) *n.* **1.** blunt refusal **2.** check —*vt.* **3.** repulse, snub

rebuke (rɪ'bjuːk) *vt.* **1.** reprove, reprimand, find fault with —*n.* **2.** reprimand, scolding

rebus ('riːbəs) *n.* riddle in which names of things *etc.* are represented by pictures standing for syllables *etc.* (*pl.* **-es**)

rebut (rɪ'bʌt) *vt.* refute, disprove (**-tt-**) —**re'buttal** *n.*

rec. **1.** receipt **2.** recipe **3.** record

recalcitrant (rɪ'kælsɪtrənt) *a./n.* wilfully disobedient (person) —**re'calcitrance** *n.*

recall (rɪ'kɔːl) *vt.* **1.** recollect, remember **2.** call, summon, order back **3.** annul, cancel **4.** revive, restore —*n.* **5.** summons to return **6.** ability to remember

recant (rɪ'kænt) *v.* withdraw (statement, opinion *etc.*) —**recan'tation** *n.*

recap ('riːkæp, riː'kæp) *v.* **1.** recapitulate (**-pp-**) —*n.* ('riːkæp) **2.** recapitulation

recapitulate (riːkə'pɪtjuleɪt) *vt.* **1.** state again briefly **2.** repeat —**recapitu'lation** *n.*

recce ('rɛkɪ) *sl. n.* **1.** reconnaissance —*v.* **2.** reconnoitre

recd. *or* **rec'd.** received

recede (rɪ'siːd) *vi.* **1.** go back **2.** become distant **3.** slope backwards **4.** start balding

receipt (rɪ'siːt) *n.* **1.** written acknowledgment of money received **2.** receiving or being received —*vt.* **3.** acknowledge payment of in writing

receive (rɪ'siːv) *vt.* **1.** take, accept, get **2.** experience **3.** greet (guests) —**re'ceivable** *a.* —**re'ceiver** *n.* **1.** officer appointed to take public money **2.** one who takes stolen goods knowing them to have been stolen **3.** equipment in telephone, radio or television that converts electrical signals into sound and light

recent ('riːsənt) *a.* **1.** that has lately happened **2.** new **3.** (**R-**) of second and most recent epoch of Quaternary period, which began 10 000 years ago (*also* '**Holocene**) —*n.* **4.** (**R-**) Recent epoch or rock series (*also* '**Holocene**) —'**recently** *adv.*

receptacle (rɪ'sɛptəkəl) *n.* vessel, place or space to contain anything

reception (rɪ'sɛpʃən) *n.* **1.** receiving **2.** manner of receiving **3.** welcome **4.** formal party **5.** area for receiving guests, clients *etc.* **6.** in

re-enter	reim'pose	re'model	re'settle
re-equip	rein'terpret	re'number	re'shuffle
re-examine	reinterpre'tation	re'occupy	re'spray *v.*
re'fill *v.*	reintro'duce	re'open	'respray *n.*
'refill *n.*	reintro'duction	re'order	re'start
re'float	re'kindle	reorgani'zation	re'stock
re'forest	re'lay *v.*	re'organize	re'surface
re-'form	'relay *n.*	re'pack	re'think *v.*
re'fuel	re'light	re'paint	'rethink *n.*
re'furnish	re'load	re'paper	re'trial
re'gain	relo'cate	re'phrase	re'try
re'gather	relo'cation	re'plant	re'type
re'grow	re'marriage	re'print *v.*	reu'nite
re'harden	re'marry	'reprint *n.*	re'use
re'heat	re'match *v.*	re'route	re'visit
re'house	'rematch *n.*	re'set	re'wind

broadcasting, quality of signals received —**re'ceptionist** n. person who receives guests, clients etc. —**reception room** 1. room in house suitable for entertaining guests 2. room in hotel suitable for receptions etc.

receptive (rɪ'sɛptɪv) a. able, quick, willing to receive new ideas, suggestions etc. —**receptivity** (riːsɛp'tɪvɪtɪ) or **re'ceptiveness** n.

recess (rɪ'sɛs, 'riːsɛs) n. 1. niche, alcove 2. hollow 3. secret, hidden place 4. remission or suspension of business 5. vacation, holiday

recession (rɪ'sɛʃən) n. 1. period of reduction in trade 2. act of receding —**re'cessive** a. receding

recessional (rɪ'sɛʃənəl) n. hymn sung while clergy retire

recherché (rə'ʃɛəʃeɪ) a. 1. of studied elegance 2. exquisite 3. choice

recidivism (rɪ'sɪdɪvɪzəm) n. habitual relapse into crime —**re'cidivist** n./a.

recipe ('rɛsɪpɪ) n. 1. directions for cooking a dish 2. prescription 3. expedient

recipient (rɪ'sɪpɪənt) a. 1. that can or does receive —n. 2. one who, that which receives —**re'cipience** or **re'cipiency** n.

reciprocal (rɪ'sɪprəkəl) a. 1. complementary 2. mutual 3. moving backwards and forwards 4. alternating —**re'ciprocally** adv. —**re'ciprocate** vt. 1. give and receive mutually 2. return —vi. 3. move backwards and forwards —**recipro'cation** n. —**reciprocity** (rɛsɪ'prɒsɪtɪ) n.

recite (rɪ'saɪt) vt. repeat aloud, esp. to audience —**re'cital** n. 1. musical performance, usu. by one person 2. act of reciting 3. narration of facts etc. 4. story 5. public entertainment of recitations etc. —**recitation** (rɛsɪ'teɪʃən) n. 1. recital, usu. from memory, of poetry or prose 2. recountal —**recitative** (rɛsɪtə'tiːv) n. musical declamation —**re'citer** n.

reckless ('rɛklɪs) a. heedless, incautious —**'recklessness** n.

reckon ('rɛkən) v. 1. count —vt. 2. include 3. consider 4. think, deem —vi. 5. make calculations —**'reckoner** n. —**'reckoning** n. 1. counting, calculating 2. settlement of account etc. 3. bill, account 4. retribution for one's actions (esp. in **day of reckoning**) 5. Navigation see **dead reckoning** at DEAD

reclaim (rɪ'kleɪm) vt. 1. make fit for cultivation 2. bring back 3. reform 4. demand the return of —**re'claimable** a.

recline (rɪ'klaɪn) v. sit, lie back or on one's side

recluse (rɪ'kluːs) n. 1. hermit —a. 2. living in complete retirement —**re'clusion** n. —**re'clusive** a.

recognize or **-ise** ('rɛkəgnaɪz) vt. 1. know again 2. treat as valid 3. notice, show appreciation of —**recognition** (rɛkəg'nɪʃən) n.

—**'recognizable** or **-isable** a. —**recognizance** or **recognisance** (rɪ'kɒgnɪzəns) n. 1. avowal 2. bond by which person undertakes before court to observe some condition 3. obs. recognition

recoil (rɪ'kɔɪl) vi. 1. draw back in horror etc. 2. go wrong so as to hurt the perpetrator 3. (esp. of gun when fired) rebound —n. (rɪ'kɔɪl, 'riːkɔɪl) 4. backward spring 5. retreat 6. recoiling

recollect (rɛkə'lɛkt) vt. call back to mind, remember —**recol'lection** n.

recommend (rɛkə'mɛnd) vt. 1. advise, counsel 2. praise, commend 3. make acceptable —**recommen'dation** n.

recompense ('rɛkəmpɛns) vt. 1. reward 2. compensate, make up for —n. 3. compensation 4. reward 5. requital

reconcile ('rɛkənsaɪl) vt. 1. bring back into friendship 2. adjust, settle, harmonize —**'reconcilable** a. —**'reconcilement** n. —**reconciliation** (rɛkənsɪlɪ'eɪʃən) n.

recondite (rɪ'kɒndaɪt, 'rɛkəndaɪt) a. obscure, abstruse, little known

recondition (riːkən'dɪʃən) vt. restore to good condition or working order

reconnoitre or U.S. **reconnoiter** (rɛkə'nɔɪtə) vt. 1. make preliminary survey of 2. survey position of (enemy) —vi. 3. make reconnaissance —**reconnaissance** (rɪ'kɒnɪsəns) n. 1. examination or survey for military or engineering purposes 2. scouting

reconstitute (riː'kɒnstɪtjuːt) vt. restore (food) to former state, esp. by addition of water to a concentrate

record ('rɛkɔːd) n. 1. being recorded 2. document or other thing that records 3. disc with indentations which gramophone transforms into sound 4. best recorded achievement 5. known facts about person's past —vt. (rɪ'kɔːd) 6. put in writing 7. register —v. (rɪ'kɔːd) 8. preserve (sound, TV programmes etc.) on plastic disc, magnetic tape etc. for reproduction on playback device —**re'corder** n. 1. one who, that which records 2. type of flute 3. judge in certain courts —**re'cording** n. 1. process of making records from sound 2. something recorded, eg radio or TV programme —**recorded delivery** Post Office service by which official record of posting and delivery is obtained for letter or package —**Record Office** institution in which official records are stored and kept (also **Public Record Office**) —**record-player** n. machine for playing gramophone records —**for the record** for the sake of strict factual accuracy —**off the record** confidential or confidentially

recount (rɪ'kaʊnt) vt. tell in detail

re-count (riː'kaʊnt) v. 1. count (votes etc.)

again —n. ('ri:kaunt) 2. second or further count, *esp.* of votes

recoup (rɪ'ku:p) *vt.* 1. recompense, compensate 2. recover (what has been expended or lost)

recourse (rɪ'kɔ:s) *n.* 1. (resorting to) source of help 2. *Law* right of action or appeal

recover (rɪ'kʌvə) *vt.* 1. regain, get back —*vi.* 2. get back health —**re'coverable** *a.* —**re'covery** *n.*

recreant ('rɛkrɪənt) *a.* 1. cowardly, disloyal —*n.* 2. recreant person 3. renegade —'**recreance** *or* '**recreancy** *n.*

recreation (rɛkrɪ'eɪʃən) *n.* agreeable or refreshing occupation, relaxation, amusement —'**recreative** *a.*

recriminate (rɪ'krɪmɪneɪt) *vi.* make countercharge or mutual accusation —**recrimi'nation** *n.* mutual abuse and blame —**re'criminative** *or* **re'criminatory** *a.*

recrudesce (ri:kru:'dɛs) *vi.* break out again —**recru'descence** *n.* —**recru'descent** *a.*

recruit (rɪ'kru:t) *n.* 1. newly-enlisted soldier 2. one newly joining society *etc.* —*vt.* 3. enlist (fresh soldiers *etc.*) —**re'cruitment** *n.*

rectangle ('rɛktæŋgəl) *n.* oblong four-sided figure with four right angles —**rec'tangular** *a.* shaped thus

rectify ('rɛktɪfaɪ) *vt.* 1. put right, correct, remedy 2. purify (**-fied, -fying**) —**rectifi'cation** *n.* 1. act of setting right 2. refining by repeated distillation 3. *Elec.* conversion of alternating current into direct current —'**rectifier** *n.* thing that rectifies

rectilinear (rɛktɪ'lɪnɪə) *or* **rectilineal** *a.* 1. in straight line 2. characterized by straight lines

rectitude ('rɛktɪtju:d) *n.* 1. moral uprightness 2. honesty of purpose

recto ('rɛktəʊ) *n.* right-hand page of book, front of leaf (*pl.* **-s**)

rector ('rɛktə) *n.* 1. clergyman with care of parish 2. head of certain institutions, chiefly academic —'**rectorship** *n.* —'**rectory** *n.* rector's house

rectum ('rɛktəm) *n.* final section of large intestine (*pl.* **-s, -ta** (-tə)) —'**rectal** *a.*

recumbent (rɪ'kʌmbənt) *a.* lying down —**re'cumbence** *or* **re'cumbency** *n.*

recuperate (rɪ'ku:pəreɪt, -'kju:-) *vi.* 1. recover from illness, convalesce —*v.* 2. restore, be restored from losses *etc.* —**recuper'ation** *n.*

recur (rɪ'kɜ:) *vi.* 1. happen again 2. return again and again 3. go or come back in mind (**-rr-**) —**re'currence** *n.* repetition —**re'current** *a.*

recusant ('rɛkjʊzənt) *n.* 1. one who refused to conform to rites of Established Anglican Church —*a.* 2. obstinate in refusal

recycle (ri:'saɪk²l) *vt.* 1. reprocess (manufactured substance) for use again 2. reuse

red (rɛd) *a.* 1. of colour varying from crimson to orange and seen in blood, rubies, glowing fire *etc.* —*n.* 2. the colour 3. *inf.* communist —'**redden** *vt.* 1. make red —*vi.* 2. become red 3. flush —'**reddish** *a.* —**red blood cell** see ERYTHROCYTE —**red-blooded** *a.* 1. vigorous 2. virile —'**redbreast** *n.* robin —'**redbrick** *a.* of provincial and relatively new university —**red carpet** 1. strip of red carpeting laid for important dignitaries to walk on 2. deferential treatment accorded to person of importance —'**redcoat** *n.* 1. *obs.* soldier 2. C *inf.* Mountie —**Red Crescent** emblem of Red Cross Society in Muslim country —**Red Cross** international humanitarian organization providing medical care for war casualties, famine relief *etc.* —**red deer** large deer formerly widely distributed in woodlands of Europe and Asia —**Red Ensign** ensign of British Merchant Navy, having Union Jack on red background at upper corner; also national flag of Canad. until 1965 —'**redfish** *n.* any of various types of fish —**red flag** 1. emblem of communist party 2. (**R- F-**) their song 3. danger signal —**red-handed** *a. inf.* (caught) in the act —**red hat** broad-brimmed crimson hat given to cardinals as symbol of rank —'**redhead** *n.* person with red hair —'**redheaded** *a.* —**red herring** topic introduced to divert attention from main issue —**red-hot** *a.* 1. (*esp.* of metal) heated to temperature at which it glows red 2. extremely hot 3. keen, excited, eager 4. furious; violent 5. very recent or topical —**red-hot poker** garden plant with tall spikes of red or orange flowers —**Red Indian** N Amer. Indian —**red lead** red poisonous insoluble oxide of lead —**red-letter day** memorably important or happy occasion —**red light** 1. signal to stop, *esp.* traffic signal 2. danger signal 3. red lamp hanging outside house indicating it is a brothel —**red-light district** district containing many brothels —**red pepper** 1. pepper plant cultivated for its hot pungent red podlike fruits 2. this fruit 3. ripe red fruit of sweet pepper 4. *see* CAYENNE PEPPER —**red rag** provocation; something that infuriates —'**redshank** *n.* large European sandpiper —**red shift** shift in spectral lines of stellar spectrum towards red end of visible region relative to wavelength of these lines in terrestrial spectrum —'**redskin** *n. inf.* Amer. Indian —'**redstart** *n.* 1. European songbird of thrush family 2. N Amer. warbler —**red tape** excessive adherence to official rules —'**redwing** *n.* small European thrush having speckled breast and reddish flanks —'**redwood** *n.* giant coniferous tree of California —**in the red** *inf.* in debt —**see red** *inf.* be angry

redeem (rɪ'di:m) *vt.* 1. buy back 2. set free 3.

free from sin **4.** make up for —re'**deemable** a. —**redemption** (rɪ'dɛmpʃən) n. —**The Redeemer** Jesus Christ

redeploy (riːdɪ'plɔɪ) v. assign new positions or tasks to (labour *etc.*) —rede'**ployment** n.

redolent ('rɛdəʊlənt) a. **1.** smelling strongly, fragrant **2.** reminiscent —'**redolence** n.

redouble (rɪ'dʌbəl) v. **1.** increase, multiply, intensify **2.** *Bridge* double a second time

redoubt (rɪ'daʊt) n. detached outwork in fortifications

redoubtable (rɪ'daʊtəbəl) a. dreaded, formidable

redound (rɪ'daʊnd) vi. **1.** contribute **2.** recoil

redress (rɪ'drɛs) vt. **1.** set right **2.** make amends for —n. **3.** compensation, amends

reduce (rɪ'djuːs) vt. **1.** bring down, lower **2.** lessen, weaken **3.** bring by force or necessity to some state or action **4.** slim **5.** simplify **6.** dilute —vi. **7.** *Chem.* separate substance from others with which it is combined —re'**ducible** a. —**reduction** (rɪ'dʌkʃən) n. —**reducing agent** substance used to deoxidize or lessen density of another substance

redundant (rɪ'dʌndənt) a. superfluous **2.** (of worker) deprived of job because it is no longer needed —re'**dundancy** n. —**redundancy payment** sum of money given to worker made redundant by employer

reduplicate (rɪ'djuːplɪkeɪt) v. **1.** make or become double; repeat **2.** repeat (sound or syllable) in word or (of sound or syllable) be repeated —a. (rɪ'djuːplɪkɪt) **3.** doubled; repeated **4.** (of petals or sepals) having margins curving outwards —redupli'**cation** n.

reed (riːd) n. **1.** any of various marsh or water plants **2.** tall straight stem of one **3.** *Mus.* vibrating cane or metal strip of certain wind instruments —'**reedy** a. **1.** full of reeds **2.** like reed instrument **3.** harsh and thin in tone —'**reedbuck** n. S Afr. antelope with buff coat —**reed bunting** common European bunting that has brown streaked plumage

reef (riːf) n. **1.** ridge of rock or coral near surface of sea **2.** vein of ore **3.** part of sail which can be rolled up to reduce area —vt. **4.** take in a reef of —'**reefer** n. **1.** sailor's jacket **2.** *sl.* hand-rolled cigarette, *esp.* containing cannabis —**reef knot** knot consisting of two overhand knots turned opposite ways (*also* **square knot**)

reek (riːk) n. **1.** strong (unpleasant) smell —vi. **2.** emit fumes **3.** smell

reel (riːl, rɪəl) n. **1.** spool on which film is wound **2.** *Cine.* portion of film **3.** winding apparatus **4.** bobbin **5.** thread wound on this **6.** lively dance **7.** music for it **8.** act of staggering —vt. **9.** wind on to reel **10.** draw (in) by means of reel —vi. **11.**

stagger, sway, rock —**reel off** recite, write fluently, quickly

re-entry (riː'ɛntrɪ) n. **1.** retaking possession of land *etc.* **2.** return of spacecraft into earth's atmosphere

reeve[1] (riːv) n. **1.** *Hist.* manorial steward or official **2.** C president of local (rural) council

reeve[2] (riːv) vt. pass (rope) through hole, in block *etc.*

reeve[3] (riːv) n. female of ruff (bird)

ref. **1.** referee **2.** reference **3.** reformed

refectory (rɪ'fɛktərɪ, -trɪ) n. room for meals in college *etc.* —re'**fection** n. meal —**refectory table** long narrow dining table supported by two trestles

refer (rɪ'fɜː) vi. **1.** relate, allude —vt. **2.** send for information **3.** trace, ascribe **4.** submit for decision (-rr-) —**referable** ('rɛfərəbəl) or re'**ferrable** a. —**referee** (rɛfə'riː) n. **1.** arbitrator **2.** person willing to testify to someone's character *etc.* **3.** umpire —v. **4.** act as referee (in) —**reference** ('rɛfərəns, 'rɛfrəns) n. **1.** act of referring **2.** citation or direction in book **3.** appeal to judgment of another **4.** testimonial **5.** one to whom inquiries as to character *etc.* may be made —**referendum** (rɛfə'rɛndəm) n. submitting of question to electorate (pl. **-s, -da** (-də)) —re'**ferral** n. act, instance of referring —**reference library** library where books may be consulted but not taken away by readers

refine (rɪ'faɪn) vt. purify —re'**fined** a. **1.** not coarse or vulgar; genteel, elegant, polite **2.** freed from impurities; purified —re'**finement** n. **1.** subtlety **2.** improvement, elaboration **3.** fineness of feeling, taste or manners —re'**finer** n. —re'**finery** n. place where sugar, oil *etc.* is refined

refit (riː'fɪt) v. **1.** make or be made ready for use again by repairing *etc.* (-tt-) —n. ('riːfɪt) **2.** repair or re-equipping, as for further use

reflation (riː'fleɪʃən) n. (steps taken to produce) increase in economic activity of country *etc.*

reflect (rɪ'flɛkt) vt. **1.** throw back, *esp.* rays of light **2.** cast (discredit *etc.*) upon —vi. **3.** meditate —re'**flection** or re'**flexion** n. **1.** act of reflecting **2.** return of rays of heat, light or waves of sound from surface **3.** image of object given back by mirror *etc.* **4.** conscious thought **5.** meditation **6.** expression of thought —re'**flective** a. **1.** meditative, quiet, contemplative **2.** throwing back images —re'**flector** n. polished surface for reflecting light *etc.*

reflex ('riːflɛks) n. **1.** reflex action **2.** reflected image **3.** reflected light, colour *etc.* —a. **4.** (of muscular action) involuntary **5.** reflected **6.** bent back —re'**flexive** a. *Gram.* denoting agent's action on himself **—reflex action** involuntary response to (nerve) stimulation

reflux ('ri:flʌks) *n.* flowing back, ebb **—refluence** ('rɛfluəns) *n.* **—refluent** ('rɛfluənt) *a.* returning, ebbing

reform (rɪ'fɔːm) *vt.* **1.** improve **2.** reconstruct **—vi.** **3.** abandon evil practices **—n.** **4.** improvement **—reformation** (rɛfə'meiʃən) *n.* **—re'formatory** *n.* institution for reforming juvenile offenders **—a.** reforming **—re'form-er** *n.*

refract (rɪ'frækt) *vt.* change course of (light *etc.*) passing from one medium to another **—re'fraction** *n.* **—re'fractive** *a.*

refractory (rɪ'fræktərɪ) *a.* **1.** unmanageable **2.** difficult to treat or work **3.** *Med.* resistant to treatment **4.** resistant to heat

refrain[1] (rɪ'freɪn) *vi.* abstain

refrain[2] (rɪ'freɪn) *n.* chorus

refresh (rɪ'frɛʃ) *vt.* **1.** give freshness to **2.** revive **3.** renew **4.** brighten **5.** provide with refreshment **—re'fresher** *n.* that which refreshes **—re'freshment** *n.* **1.** that which refreshes, *esp.* food, drink **2.** restorative

refrigerate (rɪ'frɪdʒəreɪt) *vt.* freeze **2.** cool **—re'frigerant** *n.* **1.** refrigerating substance **—a.** **2.** causing cooling or freezing **—refriger'ation** *n.* **—re'frigerator** *n.* apparatus in which foods, drinks are kept cool

refuge ('rɛfjuːdʒ) *n.* shelter, protection, retreat, sanctuary **—refu'gee** *n.* one who seeks refuge, *esp.* in foreign country

refulgent (rɪ'fʌldʒənt) *a.* shining, radiant **—re'fulgence** *n.* **—re'fulgency** *n.* splendour

refund (rɪ'fʌnd) *vt.* **1.** pay back **—n.** ('ri:fʌnd) **2.** return of money to purchaser or amount so returned

refurbish (ri:'fɜːbɪʃ) *vt.* furbish, furnish or polish anew

refuse[1] (rɪ'fjuːz) *v.* decline, deny, reject **—re'fusal** *n.* **1.** denial of anything demanded or offered **2.** option

refuse[2] ('rɛfjuːs) *n.* rubbish, useless matter

refute (rɪ'fjuːt) *vt.* disprove **—refutable** ('rɛfjutəb³l, rɪ'fjuː-) *a.* **—refutation** (rɛfju'teɪʃən) *n.*

regal ('riːg³l) *a.* of, like a king **—regalia** (rɪ'geɪlɪə) *pl.n.* (*sometimes with sing. v.*) **1.** insignia of royalty, as used at coronation *etc.* **2.** emblems of high office, an order *etc.* **—re'gality** *n.* **—'regally** *adv.*

regale (rɪ'geɪl) *vt.* **1.** give pleasure to **2.** feast **—re'galement** *n.*

regard (rɪ'gɑːd) *vt.* **1.** look at **2.** consider **3.** relate to **4.** heed **—n.** **5.** look **6.** attention **7.** particular respect **8.** esteem **—pl.** **9.** expression of good will **—re'gardful** *a.* heedful, careful **—re'garding** *prep.* in respect of; on the subject

of **—re'gardless** *a.* **1.** heedless **—adv.** **2.** in spite of everything

regatta (rɪ'gætə) *n.* meeting for yacht or boat races

regenerate (rɪ'dʒɛnəreɪt) *v.* **1.** (cause to) undergo spiritual rebirth **2.** reform morally **3.** reproduce, re-create **4.** reorganize **—a.** (rɪ'dʒɛnərɪt) **5.** born anew **—regener'ation** *n.* **—re'generative** *a.* **—re'generator** *n.*

regent ('riːdʒənt) *n.* **1.** ruler of kingdom during absence, minority *etc.*, of its monarch **—a.** **2.** ruling **—'regency** *n.* status of, (period of) office of regent

reggae ('rɛgeɪ) *n.* style of popular West Indian music with strong beat

regicide ('rɛdʒɪsaɪd) *n.* **1.** one who kills a king **2.** this crime

regime *or* **régime** (reɪ'ʒiːm) *n.* **1.** system of government, administration **2.** *see* REGIMEN (sense 1)

regimen ('rɛdʒɪmɛn) *n.* **1.** prescribed system of diet *etc.* (*also* re'gime) **2.** rule

regiment ('rɛdʒɪmənt) *n.* **1.** organized body of troops as unit of army **—vt.** ('rɛdʒɪmɛnt) **2.** discipline, organize rigidly or too strictly **—regi'mental** *a.* of regiment **—regi'mentals** *pl.n.* uniform

region ('riːdʒən) *n.* **1.** area, district **2.** stretch of country **3.** part of the body **4.** sphere, realm **5.** (*oft.* **R-**) administrative division of a country **—'regional** *a.*

register ('rɛdʒɪstə) *n.* **1.** list **2.** catalogue **3.** roll **4.** device for registering **5.** written record **6.** range of voice or instrument **—v.** **7.** show, be shown on meter, face *etc.* **—vt.** **8.** enter in register **9.** record **10.** show **11.** set down in writing **12.** *Print., photog.* cause to correspond precisely **—regis'trar** *n.* **1.** keeper of a register **2.** senior hospital doctor, junior to consultant **—regis'tration** *n.* **—'registry** *n.* **1.** registering **2.** place where registers are kept, *esp.* of births, marriages, deaths **—registered post 1.** Post Office service by which compensation is paid for loss of or damage to mail for which registration fee has been paid **2.** mail sent by this service **—registration number** sequence of numbers and letters displayed on motor vehicle to identify it

regorge (rɪ'gɔːdʒ) *vt.* vomit up

regress (rɪ'grɛs) *vi.* **1.** return, revert to former place, condition *etc.* **—n.** ('riːgrɛs) **2.** movement in backward direction **—re'gression** *n.* **1.** act of returning **2.** retrogression **—re'gressive** *a.* falling back **—re'gressively** *adv.*

regret (rɪ'grɛt) *vt.* **1.** feel sorry, distressed for loss of or on account of (**-tt-**) **—n.** **2.** sorrow, distress for thing done or left undone or lost **—re'gretful** *a.* **—re'grettable** *a.*

regular ('regjulə) a. 1. normal 2. habitual 3. done, occurring, according to rule 4. periodical 5. straight, level 6. living under rule 7. belonging to standing army —n. 8. regular soldier 9. inf. regular customer —**regu'larity** n. —**'regularize** or **-ise** v.

regulate ('regjuleɪt) vt. 1. adjust 2. arrange 3. direct 4. govern 5. put under rule —**regu'lation** n. —**'regulator** n. contrivance to produce uniformity of motion, as fly wheel, governor valve etc.

regurgitate (rɪ'gɜ:dʒɪteɪt) v. 1. vomit 2. bring back (swallowed food) into mouth —**regurgi'tation** n.

rehabilitate (ri:ə'bɪlɪteɪt) vt. 1. help (person) to readjust to society after period of illness, imprisonment etc. 2. restore to reputation or former position 3. make fit again 4. reinstate —**rehabili'tation** n.

rehash (ri:'hæʃ) vt. 1. rework, reuse —n. 2. old materials presented in new form

rehearse (rɪ'hɜːs) vt. 1. practise (play etc.) 2. repeat aloud 3. say over again 4. train, drill —**re'hearsal** n.

Reich (raɪx) n. 1. Holy Roman Empire (962-1806) (**First Reich**) 2. Hohenzollern empire in Germany from 1871 to 1918 (**Second Reich**) 3. Nazi dictatorship in Germany from 1933-45 (**Third Reich**)

reign (reɪn) n. 1. period of sovereign's rule —vi. 2. be sovereign 3. be supreme

reimburse (ri:ɪm'bɜːs) vt. 1. refund 2. pay back —**reim'bursement** n.

rein (reɪn) n. 1. (oft. pl.) narrow strap attached to bit to guide horse 2. instrument for governing —vt. 3. check, manage with reins 4. control —**give (a) free rein** remove restraints

reincarnation (ri:ɪnkɑː'neɪʃən) n. 1. rebirth of soul in successive bodies 2. one of series of such transmigrations —**re'incarnate** vt.

reindeer ('reɪndɪə) n. deer of cold regions, eg Lapland (pl. **-deer, -s**)

reinforce (ri:ɪn'fɔːs) vt. 1. strengthen with new support, material, force 2. strengthen with additional troops, ships etc. —**rein'forcement** n. —**reinforced concrete** 1. concrete strengthened internally by steel bars 2. ferroconcrete

reinstate (ri:ɪn'steɪt) vt. replace, restore, re-establish —**rein'statement** n.

reiterate (ri:'ɪtəreɪt) vt. repeat again and again —**reiter'ation** n. repetition

reject (rɪ'dʒekt) vt. 1. refuse to accept 2. put aside 3. discard 4. renounce —n. ('ri:dʒekt) 5. person or thing rejected as not up to standard —**re'jection** n. refusal

rejig (ri:'dʒɪg) vt. 1. re-equip (factory, plant) 2. inf. rearrange (**-gg-**)

rejoice (rɪ'dʒɔɪs) v. 1. make or be joyful, merry —vt. 2. exult 3. gladden

rejoin (rɪ'dʒɔɪn) vt. 1. reply 2. (ri:'dʒɔɪn) join again —**re'joinder** n. answer, retort

rejuvenate (rɪ'dʒuːvɪneɪt) vt. restore to youth —**rejuve'nation** n. —**rejuve'nescence** n. process of growing young again

relapse (rɪ'læps) v. 1. fall back (into evil, illness etc.) —n. 2. act or instance of relapsing

relate (rɪ'leɪt) vt. 1. narrate, recount 2. establish relation between —vi. 3. have reference or relation 4. form sympathetic relationship —**re'lated** a. 1. connected; associated 2. connected by kinship or marriage

relation (rɪ'leɪʃən) n. 1. relative quality or condition 2. connection by blood or marriage 3. connection (between things) 4. act of relating 5. narrative —**re'lationship** n. —**relative** ('relətɪv) a. 1. dependent on relation to something else, not absolute 2. having reference or relation —n. 3. one connected by blood or marriage 4. relative word or thing —**relatively** ('relətɪvlɪ) adv. —**relativity** (relə'tɪvɪtɪ) n. 1. state of being relative 2. subject of two theories of Albert Einstein, dealing with relationships of space, time and motion and acceleration and gravity

relax (rɪ'læks) vt. 1. make loose or slack —vi. 2. become loosened or slack 3. ease up from effort or attention 4. become more friendly, less strict —**relax'ation** n. 1. relaxing recreation 2. alleviation 3. abatement

relay ('ri:leɪ) n. 1. fresh set of people or animals relieving others 2. Elec. device for making or breaking local circuit 3. Rad., T.V. broadcasting station receiving programmes from another station —vt. (rɪ'leɪ) 4. pass on, as message (**re'layed, re'laying**) —**relay race** race between teams of which each runner races part of distance

release (rɪ'liːs) vt. 1. give up, surrender, set free 2. permit public showing of (film etc.) —n. 3. setting free 4. releasing 5. written discharge 6. permission to show publicly 7. film, record etc. newly issued

relegate ('relɪgeɪt) vt. 1. banish, consign 2. demote —**rele'gation** n.

relent (rɪ'lent) vi. give up harsh intention, become less severe —**re'lentless** a. 1. pitiless 2. merciless

relevant ('relɪvənt) a. having to do with the matter in hand, to the point —**'relevance** n.

reliable (rɪ'laɪəb²l) a. see RELY

relic ('relɪk) n. 1. thing remaining, esp. as memorial of saint 2. memento —pl. 3. remains, traces 4. obs. dead body —**'relict** n. obs. widow

relief (rɪ'liːf) n. 1. alleviation, end of pain, distress etc. 2. money, food given to victims of disaster, poverty *etc.* **3.** release from duty **4.** one who relieves another from work or duty **5.** bus, plane *etc.* that carries passengers when a scheduled service is full **6.** freeing of besieged city *etc.* **7.** projection of carved design from surface **8.** distinctness, prominence —re'**lieve** *vt.* bring or give relief to —**relief map** map showing elevations and depressions of country in relief

religion (rɪ'lɪdʒən) *n.* system of belief in, worship of a supernatural power or god —**religiose** (rɪ'lɪdʒɪəʊs) *a.* affectedly or extremely pious; sanctimoniously religious —**religiosity** (rɪlɪdʒɪ'ɒsɪtɪ) *n.* —re'**ligious** *a.* pert. to religion **2.** pious **3.** conscientious —re'**ligiously** *adv.* **1.** in religious manner **2.** scrupulously **3.** conscientiously

relinquish (rɪ'lɪŋkwɪʃ) *vt.* **1.** give up, abandon **2.** surrender or renounce (claim, right *etc.*) —re'**linquishment** *n.*

reliquary ('rɛlɪkwərɪ) *n.* case or shrine for holy relics

relish ('rɛlɪʃ) *vt.* **1.** enjoy, like —*n.* **2.** liking, gusto **3.** savoury taste **4.** taste, flavour

relive (riː'lɪv) *vt.* experience (sensation *etc.*) again, *esp.* in imagination —re'**livable** *a.*

reluctant (rɪ'lʌktənt) *a.* unwilling, loath, disinclined —re'**luctance** *n.*

rely (rɪ'laɪ) *vi.* **1.** depend **2.** (*with* on) trust (re'**lied**, re'**lying**) —relia'**bility** *n.* —re'**liable** *a.* trustworthy, dependable —re'**liance** *n.* **1.** trust **2.** confidence **3.** dependence —re'**liant** *a.* confident

REM rapid eye movement

remain (rɪ'meɪn) *vi.* **1.** stay, be left behind **2.** continue **3.** abide **4.** last —re'**mainder** *n.* **1.** rest, what is left after subtraction —*vt.* **2.** offer (end of consignment of goods, material *etc.*) at reduced prices —re'**mains** *pl.n.* **1.** relics, *esp.* of ancient buildings **2.** dead body

remand (rɪ'mɑːnd) *vt.* send back, *esp.* into custody —**remand home** or **centre** place of detention for young delinquents

remark (rɪ'mɑːk) *vi.* **1.** make casual comment —*vt.* **2.** comment, observe **3.** say **4.** take notice of —*n.* **5.** observation, comment —re'**markable** *a.* noteworthy, unusual —re'**markably** *adv.* **1.** exceedingly **2.** unusually

REME ('riːmɪ) Royal Electrical and Mechanical Engineers

remedy ('rɛmɪdɪ) *n.* **1.** means of curing, counteracting or relieving disease, trouble *etc.* —*vt.* **2.** put right (-**edied**, -**edying**) —**remediable** (rɪ'miːdɪəbəl) *a.* —**remedial** (rɪ'miːdɪəl) *a.* designed, intended to correct specific disability, handicap *etc.*

remember (rɪ'mɛmbə) *vt.* **1.** retain in, recall to memory **2.** have in mind —re'**membrance** *n.*

1. memory **2.** token **3.** souvenir **4.** reminiscence —**Remembrance Day 1.** UK Sunday closest to Nov. 11th, on which the dead of both World Wars are commemorated (*also* **Remembrance Sunday**) **2. C** statutory holiday observed on Nov. 11th in memory of the dead of both World Wars

remind (rɪ'maɪnd) *vt.* **1.** cause to remember **2.** put in mind —re'**minder** *n.*

reminisce (rɛmɪ'nɪs) *vi.* talk, write of past times, experiences *etc.* —remi'**niscence** *n.* **1.** remembering **2.** thing recollected —*pl.* **3.** memoirs —remi'**niscent** *a.* reminding, suggestive

remiss (rɪ'mɪs) *a.* negligent, careless —re'**missly** *adv.*

remit (rɪ'mɪt) *v.* **1.** send (money) for goods, services *etc.*, *esp.* by post **2.** refrain from exacting (penalty) —*vt.* **3.** give up **4.** restore, return **5.** slacken **6.** *obs.* forgive (-**tt-**) —*n.* ('riːmɪt, rɪ'mɪt) **7.** area of competence, authority —re'**missible** *a.* —re'**mission** *n.* **1.** abatement **2.** reduction in length of prison term **3.** pardon, forgiveness —re'**mittance** *n.* **1.** sending of money **2.** money sent —re'**mittence** *n.* —re'**mittent** *a.* (of symptoms of disease) characterized by periods of diminished severity —re'**mittently** *adv.*

remnant ('rɛmnənt) *n.* **1.** (*oft. pl.*) fragment or small piece remaining **2.** oddment

remonstrate ('rɛmənstreɪt) *vi.* protest, reason, argue —re'**monstrance** *n.*

remorse (rɪ'mɔːs) *n.* regret and repentance —re'**morseful** *a.* —re'**morsefully** *adv.* —re'**morseless** *a.* pitiless

remote (rɪ'məʊt) *a.* **1.** far away, distant **2.** aloof **3.** slight —re'**motely** *adv.* —**remote control** control of apparatus from a distance by electrical device

remould (riː'məʊld) *see* RETREAD

remove (rɪ'muːv) *vt.* **1.** take away or off **2.** transfer **3.** withdraw —*vi.* **4.** go away, change residence —*n.* **5.** degree of difference —re'**movable** *a.* —re'**moval** *n.*

remunerate (rɪ'mjuːnəreɪt) *vt.* reward, pay —remuner'**ation** *n.* —re'**munerative** *a.*

renaissance (rə'neɪsəns; *U.S. also* 'rɛnəsɒns) or **renascence** (rɪ'næsəns, -'neɪ-) *n.* revival, rebirth, *esp.* (**R-**) revival of learning in 14th-16th centuries

renal ('riːnəl) *a.* of the kidneys

renascent (rɪ'næsənt, -'neɪ-) *a.* springing up again into being

rend (rɛnd) *v.* **1.** tear, wrench apart **2.** burst, break, split (**rent**, '**rending**)

render ('rɛndə) *vt.* **1.** submit, present **2.** give in return, deliver up **3.** cause to become **4.** portray, represent **5.** melt down **6.** cover with plaster

rendezvous ('rɒndɪvuː) *n.* **1.** meeting place **2.**

appointment **3.** haunt **4.** assignation (*pl.* -**vous** (-vu:z)) —*vi.* **5.** meet, come together

rendition (rɛn'dɪʃən) *n.* **1.** performance **2.** translation

renegade ('rɛnɪgeɪd) *n.* **1.** deserter **2.** outlaw **3.** rebel

renege *or* **renegue** (rɪ'niːg, -'neɪg) *vi.* go back (on promise *etc.*)

renew (rɪ'njuː) *vt.* **1.** begin again **2.** reaffirm **3.** make valid again **4.** make new **5.** revive **6.** restore to former state **7.** replenish —*vi.* **8.** be made new **9.** grow again —**renewa'bility** *n.* quality of being renewable —**re'newable** *a.* —**re'newal** *n.* **1.** revival, restoration **2.** regeneration

rennet ('rɛnɪt) *n.* preparation for curdling milk

renounce (rɪ'naʊns) *vt.* **1.** give up, cast off, disown **2.** abjure **3.** resign, as title or claim —**renunci'ation** *n.* **1.** act or instance of renouncing **2.** formal declaration renouncing something

renovate ('rɛnəveɪt) *vt.* restore, repair, renew, do up —**reno'vation** *n.*

renown (rɪ'naʊn) *n.* fame

rent[1] (rɛnt) *n.* **1.** payment for use of land, buildings, machines *etc.* —*vt.* **2.** hold by lease **3.** hire **4.** let —'**rental** *n.* sum payable as rent

rent[2] (rɛnt) *n.* **1.** tear **2.** fissure —*v.* **3.** *pt./pp. of* REND

renunciation (rɪnʌnsɪ'eɪʃən) *n. see* RENOUNCE

rep[1] *or* **repp** (rɛp) *n.* fabric with corded surface for upholstery *etc.*

rep[2] (rɛp) *a./n.* repertory (company, theatre, group)

rep[3] (rɛp) *n.* representative, travelling salesman

repaid (rɪ'peɪd) *pt./pp. of* REPAY

repair[1] (rɪ'pɛə) *vt.* **1.** make whole, sound again **2.** mend **3.** patch **4.** restore —*n.* **5.** act or process of repairing —**re'pairable** *a.* —**reparation** (rɛpə'reɪʃən) *n.* **1.** repairing **2.** amends, compensation

repair[2] (rɪ'pɛə) *vi.* (*usu. with* to) resort, go

repartee (rɛpɑː'tiː) *n.* **1.** witty retort **2.** interchange of witty retorts

repast (rɪ'pɑːst) *n.* meal

repatriate (riː'pætrɪeɪt) *vt.* send (someone) back to his own country —**repatri'ation** *n.*

repay (rɪ'peɪ) *vt.* **1.** pay back, refund **2.** make return for (**re'paid, re'paying**) —**re'payable** *a.* —**re'payment** *n.*

repeal (rɪ'piːl) *vt.* **1.** revoke, annul, cancel —*n.* **2.** act of repealing

repeat (rɪ'piːt) *vt.* **1.** say, do again **2.** reproduce —*vi.* **3.** recur —*n.* **4.** act, instance of repeating, *esp.* TV show broadcast again —**re'peatedly** *adv.* **1.** again and again **2.** frequently —**re'peater** *n.* **1.** firearm that may be discharged many times without reloading **2.**

timepiece that strikes hours —**repe'tition** *n.* **1.** act of repeating **2.** thing repeated **3.** piece learnt by heart and repeated —**repetitious** (rɛpɪ'tɪʃəs) *a.* repeated unnecessarily —**re'petitive** *a.* repeated

repel (rɪ'pɛl) *vt.* **1.** drive back, ward off, refuse **2.** be repulsive to (-**ll**-) —**re'pellent** *a.* **1.** distasteful **2.** resisting (water *etc.*) —*n.* **3.** that which repels, *esp.* chemical to repel insects

repent (rɪ'pɛnt) *vi.* **1.** wish one had not done something **2.** feel regret for deed or omission —*vt.* **3.** feel regret for —**re'pentance** *n.* contrition —**re'pentant** *a.*

repercussion (riːpə'kʌʃən) *n.* **1.** (*oft. pl.*) indirect effect, oft. unpleasant **2.** recoil **3.** echo

repertory ('rɛpətərɪ, -trɪ) *n.* **1.** repertoire, collection **2.** store —**repertoire** ('rɛpətwɑː) *n.* stock of plays, songs *etc.* that player or company can give —**repertory company,** **theatre** *or* **group** (theatre *etc.* with) permanent company producing succession of plays

repetition (rɛpɪ'tɪʃən) *n. see* REPEAT

repine (rɪ'paɪn) *vi.* fret, complain

replace (rɪ'pleɪs) *vt.* **1.** substitute for **2.** put back —**re'placement** *n.*

replay ('riːpleɪ) *n.* **1.** immediate reshowing on TV of incident in sport, *esp.* in slow motion (*also* **action replay**) **2.** replaying of a match —*vt.* (riː'pleɪ) **3.** play again

replenish (rɪ'plɛnɪʃ) *vt.* fill up again —**re'plenishment** *n.*

replete (rɪ'pliːt) *a.* filled, gorged —**re'pletion** *n.* complete fullness

replica ('rɛplɪkə) *n.* **1.** exact copy **2.** facsimile, duplicate —'**replicate** *vt.* make, be a copy of

reply (rɪ'plaɪ) *v.* **1.** answer (**re'plied, re'plying**) —*n.* **2.** an answer; response

report (rɪ'pɔːt) *n.* **1.** account, statement **2.** written statement of child's progress at school **3.** rumour **4.** bang —*vt.* **5.** announce, relate **6.** make, give account of **7.** take down in writing **8.** complain about —*vi.* **9.** complain **10.** make report **11.** act as reporter **12.** present oneself (to) —**re'porter** *n.* one who reports, *esp.* for newspaper —**reported speech** *see* **indirect speech** *at* INDIRECT

repose (rɪ'pəʊz) *n.* **1.** peace **2.** composure **3.** sleep —*vi.* **4.** rest —*vt.* **5.** lay at rest **6.** place **7.** rely, lean (on) —**repository** (rɪ'pɒzɪtərɪ, -trɪ) *n.* **1.** place where valuables are deposited for safekeeping **2.** store

repossess (riːpə'zɛs) *vt.* take back possession of (property), *esp.* for nonpayment of money due under hire-purchase agreement —**repos'session** *n.*

repoussé (rə'puːseɪ) *a.* **1.** embossed **2.** hammered into relief from reverse side —*n.* **3.** metal work so produced

reprehend (reprɪ'hend) vt. find fault with —repre'hensible a. 1. deserving censure 2. unworthy —repre'hension n. censure

represent (reprɪ'zent) vt. 1. stand for 2. deputize for 3. act, play 4. symbolize 5. make out to be 6. call up by description or portrait —represen'tation n. —repre'sentative n. 1. one chosen to stand for group 2. travelling salesman —a. 3. typical

repress (rɪ'pres) vt. keep down or under, quell, check —re'pression n. restraint —re'pressive a.

reprieve (rɪ'priːv) vt. 1. suspend execution of (condemned person) 2. give temporary relief to —n. 3. postponement or cancellation of punishment 4. respite 5. last-minute intervention

reprimand ('reprɪmɑːnd) n. 1. sharp rebuke —vt. 2. rebuke sharply

reprisal (rɪ'praɪz³l) n. retaliation

reproach (rɪ'prəʊtʃ) vt. 1. blame, rebuke —n. 2. scolding, upbraiding 3. expression of this 4. thing bringing discredit —re'proachful a.

reprobate ('reprəʊbeɪt) a. 1. depraved 2. cast off by God —n. 3. depraved or disreputable person —vt. 4. disapprove of, reject —repro'bation n.

reproduce (riːprə'djuːs) vt. 1. produce copy of 2. bring (new individuals) into existence 3. re-create, produce anew —vi. 4. propagate 5. generate —repro'ducible a. —repro'duction n. 1. process of reproducing 2. that which is reproduced 3. facsimile, as of painting etc. —repro'ductive a.

reprove (rɪ'pruːv) vt. censure, rebuke —re'proof n.

reptile ('reptaɪl) n. cold-blooded, air-breathing vertebrate with horny scales or plates, as snake, tortoise etc. —reptilian (rep'tɪlɪən) a.

republic (rɪ'pʌblɪk) n. state without monarch in which supremacy of people or their elected representatives is formally acknowledged —re'publican a./n. —re'publicanism n.

repudiate (rɪ'pjuːdɪeɪt) vt. 1. reject authority or validity of 2. cast off, disown

repugnant (rɪ'pʌgnənt) a. 1. offensive 2. distasteful 3. contrary —re'pugnance n. 1. dislike, aversion 2. incompatibility

repulse (rɪ'pʌls) vt. 1. drive back 2. rebuff 3. repel —n. 4. driving back, rejection, rebuff —re'pulsion n. 1. distaste, aversion 2. Phys. force separating two objects —re'pulsive a. loathsome, disgusting

repute (rɪ'pjuːt) vt. 1. reckon, consider —n. 2. reputation, credit —reputable ('repjʊtəb³l) a. 1. of good repute 2. respectable —reputation (repjʊ'teɪʃən) n. 1. estimation in which person is held 2. character 3. good name —re'puted a.

generally reckoned or considered; supposed —re'putedly adv.

request (rɪ'kwest) n. 1. asking 2. thing asked for —vt. 3. ask

Requiem ('rekwɪem) n. 1. Mass for the dead 2. music for this

requiescat in pace (rekwɪ'eskæt ɪn 'pɑːke) Lat. may he (or she) rest in peace

require (rɪ'kwaɪə) vt. 1. want, need 2. demand —re'quirement n. 1. essential condition 2. specific need 3. want

requisite ('rekwɪzɪt) a. 1. necessary 2. essential —n. 3. something indispensable; necessity

requisition (rekwɪ'zɪʃən) n. 1. formal demand, eg for materials or supplies —vt. 2. demand (supplies) 3. press into service

requite (rɪ'kwaɪt) vt. repay —re'quital n.

reredos ('rɪədɒs) n. ornamental screen behind altar

rerun (riː'rʌn) vt. 1. broadcast or put on (film etc.) again 2. run (race etc.) again —n. ('riːrʌn) 3. film etc. that is broadcast again; repeat 4. race that is run again

resale price maintenance ('riːseɪl) practice by which manufacturer establishes fixed or minimum price for resale of brand product by retailers or other distributors

rescind (rɪ'sɪnd) vt. 1. cancel, annul —res'cindment or rescission (rɪ'sɪʒən) n.

rescue (rɪ'skjuː) vt. 1. save, deliver, extricate (-cuing, -cued) —n. 2. act or instance of rescuing —'rescuer n. —'rescuing n.

research (rɪ'sɜːtʃ) n. 1. investigation, esp. scientific study to discover facts —v. 2. carry out investigations (on, into) —re'searcher n.

resemble (rɪ'zemb³l) vt. 1. be like 2. look like —re'semblance n.

resent (rɪ'zent) vt. 1. show, feel indignation at 2. retain bitterness about —re'sentful a. —re'sentment n.

reserve (rɪ'zɜːv) vt. 1. hold back, set aside, keep for future use —n. 2. (also pl.) something, esp. money, troops etc., kept for emergencies 3. area of land reserved for particular purpose or for use by particular group of people etc. (also reser'vation) 4. reticence, concealment of feelings or friendliness —reservation (rezə'veɪʃən) n. 1. reserving 2. thing reserved 3. doubt 4. exception; limitation —re'served a. not showing feelings, lacking cordiality —re'servist n. one serving in reserve —reserve price UK minimum price acceptable to owner of property being auctioned

reservoir ('rezəvwɑː) n. 1. enclosed area for storage of water, esp. for community supplies 2. receptacle for liquid, gas etc. 3. place where anything is kept in store

reside (rɪ'zaɪd) *vi.* dwell permanently —**residence** ('rezɪdəns) *n.* 1. home 2. house —**residency** ('rezɪdənsɪ) *n.* official dwelling, *esp.*, formerly, of Brit. government agent —**resident** ('rezɪdənt) *a./n.* —**residential** (rezɪ'denʃəl) *a.* 1. (of part of town) consisting mainly of residences 2. of, connected with residence 3. providing living accommodation

residue ('rezɪdjuː) *n.* what is left, remainder —**residual** (rɪ'zɪdjuəl) *a.* —**residuary** (rɪ'zɪdjuərɪ) *a.* —**re'siduum** *n. formal* residue (*pl.* -**ua** (-juə))

resign (rɪ'zaɪn) *vt.* 1. give up 2. reconcile (oneself) —*vi.* 3. give up office, employment *etc.* —**resignation** (rezɪg'neɪʃən) *n.* 1. resigning 2. being resigned, submission —**re'signed** *a.* content to endure

resilient (rɪ'zɪlɪənt) *a.* 1. (of an object) capable of returning to normal after stretching *etc.*; elastic 2. (of a person) recovering quickly from shock *etc.* —**re'silience** *or* **re'siliency** *n.*

resin ('rezɪn) *n.* sticky substance formed in and oozing from plants, *esp.* firs and pines (*also* '**rosin**) —'**resinous** *a.* of, like resin

resist (rɪ'zɪst) *v.* 1. withstand 2. oppose —**re'sistance** *n.* 1. act of resisting 2. opposition 3. hindrance 4. *Elec.* opposition offered by circuit to passage of current through it —**re'sistant** *a.* —**re'sistible** *a.* —**resis'tivity** *n.* measure of electrical resistance —**re'sistor** *n.* component of electrical circuit producing resistance

resit (riː'sɪt) *vt.* 1. sit (examination) again —*n.* ('riːsɪt) 2. examination one must sit again

resolute ('rezəluːt) *a.* determined —'**resolutely** *adv.* —**reso'lution** *n.* 1. resolving 2. firmness 3. purpose or thing resolved upon 4. decision of court or vote of assembly

resolve (rɪ'zɒlv) *vi.* 1. make up one's mind 2. decide with effort of will —*vt.* 3. form by resolution of vote 4. separate component parts of 5. make clear —*n.* 6. resolution 7. fixed purpose —**resolu'bility**, **resolva'bility** *or* **re'solubleness, re'solvableness** *n.* —**resoluble** (rɪ'zɒljubəl, 'rezəl-) *or* **re'solvable** *a.* able to be resolved or analysed —**re'solved** *a.* fixed in purpose or intention; determined —**resolvedly** (rɪ'zɒlvɪdlɪ) *adv.* —**re'solvent** *a./n.* —**re'solver** *n.*

resonance ('rezənəns) *n.* 1. echoing, *esp.* in deep tone 2. sound produced by body vibrating in sympathy with neighbouring source of sound —'**resonant** *a.* —'**resonator** *v.* —'**resonator** *n.*

resort (rɪ'zɔːt) *vi.* 1. have recourse 2. (*with* to) frequent —*n.* 3. place of recreation, *eg* beach 4. recourse 5. frequented place 6. haunt

resound (rɪ'zaʊnd) *vi.* echo, ring, go on

sounding —**re'sounding** *a.* 1. echoing 2. thorough

resource (rɪ'zɔːs, -'sɔːs) *n.* 1. capability, ingenuity 2. that to which one resorts for support 3. expedient —*pl.* 4. source of economic wealth 5. stock that can be drawn on 6. means of support, funds —**re'sourceful** *a.* —**re'sourcefully** *adv.* —**re'sourcefulness** *n.*

respect (rɪ'spekt) *n.* 1. deference, esteem 2. point, aspect 3. reference, relation —*vt.* 4. treat with esteem 5. show consideration for —**respecta'bility** *n.* —**re'spectable** *a.* 1. worthy of respect, decent 2. fairly good —**re'specter** *n.* —**re'spectful** *a.* —**re'specting** *prep.* concerning —**re'spective** *a.* 1. relating separately to each of those in question 2. several, separate —**re'spectively** *adv.*

respire (rɪ'spaɪə) *v.* breathe —**respirable** ('respɪrəbəl) *a.* —**respiration** (respə'reɪʃən) *n.* —**respirator** ('respəreɪtə) *n.* apparatus worn over mouth and breathed through as protection against dust, poison gas *etc.* or to provide artificial respiration —**respiratory** ('respərətərɪ, -trɪ) *a.*

respite ('respɪt, -paɪt) *n.* 1. pause 2. interval 3. suspension of labour 4. delay 5. reprieve

resplendent (rɪ'splendənt) *a.* 1. brilliant, splendid 2. shining —**re'splendence** *or* **re'splendency** *n.*

respond (rɪ'spɒnd) *vi.* 1. answer 2. act in answer to any stimulus 3. react —**re'spondent** *a.* 1. replying —*n.* 2. one who answers 3. defendant —**re'sponse** *n.* answer —**re'sponsive** *a.* readily reacting to some influence —**re'sponsiveness** *n.*

responsible (rɪ'spɒnsəbəl) *a.* 1. liable to answer (for) 2. accountable 3. dependable 4. involving responsibility 5. of good credit or position —**responsi'bility** *n.* 1. state of being answerable 2. duty 3. charge 4. obligation

rest[1] (rest) *n.* 1. repose 2. freedom from exertion *etc.* 3. that on which anything rests or leans 4. pause, *esp.* in music 5. support —*vi.* 6. take rest 7. be supported —*vt.* 8. give rest to 9. place on support —'**restful** *a.* —'**restless** *a.*

rest[2] (rest) *n.* 1. remainder 2. others —*vi.* 3. remain 4. continue to be

restaurant ('restərɒŋ, 'restrɒŋ) *n.* commercial establishment serving food —**restaurateur** (restərə'tɜː) *n.* keeper of restaurant —**restaurant car** UK railway coach in which meals are served (*also* **dining car**)

restitution (restɪ'tjuːʃən) *n.* 1. giving back or making up 2. reparation, compensation

restive ('restɪv) *a.* 1. restless 2. resisting control, impatient

restore (rɪ'stɔː) *vt.* 1. build up again, repair, renew 2. re-establish 3. give back —**restoration**

(restɔˈreiʃən) n. —**restorative** (riˈstɔrɔtiv) a. 1. restoring —n. 2. medicine to strengthen etc. —re'storer n.

restrain (riˈstrein) vt. 1. check, hold back 2. prevent 3. confine —re'straint n. restraining, control, esp. self-control

restrict (riˈstrikt) vt. limit, bound —re'striction n. 1. limitation 2. restraint 3. rule —re'strictive a. —restricted area area in which speed limit for vehicles applies —restrictive practice UK 1. trading agreement against public interest 2. practice of union or other group tending to limit freedom of other workers or employers

result (riˈzʌlt) vi. 1. follow as consequence 2. happen 3. end —n. 1. effect, outcome —re'sultant a. arising as result

resume (riˈzjuːm) v. begin again —résumé ('rezjumei) n. summary, abstract —resumption (riˈzʌmpʃɔn) n. 1. resuming 2. fresh start —resumptive (riˈzʌmptiv) a.

resurgence (riˈsɜːdʒɔns) n. rising again —re'surgent a.

resurrect (rezɔˈrekt) vt. 1. restore to life, resuscitate 2. use once more (something discarded etc.) —resur'rection n. 1. rising again (esp. from dead) 2. revival

resuscitate (riˈsʌsiteit) vt. revive to life, consciousness —resusci'tation n.

retail ('riːteil) n. 1. sale of goods in small quantities —adv. 2. by retail —v. 3. sell, be sold, retail 4. (riˈteil) recount —'retailer n.

retain (riˈtein) vt. 1. keep 2. engage services of —re'tainer n. 1. fee to retain professional adviser, esp. barrister 2. Hist. follower of nobleman etc. —retention (riˈtenʃɔn) n. —retentive (riˈtentiv) a. capable of retaining, remembering —retaining wall wall constructed to hold back earth etc. (also re'vetment)

retake (riːˈteik) vt. 1. take back, capture again 2. Cine. shoot (scene) again 3. tape (recording) again —n. ('riːteik) 4. Cine. rephotographed scene 5. retaped recording

retaliate (riˈtælieit) vi. 1. repay someone in kind 2. revenge oneself —retali'ation n. —re'taliative or re'taliatory a.

retard (riˈtɑːd) vt. 1. make slow or late 2. keep back 3. impede development of —retar'dation n. —re'tarded a. underdeveloped, esp. mentally

retch (retʃ, riːtʃ) vi. try to vomit

reticent ('retisɔnt) a. 1. reserved in speech 2. uncommunicative —'reticence n.

reticulate (riˈtikjulit) a. 1. made or arranged like a net (also re'ticular) —v. (riˈtikjuleit) 2. make, be like net —reticu'lation n.

retina ('retinɔ) n. light-sensitive membrane at back of eye (pl. -s, -nae (-niː))

retinue ('retinjuː) n. band of followers or attendants

retire (riˈtaiɔ) vi. 1. give up office or work 2. go away 3. withdraw 4. go to bed —vt. 5. cause to retire —re'tired a. that has retired from office etc. —re'tirement n. —re'tiring a. unobtrusive, shy —retirement pension UK weekly payment made by government to retired man over 65 or woman over 60

retort (riˈtɔːt) vt. 1. reply 2. repay in kind, retaliate 3. hurl back (charge etc.) —vi. 4. reply with countercharge —n. 5. vigorous reply or repartee 6. vessel with bent neck used for distilling

retouch (riːˈtʌtʃ) vt. touch up, improve by new touches, esp. of paint etc.

retrace (riˈtreis) vt. go back over (a route etc.) again

retract (riˈtrækt) v. draw back, recant —re'tractable or re'tractible a. —re'tractile a. capable of being drawn in —re'traction n. drawing or taking back, esp. of statement etc. —re'tractor n. 1. muscle 2. surgical instrument

retread (riːˈtred) vt. 1. renovate (worn rubber tyre) (-'treaded, -'treading) —n. ('riːtred) 2. renovated tyre (also 'remould)

retreat (riˈtriːt) vi. 1. move back from any position 2. retire —n. 3. act of, or military signal for, retiring, withdrawal 4. place to which anyone retires 5. refuge 6. sunset call on bugle

retrench (riˈtrentʃ) v. 1. reduce (expenditure), esp. by dismissing staff —vt. 2. cut down —re'trenchment n.

retribution (retriˈbjuːʃɔn) n. 1. recompense, esp. for evil deeds 2. vengeance —retributive (riˈtribjutiv) a.

retrieve (riˈtriːv) vt. 1. fetch back again 2. restore 3. rescue from ruin 4. recover, esp. information from computer 5. regain —re'trievable a. —re'trieval n. —re'triever n. dog trained to retrieve game

retro- (comb. form) 1. back; backwards, as in retroactive 2. located behind, as in retrochoir

retroact ('retrouækt) vi. 1. react 2. act in opposite direction —retro'active a. applying or referring to the past —retro'actively adv.

retrochoir ('retroukwaiɔ) n. space in large church or cathedral behind high altar

retrograde ('retrougreid) a. 1. going backwards, reverting 2. reactionary —retro'gress vi. 1. go back to earlier, esp. worse, condition; degenerate, deteriorate 2. move backwards; recede —retro'gression n. —retro'gressive a.

retrorocket ('retrouroki t) n. rocket engine to slow or reverse spacecraft etc.

retrospect ('retrouspekt) n. looking back, survey of past —retro'spection n. —retro'spective a.

retroussé (rə'tru:seɪ) a. (of nose) turned upwards, pug

retsina (ret'si:nə) n. Gr. wine

return (rɪ'tɜːn) vi. 1. go, come back —vt. 2. give, send back 3. report officially 4. elect —n. 5. returning, being returned 6. profit 7. official report 8. return ticket —**returning officer** officer conducting election —**return ticket** ticket allowing passenger to travel to and from a place

reunion (ri:'ju:njən) n. gathering of people who have been apart

rev (rev) inf. n. 1. revolution (of engine) —v. 2. (oft. with up) increase speed of revolution (of) —**rev counter** UK inf. tachometer

Rev. 1. Bible Revelation 2. Reverend

revalue (ri:'vælju:) or U.S. **revaluate** v. adjust exchange value of (currency) upwards —**revalu'ation** n.

revamp (ri:'væmp) vt. renovate, restore

reveal (rɪ'vi:l) vt. 1. make known 2. show —**revelation** (revə'leɪʃən) n.

reveille (rɪ'vælɪ) n. morning bugle call etc. to waken soldiers

revel ('rev³l) vi. 1. take pleasure (in) 2. make merry (-ll-) —n. 3. (usu. pl.) merrymaking —'**reveller** n. —'**revelry** n. festivity

revenge (rɪ'vendʒ) n. 1. retaliation for wrong done 2. act that satisfies this 3. desire for this —vt. 4. avenge 5. make retaliation for —v.refl. 6. avenge oneself —re'**vengeful** a. 1. vindictive 2. resentful

revenue ('revɪnju:) n. income, esp. of state, as taxes etc. —**Inland Revenue** government department that administers and collects direct taxes, eg income tax

reverberate (rɪ'vɜ:bəreɪt) v. echo, resound, throw back (sound etc.) —**reverber'ation** n.

revere (rɪ'vɪə) vt. hold in great regard or religious respect —**reverence** ('revərəns) n. 1. revering 2. awe mingled with respect and esteem 3. veneration —**reverend** ('revərənd) a. (esp. as prefix to clergyman's name) worthy of reverence —**reverent** ('revərənt, 'revrənt) a. showing reverence —**reverential** (revə'renʃəl) a. marked by reverence

reverie ('revərɪ) n. daydream, absent-minded state

revers (rɪ'vɪə) n. part of garment which is turned back, eg lapel (pl. -**vers** (-'vɪəz))

reverse (rɪ'vɜ:s) v. 1. (of vehicle) (cause to) move backwards —vt. 2. turn upside down or other way round 3. change completely —n. 4. opposite, contrary 5. side opposite, obverse 6. defeat 7. reverse gear —a. 8. opposite, contrary —re'**versal** n. —re'**versible** a. —**reverse charge** telephone call made at recipient's expense —**reverse gear** mechanism enabling

vehicle to move backwards —**reversing light** light on rear of motor vehicle to provide illumination when reversing

revert (rɪ'vɜ:t) vi. 1. return to former state 2. come back to subject 3. refer (to) a second time 4. turn backwards —re'**version** n. (of property) rightful passing to owner or designated heir etc. —re'**verted** a. —re'**vertible** a.

review (rɪ'vju:) vt. 1. examine 2. look back on 3. reconsider 4. hold, make, write review of —n. 5. general survey 6. critical notice of book etc. 7. periodical with critical articles 8. inspection of troops —re'**viewer** n. writer of reviews

revile (rɪ'vaɪl) vt. be viciously scornful of, abuse —re'**viler** n.

revise (rɪ'vaɪz) vt. 1. look over and correct 2. restudy (work done previously) in preparation for examination 3. change, alter —re'**viser** n. —**revision** (rɪ'vɪʒən) n. 1. re-examination for purpose of correcting 2. revising of notes, subject for examination 3. revised copy —**revisionism** (rɪ'vɪʒənɪzəm) n. 1. (sometimes R-) moderate, nonrevolutionary version of Marxism developed in Germany around 1900 2. (sometimes R-) in Marxist-Leninist ideology, dangerous departure from true interpretation of Marx's teachings 3. advocacy of revision of some political theory etc. —**revisionist** (rɪ'vɪʒənɪst) n./a. —re'**visory** a. of revision

revive (rɪ'vaɪv) v. bring, come back to life, vigour, use etc. —re'**vival** n. reviving, esp. of religious fervour —re'**vivalist** n./a.

revoke (rɪ'vəʊk) vt. 1. take back, withdraw 2. cancel —**revocable** ('revəkəb³l) a. —**revocation** (revə'keɪʃən) n. repeal

revolt (rɪ'vəʊlt) n. 1. rebellion —vi. 2. rise in rebellion 3. feel disgust —vt. 4. affect with disgust —re'**volting** a. disgusting, horrible

revolve (rɪ'vɒlv) v. 1. turn round, rotate 2. be centred (on) —vt. 3. rotate —**revolution** (revə'lu:ʃən) n. 1. violent overthrow of government 2. great change 3. complete rotation, turning or spinning round —**revolutionary** (revə'lu:ʃənərɪ) a./n. —**revolutionize** or -**ise** (revə'lu:ʃənaɪz) vt. 1. change considerably 2. bring about revolution in —**revolving door** door that rotates about vertical axis, esp. with four leaves at right angles to each other

revolver (rɪ'vɒlvə) n. repeating pistol with revolving magazine

revue or **review** (rɪ'vju:) n. theatrical entertainment with topical sketches and songs

revulsion (rɪ'vʌlʃən) n. 1. sudden violent change of feeling 2. marked repugnance or abhorrence

reward (rɪ'wɔ:d) vt. 1. pay, make return to (someone) for service, conduct etc. —n. 2. something given in return for a deed or service rendered —**re'warding** a. giving personal satisfaction, worthwhile

rewire (riː'waɪə) vt. provide (house etc.) with new wiring

RF radio frequency

R.F.C. Rugby Football Club

R.G.S. Royal Geographical Society

Rh 1. Chem. rhodium 2. rhesus (esp. in **Rh factor** (see also **rhesus factor** at RHESUS))

rhapsody ('ræpsədɪ) n. enthusiastic or high-flown (musical) composition or utterance —**rhapsodic** (ræp'sɒdɪk) a. —**rhapsodist** n. —**rhapsodize** or **-ise** ('ræpsədaɪz) v.

rhea ('rɪə) n. S Amer. three-toed ostrich

rhebuck or **rhebok** ('riːbʌk) n. brownish-grey S Afr. antelope

rhenium ('riːnɪəm) n. dense silvery-white metallic element that has high melting point

rheostat ('rɪəstæt) n. instrument for regulating the value of the resistance in an electric circuit

rhesus ('riːsəs) n. small, long-tailed monkey of S Asia —**rhesus factor** feature distinguishing different types of human blood (also **Rh factor**)

rhetoric ('rɛtərɪk) n. 1. art of effective speaking or writing 2. artificial or exaggerated language —**rhe'torical** a. (of question) not requiring an answer —**rheto'rician** n.

rheum (ruːm) n. 1. watery discharge, mucus 2. catarrh —**rheumy** a.

rheumatism ('ruːmətɪzəm) n. painful inflammation of joints or muscles —**rheu'matic** a./n. —**rheumatoid** a. of, like rheumatism —**rheumatic fever** disease characterized by inflammation and pain in joints —**rheumatoid arthritis** chronic disease characterized by inflammation and swelling of joints

Rh factor see **rhesus factor** at RHESUS

rhinestone ('raɪnstəʊn) n. imitation gem made of paste

rhino ('raɪnəʊ) n. rhinoceros (pl. **-s**, **'rhino**)

rhino- or before vowel **rhin-** (comb. form) nose, as in rhinology

rhinoceros (raɪ'nɒsərəs, -'nɒsrəs) n. large thick-skinned animal with one or two horns on nose (**-es**, **-ros**)

rhizome ('raɪzəʊm) n. thick horizontal underground stem whose buds develop into new plants (also **'rootstock**, **'rootstalk**)

rho (rəʊ) n. 17th letter in Gr. alphabet (P, ρ) (pl. **-s**)

rhodium ('rəʊdɪəm) n. hard metal like platinum —**'rhodic** a.

rhododendron (rəʊdə'dɛndrən) n. any of various evergreen flowering shrubs

rhombus ('rɒmbəs) n. equilateral but not right-angled parallelogram, diamond-shaped figure (pl. **-es**, **-bi** (-baɪ)) —**rhombohedron** (rɒmbəʊ'hiːdrən) n. six-sided prism whose sides

are parallelograms —**'rhomboid** n./a. —**rhom-'boidal** a.

rhubarb ('ruːbɑːb) n. 1. garden plant of which the fleshy stalks are cooked and used as fruit 2. laxative from root of allied Chinese plant

rhumba ('rʌmbə, 'rʊm-) n. see RUMBA

rhumb line (rʌm) 1. imaginary line on surface of sphere that intersects all meridians at same angle 2. course navigated by vessel or aircraft that maintains uniform compass heading (also **rhumb**)

rhyme or **rime** (raɪm) n. 1. identity of sounds at ends of lines of verse, or in words 2. word or syllable identical in sound to another 3. verse marked by rhyme —vt. 4. use (word) to make rhymes —**rhymester**, **rimester** ('raɪmstə) **'rhymer** or **'rimer** n. poet, esp. one considered mediocre; poetaster, versifier —**rhyme scheme** pattern of rhymes used in piece of verse, usu. indicated by letters —**rhyming slang** slang in which word is replaced by word or phrase that rhymes with it

rhythm ('rɪðəm) n. measured beat or flow, esp. of words, music etc. —**'rhythmic(al)** a. —**'rhythmically** adv. —**rhythm-and-blues** n. kind of popular music derived from or influenced by blues —**rhythm method** method of contraception by restricting sexual intercourse to days in woman's menstrual cycle when conception is considered least likely to occur

RI Rhode Island

R.I. 1. Regina et Imperatrix (Lat., Queen and Empress) 2. Rex et Imperator (Lat., King and Emperor) 3. Royal Institution 4. religious instruction

ria ('rɪə) n. long narrow inlet of sea coast, being former valley submerged by sea

rib[1] (rɪb) n. 1. one of curved bones springing from spine and forming framework of upper part of body 2. cut of meat including rib(s) 3. curved timber of framework of boat 4. raised series of rows in knitting etc. —vt. 5. furnish, mark with ribs 6. knit to form rib pattern (**-bb-**) —**'ribbing** n.

rib[2] (rɪb) vt. inf. tease, ridicule (**-bb-**)

R.I.B.A. Royal Institute of British Architects

ribald ('rɪb³ld) a. 1. irreverent, scurrilous 2. indecent —n. 3. ribald person —**'ribaldry** n. vulgar, indecent talk

ribbon ('rɪb³n) n. 1. narrow band of fabric used for trimming, tying etc. 2. long strip or line of anything —**ribbon development** building of houses along main road leading out of town etc.

riboflavin or **riboflavine** (raɪbəʊ'fleɪvɪn) n. form of vitamin B

ribonucleic acid (raɪbəʊnjuː'kliːɪk, -'kleɪ-) see RNA

rice¹ (raɪs) n. 1. Eastern cereal plant 2. its seeds as food —**rice paper** fine, edible Chinese paper

rich (rɪtʃ) a. 1. wealthy 2. fertile 3. abounding 4. valuable 5. (of food) containing much fat or sugar 6. mellow 7. amusing —n. 8. the wealthy classes —'**riches** pl.n. wealth —'**richly** adv.

Richter scale ('rɪktə) scale for expressing intensity of earthquake

rick¹ (rɪk) n. stack of hay etc.

rick² (rɪk) vt./n. sprain, wrench

rickets ('rɪkɪts) n. disease of children marked by softening of bones, bow legs etc., caused by vitamin D deficiency —'**rickety** a. 1. shaky, insecure, unstable 2. suffering from rickets

rickshaw ('rɪkʃɔː) or **ricksha** ('rɪkʃə) n. light two-wheeled man-drawn Asian vehicle

ricochet ('rɪkəʃeɪ, 'rɪkəʃet) vi. 1. (of bullet) rebound or be deflected by solid surface or water —n. 2. bullet or shot to which this happens

rid (rɪd) vt. 1. clear, relieve 2. free 3. deliver (**rid**, '**ridding**) —'**riddance** n. 1. clearance 2. act of ridding 3. deliverance 4. relief

ridden ('rɪd°n) pp. of RIDE

-ridden (comb. form) afflicted by, affected by, as in disease-ridden

riddle¹ ('rɪd°l) n. 1. question made puzzling to test one's ingenuity 2. enigma 3. puzzling thing, person —vi. 4. speak in, make riddles

riddle² ('rɪd°l) vt. 1. pierce with many holes —n. 2. coarse sieve for gravel etc. —**riddled with** full of, esp. holes

ride (raɪd) v. 1. sit on and control or propel (horse, bicycle etc.) —vi. 2. go on horseback or in vehicle 3. lie at anchor 4. be carried on or across —vt. 5. travel over (**rode**, '**ridden**, '**riding**) —n. 6. journey on horse etc., or in any vehicle 7. riding track —'**rider** n. 1. one who rides 2. supplementary clause 3. addition to a document 4. mathematical problem on given proposition —'**riderless** a. —'**riding crop** short whip with handle at one end for opening gates —'**riding lamp** or **light** light on vessel showing it is at anchor

ridge (rɪdʒ) n. 1. long, narrow hill 2. long, narrow elevation on surface 3. line of meeting of two sloping surfaces —v. 4. form into ridges —'**ridgepole** n. 1. timber along ridge of roof, to which rafters are attached 2. horizontal pole at apex of tent

ridiculous (rɪ'dɪkjʊləs) a. deserving to be laughed at; absurd, foolish —'**ridicule** n. 1. language or behaviour intended to humiliate or mock —vt. 2. laugh at, deride

riding ('raɪdɪŋ) n. 1. (R- when part of name) former administrative district of Yorkshire 2. C parliamentary constituency

riesling ('riːzlɪŋ, 'raɪz-) n. 1. dry white wine 2. type of grape used to make this wine

rife (raɪf) a. prevalent, common

riffle ('rɪf°l) v. flick through (pages etc.) quickly

riffraff ('rɪfræf) n. disreputable people, esp. collectively; rabble

rifle ('raɪf°l) vt. 1. search and rob 2. ransack 3. make spiral grooves in (gun barrel etc.) —n. 4. firearm with long barrel —'**rifling** n. 1. arrangement of grooves in gun barrel 2. pillaging

rift (rɪft) n. crack, split, cleft —**rift valley** long narrow valley resulting from subsidence of land between two faults

rig (rɪg) vt. 1. provide (ship) with spars, ropes etc. 2. equip 3. set up, esp. as makeshift 4. arrange in dishonest way (**-gg-**) —n. 5. way ship's masts and sails are arranged 6. apparatus for drilling for oil and gas 7. US articulated lorry —'**rigger** n. —'**rigging** n. ship's spars and ropes —'**rigout** n. inf. person's clothing or costume, esp. bizarre outfit —**rig out** 1. (oft. with) equip or fit out (with) 2. dress or be dressed

right (raɪt) a. 1. just 2. in accordance with truth and duty 3. true 4. correct 5. proper 6. of side that faces east when front is turned to north 7. Pol. conservative or reactionary (also **right-wing**) 8. straight 9. upright 10. of outer or more finished side of fabric —vt. 11. bring back to vertical position 12. do justice to —vi. 13. come back to vertical position 14. claim, title etc. allowed or due 15. what is right, just or due 16. conservative political party 17. Boxing punch, blow with right hand —adv. 18. straight 19. properly 20. very 21. on or to right side —'**rightful** a. —'**rightly** adv. —**right angle** angle of 90 degrees —**right-angled triangle** triangle one angle of which is right angle —**right-hand** a. 1. of, located on or moving towards the right 2. for use by right hand —**right-handed** a. 1. using right hand with greater skill than left 2. performed with right hand 3. for use by right hand 4. turning from left to right —**right-minded** a. holding opinions or principles that accord with what is right or with opinions of speaker —**Right Reverend** title of respect for bishop —**right whale** large, grey or black whalebone whale with large head and no dorsal fin —**right-hand man** most valuable assistant —**right of way** Law 1. right to pass over someone's land 2. path used (pl. **rights of way**)

righteous ('raɪtʃəs) a. 1. just, upright 2. godly 3. virtuous 4. good 5. honest —'**righteousness** n.

rigid ('rɪdʒɪd) a. 1. inflexible 2. harsh, stiff —ri'**gidity** n.

rigmarole ('rɪɡmərəʊl) or **rigamarole**

('rɪgəmərəʊl) *n.* **1.** meaningless string of words **2.** long, complicated procedure

rigor ('raɪgɔː, 'rɪgə) *n.* sudden coldness attended by shivering —**rigor mortis** ('rɪgə 'mɔːtɪs) stiffening of body after death

rigour *or U.S.* **rigor** ('rɪgə) *n.* **1.** harshness, severity, strictness **2.** hardship —**rigorous** *a.* stern, harsh, severe

rile (raɪl) *vt. inf.* anger, annoy

rill (rɪl) *n.* small stream

rim (rɪm) *n.* **1.** edge, border, margin **2.** outer ring of wheel —**rimmed** *a.* bordered, edged

rime[1] (raɪm) *n.* hoarfrost —**rimy** *a.*

rime[2] (raɪm) *n. see* RHYME

rind (raɪnd) *n.* outer coating of fruits *etc.*

rinderpest ('rɪndəpɛst) *n.* malignant infectious disease of cattle

ring[1] (rɪŋ) *n.* **1.** circle of gold *etc.*, *esp.* for finger **2.** any circular band, coil, rim *etc.* **3.** people or things arranged so as to form circle **4.** group of people working together to advance their own interests **5.** enclosed area, *esp.* roped-in square for boxing —*vt.* **6.** put ring round **7.** mark (bird *etc.*) with ring —**ringer** *n.* **1.** one who rings bells **2.** *sl.* person, thing apparently identical to another (*esp. in* **dead ringer**) —**ringlet** *n.* curly lock of hair —**ringbark** *v.* kill (tree) by cutting bark round trunk —**ring finger** third finger, *esp.* of left hand, on which wedding ring is worn —**ringleader** *n.* instigator of mutiny, riot *etc.* —**ring main** domestic electrical supply in which outlet sockets are connected to mains supply through continuous closed circuit (**ring circuit**) —**ringmaster** *n.* master of ceremonies in circus —**ring road** main road that bypasses a town (centre) —**ringside** *n.* **1.** row of seats nearest boxing or wrestling ring **2.** any place affording close uninterrupted view —**ringworm** *n.* fungal skin disease in circular patches

ring[2] (rɪŋ) *vi.* **1.** give out clear resonant sound, as bell **2.** resound —*vt.* **3.** cause (bell) to sound **4.** call (person) by telephone (**rang** *pt.,* **rung** *pp.*) —*n.* **5.** a ringing **6.** telephone call

rink (rɪŋk) *n.* **1.** sheet of ice for skating or curling **2.** floor for roller skating

rinkhals ('rɪŋkhaʊs) *n.* S Afr. ring-necked cobra

rinse (rɪns) *vt.* **1.** remove soap from (washed clothes, hair *etc.*) by applying clean water **2.** wash lightly —*n.* **3.** a rinsing **4.** liquid to tint hair

riot ('raɪət) *n.* **1.** tumult, disorder **2.** loud revelry **3.** disorderly, unrestrained disturbance **4.** profusion —*vi.* **5.** make, engage in riot —**riotous** *a.* unruly, rebellious, wanton

rip[1] (rɪp) *vt.* **1.** cut, tear away, slash, rend (**-pp-**) —*n.* **2.** rent, tear —**ripcord** *n.* cord pulled to open parachute —**rip-roaring** *a. inf.* characterized by excitement, intensity or boisterous

behaviour —**ripsaw** *n.* handsaw with coarse teeth (used for cutting wood along grain) —**rip-off** *n. sl.* act of stealing, overcharging *etc.* —**rip off** *sl.* **1.** steal **2.** overcharge

rip[2] (rɪp) *n.* strong current, *esp.* one moving away from the shore

R.I.P. requiescat in pace

riparian (raɪ'pɛərɪən) *a.* of, on banks of river

ripe (raɪp) *a.* **1.** ready to be reaped, eaten *etc.* **2.** matured **3.** (of judgment *etc.*) sound —**ripen** *v.* **1.** make or grow ripe —*vi.* **2.** mature

riposte (rɪ'pɒst, rɪ'pəʊst) *n.* **1.** verbal retort **2.** counterstroke **3.** *Fencing* quick lunge after parry

ripple ('rɪp[ə]l) *n.* **1.** slight wave, ruffling of surface **2.** sound like ripples of water —*vi.* **3.** flow, form into little waves **4.** (of sounds) rise and fall gently —*vt.* **5.** form ripples on

rise (raɪz) *vi.* **1.** get up **2.** move upwards **3.** appear above horizon **4.** reach higher level **5.** increase in value or price **6.** rebel **7.** adjourn **8.** originate; begin (**rose, risen** ('rɪz[ə]n), **rising**) —*n.* **9.** rising **10.** slope upwards **11.** increase, *esp.* of wages —**riser** *n.* **1.** one who rises, *esp.* from bed **2.** vertical part of step —**rising** *n.* **1.** revolt —*a.* **2.** increasing in rank, maturity

risible ('rɪzɪb[ə]l) *a.* **1.** inclined to laugh **2.** laughable —**risi'bility** *n.*

risk (rɪsk) *n.* **1.** chance of disaster or loss —*vt.* **2.** venture **3.** put in jeopardy **4.** take chance of —**riskily** *adv.* —**risky** *a.* **1.** dangerous **2.** hazardous —**take** *or* **run a risk** proceed in an action regardless of danger involved

risotto (rɪ'zɒtəʊ) *n.* dish of rice cooked in stock and served with various other ingredients

risqué ('rɪskeɪ) *a.* suggestive of indecency

rissole ('rɪsəʊl) *n.* dish of fish or meat minced, coated with egg and breadcrumbs and fried

rite (raɪt) *n.* formal practice or custom, *esp.* religious —**ritual** ('rɪtjʊəl) *n.* **1.** prescribed order or book of rites **2.** regular, stereotyped action or behaviour —*a.* **3.** concerning rites —**ritualism** ('rɪtjʊəlɪzəm) *n.* practice of ritual —**ritualist** ('rɪtjʊəlɪst) *n.*

ritzy ('rɪtsɪ) *a. sl.* luxurious; elegant

rival ('raɪv[ə]l) *n.* **1.** one that competes with another for favour, success *etc.* —*vt.* **2.** vie with (**-ll-**) —*a.* **3.** in position of rival —**rivalry** *n.* keen competition

rive (raɪv) *v.* (*usu. as pp./a.* **riven**) **1.** split asunder **2.** tear apart (**rived** *pt.,* **rived, riven** *pp.,* **riving** *pr.p.*) —**riven** ('rɪv[ə]n) *a.* split

river ('rɪvə) *n.* **1.** large natural stream of water **2.** copious flow —**river basin** area drained by river and its tributaries —**riverbed** *n.* channel in which river flows or has flowed

rivet ('rɪvɪt) *n.* **1.** bolt for fastening metal plates, the end being put through holes and then beaten flat —vt. 2. fasten with rivets 3. cause to be fixed or held firmly, esp. (fig.) in surprise, horror etc. —'**riveter** n.

rivulet ('rɪvjulɪt) n. small stream

R.L. Rugby League

rly. railway

R.M. 1. Royal Mail 2. Royal Marines 3. C Rural Municipality

R.M.A. Royal Military Academy (Sandhurst)

rms or **r.m.s.** root mean square

Rn Chem. radon

R.N. Royal Navy

RNA Biochem. ribonucleic acid; any of group of nucleic acids, present in all living cells, that play essential role in synthesis of proteins

R.N.(V.)R. Royal Naval (Volunteer) Reserve

roach (rəʊtʃ) n. European freshwater fish (pl. **roach, -es**)

road (rəʊd) n. 1. track, way prepared for passengers, vehicles etc. 2. direction, way 3. street —'**roadster** n. 1. obs. touring car 2. kind of bicycle —'**roadblock** n. barricade across road to stop traffic for inspection etc. —**road-fund licence** UK licence showing that tax payable in respect of motor vehicle has been paid —**road hog** selfish, aggressive driver —'**roadholding** n. extent to which motor vehicle is stable and does not skid, esp. on sharp bends etc. —'**roadhouse** n. public house, restaurant on country route —**road metal** broken stones used in macadamizing roads —**road sense** sound judgment in driving road vehicles —**road show** 1. Rad. live programme, usu. with audience participation, transmitted from radio van taking particular show on the road 2. group of entertainers on tour —'**roadside** n./a. —'**roadstead** n. Naut. partly sheltered anchorage (also **roads**) —**road test** test to ensure that vehicle is roadworthy, esp. after repair etc., by driving it on roads —**road-test** vt. test (vehicle) in this way —'**roadway** n. 1. surface of road 2. part of road used by vehicles —'**roadworks** pl.n. repairs to road, esp. blocking part of road —'**roadworthy** a. (of vehicle) mechanically sound —**hit the road** sl. start or resume travelling —**one for the road** last alcoholic drink before leaving

roam (rəʊm) v. wander about, rove —'**roamer** n.

roan (rəʊn) a. 1. (of horses) having coat in which main colour is thickly interspersed with another, esp. bay, sorrel or chestnut mixed with white or grey —n. 2. horse having such a coat

roar (rɔː) vi. 1. make or utter loud, deep, hoarse sound, as of lion —v. 2. (of people) utter (something) with loud deep cry, as in anger or triumph —n. 3. such a sound —'**roaring** a. 1. inf. brisk and profitable —adv. 2. noisily

roast (rəʊst) v. 1. bake, cook in closed oven 2. cook by exposure to open fire 3. make, be very hot —n. 4. roasted joint —a. 5. roasted —'**roaster** n. 1. oven etc. for roasting meat 2. chicken etc. suitable for roasting —'**roasting** n. esp. inf. severe criticism, scolding

rob (rɒb) vt. 1. plunder, steal from 2. pillage, defraud (**-bb-**) —'**robber** n. —'**robbery** n.

robe (rəʊb) n. 1. any long outer garment, oft. denoting rank or office —vt. 2. dress —vi. 3. put on robes, vestments

robin ('rɒbɪn) n. small brown bird with red breast (also **robin redbreast**)

robot ('rəʊbɒt) n. 1. automated machine, esp. performing functions in human manner 2. person of machinelike efficiency 3. SA traffic lights —**ro'botic** a. of or like robot —**ro'botics** pl.n. (with sing. v.) study of use of robots

robust (rəʊ'bʌst, 'rəʊbʌst) a. sturdy, strong —**ro'bustious** a. obs. 1. rough; boisterous 2. strong, robust, stout —**ro'bustness** n.

roc (rɒk) n. monstrous bird of Arabian mythology

R.O.C. Royal Observer Corps

rock[1] (rɒk) n. 1. stone 2. large rugged mass of stone 3. hard sweet in sticks —'**rockery** n. mound or grotto of stones or rocks for plants in garden —'**rocky** a. 1. having many rocks 2. rugged —**rock bottom** lowest possible level —**rock-bound** a. hemmed in or encircled by rocks (also (poet.) **rock-girt**) —**rock cake** small cake containing dried fruit, with rough surface supposed to resemble rock —**rock crystal** transparent colourless quartz —**rock garden** garden featuring rocks or rockeries —**rock plant** plant that grows on rocks or in rocky ground —**rock rabbit** SA dassie, hyrax —**rock salmon** various food fishes, esp. dogfish —**rock salt** mineral consisting of sodium chloride in crystalline form, occurring in sedimentary beds etc.: important source of table salt (also '**halite**)

rock[2] (rɒk) v. 1. (cause to) sway to and fro 2. reel or sway or cause (someone) to reel or sway, as with shock or emotion —vi. 3. dance in rock-and-roll style —n. 4. rocking motion 5. rock-and-roll —'**rocker** n. 1. curved piece of wood etc. on which thing may rock 2. rocking chair —'**rocky** a. 1. weak, unstable 2. inf. dizzy; nauseated —**rock-and-roll** or **rock-'n'-roll** n. 1. type of pop music of 1950s as blend of rhythm-and-blues and country-and-western 2. dancing performed to such music —**rocking horse** toy horse mounted on rockers, on which child can rock to and fro in seesaw movement —**off one's rocker** inf. insane

rocket[1] ('rɒkɪt) n. 1. self-propelling device powered by burning of explosive contents, used as firework, for display, signalling, line carrying, weapon *etc.* **2.** vehicle propelled by rocket engine, as weapon or carrying spacecraft —*vi.* **3.** move fast, *esp.* upwards, as rocket —'**rocketry** *n.*

rocket² ('rɒkɪt) *n.* any of several kinds of flowering plant

rococo (rə'kəʊkəʊ) *a.* (*oft.* R-) **1.** of furniture, architecture *etc.* having much conventional decoration in style of early 18th-cent. work in France **2.** tastelessly florid

rod (rɒd) *n.* **1.** slender cylinder of metal, wood *etc.* **2.** cane **3.** unit of length equal to 5½ yards

rode (rəʊd) *pt. of* RIDE

rodent ('rəʊdənt) *n.* any gnawing animal, *eg* rat

rodeo ('rəʊdɪəʊ) *n. US, A* display of skills of cowboys, with bareback riding, cattle-handling techniques *etc.* (*pl.* -**s**)

rodomontade (rɒdəmɒn'teɪd, -'tɑːd) *Lit. n.* **1.** boastful words or behaviour —*vi.* **2.** boast; rant

roe¹ (rəʊ) *n.* small species of deer

roe² (rəʊ) *n.* mass of eggs in fish

roentgen *or* **röntgen** ('rɒntgən, -tjən, 'rɛnt-) *n.* measuring unit of radiation dose

rogation (rəʊ'geɪʃən) *n.* (*usu. pl.*) *Christianity* solemn supplication, *esp.* in form of ceremony prescribed by Church —**Rogation Days** three days preceding Ascension Day

roger ('rɒdʒə) *interj.* **1.** *Telecomm. etc.* message received and understood **2.** expression of agreement

rogue (rəʊg) *n.* **1.** rascal, knave, scoundrel **2.** mischief-loving person, *oft.* child **3.** wild beast of savage temper, living apart from herd —'**roguery** *n.* —'**roguish** *a.* —**rogues' gallery** collection of portraits of known criminals kept by police for identification purposes

roister ('rɔɪstə) *vi.* **1.** be noisy or boisterous **2.** brag, bluster or swagger —'**roisterer** *n.* reveller

role *or* **rôle** (rəʊl) *n.* **1.** actor's part **2.** specific task or function

roll (rəʊl) *v.* **1.** move by turning over and over —*vt.* **2.** wind round **3.** smooth out with roller —*vi.* **4.** move, sweep along **5.** undulate **6.** (of ship) swing from side to side **7.** (of aircraft) turn about a line from nose to tail in flight —*n.* **8.** act of lying down and turning over and over or from side to side **9.** piece of paper *etc.* rolled up **10.** any object thus shaped, as *meat roll, swiss roll, etc.* **11.** official list or register, *esp.* of names **12.** bread baked into small oval or round **13.** continuous sound, as of drums, thunder *etc.* —'**roller** *n.* **1.** cylinder of wood, stone, metal *etc.* used for pressing, crushing, smoothing, supporting thing to be moved, winding thing on *etc.* **2.** long wave of sea **3.** any of various Old World birds that have blue, green and brown plumage and erratic flight —'**rolling** *a.* **1.** having gentle rising and falling slopes **2.** reverberating **3.** that

may be turned up or down **4.** *sl.* extremely rich —*adv.* **5.** *sl.* swaying, staggering (*esp. in* **rolling drunk**) —**roll call** act, time of calling over list of names, as in schools or army —**rolled gold** metal coated with thin layer of gold —**roller bearings** bearings of hardened steel rollers —**roller coaster** *see* **big dipper** *at* BIG —**roller skate** skate with wheels instead of runner —**roller skating** —**roller towel** loop of towel on roller —**rolling mill 1.** mill or factory where ingots of heated metal are passed between rollers to produce sheets or bars of a required cross section and form **2.** machine used for this purpose —**rolling pin** cylindrical roller for pastry or dough —**rolling stock** locomotives, carriages *etc.* of railway —**rolling stone** restless or wandering person —'**rollmop** *n.* herring fillet rolled, usu. around onion slices, and pickled in spiced vinegar —**roll-on** *a.* **1.** (of deodorant *etc.*) dispensed by means of revolving ball fitted into neck of container —*n.* **2.** woman's foundation garment —**roll-top** *a.* (of desk) with flexible lid sliding in grooves —**roll on** *UK* used to express wish that eagerly anticipated event or date will come quickly —**roll up** *inf.* appear, turn up

rollick ('rɒlɪk) *vi.* **1.** behave in carefree or boisterous manner —*n.* **2.** boisterous or carefree escapade —'**rollicking** *a.*

roly-poly ('rəʊlɪ'pəʊlɪ) *n.* **1.** pudding of suet pastry covered with jam and rolled up —*a.* **2.** round, plump

ROM (rɒm) *Comp.* read only memory

rom. *Print.* roman (type)

Rom. *Bible* Romans

Roman ('rəʊmən) *a.* of Rome or Church of Rome —**Roman alphabet** alphabet evolved by ancient Romans for writing of Latin and still used for writing most of languages of Western Europe —**Roman candle** firework that produces continuous shower of sparks punctuated by coloured balls of fire —**Roman Catholic** member of that section of Christian Church which acknowledges supremacy of the Pope —**Roman nose** nose having high prominent bridge —**Roman numerals** letters I, V, X, L, C, D, M used to represent numbers in manner of Romans —**roman type** plain upright letters, ordinary style of printing

romance (rə'mæns, 'rəʊmæns) *n.* **1.** love affair, *esp.* intense and happy one **2.** mysterious or exciting quality **3.** tale of chivalry **4.** tale with scenes remote from ordinary life **5.** literature like this **6.** picturesque falsehood —*vi.* (rə'mæns) **7.** exaggerate, fantasize —**ro'mancer** *n.* —**ro'mantic** *a.* **1.** characterized by romance **2.** of or dealing with love **3.** (of literature *etc.*) preferring passion and imagination to proportion and finish —*n.* **4.** romantic person **5.** person whose tastes in art, literature *etc.* lie mainly in romanticism —ro'manticism n. —ro'manticist n. —ro'manticize or -cise v.

Romance (rə'mæns, 'rəumæns) a. **1.** of vernacular language of certain countries, developed from Latin, as French, Spanish etc. —n. **2.** this group of languages

Romanesque (rəumə'nɛsk) a./n. (in) style of round-arched vaulted architecture of period between Classical and Gothic

Romany or **Rommany** ('romənɪ, 'rəu-) n. **1.** Gypsy **2.** Gypsy language —a. **3.** of the Gypsies or their language

romp (romp) vi. **1.** run, play wildly, joyfully —n. **2.** spell of romping —'rompers pl.n. child's one-piece garment consisting of trousers and bib with straps —**come home** win easily

rondavel (ron'dɑːvəl) n. SA circular building, oft. thatched

rondo ('rondəu) n. piece of music with leading theme to which return is continually made (pl. -s)

röntgen ('rontgən, -tjən, 'rɛnt-) n. see ROENTGEN

rood (ruːd) n. **1.** the Cross **2.** crucifix **3.** quarter of acre —**rood screen** screen separating nave from choir

roof (ruːf) n. **1.** outside upper covering of building **2.** top, covering part of anything —vt. **3.** put roof on, over —'roofing n. **1.** material used to construct roof **2.** act of constructing roof —**roof rack** rack attached to roof of motor vehicle for carrying luggage etc. —'rooftree n. see ridgepole at RIDGE —**hit** (or **raise** or **go through**) **the roof** inf. become extremely angry

rooibos ('ruibos) n. S Afr. red-leafed tree

rooikat ('ruikæt) n. S Afr. lynx

rook[1] (ruk) n. **1.** bird of crow family —vt. **2.** sl. swindle, cheat —'rookery n. colony of rooks

rook[2] (ruk) n. chess piece (also 'castle)

rookie ('ruki) n. inf. recruit, esp. in army

room (ruːm, rum) n. **1.** space **2.** space enough **3.** division of house **4.** scope, opportunity —pl. **5.** lodgings —'roomy a. spacious —'roommate n. person with whom one shares room or lodging —**room service** service in hotel providing meals etc. in guests' rooms

roost (ruːst) n. **1.** perch for fowls —vi. **2.** perch —'rooster n. US domestic cock —**come home to roost** have unfavourable repercussions

root (ruːt) n. **1.** part of plant that grows down into earth and conveys nourishment to plant **2.** plant with edible root, eg carrot **3.** vital part **4.** source, origin, original cause of anything **5.** Anat. embedded portion of tooth, nail, hair etc. **6.** primitive word from which other words are derived **7.** Maths. factor of a quantity which, when multiplied by itself the number of times indicated, gives the quantity —v. **8.** (cause to)

take root —vt. **9.** pull by roots —vi. **10.** dig, burrow —'rootless a. having no roots or ties —**root mean square** square root of average of squares of set of numbers —'rootstock n. **1.** see RHIZOME **2.** see STOCK (sense 6) **3.** Biol. basic structure from which offshoots have developed —**root out** remove or eliminate completely

root for inf. cheer, applaud, encourage —'rooter n.

rope (rəup) n. **1.** thick cord —vt. **2.** secure, mark off with rope —'ropiness n. —'ropy a. **1.** inf. inferior, inadequate **2.** inf. not well **3.** (of liquid) sticky and stringy —'ropewalk n. long narrow shed where ropes are made —**know the ropes** know details or procedures, as of job

rorqual ('rɔːkwəl) n. whalebone whale with dorsal fin and series of grooves along throat and chest (also 'finback)

rosaceous (rəu'zeiʃəs) a. **1.** of Rosaceae, family of plants typically having five-petalled flowers, including rose, strawberry etc. **2.** like rose, esp. rose-coloured

rosary ('rəuzərɪ) n. R.C.Ch. series of prayers **2.** string of beads for counting these prayers as they are recited **3.** rose garden

rose[1] (rəuz) n. **1.** shrub, climbing plant usu. with prickly stems and fragrant flowers **2.** the flower **3.** perforated flat nozzle for hose etc. **4.** pink colour —a. **5.** of this colour —**roseate** ('rəuzieit) a. rose-coloured, rosy —ro'sette n. **1.** rose-shaped bunch of ribbon **2.** rose-shaped architectural ornament —'rosy a. **1.** flushed **2.** hopeful, promising —**rose-coloured** a. **1.** having colour of rose **2.** unwarrantably optimistic —**rose-water** n. **1.** scented water made by distillation of rose petals or by impregnation with oil of roses —a. **2.** elegant or delicate, esp. excessively so —**rose window** circular window with series of mullions branching from centre —'rosewood n. fragrant wood —**rose of Sharon** ('ʃærən) low, spreading shrub with yellow flowers

rose[2] (rəuz) pt. of RISE

rosé ('rəuzei) n. pink wine

rosemary ('rəuzmərɪ) n. evergreen fragrant flowering shrub

Rosh Hashanah or **Rosh Hashana** ('roʃ hə'ʃɑːnə; Hebrew 'roʃ haʃa'na) Jewish New Year

Rosicrucian (rəuzi'kruːʃən) n. **1.** member of secret order devoted to occult beliefs —a. **2.** of the Rosicrucians or Rosicrucianism —Rosi'crucianism n.

rosin ('rozɪn) n. resin

ROSPA ('rospə) UK Royal Society for Prevention of Accidents

roster ('rostə) n. **1.** list or plan showing turns of duty —vt. **2.** place on roster

rostrum ('rɒstrəm) n. 1. platform, stage, pulpit 2. beak or bill of bird (pl. -s, -tra (-trə))

rot (rɒt) v. 1. (cause to) decompose naturally —vt. 2. corrupt (-tt-) —n. 3. decay, putrefaction 4. any disease producing decomposition of tissue 5. inf. nonsense —'**rotten** a. 1. decomposed, putrid 2. corrupt —'**rotter** n. sl., chiefly UK worthless, unpleasant or despicable person

rota ('rəutə) n. roster, list

rotary ('rəutəri) a. 1. (of movement) circular 2. operated by rotary movement —**Ro'tarian** n. member of Rotary Club —**ro'tate** v. (cause to) move round centre or on pivot —**ro'tation** n. 1. rotating 2. regular succession —'**rotatory** a. —'**rotovate** vt. —'**rotovator** n. R mechanical cultivator with rotary blades —**Rotary Club** one of international association of businessmen's clubs

rote (rəut) n. mechanical repetition —**by rote** by memory

rotisserie (rəu'tisəri) n. (electrically-driven) rotating spit for cooking meat

rotor ('rəutə) n. revolving portion of a dynamo motor or turbine

rotten ('rɒtn) a. see ROT

rotund (rəu'tʌnd) a. 1. round 2. plump 3. sonorous —**ro'tundity** n.

rotunda (rəu'tʌndə) n. circular building or room, esp. with dome

rouble or **ruble** ('ru:bəl) n. monetary unit of Soviet Union

roué ('ru:ei) n. debauched or lecherous man; rake

rouge (ru:ʒ) n. 1. red powder, cream used to colour cheeks —vt. 2. colour with rouge

rough (rʌf) a. 1. not smooth, of irregular surface 2. violent, stormy, boisterous 3. rude 4. uncivil 5. lacking refinement 6. approximate 7. in preliminary form —vt. 8. make rough 9. plan out approximately 10. (with in) live without usual comforts etc. —n. 11. rough state or area 12. sketch —'**roughage** n. unassimilated portion of food promoting proper intestinal action —'**roughen** v. —'**roughly** adv. —**rough-and-ready** a. 1. crude, unpolished or hastily prepared, but sufficient for purpose 2. (of person) without formality or refinement —**rough-and-tumble** n. 1. fight or scuffle without rules —a. 2. characterized by disorderliness and disregard for rules —'**roughcast** a. 1. coated with mixture of lime and gravel —n. 2. such mixture —vt. 3. coat (wall etc.) with roughcast —**rough diamond** trustworthy but unsophisticated person —**rough-dry** a. 1. (of clothes or linen) dried ready for pressing —vt. 2. dry (clothes etc.) without ironing —**rough-hew** vt. shape roughly —'**roughhouse** n. sl. fight, row —'**roughshod** a. (of horse) shod with rough-

bottomed shoes to prevent sliding —**ride roughshod over** treat harshly and without consideration

roulette (ru:'let) n. game of chance played with revolving wheel and ball

round (raund) a. 1. spherical 2. cylindrical 3. circular 4. curved 5. full, complete 6. roughly correct 7. large, considerable 8. plump 9. positive —adv. 10. with circular or circuitous course —n. 11. thing round in shape 12. recurrent duties 13. stage in competition 14. customary course, as of milkman 15. game (of golf) 16. one of several periods in boxing match etc. 17. cartridge for firearm 18. rung 19. movement in circle —prep. 20. about 21. on all sides of —v. 22. make, become round —vt. 23. move round —'**rounders** n. ball game —'**roundly** adv. 1. plainly 2. thoroughly —'**roundabout** n. 1. revolving circular platform on which people ride for amusement 2. road junction at which traffic passes round a central island —a. 3. indirect; devious —**round dance** 1. dance in which dancers form circle 2. ballroom dance in which couples revolve —'**Roundhead** n. English hist. supporter of Parliament against Charles I during Civil War —**round robin** petition signed with names in circle to conceal order —**round-shouldered** a. denoting faulty posture characterized by drooping shoulders and slight forward bending of back —**round table** meeting of parties or people on equal terms for discussion —**round-the-clock** a. throughout day and night —**round trip** trip to place and back again —'**roundup** n. 1. act of gathering together cattle etc. for branding, counting or selling 2. inf. any similar act of bringing together —'**roundworm** n. nematode worm that is common intestinal parasite of man and pigs —**round up** 1. drive (cattle) together 2. collect and arrest criminals

roundel ('raundl) n. 1. rondeau 2. small disc —'**roundelay** n. simple song with refrain

rouse (rauz) vt. 1. wake up, stir up, excite to action 2. cause to rise —vi. 3. waken

rout[1] (raut) n. 1. overwhelming defeat, disorderly retreat 2. noisy rabble —vt. 3. scatter and put to flight

rout[2] (raut) v. 1. dig over or turn up (something), esp. (of animal) with snout; root —vt. 2. (usu. with out or up) find by searching 3. (usu. with out) drive out 4. (oft. with out) hollow or gouge out —vi. 5. search, poke, rummage

route (ru:t) n. road, chosen way —'**routemarch** n. 1. Mil. long march undertaken for training purposes 2. inf. any long exhausting walk

routine (ru:'ti:n) n. 1. regularity of procedure, unvarying round 2. regular course —a. 3. ordinary, regular

rove (rəʊv) *v.* wander, roam —**'rover** *n.* **1.** one who roves **2.** pirate

row¹ (rəʊ) *n.* **1.** number of things in a straight line **2.** rank **3.** file **4.** line

row² (rəʊ) *v.* **1.** propel (boat) by oars —*n.* **2.** spell of rowing —**rowing boat**

row³ (raʊ) *inf. n.* **1.** dispute **2.** disturbance —*vi.* **3.** quarrel noisily

rowan (ˈrəʊən, ˈraʊ-) *n.* native Brit. tree producing bright red berries (*also* (**European**) **mountain ash**)

rowdy (ˈraʊdɪ) *a.* **1.** disorderly, noisy and rough —*n.* **2.** person like this

rowel (ˈraʊəl) *n.* small wheel with points on spur

rowlock (ˈrɒlək) *n.* appliance on gunwale of boat serving as point of leverage for oar

royal (ˈrɔɪəl) *a.* **1.** of, worthy of, befitting, patronized by, king or queen **2.** splendid —**'royalist** *n.* supporter of monarchy —**'royalty** *n.* **1.** royal dignity or power **2.** royal persons **3.** payment to owner of land for right to work minerals, or to inventor for use of his invention **4.** payment to author depending on sales —**Royal Air Force** air force of Great Brit. —**royal blue** (of) deep blue colour —**royal jelly** substance secreted by pharyngeal glands of worker bees and fed to all larvae when very young or to larvae destined to become queens throughout their development —**Royal Marines** UK corps of soldiers trained in amphibious warfare —**Royal Navy** navy of Great Brit. —**royal palm** palm tree of tropical Amer. having tall trunk with tuft of feathery pinnate leaves —**royal warrant** authorization to tradesman to supply goods to royal household

r.p.m. revolutions per minute

R.R. 1. Right Reverend **2. C** Rural Route

R.S. UK Royal Society

R.S.A. 1. Republic of South Africa **2.** Royal Scottish Academy **3.** Royal Scottish Academician **4.** Royal Society of Arts **5. NZ** Returned Services Association

RSFSR Russian Soviet Federated Socialist Republic

R.S.P.C.A. UK Royal Society for the Prevention of Cruelty to Animals

R.S.V. Revised Standard Version (of the Bible)

R.S.V.P. répondez s'il vous plaît (*Fr.,* please reply)

Rt. Hon. Right Honourable

Rt. Rev. Right Reverend

Ru *Chem.* ruthenium

R.U. Rugby Union

rub (rʌb) *vt.* **1.** apply pressure to with circular or backwards and forwards movement **2.** clean, polish, dry, thus **3.** pass hand over **4.** abrade, chafe **5.** remove by friction —*vi.* **6.** come into contact accompanied by friction **7.** become frayed or worn by friction (**-bb-**) —*n.* **8.** rubbing **9.** impediment —**'rubbing** *n.* impression taken of incised or raised surface by laying paper over it and rubbing with wax *etc.*

rubato (ruːˈbɑːtəʊ) *Mus. n.* **1.** flexibility of tempo in performance (*pl.* **-s**) —*a./adv.* **2.** to be played with flexible tempo

rubber¹ (ˈrʌbə) *n.* **1.** coagulated sap of rough, elastic consistency, of certain tropical trees (*also* **India rubber, gum elastic, 'caoutchouc**) **2.** piece of rubber *etc.* used for erasing **3.** thing for rubbing **4.** person who rubs —*a.* **5.** made of rubber —**'rubberize** or **-ise** *vt.* coat, impregnate, treat with rubber —**'rubbery** *a.* —**rubber band** continuous loop of thin rubber, used to hold papers *etc.* together (*also* **elastic band**) —**'rubberneck** *sl. n.* **1.** person who gapes inquisitively **2.** sightseer, tourist —*vi.* **3.** stare in naive or foolish manner —**rubber plant 1.** plant with glossy leathery leaves, cultivated as house plant in Europe and N Amer. **2.** any of several tropical trees, sap of which yields crude rubber —**rubber stamp 1.** device for imprinting dates *etc.* **2.** automatic authorization

rubber² (ˈrʌbə) *n.* **1.** series of odd number of games or contests at various games **2.** two out of three games won

rubbish (ˈrʌbɪʃ) *n.* **1.** refuse, waste material **2.** anything worthless **3.** trash, nonsense —**'rubbishy** *a.* valueless

rubble (ˈrʌbl) *n.* **1.** fragments of stone *etc.* **2.** builders' rubbish

rubella (ruːˈbɛlə) *n.* mild contagious viral disease (*also* **German measles**)

rubicund (ˈruːbɪkənd) *a.* of reddish colour; ruddy

rubidium (ruːˈbɪdɪəm) *n.* soft highly reactive radioactive element of alkali metal group

rubric (ˈruːbrɪk) *n.* **1.** title, heading **2.** direction in liturgy **3.** instruction

ruby (ˈruːbɪ) *n.* **1.** precious red gem **2.** its colour —*a.* **3.** of this colour —**ruby wedding** fortieth wedding anniversary

ruche (ruːʃ) *n.* strip of pleated or frilled lace *etc.* used to decorate blouses *etc.*

ruck¹ (rʌk) *n.* **1.** crowd **2.** common herd **3.** rank and file **4.** *Rugby* loose scrummage or maul

ruck² (rʌk) *n.* **1.** crease —*v.* **2.** make, become wrinkled

rucksack (ˈrʌksæk) *n.* pack carried on back, knapsack (*also* **back pack**)

ruction (ˈrʌkʃən) *n. inf.* noisy disturbance

rudder (ˈrʌdə) *n.* flat piece hinged to boat's stern or rear of aircraft used to steer

ruddy (ˈrʌdɪ) *a.* **1.** of fresh or healthy red colour **2.** rosy **3.** florid

rude (ruːd) *a.* **1.** impolite **2.** coarse **3.** vulgar **4.**

primitive **5.** roughly made **6.** uneducated **7.** sudden, violent —'**rudely** adv.

rudiments ('ru:dimənts) pl.n. elements, first principles —**rudi'mentary** a.

rue[1] (ru:) v. **1.** grieve (for) —vt. **2.** regret **3.** deplore —vi. **4.** repent —n. **5.** obs. repentance —'**rueful** a. **1.** sorry **2.** regretful **3.** dejected **4.** deplorable —'**ruefully** adv.

rue[2] (ru:) n. plant with evergreen bitter leaves

ruff[1] (rʌf) n. **1.** starched and frilled collar **2.** natural collar of feathers, fur etc. on some birds and animals **3.** type of shore bird —'**ruffle** vt. **1.** rumple, disorder **2.** annoy, put out **3.** frill, pleat —n. **4.** frilled trimming

ruff[2] (rʌf) n./v. Cards trump

ruffian ('rʌfiən) n. violent, lawless person —'**ruffianism** n. —'**ruffianly** a.

rufous ('ru:fəs) a. reddish-brown

rug (rʌg) n. **1.** small, oft. shaggy or thick-piled floor mat **2.** thick woollen wrap, coverlet

rugby or **rugby football** ('rʌgbɪ) n. form of football in which the ball may be carried in the hands (also (inf.) '**rugger**)

rugged ('rʌgɪd) a. **1.** rough **2.** broken **3.** unpolished **4.** harsh, austere

ruin ('ru:ɪn) n. **1.** decay, destruction **2.** downfall **3.** fallen or broken state **4.** loss of wealth, position etc. —pl. **5.** ruined buildings etc. —vt. **6.** reduce to ruins **7.** bring to decay or destruction **8.** spoil **9.** impoverish —**rui'nation** n. —'**ruinous** a. causing or characterized by ruin or destruction —'**ruinously** adv.

rule (ru:l) n. **1.** principle **2.** precept **3.** authority **4.** government **5.** what is usual **6.** control **7.** measuring stick —vt. **8.** govern **9.** decide **10.** mark with straight lines **11.** draw (line) —'**ruler** n. **1.** one who governs **2.** stick for measuring or ruling lines —'**ruling** n. **1.** decision of someone in authority, such as judge **2.** one or more parallel ruled lines —a. **3.** controlling or exercising authority **4.** predominant —**rule of thumb** rough and practical approach, based on experience, rather than theory

rum (rʌm) n. spirit distilled from sugar cane

rumba or **rhumba** ('rʌmbə, 'rʊm-) n. **1.** rhythmic dance, orig. Cuban **2.** music for it

rumble ('rʌmbəl) vi. **1.** make noise as of distant thunder, heavy vehicle etc. —n. **2.** such noise

rumbustious (rʌm'bʌstjəs) a. boisterous, unruly

ruminate ('ru:mɪneɪt) vi. **1.** chew cud **2.** ponder, meditate —'**ruminant** a./n. cud-chewing (animal) —**rumi'nation** n. **2.** quiet meditation and reflection —'**ruminative** a.

rummage ('rʌmɪdʒ) v. **1.** search thoroughly —n. **2.** act of rummaging

rummy ('rʌmɪ) or **rum** n. card game

rumour or U.S. **rumor** ('ru:mə) n. **1.** hearsay,

common talk, unproved statement —vt. **2.** put round as, by way of, rumour

rump (rʌmp) n. **1.** hindquarters of mammal, not including legs **2.** person's buttocks

rumple ('rʌmpəl) v./n. crease, wrinkle

rumpus ('rʌmpəs) n. **1.** disturbance **2.** noise and confusion

run (rʌn) vi. **1.** move with more rapid gait than walking **2.** go quickly **3.** flow **4.** flee **5.** compete in race, contest, election **6.** revolve **7.** continue **8.** function **9.** travel according to schedule **10.** fuse **11.** melt **12.** spread **13.** have certain meaning —vt. **14.** cross by running **15.** expose oneself to (risk etc.) **16.** cause to run **17.** (of newspaper) print, publish **18.** land and dispose of (smuggled goods) **19.** manage **20.** operate (ran pt., run pp., 'running pr.p.) —n. **21.** act, spell of running **22.** rush **23.** tendency, course **24.** period **25.** sequence **26.** heavy demand **27.** enclosure for domestic fowls, animals **28.** ride in car **29.** series of unravelled stitches, ladder **30.** score of one at cricket **31.** steep snow-covered course for skiing —'**runner** n. **1.** racer **2.** messenger **3.** curved piece of wood on which sleigh slides **4.** any similar appliance **5.** slender stem of plant running along ground forming new roots at intervals **6.** strip of lace etc. placed on table for decoration **7.** strip of carpet —'**running** a. **1.** continuous **2.** consecutive **3.** flowing **4.** discharging **5.** effortless **6.** entered for race **7.** used for running —n. **8.** act of moving or flowing quickly **9.** management —'**runny** a. tending to flow or exude moisture —'**runabout** n. small light vehicle or aeroplane —'**runaway** n. **1.** person or animal that runs away **2.** act or instance of running away —a. **3.** rising rapidly, as prices **4.** (of race etc.) easily won —'**rundown** n. summary —**run-down** a. exhausted —**runner-up** n. contestant finishing race or competition in second place (pl. **runners-up**) —**running board** ledge beneath doors of old cars —**running commentary** commentary maintained continuously —**running head** or **title** Print. heading printed at top of every page of book —**running knot** knot that moves or slips easily —**running repairs** repairs that do not (greatly) interrupt operations —**run-of-the-mill** a. ordinary —**run-up** n. **1.** approach run by athlete for long jump, pole vault etc. **2.** preliminary or preparatory period —'**runway** n. level stretch where aircraft take off and land —**run about** move busily from place to place —**run away 1.** take flight; escape **2.** go away; depart **3.** (of horse) gallop away uncontrollably —**run away with 1.** abscond or elope with **2.** make off with; steal **3.** escape from control of person **4.** win easily or be assured of victory in (competition) —**run down 1.** stop working **2.** reduce **3.** exhaust **4.** denigrate —**run up 1.**

amass; incur **2.** make by sewing together quickly **3.** hoist —**in the running** having a fair chance in a competition

rune (ruːn) *n.* **1.** character of earliest Germanic alphabet **2.** magic sign —**'runic** *a.*

rung[1] (rʌŋ) *n.* crossbar or spoke, *esp.* in ladder

rung[2] (rʌŋ) *pp. of* RING[2]

runnel ('rʌnᵊl) *n.* **1.** gutter **2.** small brook or rivulet

running ('rʌnɪŋ) *see* RUN

runt (rʌnt) *n.* **1.** smallest young animal in litter **2.** *offens.* undersized person

rupee (ruːˈpiː) *n.* monetary unit of India, Pakistan, Sri Lanka *etc.*

rupture ('rʌptʃə) *n.* **1.** breaking, breach **2.** hernia —*v.* **3.** break **4.** burst, sever

rural ('rʊərᵊl) *a.* **1.** of the country **2.** rustic —**'ruralize** *or* **-ise** *v.* —**rural route** C mail service in rural area

rusbank ('rʊsbæŋk) *n.* SA wooden bench, settle

ruse (ruːz) *n.* stratagem, trick

rush[1] (rʌʃ) *vt.* **1.** impel, carry along violently and rapidly **2.** take by sudden assault —*vi.* **3.** cause to hurry **4.** move violently or rapidly —*n.* **5.** rushing, charge **6.** hurry **7.** eager demand **8.** heavy current (of air, water *etc.*) —*a.* **9.** done with speed **10.** characterized by speed —**rush hour** period at beginning and end of day when many people are travelling to and from work

rush[2] (rʌʃ) *n.* **1.** marsh plant with slender pithy stem **2.** the stems used as material for baskets —**'rushy** *a.* full of rushes

rusk (rʌsk) *n.* kind of light biscuit

Russ. Russia(n)

russet ('rʌsɪt) *a.* **1.** reddish-brown —*n.* **2.** the colour

Russian ('rʌʃən) *n.* **1.** official language of Soviet Union: Indo-European language belonging to East Slavonic branch **2.** native or inhabitant of Russia or Soviet Union —*a.* **3.** of Russia or Soviet Union —**Russian roulette 1.** act of bravado in which each person in turn spins cylinder of revolver loaded with only one cartridge and presses trigger with barrel against his own head **2.** any foolish or potentially suicidal undertaking

rust (rʌst) *n.* **1.** reddish-brown coating formed on iron by oxidation **2.** disease of plants —*v.* **3.** contract, affect with rust —**'rusty** *a.* **1.** coated with, affected by, or consisting of rust **2.** of rust colour **3.** out of practice —**'rustproof** *a.*

rustic ('rʌstɪk) *a.* **1.** of or as of country people **2.** rural **3.** of rude manufacture **4.** made of untrimmed branches —*n.* **5.** countryman, peasant —**'rusticate** *vt.* **1.** banish from university —*vi.* **2.** live a country life —**rusti'cation** *n.* —**rus'ticity** *n.*

rustle[1] ('rʌsᵊl) *vi.* **1.** make sound as of blown dead leaves *etc.* —*n.* **2.** this sound

rustle[2] ('rʌsᵊl) *vt.* US steal (cattle) —**'rustler** *n.* US cattle thief

rut[1] (rʌt) *n.* **1.** furrow made by wheel **2.** settled habit or way of living **3.** groove —**'rutty** *a.*

rut[2] (rʌt) *n.* **1.** periodic sexual excitement among animals —*vi.* **2.** be under influence of this (**-tt-**)

ruthenium (ruːˈθiːnɪəm) *n.* hard brittle white element of platinum metal group

ruthless ('ruːθlɪs) *a.* pitiless, merciless —**'ruthlessly** *adv.*

R.V. Revised Version (of the Bible)

-ry (*comb. form*) *see* -ERY

rye (raɪ) *n.* **1.** grain used for fodder and bread **2.** plant bearing it **3.** whisky made from rye —**rye bread** bread made entirely or partly from rye flour

rye-grass *n.* any of various kinds of grasses cultivated for fodder

---

S, s

s *or* **S** (ɛs) *n.* **1.** 19th letter of English alphabet **2.** speech sound represented by this letter, either voiceless, as in *sit*, or voiced, as in *dogs* **3.** something shaped like S (*pl.* **s's, S's** *or* **Ss**)

S 1. Society **2.** South(ern) **3.** *Chem.* sulphur **4.** *Phys.* entropy **5.** *Phys.* siemens **6.** *Phys.* strangeness

s. 1. second (of time) **2.** shilling **3.** singular **4.** son **5.** succeeded

-'s (*comb. form*) **1.** forming possessive singular of nouns and some pronouns, as in *man's* **2.** forming possessive plural of nouns whose plurals do not end in *-s*, as in *children's* **3.** forming plural of numbers, letters, or symbols, as in *20's*

-s' (*comb. form*) forming possessive of plural nouns, and some singular nouns, ending in sounded *s*, as in *girls'; for goodness' sake*

S.A. 1. Salvation Army **2.** South Africa **3.** South Australia **4.** *Sturmabteilung:* Nazi terrorist militia

Sabbath ('sæbəθ) *n.* **1.** Jewish and Christian day of worship and rest **2.** Sunday —**sab'batical** *a./n.* (denoting) leave granted to university staff *etc.* for study

sable ('seɪbᵊl) *n.* **1.** small weasellike Arctic animal **2.** its fur **3.** black (*pl.* **-s, 'sable**) —*a.* **4.** black

sabot ('sæbəʊ) *n.* shoe made of wood, or with wooden sole

sabotage ('sæbətɑːʒ) *n.* **1.** intentional damage done to roads, machines *etc.*, *esp.* secretly in war —*vt.* **2.** carry out sabotage on **3.** destroy, disrupt —**saboteur** (sæbə'tɜː) *n.*

sabre *or U.S.* **saber** ('seibə) *n.* curved cavalry sword —**sabre rattling** menacing display of armed force

sac (sæk) *n.* pouchlike structure in an animal or vegetable body

saccharin ('sækərɪn) *n.* artificial sweetener —**saccharine** (-ri:n) *a. lit., fig.* excessively sweet

sacerdotal (sæsə'dəʊtəl) *a.* of priests

sachet ('sæʃeɪ) *n.* small envelope or bag, *esp.* one holding liquid, as shampoo

sack[1] (sæk) *n.* **1.** large bag, *orig.* of coarse material **2.** pillaging **3.** *inf.* dismissal **4.** *sl.* bed —*vt.* **5.** pillage (captured town) **6.** *inf.* dismiss —'**sacking** *n.* material for sacks —**sackcloth** *n.* coarse fabric used for sacks —**sackcloth and ashes** public display of extreme grief

sack[2] (sæk) *n. obs.* dry white wine from SW Europe

sacrament ('sækrəmənt) *n.* one of certain ceremonies of Christian Church, *esp.* Eucharist —**sacra'mental** *a.*

sacred ('seikrɪd) *a.* **1.** dedicated, regarded as holy **2.** set apart, reserved **3.** inviolable **4.** connected with, intended for religious use —'**sacredly** *adv.* —**sacred cow** *inf.* person *etc.* held to be beyond criticism

sacrifice ('sækrɪfaɪs) *n.* **1.** giving something up for sake of something else **2.** act of giving up **3.** thing so given up **4.** making of offering to a god **5.** thing offered —*vt.* **6.** offer as sacrifice **7.** give up **8.** sell at very cheap price —**sacrificial** (sækrɪ'fɪʃəl) *a.*

sacrilege ('sækrɪlɪdʒ) *n.* misuse, desecration of something sacred —**sacrilegious** (sækrɪ'lɪdʒəs) *a.* **1.** profane **2.** desecrating

sacristan ('sækrɪstən) *or* **sacrist** ('sækrɪst, 'seɪ-) *n.* official in charge of vestments and sacred vessels of church —'**sacristy** *n.* room where sacred vessels *etc.* are kept

sacrosanct ('sækrəʊsæŋkt) *a.* **1.** preserved by religious fear against desecration or violence **2.** inviolable —**sacro'sanctity** *n.*

sacrum ('seikrəm) *n.* five vertebrae forming compound bone at base of spinal column (*pl.* -**cra** (-krə))

sad (sæd) *a.* **1.** sorrowful **2.** unsatisfactory, deplorable —'**sadden** *vt.* make sad

saddle ('sædəl) *n.* **1.** rider's seat to fasten on horse, bicycle *etc.* **2.** anything resembling a saddle **3.** joint of mutton or venison **4.** ridge of hill —*vt.* **5.** put saddle on **6.** lay burden, responsibility on *a.* **7.** resembling a saddle, as in *saddleback* —'**saddler** *n.* maker of saddles *etc.* —'**saddlery** *n.* —'**saddlebag** *n.* small bag attached to saddle of bicycle *etc.* —**saddle soap**

soft soap for preserving and cleaning leather —'**saddletree** *n.* frame of saddle

Sadducee ('sædjʊsiː) *n. Judaism* member of ancient Jewish sect, denying resurrection of dead and validity of oral tradition

sadism ('seidɪzəm) *n.* form of (sexual) perversion marked by love of inflicting pain —'**sadist** *n.* —**sadistic** (sə'dɪstɪk) *a.* —**sado-'masochism** *n.* sadistic and masochistic elements in one person —**sadomaso'chistic** *a.*

s.a.e. stamped addressed envelope

safari (sə'fɑːrɪ) *n.* (party making) overland (hunting) journey, *esp.* in Afr. (*pl.* -**s**) —**safari park** park where lions *etc.* may be viewed by public from cars

safe (seɪf) *a.* **1.** secure, protected **2.** uninjured, out of danger **3.** not involving risk **4.** trustworthy **5.** sure, reliable **6.** cautious —*n.* **7.** strong lockable container **8.** ventilated cupboard for meat *etc.* —'**safely** *adv.* —'**safety** *n.* —**safe-conduct** *n.* passport, permit to pass somewhere —**safe-deposit** *or* **safety-deposit** *n.* place with facilities for safe storage of money *etc.* —'**safeguard** *n.* **1.** protection —*vt.* **2.** protect —**safety belt 1.** *see* **seat belt** at SEAT **2.** belt worn by person working at great height —**safety curtain** fireproof curtain that can be lowered to separate auditorium and stage —**safety glass** unsplinterable glass —**safety lamp** miner's oil lamp in which flame is surrounded by metal gauze to prevent it igniting combustible gas —**safety match** match that will light only when struck against prepared surface —**safety pin** spring clasp with covering catch, designed to shield point when closed —**safety razor** razor with guard over blade —**safety valve 1.** valve in pressure vessel that allows fluid to escape at excess pressure **2.** harmless outlet for emotion *etc.*

safflower ('sæflaʊə) *n.* thistlelike plant with flowers used for dye, oil

saffron ('sæfrən) *n.* **1.** crocus **2.** orange-coloured flavouring obtained from it **3.** the colour —*a.* **4.** orange

S.Afr. South Africa(n)

sag (sæg) *vi.* **1.** sink in middle **2.** hang sideways **3.** curve downwards under pressure **4.** give way **5.** tire **6.** (of clothes) hang loosely (-**gg**-) —*n.* **7.** droop

saga ('sɑːgə) *n.* **1.** legend of Norse heroes **2.** any long (heroic) story

sagacious (sə'geɪʃəs) *a.* wise —**sa'gaciously** *adv.* —**sagacity** (sə'gæsɪtɪ) *n.*

sage[1] (seɪdʒ) *n.* **1.** very wise man —*a.* **2.** wise —'**sagely** *adv.*

sage[2] (seɪdʒ) *n.* aromatic herb

sagebrush ('seɪdʒbrʌʃ) *n.* aromatic plant of West N Amer.

Sagittarius (sædʒɪ'teərɪəs) *n.* (archer) 9th sign of zodiac, operative *c.* Nov. 22nd-Dec. 20th

sago ('seɪgəʊ) *n.* starchy cereal from powdered pith of sago palm

sahib ('sɑːhɪb) *n.* in India, form of address placed after man's name

said (sɛd) *pt./pp. of* SAY

sail (seɪl) *n.* **1.** piece of fabric stretched to catch wind for propelling ship *etc.* **2.** act of sailing **3.** journey upon the water **4.** ships collectively **5.** arm of windmill —*vi.* **6.** travel by water **7.** move smoothly **8.** begin voyage —*vt.* **9.** navigate —'**sailor** *n.* **1.** seaman **2.** one who sails —'**sailboard** *n.* floatable board, comprising sail, rudder and centreboard, used in windsurfing —'**sailcloth** *n.* **1.** fabric from which sails are made **2.** canvas-like cloth used for clothing *etc.*

saint (seɪnt; *unstressed* sənt) *n.* **1.** (title of) person formally recognized (*esp.* by R.C. Church) after death as having gained by holy deeds a special place in heaven **2.** exceptionally good person —'**sainted** *a.* **1.** canonized **2.** sacred —'**saintliness** *n.* holiness —'**saintly** *a.* —**Saint Bernard** large breed of dog with dense red-and-white coat —**Saint Leger** annual horse race run at Doncaster, England —**saintpaulia** (sənt-'pɔːlɪə) *n.* Afr. violet —**Saint Swithin's Day** July 15th; if it rains on this day it is traditionally believed it will rain for the next forty days —**Saint Valentine's Day** Feb. 14th; observed as day for sending valentines —**Saint Vitus's dance** *Pathol. see* CHOREA

saithe (seɪθ) *n.* coalfish

sake[1] (seɪk) *n.* **1.** cause, account **2.** end, purpose —**for the sake of 1.** on behalf of **2.** to please or benefit

sake[2], **saké** *or* **saki** ('sɑːkɪ) *n.* Japanese alcoholic drink made of fermented rice

salaam (sə'lɑːm) *n.* **1.** bow of salutation, mark of respect in East —*vt.* **2.** salute

salacious (sə'leɪʃəs) *a.* excessively concerned with sex, lewd —**salacity** (sə'læsɪtɪ) *n.*

salad ('sæləd) *n.* **1.** mixed vegetables, or fruit, used as food without cooking —**salad days** period of youth and inexperience —**salad dressing** oil, vinegar, herbs *etc.* mixed together as sauce for salad

salamander ('sæləmændə) *n.* **1.** variety of lizard **2.** mythical lizardlike fire spirit

salami (sə'lɑːmɪ) *n.* variety of highly-spiced sausage

salary ('sælərɪ) *n.* fixed regular payment to persons employed usu. in nonmanual work —'**salaried** *a.*

salchow ('sɔːlkəʊ) *n. Figure skating* jump from inner backward edge of one foot with full turn in air, returning to outer backward edge of opposite foot

sale (seɪl) *n.* **1.** selling **2.** selling of goods at unusually low prices **3.** auction —'**saleable** *or U.S.* '**salable** *a.* capable of being sold —**sale of work** sale of articles, proceeds of which benefit charities —'**saleroom** *n. chiefly UK* room where objects are displayed for sale, *esp.* by auction —'**salesman** *n.* **1.** shop assistant **2.** one travelling to sell goods, *esp.* as representative of firm —'**salesmanship** *n.* art of selling or presenting goods in most effective way —**sales talk** *or* **pitch** argument or other persuasion used in selling

salicin ('sælɪsɪn) *n.* substance obtained from poplars and used in medicine —**sali'cylic** *a.* —**salicylic acid** white crystalline substance used in manufacture of aspirin, and as fungicide

salient ('seɪlɪənt) *a.* **1.** prominent, noticeable **2.** jutting out —*n.* **3.** salient angle, *esp.* in fortification —'**salience** *or* '**saliency** *n.*

saline ('seɪlaɪn) *a.* **1.** containing, consisting of a chemical salt, *esp.* common salt **2.** salty —**salinity** (sə'lɪnɪtɪ) *n.*

saliva (sə'laɪvə) *n.* liquid which forms in mouth, spittle —**sa'livary** *a.* —**salivate** ('sælɪveɪt) *v.* —**saliva test** test for use of drugs in athletes, racehorses *etc.*

Salk vaccine (sɔːlk) vaccine against poliomyelitis

sallow[1] ('sæləʊ) *a.* of unhealthy pale or yellowish colour

sallow[2] ('sæləʊ) *n.* tree or low shrub allied to the willow

sally ('sælɪ) *n.* **1.** rushing out, *esp.* by troops **2.** outburst **3.** witty remark —*vi.* **4.** rush **5.** set out ('**sallied**, '**sallying**)

Sally Lunn (lʌn) flat cake made from sweet yeast dough

salmagundi (sælmə'gʌndɪ) *n.* **1.** mixed salad dish of cooked meats, eggs, beetroot *etc.* **2.** miscellany

salmon ('sæmən) *n.* **1.** large silvery fish with orange-pink flesh valued as food **2.** colour of its flesh —*a.* **3.** of this colour —**salmon ladder** series of steps designed to enable salmon to move upstream to their breeding grounds

salmonella (sælmə'nelə) *n.* any of genus of bacteria causing disease, *esp.* food poisoning (*pl.* **-lae** (-liː))

salon ('sælɒn) *n.* **1.** (reception room for) guests in fashionable household **2.** commercial premises of hairdressers, beauticians *etc.*

saloon (sə'luːn) *n.* **1.** principal cabin or public room in passenger ship **2.** public room for specified use, *eg* billiards **3.** closed car with 2 or 4 doors and 4-6 seats —**saloon bar** first-class bar in hotel *etc.*

salpiglossis (sælpɪ'glɒsɪs) *n.* plant with bright funnel-shaped flowers

salsify ('sælsıfı) *n.* purple-flowered plant with edible root

SALT (sɔːlt) Strategic Arms Limitation Talks

salt (sɔːlt) *n.* 1. white powdery or granular crystalline substance consisting mainly of sodium chloride, used to season or preserve food 2. chemical compound of acid and metal 3. wit —*vt.* 4. season, sprinkle with, preserve with salt —'**saltless** *a.* —'**saltness** *n.* —'**salty** *a.* of, like salt —'**saltbush** *n.* shrub that grows in alkaline desert regions —'**saltcellar** *n.* small vessel for salt at table —**salt lick** deposit, block of salt licked by game, cattle *etc.* —'**saltpan** *n.* depression encrusted with salt after draining away of water —**saltpetre** *or U.S.* **saltpeter** (sɔːlt'piːtə) *n.* potassium nitrate used in gunpowder —'**saltwater** *a.* —**old salt** sailor —**salt away** *or* **down** hoard or save (money, valuables *etc.*) —**with a pinch, grain, of salt** allowing for exaggeration —**worth one's salt** efficient

saltant ('sæltənt) *a.* 1. leaping 2. dancing —**sal'tation** *n.* —'**saltatory** *a.*

salubrious (sə'luːbrıəs) *a.* favourable to health, beneficial —**sa'lubrity** *n.*

Saluki (sə'luːkı) *n.* tall hound with silky coat

salutary ('sæljutərı) *a.* wholesome, resulting in good —'**salutarily** *adv.*

salute (sə'luːt) *vt.* 1. greet with words or sign 2. acknowledge with praise —*vi.* 3. perform military salute —*n.* 4. word, sign by which one person greets another 5. motion of arm as mark of respect to superior *etc.* in military usage 6. firing of guns as military greeting of honour —**salu'tation** (sælju'teıʃən) *n.*

salvage ('sælvıdʒ) *n.* 1. act of saving ship or other property from danger of loss 2. property so saved —*vt.* 3. rescue, save from wreck or ruin

salvation (sæl'veıʃən) *n.* (*esp.* of soul) fact or state of being saved —**Salvation Army** Christian body organized for evangelism and social work among poor

salve (sælv, sɑːv) *n.* 1. healing ointment —*vt.* 2. anoint with salve 3. soothe

salver ('sælvə) *n.* (silver) tray for presentation of food, letters *etc.*

salvia ('sælvıə) *n.* plant with blue or red flowers

salvo ('sælvəʊ) *n.* simultaneous discharge of guns *etc.* (*pl.* **-s, -es**)

sal volatile (sæl vɒ'lætılı) preparation of ammonia used to revive persons who faint *etc.*

SAM (sæm) surface-to-air missile

Sam. *Bible* Samuel

Samaritan (sə'mærıtən) *n.* 1. native of ancient Samaria 2. benevolent person

samarium (sə'mɛərıəm) *n.* silvery metallic element of lanthanide series

samba ('sæmbə) *n.* 1. dance of S Amer. origin 2. music for it

same (seım) *a.* (*usu. with* the) 1. identical, not different, unchanged 2. uniform 3. just mentioned previously —'**sameness** *n.* 1. similarity 2. monotony

samite ('sæmaıt) *n.* rich silk cloth

samovar ('sæməvɑː) *n.* Russian tea urn

Samoyed (sə'mɔıed) *n.* dog with thick white coat and tightly curled tail

samp (sæmp) *n.* SA crushed maize used for porridge

sampan ('sæmpæn) *n.* small oriental boat

samphire ('sæmfaıə) *n.* herb found on rocks by seashore

sample ('sɑːmpl) *n.* 1. specimen —*vt.* 2. take, give sample of 3. try 4. test 5. select —'**sampler** *n.* beginner's exercise in embroidery —'**sampling** *n.* 1. the taking of samples 2. sample

Samson ('sæmsən) *n.* 1. *O.T.* judge of Israel, who performed herculean feats of strength until he was betrayed by his mistress Delilah 2. any man of outstanding physical strength

samurai ('sæmuraı) *n.* member of ancient Japanese warrior caste (*pl.* **-rai**)

sanatorium (sænə'tɔːrıəm) *or U.S.* **sanitarium** *n.* 1. hospital, *esp.* for chronically ill 2. health resort (*pl.* **-s, -ria** (-rıə)) —'**sanatory** *or* '**sanative** *a.* curative

sanctify ('sæŋktıfaı) *vt.* 1. set apart as holy 2. free from sin (**-fied, -fying**) —**sanctifi'cation** *n.* —'**sanctity** *n.* 1. saintliness 2. sacredness 3. inviolability —'**sanctuary** *n.* 1. holy place 2. part of church nearest altar 3. formerly, place where fugitive was safe from arrest or violence 4. place protected by law where animals *etc.* can live without interference —'**sanctum** *n.* 1. sacred place or shrine 2. person's private room (*pl.* **-s, -ta**)

sanctimonious (sæŋktı'məʊnıəs) *a.* making a show of piety, holiness —'**sanctimony** *or* sancti'**moniousness** *n.*

sanction ('sæŋkʃən) *n.* 1. permission, authorization 2. penalty for breaking law —*pl.* 3. boycott or other coercive measure, *esp.* by one state against another regarded as having violated a law, right *etc.* —*vt.* 4. allow, authorize, permit

sand (sænd) *n.* 1. substance consisting of small grains of rock or mineral, *esp.* on beach or in desert —*pl.* 2. stretches or banks of this, usu. forming seashore —*vt.* 3. polish, smooth with sandpaper 4. cover, mix with sand —'**sander** *n.* power tool for smoothing surfaces —'**sandy** *a.* 1. like sand 2. sand-coloured 3. consisting of, covered with sand —'**sandbag** *n.* bag filled with sand or earth, used as protection against gunfire, floodwater *etc.*, and as weapon —**sand bar** ridge of sand in river or sea, built up by action of tides *etc.* —'**sandblast** *n.* **1.** jet of sand blown from a nozzle under pressure for cleaning, grinding *etc.* —*vt.* **2.** clean or decorate (surface) with sandblast —**sand castle** sand moulded into castle-like shape, *esp.* on seashore —'**sandman** *n.* in folklore, magical person supposed to put children to sleep by sprinkling sand in their eyes —**sand martin** small brown European songbird with white underparts —'**sandpaper** *n.* paper with sand stuck on it for scraping or polishing wood *etc.* —'**sandpiper** *n.* shore bird —'**sandpit** *n.* quantity of sand for children to play in —'**sandshoes** *pl.n.* canvas shoes for beach wear *etc.* —'**sandstone** *n.* rock composed of sand —'**sandstorm** *n.* strong wind that whips up clouds of sand —**sand yacht** wheeled boat with sails, built to be propelled over sand

sandal ('sændəl) *n.* shoe consisting of sole attached by straps

sandalwood ('sændəlwud) *or* **sandal** *n.* sweet-scented wood

sanderling ('sændəliŋ) *n.* small sandpiper that frequents sandy shores

sandwich ('sænwidʒ, -witʃ) *n.* **1.** two slices of bread with meat or other substance between —*vt.* **2.** insert between two other things —**sandwich board** one of two connected boards hung over shoulders in front of and behind person to display advertisements —**sandwich course** course consisting of alternate periods of study and industrial work —**sandwich man** man who carries sandwich board

sane (sein) *a.* **1.** of sound mind **2.** sensible, rational —**sanity** ('sæniti) *n.*

Sanforize *or* **-rise** ('sænfəraiz) *vt.* **R** preshrink (fabric) using a patented process

sang (sæŋ) *pt. of* SING

sang-froid (*Fr.* sã'frwa) *n.* composure; self-possession

Sangraal (sæŋ'greil), **Sangrail** *or* **Sangreal** ('sæŋgriəl) *n.* see Holy Grail at HOLY

sangria (sæŋ'griːə) *n.* Sp. drink of red wine and fruit juice, sometimes laced with brandy

sanguine ('sæŋgwin) *a.* **1.** cheerful, confident **2.** ruddy in complexion —'**sanguinary** *a.* **1.** accompanied by bloodshed **2.** bloodthirsty

Sanhedrin ('sænidrin) *n. Judaism* supreme judicial, ecclesiastical, and administrative council of Jews in New Testament times

sanitary ('sænitəri) *a.* helping protection of health against dirt *etc.* —**sani'tation** *n.* measures, apparatus for preservation of public health —**sanitary towel** *or esp. U.S.* **napkin** absorbent pad worn externally by women during menstruation

sank (sæŋk) *pt. of* SINK

sans (sænz) *prep.* without —**sans-culotte**

(-kju'lɒt) *n.* **1.** revolutionary of poorer class during French Revolution **2.** any revolutionary extremist

Sanskrit ('sænskrit) *n.* ancient language of India

Santa Claus ('sæntə klɔːz) legendary patron saint of children, who brings presents at Christmas (*also* **Father Christmas**)

sap[1] (sæp) *n.* **1.** moisture which circulates in plants **2.** energy —*vt.* **3.** drain of sap (-**pp-**) —'**sapless** *a.* —'**sapling** *n.* young tree

sap[2] (sæp) *vt.* **1.** undermine **2.** destroy insidiously **3.** weaken (-**pp-**) —*n.* **4.** trench dug in order to approach or undermine enemy position —'**sapper** *n.* soldier in engineering unit

sap[3] (sæp) *n. inf.* gullible person —'**sappy** *a.*

sapid ('sæpid) *a.* **1.** having pleasant taste **2.** agreeable or engaging —**sa'pidity** *n.*

sapient ('seipiənt) *a.* (*usu. ironical*) wise, discerning, shrewd, knowing —'**sapience** *n.*

saponify (sə'pɒnifai) *Chem. v.* **1.** convert (fat) into soap by treatment with alkali —*vi.* **2.** undergo reaction in which ester is hydrolysed to acid and alcohol as result of treatment with alkali —**saponifi'cation** *n.*

Sapphic ('sæfik) *a.* **1.** of Sappho, 6th-cent. B.C. Grecian poetess **2.** of metre associated with Sappho —*n.* **3.** Sapphic verse —'**sapphism** *n.* lesbianism

sapphire ('sæfaiə) *n.* **1.** (usu. blue) precious stone **2.** deep blue —*a.* **3.** of sapphire (blue) **4.** denoting 45th anniversary

saprophyte ('sæprəʊfait) *n.* plant that lives on dead organic matter

saraband *or* **sarabande** ('særəbænd) *n.* **1.** slow, stately Sp. dance **2.** music for it

Saracen ('særəsən) *n.* **1.** Arabian **2.** adherent of Mohammedanism in Syria and Palestine **3.** infidel —**Saracenic** (særə'sɛnik) *a.*

sarcasm ('sɑːkæzəm) *n.* **1.** bitter or wounding ironic remark **2.** such remarks **3.** taunt; sneer **4.** irony **5.** use of such expressions —**sar'castic** *a.* —**sar'castically** *adv.*

sarcoma (sɑː'kəʊmə) *n. Pathol.* usu. malignant tumour arising from connective tissue (*pl.* **-s**, **-mata** (-mətə)) —**sar'comatous** *a.*

sarcophagus (sɑː'kɒfəgəs) *n.* stone coffin (*pl.* **-gi** (-gai), **-es**)

sard (sɑːd) *or* **sardius** ('sɑːdiəs) *n.* precious stone, variety of chalcedony

sardine (sɑː'diːn) *n.* small fish of herring family, usu. preserved in oil

sardonic (sɑː'dɒnik) *a.* characterized by irony, mockery or derision

sardonyx ('sɑːdəniks) *n.* gemstone, variety of chalcedony

sargassum (sɑː'gæsəm) *n.* gulfweed, type of floating seaweed

sari ('sɑːrɪ) n. Hindu woman's robe (pl. **-s**)

sarong (sə'rɒŋ) n. skirtlike garment worn in Asian and Pacific countries

sarsaparilla (sɑːsəpə'rɪlə) n. (flavour of) drink, orig. made from root of plant

sartorial (sɑː'tɔːrɪəl) a. of tailor, tailoring or men's clothes

sash¹ (sæʃ) n. decorative belt or ribbon, wound around the body

sash² (sæʃ) n. wooden window frame opened by moving up and down in grooves

saskatoon (sæskə'tuːn) n. Canad. shrub with purplish berries

sassafras ('sæsəfræs) n. laurel-like tree with aromatic bark used medicinally

Sassenach ('sæsənæx) n. Scot. English person

sat (sæt) pt./pp. of SIT

Sat. 1. Saturday 2. Saturn

Satan ('seɪt³n) n. the devil —**satanic(al)** (sə'tænɪk(³l)) a. devilish, fiendish —**satanically** (sə'tænɪkəlɪ) adv. —**Satanism** n. 1. worship of Satan 2. satanic disposition —**Satanist** n./a.

satchel ('sætʃəl) n. small bag, esp. for school books

sate (seɪt) vt. satisfy (a desire or appetite) fully or excessively

sateen (sæ'tiːn) n. glossy linen or cotton fabric that resembles satin

satellite ('sætəlaɪt) n. 1. celestial body or man-made projectile orbiting planet 2. person, country etc. dependent on another

satiate ('seɪʃɪeɪt) vt. 1. satisfy to the full 2. surfeit —**'satiable** a. —**sati'ation** n. —**satiety** (sə'taɪɪtɪ) n. feeling of having had too much

satin ('sætɪn) n. fabric (of silk, rayon etc.) with glossy surface on one side —**'satiny** a. of, like satin —**'satinwood** n. any of various tropical trees that yield hard satiny wood

satire ('sætaɪə) n. 1. composition in which vice, folly or foolish person is held up to ridicule 2. use of ridicule or sarcasm to expose vice and folly —**satiric(al)** (sə'tɪrɪk(³l)) a. 1. of nature of satire 2. sarcastic 3. bitter —**satirist** ('sætərɪst) n. —**satirize** or **-rise** ('sætəraɪz) vt. 1. make object of satire 2. censure thus

satisfy ('sætɪsfaɪ) vt. 1. content, meet wishes of 2. pay 3. fulfil, supply adequately 4. convince (-**fied**, **-fying**) —**satis'faction** n. —**satis'factory** a.

satsuma (sæt'suːmə) n. kind of small orange

saturate ('sætʃəreɪt) vt. 1. soak thoroughly 2. cause to absorb maximum amount 3. Chem. cause (substance) to combine to its full capacity with another 4. shell or bomb heavily —**satu'ration** n. act, result of saturating

Saturday ('sætədɪ) n. seventh day of week

Saturn ('sætɜːn) n. 1. Roman god 2. one of planets —**Saturnalia** (sætɜː'neɪlɪə) n. 1. ancient festival of Saturn 2. (also s-) noisy revelry, orgy —**'saturnine** a. 1. gloomy 2. sluggish in temperament, dull, morose

satyr ('sætə) n. 1. woodland deity, part man, part goat 2. lustful man —**satyric** (sə'tɪrɪk) a.

sauce (sɔːs) n. 1. liquid added to food to enhance flavour 2. inf. impudence —vt. 3. add sauce to 4. inf. be cheeky, impudent to —**'saucily** adv. —**'saucy** a. impudent —**saucepan** ('sɔːspən) n. cooking pot with long handle

saucer ('sɔːsə) n. 1. curved plate put under cup 2. shallow depression

sauerkraut ('sauəkraut) n. Ger. dish of finely shredded and pickled cabbage

sauna ('sɔːnə) n. steam bath, orig. Finnish

saunter ('sɔːntə) vi. 1. walk in leisurely manner, stroll —n. 2. leisurely walk or stroll

-saur or **-saurus** (comb. form) lizard, as in dinosaur

saurian ('sɔːrɪən) n. one of the order of reptiles including the alligator, lizard etc.

sausage ('sɒsɪdʒ) n. minced meat enclosed in thin tube of animal intestine or synthetic material —**sausage roll** pastry cylinder filled with sausage

sauté ('səʊteɪ) a. fried quickly with little fat

Sauternes (səʊ'tɜːn) n. sweet white Fr. wine

savage ('sævɪdʒ) a. 1. wild 2. ferocious 3. brutal 4. uncivilized, primitive —n. 5. member of savage tribe, barbarian —vt. 6. attack ferociously —**'savagely** adv. —**'savagery** n.

savanna or **savannah** (sə'vænə) n. extensive open grassy plain

savant ('sævənt) n. man of learning

save (seɪv) vt. 1. rescue, preserve 2. protect 3. secure 4. keep for future, lay by 5. prevent need of 6. spare 7. except —vi. 8. lay by money —prep. 9. obs. except —conj. 10. obs. but —**'saving** a. 1. frugal 2. thrifty 3. delivering from sin 4. excepting 5. compensating —prep. 6. excepting —n. 7. economy —pl. 8. money, earnings put by for future use —**savings bank** bank that accepts savings of depositors and pays interest on them —**save as you earn** UK savings scheme in which monthly contributions earn tax-free interest

saveloy ('sævɪlɔɪ) n. type of smoked red sausage

saviour or U.S. **savior** ('seɪvjə) n. 1. person who rescues another 2. (S-) Christ

savoir-faire ('sævwɑː'fɛə; Fr. savwar'fɛːr) ability to do, say, the right thing in any situation

savory ('seɪvərɪ) n. aromatic herb used in cooking

savour or U.S. **savor** ('seɪvə) n. 1. characteristic taste 2. flavour 3. odour 4. distinctive quality —vi. 5. have particular smell or taste 6. (with of) have suggestion (of) —vt. 7.

give flavour to **8.** have flavour of **9.** enjoy, appreciate —**'savoury** or U.S. **'savory** a. **1.** attractive to taste or smell **2.** not sweet —n. **3.** savoury snack (before meal)

savoy (sə'vɔɪ) n. variety of cabbage

savvy ('sævɪ) sl. v. **1.** understand —n. **2.** wits, intelligence

saw[1] (sɔː) n. **1.** tool for cutting wood etc. by tearing it with toothed edge —vt. **2.** cut with saw —vi. **3.** make movements of sawing (**sawed, sawn, 'sawing**) —'**sawyer** n. one who saws timber —'**sawbones** n. sl. surgeon or doctor —'**sawdust** n. fine wood fragments made in sawing —'**sawfish** n. fish armed with toothed snout —'**sawhorse** n. stand for supporting timber during sawing —'**sawmill** n. mill where timber is sawn into planks etc.

saw[2] (sɔː) pt. of SEE[1]

saw[3] (sɔː) n. wise saying, proverb

sawn (sɔːn) pp. of SAW[1]

sax (sæks) inf. saxophone

saxe (sæks) n. shade of blue

saxhorn ('sækshɔːn) n. instrument of trumpet class

saxifrage ('sæksɪfreɪdʒ) n. Alpine or rock plant

Saxon ('sæksən) n. **1.** member of West Germanic people who settled widely in Europe in the early Middle Ages —a. **2.** of this people or their language

saxophone ('sæksəfəʊn) n. keyed wind instrument

say (seɪ) vt. **1.** speak **2.** pronounce **3.** state **4.** express **5.** take as example or as near enough **6.** make a case for (**said** pt./pp., '**saying** pr.p., **says** (sɛz) 3rd pers. sing. pres. ind.) —n. **7.** what one has to say **8.** chance of saying it **9.** share in decision —'**saying** n. maxim, proverb

S.A.Y.E. save as you earn

Sb Chem. antimony

Sc Chem. scandium

SC South Carolina

sc. 1. scale **2.** scene **3.** science **4.** screw **5.** scruple (unit of weight)

s.c. Print. small capitals

S.C. 1. A, NZ School Certificate **2.** Signal Corps **3.** C Social Credit

scab (skæb) n. **1.** crust formed over wound **2.** skin disease **3.** disease of plants **4.** offens. blackleg —'**scabby** a.

scabbard ('skæbəd) n. sheath for sword or dagger

scabies ('skeɪbiːz) n. contagious skin disease —'**scabious** a. having scabies, scabby

scabrous ('skeɪbrəs) a. **1.** having rough surface **2.** thorny **3.** indecent **4.** risky

scaffold ('skæfəld) n. **1.** temporary platform

for workmen **2.** gallows —'**scaffolding** n. (material for building) scaffold

scalar ('skeɪlə) n./a. (variable quantity, eg time) having magnitude but no direction

scalawag ('skæləwæg) n. see SCALLYWAG

scald (skɔːld) vt. **1.** burn with hot liquid or steam **2.** clean, sterilize with boiling water **3.** heat (liquid) almost to boiling point —n. **4.** injury by scalding

scale[1] (skeɪl) n. **1.** one of the thin, overlapping plates covering fishes and reptiles **2.** thin flake **3.** incrustation which forms in boilers etc. —vt. **4.** remove scales from —vi. **5.** come off in scales —'**scaly** a. resembling or covered in scales

scale[2] (skeɪl) n. (chiefly in pl.) **1.** weighing instrument —vt. **2.** weigh in scales **3.** have weight of

scale[3] (skeɪl) n. **1.** graduated table or sequence of marks at regular intervals used as reference or for fixing standards, as in making measurements, in music etc. **2.** ratio of size between a thing and a model or map of it **3.** (relative) degree, extent —vt. **4.** climb —a. **5.** proportionate —**scale up** or **down** increase or decrease proportionately in size

scalene ('skeɪliːn) a. (of triangle) with three unequal sides

scallion ('skæljən) n. onion with small bulb and long leaves

scallop ('skɒləp, 'skæl-) n. **1.** edible shellfish **2.** edging in small curves like edge of scallop shell —vt. **3.** shape like scallop shell **4.** cook in scallop shell or dish like one

scallywag ('skælɪwæg) n. inf. scamp, rascal (also '**scalawag**, '**scallawag**)

scalp (skælp) n. **1.** skin and hair of top of head —vt. **2.** cut off scalp of

scalpel ('skælpəl) n. small surgical knife

scamp (skæmp) n. **1.** mischievous person or child —vt. **2.** skimp

scamper ('skæmpə) vi. **1.** run about **2.** run hastily from place to place —n. **3.** act of scampering

scampi ('skæmpɪ) n. (with sing. or pl. v.) large prawns usu. eaten fried in batter

scan (skæn) vt. **1.** look at carefully, scrutinize **2.** measure or read (verse) by metrical feet **3.** examine, search by systematically varying the direction of a radar or sonar beam **4.** glance over quickly —vi. **5.** (of verse) conform to metrical rules (**-nn-**) —n. **6.** scanning —'**scanner** n. device, esp. electronic, which scans —'**scansion** n. analysis of metrical structure of verse

Scand. or **Scan.** Scandinavia(n)

scandal ('skændəl) n. **1.** action, event generally considered disgraceful **2.** malicious gossip —'**scandalize** or **-ise** vt. shock —'**scandalous** a.

outrageous, disgraceful —'**scandalmonger** n. person who spreads gossip etc.

Scandinavian (skændɪ'neɪvɪən) a. 1. of Scandinavia, its inhabitants or their languages —n. 2. native or inhabitant of Scandinavia

scandium ('skændɪəm) n. rare silvery-white metallic element occurring in numerous minerals

scant (skænt) a. barely sufficient or not sufficient —'**scantily** adv. —'**scanty** a.

scapegoat ('skeɪpɡəʊt) n. person bearing blame due to others

scapegrace ('skeɪpɡreɪs) n. mischievous person

scapula ('skæpjʊlə) n. shoulder blade (pl. -lae (-liː), -s) —'**scapular** a. 1. of scapula —n. 2. part of habit of certain religious orders in R.C. Church

scar[1] (skɑː) n. 1. mark left by healed wound, burn or sore 2. change resulting from emotional distress —v. 3. mark, heal with scar (-rr-)

scar[2] (skɑː) n. bare craggy rock formation

scarab ('skærəb) n. 1. sacred beetle of ancient Egypt 2. gem cut in shape of this

scarce (skɛəs) a. 1. hard to find 2. existing or available in insufficient quantity 3. uncommon —'**scarcely** adv. 1. only just 2. not quite 3. definitely or probably not —'**scarceness** or '**scarcity** n.

scare (skɛə) vt. 1. frighten —n. 2. fright, sudden panic —'**scary** a. —'**scarecrow** n. 1. thing set up to frighten birds from crops 2. badly dressed or miserable-looking person —'**scaremonger** n. one who spreads alarming rumours

scarf[1] (skɑːf) n. long narrow strip, large piece of material to put round neck, head etc. (pl. -s, **scarves**)

scarf[2] (skɑːf) n. 1. part cut away from each of two pieces of timber to be jointed longitudinally 2. joint so made (pl. -s) —vt. 3. cut or join in this way —'**scarfing** n.

scarify ('skɛərɪfaɪ, 'skærɪ-) vt. 1. scratch, cut slightly all over 2. lacerate 3. stir surface soil of 4. criticize mercilessly (-**fied**, -**fying**) —**scarifi-**'**cation** n.

scarlatina (skɑːlə'tiːnə) n. scarlet fever

scarlet ('skɑːlɪt) n. 1. brilliant red colour 2. cloth or clothing of this colour, esp. military uniform —a. 3. of this colour 4. immoral, esp. unchaste —**scarlet fever** infectious fever with scarlet rash

scarp (skɑːp) n. 1. steep slope 2. inside slope of ditch in fortifications

scarper ('skɑːpə) vi. sl. depart in haste

scarves (skɑːvz) n., pl. of SCARF

scat[1] (skæt) vi. inf. (usu. imp.) go away

scat[2] (skæt) n. Jazz singing characterized by improvised vocal sounds instead of words

scathe (skeɪð) (usu. now as pp./a. **scathed** & **un'scathed**) n. 1. injury, harm, damage —vt. 2. injure, damage —'**scathing** a. 1. harshly critical 2. cutting 3. damaging

scatology (skæ'tɒlədʒɪ) n. 1. scientific study of excrement, esp. in medicine and palaeontology 2. preoccupation with obscenity, esp. in form of references to excrement —scato'**logical** a.

scatter ('skætə) vt. 1. throw in various directions 2. put here and there 3. sprinkle —vi. 4. disperse —n. 5. sprinkling —'**scatterbrain** n. silly, careless person —'**scatty** a. inf. silly, useless

scavenge ('skævɪndʒ) v. search for (anything usable), usu. among discarded material —'**scavenger** n. 1. person who scavenges 2. animal, bird which feeds on refuse

Sc.D. Doctor of Science

S.C.E. Scottish Certificate of Education

scene (siːn) n. 1. place of action of novel, play etc. 2. place of any action 3. subdivision of play 4. view 5. episode 6. display of strong emotion —**scenario** (sɪ'nɑːrɪəʊ) n. summary of plot (of play etc.) or plan (pl. -s) —'**scenery** n. 1. natural features of district 2. constructions of wood, canvas etc. used on stage to represent a place where action is happening —'**scenic** a. 1. picturesque 2. of or on the stage

scent (sɛnt) n. 1. distinctive smell, esp. pleasant one 2. trail, clue 3. perfume —vt. 4. detect or track by or as if by smell 5. suspect, sense 6. fill with fragrance

sceptic or U.S. **skeptic** ('skɛptɪk) n. 1. one who maintains doubt or disbelief 2. agnostic 3. unbeliever —'**sceptical** or U.S. '**skeptical** a. —'**scepticism** or U.S. '**skepticism** n.

sceptre or U.S. **scepter** ('sɛptə) n. 1. ornamental staff as symbol of royal power 2. royal dignity

schedule ('ʃɛdjuːl; also, esp. U.S. 'skɛdʒʊəl) n. 1. plan of procedure for a project 2. list 3. timetable —vt. 4. enter in schedule 5. plan to occur at certain time —**on schedule** on time

schema ('skiːmə) n. overall plan or diagram (pl. -**mata** (-mətə)) —**sche'matic** a. presented as plan or diagram —'**schematize** or -**ise** vt.

scheme (skiːm) n. 1. plan, design 2. project 3. outline —v. 4. devise, plan, esp. in underhand manner —'**schemer** n.

scherzo ('skɛətsəʊ) n. Mus. light playful composition (pl. -**s**, -**zi** (-tsɪ))

schism ('sɪzəm, 'skɪz-) n. (group resulting from) division in political party, church etc. —**schis'matic** n./a.

schist (ʃɪst) n. crystalline rock which splits into layers —'**schistose** a.

schizanthus (skɪz'ænθəs) n. plant with divided leaves

schizo ('skɪtsəu) *inf. a.* 1. schizophrenic —*n.* 2. schizophrenic person (*pl.* -**s**)

schizo- *or before vowel* **schiz-** (*comb. form*) indicating cleavage, split, or division, as in *schizophrenia*

schizophrenia (skɪtsəu'fri:nɪə) *n.* mental disorder involving deterioration of, confusion about personality —'**schizoid** *a.* of schizophrenia —**schizo'phrenic** *a./n.*

schmaltz *or* **schmalz** (ʃmælts, ʃmɔːlts) *n.* excessive sentimentality —'**schmaltzy** *a.*

schnapps *or* **schnaps** (ʃnæps) *n.* 1. spirit distilled from potatoes 2. *inf.* any strong spirit

schnitzel ('ʃnɪtsəl) *n.* thin slice of meat, *esp.* veal

scholar ('skɒlə) *n. see* SCHOOL[1]

scholium ('skəʊlɪəm) *n.* 1. marginal annotation 2. note 3. comment (*pl.* -**lia** (-lɪə)) —'**scholiast** *n.* 1. commentator 2. annotator

school[1] (skuːl) *n.* 1. institution for teaching children or for giving instruction in any subject 2. buildings of such institution 3. group of thinkers, writers, artists *etc.* with principles or methods in common —*vt.* 4. educate 5. bring under control, train —'**scholar** *n.* 1. learned person 2. one taught in school 3. one quick to learn —**scholarly** ('skɒlɪlɪ) *a.* learned, erudite —**scholarship** ('skɒləʃɪp) *n.* 1. learning 2. prize, grant to student for payment of school or college fees —**scholastic** (skə'læstɪk) *a.* 1. of schools or scholars, or education 2. pedantic —'**schooling** *n.* 1. education, *esp.* when received at school 2. training of animal, *esp.* of horse for dressage —'**schoolhouse** *n.* 1. building used as school 2. house attached to school —'**schoolman** *n.* medieval philosopher —'**schoolmarm** *n. inf.* 1. woman schoolteacher 2. woman considered old-fashioned or prim —'**schoolmaster** *or* '**schoolmistress** *n.* person who teaches in or runs a school

school[2] (skuːl) *n.* shoal (of fish, whales *etc.*)

schooner ('skuːnə) *n.* 1. fore-and-aft rigged vessel with two or more masts 2. tall glass

schottische (ʃɒ'tiːʃ) *n.* 19th-century German dance 2. music for this

schwa *or* **shwa** (ʃwɑː) *n.* 1. central vowel represented in International Phonetic Alphabet by (ə), *eg* 'a' in *around* 2. symbol (ə) used to represent this sound

sciatica (saɪ'ætɪkə) *n.* 1. neuralgia of hip and thigh 2. pain in sciatic nerve —**sci'atic** *a.* 1. of the hip 2. of sciatica

science ('saɪəns) *n.* 1. systematic study and knowledge of natural or physical phenomena 2. any branch of study concerned with observed material facts —**scien'tific** *a.* 1. of the principles of science 2. systematic —**scien'tifi-cally** *adv.* —'**scientist** *n.* one versed in natural

sciences —**science fiction** stories set in the future making imaginative use of scientific knowledge

Scientology (saɪən'tɒlədʒɪ) *n.* religious cult based on belief that self-awareness is paramount

sci-fi ('saɪ'faɪ) *n. inf.* science fiction

scimitar ('sɪmɪtə) *n.* oriental curved sword

scintilla (sɪn'tɪlə) *n. rare* minute amount

scintillate ('sɪntɪleɪt) *vi.* 1. sparkle 2. be animated, witty, clever —**scintil'lation** *n.* —**scintillation counter** instrument for detecting and measuring intensity of high-energy radiation

scion ('saɪən) *n.* 1. descendant, heir 2. slip for grafting

scission ('sɪʒən) *n.* act of cutting, dividing, splitting —'**scissile** *a.*

scissors ('sɪzəz) *pl.n.* 1. cutting instrument of two blades pivoted together (*also* **pair of scissors**) —*n./a.* 2. with scissorlike action of limbs in swimming, athletics *etc.*

sclerosis (sklɪə'rəʊsɪs) *n.* a hardening of bodily organs, tissues *etc.* (*pl.* -**ses** (-siːz)) —**sclera** *n.* firm white fibrous membrane that forms outer covering of eyeball —**sclerotic** (sklɪə'rɒtɪk) *a.* 1. of sclera 2. of or having sclerosis 3. sclera

scoff[1] (skɒf) *vi.* 1. (*oft. with* at) express derision (for) —*n.* 2. derision 3. mocking words —'**scoffer** *n.*

scoff[2] (skɒf) *v. sl.* eat rapidly

scold (skəʊld) *v.* 1. find fault (with) —*vt.* 2. reprimand, be angry with —*n.* 3. one who does this

scollop ('skɒləp) *see* SCALLOP

sconce[1] (skɒns) *n.* bracket candlestick on wall

sconce[2] (skɒns) *n.* small protective fortification

scone (skəʊn, skɒn) *n.* small plain cake baked on griddle or in oven

scoop (skuːp) *n.* 1. small shovel-like tool for ladling, hollowing out *etc.* 2. *sl.* profitable deal 3. *Journalism* exclusive news item —*vt.* 4. ladle out 5. hollow out, rake in with scoop 6. make sudden profit 7. beat (rival newspaper *etc.*)

scoot (skuːt) *vi. sl.* move off quickly —'**scooter** *n.* 1. child's vehicle propelled by pushing on ground with one foot 2. light motorcycle (*also* **motor scooter**)

scope (skəʊp) *n.* 1. range of activity or application 2. opportunity

-scope (*n. comb. form*) indicating instrument for observing or detecting, as in *microscope* —**-scopic** (*a. comb. form*)

scopolamine (skə'pɒləmiːn) *n.* colourless viscous liquid alkaloid used in preventing travel sickness and as sedative and truth serum (*also* '**hyoscine**)

scorbutic (skɔː'bjuːtɪk) *or* **scorbutical** *a.* of or having scurvy —**scor'butically** *adv.*

scorch (skɔːtʃ) *v.* **1.** burn, be burnt, on surface **2.** parch **3.** shrivel **4.** wither —*n.* **5.** slight burn —**'scorcher** *n. inf.* very hot day

score (skɔː) *n.* **1.** points gained in game, competition **2.** group of 20 **3.** (*esp. pl.*) a lot **4.** musical notation **5.** mark or notch, *esp.* to keep tally **6.** reason, account **7.** grievance —*v.* **8.** gain (points) in game —*vt.* **9.** mark **10.** (*with out*) cross out **11.** arrange music for —*vi.* **12.** keep tally of points **13.** succeed —**'scorecard** *n.* **1.** card on which scores are recorded **2.** card identifying players in sports match

scoria ('skɔːrɪə) *n.* **1.** solidified lava containing many cavities **2.** refuse obtained from smelted ore (*pl.* **-riae** (-riː))

scorn (skɔːn) *n.* **1.** contempt, derision —*vt.* **2.** despise —**'scorner** *n.* —**'scornful** *a.* derisive —**'scornfully** *adv.*

Scorpio ('skɔːpɪəʊ) *n.* (scorpion) 8th sign of zodiac, operative *c.* Oct. 23rd - Nov. 21st

scorpion ('skɔːpɪən) *n.* small lobster-shaped animal with sting at end of jointed tail

Scot (skɒt) *n.* native of Scotland —**Scotch** *n.* whisky made in Scotland —**Scottish** *or* **Scots** *a.* —**Scotch broth** UK soup made from beef stock, vegetables, and pearl barley —**Scotch egg** UK hard-boiled egg enclosed in layer of sausage meat and covered in breadcrumbs —**Scotch mist 1.** heavy wet mist **2.** drizzle —**'Scotsman** *n.* —**Scots pine** *or* **Scotch pine 1.** coniferous tree of Europe and W and N Asia **2.** its wood —**Scottish Certificate of Education** Scottish examination equivalent to General Certificate of Education in England —**Scottish terrier** small long-haired breed of terrier

Scot. 1. Scotch (whisky) **2.** Scotland **3.** Scottish

scotch (skɒtʃ) *vt.* **1.** put an end to **2.** *obs.* wound

scoter ('skəʊtə) *n.* sea duck of northern regions

scot-free *a.* without harm or loss

Scotland Yard ('skɒtlənd) headquarters of police force of metropolitan London

Scottie *or* **Scotty** ('skɒtɪ) *n.* **1.** Scottish terrier **2.** *inf.* Scotsman

scoundrel ('skaʊndrəl) *n.* villain, blackguard —**'scoundrelly** *a.*

scour[1] (skaʊə) *vt.* **1.** clean, polish by rubbing **2.** clear or flush out

scour[2] (skaʊə) *v.* move rapidly along or over (territory) in search of something

scourge (skɜːdʒ) *n.* **1.** whip, lash **2.** severe affliction **3.** pest **4.** calamity —*vt.* **5.** flog **6.** punish severely

Scouse (skaʊs) UK *inf. n.* **1.** person from Liverpool **2.** dialect of such person —*a.* **3.** of or from Liverpool

scout (skaʊt) *n.* **1.** one sent out to reconnoitre **2.**

(S-) member of **Scout Association**, organization to develop character and responsibility —*vi.* **3.** go out, act as scout **4.** reconnoitre —**'scouter** *n.* leader of troop of scouts

scow (skaʊ) *n.* unpowered barge

scowl (skaʊl) *vi.* **1.** frown gloomily or sullenly —*n.* **2.** angry or gloomy expression

scrabble ('skræbəl) *vi.* **1.** scrape with hands, claws in disorderly manner —*n.* **2.** (S-) R word game

scrag (skræg) *n.* **1.** lean person or animal **2.** lean end of a neck of mutton —**'scraggy** *a.* thin, bony

scraggly ('skræglɪ) *a.* untidy

scram (skræm) *vi. inf.* (*oft. imp.*) go away hastily, get out (**-mm-**)

scramble ('skræmbəl) *vi.* **1.** move along or up by crawling, climbing *etc.* **2.** struggle with others **3.** (of aircraft, aircrew) take off hurriedly —*vt.* **4.** mix up **5.** cook (eggs) beaten up with milk **6.** render (speech) unintelligible via electronic device —*n.* **7.** scrambling **8.** rough climb **9.** disorderly proceeding **10.** motorcycle race over rough ground —**'scrambler** *n.* electronic device that renders speech unintelligible during transmission

scrap (skræp) *n.* **1.** small piece or fragment **2.** leftover material **3.** *inf.* fight —*vt.* **4.** break up, discard as useless —*vi.* **5.** *inf.* fight (**-pp-**) —**'scrappy** *a.* unequal in quality **2.** badly finished —**'scrapbook** *n.* book in which newspaper cuttings *etc.* are kept —**scrap merchant** person dealing in scrap, *esp.* scrap metal

scrape (skreɪp) *vt.* **1.** rub with something sharp **2.** clean, smooth thus **3.** grate **4.** scratch **5.** rub with harsh noise —*n.* **6.** act, sound of scraping **7.** *inf.* awkward situation, *esp.* as result of escapade —**'scraper** *n.* **1.** instrument for scraping **2.** contrivance on which mud is scraped from shoes *etc.*

scratch (skrætʃ) *vt.* **1.** score, make narrow surface wound on with claws, nails, or anything pointed **2.** make marks on with pointed instruments **3.** scrape (skin) with nails to relieve itching **4.** remove, withdraw from list, race *etc.* —*vi.* **5.** use claws or nails, *esp.* to relieve itching —*n.* **6.** wound, mark or sound made by scratching **7.** line or starting point —*a.* **8.** got together at short notice **9.** impromptu —**'scratchy** *a.*

scrawl (skrɔːl) *vt.* **1.** write, draw untidily —*n.* **2.** thing scrawled **3.** careless writing

scrawny ('skrɔːnɪ) *a.* thin, bony

scream (skriːm) *vi.* **1.** utter piercing cry, *esp.* of fear, pain *etc.* **2.** be very obvious —*vt.* **3.** utter in a scream —*n.* **4.** shrill, piercing cry **5.** *inf.* very funny person or thing

scree (skriː) n. 1. loose shifting stones 2. slope covered with these

screech (skriːtʃ) vi./n. scream —**screech owl** 1. small N Amer. owl having reddish-brown or grey plumage 2. UK any owl that utters screeching cry

screed (skriːd) n. 1. long (tedious) letter, passage or speech 2. thin layer of cement

screen (skriːn) n. 1. device to shelter from heat, light, draught, observation etc. 2. anything used for such purpose 3. mesh over doors, windows to keep out insects 4. white or silvered surface on which photographic images are projected 5. windscreen 6. wooden or stone partition in church —vt. 7. shelter, hide 8. protect from detection 9. show (film) 10. scrutinize 11. examine (group of people) for presence of disease, weapons etc. 12. examine for political motives 13. Elec. protect from stray electric or magnetic fields —**screenplay** n. script for film, including instructions for sets and camera work —**screen process** see **silk-screen** at SILK —**the screen** cinema generally

screw (skruː) n. 1. (nail-like device or cylinder with) spiral thread cut to engage similar thread or to bore into material (wood etc.) to pin or fasten 2. anything resembling a screw in shape, esp. in spiral form 3. propeller 4. twist —vt. 5. fasten with screw 6. twist around 7. inf. extort —'**screwy** a. inf. crazy, eccentric —'**screwball** US sl. n. 1. eccentric person —a. 2. odd; eccentric —'**screwdriver** n. tool for turning screws —**screw top** bottle top that screws on to bottle, allowing bottle to be resealed after use —**screw-top** a. —**screw up** 1. distort 2. inf. bungle

scribble ('skrɪbəl) v. 1. write, draw carelessly —vi. 2. make meaningless marks with pen or pencil —n. 3. something scribbled —'**scribbly** a.

scribe (skraɪb) n. 1. writer 2. copyist —v. 3. scratch a line on (a surface) with pointed instrument

scrimmage ('skrɪmɪdʒ) n. scuffle

scrimp (skrɪmp) vt. 1. make too small or short 2. treat meanly —'**scrimpy** a.

script (skrɪpt) n. 1. (system or style of) handwriting 2. written characters 3. written text of film, play, radio or television programme 4. answer paper in examination

scripture ('skrɪptʃə) n. 1. sacred writings 2. the Bible —'**scriptural** a.

scrofula ('skrɒfjʊlə) n. tuberculosis of lymphatic glands, esp. of neck —'**scrofulous** a.

scroll (skrəʊl) n. 1. roll of parchment or paper 2. list 3. ornament shaped thus

Scrooge (skruːdʒ) n. miserly person

scrotum ('skrəʊtəm) n. pouch containing testicles (pl. -ta (-tə)) —'**scrotal** a.

scrounge (skraʊndʒ) v. inf. get (something) without cost, by begging —'**scrounger** n.

scrub[1] (skrʌb) vt. 1. clean with hard brush and water 2. scour 3. inf. cancel, get rid of (-bb-) —n. 4. scrubbing —'**scrubber** n. 1. person or thing that scrubs 2. apparatus for purifying gas 3. derogatory sl. promiscuous girl

scrub[2] (skrʌb) n. 1. stunted trees 2. brushwood —'**scrubby** a. 1. covered with scrub 2. stunted 3. inf. messy

scruff (skrʌf) n. nape (of neck)

scruffy ('skrʌfɪ) a. unkempt or shabby

scrum (skrʌm) n. 1. Rugby restarting of play in which opposing packs of forwards push against each other to gain possession of the ball (also '**scrummage**) 2. crush, crowd

scrump (skrʌmp) v. UK dial. steal (apples) from orchard or garden

scrumptious ('skrʌmpʃəs) a. inf. very pleasing; delicious —'**scrumptiously** adv.

scrumpy ('skrʌmpɪ) n. rough dry cider

scrunch (skrʌntʃ) v. 1. crumple or crunch or be crumpled or crunched —n. 2. act or sound of scrunching

scruple ('skruːpəl) n. 1. doubt or hesitation about what is morally right 2. weight of 20 grains —vi. 3. hesitate —'**scrupulous** a. 1. extremely conscientious 2. thorough, attentive to small points

scrutiny ('skruːtɪnɪ) n. 1. close examination 2. critical investigation 3. official examination of votes etc. 4. searching look —scruti'**neer** n. examiner of votes —'**scrutinize** or **-nise** vt. examine closely

scuba ('skjuːbə) n./a. (relating to) self-contained underwater breathing apparatus

scud (skʌd) vi. 1. run fast 2. run before the wind (-dd-)

scuff (skʌf) vi. 1. drag, scrape with feet in walking —vt. 2. scrape with feet 3. graze —n. 4. act, sound of scuffing —pl. 5. thong sandals —**scuffed** a. (of shoes) scraped or slightly grazed

scuffle ('skʌfəl) vi. 1. fight in disorderly manner 2. shuffle —n. 3. disorderly struggle

scull (skʌl) n. 1. oar used in stern of boat 2. short oar used in pairs —v. 3. propel, move by means of scull(s)

scullery ('skʌlərɪ) n. place for washing dishes etc. —'**scullion** n. despicable person 2. obs. kitchen underservant

sculpture ('skʌlptʃə) n. 1. art of forming figures in relief or solid 2. product of this art —vt. 3. represent by sculpture —**sculpt** v. —'**sculptor** n. ('**sculptress** fem.) —'**sculptural** a. with qualities proper to sculpture

scum (skʌm) n. 1. froth or other floating matter

on liquid **2.** waste part of anything **3.** vile person(s) or thing(s) —'**scummy** a.

scunner ('skʌnə) dial., chiefly Scot. vt. **1.** produce feeling of aversion in —n. **2.** strong aversion (oft. in **take a scunner**) **3.** object of aversion

scupper ('skʌpə) n. **1.** hole in ship's side level with deck to carry off water —vt. **2.** inf. ruin, destroy, kill

scurf (skɜːf) n. flaky matter on scalp, dandruff

scurrilous ('skʌrɪləs) a. coarse, indecently abusive —**scur'rility** n.

scurry ('skʌrɪ) vi. **1.** run hastily ('**scurried**, '**scurrying**) —n. **2.** bustling haste **3.** flurry

scurvy ('skɜːvɪ) n. **1.** disease caused by lack of vitamin C —a. **2.** mean, contemptible

scut (skʌt) n. short tail of hare or other animal

scuttle¹ ('skʌtəl) n. fireside container for coal

scuttle² ('skʌtəl) vi. **1.** rush away —n. **2.** hurried pace, run

scuttle³ ('skʌtəl) vt. cause (ship) to sink by making holes in bottom

scythe (saɪð) n. **1.** manual implement with long curved blade for cutting grass —vt. **2.** cut with scythe

SD South Dakota

Se Chem. selenium

SE southeast(ern)

sea (siː) n. **1.** mass of salt water covering greater part of earth **2.** broad tract of this **3.** waves **4.** swell **5.** large quantity **6.** vast expanse —**sea anchor** Naut. device dragged in water to slow vessel —**sea anemone** sea animal with suckers like petals —'**seaboard** n. chiefly US coast —**sea cow 1.** dugong or manatee **2.** obs. walrus —**sea dog** experienced or old sailor —'**seafaring** a. occupied in sea voyages —'**seafood** n. edible saltwater fish or shellfish —**sea-girt** a. Lit. surrounded by sea —**sea gull** gull —**sea horse** fish with bony plated body and horselike head —**sea kale** European coastal plant with edible asparagus-like shoots —**sea legs** inf. **1.** ability to maintain one's balance on board ship **2.** ability to resist seasickness —**sea level** level of surface of sea, taken to be mean level between high and low tide —**sea lion** kind of large seal —'**seaman** n. sailor —'**seamanship** n. skill in navigating, maintaining and operating vessel —'**seaplane** n. aircraft that lands on and takes off from water —**Sea Scout** Scout belonging to any of number of Scout troops whose main activities are sailing etc. —'**seashell** n. empty shell of marine mollusc —'**seasick** a. —**seasickness** n. nausea caused by motion of ship —'**seaside** n. place, esp. holiday resort, on coast —**sea urchin** marine animal with globular body enclosed in rigid,

spiny test —'**seaweed** n. plant growing in sea —'**seaworthy** a. in fit condition to put to sea

seal¹ (siːl) n. **1.** device impressed on piece of wax etc., fixed to letter etc. as mark of authentication **2.** impression thus made **3.** device, material preventing passage of water, air, oil etc. (also '**sealer**) —vt. **4.** affix seal to **5.** ratify, authorize **6.** mark with stamp as evidence of some quality **7.** keep close or secret **8.** settle **9.** make watertight, airtight etc. —**sealing wax** hard material made of shellac and turpentine that softens when heated

seal² (siːl) n. **1.** amphibious furred carnivorous mammal with flippers as limbs —vi. **2.** hunt seals —'**sealer** n. man or ship engaged in sealing —'**sealskin** n. skin, fur of seals

seam (siːm) n. **1.** line of junction of two edges, eg of two pieces of cloth, or two planks **2.** thin layer, stratum —vt. **3.** mark with furrows or wrinkles —'**seamless** a. —**seamstress** ('sɛmstrɪs) or **sempstress** ('sɛmpstrɪs) n. woman who sews and makes clothes, esp. professionally —'**seamy** a. **1.** sordid **2.** marked with seams

seance ('seɪɒns) n. meeting of spiritualists

sear (sɪə) vt. **1.** scorch, brand with hot iron **2.** deaden

search (sɜːtʃ) v. **1.** look over or through (a place etc.) to find something —vt. **2.** probe into, examine —n. **3.** act of searching **4.** quest —'**searcher** n. —'**searching** a. **1.** keen **2.** thorough **3.** severe —'**searchlight** n. powerful electric light with concentrated beam —**search warrant** legal document authorizing search of premises for stolen goods etc.

season ('siːzən) n. **1.** one of four divisions of year (spring, summer, autumn and winter), which have characteristic weather conditions **2.** period during which thing takes place, grows, is active etc. **3.** proper time —vt. **4.** flavour with salt, herbs etc. **5.** make reliable or ready for use **6.** make experienced —'**seasonable** a. **1.** appropriate for the season **2.** opportune **3.** fit —'**seasonal** a. depending on, varying with seasons —'**seasoning** n. flavouring —**season ticket** ticket for series of journeys, events etc. within a certain time

seat (siːt) n. **1.** thing for sitting on **2.** buttocks **3.** base **4.** right to sit (eg in council etc.) **5.** place where something is located, centred **6.** locality of disease, trouble etc. **7.** country house —vt. **8.** bring to or place on seat **9.** provide sitting accommodation for **10.** install firmly —**seat belt** belt worn in car, aircraft etc. to secure seated passenger (also **safety belt**)

SEATO ('siːtəʊ) South East Asia Treaty Organization

sebaceous (sɪ'beɪʃəs) a. 1. of, pert. to fat 2. secreting fat, oil

sec¹ (sɛk) a. 1. (of wines) dry 2. (of champagne) of medium sweetness

sec² (sɛk) inf. second (of time)

sec³ (sɛk) secant

sec. 1. second (of time) 2. secondary 3. secretary 4. section 5. sector

secant ('siːkənt) n. Maths. 1. (of angle) the reciprocal of its cosine 2. line that intersects a curve

secateurs ('sɛkətəz) pl.n. small pruning shears

secede (sɪ'siːd) vi. withdraw formally from federation, Church etc. —**secession** (sɪ'sɛʃən) n. —**secessionist** (sɪ'sɛʃənɪst) n.

seclude (sɪ'kluːd) vt. guard from, remove from sight, view, contact with others —**se'cluded** a. 1. remote 2. private —**se'clusion** n.

second¹ ('sɛkənd) a. 1. next after first 2. alternate 3. additional 4. of lower quality —n. 5. person or thing coming second 6. attendant 7. sixtieth part of minute 8. SI unit of time 9. moment 10. (esp. pl.) inferior goods —vt. 11. support 12. support (motion in meeting) so that discussion may be in order —**'seconder** n. —**'secondly** adv. —**second-best** a. next to best —**second chamber** upper house of bicameral legislative assembly —**second class** class next in value etc. to first —**second-class** a. 1. of grade next to best in quality etc. 2. shoddy or inferior 3. (of accommodation in hotel, on aircraft etc.) next in quality to first class 4. UK (of letters) handled more slowly than first-class letters —adv. 5. by second-class mail etc. —**Second Coming** or **Advent** Christian theol. prophesied return of Christ to earth at Last Judgment —**second cousin** child of first cousin of either of one's parents —**second fiddle** inf. 1. second violin in string quartet 2. person who has secondary status —**second hand** pointer on face of timepiece that indicates seconds —**second-hand** a. 1. bought after use by another 2. not original 3. dealing in goods that are not new —adv. 4. not directly —**second lieutenant** officer holding lowest commissioned rank in armed forces of certain nations —**second nature** habit etc. long practised so as to seem innate —**second person** grammatical category of pronouns and verbs used when referring to individual(s) being addressed —**second-rate** a. 1. mediocre 2. second in importance etc. —**second sight** faculty of seeing events before they occur —**second thought** revised opinion on matter already considered —**second wind** 1. return of breath at normal rate, esp. following exertion 2. renewed ability to continue in effort —**come off second best** inf. be defeated in competition

second² (sə'kɒnd) vt. transfer (employee, officer) temporarily

secondary ('sɛkəndərɪ) a. 1. subsidiary, of less importance 2. developed from, or dependent on, something else —**'secondarily** adv. —**secondary education** education of young people between ages of 11 and 18 —**secondary picketing** picketing by striking workers of distribution outlet etc. that supplies goods to or distributes goods from their employer

secret ('siːkrɪt) a. 1. kept, meant to be kept from knowledge of others 2. hidden 3. private —n. 4. thing kept secret —**'secrecy** n. keeping or being kept secret —**'secretive** a. given to having secrets; uncommunicative, reticent —**'secretiveness** n. —**'secretly** adv. —**secret agent** person employed in espionage —**secret police** police force that operates secretly to check subversion —**secret service** government department that conducts intelligence or counterintelligence operations

secretary ('sɛkrətrɪ) n. 1. one employed by individual or organization to deal with papers and correspondence, keep records, prepare business etc. 2. head of a state department —**secre'tarial** a. —**secre'tariat** n. 1. body of secretaries 2. building occupied by secretarial staff —**'secretaryship** n. —**secretary bird** large Afr. bird of prey

secrete (sɪ'kriːt) vt. 1. hide, conceal 2. (of gland etc.) collect and supply (particular substance in body) —**se'cretion** n. —**se'cretory** a.

sect (sɛkt) n. 1. group of people (within religious body etc.) with common interest 2. faction —**sec'tarian** a. 1. of a sect 2. narrow-minded

section ('sɛkʃən) n. 1. part cut off 2. division 3. portion 4. distinct part of city, country, people etc. 5. cutting 6. drawing of anything as if cut through 7. smallest military unit —**'sectional** a.

sector ('sɛktə) n. 1. part, subdivision 2. part of circle enclosed by two radii and the arc which they cut off

secular ('sɛkjʊlə) a. 1. worldly 2. lay, not religious 3. not monastic 4. lasting for, or occurring once in, an age 5. centuries old —**'secularism** n. —**'secularist** n. one who believes that religion should have no place in civil affairs —**seculari'zation** or **-ri'sation** n. —**'secularize** or **-rise** vt. transfer from religious to lay possession or use

secure (sɪ'kjʊə) a. 1. safe 2. free from fear, anxiety 3. firmly fixed 4. certain 5. sure, confident —vt. 6. gain possession of 7. make safe 8. free (creditor) from risk of loss 9. make firm —**se'curely** adv. —**se'curity** n. 1. state of safety 2. protection 3. that which secures 4. assurance 5. anything given as bond, caution or pledge 6.

one that becomes surety for another —**security risk** person deemed to be threat to state security

sedan (sɪ'dæn) n. US saloon car —**sedan chair** Hist. closed chair for one person, carried on poles by bearers

sedate[1] (sɪ'deɪt) a. 1. calm, collected 2. serious

sedate[2] (sɪ'deɪt) vt. make calm by sedative —**se'dation** n. —**sedative** ('sedətɪv) a. 1. having soothing or calming effect —n. 2. sedative drug

sedentary ('sedntərɪ) a. 1. done sitting down 2. sitting much 3. (of birds) not migratory

sedge (sedʒ) n. plant like coarse grass growing in swampy ground —**sedge warbler** European songbird having streaked brownish plumage with white eye stripes

sedilia (se'dɪlɪə) n. (with sing. v.) stone seats on south side of altar for priests

sediment ('sedɪmənt) n. 1. matter which settles to the bottom of liquid 2. matter deposited from water, ice or wind —**sedi'mentary** a.

sedition (sɪ'dɪʃən) n. speech or action threatening authority of a state —**se'ditious** a.

seduce (sɪ'djuːs) vt. 1. persuade to commit some (wrong) deed, esp. sexual intercourse 2. tempt 3. attract —**se'ducer** n. (**seductress** (sɪ'dʌktrɪs) fem.) —**seduction** (sɪ'dʌkʃən) n. —**seductive** (sɪ'dʌktɪv) a. 1. alluring 2. winning

sedulous ('sedjʊləs) a. 1. diligent 2. industrious 3. persevering, persistent —**se'dulity** n.

sedum ('siːdəm) n. rock plant

see[1] (siː) vt. 1. perceive with eyes or mentally 2. observe 3. watch 4. find out 5. consider 6. have experience of 7. interview 8. make sure 9. accompany —vi. 10. have power of sight 11. consider 12. understand (**saw**, **seen**, '**seeing**) —'**seeing** conj. since, in view of the fact that

see[2] (siː) n. diocese, office or jurisdiction of bishop

seed (siːd) n. 1. reproductive germs of plants 2. one grain of this 3. such grains saved or used for sowing 4. origin 5. sperm 6. obs. offspring —vt. 7. sow with seed 8. arrange (draw for lawn tennis or other tournament) so that best players do not meet in early rounds —vi. 9. produce seed —'**seedling** n. young plant raised from seed —'**seedy** a. 1. shabby 2. (of plant) at seed-producing stage 3. inf. unwell, ill —**seed pearl** tiny pearl weighing less than a quarter of a grain

seek (siːk) vt. 1. make search or enquiry for —vi. 2. search (**sought**, '**seeking**)

seem (siːm) vi. 1. appear (to be or to do) 2. look 3. appear to one's judgment —'**seeming** a. apparent but not real —'**seemingly** adv.

seemly ('siːmlɪ) a. becoming and proper —'**seemliness** n.

seen (siːn) pp. of SEE[1]

seep (siːp) vi. trickle through slowly, as water, ooze

seer (sɪə) n. prophet

seersucker ('sɪəsʌkə) n. light cotton fabric with slightly crinkled surface

seesaw ('siːsɔː) n. 1. game in which children sit at opposite ends of plank supported in middle and swing up and down 2. plank used for this —vi. 3. move up and down

seethe (siːð) vi. 1. boil, foam 2. be very agitated 3. be in constant movement (as large crowd etc.) (**seethed**, '**seething**)

segment ('segmənt) n. 1. piece cut off 2. section —v. (seg'ment) 3. divide into segments —**seg'mental** a. —**segmen'tation** n.

segregate ('segrɪgeɪt) vt. set apart from the rest —**segre'gation** n.

seigneur (se'njɜː; Fr. sɛ'nœːr) n. feudal lord, esp. in France —**sei'gneurial** a. —'**seigneury** n. estate of seigneur

seignior ('seɪnjə) n. 1. less common name for seigneur 2. in England, lord of seigniory —**sei'gniorial** a. —'**seigniory** or '**signory** n. 1. less common names for seigneury 2. in England, fee or manor of seignior 3. authority of seignior

seine (seɪn) n. type of large fishing net

seismic ('saɪzmɪk) a. pert. to earthquakes —'**seismograph** n. instrument that records earthquakes (also **seis'mometer**) —**seismo'logic(al)** a. pert. to seismology —**seis'mologist** n. one versed in seismology —**seis'mology** n. science of earthquakes

seismo- or before vowel **seism-** (comb. form) earthquake, as in seismology

seize (siːz) vt. 1. grasp 2. lay hold of 3. capture —vi. 4. (of mechanical parts) stick tightly through overheating —'**seizable** a. —'**seizure** n. 1. act of taking, esp. by warrant, as goods 2. sudden onset of disease

seldom ('seldəm) adv. not often, rarely

select (sɪ'lekt) vt. 1. pick out, choose —a. 2. choice, picked 3. exclusive —**se'lection** n. —**se'lective** a. —**selec'tivity** n. —**se'lector** n.

selenium (sɪ'liːnɪəm) n. nonmetallic element with photoelectric properties —**se'lenic** a.

self (self) pron. 1. used reflexively or to express emphasis (pl. **selves**) 2. (of colour) same throughout, uniform —n. 3. one's own person or individuality (pl. **selves**) —'**selfish** a. 1. concerned unduly over personal profit or pleasure 2. lacking consideration for others 3. greedy —'**selfishly** adv. —'**selfless** a. 1. having no regard to self 2. unselfish

self- (comb. form) of oneself or itself. See the list on page 449

self-abnegation n. denial of one's own interests

self-abuse n. 1. misuse of one's own abilities etc. 2. euphemistic masturbation

self-aggrandizement n. act of increasing one's own power etc. —**self-aggrandizing** a.

self-assertion n. act of putting forward one's own opinions etc., esp. in aggressive manner —**self-asserting** a. —**self-assertive** a.

self-assurance n. confidence in validity etc. of one's own opinions etc. —**self-assured** a.

self-conscious a. 1. unduly aware of oneself 2. conscious of one's acts or states

self-determination n. the right of person or nation to decide for himself or itself

self-discipline n. disciplining of one's own feelings, desires etc. —**self-disciplined** a.

self-educated a. educated through one's own efforts without formal instruction

self-effacement n. act of making oneself, one's actions etc. inconspicuous —**self-effacing** a.

self-employed a. earning one's living in one's own business —**self-employment** n.

self-expression n. expression of one's own personality etc. as in painting etc. —**self-expressive** a.

self-government n. government of country etc. by its own people —**self-governed** a. —**self-governing** a.

selfheal ('sclfhi:l) n. European herbaceous plant reputedly having healing powers

self-important a. having unduly high opinion of one's own importance etc. —**self-importance** n.

self-improvement n. improvement of one's status, education etc. by one's own efforts

self-induced a. induced by oneself or itself

self-interest n. 1. one's personal interest or advantage 2. act of pursuing one's own interest

self-made a. having achieved wealth, status etc. by one's own efforts

self-opinionated a. 1. having unduly high regard for oneself or one's own opinions 2. clinging stubbornly to one's own opinions

self-possessed a. calm, composed —**self-possession** n.

self-propelled a. (of vehicle) provided with its own source of tractive power

self-raising a. (of flour) having raising agent already added

self-respect n. proper sense of one's own dignity and integrity

self-righteous a. smugly sure of one's own virtue

self-sacrifice n. sacrifice of one's own desires etc. for sake of well-being of others —**self-sacrificing** a.

selfsame ('sclfseim) a. very same

self-satisfied a. having or showing complacent satisfaction with oneself, one's own actions etc. —**self-satisfaction** n.

self-sealing a. (esp. of envelope) designed to become sealed by pressure only

self-seeking n. 1. act of seeking one's own profit or interest —a. 2. having exclusive preoccupation with one's own profit or interest —**self-seeker** n.

self-service a./n. (of) shop or restaurant where customers serve themselves

self-starter n. 1. electric motor used to start internal-combustion engine 2. switch that operates this motor

self-styled a. claiming to be of specified nature, profession etc.

self-sufficient or **self-sufficing** a. 1. sufficient in itself 2. relying on one's own powers

self-will n. 1. obstinacy 2. wilfulness —**self-willed** a. headstrong

self-winding a. (of wrist watch) winding automatically

sell (sɛl) vt. 1. hand over for a price 2. stock, have for sale 3. make (someone) accept 4. inf. betray, cheat —vi. 5. find purchasers (**sold**, **'selling**) —n. inf. 6. hoax —**'seller** n. —**selling race** or **plate** horse race in which winner must be offered for sale at auction —'**sellout** n. 1. disposing of completely by selling 2. betrayal

self-abasement	self-confidence	self-evident	self-raising
self-absorbed	self-confident	self-explanatory	self-realization
self-absorption	self-contained	self-help	self-regard
self-addressed	self-control	self-indulgence	self-reliance
self-adhesive	self-deception	self-indulgent	self-reliant
self-appointed	self-defeating	self-inflicted	self-reproach
self-assurance	self-defence	self-interest	self-restraint
self-assured	self-delusion	self-justification	self-righting
self-catering	self-denial	self-knowledge	self-sacrifice
self-centred	self-doubt	self-pity	self-satisfied
self-complacent	self-employed	self-portrait	self-supporting
self-confessed	self-esteem	self-preservation	self-taught

Sellotape ('sɛləteɪp) *n.* **1. R** type of adhesive tape —*vt.* **2.** seal using adhesive tape

Seltzer ('sɛltsə) *n.* aerated mineral water

selvage *or* **selvedge** ('sɛlvɪdʒ) *n.* finished, nonfraying edge of cloth

selves (sɛlvz) *n., pl. of* SELF

Sem. 1. Seminary **2.** Semitic

semantic (sɪ'mæntɪk) *a.* relating to meaning of words or symbols —**se'mantics** *pl.n.* (*with sing. v.*) study of linguistic meaning

semaphore ('sɛməfɔː) *n.* **1.** post with movable arms for signalling **2.** system of signalling by human or mechanical arms

semblance ('sɛmbləns) *n.* **1.** (false) appearance **2.** image, likeness

semen ('siːmɛn) *n.* **1.** fluid carrying sperm of male animals **2.** sperm

semester (sɪ'mɛstə) *n.* US half-year session in many universities, colleges

semi ('sɛmɪ) *inf.* semidetached house

semi- (*comb. form*) half, partly, not completely, as in *semicircle*

semiannual (sɛmɪ'ænjʊəl) *a.* **1.** occurring every half-year **2.** lasting for half a year —**semi'annually** *adv.*

semibreve ('sɛmɪbriːv) *n.* musical note half length of breve

semicircle ('sɛmɪsɜːkəl) *n.* half of circle —**semi'circular** *a.* —**semicircular canal** *Anat.* any of three looped fluid-filled membranous tubes that comprise labyrinth of ear

semicolon (sɛmɪ'kəʊlən) *n.* punctuation mark (;)

semiconductor (sɛmɪkən'dʌktə) *n.* **1.** substance, as silicon, having electrical conductivity that increases with temperature **2.** device, as transistor, dependent on properties of such substance

semidetached (sɛmɪdɪ'tætʃt) *a./n.* (of) house joined to another on one side only

semifinal (sɛmɪ'faɪnəl) *n.* match, round *etc.* before final

seminal ('sɛmɪnəl) *a.* **1.** capable of developing **2.** influential, important **3.** rudimentary **4.** of semen or seed

seminar ('sɛmɪnɑː) *n.* meeting of group (of students) for discussion

seminary ('sɛmɪnərɪ) *n.* college for priests

semiprecious (sɛmɪ'prɛʃəs) *a.* (of gemstones) having less value than precious stones

semiprofessional (sɛmɪprə'fɛʃənəl) *a.* **1.** (of person) engaged in activity or sport part-time but for pay **2.** (of activity or sport) engaged in by semiprofessionals **3.** of person whose activities are professional in some respects —*n.* **4.** semiprofessional person

semiquaver ('sɛmɪkweɪvə) *n. Mus.* note having time value of one-sixteenth of semibreve

semiskilled (sɛmɪ'skɪld) *a.* partly skilled, trained but not for specialized work

Semite ('siːmaɪt) *n.* member of race including Jews and Arabs —**Semitic** (sɪ'mɪtɪk) *a.* **1.** denoting a Semite **2.** Jewish

semitone ('sɛmɪtəʊn) *n.* musical halftone

semitrailer (sɛmɪ'treɪlə) *n.* type of trailer that has wheels only at rear, front end being supported by towing vehicle

semivowel ('sɛmɪvaʊəl) *n. Phonet.* vowel-like sound that acts like consonant, as (w) in *well* and (j), represented as *y*, in *yell* (*also* **glide**)

semolina (sɛmə'liːnə) *n.* hard grains left after sifting of flour, used for puddings *etc.*

sempervivum (sɛmpə'vaɪvəm) *n.* plant with ornamental rosettes of leaves

sempre ('sɛmprɪ) *adv. Mus.* always; consistently

S.E.N. State Enrolled Nurse

Sen. *or* **sen. 1.** senate **2.** senator **3.** senior

senate ('sɛnɪt) *n.* upper council of state, university *etc.* —**'senator** *n.* —**sena'torial** *a.*

send (sɛnd) *vt.* **1.** cause to go or be conveyed **2.** dispatch **3.** transmit (by radio) (**sent, 'sending**) —**'sendoff** *n. inf.* demonstration of good wishes to person about to set off on journey *etc.* —**send-up** *n.* UK parody or imitation —**send off 1.** cause to depart **2.** *Soccer, rugby etc.* (of referee) dismiss (player) from field of play for some offence —**send up** *sl.* **1.** send to prison **2.** UK make fun of, parody

senescent (sɪ'nɛsənt) *a.* **1.** growing old **2.** characteristic of old age —**se'nescence** *n.*

senile ('siːnaɪl) *a.* showing weakness of old age —**senility** (sɪ'nɪlɪtɪ) *n.*

senior ('siːnjə) *a.* **1.** superior in rank or standing **2.** older —*n.* **3.** superior **4.** elder person —**seni'ority** *n.* —**senior aircraftman** rank in Royal Air Force comparable to that of private in army, though not lowest rank in Royal Air Force —**senior citizen** UK, A, NZ, *euphemistic* elderly person —**senior service** UK Royal Navy

senna ('sɛnə) *n.* **1.** tropical plant **2.** its dried leaves or pods, used as laxative

señor (sɛ'njɔː; *Sp.* se'ɲor) *n.* Sp. title of respect, like Mr. (*pl.* **-s, -ñores** (*Sp.* -'ɲores)) —**se'ñora** *n.* Mrs. —**seño'rita** *n.* Miss

sensation (sɛn'seɪʃən) *n.* **1.** operation of sense, feeling, awareness **2.** excited feeling, state of excitement **3.** exciting event **4.** strong impression **5.** commotion —**sen'sational** *a.* **1.** producing great excitement **2.** melodramatic **3.** of perception by senses —**sen'sationalism** *n.* **1.** use of sensational language *etc.* to arouse intense emotional excitement **2.** doctrine that sensations are basis of all knowledge

sense (sɛns) *n.* **1.** any of bodily faculties of perception or feeling **2.** sensitiveness of any or all of these faculties **3.** ability to perceive, mental alertness **4.** consciousness **5.** meaning **6.** coherence, intelligible meaning **7.** sound practical judgment —*vt.* **8.** perceive **9.** understand —'**senseless** *a.* —'**senselessly** *adv.* —**sense organ** structure in animals that is specialized for receiving external stimuli and transmitting them to brain

sensible ('sɛnsɪbəl) *a.* **1.** reasonable, wise **2.** perceptible by senses **3.** aware, mindful **4.** considerable, appreciable —**sensi'bility** *n.* ability to feel, *esp.* emotional or moral feelings —'**sensibly** *adv.*

sensitive ('sɛnsɪtɪv) *a.* **1.** open to, acutely affected by, external impressions **2.** easily affected or altered **3.** easily upset by criticism **4.** responsive to slight changes —'**sensitively** *adv.* —**sensi'tivity** *or* '**sensitiveness** *n.* —'**sensitize** *or* **-tise** *vt.* make sensitive, *esp.* make (photographic film *etc.*) sensitive to light

sensor ('sɛnsə) *n.* device that responds to stimulus

sensory ('sɛnsərɪ) *or* **sensorial** (sɛn'sɔːrɪəl) *a.* relating to organs, operation, of senses

sensual ('sɛnsjuəl) *a.* **1.** of senses only and not of mind **2.** given to pursuit of pleasures of sense **3.** self-indulgent **4.** licentious —'**sensualism** *n.* —'**sensualist** *n.* —**sensu'ality** *n.*

sensuous ('sɛnsjuəs) *a.* stimulating, or apprehended by senses, *esp.* in aesthetic manner

sent (sɛnt) *pt./pp. of* SEND

sentence ('sɛntəns) *n.* **1.** combination of words, which is complete as expressing a thought **2.** judgment passed on criminal by court or judge —*vt.* **3.** pass sentence on, condemn —**sen'tential** *a.* of sentence —**sen'tentious** *a.* **1.** full of axioms and maxims **2.** pithy **3.** pompously moralizing —**sen'tentiously** *adv.* —**sen'tentiousness** *n.*

sentient ('sɛntɪənt) *a.* **1.** capable of feeling **2.** feeling **3.** thinking —'**sentience** *or* '**sentiency** *n.*

sentiment ('sɛntɪmənt) *n.* **1.** tendency to be moved by feeling rather than reason **2.** verbal expression of feeling **3.** mental feeling, emotion **4.** opinion —**senti'mental** *a.* **1.** given to indulgence in sentiment and in its expression **2.** weak **3.** sloppy —**senti'mentalist** *n.* —**senti'mental** *n.* —**senti'mentalize** *or* **-lise** *v.*

sentinel ('sɛntɪnəl) *n.* sentry

sentry ('sɛntrɪ) *n.* soldier on watch —**sentry box** small shelter in which sentry may stand to be sheltered from weather

sepal ('sɛpəl) *n.* leaf or division of the calyx of a flower

separate ('sɛpəreɪt) *vt.* **1.** part **2.** divide **3.** sever **4.** put apart **5.** occupy place between —*vi.* **6.** withdraw, become parted —*a.* ('sɛprɪt,

'sɛpərɪt) **7.** disconnected, apart **8.** distinct, individual —'**separable** *a.* —'**separately** ('sɛprɪtlɪ, 'sɛpərɪtlɪ) *adv.* —**sepa'ration** *n.* **1.** disconnection **2.** *Law* living apart of married people without divorce —'**separatism** *n.* —'**separatist** *n.* person who advocates secession from organization, union *etc.* —'**separator** *n.* **1.** that which separates **2.** apparatus for separating cream from milk —**separate school** C school for a large religious minority

sepia ('siːpɪə) *n.* **1.** reddish-brown pigment made from a fluid secreted by the cuttlefish —*a.* **2.** of this colour

sepoy ('siːpɔɪ) *n.* formerly, Indian soldier in service of Brit.

sepsis ('sɛpsɪs) *n.* presence of pus-forming bacteria in body

Sept. September

September (sɛp'tɛmbə) *n.* 9th month

septennial (sɛp'tɛnɪəl) *a.* lasting, occurring every seven years

septet (sɛp'tɛt) *n.* **1.** music for seven instruments or voices **2.** group of seven performers

septic ('sɛptɪk) *a.* **1.** of, caused by, sepsis **2.** (of wound) infected —**septicaemia** *or* **septicemia** (sɛptɪ'siːmɪə) *n.* blood poisoning —**septic tank** tank for containing sewage to be decomposed by anaerobic bacteria

septuagenarian (sɛptjuədʒɪ'nɛərɪən) *a.* **1.** aged between seventy and eighty —*n.* **2.** person of this age

Septuagesima (sɛptjuə'dʒɛsɪmə) *n.* third Sunday before Lent

septum ('sɛptəm) *n. Biol., anat.* dividing partition between two tissues or cavities (*pl.* **-ta** (-tə))

septuple ('sɛptjupəl) *a.* **1.** seven times as much or many **2.** consisting of seven parts or members —*vt.* **3.** multiply by seven —**septuplicate** (sɛp'tjuːplɪkət) *n./a.*

sepulchre *or U.S.* **sepulcher** ('sɛpəlkə) *n.* tomb, burial vault —**se'pulchral** *a.* **1.** of burial, or the grave **2.** mournful **3.** gloomy —'**sepulture** *n.* burial

sequel ('siːkwəl) *n.* **1.** consequence **2.** continuation, *eg* of story

sequence ('siːkwəns) *n.* **1.** arrangement of things in successive order **2.** section, episode of film —'**sequent** *or* **se'quential** *a.*

sequester (sɪ'kwɛstə) *vt.* **1.** separate **2.** seclude **3.** put aside —**se'questrate** *vt.* **1.** confiscate **2.** divert or appropriate income of (property) to satisfy claims against its owner —**sequestration** (siːkwɛ'streɪʃən) *n.*

sequin ('siːkwɪn) *n.* **1.** small ornamental metal disc on dresses *etc.* **2.** formerly, Venetian gold coin

sequoia (sɪ'kwɔɪə) *n.* giant Californian coniferous tree

seraglio (se'rɑːlɪəʊ) *or* **serail** (se'raɪ) *n.* harem, palace, of Turkish sultan (*pl.* -s)

seraph ('serəf) *n.* member of highest order of angels (*pl.* -s, -aphim (-əfɪm)) —se'raphic *a.*

Serbian ('sɜːbɪən) *a.* 1. of Serbia, its people or their dialect of Serbo-Croatian —*n.* 2. dialect of Serbo-Croatian spoken in Serbia 3. native or inhabitant of Serbia (*also* **Serb**) —**Serbo-Croatian** *or* **Serbo-Croat** *n.* 1. chief official language of Yugoslavia —*a.* 2. of this language

serenade (serɪ'neɪd) *n.* 1. sentimental piece of music or song of type addressed to woman by lover, *esp.* at evening —*v.* 2. sing serenade (to)

serendipity (serən'dɪpɪtɪ) *n.* faculty of making fortunate discoveries by accident

serene (sɪ'riːn) *a.* 1. calm, tranquil 2. unclouded 3. quiet, placid —se'renely *adv.* —serenity (sɪ'renɪtɪ) *n.*

serf (sɜːf) *n.* one of class of medieval labourers bound to, and transferred with, land —'serfdom *or* 'serfhood *n.*

serge (sɜːdʒ) *n.* strong hard-wearing twilled worsted fabric

sergeant ('sɑːdʒənt) *n.* 1. noncommissioned officer in army 2. police officer above constable —**sergeant major** highest noncommissioned officer in regiment —**sergeant at arms** parliamentary, court officer with ceremonial duties

series ('sɪəriːz) *n.* 1. sequence 2. succession, set (*eg* of radio, TV programmes with same characters, setting, but different stories) (*pl.* -ries) —'serial *n.* 1. story or play produced in successive episodes or instalments 2. periodical publication —*a.* 3. of, in or forming a series —'serialize *or* -lise *vt.* publish, present as serial —seriatim (sɪərɪ'ætɪm) *adv.* one after another

serif *or* **seriph** ('serɪf) *n.* Print. small line finishing off stroke of letter

seriocomic (sɪərɪəʊ'kɒmɪk) *a.* mixing serious and comic elements —serio'comically *adv.*

serious ('sɪərɪəs) *a.* 1. thoughtful, solemn 2. earnest, sincere 3. of importance 4. giving cause for concern —'seriously *adv.*

sermon ('sɜːmən) *n.* 1. discourse of religious instruction or exhortation spoken or read from pulpit 2. any similar discourse —'sermonize *or* -ise *vi.* 1. talk like preacher 2. compose sermons

serpent ('sɜːpənt) *n.* Lit. snake —'serpentine *a.* 1. like, shaped like, serpent —*n.* 2. any of several kinds of green to black rock

serrate ('serɪt, -eɪt) *a.* having notched, sawlike edge —ser'rated *a.* —ser'ration *n.*

serried ('serɪd) *a.* in close order, shoulder to shoulder

serum ('sɪərəm) *n.* watery animal fluid, *esp.*

thin part of blood as used for inoculation or vaccination (*pl.* -s, -ra (-rə)) —se'rosity *n.* —'serous *a.* of or producing serum

serval ('sɜːvəl) *n.* feline Afr. mammal

serve (sɜːv) *vt.* 1. work for, under 2. attend to (customers) in shop *etc.* 3. provide 4. provide (guests) with (food *etc.*) 5. present (food *etc.*) in particular way 6. provide with regular supply of 7. pay homage to 8. go through (period of service *etc.*) 9. suit 10. *Tennis etc.* put (ball) into play —*vi.* 11. be member of military unit —*n.* 12. *Tennis etc.* act of serving ball —'servant *n.* personal or domestic attendant —'service *n.* 1. the act of serving, helping, assisting 2. system organized to provide for needs of public 3. maintenance of vehicle 4. use 5. readiness, availability for use 6. department of State employ 7. employment of persons engaged in this 8. set of dishes *etc.* 9. form, session, of public worship —*pl.* 10. armed forces —*vt.* 11. overhaul —'serviceable *a.* 1. in working order, usable 2. durable —'serving *n.* portion of food or drink —**service area** place on motorway providing facilities as garage, restaurant *etc.* —**service charge** percentage of bill added to total to pay for service —**service flat** rented flat where landlord provides services such as cleaning *etc.* —'serviceman *n.* member of the armed forces —**service road** narrow road giving access to houses, shops *etc.* —**service station** place supplying fuel, oil, maintenance for motor vehicles —**service tree** Eurasian rosaceous tree with white flowers and brown edible apple-like fruits

serviette (sɜːvɪ'et) *n.* table napkin

servile ('sɜːvaɪl) *a.* 1. slavish, without independence 2. cringing, fawning 3. menial —**servility** (sɜː'vɪlɪtɪ) *n.*

servitude ('sɜːvɪtjuːd) *n.* bondage, slavery

servomechanism ('sɜːvəʊmekənɪzəm) *n.* device for converting small mechanical force into larger force, *esp.* in steering mechanisms

servomotor ('sɜːvəʊməʊtə) *n.* motor that supplies power to servomechanism

sesame ('sesəmɪ) *n.* plant with seeds used as herbs and for making oil

sesqui- (*comb. form*) one and a half, as in *sesquicentennial*

sessile ('sesaɪl) *a.* 1. (of flowers or leaves) having no stalk 2. (of animals such as barnacle) permanently attached —**sessility** (se'sɪlɪtɪ) *n.*

session ('seʃən) *n.* 1. meeting of court *etc.* 2. assembly 3. continuous series of such meetings 4. any period devoted to an activity 5. school or university term or year

sestet (se'stet) *n.* 1. *Prosody* last six lines of sonnet 2. *see* SEXTET (sense 1)

set (set) *vt.* 1. put or place in specified position

or condition **2.** cause to sit **3.** fix **4.** point **5.** put up **6.** make ready **7.** establish **8.** prescribe, allot **9.** put to music **10.** (of hair) arrange while wet, so that it dries in position —*vi.* **11.** become firm or fixed **12.** (of sun) go down **13.** have direction (**set, 'setting**) —*a.* **14.** fixed, established **15.** deliberate **16.** formal **17.** arranged beforehand **18.** unvarying —*n.* **19.** act or state of being set **20.** bearing, posture **21.** *Rad., T.V.* complete apparatus for reception or transmission **22.** *Theat., cine.* organized settings and equipment to form ensemble of scene **23.** number of things, persons associated as being similar, complementary or used together **24.** *Maths.* group of numbers, objects *etc.* with at least one common property —**'setback** *n.* anything that hinders or impedes —**set piece 1.** work of literature *etc.* intended to create impressive effect **2.** display of fireworks —**'setscrew** *n.* screw that fits into coupling, cam *etc.* and prevents motion of part relative to shaft on which it is mounted —**set square** thin flat piece of plastic *etc.* in shape of right-angled triangle, used in technical drawing —**set-to** *n. inf.* brief disagreement or fight —**'setup** *n.* **1.** position **2.** organization —**set to 1.** begin working **2.** start fighting —**set up** establish

sett *or* **set** (sɛt) *n.* badger's burrow

settee (sɛ'tiː) *n.* couch

setter ('sɛtə) *n.* any of various breeds of gun dog

setting ('sɛtɪŋ) *n.* **1.** background **2.** surroundings **3.** scenery and other stage accessories **4.** act of fixing **5.** decorative metalwork holding precious stone *etc.* in position **6.** tableware and cutlery for (single place at) table **7.** descending below horizon of sun **8.** music for song

settle[1] ('sɛtl) *vt.* **1.** arrange, put in order **2.** establish, make firm or secure **3.** make quiet or calm **4.** decide upon **5.** end (dispute *etc.*) **6.** pay **7.** bestow (property) by legal deed —*vi.* **8.** come to rest **9.** subside **10.** become clear **11.** take up residence **12.** sink to bottom **13.** come to agreement —**'settlement** *n.* **1.** act of settling **2.** place newly inhabited **3.** money bestowed legally **4.** subsidence (of building) —**'settler** *n.* colonist

settle[2] ('sɛtl) *n.* seat, usu. made of wood with high back and arms

seven ('sɛvn) *a./n.* cardinal number, next after six —**'seven'teen** *a./n.* ten and seven —**'seventh** *a.* ordinal number of seven —**'seventy** *a./n.* ten times seven —**seven seas** all the oceans of the world —**seventh heaven 1.** final state of eternal bliss **2.** state of supreme happiness

sever ('sɛvə) *v.* **1.** separate, divide —*vt.* **2.** cut off —**'severance** *n.* —**severance pay** compensa-

tion paid by a firm to employee for loss of employment

several ('sɛvrəl) *a.* **1.** some, a few **2.** separate; individual **3.** various **4.** different —*pron.* **5.** indefinite small number —**'severally** *adv.* apart from others

severe (sɪ'vɪə) *a.* **1.** strict; rigorous **2.** hard to do **3.** harsh **4.** austere **5.** extreme —**se'verely** *adv.* —**severity** (sɪ'vɛrɪtɪ) *n.*

Seville orange (sə'vɪl) **1.** orange tree grown for its bitter fruit, used *esp.* to make marmalade **2.** its fruit

sew (səʊ) *v.* **1.** join (pieces of fabric *etc.*) with needle and thread —*vt.* **2.** make by sewing (**sewed** *pt.,* **sewed, sewn** *pp.,* **'sewing** *pr.p.*) —**'sewing** *n.*

sewage ('suːɪdʒ) *n.* refuse, waste matter, excrement conveyed in sewer —**'sewer** *n.* underground drain to remove waste water and refuse —**'sewerage** *n.* **1.** arrangement of sewers **2.** sewage —**sewage farm** place where sewage is treated, *esp.* for use as manure

sex (sɛks) *n.* **1.** state of being male or female **2.** males or females collectively **3.** sexual intercourse —*a.* **4.** concerning sex —*vt.* **5.** ascertain sex of —**'sexism** *n.* discrimination on basis of sex —**'sexist** *n./a.* —**'sexless** *a.* **1.** having no sexual differentiation **2.** having no sexual appeal or desires —**'sexual** *a.* —**'sexually** *adv.* —**'sexy** *a. inf.* provoking or intended to provoke sexual interest —**sex appeal** quality of attracting opposite sex —**sex change** change of sex, *esp.* involving medical or surgical treatment to alter sexual characteristics to those of opposite sex —**sex chromosome** either of chromosomes determining sex of animals —**sexual intercourse** act of procreation in which male's penis is inserted into female's vagina

sex- (*comb. form*) six, as in *sexcentenary*

sexagenarian (sɛksədʒɪ'nɛərɪən) *a./n.* (person) sixty years old

Sexagesima (sɛksə'dʒɛsɪmə) *n.* the second Sunday before Lent

sexennial (sɛk'sɛnɪəl) *a.* lasting, occurring every six years

sextant ('sɛkstənt) *n.* navigator's instrument for measuring elevations of heavenly body *etc.*

sextet *or* **sextette** (sɛks'tɛt) *n.* **1.** (composition for) six singers or players **2.** group of six

sexton ('sɛkstən) *n.* official in charge of a church, oft. acting as gravedigger

sextuple ('sɛkstjʊpl) *n.* **1.** quantity or number six times as great as another —*a.* **2.** six times as much or as many **3.** consisting of six parts or members —**'sextuplet** *n.* **1.** one of six offspring born at one birth **2.** *Mus.* group of six notes played in time value of four

SF *or* **sf** science fiction

SFA Scottish Football Association

sforzando (sfɔː'tsɑːndəʊ) *or* **sforzato** (sfɔː-'tsɑːtəʊ) *Mus. a./adv.* **1.** to be played with emphasis —*n.* **2.** symbol, mark *etc.* indicating this

S. Glam South Glamorgan

Sgt. Sergeant

sh (*spelling pron.* ʃʃʃ) *interj.* exclamation to request silence or quiet

shabby ('ʃæbɪ) *a.* **1.** faded, worn, ragged **2.** poorly dressed **3.** mean, dishonourable **4.** stingy —'**shabbily** *adv.* —'**shabbiness** *n.*

shack (ʃæk) *n.* rough hut —**shack up** (*usu. with* with) *sl.* live (*esp.* with lover)

shackle ('ʃækəl) *n.* (*oft. pl.*) **1.** metal ring or fastening for prisoner's wrist or ankle **2.** anything that confines —*vt.* **3.** fasten with shackles **4.** hamper

shad (ʃæd) *n.* herringlike fish

shade (ʃeɪd) *n.* **1.** partial darkness **2.** shelter, place sheltered from light, heat *etc.* **3.** darker part of anything **4.** depth of colour **5.** tinge **6.** ghost **7.** screen **8.** anything used to screen **9.** US windowblind —*pl.* **10.** US *sl.* sunglasses —*vt.* **11.** screen from light, darken **12.** represent (shades) in (drawing) —'**shady** *a.* **1.** shielded from sun **2.** dim **3.** dubious **4.** dishonest **5.** dishonourable

shadow ('ʃædəʊ) *n.* **1.** dark figure projected by anything that intercepts rays of light **2.** patch of shade **3.** slight trace **4.** indistinct image **5.** gloom **6.** inseparable companion —*vt.* **7.** cast shadow over **8.** follow and watch closely —'**shadowy** *a.* —**shadow cabinet** (in Brit. Parliament) members of opposition party, who would hold ministerial office if their party were in power

shaft (ʃɑːft) *n.* **1.** straight rod, stem **2.** handle **3.** arrow **4.** ray, beam (of light) **5.** revolving rod for transmitting power **6.** one of the bars between which horse is harnessed **7.** entrance boring of mine

shag[1] (ʃæg) *n.* **1.** matted wool or hair **2.** long-napped cloth **3.** coarse shredded tobacco —'**shaggy** *a.* **1.** covered with rough hair or wool **2.** tousled, unkempt

shag[2] (ʃæg) *n.* any of various varieties of cormorant

shagreen (ʃæ'griːn) *n.* **1.** rough skin of certain sharks and rays **2.** rough grainy leather made from certain animal hides

shah (ʃɑː) *n.* formerly, ruler of Iran

shake (ʃeɪk) *v.* **1.** (cause to) move with quick vibrations **2.** grasp the hand (of another) in greeting —*vi.* **3.** tremble —*vt.* **4.** upset **5.** wave, brandish (**shook, 'shaken**) —*n.* **6.** act of shaking **7.** vibration **8.** jolt **9.** *inf.* short period of time, jiffy —'**shaker** *n.* **1.** person or thing that shakes **2.** container from which condiment is shaken **3.**

container in which ingredients of alcoholic drinks are shaken together —'**shakily** *adv.* —'**shaky** *a.* unsteady, insecure

shale (ʃeɪl) *n.* flaky, sedimentary rock

shall (ʃæl; *unstressed* ʃəl) *v. aux.* makes compound tenses or moods to express obligation, command, condition or intention (**should** *pt.*)

shallot (ʃə'lɒt) *n.* kind of small onion

shallow ('ʃæləʊ) *a.* **1.** not deep **2.** having little depth of water **3.** superficial **4.** not sincere —*n.* **5.** shallow place —'**shallowness** *n.*

shalom aleichem (ʃa'lɒm a'lexɛm) *Hebrew* peace be to you: used by Jews as greeting or farewell (*oft. also* **sha'lom**)

sham (ʃæm) *a./n.* **1.** imitation, counterfeit —*vi.* **2.** pretend —*v.* **3.** feign (**-mm-**)

shaman (ʃæmən) *n.* **1.** priest of shamanism **2.** medicine man of similar religion —'**shamanism** *n.* religion of certain peoples of northern Asia, based on belief in good and evil spirits who can be controlled only by shamans

shamble ('ʃæmbəl) *vi.* walk in shuffling, awkward way

shambles ('ʃæmbəlz) *pl.n.* (*with sing. v.*) messy, disorderly ruined place

shame (ʃeɪm) *n.* **1.** emotion caused by consciousness of guilt or dishonour in one's conduct or state **2.** cause of disgrace **3.** ignominy **4.** pity, hard luck —*vt.* **5.** cause to feel shame **6.** disgrace **7.** force by shame —'**shameful** *a.* disgraceful —'**shamefully** *adv.* —'**shameless** *a.* **1.** with no sense of shame **2.** indecent —'**shamefaced** *a.* ashamed

shammy ('ʃæmɪ) *inf.* chamois leather

shampoo (ʃæm'puː) *n.* **1.** any of various preparations of liquid soap for washing hair, carpets *etc.* **2.** this process —*vt.* **3.** use shampoo to wash

shamrock ('ʃæmrɒk) *n.* clover leaf, *esp.* as Irish emblem

shandy ('ʃændɪ) *or* U.S. **shandygaff** ('ʃændɪgæf) *n.* mixed drink, *esp.* beer diluted with soft drink

shanghai ('ʃæŋhaɪ, ʃæŋ'haɪ) *vt.* force, trick (someone) to do something

shank (ʃæŋk) *n.* **1.** lower leg **2.** shinbone **3.** stem of thing

shantung (ʃæn'tʌŋ) *n.* soft, natural Chinese silk

shanty[1] ('ʃæntɪ) *n.* **1.** temporary wooden building **2.** crude dwelling

shanty[2] ('ʃæntɪ) *n.* sailor's song with chorus

shape (ʃeɪp) *n.* **1.** external form or appearance **2.** mould, pattern **3.** *inf.* condition, *esp.* of physical fitness —*vt.* **4.** form, mould, fashion, make —*vi.* **5.** develop (**shaped, 'shaping**) —'**shapeless** *a.* —'**shapely** *a.* well-proportioned

SHAPE (ʃeip) Supreme Headquarters Allied Powers Europe

shard (ʃɑːd) or **sherd** n. broken fragment, esp. of earthenware

share[1] (ʃeə) n. 1. portion, quota, lot 2. unit of ownership in public company —v. 3. give, take a share (of) 4. join with others in doing, using (something) —'**shareholder** n.

share[2] (ʃeə) n. blade of plough

shark (ʃɑːk) n. 1. large usu. predatory sea fish 2. person who cheats others

sharkskin (ʃɑːkskɪn) n. stiff rayon fabric

sharp (ʃɑːp) a. 1. having keen cutting edge or fine point 2. keen 3. not gradual or gentle 4. brisk 5. clever 6. harsh 7. dealing cleverly but unfairly 8. shrill 9. strongly marked, esp. in outline —adv. 10. promptly —n. 11. Mus. note half a tone above natural pitch 12. sl. cheat, swindler —'**sharpen** vt. make sharp —'**sharper** n. person who cheats or swindles —'**sharply** adv. —'**sharpness** n. —**sharp practice** dishonest dealings —**sharp-set** a. 1. set to give acute cutting angle 2. keenly hungry —'**sharpshooter** n. marksman —**sharp-witted** a. having or showing keen intelligence

shatter ('ʃætə) v. 1. break in pieces —vt. 2. ruin (plans etc.) 3. disturb (person) greatly

shave (ʃeiv) v. 1. cut close (esp. hair of face or head) —vt. 2. pare away 3. graze 4. reduce (**shaved**, '**shaven**, '**shaving**) —n. 5. shaving —'**shaver** n. 1. person or thing that shaves 2. electrical implement for shaving —'**shavings** pl.n. parings —**close** or **near shave** narrow escape

Shavian ('ʃeiviən) a. 1. of or like George Bernard Shaw, his works, ideas etc. —n. 2. admirer of Shaw or his works

shawl (ʃɔːl) n. piece of fabric to cover woman's shoulders or wrap baby

she (ʃiː) pron. 3rd person singular feminine pronoun

sheaf (ʃiːf) n. 1. bundle, esp. corn 2. loose leaves of paper (pl. **sheaves**)

shear (ʃiə) vt. 1. clip hair, wool from 2. cut (through) 3. fracture (**sheared** pt., **shorn**, **sheared** pp., '**shearing** pr.p.) —'**shearer** n. —**shears** pl.n. 1. large pair of scissors 2. any of various analogous cutting instruments

shearwater ('ʃiəwɔːtə) n. any of various sea birds

sheath (ʃiːθ) n. 1. close-fitting cover, esp. for knife or sword 2. scabbard 3. condom (pl. **sheaths** (ʃiːðz)) —**sheathe** vt. put into sheath

sheave (ʃiːv) n. wheel with grooved rim, esp. one used as pulley

sheaves (ʃiːvz) n., pl. of SHEAF

shebang (ʃiˈbæŋ) n. sl. situation, matter (esp. in **the whole shebang**)

shebeen or **shebean** (ʃəˈbiːn) n. 1. Irish, Scot., SA place where alcohol is sold illegally 2. in S Afr., place where Black Afr. men engage in social drinking

shed[1] (ʃed) n. roofed shelter used as store or workshop

shed[2] (ʃed) v. 1. (cause to) pour forth (eg tears, blood) —vt. 2. cast off (**shed**, '**shedding**)

sheen (ʃiːn) n. gloss —'**sheeny** a.

sheep (ʃiːp) n. ruminant animal bred for wool and meat (pl. **sheep**) —'**sheepish** a. embarrassed, shy —**sheep-dip** n. (deep trough containing) solution in which sheep are immersed to kill vermin and germs in fleece —'**sheepdog** n. any of various breeds of dog, orig. for herding sheep —'**sheepfold** n. pen or enclosure for sheep —'**sheepshank** n. knot etc. made in rope to shorten it temporarily

sheer[1] (ʃiə) a. 1. perpendicular 2. (of material) very fine, transparent 3. absolute, unmitigated

sheer[2] (ʃiə) vi. deviate from course, swerve, turn aside

sheet[1] (ʃiːt) n. 1. large piece of cotton etc. to cover bed 2. broad piece of any thin material 3. large expanse —vt. 4. cover with sheet —**sheet music** printed copy of short composition or piece

sheet[2] (ʃiːt) n. rope fastened in corner of sail —**sheet anchor** large anchor for emergency

sheik or **sheikh** (ʃeik) n. Arab chief

shekel ('ʃekl) n. 1. Jewish weight and silver coin 2. (oft. pl.) inf. money, cash

shelf (ʃelf) n. 1. board fixed horizontally (on wall etc.) for holding things 2. ledge (pl. **shelves**) —**shelf life** length of time packaged food etc. will last without deteriorating

shell (ʃel) n. 1. hard outer case (esp. of egg, nut etc.) 2. husk 3. explosive projectile 4. outer part of structure left when interior is removed —vt. 5. take shell from 6. take out of shell 7. fire at with shells —'**shellfish** n. 1. mollusc 2. crustacean —**shell shock** nervous disorder caused by bursting of shells or bombs —**shell out** inf. pay up

shellac (ʃəˈlæk, ˈʃelæk) n. 1. resin usu. produced in thin plates for use as varnish —vt. 2. coat with shellac (-'**lacked**, -'**lacking**)

shelter ('ʃeltə) n. 1. place, structure giving protection 2. protection 3. refuge; haven —vt. 4. give protection to 5. screen —vi. 6. take shelter

shelve (ʃelv) vt. 1. put on a shelf 2. put off, defer indefinitely 3. cease to employ —vi. 4. slope gradually —'**shelving** n. 1. material for making shelves 2. set of shelves

shelves (ʃelvz) n., pl. of SHELF

shenanigan (ʃiˈnænigən) n. sl. 1. frolicking 2. act of playing tricks etc.

shepherd ('ʃepəd) n. 1. man who tends sheep

('**shepherdess** *fem.*) —*vt.* **2.** guide, watch over —**shepherd's pie** *chiefly* UK dish of minced meat covered with mashed potato —**shepherd's-purse** *n.* plant with white flowers

sherbet ('ʃɜːbət) *n.* fruit-flavoured effervescent powder, eaten as sweet or used in drinks

sherd (ʃɜːd) *n. see* SHARD

sheriff ('ʃɛrɪf) *n.* **1.** US law enforcement officer **2.** in England and Wales, chief executive representative of the crown in a county **3.** in Scotland, chief judge of a district **4.** C municipal officer who enforces court orders *etc.* —'**sheriffdom** *n.*

Sherpa ('ʃɜːpə) *n.* member of a Tibetan people (*pl.* **-s,** '**Sherpa**)

sherry ('ʃɛrɪ) *n.* fortified wine

Shetland pony ('ʃɛtlənd) very small sturdy breed of pony

shewbread *or* **showbread** ('ʃəʊbrɛd) *n.* unleavened bread used in Jewish ritual

shield (ʃiːld) *n.* **1.** piece of armour carried on arm **2.** any protection used to stop blows, missiles *etc.* **3.** any protective device **4.** sports trophy —*vt.* **5.** cover, protect

shieling ('ʃiːlɪŋ) *n. chiefly Scot.* **1.** temporary shelter used by people tending cattle on high ground **2.** grazing ground

shift (ʃɪft) *v.* **1.** (cause to) move, change position —*n.* **2.** relay of workers **3.** time of their working **4.** evasion **5.** expedient **6.** removal **7.** woman's undershirt or dress —'**shiftiness** *n.* —'**shiftless** *a.* lacking in resource or character —'**shifty** *a.* **1.** evasive **2.** of dubious character

shillelagh *or* **shillala** (ʃə'leɪlə, -lɪ) *n.* in Ireland, cudgel

shilling ('ʃɪlɪŋ) *n.* **1.** former Brit. coin, now 5p **2.** monetary unit in various countries

shillyshally ('ʃɪlɪʃælɪ) *vi.* **1.** waver —*n.* **2.** wavering, indecision

shim (ʃɪm) *n.* **1.** thin washer used to adjust clearance for gears *etc.* —*vt.* **2.** modify clearance on (gear *etc.*) by use of shims (**-mm-**)

shimmer ('ʃɪmə) *vi.* **1.** shine with quivering light —*n.* **2.** such light **3.** glimmer

shimmy ('ʃɪmɪ) *n.* **1.** Amer. ragtime dance with much shaking of hips and shoulders **2.** abnormal wobbling motion in motor vehicle

shin (ʃɪn) *n.* **1.** front of lower leg —*v.* **2.** climb with arms and legs —*vt.* **3.** kick on shin (**-nn-**) —'**shinbone** *n. see* TIBIA

shindig ('ʃɪndɪg) *or* **shindy** ('ʃɪndɪ) *n. inf.* row; noisy disturbance

shine (ʃaɪn) *vi.* **1.** give out, reflect light **2.** perform very well, excel —*vt.* **3.** cause to shine by polishing (**shone,** '**shining**) —*n.* **4.** brightness, lustre **5.** polishing —'**shiner** *n.* **1.** something that shines, such as polishing device **2.** small N

Amer. freshwater cyprinid fish **3.** *inf.* black eye —'**shiny** *a.*

shingle[1] ('ʃɪŋgəl) *n.* **1.** wooden roof tile —*vt.* **2.** cover with shingles

shingle[2] ('ʃɪŋgəl) *n.* mass of pebbles

shingles ('ʃɪŋgəlz) *n.* disease causing inflammation along a nerve

Shinto ('ʃɪntəʊ) *n.* native Japanese religion —'**Shintoism** *n.*

shinty ('ʃɪntɪ) *n.* **1.** simple form of hockey played with ball and sticks curved at lower end **2.** stick used in this game

ship (ʃɪp) *n.* **1.** large seagoing vessel —*vt.* **2.** put on or send by ship —*vi.* **3.** embark **4.** take service in ship (**-pp-**) —'**shipment** *n.* **1.** act of shipping **2.** goods shipped —'**shipper** *n.* company *etc.* in business of shipping freight —'**shipping** *n.* **1.** freight transport business **2.** ships collectively —'**shipboard** *a.* taking place, used, or intended for use aboard ship —'**shipmate** *n.* sailor who serves on same ship as another —'**shipshape** *a.* orderly, trim —'**shipwreck** *n.* **1.** destruction of ship through storm, collision *etc.* —*vt.* **2.** cause to undergo shipwreck —'**shipwright** *n.* artisan skilled in tasks required to build vessels —'**shipyard** *n.* place for building and repair of ships

-ship (*comb. form*) **1.** state, condition, as in *fellowship* **2.** rank, office, position, as in *lordship* **3.** craft, skill, as in *scholarship*

shire (ʃaɪə) *n.* county —**shire horse** large heavy breed of carthorse

shirk (ʃɜːk) *vt.* evade, try to avoid (duty *etc.*)

shirr (ʃɜː) *vt.* **1.** gather (fabric) into parallel rows —*n.* **2.** series of gathered rows decorating dress *etc.*

shirt (ʃɜːt) *n.* garment for upper part of body —'**shirty** *a. sl.* annoyed —**shirt-tail** *n.* part of shirt that extends below waist —'**shirtwaister** *or U.S.* '**shirtwaist** *n.* woman's dress with bodice resembling shirt

shish kebab ('ʃiːʃ kə'bæb) *see* KEBAB

shiver[1] ('ʃɪvə) *vi.* **1.** tremble, usu. with cold or fear; shudder; vibrate —*n.* **2.** act, state of shivering

shiver[2] ('ʃɪvə) *v.* **1.** splinter, break in pieces —*n.* **2.** splinter

shoal[1] (ʃəʊl) *n.* **1.** stretch of shallow water **2.** sandbank, sandbar —*v.* **3.** make, become shallow

shoal[2] (ʃəʊl) *n.* **1.** large number of fish swimming together —*vi.* **2.** form shoal

shock[1] (ʃɒk) *vt.* **1.** horrify, scandalize —*n.* **2.** violent or damaging blow **3.** emotional disturbance **4.** state of weakness, illness, caused by physical or mental shock **5.** paralytical stroke **6.** collision **7.** effect on sensory nerves of electric discharge —'**shocker** *n.* person or thing which shocks or distresses —'**shocking** *a.* **1.** causing shock, disgust *etc.* **2.** *inf.* very bad or terrible —**shock absorber** device, *esp.* in cars, to absorb shocks —**shock therapy** *or* **treatment** treatment of certain psychotic conditions by injecting drugs or by passing electric current through brain

shock[2] (ʃɒk) *n.* group of corn sheaves placed together

shock[3] (ʃɒk) *n.* **1.** mass of hair —*a.* **2.** shaggy —'**shockheaded** *a.*

shod (ʃɒd) *pt./pp.* of SHOE

shoddy ('ʃɒdɪ) *a.* **1.** worthless, trashy **2.** second-rate **3.** made of poor material

shoe (ʃuː) *n.* **1.** covering for foot, not enclosing ankle **2.** metal rim or curved bar put on horse's hoof **3.** any of various protective plates or undercoverings —*vt.* **4.** protect, furnish with shoe or shoes (**shod** *pt./pp.*, '**shoeing** *pr.p.*) —'**shoehorn** *n.* curved plastic or metal implement, inserted at back of shoe, used to ease in heel —'**shoestring** *a./n.* very small (amount of money *etc.*) —'**shoetree** *n.* wooden or metal block inserted into shoe to preserve shape

shone (ʃɒn; *U.S.* ʃoʊn) *pt./pp.* of SHINE

shoo (ʃuː) *interj.* **1.** go away —*vt.* **2.** drive away

shook (ʃʊk) *pt.* of SHAKE

shoot (ʃuːt) *vt.* **1.** hit, wound, kill with missile fired from weapon **2.** send, slide, push rapidly —*v.* **3.** discharge (weapon) **4.** photograph, film —*vi.* **5.** hunt **6.** sprout (**shot**, '**shooting**) —*n.* **7.** young branch, sprout **8.** shooting competition **9.** hunting expedition —'**shooter** *n.* —**shooting brake** UK estate car —**shooting star** *inf.* meteor —**shooting stick** device resembling walking stick, having spike at one end and folding seat at other

shop (ʃɒp) *n.* **1.** place for retail sale of goods and services **2.** workshop, works building —*vi.* **3.** visit shops to buy —*vt.* **4.** *sl.* inform against (-**pp**-) —**shop floor 1.** part of factory housing machines **2.** workers in factory —'**shopkeeper** *n.* person who owns or manages shop —'**shoplifter** *n.* one who steals from shop —'**shopping centre 1.** area of town where most of shops are situated **2.** complex of stores, restaurants *etc.* with adjoining car park —'**shopsoiled** *a.* faded *etc.* from being displayed in shop —**shop steward** trade union representative of workers in factory *etc.* —'**shoptalk** *n.* conversation concerning one's work, *esp.* outside business hours —'**shopwalker** *n.* overseer who directs customers *etc.* —**talk shop** talk of one's business *etc.* at unsuitable moments

shore[1] (ʃɔː) *n.* edge of sea or lake

shore[2] (ʃɔː) *vt.* (*oft.* with **up**) prop (up)

shorn (ʃɔːn) *pp.* of SHEAR

short (ʃɔːt) *a.* **1.** not long **2.** not tall **3.** brief, hasty **4.** not reaching quantity or standard required **5.** wanting, lacking **6.** abrupt, rude **7.** friable —*adv.* **8.** suddenly, abruptly **9.** without reaching end —*n.* **10.** drink of spirits, as opposed to beer *etc.* **11.** short film —*pl.* **12.** short trousers —'**shortage** *n.* deficiency —'**shorten** *v.* —'**shortening** *n.* butter, lard or other fat, used in cake mixture *etc.* to make pastry light —'**shortly** *adv.* **1.** soon **2.** briefly —'**shortcake** *or* '**shortbread** *n.* sweet, brittle cake made of butter, flour and sugar —**short-change** *vt.* **1.** give less than correct change to **2.** *sl.* cheat, swindle —**short circuit** faulty connection between two points in electric circuit, establishing path of low resistance through which excessive current can flow —**short-circuit** *v.* **1.** develop or cause to develop short circuit —*vt.* **2.** bypass (procedure *etc.*) —'**shortcoming** *n.* failing, defect —**short cut 1.** shorter route than usual one **2.** means of saving time or effort —**short-cut** *vi.* use short cut —'**shortfall** *n.* failure to meet requirement —'**shorthand** *n.* method of rapid writing by signs or contractions —**short-handed** *a.* lacking the usual or necessary number of workers, helpers —'**shorthorn** *n.* short-horned breed of cattle with several regional varieties —**short list** selected list of candidates (*esp.* for job) from which final selection will be made —**short-lived** *a.* living or lasting only for a short time —**short-range** *a.* of limited extent in time or distance —**short shrift** summary treatment —**short-sighted** *a.* **1.** relating to or suffering from myopia **2.** lacking foresight —**short-tempered** *a.* easily moved to anger —**short-term** *a.* **1.** extending over limited period **2.** *Fin.* extending over or maturing within short period of time —**short ton** *US* ton (2000 lbs.) —**short wave** radio wave between 10 and 50 metres —**short-winded** *a.* **1.** tending to run out of breath, *esp.* after exertion **2.** (of speech or writing) abrupt

shot (ʃɒt) *n.* **1.** act of shooting **2.** missile **3.** lead in small pellets **4.** marksman, shooter **5.** try, attempt **6.** photograph **7.** short film sequence **8.** dose **9.** *inf.* injection —*a.* **10.** woven so that colour is different, according to angle of light —*v.* **11.** *pt./pp.* of SHOOT —'**shotgun** *n.* **1.** firearm with unrifled bore used mainly for hunting small game —*a.* **2.** *chiefly US* involving coercion or duress —**shot put** athletic event in which contestants hurl heavy metal ball as far as possible

should (ʃʊd) *pt.* of SHALL

shoulder ('ʃəʊldə) *n.* **1.** part of body to which arm or foreleg is attached **2.** anything resembling shoulder **3.** side of road —*vt.* **4.** undertake **5.** bear (burden) **6.** accept (responsibility) **7.** put on one's shoulder —*vi.* **8.** make way by pushing —**shoulder blade** shoulder bone

shout (ʃaʊt) *n.* **1.** loud cry —*v.* **2.** utter (cry *etc.*) with loud voice

shove (ʃʌv) *vt.* **1.** push **2.** *inf.* put —*n.* **3.** push —**shove off** *inf.* go away

shovel (ˈʃʌvəl) *n.* **1.** instrument for scooping, lifting earth *etc.* —*vt.* **2.** lift, move (as) with shovel (**-ll-**) —**ˈshoveler** *n.* duck with spoon-shaped bill

show (ʃəʊ) *vt.* **1.** expose to view **2.** point out **3.** display, exhibit **4.** explain; prove **5.** guide **6.** accord (favour *etc.*) —*vi.* **7.** appear **8.** be noticeable (**showed**, **shown**, ˈ**showing**) —*n.* **9.** display, exhibition **10.** spectacle **11.** theatrical or other entertainment **12.** indication **13.** competitive event **14.** ostentation **15.** semblance **16.** pretence —ˈ**showily** *adv.* —ˈ**showy** *a.* **1.** gaudy **2.** ostentatious —**show business** entertainment industry (*also* (*inf.*) **show biz**) —ˈ**showcase** *n.* **1.** glass case used for displaying and protecting objects in museum *etc.* **2.** setting in which anything may be displayed to best advantage —ˈ**showdown** *n.* **1.** confrontation **2.** final test —ˈ**showjumping** *n.* horse-riding competition to demonstrate skill in jumping obstacles —ˈ**showman** *n.* **1.** one employed in, or owning, show at fair *etc.* **2.** one skilled at presenting anything in effective way —**show-off** *n.* —ˈ**showpiece** *n.* **1.** anything exhibited **2.** anything prized as fine example of its type —**show off 1.** exhibit to invite admiration **2.** behave in such a way as to make an impression —**show up 1.** reveal **2.** expose **3.** *inf.* embarrass **4.** *inf.* arrive

shower (ˈʃaʊə) *n.* **1.** short fall of rain **2.** anything coming down like rain **3.** kind of bath in which person stands while being sprayed with water **4.** US to present gifts to a person, such as a prospective bride —*vt.* **5.** bestow liberally —*vi.* **6.** take bath in shower —ˈ**showery** *a.*

shrank (ʃræŋk) *pt. of* SHRINK

shrapnel (ˈʃræpnəl) *n.* **1.** shell filled with pellets which scatter on bursting **2.** shell splinters

shred (ʃred) *n.* **1.** fragment, torn strip **2.** small amount —*vt.* **3.** cut, tear to shreds (**shred** *or* ˈ**shredded**, ˈ**shredding**)

shrew (ʃruː) *n.* **1.** animal like mouse **2.** bad-tempered woman **3.** scold —ˈ**shrewish** *a.* nagging

shrewd (ʃruːd) *a.* **1.** astute, intelligent **2.** crafty

shriek (ʃriːk) *n.* **1.** shrill cry **2.** piercing scream —*v.* **3.** screech

shrift (ʃrɪft) *n.* **1.** confession **2.** absolution

shrike (ʃraɪk) *n.* bird of prey

shrill (ʃrɪl) *a.* **1.** piercing, sharp in tone —*v.* **2.** utter (words *etc.*) in such tone —ˈ**shrilly** *adv.*

shrimp (ʃrɪmp) *n.* **1.** small edible crustacean **2.** *inf.* undersized person —*vi.* **3.** fish for shrimps

shrine (ʃraɪn) *n.* place (building, tomb, alcove) of worship, usu. associated with saint

shrink (ʃrɪŋk) *vi.* **1.** become smaller **2.** retire, flinch, recoil —*vt.* **3.** make smaller (**shrank** *pt.*, ˈ**shrunken**, **shrunk** *pp.*, ˈ**shrinking** *pr.p.*) —*n.* **4.** *sl.* psychiatrist —ˈ**shrinkage** *n.* —**shrink-wrap** *vt.* package (product) in flexible plastic wrapping designed to shrink about its contours

shrivel (ˈʃrɪvəl) *vi.* shrink and wither (**-ll-**)

shroud (ʃraʊd) *n.* **1.** sheet, wrapping, for corpse **2.** anything which covers, envelops like shroud —*pl.* **3.** set of ropes to masthead —*vt.* **4.** put shroud on **5.** screen, veil **6.** wrap up

Shrovetide (ˈʃrəʊvtaɪd) *n.* the three days preceding Lent —**Shrove Tuesday** day before Ash Wednesday

shrub (ʃrʌb) *n.* bushy plant —ˈ**shrubbery** *n.* plantation, part of garden, filled with shrubs

shrug (ʃrʌg) *vi.* **1.** raise shoulders, as sign of indifference, ignorance *etc.* —*vt.* **2.** move (shoulders) thus **3.** (*with off*) dismiss as unimportant (**-gg-**) —*n.* **4.** shrugging

shrunk (ʃrʌŋk) *pp. of* SHRINK

shuck (ʃʌk) *n.* shell, husk, pod

shudder (ˈʃʌdə) *vi.* **1.** shake, tremble violently, *esp.* with horror —*n.* **2.** shuddering, tremor

shuffle (ˈʃʌfəl) *vi.* **1.** move feet without lifting them **2.** act evasively —*vt.* **3.** mix (cards) **4.** (*with off*) evade, pass to another —*n.* **5.** shuffling **6.** rearrangement —ˈ**shuffler** *n.*

shun (ʃʌn) *vt.* **1.** avoid **2.** keep away from (**-nn-**)

shunt (ʃʌnt) *vt.* **1.** push aside **2.** divert **3.** move (train) from one line to another

shush (ʃʊʃ) *interj.* **1.** be quiet, hush —*vt.* **2.** silence or calm by saying 'shush'

shut (ʃʌt) *v.* **1.** close —*vt.* **2.** bar **3.** forbid entrance to (**shut**, ˈ**shutting**) —ˈ**shutter** *n.* **1.** movable window screen, usu. hinged to frame **2.** device in camera admitting light as required to film or plate —ˈ**shuteye** *n. sl.* sleep —**shut down** close or stop (factory, machine *etc.*)

shuttle (ˈʃʌtəl) *n.* **1.** instrument which threads weft between threads of warp in weaving **2.** similar appliance in sewing machine **3.** plane, bus *etc.* travelling to and fro over short distance —ˈ**shuttlecock** *n.* small, light cone with cork stub and fan of feathers used as a ball in badminton

shy[1] (ʃaɪ) *a.* **1.** awkward in company **2.** timid, bashful **3.** reluctant **4.** scarce, lacking (*esp.* in card games, not having enough money for bet *etc.*) —*vi.* **5.** start back in fear **6.** show sudden reluctance (**shied**, ˈ**shying**) —*n.* **7.** start of fear by horse —ˈ**shyly** *adv.* —ˈ**shyness** *n.*

shy[2] (ʃaɪ) *vt./n.* throw (**shied**, ˈ**shying**)

Shylock (ˈʃaɪlɒk) *n.* heartless or demanding creditor

shyster ('ʃaɪstə) *n. sl.* dishonest, deceitful person

si (siː) *n. Mus. see* TE

Si *Chem.* silicon

SI *Fr.* Système International (d'Unités), international system of units of measurement based on units of ten

Siamese (saɪə'miːz) *a.* of Siam, former name of Thailand —**Siamese cat** breed of cat with blue eyes —**Siamese twins** twins born joined to each other by some part of body

sibilant ('sɪbɪlənt) *a.* 1. hissing —*n.* 2. speech sound with hissing effect

sibling ('sɪblɪŋ) *n.* person's brother or sister

sibyl ('sɪbɪl) *n.* woman endowed with spirit of prophecy —**sibylline** ('sɪbɪlaɪn) *a.* occult

sic (sɪk) *Lat.* thus: oft. used to call attention to a quoted mistake

sick (sɪk) *a.* 1. inclined to vomit, vomiting 2. not well or healthy, physically or mentally 3. *inf.* macabre, sadistic, morbid 4. *inf.* bored, tired 5. *inf.* disgusted —**sicken** *v.* 1. make, become sick —*vt.* 2. disgust; nauseate —**sickening** *a.* 1. causing sickness or revulsion 2. *inf.* extremely annoying —**sickly** *a.* 1. unhealthy, weakly 2. inducing nausea —**sickness** *n.* —**sickbay** *n.* place set aside for treating sick people, *esp.* in ships

sickle ('sɪkəl) *n.* reaping hook —**sickle cell anaemia** inherited form of anaemia in which large number of red blood cells become sickle-shaped

side (saɪd) *n.* 1. one of the surfaces of object, *esp.* upright inner or outer surface 2. either surface of thing having only two 3. part of body that is to right or left 4. region nearer or farther than, or right or left of, dividing line *etc.* 5. region 6. aspect or part 7. one of two parties or sets of opponents 8. sect, faction 9. line of descent traced through one parent 10. *sl.* swank, conceit —*a.* 11. at, in the side 12. subordinate, incidental —*vi.* 13. (*usu. with* with) take up cause (of) —**siding** *n.* short line of rails on which trains or wagons are shunted from main line —**side arms** weapons carried on person, by belt or holster, such as sword, pistol *etc.* —**sideboard** *n.* piece of furniture for holding dishes *etc.* in dining room —**sideboards** *pl.n.* UK man's whiskers grown down either side of face in front of ears (*also* US **'sideburns**) —**sidecar** *n.* small car attached to side of motorcycle —**sidekick** *n. sl., chiefly* US close friend or follower —**sidelight** *n.* either of two small lights on front of motor vehicle —**sideline** *n.* 1. *Sport* boundary of playing area 2. subsidiary interest or activity —**sidelong** *a.* 1. lateral, not directly forward —*adv.* 2. obliquely —**side-saddle** *n.* riding saddle orig. designed for women riders in skirts, who sit with both legs on near side of horse —**sideshow** *n.* 1. small show offered in conjunction with larger attraction, as at circus 2. subordinate event —**sideslip** *n.* skid —**sidesman** *n. Anglican Ch.* man elected to help parish churchwarden —**side-splitting** *a.* 1. producing great mirth 2. (of laughter) very hearty —**sidestep** *v.* 1. step aside from or out of way of (something) —*vt.* 2. dodge —**side step** movement to one side, as in boxing *etc.* —**sidetrack** *v.* 1. distract or be distracted from main topic —*n.* 2. digression —**sidewalk** *n.* US footpath beside road —**sideways** *adv.* 1. to or from the side 2. laterally

sidereal (saɪ'dɪərɪəl) *a.* relating to, fixed by, stars

sidle ('saɪdəl) *vi.* 1. move in furtive or stealthy manner 2. move sideways

SIDS sudden infant death syndrome

siege (siːdʒ) *n.* besieging of town or fortified place

siemens ('siːmənz) *n.* derived SI unit of electrical conductance

sienna (sɪ'ɛnə) *n.* (pigment of) brownish-yellow colour

sierra (sɪ'ɛərə) *n.* range of mountains with jagged peaks

siesta (sɪ'ɛstə) *n.* rest, sleep in afternoon

sieve (sɪv) *n.* 1. device with network or perforated bottom used for sifting —*vt.* 2. sift 3. strain

sift (sɪft) *vt.* 1. separate (*eg* with sieve) coarser portion from finer 2. examine closely

sigh (saɪ) *vi./v.* 1. (utter) long audible breath —**sigh for** yearn for, grieve for

sight (saɪt) *n.* 1. faculty of seeing 2. seeing 3. thing seen 4. view 5. glimpse 6. device for guiding eye 7. spectacle 8. *inf.* pitiful or ridiculous object 9. *inf.* large number, great deal —*vt.* 10. catch sight of 11. adjust sights of (gun *etc.*) —**sightless** *a.* —**sight-read** *v.* play, sing (music) without previous preparation —**sightscreen** *n. Cricket* white screen placed near boundary behind bowler to help batsman see ball —**sightsee** *v.* visit (place) to look at interesting sights —**sightseeing** *n.*

sigma ('sɪgmə) *n.* 1. 18th letter in Gr. alphabet (Σ, σ or, when final, ς), consonant, transliterated as *S* 2. *Maths.* symbol Σ, indicating summation

sign (saɪn) *n.* 1. mark, gesture *etc.* to convey some meaning 2. (board, placard bearing) notice, warning *etc.* 3. symbol 4. omen 5. evidence —*vt.* 6. put one's signature to 7. ratify —*vi.* 8. make sign or gesture 9. affix signature —**sign language** any system of communication by signs, *esp.* used by deaf —**signpost** *n.* 1. post bearing sign that shows way, as at roadside 2. something that serves as indication —*vt.* 3. mark with signposts

signal ('sɪgnəl) n. 1. sign to convey order or information, *esp.* on railway 2. that which in first place impels any action 3. *Rad. etc.* sequence of electrical impulses transmitted or received —a. 4. remarkable, striking —vt. 5. make signals to —vi. 6. give orders *etc.* by signals (**-ll-**) —'**signalize** *or* **-lise** vt. make notable —'**signally** adv. —**signal box** 1. building containing signal levers for railway lines 2. control point for large area of railway system —'**signalman** n. railway employee in charge of signals

signatory ('sɪgnətərɪ) n. one of those who sign agreements, treaties

signature ('sɪgnɪtʃə) n. 1. person's name written by himself 2. act of writing it —**signature tune** tune associated with particular programme, person *etc.*

signet ('sɪgnɪt) n. small seal —**signet ring** finger ring bearing signet

significant (sɪg'nɪfɪkənt) a. 1. revealing 2. designed to make something known 3. important —**sig'nificance** n. 1. import, weight 2. meaning —**sig'nificantly** adv. —**signifi'cation** n. meaning —**significant figures** 1. figures of number that express magnitude to specified degree of accuracy 2. number of such figures

signify ('sɪgnɪfaɪ) vt. 1. mean 2. indicate 3. denote 4. imply —vi. 5. be of importance ('**signified,** '**signifying**)

signor *or* **signior** ('siːnjɔː; *It.* siɲ'ɲoːr) n. *It.* title of respect, like Mr. (*pl.* **-s, -gnori** (*It.* -'ɲoːri)) —**signora** (siːn'jɔːrə; *It.* siɲ'ɲoːra) n. Mrs. (*pl.* **-s, -re** (*It.* -re)) —**signorina** (siːnjɔː'riːnə; *It.* siɲɲo'riːna) n. Miss (*pl.* **-s, -ne** (*It.* -ne))

Sikh (siːk) n. member of Indian religious sect

silage ('saɪlɪdʒ) n. fodder crop harvested while green and stored in state of partial fermentation

silence ('saɪləns) n. 1. absence of noise 2. refraining from speech —vt. 3. make silent 4. put a stop to —'**silencer** n. device to reduce noise of engine exhaust, firearm —'**silent** a.

silhouette (sɪluː'ɛt) n. 1. outline of object seen against light 2. profile portrait in black

silica ('sɪlɪkə) n. naturally occurring dioxide of silicon —**siliceous** *or* **silicious** (sɪ'lɪʃəs) a. —**sili'cosis** n. lung disease caused by inhaling silica dust over a long period

silicon ('sɪlɪkən) n. brittle metalloid element found in sand, clay, stone, widely used in chemistry, industry —'**silicone** n. large class of synthetic substances, related to silicon and used in chemistry, industry and medicine —**silicon chip** *see* CHIP (sense 4)

silk (sɪlk) n. 1. fibre made by larvae (**silkworm**) of certain moth 2. thread, fabric made from this —'**silken** a. 1. made of, like silk 2. soft 3. smooth 4. dressed in silk —'**silkily** adv. —'**silkiness** n. —'**silky** a. —**silk hat** man's top hat covered with silk —**silk-screen** n. stencil process of printing a design through screen of fine mesh cloth

sill (sɪl) n. 1. ledge beneath window 2. bottom part of door or window frame

sillabub ('sɪləbʌb) n. *see* SYLLABUB

silly ('sɪlɪ) a. 1. foolish 2. trivial 3. feeble-minded —'**silliness** n.

silo ('saɪləʊ) n. 1. pit, tower for storing fodder or grain 2. underground missile launching site (*pl.* **-s**)

silt (sɪlt) n. 1. mud deposited by water —v. 2. fill, be choked with silt —**sil'tation** n. —'**silty** a.

Silurian (saɪ'lʊərɪən) a. 1. of or formed in third period of Palaeozoic era, during which fishes first appeared —n. 2. Silurian period or rock system

silvan ('sɪlvən) a. *see* SYLVAN

silver ('sɪlvə) n. 1. white precious metal 2. things made of it 3. silver coins 4. cutlery —a. 5. made of silver 6. resembling silver or its colour 7. having pale lustre, as moon 8. soft, melodious, as sound 9. bright —vt. 10. coat with silver —'**silvery** a. —**silver birch** tree having silvery-white peeling bark —**silver jubilee** 25th anniversary —**silver lining** hopeful aspect of otherwise desperate situation —**silver plate** 1. thin layer of silver deposited on base metal 2. articles, *esp.* tableware, made of silver plate —**silver-plate** vt. coat (metal *etc.*) with silver —**silver screen** *inf.* 1. films collectively 2. screen on to which films are projected —'**silverside** n. UK cut of beef below aitchbone and above leg —'**silversmith** n. craftsman who makes articles of silver —**silver wedding** 25th wedding anniversary

silviculture ('sɪlvɪkʌltʃə) n. branch of forestry concerned with cultivation of trees

simian ('sɪmɪən) a. of, like apes

similar ('sɪmɪlə) a. resembling, like —**simi'larity** n. likeness, close resemblance

simile ('sɪmɪlɪ) n. comparison of one thing with another, using *as* or *like*, *esp.* in poetry

similitude (sɪ'mɪlɪtjuːd) n. 1. outward appearance, likeness 2. guise

simmer ('sɪmə) v. 1. keep or be just bubbling or just below boiling point —vi. 2. be in state of suppressed anger or laughter

simnel cake ('sɪmnəl) UK fruit cake covered with layer of marzipan

simper ('sɪmpə) v. 1. smile, utter in silly or affected way —n. 2. simpering smile

simple ('sɪmpəl) a. 1. not complicated 2. plain 3. not combined or complex 4. ordinary, mere 5. guileless 6. stupid —'**simpleton** n. foolish person —**sim'plicity** n. 1. simpleness 2. clearness 3.

artlessness —**simplifi'cation** *n.* —'**simplify** *vt.* make simple, plain or easy (**-plified, -plifying**) —**sim'plistic** *a.* very simple, naive —'**simply** *adv.* —**simple fraction** fraction in which both the numerator and the denominator are integers —**simple fracture** fracture in which broken bone does not pierce skin —**simple interest** interest paid on principal alone —**simple-minded** *a.* **1.** stupid; feeble-minded **2.** mentally defective **3.** unsophisticated —**simple-mindedness** *n.* —**simple sentence** sentence consisting of single main clause

simulate ('simjuleit) *vt.* **1.** make pretence of **2.** reproduce, copy (*esp.* conditions of particular situation) —**simu'lation** *n.* —'**simulator** *n.*

simultaneous (siməl'teiniəs) *a.* occurring at the same time —**simultaneity** (siməltə'ni:iti) *or* **simul'taneousness** *n.* —**simul'taneously** *adv.*

sin[1] (sin) *n.* **1.** transgression of divine or moral law, *esp.* committed consciously **2.** offence against principle or standard —*vi.* **3.** commit sin (**-nn-**) —'**sinful** *a.* **1.** of nature of sin **2.** guilty of sin —'**sinfully** *adv.* —'**sinner** *n.* —**sin bin** C *sl.* penalty box used in ice hockey

sin[2] Maths. sine

SIN C Social Insurance Number

since (sins) *prep.* **1.** during or throughout period of time after —*conj.* **2.** from time when **3.** because —*adv.* **4.** from that time

sincere (sin'siə) *a.* **1.** not hypocritical, actually moved by or feeling apparent emotions **2.** true, genuine **3.** unaffected —**sin'cerely** *adv.* —**sincerity** (sin'seriti) *n.*

sine (sain) *n.* mathematical function, *esp.* ratio of length of hypotenuse to opposite side in right-angled triangle

sinecure ('sainikjuə) *n.* office with pay but minimal duties

sine die ('saini 'daii) *Lat.* with no date, indefinitely postponed

sine qua non ('saini kwei 'nɒn) *Lat.* essential condition or requirement

sinew ('sinju:) *n.* **1.** tough, fibrous cord joining muscle to bone —*pl.* **2.** muscles, strength —'**sinewy** *a.* **1.** stringy **2.** muscular

sing (siŋ) *vi.* **1.** utter musical sounds **2.** hum, whistle, ring —*vt.* **3.** utter (words) with musical modulation **4.** celebrate in song or poetry (**sang, sung,** '**singing**) —'**singer** *n.* —'**singsong** *n.* informal singing session —*a.* **2.** monotonously regular in tone, rhythm

singe (sindʒ) *vt.* **1.** burn surface of (**singed,** '**singeing**) —*n.* **2.** act or effect of singeing

Singh (siŋ) *n.* title assumed by Sikh on becoming full member of community

single ('siŋgəl) *a.* **1.** one only **2.** alone, separate **3.** unmarried **4.** for one **5.** formed of only one part, fold *etc.* **6.** denoting ticket for train *etc.*

valid for outward journey only **7.** whole-hearted, straightforward —*n.* **8.** single thing **9.** gramophone record with one short item on each side **10.** single ticket —*vt.* **11.** (*with* out) pick (out) —'**singleton** *n.* **1.** *Bridge etc.* original holding of one card only in suit **2.** single object as distinguished from pair or group **3.** *Maths.* set containing only one member —'**singly** *adv.* —**single-breasted** *a.* (of garment) overlapping only slightly and with one row of fastenings —**single entry** *Book-keeping* entered in one account only —**single file** persons, things arranged in one line —**single-handed** *a./adv.* without assistance —**single-minded** *a.* having but one aim or purpose —**single-mindedness** *n.*

singlet ('siŋlit) *n.* sleeveless undervest

singular ('siŋgjulə) *a.* **1.** remarkable **2.** unusual **3.** unique **4.** denoting one person or thing —**singu'larity** *n.* something unusual —'**singularly** *adv.* **1.** particularly **2.** peculiarly

Sinhalese (sinhə'li:z) *or* **Singhalese** (siŋə'li:z) *n.* **1.** member of people living chiefly in Sri Lanka **2.** language of this people —*a.* **3.** of this people or their language

sinister ('sinistə) *a.* **1.** threatening **2.** evil-looking **3.** wicked **4.** unlucky **5.** *Her.* on left-hand side

sink (siŋk) *vi.* **1.** become submerged (in water) **2.** drop, give way **3.** decline in value, health *etc.* **4.** penetrate —*vt.* **5.** cause to sink **6.** make by digging out **7.** invest (**sank** *pt.,* **sunk,** '**sunken** *pp.,* '**sinking** *pr.p.*) —*n.* **8.** receptacle with pipe for carrying away waste water **9.** cesspool **10.** place of corruption, vice —'**sinker** *n.* weight for fishing line —**sinking fund** money set aside at intervals for payment of particular liability at fixed date

Sinn Fein ('ʃin 'fein) Irish republican political movement

Sino- (*comb. form*) Chinese, of China, as in *Sino-Tibetan*

Sinology (sai'nɒlədʒi) *n.* study of Chinese history, language, culture *etc.* —**Sinological** (sainə'lɒdʒikəl) *a.* —**Si'nologist** *n.*

sinuous ('sinjuəs) *a.* **1.** curving **2.** devious **3.** lithe —'**sinuate** *a.* —**sinu'osity** *n.*

sinus ('sainəs) *n.* cavity, *esp.* any of air passages in bones of skull —**sinu'sitis** *n.* inflammation of sinus

Sion ('saiən) *n. see* ZION

sip (sip) *v.* **1.** drink in very small portions (**-pp-**) —*n.* **2.** small drink

siphon *or* **syphon** ('saifən) *n.* **1.** device, *esp.* bent tube, which uses atmospheric or gaseous pressure to draw liquid from container —*vt.* **2.** draw off thus **3.** draw off in small amounts

sir (sɜ:) *n.* **1.** polite term of address for a man **2.** (**S-**) title of knight or baronet

sire (saɪə) n. 1. male parent, esp. of horse or domestic animal 2. term of address to king —vt. 3. beget

siren ('saɪərən) n. 1. device making loud wailing noise, esp. giving warning of danger 2. legendary sea nymph who lured sailors to destruction 3. alluring woman

Sirius ('sɪrɪəs) n. brightest star in sky, lying in constellation Canis Major (also **Dog Star**)

sirloin ('sɜːlɔɪn) n. prime cut of loin of beef

sirocco (sɪ'rɒkəʊ) n. hot oppressive wind beginning in N Afr. and reaching S Europe (pl. -s)

sisal ('saɪsəl) n. (fibre of) plant used in making ropes

siskin ('sɪskɪn) n. small olive-green bird of finch family

sissy ('sɪsɪ) a./n. weak, cowardly (person)

sister ('sɪstə) n. 1. daughter of same parents 2. woman fellow-member, esp. of religious body 3. senior nurse —a. 4. closely related, similar —'**sisterhood** n. 1. relation of sister 2. order, band of women —'**sisterly** a. —**sister-in-law** n. 1. sister of husband or wife 2. brother's wife

sit (sɪt) vi. 1. adopt posture or rest on buttocks, thighs 2. perch 3. (of bird) cover eggs to hatch them 4. pose for portrait 5. occupy official position 6. hold session 7. remain 8. keep watch over baby etc. —vt. 9. take (examination) (**sat**, '**sitting**) —'**sitter** n. 1. person or animal that sits 2. person who is posing for portrait 3. one **baby-sitter** at BABY —'**sitting** n. 1. continuous period of being seated 2. in canteen etc., such period during which one of two or more meals is served 3. meeting, esp. of official body 4. incubation period of bird's eggs during which mother sits on them —**sit-down** a. (of meal etc.) eaten while sitting down at table —**sit-down strike** strike in which employees refuse to leave their place of employment —**sit-in** n. protest involving refusal to move from place —**sitting duck** inf. person or thing in defenceless position —**sitting tenant** tenant already occupying flat etc. —**sit down** 1. adopt sitting posture 2. (with under) suffer (insults etc.) without protest —**sit in** protest by sit-in

sitar (sɪ'tɑː) n. stringed musical instrument, esp. of India

site (saɪt) n. 1. place, location 2. space for, with, a building —vt. 3. locate in specific place

situate ('sɪtjʊeɪt) vt. place, locate —situ'ation n. 1. place, position 2. state of affairs 3. employment, post —**situation comedy** comedy based on humorous situations that could arise in day-to-day life

six (sɪks) a./n. cardinal number one more than five —'**six'teen** n./a. six and ten —**sixth** a. 1. ordinal number of six —n. 2. sixth part —'**sixty**

n./a. six times ten —**six-shooter** n. US inf. revolver with six chambers —**sixth sense** any supposed means of perception, such as intuition

size[1] (saɪz) n. 1. bigness, dimensions 2. one of series of standard measurements of clothes etc. 3. inf. state of affairs —vt. 4. arrange according to size —'**sizable** or '**sizeable** a. quite large —**size up** inf. assess (person, situation etc.)

size[2] (saɪz) n. 1. gluelike sealer, filler —vt. 2. coat, treat with size

sizzle ('sɪzəl) vi./n. (make) hissing, spluttering sound, as of frying —'**sizzler** n. inf. hot day

SJA Saint John's Ambulance (Brigade or Association)

SK Saskatchewan

skate[1] (skeɪt) n. 1. steel blade attached to boot, for gliding over ice —vi. 2. glide as on skates —'**skateboard** n. small board mounted on roller-skate wheels

skate[2] (skeɪt) n. large marine ray

skean-dhu (skiːən'duː) n. dagger worn in stocking as part of Highland dress

skedaddle (skɪ'dædəl) vi. inf. scamper off

skein (skeɪn) n. 1. quantity of yarn, wool etc. in loose knot 2. flight of wildfowl

skeleton ('skelɪtən) n. 1. bones of animal 2. bones separated from flesh and preserved in their natural position 3. very thin person 4. outline, draft, framework 5. nucleus —a. 6. reduced to a minimum 7. drawn in outline 8. not in detail —'**skeletal** a. —**skeleton key** key filed down so as to open many different locks

skeptic ('skeptɪk) n. US see SCEPTIC

skerry ('skerɪ) n. rocky island or reef

sketch (sketʃ) n. 1. rough drawing 2. brief account 3. essay 4. short humorous play —v. 5. make sketch (of) —'**sketchy** a. 1. omitting detail 2. incomplete 3. inadequate

skew (skjuː) vi. 1. move obliquely —a. 2. slanting 3. crooked —'**skew'whiff** a. inf. 1. aslant 2. crooked

skewbald ('skjuːbɔːld) a. (esp. of horse) white and any other colour (except black) in patches

skewer ('skjʊə) n. 1. pin to fasten meat together —vt. 2. pierce or fasten with skewer

ski (skiː) n. 1. long runner fastened to foot for sliding over snow or water (pl. -s, ski) —vi. 2. slide on skis (**skied**, '**skiing**) —**ski jump** ramp overhanging slope from which skiers compete to make longest jump —**ski-jump** vi.

skid (skɪd) v. 1. (cause (esp. vehicle) to) slide (sideways) out of control with wheels not revolving (**-dd-**) —n. 2. instance of this 3. device to facilitate sliding, eg in moving heavy objects —'**skidpan** n. area made slippery so that drivers can practise controlling skids —**skid row** or **road** sl., chiefly US dilapidated section of city inhabited by vagrants etc.

skidoo ('skɪduː) n. C snowmobile

skiff (skɪf) n. small boat

skill (skɪl) n. practical ability, cleverness, dexterity —'**skilful** or U.S. '**skillful** a. expert, masterly, adroit —'**skilfully** or U.S. '**skillfully** adv. —**skilled** a. having, requiring knowledge, united with readiness and dexterity

skillet ('skɪlɪt) n. small frying pan

skim (skɪm) vt. 1. remove floating matter from surface of (liquid) 2. glide over lightly and rapidly 3. read thus —vi. 4. move thus (-**mm**-) —**skim** or **skimmed milk** milk from which cream has been removed

skimp (skɪmp) v. 1. give short measure (on) 2. do (thing) imperfectly —'**skimpy** a. 1. meagre 2. scanty

skin (skɪn) n. 1. outer covering of vertebrate body, lower animal or fruit 2. animal skin used as material or container 3. film on surface of cooling liquid etc. 4. complexion —vt. 5. remove skin of (-**nn**-) —'**skinless** a. —'**skinned** a. 1. stripped of skin 2. having skin of specified kind —'**skinner** n. 1. dealer in hides 2. furrier —'**skinny** a. thin —**skin-deep** a. superficial 2. slight —**skin diving** underwater swimming using breathing apparatus —**skin flick** film containing much nudity and explicit sex scenes —'**skinflint** n. miser, niggard —**skin graft** transplant of piece of healthy skin to wound to form new skin —'**skin'tight** a. fitting close to skin —**keep one's eyes skinned** watch carefully

skint (skɪnt) a. sl. without money

skip[1] (skɪp) vi. 1. leap lightly 2. jump a rope as it is swung under one —vt. 3. pass over, omit (-**pp**-) —n. 4. act of skipping —**skipping-rope** n. UK cord that is held in hands and swung round so that holder or others can jump over it

skip[2] (skɪp) n. 1. large open container for builders' rubbish etc. 2. large bucket, container for transporting men, materials in mines etc.

skipper ('skɪpə) n. 1. captain of ship, plane or team —vt. 2. captain

skirl (skɜːl) n. sound of bagpipes

skirmish ('skɜːmɪʃ) n. 1. fight between small parties, small battle —vi. 2. fight briefly or irregularly

skirt (skɜːt) n. 1. woman's garment hanging from waist 2. lower part of woman's dress, coat etc. 3. outlying part 4. sl. woman —vt. 5. border 6. go round —'**skirting** n. 1. vertical board round margin of floor (also **skirting board**) 2. material for women's skirts

skit (skɪt) n. satire, esp. theatrical burlesque

skittish ('skɪtɪʃ) a. frisky, frivolous

skittles ('skɪt²lz) pl.n. ninepins

skive (skaɪv) v. evade (work or responsibility)

skivvy ('skɪvɪ) n. female servant who does menial work

skokiaan ('skɔːkɪɑːn) n. SA potent alcoholic beverage

skua ('skjuːə) n. large predatory gull

skulduggery or U.S. **skullduggery** (skʌl-'dʌɡərɪ) n. inf. trickery

skulk (skʌlk) vi. 1. sneak out of the way 2. lurk

skull (skʌl) n. bony case that encloses brain —**skull and crossbones** picture of human skull above two crossed thighbones, used as warning of danger or death —'**skullcap** n. close-fitting cap

skunk (skʌŋk) n. 1. small N Amer. animal which emits evil-smelling fluid 2. sl. mean person

sky (skaɪ) n. 1. apparently dome-shaped expanse extending upwards from the horizon 2. outer space 3. heavenly regions (pl. **skies**) —vt. 4. hit (cricket ball) high —'**skydiving** n. parachute jumping with delayed opening of parachute —**sky-high** a./adv. 1. at or to unprecedented level —adv. 2. high into air —'**skyjack** vt. hijack (an aircraft) —'**skylark** n. lark, noted for singing while hovering at great height —vi. 2. inf. romp or play jokes —'**skylight** n. window in roof or ceiling —'**skyline** n. 1. line at which earth and sky appear to meet 2. outline of trees etc. seen against sky —'**skyscraper** n. very tall building —**blow sky-high** destroy

Skye terrier (skaɪ) short-legged breed of terrier with long wiry hair

slab (slæb) n. thick, broad piece

slack[1] (slæk) a. 1. loose 2. sluggish 3. careless, negligent 4. not busy —n. 5. loose part, as of rope —vi. 6. be idle or lazy —'**slacken** v. 1. make or become looser 2. make or become slower —'**slacker** n. person who evades work —'**slackly** adv. —**slack water** period of still water around turn of tide

slack[2] (slæk) n. coal dust, small pieces of coal

slacks (slæks) pl.n. informal trousers worn by men or women

slag (slæg) n. 1. refuse of smelted metal 2. sl. coarse woman —**slag heap** hillock of waste matter from coal-mining etc.

slain (sleɪn) pp. of SLAY

slake (sleɪk) vt. 1. satisfy (thirst, desire etc.) 2. combine (lime) with water to produce calcium hydroxide

slalom ('slɑːləm) n. race over winding course in skiing etc.

slam (slæm) v. 1. shut noisily 2. bang —vt. 3. hit 4. dash down 5. inf. criticize harshly (-**mm**-) —n. 6. (noise of) this action —**grand slam** Cards winning of all tricks

slander ('slɑːndə) n. 1. false or malicious statement about person —v. 2. utter such statement (about) —'**slanderer** n. —'**slanderous** a.

slang (slæŋ) n. 1. colloquial language —vt. 2. sl. scold, abuse violently

slant (slɑ:nt) v. 1. slope —vt. 2. put at angle 3. write, present (news etc.) with bias —n. 4. slope 5. point of view 6. idea —a. 7. sloping, oblique —'**slantwise** or '**slantways** adv.

slap (slæp) n. 1. blow with open hand or flat instrument —vt. 2. strike thus 3. inf. put (on, down) carelessly or messily (-pp-) —'**slapdash** a. careless and abrupt —'**slaphappy** a. inf. 1. cheerfully irresponsible 2. dazed as if from repeated blows —'**slapstick** n. boisterous knockabout comedy —**slap-up** a. UK inf. (esp. of meals) lavish

slash (slæʃ) vt. 1. gash 2. lash 3. cut, slit 4. criticize unmercifully —n. 5. gash 6. cutting stroke

slat (slæt) n. narrow strip of wood or metal as in blinds etc.

slate (sleɪt) n. 1. kind of stone which splits easily in flat sheets 2. piece of this for covering roof or, formerly, for writing on —vt. 3. cover with slates 4. abuse —'**slating** n. severe reprimand

slater ('sleɪtə) n. woodlouse

slattern ('slætən) n. slut —'**slatternly** a. slovenly, untidy

slaughter ('slɔ:tə) n. 1. killing —vt. 2. kill —'**slaughterous** a. —'**slaughterhouse** n. place for killing animals for food

Slav (slɑ:v) n. member of any of peoples of E Europe or Soviet Asia who speak Slavonic language —**Sla'vonic** or '**Slavic** n. 1. branch of Indo-European family of languages, including Bulgarian, Russian, Polish, Czech etc. —a. 2. of this group of languages

slave (sleɪv) n. 1. captive, person without freedom or personal rights 2. person dominated by another or by a habit etc. —vi. 3. work like slave —'**slaver** n. person, ship engaged in slave traffic —'**slavery** n. —'**slavish** a. servile —**slave-driver** n. 1. esp. formerly, person forcing slaves to work 2. employer demanding excessively hard work from employees

slaver ('slævə) vi. 1. dribble saliva from mouth 2. fawn —n. 3. saliva running from mouth

slaw (slɔ:) n. chiefly US short for COLESLAW

slay (sleɪ) vt. 1. kill 2. inf. impress, esp. by being very funny (**slew, slain,** '**slaying**)

sleazy ('sli:zɪ) a. sordid

sledge[1] (sledʒ) or (esp. U.S.) **sled** (sled) n. 1. carriage on runners for sliding on snow 2. toboggan —v. 3. convey, travel by sledge

sledge[2] (sledʒ) n. heavy hammer with long handle (also '**sledgehammer**)

sleek (sli:k) a. glossy, smooth, shiny

sleep (sli:p) n. 1. unconscious state regularly occurring in man and animals 2. slumber, repose 3. inf. dried particles oft. found in corners of eyes after sleeping —vi. 4. take rest in sleep, slumber (**slept,** '**sleeping**) —'**sleeper** n. 1. one who sleeps 2. beam supporting rails of railway 3. railway sleeping car —'**sleepily** adv. —'**sleepiness** n. —'**sleepless** a. —'**sleepy** a. —**sleeping bag** large well-padded bag for sleeping in, esp. outdoors —**sleeping car** railway car fitted with compartments containing bunks for sleeping in —**sleeping partner** partner in business who does not play active role (also **silent partner**) —**sleeping policeman** protuberance built across roads to deter motorists from speeding —**sleeping sickness** Afr. disease spread by tsetse fly —'**sleepwalk** vi. walk while asleep

sleet (sli:t) n. rain and snow or hail falling together

sleeve (sli:v) n. 1. part of garment which covers arm 2. case surrounding shaft 3. gramophone record cover —vt. 4. furnish with sleeves —**sleeved** a. —'**sleeveless** a. —**have** (**something**) **up one's sleeve** have (something) prepared secretly for emergency

sleigh (sleɪ) n. sledge

sleight (slaɪt) n. 1. dexterity 2. trickery 3. deviousness —**sleight of hand** 1. (manual dexterity in) conjuring, juggling 2. legerdemain

slender ('slendə) a. 1. slim, slight 2. feeble

slept (slept) pt./pp. of SLEEP

sleuth (slu:θ) n. 1. detective 2. tracking dog (also '**sleuthhound**) —vt. 3. track

slew[1] (slu:) pt. of SLAY

slew[2] or esp. U.S. **slue** (slu:) v. swing round

slice (slaɪs) n. 1. thin flat piece cut off 2. share 3. flat culinary tool —vt. 4. cut into slices 5. cut cleanly 6. hit (ball) with bat etc. at angle

slick (slɪk) a. 1. smooth 2. smooth-tongued 3. flattering 4. superficially attractive 5. sly —vt. 6. make glossy, smooth —n. 7. slippery area 8. patch of oil on water

slide (slaɪd) vi. 1. slip smoothly along 2. glide, as over ice 3. deteriorate morally —v. 4. pass imperceptibly (**slid** (slɪd) pt., **slid, slidden** ('slɪdⁿn) pp., '**sliding** pr.p.) —n. 5. sliding 6. surface, track for sliding 7. sliding part of mechanism 8. piece of glass holding object to be viewed under microscope 9. photographic transparency 10. ornamental clip to hold hair in place, hair slide —**slide rule** mathematical instrument of two parts, one of which slides upon the other, for rapid calculations —**sliding scale** schedule for automatically varying one thing (eg wages) according to fluctuations of another (eg cost of living)

slight (slaɪt) a. 1. small, trifling 2. not substantial, fragile 3. slim, slender —vt. 4. disregard 5. neglect —n. 6. indifference 7. act of discourtesy —'**slightly** adv.

slim (slɪm) a. 1. thin 2. slight —v. 3. make or become slim by diet and exercise (**-mm-**)

slime (slaɪm) n. greasy, thick, liquid mud or similar substance —'**slimy** a. 1. like slime 2. fawning

sling (slɪŋ) n. 1. strap, loop with string attached at each end for hurling stone 2. bandage for supporting wounded limb 3. rope, belt etc. for hoisting, carrying weights —vt. 4. throw 5. hoist, swing by rope (**slung**, '**slinging**) —'**slingback** n. shoe with strap instead of full covering for heel

slink (slɪŋk) vi. move stealthily, sneak (**slunk**, '**slinking**) —'**slinky** a. 1. sinuously graceful a. (of clothes etc.) figure-hugging

slip[1] (slɪp) v. 1. (cause to) move smoothly, easily, quietly 2. pass out of (mind etc.) 3. (of motor vehicle clutch) engage partially, fail —vi. 4. lose balance by sliding 5. fall from person's grasp 6. (usu. with up) make mistake 7. decline in health, morals —vt. 8. put on or take off easily, quickly 9. let go (anchor etc.) 10. dislocate (bone) (**-pp-**) —n. 11. act or occasion of slipping 12. mistake 13. petticoat 14. small piece of paper 15. plant cutting 16. launching slope on which ships are built 17. Cricket (fieldsman in) position offside and a little behind wicket 18. covering for pillow —'**slippy** a. 1. see SLIPPERY (sense 1) UK inf. alert —'**slipknot** n. knot tied so that it will slip along rope round which it is made (also **running knot**) —**slip-on** a. 1. (of garment or shoe) easily put on or removed —n. 2. slip-on garment or shoe —**slipped disc** Pathol. herniated intervertebral disc, oft. resulting in pain due to pressure on spinal nerves —**slip road** narrow road giving access to motorway etc. —'**slipshod** a. slovenly, careless —'**slipstream** n. Aviation stream of air driven astern by engine —**slip-up** n. inf. mistake or mishap —'**slipway** n. incline for launching ships —**slip up** inf. blunder

slip[2] (slɪp) n. clay mixed with water to creamy consistency, used for decorating ceramic ware

slipper ('slɪpə) n. light shoe for indoor use

slippery ('slɪpərɪ, -prɪ) a. 1. so smooth as to cause slipping or to be difficult to hold or catch 2. changeable 3. unreliable 4. crafty, wily

slit (slɪt) vt. 1. make long straight cut in 2. cut in strips (**slit**, '**slitting**) —n. 3. long narrow cut or opening

slither ('slɪðə) vi. slide unsteadily (down slope etc.)

sliver ('slɪvə) n. 1. thin small piece torn off something 2. splinter

slob (slɒb) n. inf. stupid, coarse person

slobber ('slɒbə) or **slabber** ('slæbə) vi. 1. slaver 2. be weakly and excessively demonstrative —n. 3. running saliva 4. maudlin speech —'**slobbery** or '**slabbery** a.

slob ice C sludgy masses of floating ice

sloe (sləʊ) n. blue-black, sour fruit of blackthorn —**sloe-eyed** a. having dark slanted or almond-shaped eyes

slog (slɒg) vt. 1. hit vigorously, esp. at cricket —vi. 2. work or study with dogged determination 3. move, work with difficulty (**-gg-**) —n. 4. tiring walk 5. long exhausting work 6. heavy blow

slogan ('sləʊgən) n. distinctive phrase (in advertising etc.)

sloop (slu:p) n. 1. small one-masted vessel 2. Hist. small warship

sloot (slu:t) n. SA ditch for irrigation or drainage

slop (slɒp) vi. 1. spill —vt. 2. spill, splash (**-pp-**) —n. 3. liquid spilt 4. liquid food 5. dirty liquid —pl. 6. liquid refuse —'**sloppy** a. 1. careless, untidy 2. sentimental 3. wet, muddy

slope (sləʊp) vt. 1. place slanting —vi. 2. lie in, follow an inclined course 3. go furtively —n. 4. slant 5. upward, downward inclination

slosh (slɒʃ) n. 1. watery mud, snow etc. 2. sl. heavy blow —v. 3. splash —vt. 4. hit —**sloshed** a. sl. drunk

slot (slɒt) n. 1. narrow hole or depression 2. slit for coins —vt. 3. put in slot 4. sort 5. inf. place in series, organization (**-tt-**) —**slot machine** automatic machine worked by insertion of coin

sloth (sləʊθ) n. 1. sluggish S Amer. animal 2. sluggishness —'**slothful** a. lazy, idle

slouch (slaʊtʃ) vi. 1. walk, sit etc. in lazy or ungainly, drooping manner —n. 2. drooping bearing 3. incompetent or slovenly person —a. 4. (of hat) with wide, flexible brim

slough[1] (slaʊ) n. 1. bog 2. (slu:) C hole where water collects

slough[2] (slʌf) n. 1. skin shed by snake —v. 2. shed (skin) —**slough off** cast off (cares etc.)

sloven ('slʌvən) n. dirty, untidy person —'**slovenly** a. 1. untidy 2. careless 3. disorderly —adv. 4. in slovenly manner

slow (sləʊ) a. 1. lasting a long time 2. moving at low speed 3. behind the true time 4. dull —v. 5. (cause to) decrease in speed —'**slowly** adv. —'**slowness** n. —'**slowcoach** n. person slow in moving, acting, deciding etc. —**slow-motion** a. (of film) showing movement greatly slowed down

slowworm ('sləʊwɜ:m) n. small legless lizard, blindworm

sludge (slʌdʒ) n. 1. slush, ooze 2. sewage

slue[1] (slu:) v. esp. US see SLEW[2]

slue[2] (slu:) n. see SLOUGH[1] (sense 2)

slug[1] (slʌg) n. 1. land snail with no shell 2. bullet —'**sluggard** n. lazy, idle person —'**sluggish** a. 1. slow 2. lazy, inert 3. not functioning well

slug[2] (slʌg) vt. 1. hit, slog (**-gg-**) —n. 2. heavy

blow **3.** portion of spirits —**'slugger** *n.* hard-hitting boxer, slogger

sluice (slu:s) *n.* **1.** gate, door to control flow of water —*vt.* **2.** pour water over, through

slum (slʌm) *n.* **1.** squalid street or neighbourhood —*vi.* **2.** visit slums (**-mm-**)

slumber ('slʌmbə) *vi./n.* sleep —**'slumberer** *n.*

slump (slʌmp) *vi.* **1.** fall heavily **2.** relax ungracefully **3.** decline suddenly in value, volume or esteem —*n.* **4.** sudden decline **5.** (of prices *etc.*) sharp fall **6.** depression

slung (slʌŋ) *pt./pp. of* SLING

slunk (slʌŋk) *pt./pp. of* SLINK

slur (slɜ:) *vt.* **1.** pass over lightly **2.** run together (words, musical notes) **3.** disparage (**-rr-**) —*n.* **4.** slight, stigma **5.** *Mus.* curved line above or below notes to be slurred

slurp (slɜ:p) *v. inf.* eat, drink noisily

slurry ('slʌrı) *n.* muddy liquid mixture, such as cement, mud *etc.*

slush (slʌʃ) *n.* **1.** watery, muddy substance **2.** excess sentimentality —**slush fund** *US* fund for financing bribery, corruption

slut (slʌt) *n.* dirty (immoral) woman —**'sluttish** *a.* —**'sluttishness** *n.*

sly (slaı) *a.* **1.** cunning, wily, knowing **2.** secret, deceitful —**'slyly** *or* **'slily** *adv.* —**'slyness** *n.*

Sm *Chem.* samarium

smack[1] (smæk) *n.* **1.** taste, flavour **2.** *sl.* heroin —*vi.* (*with* of) **3.** have taste (of) **4.** be suggestive (of)

smack[2] (smæk) *vt.* **1.** slap **2.** open and close (lips) with loud sound —*n.* **3.** smacking slap **4.** crack **5.** such sound **6.** loud kiss —*adv.* **7.** *inf.* squarely; directly —**'smacker** *n. sl.* **1.** loud kiss **2.** pound note or dollar bill

smack[3] (smæk) *n.* small sailing vessel, usu. for fishing

small (smɔ:l) *a.* **1.** little **2.** unimportant; petty **3.** short **4.** weak **5.** mean —*n.* **6.** small slender part, *esp.* of the back —*pl.* **7.** *inf.* personal laundry, underwear —**'smallness** *n.* —**small beer** *inf.*, *chiefly* UK people or things of no importance —**small change 1.** coins, *esp.* those of low value **2.** *rare* person or thing of little importance —**'smallholding** *n.* small area of farming land —**small hours** hours just after midnight —**small-minded** *a.* having narrow views; petty —**'smallpox** *n.* contagious disease —**small-scale** *a.* **1.** of limited size **2.** (of map *etc.*) giving small representation of something —**small talk** light, polite conversation —**small-time** *a. inf.* insignificant —**small-timer** *n.*

smarm (smɑ:m) *vi. inf.* fawn —**'smarmy** *a. inf.* unpleasantly suave; fawning

smart (smɑ:t) *a.* **1.** astute **2.** brisk **3.** clever, witty **4.** impertinent **5.** trim, well dressed **6.** fashionable **7.** causing stinging pain —*v.* **8.** feel,

cause pain —*n.* **9.** sharp pain —**'smarten** *v.* —**'smartness** *n.* —**smart aleck** ('ælık) *or* **'smarty** *inf.* conceited person, know-all

smash (smæʃ) *vt.* **1.** break violently **2.** strike hard **3.** ruin **4.** destroy —*vi.* **5.** break **6.** dash violently —*n.* **7.** heavy blow **8.** collision (of vehicles *etc.*) **9.** total financial failure **10.** *inf.* popular success —**smashed** *a. sl.* very drunk or affected by drugs —**'smasher** *n. inf.* attractive person, thing —**'smashing** *a. inf., chiefly* UK excellent —**smash-and-grab** *a. inf.* of robbery in which shop window is broken and contents removed

smattering ('smætərıŋ) *n.* slight superficial knowledge

smear (smıə) *vt.* **1.** rub with grease *etc.* **2.** smudge, spread with dirt, grease *etc.* —*n.* **3.** mark made thus **4.** sample of secretion for medical examination **5.** slander

smell (smɛl) *vt.* **1.** perceive by nose **2.** *fig.* suspect —*vi.* **3.** give out odour **4.** use nose (**smelt** *or* **smelled**, **'smelling**) —*n.* **5.** faculty of perceiving odours by nose **6.** anything detected by sense of smell —**'smelly** *a.* with strong (unpleasant) smell —**smelling salts** preparation of ammonium carbonate that has stimulant action when sniffed in cases of faintness *etc.*

smelt[1] (smɛlt) *vt.* extract (metal) from (ore) —**'smeltery** *n.*

smelt[2] (smɛlt) *n.* fish of salmon family

smew (smju:) *n.* type of duck

smilax ('smaɪlæks) *n.* **1.** climbing shrub having slightly lobed leaves and berry-like fruits **2.** much branched vine of S Afr. with glossy green foliage

smile (smaɪl) *n.* **1.** curving or parting of lips in pleased or amused expression —*vi.* **2.** wear, assume a smile **3.** (*with* on) approve, favour

smirch (smɜ:tʃ) *vt.* **1.** dirty, sully **2.** disgrace, discredit —*n.* **3.** stain **4.** disgrace

smirk (smɜ:k) *n.* **1.** smile expressing scorn, smugness —*vi.* **2.** give such smile

smite (smaɪt) *vt.* **1.** strike **2.** attack **3.** afflict **4.** affect, *esp.* with love or fear (**smote**, **'smitten**, **'smiting**)

smith (smıθ) *n.* worker in iron, gold *etc.* —**smithy** ('smıðı) *n.* blacksmith's workshop

smithereens (smıðə'ri:nz) *pl.n.* small bits

smitten ('smıt²n) *pp. of* SMITE

smock (smɒk) *n.* **1.** loose outer garment —*vt.* **2.** gather by sewing in honeycomb pattern

smog (smɒg) *n.* mixture of smoke and fog

smoke (sməʊk) *n.* **1.** cloudy mass of suspended particles that rises from fire or anything burning **2.** spell of tobacco smoking —*vi.* **3.** give off smoke **4.** inhale and expel tobacco smoke —*vt.* **5.** use (tobacco) by smoking **6.** expose to smoke (*esp.* in curing fish *etc.*) —'smoker *n.* —'smokily *adv.* —'smoky *a.* —smoke screen 1. *Mil.* cloud of smoke produced to obscure movements 2. something said or done to conceal truth —'smokestack *n.* chimney that conveys smoke into air

smolt (sməʊlt) *n.* young salmon at stage when it migrates from fresh water to sea

smooch (smuːtʃ) *vi./n. inf.* kiss, cuddle

smooth (smuːð) *a.* 1. not rough, even of surface or texture 2. sinuous 3. flowing 4. calm, soft, soothing 5. suave, plausible 6. free from jolts —*vt.* 7. make smooth 8. quieten —'smoothly *adv.* —smooth-spoken *a.* speaking in gently persuasive manner —smooth-tongued *a.* suave or persuasive in speech

smorgasbord ('smɔːɡəsbɔːd) *n.* buffet meal of assorted dishes

smote (sməʊt) *pt.* of SMITE

smother ('smʌðə) *vt.* 1. suffocate 2. envelop 3. suppress —*vi.* 4. be suffocated

smoulder or *U.S.* smolder ('sməʊldə) *vi.* 1. burn slowly without flame 2. (of feelings) exist in suppressed state

smudge (smʌdʒ) *n.* 1. make smear, stain, dirty mark on —*n.* 2. smear or dirty mark

smug (smʌɡ) *a.* self-satisfied, complacent

smuggle ('smʌɡəl) *vt.* 1. import, export without paying customs duties 2. conceal, take secretly

smut (smʌt) *n.* 1. piece of soot, particle of dirt 2. lewd or obscene talk —*vt.* 3. disease of grain 4. blacken, smudge (-tt-) —'smutty *a.* soiled with smut, soot 2. obscene, lewd

Sn *Chem.* tin

snack (snæk) *n.* light, hasty meal —snack bar bar at which snacks are served

snaffle ('snæfəl) *n.* 1. light bit for horse —*vt.* 2. *sl.* appropriate, scrounge 3. put snaffle on

snag (snæɡ) *n.* 1. difficulty 2. sharp protuberance 3. hole, loop in fabric caused by sharp object 4. obstacle (eg tree branch *etc.* in river bed) —*vt.* 5. catch, damage on snag

snail (sneɪl) *n.* 1. slow-moving mollusc with shell 2. slow, sluggish person —snail-like *a.* —snail's pace very slow rate

snake (sneɪk) *n.* 1. long scaly limbless reptile, serpent —*vi.* 2. move like snake —'snaky *a.* of, like snakes —snake charmer entertainer who appears to charm snakes by playing music —snakes and ladders board game in which tossed dice determine how far counters move either to climb up ladders or slide down snakes

snap (snæp) *v.* 1. break suddenly 2. (cause to) make cracking sound 3. bite (at) suddenly 4. speak (words) suddenly, angrily —*n.* 5. act of snapping 6. fastener 7. *inf.* snapshot 8. *inf.* easy task 9. brief period, *esp.* of cold weather —*a.* 10. sudden, unplanned, arranged quickly —'snap-

per *n.* perchlike fish —'snappy *a.* 1. irritable 2. *sl.* quick 3. *sl.* well-dressed, fashionable —'snapdragon *n.* plant with flowers that can be opened like a mouth —snap fastener press stud —'snapshot *n.* photograph

snare¹ (snɛə) *n.* 1. (noose used as) trap —*vt.* 2. catch with one

snare² (snɛə) *n. Mus.* set of gut strings wound with wire fitted across bottom of drum to increase vibration —snare drum *Mus.* cylindrical double-headed drum with snares

snarl (snɑːl) *n.* 1. growl of angry dog 2. tangle, knot —*vi.* 3. utter snarl 4. grumble —snarl-up *n. inf.* confusion, obstruction, *esp.* traffic jam

snatch (snætʃ) *vt.* 1. make quick grab or bite at 2. seize, catch —*n.* 3. grab 4. fragment 5. short spell

snazzy ('snæzɪ) *a. inf.* stylish, flashy

sneak (sniːk) *vi.* 1. slink 2. move about furtively 3. act in mean, underhand manner —*n.* 4. mean, treacherous person 5. petty informer —'sneaking *a.* secret but persistent —sneak thief person who steals articles from premises which he enters through open windows *etc.*

sneakers ('sniːkəz) *pl.n. chiefly US* flexible, informal sports shoes

sneer (snɪə) *n.* 1. scornful, contemptuous expression or remark —*vi.* 2. assume scornful expression —*v.* 3. speak or utter contemptuously

sneeze (sniːz) *vi.* 1. emit breath through nose with sudden involuntary spasm and noise —*n.* 2. sound or act of sneezing

snick (snɪk) *n.* 1. small cut or notch, nick —*vt.* 2. cut; clip; nick

snicker ('snɪkə) *see* SNIGGER

snide (snaɪd) *a.* malicious, supercilious

sniff (snɪf) *vi.* 1. inhale through nose with sharp hiss 2. (with at) express disapproval *etc.* by sniffing —*vt.* 3. take up through nose 4. smell —*n.* 5. act or sound of sniffing —'sniffle *vi.* sniff noisily through nose, *esp.* when suffering from a cold in the head, snuffle

snifter ('snɪftə) *n.* 1. pear-shaped glass with bowl that narrows towards the top so that aroma of brandy *etc.* is retained 2. *inf.* small alcoholic drink

snigger ('snɪɡə) *n.* 1. sly, disrespectful laugh, *esp.* partly stifled —*vi.* 2. utter such laugh

snip (snɪp) *v.* 1. cut (bits off) (-pp-) —*n.* 2. act, sound of snipping 3. bit cut off 4. *inf.* bargain 5. *inf.* certainty —'snippet *n.* shred, fragment, clipping —snips *pl.n.* tool for cutting

snipe (snaɪp) *n.* 1. wading bird —*v.* 2. shoot at (enemy) from cover 3. (with at) criticize, attack (person) slyly —'sniper *n.*

snitch (snɪtʃ) *inf. vt.* 1. steal —*vi.* 2. inform on someone —*n.* 3. telltale

snivel ('snɪvᵊl) vi. 1. sniffle to show distress 2. whine (-ll-)

snob (snɒb) n. one who pretentiously judges others by social rank etc. —'**snobbery** n. —'**snobbish** a. of, like snob —'**snobbishly** adv.

snoek (snʊk) n. SA barracouta

snood (snu:d) n. 1. pouchlike hat, worn at back of head to hold woman's hair 2. Scot. headband, esp. formerly worn by young unmarried women

snook (snu:k) n. UK rude gesture, made by putting one thumb to nose with fingers outstretched (esp. in **cock a snook at**)

snooker ('snu:kə) n. 1. game played on billiard table —vt. 2. leave (opponent) in unfavourable position 3. place (someone) in difficult situation

snoop (snu:p) vi. 1. pry, meddle 2. peer —n. 3. one who acts thus 4. act or instance of snooping

snooty ('snu:tɪ) a. sl. haughty

snooze (snu:z) vi. 1. take short sleep, be half asleep —n. 2. nap

snore (snɔ:) vi. 1. breathe noisily when asleep —n. 2. noise of snoring

snorkel ('snɔ:kᵊl) n. 1. tube for breathing underwater —vi. 2. swim, fish using this (-ll-)

snort (snɔ:t) vi. 1. make (contemptuous) noise by driving breath through nostrils —n. 2. such noise

snot (snɒt) n. vulg. mucus from nose

snout (snaʊt) n. animal's nose

snow (snəʊ) n. 1. frozen vapour which falls in flakes 2. sl. cocaine —v. 3. fall, sprinkle as snow —vt. 4. let fall, throw down like snow 5. cover with snow —'**snowy** a. 1. of, like snow 2. covered with snow 3. very white —'**snowball** n. 1. snow pressed into hard ball for throwing —vi. 2. increase rapidly in importance etc. 3. play, fight with snowballs —'**snowberry** n. shrub with small pink flowers and white berries —**snow blindness** temporary blindness due to brightness of snow —'**snowdrift** n. bank of deep snow —'**snowdrop** n. small, white, bell-shaped spring flower —'**snowfall** n. 1. fall of snow 2. Met. amount of snow received in specified place and time —**snow fence** C fence erected in winter beside exposed road —'**snowflake** n. 1. one of mass of ice crystals that fall as snow 2. any of various European plants that have white bell-shaped flowers —**snow goose** white N Amer. goose —**snow-in-summer** n. rock plant with white flowers —**snow line** elevation above which snow does not melt —'**snowman** n. figure shaped out of snow —'**snowmobile** n. C motor vehicle with caterpillar tracks and front skis —'**snowplough** n. implement or vehicle for clearing away snow —'**snowshoes** pl.n. shoes like rackets for travelling on snow —**snow under** 1. cover and block with snow 2. fig. overwhelm

SNP Scottish National Party

snub (snʌb) vt. 1. insult (esp. by ignoring) intentionally (-bb-) —n. 2. snubbing, rebuff —a. 3. short and blunt

snuff¹ (snʌf) n. powdered tobacco for inhaling through nose

snuff² (snʌf) vt. extinguish (esp. light from candle) —'**snuffer** n. 1. cone-shaped implement for extinguishing candles —pl. 2. instrument resembling scissors for trimming wick of candle —**snuff it** sl. die

snuffle ('snʌfᵊl) vi. breathe noisily or with difficulty

snug (snʌg) a. warm, comfortable —'**snuggle** v. lie close to, for warmth or affection —'**snugly** adv.

snye (snaɪ) n. C side channel of river

so¹ (səʊ) adv. 1. to such an extent 2. in such a manner 3. very 4. the case being such 5. accordingly —conj. 6. therefore 7. in order that 8. with the result that —interj. 9. well —**so-and-so** n. inf. 1. person whose name is forgotten or ignored 2. euphemistic person or thing regarded as unpleasant —**so-called** a. called by but doubtfully deserving the name —**so long** interj. 1. inf. farewell; goodbye —adv. 2. SA sl. in the meantime, for the time being

so² (səʊ) n. Mus. see SOH

So. south(ern)

soak (səʊk) v. 1. steep —vt. 2. absorb 3. drench —vi. 4. lie in liquid —n. 5. soaking 6. sl. habitual drunkard

soap (səʊp) n. 1. compound of alkali and oil used in washing —vt. 2. apply soap to —'**soapy** a. —'**soapbox** n. crate used as platform for speech-making —**soap opera** radio or television serial of domestic life —'**soapstone** n. massive compact variety of talc, used for making hearths etc. (also '**steatite**)

soar (sɔ:) vi. 1. fly high 2. increase, rise (in price etc.)

sob (sɒb) vi. 1. catch breath, esp. in weeping (-bb-) —n. 2. sobbing —**sob story** tale of personal distress told to arouse sympathy

sober ('səʊbə) a. 1. not drunk 2. temperate 3. subdued 4. dull, plain 5. solemn —v. 6. make, become sober —'**soberly** adv. —so'**briety** n. state of being sober

sobriquet or **soubriquet** ('səʊbrɪkeɪ) n. 1. nickname 2. assumed name

Soc. or **soc.** Society

soccer ('sɒkə) n. game of football played with spherical ball

sociable ('səʊʃəbᵊl) a. 1. friendly 2. convivial —socia'**bility** n. —'**sociably** adv.

social ('səʊʃᵊl) a. 1. living in communities 2. relating to society 3. sociable —n. 4. informal gathering —'**socialite** n. member of fashionable society —**sociali'zation** or **-li'sation** n. —**socialize** or **-lise** v. —**socially** adv. —**social contract** or **compact** agreement entered into by individuals, that results in formation of state and entails surrender of some personal liberties —**social science** study of society and of relationship of individual members within society, including economics, history, psychology etc. —**social security** state provision for the unemployed, aged etc. —**social services** welfare activities organized by state —**social studies** (with sing. v.) study of how people live and organize themselves in society, embracing geography, economics etc. —**social work** work to improve welfare of others

socialism ('səʊʃəlɪzəm) n. political system which advocates public ownership of means of production, distribution and exchange —**social-ist** n./a. —**socia'listic** a.

society (sə'saɪətɪ) n. **1.** living associated with others **2.** those so living **3.** companionship **4.** company **5.** association **6.** club **7.** fashionable people collectively

socio- (comb. form) denoting social or society, as in socioeconomic

socioeconomic (səʊsɪəʊiːkə'nɒmɪk) a. of or involving both economic and social factors

sociology (səʊsɪ'ɒlədʒɪ) n. study of societies

sociopolitical (səʊsɪəʊpə'lɪtɪk°l) a. of or involving both political and social factors

sock[1] (sɒk) n. cloth covering for foot

sock[2] (sɒk) sl. vt. **1.** hit —n. **2.** blow

socket ('sɒkɪt) n. hole or recess for something to fit into

Socratic (sɒ'krætɪk) a. of, like Gr. philosopher Socrates

sod (sɒd) n. **1.** lump of earth with grass **2.** sl. person considered obnoxious **3.** sl. person, as specified

soda ('səʊdə) n. **1.** compound of sodium **2.** soda water —**soda fountain** US **1.** counter that serves drinks, snacks etc. **2.** apparatus dispensing soda water —**soda water** water charged with carbon dioxide

sodden ('sɒd°n) a. **1.** soaked **2.** drunk **3.** heavy and doughy

sodium ('səʊdɪəm) n. metallic alkaline element —**sodium bicarbonate** white crystalline soluble compound used in baking powder etc. (also **bicarbonate of soda**) —**sodium carbonate** soluble crystalline compound used in manufacture of glass, ceramics, soap and paper, and as cleansing agent —**sodium chloride** common table salt

Sodom ('sɒdəm) n. **1.** O.T. city that, with Gomorrah, traditionally typifies depravity **2.** this city as representing homosexuality **3.** any place notorious for depravity

sodomy ('sɒdəmɪ) n. anal intercourse —**sodo-mite** n.

sofa ('səʊfə) n. upholstered seat with back and arms, for two or more people

soft (sɒft) a. **1.** yielding easily to pressure **2.** mild **3.** easy **4.** subdued **5.** quiet, gentle **6.** (too) lenient **7.** oversentimental **8.** feeble-minded **9.** (of water) containing few mineral salts **10.** (of drugs) not liable to cause addiction —**soften** ('sɒf°n) v. **1.** make, become soft or softer —vt. **2.** mollify **3.** lighten **4.** mitigate **5.** make less loud —**softly** adv. gently, quietly —**softy** or **softie** n. inf. person who is sentimental, weakly foolish or lacking in physical endurance —**soft-boiled** a. (of egg) boiled for a short time so that yolk remains soft —**soft drink** drink that is nonalcoholic —**soft furnishings** curtains, rugs etc. —**soft'hearted** a. easily moved to pity —**soft palate** posterior fleshy portion of roof of mouth —**soft-pedal** vt. **1.** mute tone of (piano) **2.** inf. make (something) less obvious by deliberately failing to emphasize it —**soft pedal** foot-operated lever on piano that causes fewer of strings to sound —**soft sell** chiefly US method of selling based on indirect suggestion or inducement —**soft shoe** (of tap dancing) shoe without metal taps on shoes —**soft soap** flattery —**soft spot** sentimental fondness —**'software** n. computer programs, tapes etc. for a particular computer system —**'softwood** n. wood of coniferous tree

SOGAT ('səʊgæt) UK Society of Graphical and Allied Trades

soggy ('sɒgɪ) a. **1.** soaked with liquid **2.** damp and heavy

soh or **so** (səʊ) n. Mus. in tonic sol-fa, name used for fifth note or dominant of any scale

soigné or (fem.) **soignée** ('swɑːnjeɪ) a. well-groomed

soil[1] (sɔɪl) n. **1.** earth, ground **2.** country, territory

soil[2] (sɔɪl) v. **1.** make, become dirty —vt. **2.** tarnish, defile —n. **3.** dirt **4.** sewage **5.** stain

soiree ('swɑːreɪ) n. private evening party, esp. with music

sojourn ('sɒdʒɜːn, 'sʌdʒ-) vi. **1.** stay for a time —n. **2.** short stay —'**sojourner** n.

sol (sɒl) n. Mus. see SOH

solace ('sɒlɪs) n./vt. comfort in distress

solar ('səʊlə) a. of the sun —**solari'zation** or **-i'sation** n. —**'solarize** or **-ise** vt. affect by sunlight —**solar cell** cell that produces electricity from sun's rays —**solar plexus** ('plɛksəs) network of nerves at pit of stomach —**solar system** system containing sun and heavenly bodies held in its gravitational field

solarium (səʊ'lɛərɪəm) n. **1.** room built mainly

of glass to give exposure to sun **2.** (place with) bed for acquiring suntan by artificial means

sold (səʊld) *pt./pp. of* SELL

solder ('səʊldə; *U.S.* 'spdər) *n.* **1.** easily-melted alloy used for joining metal —*vt.* **2.** join with solder —**soldering iron**

soldier ('səʊldʒə) *n.* **1.** one serving in army —*vi.* **2.** serve in army **3.** (*with* on) persist doggedly —'**soldierly** *a.* —'**soldiery** *n.* troops —**soldier of fortune** man who seeks money or adventure as soldier

sole¹ (səʊl) *a.* **1.** one and only, unique **2.** solitary —'**solely** *adv.* **1.** alone **2.** only **3.** entirely

sole² (səʊl) *n.* **1.** underside of foot **2.** underpart of boot *etc.* —*vt.* **3.** fit with sole

sole³ (səʊl) *n.* small edible flatfish

solecism ('spltsizəm) *n.* breach of grammar or etiquette

solemn ('spləm) *a.* **1.** serious **2.** formal **3.** impressive —**solemnity** (sə'lemnɪtɪ) *n.* —**solemnization** *or* **-isation** (spləmnaɪ'zeɪʃən) *n.* —'**solemnize** *or* **-ise** ('spləmnaɪz) *vt.* **1.** celebrate, perform **2.** make solemn —'**solemnly** *adv.*

solenoid ('səʊlɪnɔɪd) *n.* coil of wire as part of electrical apparatus

sol-fa ('spl'fɑː) *n. Mus.* system of syllables sol, fa *etc.* sung in scale

solicit (sə'lɪsɪt) *vt.* **1.** request **2.** accost **3.** urge **4.** entice —**solici'tation** *n.* —**so'licitor** *n.* lawyer who prepares documents, advises clients, but represents them in lower courts only —**so'licitous** *a.* **1.** anxious **2.** eager **3.** earnest —**so'licitude** *n.* —**Solicitor General** UK law officer of Crown ranking next to Attorney General

solid ('splɪd) *a.* **1.** not hollow **2.** compact **3.** composed of one substance **4.** firm **5.** massive **6.** reliable, sound —*n.* **7.** body of three dimensions **8.** substance not liquid or gas —**soli'darity** *n.* **1.** unity of interests **2.** united state —**solidifi'cation** *n.* —**so'lidify** *v.* **1.** make, become solid or firm **2.** harden (**-ified, -ifying**) —**so'lidity** *n.* —'**solidly** *adv.* —**solid geometry** branch of geometry concerned with solid geometric figures —**solid-state** *a.* (of electronic device) consisting chiefly of semiconductor materials and controlled by means of their electrical properties

solidus ('splɪdəs) *n.* short stroke (/) used in text to separate items (*pl.* **-di** (-daɪ))

soliloquy (sə'lɪləkwɪ) *n. esp.* in drama, thoughts spoken by person while alone —**so'liloquize** *or* **-ise** *v.*

solipsism ('splɪpsɪzəm) *n.* doctrine that self is the only thing known to exist —'**solipsist** *n.*

solitary ('splɪtərɪ, -trɪ) *a.* **1.** alone, single —*n.* **2.** hermit —**soli'taire** *n.* **1.** game for one person

played with pegs set in board **2.** single precious stone, *esp.* diamond, set by itself —'**solitude** *n.* **1.** state of being alone **2.** loneliness —**solitary confinement** isolation imposed on prisoner

solo ('səʊləʊ) *n.* **1.** music for one performer (*pl.* **-s, -li** (-liː)) **2.** card game like whist (*pl.* **-s**) —*a.* **3.** not concerted **4.** unaccompanied, alone **5.** piloting aeroplane alone —'**soloist** *n.*

solstice ('splstɪs) *n.* either shortest (winter) or longest (summer) day of year —**solstitial** (spl'stɪʃəl) *a.*

solve (splv) *vt.* **1.** work out, explain **2.** find answer to —**solubility** (spljʊ'bɪlɪtɪ) *n.* —**soluble** ('spljʊbᵊl) *a.* **1.** capable of being dissolved in liquid **2.** able to be solved or explained —**so'lute** *n.* **1.** substance dissolved in solution —*a.* **2.** *Bot.* unattached —**solution** (sə'luːʃən) *n.* **1.** answer to problem **2.** dissolving **3.** liquid with something dissolved in it —'**solvable** *a.* —'**solvency** *n.* —'**solvent** *a.* **1.** able to meet financial obligations —*n.* **2.** liquid with power of dissolving

Som. Somerset

somatic (səʊ'mætɪk) *a.* **1.** of the body, as distinct from the mind **2.** of animal body or body wall as distinct from viscera, limbs and head

sombre *or U.S.* **somber** ('spmbə) *a.* dark, gloomy

sombrero (spm'breərəʊ) *n.* wide-brimmed hat (*pl.* **-s**)

some (sʌm; *unstressed* səm) *a.* **1.** denoting an indefinite number, amount or extent **2.** one or other **3.** amount of **4.** certain **5.** approximately —*pron.* **6.** portion, quantity —'**somebody** *pron.* **1.** some person —*n.* **2.** important person —'**somehow** *adv.* by some means unknown —'**someone** *pron.* some person —'**something** *pron.* **1.** thing not clearly defined **2.** indefinite amount, quantity or degree —'**sometime** *adv.* **1.** formerly **2.** at some (past or future) time —*a.* **3.** former —'**sometimes** *adv.* **1.** occasionally **2.** now and then —'**somewhat** *adv.* to some extent, rather —'**somewhere** *adv.*

somersault *or* **summersault** ('sʌməsɔːlt) *n.* tumbling head over heels

somnambulism (spm'næmbjʊlɪst) *n.* sleepwalker —som'nambulism *n.* —**somnambu'listic** *a.*

somnolent ('spmnələnt) *a.* **1.** drowsy **2.** causing sleep —'**somnolence** *or* '**somnolency** *n.*

son (sʌn) *n.* male child —'**sonny** *n.* familiar term of address to boy or man —**son-in-law** *n.* daughter's husband

sonar ('səʊnɑː) *n.* device like echo sounder

sonata (sə'nɑːtə) *n.* piece of music in several movements —**sonatina** (spnə'tiːnə) *n.* short sonata

son et lumière ('spn eɪ 'luːmɪeə) *Fr.*

entertainment staged at night at famous place, building, giving dramatic history of it with lighting and sound effects

song (sɒŋ) n. 1. singing 2. poem etc. for singing —'**songster** n. 1. singer 2. songbird ('**songstress** fem.)

sonic ('sɒnɪk) a. pert. to sound waves —**sonic barrier** see **sound barrier** at SOUND¹ —**sonic boom** explosive sound caused by aircraft travelling at supersonic speed

sonnet ('sɒnɪt) n. fourteen-line poem with definite rhyme scheme —**sonne'teer** n. writer of this

sonorous (sə'nɔːrəs, 'sɒnərəs) a. giving out (deep) sound, resonant —**sonority** (sə'nɒrɪtɪ) n. —so'norously adv.

soon (suːn) adv. 1. in a short time 2. before long 3. early, quickly

soot (sʊt) n. black powdery substance formed by burning of coal etc. —'**sooty** a. of, like soot

sooth (suːθ) n. truth —'**soothsayer** n. one who foretells future, diviner

soothe (suːð) vt. 1. make calm, tranquil 2. relieve (pain etc.)

sop (sɒp) n. 1. piece of bread etc. soaked in liquid 2. concession, bribe —vt. 3. steep in water etc. 4. soak (up) (**-pp-**) —'**sopping** a. completely soaked —'**soppy** a. inf. oversentimental

sophist ('sɒfɪst) n. fallacious reasoner, quibbler —'**sophism** n. specious argument —so'**phistical** a. —'**sophistry** n.

sophisticate (sə'fɪstɪkeɪt) vt. 1. make artificial, spoil, falsify, corrupt —n. (sə'fɪstɪkeɪt, -kɪt) 2. sophisticated person —so'**phisticated** a. 1. having refined or cultured tastes, habits 2. worldly-wise 3. superficially clever 4. complex —sophisti'cation n.

sophomore ('sɒfəmɔː) n. US student in second year at college

-sophy (n. comb. form) indicating knowledge or intellectual system, as in philosophy —**-sophic** or **-sophical** (a. comb. form)

soporific (sɒpə'rɪfɪk) a. 1. causing sleep (esp. by drugs) —n. 2. drug or other agent that induces sleep

soprano (sə'prɑːnəʊ) n. 1. highest voice in women and boys 2. singer with this voice 3. musical part for it (pl. **-s**)

sorbet ('sɔːbɪt, -beɪ) n. (fruit-flavoured) water ice

sorcerer ('sɔːsərə) or (fem.) **sorceress** ('sɔːsərɪs) n. magician —'**sorcery** n. witchcraft, magic

sordid ('sɔːdɪd) a. 1. mean, squalid 2. ignoble, base —'**sordidly** adv. —'**sordidness** n.

sore (sɔː) a. 1. painful 2. causing annoyance 3. severe 4. distressed 5. annoyed —adv. 6. obs.

grievously, intensely —n. 7. sore place, ulcer, boil etc. —'**sorely** adv. 1. grievously 2. greatly

sorghum ('sɔːgəm) n. kind of grass cultivated for grain

sorority (sə'rɒrɪtɪ) n. chiefly US social club or society for university women

sorrel ('sɒrəl) n. 1. plant 2. reddish-brown colour 3. horse of this colour —a. 4. of this colour

sorrow ('sɒrəʊ) n. 1. pain of mind, grief, sadness —vi. 2. grieve —'**sorrowful** a.

sorry ('sɒrɪ) a. 1. feeling pity or regret 2. distressed 3. miserable, wretched 4. mean, poor —'**sorrily** adv. —'**sorriness** n.

sort (sɔːt) n. 1. kind or class —vt. 2. classify

sortie ('sɔːtɪ) n. sally by besieged forces

SOS 1. international code signal of distress 2. call for help

so-so a. inf. mediocre

sostenuto (sɒstə'nuːtəʊ) a./adv. Mus. in smooth sustained manner

sot (sɒt) n. habitual drunkard

sotto voce ('sɒtəʊ 'vəʊtʃɪ) It. in an undertone

sou (suː) n. 1. former French coin 2. small amount of money

soubrette (suː'brɛt) n. 1. minor female role in comedy 2. any flirtatious girl

soufflé ('suːfleɪ) n. dish of eggs beaten to froth, flavoured and baked

sough (saʊ) n. low murmuring sound as of wind in trees

sought (sɔːt) pt./pp. of SEEK

souk (suːk) n. open-air marketplace, esp. in N Afr. and Middle East

soul (səʊl) n. 1. spiritual and immortal part of human being 2. example, pattern 3. person —'**soulful** a. full of emotion or sentiment —'**soulless** a. 1. mechanical 2. lacking sensitivity or nobility 3. heartless, cruel —**soul-destroying** a. (of occupation etc.) monotonous —**soul food** inf. food, as yams etc., traditionally eaten by U.S. Negroes —**soul mate** person for whom one has deep affinity —**soul music** type of Black music resulting from addition of jazz and gospel to urban blues style —**soul-searching** n. deep or critical examination of one's motives, actions etc.

sound (saʊnd) n. 1. what is heard 2. noise —vi. 3. make sound 4. seem 5. resonate with a certain quality —vt. 6. cause to sound 7. utter —**sound barrier** large increase in resistance encountered by aircraft approaching speed of sound —**sound effect** sound artificially produced to create theatrical effect, as in plays, films etc. —**sounding board** 1. thin wooden board in violin etc. designed to reflect sound 2. person etc. used to test new idea etc. —**sound track** recorded sound accompaniment of film *etc.* —**sound wave** wave that propagates sound

sound² (saund) *a.* **1.** in good condition **2.** solid **3.** of good judgment **4.** legal **5.** solvent **6.** thorough **7.** effective **8.** watertight **9.** deep —**'soundly** *adv.* thoroughly

sound³ (saund) *vt.* **1.** measure depth of (well, sea *etc.*) **2.** probe —**'soundings** *pl.n.* measurements taken by sounding —**sound out** ascertain views of

sound⁴ (saund) *n.* channel, strait

soup (suːp) *n.* liquid food made by boiling meat, vegetables *etc.* —**'soupy** *a.* **1.** like soup **2.** murky **3.** sentimental —**soup kitchen 1.** place where food, *esp.* soup, is served to destitute people **2.** *Mil.* mobile kitchen

soupçon (sup'sɔ̃) *Fr.* small amount

sour (sauə) *a.* **1.** acid **2.** gone bad **3.** rancid **4.** peevish **5.** disagreeable —*v.* **6.** make, become sour —**'sourly** *adv.* —**'sourness** *n.* —**sour grapes** attitude of despising something because one cannot have it oneself —**'sourpuss** *n.* sullen, sour-faced person

source (sɔːs) *n.* **1.** origin, starting point **2.** spring

souse (saus) *v.* **1.** plunge, drench or be drenched **2.** pickle —*n.* **3.** sousing **4.** brine for pickling

soutane (suː'tæn) *n.* priest's cassock

south (sauθ) *n.* **1.** cardinal point opposite north **2.** region, part of country *etc.* lying to that side —*a./adv.* **3.** (that is) towards south —**southerly** ('sʌðəlɪ) *a.* **1.** towards south —*n.* **2.** wind from the south —**southern** ('sʌðən) *a.* in south —**'Southerner** *n.* (*sometimes* s-) native or inhabitant of south of any specified region —**'southwards** *adv.* —**'Southdown** *n.* breed of sheep —**south'east** *n.* **1.** point of compass midway between south and east —*a.* **2.** (*sometimes* S-) denoting southeastern part of specified country *etc.* **3.** in, towards or facing southeast —*adv.* **4.** in, to, towards or (*esp.* of wind) from southeast —**South'east** *n.* (*usu.* *with* the) southeastern part of Britain —**Southern Cross** small constellation in S hemisphere whose four brightest stars form cross —**southern hemisphere** (*oft.* S- H-) that half of earth lying south of equator —**southern lights** aurora australis —**'southpaw** *inf.* *n.* **1.** any left-handed person, *esp.* a boxer —*a.* **2.** of or relating to southpaw —**South Pole** southernmost point on earth's axis —**South Seas** seas south of equator —**south-southeast** *n.* **1.** point on compass midway between southeast and south —*a./adv.* **2.** in, from or towards this direction —**south-southwest** *n.* **1.** point on compass midway between south and southwest —*a./adv.* **2.** in, from or towards this direction —**south'west** *n.* **1.** point on compass midway between west and south —*a.* **2.** (*sometimes* S-)

of or denoting southwestern part of specified country *etc.* **3.** in or towards southwest —*adv.* **4.** in, to, towards or (*esp.* of wind) from southwest —**South'west** *n.* (*usu.* *with* the) southwestern part of Britain

souvenir (suːvə'nɪə, 'suːvəniə) *n.* keepsake, memento

sou'wester (sau'wɛstə) *n.* waterproof hat

sovereign ('sɒvrɪn) *n.* **1.** king, queen **2.** former Brit. gold coin worth 20 shillings —*a.* **3.** supreme **4.** efficacious —**'sovereignty** *n.* **1.** supreme power and right to exercise it **2.** dominion **3.** independent state

soviet ('səuvɪət, 'sɒv-) *n.* **1.** elected council at various levels of government in U.S.S.R. **2.** (S-) citizen of U.S.S.R. —*a.* **3.** (S-) of U.S.S.R., its people or its government —**'sovietism** *n.*

sow¹ (səu) *vi.* **1.** scatter, plant seed —*vt.* **2.** scatter, deposit (seed) **3.** spread abroad (**sowed** *pt.,* **sown** *or* **sowed** *pp.,* **'sowing** *pr.p.*)

sow² (sau) *n.* female adult pig

soya bean ('sɔɪə) *or U.S.* **soybean** ('sɔɪbiːn) *n.* edible bean used as meat substitute in making soy sauce *etc.* —**soy sauce** (sɔɪ) salty, dark brown sauce made from fermented soya beans, used *esp.* in Chinese cookery (*also* **soya sauce**)

sozzled ('sɒzəld) *a. sl.* drunk

sp. 1. special **2.** species (*pl.* **spp.**) **3.** specific **4.** specimen **5.** spelling

spa (spɑ:) *n.* **1.** medicinal spring **2.** place or resort with such a spring

space (speɪs) *n.* **1.** extent **2.** room **3.** period **4.** empty place **5.** area **6.** expanse **7.** region beyond earth's atmosphere —*vt.* **8.** place at intervals —**spacious** ('speɪʃəs) *a.* roomy, extensive —**space age** period in which exploration of space has become possible —**space-age** *a.* ultramodern —**'spacecraft** *or* **'spaceship** *n.* vehicle for travel beyond earth's atmosphere —**'spaceman** *n.* —**space shuttle** vehicle designed to carry men and materials to space stations *etc.* —**space station** any manned artificial satellite designed to orbit earth and provide base for scientific research in space —**'spacesuit** *n.* sealed, pressurized suit worn by astronaut —**space-time** *n. Phys.* continuum having three spatial coordinates and one time coordinate that together specify location of particle or event (*also* **space-time continuum**)

spade¹ (speɪd) *n.* tool for digging —**'spadework** *n.* arduous preparatory work

spade² (speɪd) *n.* leaf-shaped black symbol on playing card

spadix ('speɪdɪks) *n.* spike of small flowers on fleshy stem, whole being enclosed in spathe (*pl.* **spadices** (speɪ'daɪsiːz))

spaghetti (spə'gɛtɪ) *n.* pasta in form of long strings

Spam (spæm) *n.* **R** kind of tinned luncheon meat

span (spæn) *n.* **1.** space from thumb to little finger as measure **2.** extent, space **3.** stretch of arch *etc.* **4.** distance from wingtip to wingtip (*also* '**wingspan**) —*vt.* **5.** stretch over **6.** measure with hand (**-nn-**)

spangle ('spæŋgəl) *n.* **1.** small shiny metallic ornament —*vt.* **2.** decorate with spangles

spaniel ('spænjəl) *n.* breed of dog with long ears and silky hair

Spanish ('spænɪʃ) *n.* **1.** official language of Spain, Mexico and most countries of S and Central Amer., except Brazil —*a.* **2.** of Spanish language or its speakers **3.** of Spain or Spaniards —'**Spaniard** *n.* native or inhabitant of Spain —**Spanish America** parts of America colonized by Spaniards and now chiefly Spanish-speaking —**Spanish fly 1.** European blister beetle, the dried bodies of which yield cantharides **2.** cantharides —**Spanish Main 1.** mainland of Spanish America **2.** Caribbean Sea

spank (spæŋk) *vt.* **1.** slap with flat of hand, *esp.* on buttocks —*n.* **2.** one or series of these slaps —'**spanking** *n.* **1.** series of spanks —*a.* **2.** quick, lively **3.** large, fine

spanner ('spænə) *n.* tool for gripping nut or bolt head

spanspek ('spænspɛk) *n.* **SA** sweet melon

spar[1] (spɑː) *n.* pole, beam, *esp.* as part of ship's rigging

spar[2] (spɑː) *vi.* **1.** box **2.** dispute, *esp.* in fun (**-rr-**) —*n.* **3.** sparring —**sparring partner** person who practises with boxer during training

spar[3] (spɑː) *n.* any of various kinds of crystalline mineral

spare (spɛə) *vt.* **1.** leave unhurt **2.** show mercy **3.** abstain from using **4.** do without **5.** give away —*a.* **6.** additional **7.** in reserve **8.** thin, lean **9.** scanty —*n.* **10.** spare part (for machine) —'**sparing** *a.* economical, careful —'**sparerib** *n.* cut of pork ribs with most of meat trimmed off —**spare tyre UK** *sl.* roll of fat just above waist

spark (spɑːk) *n.* **1.** small glowing or burning particle **2.** flash of light produced by electrical discharge **3.** vivacity, humour **4.** trace **5.** in internal-combustion engines, electric spark (in sparking plug) which ignites explosive mixture in cylinder —*vi.* **6.** emit sparks —*vt.* **7.** (*oft.* with off) kindle, excite —**sparking plug** device screwed into cylinder head of internal-combustion engine to ignite explosive mixture by means of electric spark (*also* **spark plug**)

sparkle ('spɑːkəl) *vi.* **1.** glitter **2.** effervesce **3.** scintillate —*n.* **4.** small spark **5.** glitter **6.** flash **7.**

lustre —'**sparkler** *n.* **1.** type of firework that throws out sparks **2.** *inf.* sparkling gem

sparrow ('spærəʊ) *n.* small brownish bird —**sparrow hawk** hawk that hunts small birds

sparse (spɑːs) *a.* thinly scattered

Spartan ('spɑːtən) *a.* **1.** of ancient Gk. city of Sparta, its inhabitants or their culture **2.** (*sometimes* **s-**) very strict or austere **3.** (*sometimes* **s-**) possessing courage and resolve

spasm ('spæzəm) *n.* **1.** sudden convulsive (muscular) contraction **2.** sudden burst of activity *etc.* —**spas'modic** *a.* occurring in spasms

spastic ('spæstɪk) *a.* affected by spasms, suffering cerebral palsy —*n.* **2.** person who has cerebral palsy

spat[1] (spæt) *pt./pp.* of SPIT[1]

spat[2] (spæt) *n.* short gaiter

spat[3] (spæt) *n.* slight quarrel

spate (speɪt) *n.* **1.** rush, outpouring **2.** flood

spathe (speɪð) *n.* large sheathlike leaf enclosing flower cluster

spatial *or* **spacial** ('speɪʃəl) *a.* of, in space

spatter ('spætə) *vt.* **1.** splash, cast drops over —*vi.* **2.** be scattered in drops —*n.* **3.** slight splash **4.** sprinkling

spatula ('spætjʊlə) *n.* utensil with broad, flat blade used for various purposes

spawn (spɔːn) *n.* **1.** eggs of fish or frog **2.** *oft. offens.* offspring —*vi.* **3.** (of fish or frog) cast eggs —*vt.* **4.** produce, engender

spay (speɪ) *vt.* remove ovaries from (animal)

speak (spiːk) *vi.* **1.** utter words **2.** converse **3.** deliver discourse —*vt.* **4.** utter **5.** pronounce **6.** express **7.** communicate in (**spoke,** '**spoken,** '**speaking**) —'**speakable** *a.* —'**speaker** *n.* **1.** one who speaks **2.** one who specializes in speech-making **3.** (*oft.* **S-**) official chairman of many legislative bodies **4.** loudspeaker —'**speakeasy** *n.* **US** place where alcoholic drink was sold illicitly during Prohibition —**speaking clock UK** telephone service giving verbal statement of time

spear (spɪə) *n.* **1.** long pointed weapon **2.** slender shoot, as of asparagus —*vt.* **3.** transfix, pierce, wound with spear —'**spearhead** *n.* **1.** leading force in attack, campaign —*vt.* **2.** lead, initiate (attack, campaign *etc.*)

spearmint ('spɪəmɪnt) *n.* type of mint

spec (spɛk) *n. inf.* speculation, gamble (*esp.* in **on spec**)

spec. **1.** special **2.** specification **3.** speculation

special ('spɛʃəl) *a.* **1.** beyond the usual **2.** particular, individual **3.** distinct **4.** limited —'**specialism** *n.* —'**specialist** *n.* one who devotes himself to special subject or branch of subject —**speci'ality** *n.* special product, skill, characteristic *etc.* —**speciali'zation** *or* **-i'sation**

n. —'**specialize** *or* **-ise** *vi.* 1. be specialist —*vt.* 2. make special —'**specially** *adv.* —**Special Branch** UK department of police force concerned with political security —**special constable** person recruited for temporary police duties, *esp.* in time of emergency —**special delivery** delivery of mail outside time of scheduled delivery —**special licence** UK licence permitting marriage to take place without usual legal conditions

specie ('spi:ʃi:) *n.* coined, as distinct from paper, money

species ('spi:ʃi:z; *Lat.* 'spi:ʃii:z) *n.* 1. sort, kind, *esp.* of animals *etc.* 2. class 3. subdivision (*pl.* **-cies**)

specific (spɪ'sɪfɪk) *a.* 1. definite 2. exact in detail 3. characteristic of a thing or kind —spe'**cifically** *adv.* —**specifi'cation** *n.* detailed description of something to be made, done —'**specify** *vt.* state definitely or in detail (**-ified, -ifying**) —**specific gravity** ratio of density of substance to that of water

specimen ('spesɪmɪn) *n.* 1. part typifying whole 2. individual example 3. *Med.* sample of tissue, urine *etc.* taken for diagnostic examination

specious ('spi:ʃəs) *a.* deceptively plausible, but false —'**speciously** *adv.* —'**speciousness** *n.*

speck (spɛk) *n.* 1. small spot, particle —*vt.* 2. spot —'**speckle** *n./vt.* speck

specs (spɛks) *pl.n. inf.* spectacles

spectacle ('spɛktək²l) *n.* 1. show 2. thing exhibited 3. ridiculous sight —*pl.* 4. pair of lenses for correcting defective sight —spec'**tacular** *a.* 1. impressive 2. showy 3. grand 4. magnificent —*n.* 5. lavishly produced performance —spec'**tator** *n.* one who looks on

spectra ('spɛktrə) *n.*, *pl. of* SPECTRUM

spectre *or U.S.* **specter** ('spɛktə) *n.* 1. ghost 2. image of something unpleasant —'**spectral** *a.* ghostly

spectrum ('spɛktrəm) *n.* band of colours into which beam of light can be decomposed, *eg* by prism (*pl.* **-tra**) —'**spectroscope** *n.* instrument for producing, examining spectra —spec'**troscopist** *n.* —spec'**troscopy** *n.* study of spectra by use of spectroscopes *etc.*

speculate ('spɛkjʊleɪt) *vi.* 1. guess, conjecture 2. engage in (risky) commercial transactions —specu'**lation** *n.* —'**speculative** *a.* given to, characterized by speculation —'**speculator** *n.*

speculum ('spɛkjʊləm) *n.* 1. mirror 2. reflector of polished metal, *esp.* in reflecting telescopes (*pl.* **-la** (-lə), **-s**) —'**specular** *a.*

sped (spɛd) *pt./pp. of* SPEED

speech (spi:tʃ) *n.* 1. act, faculty of speaking 2. words, language 3. conversation 4. discourse 5. (formal) talk given before audience —'**speechi-**

fy *vi.* make speech, *esp.* long and tedious one (**-ified, -ifying**) —'**speechless** *a.* 1. dumb 2. at a loss for words —**speech day** UK in schools, annual prize-giving day at which speeches are made

speed (spi:d) *n.* 1. swiftness 2. rate of progress 3. degree of sensitivity of photographic film 4. *sl.* amphetamine —*vi.* 5. move quickly 6. drive vehicle at high speed 7. *obs.* succeed —*vt.* 8. further 9. expedite (**sped** *or* '**speeded** *pt./pp.*) —'**speedily** *adv.* —'**speeding** *n.* driving (vehicle) at high speed, *esp.* over legal limit —'**speedo** *n. inf.* speedometer (*pl.* **-s**) —'**speedy** *a.* 1. quick 2. rapid 3. nimble 4. prompt —'**speedboat** *n.* light, fast motorboat —**speed limit** maximum permitted speed at which vehicle may travel on certain roads —**speed-'ometer** *n.* instrument to show speed of vehicle —'**speedway** *n.* track for motorcycle racing —'**speedwell** *n.* plant with small, *usu.* blue flowers

spek (spɛk) *n.* SA bacon

speleology *or* **spelaeology** (spi:lɪ'ɒlədʒɪ) *n.* study, exploring of caves —speleo'**logical** *or* spelaeo'**logical** *a.*

spell[1] (spɛl) *vt.* 1. give letters of in order 2. read letter by letter 3. indicate, result in (**spelled** *or* **spelt** *pt./pp.*, '**spelling** *pr.p.*) —'**spelling** *n.* —**spell out** make explicit

spell[2] (spɛl) *n.* 1. magic formula 2. enchantment —'**spellbound** *a.* enchanted, entranced

spell[3] (spɛl) *n.* (short) period of time, work

spelt (spɛlt) *pt./pp. of* SPELL[1]

spend (spɛnd) *vt.* 1. pay out 2. pass (time) on activity *etc.* 3. use up completely (**spent** *pt./pp.*, '**spending** *pr.p.*) —'**spender** *n.* —**spent** *a.* used up, exhausted —'**spendthrift** *n.* wasteful person

sperm (spɜ:m) *n.* 1. male reproductive cell 2. semen —**spermaceti** (spɜ:mə'sɛtɪ, -'si:tɪ) *n.* white, waxy substance obtained from oil from head of sperm whale —sper'**matic** *a.* of sperm —**spermatozoon** (spɜ:mətəʊ'zəʊən) *n.* any of male reproductive cells released in semen during ejaculation (*pl.* **-zoa** (-'zəʊə)) (*also* **sperm**, '**zoosperm**) —'**spermicide** *n.* drug *etc.* that kills sperm —**sperm whale** large, toothed whale hunted for sperm oil, spermaceti and ambergris (*also* '**cachalot**)

spew (spju:) *v.* vomit

sphagnum ('sfægnəm) *n.* moss that grows in bogs

sphere (sfɪə) *n.* 1. ball, globe 2. range 3. field of action 4. status 5. position 6. province —'**spherical** ('sfɛrɪk²l) *a.* —'**spheroid** *n.* 1. geometric surface produced by rotating ellipse about one of its two axes —*a.* 2. shaped like but not exactly a sphere

sphincter ('sfɪŋktə) n. ring of muscle surrounding opening of hollow bodily organ

sphinx (sfɪŋks) n. 1. statue in Egypt with lion's body and human head 2. (S-) monster with woman's head and lion's body 3. enigmatic person (pl. -es, **sphinges** ('sfɪndʒiːz))

spice (spaɪs) n. 1. aromatic or pungent vegetable substance 2. spices collectively 3. anything that adds flavour, relish, piquancy, interest etc. —vt. 4. season with spices, flavour —'**spicily** adv. —'**spicy** a. 1. flavoured with spices 2. inf. slightly indecent, risqué

spick-and-span or **spic-and-span** ('spɪk-ən'spæn) a. 1. neat, smart 2. new-looking

spider ('spaɪdə) n. small eight-legged creature which spins web to catch prey —'**spidery** a. —**spider plant** hardy house plant with long thin leaves

spiel (ʃpiːl) inf. n. 1. glib (sales) talk —vi. 2. deliver spiel, recite —'**spieler** n.

spigot ('spɪgət) n. peg, plug

spike (spaɪk) n. 1. sharp point 2. sharp pointed object 3. long flower cluster with flowers attached directly to the stalk —vt. 4. pierce, fasten with spike 5. render ineffective 6. add alcohol to (drink) —'**spiky** a. —'**spikenard** n. 1. aromatic Indian plant with rose-purple flowers 2. aromatic ointment obtained from this plant

spill[1] (spɪl) v. 1. (cause to) pour, flow over, fall out, esp. unintentionally 2. upset —vi. 3. be lost or wasted (**spilt** (spɪlt) or **spilled** pt./pp.) —n. 4. fall 5. amount spilt —'**spillage** n.

spill[2] (spɪl) n. thin strip of wood, twisted paper etc. for lighting fires etc.

spin (spɪn) v. 1. (cause to) revolve rapidly 2. whirl —vt. 3. twist into thread 4. (with out) prolong 5. inf. tell (a story) —vi. 6. fish with lure (**spun**, obs. **span** (spæn) pt., **spun** pp., '**spinning** pr.p.) —n. 7. spinning 8. (of aircraft) descent in dive with continued rotation 9. rapid run or ride 10. in skating, rapid turning on the spot 11. angular momentum of elementary particle —'**spinner** n. 1. person or thing that spins 2. Cricket ball that is bowled with spinning motion; spin bowler 3. fishing lure with fin or wing that revolves —'**spinneret** n. any of several organs in spiders etc. through which silk threads are exuded —'**spinning** n. act, process of drawing out and twisting into threads, as wool, cotton, flax etc. —**spin bowler** Cricket bowler who specializes in bowling balls with spinning motion —**spin-dry** vt. spin (clothes) in spin-dryer —**spin-dryer** n. device that extracts water from clothes etc. by spinning them in perforated drum —**spinning jenny** early type of spinning frame with several spindles —**spinning wheel** household machine with large wheel turned by treadle for spinning wool etc. into thread

—**spin-off** n. any product or development derived incidentally from application of existing knowledge or enterprise

spina bifida ('spaɪnə 'bɪfɪdə) congenital condition in which meninges of spinal cord protrude through gap in backbone

spinach ('spɪnɪdʒ, -ɪtʃ) n. 1. annual plant with edible leaves 2. the leaves, eaten boiled as vegetable

spindle ('spɪnd³l) n. rod, axis for spinning —'**spindly** a. 1. long and slender 2. attenuated —'**spindlelegs** or '**spindleshanks** pl.n. 1. long thin legs 2. person who has such legs

spindrift ('spɪndrɪft) or **spoondrift** ('spuːn-drɪft) n. spray blown along surface of sea

spine (spaɪn) n. 1. backbone 2. thin spike, esp. on fish etc. 3. ridge 4. back of book —**spinal** a. —'**spineless** a. 1. lacking spine 2. cowardly —'**spiny** a. 1. (of animals) having or covered with quills or spines 2. (of plants) covered with spines 3. troublesome —**spinal column** series of contiguous bony segments that surround spinal cord (also **spine**, **vertebral column**) —**spinal cord** cord of nerve tissue within spinal canal, which together with brain forms central nervous system —**spine-chiller** n. film etc. that arouses terror

spinet (spɪ'nɛt, 'spɪnɪt) n. keyboard instrument like harpsichord

spinnaker ('spɪnəkə; Naut. 'spæŋkə) n. large yacht sail

spinney ('spɪnɪ) n. small wood

spinster ('spɪnstə) n. unmarried woman

spiracle ('spaɪərək³l, 'spaɪrə-) n. Zool. opening for breathing

spiraea or esp. U.S. **spirea** (spaɪ'rɪə) n. any of various plants with small white or pink flower sprays

spiral ('spaɪərəl) n. 1. continuous curve drawn at ever-increasing distance from fixed point 2. anything resembling this —a. 3. having shape of spiral —'**spirally** adv.

spirant ('spaɪrənt) a. 1. Phonet. see FRICATIVE —n. 2. fricative consonant

spire (spaɪə) n. 1. pointed part of steeple 2. pointed stem

spirit ('spɪrɪt) n. 1. life principle animating body 2. disposition 3. liveliness 4. courage 5. frame of mind 6. essential character or meaning 7. soul 8. ghost 9. liquid got by distillation, alcohol —pl. 10. emotional state 11. strong alcoholic drink, eg whisky —vt. 12. (usu. with away or off) carry away mysteriously —'**spirited** a. lively —'**spiritless** a. listless, apathetic —'**spiritual** a. 1. given to, concerned in things of the spirit —n. 2. Negro sacred song, hymn —'**spiritualism** n. belief that spirits of the dead communicate with the living —'**spiritual-**

ist n. —spiritu'ality n. —'spiritually adv. —'spirituous a. alcoholic —spirit gum glue made from gum dissolved in ether —spirit lamp lamp that burns methylated or other spirits —spirit level glass tube containing bubble in liquid, used to check horizontal, vertical surfaces —spirits of salts hydrochloric acid

spirt (sp3:t) see SPURT

spit¹ (spit) vi. 1. eject saliva —vt. 2. eject from mouth (spat, spit pt./pp., 'spitting pr.p.) —n. 3. spitting, saliva —'spittle n. saliva —spit'toon n. vessel to spit into —'spitfire n. person with fiery temper —spitting image inf. person who bears physical resemblance to another —spit and polish inf. punctilious attention to neatness, discipline etc., esp. in armed forces

spit² (spit) n. 1. sharp rod to put through meat for roasting 2. sandy point projecting into the sea —vt. 3. thrust through (-tt-)

spite (spait) n. 1. malice —vt. 2. thwart spitefully —'spiteful a. —'spitefully adv. —in spite of regardless of; notwithstanding

spiv (spiv) n. smartly dressed man, esp. one who makes living by shady dealings

splake (spleik) n. type of hybrid Canad. trout

splash (splæʃ) v. 1. scatter (liquid) about, on or over (something) —vt. 2. print, display prominently —n. 3. sound of water being scattered 4. patch, esp. of colour 5. (effect of) extravagant display 6. small amount —'splash-down n. 1. controlled landing of spacecraft on water 2. time scheduled for this event —splash down

splat (splæt) n. wet, slapping sound

splatter ('splætə) v./n. spatter

splay (splei) v. 1. spread out 2. slanting 3. turned outwards —v. 4. spread out 5. twist outwards —n. 6. slant surface 7. spread —'splayfooted a. flat and broad (of foot)

spleen (spli:n) n. 1. organ in abdomen 2. anger 3. irritable or morose temper —splenetic (spli'netik) a. —'spleenwort n. any of various ferns

splendid ('splendid) a. 1. magnificent 2. brilliant 3. excellent —'splendidly adv. —'splendour or U.S. 'splendor n.

splice (splais) vt. 1. join by interweaving strands 2. join (wood) by overlapping 3. sl. join in marriage —n. 4. spliced joint

spline (splain) n. narrow groove, ridge, strip, esp. joining wood etc.

splint (splint) n. rigid support for broken limb etc.

splinter ('splintə) n. 1. thin fragment of glass, wood etc. —v. 2. break into fragments, shiver —splinter group group that separates from main party, organization, oft. after disagreement

split (split) v. 1. break asunder 2. separate 3. divide —vi. 4. sl. depart; leave (split, 'splitting) —n. 5. crack, fissure 6. dessert of fruit and ice cream —'splitting a. 1. (of headache) acute 2. (of head) assailed by overpowering unbearable pain —split infinitive in English grammar, infinitive used with another word between to and verb —split-level a. (of house etc.) having floor level of one part about half storey above floor level of adjoining part —split pea pea dried and split and used in soups etc. —split personality 1. tendency to change rapidly in mood or temperament 2. schizophrenia —split second infinitely small period of time —split-second a. made or arrived at in infinitely short time

splotch (splotʃ) or splodge (splodʒ) n./vt. splash, daub —'splotchy or 'splodgy a.

splurge (spl3:dʒ) v. 1. spend (money) extravagantly —n. 2. ostentatious display, esp. of wealth 3. bout of unrestrained extravagance

splutter ('splʌtə) vi. 1. make hissing, spitting sounds —vt. 2. utter incoherently with spitting sounds —n. 3. process or noise of spluttering 4. spluttering incoherent speech

spode (spəud) n. (sometimes S-) china or porcelain manufactured by Josiah Spode, English potter, or his company

spoil (spoil) vt. 1. damage, injure 2. damage manners or behaviour of (esp. child) by indulgence 3. pillage —vi. 4. go bad (spoiled or spoilt pt./pp., 'spoiling pr.p.) —n. 5. booty 6. waste material, esp. in mining (also 'spoilage) —'spoiler n. slowing device on aircraft wing etc. —'spoilsport n. inf. one who spoils pleasure of other people —spoiling for eager for

spoke¹ (spəuk) pt. of SPEAK —'spoken pp. of SPEAK —'spokesman n. one deputed to speak for others

spoke² (spəuk) n. radial bar of wheel

spoliation (spəuli'eiʃən) n. 1. act of spoiling 2. robbery 3. destruction

spondee ('spondi:) n. metrical foot consisting of two long syllables (ˉ ˉ)

sponge (spʌndʒ) n. 1. marine animal 2. its skeleton, or a synthetic substance like it, used to absorb liquids 3. type of light cake —vt. 4. wipe with sponge —vi. 5. live meanly at expense of others —v. 6. cadge —'sponger n. sl. one who cadges or lives at expense of others —'spongy a. 1. spongelike 2. wet and soft —sponge bag small bag usu. of plastic that holds toilet articles

sponsor ('sponsə) n. 1. one promoting, advertising something 2. one who agrees to give money to a charity on completion of specified activity by another 3. one taking responsibility (esp. for welfare of child at baptism, ie godparent) **4.** guarantor —*vt.* **5.** act as sponsor for —'**sponsorship** *n.*

spontaneous (spon'teɪnɪəs) *a.* **1.** voluntary **2.** natural **3.** not forced **4.** produced without external force —**spontaneity** (sponto'niːɪtɪ, -'neɪ-) *n.* —**spon'taneously** *adv.* —**spon'taneousness** *n.* —**spontaneous combustion** ignition of substance as result of internal oxidation processes

spoof (spuːf) *n.* **1.** mild satirical mockery **2.** trick, hoax

spook (spuːk) *n.* ghost —'**spooky** *a.*

spool (spuːl) *n.* reel, bobbin

spoon (spuːn) *n.* **1.** implement with shallow bowl at end of handle for eating or serving food *etc.* —*vt.* **2.** lift with spoon —'**spoonful** *n.* —'**spoonbill** *n.* any of several wading birds having long horizontally flattened bill —**spoonfeed** *vt.* **1.** feed with spoon **2.** spoil **3.** provide (person) with ready-made opinions *etc.*

spoonerism ('spuːnərɪzəm) *n.* amusing transposition of initial consonants, *eg* 'half-warmed fish' for 'half-formed wish'

spoor (spuə, spɔː) *n.* **1.** trail of wild animals —*v.* **2.** follow spoor (of)

sporadic (spə'rædɪk) *or* **sporadical** *a.* **1.** intermittent **2.** scattered —**spo'radically** *adv.*

spore (spɔː) *n.* minute reproductive organism of some plants and protozoans

sporran ('spɒrən) *n.* pouch worn in front of kilt

sport (spɔːt) *n.* **1.** game, activity for pleasure, competition, exercise **2.** enjoyment **3.** mockery **4.** cheerful person, good loser —*vt.* **5.** wear, *esp.* ostentatiously —*vi.* **6.** frolic **7.** play (sport) —'**sportiness** *n.* —'**sporting** *a.* **1.** of sport **2.** behaving with fairness, generosity —'**sportive** *a.* playful —'**sporty** *a.* **1.** stylish, loud or gay **2.** relating to or appropriate to sportsman —**sporting chance** sufficient prospect of success to justify the attempt —**sports car** fast (open) car —**sports jacket** man's casual jacket —'**sportsman** *n.* **1.** one who engages in sport **2.** good loser

spot (spɒt) *n.* **1.** small mark, stain **2.** blemish **3.** pimple **4.** place **5.** (difficult) situation **6.** *inf.* small quantity —*vt.* **7.** mark with spots **8.** detect **9.** observe (-tt-) —'**spotless** *a.* unblemished **2.** pure —'**spotlessly** *adv.* —'**spotty** *a.* **1.** with spots **2.** uneven —**spot check** random examination —'**spotlight** *n.* **1.** powerful light illuminating small area **2.** centre of attention —**spot-on** *a.* UK *inf.* absolutely correct —**spotted dick** *or* **dog** UK steamed or boiled suet pudding containing dried fruit —**spot-weld** *vt.* **1.** join (two pieces of metal) by electrically generated heat —*n.* **2.** weld so formed

spouse (spaʊs, spaʊz) *n.* husband or wife —**spousal** ('spaʊzəl) *n.* marriage

spout (spaʊt) *v.* **1.** pour out —*vi.* **2.** *sl.* speechify —*n.* **3.** projecting tube or lip for pouring liquids **4.** copious discharge —**up the spout** *sl.* **1.** ruined; lost **2.** pregnant

SPQR Senatus Populusque Romanus (*Lat.,* the Senate and people of Rome)

sprain (spreɪn) *n./vt.* wrench or twist (of muscle *etc.*)

sprang (spræŋ) *pt.* of SPRING

sprat (spræt) *n.* small sea fish

sprawl (sprɔːl) *vi.* **1.** lie or sit about awkwardly —*v.* **2.** spread in rambling, unplanned way —*n.* **3.** sprawling

spray¹ (spreɪ) *n.* **1.** (device for producing) fine drops of liquid —*vt.* **2.** sprinkle with shower of fine drops —**spray gun** device that sprays fluid in finely divided form by atomizing it in air jet

spray² (spreɪ) *n.* **1.** branch, twig with buds, flowers *etc.* **2.** floral ornament, brooch *etc.* like this

spread (spred) *v.* **1.** extend **2.** stretch out **3.** open out **4.** scatter **5.** distribute or be distributed **6.** unfold —*vt.* **7.** cover (**spread,** '**spreading**) —*n.* **8.** extent **9.** increase **10.** ample meal **11.** food which can be spread on bread *etc.* —**spreadeagle** *a.* with arms and legs outstretched (*also* **spread-eagled**)

spree (spriː) *n.* **1.** session of overindulgence **2.** romp

sprig (sprɪg) *n.* **1.** small twig **2.** ornamental design like this **3.** small nail

sprightly ('spraɪtlɪ) *a.* lively, brisk —'**sprightliness** *n.*

spring (sprɪŋ) *vi.* **1.** leap **2.** shoot up or forth **3.** come into being **4.** appear **5.** grow **6.** become bent or split —*vt.* **7.** produce unexpectedly **8.** set off (trap) (**sprang, sprung,** '**springing**) —*n.* **9.** leap **10.** recoil **11.** piece of coiled or bent metal with much resilience **12.** flow of water from earth **13.** first season of year —'**springy** *a.* elastic —**spring balance** device in which object to be weighed is attached to end of helical spring, extension of which indicates weight on calibrated scale —'**springboard** *n.* flexible board for diving —**spring-clean** *v.* clean (house) thoroughly —**spring-cleaning** *n.* —'**springer spaniel** breed of spaniel with silky coat, used for flushing or springing game —**spring onion** immature onion cultivated for its tiny bulb and long green leaves which are eaten in salads *etc.* —**spring tide** high tide at new or full moon

springbok *or* **springbuck** ('sprɪŋbʌk) *n.* **1.** S Afr. antelope **2.** (S-) South African national sportsman

sprinkle ('sprɪŋkəl) *vt.* scatter small drops on, strew —'**sprinkler** *n.* —'**sprinkling** *n.* small quantity or number

sprint (sprɪnt) *vi.* **1.** run short distance at great speed —*n.* **2.** such run, race

sprit (sprɪt) *n.* small spar set diagonally across fore-and-aft sail in order to extend it —**spritsail** ('sprɪtseɪl; *Naut.* 'sprɪtsəl) *n.* sail extended by sprit

sprite (spraɪt) *n.* fairy, elf

sprocket ('sprɒkɪt) *n.* **1.** projection on wheel or capstan for engaging chain **2.** wheel with sprockets (*also* **sprocket wheel**)

sprout (spraʊt) *v.* **1.** put forth (shoots) —*vi.* **2.** spring up —*n.* **3.** shoot

spruce¹ (spruːs) *n.* variety of fir

spruce² (spruːs) *a.* neat in dress

sprung (sprʌŋ) *pp. of* SPRING

spry (spraɪ) *a.* nimble, vigorous

spud (spʌd) *n. inf.* potato

spume (spjuːm) *n./vi.* foam, froth

spun (spʌn) *pt./pp. of* SPIN

spunk (spʌŋk) *n.* courage, spirit

spur (spɜː) *n.* **1.** pricking instrument attached to horseman's heel **2.** incitement **3.** stimulus **4.** projection on cock's leg **5.** projecting mountain range **6.** railway branch line or siding —*vt.* **7.** ride hard (**-rr-**)

spurious ('spjʊərɪəs) *a.* not genuine

spurn (spɜːn) *vt.* reject with scorn, thrust aside

spurt *or* **spirt** (spɜːt) *v.* **1.** send, come out in jet —*vi.* **2.** rush suddenly —*n.* **3.** jet **4.** short sudden effort, *esp.* in race

sputnik ('spʊtnɪk, 'spʌt-) *n.* any of series of Russian satellites

sputter ('spʌtə) *v.* splutter

sputum ('spjuːtəm) *n.* spittle (*pl.* **-ta** (-tə))

spy (spaɪ) *n.* **1.** one who watches (*esp.* in rival countries, companies *etc.*) and reports secretly —*vi.* **2.** act as spy —*vt.* **3.** catch sight of (**spied**, **'spying**) —**'spyglass** *n.* small telescope

Sq. 1. Square **2.** Squadron

squab (skwɒb) *n.* **1.** young unfledged bird, *esp.* pigeon **2.** short fat person **3.** well-stuffed cushion —*a.* **4.** (of birds) unfledged **5.** short and fat

squabble ('skwɒbᵊl) *vi.* **1.** engage in petty, noisy quarrel, bicker —*n.* **2.** petty quarrel

squad (skwɒd) *n.* small party, *esp.* of soldiers —**'squadron** *n.* division of cavalry regiment, fleet or air force —**squadron leader** officer holding commissioned rank, between flight lieutenant and wing commander in air forces of Brit. and certain other countries

squalid ('skwɒlɪd) *a.* mean and dirty —**'squalor** *n.*

squall (skwɔːl) *n.* **1.** harsh cry **2.** sudden gust of wind **3.** short storm —*vi.* **4.** yell

squander ('skwɒndə) *vt.* spend wastefully, dissipate

square (skwɛə) *n.* **1.** equilateral rectangle **2.**

area of this shape **3.** in town, open space (of this shape) **4.** product of a number multiplied by itself **5.** instrument for drawing right angles —*a.* **6.** square in form **7.** honest **8.** straight, even **9.** level, equal **10.** denoting a measure of area **11.** *inf.* old-fashioned, conservative —*vt.* **12.** make square **13.** find square of **14.** pay **15.** bribe —*vi.* **16.** fit, suit —'**squarely** *adv.* —**square-bashing** *n.* UK *Mil. sl.* drill on barrack square —**square dance** any of various formation dances in which couples form squares —**square-dance** *vi.* perform such dance —**square deal** any transaction *etc.* that is honest and fair —**square leg** *Cricket* **1.** fielding position on on side approximately at right angles to batsman **2.** person who fields in this position —**square measure** unit or system of units for measuring areas —**square metre** *etc.* area equal to that of square with sides one metre *etc.* long —**square root** number that, multiplied by itself, gives number of which it is factor

squash (skwɒʃ) *vt.* **1.** crush flat **2.** pulp **3.** suppress **4.** humiliate —*n.* **5.** juice of crushed fruit **6.** crowd **7.** game played with rackets and soft balls in walled court **8.** marrowlike plant

squat (skwɒt) *vi.* **1.** sit on heels **2.** act as squatter (**-tt-**) —*a.* **3.** short and thick —'**squatter** *n.* one who settles on land or occupies house without permission

squaw (skwɔː) *n.* N Amer. Indian woman

squawk (skwɔːk) *n.* **1.** short harsh cry, *esp.* of bird —*vi.* **2.** utter this cry

squeak (skwiːk) *vi./n.* (make) short shrill sound

squeal (skwiːl) *n.* **1.** long piercing squeak —*vi.* **2.** make one **3.** *sl.* confess information (about another)

squeamish ('skwiːmɪʃ) *a.* **1.** easily made sick **2.** easily shocked **3.** overscrupulous

squeegee ('skwiːdʒiː) *or* **squilgee** ('skwɪldʒiː) *n.* **1.** tool with rubber blade for clearing water (from glass *etc.*), spreading wet paper *etc.* —*vt.* **2.** press, smooth with squeegee

squeeze (skwiːz) *vt.* **1.** press **2.** wring **3.** force **4.** hug **5.** subject to extortion —*n.* **6.** act of squeezing **7.** period of hardship, difficulty caused by financial weakness

squelch (skwɛltʃ) *vi.* **1.** make, walk with wet sucking sound, as in walking through mud —*n.* **2.** squelching sound

squib (skwɪb) *n.* **1.** small firework that hisses before exploding **2.** insignificant person

squid (skwɪd) *n.* type of cuttlefish

squiffy ('skwɪfɪ) *a.* UK *inf.* slightly drunk

squiggle ('skwɪgᵊl) *n.* **1.** wavy, wriggling mark —*vi.* **2.** wriggle **3.** draw squiggle

squill (skwɪl) *n.* **1.** Mediterranean plant of lily

family **2.** its bulb, used medicinally as expectorant

squint (skwɪnt) *vi.* **1.** have the eyes turned in different directions **2.** glance sideways —*n.* **3.** this eye disorder **4.** glance —*a.* **5.** having a squint

squire (skwaɪə) *n.* country gentleman

squirm (skwɜːm) *vi.* **1.** wriggle **2.** be embarrassed —*n.* **3.** squirming movement

squirrel ('skwɪrəl) *n.* small graceful bushy-tailed tree animal

squirt (skwɜːt) *v.* **1.** force (liquid) or (of liquid) be forced through narrow opening —*n.* jet **3.** *inf.* short or insignificant person

Sr *Chem.* strontium

Sr. *or* **Sr 1.** Senior **2.** Sister

S.R.C. UK Science Research Council

S.R.N. State Registered Nurse

SS 1. Saints **2.** paramilitary organization within Nazi party that provided Hitler's bodyguard, security forces, concentration camp guards *etc.* **3.** (*also* **S.S.**) steamship

SSE south-southeast

SSR Soviet Socialist Republic

S.S.R.C. UK Social Science Research Council

SSW south-southwest

st. stone (weight)

St. *or* **St 1.** Saint **2.** Strait **3.** Street

stab (stæb) *v.* **1.** pierce, strike (at) with pointed weapon (**-bb-**) —*n.* **2.** blow, wound so inflicted **3.** sudden sensation, *eg* of fear **4.** attempt

stabilize *or* **-ise** ('steɪbɪlaɪz) *vt.* make steady, restore to equilibrium, *esp.* of money values, prices and wages —**stabili'zation** *or* **-i'sation** *n.* —'**stabilizer** *or* **-iser** *n.* device to maintain equilibrium of ship, aircraft *etc.*

stable[1] ('steɪbəl) *n.* **1.** building for horses **2.** racehorses of particular owner, establishment **3.** such establishment —*vt.* **4.** put into stable

stable[2] ('steɪbəl) *a.* **1.** firmly fixed **2.** steadfast, resolute —**stability** (stə'bɪlɪtɪ) *n.* **1.** steadiness **2.** ability to resist change of any kind —'**stably** *adv.*

staccato (stə'kɑːtəʊ) *a.* **1.** *Mus.* with notes sharply separated **2.** abrupt

stack (stæk) *n.* **1.** ordered pile, heap **2.** chimney —*vt.* **3.** pile in stack **4.** control (aircraft waiting to land) so that they fly at different altitudes

stadium ('steɪdɪəm) *n.* open-air arena for athletics *etc.* (*pl.* **-s, -dia** (-dɪə))

staff (stɑːf) *n.* **1.** body of officers or workers employed by a company *etc.*; personnel (*pl.* **-s**) **2.** pole (*pl.* **-s, staves**) **3.** set of five lines on which music is written (*pl.* **-s, staves**) —*vt.* **4.** supply with personnel —**staff nurse** qualified nurse ranking immediately below sister —**staff sergeant** *Mil.* **1.** UK noncommissioned officer holding sergeant's rank and carrying out certain special duties **2.** US noncommissioned officer who ranks: in Army, above sergeant and below sergeant first class; in Air Force, above airman first class and below technical sergeant; in Marine Corps, above sergeant and below gunnery sergeant

Staffs. (stæfs) Staffordshire

stag (stæg) *n.* **1.** male deer —*a.* **2.** for men only

stage (steɪdʒ) *n.* **1.** period, division of development **2.** raised floor or platform **3.** (platform of) theatre **4.** scene of action **5.** stopping-place on road, distance between two of them **6.** separate unit of space rocket that can be jettisoned —*vt.* **7.** put (play) on stage **8.** arrange, bring about —'**staging** *n.* any temporary structure used in building, *esp.* platforms supported by scaffolding —'**stagy** *a.* theatrical —'**stagecoach** *n.* formerly, four-wheeled horse-drawn vehicle used to carry passengers *etc.* on regular route —**stage fright** panic that may beset person about to appear in front of audience —'**stagehand** *n.* person who sets stage, moves props *etc.* in theatrical production —**stage-manage** *v.* **1.** work as stage manager for (play *etc.*) —*vt.* **2.** arrange or supervise from behind the scenes —**stage manager** person who supervises stage arrangements of theatrical production —**stage-struck** *a.* infatuated with glamour of theatrical life —**stage whisper** loud whisper intended to be heard by audience

stagflation (stæg'fleɪʃən) *n.* inflationary economic situation characterized by decline in industrial output

stagger ('stægə) *vi.* **1.** walk unsteadily —*vt.* **2.** astound **3.** arrange in overlapping or alternating positions, times **4.** distribute over a period —*n.* **5.** act of staggering —*pl.* **6.** form of vertigo **7.** disease of horses —'**staggering** *a.* astounding

stagnate (stæg'neɪt) *vi.* cease to flow or develop —'**stagnant** *a.* **1.** sluggish **2.** not flowing **3.** foul, impure —**stag'nation** *n.*

staid (steɪd) *a.* of sober and quiet character, sedate —'**staidly** *adv.* —'**staidness** *n.*

stain (steɪn) *vt.* **1.** spot, mark **2.** apply liquid colouring to (wood *etc.*) **3.** bring disgrace upon —*n.* **4.** spot, mark, discoloration **5.** moral taint —'**stainless** *a.* —**stainless steel** rustless steel alloy

stairs (steəz) *pl.n.* set of steps, *esp.* as part of house —'**staircase** *or* '**stairway** *n.* **1.** structure enclosing stairs **2.** stairs —'**stairwell** *n.* vertical shaft that contains staircase

stake (steɪk) *n.* **1.** sharpened stick or post **2.** money wagered or contended for —*vt.* **3.** secure, mark out with stakes **4.** wager, risk —**stake out** US *sl.* keep under surveillance

stalactite 480 star

stalactite ('stæləktaɪt) *n.* lime deposit like icicle on roof of cave

stalagmite ('stæləgmaɪt) *n.* lime deposit like pillar on floor of cave

stale (steɪl) *a.* 1. old, lacking freshness 2. hackneyed 3. lacking energy, interest through monotony —'**stalemate** *n.* 1. *Chess* draw through one player being unable to move 2. deadlock, impasse

stalk¹ (stɔːk) *n.* 1. plant's stem 2. anything like this

stalk² (stɔːk) *v.* 1. follow, approach (game *etc.*) stealthily —*vi.* 2. walk in stiff and stately manner —*n.* 3. stalking —**stalking-horse** *n.* pretext

stall (stɔːl) *n.* 1. compartment in stable *etc.* 2. erection for display and sale of goods 3. seat in chancel of church 4. finger sheath —*pl.* 5. area of seats on ground floor of theatre or cinema, nearest to orchestra pit or screen —*vt.* 6. put in stall 7. hinder 8. stick fast —*v.* 9. delay 10. stop unintentionally (motor engine) 11. lose flying speed (of aircraft) —*vi.* 12. prevaricate

stallion ('stæljən) *n.* uncastrated male horse, *esp.* one used for breeding

stalwart ('stɔːlwət) *a.* 1. strong 2. brave 3. staunch —*n.* 4. stalwart person

stamen ('steɪmən) *n.* male organ of flowering plant (*pl.* **-s, stamina** ('stæmɪnə))

stamina ('stæmɪnə) *n.* power of endurance, vitality

stammer ('stæmə) *v.* 1. speak, say with repetition of syllables, stutter —*n.* 2. habit of so speaking —'**stammerer** *n.*

stamp (stæmp) *vi.* 1. put down foot with force —*vt.* 2. impress mark on 3. affix postage stamp to 4. fix (in memory) 5. reveal, characterize —*n.* 6. stamping with foot 7. imprinted mark 8. appliance for marking 9. piece of gummed paper printed with device as evidence of postage *etc.* 10. character —**stamping ground** habitual meeting or gathering place

stampede (stæm'piːd) *n.* 1. sudden frightened rush, *esp.* of herd of cattle 2. headlong rush of a crowd 3. C rodeo —*vi.* 4. cause, take part in stampede

stance (stæns, stɑːns) *n.* 1. manner, position of standing 2. attitude 3. point of view

stanch (stɑːntʃ) *vt. see* STAUNCH

stanchion ('stɑːnʃən) *n.* 1. upright bar, support —*vt.* 2. support

stand (stænd) *v.* 1. have, take, set in upright position —*vi.* 2. remain 3. be situated 4. remain firm or stationary 5. cease to move 6. adhere to principles 7. offer oneself as a candidate 8. (*with* for) be symbol *etc.* (of) —*vt.* 9. endure 10. *inf.* provide free, treat to (**stood, 'standing**) —*n.* 11. holding firm 12. position 13. halt 14. something

on which thing may be placed 15. structure from which spectators watch sport *etc.* 16. stop made by pop group *etc.* —'**standing** *n.* 1. reputation, status 2. duration —*a.* 3. erect 4. permanent, lasting 5. stagnant 6. performed from stationary position, as in *standing jump* —**stand-by** *n.* person or thing that is ready for use or can be relied on in emergency —**stand-in** *n.* person, thing that acts as substitute —**standing order** 1. instruction to bank by depositor to pay stated amount at regular intervals 2. rule governing procedure *etc.* of legislative body 3. *Mil.* one of number of orders which have long-term validity —**stand'offish** *a.* reserved or aloof —'**standstill** *n.* complete cessation of movement —**stand by** 1. be available and ready to act if needed 2. be present as onlooker 3. be faithful to —**stand in** deputize —**stand over** 1. watch closely 2. postpone

standard ('stændəd) *n.* 1. accepted example of something against which others are judged 2. degree, quality 3. flag 4. weight or measure to which others must conform 5. post 6. SA school form or grade —*a.* 7. usual, regular 8. average 9. of recognized authority, competence 10. accepted as correct —**standardi'zation** *or* **-i'sation** *n.* —'**standardize** *or* **-ise** *vt.* regulate by a standard —**standard-bearer** *n.* 1. man who carries a standard 2. leader of party *etc.* —**standard gauge** railway track with distance of 56½ inches between lines —**standard-gauge** *or* **standard-gauged** *a.* of or denoting railway with standard gauge —**standard lamp** electric light fixed to tall support standing on floor —**standard time** official local time of region or country determined by distance from Greenwich of line of longitude passing through area —**standard of living** level of subsistence or material welfare of community, person *etc.*

standpoint ('stændpɔɪnt) *n.* 1. point of view, opinion 2. mental attitude

stank (stæŋk) *pt. of* STINK

stannary ('stænərɪ) *n.* place or region where tin is mined or worked

stannous ('stænəs) *a.* of, containing tin

stanza ('stænzə) *n.* group of lines of verse

staple ('steɪpəl) *n.* 1. U-shaped piece of wire used to fasten papers, cloth *etc.* 2. short length of stiff wire formed into U-shape with pointed ends, used for holding hasp to post, securing electrical cables *etc.* 3. main product 4. fibre 5. pile of wool *etc.* —*a.* 6. principal 7. regularly produced or made for market —*vt.* 8. fasten with staple 9. sort, classify (wool *etc.*) according to length of fibre —'**stapler** *n.* small device for fastening papers together

star (stɑː) *n.* 1. celestial body, seen as twinkling point of light 2. asterisk (*) 3. celebrated player, actor *etc.* **4.** medal, jewel *etc.* of apparent shape of star —*vt.* **5.** adorn with stars **6.** mark (with asterisk) **7.** feature as star performer —*vi.* **8.** play leading role (in film *etc.*) (**-rr-**) —*a.* **9.** leading, most important, famous —'**stardom** *n.* —'**starlet** *n.* young actress who is projected as potential star —'**starry** *a.* covered with stars —**star-crossed** *a.* dogged by ill luck —'**starfish** *n.* small star-shaped sea creature —'**stargaze** *vi.* **1.** observe stars **2.** daydream —'**stargazing** *n./a.* —**starry-eyed** *a.* given to naive wishes, judgments *etc.* —**Star-Spangled Banner 1.** national anthem of the United States **2.** Stars and Stripes —**star-studded** *a.* featuring large proportion of well-known performers —**Star of David** emblem symbolizing Judaism, consisting of six-pointed star formed by superimposing one equilateral triangle upon another —**Stars and Stripes** national flag of the United States, consisting of 50 white stars and seven red and six white horizontal stripes

starboard ('stɑːbəd, -bɔːd) *n.* **1.** right-hand side of ship, looking forward —*a.* **2.** of, on this side

starch (stɑːtʃ) *n.* **1.** substance forming the main food element in bread, potatoes *etc.*, and used mixed with water, for stiffening linen *etc.* —*vt.* **2.** stiffen thus —'**starchy** *a.* **1.** containing starch **2.** stiff **3.** formal **4.** prim

stare (stɛə) *vi.* **1.** look fixedly **2.** gaze with wide-open eyes —*n.* **3.** staring, fixed gaze —**stare one in the face** be obvious or visible to one —**stare out** abash by staring at

stark (stɑːk) *a.* **1.** blunt, bare **2.** desolate **3.** absolute —*adv.* **4.** completely

starling ('stɑːlɪŋ) *n.* glossy black speckled songbird

start (stɑːt) *vt.* **1.** begin **2.** set going —*vi.* **3.** begin, *esp.* journey **4.** make sudden movement —*n.* **5.** beginning **6.** abrupt movement **7.** advantage of a lead in a race —'**starter** *n.* **1.** electric motor starting car engine **2.** competitor in, supervisor of, start of race

startle ('stɑːt^əl) *vt.* surprise, frighten or alarm suddenly

starve (stɑːv) *v.* (cause to) suffer or die from hunger —**star'vation** *n.*

stash (stæʃ) *vt. inf.* put away, hide

-stat (*comb. form*) device that causes something to remain stationary or constant, as in *thermostat*

state (steɪt) *n.* **1.** condition **2.** place, situation **3.** politically organized people **4.** government **5.** rank **6.** pomp —*vt.* **7.** express in words —'**stated** *a.* **1.** fixed **2.** regular **3.** settled —'**stateless** *a.* without nationality **2.** without state or states —'**stately** *a.* dignified, lofty —'**statement** *n.* **1.** expression in words **2.** account —**State Enrolled Nurse** nurse who has passed examinations

enabling him or her to perform many nursing services —**stately home** UK large mansion, *esp.* one open to public —**state-of-the-art** *a.* (of hi-fi equipment *etc.*) up-to-the-minute —**State Registered Nurse** nurse who has passed examinations enabling him or her to perform all nursing services —'**stateroom** *n.* **1.** private cabin on ship **2.** large room in palace, mansion, used for ceremonial occasions —**state school** any school maintained by the state —'**statesman** *n.* respected political leader

static ('stætɪk) *a.* **1.** motionless, inactive **2.** pert. to bodies at rest or in equilibrium **3.** *Comp.* (of a memory) not needing its contents refreshed periodically —*n.* **4.** electrical interference in radio reception —*pl.* **5.** (*with sing. v.*) branch of physics —'**statically** *adv.*

station ('steɪʃən) *n.* **1.** place where thing stops or is placed **2.** stopping place for railway trains **3.** local office for police force, fire brigade *etc.* **4.** place equipped for radio or television transmission **5.** bus garage **6.** post, employment **7.** status **8.** position in life —*vt.* **9.** put in position —'**stationary** *a.* **1.** not moving, fixed **2.** not changing —**station wagon** estate car

stationer ('steɪʃənə) *n.* dealer in writing materials *etc.* —'**stationery** *n.*

statistics (stə'tɪstɪks) *pl.n.* **1.** numerical facts collected systematically and arranged **2.** (*with sing. v.*) the study of them —sta'tistical *a.* —sta'tistically *adv.* —statis'tician *n.* one who compiles and studies statistics

statue ('stætjuː) *n.* solid carved or cast image of person, animal *etc.* —'**statuary** *n.* statues collectively —**statuesque** (stætjuˈɛsk) *a.* **1.** like statue **2.** dignified —statu'ette *n.* small statue

stature ('stætʃə) *n.* **1.** bodily height **2.** greatness

status ('steɪtəs) *n.* **1.** position, rank **2.** prestige **3.** relation to others —**status quo** (kwəʊ) existing state of affairs —**status symbol** possession regarded as proof of owner's wealth *etc.*

statute ('stætjuːt) *n.* written law —'**statutory** *a.* enacted, defined or authorized by statute

staunch (stɔːntʃ) *vt.* **1.** stop flow of (blood) (*also* **stanch**) —*a.* **2.** trustworthy, loyal

stave (steɪv) *n.* **1.** one of the pieces forming barrel **2.** verse, stanza **3.** *Mus.* staff —*vt.* **4.** (*usu. with* in) burst or force (hole in something) **5.** (*with* off) ward (off) (**stove, staved** *pt./pp.*, '**staving** *pr.p.*)

staves (steɪvz) *n., pl. of* STAFF, STAVE

stay¹ (steɪ) *vi.* **1.** remain **2.** sojourn **3.** pause **4.** wait **5.** endure —*vt.* **6.** stop **7.** hinder **8.** postpone (**stayed, 'staying**) —*n.* **9.** remaining, sojourning **10.** check **11.** restraint **12.** deterrent **13.** postponement —**stay-at-home** *a./n.* (person) enjoying quiet and unadventurous use of leisure —**staying power** endurance

stay² (steɪ) n. 1. support, prop 2. rope supporting mast etc. —pl. 3. formerly, laced corsets

S.T.D. subscriber trunk dialling

stead (stɛd) n. rare place —**stand (someone) in good stead** be useful or of good service to (someone)

steady ('stɛdɪ) a. 1. firm 2. regular 3. temperate 4. industrious 5. reliable —vt. 6. make steady —'**steadily** adv. —'**steadiness** n. —'**steadfast** a. firm, fixed, unyielding —'**steadfastly** adv. —**steady state** Phys. condition of system when some or all of quantities describing it are independent of time —**steady (on)** be careful

steak (steɪk) n. 1. thick slice of meat, esp. beef 2. slice of fish

steal (stiːl) v. 1. take (something) without right or leave —vi. 2. move silently (**stole, 'stolen, 'stealing**)

stealth (stɛlθ) n. secret or underhand procedure, behaviour —'**stealthily** adv. —'**stealthy** a.

steam (stiːm) n. 1. vapour of boiling water 2. inf. power, energy —vi. 3. give off steam 4. rise in vapour 5. move by steam power —vt. 6. cook or treat with steam —'**steamer** n. 1. steam-propelled ship 2. vessel for cooking or treating with steam —'**steamy** a. 1. of, full of, or covered with steam 2. inf. lustful —**steam-engine** n. engine worked or propelled by steam —**steam iron** electric iron that emits steam to facilitate pressing and ironing —'**steamroller** n. 1. large roller, orig. moved by steam, for levelling road surfaces etc. 2. any great power used to crush opposition —vt. 3. crush

stearin or **stearine** ('stɪərɪn) n. 1. colourless crystalline ester, present in fats and used in soap and candles (also **tri'stearin**) 2. fat in its solid form

steatite ('stɪətaɪt) n. soapstone

steed (stiːd) n. Poet. horse

steel (stiːl) n. 1. hard and malleable metal made by mixing carbon in iron 2. tool, weapon of steel 3. C railway track, line —vt. 4. harden —'**steely** a. —**steel band** type of band consisting mainly of percussion instruments made from oildrums —**steel wool** woven mass of fine steel fibres, used for cleaning or polishing

steelyard ('stiːljɑːd) n. kind of balance with unequal arms

steep¹ (stiːp) a. 1. rising, sloping abruptly 2. precipitous 3. inf. difficult 4. (of prices) very high or exorbitant 5. inf. unreasonable —'**steepen** v. —'**steeply** adv.

steep² (stiːp) vt. 1. soak, saturate —vi. 2. be soaked —n. 3. act or process of steeping 4. the liquid used for this purpose

steeple ('stiːpəl) n. church tower with spire —'**steeplechase** n. 1. horse race with ditches and fences to jump 2. foot race with hurdles etc. to jump —'**steeplejack** n. one who builds, repairs chimneys, steeples etc.

steer¹ (stɪə) vt. 1. guide, direct course of (vessel, motor vehicle etc.) —vi. 2. direct one's course —'**steerage** n. 1. effect of a helm 2. formerly, cheapest accommodation on ship —**steering committee** committee set up to prepare topics to be discussed, order of business etc. for legislative assembly etc. —**steering gear, wheel** etc. mechanism for steering —'**steersman** n. helmsman of vessel

steer² (stɪə) n. castrated male ox

stein (staɪn) n. earthenware beer mug

stele ('stiːlɪ, stiːl) n. ancient carved stone pillar or slab (pl. **stelae** ('stiːliː), **steles** ('stiːlɪz, stiːlz))

stellar ('stɛlə) a. of stars

stem¹ (stɛm) n. 1. stalk, trunk 2. long slender part, as in tobacco pipe 3. part of word to which inflections are added 4. foremost part of ship —vi. 5. (with **from**) originate

stem² (stɛm) vt. check, stop, dam up (**-mm-**)

stench (stɛntʃ) n. offensive smell

stencil ('stɛnsəl) n. 1. thin sheet of plastic or metal pierced with pattern, which is brushed over with paint or ink, leaving pattern on surface under it 2. pattern produced by this process —vt. 3. mark (surface) with stencil (**-ll-**)

Sten gun (stɛn) light sub-machine-gun

stenography (stə'nɒgrəfɪ) n. shorthand writing —**ste'nographer** n. —**steno'graphic** a.

stentorian (stɛn'tɔːrɪən) a. (of voice) very loud

step (stɛp) vi. 1. move and set down foot 2. proceed (in this way) —vt. 3. measure in paces (**-pp-**) —n. 4. act of stepping 5. sound made by stepping 6. mark made by foot 7. manner of walking 8. series of foot movements forming part of dance 9. gait 10. pace 11. measure, act, stage in proceeding 12. board, rung etc. to put foot on 13. degree in scale 14. mast socket 15. promotion —pl. 16. stepladder (also **pair of steps**) —'**stepladder** n. four-legged ladder having broad flat steps —**stepping stone 1.** one of series of stones acting as footrests for crossing streams etc. 2. circumstance that assists progress towards any goal

stepchild ('stɛptʃaɪld) n. child of husband or wife by former marriage —'**stepbrother** n. —'**stepfather** n. —'**stepmother** n. —'**stepsister** n.

stephanotis (stɛfə'nəʊtɪs) n. climbing shrub with fragrant waxy flowers

steppe (stɛp) n. (oft. pl.) extensive treeless plain in European and Asiatic Russia

-ster (comb. form) 1. indicating person who is engaged in certain activity, as in prankster 2. indicating person associated with or being something specified, as in mobster, youngster

stere (stɪə) *n.* cubic metre

stereo- *or sometimes before vowel* **stere-** (*comb. form*) three-dimensional quality or solidity, as in *stereoscope*

stereophonic (sterɪə'fɒnɪk, stɪər-) *a.* (of sound reproduction) using two or more separate microphones to feed two or more loudspeakers through separate channels in order to give spatial effect to sound —'**stereo** *a./n.* (of, for) stereophonic gramophone *etc.*

stereoscope ('sterɪəskəʊp, 'stɪər-) *n.* optical instrument for viewing two-dimensional pictures, giving illusion of depth and relief —**stereoscopic** (sterɪə'skɒpɪk, stɪər-) *a.*

stereotype ('sterɪətaɪp, 'stɪər-) *n.* 1. metal plate for printing cast from set-up type 2. something (monotonously) familiar, conventional, predictable —*vt.* 3. make stereotype of —'**stereotyped** *a.* 1. lacking originality or individuality 2. reproduced from or on stereotype printing plate

sterile ('steraɪl) *a.* 1. unable to produce fruit, crops, young *etc.* 2. free from (harmful) germs —**sterility** (ste'rɪlɪtɪ) *n.* —**sterilization** *or* **-isation** (sterɪlaɪ'zeɪʃən) *n.* process or act of making sterile —**sterilize** *or* **-ise** ('sterɪlaɪz) *vt.* render sterile

sterling ('stɜːlɪŋ) *a.* 1. genuine, true 2. of solid worth, dependable 3. in British money —*n.* 4. British money

stern¹ (stɜːn) *a.* severe, strict

stern² (stɜːn) *n.* rear part of ship

sternum ('stɜːnəm) *n.* breastbone (*pl.* **-na** (-nə), **-s**)

sterols ('sterɒlz) *pl.n.* class of complex organic alcohols, including ergosterol, cholesterol —'**steroid** *n. Biochem.* any of group of organic compounds including sterols, bile acids, many hormones, and D vitamins

stertorous ('stɜːtərəs) *a.* with sound of heavy snoring 2. breathing in this way

stet (stet) *Lat.*, let it stand (proofreader's direction to cancel alteration previously made)

stethoscope ('steθəskəʊp) *n.* instrument for listening to action of heart, lungs *etc.*

stetson ('stetsən) *n.* type of broad-brimmed felt hat

stevedore ('stiːvɪdɔː) *n.* one who loads or unloads ships

stew (stjuː) *n.* 1. food cooked slowly in closed vessel 2. state of excitement, agitation or worry —*v.* 3. cook by stewing —**stewed** *a.* 1. (of fish *etc.*) cooked by stewing 2. UK (of tea) bitter through having been left to infuse for too long 3. *sl.* drunk

steward ('stjʊəd) *n.* 1. one who manages another's property 2. official managing race

meeting, assembly *etc.* 3. attendant on ship's or aircraft's passengers ('**stewardess** *fem.*)

stick (stɪk) *n.* 1. long, thin piece of wood 2. anything shaped like a stick 3. *inf.* person, as in *good stick* —*vt.* 4. pierce, stab 5. place, fasten, as by pins, glue 6. (*with out*) protrude 7. *inf.* tolerate, abide —*vi.* 8. adhere 9. come to stop, jam 10. remain 11. be fastened 12. (*with out*) protrude (**stuck** *pt./pp.*) —'**sticker** *n.* adhesive label, poster —'**sticky** *a.* 1. covered with, like adhesive substance 2. (of weather) warm, humid 3. *inf.* difficult, unpleasant —**sticking plaster** thin cloth with adhesive substance on one side, used for covering slight wounds —**stick insect** insect that resembles a twig —**stick-in-the-mud** *n. inf.* person who lacks initiative or imagination —**stick-up** *n. sl.*, *chiefly US* robbery at gunpoint —**sticky wicket** 1. cricket pitch rapidly dried by sun after rain and particularly conducive to spin 2. *inf.* difficult situation —**stick up** *sl.*, *chiefly US* rob, *esp.* at gunpoint —**stick up for** *inf.* support or defend

stickleback ('stɪkᵊlbæk) *n.* small fish with sharp spines on back

stickler ('stɪklə) *n.* (*usu. with* for) person who insists on something

stiff (stɪf) *a.* 1. not easily bent or moved 2. rigid 3. awkward 4. difficult 5. thick, not fluid 6. formal 7. stubborn 8. unnatural 9. strong or fresh, as breeze 10. *inf.* excessive —*n.* 11. *sl.* corpse —'**stiffen** *v.* —'**stiffly** *adv.* —'**stiffness** *n.* —**stiff-necked** *a.* obstinate, stubborn

stifle ('staɪfᵊl) *vt.* smother, suppress

stigma ('stɪgmə) *n.* distinguishing mark, *esp.* of disgrace (*pl.* **-s**, **stigmata** ('stɪgmətə, stɪg'mɑːtə)) —'**stigmatism** *n.* —'**stigmatize** *or* **-ise** *vt.* mark with stigma

stile (staɪl) *n.* arrangement of steps for climbing a fence

stiletto (stɪ'letəʊ) *n.* 1. small dagger 2. small boring tool 3. very high heel on woman's shoe, tapering to very narrow tip (*pl.* **-s**) —*a.* 4. thin, pointed like stiletto

still¹ (stɪl) *a.* 1. motionless 2. noiseless 3. at rest —*vt.* 4. quiet —*adv.* 5. to this time 6. yet 7. even —*n.* 8. photograph, *esp.* of film scene —'**stillness** *n.* —'**stillborn** *a.* born dead —**still life** painting of inanimate objects

still² (stɪl) *n.* apparatus for distilling —**still room** pantry, storeroom in large house

stilt (stɪlt) *n.* 1. pole with footrests for walking raised from ground 2. long post supporting building *etc.* 3. shore bird similar to avocet but having straight bill —'**stilted** *a.* stiff in manner, pompous —'**stiltedly** *adv.*

Stilton ('stɪltən) *n.* either of two rich cheeses, blue-veined or white

stimulus ('stɪmjʊləs) *n.* 1. something that

rouses to activity **2.** incentive (*pl.* **-uli** (-julaı, -juliː)) —'**stimulant** *n.* drug *etc.* acting as a stimulus —'**stimulate** *vt.* rouse up, spur —'**stimulating** *a.* acting as stimulus —**stimu'lation** *n.* —'**stimulative** *a./n.*

sting (stıŋ) *vt.* **1.** thrust sting into **2.** cause sharp pain to **3.** *sl.* impose upon by asking for money **4.** overcharge —*vi.* **5.** feel sharp pain (**stung**, '**stinging**) —*n.* **6.** (wound, pain, caused by) sharp pointed organ, oft. poisonous, of certain insects and animals —'**stingray** *n.* ray having whiplike tail bearing serrated venomous spine capable of inflicting painful weals

stingy ('stındʒı) *a.* **1.** mean **2.** avaricious **3.** niggardly —'**stingily** *adv.* —'**stinginess** *n.*

stink (stıŋk) *vi.* **1.** give out strongly offensive smell **2.** *sl.* be abhorrent (**stank, stunk,** '**stinking**) —*n.* **3.** such smell, stench **4.** *inf.* fuss, bother —'**stinker** *n. sl.* **1.** difficult or unpleasant person or thing **2.** something of very poor quality —**stink bomb** small bomb containing liquid with offensive smell

stint (stınt) *v.* **1.** be frugal, miserly to (someone) with (something) —*n.* **2.** allotted amount of work or time **3.** limitation, restriction

stipend ('staıpend) *n.* salary, *esp.* of clergyman —sti'**pendiary** *a.* receiving stipend

stipple ('stıpəl) *vt.* **1.** engrave, paint in dots —*n.* **2.** this process

stipulate ('stıpjuleıt) *vt.* specify in making a bargain —stipu'**lation** *n.* proviso, condition —'**stipulator** *n.*

stipule ('stıpjuːl) *n.* small paired outgrowth occurring at base of leaf or its stalk —'**stipular** *a.*

stir (stɜː) *v.* **1.** (begin to) move —*vt.* **2.** set, keep in motion **3.** excite; rouse **4.** (*with* up) cause (trouble) (**-rr-**) —*n.* **5.** commotion, disturbance —'**stirring** *a.* **1.** exciting emotions; stimulating **2.** active or busy

stir² (stɜː) *n.* **1.** *sl.* prison **2.** *NZ sl.* noisy party —**stir-crazy** *a. US sl.* mentally disturbed as result of being in prison

stirk (stɜːk) *n.* **1.** heifer of 6 to 12 months old **2.** yearling heifer or bullock

stirrup ('stırəp) *n.* metal loop hung from strap for supporting foot of rider on horse (*also* **stirrup iron**) —**stirrup cup** cup containing alcoholic drink offered to horseman ready to depart —**stirrup pump** hand-operated pump, base of cylinder of which is placed in bucket of water: used in fighting fires

stitch (stıtʃ) *n.* **1.** movement of needle in sewing *etc.* **2.** its result in the work **3.** sharp pain in side **4.** least fragment (of clothing) —*vt.* **5.** sew, fasten *etc.* with stitches

stoat (stəʊt) *n.* small mammal with brown coat and black-tipped tail

stock (stɒk) *n.* **1.** goods, material stored, *esp.* for sale or later use **2.** reserve, fund **3.** financial shares in, or capital of, company *etc.* **4.** standing, reputation **5.** farm animals, livestock **6.** plant, stem from which cuttings are taken **7.** handle of gun, tool *etc.* **8.** liquid broth produced by boiling meat *etc.* **9.** flowering plant **10.** lineage —*pl.* **11.** *Hist.* frame to secure feet, hands (of offender) **12.** frame to support ship during construction —*a.* **13.** kept in stock **14.** standard, hackneyed —*vt.* **15.** keep, store **16.** supply with livestock, fish *etc.* —'**stockist** *n.* dealer who maintains stocks of specified product —'**stocky** *a.* thickset —'**stockbreeder** *n.* person who breeds livestock as occupation —'**stockbroker** *n.* agent for buying, selling shares in companies —**stock car** ordinary car strengthened and modified for a form of racing in which cars often collide —**stock exchange** institution for buying and selling shares —'**stockjobber** *n.* dealer on a stock exchange —'**stockman** *n.* man experienced in driving, handling cattle, sheep —**stock market** stock exchange —'**stockpile** *v.* acquire and store large quantity of (something) —**stock-still** *a.* motionless —'**stocktaking** *n.* examination, counting and valuing of goods in shop *etc.* —'**stockyard** *n.* yard with pens or covered buildings where farm animals are assembled, sold *etc.* —**stock in trade 1.** goods necessary for carrying on business **2.** anything constantly used by someone as part of his occupation, trade *etc.*

stockade (stɒ'keıd) *n.* enclosure of stakes, barrier

stockinet (stɒkı'nɛt) *n.* machine-knitted elastic fabric

stocking ('stɒkıŋ) *n.* one of pair of close-fitting coverings for legs and feet —'**stockinged** *a.*

stodgy ('stɒdʒı) *a.* (*esp.* of food) heavy, dull —**stodge** *n.* heavy, solid food

stoep (stuːp) *n. SA* veranda

stoic ('stəʊık) *a.* **1.** capable of much self-control, great endurance without complaint —*n.* **2.** stoical person —'**stoical** *a.* —**stoicism** ('stəʊısızəm) *n.*

stoke (stəʊk) *v.* feed, tend (fire or furnace) —'**stoker** *n.* —'**stokehold** *n. Naut.* **1.** coal bunker for ship's furnace **2.** hold for ship's boilers; fire room —'**stokehole** *n.* **1.** stokehold **2.** hole in furnace through which it is stoked

stole¹ (stəʊl) *pt. of* STEAL —'**stolen** *pp. of* STEAL

stole² (stəʊl) *n.* long scarf or shawl

stolid ('stɒlıd) *a.* **1.** hard to excite **2.** heavy, slow, apathetic —sto'**lidity** *n.* —'**stolidly** *adv.*

stoma ('stəʊmə) *n.* **1.** *Bot.* epidermal pore in plant leaves, that controls passage of gases through plant **2.** *Zool., anat.* mouth or mouthlike part (*pl.* **stomata** ('stəʊmətə, 'stɒm-, stəʊ'mɑːtə))

stomach ('stʌmək) *n.* **1.** sac forming chief digestive organ in any animal **2.** appetite **3.** desire, inclination —*vt.* **4.** put up with —**stomach pump** *Med.* suction device for removing stomach contents —**stomach upset** slight digestive disorder

stomp (stɒmp) *vi. inf.* stamp

stone (stəʊn) *n.* **1.** (piece of) rock **2.** gem **3.** hard seed of fruit **4.** hard deposit formed in kidneys, bladder **5.** weight, 14 lbs. —*vt.* **6.** throw stones at **7.** free (fruit) from stones —**stoned** *a. sl.* stupefied by alcohol or drugs —**stonily** *adv.* —'**stony** *or* '**stoney** *a.* **1.** of, like stone **2.** hard **3.** cold —**Stone Age** period in human culture identified by use of stone implements —**stoneblind** *a.* completely blind —**stonechat** *n.* black songbird with reddish-brown breast —**stone-cold** *a.* completely cold —**stone-cold sober** completely sober —'**stonecrop** *n.* N temperate plant having fleshy leaves and typically red, yellow or white flowers —**stone deaf** completely deaf —'**stonemason** *n.* person skilled in preparing stone for building —**stone's throw** short distance —**stone'wall** *vi.* **1.** obstruct business **2.** play slow game, *esp.* in cricket —'**stoneware** *n.* heavy common pottery —**stony-broke** *a. sl.* with no money left

stood (stʊd) *pt./pp. of* STAND

stooge (stuːdʒ) *n.* **1.** *Theat. etc.* performer who is always the butt of another's jokes **2.** *sl.* one taken advantage of by another

stook (stuːk) *n.* group of sheaves set upright in field to dry

stool (stuːl) *n.* **1.** backless chair **2.** excrement —**stool ball** game resembling cricket —**stool pigeon 1.** living or dummy pigeon used as decoy **2.** police informer

stoop (stuːp) *vi.* **1.** lean forward or down, bend **2.** swoop **3.** abase, degrade oneself —*n.* **4.** stooping carriage of the body

stop (stɒp) *vt.* **1.** check, bring to halt **2.** prevent **3.** interrupt **4.** suspend **5.** desist from **6.** fill up (an opening) —*vi.* **7.** cease, come to a halt **8.** stay (-**pp-**) —*n.* **9.** stopping or becoming stopped **10.** punctuation mark, *esp.* full stop **11.** any device for altering or regulating pitch **12.** set of pipes in organ having tones of a distinct quality —'**stoppage** *n.* —'**stopper** *n.* plug for closing bottle *etc.* —'**stopcock** *n.* valve to control or stop flow of fluid in pipe —'**stopgap** *n.* temporary substitute —'**stopoff** *or* '**stopover** *n.* short break in journey —**stop press** news put into a newspaper at the last minute —'**stopwatch** *n.* watch which can be stopped for exact timing of race

store (stɔː) *vt.* **1.** stock, furnish, keep —*n.* **2.** shop

3. abundance **4.** stock **5.** department store **6.** place for keeping goods **7.** warehouse —*pl.* **8.** stocks of goods, provisions —'**storage** *n.* —**storage battery** *esp.* US accumulator —**storage heater** electric device which accumulates and radiates heat generated by off-peak electricity —**store cattle** cattle bought lean to be fattened for market

storey *or U.S.* **story** ('stɔːrɪ) *n.* horizontal division of a building

stork (stɔːk) *n.* large wading bird

storm (stɔːm) *n.* **1.** violent weather with wind, rain, hail, sand, snow *etc.* **2.** assault on fortress **3.** violent outbreak, discharge —*vt.* **4.** assault **5.** take by storm —*vi.* **6.** rage —'**stormy** *a.* **1.** like storm **2.** (emotionally) violent —**storm centre 1.** centre of cyclonic storm *etc.* where pressure is lowest **2.** centre of disturbance or trouble —**storm door** additional door outside ordinary door, providing extra insulation against wind *etc.* —**storm-trooper** *n.* **1.** member of Nazi S.A. **2.** member of shock troops —**stormy petrel 1.** any of various small petrels typically having dark plumage and paler underparts **2.** person who brings trouble

story ('stɔːrɪ) *n.* **1.** (book, piece of prose *etc.*) telling about events, happenings **2.** *inf.* lie **3.** US *see* STOREY —'**storybook** *n.* book containing stories, *esp.* for children

stoup *or* **stoop** (stuːp) *n.* small basin for holy water

stout (staʊt) *a.* **1.** fat **2.** sturdy **3.** resolute —*n.* **4.** kind of beer —'**stoutly** *adv.* —'**stoutness** *n.* —**stout'hearted** *a.* brave

stove[1] (stəʊv) *n.* apparatus for cooking, heating *etc.* —'**stovepipe** *n.* **1.** pipe that serves as flue to stove **2.** man's tall silk hat

stove[2] (stəʊv) *pt./pp. of* STAVE

stow (stəʊ) *vt.* pack away —'**stowage** *n.* —'**stowaway** *n.* one who hides in ship to obtain free passage

strabismus (strəˈbɪzməs) *n.* abnormal parallel alignment of one or both eyes, characterized by turning inwards or outwards from nose (*also* squint)

straddle ('strædəl) *vt.* **1.** bestride —*vi.* **2.** spread legs wide —*n.* **3.** act or position of straddling

Stradivarius (strædɪˈvɑːrɪəs) *n.* violin manu-factured in Italy by Antonio Stradivari or his family

strafe (streɪf, strɑːf) *vt.* attack (*esp.* with bullets, rockets) from air

straggle ('strægəl) *vi.* stray, get dispersed, linger —'**straggler** *n.*

straight (streɪt) *a.* **1.** without bend **2.** honest **3.** level **4.** in order **5.** (of spirits) undiluted, neat **6.** expressionless **7.** (of drama, actor *etc.*) serious **8.** *sl.* heterosexual —*n.* **9.** straight state or part

—*adv.* **10.** direct —'**straighten** *v.* —**straight·a'way** *adv.* immediately (*also* **straight away**) —**straight face** serious facial expression, *esp.* one that conceals impulse to laugh —**straight-faced** *a.* —**straight'forward** *a.* **1.** open, frank **2.** simple **3.** honest —**straight·'forwardly** *adv.* —**straight man** subsidiary actor who acts as stooge to comedian

strain¹ (strein) *vt.* **1.** stretch tightly **2.** stretch to full or to excess **3.** filter —*vi.* **4.** make great effort —*n.* **5.** stretching force **6.** violent effort **7.** injury from being strained **8.** burst of music or poetry **9.** great demand **10.** (condition caused by) overwork, worry *etc.* **11.** tone of speaking or writing —**strained** *a.* —'**strainer** *n.* filter, sieve

strain² (strein) *n.* **1.** breed or race **2.** *esp. Biol.* type **3.** trace, streak

strait (streit) *n.* **1.** channel of water connecting two larger areas of water —*pl.* **2.** position of difficulty or distress —*a.* **3.** narrow **4.** strict —'**straiten** *vt.* **1.** make strait, narrow **2.** press with poverty —'**strait·jacket** *or* '**straight·jacket** *n.* jacket to confine arms of violent person —**strait-laced** *a.* austere, strict **2.** puritanical

strand¹ (strænd) *v.* **1.** run aground **2.** leave, be left helpless or in difficulties —*n.* **3.** *Poet.* shore

strand² (strænd) *n.* one of individual fibres or threads of string, wire *etc.*

strange (streindʒ) *a.* **1.** odd, queer **2.** unaccustomed **3.** foreign **4.** uncommon **5.** wonderful **6.** singular —'**strangely** *adv.* —'**strangeness** *n.* —'**stranger** *n.* **1.** unknown person **2.** foreigner **3.** (*with* to) one unaccustomed (to)

strangle ('stræŋgᵊl) *vt.* **1.** kill by squeezing windpipe **2.** suppress —**strangu'lation** *n.* strangling —'**stranglehold** *n.* **1.** wrestling hold in which wrestler's arms are pressed against opponent's windpipe **2.** complete control over person or situation

strap (stræp) *n.* **1.** strip, *esp.* of leather —*vt.* **2.** fasten, beat with strap (**-pp-**) —'**strapping** *a.* tall and well-made —'**straphanger** *n.* in bus, train, one who has to stand, steadying himself with strap provided for this

strata ('stra:tə) *n., pl. of* STRATUM

stratagem ('strætidʒəm) *n.* plan, trick —**strategic(al)** (strə'ti:dʒɪk(ᵊl)) *a.* —'**strategist** *n.* —'**strategy** *n.* **1.** art of war **2.** overall plan

strathspey (stræθ'spei) *n.* type of Scottish dance with gliding steps

stratosphere ('strætəsfiə) *n.* upper part of the atmosphere, approx. 11 kms above earth's surface

stratum ('stra:təm) *n.* **1.** layer, *esp.* of rock **2.** class in society (*pl.* **-s, -ta**) —**strati·fi'cation** *n.* —'**stratify** *v.* form, deposit in layers (**-ified, -ifying**)

stratus ('streitəs) *n.* grey layer cloud (*pl.* **-ti** (-tai))

straw (strɔː) *n.* **1.** stalks of grain **2.** single stalk **3.** long, narrow tube used to suck up liquid —**strawberry** ('strɔːbəri, -bri) *n.* **1.** creeping plant producing red, juicy fruit **2.** the fruit —**strawberry blonde** (of hair) reddish blonde —**strawberry mark** soft vascular red birthmark

stray (strei) *vi.* **1.** wander **2.** digress **3.** get lost —*a.* **4.** strayed **5.** occasional, scattered —*n.* **6.** stray animal

streak (stri:k) *n.* **1.** long line or band **2.** element, trace —*vt.* **3.** mark with streaks —*vi.* **4.** move fast **5.** *inf.* run naked in public —'**streaky** *a.* **1.** having streaks **2.** striped —**streaky bacon** bacon having alternating strips of fat and lean meat

stream (stri:m) *n.* **1.** flowing body of water or other liquid **2.** steady flow **3.** class, division of schoolchildren grouped together because of similar ability —*vi.* **4.** flow **5.** run with liquid **6.** float, wave in the air —*vt.* **7.** group (schoolchildren) in streams —'**streamer** *n.* **1.** (paper) ribbon **2.** narrow flag —**stream of consciousness 1.** *Psychol.* continuous flow of ideas, feelings *etc.* forming content of individual's consciousness **2.** literary technique that reveals flow of thoughts and feelings of characters through long passages of soliloquy

streamlined ('stri:mlaind) *a.* (of car, plane *etc.*) built so as to offer least resistance to air

street (stri:t) *n.* road in town or village, usu. lined with houses —'**streetwalker** *n.* prostitute

strength (strɛŋθ) *n.* **1.** quality of being strong **2.** power **3.** capacity for exertion or endurance **4.** vehemence **5.** force **6.** full or necessary number of people —'**strengthen** *v.* make or become stronger —**on the strength of 1.** relying on **2.** because of

strenuous ('strɛnjʊəs) *a.* **1.** energetic **2.** earnest —'**strenuously** *adv.*

streptomycin (strɛptəʊ'maisin) *n.* antibiotic drug

stress (strɛs) *n.* **1.** emphasis **2.** strain **3.** impelling force **4.** effort **5.** tension —*vt.* **6.** emphasize **7.** accent **8.** put mechanical stress on

stretch (strɛtʃ) *vt.* **1.** extend **2.** exert to utmost **3.** tighten, pull out **4.** reach out —*vi.* **5.** reach **6.** have elasticity —*n.* **7.** stretching, being stretched, expanse **8.** spell —'**stretcher** *n.* **1.** person, thing that stretches **2.** appliance on which ill, wounded or dead person is carried

strew (stru:) *vt.* scatter over surface, spread (**strewed** *pt.,* **strewn** *or* **strewed** *pp.,* '**strewing** *pr.p.*)

strewth (stru:θ) *interj.* expression of surprise or dismay

stria ('straiə) *n.* small channel or threadlike line in surface of shell or other object (*pl.* **striae**

('straɪɪ)) —**striate** ('straɪɪt) a. 1. streaked, furrowed, grooved (also **stri'ated**) —vt. ('straɪeɪt) 2. mark with streaks 3. score —**stri'ation** n.

stricken ('strɪkən) a. 1. seriously affected by disease, grief, famine 2. afflicted —v. 3. pp. of STRIKE

strict (strɪkt) a. 1. stern, not lax or indulgent 2. defined 3. without exception

stricture ('strɪktʃə) n. 1. critical remark 2. constriction

stride (straɪd) vi. 1. walk with long steps (**strode, stridden** ('strɪdən), 'striding) —n. 2. single step 3. its length 4. regular pace

strident ('straɪdənt) a. 1. harsh in tone 2. loud 3. urgent

strife (straɪf) n. 1. conflict 2. quarrelling

strike (straɪk) v. 1. hit (against) 2. ignite 3. (of snake) bite 4. (of plants) (cause to) take root 5. attack 6. hook (fish) 7. sound (time) as bell in clock etc. —vt. 8. affect 9. arrive at, come upon 10. enter mind of 11. discover (gold, oil etc.) 12. dismantle, remove 13. make (coin) —vi. 14. cease work as protest or to make demands (**struck** pt., 'stricken, struck pp., 'striking pr.p.) —n. 15. act of striking —'striker n. —'striking a. noteworthy, impressive —'strike-breaker n. person who tries to make strike ineffectual by working —'strikebreaking n./a. —strike pay allowance paid by trade union to members on strike —strike off remove

Strine (straɪn) n. humorous transliteration of Australian pronunciation

string (strɪŋ) n. 1. (length of) thin cord or other material 2. strand, row 3. series 4. fibre in plants —pl. 5. conditions —vt. 6. provide with, thread on string 7. form in line, series (**strung,** 'stringing) —**stringed** a. (of musical instruments) furnished with strings —'stringer n. 1. Archit. horizontal timber beam used for structural purposes 2. Naut. longitudinal structural brace for strengthening hull of vessel 3. part-time journalist retained by newspaper to cover particular area —'stringy a. 1. like string 2. fibrous —string course Archit. ornamental projecting band or continuous moulding along wall (also 'cordon) —string vest undergarment made from large-meshed material

stringent ('strɪndʒənt) a. strict, rigid, binding —'stringency n. severity —'stringently adv.

strip (strɪp) vt. 1. lay bare, take covering off 2. dismantle 3. deprive —vi. 4. undress (-pp-) —n. 5. long, narrow piece 6. act of undressing or performing striptease —'stripper n. —strip cartoon see comic strip at COMIC —strip lighting electric lighting by means of long glass tubes that are fluorescent lamps —'striptease n. cabaret or theatre act in which person undresses

stripe (straɪp) n. 1. narrow mark, band 2. chevron as symbol of military rank —'stripy a.

stripling ('strɪplɪŋ) n. youth

strive (straɪv) vi. try hard, struggle, contend (**strove, striven** ('strɪvən), 'striving)

strobe (strəʊb) n. apparatus which produces high-intensity flashing light

stroboscope ('strəʊbəskəʊp) n. 1. instrument producing intense flashing light 2. similar device synchronized with shutter of camera so that series of still photographs can be taken of moving object —strobo'scopic(al) a.

strode (strəʊd) pt. of STRIDE

stroke (strəʊk) n. 1. blow 2. sudden action, occurrence 3. apoplexy 4. mark of pen, pencil, brush etc. 5. chime of clock 6. completed movement in series 7. act, manner of striking (ball etc.) 8. style, method of swimming 9. rower sitting nearest stern setting the rate of rowing 10. act of stroking —vt. 11. set stroke for (rowing crew) 12. pass hand lightly over

stroll (strəʊl) vi. 1. walk in leisurely or idle manner —n. 2. leisurely walk

strong (strɒŋ) a. 1. powerful 2. robust 3. healthy 4. difficult to break 5. noticeable 6. intense 7. emphatic 8. not diluted 9. having a certain number —'strongly adv. —strong-arm inf. a. 1. of or involving physical force or violence —vt. 2. show violence towards —'strongbox n. box or safe in which valuables are locked for safety —strong drink alcoholic drink —'stronghold n. fortress —strong language swearing —'strongroom n. specially designed room for storing valuables

strontium ('strɒntɪəm) n. silvery-white chemical element —strontium 90 radioactive isotope of strontium present in fallout of nuclear explosions

strop (strɒp) n. 1. leather for sharpening razors —vt. 2. sharpen on strop (-pp-) —'stroppy a. sl. angry, awkward

strophe ('strəʊfɪ) n. division of ode —strophic ('strɒfɪk, 'strəʊ-) a.

strove (strəʊv) pt. of STRIVE

struck (strʌk) pt./pp. of STRIKE

structure ('strʌktʃə) n. 1. (arrangement of parts in) construction, building etc. 2. form 3. organization —vt. 4. give structure to —'structural a.

strudel ('struːdəl) n. thin sheet of dough usu. filled with apple and baked

struggle ('strʌgəl) vi. 1. contend 2. fight 3. proceed, work, move with difficulty and effort —n. 4. act of struggling

strum (strʌm) v. strike strings of (guitar etc.) (-mm-)

strumpet ('strʌmpɪt) *n. obs.* promiscuous woman

strung (strʌŋ) *pt./pp.* of STRING

strut (strʌt) *vi.* **1.** walk affectedly or pompously (**-tt-**) *—n.* **2.** brace **3.** rigid support, usu. set obliquely **4.** strutting gait

strychnine ('strɪkniːn) *n.* poison obtained from nux vomica seeds —'**strychnic** *a.*

stub (stʌb) *n.* **1.** remnant of anything, *eg* pencil, cigarette *etc.* **2.** counterfoil of cheque *etc. —vt.* **3.** strike (toes) against fixed object **4.** extinguish by pressing against surface (**-bb-**) —'**stubby** *a.* short, broad

stubble ('stʌbᵊl) *n.* **1.** stumps of cut grain after reaping **2.** short growth of beard

stubborn ('stʌbən) *a.* unyielding, obstinate

stucco ('stʌkəʊ) *n.* plaster (*pl.* **-s, -es**) —'**stuccoed** *a.*

stuck (stʌk) *pt./pp.* of STICK —**stuck-up** *a. inf.* conceited; snobbish

stud¹ (stʌd) *n.* **1.** nail with large head **2.** removable double-headed button **3.** vertical wall support —*vt.* **4.** set with studs (**-dd-**)

stud² (stʌd) *n.* set of animals, *esp.* horses, kept for breeding —'**studbook** *n.* book giving pedigree of noted or thoroughbred animals, *esp.* horses —**stud farm**

studio ('stjuːdɪəʊ) *n.* **1.** workroom of artist, photographer *etc.* **2.** building, room where film, television or radio shows are made, broadcast (*pl.* **-s**) —**studio couch** upholstered couch that can be converted into double bed

study ('stʌdɪ) *vi.* **1.** be engaged in learning —*vt.* **2.** make study of **3.** try constantly to do **4.** consider **5.** scrutinize ('**studied, 'studying**) —*n.* **6.** effort to acquire knowledge **7.** subject of this **8.** room to study in **9.** book, report *etc.* produced as result of study **10.** sketch —**student** ('stjuːdᵊnt) *n.* one who studies, *esp.* at university *etc.* —'**studied** *a.* carefully designed, premeditated —'**studious** ('stjuːdɪəs) *a.* **1.** fond of study **2.** thoughtful **3.** painstaking **4.** deliberate

stuff (stʌf) *n.* **1.** eat (large amount) —*vt.* **2.** pack, cram, fill (completely) **3.** fill with seasoned mixture **4.** fill (animal's skin) with material to preserve lifelike form —*n.* **5.** material, fabric **6.** any substance —'**stuffing** *n.* material for stuffing, *esp.* seasoned mixture for inserting in poultry *etc.* before cooking —'**stuffy** *a.* **1.** lacking fresh air **2.** *inf.* dull, conventional —**do your stuff** *inf.* do what is required or expected of you

stultify ('stʌltɪfaɪ) *vt.* make ineffectual (**-ified, -ifying**) —**stultifiʹcation** *n.*

stumble ('stʌmbᵊl) *vi.* **1.** trip and nearly fall **2.** falter —*n.* **3.** act of stumbling —**stumbling block** obstacle

stump (stʌmp) *n.* **1.** remnant of tree, tooth *etc.*

when main part has been cut away **2.** one of uprights of wicket in cricket —*vt.* **3.** confuse, puzzle **4.** break wicket of (batsman out of his ground in playing ball) —*vi.* **5.** walk heavily, noisily —'**stumpy** *a.* short and thickset

stun (stʌn) *vt.* **1.** knock senseless **2.** amaze (**-nn-**) —'**stunner** *n. inf.* person or thing of great beauty, quality *etc.* —'**stunning** *a.*

stung (stʌŋ) *pt./pp.* of STING

stunk (stʌŋk) *pp.* of STINK

stunt¹ (stʌnt) *vt.* check growth of, dwarf —'**stunted** *a.* **1.** underdeveloped **2.** undersized

stunt² (stʌnt) *n.* **1.** feat of dexterity or daring **2.** anything spectacular, unusual, done to gain publicity —**stunt man** professional acrobat substituted for actor when dangerous scenes are filmed

stupefy ('stjuːpɪfaɪ) *vt.* **1.** make insensitive, lethargic **2.** astound (**-efied, -efying**) —**stupeʹfaction** *n.*

stupendous (stjuːˈpɛndəs) *a.* **1.** astonishing, amazing **2.** huge

stupid ('stjuːpɪd) *a.* **1.** slow-witted **2.** silly **3.** dazed or stupefied

stupor ('stjuːpə) *n.* **1.** dazed state **2.** insensibility

sturdy ('stɜːdɪ) *a.* **1.** robust **2.** strongly built **3.** vigorous —'**sturdily** *adv.* —'**sturdiness** *n.*

sturgeon ('stɜːdʒən) *n.* fish yielding caviar and isinglass

stutter ('stʌtə) *v.* **1.** speak (word *etc.*) with difficulty **2.** stammer —*n.* **3.** act or habit of stuttering

sty¹ (staɪ) *n.* **1.** place in which pigs are kept **2.** hovel, dirty place

sty² or **stye** (staɪ) *n.* inflammation on edge of eyelid

Stygian ('stɪdʒɪən) *a.* **1.** of river Styx in Hades **2.** gloomy **3.** infernal

style (staɪl) *n.* **1.** manner of writing, doing *etc.* **2.** designation **3.** sort **4.** elegance, refinement **5.** superior manner, quality **6.** design —*vt.* **7.** shape, design **8.** adapt **9.** designate —'**stylish** *a.* fashionable —'**stylishly** *adv.* —'**stylist** *n.* **1.** one cultivating style in literary or other execution **2.** designer **3.** hairdresser —**styʹlistic** *a.* —'**stylize** *or* **-ise** *vt.* give conventional stylistic form to

stylus ('staɪləs) *n.* **1.** writing instrument **2.** in record-player, tiny point running in groove of record (*pl.* **-li** (-laɪ), **-es**)

stymie *or* **stymy** ('staɪmɪ) *vt.* hinder, thwart

styptic ('stɪptɪk) *a./n.* (designating) a substance that stops bleeding

styrene ('staɪriːn) *n.* colourless liquid used in making synthetic rubber, plastics

suave (swɑːv) *a.* smoothly polite, affable, bland —'**suavity** *n.*

sub (sʌb) *n.* **1.** subeditor **2.** submarine **3.** subscription **4.** substitute **5.** *inf.* advance payment of wages, salary —*vi.* **6.** *inf.* serve as substitute —*v.* **7.** *inf.* grant or receive (advance payment) —*vt.* **8.** subedit (**-bb-**)

sub- (*comb. form*) under, less than, in lower position, subordinate, forming subdivision, as in *subaqua, subeditor, subheading, subnormal, subsoil.* Such words are not given here where the meaning may be easily inferred from the simple word

subaltern ('sʌb^əltən) *n.* army officer below rank of captain

subcommittee (sʌbkə'mɪtɪ) *n.* section of committee functioning separately from main body

subconscious (sʌb'kɒnʃəs) *a.* **1.** acting, existing without one's awareness —*n.* **2.** *Psychol.* that part of human mind unknown, or only partly known, to possessor

subcontinent (sʌb'kɒntɪnənt) *n.* large land mass that is distinct part of continent —**subconti'nental** *a.*

subcontract (sʌb'kɒntrækt) *n.* **1.** subordinate contract under which supply of materials or labour is let out to someone other than party to main contract —*vi.* (sʌbkən'trækt) **2.** (*oft.* with *for*) enter into subcontract —*vt.* (sʌbkən'trækt) **3.** let out (work) on subcontract —**subcon'tractor** *n.*

subculture ('sʌbkʌltʃə) *n.* subdivision of national culture with distinct integrated network of behaviour, beliefs and attitudes

subcutaneous (sʌbkjuː'teɪnɪəs) *a.* under the skin

subdivide (sʌbdɪ'vaɪd, 'sʌbdɪvaɪd) *vt.* divide again —**subdivision** ('sʌbdɪvɪʒən) *n.*

subdominant (sʌb'dɒmɪnənt) *Mus. n.* **1.** fourth degree of major or minor scale **2.** key or chord based on this —*a.* **3.** of the subdominant

subdue (səb'djuː) *vt.* **1.** win control over; conquer **2.** overcome **3.** render less intense or less conspicuous (**-'dued,** -**'duing**)

subfusc ('sʌbfʌsk) *a.* devoid of brightness; drab, dull or dark

subject ('sʌbdʒɪkt) *n.* **1.** theme, topic **2.** that about which something is predicated **3.** conscious self **4.** one under power of another —*a.* **5.** owing allegiance **6.** subordinate **7.** dependent **8.** liable —*vt.* (səb'dʒɛkt) **9.** cause to undergo **10.** make liable **11.** subdue —**sub'jection** *n.* act of bringing, or state of being, under control —**sub'jective** *a.* **1.** based on personal feelings, not impartial **2.** of the self **3.** existing in the mind **4.** displaying artist's individuality —**subjec'tivity** *n.*

subjoin (sʌb'dʒɔɪn) *vt.* add to end of something written *etc.*

sub judice ('dʒuːdɪsɪ) *Lat.* under judicial consideration

subjugate ('sʌbdʒugeɪt) *vt.* **1.** force to submit **2.** conquer —**subju'gation** *n.* —'**subjugator** *n.*

subjunctive (səb'dʒʌŋktɪv) *Gram. n.* **1.** mood used mainly in subordinate clauses expressing wish, possibility —*a.* **2.** in, of that mood

sublease ('sʌbliːs) *n.* **1.** lease of property made by lessee of that property —*v.* (sʌb'liːs) **2.** grant sublease of (property); sublet

sublet (sʌb'lɛt) *vt.* (of tenant) let whole or part of what he has rented to another

sublieutenant (sʌblə'tɛnənt) *n.* most junior commissioned officer in Royal Navy and certain other navies —**sublieu'tenancy** *n.*

sublimate ('sʌblɪmeɪt) *vt.* **1.** *Psychol.* direct energy (*esp.* sexual) into activities considered more socially acceptable **2.** refine —*n.* **3.** *Chem.* material obtained when substance is sublimed —**subli'mation** *n.*

sublime (sə'blaɪm) *a.* **1.** elevated **2.** eminent **3.** majestic **4.** inspiring awe **5.** exalted —*v.* **6.** *Chem.* (cause) to change from solid to vapour —**sub'limely** *adv.* —**sublimity** (sə'blɪmɪtɪ) *or* **su'blimeness** *n.*

subliminal (sʌb'lɪmɪn^əl) *a.* resulting from processes of which the individual is not aware

sub-machine-gun *n.* portable automatic gun with short barrel

submarine (sʌbmə'riːn, 'sʌbmə'riːn) *n.* **1.** (war)ship which can travel (and attack from) below surface of sea and remain submerged for long periods —*a.* **2.** below surface of sea

submerge (səb'mɜːdʒ) *or* **submerse** (səb'mɜːs) *v.* place, go under water —**sub'mergence** *or* **sub'mersion** *n.* —**sub'mersible** *or* **sub'mergible** *a.* **1.** able to be submerged **2.** capable of operating under water *etc.* —*n.* **3.** warship designed to operate under water

submit (səb'mɪt) *vt.* **1.** surrender **2.** put forward for consideration —*vi.* **3.** surrender **4.** defer (**-tt-**) —**sub'mission** *n.* —**sub'missive** *a.* meek, obedient

subordinate (sə'bɔːdɪnət) *a.* **1.** of lower rank or less importance —*n.* **2.** inferior **3.** one under order of another —*vt.* (sə'bɔːdɪneɪt) **4.** make, treat as subordinate —**sub'ordinately** *adv.* —**subordi'nation** *n.* —**subordinate clause** *Gram.* clause with adjectival, adverbial or nominal function, rather than one that functions as separate sentence in its own right

suborn (sə'bɔːn) *vt.* bribe to do evil —**subornation** (sʌbɔː'neɪʃən) *n.* —**sub'orner** *n.*

subplot ('sʌbplɒt) *n.* subordinate plot in novel, film *etc.*

subpoena (səb'piːnə) *n.* **1.** writ requiring attendance at court of law —*vt.* **2.** summon by such order (**-naed, -naing**)

sub rosa ('rəuzə) in secret

subscribe (səb'skraɪb) *vt.* **1.** pay, promise to

pay (contribution) —v. **2.** write (one's name) at end of document —**sub'scriber** n. —**subscription** (səb'skrıpʃən) n. **1.** subscribing **2.** money paid —**subscriber trunk dialling UK** service by which telephone subscribers can obtain trunk calls by dialling direct without aid of operator

subscript ('sʌbskrıpt) a. **1.** *Print.* (of character) printed below base line —n. **2.** subscript character (*also* **sub'index**)

subsection (sʌb'sɛkʃən) n. division of a section

subsequent ('sʌbsıkwənt) a. later, following or coming after in time —**'subsequence** n.

subservient (səb'sɜːvıənt) a. submissive, servile —**sub'servience** n.

subset ('sʌbsɛt) n. mathematical set contained within larger set

subside (səb'saıd) vi. **1.** abate, come to an end **2.** sink **3.** settle **4.** collapse —**subsidence** (səb'saıdəns, 'sʌbsıdəns) n.

subsidiary (səb'sıdıərı) a. **1.** supplementing **2.** secondary **3.** auxiliary —n. **4.** subsidiary person or thing

subsidize or **-ise** ('sʌbsıdaız) vt. **1.** help financially **2.** pay grant to —**'subsidy** n. money granted

subsist (səb'sıst) vi. exist, sustain life —**sub'sistence** n. **1.** the means by which one supports life **2.** livelihood

subsonic (sʌb'sɒnık) a. concerning speeds less than that of sound

substance ('sʌbstəns) n. **1.** matter **2.** particular kind of matter **3.** chief part, essence **4.** wealth —**sub'stantial** a. **1.** considerable **2.** of real value **3.** solid, big **4.** important **5.** really existing —**substanti'ality** n. —**sub'stantially** adv. —**sub'stantiate** vt. bring evidence for, confirm, prove —**substanti'ation** n. —**'substantive** a. **1.** having independent existence **2.** real, fixed —n. **3.** noun

substitute ('sʌbstıtjuːt) v. **1.** put, serve in exchange (for) —n. **2.** thing, person put in place of another **3.** deputy —**substi'tution** n.

substratum (sʌb'strɑːtəm, -'streı-) n. **1.** that which is laid or spread under **2.** layer of earth lying under another **3.** basis (*pl.* **-ta** (-tə), **-s**)

subsume (səb'sjuːm) vt. incorporate (idea, case *etc.*) under comprehensive heading, classification

subtenant (sʌb'tɛnənt) n. person who rents property from tenant —**sub'tenancy** n.

subtend (səb'tɛnd) vt. *Geom.* be opposite to and delimit

subterfuge ('sʌbtəfjuːdʒ) n. trick, lying excuse used to evade something

subterranean (sʌbtə'reınıən) a. underground (*also* **subter'restrial**)

subtitle ('sʌbtaıtəl) n. **1.** secondary title of book

2. (*oft. pl.*) written translation of film dialogue superimposed on film

subtle ('sʌtəl) a. **1.** not immediately obvious **2.** ingenious, acute **3.** crafty **4.** intricate **5.** delicate **6.** making fine distinctions —**'subtlety** n. —**'subtly** adv.

subtonic (sʌb'tɒnık) n. *Mus.* seventh degree of major or minor scale

subtract (səb'trækt) vt. take away, deduct —**sub'traction** n.

subtrahend ('sʌbtrəhɛnd) n. number to be subtracted from another number (**minuend**)

subtropical (sʌb'trɒpıkəl) a. of regions bordering on the tropics

suburb ('sʌbɜːb) n. residential area on outskirts of city —**su'burban** a./n. —**su'burbia** n. **1.** suburbs or people living in them considered as an identifiable community or class in society **2.** life, customs *etc.* of suburban people

subvention (səb'vɛnʃən) n. subsidy

subvert (səb'vɜːt) vt. **1.** overthrow **2.** corrupt —**sub'version** n. —**sub'versive** a.

subway ('sʌbweı) n. **1.** underground passage **2.** underground railway

succeed (sək'siːd) vi. **1.** accomplish purpose **2.** turn out satisfactorily **3.** follow —vt. **4.** follow, take place of —**success** (sək'sɛs) n. **1.** favourable accomplishment, attainment, issue or outcome **2.** successful person or thing —**successful** (sək'sɛsful) a. —**successfully** (sək'sɛsfəlı) adv. —**succession** (sək'sɛʃən) n. **1.** following **2.** series **3.** succeeding —**successive** (sək'sɛsıv) a. following in order, consecutive —**successively** (sək'sɛsıvlı) adv. —**successor** (sək'sɛsə) n.

succinct (sək'sıŋkt) a. terse, concise

succour or *U.S.* **succor** ('sʌkə) vt./n. help in distress

succubus ('sʌkjubəs) n. female demon fabled to have sexual intercourse with sleeping men (*pl.* **-bi** (-baı))

succulent ('sʌkjulənt) a. **1.** juicy, full of juice **2.** (of plant) having thick, fleshy leaves —n. **3.** such plant —**'succulence** or **'succulency** n.

succumb (sə'kʌm) vi. **1.** yield, give way **2.** die

such (sʌtʃ) a. **1.** of the kind or degree mentioned **2.** so great, so much **3.** so made *etc.* **4.** of the same kind —**such and such** particular thing that is unspecified —**'suchlike** inf. a. **1.** such —pron. **2.** other such things

suck (sʌk) vt. **1.** draw into mouth **2.** hold, dissolve in mouth **3.** draw in —n. **4.** sucking —**'sucker** n. **1.** person, thing that sucks **2.** organ, appliance which adheres by suction **3.** shoot coming from root or base of stem of plant **4.** inf. person easily deceived or taken in

suckle ('sʌkəl) v. feed from the breast —**'suckling** n. unweaned infant

sucrose ('sju:krəuz, -krəus) n. sugar

suction ('sʌkʃən) n. 1. drawing or sucking of air or fluid 2. force produced by difference in pressure

Sudanese (su:də'ni:z) a. 1. of Sudan, in NE Afr. —n. 2. native or inhabitant of Sudan

sudden ('sʌdən) a. 1. done, occurring unexpectedly 2. abrupt, hurried —'suddenly adv. —'suddenness n. —sudden infant death syndrome unexplained death of infant during sleep

sudorific (sju:də'rɪfɪk) a. 1. causing perspiration —n. 2. medicine that produces sweat

suds (sʌdz) pl.n. froth of soap and water, lather

sue (sju:, su:) vt. 1. prosecute 2. seek justice from 3. beseech —vi. 4. make application or entreaty (sued, 'suing)

suede (sweɪd) n. leather with soft, velvety finish

suet ('su:ɪt, 'sju:ɪt) n. hard animal fat from sheep, ox etc.

suffer ('sʌfə) v. 1. undergo, endure, experience (pain etc.) —vt. 2. obs. allow —'sufferable a. —'sufferance n. toleration —'sufferer n.

suffice (sə'faɪs) v. be adequate, satisfactory (for) —sufficiency (sə'fɪʃənsɪ) n. adequate amount —sufficient (sə'fɪʃənt) a. enough, adequate

suffix ('sʌfɪks) n. 1. letter or word added to end of word —vt. ('sʌfɪks, sə'fɪks) 2. add, annex to the end

suffocate ('sʌfəkeɪt) v. 1. kill, be killed by deprivation of oxygen 2. smother —suffo'cation n.

suffrage ('sʌfrɪdʒ) n. vote or right of voting —'suffragist n. one claiming a right of voting (suffra'gette fem.)

suffuse (sə'fju:z) vt. well up and spread over —suf'fusion n.

sugar ('ʃugə) n. 1. sweet crystalline vegetable substance —vt. 2. sweeten, make pleasant (with sugar) —'sugary a. —sugar beet variety of common beet grown for sugar —sugar cane plant from whose juice sugar is obtained —sugar daddy sl. wealthy (elderly) man who pays for (esp. sexual) favours of younger person —sugar loaf conical mass of hard refined sugar

suggest (sə'dʒest) vt. 1. propose 2. call up the idea of —suggesti'bility n. —sug'gestible a. easily influenced —sug'gestion n. 1. hint 2. proposal 3. insinuation of impression, belief etc. into mind —sug'gestive a. containing, open to suggestion, esp. of something indecent

suicide ('sju:ɪsaɪd, 'su:-) n. 1. act or instance of killing oneself intentionally 2. person who does this —sui'cidal a.

suit (su:t, sju:t) n. 1. set of clothing 2. garment worn for particular event, purpose 3. one of four sets in pack of cards 4. action at law —v. 5.

make, be fit or appropriate (for) 6. be acceptable (to) —suita'bility n. —'suitable a. 1. fitting, proper 2. convenient 3. becoming —'suitably adv. —'suitcase n. flat rectangular travelling case

suite (swi:t) n. 1. matched set, esp. of furniture 2. set of rooms 3. retinue

suitor ('su:tə, 'sju:t-) n. 1. wooer 2. one who sues 3. petitioner

sulk (sʌlk) vi. 1. be silent, resentful, esp. to draw attention to oneself —n. 2. sulky mood —'sulkily adv. —'sulky a.

sullen ('sʌlən) a. 1. unwilling to talk or be sociable; morose 2. dismal, dull —'sullenly adv.

sully ('sʌlɪ) vt. stain, tarnish, disgrace ('sullied, 'sullying)

sulpha drug ('sʌlfə) sulphonamide used to treat bacterial infections

sulphate ('sʌlfeɪt) n. salt formed by sulphuric acid in combination with any base

sulphonamide (sʌl'fɒnəmaɪd) n. any of group of drugs used as internal germicides in treatment of many bacterial diseases

sulphur or U.S. **sulfur** ('sʌlfə) n. pale yellow nonmetallic element —'sulphide n. compound of sulphur with more electropositive element —'sulphite n. salt or ester of acid —sulphitic (sʌl'fɪtɪk) a. —sulphuric or U.S. sulfuric (sʌl'fjʊərɪk) a. —'sulphurous a. —sulphur dioxide colourless soluble pungent gas used in manufacture of sulphuric acid, preservation of foodstuffs, bleaching and disinfecting —sulphuric acid colourless oily corrosive liquid used in manufacture of fertilizers, dyes and explosives

sultan ('sʌltən) n. ruler of Muslim country —sul'tana n. 1. sultan's wife 2. kind of raisin —'sultanate n. 1. territory or country ruled by sultan 2. office, rank or jurisdiction of sultan

sultry ('sʌltrɪ) a. 1. (of weather) hot, humid 2. (of person) looking sensual

sum (sʌm) n. 1. amount, total 2. problem in arithmetic —v. 3. add up 4. (with up) make summary of (main parts) (-mm-) —summing-up n. summary of main points of speech etc. —sum total 1. total obtained by adding up sum or sums 2. everything included

sumach or U.S. **sumac** ('su:mæk, 'ʃu:-) n. shrub with clusters of green flowers and red hairy fruits

summary ('sʌmərɪ) n. 1. abridgment or statement of chief points of longer document, speech etc. 2. abstract —a. 3. done quickly —'summarily adv. 1. speedily 2. abruptly —'summarize or -ise vt. 1. make summary of 2. present briefly and concisely —sum'mation n. adding up

summer ('sʌmə) n. 1. second, warmest season —vi. 2. pass the summer —'summery a.

—'**summerhouse** *n.* small building in garden or park, used for shade in summer —**summer school** academic course *etc.* held during summer —**summer solstice 1.** time at which sun is at its northernmost point in sky; June 21st **2.** *Astron.* point on celestial sphere at which ecliptic is furthest north from celestial equator —'**summertime** *n.* daylight-saving time, *ie* time shown by clocks *etc.* put forward one hour during certain period of year

summit ('sʌmɪt) *n.* top, peak —**summit conference** meeting of heads of governments

summon ('sʌmən) *vt.* **1.** demand attendance of **2.** call on **3.** bid (witness) appear in court **4.** gather up (energies *etc.*) —'**summons** *n.* **1.** call **2.** authoritative demand

sump (sʌmp) *n.* place or receptacle (*esp.* as oil reservoir in engine) where fluid collects

sumptuous ('sʌmptjʊəs) *a.* **1.** lavish, magnificent **2.** costly —'**sumptuary** *a.* pert. to or regulating expenditure —'**sumptuously** *adv.* —'**sumptuousness** *n.*

sun (sʌn) *n.* **1.** luminous body round which earth and other planets revolve **2.** its rays —*vt.* **3.** expose to sun's rays (**-nn-**) —'**sunless** *a.* —'**sunny** *a.* **1.** like the sun **2.** warm **3.** cheerful —'**sunbathing** *n.* exposure of whole or part of body to sun's rays —'**sunbeam** *n.* ray of sun —'**sunburn** *n.* inflammation of skin due to excessive exposure to sun —'**sundial** *n.* device indicating time during hours of sunlight by means of pointer that casts shadow on to surface marked in hours —'**sundown** *n.* sunset —'**sunfish** *n.* sea fish with large rounded body —'**sunflower** *n.* plant with large golden flowers —'**sunglasses** *pl.n.* glasses with darkened or polarizing lenses that protect eyes from sun's glare —**sun-god** *n.* sun considered as personal deity —**sun lamp** lamp that generates ultraviolet rays —'**sunrise** *n.* **1.** daily appearance of sun above horizon **2.** atmospheric phenomena accompanying this appearance **3.** time at which sun rises at particular locality —'**sunset** *n.* **1.** daily disappearance of sun below horizon **2.** atmospheric phenomena accompanying this disappearance **3.** time at which sun sets at particular locality —'**sunshade** *n.* device, *esp.* parasol or awning, serving to shade from sun —'**sunshine** *n.* **1.** light or warmth received directly from sun **2.** light-hearted term of affection —'**sunshiny** *a.* —'**sunspot** *n.* dark patch appearing temporarily on sun's surface —'**sunstroke** *n.* illness caused by prolonged exposure to intensely hot sun —'**suntan** *n.* colouring of skin by exposure to sun

Sun. Sunday

sundae ('sʌndɪː, -deɪ) *n.* ice cream topped with fruit *etc.*

Sunday ('sʌndɪ) *n.* **1.** first day of week **2.** Christian Sabbath —**Sunday best** one's best clothes —**Sunday school** school for religious instruction of children

sunder ('sʌndə) *vt.* separate, sever

sundry ('sʌndrɪ) *a.* several, various —'**sundries** *pl.n.* odd items not mentioned in detail

sung (sʌŋ) *pp. of* SING

sunk (sʌŋk) *pp. of* SINK

sup (sʌp) *vt.* **1.** take by sips —*vi.* **2.** take supper (**-pp-**) —*n.* **3.** mouthful of liquid

sup. 1. above **2.** superior **3.** *Gram.* superlative **4.** supplement **5.** supplementary **6.** supply

super ('suːpə, 'sjuːpə) *a. inf.* very good

super- (*comb. form*) above, greater, exceeding- (ly), as in **superhuman, superman, superstore, supertanker.** Such compounds are not given here where the meaning may be inferred from the simple word

superable ('suːpərəbəl, 'sjuː-) *a.* **1.** capable of being overcome **2.** surmountable

superannuate (suːpər'ænjʊeɪt, sjuː-) *vt.* **1.** pension off **2.** discharge or dismiss as too old —**super'annuated** *a.* —**superannu'ation** *n.* **1.** pension given on retirement **2.** contribution by employee to pension

superb (sʊ'pɜːb, sjuː-) *a.* **1.** splendid **2.** grand **3.** impressive —**su'perbly** *adv.*

supercargo (suːpə'kɑːgəʊ, sjuː-) *n.* officer on merchant ship in charge of cargo

supercharge ('suːpətʃɑːdʒ, 'sjuː-) *vt.* charge, fill to excess —'**supercharged** *a.* —'**supercharger** *n.* in internal-combustion engine, device to ensure complete filling of cylinder with explosive mixture when running at high speed

supercilious (suːpə'sɪlɪəs, sjuː-) *a.* displaying arrogant pride, scorn, indifference

superconductivity (suːpəkɒndʌk'tɪvɪtɪ, sjuː-) *n. Phys.* property of certain substances that have almost no electrical resistance at temperatures close to absolute zero —**supercon'ductive** *or* **supercon'ducting** *a.* —**supercon'ductor** *n.*

supercool (suːpə'kuːl, sjuː-) *v. Chem.* cool without freezing or crystallization to temperature below that at which freezing or crystallization should occur

superego (suːpər'iːgəʊ, -'ɛgəʊ, sjuː-) *n. Psychoanal.* that part of the unconscious mind that acts as conscience for the ego

supererogation (suːpərɛrə'geɪʃən, sjuː-) *n.* **1.** performance of work in excess of that required **2.** *R.C.Ch.* prayers, devotions *etc.* beyond those prescribed as obligatory

superficial (suːpə'fɪʃəl, sjuː-) *a.* **1.** of or on surface **2.** not careful or thorough **3.** without depth, shallow —**superfici'ality** *n.*

superfluous (suː'pɜːflʊəs, sjuː-) *a.* **1.** extra,

unnecessary **2.** excessive **3.** left over —**super-**
fluity n. **1.** superabundance **2.** unnecessary
amount —**su'perfluously** adv.

supergrass ('suːpəgrɑːs) n. person who acts
as police informer on a large scale

superheat (suːpə'hiːt, sjuː-) vt. **1.** heat (vapour,
esp. steam) to temperature above its saturation
point for given pressure **2.** heat (liquid) to
temperature above its boiling point without
boiling occurring **3.** overheat —**super'heater** n.

superheterodyne receiver (suːpə'hetərə-
dain, sjuː-) radio receiver that combines two
radio-frequency signals by heterodyne action to
produce signal above audible frequency limit

superimpose (suːpərɪm'pəʊz, sjuː-) vt. **1.** set
or place on or over something else **2.** (usu. with
on or upon) add (to) —**superimpo'sition** n.

superintend (suːpərɪn'tɛnd, sjuː-) vt. **1.** have
charge of **2.** overlook **3.** supervise —**superin-**
'tendence n. —**superin'tendent** n. senior police
officer

superior (suː'pɪərɪə, sjuː-) a. **1.** greater in
quality or quantity **2.** upper, higher in position,
rank or quality **3.** showing consciousness of
being so —**superi'ority** n. quality of being
higher, greater or more excellent

superlative (suː'pɜːlətɪv, sjuː-) a. **1.** of, in
highest degree of quality **2.** surpassing **3.** Gram.
denoting form of adjective, adverb meaning
'most' —n. **4.** Gram. superlative degree of
adjective or adverb

supermarket ('suːpəmɑːkɪt, 'sjuː-) n. large
self-service store selling chiefly food and
household goods

supernatural (suːpə'nætʃərəl, sjuː-) a. being
beyond the powers or laws of nature **2.**
miraculous —**super'naturally** adv.

supernova (suːpə'nəʊvə, sjuː-) n. star that
explodes and is for a few days up to one hundred
million times brighter than sun (pl. **-vae** (-viː),
-s)

supernumerary (suːpə'njuːmərərɪ, sjuː-) a. **1.**
in excess of normal number, extra —n. **2.** extra
person or thing

superphosphate (suːpə'fɒsfeɪt, sjuː-) n.
chemical fertilizer

superpose (suːpə'pəʊz, sjuː-) vt. Geom. place
(one figure) upon another so that their
perimeters coincide

superpower ('suːpəpaʊə, 'sjuː-) n. **1.** an
extremely powerful state, such as U.S.A. **2.**
extremely high power, esp. electrical —**'super-**
powered a.

superscribe (suːpə'skraɪb, sjuː-) vt. write
(inscription etc.) above, on top of or outside
—**superscription** (suːpə'skrɪpʃən, sjuː-) n.

superscript ('suːpəskrɪpt, 'sjuː-) n./a. (character) printed, written above the line

supersede (suːpə'siːd, sjuː-) vt. **1.** take the
place of **2.** set aside, discard, supplant
—**supersession** (suːpə'sɛʃən, sjuː-) n.

supersonic (suːpə'sɒnɪk, sjuː-) a. denoting
speed greater than that of sound

superstition (suːpə'stɪʃən, sjuː-) n. religion,
opinion or practice based on belief in luck or
magic —**super'stitious** a. —**super'stitiously**
adv.

superstructure ('suːpəstrʌktʃə, 'sjuː-) n. **1.**
structure above foundations **2.** part of ship
above deck

supertax ('suːpətæks, 'sjuː-) n. tax on large
incomes in addition to usual income tax

supervene (suːpə'viːn, sjuː-) vi. happen, as an
interruption or change —**supervention**
(suːpə'vɛnʃən, sjuː-) n.

supervise ('suːpəvaɪz, 'sjuː-) vt. **1.** oversee **2.**
direct **3.** inspect and control **4.** superintend
—**supervision** (suːpə'vɪʒən, sjuː-) n. —**'supervi-**
sor n. —**'supervisory** a.

supine (suː'paɪn, sjuː-; 'suːpaɪn, 'sjuː-) a. **1.**
lying on back with face upwards **2.** indolent —n.
('suːpaɪn, 'sjuː-) **3.** Latin verbal noun

supper ('sʌpə) n. (light) evening meal

supplant (sə'plɑːnt) vt. **1.** take the place of,
esp. unfairly **2.** oust —**sup'planter** n.

supple ('sʌpl) a. **1.** pliable **2.** flexible **3.**
compliant —**'supply** or **'supplely** adv.

supplement ('sʌplɪmənt) n. **1.** thing added to
fill up, supply deficiency, esp. extra part added
to book etc. **2.** additional number of periodical,
usu. on special subject **3.** separate, oft.
illustrated section published periodically with
newspaper —vt. ('sʌplɪment) **4.** add to **5.**
remedy deficiency of —**supple'mentary** a.
additional —**supplementary angle** either of two
angles whose sum is 180° —**supplementary**
benefit UK allowance paid to various groups of
people by state to bring their incomes up to
minimum levels established by law

suppliant ('sʌplɪənt) a. **1.** petitioning —n. **2.**
petitioner

supplicate ('sʌplɪkeɪt) v. **1.** beg humbly —vt. **2.**
entreat —**suppli'cation** n. —**'supplicatory** a.

supply (sə'plaɪ) vt. **1.** furnish **2.** make available
3. provide (**sup'plied, sup'plying**) —n. **4.**
supplying, substitute **5.** stock, store

support (sə'pɔːt) vt. **1.** hold up **2.** sustain **3.**
assist —n. **4.** supporting, being supported **5.**
means of support —**sup'portable** a. —**sup'port-**
er n. adherent —**sup'porting** a. (of film etc.
role) less important —**sup'portive** a.

suppose (sə'pəʊz) vt. **1.** assume as theory **2.**
take for granted **3.** accept as likely **4.** (in
passive) be expected, obliged **5.** (in passive)
ought —**supposed** (sə'pəʊzd, -'pəʊzɪd) a.
—**supposedly** (sə'pəʊzɪdlɪ) adv. —**suppo'sition**

n. 1. assumption 2. belief without proof 3. conjecture —**suppo'sitious** *or* **supposititious** (səpɒzɪˈtɪʃəs) *a.* sham, spurious, counterfeit

suppository (səˈpɒzɪtərɪ, -trɪ) *n.* medication (in capsule) for insertion in orifice of body

suppress (səˈprɛs) *vt.* 1. put down, restrain 2. crush, stifle 3. keep or withdraw from publication —**sup'pression** *n.*

suppurate (ˈsʌpjʊreɪt) *vi.* fester, form pus —**suppu'ration** *n.*

supra- (*comb. form*) above, over, as in **supranational**. Such words are not given here where the meaning may easily be inferred from the simple word

supreme (suˈpriːm, sjʊ-) *a.* 1. highest in authority or rank 2. utmost —**supremacy** (sʊˈprɛməsɪ, sjʊ-) *n.* position of being supreme —**su'premely** *adv.* —**su'premo** *n.* person with overall authority (*pl.* -s) —**Supreme Being** God

Supt. *or* **supt.** superintendent

sur-¹ (*comb. form*) over, above; beyond, as in **surcharge**

sur-² (*comb. form*) *see* SUB-

surcease (sɜːˈsiːs) *v.* 1. (cause to) cease —*n.* 2. cessation

surcharge (ˈsɜːtʃɑːdʒ) *n.* 1. additional charge —*vt.* (sɜːˈtʃɑːdʒ, ˈsɜːtʃɑːdʒ) 2. subject to additional charge

surd (sɜːd) *n.* 1. *Maths.* sum containing one or more irrational roots of numbers 2. *Phonet.* voiceless consonant —*a.* 3. of or relating to surd

sure (ʃʊə, ʃɔː) *a.* 1. certain 2. trustworthy 3. without doubt —*a., inf.* certainly —**'surely** *adv.* —**surety** (ˈʃʊətɪ, ˈʃʊərɪtɪ) *n.* one who makes himself responsible for another's obligations —**sure-fire** *a. inf.* certain to succeed or meet expectations —**sure-footed** *a.* 1. unlikely to fall, slip or stumble 2. not likely to err or fall

surf (sɜːf) *n.* 1. waves breaking on shore —*vi.* 2. swim in, ride surf —**'surfer** *n.* —**'surfboard** *n.* board used in sport of riding over surf

surface (ˈsɜːfɪs) *n.* 1. outside face of body 2. exterior 3. plane 4. top, visible side 5. superficial appearance, outward impression —*a.* 6. involving the surface only 7. going no deeper than surface —*v.* 8. (cause to) come to surface —*vt.* 9. put a surface on —**surface tension** property of liquids caused by intermolecular forces near surface leading to apparent presence of surface film

surfeit (ˈsɜːfɪt) *n.* 1. excess 2. disgust caused by excess —*vt.* 3. feed to excess

surge (sɜːdʒ) *n.* 1. wave 2. sudden increase 3. *Elec.* sudden rush of current in circuit —*vi.* 4. move in large waves 5. swell, billow

surgeon (ˈsɜːdʒən) *n.* medical expert who performs operations —**'surgery** *n.* 1. medical treatment by operation 2. doctor's, dentist's

consulting room —**'surgical** *a.* —**'surgically** *adv.* —**surgical spirit** methylated spirit

surly (ˈsɜːlɪ) *a.* 1. gloomily morose 2. ill-natured 3. cross and rude —**'surlily** *adv.* —**'surliness** *n.*

surmise (sɜːˈmaɪz) *v./n.* guess, conjecture

surmount (sɜːˈmaʊnt) *vt.* get over, overcome —**sur'mountable** *a.*

surname (ˈsɜːneɪm) *n.* family name

surpass (sɜːˈpɑːs) *vt.* 1. go beyond 2. excel 3. outstrip —**sur'passable** *a.* —**sur'passing** *a.* 1. excellent 2. exceeding others

surplice (ˈsɜːplɪs) *n.* loose white vestment worn by clergy and choristers

surplus (ˈsɜːpləs) *n.* what remains over in excess

surprise (səˈpraɪz) *vt.* 1. cause surprise to 2. astonish 3. take, come upon unexpectedly 4. startle (someone) into action thus —*n.* 5. what takes unawares 6. something unexpected 7. emotion aroused by being taken unawares

surrealism (səˈrɪəlɪzəm) *n.* movement in art and literature emphasizing expression of the unconscious —**sur'real** *a.* —**sur'realist** *n./a.*

surrender (səˈrɛndə) *vt.* 1. hand over, give up —*vi.* 2. yield 3. cease resistance 4. capitulate —*n.* 5. act of surrendering

surreptitious (sʌrəpˈtɪʃəs) *a.* 1. done secretly or stealthily 2. furtive —**surrep'titiously** *adv.*

surrogate (ˈsʌrəgɪt) *n.* 1. deputy, *esp.* of bishop 2. substitute

surround (səˈraʊnd) *vt.* 1. be, come all round, encompass 2. encircle 3. hem in —*n.* 4. border, edging —**sur'roundings** *pl.n.* conditions, scenery *etc.* around a person, place, environment

surtax (ˈsɜːtæks) *n.* additional tax

surveillance (sɜːˈveɪləns) *n.* close watch, supervision —**sur'veillant** *a./n.*

survey (sɜːˈveɪ, ˈsɜːveɪ) *vt.* 1. view, scrutinize 2. inspect, examine 3. measure, map (land) —*n.* (ˈsɜːveɪ) 4. a surveying 5. inspection 6. report incorporating results of survey —**sur'veyor** *n.*

survive (səˈvaɪv) *vt.* 1. outlive 2. come through alive —*vi.* 3. continue to live or exist —**sur'vival** *n.* continuation of existence of persons, things *etc.* —**sur'vivor** *n.* one left alive when others have died —**survival of the fittest** natural selection

sus (sʌs) *n. sl.* 1. suspect 2. suspicion

susceptible (səˈsɛptəbʰl) *a.* 1. yielding readily 2. capable 3. impressionable —**suscepti'bility** *n.*

suspect (səˈspɛkt) *vt.* 1. doubt innocence of 2. have impression of existence or presence of 3. be inclined to believe 4. mistrust —*a.* (ˈsʌspɛkt) 5. of suspected character —*n.* (ˈsʌspɛkt) 6. suspected person

suspend (səˈspɛnd) *vt.* 1. hang up 2. cause to cease for a time 3. debar from an office or privilege 4. keep inoperative 5. sustain in fluid

—**sus'penders** *pl.n.* straps for supporting stockings —**suspended animation** temporary cessation of vital functions —**suspended sentence** prison sentence that is not served by offender unless he commits further offence during its currency —**suspender belt** belt with suspenders hanging from it to hold up women's stockings

suspense (sə'spɛns) *n.* 1. state of uncertainty, *esp.* while awaiting news, an event *etc.* 2. anxiety, worry —**sus'pension** *n.* 1. state of being suspended 2. springs on axle of body of vehicle —**sus'pensory** *a.* —**suspension bridge** bridge suspended from cables that hang between two towers and are anchored at both ends

suspicion (sə'spiʃən) *n.* 1. suspecting, being suspected 2. slight trace —**sus'picious** *a.*

suss (sʌs) *vt.* 1. suspect 2. (*oft. with* out) investigate, find (out)

sustain (sə'steɪn) *vt.* 1. keep, hold up 2. endure 3. keep alive 4. confirm —**sus'tainable** *a.* —**sustenance** ('sʌstɪnəns) *n.* food

suture ('suːtʃə) *n.* 1. act of sewing 2. sewing up of a wound 3. material used for this 4. a joining of the bones of the skull —**sutural** *a.*

suzerain ('suːzəreɪn) *n.* 1. sovereign with rights over autonomous state 2. feudal lord —**suzerainty** ('suːzərəntɪ) *n.*

svelte (svɛlt, sfɛlt) *a.* 1. lightly built, slender 2. sophisticated

SW *or* **S.W.** southwest(ern)

Sw. 1. Sweden 2. Swedish

swab (swɒb) *n.* 1. mop 2. pad of surgical wool *etc.* for cleaning, taking specimen *etc.* 3. *sl.* low or unmannerly fellow —*vt.* 4. clean with swab (-**bb-**) —**'swabber** *n.*

swaddle ('swɒdᵊl) *vt.* swathe —**swaddling clothes** *Hist.* long strips of cloth for wrapping newborn baby

swag (swæg) *n.* 1. *sl.* stolen property 2. A *inf.* bag carried by swagman —**'swagman** *n.* A itinerant tramp

swagger ('swægə) *vi.* 1. strut 2. boast —*n.* 3. strutting gait 4. boastful, overconfident manner —**swagger stick** *or esp.* *U.K.* **swagger cane** short cane or stick carried on occasion by army officers

Swahili (swɑː'hiːlɪ) *n.* 1. Bantu language widely used as lingua franca throughout E and central Afr. 2. member of people speaking this language (*pl.* **-s, -li**) —**Swa'hilian** *a.*

swain (sweɪn) *n.* rustic lover

swallow[1] ('swɒləʊ) *vt.* 1. cause, allow to pass down gullet 2. engulf 3. suppress, keep back 4. *inf.* believe gullibly —*n.* 5. act of swallowing

swallow[2] ('swɒləʊ) *n.* migratory bird with forked tail and skimming manner of flight —**swallow dive** dive in which diver arches back,

keeping his legs straight and his arms outstretched —**'swallowtail** *n.* 1. butterfly having tail-like extension of each hind wing 2. forked tail of swallow or similar bird

swam (swæm) *pt. of* SWIM

swami ('swɑːmɪ) *n.* in India, title of respect for Hindu saint or religious teacher (*pl.* **-es, -s**)

swamp (swɒmp) *n.* 1. bog —*vt.* 2. entangle in swamp 3. overwhelm 4. flood —**'swampy** *a.*

swan (swɒn) *n.* 1. large, webfooted water bird with graceful curved neck —*vi.* 2. *inf.* stroll idly (-**nn-**) —**'swannery** *n.* —**swan's-down** *n.* 1. fine soft down feathers of swan, used to trim clothes *etc.* 2. thick soft fabric of wool with silk, cotton or rayon 3. cotton fabric with heavy nap —**swan song** 1. fabled song of a swan before death 2. last act *etc.* before death —**swan-upping** *n.* UK practice of marking nicks in swans' beaks as sign of ownership

swank (swæŋk) *vi. sl.* 1. swagger 2. show off —**'swanky** *a. sl.* 1. smart 2. showy

swap *or* **swop** (swɒp) *n./v. inf.* 1. exchange 2. barter (-**pp-**)

sward (swɔːd) *or* **swarth** (swɔːθ) *n.* green turf

swarm[1] (swɔːm) *n.* 1. large cluster of insects 2. vast crowd —*vi.* 3. (of bees) be on the move in swarm 4. gather in large numbers

swarm[2] (swɔːm) *v.* climb (rope *etc.*) by grasping with hands and knees

swarthy ('swɔːðɪ) *a.* dark-complexioned

swashbuckler ('swɒʃbʌklə) *n.* swaggering daredevil person —**'swashbuckling** *a.*

swastika ('swɒstɪkə) *n.* form of cross with arms bent at right angles, used as badge by Nazis

swat (swɒt) *vt.* 1. hit smartly 2. kill, *esp.* insects (-**tt-**)

swatch (swɒtʃ) *n.* 1. sample of cloth or other material 2. a number of such samples, usu. fastened together in book form

swathe (sweɪð) *vt.* cover with wraps or bandages

sway (sweɪ) *v.* 1. swing unsteadily 2. (cause to) vacillate in opinion *etc.* —*vt.* 3. influence opinion *etc.* of —*n.* 4. control 5. power 6. swaying motion

swear (sweə) *vt.* 1. promise on oath 2. cause to take an oath —*vi.* 3. declare 4. curse (**swore, sworn, 'swearing**) —**'swearword** *n.* socially taboo word of a profane, obscene or insulting character

sweat (swɛt) *n.* 1. moisture oozing from, forming on skin, *esp.* in humans —*v.* 2. (cause to) exude sweat —*vi.* 3. toil 4. *inf.* worry —*vt.* 5. employ at wrongfully low wages (**sweat** *or* **'sweated** *pt./pp.,* **'sweating** *pr.p.*) —**'sweaty** *a.* —**'sweatband** *n.* 1. band of material set in hat to protect it from sweat 2. piece of cloth tied around forehead to keep sweat out of eyes or around wrist to keep hands dry, as in sports —**sweat shirt** long-sleeved knitted cotton sweater —'**sweatshop** n. workshop where employees work long hours for low wages

sweater ('swɛtə) n. woollen jersey

Swede (swi:d) n. 1. native of Sweden 2. (s-) variety of turnip —'**Swedish** a. 1. of Sweden, its people or their language —n. 2. official language of Sweden

sweep (swi:p) vi. 1. effect cleaning with broom 2. pass quickly or magnificently 3. extend in continuous curve —vt. 4. clean with broom 5. carry impetuously (**swept**, '**sweeping**) —n. 6. act of cleaning with broom 7. sweeping motion 8. wide curve 9. range 10. long oar 11. one who cleans chimneys —'**sweeping** a. 1. wide-ranging 2. without limitations, reservations —**sweep** or '**sweepstake** n. gamble in which winner takes stakes contributed by all

sweet (swi:t) a. 1. tasting like sugar 2. agreeable 3. kind, charming 4. fresh, fragrant 5. in good condition 6. tuneful 7. gentle, dear, beloved —n. 8. small piece of sweet food 9. sweet course served at end of meal —'**sweeten** v. —'**sweetener** n. 1. sweetening agent, esp. one that is sugar-free 2. sl. bribe —'**sweetish** a. —'**sweetly** adv. —'**sweetbread** n. animal's pancreas used as food —'**sweetbrier** n. wild rose —**sweet corn** variety of maize whose kernels are rich in sugar and eaten as vegetable when young —'**sweetheart** n. lover —'**sweetmeat** n. sweetened delicacy, eg small cake, sweet —**sweet pea** plant of pea family with bright flowers —**sweet potato** 1. trailing plant 2. its edible, sweetish, starchy tubers —**sweet-talk** vt. inf. coax, flatter —**sweet tooth** strong liking for sweet foods —**sweet william** ('wɪljəm) garden plant with flat flower clusters

swell (swɛl) v. 1. expand —vi. 2. be greatly filled with pride, emotion (**swelled**, '**swollen**, '**swelling**) —n. 3. act of swelling or being swollen 4. wave of sea 5. mechanism in organ to vary volume of sound 6. sl. person of high social standing —a. 7. sl. smart, fine —**swelled head** or **swollen head** inf. inflated view of one's own worth

swelter ('swɛltə) vi. be oppressed with heat

swept (swɛpt) pt./pp. of SWEEP —'**sweptwing** a. (of aircraft etc.) having wings swept backwards

swerve (swɜːv) vi. 1. swing round, change direction during motion 2. turn aside (from duty etc.) —n. 3. swerving

swift (swɪft) a. 1. rapid, quick, ready —n. 2. bird like a swallow —'**swiftly** adv.

swig (swɪg) n. 1. large swallow of drink —v. 2. drink thus (**-gg-**)

swill (swɪl) v. 1. drink greedily —vt. 2. pour water over or through —n. 3. liquid pig food 4. greedy drinking 5. rinsing

swim (swɪm) vi. 1. support and move oneself in water 2. float 3. be flooded 4. have feeling of dizziness —vt. 5. cross by swimming 6. compete in by swimming (**swam**, **swum**, '**swimming**) —n. 7. spell of swimming —'**swimmer** n. —'**swimmingly** adv. successfully, effortlessly —**swimming pool** artificial pool for swimming —'**swimsuit** n. woman's one-piece swimming garment

swindle ('swɪndl) n./v. cheat —'**swindler** n.

swine (swaɪn) n. 1. pig 2. contemptible person (pl. **swine**) —'**swinish** a. —**swine fever** infectious viral disease of pigs —'**swineherd** n.

swing (swɪŋ) v. 1. (cause to) move to and fro 2. (cause to) pivot, turn 3. hang 4. arrange, play (music) with (jazz) rhythm —vi. 5. be hanged 6. hit out (at) (**swung** pt./pp.) —n. 7. act, instance of swinging 8. seat hung to swing on 9. fluctuation (esp. in voting pattern) 10. C train of freight sleighs, canoes —'**swinger** n. inf. person regarded as modern, lively —'**swingboat** n. piece of fairground equipment consisting of boat-shaped carriage for swinging in

swingeing ('swɪndʒɪŋ) a. 1. severe 2. huge

swingletree ('swɪŋgltriː) n. crossbar in horse's harness to which ends of traces are attached (also '**whiffletree**)

swipe (swaɪp) v. 1. (sometimes with at) strike with wide, sweeping or glancing blow —vt. 2. sl. steal

swirl (swɜːl) v. 1. (cause to) move with eddying motion —n. 2. such motion

swish (swɪʃ) v. 1. (cause to) move with audible hissing sound —n. 2. the sound —a. 3. inf. fashionable, smart

Swiss (swɪs) n. 1. native of Switzerland —a. 2. of Switzerland —**swiss roll** type of rolled-up sponge cake

switch (swɪtʃ) n. 1. mechanism to complete or interrupt electric circuit etc. 2. abrupt change 3. flexible stick or twig 4. tufted end of animal's tail 5. tress of false hair —vi. 6. shift, change 7. swing —vt. 8. affect (current etc.) with switch 9. change abruptly 10. strike with switch —'**switchback** n. road, railway with steep rises and descents —'**switchboard** n. installation for establishing or varying connections in telephone and electric circuits

swither ('swɪðə) Scot. dial. vi. 1. hesitate; be perplexed —n. 2. hesitation; perplexity; agitation

swivel ('swɪvl) n. 1. mechanism of two parts which can revolve the one on the other —v. 2. turn (on swivel) (**-ll-**)

swizzle ('swɪzl) n. 1. an alcoholic drink

containing gin or rum **2.** *inf.* UK swindle or disappointment (*also* **swizz**) **—swizzle stick** small rod used to agitate effervescent drink to facilitate escape of carbon dioxide

swob (swob) *see* SWAB

swollen ('swəʊlən) *pp. of* SWELL

swoon (swuːn) *vi./n.* faint

swoop (swuːp) *vi.* **1.** dive, as hawk *—n.* **2.** act of swooping **3.** sudden attack

swoosh (swuʃ) *vi.* **1.** make rustling, swirling sound, *esp.* when moving, pouring out *—n.* **2.** swirling, rustling sound or movement

swop (swop) *see* SWAP

sword (sɔːd) *n.* weapon with long blade for cutting or thrusting **—sword dance** dance in which performers dance nimbly over swords on ground or brandish them in the air —'**swordfish** *n.* fish with elongated sharp upper jaw, like sword —'**swordplay** *n.* **1.** action or art of fighting with sword **2.** verbal sparring **—sword swallower** person who swallows or appears to swallow swords, in a circus *etc.*

swore (swɔː) *pt. of* SWEAR **—sworn** *pp. of* SWEAR

swot (swot) *inf. v.* **1.** study hard (**-tt-**) *—n.* **2.** one who works hard at lessons or studies

swum (swʌm) *pp. of* SWIM

swung (swʌŋ) *pt./pp. of* SWING

sybarite ('sɪbəraɪt) *n.* person who loves luxury —**sybaritic** (sɪbə'rɪtɪk) *a.*

sycamore ('sɪkəmɔː) *n.* tree allied to plane tree and maple

sycophant ('sɪkəfənt) *n.* one using flattery to gain favours —'**sycophancy** *n.* —syco'**phantic** *a.*

syllable ('sɪləb^əl) *n.* division of word as unit for pronunciation —syl'**labic** *a.* —syl'**labify** *vt.*

syllabub *or* **sillabub** ('sɪləbʌb) *n.* **1.** sweet frothy dish of cream, sugar and wine **2.** something insubstantial

syllabus ('sɪləbəs) *n.* **1.** outline of a course of study **2.** programme, list of subjects studied on course (*pl.* **-es, -bi** (-baɪ))

syllogism ('sɪlədʒɪzəm) *n.* form of logical reasoning consisting of two premisses and conclusion —syllo'**gistic** *a.*

sylph (sɪlf) *n.* **1.** slender, graceful woman **2.** sprite —'**sylphlike** *a.*

sylvan *or* **silvan** ('sɪlvən) *a.* of forests, trees

sym- *see* SYN-

symbiosis (sɪmbɪ'əʊsɪs) *n.* living together of two organisms of different kinds, *esp.* to their mutual benefit —**symbiotic** (sɪmbɪ'ɒtɪk) *a.*

symbol ('sɪmb^əl) *n.* **1.** sign **2.** thing representing or typifying something —sym'**bolic** *a.* —sym-'**bolically** *adv.* —'**symbolism** *n.* **1.** use of, representation by symbols **2.** movement in art holding that work of art should express idea in

symbolic form —'**symbolist** *n./a.* —'**symbolize** *or* **-ise** *v.*

symmetry ('sɪmɪtrɪ) *n.* **1.** proportion between parts **2.** balance of arrangement between two sides **3.** order —sym'**metrical** *a.* **1.** having due proportion in parts **2.** harmonious **3.** regular

sympathy ('sɪmpəθɪ) *n.* **1.** feeling for another in pain *etc.* **2.** compassion, pity **3.** sharing of emotion, interest, desire *etc.* **4.** fellow feeling **—sympa'thetic** *a.* —sympa'**thetically** *adv.* —'**sympathize** *or* **-ise** *vi.* —**sympathetic magic** type of magic in which it is sought to produce large-scale effect by performing some small-scale ceremony resembling it, as pouring of water on altar to induce rainfall

symphony ('sɪmfənɪ) *n.* **1.** composition for full orchestra **2.** harmony of sounds —**symphonic** (sɪm'fɒnɪk) *a.* —sym'**phonious** *a.* harmonious —**symphonic poem** extended orchestral composition, based on nonmusical material, such as work of literature or folk tale —**symphony orchestra** large orchestra comprising strings, brass, woodwind, harp and percussion

symposium (sɪm'pəʊzɪəm) *n.* **1.** conference, meeting **2.** discussion, writings on a given topic (*pl.* **-s, -sia** (-zɪə))

symptom ('sɪmptəm) *n.* **1.** change in body indicating its state of health or disease **2.** sign, token —sympto'**matic** *a.*

syn- *or* **sym-** (*comb. form*) with, together, alike

synagogue ('sɪnəgɒg) *n.* (place of worship of) Jewish congregation

synchromesh ('sɪŋkrəʊmeʃ) *a.* (of gearbox) having device that synchronizes speeds of gears before they engage

synchronize *or* **-ise** ('sɪŋkrənaɪz) *vt.* **1.** make agree in time *—vi.* **2.** happen at same time —'**synchronism** *n.* —**synchroni'zation** *or* **-i'sation** *n.* —'**synchronous** *a.* simultaneous

synchrotron ('sɪŋkrətrɒn) *n.* device for acceleration of stream of electrons

syncopate ('sɪŋkəpeɪt) *vt.* accentuate (weak beat in bar of music) —synco'**pation** *n.*

syncope ('sɪŋkəpɪ) *n.* **1.** fainting **2.** elision of letter(s) from middle of word

syncretize *or* **-ise** ('sɪŋkrɪtaɪz) *v.* attempt to combine characteristic teachings, beliefs, or practices of (differing systems of religion or philosophy) —syncreti'**zation** *or* **-i'sation** *n.*

syndicate ('sɪndɪkɪt) *n.* **1.** body of people, delegates associated for some enterprise *—vt.* ('sɪndɪkeɪt) **2.** form into syndicate **3.** publish in many newspapers at the same time —'**syndicalism** *n.* economic movement aiming at combination of workers in all trades to enforce demands of labour

syndrome ('sɪndrəʊm) *n.* **1.** combination of

several symptoms in disease **2.** symptom, set of symptoms or characteristics

synecdoche (sɪn'ɛkdəkɪ) n. figure of speech by which whole of thing is put for part or part for whole, *eg* sail for *ship*

synod ('sɪnəd, 'sɪnɒd) n. **1.** church council **2.** convention

synonym ('sɪnənɪm) n. word with same meaning as another —**syno'nymity** n. —**synonymous** (sɪ'nɒnɪməs) a.

synopsis (sɪ'nɒpsɪs) n. summary, outline (*pl.* **-ses** (-siːz)) —**syn'optic** a. **1.** of, like synopsis **2.** having same viewpoint

syntax ('sɪntæks) n. part of grammar treating of arrangement of words in sentence —**syn'tactic** a. —**syn'tactically** adv.

synthesis ('sɪnθɪsɪs) n. putting together, combination (*pl.* **-theses** (-θɪsiːz)) —**'synthesize** or **-ise** v. (cause to) combine into a whole —**'synthesizer** n. **1.** see MOOG SYNTHESIZER **2.** person or thing that synthesizes —**synthetic** (sɪn'θɛtɪk) a. **1.** artificial **2.** of synthesis

syphilis ('sɪfɪlɪs) n. contagious venereal disease —**syphi'litic** a.

syphon ('saɪfən) see SIPHON

Syrian ('sɪrɪən) a. **1.** of Syria, republic in W Asia, its people or their dialect of Arabic —n. **2.** native or inhabitant of Syria

syringe ('sɪrɪndʒ, sɪ'rɪndʒ) n. **1.** instrument for drawing in liquid by piston and forcing it out in fine stream or spray **2.** squirt —vt. **3.** spray, cleanse with syringe

syrup ('sɪrəp) n. **1.** thick solution obtained in process of refining sugar **2.** any liquid like this, *esp.* in consistency —**'syrupy** a.

system ('sɪstəm) n. **1.** complex whole, organization **2.** method **3.** classification —**syste'matic** a. methodical —**syste'matically** adv. —**'systematize** or **-ise** vt. **1.** reduce to system **2.** arrange methodically —**systemic** (sɪ'stɛmɪk, -'stiː-) a. affecting entire body or organism —**systems analysis** analysis of methods involved in scientific and industrial operations, usu. with computer so that improved system can be designed

systole ('sɪstəlɪ) n. contraction of heart and arteries for expelling blood and carrying on circulation —**systolic** (sɪ'stɒlɪk) a. **1.** contracting **2.** of systole

---

T,t

t *or* **T** (tiː) n. **1.** 20th letter of English alphabet **2.** speech sound represented by this letter **3.** something shaped like T (*pl.* **t's, T's** *or* **Ts**) —**to a T** in every detail; perfectly

t 1. tense **2.** ton

T 1. absolute temperature **2.** Chem. tritium **3.** surface tension **4.** tablespoon

ta (tɑː) interj. UK inf. thank you

Ta Chem. tantalum

TA Territorial Army

Taal (tɑːl) n. SA language, *esp.* Afrikaans

tab[1] (tæb) n. tag, label, short strap —**keep tabs on** inf. keep watchful eye on

tab[2] (tæb) **1.** tabulator **2.** tablet

tabard ('tæbəd) n. (herald's) short tunic open at sides

tabby ('tæbɪ) n./a. (cat) with markings of stripes *etc.* on lighter background

tabernacle ('tæbənækəl) n. **1.** portable shrine of Israelites **2.** R.C.Ch. receptacle containing consecrated Host **3.** place of worship not called a church

table ('teɪbəl) n. **1.** piece of furniture consisting of flat board supported by legs **2.** food **3.** set of facts, figures arranged in lines or columns —vt. **4.** lay on table **5.** submit (motion *etc.*) for consideration by meeting **6.** suspend discussion of (bill *etc.*) indefinitely —**'tablecloth** n. cloth for covering table —**'tableland** n. plateau, high flat area —**table licence** licence authorizing sale of alcoholic drinks with meals only —**'tablespoon** n. spoon used for serving food *etc.* —**table tennis** ball game played on table with small bats and light hollow ball

tableau ('tæbləʊ) n. **1.** group of persons, silent and motionless, arranged to represent some scene **2.** dramatic scene (*pl.* **-leaux** (-ləʊ, -ləʊz))

table d'hôte ('tɑːbəl 'dəʊt) Fr. (meal) with limited choice of dishes, at a fixed price

tablet ('tæblɪt) n. **1.** pill of compressed powdered medicinal substance **2.** flattish cake of soap *etc.* **3.** slab of stone, wood *etc.*, *esp.* used formerly for writing on

tabloid ('tæblɔɪd) n. illustrated popular small-sized newspaper with terse, sensational headlines

taboo *or* **tabu** (tə'buː) a. **1.** forbidden; disapproved of —n. **2.** prohibition resulting from social conventions *etc.* **3.** thing prohibited —vt. **4.** place under taboo

tabor *or* **tabour** ('teɪbə) n. small drum, used *esp.* in Middle Ages, struck with one hand while other held pipe

tabular ('tæbjʊlə) a. shaped, arranged like a

table —'**tabulate** vt. arrange (figures, facts etc.) in tables —**tabu**'**lation** n. —'**tabulator** n. device for setting stops that locate column margins on typewriter **2.** Comp. machine that reads data from punched cards etc., producing lists, tabulations or totals

tacho- (comb. form) speed, as in tachometer

tachograph ('tækəgrɑːf) n. device for recording speed and distance travelled by lorries

tachometer (tæ'kɒmɪtə) n. device for measuring speed, esp. of revolving shaft (in car) and hence revolutions per minute

tacit ('tæsɪt) a. **1.** implied but not spoken **2.** silent —'**tacitly** adv. —'**taciturn** a. **1.** talking little **2.** habitually silent —**taci**'**turnity** n.

tack[1] (tæk) n. **1.** small nail **2.** long, loose, temporary stitch **3.** Naut. course of ship obliquely to windward **4.** course, direction **5.** inf. food —vt. **6.** nail with tacks **7.** stitch (garment) with long, loose temporary stitches **8.** append, attach —v. **9.** sail to windward —**on the wrong tack** under false impression

tack[2] (tæk) n. riding harness for horses

tackies ('tækɪz) pl.n. SA plimsolls

tackle ('tækəl) n. **1.** equipment, apparatus, esp. lifting appliances with ropes **2.** Sport physical challenge of opponent —vt. **3.** take in hand **4.** grapple with **5.** challenge

tacky[1] ('tækɪ) a. sticky, not quite dry —'**tackiness** n.

tacky[2] ('tækɪ) a. US inf. **1.** shabby, shoddy **2.** ostentatious and vulgar **3.** (of person) eccentric; crazy

tact (tækt) n. **1.** skill in dealing with people or situations **2.** delicate perception of the feelings of others —'**tactful** a. —'**tactfully** adv. —'**tactless** a. —'**tactlessly** adv.

tactics ('tæktɪks) pl.n. **1.** (with sing. v.) art of handling troops, ships in battle **2.** adroit management of a situation **3.** plans for this —'**tactical** a. —tac'**tician** n.

tactile ('tæktaɪl) a. of the sense of touch

tadpole ('tædpəʊl) n. immature frog, in its first state before gills and tail are absorbed

taffeta ('tæfɪtə) n. smooth, stiff fabric of silk, rayon etc.

taffrail ('tæfreɪl) n. **1.** rail at stern of ship **2.** flat ornamental part of stern

Taffy ('tæfɪ) n. sl. Welshman

tag[1] (tæg) n. **1.** label identifying or showing price of something **2.** ragged, hanging end **3.** pointed end of shoelace etc. **4.** trite quotation **5.** any appendage —vt. **6.** append, add (on) —vi. **7.** (usu. with on or along) trail behind (-gg-)

tag[2] (tæg) n. **1.** children's game where one being chased becomes the chaser upon being touched by chaser —vt. **2.** touch (-gg-) —**tag wrestling**

wrestling match for teams of two, where one partner may replace the other upon being touched on hand

tagetes (tæ'dʒiːtiːz) n. plant with yellow or orange flowers

tail (teɪl) n. **1.** flexible prolongation of animal's spine **2.** lower or inferior part of anything **3.** appendage **4.** rear part of aircraft **5.** inf. person employed to follow and spy on another —pl. **6.** reverse side of coin **7.** inf. tail coat —vt. **8.** remove tail of **9.** inf. follow closely, trail —**tailed** a. —'**tailings** pl.n. waste left over from some (eg industrial) process —'**tailless** a. —'**tailback** n. queue of traffic stretching back from an obstruction —'**tailboard** n. removable or hinged rear board on lorry etc. —**tail coat** man's evening dress jacket —**tail end** last part —**tail gate** gate to control flow of water at lower end of lock —'**tailgate** n. **1.** esp. US tailboard —v. **2.** US drive very close behind (vehicle) —'**taillight** or '**tailamp** n. light at rear of vehicle —'**tailpiece** n. **1.** extension or appendage that lengthens or completes something **2.** decorative design at foot of page etc. **3.** piece of wood to which strings of violin etc. are attached at lower end **4.** short beam or rafter with one end embedded in wall —'**tailpipe** n. pipe from which exhaust gases are discharged, esp. at rear of motor vehicle —'**tailplane** n. stabilizing surface at rear of aircraft —'**tailspin** n. spinning dive of aircraft —'**tailwind** n. wind blowing in same direction as course of aircraft or ship —**tail off** diminish gradually, dwindle —**turn tail** run away

tailor ('teɪlə) n. maker of outer clothing, esp. for men —'**tailored** a. **1.** having simple lines, as some women's garments **2.** specially fitted —'**tailorbird** n. tropical Asian warbler that builds nest by sewing together large leaves using plant fibres —**tailor-made** a. **1.** made by tailor **2.** well-fitting **3.** appropriate —n. **4.** inf. factory-made cigarettes

taint (teɪnt) v. **1.** affect or be affected by pollution etc. —n. **2.** defect, flaw **3.** infection, contamination

take (teɪk) vt. **1.** grasp, get hold of **2.** get, receive **3.** assume **4.** adopt **5.** accept **6.** understand **7.** consider **8.** carry, conduct **9.** use **10.** capture **11.** consume **12.** require —vi. **13.** be effective **14.** please **15.** go (**took**, '**taken**, '**taking**) —n. **16.** esp. Cine. (recording of) scene, sequence photographed without interruption —'**taking** a. charming —'**takings** pl.n. earnings, receipts —'**takeaway** UK, A, NZ a. **1.** sold for consumption away from premises **2.** selling food for consumption away from premises —n. **3.** shop or restaurant that sells such food —**take-home pay** remainder of one's pay after all income tax and other compulsory deductions have been made —**take-off** n. 1. instant at which aircraft becomes airborne 2. commencement of flight 3. *inf.* act of mimicry —**'takeover** n. act of assuming power, control *etc.* —**take after** resemble in appearance or character —**take down** 1. write down 2. dismantle 3. humiliate —**take in** 1. understand 2. make (garment *etc.*) smaller 3. deceive —**take in vain** 1. blaspheme 2. mention (person's name) —**take off** 1. (of aircraft) leave ground 2. *inf.* go away 3. *inf.* mimic —**take over** 1. assume control or management (of) 2. *Print.* move (copy) to next line —**take to** become fond of

talc (tælk) n. 1. soft mineral of magnesium silicate 2. talcum powder —**talcum powder** powder, *usu.* scented, to absorb body moisture, deodorize *etc.*

tale (teɪl) n. 1. story, narrative, report 2. fictitious story —**tell tales** 1. tell fanciful lies 2. report malicious stories *etc., esp.* to someone in authority

talent ('tælənt) n. 1. natural ability or power 2. ancient weight or money 3. *inf.* (*esp.* attractive) members of opposite sex —**talented** a. gifted —**talent scout** person whose occupation is searching for talented sportsmen, performers *etc.* for engagement as professionals

talisman ('tælɪzmən) n. 1. object supposed to have magic power 2. amulet (*pl.* **-s**) —**talis'manic** a.

talk (tɔːk) vi. 1. express, exchange ideas *etc.* in words 2. spread rumours or gossip —vt. 3. express in speech, utter 4. discuss —n. 5. speech, lecture 6. conversation 7. rumour —**'talkative** a. fond of talking —**'talker** n. —**talking book** recording of book, designed to be used by blind —**talking-to** n. *inf.* reproof —**talk back** answer boldly or impudently —**talk into** persuade to by talking —**talk out of** dissuade from by talking

tall (tɔːl) a. 1. high, of great stature 2. incredible, untrue (*esp. in* **tall story**) —**'tallboy** n. high chest of drawers —**tall order** demand which is difficult to accomplish

tallow ('tæləʊ) n. 1. melted and clarified animal fat —vt. 2. smear with this

tally ('tælɪ) vi. 1. correspond one with the other 2. keep score (**-lied, -lying**) —n. 3. record, account, total number —**'tallier** n.

tally-ho (tælɪ'həʊ) interj. huntsman's cry to urge on hounds

Talmud ('tælmʊd) n. body of Jewish law —**Tal'mudic** a.

talon ('tælən) n. claw

tamarind ('tæmərɪnd) n. 1. tropical tree 2. its pods containing sour brownish pulp

tamarisk ('tæmərɪsk) n. ornamental, ever-green tree or shrub with slender branches, very small leaves and spiky flowers

tambour ('tæmbʊə) n. 1. *Real tennis* sloping buttress on one side of receiver's end of court 2. embroidery frame consisting of two hoops over which fabric is stretched while being worked 3. embroidered work done on such frame 4. sliding door on desks *etc.*, made of thin strips of wood glued on to canvas backing 5. *Archit.* wall that is circular in plan, *esp.* supporting dome or surrounded by colonnade 6. drum —v. 7. embroider on tambour

tambourine (tæmbə'riːn) n. flat half-drum with jingling discs of metal attached

tame (teɪm) a. 1. not wild, domesticated 2. subdued 3. uninteresting —vt. 4. make tame —**'tamely** adv. 1. in a tame manner 2. without resisting —**'tamer** n.

Tamil ('tæmɪl) n. 1. member of a people of S India and Sri Lanka 2. language of this people (*pl.* **-s**, **'Tamil**) —a. 3. of this people

tam-o'-shanter (tæmə'ʃæntə) n. Scottish brimless wool cap with bobble in centre

tamp (tæmp) vt. pack, force down by repeated blows

tamper ('tæmpə) vi. (*usu. with* with) interfere improperly, meddle

tampon ('tæmpon) n. plug of lint, cotton *etc.* inserted in wound, body cavity, to stop flow of blood, absorb secretions *etc.*

tan[1] (tæn) a./n. 1. (of) brown colour of skin after long exposure to rays of sun *etc.* —v. 2. (cause to) go brown —vt. 3. (of animal hide) convert to leather by chemical treatment 4. *inf.* beat, flog (**-nn-**) —**'tanner** n. —**'tannery** n. place where hides are tanned —**'tannic** a. of tan, tannin or tannic acid —**'tannin** n. vegetable substance used as tanning agent —**'tanbark** n. bark of certain trees, yielding tannin —**tannic acid** astringent derived from oak bark *etc.*, used in tanning *etc.*

tan[2] (tæn) *Trig.* tangent

tanager ('tænɪdʒə) n. any of family of Amer. songbirds having short thick bill and, in male, brilliantly coloured plumage

tandem ('tændəm) n. bicycle for two riders, one behind the other

tandoori (tæn'dʊərɪ) n. Indian method of cooking meat or vegetables on a spit in clay oven

tang (tæŋ) n. 1. strong pungent taste or smell 2. trace, hint 3. spike, barb —**'tangy** a.

tangent ('tændʒənt) n. 1. line that touches a curve without cutting 2. divergent course 3. *Trig.* ratio of side opposite given acute angle in right-angled triangle to adjacent side —a. 4. touching, meeting without cutting —**tan'gential** a. —**tan'gentially** adv.

tangerine (tændʒə'riːn) n. 1. Asian citrus tree

2. its fruit, a variety of orange **3.** reddish-orange colour

tangible ('tændʒəbəl) *a.* **1.** that can be touched **2.** definite **3.** palpable; concrete —**tangi'bility** *n.*

tangle ('tæŋgəl) *n.* **1.** confused mass or situation —*vt.* **2.** twist together in muddle —*vi.* **3.** contend

tango ('tæŋgəʊ) *n.* dance of S Amer. origin (*pl.* -**s**)

tank (tæŋk) *n.* **1.** storage vessel for liquids or gas **2.** armoured motor vehicle moving on tracks **3.** cistern **4.** UK, US *dial.* reservoir —'**tanker** *n.* ship, lorry *etc.* for carrying liquid in bulk —**tank farming** *see* HYDROPONICS —**tank up** *chiefly* UK *sl.* imbibe large quantity of alcoholic drink

tankard ('tæŋkəd) *n.* **1.** large drinking cup of metal or glass **2.** its contents, *esp.* beer

tanner ('tænə) *n.* UK *inf.* sixpence

tannin ('tænɪn) *n. see* TAN[1]

Tannoy ('tænɔɪ) *n.* **R** type of public-address system

tansy ('tænzɪ) *n.* yellow-flowered aromatic herb

tantalize *or* -**ise** ('tæntəlaɪz) *vt.* torment by appearing to offer something desired, tease —'**tantalus** *n.* UK case in which bottles may be locked with their contents visible

tantalum ('tæntələm) *n.* hard greyish-white metallic element

tantamount ('tæntəmaʊnt) *a.* **1.** equivalent in value or signification **2.** equal, amounting

tantrum ('tæntrəm) *n.* childish outburst of temper

Taoism ('taːʊɪzəm) *n.* system of religion and philosophy based on teachings of Lao-tse, Chinese philosopher, and advocating simple, honest life and noninterference with course of natural events —'**Taoist** *n./a.* —**Tao'istic** *a.*

tap[1] (tæp) *v.* **1.** strike lightly but with some noise (-**pp**-) —*n.* **2.** slight blow, rap —**tap dance** step dance in which performer wears shoes equipped with taps that make rhythmic sound on stage as he dances —**tap-dance** *vi.* perform tap dance —**tap-dancer** *n.* —**tap-dancing** *n.*

tap[2] (tæp) *n.* **1.** valve with handle to regulate or stop flow of fluid in pipe *etc.* **2.** stopper, plug permitting liquid to be drawn from cask *etc.* **3.** steel tool for forming internal screw threads —*vt.* **4.** put tap in **5.** draw off (as) with tap **6.** make secret connection to (telephone wire) to overhear conversation on it **7.** make connection to (pipe, drain *etc.*) **8.** form internal threads in **9.** UK *sl.* ask (someone) for money; obtain (money) from someone (-**pp**-) —'**taproom** *n.* bar, as in hotel or pub

tape (teɪp) *n.* **1.** narrow long strip of fabric, paper *etc.* **2.** magnetic recording of music *etc.* —*vt.* **3.** record (speech, music *etc.*) —**tape deck** platform supporting spools *etc.* of tape recorder, incorporating motor and playback, recording

and erasing heads —**tape machine** telegraphic device that records current stock quotations electronically or on ticker tape —**tape measure** tape of fabric or metal, marked off in centimetres, inches *etc.* —**tape recorder** apparatus for recording sound on magnetized tape and playing it back —**tape recording 1.** act of recording on magnetic tape **2.** magnetized tape used for this **3.** music *etc.* so recorded —'**tapeworm** *n.* long flat worm parasitic in animals and man —**have (someone) taped** *inf.* have (someone) sized up, have measure of (someone)

taper ('teɪpə) *vi.* **1.** become gradually thinner towards one end —*n.* **2.** thin candle **3.** long wick covered with wax; spill **4.** a narrowing

tapestry ('tæpɪstrɪ) *n.* fabric decorated with designs in colours woven by needles, not in shuttles —'**tapestried** *a.*

tapioca (tæpɪ'əʊkə) *n.* beadlike starch made from cassava root, used *esp.* in puddings

tapir ('teɪpə) *n.* Amer. animal with elongated snout, allied to pig

tappet ('tæpɪt) *n.* in internal-combustion engine, short steel rod conveying movement imparted by the lift of a cam to the valve stem

taproot ('tæpruːt) *n.* large single root growing straight down

tar[1] (taː) *n.* **1.** thick black liquid distilled from coal *etc.* —*vt.* **2.** coat, treat with tar (-**rr**-)

tar[2] (taː) *n.* *inf.* sailor

tarantella (tærən'tɛlə) *n.* **1.** lively It. dance **2.** music for it

tarantula (tə'ræntjʊlə) *n.* any of various large (poisonous) hairy spiders (*pl.* -**s**, -**lae** (-liː))

tarboosh (taː'buːʃ) *n.* felt brimless cap, usu. red and oft. with silk tassel, worn by Muslim men

tardy ('taːdɪ) *a.* **1.** slow **2.** late —'**tardily** *adv.*

tare[1] (tɛə) *n.* **1.** weight of wrapping or container for goods **2.** unladen weight of vehicle

tare[2] (tɛə) *n.* **1.** vetch **2.** weed

target ('taːgɪt) *n.* **1.** mark to aim at in shooting *etc.* **2.** thing aimed at **3.** object of criticism **4.** butt —**target language** language into which text *etc.* is translated

tariff ('tærɪf) *n.* **1.** tax levied on imports *etc.* **2.** list of charges **3.** method of charging for supply of services, *eg* electricity

Tarmac ('taːmæk) *n.* **R** mixture of tar, bitumen and crushed stones rolled to give hard, smooth surface *esp.* as used for road, airport runway *etc.* (*also* **Tarma'cadam**)

tarn (taːn) *n.* small mountain lake

tarnish ('taːnɪʃ) *v.* **1.** (cause to) become stained, lose shine or become dimmed or sullied —*n.* **2.** discoloration, blemish

taro ('tɑːrəʊ) *n.* 1. plant of Pacific islands 2. its edible roots

tarot ('tærəʊ) *n.* one of special pack of cards now used mainly in fortune-telling

tarpaulin (tɑː'pɔːlɪn) *n.* (sheet of) heavy hard-wearing waterproof fabric

tarragon ('tærəgən) *n.* aromatic herb

tarry ('tærɪ) *vi.* 1. linger, delay 2. stay behind (-ried, -rying)

tarsier ('tɑːsɪə) *n.* nocturnal tree-dwelling mammal of Indonesia

tarsus ('tɑːsəs) *n.* 1. bones of ankle and heel collectively 2. corresponding part in other mammals *etc.* 3. connective tissue supporting free edge of each eyelid (*pl.* **-si** (-saɪ)) —'**tarsal** *a.* 1. of tarsus or tarsi —*n.* 2. tarsal bone

tart[1] (tɑːt) *n.* 1. pie or flan filled with fruit, jam *etc.* 2. *inf., offens.* promiscuous woman, *esp.* prostitute —**tart up** UK *sl.* 1. dress and make (oneself) up in provocative or promiscuous way 2. reissue or decorate in cheap and flashy way

tart[2] (tɑːt) *a.* 1. sour, bitter 2. sharp

tartan ('tɑːtᵊn) *n.* 1. woollen cloth woven in pattern of coloured checks, *esp.* in colours, patterns associated with Scottish clans 2. such pattern

tartar[1] ('tɑːtə) *n.* 1. crust deposited on teeth 2. deposit formed during fermentation of wine —**tar'taric** *a.* —**tartaric acid** colourless crystalline acid found in many fruits

tartar[2] ('tɑːtə) *n.* vicious-tempered person, difficult to deal with

Tartar ('tɑːtə) *see* TATAR

tartar sauce mayonnaise sauce mixed with chopped herbs, capers *etc.*

Tas. Tasmania

task (tɑːsk) *n.* 1. piece of work (*esp.* unpleasant or difficult) set or undertaken —*vt.* 2. assign task to 3. exact —**task force** naval or military unit dispatched to carry out specific undertaking —'**taskmaster** *n.* overseer —**take to task** reprove

Tasmanian devil (tæz'meɪnɪən) small, ferocious, carnivorous marsupial of Tasmania

Tass (tæs) *n.* principal news agency of Soviet Union

tassel ('tæsᵊl) *n.* 1. ornament of fringed knot of threads *etc.* 2. tuft

taste (teɪst) *n.* 1. sense by which flavour, quality of substance is detected by the tongue 2. this act or sensation 3. (brief) experience of something 4. small amount 5. preference, liking 6. power of discerning, judging 7. discretion, delicacy —*v.* 8. observe or distinguish the taste of (a substance) 9. take small amount of (food *etc.*) into mouth —*vt.* 10. experience —*vi.* 11. have specific flavour —'**tasteful** *a.* 1. in good style 2. with, showing good taste —'**tastefully** *adv.* —'**taste-**less *a.* —'**taster** *n.* 1. person who samples food or drink for quality 2. device used in tasting or sampling 3. *esp.* formerly, person employed to taste food and drink prepared for king *etc.* to test for poison —'**tasty** *a.* pleasantly or highly flavoured —**taste bud** small organ of taste on tongue

tat[1] (tæt) *v.* make (something) by tatting (-**tt**-) —'**tatter** *n.* —'**tatting** *n.* type of handmade lace

tat[2] (tæt) *n.* 1. ragged, shoddy article 2. tattiness

ta-ta (tæ'tɑː) *interj.* UK *inf.* goodbye; farewell

Tatar *or* **Tartar** ('tɑːtə) *n.* 1. member of Mongoloid people who established powerful state in central Asia in 13th century 2. descendant of this people, now scattered throughout Soviet Union 3. Turkic language or dialect spoken by this people —*a.* 4. of Tatars

tater ('teɪtə) *n. dial.* potato

tatter ('tætə) *v.* 1. make or become ragged, worn to shreds —*n.* 2. ragged piece

tattle ('tætᵊl) *vi./n.* gossip, chatter —'**tattletale** *chiefly* US *n.* 1. scandalmonger, gossip —*a.* 2. telltale

tattoo[1] (tæ'tuː) *n.* 1. formerly, beat of drum and bugle call 2. military spectacle or pageant

tattoo[2] (tæ'tuː) *vt.* 1. mark (skin) in patterns *etc.* by pricking and filling punctures with indelible coloured inks (-'**tooed**, -'**tooing**) —*n.* 2. mark so made

tatty ('tætɪ) *a.* shabby, worn-out —'**tattiness** *n.*

tau (tɔː, taʊ) *n.* 19th letter in Gr. alphabet (T, τ)

taught (tɔːt) *pt./pp. of* TEACH

taunt (tɔːnt) *vt.* 1. provoke, deride with insulting words *etc.* 2. tease; tantalize —*n.* 3. instance of this

taupe (təʊp) *n.* brownish-grey colour

Taurus ('tɔːrəs) *n.* (bull) 2nd sign of zodiac, operative *c.* Apr. 21st-May 20th

taut (tɔːt) *a.* 1. drawn tight 2. under strain —'**tauten** *vt.* make tight or tense

tauto- *or before vowel* **taut-** (*comb. form*) identical, same, as in *tautology*

tautology (tɔː'tɒlədʒɪ) *n.* repetition of same thing in other words in same sentence —**tauto'logical** *a.*

tavern ('tævən) *n.* inn, public house

tawdry ('tɔːdrɪ) *a.* showy, but cheap and without taste, flashy —'**tawdrily** *adv.* —'**taw-driness** *n.*

tawny ('tɔːnɪ) *a./n.* (of) light (yellowish) brown —**tawny owl** European owl having reddish-brown plumage and round head

tawse *or* **taws** (tɔːz) *n.* in Scotland, leather strap used *esp.* formerly by schoolteacher to punish pupils

tax (tæks) *n.* 1. compulsory payments by wage earners, companies *etc.* imposed by government to raise revenue 2. heavy demand (on something) —vt. **3.** impose tax on **4.** strain **5.** accuse, blame —**'taxable** a. —**tax'ation** n. levying of taxes —**tax-deductible** a. legally deductible from income before tax assessment —**tax exile** person who lives abroad to avoid paying high taxes —**tax-free** a. exempt from taxation —**'taxpayer** n. —**tax return** statement of personal income for tax purposes

taxi ('tæksɪ) n. **1.** motor vehicle for hire with driver (pl. -s) (also **cab, 'taxicab**) —vi. **2.** (of aircraft) run along ground under its own power **3.** go in taxi ('**taxied** pt./pp., '**taxying, 'taxiing** pr.p.) —'**taximeter** n. meter fitted to taxi to register fare, based on length of journey —**taxi rank** place where taxis wait to be hired

taxidermy ('tæksɪdɜːmɪ) n. art of stuffing, mounting animal skins to give them lifelike appearance —**taxi'dermal** or **taxi'dermic** a. —'**taxidermist** n.

taxonomy (tæk'sɒnəmɪ) n. science, practice of classification, esp. of biological organisms

Tb Chem. terbium

T.B. or **t.b.** tuberculosis

T-bone steak steak cut from sirloin of beef, containing T-shaped bone

tbs. or **tbsp.** tablespoon(ful)

Tc Chem. technetium

tch interj./n. **1.** clicking sound made with tongue, to express disapproval etc. —vi. **2.** utter tch's

te or **ti** (tiː) n. Mus. in tonic sol-fa, syllable used for seventh note or subtonic of any scale

Te Chem. tellurium

tea (tiː) n. **1.** dried leaves of plant cultivated esp. in (sub)tropical Asia **2.** infusion of it as beverage **3.** any of various herbal infusions **4.** tea, cakes etc. as light afternoon meal **5.** main evening meal —**tea bag** small porous bag of paper containing tea leaves —**tea ball** chiefly US perforated metal ball filled with tea leaves and used to make tea —'**teacake** n. UK flat bun, usu. eaten toasted and buttered —**tea-chest** n. square wooden box lined with foil for exporting tea etc. —**tea cosy** covering for teapot to keep contents hot —'**teacup** n. **1.** cup out of which tea may be drunk **2.** amount teacup will hold, about four fluid ounces (also '**teacupful**) —'**teahouse** n. restaurant, esp. in Japan or China, where tea and light refreshments are served —**tea leaf 1.** dried leaf of tea shrub, used to make tea **2.** (usu. pl.) shredded parts of these leaves, esp. after infusion —**tea party** social gathering at which tea is served —'**teapot** n. container with lid, spout and handle, in which tea is made —'**tearoom** n. UK restaurant where tea and light refreshments are served (also '**teashop**) —'**teaspoon** n. small spoon for stirring tea etc. —**tea tree** Aust., N.Z. tree

teach (tiːtʃ) vt. **1.** instruct **2.** educate **3.** train **4.** impart knowledge of —vi. **5.** act as teacher (**taught, 'teaching**) —'**teacher** n. —'**teaching** n. —**teaching machine** machine that presents information and questions to user, registers answers, and indicates whether these are correct or acceptable

teak (tiːk) n. **1.** E Indian tree **2.** very hard wood obtained from it

teal (tiːl) n. **1.** type of small duck **2.** greenish-blue colour

team (tiːm) n. **1.** set of animals, players of game etc. associated in activity —v. **2.** (usu. with up) (cause to) make a team —'**teamster** n. driver of team of draught animals —**team-mate** n. fellow member of team —**team spirit** subordination of individual desire for good of team —'**teamwork** n. cooperative work by team acting as unit

tear¹ (tɪə) n. drop of fluid appearing in and falling from eye —'**tearful** a. **1.** inclined to weep **2.** involving tears —'**tearless** a. —'**teardrop** n. —**tear gas** irritant gas causing abnormal watering of eyes and temporary blindness —**tear-jerker** n. inf. excessively sentimental film etc.

tear² (tɛə) vt. **1.** pull apart, rend —vi. **2.** become torn **3.** rush (**tore, torn, 'tearing**) —n. **4.** hole, cut; split —'**tearaway** n. UK reckless impetuous person —**tear away** persuade (oneself or someone else) to leave

tease (tiːz) vt. **1.** tantalize, torment, irritate, bait **2.** pull apart fibres of —n. **3.** one who teases —'**teaser** n. annoying or puzzling problem —'**teasing** a.

teasel, teazel, or **teazle** ('tiːzəl) n. plant with prickly leaves and head

teat (tiːt) n. **1.** nipple of female breast **2.** rubber nipple of baby's feeding bottle

tech (tɛk) a./n. inf. technical (college)

tech. 1. technical **2.** technology

technetium (tɛk'niːʃɪəm) n. silvery-grey metallic element, artificially produced by bombardment of molybdenum by deuterons

technical ('tɛknɪkəl) a. **1.** of, specializing in industrial, practical or mechanical arts and applied sciences **2.** skilled in practical and mechanical arts **3.** belonging to particular art or science **4.** according to letter of the law —**techni'cality** n. **1.** point of procedure **2.** state of being technical —'**technically** adv. —**tech-'nician** n. one skilled in technique of an art —**technique** (tɛk'niːk) n. **1.** method of performance in an art **2.** skill required for mastery of subject —**technical college** higher educational institution, with courses in art, technology etc. —**technical drawing** drawing done with T-squares, scales etc. —**technical knockout** Boxing judgment of knockout given when boxer is in referee's opinion too badly beaten to continue

Technicolor ('tɛknɪkʌlə) n. **R** colour photography, esp. in cinema

techno- (comb. form) **1.** craft; art, as in technology, technography **2.** technological; technical, as in technocracy

technocracy (tɛk'nɒkrəsɪ) n. **1.** government by technical experts **2.** group of these experts

technology (tɛk'nɒlədʒɪ) n. **1.** application of practical, mechanical sciences to industry, commerce **2.** technical methods, skills, knowledge —techno'logical a. —tech'nologist n.

tectonic (tɛk'tɒnɪk) a. of construction or building —tec'tonics pl.n. (with sing. v.) art, science of building

ted (tɛd) inf. teddy boy

teddy bear ('tɛdɪ) child's soft toy bear (also 'teddy)

teddy boy 1. UK esp. in mid-1950s, one of cult of youths who wore mock Edwardian fashions **2.** any tough or delinquent youth

Te Deum (tiː 'diːəm) **1.** ancient Latin hymn in rhythmic prose **2.** musical setting of this hymn **3.** service of thanksgiving in which recital of this hymn forms central part

tedious ('tiːdɪəs) a. causing fatigue or boredom, monotonous —'tedium n. monotony

tee (tiː) n. **1.** Golf slightly raised ground from which first stroke of hole is made **2.** small peg supporting ball for this stroke **3.** target in some games (eg quoits) —tee off make first stroke of hole in golf

teem (tiːm) vi. **1.** abound, swarm, be prolific **2.** pour, rain heavily

teens (tiːnz) pl.n. years of life from 13 to 19 —'teenage a. —'teenager n. young person between 13 and 19 —'teenybopper n. sl. young teenager, usu. girl, who avidly follows fashions

teeny ('tiːnɪ) a. extremely small; tiny (also teeny-weeny ('tiːnɪ'wiːnɪ), teensy-weensy ('tiːnzɪ'wiːnzɪ))

teepee ('tiːpiː) n. see TEEPEE

tee shirt see T-SHIRT

teeter ('tiːtə) vi. **1.** seesaw or make similar movements **2.** vacillate

teeth (tiːθ) n., pl. of TOOTH —teethe (tiːð) vi. (of baby) grow first teeth —teething ring hard ring on which babies may bite while teething —teething troubles problems, difficulties at first stage of something

teetotal (tiː'təʊtᵊl) a. pledged to abstain from alcohol —tee'totalism n. —tee'totaller n.

Teflon ('tɛflɒn) n. **R** polymer used to make nonstick coatings on cooking utensils

tel. 1. telegram **2.** telegraph(ic) **3.** telephone

tel- (comb. form) see TELE-

tele- (comb. form) at a distance, from far off, as in telescope

telecast ('tɛlɪkɑːst) vi./n. (broadcast) television programme

telecommunications (tɛlɪkəmjuːnɪ'keɪʃənz) pl.n. (with sing. v.) science and technology of communications by telephony, radio, television etc.

telegram ('tɛlɪgræm) n. message sent by telegraph

telegraph ('tɛlɪgrɑːf) n. **1.** electrical apparatus for transmitting messages to a distance **2.** any signalling device for transmitting messages —v. **3.** communicate by telegraph —vt. **4.** C cast (votes) illegally by impersonating registered voters —tele'graphic a. —tele'graphically adv. —te'legraphist n. one who works telegraph —te'legraphy n. **1.** science of telegraph **2.** use of telegraph

telekinesis (tɛlɪkaɪ'niːsɪs) n. **1.** movement of a body caused by thought or willpower **2.** ability to cause such movement —telekinetic (tɛlɪkɪ'nɛtɪk) a.

teleology (tɛlɪ'ɒlədʒɪ, tiːlɪ-) n. **1.** doctrine of final causes **2.** belief that things happen because of the purpose or design that will be fulfilled by them —teleo'logic(al) a.

telepathy (tɪ'lɛpəθɪ) n. action of one mind on another at a distance —tele'pathic a. —tele'pathically adv.

telephone ('tɛlɪfəʊn) n. **1.** apparatus for communicating sound to hearer at a distance —v. **2.** communicate, speak by telephone —telephonic (tɛlɪ'fɒnɪk) a. —te'lephonist n. person operating telephone switchboard —te'lephony n. —telephone box soundproof enclosure from which paid telephone call can be made (also telephone kiosk, telephone booth) —telephone directory book listing names, addresses and telephone numbers of subscribers in particular area

telephoto ('tɛlɪfəʊtəʊ) a. (of lens) producing magnified image of distant object —telepho'tography n. process or technique of photographing distant objects using telephoto lens

teleprinter ('tɛlɪprɪntə) n. apparatus like typewriter, by which typed messages are sent and received by wire

Teleprompter ('tɛlɪprɒmptə) n. **R** T.V. device to enable speaker to refer to his script out of sight of the cameras

telescope ('tɛlɪskəʊp) n. **1.** optical instrument for magnifying distant objects —v. **2.** slide or drive together, esp. parts designed to fit one inside the other **3.** make smaller, shorter —telescopic (tɛlɪ'skɒpɪk) a.

teletext ('tɛlɪtɛkst) n. electronic system which

shows information, news on subscribers' television screens

television ('tɛlɪvɪʒən) *n.* 1. system of producing on screen images of distant objects, events *etc.* by electromagnetic radiation 2. device for receiving this transmission and converting it to optical images 3. programmes *etc.* viewed on television set —**televise** *vt.* 1. transmit by television 2. make, produce as television programme

telex ('tɛlɛks) *n.* 1. international telegraph service using teleprinters —*v.* 2. transmit (message) to (person *etc.*) by telex

tell (tɛl) *vt.* 1. let know 2. order, direct 3. narrate, make known 4. discern 5. distinguish 6. count —*vi.* 7. give account 8. be of weight, importance (**told, 'telling**) —**'teller** *n.* 1. narrator 2. bank cashier —**'telling** *a.* effective, striking —**'telltale** *n.* 1. sneak 2. automatic indicator —*a.* 3. revealing

tellurian (tɛ'lʊərɪən) *a.* of the earth —**tel'luric** *a.* —**tel'lurium** *n.* nonmetallic bluish-white element —**tellurous** ('tɛljʊrəs, tɛ'lʊərəs) *a.*

telly ('tɛlɪ) *inf.* television (set)

temerity (tɪ'mɛrɪtɪ) *n.* boldness, audacity

temp (tɛmp) *inf. n.* 1. one employed on temporary basis —*vi.* 2. work as temp

temp. 1. temperature 2. temporary

temper ('tɛmpə) *n.* 1. frame of mind 2. anger, oft. noisy 3. mental constitution 4. degree of hardness of steel *etc.* —*vt.* 5. restrain, qualify, moderate 6. harden 7. bring to proper condition —**'tempered** *a.* having temper or temperament as specified, as in *ill-tempered*

tempera ('tɛmpərə) *n.* emulsion used as painting medium

temperament ('tɛmpərəmənt) *n.* 1. natural disposition 2. excitability; moodiness; anger —**tempera'mental** *a.* 1. given to extremes of temperament, moody 2. of, occasioned by temperament 3. *inf.* working erratically and inconsistently; unreliable —**tempera'mentally** *adv.*

temperate ('tɛmpərɪt) *a.* 1. not extreme 2. showing, practising moderation —**'temperance** *n.* 1. moderation 2. abstinence, *esp.* from alcohol —**'temperately** *adv.* —**Temperate Zone** parts of earth's surface lying between Arctic Circle and tropic of Cancer and between Antarctic Circle and tropic of Capricorn

temperature ('tɛmprɪtʃə) *n.* 1. degree of heat or coldness 2. *inf.* (abnormally) high body temperature

tempest ('tɛmpɪst) *n.* violent storm —**tem'pestuous** *a.* 1. turbulent 2. violent, stormy —**tem'pestuously** *adv.*

template *or* **templet** ('tɛmplɪt) *n.* mould, pattern to help shape something accurately

temple ('tɛmpəl) *n.* 1. building for worship 2. shrine

temple ('tɛmpəl) *n.* flat part on either side of forehead

tempo ('tɛmpəʊ) *n.* rate, rhythm, *esp.* in music (*pl.* **-s, -pi** (-piː))

temporal ('tɛmpərəl) *a.* 1. of time 2. of this life or world, secular 3. *Gram.* of tense or linguistic expression of time —**tempo'rality** *n.*

temporal ('tɛmpərəl) *a. Anat.* of temple or temples —**temporal bone** either of two compound bones forming sides of skull

temporary ('tɛmpərərɪ) *a.* lasting, used only for a time —**'temporarily** *adv.*

temporize *or* **-ise** ('tɛmpəraɪz) *vi.* 1. use evasive action; hedge; gain time by negotiation *etc.* 2. conform to circumstances —**'temporizer** *or* **-iser** *n.*

tempt (tɛmpt) *vt.* 1. try to persuade, entice, *esp.* to something wrong or unwise 2. dispose, cause to be inclined —**temp'tation** *n.* 1. act of tempting 2. thing that tempts —**'tempter** *n.* ('temptress *fem.*) —**'tempting** *a.* attractive, inviting

tempus fugit ('tɛmpəs 'fjuːdʒɪt) *Lat.* time flies

ten (tɛn) *n./a.* cardinal number next after nine —**tenth** *a./n.* ordinal number —**ten-gallon hat** US cowboy's broad-brimmed felt hat with high crown —**tenpin bowling** ('tɛnpɪn) bowling game in which bowls are rolled down lane to knock over ten target pins (*also* (*esp.* US) **'tenpins**) —**the Ten Commandments** *O.T.* commandments summarizing basic obligations of man towards God and his fellow men

ten. *Mus.* 1. tenor 2. tenuto

tenable ('tɛnəbl) *a.* able to be held, defended, maintained

tenacious (tɪ'neɪʃəs) *a.* 1. holding fast 2. retentive 3. stubborn —**tenacity** (tɪ'næsɪtɪ) *n.*

tenant ('tɛnənt) *n.* one who holds lands, house *etc.* on rent or lease —**'tenancy** *n.* —**'tenantry** *n.* body of tenants —**tenant farmer** person who farms land rented from another, rent usu. taking form of crops *etc.*

tench (tɛntʃ) *n.* freshwater game fish

tend (tɛnd) *vi.* 1. be inclined 2. be conducive 3. go or move (in particular direction) —**'tendency** *n.* inclination, bent —**ten'dentious** *or* **ten'dencious** *a.* having, showing tendency or bias, controversial

tend (tɛnd) *vt.* take care of, watch over —**'tender** *n.* 1. small boat carried by yacht or ship 2. carriage for fuel and water attached to steam locomotive 3. one who tends, *eg* bar tender

tender ('tɛndə) *a.* 1. not tough or hard 2. easily injured 3. gentle, loving, affectionate 4. delicate, soft —'**tenderize** or -**ise** vt. soften (meat) by pounding or by treating with substance made for this purpose —'**tenderly** adv. —'**tenderness** n. —'**tenderfoot** n. newcomer, esp. to ranch etc. —'**tenderloin** n. tender cut of pork etc. from between sirloin and ribs

tender² ('tendə) vt. 1. offer —vi. 2. make offer or estimate —n. 3. offer 4. offer or estimate for contract to undertake specific work 5. what may legally be offered in payment

tendon ('tendən) n. sinew attaching muscle to bone etc.

tendril ('tendril) n. 1. slender curling stem by which climbing plant clings to anything 2. curl, as of hair

tenement ('tenəmənt) n. building divided into separate flats (also **tenement building**)

tenet ('tenɪt, 'tiːnɪt) n. doctrine, belief

tenner ('tenə) inf. ten-pound note

tennis ('tenɪs) n. game in which ball is struck with racket by players on opposite sides of net, lawn tennis —**tennis elbow** strained muscle as a result of playing tennis —**tennis shoe** rubber-soled canvas shoe tied with laces

tenon ('tenən) n. tongue put on end of piece of wood etc. to fit into a mortise —**tenon saw**

tenor ('tenə) n. 1. male voice between alto and bass 2. music for, singer with this 3. saxophone etc. intermediate between alto and baritone or bass 4. general course, meaning

tense¹ (tens) n. modification of verb to show time of action

tense² (tens) a. 1. stretched tight, strained; taut 2. emotionally strained —v. 3. make, become tense —'**tensile** a. 1. of tension 2. capable of being stretched —'**tension** n. 1. stretching 2. strain when stretched 3. emotional strain or excitement 4. hostility 5. suspense 6. Elec. voltage —**tensile strength** measure of ability of material to withstand longitudinal stress

tent (tent) n. portable shelter of canvas —**tent stitch** see petit point at PETIT

tentacle ('tentəkl) n. elongated, flexible organ of some animals (eg octopus) used for grasping, feeding etc.

tentative ('tentətɪv) a. 1. done as a trial 2. experimental, cautious —'**tentatively** adv.

tenterhooks ('tentəhuks) pl.n. —**on tenter-hooks** in anxious suspense

tenuous ('tenjʊəs) a. 1. flimsy, uncertain 2. thin, fine, slender —te'**nuity** n.

tenure ('tenjʊə, 'tenjə) n. (length of time of) possession, holding of office, position etc.

tenuto (tɪ'njuːtəu) a./adv. Mus. (of note) to be held for or beyond its full time value

tepee or **teepee** ('tiːpiː) n. N Amer. Indian cone-shaped tent of animal skins

tepid ('tepɪd) a. 1. moderately warm, lukewarm 2. half-hearted

tequila (tɪ'kiːlə) n. Mexican alcoholic spirit

ter. 1. terrace 2. territory

terbium ('tɜːbɪəm) n. rare metallic element

tercel ('tɜːsəl) or **tiercel** n. male falcon or hawk, esp. as used in falconry

tercentenary (tɜːsɛn'tiːnərɪ) or **tercenten-nial** a./n. (of) three hundredth anniversary

tergiversate ('tɜːdʒɪvəseɪt) vi. 1. change sides or loyalties 2. be evasive or ambiguous —tergiver'**sation** n.

term (tɜːm) n. 1. word; expression 2. limited period of time 3. period during which courts sit, schools are open etc. 4. limit, end —pl. 5. conditions 6. mutual relationship —vt. 7. name, designate —**terms of reference** specific limits of responsibility that determine activities of investigating body etc. —**terms of trade** UK Econ. ratio of export prices to import prices

termagant ('tɜːməgənt) n. rare shrewish woman; scold

terminal ('tɜːmɪnl) a. 1. at, forming an end 2. pert. to, forming a terminus 3. (of disease) ending in death —n. 4. terminal part or structure 5. extremity 6. point where current enters, leaves electrical device (eg battery) 7. device permitting operation of computer at some distance from it —**terminal velocity** 1. constant maximum velocity reached by body falling under gravity through fluid, esp. atmosphere 2. velocity of missile or projectile when it reaches target 3. maximum velocity attained by rocket etc. flying in parabolic flight path 4. maximum velocity that aircraft can attain

terminate ('tɜːmɪneɪt) v. bring, come to an end —'**terminable** a. —termi'**nation** n.

terminology (tɜːmɪ'nɒlədʒɪ) n. 1. set of technical terms or vocabulary 2. study of terms —termino'**logical** a.

terminus ('tɜːmɪnəs) n. 1. finishing point 2. farthest limit 3. railway station, bus station etc. at end of long-distance line (pl. -**ni** (-naɪ), -**es**)

termite ('tɜːmaɪt) n. insect, some species of which feed on and damage wood (also **white ant**)

tern (tɜːn) n. sea bird like gull

ternary ('tɜːnərɪ) a. 1. consisting of three 2. proceeding in threes

Terpsichore (tɜːp'sɪkərɪ) n. Muse of dance and choral song —**Terpsichorean** (tɜːpsɪkə'rɪən, -'kɔːrɪən) oft. jocular a. 1. of dancing (also **Terpsicho'real**) —n. 2. dancer

Terr. 1. Terrace 2. Territory

terrace ('terəs) n. 1. raised level place 2. level cut out of hill 3. row, street of houses built as one block 4. (oft. pl.) unroofed tier for spectators at football stadium —*vt.* **5.** form into, furnish with terrace

terra cotta ('tɛrə 'kɒtə) **1.** hard unglazed pottery **2.** its colour, brownish red

terra firma ('fɜːmə) *Lat.* firm ground; dry land

terrain (tə'reɪn) *n.* area of ground, *esp.* with reference to its physical character

terra incognita (ɪn'kɒgnɪtə) *Lat.* unexplored or unknown area

terrapin ('tɛrəpɪn) *n.* type of aquatic tortoise

terrazzo (tɛ'rætsəʊ) *n.* floor, wall finish of chips of stone set in mortar and polished

terrene (tɛ'riːn) *a.* **1.** of earth; worldly; mundane **2.** *rare* of earth; earthy —*n.* **3.** land **4.** *rare* earth

terrestrial (tə'rɛstrɪəl) *a.* **1.** of the earth **2.** of, living on land

terrible ('tɛrəbl) *a.* **1.** serious **2.** dreadful, frightful **3.** excessive **4.** causing fear —'**terribly** *adv.*

terrier ('tɛrɪə) *n.* small dog of various breeds, *orig.* for following quarry into burrow

terrific (tə'rɪfɪk) *a.* **1.** very great **2.** *inf.* good, excellent **3.** terrible, awe-inspiring

terrify ('tɛrɪfaɪ) *vt.* fill with fear, dread

terrine (tɛ'riːn) *n.* **1.** oval earthenware cooking dish **2.** food cooked or served in such dish, *esp.* paté

territory ('tɛrɪtərɪ) *n.* **1.** region **2.** geographical area under control of a political unit, *esp.* a sovereign state **3.** area of knowledge —**terri'torial** *a.* of territory —**Territorial Army** locally recruited volunteer force —**territorial waters** waters over which nation exercises jurisdiction

terror ('tɛrə) *n.* **1.** great fear **2.** *inf.* troublesome person or thing —'**terrorism** *n.* **1.** use of violence, intimidation to achieve ends **2.** state of terror —'**terrorist** *n./a.* —'**terrorize** or **-ise** *vt.* force, oppress by fear, violence

terry ('tɛrɪ) *n./a.* (pile fabric) with the loops uncut

terse (tɜːs) *a.* **1.** expressed in few words, concise **2.** abrupt

tertiary ('tɜːʃərɪ) *a.* **1.** third in degree, order *etc.* **2.** (T-) of Tertiary period or rock system —*n.* **3.** (T-) geological period before Quaternary

Terylene ('tɛrɪliːn) *n.* **R 1.** synthetic yarn **2.** fabric made of it

tessellate ('tɛsɪleɪt) *vt.* **1.** make, pave, inlay with mosaic of small tiles **2.** (of identical shapes) fit together exactly —'**tessellated** *a.* —**tessel-'lation** *n.* —**tessera** ('tɛsərə) *n.* stone used in mosaic (*pl.* **-ae** (-iː))

test (tɛst) *vt.* **1.** try, put to the proof **2.** carry out test(s) on —*n.* **3.** critical examination **4.** means of trial —'**testing** *a.* difficult —**test case** lawsuit viewed as means of establishing precedent

—**test match** one of series of international sports contests, *esp.* cricket —**test paper 1.** *Chem.* paper impregnated with indicator for chemical tests **2.** question sheet of test **3.** paper completed by test candidate —**test pilot** pilot who flies aircraft of new design to test performance in air —**test tube** narrow cylindrical glass vessel used in scientific experiments —**test-tube baby** baby conceived in artificial womb

testament ('tɛstəmənt) *n.* **1.** *Law* will **2.** declaration **3.** (T-) one of the two main divisions of the Bible —**testa'mentary** *a.*

testate ('tɛsteɪt, 'tɛstɪt) *a.* having left a valid will —'**testacy** *n.* state of being testate —**tes'tator** *n.* maker of will (**tes'tatrix** *fem.*)

testicle ('tɛstɪkl) *n.* either of two male reproductive glands

testify ('tɛstɪfaɪ) *v.* **1.** declare **2.** bear witness (to) —'**fied, -fying**)

testimony ('tɛstɪmənɪ) *n.* **1.** affirmation **2.** evidence —**testi'monial** *n.* **1.** certificate of character, ability *etc.* **2.** tribute given by person expressing regard for recipient —*a.* **3.** of testimony or testimonial

testis ('tɛstɪs) *n.* testicle (*pl.* **testes** ('tɛstiːz)) —**tes'tosterone** *n.* hormone secreted mainly by testes

testy ('tɛstɪ) *a.* irritable, short-tempered —'**testily** *adv.*

tetanus ('tɛtənəs) *n.* acute infectious disease producing muscular spasms, contractions (*also* '**lockjaw**)

tetchy ('tɛtʃɪ) *a.* cross, irritable, touchy —'**tetchiness** *n.*

tête-à-tête (teɪtə'teɪt) *n.* **1.** private conversation between two people **2.** small sofa for two people, *esp.* S-shaped (*pl.* **-s, -tête**) —*adv.* **3.** intimately; in private

tether ('tɛðə) *n.* **1.** rope or chain for fastening (grazing) animal —*vt.* **2.** tie up with rope —**be at the end of one's tether** have reached limit of one's endurance

tetra- or *before vowel* **tetr-** (*comb. form*) four, as in *tetrameter*

tetrad ('tɛtræd) *n.* group or series of four

tetraethyl lead (tɛtrə'iːθaɪl lɛd) colourless oily insoluble liquid used in petrol to prevent knocking

tetragon ('tɛtrəgɒn) *n.* figure with four angles and four sides —**te'tragonal** *a.* —**tetra'hedron** *n.* solid contained by four plane faces

tetralogy (tɛ'trælədʒɪ) *n.* series of four related works, as in drama or opera

tetrameter (tɛ'træmɪtə) *n. Prosody* **1.** line of verse consisting of four metrical feet **2.** verse composed of such lines

Teuton ('tjuːtɒn) *n.* **1.** member of ancient

Germanic people from Jutland who migrated to S Gaul in 2nd century B.C. **2.** member of any Germanic-speaking people, *esp.* German —*a.* **3.** Teutonic —**Teu'tonic** *a.* **1.** German **2.** of ancient Teutons

text (tɛkst) *n.* **1.** (actual words of) book, passage *etc.* **2.** passage of Scriptures *etc.*, *esp.* as subject of discourse —**'textual** *a.* of, in a text —**'textbook** *n.* book of instruction on particular subject —**textual criticism** **1.** scholarly study of manuscripts, *esp.* of Bible, to establish original text **2.** literary criticism emphasizing close analysis of text

textile ('tɛkstaɪl) *n.* **1.** any fabric or cloth, *esp.* woven —*a.* **2.** of (the making of) fabrics

texture ('tɛkstʃə) *n.* **1.** surface of material, *esp.* as perceived by sense of touch **2.** character, structure **3.** consistency —*vt.* **4.** give distinctive texture to

T.G.W.U. Transport and General Workers' Union

Th *Chem.* thorium

-th¹ (*comb. form*) **1.** action or its consequence, as in *growth* **2.** quality, as in *width*

-th² or **-eth** (*comb. form*) forming ordinal numbers, as in *fourth, thousandth*

Thai (taɪ) *a.* **1.** of Thailand —*n.* **2.** native of Thailand (*pl.* **-s, Thai**) **3.** language of Thailand

thalidomide (θə'lɪdəmaɪd) *n.* drug formerly used as sedative, but found to cause abnormalities in developing foetus

thallium ('θælɪəm) *n.* highly toxic metallic element —**'thallic** *a.*

than (ðæn; *unstressed* ðən) *conj.* introduces second part of comparison

thane or **thegn** (θeɪn) *n. Hist.* nobleman holding lands in return for certain services

thank (θæŋk) *vt.* **1.** express gratitude to **2.** say thanks to **3.** hold responsible —**'thankful** *a.* grateful, appreciative —**'thankless** *a.* **1.** having, bringing no thanks **2.** unprofitable —**thanks** *pl.n.* words of gratitude —**Thanksgiving Day** public holiday in Canad. and U.S.A.

that (ðæt; *unstressed* ðət) *a.* **1.** demonstrates or particularizes (*pl.* **those**) —*demonstrative pron.* **2.** particular thing meant (*pl.* **those**) —*adv.* **3.** as —*relative pron.* **4.** which, who —*conj.* **5.** introduces noun or adverbial clauses

thatch (θætʃ) *n.* **1.** reeds, straw *etc.* used as roofing material —*vt.* **2.** roof (a house) with reeds, straw *etc.* —**'thatcher** *n.*

thaw (θɔː) *v.* **1.** melt **2.** (cause to) unfreeze **3.** defrost —*vi.* **4.** become warmer or more genial —*n.* **5.** a melting (of frost *etc.*)

Th.D. Doctor of Theology

the (*stressed or emphatic* ðiː; *unstressed before consonant* ðə; *unstressed before vowel* ðɪ) the definite article

theatre or *U.S.* **theater** ('θɪətə) *n.* **1.** place where plays *etc.* are performed **2.** drama, dramatic works generally **3.** large room with (tiered) seats, used for lectures *etc.* **4.** surgical operating room —**theatrical** (θɪ'ætrɪk°l) *a.* **1.** of, for the theatre **2.** exaggerated, affected —**theatrically** (θɪ'ætrɪkəlɪ) *adv.* —**theatricals** (θɪ'ætrɪk°lz) *pl.n.* amateur dramatic performances

thee (ðiː) *pron. obs.* objective and dative of THOU¹

theft (θɛft) *n.* stealing

their (ðɛə) *a.* belonging to them —**theirs** *pron.* something or someone belonging to them

theism ('θiːɪzəm) *n.* belief in creation of universe by one god —**'theist** *n.* —**the'istic(al)** *a.*

them (ðɛm; *unstressed* ðəm) *pron.* **1.** objective case of THEY **2.** those persons or things —**them'selves** *pron.* emphatic and reflexive form of THEY

theme (θiːm) *n.* **1.** main idea or topic of conversation, book *etc.* **2.** subject of composition **3.** recurring melody in music —**the'matic** *a.*

then (ðɛn) *adv.* **1.** at that time **2.** next **3.** that being so

thence (ðɛns) *adv.* from that place, point of reasoning *etc.*

theo- or *before vowel* **the-** (*comb. form*) God; gods, as in *theology*

theocracy (θɪ'ɒkrəsɪ) *n.* government by a deity or a priesthood —**theo'cratic** *a.*

theodolite (θɪ'ɒdəlaɪt) *n.* surveying instrument for measuring angles

theology (θɪ'ɒlədʒɪ) *n.* systematic study of religion(s) and religious belief(s) —**theologian** (θɪə'ləʊdʒɪən) *n.* —**theo'logical** *a.* —**theo'logically** *adv.*

theorem ('θɪərəm) *n.* proposition which can be demonstrated by argument —**theore'matic** or **theo'remic** *a.*

theory ('θɪərɪ) *n.* **1.** supposition to account for something **2.** system of rules and principles **3.** rules and reasoning *etc.* as distinguished from practice —**theo'retic(al)** *a.* **1.** based on theory **2.** speculative, as opposed to practical —**theo'retically** *adv.* —**theore'tician** *n.* student or user of theory rather than practical aspects of subject —**'theorist** *n.* —**'theorize** or **-ise** *vi.* form theories, speculate

theosophy (θɪ'ɒsəfɪ) *n.* any of various religious, philosophical systems claiming possibility of intuitive insight into divine nature

therapy ('θɛrəpɪ) *n.* healing treatment (*usu.* in *comb. forms* as *radiotherapy*) —**therapeutic** (θɛrə'pjuːtɪk) *a.* **1.** of healing **2.** serving to improve or maintain health —**therapeutics**

(θεrə'pjuːtiks) *pl.n.* (*with sing. v.*) art of healing —'**therapist** *n.*

there (δεə) *adv.* **1.** in that place **2.** to that point —'**thereabouts** *or* '**thereabout** *adv.* near that place, time *etc.* —**there**'**after** *adv.* from that time on; after that time —**there**'**by** *adv.* by that means —'**therefore** *adv.* in consequence, that being so —**there**'**in** *adv. Formal, law* in or into that place *etc.* —**there**'**of** *adv. Formal, law* **1.** of or concerning that or it **2.** from or because of that —**there**'**to** *adv. Formal, law* to that or it **2.** *obs.* in addition to that —**there**'**under** *adv. Formal, law* **1.** in documents *etc.*, below that or it; subsequently in that; thereafter **2.** under terms or authority of that —**thereu**'**pon** *adv.* at that point, immediately afterwards —**there**'**with** *or* **therewith**'**al** *adv.* **1.** *Formal, law* with or in addition to that **2.** *rare* thereupon **3.** *obs.* by means of or on account of that

therm (θɜːm) *n.* unit of measurement of heat —'**thermal** *or* '**thermic** *a.* **1.** of, pert. to heat **2.** hot, warm (*esp.* of spring *etc.*) **3.** (of garments) specially made so as to have exceptional heat-retaining qualities

thermion ('θɜːmɪən) *n. Phys.* ion emitted by incandescent body —**thermi**'**onic** *a.* pert. to thermion —**thermionic valve** electronic valve in which electrons are emitted from a heated rather than a cold cathode

thermo- *or before vowel* **therm-** (*comb. form*) related to, caused by or producing heat, as in *thermopile*

thermocouple ('θɜːməʊkʌpəl) *n.* **1.** device for measuring temperature consisting of pair of wires of different metals joined at both ends **2.** similar device with only one junction between two dissimilar metals

thermodynamics (θɜːməʊdaɪ'næmɪks) *pl.n.* (*with sing. v.*) the science that deals with the interrelationship and interconversion of different forms of energy

thermoelectricity (θɜːməʊɪlek'trɪsɪtɪ) *n.* electricity developed by the action of heat —**thermoe**'**lectric(al)** *a.* **1.** of conversion of heat energy to electrical energy **2.** of conversion of electrical energy

thermometer (θə'mɒmɪtə) *n.* instrument to measure temperature —**thermo**'**metric** *a.*

thermonuclear (θɜːməʊ'njuːklɪə) *a.* involving nuclear fusion

thermoplastic (θɜːməʊ'plæstɪk) *n.* **1.** plastic that retains its properties after being melted and solidified —*a.* **2.** (of plastic *etc.*) becoming soft when heated and rehardening on cooling without appreciable change of properties

Thermos *or* **Thermos flask** ('θɜːməs) *n.* **R** vacuum flask

thermosetting (θɜːməʊ'setɪŋ) *a.* (of material,

esp. synthetic plastic) hardening permanently after one application of heat and pressure

thermostat ('θɜːməstæt) *n.* apparatus for automatically regulating temperature —**ther-mo**'**static** *a.*

thesaurus (θɪ'sɔːrəs) *n.* **1.** book containing lists of synonyms and sometimes antonyms **2.** dictionary of selected words, topics (*pl.* **-es, -ri** (-raɪ))

these (δiːz) *pron., pl. of* THIS

thesis ('θiːsɪs) *n.* **1.** written work submitted for degree, diploma **2.** theory maintained in argument (*pl.* **theses** ('θiːsiːz))

Thespian ('θεspɪən) *a.* **1.** theatrical —*n.* **2.** actor, actress

Thess. *Bible* Thessalonians

theta ('θiːtə) *n.* eighth letter in Gr. alphabet (Θ, θ)

they (δeɪ) *pron.* the third person plural pronoun

thick (θɪk) *a.* **1.** having great thickness, not thin **2.** dense, crowded **3.** viscous **4.** (of voice) throaty **5.** *inf.* stupid, insensitive **6.** *inf.* friendly (*esp. in* **thick as thieves**) —*n.* **7.** busiest, most intense part —'**thicken** *v.* **1.** make, become thick —*vi.* **2.** become more involved, complicated —'**thickening** *n.* **1.** something added to liquid to thicken it **2.** thickened part or piece —'**thicket** *n.* thick growth of small trees —'**thickly** *adv.* —'**thickness** *n.* **1.** dimensions of anything measured through it, at right angles to length and breadth **2.** state of being thick **3.** layer —'**thickhead** *n.* **1.** stupid or ignorant person; fool **2.** Aust. *or* SE Asian songbird —**thick**'**headed** *a.* —**thick**'**headedness** *n.* —**thick**'**set** *a.* **1.** sturdy and solid of body **2.** set closely together —**thick-skinned** *a.* insensitive to criticism or hints; not easily upset or affected

thief (θiːf) *n.* one who steals (*pl.* **thieves** (θiːvz)) —**thieve** *v.* steal —'**thievish** *a.*

thigh (θaɪ) *n.* upper part of leg

thimble ('θɪmbəl) *n.* cap protecting end of finger when sewing

thin (θɪn) *a.* **1.** of little thickness **2.** slim, lean **3.** of little density **4.** sparse; fine **5.** loose, not close-packed **6.** *inf.* unlikely —*v.* **7.** make, become thin (**-nn-**) —'**thinner** *n.* —'**thinness** *n.* —**thin-skinned** *a.* sensitive to criticism or hints; easily upset or affected

thine (δaɪn) *pron./a.* (thing) belonging to thee

thing (θɪŋ) *n.* **1.** material object **2.** any possible object of thought **3.** preoccupation, obsession (*esp. in* **have a thing about**) —**thingumabob** *or* **thingamabob** ('θɪŋəməbɒb) *n. inf.* person or thing the name of which is unknown, temporarily forgotten or deliberately overlooked (*also* '**thingumajig,** '**thingamajig** *or* '**thingummy**)

think (θɪŋk) *vi.* **1.** have one's mind at work **2.**

reflect, meditate **3.** reason **4.** deliberate **5.** imagine **6.** hold opinion —*vt.* **7.** conceive, consider in the mind **8.** believe **9.** esteem (**thought**, '**thinking**) —'**thinkable** *a.* able to be conceived, considered, possible, feasible —'**thinker** *n.* —'**thinking** *a.* reflecting —**think-tank** *n.* group of experts studying specific problems

thio- *or before vowel* **thi-** (*comb. form*) sulphur, *esp.* denoting replacement of oxygen atom with sulphur atom, as in *thiol, thiosulphate*

thiopentone sodium (θaɪəʊ'pɛntəʊn) *or* **thiopental sodium** (θaɪəʊ'pɛntæl) barbiturate drug used as intravenous general anaesthetic (*also* **sodium pentothal**)

third (θɜːd) *a.* **1.** ordinal number corresponding to *three* —*n.* **2.** third part —**third degree** *see* DEGREE —**third dimension** dimension of depth by which solid object may be distinguished from two-dimensional drawing or picture of it —**third man** *Cricket* fielding position on off side near boundary behind batsman's wicket —**third party** *Law, insurance etc.* person involved by chance or only incidentally in legal proceedings *etc.* —**third person** grammatical category of pronouns and verbs used when referring to objects or individuals other than speaker or his addressee(s) —**third-rate** *a.* mediocre, inferior —**Third World** developing countries of Afr., Asia, Latin Amer.

thirst (θɜːst) *n.* **1.** desire to drink **2.** feeling caused by lack of drink **3.** craving, yearning —*vi.* **4.** feel lack of drink —'**thirstily** *adv.* —'**thirsty** *a.*

thirteen ('θɜː'tiːn) *n./a.* three plus ten —'**thirty** *n./a.* three times ten

this (ðɪs) *demonstrative a./pron.* denotes thing, person near, or just mentioned (*pl.* **these**)

thistle ('θɪsəl) *n.* prickly plant with dense flower heads —'**thistledown** *n.* mass of feathery plumed seeds produced by thistle

thither ('ðɪðə) *or* **thitherward** *adv. obs.* to or towards that place

thixotropic (θɪksə'trɒpɪk) *a.* (of certain liquids, as paints) having property of thickening if left undisturbed but becoming less viscous when stirred

tho *or* **tho'** (ðəʊ) *US, poet. see* THOUGH

thole[1] (θəʊl) *or* **tholepin** ('θəʊlpɪn) *n.* wooden pin set upright in gunwale of rowing boat to serve as fulcrum in rowing

thole[2] (θəʊl) *vt.* **1.** *dial.* put up with; bear **2.** suffer

thong (θɒŋ) *n.* **1.** narrow strip of leather, strap **2.** *chiefly US, A, NZ* flip-flop (sandal)

thorax ('θɔːræks) *n.* part of body between neck and belly —**thoracic** (θɔː'ræsɪk) *a.*

thorium ('θɔːrɪəm) *n.* radioactive metallic element

thorn (θɔːn) *n.* **1.** prickle on plant **2.** spine **3.** bush noted for its thorns **4.** *fig.* anything which causes trouble or annoyance (*esp. in* **thorn in one's side** *or* **flesh**) —'**thorny** *a.*

thorough ('θʌrə) *a.* **1.** careful, methodical **2.** complete, entire —'**thoroughly** *adv.* —'**thoroughbred** *a.* **1.** of pure breed —*n.* **2.** purebred animal, *esp.* horse —'**thoroughfare** *n.* **1.** road or passage open at both ends **2.** right of way —'**thoroughgoing** *a.* **1.** extremely thorough **2.** absolute; complete

those (ðəʊz) *pron., pl. of* THAT

thou[1] (ðaʊ) *pron. obs.* the second person singular pronoun (*pl.* **ye, you**)

thou[2] (θaʊ) *n.* **1.** thousandth of inch **2.** *inf.* thousand (*pl.* **-s, thou**)

though (ðəʊ) *conj.* **1.** in spite of the fact that, even if —*adv.* **2.** nevertheless

thought (θɔːt) *n.* **1.** process of thinking **2.** what one thinks **3.** product of thinking **4.** meditation —*v.* **5.** *pt./pp. of* THINK —'**thoughtful** *a.* **1.** considerate **2.** showing careful thought **3.** engaged in meditation **4.** attentive —'**thoughtless** *a.* inconsiderate, careless, heedless —**thought transference** *Psychol. see* TELEPATHY

thousand ('θaʊzənd) *n./a.* cardinal number, ten hundred

thrall (θrɔːl) *n.* **1.** slavery **2.** slave, bondsman —*vt.* **3.** enslave —'**thralldom** *or* '**thraldom** *n.* bondage

thrash (θræʃ) *vt.* **1.** beat, whip soundly **2.** defeat soundly **3.** thresh —*vi.* **4.** move, plunge, *esp.* arms, legs in wild manner —**thrash out 1.** argue about from every angle **2.** solve by exhaustive discussion

thread (θrɛd) *n.* **1.** fine cord **2.** yarn **3.** ridge cut spirally on screw **4.** theme, meaning —*vt.* **5.** put thread into **6.** fit form, magnetic tape *etc.* into (machine) **7.** put on thread **8.** pick (one's way *etc.*) —'**threadbare** *a.* **1.** worn, with nap rubbed off **2.** meagre **3.** shabby

threat (θrɛt) *n.* **1.** declaration of intention to harm, injure *etc.* **2.** person or thing regarded as dangerous —'**threaten** *vt.* **1.** utter threats against **2.** menace

three (θriː) *n./a.* cardinal number, one more than two —'**threesome** *n.* group of three —**three-D** *or* **3-D** *n.* three-dimensional effect —**three-dimensional** *a.* **1.** having three dimensions **2.** simulating the effect of depth —**three-legged race** race in which pairs of competitors run with adjacent legs tied together —**threepenny bit** *or* **thrupenny bit** ('θrʌpnɪ, -ɒnɪ, 'θrɛp-) former twelve-sided Brit. coin valued at three old pence —**three-ply** *a.* having three layers (as wood) or strands (as wool) —**three-point turn** complete turn of motor vehicle using forward and reverse gears —**three-quarter** a. 1. being three quarters of something 2. being of three quarters the normal length —n. 3. *Rugby* any of players between full back and forwards —'**three**'**score** n./a. *obs.* sixty

threnody ('θrɛnədi, 'θriː-) *or* **threnode** ('θriːnəʊd, 'θrɛn-) n. ode, song or speech of lamentation, esp. for dead —'**threnodist** n.

thresh (θrɛʃ) v. 1. beat, rub (wheat, *etc.*) to separate grain from husks and straw 2. thrash

threshold ('θrɛʃəʊld, 'θrɛʃhəʊld) n. 1. bar of stone or wood forming bottom of doorway 2. entrance 3. starting point 4. point at which a stimulus is perceived, or produces a response

threw (θruː) *pt. of* THROW

thrice (θraɪs) *adv.* three times

thrift (θrɪft) n. 1. saving, economy 2. genus of plant, sea pink —'**thrifty** a. economical, frugal, sparing

thrill (θrɪl) n. 1. sudden sensation of excitement and pleasure —v. 2. (cause to) feel a thrill —vi. 3. vibrate, tremble —'**thriller** n. book, film *etc.* with story of mystery, suspense —'**thrilling** a. exciting

thrips (θrɪps) n. small slender-bodied insect that feeds on plant sap (*pl.* **thrips**)

thrive (θraɪv) vi. 1. grow well 2. flourish, prosper (**throve, thrived** *pt.*, **thriven** ('θrɪvən), **thrived** *pp.*, '**thriving** *pr.p.*)

thro' *or* **thro** (θruː) *Poet.* see THROUGH

throat (θrəʊt) n. 1. front of neck 2. either or both of passages through it —'**throaty** a. (of voice) hoarse

throb (θrɒb) vi. 1. beat, quiver strongly, pulsate (**-bb-**) —n. 2. pulsation, beat; vibration

throes (θrəʊz) *pl.n.* condition of violent pangs, pain *etc.* —**in the throes of** *inf.* in the process of

thrombosis (θrɒm'bəʊsɪs) n. formation of clot of coagulated blood in blood vessel or heart

throne (θrəʊn) n. 1. ceremonial seat, powers and duties of king or queen —vt. 2. place on throne, declare king *etc.*

throng (θrɒŋ) n./v. crowd

throstle ('θrɒsəl) n. thrush

throttle ('θrɒtəl) n. 1. device controlling amount of fuel entering engine and thereby its speed —vt. 2. strangle 3. suppress 4. restrict (flow of liquid *etc.*)

through (θruː) *prep.* 1. from end to end, from side to side of 2. between the sides of 3. in consequence of 4. by means or fault of —*adv.* 5. from end to end 6. to the end —a. 7. completed 8. *inf.* finished 9. continuous 10. (of transport, traffic) not stopping —**through**'**out** *adv./prep.* in every part (of) —'**throughput** n. quantity of material processed, esp. by computer —**through ticket** ticket for whole of journey —**through train, bus** *etc.* train, bus *etc.* which travels

whole (unbroken) length of long journey —**carry through** accomplish

throve (θrəʊv) *pt. of* THRIVE

throw (θrəʊ) vt. 1. fling, cast 2. move, put abruptly, carelessly 3. give, hold (party *etc.*) 4. cause to fall 5. shape on potter's wheel 6. move (switch, lever *etc.*) 7. *inf.* baffle, disconcert (**threw, thrown,** '**throwing**) —n. 8. act or distance of throwing —'**throwaway** a. 1. *chiefly UK* said incidentally, *esp.* for rhetorical effect; casual —n. 2. anything that can be thrown away or discarded 3. *chiefly US* handbill —**throw away** 1. get rid of; discard 2. fail to make good use of; waste —'**throwback** n. 1. one who, that which reverts to character of an ancestor 2. this process

thrum (θrʌm) v. 1. strum rhythmically but without expression on (musical instrument) —vi. 2. drum incessantly (**-mm-**) —n. 3. repetitive strumming

thrush[1] (θrʌʃ) n. songbird

thrush[2] (θrʌʃ) n. 1. fungal disease of mouth, *esp.* in infants 2. vaginal infection caused by same fungus 3. foot disease of horses

thrust (θrʌst) vt. 1. push, drive —v. 2. (make a) stab —vi. 3. push one's way (**thrust,** '**thrusting**) —n. 4. lunge, stab with pointed weapon *etc.* 5. cutting remark 6. propulsive force or power

thud (θʌd) n. 1. dull heavy sound —vi. 2. make thud (**-dd-**)

thug (θʌg) n. brutal, violent person —'**thuggery** n. —'**thuggish** a.

thuja *or* **thuya** ('θuːjə) n. any of various coniferous trees of N Amer. and E Asia

thulium ('θjuːlɪəm) n. malleable ductile silvery-grey element

thumb (θʌm) n. 1. first, shortest, thickest finger of hand —vt. 2. handle, dirty with thumb 3. signal for (lift in vehicle) 4. flick through (pages of book *etc.*) —**thumb index** series of indentations cut into fore-edge of book to facilitate quick reference —**thumb-index** vt. furnish with thumb index —'**thumbnail** n. 1. nail of thumb —a. 2. concise and brief —'**thumbscrew** n. 1. instrument of torture that pinches or crushes thumbs 2. screw with projections on head enabling it to be turned by thumb and forefinger

thump (θʌmp) n. 1. dull heavy blow 2. sound of one —vt. 3. strike heavily —vi. 4. throb, beat or pound violently —'**thumping** a. *sl.* huge; excessive

thunder ('θʌndə) n. 1. loud noise accompanying lightning —vi. 2. rumble with thunder 3. make noise like thunder —vt. 4. utter loudly —'**thundering** a. *sl.* very great; excessive —'**thunderous** a. —'**thundery** a. sultry —'**thunderbolt** *or* '**thunderclap** n. 1. lightning flash followed by peal of thunder **2.** anything totally unexpected and unpleasant —'**thundercloud** n. electrically charged cumulonimbus cloud associated with thunderstorms —'**thunderstorm** n. storm with thunder and lightning and usu. heavy rain or hail —'**thunderstruck** a. amazed

thurible ('θjʊərɪbᵊl) n. see CENSER

Thurs. Thursday

Thursday ('θɜːzdɪ) n. fifth day of week

thus (ðʌs) adv. **1.** in this way **2.** therefore

thwack (θwæk) vt./n. whack

thwart (θwɔːt) vt. **1.** foil, frustrate —adv. **2.** obs. across —n. **3.** seat across a boat

thy (ðaɪ) a. belonging to thee —**thy'self** pron. emphatic form of THOU¹

thyme (taɪm) n. aromatic herb

thymol ('θaɪmɒl) n. white crystalline substance obtained from thyme and used as antiseptic etc.

thymus ('θaɪməs) n. small ductless gland in upper part of chest (pl. **-es, -mi** (-maɪ))

thyroid ('θaɪrɔɪd) a. **1.** of thyroid gland **2.** of largest cartilage of larynx —n. **3.** thyroid gland **4.** preparation of thyroid gland of certain animals, used to treat hypothyroidism —**thyroid gland** endocrine gland controlling body growth, situated (in man) at base of neck

ti (tiː) n. Mus. see TE

Ti Chem. titanium

tiara (tɪ'ɑːrə) n. jewelled head ornament, coronet

tibia ('tɪbɪə) n. inner and thicker of two bones of the leg below the knee (pl. **-biae** (-biː), **-s**) —'**tibial** a.

tic (tɪk) n. spasmodic twitch in muscles, esp. of face

tick¹ (tɪk) n. **1.** slight tapping sound, as of watch movement **2.** small mark (√) **3.** inf. moment —vt. **4.** mark with tick —vi. **5.** make ticking sound —'**ticker** n. **1.** sl. heart **2.** sl. watch **3.** person or thing that ticks **4.** US tape machine —**ticker tape** continuous paper ribbon —'**ticktack** n. UK system of sign language, mainly using hands, by which bookmakers transmit their odds to each other at racecourses **2.** US ticking sound —'**ticktock** n. **1.** ticking sound as made by clock —vi. **2.** make ticking sound —**tick off 1.** mark off **2.** reprimand —**tick over 1.** (of engine) idle **2.** continue to function smoothly

tick² (tɪk) n. small insectlike parasite living on and sucking blood of warm-blooded animals

tick³ (tɪk) n. mattress case —'**ticking** n. strong material for mattress covers

tick⁴ (tɪk) n. inf. credit, account

ticket ('tɪkɪt) n. **1.** card, paper entitling holder to admission, travel etc. **2.** label **3.** summons served for parking or traffic offence **4.** US list of candidates of one party for election —vt. **5.** attach label to **6.** issue tickets to

tickle ('tɪkᵊl) vt. **1.** touch, stroke, poke (person, part of body etc.) to produce laughter etc. **2.** please, amuse (oft. in tickle one's fancy) —vi. **3.** be irritated, itch —n. **4.** act, instance of this **5.** C narrow strait —'**ticklish** a. **1.** sensitive to tickling **2.** requiring care or tact

tiddler ('tɪdlə) n. inf. very small fish etc. —'**tiddly** a. tiny

tiddly ('tɪdlɪ) a. inf. slightly drunk

tiddlywinks ('tɪdlɪwɪŋks) pl.n. game of trying to flip small plastic discs into cup

tide (taɪd) n. **1.** rise and fall of sea happening twice each lunar day **2.** stream **3.** season, time —'**tidal** a. of, like tide —**tidal wave** great wave, esp. produced by earthquake —'**tidemark** n. **1.** mark left by highest or lowest point of tide **2.** inf., chiefly UK mark showing level reached by liquid **3.** inf., chiefly UK dirty mark on skin, indicating extent to which someone has washed —**tide someone over** help someone for a while, esp. by loan etc.

tidings ('taɪdɪŋz) pl.n. news

tidy ('taɪdɪ) a. **1.** orderly, neat **2.** inf. of fair size —vt. **3.** put in order

tie (taɪ) vi. **1.** make an equal score —vt. **2.** fasten, bind, secure **3.** restrict (**tied, 'tying**) —n. **4.** that with which anything is bound **5.** restriction, restraint **6.** long, narrow piece of material worn knotted round neck **7.** bond, link **8.** drawn game, contest **9.** match, game in eliminating competition —**tied** a. **1.** of (public house) obliged to sell beer etc. of only one brewer **2.** (of cottage etc.) rented to tenant only as long as he is employed by owner —**tie-dyeing** n. way of dyeing cloth in patterns by tying sections tightly so they will not absorb dye —'**tiepin** n. ornamental pin used to pin ends of tie to shirt —**tie-up** n. **1.** link, connection **2.** chiefly US standstill **3.** chiefly US inf. traffic jam —**tie up 1.** bind securely (as if) with string etc. **2.** moor (vessel) **3.** engage attentions of **4.** conclude (organization of something) **5.** come or bring to complete standstill **6.** commit (funds etc.) and so make unavailable for other uses **7.** subject (property) to conditions that prevent sale etc.

tier (tɪə) n. row, rank, layer

tiercel ('tɪəsᵊl) n. see TERCEL

tiff (tɪf) n. petty quarrel

tiffin ('tɪfɪn) n. in India, light meal, esp. at midday

tiger ('taɪgə) n. large carnivorous feline animal —'**tigress** n. **1.** female tiger **2.** fierce, cruel or wildly passionate woman —**tiger lily** lily plant cultivated for its flowers, which have black-spotted orange petals —**tiger moth** moth with wings conspicuously marked with stripes and spots —**tiger's-eye** or '**tigereye** n. semiprecious golden-brown stone

tight (taɪt) *a.* 1. taut, tense 2. closely fitting 3. secure, firm 4. not allowing passage of water *etc.* 5. cramped 6. *inf.* mean 7. *inf.* drunk —'**tighten** *v.* —'**tightly** *adv.* —**tights** *pl.n.* one-piece clinging garment covering body from waist to feet —**tight**'**fisted** *a.* mean; miserly —**tight**'**knit** 1. closely integrated 2. organized carefully —**tight-lipped** *a.* 1. secretive; taciturn 2. with lips pressed tightly together, as through anger —'**tightrope** *n.* rope stretched taut above the ground, on which acrobats perform

tigon ('taɪgən) *or* **tiglon** ('tɪglən) *n.* offspring of tiger and lioness

tike (taɪk) *n. see* TYKE

tiki ('tiːkɪ) *n.* amulet, figurine of Maori cultures

tilde ('tɪldə) *n.* diacritical mark (˜) placed over letter to indicate nasal sound, as in Sp. *señor*

tile (taɪl) *n.* 1. flat piece of ceramic, plastic *etc.* material used for roofs, walls, floors, fireplaces *etc.* —*vt.* 2. cover with tiles —**tiled** *a.* —'**tiling** *n.* —**on the tiles** *inf.* on a spree, *esp.* of drinking or debauchery

till¹ (tɪl) *prep.* 1. up to the time of —*conj.* 2. to the time that

till² (tɪl) *vt.* cultivate —'**tillage** *n.* —'**tiller** *n.*

till³ (tɪl) *n.* 1. drawer for money in shop counter 2. cash register

tiller ('tɪlə) *n.* lever to move rudder of boat

tilt (tɪlt) *v.* 1. incline, slope, slant 2. tip up —*vi.* 3. take part in medieval combat with lances 4. thrust, aim —*n.* 5. slope, incline 6. *Hist.* combat for mounted men with lances, joust

tilth (tɪlθ) *n.* 1. tilled land 2. condition of soil

Tim. *Bible* Timothy

timber ('tɪmbə) *n.* 1. wood for building *etc.* 2. trees suitable for the sawmill —'**timbered** *a.* 1. made of wood 2. covered with trees —**timber limit** 1. C area to which rights of cutting trees are limited 2. timber line —**timber line** geographical limit beyond which trees will not grow

timbre ('tɪmbə, 'tæmbə) *n.* 1. *Mus.* quality of sound 2. *Phonet.* tone differentiating one vowel *etc.* from another

time (taɪm) *n.* 1. existence as a succession of states 2. hour 3. duration 4. period 5. point in duration 6. opportunity 7. occasion 8. leisure 9. tempo —*vt.* 10. choose time for 11. note time taken by —'**timeless** *a.* 1. unaffected or unchanged by time; ageless 2. eternal —'**timely** *a.* at opportune or appropriate time —'**timer** *n.* person, device for recording or indicating time —'**timing** *n.* regulation of actions or remarks in relation to others to produce best effect, as in theatre *etc.* —**time and motion study** analysis of industrial or work procedures to determine most efficient methods of operation (*also* **time and motion, time study, motion study**) —**time**

bomb bomb designed to explode at prearranged time —**time clock** clock which records, by punching or stamping **timecards** inserted into it, time of arrival or departure of employees —**time exposure** 1. exposure of photographic film for a relatively long period, usu. a few seconds 2. photograph produced by such exposure —**time-honoured** *a.* respectable because old —**time-lag** *n.* period of time between cause and effect —**time off** period when one is absent from work for holiday, through sickness *etc.* —**time-out** *n. chiefly US* 1. *Sport* interruption in play during which players rest, discuss tactics *etc.* 2. period of rest; break —'**timepiece** *n.* watch or clock —'**timeserver** *n.* person who compromises and changes his opinions *etc.* to suit current fashions —**time sharing** 1. system by which users at different terminals of computer can apparently communicate with it at same time 2. system of part-ownership of holiday home, whereby each participant owns property for particular period every year for specified number of years —**time signature** *Mus.* sign, usu. consisting of two figures, one above other, after key signature, indicating tempo —'**timetable** *n.* plan showing hours of work, times of arrival and departure *etc.* —'**timeworn** *a.* 1. showing adverse effects of overlong use or of old age 2. hackneyed; trite —**time zone** region throughout which same standard time is used —**Greenwich Mean Time** world standard time, time as settled by passage of sun over the meridian at Greenwich —**time and a half** rate of pay equalling one and a half times normal rate, oft. for overtime

timid ('tɪmɪd) *a.* 1. easily frightened 2. lacking self-confidence —ti'**midity** *or* '**timidness** *n.* —'**timidly** *adv.* —'**timorous** *a.* 1. timid 2. indicating fear

timpani *or* **tympani** ('tɪmpənɪ) *pl.n.* set of kettledrums —'**timpanist** *or* '**tympanist** *n.*

tin (tɪn) *n.* 1. malleable metal 2. container made of tin or tinned iron —*vt.* 3. put in tin, *esp.* for preserving (food) 4. coat with tin (-**nn**-) —'**tinny** *a.* 1. (of sound) thin, metallic 2. cheap, shoddy —'**tin'foil** *n.* 1. thin foil made of tin or alloy of tin and lead 2. thin foil made of aluminium; used for wrapping foodstuffs —**tin god** 1. self-important person 2. person erroneously regarded as holy or venerable —**tin lizzie** ('lɪzɪ) *inf.* old or decrepit car —**tin plate** thin steel sheet coated with layer of tin that protects steel from corrosion —**tin-plate** *vt.* coat with layer of tin —'**tinpot** *a. inf.* inferior, worthless —'**tinsmith** *n.* person who works with tin or tin plate

tincture ('tɪŋktʃə) *n.* 1. solution of medicinal substance in alcohol 2. colour, stain —*vt.* 3. colour, tint

tinder ('tɪndə) n. dry, easily-burning material used to start fire —'**tinderbox** n. **1.** formerly, box for holding tinder, *esp.* one fitted with flint and steel **2.** touchy or explosive person or thing

tine (taɪn) n. tooth, spike of fork, antler, harrow *etc.*

tinea ('tɪnɪə) n. fungal skin disease

ting (tɪŋ) n. **1.** sharp sound, as of bell **2.** tinkling —*vi.* **3.** tinkle —**ting-a-ling** n. sound of small bell

tinge (tɪndʒ) n. **1.** slight trace, flavour —*vt.* **2.** colour, flavour slightly

tingle ('tɪŋɡəl) *vi.* **1.** feel thrill or pricking sensation —*n.* **2.** sensation of tingling

tinker ('tɪŋkə) n. **1.** formerly, travelling mender of pots and pans —*vi.* **2.** fiddle, meddle (*eg* with machinery), oft. inexpertly —**tinker's damn** *or* **cuss** *sl.* slightest heed (*esp. in* **not give a tinker's damn** *or* **cuss**)

tinkle ('tɪŋkəl) *v.* **1.** (cause to) give out series of light sounds like small bell —*n.* **2.** this sound or action

tinsel ('tɪnsəl) n. **1.** glittering, metallic substance for decoration **2.** anything sham and showy

tint (tɪnt) n. **1.** colour **2.** shade of colour **3.** tinge —*vt.* **4.** dye, give tint to

tintinnabulation (ˌtɪntɪnæbjʊˈleɪʃən) n. act or instance of ringing or pealing of bells

tiny ('taɪnɪ) a. very small, minute

-**tion** (*comb. form*) state, condition, action, process, result, as in *election, prohibition*

tip[1] (tɪp) n. **1.** slender or pointed end of anything **2.** piece of metal, leather *etc.* protecting an extremity —*vt.* **3.** put a tip on (-**pp**-) —'**tipstaff** n. **1.** court official **2.** metal-tipped staff formerly used as symbol of office

tip[2] (tɪp) n. **1.** small present of money given for service rendered **2.** helpful piece of information **3.** warning, hint —*vt.* **4.** give tip to (-**pp**-) —'**tipster** n. one who sells tips about races —**tip-off** n. warning or hint, *esp.* given confidentially and based on inside information —**tip off**

tip[3] (tɪp) *vt.* **1.** tilt, upset **2.** touch lightly —*vi.* **3.** topple over (-**pp**-) —*n.* **4.** place where rubbish is dumped

tippet ('tɪpɪt) n. covering for the neck and shoulders

tipple ('tɪpəl) *v.* **1.** drink (alcohol) habitually, *esp.* in small quantities —*n.* **2.** alcoholic drink —'**tippler** n.

tipsy ('tɪpsɪ) a. (slightly) drunk

tiptoe ('tɪptəʊ) *vi.* **1.** walk on ball of foot and toes **2.** walk softly

tiptop (tɪp'tɒp) a. of the best quality or highest degree

TIR Transports Internationaux Routiers (*Fr.*, International Road Transport)

tirade (taɪ'reɪd) n. long speech, generally vigorous and hostile, denunciation

tire[1] (taɪə) *vt.* **1.** reduce energy of, *esp.* by exertion **2.** bore **3.** irritate —*vi.* **4.** become tired, wearied, bored —**tired** a. **1.** weary; fatigued **2.** no longer fresh; hackneyed —'**tireless** a. unable to be tired —'**tirelessly** *adv.* —'**tiresome** a. wearisome, irritating, tedious —'**tiring** a.

tire[2] (taɪə) n. *US* tyre

tiro ('taɪrəʊ) n. *see* TYRO

tissue ('tɪsjuː, 'tɪʃuː) n. **1.** substance of animal body, plant *etc.* **2.** fine, soft paper, *esp.* used as handkerchief *etc.* **3.** fine woven fabric

tit[1] (tɪt) n. any of numerous small, active Old World songbirds *esp.* bluetit, tomtit *etc.*

tit[2] (tɪt) n. **1.** *vulg. sl.* female breast **2.** *sl.* despicable, stupid person

Tit. *Bible* Titus

titan ('taɪtən) n. person of great strength or size —ti'**tanic** a. huge, epic

titanium (taɪ'teɪnɪəm) n. rare metal of great strength and rust-resisting qualities

titbit ('tɪtbɪt) *or esp. U.S.* **tidbit** ('tɪdbɪt) n. **1.** tasty morsel of food **2.** pleasing scrap (of scandal *etc.*)

tit for tat blow for blow, retaliation

tithe (taɪð) n. **1.** *esp. Hist.* tenth part of agricultural produce paid for the upkeep of the clergy or as tax —*vt.* **2.** exact tithes from —**tithe barn** formerly, large barn where agricultural tithe of parish was stored

Titian red ('tɪʃən) a. (of hair) reddish-gold, auburn

titillate ('tɪtɪleɪt) *vt.* tickle, stimulate agreeably —titil'**lation** n. —'**titillator** n.

titivate *or* **tittivate** ('tɪtɪveɪt) *v.* dress or smarten up —titi'**vation** *or* titti'**vation** n.

title ('taɪtəl) n. **1.** name of book **2.** heading **3.** name **4.** appellation denoting rank **5.** legal right or document proving it **6.** *Sport* championship —'**titled** a. of the aristocracy —**title deed** legal document as proof of ownership —'**titleholder** n. person who holds title, *esp.* sporting championship —**title page** page in book that gives title, author, publisher *etc.* —**title role** role of character after whom play *etc.* is named

titration (taɪ'treɪʃən) n. operation in which measured amount of one solution is added to known quantity of another solution until reaction between the two is complete —'**titrate** *vt.* measure volume or concentration of (solution) by titration

titter ('tɪtə) *vi.* **1.** laugh in suppressed way —*n.* **2.** such laugh

tittle ('tɪtəl) n. whit, detail

tittle-tattle n./vi. gossip

titular ('tɪtjʊlə) a. **1.** pert. to title **2.** nominal **3.** held by virtue of a title

tizzy ('tɪzɪ) *n. inf.* state of confusion, anxiety

Tl *Chem.* thallium

Tm *Chem.* thulium

TN Tennessee

tn. ton(s)

TNT trinitrotoluene

to (tuː; *unstressed* tu, tə) *prep.* 1. towards, in the direction of 2. as far as 3. used to introduce a comparison, ratio, indirect object, infinitive mood *etc.* —*adv.* 4. to the required or normal state or position —**to and fro** 1. back and forth 2. here and there —**toing and froing**

toad (təʊd) *n.* animal like large frog —**toad-in-the-hole** *n.* sausages baked in batter

toadflax ('təʊdflæks) *n.* perennial plant having yellow-orange flowers (*also* **butter-and-eggs**)

toadstool ('təʊdstuːl) *n.* fungus like mushroom, but usu. poisonous

toady ('təʊdɪ) *n.* 1. one who flatters, ingratiates himself —*vi.* 2. do this (**toadied, 'toadying**)

toast (təʊst) *n.* 1. slice of bread crisped and browned on both sides by heat 2. tribute, proposal of health, success *etc.* made by company of people and marked by drinking together (as bread) 3. person toasted —*vt.* 4. crisp and brown (as bread) 5. drink toast to 6. dry or warm at fire —**'toaster** *n.* electrical device for toasting bread —**'toastmaster** *n.* person who introduces speakers, proposes toasts *etc.* at public dinners (**'toastmistress** *fem.*) —**'toast-rack** *n.* small, partitioned stand of metal *etc.* for serving toasted bread

tobacco (tə'bækəʊ) *n.* 1. plant with leaves used for smoking 2. the prepared leaves (*pl.* **-s, -es**) —**to'bacconist** *n.* one who sells tobacco products

toboggan (tə'bɒgən) *n.* 1. sledge for sliding down slope of snow —*vi.* 2. slide on toboggan

toby jug ('təʊbɪ) mug in form of stout, seated man

toccata (tə'kɑːtə) *n.* rapid piece of music for keyboard instrument

tocsin ('tɒksɪn) *n.* alarm signal, bell

today (tə'deɪ) *n.* 1. this day —*adv.* 2. on this day 3. nowadays

toddle ('tɒdəl) *vi.* 1. walk with unsteady, short steps 2. *inf.* stroll —*n.* 3. toddling —**'toddler** *n.* child beginning to walk

toddy ('tɒdɪ) *n.* sweetened mixture of alcoholic spirit, hot water *etc.*

to-do *n. inf.* fuss, commotion (*pl.* **-s**)

toe (təʊ) *n.* 1. digit of foot 2. anything resembling toe in shape or position —*vt.* 3. reach, touch or kick with toe —**'toecap** *n.* reinforced covering for toe of shoe —**'toehold** *n.* 1. small foothold to facilitate climbing 2. any means of gaining access, support *etc.* 3. wrestling hold in which opponent's toe is held and leg twisted —**toe the line** conform

toff (tɒf) *n. sl.* well-dressed or upper-class person

toffee *or* **toffy** ('tɒfɪ) *n.* chewy sweet made of boiled sugar *etc.* —**toffee-apple** *n.* apple fixed on stick and coated with toffee —**toffee-nosed** *a. sl., chiefly UK* pretentious; supercilious; snobbish

tofu ('təʊfuː) *n.* unfermented soya bean curd

tog (tɒg) *n.* unit of measurement of warmth of continental quilts *etc.* —**tog rating** *or* **value**

toga ('təʊgə) *n.* loose outer garment worn by ancient Romans

together (tə'gɛðə) *adv.* 1. in company 2. simultaneously —*a./adv.* 3. *inf.* (well) organized —**to'getherness** *n.* feeling of closeness or affection from being united with other people

toggle ('tɒgəl) *n.* 1. small wooden, metal peg fixed crosswise on cord, wire *etc.* and used for fastening as button 2. any similar device —**toggle joint** device consisting of two arms pivoted at common joint and at outer ends, and used to apply pressure by straightening angle between two arms —**toggle switch** electric switch having projecting lever that is manipulated in particular way to open or close circuit

togs (tɒgz) *pl.n. inf.* clothes

toil (tɔɪl) *n.* 1. heavy work or task —*vi.* 2. labour —**'toilsome** *or* **'toilful** *a.* laborious —**'toilworn** *a.* 1. weary with toil 2. hard and lined

toilet ('tɔɪlɪt) *n.* 1. lavatory 2. process of washing, dressing 3. articles used for this —**'toiletry** *n.* object or cosmetic used in making up *etc.* —**toilet paper** *or* **tissue** thin absorbent paper, oft. wound in roll round cardboard cylinder (**toilet roll**), used for cleaning oneself after defecation or urination —**toilet training** training of young child to use toilet when he needs to discharge bodily waste —**toilet water** form of liquid perfume lighter than cologne

token ('təʊkən) *n.* 1. sign or object used as evidence 2. symbol 3. disc used as money 4. gift card, voucher exchangeable for goods of a certain value —*a.* 5. nominal, slight —**'tokenism** *n.* practice of making only token effort or doing no more than minimum, *esp.* to comply with law

tokoloshe (tokə'lɒʃ, -'lɒʃɪ) *n. SA* malevolent imp in Bantu folklore

told (təʊld) *pt./pp.* of TELL

tolerate ('tɒləreɪt) *vt.* 1. put up with 2. permit —**'tolerable** *a.* 1. bearable 2. fair, moderate —**'tolerably** *adv.* —**'tolerance** *n.* (degree of) ability to endure stress, pain, radiation *etc.* —**'tolerant** *a.* 1. disinclined to interfere with others' ways or opinions 2. forbearing 3. broad-minded —**'tolerantly** *adv.* —**tole'ration** *n.*

toll¹ (tɔul) vt. 1. make (bell) ring slowly at regular intervals 2. announce death thus —vi. 3. ring thus —n. 4. tolling sound

toll² (tɔul, tol) n. 1. tax, esp. for the use of bridge or road 2. loss, damage incurred through accident, disaster etc.

tollie ('tolɪ) n. SA steer calf

toluene ('toljuːn) n. colourless volatile flammable liquid obtained from petroleum and coal tar

tom (tom) n. male of some animals, esp. cat

tomahawk ('tomǝhɔːk) n. 1. fighting axe of N Amer. Indians —vt. 2. strike, kill with tomahawk

tomato (tǝ'mɑːtǝu) n. 1. plant with red fruit 2. the fruit, used in salads etc. (pl. **-es**)

tomb (tuːm) n. 1. grave 2. monument over grave —'**tombstone** n. gravestone

tombola (tom'bǝulǝ) n. lottery with tickets drawn to win prizes

tomboy ('tombɔɪ) n. girl who acts, dresses in boyish way

Tom, Dick, and (or) Harry ordinary, undistinguished or common person (esp. in **every Tom, Dick, and Harry; any Tom, Dick, or Harry**)

tome (tǝum) n. large book or volume

tomfoolery (tom'fuːlǝrɪ) n. nonsense, silly behaviour

tommy ('tomɪ) n. sl. private soldier in Brit. army —**Tommy gun** type of sub-machine-gun —'**tommyrot** n. utter nonsense

tomorrow (tǝ'mɒrǝu) adv./n. (on) the day after today

tom-tom or **tam-tam** n. drum associated with N Amer. Indians or with Asia

ton (tʌn) n. 1. measure of weight, 1016 kg (2240 lbs) (also **long ton**) 2. US measure of weight, 907 kg (2000 lbs) (also **short ton**) —'**tonnage** n. 1. carrying capacity 2. charge per ton 3. ships collectively —**ton-up** UK inf. a. 1. (esp. of motorcycle) capable of speeds of a hundred miles per hour or more 2. liking to travel at such speeds —n. 3. person who habitually rides at such speeds

tone (tǝun) n. 1. quality of musical sound 2. quality of voice, colour etc. 3. general character, style 4. healthy condition —vt. 5. give tone to —v. 6. blend, harmonize —'**tonal** a. —to'**nality** n. —**tone-deaf** a. unable to distinguish subtle differences in musical pitch —**tone deafness** —**tone poem** orchestral work based on story, legend etc.

tong (toŋ) n. formerly, secret society of Chinese Americans

tongs (toŋz) pl.n. large pincers, esp. for handling coal, sugar

tongue (tʌŋ) n. 1. muscular organ inside mouth, used for speech, taste etc. 2. various things

shaped like this 3. language; speech; voice —**tongue-and-groove joint** joint made by means of tongue along edge of one board that fits into groove along edge of another board —**tongue-lash** vt. reprimand severely; scold —**tongue-lashing** n./a. —**tongue-tie** n. congenital condition in which tongue has restricted mobility as result of abnormally short fold of skin under tongue —**tongue-tied** a. 1. speechless, esp. with embarrassment or shyness 2. having condition of tongue-tie —**tongue twister** sentence or phrase difficult to articulate clearly and quickly

tonic ('tonɪk) n. 1. medicine to improve bodily tone or condition 2. Mus. first keynote of scale —a. 3. invigorating, restorative 4. of tone —**tonic sol-fa** method of teaching music, by which syllables are used as names for notes of major scale in any key —**tonic water** or **tonic** n. mineral water oft. containing quinine

tonight (tǝ'naɪt) n. 1. this night 2. the coming night —adv. 3. on this night

tonne (tʌn) n. metric ton, 1000 kg

tonsil ('tonsɪl) n. gland in throat —'**tonsillar** a. —**tonsil'lectomy** n. surgical removal of tonsils —**tonsil'litis** n. inflammation of tonsils

tonsorial (ton'sɔːrɪǝl) a. oft. jocular of barbering or hairdressing

tonsure ('tonʃǝ) n. 1. shaving of part of head as religious or monastic practice 2. part shaved —vt. 3. shave thus

too (tuː) adv. 1. also, in addition 2. in excess, overmuch

took (tuk) pt. of TAKE

tool (tuːl) n. 1. implement or appliance for mechanical operations 2. servile helper 3. means to an end —vt. 4. work on with tool 5. indent design on (leather book cover etc.) —'**tooling** n. 1. decorative work 2. setting up etc. of tools, esp. for machine operation

toot (tuːt) v. 1. (cause to) give short blast, hoot or whistle —n. 2. short sound of horn, trumpet etc.

tooth (tuːθ) n. 1. bonelike projection in gums of upper and lower jaws of vertebrates 2. various pointed things like this 3. prong, cog (pl. **teeth**) —'**toothsome** a. of delicious or appetizing appearance, flavour or smell —'**toothy** a. having or showing numerous, large or projecting teeth —'**toothache** n. pain in or about tooth —'**toothbrush** n. small brush, usu. with long handle, for cleaning teeth —**tooth-comb** n. small comb with teeth close together —'**toothpaste** n. paste for cleaning teeth, applied with toothbrush —'**toothpick** n. small sharp sliver of wood etc. for extracting pieces of food from between teeth

tootle ('tuːtl) *inf. v.* 1. toot —*n.* 2. soft hoot or series of hoots

top¹ (top) *n.* 1. highest part, summit 2. highest rank 3. first in merit 4. garment for upper part of body 5. lid, stopper of bottle *etc.* 6. platform on ship's mast —*vt.* 7. cut off, pass, reach, surpass top of 8. provide top for (-**pp-**) —'**topless** *a.* (of costume, woman) with no covering for breasts —'**topmost** *a.* 1. supreme 2. highest —'**topper** *n.* 1. *inf.* top hat 2. person or thing that tops or excels —'**topping** *n.* 1. something that tops something else, *esp.* sauce or garnish for food —*a.* 2. high or superior in rank, degree *etc.* 3. *UK sl.* excellent; splendid —**top brass** *inf.* 1. high-ranking army officers 2. important officials —'**topcoat** *n.* outdoor coat worn over suit *etc.* —**top dog** *inf.* leader or chief of group —**top-drawer** *a.* of highest standing, *esp.* socially —**top-dress** *vt.* spread soil, fertilizer *etc.* on surface of (land) —**top dressing** —**top-flight** *a.* of superior or excellent quality —**topgallant** (top'gælənt; *Naut.* tə'gælənt) *n.* 1. mast on square-rigger above topmast or extension of topmast 2. sail set on yard of topgallant mast —*a.* 3. of topgallant —**top gear** 1. highest forward ratio of gearbox in motor vehicle 2. highest speed, greatest energy *etc.* (*also* **top**) —**top hat** man's hat with tall cylindrical crown —**top-heavy** *a.* 1. unbalanced 2. with too heavy for base —**top-hole** *interj./a. UK inf.* excellent; splendid —'**topknot** *n.* 1. crest, tuft, chignon *etc.* on top of head 2. European flatfish —**top-level** *a.* of those on highest level of influence or authority —**topmast** ('topmɑːst; *Naut.* 'topməst) *n.* mast next above lower mast on sailing vessel —'**top'notch** *a.* excellent, first-class —**topsail** ('topseil; *Naut.* 'topsl) *n.* square sail carried on yard set on topmast —**top-secret** *a.* needing highest level of secrecy, security —**topside** *n.* 1. uppermost side 2. *UK* lean cut of beef from thigh, containing no bone 3. (*oft. pl.*) part of ship's sides above waterline 4. (*oft. pl.*) part of ship above decks —'**topsoil** *n.* surface layer of soil

top² (top) *n.* toy which spins on tapering point

topaz ('təupæz) *n.* precious stone of various colours

tope¹ (təup) *v.* consume (alcoholic drink) as regular habit, usu. in large quantities —'**toper** *n.*

tope² (təup) *n.* small grey shark of European coastal waters

topee *or* **topi** ('təupiː, -pɪ) *n.* lightweight hat made of pith (*pl.* -**s**)

topiary ('təupɪərɪ) *a.* 1. (of shrubs) shaped by cutting or pruning, made ornamental by trimming or training —*n.* 2. topiary work 3. topiary garden —'**topiarist** *n.*

topic ('topɪk) *n.* subject of discourse, conversation *etc.* —'**topical** *a.* 1. up-to-date, having news value 2. of topic

topography (tə'pogrəfɪ) *n.* (description of) surface features of a place —to'**pographer** *n.* —topo'**graphic** *a.* —topo'**graphically** *adv.*

topology (tə'polədʒɪ) *n.* 1. branch of mathematics concerned with generalization of concepts of continuity, limit *etc.* 2. branch of geometry describing properties of figure that are unaffected by continuous distortion 3. *Maths.* family of subsets of given set *S*, such that *S* is topological space 4. study of topography of given place 5. anatomy of any specific bodily area, structure or part —topo'**logic(al)** *a.* —to'**pologist** *n.*

topple ('topl) *v.* (cause to) fall over, collapse

topsy-turvy ('topsɪ'tɜːvɪ) *a.* 1. upside down 2. in confusion

toque (təuk) *n.* 1. small round hat 2. C knitted cap

tor (tɔː) *n.* high, rocky hill

Torah ('tɔurə) *n.* 1. the Pentateuch 2. scroll on which this is written 3. whole body of Jewish sacred writings and tradition, including oral expositions of the Law

torch (tɔːtʃ) *n.* 1. portable hand light containing electric battery and bulb 2. burning brand *etc.* 3. any apparatus burning with hot flame (*eg* for welding) —'**torchbearer** *n.* —**torch singer** —**torch song** sentimental song, usu. sung by woman —**carry a torch for** be in love with, *esp.* unrequitedly

tore (tɔː) *pt. of* TEAR² —**torn** *pp. of* TEAR²

toreador ('tɒrɪədɔː) *n.* bullfighter

torment (tɔː'ment) *vt.* 1. torture in body or mind 2. afflict 3. tease —*n.* ('tɔːment) 4. suffering, torture, agony of body or mind —tor'**mentor** *n.*

tornado (tɔː'neɪdəu) *n.* 1. whirlwind 2. violent storm (*pl.* -**es**, -**s**)

torpedo (tɔː'piːdəu) *n.* 1. cylindrical, self-propelled underwater missile with explosive warhead, fired *esp.* from submarine (*pl.* -**es**) —*vt.* 2. strike, sink with, as with, torpedo

torpid ('tɔːpɪd) *a.* sluggish, apathetic —tor'**pidity** *or* '**torpidness** *n.* —'**torpor** *n.* torpid state

torque (tɔːk) *n.* 1. collar, similar ornament of twisted gold or other metal 2. *Mech.* any rotating or twisting force

torr (tɔː) *n.* unit of pressure equal to one millimetre of mercury (133.322 newtons per square metre)

torrent ('tɒrənt) *n.* 1. rushing stream 2. downpour —tor'**rential** *a.* 1. resembling a torrent 2. overwhelming

torrid ('torɪd) *a.* **1.** parched, dried with heat **2.** highly emotional —**tor'ridity** *or* **'torridness** *n.* —**Torrid Zone** land between tropics

torsion ('tɔːʃən) *n.* twist, twisting

torso ('tɔːsəʊ) *n.* **1.** (statue of) body without head or limbs **2.** trunk (*pl.* **-s, -si** (-sɪ))

tort (tɔːt) *n. Law* private or civil wrong

tortilla (tɔː'tiːə) *n.* thin Mexican pancake

tortoise ('tɔːtəs) *n.* four-footed reptile covered with shell of horny plates —**'tortoiseshell** *n.* **1.** mottled brown shell of hawksbill turtle used commercially —*a.* **2.** of yellowish-brown mottled colour **3.** made of tortoiseshell

tortuous ('tɔːtjʊəs) *a.* **1.** winding, twisting **2.** involved, not straightforward —**tortu'osity** *n.*

torture ('tɔːtʃə) *n.* **1.** infliction of severe pain —*vt.* **2.** subject to torture —**'torturer** *n.* —**torture chamber**

Tory ('tɔːrɪ) *n.* **1.** member of Brit., Canad. conservative party **2.** politically reactionary person

toss (tɒs) *vt.* **1.** throw up, about —*vi.* **2.** be thrown, fling oneself about —*n.* **3.** act of tossing —**toss-up** *n.* **1.** instance of tossing up coin **2.** *inf.* even chance or risk —**toss up** spin (coin) in air to decide between alternatives by guessing which side will fall uppermost

tot¹ (tɒt) *n.* **1.** very small child **2.** small quantity, *esp.* of drink

tot² (tɒt) *v.* (*with* up) total; add (**-tt-**)

total ('təʊt(ə)l) *n.* **1.** whole amount **2.** sum, aggregate —*a.* **3.** complete, entire, full, absolute —*v.* **4.** (*sometimes with* to) amount —*vt.* **5.** add up (**-ll-**) —**to'tality** *n.* —**'totalizator, 'totalizer** *or* **'totalisator, 'totaliser** *n.* machine to operate system of betting on racecourse in which money is paid out to winners in proportion to their stakes —**total allergy syndrome** combination of symptoms produced by allergic reaction to various elements of modern everyday life

totalitarian (təʊtælɪ'tɛərɪən) *a.* of dictatorial, one-party government

tote¹ (təʊt) *n.* totalizator

tote² (təʊt) *vt.* haul, carry —**tote bag** large handbag or shopping bag

totem ('təʊtəm) *n.* tribal badge or emblem —**to'temic** *a.* —**totem pole** post carved, painted with totems, *esp.* by Amer. Indians

totter ('tɒtə) *vi.* **1.** walk unsteadily **2.** begin to fall

toucan ('tuːkən) *n.* tropical Amer. bird with large bill

touch (tʌtʃ) *n.* **1.** sense by which qualities of object *etc.* are perceived by touching **2.** characteristic manner or ability **3.** touching **4.** slight blow, stroke, contact, amount *etc.* —*vt.* **5.** come into contact with **6.** put hand on **7.** reach **8.** affect emotions of **9.** deal with, handle **10.** eat,

drink **11.** *inf.* (try to) borrow from —*vi.* **12.** be in contact **13.** (*with* on) refer (to) —**touched** *a.* **1.** moved to sympathy or emotion **2.** showing slight insanity —**'touching** *a.* **1.** emotionally moving —*prep.* **2.** concerning —**'touchy** *a.* easily offended, sensitive —**'touchdown** *n.* **1.** moment at which landing aircraft or spacecraft comes into contact with landing surface **2.** *Rugby* act of placing or touching ball on ground behind goal line, as in scoring try **3.** *American football* scoring play for six points achieved by being in possession of ball in opponents' end zone —**touch judge** one of two linesmen in rugby —**'touchline** *n.* side line of pitch in some games —**'touchpaper** *n.* paper soaked in saltpetre for firing gunpowder —**'touchstone** *n.* criterion —**touch-type** *vi.* type without looking at keyboard —**touch-typist** *n.* —**'touchwood** *n.* tinder —**touch and go** precarious (situation) —**touch down 1.** (of aircraft *etc.*) land **2.** *Rugby* place ball behind goal line, as when scoring try

touché (tuː'ʃeɪ) *interj. orig.* in fencing, acknowledgment that blow, witty remark *etc.* has been successful

tough (tʌf) *a.* **1.** strong, resilient, not brittle **2.** sturdy **3.** able to bear hardship, strain **4.** difficult **5.** needing effort to chew **6.** *sl.* rough, uncivilized, violent **7.** *inf.* unlucky, unfair —*n.* **8.** *inf.* rough, violent person —**'toughen** *v.* —**'toughness** *n.*

toupee ('tuːpeɪ) *n.* hairpiece

tour (tʊə) *n.* **1.** travelling round **2.** journey to one place after another **3.** excursion —*v.* **4.** make tour (of) —**'tourism** *n.* **1.** tourist travel **2.** this as an industry —**'tourist** *n.* one who travels for pleasure —**'touristy** *a. inf., oft.* derogatory abounding in or designed for tourists

tour de force (tur də 'fɔrs) *Fr.* brilliant stroke, achievement

tourmaline ('tʊəməliːn) *n.* crystalline mineral used for optical instruments and as gem

tournament ('tʊənəmənt) *n.* **1.** competition, contest usu. with several stages to decide overall winner **2.** *Hist.* contest between knights on horseback —**'tourney** *n. Hist.* knightly tournament

tourniquet ('tʊənɪkeɪ) *n. Med.* bandage, surgical instrument to constrict artery and stop bleeding

tousle ('taʊz(ə)l) *vt.* **1.** tangle, ruffle **2.** treat roughly —*n.* **3.** disorderly, tangled or rumpled state **4.** dishevelled or disordered mass, *esp.* of hair

tout (taʊt) *vi.* **1.** solicit custom (usu. in undesirable fashion) **2.** obtain and sell information about racehorses —*n.* **3.** one who touts

tow¹ (təʊ) *vt.* **1.** drag along behind, *esp.* at end of rope —*n.* **2.** towing or being towed **3.** vessel, vehicle in tow —**'towage** n. —**'towbar** n. metal bar attached to car for towing caravan etc. —**'towpath** n. path beside canal, river, orig. for towing —**'towrope** n. rope or cable used for towing vehicle or vessel (also **'towline**)

tow[2] (təʊ) n. fibre of hemp, flax —**tow-headed** a. with pale-coloured or rumpled hair

towards (təˈwɔːdz, tɔːdz) prep. 1. in direction of 2. with regard to 3. as contribution to (also **to'ward**)

towel ('taʊəl) n. 1. cloth for wiping off moisture after washing —vt. 2. dry or wipe with towel (-ll-) —**'towelling** n. material used for making towels —**throw in the towel** give up completely

tower ('taʊə) n. 1. tall strong structure oft. forming part of church or other large building 2. fortress —vi. 3. stand very high 4. loom —**'towering** a. 1. very tall; lofty 2. outstanding, as in importance or stature 3. very intense —**tower block** a building of many storeys, as for offices or flats

town (taʊn) n. collection of dwellings etc., larger than village and smaller than city —**'township** n. 1. small town 2. C land-survey area —**town clerk** chief administrative officer of town —**town crier** person employed to make public announcements in streets —**town hall** chief building in which municipal business is transacted, oft. with hall for public meetings —**town planning** comprehensive planning of physical and social development of town —**'townspeople** pl.n.

toxic ('tɒksɪk) a. 1. poisonous 2. due to poison —**toxaemia** or U.S. **toxemia** (tɒkˈsiːmɪə) n. blood poisoning —**tox'icity** n. strength of a poison —**toxi'cology** n. study of poisons —**'toxin** n. poison of bacterial origin

toy (tɔɪ) n. 1. something designed to be played with 2. (miniature) replica —a. 3. very small —vi. 4. act idly, trifle

trace[1] (treɪs) n. 1. track left by anything 2. indication 3. minute quantity —vt. 4. follow course, track of 5. find out 6. make plan of 7. draw or copy exactly, esp. using tracing paper —**'tracer** n. 1. person or thing that traces 2. ammunition that can be observed when in flight by burning of chemical substances in base of projectile 3. Med. radioactive isotope introduced into body to study metabolic processes etc. by following its progress with Geiger counter or other detector 4. investigation to trace missing cargo etc. —**'tracery** n. interlaced ornament, esp. stonework of Gothic window —**'tracing** n. traced copy of drawing —**trace element** chemical element occurring in very small quantity in soil etc. —**tracer bullet** bullet which leaves visible trail so that aim can be checked —**tracing paper** transparent paper placed over

drawing, map etc. to enable exact copy to be taken

trace[2] (treɪs) n. 1. chain, strap by which horse pulls vehicle 2. Angling short piece of gut, nylon attaching hook or fly to line

trachea (trəˈkiːə) n. windpipe (pl. **tracheae** (trəˈkiːiː)) —**tra'cheal** or **tra'cheate** a. —**trache'otomy** n. surgical incision into trachea

track (træk) n. 1. mark, line of marks, left by passage of anything 2. path, rough road 3. course 4. railway line 5. distance between two road wheels on same axle 6. circular jointed metal band driven by wheels as on tank, bulldozer etc. 7. course for running or racing 8. separate section on gramophone record —vt. 9. follow trail or path of 10. (with down) find thus —**track events** athletic sports held on a track —**track record** past accomplishments of person, company etc. —**track shoe** light running shoe fitted with steel spikes for better grip —**'tracksuit** n. warm, two-piece garment worn esp. by athletes

tract[1] (trækt) n. 1. wide expanse, area 2. Anat. system of organs etc. with particular function

tract[2] (trækt) n. treatise or pamphlet, esp. religious one —**'tractate** n. short tract

tractable ('træktəbᵊl) a. easy to manage, docile, amenable

traction ('trækʃən) n. action of drawing, pulling —**traction engine** steam-powered locomotive used, esp. formerly, for drawing heavy loads along roads or over rough ground

tractor ('træktə) n. motor vehicle for hauling, pulling etc.

trad (træd) n. 1. chiefly UK traditional jazz —a. 2. traditional

trade (treɪd) n. 1. commerce, business 2. buying and selling 3. any profitable pursuit 4. those engaged in trade —vi. 5. engage in trade —vt. 6. buy and sell 7. barter 8. exchange (one thing) for another —**'trader** n. **trade-in** n. used article given in part payment for new —**'trademark** or **trade name** n. distinctive mark (secured by legal registration) on maker's goods —**trade price** price of commodities as sold by wholesalers to retailers —**trade secret** secret formula, process etc. known and used to advantage by only one manufacturer —**'tradesman** n. 1. shopkeeper 2. skilled worker —**Trades Union Congress** major association of British trade unions —**trade union** or **trades union** society of workers for protection of their interests —**trade wind** wind blowing constantly towards equator in certain parts of globe —**trading estate** chiefly UK large area in which a number of commercial or industrial firms are situated —**trading stamp** stamp given by some retail organizations to customers, redeemable for merchandise or cash

tradescantia (trædɛs'kænʃɪə) n. widely cultivated plant with striped variegated leaves

tradition (trə'dɪʃən) n. **1.** unwritten body of beliefs, facts etc. handed down from generation to generation **2.** custom, practice of long standing **3.** process of handing down —**tra'ditional** a. —**tra'ditionally** adv.

traduce (trə'djuːs) vt. slander

traffic ('træfɪk) n. **1.** vehicles passing to and fro in street, town etc. **2.** (illicit) trade —vi. **3.** trade, esp. in illicit goods (eg drugs) ('**trafficked**, '**trafficking**) —'**trafficker** n. trader —**traffic island** see ISLAND (sense 2) —**traffic lights** set of coloured lights at road junctions etc. to control flow of traffic —**traffic warden** one employed to supervise road traffic, parking etc.

tragedy ('trædʒɪdɪ) n. **1.** sad or calamitous event **2.** dramatic, literary work dealing with serious, sad topic and with ending marked by (inevitable) disaster —**tra'gedian** n. actor in, writer of tragedies (**tragedi'enne** fem.) —'**tragic** a. **1.** of, in manner of tragedy **2.** disastrous **3.** appalling —'**tragically** adv. —**tragi'comedy** n. play with both tragic and comic elements

trail (treɪl) vt. **1.** drag behind one —vi. **2.** be drawn behind **3.** hang, grow loosely —n. **4.** track, trace **5.** thing that trails **6.** rough, ill-defined track in wild country —'**trailer** n. **1.** vehicle towed by another vehicle **2.** Cine. advertisement of forthcoming film **3.** trailing plant —'**trailblazer** n. **1.** pioneer in particular field **2.** person who blazes trail

train (treɪn) vt. **1.** educate, instruct, exercise **2.** cause to grow in particular way **3.** aim (gun etc.) —vi. **4.** follow course of training, esp. to achieve physical fitness for athletics —n. **5.** line of railway vehicles joined to locomotive **6.** succession, esp. of thoughts, events etc. **7.** procession of animals, vehicles etc. travelling together **8.** trailing part of dress **9.** body of attendants —**trai'nee** n. one training to be skilled worker, esp. in industry —'**trainer** n. **1.** person who trains athletes **2.** piece of equipment employed in training, such as simulated aircraft cockpit **3.** person who schools racehorses —'**training** n. —'**trainbearer** n. attendant who holds up train of dignitary's robe —**train spotter** person who collects numbers of railway locomotives

traipse or **trapes** (treɪps) vi. inf. walk wearily

trait (treɪt, treɪ) n. characteristic feature

traitor ('treɪtə) n. one who betrays or is guilty of treason —'**traitorous** a. **1.** disloyal **2.** guilty of treachery —'**traitorously** adv.

trajectory (trə'dʒɛktərɪ) n. line of flight, (curved) path of projectile

tram (træm) n. vehicle (esp. electrically driven and for public transport) running on rails laid on roadway (also '**tramcar**) —'**tramway** n. rails for trams in street

trammel ('træməl) n. **1.** anything that restrains or holds captive **2.** type of compasses —vt. **3.** restrain, hinder (-**ll**-)

tramp (træmp) vi. **1.** travel on foot, esp. as vagabond or for pleasure **2.** walk heavily —n. **3.** (homeless) person who travels about on foot **4.** walk **5.** tramping **6.** vessel that takes cargo wherever shippers desire **7.** sl., chiefly US prostitute; promiscuous woman

trample ('træmp'l) v. tread (on) and crush under foot

trampoline ('træmpəlɪn, -liːn) n. tough canvas sheet stretched horizontally with elastic cords etc. to frame, for gymnastic, acrobatic use

trance (trɑːns) n. **1.** unconscious or dazed state **2.** state of ecstasy or total absorption

trannie or **tranny** ('trænɪ) inf. transistor radio

tranquil ('træŋkwɪl) a. calm, quiet, serene —**tran'quillity** or U.S. (sometimes) **tran'quility** n. —'**tranquillize**, -**ise** or U.S. '**tranquilize** vt. make calm —'**tranquillizer** or -**iser** n. drug which induces calm, tranquil state —'**tranquilly** adv.

trans. **1.** transaction **2.** transferred **3.** transitive **4.** translated **5.** translator **6.** transport(ation) **7.** transverse

trans- (comb. form) across, through, beyond, on the other side, as in transatlantic

transact (træn'zækt) vt. **1.** carry through **2.** negotiate **3.** conduct (affair etc.) —**trans'action** n. **1.** performing of any business **2.** that which is performed **3.** single sale or purchase —pl. **4.** proceedings **5.** reports of a society

transatlantic (trænzət'læntɪk) a. **1.** on or from the other side of the Atlantic **2.** crossing the Atlantic

transceiver (træn'siːvə) n. combined radio transmitter and receiver

transcend (træn'sɛnd) vt. **1.** rise above **2.** exceed, surpass —**tran'scendence** n. —**tran'scendent** a. —**transcen'dental** a. **1.** surpassing experience **2.** supernatural **3.** abstruse —**transcen'dentalism** n. —**transcendental meditation** technique, based on Hindu traditions, for relaxing and refreshing mind and body through silent repetition of mantra

transcribe (træn'skraɪb) vt. **1.** copy out **2.** transliterate, translate **3.** record for later broadcast **4.** arrange (music) for different instrument —'**transcript** n. copy —**tran'scription** n. **1.** act or instance of transcribing or state of being transcribed **2.** something transcribed **3.** representation in writing of actual pronunciation of word *etc.* using phonetic symbols

transducer (trænz'djuːsə) *n.* any device that converts one form of energy into another

transept ('trænsept) *n.* **1.** transverse part of cruciform church **2.** either of its arms

transfer (træns'fɜː) *v.* **1.** move, send from one person, place *etc.* to another (**-rr-**) —*n.* ('trænsfɜː) **2.** removal of person or thing from one place to another **3.** design which can be transferred from one surface to another by pressure, heat *etc.* —**trans'ferable** *or* **trans'ferrable** *a.* —**transference** ('trænsfərəns) *n.* transfer

transfigure (træns'fɪgə) *vt.* alter appearance of —**transfiguration** (trænsfɪgjʊ'reɪʃən) *n.*

transfix (træns'fɪks) *vt.* **1.** astound, stun **2.** pierce

transform (træns'fɔːm) *vt.* change shape, character of —**transfor'mation** *n.* —**trans'former** *n. Elec.* apparatus for changing voltage of alternating current

transfuse (træns'fjuːz) *vt.* convey from one vessel to another, *esp.* blood from healthy person to one injured or ill —**trans'fusion** *n.*

transgress (trænz'grɛs) *vt.* **1.** break (law) —*vi.* **2.** sin —**trans'gression** *n.* —**trans'gressor** *n.*

tranship (træn'ʃɪp) *v. see* TRANSSHIP

transient ('trænzɪənt) *a.* fleeting, not permanent —'**transience** *n.*

transistor (træn'zɪstə) *n.* **1.** *Electron.* small, semiconducting device used to amplify electric currents **2.** portable radio using transistors —**tran'sistorize** *or* **-ise** *v.* **1.** convert to use or manufacture of transistors and other solid-state components —*vt.* **2.** equip with transistors and other solid-state components

transit ('trænsɪt, 'trænz-) *n.* passage, crossing —**transition** (træn'zɪʃən) *n.* change from one state to another —**transitional** (træn'zɪʃənˀl) *a.* —'**transitive** *a.* (of verb) requiring direct object —'**transitory** *a.* not lasting long, transient —**transit camp** camp in which refugees *etc.* live temporarily

translate (træns'leɪt, trænz-) *vt.* **1.** turn from one language into another **2.** interpret —**trans'lation** *n.* —**trans'lator** *n.*

transliterate (trænz'lɪtəreɪt) *vt.* write in the letters of another alphabet —**transliter'ation** *n.*

translucent (trænz'luːsˀnt) *a.* letting light pass through, semitransparent —**trans'lucence** *n.*

transmigrate (trænzmaɪ'greɪt) *vi.* (of soul) pass into another body —**transmi'gration** *n.*

transmit (trænz'mɪt) *vt.* **1.** send, cause to pass to another place, person *etc.* **2.** communicate **3.**

send out (signals) by means of radio waves **4.** broadcast (radio, television programme) (**-tt-**) —**trans'mission** *n.* **1.** transference **2.** gear by which power is communicated from engine to road wheels —**trans'mitter** *n.* **1.** person or thing that transmits **2.** equipment used for generating and amplifying radio-frequency carrier, modulating carrier with information and feeding it to aerial for transmission **3.** microphone in telephone that converts sound waves into audio-frequency electrical signals **4.** device that converts mechanical movements into coded electrical signals transmitted along telegraph circuit

transmogrify (trænz'mɒgrɪfaɪ) *vt. inf.* change completely *esp.* into bizarre form

transmute (trænz'mjuːt) *vt.* change in form, properties or nature —**transmu'tation** *n.*

transom ('trænzəm) *n.* **1.** crosspiece **2.** lintel

transparent (træns'pærənt) *a.* **1.** letting light pass without distortion **2.** that can be seen through distinctly **3.** obvious —**trans'parence** *n.* —**trans'parency** *n.* **1.** quality of being transparent **2.** photographic slide **3.** picture made visible by light behind it —**trans'parently** *adv.*

transpire (træn'spaɪə) *vi.* **1.** become known **2.** *inf.* happen **3.** (of plants) give off water vapour through leaves —**transpiration** (trænspə'reɪʃən) *n.*

transplant (træns'plɑːnt) *vt.* **1.** move and plant again in another place **2.** transfer (organ) surgically from one body to another —*n.* ('trænsplɑːnt) **3.** surgical transplanting of organ **4.** anything transplanted —**transplan'tation** *n.*

transponder (træn'spɒndə) *n.* radio or radar transmitter-receiver that transmits signals automatically when it receives predetermined signals

transport (træns'pɔːt) *vt.* **1.** convey from one place to another **2.** *Hist.* banish, as criminal, to penal colony **3.** enrapture —*n.* ('trænspɔːt) **4.** means of conveyance **5.** ships, aircraft *etc.* used in transporting stores, troops *etc.* **6.** a ship *etc.* so used **7.** ecstasy, rapture or any powerful emotion —**transpor'tation** *n.* **1.** transporting **2.** *Hist.* deportation to penal colony —**transport café** *UK* inexpensive eating place on main route, used mainly by long-distance lorry drivers

transpose (træns'pəʊz) *vt.* **1.** change order of, interchange **2.** put (music) into different key —**trans'posal** *n.* —**transpo'sition** *n.*

transsexual (trænz'sɛksjʊəl) *n.* **1.** person who is completely identified with opposite sex **2.** person who has undergone medical procedures to alter sexual characteristics to those of opposite sex

transship (trænsˈʃɪp) *or* **tranship** *v.* move from one ship, train *etc.* to another

transubstantiation (trænsəbstænʃɪˈeɪʃən) *n.* doctrine that substance of bread and wine changes into substance of Christ's body when consecrated in Eucharist

transuranic (trænzjuˈrænɪk), **transuranian** (trænzjuˈreɪnɪən), *or* **transuranium** *a.* 1. (of element) having atomic number greater than that of uranium 2. of behaviour of transuranic elements

transverse (trænzˈvɜːs) *a.* 1. lying across 2. at right angles

transvestite (trænzˈvɛstaɪt) *n.* person seeking sexual pleasure by wearing clothes normally worn by opposite sex

trap[1] (træp) *n.* 1. snare, device for catching game *etc.* 2. anything planned to deceive, betray *etc.* 3. arrangement of pipes to prevent escape of gas 4. movable opening, *esp.* through ceiling *etc.* 5. *Hist.* two-wheeled carriage 6. *sl.* mouth —*vt.* 7. catch, ensnare (**-pp-**) —ˈ**trapper** *n.* one who traps animals for their fur —**trap door** door in floor or roof

trap[2] (træp) *vt.* (*oft. with* out) dress, adorn (**-pp-**)

trapeze (trəˈpiːz) *n.* horizontal bar suspended from two ropes for use in gymnastics, acrobatic exhibitions *etc.*

trapezium (trəˈpiːzɪəm) *n.* quadrilateral figure with only two sides parallel (*pl.* **-s**, **-zia** (-zɪə)) —ˈ**trapezoid** *n.* quadrilateral with no parallel sides

trappings (ˈtræpɪŋz) *pl.n.* equipment, ornaments

Trappist (ˈtræpɪst) *n.* member of Cistercian order of monks who observe strict silence

trash (træʃ) *n.* 1. *chiefly US* rubbish 2. nonsense —ˈ**trashy** *a.* worthless, cheap

trauma (ˈtrɔːmə) *n.* 1. nervous shock 2. injury (*pl.* **-ta** (-tə), **-s**) —trauˈmatic *a.* of, causing, caused by trauma

travail (ˈtræveɪl) *vi./n.* labour, toil

travel (ˈtrævl) *vi.* 1. go, move from one place to another (**-ll-**) —*v.* 2. act of travelling, *esp.* as tourist 3. *Machinery* distance component is permitted to move —*pl.* 4. (account of) travelling —ˈ**traveller** *n.* —ˈ**travelogue** *or U.S.* (*sometimes*) ˈ**travelog** *n.* film *etc.* about travels —**travel agency** *or* **bureau** agency that arranges and negotiates holidays *etc.* for travellers —**travel agent** —**traveller's cheque** cheque sold by bank *etc.* to bearer, who signs it on purchase and can cash it abroad by signing it again —**travelling salesman** salesman who travels within assigned territory to sell merchandise or solicit orders for commercial enterprise he represents by direct personal contact with (potential) customers

traverse (ˈtrævɜːs) *vt.* 1. cross, go through or over —*vi.* 2. (of gun) move laterally —*n.* 3. anything set across 4. partition 5. *Mountaineering* face, steep slope to be crossed from side to side —*a.* 6. being, lying across

travesty (ˈtrævɪstɪ) *n.* 1. farcical, grotesque imitation 2. mockery —*vt.* 3. make, be a travesty of (**-estied**, **-estying**)

trawl (trɔːl) *n.* 1. net dragged at deep levels behind special boat, to catch fish —*vi.* 2. fish with one —ˈ**trawler** *n.* trawling vessel

tray (treɪ) *n.* 1. flat board, usu. with rim, for carrying things 2. any similar utensil

treachery (ˈtrɛtʃərɪ) *n.* deceit, betrayal —ˈ**treacherous** *a.* 1. disloyal 2. unreliable, dangerous —ˈ**treacherously** *adv.*

treacle (ˈtriːkəl) *n.* thick syrup produced when sugar is refined —ˈ**treacly** *a.*

tread (trɛd) *vt.* 1. set foot on 2. trample —*vi.* 3. walk 4. (*sometimes with* on) repress (**trod** *pt.*, ˈ**trodden** *or* **trod** *pp.*, ˈ**treading** *pr.p.*) —*n.* 5. treading 6. fashion of walking 7. upper surface of step 8. part of rubber tyre in contact with ground —ˈ**treadmill** *n.* 1. *Hist.* cylinder turned by treading on steps projecting from it 2. dreary routine *etc.*

treadle (ˈtrɛdəl) *n.* lever worked by foot to turn wheel

treason (ˈtriːzən) *n.* 1. violation by subject of allegiance to sovereign or state 2. treachery; disloyalty —ˈ**treasonable** *or* ˈ**treasonous** *a.* constituting treason —ˈ**treasonably** *adv.*

treasure (ˈtrɛʒə) *n.* 1. riches 2. stored wealth or valuables —*vt.* 3. prize, cherish 4. store up —ˈ**treasurer** *n.* official in charge of funds —ˈ**treasury** *n.* place for treasure 2. (**T-**) government department in charge of finance —**treasure-trove** *n.* treasure found hidden with no evidence of ownership

treat (triːt) *n.* 1. pleasure, entertainment given —*vt.* 2. deal with, act towards 3. give medical treatment to 4. give (someone) gift, food *etc.* at one's own expense —*vi.* 5. negotiate 6. (*with of*) discourse (on) —ˈ**treatment** *n.* 1. method of counteracting a disease 2. act or mode of treating 3. manner of handling an artistic medium

treatise (ˈtriːtɪz) *n.* book discussing a subject, formal essay

treaty (ˈtriːtɪ) *n.* signed contract between states *etc.*

treble (ˈtrɛbəl) *a.* 1. threefold, triple 2. *Mus.* high-pitched —*n.* 3. soprano voice 4. part of music for it 5. singer with such voice —*v.* 6. increase threefold —ˈ**trebly** *adv.* —**treble chance** method of betting in football pools in which chances of winning are related to number of draws and number of home and away wins forecast by competitor —**treble clef** *Mus.* clef that establishes G fifth above middle C as being on second line of staff

tree (triː) *n.* 1. large perennial plant with woody trunk 2. beam 3. anything (*eg* genealogical chart) resembling tree or tree's structure —*vt.* 4. force, drive up tree —**tree creeper** small songbird

trefoil ('trɛfɔil) *n.* 1. plant with three-lobed leaf, clover 2. carved ornament like this

trek (trɛk) *n.* 1. long difficult journey, *esp.* on foot 2. SA journey or stage of journey, *esp.* migration by ox wagon —*vi.* 3. make a trek (-kk-) —'**trekker** *n.*

trellis ('trɛlɪs) *n.* 1. lattice or grating of light bars fixed crosswise —*vt.* 2. screen, supply with one

tremble ('trɛmb°l) *vi.* 1. quiver, shake 2. feel fear, anxiety —*n.* 3. involuntary shaking, quiver, tremor —'**trembler** *n.* trembling spring that makes electrical contact when shaken

tremendous (trɪ'mɛndəs) *a.* 1. vast, immense 2. *inf.* exciting, unusual 3. *inf.* excellent

tremolo ('trɛmələu) *n.* quivering or vibrating effect in singing or playing (*pl.* -s)

tremor ('trɛmə) *n.* 1. quiver 2. shaking 3. minor earthquake

tremulous ('trɛmjuləs) *a.* 1. quivering slightly 2. timorous, agitated

trench (trɛntʃ) *n.* 1. long narrow ditch, *esp.* as shelter in war —*vt.* 2. cut grooves or ditches in —**trench coat** double-breasted waterproof coat

trenchant ('trɛntʃənt) *a.* cutting, incisive, biting

trencher ('trɛntʃə) *n. Hist.* wooden plate on which food was served —'**trencherman** *n.* person who enjoys food; hearty eater

trend (trɛnd) *n.* 1. direction, tendency, inclination, drift 2. fashion; mode —'**trendiness** *n.* —'**trendy** *a./n. inf.* consciously fashionable (person) —'**trendsetter** *n.* person or thing that creates or may create new fashion —'**trendsetting** *a.*

trephine (trɪ'fiːn) *or* **trepan** (trɪ'pæn) *n.* 1. instrument for cutting circular pieces, *esp.* from skull —*vt.* 2. remove circular section of bone, *esp.* from skull, of (someone)

trepidation (trɛpɪ'deɪʃən) *n.* fear, anxiety

trespass ('trɛspəs) *vi.* 1. intrude (on property *etc.* of another) 2. transgress, sin —*n.* 3. wrongful entering on another's land 4. wrongdoing —'**trespasser** *n.*

tress (trɛs) *n.* long lock of hair

trestle ('trɛs°l) *n.* board fixed on pairs of spreading legs and used as support

trews (truːz) *pl.n.* close-fitting trousers, orig. of tartan

tri- (*comb. form*) three, as in *trisect*

triad ('traɪæd) *n.* 1. group of three 2. *Chem.* element, radical with valency of three

trial ('traɪəl, trail) *n.* 1. act of trying, testing 2. experimental examination 3. *Law* investigation of case before judge 4. thing, person that strains endurance or patience —**trial and error** method of discovery *etc.* based on practical experiment and experience rather than theory —**trial balance** *Book-keeping* statement of all debit and credit balances in ledger of double-entry system

triangle ('traɪæŋg°l) *n.* 1. figure with three angles 2. percussion musical instrument —**tri'angular** *a.* —**triangulate** (traɪ'æŋgjuleɪt) *vt.* 1. survey by method of triangulation 2. calculate trigonometrically 3. divide into triangles 4. make triangular —*a.* (traɪ'æŋgjulɪt, -leɪt) 5. marked with or composed of triangles —**triangu'lation** *n.* method of surveying in which area is divided into triangles, one side and all angles of which are measured and lengths of other lines calculated trigonometrically

Triassic (traɪ'æsɪk) *a.* 1. of first period of Mesozoic era —*n.* 2. Triassic period or rock system (*also* '**Trias**)

tribe (traɪb) *n.* 1. race 2. subdivision of race of people —'**tribal** *a.*

tribulation (trɪbju'leɪʃən) *n.* 1. misery, trouble, affliction, distress 2. cause of this

tribune ('trɪbjuːn) *n.* person or institution upholding public rights —**tribunal** (traɪ'bjuːn°l, trɪ-) *n.* 1. lawcourt 2. body appointed to inquire into and decide specific matter 3. seat of judge

tributary ('trɪbjutərɪ) *n.* 1. stream flowing into another —*a.* 2. auxiliary 3. contributory 4. paying tribute

tribute ('trɪbjuːt) *n.* 1. sign of honour or recognition 2. tax paid by one state to another

trice (traɪs) *n.* moment —**in a trice** instantly

triceps ('traɪsɛps) *n.* muscle having three heads, *esp.* one that extends forearm (*pl.* -es, -ceps)

trichina (trɪ'kaɪnə) *n.* minute parasitic worm (*pl.* -nae (-niː)) —**trichinosis** (trɪkɪ'nəusɪs) *n.* disease caused by this

trichromatic (traɪkrəu'mætɪk) *or* **trichromic** (traɪ'krəumɪk) *a.* 1. involving combination of three primary colours 2. of normal colour vision 3. having three colours —**tri'chromatism** *n.*

trick (trɪk) *n.* 1. deception 2. prank 3. mannerism 4. illusion 5. feat of skill or cunning 6. knack 7. cards played in one round 8. spell of duty —*vt.* 9. cheat, hoax, deceive —'**trickery** *n.* —'**trickster** *n.* —'**tricky** *a.* 1. difficult, needing careful handling 2. crafty

trickle ('trɪk°l) *v.* (cause to) run, flow, move in thin stream or drops

tricolour *or U.S.* **tricolor** ('trɪkələ, 'traɪkʌlə) *a.* **1.** three-coloured —*n.* **2.** tricolour flag (*eg* of France)

tricot ('trɪkəʊ, 'triː-) *n.* **1.** thin rayon or nylon fabric knitted or resembling knitting **2.** ribbed dress fabric

tricycle ('traɪsɪkəl) *n.* three-wheeled cycle

trident ('traɪdənt) *n.* three-pronged fork or spear

triennial (traɪ'ɛnɪəl) *a.* happening every, or lasting, three years

trifle ('traɪfəl) *n.* **1.** insignificant thing or matter **2.** small amount **3.** pudding of sponge cake, whipped cream *etc.* —*vi.* **4.** toy **5.** act, speak idly —'**trifler** *n.* —'**trifling** *a.* **1.** insignificant, petty **2.** frivolous; idle

trig. 1. trigonometry **2.** trigonometrical —**trig station** *or* **point** landmark which surveyor uses

trigger ('trɪgə) *n.* **1.** catch which releases spring, *esp.* to fire gun —*vt.* **2.** (*oft. with* off) start, set in action *etc.* —**trigger-happy** *a.* tending to irresponsible, ill-considered behaviour, *esp.* in use of firearms

trigonometry (trɪgə'nɒmɪtrɪ) *n.* branch of mathematics dealing with relations of sides and angles of triangles —**trigono'metrical** *a.*

trike (traɪk) tricycle

trilateral (traɪ'lætərəl) *a.* having three sides —tri'**laterally** *adv.*

trilby ('trɪlbɪ) *n.* man's soft felt hat

trill (trɪl) *vi.* **1.** sing with quavering voice **2.** sing lightly **3.** warble —*n.* **4.** such singing or sound

trillion ('trɪljən) *n.* **1.** one million million million, 10¹⁸ **2.** *US* one million million, 10¹²

trilobite ('traɪləbaɪt) *n.* extinct marine arthropod abundant in Palaeozoic times, having segmented exoskeleton divided into three parts —**trilobitic** (traɪlə'bɪtɪk) *a.*

trilogy ('trɪlədʒɪ) *n.* series of three related (literary) works

trim (trɪm) *a.* **1.** neat, smart **2.** slender **3.** in good order —*vt.* **4.** shorten slightly by cutting, prune **5.** decorate **6.** adjust **7.** put in good order **8.** adjust balance of (ship, aircraft) (-**mm**-) —*n.* **9.** decoration **10.** order, state of being trim **11.** haircut that neatens existing style **12.** upholstery, accessories in car **13.** edging material, as inside woodwork round doors, windows *etc.* —'**trimming** *n.* (*oft. pl.*) decoration, addition

trimaran ('traɪmərxn) *n.* three-hulled vessel

trinitrotoluene (traɪnaɪtrəʊ'tɒljuːin) *or* **trinitrotoluol** (traɪnaɪtrəʊ'tɒljʊɒl) *n.* a high explosive derived from toluene

trinity ('trɪnɪtɪ) *n.* **1.** the state of being threefold **2.** (**T-**) the three persons of the Godhead —**trini'tarian** *n./a.* —**Trinity Sunday** Sunday after Whit Sunday

trinket ('trɪŋkɪt) *n.* small ornament, trifle —'**trinketry** *n.*

trio ('triːəʊ) *n.* **1.** group of three **2.** music for three parts (*pl.* **-s**)

triode ('traɪəʊd) *n. Electron.* three-electrode valve

trip (trɪp) *n.* **1.** (short) journey for pleasure **2.** stumble **3.** switch **4.** *inf.* hallucinatory experience caused by drug —*v.* **5.** (*oft. with* up) (cause to) stumble **6.** (cause to) make false step, mistake —*vi.* **7.** run lightly; skip; dance **8.** *inf.* take hallucinatory drugs —*vt.* **9.** operate (switch) (-**pp**-) —'**tripper** *n.* tourist

tripartite (traɪ'pɑːtaɪt) *a.* having, divided into three parts

tripe (traɪp) *n.* **1.** stomach of cow *etc.* prepared for food **2.** *inf.* nonsense

triplane ('traɪpleɪn) *n.* aeroplane with three wings one above another

triple ('trɪpəl) *a.* **1.** threefold —*v.* **2.** treble —'**triplet** *n.* **1.** three of a kind **2.** one of three offspring born at one birth —'**triply** *adv.* —**triple jump** athletic event in which competitor has to perform hop, step and jump in continuous movement —**triple point** *Chem.* temperature and pressure at which three phases of substance are in equilibrium

triplicate ('trɪplɪkɪt) *a.* **1.** threefold —*vt.* ('trɪplɪkeɪt) **2.** make threefold —*n.* **3.** state of being triplicate **4.** one of set of three copies —**tripli'cation** *n.*

tripod ('traɪpɒd) *n.* stool, stand *etc.* with three feet

tripos ('traɪpɒs) *n.* degree examination at Cambridge University

triptych ('trɪptɪk) *n.* carving, set of pictures, *esp.* altarpiece, on three panels hinged side by side

trireme ('traɪriːm) *n.* ancient Gr. galley with three banks of oars on each side

trisect (traɪ'sɛkt) *vt.* divide into three (equal) parts —**tri'section** *n.*

trite (traɪt) *a.* hackneyed, banal

tritium ('trɪtɪəm) *n.* radioactive isotope of hydrogen

triumph ('traɪəmf) *n.* **1.** great success **2.** victory **3.** exultation —*vi.* **4.** achieve great success or victory **5.** exult —tri'**umphal** *a.* —tri'**umphant** *a.* victorious

triumvirate (traɪ'ʌmvɪrɪt) *n.* joint rule by three persons

trivalent (traɪ'veɪlənt, 'trɪvələnt) *a. Chem.* **1.** having valency of three **2.** having three valencies (*also* **ter'valent**) —tri'**valency** *n.*

trivet ('trɪvɪt) *n.* metal bracket or stand for pot or kettle

trivia ('trɪvɪə) *pl.n.* petty, unimportant things,

details —'**trivial** a. 1. of little consequence 2. commonplace —**trivi'ality** n.

trochee ('trəʊkiː) n. in verse, foot of two syllables, first long and second short —**tro'chaic** a.

trod (trɒd) pt. of TREAD —'**trodden** or **trod** pp. of TREAD

troglodyte ('trɒglədaɪt) n. cave dweller

troika ('trɔɪkə) n. 1. Russian vehicle drawn by three horses abreast 2. three horses harnessed abreast 3. triumvirate

Trojan ('trəʊdʒən) n./a. 1. (inhabitant) of ancient Troy 2. steadfast or persevering (person) —**Trojan Horse** 1. Gr. myth. hollow wooden figure of horse left outside Troy by Greeks and dragged inside by Trojans. Men concealed inside opened city to final Greek assault 2. trap intended to undermine enemy

troll[1] (trəʊl) vt. fish for by dragging baited hook or lure through water

troll[2] (trəʊl) n. supernatural being in Scandinavian mythology and folklore

trolley ('trɒlɪ) n. 1. small wheeled table for food and drink 2. wheeled cart for moving goods etc. 3. US tram —**trolley bus** bus deriving power from overhead electric wire but not running on rails

trollop ('trɒləp) n. promiscuous or slovenly woman

trombone (trɒm'bəʊn) n. deep-toned brass wind instrument with sliding tube —**trom'bonist** n.

troop (truːp) n. 1. group or crowd of persons or animals 2. unit of cavalry —pl. 3. soldiers —vi. 4. move in a troop, flock —'**trooper** n. cavalry soldier

trope (trəʊp) n. figure of speech

trophy ('trəʊfɪ) n. 1. prize, award, as shield, cup 2. memorial of victory, hunt etc.

-trophy (n. comb. form) certain type of nourishment or growth, as in dystrophy —**-trophic** (a. comb. form)

tropic ('trɒpɪk) n. 1. either of two lines of latitude at 23½° N (**tropic of Cancer**) or 23½° S (**tropic of Capricorn**) —pl. 2. area of earth's surface between these lines —'**tropical** a. 1. pert. to, within tropics 2. (of climate) very hot —'**tropicbird** n. tropical aquatic bird having long tail feathers and white plumage with black markings

tropism ('trəʊpɪzəm) n. response of organism, esp. plant, to external stimulus by growth in direction determined by stimulus

troposphere ('trɒpəsfɪə) n. lowest atmospheric layer, in which air temperature decreases normally with height at about 6.5° C per km

trot (trɒt) vi. 1. (of horse) move at medium pace, lifting feet in diagonal pairs 2. (of person) run easily with short strides (-tt-) —n. 3. trotting, jog —'**trotter** n. 1. horse trained to trot in race 2. foot of certain animals, esp. pig

Trot (trɒt) n. inf. follower of Trotsky; Trotskyite

troth (trəʊθ) n. obs. fidelity, truth

Trotskyism ('trɒtskɪɪzəm) n. theory of communism of Leon Trotsky, Russian revolutionary and writer, in which he called for immediate worldwide revolution by proletariat —'**Trotskyite** or '**Trotskyist** n./a.

troubadour ('truːbədʊə) n. one of school of early poets and singers

trouble ('trʌbəl) n. 1. state or cause of mental distress, pain, inconvenience etc. 2. care, effort —vt. 3. be trouble to —vi. 4. be inconvenienced, concerned 5. be agitated 6. take pains; exert oneself —'**troublesome** a. —'**troubleshooter** n. person who locates cause of trouble and removes or treats it, as in running of machine —'**troubleshooting** n./a.

trough (trɒf) n. 1. long open vessel, esp. for animals' food or water 2. hollow between two waves 3. Met. area of low pressure

trounce (traʊns) vt. beat thoroughly, thrash

troupe (truːp) n. company of performers —'**trouper** n. 1. member of troupe 2. dependable worker or associate

trousers ('traʊzəz) pl.n. two-legged outer garment with legs reaching to the ankles

trousseau ('truːsəʊ) n. bride's outfit of clothing (pl. **-seaux** (-səʊz), **-s**)

trout (traʊt) n. freshwater sport and food fish

trowel ('traʊəl) n. small tool like spade for spreading mortar, lifting plants etc.

troy weight or **troy** (trɔɪ) n. system of weights used for gold, silver and gems

truant ('truːənt) n. 1. one absent without leave, esp. child so absenting himself or herself from school —a. 2. being or relating to truant —'**truancy** n.

truce (truːs) n. 1. temporary cessation of fighting 2. respite, lull

truck[1] (trʌk) n. wheeled (motor) vehicle for moving goods

truck[2] (trʌk) n. 1. barter 2. dealing (esp. in have no truck with) 3. payment of workmen in goods 4. inf. rubbish

truckle ('trʌkəl) vi. yield weakly

truckle bed low bed on wheels, stored under larger bed

truculent ('trʌkjʊlənt) a. aggressive, defiant

trudge (trʌdʒ) vi. 1. walk laboriously —n. 2. laborious or wearisome walk

true (truː) a. 1. in accordance with facts 2. faithful 3. exact, correct 4. genuine —'**truism** n. self-evident truth —'**truly** adv. 1. exactly 2. really 3. sincerely —**truth** n. 1. state of being true 2. something that is true —'**truthful** a. 1.

accustomed to speak the truth **2.** accurate, exact —'**truthfully** adv. —**true-blue** a. unwaveringly or staunchly loyal —**true blue** chiefly UK staunch royalist or conservative

truffle ('trʌf°l) n. **1.** edible fungus growing underground **2.** sweet resembling this

trug (trʌg) n. long shallow basket used by gardeners

truism ('tru:ɪzəm) n. see TRUE

trump[1] (trʌmp) n. **1.** card of suit temporarily ranking above others —v. **2.** play trump card on (plain suit) —**trump up** invent, concoct —**turn up** or **out trumps** turn out (unexpectedly) well, successfully

trump[2] (trʌmp) n. **1.** trumpet **2.** blast on trumpet —**the last trump** final trumpet call on Day of Judgment

trumpery ('trʌmpərɪ) a. **1.** showy but worthless —n. **2.** worthless finery **3.** trash, rubbish

trumpet ('trʌmpɪt) n. **1.** metal wind instrument like horn —vi. **2.** blow trumpet **3.** make sound like one, as elephant —vt. **4.** proclaim, make widely known

truncate (trʌŋ'keɪt, 'trʌŋkeɪt) vt. cut short —'**truncated** a. **1.** (of cone etc.) having apex or end removed by plane intersection **2.** shortened (as if) by cutting off (also '**truncate**)

truncheon ('trʌntʃən) n. **1.** short thick club or baton **2.** staff of office or authority —vt. **3.** cudgel

trundle ('trʌnd°l) vt. roll, as a thing on little wheels

trunk (trʌŋk) n. **1.** main stem of tree **2.** person's body without or excluding head and limbs **3.** box for clothes etc. **4.** elephant's proboscis —pl. **5.** man's swimming costume —**trunk call** long-distance telephone call —**trunk line** main line of railway, canal, telephone etc. —**trunk road** main road

truss (trʌs) vt. **1.** (oft. with up) fasten, tie —n. **2.** support **3.** medical device of belt etc. to hold hernia in place **4.** package, bundle (of hay etc.) **5.** cluster of flowers at end of single stalk

trust (trʌst) n. **1.** confidence **2.** firm belief **3.** reliance **4.** combination of producers to reduce competition and keep up prices **5.** care, responsibility **6.** property held for another —vt. **7.** rely on **8.** believe in **9.** consign to care —v. **10.** expect, hope —**trus'tee** n. one legally holding property on another's behalf —**trus'teeship** n. —'**trustful** a. **1.** inclined to trust **2.** credulous —'**trustworthy** a. **1.** reliable, dependable, honest **2.** safe —'**trusty** a. **1.** faithful **2.** reliable —**trust fund** money, securities etc. held in trust

truth (tru:θ) n. see TRUE

try (traɪ) vi. **1.** attempt, endeavour —vt. **2.** attempt **3.** test **4.** make demands upon **5.**

investigate (case) **6.** examine (person) in court of law **7.** purify; refine (as metals) (**tried**, '**trying**) —n. **8.** attempt, effort **9.** Rugby score gained by touching ball down over opponent's goal line —**tried** a. **1.** proved **2.** afflicted —'**trying** a. **1.** upsetting, annoying **2.** difficult —**try-on** n. UK inf. something done to test out person's tolerance etc. —'**tryout** n. —**trysail** ('traɪseɪl; Naut. 'traɪs°l) n. small fore-and-aft sail set on sailing vessel in foul weather to help keep her head to wind —**try on 1.** put on (garment) to find out whether it fits etc. **2.** inf. attempt to deceive or fool (esp. in **try it on**) —**try out 1.** test; put to experimental use **2.** (usu. with for) US (of actor etc.) undergo test; submit (actor etc.) to test to determine suitability for role etc.

tryst (trɪst, traɪst) n. **1.** appointment to meet **2.** place appointed

tsar (zɑː) n. see CZAR

tsetse fly or **tzetze fly** ('tsɛtsɪ) Afr. bloodsucking fly whose bite transmits various diseases to man and animals

T-shirt or **tee-shirt** n. informal (short-sleeved) sweater, usu. of cotton

tsp. teaspoon

T-square n. T-shaped ruler for drawing parallel lines, right angles etc.

TT or **T.T. 1.** teetotal **2.** Tourist Trophy **3.** tuberculin tested

tub (tʌb) n. **1.** open wooden vessel like bottom half of barrel **2.** small round container **3.** bath **4.** inf. old, slow ship etc. —'**tubby** a. **1.** plump **2.** shaped like tub

tuba ('tju:bə) n. valved brass wind instrument of low pitch

tube (tju:b) n. **1.** long, narrow, hollow cylinder **2.** flexible cylinder with cap to hold liquids, pastes **3.** (sometimes T-) underground electric railway, esp. in London **4.** sl., chiefly US television set —'**tubing** n. **1.** tubes collectively **2.** length of tube **3.** system of tubes **4.** fabric in form of tube —'**tubular** a. like tube

tuber ('tju:bə) n. fleshy underground stem of some plants, eg potato —'**tuberous** a.

tubercle ('tju:bək°l) n. **1.** any small rounded nodule on skin etc. **2.** small lesion of tissue, esp. produced by tuberculosis —**tu'bercular** a. —**tu'berculin** n. extraction from bacillus used to test for and treat tuberculosis —**tubercu'losis** n. communicable disease, esp. of lungs —**tuberculin tested** (of milk) produced by cows certified as free of tuberculosis

T.U.C. Trades Union Congress

tuck (tʌk) vt. **1.** push, fold into small space **2.** gather, stitch in folds **3.** draw, roll together —n. **4.** stitched fold **5.** inf. food —'**tucker** n. strip of linen or lace formerly worn across bosom by women —**tuck-in** n. UK inf. meal, esp. large

—**tuck shop** *chiefly UK* shop, *esp.* near school, where cakes and sweets are sold —**tuck in 1.** put to bed and make snug **2.** thrust loose ends or sides of (something) into confining space **3.** *inf.* eat, *esp.* heartily

Tudor ('tjuːdə) *a.* **1.** of the English royal house ruling 1485-1603 **2.** in, resembling style of this period, *esp.* of architecture

Tues. Tuesday

Tuesday ('tjuːzdɪ) *n.* third day of week

tufa ('tjuːfə) *n.* porous rock formed as deposit from springs *etc.*

tuff (tʌf) *n.* hard volcanic rock consisting of consolidated fragments of lava

tuffet ('tʌfɪt) *n.* small mound or seat

tuft (tʌft) *n.* bunch of feathers, threads *etc.*

tug (tʌg) *vt.* **1.** pull hard or violently **2.** haul **3.** jerk forward (**-gg-**) —*n.* **4.** violent pull **5.** ship used to tow other vessels —**tug of war** contest in which two teams pull against one another on a rope

tuition (tjuːˈɪʃən) *n.* **1.** teaching, instruction **2.** private coaching —**tuˈitional** *a.*

tulip ('tjuːlɪp) *n.* plant with bright cup-shaped flowers

tulle (tjuːl) *n.* kind of fine thin silk or lace

tullibee ('tʌlɪbiː) *n.* Canad. whitefish

tumble ('tʌmbᵊl) *v.* **1.** (cause to) fall, roll, twist *etc.*, *esp.* in play —*vt.* **2.** rumple, disturb *etc.* **3.** fall **4.** somersault —**ˈtumbler** *n.* **1.** stemless drinking glass **2.** acrobat **3.** spring catch in lock —**tumble-down** *a.* dilapidated —**tumble drier** *or* **tumbler drier** machine that dries clothes *etc.* by tumbling in warm air —**tumble to** *inf.* realize, understand

tumbrel *or* **tumbril** ('tʌmbrəl) *n.* open cart for taking victims of French Revolution to guillotine

tumefy ('tjuːmɪfaɪ) *v.* (cause to) swell —**tuˈmescence** *n.* —**tuˈmescent** *a.* (becoming) swollen

tummy ('tʌmɪ) *n. inf. childish word for* stomach

tumour *or U.S.* **tumor** ('tjuːmə) *n.* abnormal growth in or on body

tumult ('tjuːmʌlt) *n.* violent uproar, commotion —**tuˈmultuous** *a.*

tumulus ('tjuːmjʊləs) *n.* burial mound, barrow (*pl.* **-li** (-laɪ))

tun (tʌn) *n.* **1.** large cask **2.** measure of liquid

tuna ('tjuːnə) *n. see* TUNNY

tundra ('tʌndrə) *n.* vast treeless zone between icecap and timber line of N Amer. and Eurasia

tune (tjuːn) *n.* **1.** melody **2.** quality of being in pitch **3.** adjustment of musical instrument **4.** concord **5.** frame of mind —*vt.* **6.** put in tune **7.** adjust (machine) to obtain most efficient running **8.** adjust (radio circuit) —**ˈtuneful** *a.*

—**ˈtunefully** *adv.* —**ˈtuner** *n.* —**tune-up** *n.* adjustments to engine to improve performance —**tuning fork** two-pronged metal fork that when struck produces pure note of constant specified pitch —**tune in** adjust (radio, television) to receive (a station, programme) —**tune up 1.** adjust (musical instrument) to particular pitch **2.** tune (instruments) to common pitch **3.** adjust (engine) in (car *etc.*) to improve performance

tungsten ('tʌŋstən) *n.* greyish-white metal, used in lamp filaments, some steels *etc.*

tunic ('tjuːnɪk) *n.* **1.** close-fitting jacket forming part of uniform **2.** loose hiplength or kneelength garment

tunnel ('tʌnᵊl) *n.* **1.** underground passage, *esp.* as track for railway line **2.** burrow of a mole *etc.* —*vt.* **3.** make tunnel through —*vi.* **4.** (*with* through, under *etc.*) make or force a way (through or under something) (**-ll-**) —**ˈtunneller** *n.*

tunny ('tʌnɪ) *n.* large marine food and game fish

tup (tʌp) *n.* male sheep, ram

tupik ('tuːpɪk) *n. C* tent used as summer shelter by Eskimos

tuppence ('tʌpəns) *n. see* **twopence** *at* TWO

tuque (tuːk) *n. C* knitted cap with tapering end

turban ('tɜːbən) *n.* **1.** in certain countries, man's headdress, made by coiling length of cloth round head or a cap **2.** woman's hat like this

turbid ('tɜːbɪd) *a.* **1.** muddy, not clear **2.** disturbed —**turˈbidity** *or* **ˈturbidness** *n.*

turbine ('tɜːbɪn, -baɪn) *n.* rotary engine driven by steam, gas, water or air playing on blades

turbo- (*comb. form*) of, relating to, or driven by a turbine, as in *turbofan*

turbofan ('tɜːbəʊˈfæn) *n.* **1.** bypass engine in which large fan driven by turbine forces air rearwards around exhaust gases to increase propulsive thrust **2.** aircraft driven by turbofans **3.** fan in such engine

turbojet ('tɜːbəʊˈdʒet) *n.* **1.** turbojet engine **2.** aircraft powered by turbojet engines, in which exhaust gasses provide propulsion

turboprop ('tɜːbəʊˈprɒp) *n.* **1.** gas turbine for driving aircraft propeller **2.** aircraft powered by turboprops

turbot ('tɜːbət) *n.* large European flatfish

turbulent ('tɜːbjʊlənt) *a.* **1.** in commotion **2.** swirling **3.** riotous —**ˈturbulence** *n. Met.* instability of atmosphere causing gusty air currents *etc.*

tureen (təˈriːn) *n.* serving dish for soup

turf (tɜːf) *n.* **1.** short grass with earth bound to it by matted roots **2.** grass, *esp.* as lawn (*pl.* **-s, turves**) —*vt.* **3.** lay with turf —**turf accountant**

bookmaker —**the turf** 1. horse racing 2. racecourse —**turf out** *inf.* dismiss, throw out

turgid ('tɜːdʒɪd) *a.* 1. swollen, inflated 2. bombastic —**tur'gescent** *a.* —**tur'gidity** *n.*

turkey ('tɜːkɪ) *n.* large bird reared for its flesh

Turkish ('tɜːkɪʃ) *a.* of, pert. to Turkey, the Turks —**Turk** *n.* 1. native of Turkey 2. native speaker of any Turkic language 3. brutal or domineering person —'**Turkic** *n.* branch of Altaic family of languages, including Turkish —**Turkish bath** steam bath —**Turkish coffee** very strong black coffee —**Turkish delight** gelatin flavoured and coated with powdered sugar —**Turkish towel** rough, loose-piled towel

turmeric ('tɜːmərɪk) *n.* 1. Asian plant 2. powdered root of this used as dye, medicine and condiment

turmoil ('tɜːmɔɪl) *n.* confusion and bustle, commotion

turn (tɜːn) *v.* 1. move around, rotate 2. change, reverse, alter position or direction (of) —*vi.* 3. (*oft. with* into) change in nature, character *etc.* 4. (of milk) become rancid or sour —*vt.* 5. make, shape on lathe —*n.* 6. act of turning 7. inclination 8. period, spell 9. turning 10. short walk 11. (part of) rotation 12. performance —'**turner** *n.* —'**turning** *n.* road, path leading off main route —'**turnabout** *n.* 1. act of turning so as to face different direction 2. reversal of opinion *etc.* —'**turncoat** *n.* one who forsakes his party or principles —**turning circle** smallest circle in which vehicle can turn —**turning point** 1. moment when course of events is changed 2. point at which there is change in direction or motion —'**turnkey** *n. obs.* keeper of keys, *esp.* in prison; warder, jailer —**turn-off** *n.* 1. road *etc.* branching off from main thoroughfare 2. something or someone that turns one off —**turn-on** *n.* something or someone that turns one on —'**turnout** *n.* 1. number of people appearing for some purpose, occasion 2. way in which person is dressed, equipped —'**turnover** *n.* 1. total sales made by business over certain period 2. rate at which staff leave and are replaced 3. small pasty —'**turnpike** *n. Hist.* (gate across) road where toll was paid —'**turnstile** *n.* revolving gate for controlling admission of people —'**turnstone** *n.* shore bird that lifts up stones in search of food —'**turntable** *n.* revolving platform, *esp.* on record-player —**turn-up** *n.* 1. turned-up fold at bottom of trouser leg 2. unexpected or chance occurrence —**turn down** refuse —**turn off** 1. leave (road *etc.*) 2. (of road *etc.*) deviate from (another road *etc.*) 3. cause (something) to cease operating by turning knob *etc.* 4. *inf.* cause (person *etc.*) to feel dislike or distaste for (something) —**turn on** 1. cause (something) to operate by turning knob *etc.* 2. depend or hinge on 3. become hostile; retaliate

4. *inf.* produce (charm *etc.*) suddenly or automatically 5. *sl.* arouse emotionally or sexually 6. *sl.* take or become intoxicated by drugs 7. *sl.* introduce to drugs —**turn up** 1. appear 2. be found 3. increase (flow, volume)

turnip ('tɜːnɪp) *n.* plant with globular root used as food

turpentine ('tɜːpəntaɪn) *n.* 1. resin got from certain trees 2. oil, spirits made from this

turpitude ('tɜːpɪtjuːd) *n.* depravity

turps (tɜːps) turpentine

turquoise ('tɜːkwɔɪz, -kwɑːz) *n.* 1. bluish-green precious stone 2. this colour —*a.* 3. bluish-green

turret ('tʌrɪt) *n.* 1. small tower 2. revolving armoured tower for guns on warship, tank *etc.*

turtle ('tɜːtəl) *n.* sea tortoise —'**turtleneck** *n.* 1. round high close-fitting neck on sweater 2. sweater itself

turtledove ('tɜːtəldʌv) *n.* 1. Old World dove having brown plumage with speckled wings and long dark tail 2. gentle or loving person

tusk (tʌsk) *n.* long pointed side tooth of certain animals (*eg* elephant, wild boar *etc.*) —'**tusker** *n.* animal with tusks fully developed

tussle ('tʌsəl) *n./vi.* fight, wrestle, struggle

tussock ('tʌsək) *n.* 1. clump of grass 2. tuft —'**tussocky** *a.*

tutelage ('tjuːtɪlɪdʒ) *n.* act, office of tutor or guardian —'**tutelary** or '**tutelar** *a.*

tutor ('tjuːtə) *n.* 1. one teaching individuals or small groups —*v.* 2. teach thus —**tu'torial** *n.* period of instruction with tutor

tutti ('tʊtɪ) *a./adv. Mus.* to be performed by whole orchestra, choir *etc.*

tutti-frutti ('tʊtɪ'fruːtɪ) *n.* 1. ice cream or confection containing small pieces of candied or fresh fruits 2. preserve of chopped mixed fruits 3. flavour like that of many fruits combined

tutu ('tuːtuː) *n.* short, stiff skirt worn by ballerinas

tu-whit tu-whoo (təˈwɪt təˈwuː) imitation of sound made by owl

tuxedo (tʌkˈsiːdəʊ) *n.* US dinner jacket (*pl.* -s)

TV television

twaddle ('twɒdəl) *n.* silly talk

twain (tweɪn) *n. obs.* two —**in twain** asunder

twang (twæŋ) *n.* 1. vibrating metallic sound 2. nasal speech —*v.* 3. (cause to) make such sounds

tweak (twiːk) *vt.* 1. pinch and twist or pull —*n.* 2. a tweaking

twee (twiː) *a. inf.* excessively sentimental, sweet, pretty

tweed (twiːd) *n.* 1. rough-surfaced cloth used for clothing —*pl.* 2. suit of tweed —'**tweedy** *a.* 1. of tweed 2. showing fondness for hearty outdoor life, usu. associated with wearers of tweeds

tweet (twiːt) *n./vi.* chirp —'**tweeter** *n.* loudspeaker reproducing high-frequency sounds

tweezers ('twiːzəz) *pl.n.* small forceps or tongs

twelve (twelv) *n./a.* cardinal number two more than ten —**twelfth** *a./n.* ordinal number —**Twelfth Day** Jan. 6th, twelfth day after Christmas; feast of Epiphany —**twelve-tone** *a.* of type of serial music which uses as musical material tone row formed by 12 semitones of chromatic scale

twenty ('twentɪ) *n./a.* cardinal number, twice ten —'**twentieth** *a./n.* ordinal number

twerp *or* **twirp** (twɜːp) *n. inf.* silly person

twice (twaɪs) *adv.* two times

twiddle ('twɪdªl) *v.* **1.** fiddle —*vt.* **2.** twist

twig[1] (twɪg) *n.* small branch, shoot

twig[2] (twɪg) *v. inf.* notice; understand (-**gg**-)

twilight ('twaɪlaɪt) *n.* soft light after sunset —'**twilit** *a.* —**twilight zone 1.** inner-city area where houses have become dilapidated **2.** any indefinite or transitional condition or area

twill (twɪl) *n.* fabric woven so as to have surface of parallel ridges

twin (twɪn) *n.* **1.** one of pair, *esp.* of two children born together —*a.* **2.** being a twin —*v.* **3.** pair, be paired —**twin-set** *n.* UK matching jumper and cardigan —**twin town** UK town that has civic associations with foreign town

twine (twaɪn) *v.* **1.** twist, coil round —*n.* **2.** string, cord

twinge (twɪndʒ) *n.* **1.** momentary sharp, shooting pain **2.** qualm

twinkle ('twɪŋkªl) *vi.* **1.** shine with dancing or quivering light, sparkle —*n.* **2.** twinkling **3.** flash **4.** gleam of amusement in eyes —'**twinkling** *n.* very brief time

twirl (twɜːl) *v.* **1.** turn or twist round quickly **2.** whirl —*vt.* **3.** twiddle —*n.* **4.** rotating; being rotated; whirl, twist **5.** something wound around or twisted; coil **6.** written flourish

twist (twɪst) *v.* **1.** make, become spiral, by turning with one end fast **2.** distort, change **3.** wind —*n.* **4.** thing twisted **5.** dance popular in 1960s, in which dancers vigorously twist the hips —'**twister** *n. inf.* swindler —'**twisty** *a.*

twit (twɪt) *n.* **1.** *inf.* foolish person —*vt.* **2.** taunt (**-tt-**)

twitch (twɪtʃ) *v.* **1.** give momentary sharp pull or jerk (to) —*n.* **2.** such pull or jerk **3.** spasmodic jerk, spasm

twitter ('twɪtə) *vi.* **1.** (of birds) utter succession of tremulous sounds —*n.* **2.** such succession of notes

two (tuː) *n./a.* cardinal number, one more than one —'**twofold** *a./adv.* —'**twosome** *n.* **1.** two together, *esp.* two people **2.** match between two people —**two-edged** *a.* **1.** having two cutting edges **2.** (*esp.* of remark) having two interpretations —**two-faced** *a.* **1.** double-dealing, deceitful **2.** with two faces —**twopence** *or* **tuppence** ('tʌpəns) *n.* UK **1.** sum of two pennies **2.** something of little value (*esp. in* **not care** *or* **give twopence**) **3.** formerly, Brit. silver coin —**twopenny** *or* **tuppenny** ('tʌpnɪ) *a. chiefly* UK **1.** cheap, tawdry (*also* **twopenny-halfpenny**) **2.** worth two pence —**two-ply** *a.* **1.** made of two layers, strands *etc.* —*n.* **2.** two-ply knitting yarn *etc.* —**two-step** *n.* **1.** ballroom dance in duple time **2.** music for such dance —**two-stroke** *a.* (of internal combustion engine) making one explosion to every two strokes of piston —**two-time** *v. inf.* deceive (someone, *esp.* lover) by carrying on relationship with another —**two-timer** *n.*

TX Texas

-ty[1] (*comb. form*) multiple of ten, as in *sixty, seventy*

-ty[2] (*comb. form*) state, condition, quality, as in *cruelty*

tycoon (taɪ'kuːn) *n.* powerful, influential businessman

tyke *or* **tike** (taɪk) *n.* **1.** *inf.* small, cheeky child **2.** small (mongrel) dog

tympani ('tɪmpənɪ) *pl.n. see* TIMPANI

tympanum ('tɪmpənəm) *n.* **1.** cavity of middle ear **2.** tympanic membrane **3.** any diaphragm resembling that in middle ear in function **4.** *Archit.* recessed space, *esp.* triangular, bounded by cornices of pediment **5.** recessed space bounded by arch and lintel of doorway or window below it **6.** *Mus.* drum **7.** scoop wheel for raising water (*pl.* **-s, -na** (-nə)) —**tym'panic** *a.* —**tympanic membrane** thin membrane separating external ear from middle ear

Tynwald ('tɪnwəld, 'taɪn-) *n.* Parliament of Isle of Man

type (taɪp) *n.* **1.** class, sort **2.** model; pattern **3.** characteristic build **4.** specimen **5.** block bearing letter used for printing **6.** such pieces collectively —*vt.* **7.** print with typewriter **8.** typify **9.** classify —'**typist** *n.* one who operates typewriter —'**typo** *n. inf.* error in typing —'**typecast** *vt.* cast (actor) in same kind of role continually —'**typeface** *n.* **1.** printing surface of any type character **2.** style or design of character on type (*also* **face**) —'**typescript** *n.* typewritten document or copy —'**typesetter** *n.* **1.** person who sets type; compositor **2.** typesetting machine —'**typewrite** *v.* —'**typewriter** *n.* keyed writing machine

-type (*comb. form*) **1.** type, form, as in *archetype* **2.** printing type; photographic process, as in *collotype*

typhoid ('taɪfɔɪd) *n.* **1.** acute infectious disease, affecting *esp.* intestines —*a.,* also **ty'phoidal 2.**

resembling typhus —**'typhus** *n.* infectious disease

typhoon (taɪˈfuːn) *n.* violent tropical storm or cyclone —**typhonic** (taɪˈfɒnɪk) *a.*

typical (ˈtɪpɪkˈl) *or* **typic** *a.* 1. true to type 2. characteristic —**typically** *adv.*

typify (ˈtɪpɪfaɪ) *vt.* serve as type or model of (**-ified, -ifying**)

typography (taɪˈpɒɡrəfɪ) *n.* 1. art of printing 2. style of printing —**ty'pographer** *n.* —**typo'graphical** *a.*

tyrannosaur (tɪˈrænəsɔː) *or* **tyrannosaurus** (tɪrænəˈsɔːrəs) *n.* large carnivorous two-footed dinosaur common in N Amer. in Upper Jurassic and Cretaceous times

tyrant (ˈtaɪrənt) *n.* 1. oppressive or cruel ruler 2. one who forces his will on others cruelly and arbitrarily —**tyrannical** (tɪˈrænɪkˈl) *a.* 1. despotic 2. ruthless —**tyrannically** (tɪˈrænɪkəlɪ) *adv.* —**tyrannicide** (tɪˈrænɪsaɪd) *n.* 1. slayer of tyrant 2. his deed —**tyrannize** *or* **-ise** (ˈtɪrənaɪz) *v.* exert ruthless or tyrannical authority (over) —**tyrannous** (ˈtɪrənəs) *a.* —**tyranny** (ˈtɪrənɪ) *n.* despotism

tyre *or* *U.S.* **tire** (taɪə) *n.* 1. (inflated) rubber ring over rim of road vehicle 2. metal band on rim of cart wheel

Tyrian (ˈtɪrɪən) *n.* 1. native of ancient Tyre, port in S Lebanon and centre of ancient Phoenician culture —*a.* 2. of ancient Tyre

tyro *or* **tiro** (ˈtaɪrəʊ) *n.* novice, beginner (*pl.* **-s**)

tzar (zɑː) *n. see* CZAR

tzetze fly (ˈtsɛtsɪ) *see* TSETSE FLY

U,u

u *or* **U** (juː) *n.* 1. 21st letter of English alphabet 2. any of several speech sounds represented by this letter, as in *mute, cut* or *minus* 3. something shaped like U (*pl.* **u's, U's** *or* **Us**)

U 1. united 2. unionist 3. university 4. UK universal (used to describe category of film certified as suitable for viewing by anyone) 5. *Chem.* uranium

U.A.E. United Arab Emirates

ubiquitous (juːˈbɪkwɪtəs) *a.* 1. everywhere at once 2. omnipresent —**u'biquity** *n.*

U-boat *n.* German submarine

u.c. *Print.* upper case

udder (ˈʌdə) *n.* milk-secreting organ of cow *etc.*

UDI Unilateral Declaration of Independence

UEFA (juːˈeɪfə, ˈjuːfə) Union of European Football Associations

UFO (*sometimes* ˈjuːfəʊ) unidentified flying object

ugh (ʊx, ʊh, ʌh) *interj.* exclamation of disgust, annoyance *etc.*

ugly (ˈʌɡlɪ) *a.* 1. unpleasant or repulsive to the sight, hideous 2. ill-omened 3. threatening —**'ugliness** *n.* —**ugly duckling** person or thing, initially ugly or unpromising, that changes into something beautiful or admirable

UHF ultrahigh frequency

UHT ultra heat treated

U.K. United Kingdom

ukase (juːˈkeɪz) *n.* in imperial Russia, edict of Czar

Ukrainian (juːˈkreɪnɪən) *a.* 1. of Ukraine —*n.* 2. East Slavonic language of Ukrainians 3. native or inhabitant of Ukraine

ukulele *or* **ukelele** (juːkəˈleɪlɪ) *n.* small four-stringed guitar, *esp.* of Hawaii

ulcer (ˈʌlsə) *n.* open sore on skin, mucous membrane that is slow to heal —**'ulcerate** *v.* make, form ulcer(s) —**'ulcerated** *a.* —**ulce'ration** *n.* —**'ulcerous** *a.*

ulna (ˈʌlnə) *n.* longer of two bones of forearm (*pl.* **ulnae** (ˈʌlniː), **-s**)

ulster (ˈʌlstə) *n.* man's heavy double-breasted overcoat

ult. 1. ultimate 2. ultimo

ulterior (ʌlˈtɪərɪə) *a.* 1. lying beneath, beyond what is revealed or evident (*eg* motives) 2. situated beyond

ultimate (ˈʌltɪmɪt) *a.* 1. last 2. highest 3. most significant 4. fundamental —**'ultimately** *adv.* —**ultimatum** (ʌltɪˈmeɪtəm) *n.* 1. final proposition 2. final terms offered (*pl.* **-s, -ta** (-tə)) —**'ultimo** *adv.* in last month

ultra (ˈʌltrə) *a.* 1. extreme, *esp.* in beliefs or opinions —*n.* 2. extremist

ultra- (*comb. form*) beyond, excessive(ly), extreme(ly) as in *ultramodern*

ultrahigh frequency (ˈʌltrəhaɪ) (band of) radio waves of very short wavelength

ultramarine (ʌltrəməˈriːn) *n.* blue pigment

ultrasonic (ʌltrəˈsɒnɪk) *a.* of sound waves beyond the range of human ear —**ultra'sonics** *pl.n.* (*with sing. v.*) branch of physics concerned with ultrasonic waves (*also* **super'sonics**)

ultrasound (ʌltrəˈsaʊnd) *n.* ultrasonic waves, used in cleaning metallic parts, echo sounding, medical diagnosis *etc.*

ultraviolet (ʌltrəˈvaɪəlɪt) *a.* of electromagnetic radiation, *eg* of sun *etc.*, beyond limit of visibility at violet end of spectrum

ululate (ˈjuːljʊleɪt) *vi.* howl, wail —**'ululant** *a.* —**ulu'lation** *n.*

umbel (ˈʌmbˈl) *n.* umbrellalike flower cluster with stalks springing from central point —**umbel'liferous** *a.*

umber (ˈʌmbə) *n.* dark brown pigment

umbilical (ʌmˈbɪlɪkəl, ʌmbɪˈlaɪkəl) a. of (region of) navel —**umˈbilicus** n. 1. Biol. hollow structure, such as cavity at base of gastropod shell 2. Anat. navel (pl. **-bilici** (-ˈbɪlɪsaɪ, -bəˈlaɪsaɪ)) —**umbilical cord** 1. cordlike structure connecting foetus with placenta of mother 2. cord joining astronaut to spacecraft etc.

umbra (ˈʌmbrə) n. 1. region of complete shadow due to obstruction of light by opaque object, esp. shadow cast by moon onto earth during solar eclipse 2. darker inner region of sunspot (pl. **-brae** (-briː), **-s**) —**ˈumbral** a.

umbrage (ˈʌmbrɪdʒ) n. offence, resentment (esp. in give or take umbrage)

umbrella (ʌmˈbrelə) n. 1. folding circular cover of nylon etc. on stick, carried in hand to protect against rain, heat of sun 2. anything shaped or functioning like an umbrella

umiak or **oomiak** (ˈuːmɪæk) n. Eskimo boat made of skins

umlaut (ˈʊmlaʊt) n. 1. mark (¨) placed over vowel in some languages, such as German 2. esp. in Germanic languages, change of vowel within word caused by assimilating influence of vowel or semivowel in preceding or following syllable

umpire (ˈʌmpaɪə) n. 1. person chosen to decide question, or to decide disputes and enforce rules in a game —v. 2. act as umpire in or for (game etc.)

umpteen (ʌmpˈtiːn) a. inf. many —**umpˈteenth** n./a.

UN or **U.N.** United Nations

un- (comb. form) not, contrary to, opposite of, reversal of an action, removal from, release, deprivation. See the list on pages 532-536

unaccountable (ʌnəˈkaʊntəbəl) a. that cannot be explained

unaffected[1] (ʌnəˈfektɪd) a. unpretentious, natural, sincere —**unafˈfectedly** adv.

unaffected[2] (ʌnəˈfektɪd) a. not affected

unanimous (juːˈnænɪməs) a. 1. in complete agreement 2. agreed by all —**unaˈnimity** n. —**uˈnanimously** adv.

unassailable (ʌnəˈseɪləbəl) a. 1. able to withstand attack 2. irrefutable —**unasˈsailably** adv.

unassuming (ʌnəˈsjuːmɪŋ) a. not pretentious, modest

unattached (ʌnəˈtætʃt) a. 1. not connected with any specific thing, group etc. 2. not engaged or married

unavailing (ʌnəˈveɪlɪŋ) a. useless, futile

unaware (ʌnəˈwɛə) a. not aware, uninformed —**unaˈwares** adv. 1. without previous warning 2. unexpectedly

unbend (ʌnˈbend) v. 1. release or be released

from restraints of formality 2. inf. relax (mind) or (of mind) become relaxed 3. make or become straight from original bent shape (-ˈbent, -ˈbending) —**unˈbending** a. rigid, inflexible 2. characterized by sternness or severity

unbidden (ʌnˈbɪdən) a. 1. not commanded; voluntary, spontaneous 2. not invited

unbosom (ʌnˈbʊzəm) vt. tell or reveal (one's secrets etc.)

unbounded (ʌnˈbaʊndɪd) a. having no boundaries or limits —**unˈboundedly** adv.

unbridled (ʌnˈbraɪdəld) a. 1. with all restraints removed 2. (of horse etc.) wearing no bridle

unburden (ʌnˈbɜːdən) vt. 1. remove load or burden from 2. relieve, make free (one's mind, oneself etc.) of worry etc. by revelation or confession

uncalled-for a. unnecessary; unwarranted

uncanny (ʌnˈkænɪ) a. weird, mysterious

uncial (ˈʌnsɪəl) a. 1. of majuscule letters, as used in Greek and Latin manuscripts of third to ninth centuries, that resemble modern capitals but are more rounded —n. 2. uncial letter or manuscript —**ˈuncially** adv.

uncle (ˈʌŋkəl) n. 1. brother of father or mother 2. husband of aunt

uncompromising (ʌnˈkɒmprəmaɪzɪŋ) a. not prepared to compromise —**unˈcompromisingly** adv.

unconscionable (ʌnˈkɒnʃənəbəl) a. 1. unscrupulous, unprincipled 2. excessive

unconscious (ʌnˈkɒnʃəs) a. 1. insensible 2. not aware 3. not knowing 4. of thoughts, memories etc. of which one is not normally aware —n. 5. these thoughts —**unˈconsciously** adv. —**unˈconsciousness** n.

uncounted (ʌnˈkaʊntɪd) a. 1. innumerable 2. not counted

uncouth (ʌnˈkuːθ) a. 1. clumsy, boorish 2. without ease or polish

uncover (ʌnˈkʌvə) vt. 1. remove cover, top etc. from 2. reveal, disclose —v. 3. take off (one's head covering), esp. as mark of respect

unction (ˈʌŋkʃən) n. 1. anointing 2. excessive politeness 3. soothing words or thoughts —**ˈunctuous** a. 1. slippery, greasy 2. oily in manner, ingratiating

undeceive (ʌndɪˈsiːv) vt. reveal truth to (someone mistaken, misled)

under (ˈʌndə) prep. 1. below, beneath 2. bound by, included in 3. less than 4. subjected to 5. known by 6. in the time of —adv. 7. in lower place or condition —a. 8. lower —**under way** 1. in progress 2. Naut. in motion in direction headed

under- (comb. form) beneath, below, lower, too little, as in underground, underbid. Such words are not given where the meaning can be deduced from the meaning(s) of the simple word

under·chieve	·underpants
under·bid v.	·underpart
·underbid n.	under·priced
·underclothes	under·sea
under·do	under·sexed
under·done	·undershirt
underem·ployed	under·sized
under·foot	·underskirt
·undergarment	under·staffed
under·lie	under·state
under·manned	under·value
under·nourish	under·water
under·paid	under·weight

underage (ʌndər'eidʒ) a. below required age, *esp.* below legal age for voting or drinking

undercarriage ('ʌndəkæridʒ) n. landing gear of aircraft

undercoat ('ʌndəkəut) n. coat of paint applied before top coat

undercover (ʌndə'kʌvə) a. done or acting in secret

undercurrent ('ʌndəkʌrənt) n. **1.** current that lies beneath another current **2.** opinion, emotion *etc.* lying beneath apparent feeling or meaning (*also* '**underflow**)

undercut (ʌndə'kʌt) v. **1.** charge less than (competitor) in order to obtain trade **2.** cut away under part of (something) **3.** *Sport* hit (ball) in such a way as to impart backspin —n. ('ʌndəkʌt) **4.** act of cutting underneath **5.** tenderloin of beef **6.** *Sport* stroke that imparts backspin to ball

underdeveloped (ʌndədɪ'veləpt) a. **1.** immature; undersized **2.** relating to societies lacking economical and industrial development neces-

sary to advance **3.** *Photog.* (of film *etc.*) processed in developer for less than required time

underdog ('ʌndədɒg) n. **1.** losing competitor in contest *etc.* **2.** person in position of inferiority

underestimate (ʌndər'estimeit) vt. **1.** make too low an estimate of **2.** think insufficiently highly of —n. (ʌndər'estimit) **3.** too low an estimate —underesti'mation n.

underexpose (ʌndərik'spəuz) vt. **1.** *Photog.* expose (film *etc.*) for too short a period or with insufficient light **2.** fail to subject to appropriate publicity —underex'posure n.

undergo (ʌndə'gəu) vt. experience, endure, sustain (-'went, -'gone, -'going)

undergraduate (ʌndə'grædjuit) n. student member of university or college who has not taken degree

underground ('ʌndəgraund) a. **1.** under the ground **2.** secret —adv. (ʌndə'graund) **3.** under earth's surface **4.** secretly —n. **5.** secret but organized resistance to government in power **6.** railway system under the ground

undergrowth ('ʌndəgrəuθ) n. small trees, bushes *etc.* growing beneath taller trees in wood or forest

underhand ('ʌndəhænd) a. **1.** secret, sly **2.** *Sport* underarm

underlay (ʌndə'lei) vt. **1.** place (something) under or beneath **2.** support by something laid beneath (-'laid, -'laying) —n. ('ʌndəlei) **3.** lining, support *etc.* laid underneath something else **4.** felt, rubber *etc.* laid beneath carpet to increase insulation

underline (ʌndə'lain) vt. **1.** put line under **2.** emphasize

underling ('ʌndəliŋ) n. subordinate

una·bated	unap·preciated
una·bridged	unap·proachable
unac·ceptable	un·armed
unac·companied	una·shamed
unac·customed	un·asked
unac·knowledged	unat·tainable
unac·quainted	unat·tended
una·dorned	unat·tractive
una·dulterated	un·authorized
unad·venturous	una·vailable
una·fraid	un·balanced
un·aided	un·bearable
unal·loyed	un·beaten
un·alterable	unbe·coming
unam·biguous	unbe·lievable
un·answerable	unbe·liever
unap·pealing	unbe·lieving
un·appetizing	un·bias(s)ed
un·bind	un·christian
un·blemished	un·circumcised
un·blinking	un·civil
un·block	un·claimed
un·bolt	un·clear
un·born	un·clothe
un·breakable	un·cluttered
un·broken	un·coil
un·buckle	un·combed
uncared-for	un·comfortable
un·ceasing	uncom·mitted
un·censored	un·common
un·censured	uncom·municative
un·certain	uncom·plaining
un·challenged	un·complicated
uncharacte·ristic	uncompli·mentary
un·charitable	uncon·cerned
un·checked	uncon·ditional

underlying (ʌndəˈlaɪɪŋ) a. 1. concealed but detectable 2. fundamental; basic 3. lying under

undermine (ʌndəˈmaɪn) vt. 1. wear away base, support of 2. weaken insidiously

underneath (ʌndəˈniːθ) adv. 1. below —prep. 2. under —a. 3. lower —n. 4. lower part, surface etc.

underpass (ˈʌndəpɑːs) n. section of road passing under another road, railway line etc.

underpin (ʌndəˈpɪn) vt. 1. support from beneath, esp. by prop 2. give corroboration or support to (-nn-)

underprivileged (ʌndəˈprɪvɪlɪdʒd) a. lacking rights and advantages of other members of society

underseal (ˈʌndəsiːl) n. UK coating of tar etc., applied to underside of motor vehicle to retard corrosion

underside (ˈʌndəsaɪd) n. bottom or lower surface

understand (ʌndəˈstænd) v. 1. know and comprehend 2. realize —vt. 3. infer 4. take for granted (-ˈstood, -ˈstanding) —underˈstandable a. —underˈstandably adv. —underˈstanding n. 1. intelligence 2. opinion 3. agreement —a. 4. sympathetic

understudy (ˈʌndəstʌdɪ) n. 1. one prepared to take over theatrical part from performer if necessary —vt. 2. act as understudy (to) or learn (part) thus

undertake (ʌndəˈteɪk) vt. 1. make oneself responsible for 2. enter upon 3. promise (-ˈtook, -ˈtaken, -ˈtaking) —ˈundertaker n. one who arranges funerals —ˈundertaking n. 1. that which is undertaken 2. project 3. guarantee

undertone (ˈʌndətəʊn) n. 1. quiet, dropped tone of voice 2. underlying tone or suggestion

undertow (ˈʌndətəʊ) n. backwash of wave 2.

current beneath surface moving in different direction from surface current

underwear (ˈʌndəwɛə) n. garments worn next to skin (also ˈunderclothes)

underworld (ˈʌndəwɜːld) n. 1. criminals and their associates 2. Myth. abode of the dead

underwrite (ˈʌndəraɪt, ʌndəˈraɪt) vt. 1. agree to pay 2. accept liability in (insurance policy) (-ˈwrote, -ˈwritten, -ˈwriting) —ˈunderwriter n. 1. one that underwrites 2. agent for insurance company who assesses risks

undies (ˈʌndɪz) pl.n. inf. women's underwear

undo (ʌnˈduː) vt. 1. untie, unfasten 2. reverse 3. cause downfall of (-ˈdid, -ˈdone, -ˈdoing) —unˈdoing n. —unˈdone a. 1. ruined 2. not performed

undoubted (ʌnˈdaʊtɪd) a. certain; indisputable —unˈdoubtedly adv.

undue (ʌnˈdjuː) a. 1. excessive 2. improper; illegal —unˈduly adv. immoderately

undulate (ˈʌndjʊleɪt) v. move up and down like waves —unduˈlation n. —ˈundulatory a.

unearth (ʌnˈɜːθ) vt. 1. dig up 2. discover

unearthly (ʌnˈɜːθlɪ) a. 1. ghostly; eerie 2. heavenly; sublime 3. ridiculous or unreasonable (esp. in unearthly hour) —unˈearthliness n.

uneasy (ʌnˈiːzɪ) a. 1. anxious 2. uncomfortable

unemployed (ʌnɪmˈplɔɪd) a. having no paid employment, out of work —unemˈployment n.

unerring (ʌnˈɜːrɪŋ) a. 1. not missing the mark 2. consistently accurate

UNESCO (juːˈnɛskəʊ) United Nations Educational, Scientific and Cultural Organization

unexceptionable (ʌnɪkˈsɛpʃənəbəl) a. beyond criticism or objection —unexˈceptionably adv.

unexceptional (ʌnɪkˈsɛpʃənəl) a. 1. ordinary or normal 2. subject to or allowing no exceptions —unexˈceptionally adv.

unconˈfirmed	unˈcurl	undisˈcovered
unconˈnected	unˈdamaged	undisˈputed
unˈconquered	unˈdaunted	undisˈturbed
unconˈtrollable	undeˈcided	unˈdrinkable
unconˈtrolled	undeˈfeated	unˈdying
uncontroˈversial	undeˈfended	unˈearned
unconˈventional	undeˈmanding	unˈeatable
unconˈvincing	undemoˈcratic	unecoˈnomic
uncoˈoperative	undeˈmonstrative	unˈeducated
uncoˈordinated	undeˈniable	uneˈmotional
unˈcork	undeˈserved	unˈending
uncorˈroborated	undeˈserving	unˈequal
unˈcouple	undeˈsirable	unˈequalled
unˈcritical	undeˈtected	uneˈquivocal
unˈcrowned	undeˈterred	unˈethical
unˈcultivated	undeˈveloped	unˈeven
unˈcultured	undiˈminished	unˈeventful
unˈcurbed	unˈdisciplined	unexˈpected
		unexˈplained
		unˈfailing
		unˈfair
		unˈfaithful
		unfaˈmiliar
		unˈfashionable
		unˈfavourable
		unˈfeeling
		unˈfeigned
		unˈfinished
		unˈfit
		unˈflinching
		unˈfold
		unforeˈseen
		unforˈgettable
		unforˈgivable
		unˈfortunate
		unˈfounded

unfortunate (ʌnˈfɔːtʃənɪt) a. 1. causing or attended by misfortune 2. unlucky or unhappy 3. regrettable; unsuitable —n. 4. unlucky person —unˈfortunately adv.

unfounded (ʌnˈfaʊndɪd) a. 1. (of ideas, allegations etc.) baseless 2. not yet established —unˈfoundedly adv.

unfrock (ʌnˈfrɒk) vt. deprive (person in holy orders) of ecclesiastical status

ungainly (ʌnˈɡeɪnlɪ) a. awkward, clumsy

unguarded (ʌnˈɡɑːdɪd) a. 1. unprotected; vulnerable 2. open; frank 3. incautious

unguent (ˈʌnɡwənt) n. ointment

ungulate (ˈʌnɡjʊlɪt, -leɪt) n. any of large group of mammals all of which have hooves

unhinge (ʌnˈhɪndʒ) vt. 1. remove (door etc.) from its hinges 2. unbalance (person, his mind etc.)

unholy (ʌnˈhəʊlɪ) a. 1. not holy or sacred 2. immoral or depraved 3. inf. outrageous; unnatural

uni- (comb. form) one, as in unicorn, uniform. Such words are not given here where the meanings may easily be inferred from the simple word

UNICEF (ˈjuːnɪsɛf) United Nations International Children's Emergency Fund

unicellular (juːnɪˈsɛljʊlə) a. (of organisms and certain algae) consisting of single cell —unicelluˈlarity n.

unicorn (ˈjuːnɪkɔːn) n. mythical horselike animal with single long horn

uniform (ˈjuːnɪfɔːm) n. 1. identifying clothes worn by members of same group, eg soldiers, nurses etc. —a. 2. not changing, unvarying 3. regular, consistent 4. conforming to same standard or rule —uniˈformity n. sameness —ˈuniformly adv.

unify (ˈjuːnɪfaɪ) v. make or become one (-ified, -ifying) —unifiˈcation n. —Unification Church religious sect founded by Rev. Sun Myung Moon, S Korean industrialist and religious leader

unilateral (juːnɪˈlætərəl) a. 1. one-sided 2. (of contract) binding one party only —uniˈlaterally adv.

unimpeachable (ʌnɪmˈpiːtʃəbəl) a. unquestionable as to honesty, truth etc.

union (ˈjuːnjən) n. 1. joining into one 2. state of being joined 3. result of being joined 4. federation, combination of societies etc. 5. trade union —ˈunionism n. —ˈunionist n. supporter of union —ˈunionize or -nise v. organize (workers) into trade union —Union Jack national flag of United Kingdom

unique (juːˈniːk) a. 1. being only one of its kind 2. unparalleled

unisex (ˈjuːnɪsɛks) a. of clothing, hair style, hairdressers etc. that can be worn or used by either sex

unison (ˈjuːnɪsən) n. 1. Mus. singing etc. of same note as others 2. agreement, harmony, concord

unit (ˈjuːnɪt) n. 1. single thing or person 2. standard quantity 3. group of people or things with one purpose —Uniˈtarian n. member of Christian body that denies doctrine of the Trinity —Uniˈtarianism n. —ˈunitary a. —unit trust UK investment trust that issues units for public sale, holders of which are creditors with their interests represented by independent trust company

unite (juːˈnaɪt) vt. 1. join into one, connect 2. associate 3. cause to adhere —vi. 4. become one 5. combine —ˈunity n. 1. state of being one 2. harmony 3. agreement, uniformity 4. combination of separate parts into connected whole 5. Maths. the number one —United Empire

un'freeze	unhy'gienic	uninter'rupted	unlooked-for
un'furl	uni'dentified	unin'vited	un'lucky
un'godly	uni'maginable	unin'viting	un'made
un'governable	uni'maginative	un'justified	un'make
un'gracious	unim'paired	un'kind	un'manageable
ungram'matical	unim'portant	un'known	un'manned
un'grateful	unim'pressed	un'labelled	un'mannerly
un'hallowed	unin'formed	un'ladylike	un'marked
un'happy	unin'habited	un'lawful	un'married
un'harmed	unin'hibited	un'learned	un'mask
un'healthy	un'injured	un'leash	un'mentionable
un'heard	unin'spired	un'lettered	un'merciful
unheard-of	unin'sured	un'like	un'merited
un'heated	unin'telligent	un'likely	unmis'tak(e)able
un'heeded	unin'telligible	un'limited	un'moved
un'helpful	unin'tended	un'lined	un'musical
un'hurried	unin'tentional	un'load	un'named
un'hurt	un'interesting	un'lock	un'natural

Loyalist American colonist who settled in Canada in War of Amer. Independence from loyalty to Britain —**United Kingdom** island of Great Britain together with Northern Ireland —**United Nations Organization** organization formed in 1945 to promote peace and international cooperation

Univ. University

univalent (juːnɪ'veɪlənt; juː'nɪvələnt) a. 1. (of chromosome during meiosis) not paired with its homologue 2. *Chem. see* MONOVALENT —**uni'valency** n.

universe ('juːnɪvɜːs) n. 1. all existing things considered as constituting systematic whole 2. the world —**uni'versal** a. 1. relating to all things or all people 2. applying to all members of a community —**univer'sality** n. —**uni'versally** adv. —**universal joint** *or* **coupling** form of coupling between two rotating shafts allowing freedom of movement in all directions

university (juːnɪ'vɜːsɪtɪ) n. educational institution for study, examination and conferment of degrees in various branches of learning

unjust (ʌn'dʒʌst) a. not in accordance with accepted standards of justice; unfair —**un'justly** adv.

unkempt (ʌn'kɛmpt) a. of rough or uncared-for appearance

unless (ʌn'lɛs) conj. except under the circumstances that

unloose (ʌn'luːs) *or* **unloosen** vt. 1. release 2. loosen (hold, grip *etc.*) 3. unfasten, untie

unman (ʌn'mæn) vt. 1. cause to lose nerve *etc.* 2. make effeminate 3. remove men from (-**nn-**)

unmitigated (ʌn'mɪtɪgeɪtɪd) a. not diminished in intensity, severity *etc.*

unnatural (ʌn'nætʃərəl) a. 1. abnormal 2. not in accordance with accepted standards of behaviour 3. uncanny; supernatural 4. affected; forced 5. inhuman, monstrous —**un'naturally** adv.

unnerve (ʌn'nɜːv) vt. cause to lose courage, confidence *etc.*

U.N.O. United Nations Organization

unparalleled (ʌn'pærəleld) a. unmatched; unequalled

unprincipled (ʌn'prɪnsɪpəld) a. lacking moral principles

unquote (ʌn'kwəʊt) interj. expression used parenthetically to indicate that preceding quotation is finished

unravel (ʌn'rævəl) vt. undo, untangle (-**ll-**)

unread (ʌn'rɛd) a. 1. (of book *etc.*)'not yet read 2. (of person) having read little

unregenerate (ʌnrɪ'dʒɛnərɪt) a. 1. unrepentant; unreformed 2. obstinately adhering to one's own views —**unre'generacy** n. —**unre'generately** adv.

unremitting (ʌnrɪ'mɪtɪŋ) a. never slackening or stopping

unrest (ʌn'rɛst) n. troubled or rebellious state of discontent

unroll (ʌn'rəʊl) v. 1. open out (something rolled or folded) or (of something rolled *etc.*) become unwound —vi. 2. become visible or apparent, *esp.* gradually

unruly (ʌn'ruːlɪ) a. badly behaved, ungovernable, disorderly

unsaturated (ʌn'sætʃəreɪtɪd) a. 1. not saturated 2. (of chemical compound, *esp.* organic compound) containing one or more double or triple bonds and thus capable of undergoing addition reactions —**unsatu'ration** n.

unsavoury *or U.S.* **unsavory** (ʌn'seɪvərɪ) a. distasteful, disagreeable

unsightly (ʌn'saɪtlɪ) a. ugly

unspeakable (ʌn'spiːkəbəl) a. 1. incapable of

un'necessary	un'pleasant
un'noticed	un'pleasing
unob'servant	un'plumbed
unob'served	un'popular
unob'tainable	un'practised
unob'trusive	un'precedented
un'occupied	unpre'dictable
unof'ficial	unpre'pared
un'opened	unprepos'sessing
unop'posed	unpre'tentious
un'organized	un'printable
un'orthodox	unpro'ductive
un'pack	unpro'fessional
un'paid	un'profitable
unpardonable	un'promising
un'pick	unpro'pitious
un'pin	unpro'tected
un'playable	unpro'voked

un'qualified	un'saddle
un'questionable	un'safe
un'real	un'said
unrea'listic	un'saleable
un'reasonable	unsatis'factory
un'registered	un'scathed
unre'lenting	un'scheduled
unre'liable	unscien'tific
unre'pentent	un'scramble
unrepre'sentative	un'screw
unre'quited	un'scrupulous
unre'served	un'seasonable
unre'solved	un'seat
unre'strained	un'seemly
un'righteous	unself'conscious
un'ripe	un'selfish
un'rivalled	un'settle
un'ruffled	un'shak(e)able

expression in words **2.** indescribably bad or evil **3.** not to be uttered —**un'speakably** adv.

unstructured (ʌn'strʌktʃəd) a. without formal or systematic organization

unstrung (ʌn'strʌŋ) a. **1.** emotionally distressed **2.** (of stringed instrument) with strings detached

unstudied (ʌn'stʌdɪd) a. **1.** natural **2.** (with in) without knowledge or training

unsung (ʌn'sʌŋ) a. **1.** not acclaimed or honoured **2.** not yet sung

untenable (ʌn'tɛnəbəl) a. (of theories etc.) incapable of being maintained, defended

unthinkable (ʌn'θɪŋkəbəl) a. **1.** out of the question **2.** inconceivable **3.** unreasonable

untie (ʌn'taɪ) v. **1.** unfasten or free (knot or something that is tied) or (of knot etc.) become unfastened —vt. **2.** free from restriction (-'tied, -'tying)

until (ʌn'tɪl) conj. **1.** to the time that **2.** (with a negative) before —prep. **3.** up to the time of

unto ('ʌntuː) prep. obs. to

untold (ʌn'təʊld) a. **1.** incapable of description **2.** incalculably great in number or quantity **3.** not told

untouched (ʌn'tʌtʃt) a. **1.** not touched **2.** not harmed —**un'touchable** a. **1.** not able to be touched —n. **2.** esp. formerly, non-caste Hindu, forbidden to be touched by one of caste

untoward (ʌntə'wɔːd) a. awkward, inconvenient

unutterable (ʌn'ʌtərəbəl) a. incapable of being expressed in words —**un'utterably** adv.

unwell (ʌn'wɛl) a. not well, ill

unwieldy (ʌn'wiːldɪ) a. **1.** awkward, big, heavy to handle **2.** clumsy

unwitting (ʌn'wɪtɪŋ) a. **1.** not knowing **2.** not intentional

up (ʌp) prep. **1.** from lower to higher position **2.** along —adv. **3.** in or to higher position, source, activity etc. **4.** indicating completion ('**upper** comp., '**uppermost** sup.) —'**upward** a./adv. —'**upwards** or '**upward** adv. —**up-and-coming** a. promising continued or future success; enterprising —'**up'hill** a. **1.** inclining; sloping **2.** requiring protracted effort —adv. **3.** up incline or slope **4.** against difficulties —n. **5.** rising incline —**up-to-date** a. modern; fashionable —**up against** confronted with

up- (comb. form) up, upper, upwards as in uproot, upgrade. Such words are not given here where the meaning may easily be inferred from the simple word

upbeat ('ʌpbiːt) n. **1.** Mus. unaccented beat; upward gesture of conductor's baton indicating this —a. **2.** inf. cheerful; optimistic

upbraid (ʌp'breɪd) vt. scold, reproach

upbringing ('ʌpbrɪŋɪŋ) n. rearing and education of children

update (ʌp'deɪt) vt. bring up to date

upgrade (ʌp'greɪd) vt. **1.** promote to higher position **2.** improve

upheaval (ʌp'hiːvəl) n. sudden or violent disturbance

uphill see UP

uphold (ʌp'həʊld) vt. **1.** maintain **2.** support (**up'held, up'holding**)

upholster (ʌp'həʊlstə) vt. fit springs, padding and coverings on (chairs etc.) —**up'holsterer** n. —**up'holstery** n.

upkeep ('ʌpkiːp) n. act, process or cost of keeping something in good repair

upland ('ʌplənd) n. high land

uplift (ʌp'lɪft) vt. **1.** raise aloft **2.** Scot., NZ collect; pick up (documents etc.) —n. ('ʌplɪft) **3.** a lifting up **4.** mental, social or emotional improvement —a. ('ʌplɪft) **5.** designating brassiere for lifting and supporting breasts

upon (ə'pɒn) prep. on

un'sheathe	unsub'stantiated
un'skilful	unsuc'cessful
un'skilled	un'suitable
un'sociable	un'sure
un'social	unsur'passed
unso'licited	unsus'pected
un'solved	unsus'pecting
unso'phisticated	un'sweetened
un'sound	unsympa'thetic
un'sparing	unsyste'matic
un'specified	un'tainted
un'spoken	un'tamed
un'sporting	un'tangle
un'stable	un'tapped
un'steady	un'taught
un'stinted	un'taxed
un'string	un'thinking
un'strung	un'throne

un'tidy	un'warranted
un'timely	un'wary
un'trained	un'washed
un'troubled	un'wavering
un'true	un'welcome
un'trustworthy	un'wept
un'truthful	un'wholesome
un'tutored	un'willing
un'twist	un'wind
un'typical	un'wise
un'usable	un'workable
un'used	un'worldly
un'usual	un'worn
un'utterable	un'worthy
un'veil	un'wrap
un'verified	un'written
un'voiced	un'yielding
un'wanted	un'zip

upper ('ʌpə) a. comp. of UP **1.** higher, situated above —n. **2.** upper part of boot or shoe —'**uppermost** a. sup. of UP —**upper-case** a. of or relating to capital letters used in setting or production of printed or typed matter —'**uppercut** n. short-arm upward blow —**the upper hand** position of control

uppish ('ʌpɪʃ) a. inf. **1.** self-assertive **2.** arrogant **3.** affectedly superior

upright ('ʌpraɪt) a. **1.** erect **2.** honest, just —adv. **3.** vertically —n. **4.** thing standing upright, eg post in framework **5.** upright piano —**upright piano** piano with rectangular vertical case

uprising ('ʌpraɪzɪŋ, ʌp'raɪzɪŋ) n. rebellion, revolt

uproar ('ʌprɔː) n. tumult, disturbance —**up-'roarious** a. rowdy —**up'roariously** adv.

uproot (ʌp'ruːt) vt. **1.** pull up by or as if by the roots **2.** displace (person or persons) from native or habitual surroundings

upset (ʌp'sɛt) vt. **1.** overturn **2.** distress **3.** disrupt **4.** make ill (**up'set, up'setting**) —n. ('ʌpset) **5.** unexpected defeat **6.** confusion **7.** trouble **8.** overturning

upshot ('ʌpʃot) n. outcome, end

upside down ('ʌpsaɪd) **1.** turned over completely; inverted **2.** in disorder or chaos

upsilon ('ʌpsɪlɒn) n. 20th letter in Gr. alphabet (Υ, υ), vowel transliterated as y or u

upstage ('ʌp'steɪdʒ) a. of back of stage —vt. **2.** inf. draw attention away from (another) to oneself

upstanding (ʌp'stændɪŋ) a. **1.** of good character **2.** upright and vigorous in build

upstart ('ʌpstɑːt) n. one suddenly raised to wealth, power etc.

uptake ('ʌpteɪk) n. **1.** shaft etc. used to convey smoke or gases, esp. one that connects furnace to chimney **2.** lifting up —**quick** (or **slow**) **on the uptake** inf. quick (or slow) to understand or learn

uptight (ʌp'taɪt) a. inf. **1.** displaying tense nervousness, irritability **2.** repressed

upturn (ʌp'tɜːn) v. **1.** turn or cause to turn over or upside down —vt. **2.** create disorder in **3.** direct upwards —n. ('ʌptɜːn) **4.** upward trend or improvement

uranium (ju'reɪnɪəm) n. white radioactive metallic element, used as chief source of nuclear energy

urban ('ɜːbən) a. relating to town or city —'**urbanize** or **-nise** vt. change (countryside) to residential or industrial area

urbane (ɜː'beɪn) a. elegant, sophisticated —**urbanity** (ɜː'bænɪtɪ) n.

urchin ('ɜːtʃɪn) n. mischievous, unkempt child

Urdu ('ʊəduː, 'ɜː-) n. official language of Pakistan, belonging to Indic branch of Indo-European family of languages, closely related to Hindi

urea ('jʊərɪə) n. substance occurring in urine

ureter (ju'riːtə) n. tube that conveys urine from kidney to urinary bladder or cloaca —u'reteral or ureteric (jʊərɪ'tɛrɪk) a.

urethra (ju'riːθrə) n. canal conveying urine from bladder out of body (pl. **-thrae** (-θriː), **-s**)

urge (ɜːdʒ) vt. **1.** exhort earnestly **2.** entreat **3.** drive on —n. **4.** strong desire —'**urgency** n. —'**urgent** a. **1.** pressing **2.** needing attention at once —'**urgently** adv.

urine ('jʊərɪn) n. fluid excreted by kidneys to bladder and passed as waste from body —'**uric** a. —**urinal** (ju'raɪnəl, 'jʊərɪ-) n. (place with) sanitary fitting(s) used by men for urination —'**urinary** a. —'**urinate** vi. discharge urine —uri'nation n.

urn (ɜːn) n. **1.** vessel like vase, esp. for ashes of the dead **2.** large container with tap for making and dispensing tea, coffee etc.

urogenital (jʊərəʊ'dʒɛnɪtl) or **urinogenital** a. of urinary and genital organs and their functions (also **genito'urinary**)

Ursa Major ('ɜːsə 'meɪdʒə) extensive conspicuous constellation in N hemisphere. The seven brightest stars form Plough (also **the Great Bear, the Bear**)

Ursa Minor ('ɜːsə 'maɪnə) small faint constellation, brightest star of which is Pole Star (also **the Little Bear, the Bear**)

ursine ('ɜːsaɪn) a. of, like a bear

us (ʌs) pron. pl. the objective case of WE

U.S. United States (of America)

use (juːz) vt. **1.** employ, avail oneself of **2.** exercise **3.** exploit **4.** consume —n. (juːs) **5.** employment, application to a purpose **6.** need to employ **7.** serviceableness **8.** profit **9.** habit —'**usable** or '**useable** a. fit for use —**usage** ('juːsɪdʒ, -zɪdʒ) n. **1.** act of using **2.** custom **3.** customary way of using —**used** a. second-hand, not new —**useful** ('juːsful) a. **1.** of use **2.** helpful **3.** serviceable —**usefully** ('juːsfəlɪ) adv. —**usefulness** ('juːsfulnɪs) n. —**useless** ('juːslɪs) a. —**uselessly** ('juːslɪslɪ) adv. —**uselessness** ('juːslɪsnɪs) n. —**user-friendly** a. (of computers) easy to operate —**used to** (juːst) a. **1.** accustomed to —vt. **2.** did so formerly

usher ('ʌʃə) n. **1.** doorkeeper, one showing people to seats etc. (**ushe'rette** fem.) —vt. **2.** introduce, announce **3.** inaugurate

U.S.S.R. Union of Soviet Socialist Republics

usual ('juːʒʊəl) a. habitual, ordinary —'**usually** adv. **1.** as a rule **2.** generally, commonly

usurp (juː'zɜːp) vt. seize wrongfully —**usur'pation** n. violent or unlawful seizing of power —u'surper n.

usury ('juːʒəri) n. **1.** lending of money at excessive interest **2.** such interest —'**usurer** n. money lender —u'**surious** a.

UT Utah

utensil (juːˈtɛnsəl) n. vessel, implement, esp. in domestic use

uterus ('juːtərəs) n. womb (pl. **uteri** ('juːtəraɪ)) —**uterine** ('juːtəraɪn) a. of the uterus

utilidor (juːˈtɪlɪdɔː; Canad. ˈdɒr) n. C above-ground insulated casing for pipes

utility (juːˈtɪlɪti) n. **1.** usefulness **2.** benefit **3.** useful thing —a. **4.** made for practical purposes —**utili'tarian** a. **1.** useful rather than beautiful **2.** of utilitarianism —n. **3.** believer in utilitarianism —**utili'tarianism** n. doctrine that morality of actions is to be tested by their utility, esp. that the greatest good of the greatest number should be the sole end of public action —**utili'zation** or **-li'sation** n. —**utilize** or **-lise** vt. make use of —**utility room** room used for storage, laundry etc. —**utility truck A, NZ** small truck with open body and low sides

utmost ('ʌtməʊst) or **uttermost** a. **1.** to the highest degree **2.** extreme, furthest —n. **3.** greatest possible amount

Utopia (juːˈtəʊpɪə) n. (sometimes u-) imaginary state with perfect political and social conditions or constitution —U'**topian** a. (sometimes u-) ideally perfect but impracticable

utter[1] ('ʌtə) vt. **1.** express, emit audibly, say **2.** put in circulation (forged banknotes, counterfeit coin) —'**utterance** n. **1.** act of speaking **2.** expression in words **3.** spoken words

utter[2] ('ʌtə) a. complete, total, absolute —'**utterly** adv.

uttermost ('ʌtəməʊst) see UTMOST

U-turn n. **1.** U-shaped turn by vehicle in order to go in opposite direction **2.** reversal of political policy

U.V. ultraviolet

uvula ('juːvjʊlə) n. pendent fleshy part of soft palate (pl. **-lae** (-liː), **-s**) —'**uvular** a.

uxorious (ʌkˈsɔːrɪəs) a. excessively fond of one's wife

V, v

v or **V** (viː) n. **1.** 22nd letter of English alphabet **2.** speech sound represented by this letter, as in vote **3.** something shaped like V (pl. **v's, V's** or **Vs**)

v volt

V Chem. vanadium

v. 1. verb **2.** verso **3.** versus **4.** very **5.** vide

V-1 n. flying robot bomb invented by Germans in World War II (also '**doodlebug**, '**buzzbomb**)

VA Virginia

V.A. 1. Vicar Apostolic **2.** (Order of) Victoria and Albert

vacant ('veɪkənt) a. **1.** without thought, empty **2.** unoccupied —'**vacancy** n. **1.** state of being unoccupied **2.** unfilled post, accommodation etc. —'**vacantly** adv.

vacate (vəˈkeɪt) vt. quit, leave empty —**va'cation** n. **1.** time when universities and law courts are closed **2.** US holidays **3.** act of vacating

vaccinate ('væksɪneɪt) vt. inoculate with vaccine as protection against a specific disease —**vacci'nation** n. —'**vaccinator** n. —**vaccine** ('væksiːn) n. any substance used for inoculation against disease

vacillate ('væsɪleɪt) vi. **1.** fluctuate in opinion **2.** waver **3.** move to and fro —**vacil'lation** n. **1.** indecision **2.** wavering **3.** unsteadiness

vacuum ('vækjʊəm) n. **1.** place, region containing no matter and from which all or most air, gas has been removed (pl. **-s, -ua** (-jʊə)) —v. **2.** clean with vacuum cleaner —**va'cuity** n. —'**vacuous** a. **1.** vacant **2.** expressionless **3.** unintelligent —**vacuum cleaner** apparatus for removing dust by suction —**vacuum flask** double-walled flask with vacuum between walls, for keeping contents of inner flask at temperature at which they were inserted —**vacuum-packed** a. packed in airtight container to maintain freshness etc. —**vacuum pump** pump for producing low gas pressure —**vacuum tube** or **valve** see VALVE (sense 3)

vade mecum ('vɑːdɪ 'meɪkʊm) handbook etc. carried on person for immediate use when needed

vagabond ('vægəbɒnd) n. **1.** person with no fixed home **2.** wandering beggar or thief —a. **3.** like a vagabond

vagary ('veɪgəri, vəˈgɛəri) n. **1.** something unusual, erratic **2.** whim

vagina (vəˈdʒaɪnə) n. passage from womb to exterior —va'**ginal** a.

vagrant ('veɪgrənt) n. **1.** vagabond, tramp —a. **2.** wandering, esp. without purpose —'**vagrancy** n.

vague (veɪg) a. **1.** indefinite, uncertain **2.** indistinct **3.** not clearly expressed **4.** absent-minded

vain (veɪn) a. **1.** conceited **2.** worthless, useless **3.** unavailing **4.** foolish —'**vainly** adv.

vainglory (veɪnˈglɔːri) n. boastfulness, vanity —**vain'glorious** a.

valance ('væləns) n. short curtain round base of bed etc.

vale (veɪl) n. Poet. valley

valediction (vælɪ'dɪkʃən) *n.* farewell —**vale'dictory** *n.* **1.** farewell address —*a.* **2.** parting, farewell

valency ('veɪlənsɪ) *or esp. U.S.* **valence** ('veɪləns) *n. Chem.* combining power of element or atom

valentine ('væləntaɪn) *n.* (one receiving) card, gift, expressing affection on Saint Valentine's Day, Feb. 14th

valet ('vælɪt, 'væleɪ) *n.* gentleman's personal servant

valetudinarian (vælɪtjuːdɪ'nɛərɪən) *or* **valetudinary** (vælɪ'tjuːdɪnərɪ) *a.* **1.** sickly **2.** infirm —*n.* **3.** person obliged or disposed to live the life of an invalid

valiant ('væljənt) *a.* brave, courageous

valid ('vælɪd) *a.* **1.** sound **2.** capable of being justified **3.** of binding force in law —**va'lidity** *n.* **1.** soundness **2.** power to convince **3.** legal force —'**validate** *vt.* make valid

valise (vɔ'liːz) *n.* travelling bag

valley ('vælɪ) *n.* **1.** low area between hills **2.** river basin

valour *or U.S.* **valor** ('vælə) *n.* bravery —'**valorous** *a.*

value ('væljuː) *n.* **1.** worth **2.** utility **3.** equivalent **4.** importance —*pl.* **5.** principles, standards —*vt.* **6.** estimate value of **7.** hold in respect **8.** prize —'**valuable** *a.* **1.** precious **2.** worthy **3.** capable of being valued —*n.* **4.** (*usu. pl.*) valuable thing —**valu'ation** *n.* estimated worth —'**valued** *a.* **1.** estimated; appraised **2.** highly thought of —'**valueless** *a.* worthless —'**valuer** *n.* —**value added tax** tax on difference between cost of basic materials and cost of article made from them —**value judgment** subjective assessment based on one's own values or those of one's class

valve (vælv) *n.* **1.** device to control passage of fluid *etc.* through pipe **2.** *Anat.* part of body allowing one-way passage of fluids **3.** part of radio or television which controls flow of current **4.** any of separable parts of shell of mollusc **5.** *Mus.* device on brass instrument for lengthening tube —'**valvular** *a.* of, like valves

vamoose (vɔ'muːs) *vi. sl.* depart quickly

vamp[1] (væmp) *inf. n.* **1.** woman who deliberately allures men —*v.* **2.** exploit (man) as vamp

vamp[2] (væmp) *n.* **1.** something patched up (*also* re'**vamp**) **2.** front part of shoe upper —*vt.* **3.** patch up, rework

vampire ('væmpaɪə) *n.* in folklore, corpse that rises from dead to drink blood of the living —**vampire bat** bat that sucks blood of animals

van[1] (væn) *n.* **1.** covered vehicle, *esp.* for goods **2.** railway carriage for goods and use of guard

van[2] (væn) *n.* vanguard

vanadium (vɔ'neɪdɪəm) *n.* metallic element used in manufacture of hard steel

vandal ('vændəl) *n.* one who wantonly and deliberately damages or destroys —'**vandalism** *n.* —'**vandalize** *or* -**lise** *vt.*

Vandyke beard (væn'daɪk) short pointed beard (*also* '**Vandyke**)

vane (veɪn) *n.* **1.** weathercock **2.** blade of propeller **3.** fin on bomb *etc.* **4.** sight on quadrant

vanguard ('vængɑːd) *n.* leading, foremost group, position *etc.*

vanilla (vɔ'nɪlə) *n.* **1.** tropical climbing orchid **2.** its seed(pod) **3.** essence of this for flavouring

vanish ('vænɪʃ) *vi.* **1.** disappear **2.** fade away —**vanishing cream** cosmetic cream that is colourless once applied, used as foundation or cleansing cream —**vanishing point 1.** point to which parallel lines appear to converge **2.** point at which something disappears

vanity ('vænɪtɪ) *n.* **1.** excessive pride or conceit **2.** ostentation —**vanity case** *or* **box** woman's small hand case for carrying cosmetics *etc.*

vanquish ('væŋkwɪʃ) *vt.* **1.** subdue in battle **2.** conquer, overcome —'**vanquishable** *a.* —'**vanquisher** *n.*

vantage ('vɑːntɪdʒ) *n.* advantage

vapid ('væpɪd) *a.* flat, dull, insipid —va'**pidity** *n.*

vapour *or U.S.* **vapor** ('veɪpə) *n.* **1.** gaseous form of a substance more familiar as liquid or solid **2.** steam, mist **3.** invisible moisture in air —'**vaporize** *or* -**rise** *v.* convert into, pass off in, vapour —'**vaporizer** *or* -**riser** *n.* —'**vaporous** *a.*

variable ('vɛərɪəbəl) *see* VARY

varicose ('værɪkəʊs) *a.* (of vein), swollen, twisted

variegate ('vɛərɪgeɪt) *vt.* diversify by patches of different colours —'**variegated** *a.* streaked, spotted, dappled —**varie'gation** *n.*

variety (vɔ'raɪɪtɪ) *n.* **1.** state of being varied or various **2.** diversity **3.** varied assortment **4.** sort, kind

various ('vɛərɪəs) *a.* manifold, diverse, of several kinds

varlet ('vɑːlɪt) *n.* formerly, menial servant, rascal

varmint ('vɑːmɪnt) *n. inf.* obnoxious person or animal

varnish ('vɑːnɪʃ) *n.* **1.** resinous solution put on a surface to make it hard and shiny —*vt.* **2.** apply varnish to

varsity ('vɑːsɪtɪ) *n. UK inf.* university

vary ('vɛərɪ) *v.* (cause to) change, diversify, differ, deviate ('**varied**, '**varying**) —**varia'bility** *n.* —'**variable** *a.* **1.** changeable **2.** unsteady; fickle —*n.* **3.** something subject to variation —'**variance** *n.* state of discord, discrepancy —'**variant** *a.* **1.** different —*n.* **2.** difference in form **3.** alternative form or reading —**vari'ation** *n.* **1.** alteration **2.** extent to which thing varies **3.** modification —**vari'ational** *a.* —**'varied** *a.* **1.** diverse **2.** modified **3.** variegated

vas (væs) *n. Anat.* vessel, tube carrying bodily fluid (*pl.* **vasa** ('veɪsə)) —**vas deferens** ('dɛfərɛnz) duct within each testis that conveys spermatozoa to ejaculatory duct (*pl.* **vasa deferentia** (dɛfə'rɛnʃɪə))

vascular ('væskjulə) *a.* of, with vessels for conveying sap, blood *etc.*

vase (vɑːz) *n.* vessel, jar as ornament or for holding flowers

vasectomy (væ'sɛktəmɪ) *n.* contraceptive measure of surgical removal of part of vas bearing sperm from testicle

Vaseline ('væsɪliːn) *n.* **R** jellylike petroleum product

vassal ('væsəl) *n.* **1.** holder of land by feudal tenure **2.** dependant —**'vassalage** *n.*

vast (vɑːst) *a.* very large —**'vastly** *adv.* —**'vastness** *n.*

vat (væt) *n.* large tub, tank

VAT (*sometimes* væt) value added tax

Vatican ('vætɪkən) *n.* **1.** Pope's palace **2.** papal authority

vaudeville ('vɔːdəvɪl, 'vəʊ-) *n.* theatrical entertainment with songs, juggling acts, dance *etc.*

vault[1] (vɔːlt) *n.* **1.** arched roof **2.** arched apartment **3.** cellar **4.** burial chamber **5.** place for storing valuables —*vt.* **6.** build with arched roof —**'vaulting** *n.* one or more vaults in building or such structures collectively

vault[2] (vɔːlt) *v.* **1.** spring, jump over (object) with the hands resting on something —*n.* **2.** such jump —**'vaulting** *a.* **1.** excessively confident **2.** used to vault

vaunt (vɔːnt) *v./n.* boast

vb. verb

V.C. 1. Vice Chairman **2.** Vice Chancellor **3.** Victoria Cross **4.** Viet Cong

VD venereal disease

VDU visual display unit

veal (viːl) *n.* calf flesh as food

vector ('vɛktə) *n.* **1.** quantity (*eg* force) having both magnitude and direction **2.** disease-carrying organism, *esp.* insect **3.** compass direction, course

V-E Day day marking Allied victory in Europe in World War II (May 8th, 1945)

veer (vɪə) *vi.* **1.** change direction **2.** change one's mind

vegan ('viːgən) *n.* strict vegetarian, who does not eat animal products

vegetable ('vɛdʒtəbəl) *n.* **1.** plant, *esp.* edible one **2.** *inf.* person who has lost use of his mental faculties, limbs *etc.* **3.** *inf.* dull person —*a.* **4.** of,

from, concerned with plants —**vegetable marrow** plant with long, green-striped fruit, eaten as vegetable —**vegetable oil** any of group of oils obtained from plants

vegetarian (vɛdʒɪ'tɛərɪən) *n.* **1.** one who does not eat meat —*a.* **2.** not eating meat; without meat —**vege'tarianism** *n.*

vegetate ('vɛdʒɪteɪt) *vi.* **1.** (of plants) grow, develop **2.** (of person) live dull, unproductive life —**vege'tation** *n.* **1.** plants collectively **2.** plants growing in a place **3.** process of plant growth —**vegetative** ('vɛdʒɪtətɪv) *a.*

vehement ('viːɪmənt) *a.* **1.** marked by intensity of feeling **2.** vigorous **3.** forcible —**'vehemence** *n.* —**'vehemently** *adv.*

vehicle ('viːɪkəl) *n.* **1.** means of conveying **2.** means of expression **3.** medium —**vehicular** (vɪ'hɪkjulə) *a.*

veil (veɪl) *n.* **1.** light material to cover face or head **2.** mask, cover —*vt.* **3.** cover with, as with, veil —**veiled** *a.* disguised —**take the veil** become a nun

vein (veɪn) *n.* **1.** tube in body taking blood to heart **2.** rib of leaf or insect's wing **3.** fissure in rock filled with ore **4.** streak **5.** distinctive trait, strain *etc.* **6.** mood —*vt.* **7.** mark with streaks —**'veiny** *a.* —**venation** (viː'neɪʃən) *n.* **1.** arrangement of veins in leaf *etc.* **2.** such veins collectively —**'venous** *a.* of veins

Velcro ('vɛlkrəʊ) *n.* **R** fastening consisting of two strips of nylon fabric, one having tiny hooked threads and the other a coarse surface, that form strong bond when pressed together

veld *or* **veldt** (fɛlt, vɛlt) *n.* elevated grassland in S Afr. —**veldskoen** (fɛltskun, 'vɛlt-) *n.* SA ankle-length boot *orig.* of raw hide

veleta *or* **valeta** (və'liːtə) *n.* ballroom dance in triple time

vellum ('vɛləm) *n.* **1.** parchment of calfskin used for manuscripts or bindings **2.** paper resembling this

velocipede (vɪ'lɒsɪpiːd) *n.* early form of bicycle

velocity (vɪ'lɒsɪtɪ) *n.* **1.** rate of motion in given direction, *esp.* of inanimate things **2.** speed

velodrome ('viːlədrəʊm, 'vɛl-) *n.* area with banked track for cycle racing

velours *or* **velour** (və'lʊə) *n.* fabric with velvety finish

velum ('viːləm) *n.* **1.** *Zool.* membranous covering or organ **2.** soft palate (*pl.* **vela** ('viːlə))

velvet ('vɛlvɪt) *n.* silk or cotton fabric with thick, short pile —**velve'teen** *n.* cotton fabric resembling velvet —**'velvety** *a.* **1.** of, like velvet **2.** soft and smooth

vena cava ('viːnə 'keɪvə) either of two large veins that convey oxygen-depleted blood to heart (*pl.* **venae cavae** ('viːniː 'keɪviː))

venal ('vi:nəl) *a.* **1.** guilty of taking, prepared to take, bribes **2.** corrupt —**ve'nality** *n.*

vend (vɛnd) *vt.* sell —**'vendible** *a.* **1.** saleable, marketable **2.** (*usu. pl.*) *rare* saleable object —**'vendor** *n.* —**vending machine** machine that automatically dispenses goods when money is inserted

vendetta (vɛn'dɛtə) *n.* bitter, prolonged feud

veneer (vɪ'nɪə) *n.* **1.** thin layer of fine wood **2.** superficial appearance —*vt.* **3.** cover with veneer

venerable ('vɛnərəbəl) *a.* worthy of reverence —**'venerate** *vt.* look up to, respect, revere —**vener'ation** *n.*

venereal (vɪ'nɪərɪəl) *a.* **1.** (of disease) transmitted by sexual intercourse **2.** infected with venereal disease **3.** of genitals or sexual intercourse

venery[1] ('vɛnərɪ, 'vi:-) *n. obs.* pursuit of sexual gratification

venery[2] ('vɛnərɪ, 'vi:-) *n. Hist.* art, practice of hunting

Venetian (vɪ'ni:ʃən) *a.* **1.** of Venice, port in NE Italy —*n.* **2.** native or inhabitant of Venice —**Venetian blind** window blind made of thin horizontal slats arranged to turn so as to admit or exclude light

vengeance ('vɛndʒəns) *n.* **1.** revenge **2.** retribution for wrong done —**'vengeful** *a.*

venial ('vi:nɪəl) *a.* pardonable

venison ('vɛnɪzən, -sən) *n.* flesh of deer as food

venom ('vɛnəm) *n.* **1.** poison **2.** spite —**'venomous** *a.* poisonous

venous ('vi:nəs) *a. see* VEIN

vent[1] (vɛnt) *n.* **1.** small hole or outlet —*vt.* **2.** give outlet to **3.** utter **4.** pour forth

vent[2] (vɛnt) *n.* vertical slit in garment, *esp.* at back of jacket

ventilate ('vɛntɪleɪt) *vt.* **1.** supply with fresh air **2.** bring into discussion —**venti'lation** *n.* —**'ventilator** *n.*

ventral ('vɛntrəl) *a.* abdominal

ventricle ('vɛntrɪkəl) *n.* cavity, hollow in body, *esp.* in heart or brain —**ven'tricular** *a.*

ventriloquist (vɛn'trɪləkwɪst) *n.* one who can so speak that the sounds seem to come from some other person or place —**ven'triloquism** *n.*

venture ('vɛntʃə) *vt.* **1.** expose to hazard **2.** risk —*vi.* **3.** dare **4.** have courage (to do something or go somewhere) —*n.* **5.** risky undertaking **6.** speculative commercial undertaking —**'venturesome** *or* **'venturous** *a.*

venue ('vɛnju:) *n.* **1.** *Law* district in which case is tried **2.** meeting place **3.** location

Venus ('vi:nəs) *n.* **1.** Roman goddess of love **2.** planet between earth and Mercury —**Venus's flytrap** insect-eating plant

veracious (vɛ'reɪʃəs) *a.* **1.** truthful **2.** true —**veracity** (vɛ'ræsɪtɪ) *n.*

veranda *or* **verandah** (və'rændə) *n.* open or partly enclosed porch on outside of house

verb (vɜ:b) *n.* part of speech used to express action or being —**'verbal** *a.* **1.** of, by, or relating to words spoken rather than written **2.** of, like a verb —**'verbalism** *n.* **1.** verbal expression; phrase; word **2.** exaggerated emphasis on importance of words **3.** statement lacking real content —**'verbalize** *or* **-lise** *vt.* **1.** put into words —*vi.* **2.** speak —**'verbally** *adv.* —**verbatim** (vɜ:'beɪtɪm) *adv./a.* word for word, literal(ly) —**verbal noun** noun derived from verb

verbascum (vɜ:'bæskəm) *n.* perennial garden plant

verbena (vɜ:'bi:nə) *n.* **1.** genus of fragrant, beautiful plants **2.** their characteristic scent

verbiage ('vɜ:bɪɪdʒ) *n.* excess of words —**verbose** (vɜ:'bəus) *a.* wordy, long-winded —**verbosity** (vɜ:'bɒsɪtɪ) *n.*

verdant ('vɜ:dənt) *a.* green and fresh —**'verdure** *n.* **1.** greenery **2.** freshness —**'verdurous** *a.*

verdict ('vɜ:dɪkt) *n.* **1.** decision of a jury **2.** opinion reached after examination of facts

verdigris ('vɜ:dɪgrɪs) *n.* green film on copper

verdure ('vɜ:dʒə) *n. see* VERDANT

verge (vɜ:dʒ) *n.* **1.** edge **2.** brink **3.** grass border along a road —*vi.* **4.** (*with* on) come close (to) **5.** (*sometimes with* on) be on the border (of)

verger ('vɜ:dʒə) *n.* **1.** caretaker and attendant in church **2.** bearer of wand of office

verify ('vɛrɪfaɪ) *vt.* **1.** prove, confirm truth of **2.** test accuracy of (**-ified, -ifying**) —**'verifiable** *a.* —**verifi'cation** *n.*

verily ('vɛrɪlɪ) *adv. obs.* **1.** truly **2.** in truth

verisimilitude (vɛrɪsɪ'mɪlɪtju:d) *n.* **1.** appearance of truth **2.** likelihood —**veri'similar** *a.* probable; likely

veritable ('vɛrɪtəbəl) *a.* actual, true, genuine —**'veritably** *adv.*

verity ('vɛrɪtɪ) *n.* **1.** truth **2.** reality **3.** true assertion

verkrampte (fə'krɑmtə) *n.* SA Afrikaner Nationalist opposed to liberal trends in government policy, particularly those related to race

verligte (fə'lɔxtə) *n.* SA member of any white political party who supports more liberal trends in government policy

vermi- (*comb. form*) worm, as in *vermicide, vermiform, vermifuge*

vermicelli (vɜ:mɪ'sɛlɪ, -'tʃɛlɪ) *n.* **1.** pasta in fine strands, used in soups **2.** tiny chocolate strands used to coat cakes *etc.*

vermicide ('vɜ:mɪsaɪd) *n.* substance to

destroy worms —**ver'micular** a. **1.** resembling form, motion or tracks of worms **2.** of worms —**'vermiform** a. shaped like a worm (eg **vermiform appendix**)

vermilion (vəˈmiljən) a./n. (of) bright red colour or pigment

vermin (ˈvɜːmin) n. (with pl. v.) injurious animals, parasites etc. —**'verminous** a.

vermouth (ˈvɜːməθ) n. wine flavoured with aromatic herbs etc.

vernacular (vəˈnækjulə) n. **1.** commonly spoken language or dialect of particular country or place —a. **2.** of vernacular **3.** native

vernal (ˈvɜːnəl) a. of spring

vernier (ˈvɜːniə) n. sliding scale for obtaining fractional parts of subdivision of graduated scale

veronica (vəˈrɒnikə) n. genus of plants including speedwell

verruca (veˈruːkə) n. wart, esp. on foot

versatile (ˈvɜːsətail) a. **1.** capable of or adapted to many different uses, skills etc. **2.** liable to change —**versatility** (vɜːsəˈtiliti) n.

verse (vɜːs) n. **1.** stanza or short subdivision of poem or the Bible **2.** poetry **3.** line of poetry —**versifi'cation** n. —**'versify** v. turn (something) into verse (**-ified, -ifying**) —**versed** in skilled in

version (ˈvɜːʃən) n. **1.** description from certain point of view **2.** translation **3.** adaptation

verso (ˈvɜːsəu) n. back of sheet of printed paper, left-hand page (pl. **-s**)

versus (ˈvɜːsəs) prep. against

vertebra (ˈvɜːtibrə) n. single section of backbone (pl. **-brae** (-briː), **-s**) —**'vertebral** a. of the spine —**'vertebrate** n. **1.** animal with backbone —a. **2.** having a backbone

vertex (ˈvɜːteks) n. summit (pl. **-es, vertices** (ˈvɜːtisiːz))

vertical (ˈvɜːtikəl) a. **1.** at right angles to the horizon **2.** upright **3.** overhead

vertigo (ˈvɜːtigəu) n. giddiness (pl. **-es, vertigines** (vɜːˈtidʒiniːz)) —**vertiginous** (vɜːˈtidʒinəs) a. dizzy

vertu (vɜːˈtuː) n. see VIRTU

verve (vɜːv) n. **1.** enthusiasm **2.** spirit **3.** energy, vigour

very (ˈveri) a. **1.** exact, ideal **2.** same **3.** complete **4.** actual —adv. **5.** extremely, to great extent —**very high frequency** radio frequency or band lying between 300 and 30 megahertz —**very low frequency** radio frequency band or radio frequency lying between 30 and 3 kilohertz

vesicle (ˈvesikəl) n. small blister, bubble or cavity —**ve'sicular** a.

vespers (ˈvespəz) n. **1.** evening church service **2.** evensong

vessel (ˈvesəl) n. **1.** any object used as container, esp. for liquids **2.** ship, large boat **3.** tubular structure conveying liquids (eg blood) in body

vest (vest) n. **1.** undergarment for the trunk —vt. **2.** place **3.** bestow **4.** confer **5.** clothe —**'vestment** n. robe or official garment —**vested interest** strong personal interest in particular state of affairs

vestal (ˈvestəl) a. pure, chaste —**vestal virgin** in ancient Rome, one of virgin priestesses whose lives were dedicated to Vesta and to maintaining sacred fire in her temple

vestibule (ˈvestibjuːl) n. entrance hall, lobby

vestige (ˈvestidʒ) n. small trace, amount —**ves'tigial** a.

vestry (ˈvestri) n. room in church for keeping vestments, holding meetings etc.

vet (vet) n. **1.** veterinary surgeon —vt. **2.** examine **3.** check (**-tt-**)

vet. **1.** veteran **2.** veterinary

vetch (vetʃ) n. plant of bean family

veteran (ˈvetərən) n. **1.** one who has served a long time, esp. in fighting services —a. **2.** long-serving —**veteran car** UK car constructed before 1919, esp. before 1905

veterinary (ˈvetərinəri) a. of, concerning the health of animals —**veterinary surgeon** surgeon qualified to treat animal ailments

veto (ˈviːtəu) n. **1.** power of rejecting piece of legislation or preventing it from coming into effect **2.** any prohibition (pl. **-es**) —vt. **3.** enforce veto against **4.** forbid with authority

vex (veks) vt. **1.** annoy **2.** distress —**vex'ation** n. **1.** cause of irritation **2.** state of distress —**vex'atious** a. —**vexed** a. **1.** cross, annoyed **2.** much discussed

VHF or **vhf** very high frequency

V.I. Vancouver Island

via (ˈvaiə) prep. by way of

viable (ˈvaiəbəl) a. **1.** practicable **2.** able to live and grow independently —**via'bility** n.

viaduct (ˈvaiədʌkt) n. bridge over valley for a road or railway

vial (ˈvaiəl) n. see PHIAL

viands (ˈvaiəndz) pl.n. food

viaticum (vaiˈætikəm) n. **1.** Holy Communion as administered to person dying or in danger of death **2.** rare provisions or travel allowance for journey (pl. **-ca** (-kə), **-s**)

vibes (vaibz) pl.n. inf. **1.** vibrations **2.** vibraphone

vibraphone (ˈvaibrəfəun) n. musical instrument like xylophone, but with electronic resonators, that produces a gentle vibrato

vibrate (vaiˈbreit) v. **1.** (cause to) move to and fro rapidly and continuously **2.** give off (light or sound) by vibration —vi. **3.** oscillate **4.** quiver

—'**vibrant** *a.* **1.** throbbing **2.** vibrating **3.** appearing vigorous, lively —**vi'bration** *n.* **1.** a vibrating —*pl.* **2.** *inf.* instinctive feelings about a place, person *etc.* —**vibrato** (vɪ'brɑːtəʊ) *n.* vibrating effect in music (*pl.* **-s**) —**vi'brator** *n.* —'**vibratory** *a.*

viburnum (vaɪ'bɜːnəm) *n.* subtropical shrub with white flowers and berrylike fruits

Vic. A Victoria (state)

vicar ('vɪkə) *n.* clergyman in charge of parish —'**vicarage** *n.* vicar's house —**vicarial** (vɪ'kɛərɪəl) *a.* of vicar —**vicar apostolic** *R.C. Ch.* titular bishop having jurisdiction in missionary countries —**vicar general** official appointed to assist bishop of diocese in administrative or judicial duties (*pl.* **vicars general**) —**Vicar of Christ** *R.C.Ch.* the Pope

vicarious (vɪ'kɛərɪəs, vaɪ-) *a.* **1.** obtained, enjoyed or undergone at second hand through sympathetic participation in another's experiences **2.** suffered, done *etc.* as substitute for another —**vi'cariously** *adv.*

vice[1] (vaɪs) *n.* **1.** evil or immoral habit or practice **2.** criminal immorality, *esp.* prostitution **3.** fault, imperfection —**vice squad** police division which deals with enforcement of gaming and prostitution laws

vice[2] *or U.S.* (oft.) **vise** (vaɪs) *n.* appliance with screw jaw for holding things while working on them

vice[3] (vaɪs) *n. inf.* person who serves as deputy to another

vice- (*comb. form*) in place of, second to, as in *vice-chairman, viceroy.* Such compounds are not given here where meaning may be inferred from simple word

vice admiral commissioned officer of flag rank in certain navies, junior to admiral and senior to rear admiral

vicegerent (vaɪs'dʒɛrənt) *n.* **1.** person appointed to exercise all or some of authority of another **2.** *R.C.Ch.* representative of God or Christ on earth, such as pope —*a.* **3.** invested with or characterized by delegated authority —**vice'gerency** *n.*

vice president officer ranking immediately below president and serving as his deputy —**vice-presidency** *n.*

viceroy ('vaɪsrɔɪ) *n.* ruler acting for king in province or dependency (**vicereine** (vaɪs'reɪn) *fem.*) —**vice'regal** *a.* of viceroy —**vice'royalty** *n.*

vice versa ('vaɪsɪ 'vɜːsə) *Lat.* conversely, the other way round

vichy water ('vɪʃɪ) **1.** (*sometimes* V-) mineral water from Vichy in France, reputed to be beneficial to health **2.** any sparkling mineral water resembling this

vicinage ('vɪsɪnɪdʒ) *n. rare* **1.** residents of particular neighbourhood **2.** vicinity

vicinity (vɪ'sɪnɪtɪ) *n.* neighbourhood

vicious ('vɪʃəs) *a.* **1.** wicked, cruel **2.** ferocious, dangerous **3.** leading to vice —'**viciously** *adv.* —**vicious circle 1.** situation in which attempt to resolve one problem creates new problems that lead back to original situation **2.** *Logic* invalid form of reasoning in which conclusion is derived from premiss orig. deduced from same conclusion **3.** *Logic* circular definition

vicissitude (vɪ'sɪsɪtjuːd) *n.* **1.** change of fortune —*pl.* **2.** ups and downs of fortune —**vicissi'tudinous** *a.*

victim ('vɪktɪm) *n.* **1.** person or thing killed, injured *etc.* as result of another's deed, or accident, circumstances *etc.* **2.** person cheated **3.** sacrifice —**victimi'zation** *or* **-mi'sation** *n.* —'**victimize** *or* **-mise** *vt.* **1.** punish unfairly **2.** make victim of

victor ('vɪktə) *n.* **1.** conqueror **2.** winner —**vic'torious** *a.* **1.** winning **2.** triumphant —'**victory** *n.* winning of battle *etc.*

victoria (vɪk'tɔːrɪə) *n.* **1.** four-wheeled horse-drawn carriage with folding hood **2. UK** large sweet plum, red and yellow in colour (*also* **victoria plum**)

Victorian (vɪk'tɔːrɪən) *a.* **1.** of Victoria, queen of Great Brit. and Ireland, or period of her reign **2.** exhibiting characteristics popularly attributed to Victorians, *esp.* prudery *etc.* **3.** of Victoria (state in Aust. or any of the cities) —*n.* **4.** person who lived during reign of Queen Victoria **5.** inhabitant of Victoria (state or any of the cities) —**Victoria Cross** highest decoration for gallantry in face of enemy awarded to Brit. and Commonwealth armed forces —**Victoria Day** Monday preceding May 24th: national holiday in Canad. in commemoration of Queen Victoria's birthday

victual ('vɪtl) *n.* **1.** (*usu. pl.*) food —*v.* **2.** supply with or obtain food (**-ll-**) —'**victualler** *n.*

vicuña (vɪ'kjuːnə, -'kuːnjə) *n.* **1.** S Amer. animal like llama **2.** fine, light cloth made from its wool

vide ('vaɪdɪ) *Lat.* see —**vide infra** see below —**vide supra** see above

videlicet (vɪ'diːlɪset) *Lat.* namely

video ('vɪdɪəʊ) *a.* **1.** relating to or used in transmission or production of television image —*n.* **2.** apparatus for recording television programmes *etc.* —**video disc** *or* '**videodisc** *n.* disc stored with information, which one plays like a gramophone record, the result being translated, in sound and vision, on to TV set —'**videophone** *n.* telephonic device in which there is both verbal and visual communication between parties —**video tape** magnetic tape on which to record television programme

vie (vaɪ) *vi.* (*with* with *or* for) contend, compete (against or for someone, something) (**vied, 'vying**)

Vietnamese (vjɛtnə'miːz) *a.* 1. of Vietnam, in SE Asia —*n.* 2. native of Vietnam (*pl.* **-ese**) 3. language of Vietnam

view (vjuː) *n.* 1. survey by eyes or mind 2. range of vision 3. picture 4. scene 5. opinion 6. purpose —*vt.* 7. look at 8. survey 9. consider —'**viewer** *n.* 1. one who views 2. one who watches television 3. optical device to assist viewing of photographic slides —'**viewfinder** *n.* device on camera enabling user to see what will be included in photograph —'**viewpoint** *n.* 1. way of regarding a subject 2. position commanding view of landscape

viewdata ('vjuːdeɪtə) *n. see* TELETEXT

vigil ('vɪdʒɪl) *n.* 1. a keeping awake, watch 2. eve of feast day —'**vigilance** *n.* —'**vigilant** *a.* watchful, alert —**vigilance committee** US self-appointed body of citizens organized to maintain order *etc.*

vigilante (vɪdʒɪ'læntɪ) *n.* one, *esp.* as member of group, who unofficially takes it upon himself to enforce law

vignette (vɪ'njɛt) *n.* 1. short literary essay, sketch 2. photograph or portrait with the background shaded off

vigour *or U.S.* **vigor** ('vɪgə) *n.* 1. force, strength 2. energy, activity —'**vigorous** *a.* 1. strong 2. energetic 3. flourishing —'**vigorously** *adv.*

Viking ('vaɪkɪŋ) *n.* medieval Scandinavian seafarer, raider, settler

vile (vaɪl) *a.* 1. very wicked, shameful 2. disgusting 3. despicable —'**vilely** *adv.* —'**vileness** *n.* —**vilification** (vɪlɪfɪ'keɪʃən) *n.* —**vilify** ('vɪlɪfaɪ) *vt.* 1. speak ill of 2. slander (**-ified, -ifying**)

villa ('vɪlə) *n.* 1. large, luxurious, country house 2. detached or semidetached suburban house

village ('vɪlɪdʒ) *n.* small group of houses in country area —'**villager** *n.*

villain ('vɪlən) *n.* 1. wicked person 2. *inf.* mischievous person —'**villainous** *a.* 1. wicked 2. vile —'**villainy** *n.*

villein ('vɪlən) *n.* in medieval Europe, peasant personally bound to his lord, to whom he paid dues and services in return for land —'**villeinage** *n.*

vim (vɪm) *n. inf.* force, energy

vinaigrette (vɪneɪ'grɛt) *n.* 1. small bottle of smelling salts 2. type of salad dressing

vinculum ('vɪŋkjʊləm) *n.* 1. line drawn above group of mathematical terms, used as sign of aggregation in mathematical expressions, as in $\overline{x+y}$ 2. *Anat.* bandlike structure, *esp.* uniting two or more parts (*pl.* **-la** (-lə))

vindicate ('vɪndɪkeɪt) *vt.* 1. clear of charges 2. justify 3. establish the truth or merit of —'**vindicable** *a.* capable of being vindicated; justifiable —**vindi'cation** *n.* —'**vindicator** *n.* —'**vindicatory** *n.*

vindictive (vɪn'dɪktɪv) *a.* 1. revengeful 2. inspired by resentment

vine (vaɪn) *n.* climbing plant bearing grapes —'**vinery** *n.* 1. hothouse for growing grapes 2. vineyard 3. vines collectively —**vinosity** (vɪ'nɒsɪtɪ) *n.* distinctive and essential quality and flavour of wine —**vintage** ('vɪntɪdʒ) *n.* 1. gathering of the grapes 2. the yield 3. wine of particular year 4. time of origin —*a.* 5. best and most typical —**vintner** ('vɪntnə) *n.* dealer in wine —**vintage car** *chiefly* UK old car, *esp.* constructed between 1919 and 1930 —**vineyard** ('vɪnjəd) *n.* plantation of vines

vinegar ('vɪnɪgə) *n.* acid liquid obtained from wine and other alcoholic liquors —'**vinegary** *a.* 1. like vinegar 2. sour 3. bad-tempered

vingt-et-un (vɛ̃te'œ̃) *Fr. see* PONTOON[2]

vini- *or before vowel* **vin-** (*comb. form*) wine, as in *viniculture*

viniculture ('vɪnɪkʌltʃə) *n.* process or business of growing grapes and making wine

vinyl ('vaɪnɪl) *n.* plastic material with variety of domestic and industrial uses

viol ('vaɪəl) *n.* early stringed instrument preceding violin —'**violist** *n.* person who plays viol

viola[2] (vɪ'əʊlə) *n. see* VIOLIN

viola[2] ('vaɪələ, vaɪ'əʊ-) *n.* single-coloured variety of pansy

violate ('vaɪəleɪt) *vt.* 1. break (law, agreement *etc.*), infringe 2. rape 3. outrage, desecrate —'**violable** *a.* —**vio'lation** *n.* —'**violator** *n.*

violent ('vaɪələnt) *a.* 1. marked by, due to, extreme force, passion or fierceness 2. of great force 3. intense —'**violence** *n.* —'**violently** *adv.*

violet ('vaɪəlɪt) *n.* 1. plant with small bluish-purple or white flowers 2. the flower 3. bluish-purple colour —*a.* 4. of this colour

violin (vaɪə'lɪn) *n.* small four-stringed musical instrument —**vi'ola** *n.* large violin with lower range —**vio'linist** *n.* —**violoncello** (vaɪələn'tʃɛləʊ) *n. see* CELLO —**viola da gamba** (vɪ'əʊlə də 'gæmbə) second largest and lowest member of viol family

V.I.P. very important person

viper ('vaɪpə) *n.* venomous snake

virago (vɪ'rɑːgəʊ) *n.* abusive woman (*pl.* **-es, -s**)

virgin ('vɜːdʒɪn) *n.* 1. one who has not had sexual intercourse 2. without experience of sexual intercourse 3. unsullied, fresh 4. (of land) untilled —'**virginal** *a.* 1. of, like virgin —*n.* 2. (*oft. pl.*) type of spinet —**vir'ginity** *n.* —**Virgin**

Birth doctrine that Jesus Christ was conceived solely by direct intervention of Holy Spirit so that Mary remained a virgin after his birth —**Virgin Mary** Mary, mother of Christ (*also* **the Virgin**)

Virginia creeper (vɔ'dʒɪnɪə) climbing plant that turns red in autumn

Virgo ('vɜːgəʊ) n. (virgin) 6th sign of the zodiac operative c. Aug. 22nd–Sept. 21st

virgule ('vɜːgjuːl) n. Print. see SOLIDUS

virile ('vɪraɪl) a. 1. (of male) capable of copulation or procreation 2. strong, forceful —**virility** (vɪ'rɪlɪtɪ) n.

virology (vaɪ'rolədʒɪ) n. see VIRUS

virtu or **vertu** (vɜː'tuː) n. 1. taste or love for curios or works of fine art 2. such objects collectively 3. quality of being appealing to connoisseur (*esp. in* **articles of virtu, objects of virtu**)

virtual ('vɜːtʃʊəl) a. so in effect, though not in appearance or name —**virtually** adv. practically, almost

virtue ('vɜːtjuː) n. 1. moral goodness 2. good quality 3. merit 4. inherent power —**virtuous** a. 1. morally good 2. chaste —**virtuously** adv.

virtuoso (vɜːtjʊ'əʊzəʊ) n. one with special skill, esp. in a fine art (pl. **-s, -si** (-ziː)) —**virtuosity** (vɜːtjʊ'osɪtɪ) n. great technical skill, esp. in a fine art, as music

virulent ('vɪrʊlənt) a. 1. very infectious, poisonous etc. 2. malicious

virus ('vaɪrəs) n. any of various submicroscopic organisms, some causing disease —**viral** a. of virus —**vi'rology** n. study of viruses

visa ('viːzə) n. endorsement on passport permitting the bearer to travel into country of issuing government —**visaed** a.

visage ('vɪzɪdʒ) n. face

vis-à-vis (viːzɑː'viː) Fr. 1. in relation to, regarding 2. opposite to

Visc. Viscount

viscera ('vɪsərə) pl.n. large internal organs of body, esp. of abdomen (sing. **viscus** ('vɪskəs)) —**visceral** a.

viscid ('vɪsɪd) a. sticky, of a consistency like treacle —**vis'cidity** n.

viscose ('vɪskəʊs) n. (substance used to produce) synthetic fabric

viscount ('vaɪkaʊnt) n. Brit. nobleman ranking below earl and above baron ('**viscountess** fem.)

viscous ('vɪskəs) a. thick and sticky —**vis'cosity** n.

visible ('vɪzɪbᵊl) a. that can be seen —**visi'bility** n. degree of clarity of atmosphere, esp. for navigation —'**visibly** adv.

vision ('vɪʒən) n. 1. sight 2. insight 3. dream 4. phantom 5. imagination —'**visionary** a. 1.

marked by vision 2. impractical —n. 3. mystic 4. impractical person

visit ('vɪzɪt) v. 1. go, come and see, stay temporarily with (someone) —n. 2. stay 3. call at person's home etc. 4. official call —'**visitant** n. 1. ghost; apparition 2. visitor or guest, usu. from far away 3. migratory bird that is present in particular region only at certain times (also '**visitor**) —**visi'tation** n. 1. formal visit or inspection 2. affliction or plague —'**visitor** n.

visor or **vizor** ('vaɪzə) n. 1. front part of helmet made to move up and down before face 2. eyeshade, esp. on car 3. peak on cap

vista ('vɪstə) n. view, esp. distant view

visual ('vɪʒʊəl, -zjʊ-) a. 1. of sight 2. visible —**visuali'zation** or **-li'sation** n. —'**visualize** or **-lise** vt. form mental image of —**visual aids** devices, such as films, slides etc., that display in visual form material to be understood or remembered

vital ('vaɪtᵊl) a. 1. necessary to, affecting life 2. lively, animated 3. essential 4. highly important —**vi'tality** n. life, vigour —'**vitalize** or **-lise** vt. 1. give life to 2. lend vigour to —'**vitally** adv. —'**vitals** pl.n. vital organs of body —**vital statistics** 1. data concerning human life or conditions affecting it, such as death rate 2. inf. measurements of woman's bust, waist and hips

vitamin ('vɪtəmɪn, 'vaɪ-) n. any of group of substances occurring in foodstuffs and essential to health

vitiate ('vɪʃɪeɪt) vt. 1. spoil 2. deprive of efficacy 3. invalidate —**viti'ation** n.

viticulture ('vɪtɪkʌltʃə) n. 1. science, art or process of cultivating grapevines 2. study of (growing of) grapes —**viti'culturist** n.

vitreous ('vɪtrɪəs) a. 1. of glass 2. glassy —**vitrifi'cation** n. —'**vitrify** v. convert or be converted into glass, or glassy substance (**-ified, -ifying**) —**vitreous humour** or **body** transparent gelatinous substance that fills eyeball between lens and retina

vitriol ('vɪtrɪol) n. 1. sulphuric acid 2. caustic speech —**vitri'olic** a.

vituperate (vɪ'tjuːpəreɪt) vt. abuse in words, revile —**vituper'ation** n. —**vi'tuperative** a.

viva ('viːvə) interj. long live; up with (specified person or thing)

vivace (vɪ'vɑːtʃɪ) a./adv. Mus. to be performed in brisk lively manner

vivacious (vɪ'veɪʃəs) a. lively, gay, sprightly —**vivacity** (vɪ'væsɪtɪ) n.

vivarium (vaɪ'veərɪəm) n. place where animals are kept under natural conditions for study etc. (pl. **-s, -ia** (-ɪə))

viva voce ('vaɪvə 'vəʊtʃɪ) Lat. adv. 1. by word of mouth —n. 2. oral examination (oft. '**viva**)

vivid ('vɪvɪd) a. 1. bright, intense 2. clear 3. lively, animated 4. graphic —'**vividly** adv.

vivify ('vɪvɪfaɪ) vt. animate, inspire (-**ified, -ifying**)

viviparous (vɪ'vɪpərəs) a. bringing forth young alive

vivisection (vɪvɪ'sɛkʃən) n. dissection of, or operating on, living animals —'**vivisect** v. subject (animal) to vivisection —**vivi'sectionist** n. —'**vivisector** n.

vixen ('vɪksən) n. 1. female fox 2. spiteful woman —'**vixenish** a.

viz. videlicet

vizier (vɪ'zɪə) n. high official in some Muslim countries

vizor ('vaɪzə) n. see VISOR

V-J Day day marking Allied victory over Japan in World War II (Aug. 15th, 1945)

V.L. Vulgar Latin

vlei (fleɪ, vleɪ) n. SA low, marshy ground

VLF or **vlf** Rad. very low frequency

V neck neck on garment resembling shape of letter 'V' —**V-neck** or **V-necked** a.

voc. or **vocat.** vocative

vocable ('vəʊkəbəl) n. word regarded as sequence of letters or spoken sounds

vocabulary (və'kæbjʊlərɪ) n. 1. list of words, usu. in alphabetical order 2. stock of words used in particular language etc.

vocal ('vəʊkəl) a. 1. of, with, or giving out voice 2. outspoken, articulate —n. 3. piece of popular music that is sung —'**vocalist** n. singer —'**vocalize** or **-ise** vt. utter with voice —'**vocally** adv. —**vocal cords** either of two pairs of membranous folds in larynx.

vocalic (vəʊ'kælɪk) a. of vowel(s)

vocation (vəʊ'keɪʃən) n. (urge, inclination, predisposition to) particular career, profession etc. —vo'**cational** a. —**vocational guidance** guidance service based on psychological tests and interviews to find out what career may best suit person

vocative ('vɒkətɪv) n. in some languages, case of nouns used in addressing a person

vociferate (vəʊ'sɪfəreɪt) v. exclaim, cry out —**vocifer'ation** n. —vo'**ciferous** a. shouting, noisy

vodka ('vɒdkə) n. Russian spirit distilled from grain, potatoes etc.

vogue (vəʊg) n. 1. fashion, style 2. popularity

voice (vɔɪs) n. 1. sound given out by person in speaking, singing etc. 2. quality of the sound 3. expressed opinion 4. (right to) share in discussion 5. verbal form proper to relation of subject and action —vt. 6. give utterance to, express —'**voiceless** a. —**voice-over** n. voice of unseen commentator heard during film etc.

—'**voiceprint** n. graphic representation of person's voice recorded electronically

void (vɔɪd) a. 1. empty 2. destitute 3. not legally binding —n. 4. empty space —vt. 5. make ineffectual or invalid 6. empty out

voile (vɔɪl) n. light semitransparent fabric

vol. volume

volatile ('vɒlətaɪl) a. 1. evaporating quickly 2. lively 3. fickle, changeable —**volatility** (vɒlə'tɪlɪtɪ) n. —**volatilization** or **-lisation** (vɒlætɪlaɪ'zeɪʃən) n. —**volatilize** or **-lise** (vɒ'lætɪlaɪz) v. (cause to) evaporate

vol-au-vent (Fr. vɔlo'vɑ̃) n. small, light pastry case with savoury filling

volcano (vɒl'keɪnəʊ) n. 1. hole in earth's crust through which lava, ashes, smoke etc. are discharged 2. mountain so formed (pl. **-es, -s**) —**volcanic** (vɒl'kænɪk) a. —**volcanology** (vɒlkə'nɒlədʒɪ) or **vulca'nology** n. study of volcanoes and volcanic phenomena

vole (vəʊl) n. small rodent

volition (və'lɪʃən) n. 1. act, power of willing 2. exercise of the will —vo'**litional** a.

Volk (fɒlk) n. SA Afrikaner people

volley ('vɒlɪ) n. 1. simultaneous discharge of weapons or missiles 2. rush of oaths, questions etc. 3. Sport kick, stroke etc. at moving ball before it touches ground —vt. 4. discharge or be discharged —vt. 5. utter 6. fly, strike etc. in volley —'**volleyball** n. team game where large ball is hit by hand over high net

volt (vəʊlt) n. unit of electric potential —'**voltage** n. electric potential difference expressed in volts —'**voltmeter** n.

voltaic (vɒl'teɪɪk) a. see GALVANIC (sense 1)

volte-face ('vɒlt'fɑːs) Fr. n. complete reversal of opinion or direction (pl. **volte-face**)

voluble ('vɒljʊbəl) a. talking easily, readily and at length —**volu'bility** n. —'**volubly** adv.

volume ('vɒljuːm) n. 1. space occupied 2. bulk, mass 3. amount 4. power, fullness of voice or sound 5. control on radio etc. for adjusting this 6. book 7. part of book bound in one cover —**volu'metric** a. pert. to measurement by volume —**voluminous** (və'luːmɪnəs) a. bulky, copious

voluntary ('vɒləntərɪ) a. 1. having, done by free will 2. done without payment 3. supported by freewill contributions 4. spontaneous —n. 5. organ solo in church service —'**voluntarily** adv. —**volun'teer** n. 1. one who offers service, joins force etc. of his own free will —v. 2. offer oneself or one's services

voluptuous (və'lʌptjʊəs) a. of, contributing to pleasures of the senses —vo'**luptuary** n. one given to luxury and sensual pleasures

volute ('vɒljuːt, vɒ'luːt) n. spiral or twisting turn, form or object

vomit ('vomɪt) v. 1. eject (contents of stomach) through mouth —n. 2. matter vomited

voodoo ('vu:du:) n. 1. practice of black magic, *esp.* in W Indies, witchcraft —vt. 2. affect by voodoo

voorkamer ('fʊəka:mə) n. SA front room of a house

voorlaaier ('fʊəla:ə) n. SA muzzle-loading gun

voorskot ('fʊəskɒt) n. SA advance payment made to farmers' cooperative for a crop or wool clip

Voortrekker ('fʊətrɛkə) n. SA 1. one of original Afrikaner settlers of Transvaal and Orange Free State who migrated from Cape Colony in 1830s 2. member of Afrikaner youth movement founded in 1931

voracious (vɒ'reɪʃəs) a. greedy, ravenous —vo'raciously adv. —voracity (vɒ'ræsɪtɪ) n.

-vorous (a. comb. form) feeding on; devouring, as in *carnivorous* —-vore (n. comb. form)

vortex ('vɔ:tɛks) n. 1. whirlpool 2. whirling motion (pl. -es, vortices ('vɔ:tɪsi:z))

votary ('vəʊtərɪ) n. one vowed to service or pursuit —'votaress fem. —'votive a. given, consecrated by vow

vote (vəʊt) n. 1. formal expression of choice 2. individual pronouncement 3. right to give it, in question or election 4. result of voting 5. that which is given or allowed by vote —v. 6. express, declare opinion, choice, preference *etc.* by vote 7. authorize, enact *etc.* by vote —'voter n.

vouch (vaʊtʃ) vi. (usu. with for) guarantee, make oneself responsible (for) —'voucher n. 1. document proving correctness of item in accounts, or to establish facts 2. ticket as substitute for cash —vouch'safe vt. condescend to grant or do

vow (vaʊ) n. 1. solemn promise, *esp.* religious one —vt. 2. promise, threaten by vow

vowel ('vaʊəl) n. 1. any speech sound pronounced without stoppage or friction of the breath 2. letter standing for such sound, as a, e, i, o, u

vox (vɒks) n. voice; sound (pl. **voces** ('vəʊsi:z)) —**vox populi** ('pɒpjʊlaɪ) voice of the people; popular or public opinion

voyage ('vɔɪɪdʒ) n. 1. journey, *esp.* long one, by sea or air —vi. 2. make voyage —'voyager n. —voyageur (vwa:jɑ:'ʒɜ:; Fr. vwaja'ʒœːr) n. C guide, trapper in N regions

voyeur (vwa:'ɜ:) n. one obtaining sexual pleasure by watching sexual activities of others

V. Rev. Very Reverend

vs. versus

V.S. Veterinary Surgeon

V-sign n. 1. UK offensive gesture made by sticking up index and middle fingers with palm of hand inwards 2. similar gesture with palm outwards meaning victory or peace

V.S.O. Voluntary Service Overseas

V.S.O.P. very superior old pale

VT Vermont

VTOL ('vi:tɒl) vertical takeoff and landing

VTR video tape recorder

vulcanize or **-nise** ('vʌlkənaɪz) vt. treat (rubber) with sulphur at high temperature to increase its durability —'vulcanite n. rubber so hardened —vulcani'zation or -ni'sation n. —vulca'nology n. see volcanology at VOLCANO

Vulg. Vulgate

vulgar ('vʌlgə) a. 1. offending against good taste 2. coarse 3. common —vulgarian (vʌl'gɛərɪən) n. vulgar (rich) person —'vulgarism n. coarse, obscene word, phrase —vulgarity (vʌl'gærɪtɪ) n. —vulgari'zation or -ri'sation n. —'vulgarize or -rise vt. make vulgar or too common —'vulgarly adv. —vulgar fraction simple fraction —Vulgar Latin any of dialects of Latin spoken in Roman Empire other than classical Latin

Vulgate ('vʌlgeɪt, -gɪt) n. fourth-century Latin version of the Bible

vulnerable ('vʌlnərəbᵊl) a. 1. capable of being physically or emotionally wounded or hurt 2. exposed, open to attack, persuasion *etc.* —vulnera'bility n.

vulpine ('vʌlpaɪn) a. 1. of foxes 2. foxy

vulture ('vʌltʃə) n. large bird which feeds on carrion —'vulturine or 'vulturous a. 1. of vulture 2. rapacious

vulva ('vʌlvə) n. external genitals of human female

vv. 1. versus 2. *Mus.* volumes

v.v. vice versa

vying ('vaɪɪŋ) pr.p. of VIE

W,w

w or **W** ('dʌbᵊlju:) n. 1. 23rd letter of English alphabet 2. speech sound represented by this letter, usu. bilabial semivowel, as in *web* (pl. **w's, W's** or **Ws**)

W 1. Chem. tungsten 2. watt 3. Wednesday 4. west(ern)

w. 1. week 2. weight 3. width

W. 1. Wales 2. Welsh

WA Washington

W.A. 1. West Africa 2. Western Australia

WAAC (wæk) n. 1. Women's Army Auxiliary Corps 2. member of this corps (*also* waac)

WAAF (wæf) n. 1. Women's Auxiliary Air Force 2. member of this force (*also* Waaf)

wacky ('wækı) *a. sl.* eccentric or unpredictable

wad (wɒd) *n.* 1. small pad of fibrous material 2. thick roll of banknotes 3. sum of money —*vt.* 4. line, pad, stuff *etc.* with wad (-**dd**-) —'**wadding** *n.* stuffing

waddle ('wɒdªl) *vi.* 1. walk like duck —*n.* 2. this gait

wade (weɪd) *vi.* 1. walk through something that hampers movement, *esp.* water 2. proceed with difficulty —'**wader** *n.* 1. person or bird that wades —*pl.* 2. angler's high waterproof boots

wafer ('weɪfə) *n.* 1. thin, crisp biscuit 2. thin slice of anything

waffle[1] ('wɒfªl) *n.* kind of pancake with deep indentations on both sides —**waffle iron** utensil for cooking waffles, having two flat, studded plates hinged together

waffle[2] ('wɒfªl) *inf. vi.* 1. speak, write in vague wordy manner —*n.* 2. vague speech *etc.* 3. nonsense

waft (wɑːft, wɒft) *vt.* 1. convey smoothly through air or water —*n.* 2. breath of wind 3. odour, whiff

wag (wæg) *v.* 1. (cause to) move rapidly from side to side (-**gg**-) —*n.* 2. instance of wagging 3. *inf.* humorous, witty person —'**waggish** *a.* —'**wagtail** *n.* small bird with wagging tail

wage (weɪdʒ) *n.* 1. (*oft. pl.*) payment for work done —*vt.* 2. engage in

wager ('weɪdʒə) *n./v.* bet

waggle ('wægªl) *v.* wag —'**waggly** *a.*

Wagnerian (vɑːgˈnɪərɪən) *a.* pert. to German composer Richard Wagner, his music or his theories

wagon *or* **waggon** ('wægən) *n.* 1. four-wheeled vehicle for heavy loads 2. railway freight truck —'**wagoner** *or* '**waggoner** *n.* —wago'**nette** *or* waggo'**nette** *n.* four-wheeled horse-drawn vehicle with two lengthwise seats facing each other behind driver's seat

waif (weɪf) *n.* homeless person, *esp.* child

wail (weɪl) *v.* 1. cry out —*vt.* 2. lament —*n.* 3. mournful cry

wainscot ('weɪnskət) *n.* 1. wooden lining of walls of room —*vt.* 2. line thus

waist (weɪst) *n.* 1. part of body between hips and ribs 2. various narrow central parts —'**waistband** *n.* encircling band of material to finish and strengthen skirt *etc.* at waist —**waistcoat** ('weɪskəut) *n.* sleeveless garment worn under jacket or coat —'**waistline** *n.* line, size of waist (of person, garment)

wait (weɪt) *v.* 1. stay in one place, remain inactive in expectation (of something) 2. be prepared (for something) 3. delay —*vi.* 4. serve in restaurant *etc.* —*n.* 5. act or period of waiting —*pl.* 6. street musicians, carol singers —'**waiter** *n.* 1. attendant on guests at hotel, restaurant *etc.*

('**waitress** *fem.*) 2. one who waits —**waiting game** postponement of action in order to gain advantage —**waiting list** list of people waiting to obtain some object, treatment *etc.*

waive (weɪv) *vt.* 1. forgo 2. not insist on —'**waiver** *n.* (written statement of) this act

wake[1] (weɪk) *v.* 1. rouse from sleep 2. stir (up) (**woke**, '**woken**, '**waking**) —*n.* 3. vigil 4. watch beside corpse 5. (*oft. pl.*) annual holiday in parts of N England —'**wakeful** *a.* —'**waken** *v.* wake

wake[2] (weɪk) *n.* track or path left by anything that has passed, as track of turbulent water behind ship

wale (weɪl) *n.* 1. raised mark left on skin after stroke of whip 2. weave of fabric, such as ribs in corduroy 3. *Naut.* ridge of planking along rail of ship —*v.* 4. raise wales (on) by striking 5. weave with wale

walk (wɔːk) *v.* 1. (cause, assist to) move, travel on foot at ordinary pace —*vt.* 2. cross, pass through by walking 3. escort, conduct by walking —*n.* 4. act, instance of walking 5. path or other place or route for walking 6. manner of walking 7. occupation, career —'**walker** *n.* —'**walkabout** *n.* informal walk among crowd by royalty *etc.* —**walkie-talkie** *or* **walky-talky** *n.* portable radio set containing both transmission and receiver units —**walking stick** stick, cane carried to assist walking —**walk-on** *n.* small part in play *etc.*, *esp.* one without lines —'**walkout** *n.* 1. strike 2. act of leaving as a protest —'**walkover** *n.* unopposed or easy victory

wall (wɔːl) *n.* 1. structure of brick, stone *etc.* serving as fence, side of building *etc.* 2. surface of one 3. anything resembling this —*vt.* 4. enclose with wall 5. block up with wall —'**wallboard** *n.* thin board made of materials, such as compressed wood fibres or gypsum plaster, used to cover walls *etc.* —'**wallflower** *n.* 1. garden flower, oft. growing on walls 2. woman who remains seated at dance *etc.* for lack of partner —'**wallpaper** *n.* paper, usu. patterned, to cover interior walls

wallaby ('wɒləbı) *n.* Aust. marsupial similar to and smaller than kangaroo

wallet ('wɒlɪt) *n.* small folding case, *esp.* for paper money, documents *etc.*

walleyed ('wɔːlaɪd) *a.* 1. squinting 2. having eyes with pale irises

Walloon (wɒˈluːn) *n.* 1. member of French-speaking people living chiefly in S and SE Belgium 2. French dialect of Belgium —*a.* 3. of Walloons or their dialect

wallop ('wɒləp) *inf. vt.* 1. beat soundly 2. strike hard —*n.* 3. stroke or blow —'**walloper** *n. inf.* one who wallops —'**walloping** *inf. n.* 1. thrashing —*adv.* 2. very, greatly *a.* 3. great

wallow ('wɒləu) *vi.* 1. roll (in liquid or mud) 2.

revel —n. **3.** act or instance of wallowing **4.** muddy place where animals wallow

Wall Street street in New York, where Stock Exchange and major banks are situated

walnut ('wɔːlnʌt) n. **1.** large nut with crinkled shell splitting easily into two halves **2.** the tree **3.** its wood

walrus ('wɔːlrəs, 'wɒl-) n. large sea mammal with long tusks (pl. **-es, -rus**)

waltz (wɔːls) n. **1.** ballroom dance **2.** music for it —v. **3.** dance or lead (someone) in or as in a wɔːltz

wampum ('wɒmpəm) n. beads made of shells, formerly used by N Amer. Indians as money and for ornament

wan (wɒn) a. pale, sickly complexioned, pallid

wand (wɒnd) n. stick, usu. straight and slender, esp. as carried by magician etc.

wander ('wɒndə) v. **1.** roam, ramble —vi. **2.** go astray, deviate **3.** stroll —'**wanderer** n. —'**wanderlust** n. irrepressible urge to wander or travel

wane (weɪn) vi./n. **1.** decline **2.** (of moon) decrease in size

wangle ('wæŋgəl) inf. vt. **1.** manipulate, manage in skilful way —n. **2.** intrigue, trickery, something obtained by craft

Wankel engine ('wæŋkəl) type of rotary four-stroke internal-combustion engine without reciprocating parts

want (wɒnt) v. **1.** desire —vt. **2.** lack —n. **3.** desire **4.** need **5.** deficiency —'**wanted** a. being sought, esp. by the police —'**wanting** a. **1.** lacking **2.** below standard

wanton ('wɒntən) a. **1.** dissolute **2.** without motive, thoughtless **3.** unrestrained —n. **4.** wanton person esp. woman

war (wɔː) n. **1.** fighting between nations **2.** state of hostility **3.** conflict, contest —vi. **4.** make war (**-rr-**) —'**warlike** a. **1.** of, for war **2.** fond of war —'**warrior** n. fighter —**war crime** crime committed in wartime in violation of accepted customs of war —**war cry 1.** cry used by attacking troops in war **2.** distinctive word, phrase used by political party etc. —'**warfare** n. hostilities —**war game 1.** notional tactical exercise for training military commanders, in which no military units are actually deployed **2.** game in which model soldiers are used to create battles in order to study tactics —'**warhead** n. part of missile etc. containing explosives —'**warhorse** n. **1.** horse used in battle **2.** inf. veteran soldier or politician —**war memorial** monument to those who die in war —'**warmonger** n. one fostering, encouraging war —**war paint 1.** painted decoration of face and body applied by certain N Amer. Indians before battle **2.** inf. cosmetics —'**warpath** n.

route taken by N Amer. Indians on warlike expedition —'**warship** n. vessel armed, armoured for naval warfare —**on the warpath** inf. in a state of anger

War. Warwickshire

warble ('wɔːbəl) v. sing with trills —'**warbler** n. **1.** person or bird that warbles **2.** kind of small songbird

ward (wɔːd) n. **1.** division of city, hospital etc. **2.** minor under care of guardian **3.** guardianship **4.** bar in lock, groove in key that prevents incorrectly cut key opening lock —'**warder** n. jailer ('**wardress** fem.) —'**wardship** n. **1.** office of guardian **2.** state of being under guardian —'**wardroom** n. senior officers' mess on warship —**ward off** avert, repel

-ward (comb. form) **1.** indicating direction towards, as in backward step **2.** esp. US see -WARDS

warden ('wɔːdən) n. person, officer in charge of building, institution, college etc.

wardrobe ('wɔːdrəʊb) n. **1.** piece of furniture for hanging clothes in **2.** person's supply of clothes **3.** costumes of theatrical company

-wards or **-ward** (comb. form) indicating direction towards, as in step backwards

ware (weə) n. **1.** goods **2.** articles collectively —pl. **3.** goods for sale **4.** commodities **5.** merchandise —'**warehouse** n. storehouse for goods prior to distribution and sale

warlock ('wɔːlɒk) n. wizard, sorcerer

warm (wɔːm) a. **1.** moderately hot **2.** serving to maintain heat **3.** affectionate **4.** ardent **5.** earnest **6.** hearty **7.** (of colour) having yellow or red base —v. **8.** make, become warm —'**warmly** adv. —'**warmth** n. **1.** mild heat **2.** cordiality **3.** vehemence, anger —**warm-blooded** a. ardent —**warm-bloodedness** n. —**warm front** Met. boundary between warm air mass and cold air above

warn (wɔːn) vt. **1.** put on guard **2.** caution, admonish **3.** give advance information to **4.** notify authoritatively —'**warning** n. **1.** hint of harm etc. **2.** admonition **3.** advance notice

warp (wɔːp) v. **1.** (cause to) twist (out of shape) **2.** pervert or be perverted —n. **3.** state, condition of being warped **4.** lengthwise threads on loom

warrant ('wɒrənt) n. **1.** authority **2.** document giving authority —vt. **3.** guarantee **4.** authorize, justify —**warran'tee** n. person given warranty —'**warrantor** n. person, company giving warranty —'**warranty** n. **1.** guarantee of quality of goods **2.** security —**warrant officer** officer in certain armed services who holds a rank between those of commissioned and noncommissioned officers.

warren ('wɒrən) n. (burrows inhabited by) colony of rabbits

wart (wɔːt) n. small hard growth on skin —**wart hog** kind of Afr. wild pig

wary ('wɛərɪ) a. watchful, cautious, alert

was (wɒz; *unstressed* wəz) *pt.* first and third person sing. of BE

wash (wɒʃ) v. 1. clean (oneself, clothes *etc.*), *esp.* with water, soap *etc.* 2. move, be moved by water —vi. 3. be washable 4. *inf.* be able to be proved true —vt. 5. flow, sweep over, against —n. 6. act of washing 7. clothes washed at one time 8. sweep of water, *esp.* set up by moving ship 9. thin coat of colour —'**washable** a. capable of being washed without damage *etc.* —'**washer** n. one who, that which, washes 2. ring put under a nut —'**washing** n. clothes to be washed —'**washy** a. 1. dilute 2. watery 3. insipid —'**washboard** n. 1. board having surface, usu. of corrugated metal, on which, *esp.* formerly, clothes are scrubbed 2. *Naut.* planklike shield fastened to gunwales of boat to prevent water from splashing over side —**wash drawing** pen-and-ink drawing that has been lightly brushed over with water —**washing-up** n. UK 1. washing of dishes, cutlery *etc.* after meal 2. dishes, cutlery *etc.* waiting to be washed up —**wash leather** piece of leather, usu. chamois, used for washing windows *etc.* —'**washout** n. *inf.* complete failure —**washed out** 1. faded or colourless 2. exhausted, pale

wasp (wɒsp) n. striped stinging insect resembling bee —'**waspish** a. irritable, snappish —**wasp waist** very small waist

Wasp *or* **WASP** (wɒsp) n. US *usu.* derogatory person descended from N European Protestant stock

wassail ('wɒseɪl) n. 1. formerly, toast made to person at festivities 2. festivity when much drinking takes place 3. alcoholic drink drunk at such festivity, *esp.* spiced beer —v. 4. drink health of (person) at wassail —vi. 5. go from house to house singing carols at Christmas

waste (weɪst) vt. 1. expend uselessly, use extravagantly 2. fail to take advantage of 3. lay desolate —vi. 4. dwindle 5. pine away —n. 6. act of wasting 7. what is wasted 8. desert —a. 9. worthless, useless 10. desert 11. wasted —'**wastage** n. 1. loss by use or decay 2. reduction in numbers, *esp.* of workforce —'**wasteful** a. extravagant —'**wastefully** adv. —'**wasting** a. reducing vitality, strength, or robustness of body —'**wastrel** n. wasteful person, idler —'**wasteland** n. barren or desolate area of land

watch (wɒtʃ) vt. 1. observe closely 2. guard —vi. 3. wait expectantly 4. be on watch —n. 5. portable timepiece for wrist, pocket *etc.* 6. state of being on the lookout 7. guard 8. spell of duty —'**watchful** a. —'**watchfully** adv. —'**watchdog**

n. 1. dog trained to guard property 2. person or group that acts as protector against inefficiency *etc.* —'**watchmaker** n. one skilled in making and repairing watches —'**watchman** n. man guarding building *etc.*, *esp.* at night —**watch night** in Protestant churches, service held on night of Dec. 31st, to mark passing of old year —'**watchword** n. 1. password 2. rallying cry

water ('wɔːtə) n. 1. transparent, colourless, odourless, tasteless liquid, substance of rain, river *etc.* 2. body of water 3. river 4. lake 5. sea 6. tear 7. urine —vt. 8. put water on or into 9. irrigate, provide with water —vi. 10. salivate 11. (of eyes) fill with tears 12. take in or obtain water —'**watery** a. —**water bed** waterproof mattress filled with water —**water biscuit** thin crisp plain biscuit —'**waterbuck** n. Afr. antelope —**water buffalo** oxlike Asian animal —**water butt** barrel with one end open, used for collecting and storing rainwater —**water chestnut** floating aquatic plant of Asia, having edible nutlike fruits —**water closet** sanitary convenience flushed by water —'**watercolour** *or U.S.* '**watercolor** n. 1. pigment mixed with water 2. painting in this —'**watercourse** n. stream —'**watercress** n. plant growing in clear ponds and streams —'**waterfall** n. perpendicular descent of waters of river —'**waterfront** n. area of town alongside body of water, such as harbour —**water gauge** instrument that indicates presence or quantity of water in tank *etc.* (*also* **water glass**) —**water glass** 1. syrupy solution of sodium silicate dissolved in water, used as preservative, *esp.* for eggs 2. water gauge —**water hole** depression, such as pool, containing water, *esp.* one used by animals as drinking place —**water ice** ice cream made from frozen sugar syrup flavoured with fruit juice *etc.* —**watering place** 1. place where drinking water may be obtained 2. UK spa 3. UK seaside resort —**water jump** ditch over which athletes or horses must jump, as in steeplechase —**water lily** plant that floats on surface of fresh water —**water line** 1. line marked at level around vessel's hull to which vessel will be immersed when afloat 2. line marking level reached by body of water —'**waterlogged** a. saturated, filled with water —**water main** principal supply pipe in arrangement of water pipes —'**watermark** n. faint translucent design stamped on substance of sheet of paper —**water meadow** meadow that remains fertile due to periodic flooding by stream —'**watermelon** n. large edible fruit which has hard green rind and sweet watery reddish flesh —**water pistol** toy pistol that squirts stream of water —**water power** 1. power latent in dynamic or static head of water as used to drive machinery 2. source of such power, such as drop in level of river *etc.*

—'**waterproof** a. 1. not letting water through —vt. 2. make waterproof —n. 3. waterproof garment —**water rate** charge levied for use of public water supply —**water-repellent** a. (of garments etc.) having water-resistant finish —'**watershed** n. 1. line separating two river systems 2. divide —**water-ski** n. 1. type of ski used for gliding over water —vi. 2. ride over water on water-skis, while holding rope towed by speedboat —'**waterspout** n. 1. Met. tornado occurring over water, that forms column of water and mist; sudden heavy rainfall 2. pipe or channel through which water is discharged —**water table** level below which ground is saturated with water —'**watertight** a. 1. so fitted as to prevent water entering or escaping 2. with no loopholes or weak points —**water tower** storage tank mounted on towerlike structure so that water can be distributed at uniform pressure —**water vapour** water in gaseous state, esp. when due to evaporation at temperature below boiling point —**water wheel** 1. water-driven turbine consisting of wheel having vanes set axially across its rim, used to drive machinery 2. wheel with buckets attached to its rim for raising water from pond etc. —**water wings** inflatable rubber device, placed under arms of person learning to swim —'**waterworks** pl.n. 1. (with sing. v.) establishment for storing, purifying, and distributing water for community supply 2. (with pl. v.) display of water in movement, as in fountains 3. (with pl. v.) sl. crying; tears

Watergate ('wɔːtəgeɪt) n. political scandal when agents employed by U.S. President Richard Nixon's re-election organization were caught breaking into Democratic Party headquarters in Watergate building, Washington, D.C.; exacerbated by attempts to conceal the fact that White House officials had approved the burglary

Waterloo (wɔːtə'luː) n. 1. town in Belgium, site of battle where Napoleon met his final defeat 2. total or crushing defeat (esp. in **meet one's Waterloo**)

watt (wɒt) n. unit of electric power —'**wattage** n. electric power expressed in watts

wattle ('wɒtəl) n. 1. frame of woven branches etc. as fence 2. fleshy pendent lobe of neck of certain birds, eg turkey —**wattle and daub** form of wall construction consisting of interwoven twigs plastered with mixture of clay and water

waul or **wawl** (wɔːl) vi. cry or wail plaintively like cat

wave (weɪv) v. 1. move to and fro, as hand in greeting or farewell 2. signal by waving 3. give, take shape of waves (as hair etc.) —n. 4. ridge and trough on water etc. 5. act, gesture of waving 6. vibration, as in radio waves, of

electric and magnetic forces alternating in direction 7. prolonged spell of something 8. upsurge 9. wavelike shape in the hair etc. —'**wavy** a. —'**waveband** n. range of wavelengths or frequencies used for particular type of radio transmission —'**wavelength** n. distance between same points of two successive sound waves

waver ('weɪvə) vi. 1. hesitate, be irresolute 2. be, become unsteady —'**waverer** n.

wax[1] (wæks) n. 1. yellow, soft, pliable material made by bees 2. this or similar substance used for sealing, making candles etc. 3. waxy secretion of ear —vt. 4. put wax on —'**waxen** a. 1. made of, treated with, or covered with wax 2. resembling wax in colour or texture —'**waxy** a. like wax —'**waxbill** n. Afr. finchlike weaverbird —**wax paper** paper coated with wax or paraffin to make it waterproof —'**waxwing** n. small songbird —'**waxwork** n. lifelike figure, esp. of famous person, reproduced in wax

wax[2] (wæks) vi. grow, increase

way (weɪ) n. 1. manner 2. method, means 3. track 4. direction 5. path 6. passage 7. course 8. route 9. progress 10. state or condition —'**waybill** n. document attached to goods in transit specifying their nature, point of origin, destination and rate to be charged —'**wayfarer** n. traveller, esp. on foot —**way'lay** vt. lie in wait for and accost, attack (-'**laid**, -'**laying**) —**way-out** a. inf. 1. extremely unconventional or experimental 2. excellent or amazing —'**wayside** n. 1. side or edge of a road —a. 2. situated by the wayside —'**wayward** a. capricious, perverse, wilful —'**waywardly** adv. —'**waywardness** n. —**ways and means** 1. revenues and methods of raising revenues needed for functioning of state etc. 2. methods and resources for accomplishing some purpose

-**ways** (comb. form) indicating direction or manner, as in sideways

Wb Phys. weber

w.b. 1. water ballast 2. waybill (also **W/B, W.B.**) 3. westbound

W.C. or **WC** water closet

we (wiː) pron. first person plural pronoun

weak (wiːk) a. 1. lacking strength 2. feeble 3. fragile 4. defenceless 5. easily influenced 6. faint —'**weaken** v. —'**weakling** n. feeble creature —'**weakly** a. 1. sickly —adv. 3. in a weak or feeble manner —'**weakness** n. —**weak-kneed** a. inf. yielding readily to force, intimidation etc.

weal[1] (wiːl) n. streak left on flesh by blow of stick or whip

weal[2] (wiːl) n. obs. prosperity or wellbeing (esp. in the **public weal, common weal**)

weald (wiːld) n. obs. forested country

wealth (wɛlθ) n. **1.** riches **2.** abundance —'**wealthiness** n. —'**wealthy** a.

wean (wiːn) vt. **1.** accustom to food other than mother's milk **2.** win over, coax away

weapon ('wɛpən) n. **1.** implement to fight with **2.** anything used to get the better of an opponent

wear (wɛə) vt. **1.** have on the body **2.** show **3.** produce (hole etc.) by rubbing etc. **4.** harass; weaken **5.** inf. allow, tolerate —vi. **6.** last **7.** become impaired by use **8.** (with on) (of time) pass slowly (**wore, worn, 'wearing**) —n. **9.** act of wearing **10.** things to wear **11.** damage caused by use **12.** ability to resist effects of constant use —'**wearer** n. —**wear and tear** depreciation or loss resulting from ordinary use

weary ('wɪərɪ) a. **1.** tired, exhausted, jaded **2.** tiring **3.** tedious —v. **4.** make, become weary ('**wearied, 'wearying**) —'**wearily** adv. —'**weariness** n. —'**wearisome** a. causing weariness

weasel ('wiːzªl) n. small carnivorous mammal with long body and short legs

weather ('wɛðə) n. **1.** day-to-day meteorological conditions, esp. temperature, cloudiness etc. of a place —a. **2.** towards the wind —v. **3.** affect or be affected by weather —vt. **4.** endure **5.** resist **6.** come safely through **7.** sail to windward of —'**weathering** n. mechanical and chemical breakdown of rocks by action of rain, cold etc. —**weather-beaten** a. showing signs of exposure to weather —'**weatherboard** n. timber boards used as external cladding of house —**weather-bound** a. (of vessel, aircraft etc.) delayed by bad weather —'**weathercock** n. revolving vane to show which way wind blows —**weather eye 1.** vision of person trained to observe changes in weather **2.** inf. alert or observant gaze —**weather house** model house, usu. with two human figures, one that enters to foretell bad weather and one that enters to foretell good weather —**weather strip** thin strip of metal, felt etc. fitted between frame of door or window and opening part to exclude draughts and rain —**weather vane** designed to indicate direction in which wind is blowing

weave (wiːv) vt. **1.** form into texture or fabric by interlacing, esp. on loom **2.** fashion, construct —vi. **3.** practise weaving **4.** make one's way, esp. with side to side motion (**wove** or **weaved, 'woven** or **weaved, 'weaving**) —'**weaver** n.

web (wɛb) n. **1.** woven fabric **2.** net spun by spider **3.** membrane between toes of waterfowl, frogs etc. —'**webbing** n. strong fabric woven in strips

weber ('veɪbə) n. SI unit of magnetic flux

wed (wɛd) v. **1.** marry —vt. **2.** unite closely ('**wedded, wed** pt./pp., '**wedding**) —'**wedding** n. act of marrying, nuptial ceremony —'**wedlock** n. marriage

Wed. Wednesday

wedge (wɛdʒ) n. **1.** piece of wood, metal etc., thick at one end, tapering to a thin edge —vt. **2.** fasten, split with wedge **3.** stick by compression or crowding

Wedgwood ('wɛdʒwʊd) n. **R** kind of pottery with ornamental reliefs

Wednesday ('wɛnzdɪ) n. fourth day of week

wee (wiː) a. small, little

weed (wiːd) n. **1.** plant growing where undesired **2.** inf. tobacco **3.** inf. marijuana **4.** inf. thin, sickly person, animal —vt. **5.** clear of weeds —'**weedy** a. **1.** full of weeds **2.** inf. thin, weakly —**weed out** remove, eliminate what is unwanted

weeds (wiːdz) pl.n. (widow's) mourning clothes

week (wiːk) n. **1.** period of seven days, esp. one beginning on Sunday and ending on Saturday **2.** hours, days of work in seven-day period —'**weekly** a./adv. **1.** (happening, done, published etc.) once a week —n. **2.** newspaper or magazine issued every week —'**weekday** n. any day of week except Sunday and usu. Saturday —**week'end** n. Saturday and Sunday, esp. considered as rest period

weep (wiːp) v. **1.** shed (tears) **2.** grieve (**wept, 'weeping**) —'**weepy** a. —**weeping willow** willow with drooping branches

weevil ('wiːvɪl) n. small beetle harmful to grain etc.

weft (wɛft) n. cross threads in weaving, woof

weigh (weɪ) vt. **1.** find weight of **2.** consider **3.** raise (anchor) —vi. **4.** have weight **5.** be burdensome —'**weight** n. **1.** measure of the heaviness of an object **2.** quality of heaviness **3.** heavy mass **4.** object of known mass for weighing **5.** unit of measurement of weight **6.** importance, influence —vt. **7.** add weight to —'**weightily** adv. —'**weighting** n. additional allowance payable in particular circumstances —'**weightlessness** n. having little or no weight, experienced esp. at great distances from earth because of reduced gravitational attraction (also **zero gravity**) —'**weighty** a. **1.** heavy **2.** onerous **3.** important **4.** momentous —'**weighbridge** n. machine for weighing vehicles etc. by means of metal plate set into road —'**weightlifting** n. sport of lifting barbells of specified weights in prescribed manner

weir (wɪə) n. river dam

weird (wɪəd) a. **1.** unearthly, uncanny **2.** strange, bizarre

welch (wɛlʃ) vi. see WELSH

welcome ('wɛlkəm) a. **1.** received gladly **2.** freely permitted —n. **3.** kindly greeting —vt. **4.** greet with pleasure **5.** receive gladly (-**comed,** -**coming**)

weld (wɛld) vt. **1.** unite (metal) by softening

with heat **2.** unite closely —*n.* **3.** welded joint —'**welder** *n.* **1.** tradesman who welds **2.** machine used in welding

welfare ('wɛlfɛə) *n.* wellbeing —**welfare state** system in which the government takes responsibility for the social, economic *etc.* security of its citizens

well[1] (wɛl) *adv.* **1.** in good manner or degree **2.** suitably **3.** intimately **4.** fully **5.** favourably, kindly **6.** to a considerable degree —*a.* **7.** in good health **8.** suitable ('**better** *comp.*, **best** *sup.*) —*interj.* **9.** exclamation of surprise, interrogation *etc.* —**well-appointed** *a.* well equipped or furnished —**well-balanced** *a.* **1.** having good balance or proportions **2.** sane or sensible —'**well'being** *n.* state of being well, happy, or prosperous —**well-connected** *a.* having influential or important relatives or friends —**well-disposed** *a.* inclined to be friendly, kindly (towards) —**well-done** *a.* **1.** (of food, *esp.* meat) cooked thoroughly **2.** accomplished satisfactorily —**well-grounded** *a.* **1.** well instructed in basic elements of subject **2.** based on good reasons —**well-heeled** *a. sl.* rich; wealthy —**well-intentioned** *a.* having benevolent intentions, usu. with unfortunate results —**well-mannered** *a.* having good manners —**well-nigh** *adv. poet.* nearly; almost —**well-off** *a.* fairly rich —**well-read** *a.* having read much —**well-spoken** *a.* speaking fluently, graciously, aptly —**well-to-do** *a.* moderately wealthy —**well tried** proved to be satisfactory by long experience —**well-wisher** *n.* person who shows benevolence towards person, cause *etc.* —**well-wishing** *a./n.* —**well-worn** *a.* **1.** so much used as to be affected by wear **2.** hackneyed

well[2] (wɛl) *n.* **1.** hole sunk into the earth to reach water, gas, oil *etc.* **2.** spring **3.** any shaft like a well **4.** space in a lawcourt where solicitors sit —*vi.* **5.** spring, gush —'**wellhead** *n.* **1.** source of well or stream **2.** source, fountainhead or origin —'**wellspring** *n.* **1.** source of spring or stream **2.** source of abundant supply

Wellington boots ('wɛlɪŋtən) high waterproof boots (*also* 'Wellingtons, 'wellies)

welsh *or* **welch** (wɛlʃ) *vi.* fail to pay debt or fulfil obligation —'**welsher** *or* '**welcher** *n.*

Welsh (wɛlʃ) *a.* **1.** of Wales —*n.* **2.** language, natives or inhabitants of Wales —**Welsh rabbit** *or* **rarebit** savoury dish of melted cheese on toast —**Welsh terrier** wire-haired breed of terrier with black-and-tan coat

welt (wɛlt) *n.* **1.** raised, strengthened seam **2.** weal —*vt.* **3.** provide with welt **4.** thrash

welter ('wɛltə) *vi.* **1.** roll or tumble —*n.* **2.** turmoil, disorder

welterweight ('wɛltəweɪt) *n.* **1.** professional boxer weighing 140-147 lbs (63.5-66.5 kg);

amateur boxer weighing 63.5-67 kg (140-148 kg) **2.** wrestler weighing usu. 154-172 lbs (70-78 kg)

wen (wɛn) *n.* cyst, *esp.* on scalp

wench (wɛntʃ) *n.* now oft. facetious young woman

wend (wɛnd) *v.* go, travel

wendigo ('wɛndɪgəʊ) *n.* **C** *see* SPLAKE

wensleydale ('wɛnzlɪdeɪl) *n.* **1.** type of white cheese with flaky texture **2.** breed of sheep with long woolly fleece

went (wɛnt) *pt.* of GO

wept (wɛpt) *pt./pp.* of WEEP

were (wɜː; *unstressed* wə) imperfect indicative plural and subjunctive sing. and pl. of BE

werewolf ('wɪəwʊlf, 'wɛə-) *n.* in folklore, human being turned into wolf

Wesleyan ('wɛzlɪən) *a.* **1.** pert. to English preacher, John Wesley (1703-91), who founded Methodism **2.** of Methodism, *esp.* in its original form —*n.* **3.** follower of John Wesley **4.** member of Methodist Church —'**Wesleyanism** *n.*

west (wɛst) *n.* **1.** part of sky where sun sets **2.** part of country *etc.* lying to this side **3.** occident —*a.* **4.** that is toward or in this region —*adv.* **5.** to the west —'**westerly** *a.* —'**western** *a.* **1.** of, in the west —*n.* **2.** film, story *etc.* about cowboys or frontiersmen in western U.S. —'**westernize** *or* **-ise** *vt.* influence with customs, practices *etc.* of West —'**westward** *a./adv.* —'**westwards** *adv.* towards the west —**western hemisphere** (*oft.* **W- H-**) that half of the globe containing N and S Amer. —**go west** *inf.* **1.** disappear **2.** die **3.** be lost —**the West Country** southwest of England, *esp.* Cornwall, Devon and Somerset —**the West End** part of W central London containing main shopping and entertainment areas

Westminster ('wɛstmɪnstə) *n.* British Houses of Parliament

wet (wɛt) *a.* **1.** having water or other liquid on a surface or being soaked in it **2.** rainy **3.** not yet dry (paint, ink *etc.*) **4.** *inf.* (of person) feeble, dull *etc.* ('**wetter** *comp.*, '**wettest** *sup.*) —*vt.* **5.** make wet (**wet,** '**wetted** *pt./pp.*, '**wetting** *pr.p.*) —*n.* **6.** moisture, rain **7.** (*oft.* **W-**) UK *inf.* Conservative politician who is not a hardliner —**wet blanket** *inf.* one depressing spirits of others —**wet dream** erotic dream accompanied by emission of semen —**wet nurse** woman suckling another's child —**wet suit** close-fitting rubber suit worn by divers *etc.*

wether ('wɛðə) *n.* castrated ram

W. Glam. West Glamorgan

whack (wæk) *vt.* **1.** strike with sharp resounding blow —*n.* **2.** such blow **3.** *inf.* share **4.** *inf.* attempt —**whacked** *a.* exhausted —'**whacking** *a. inf.* big, enormous

whale (weɪl) *n.* large fish-shaped sea mammal —'**whaler** *n.* man, ship employed in hunting whales —'**whaling** n. work or industry of hunting and processing whales for food, oil etc. —'**whalebone** n. horny elastic substance from projections of upper jaw of certain whales

wham (wæm) n. 1. forceful blow or sound produced by it —v. 2. strike or cause to strike with great force (-mm-)

wharf (wɔːf) n. platform at harbour, on river etc. for loading and unloading ships (pl. **wharves** (wɔːvz), **-s**)

what (wɒt; unstressed wət) pron. 1. which thing 2. that which 3. request for statement to be repeated —a. 4. which 5. as much as 6. how great, surprising etc. —interj. 7. exclamation of surprise, anger etc. —**what'ever** pron. 1. anything which 2. of what kind it may be —**whatso'ever** a. 1. at all: used as intensifier with indefinite pronouns and determiners such as none, anybody etc. —pron. 2. rare whatever —'**whatnot** n. 1. inf. person, thing whose name is unknown, forgotten etc. 2. small stand with shelves

wheat (wiːt) n. cereal plant with thick four-sided seed spikes of which bread is chiefly made —'**wheaten** a. —'**wheatear** n. small songbird —**wheat germ** embryo of wheat kernel —'**wheatmeal** n. wholemeal flour made from wheat

wheedle ('wiːdəl) v. coax, cajole

wheel (wiːl) n. 1. circular frame or disc (with spokes) revolving on axle 2. anything like a wheel in shape or function 3. act of turning 4. steering wheel —v. 5. (cause to) turn as if on axis 6. (cause to) move on or as if on wheels 7. (cause to) change course, esp. in opposite direction —'**wheelbarrow** n. barrow with one wheel —'**wheelbase** n. distance between front and rear hubs of vehicle —'**wheelchair** n. chair mounted on large wheels, used by people who cannot walk —'**wheelhouse** n. enclosed structure on vessel's bridge for steersman —'**wheelspin** n. revolution of wheels without full grip of road —'**wheelwright** n. person who makes or mends wheels as trade

wheeze (wiːz) vi. 1. breathe with difficulty and whistling noise —n. 2. this sound 3. inf. trick, idea, plan —'**wheezy** a.

whelk (wɛlk) n. sea snail, esp. edible variety

whelp (wɛlp) n. 1. young of certain animals, esp. of wolf or dog 2. disparaging youth 3. jocular child —v. 4. give birth to (whelps)

when (wɛn) adv. 1. at what time —conj. 2. at the time that 3. although 4. since —pron. 5. at which (time) —**when'ever** adv./conj. at whatever time —**whenso'ever** conj./adv. rare whenever

whence (wɛns) adv./conj. formal 1. from what place or source 2. how

where (wɛə) adv./conj. 1. at what place 2. at or

to the place in which —'**whereabouts** adv./conj. 1. in what, which place —n. 2. present position —where'as conj. 1. considering that 2. while, on the contrary —where'by conj. by which —'**wherefore** adv. obs. 1. why 2. consequently —where'of conj. 1. of what or which person or thing? —pron. 2. of which (person or thing) —where'upon conj. at which point —wher'ever adv. at whatever place —'**wherewithal** n. necessary funds, resources etc.

whet (wɛt) vt. 1. sharpen 2. stimulate (-tt-) —'**whetstone** n. stone for sharpening tools

whether ('wɛðə) conj. introduces the first of two alternatives, of which the second may be expressed or implied

whew (hwjuː) interj. exclamation expressing relief, delight etc.

whey (weɪ) n. watery part of milk left after separation of curd in cheese making

which (wɪtʃ) a. 1. used in requests for a selection from alternatives —pron. 2. which person or thing 3. the thing 'who' —which'ever pron.

whiff (wɪf) n. 1. brief smell or suggestion of 2. puff of air —vt. 3. smell

Whig (wɪg) n. member of British political party that preceded the Liberal Party

while (waɪl) conj. 1. in the time that 2. in spite of the fact that, although 3. whereas —vt. 4. pass (time, usu. idly) —n. 5. period of time —**whilst** conj. while

whim (wɪm) n. sudden, passing fancy —'**whimsical** a. 1. fanciful 2. full of whims —**whimsi'cality** n. —'**whimsy** or '**whimsey** n. 1. whim 2. caprice —a. 3. quaint, comical or unusual, oft. in tasteless way

whimper ('wɪmpə) vi. 1. cry or whine softly 2. complain in this way —n. 3. such cry or complaint

whin (wɪn) n. gorse

whine (waɪn) n. 1. high-pitched plaintive cry 2. peevish complaint —vi. 3. utter this

whinge (wɪndʒ) inf. vi. 1. whine, complain n. 2. complaint

whinny ('wɪnɪ) vi. 1. neigh softly ('**whinnied, 'whinnying**) —n. 2. gentle neigh

whip (wɪp) vt. 1. strike with whip 2. thrash 3. beat (cream, eggs) to a froth 4. lash 5. inf. pull, remove, insert etc. quickly 6. inf. steal —vi. 7. dart (-pp-) —n. 8. lash attached to handle for urging or punishing 9. one who enforces attendance of political party 10. call made on members of Parliament to attend for important divisions 11. elastic quality permitting bending in mast, fishing rod etc. 12. whipped dessert —'**whipping** n. 1. thrashing with whip or similar implement 2. cord used for binding or lashing 3. binding formed by wrapping rope etc. with cord or twine —'**whipcord** n. **1.** strong worsted fabric with diagonally ribbed surface **2.** hard twisted cord used for lashes of whips *etc.* —**whip hand** (*usu.* with the) **1.** in driving horses *etc.,* hand holding whip **2.** advantage or dominating position —'**whiplash** n. quick lash of whip or like that of whip —**whiplash injury** injury to neck as result of sudden jerking of unsupported head —'**whippersnapper** n. insignificant but pretentious or cheeky person, oft. young one. (*also* '**whipster**) —**whipping boy** scapegoat —**whip-round** n. *inf.* collection of money

whippet ('wɪpɪt) n. racing dog like small greyhound

whir *or* **whirr** (wɜ:) v. **1.** (cause to) fly, spin *etc.* with buzzing or whizzing sound —*vi.* **2.** bustle —*n.* **3.** this sound **4.** bustle

whirl (wɜ:l) v. **1.** swing rapidly round **2** drive or be driven at high speed —*vi.* **3.** move rapidly in a circular course —*n.* **4.** whirling movement **5.** confusion, bustle, giddiness —'**whirligig** n. **1.** spinning toy **2.** merry-go-round —'**whirlpool** n. circular current, eddy —'**whirlwind** n. **1.** wind whirling round while moving forwards —*a.* **2.** rapid or sudden —'**whirlybird** n. *inf.* helicopter

whisk (wɪsk) vt. **1.** brush, sweep, beat lightly **2.** beat to a froth —v. **3.** move, remove, quickly —n. **4.** light brush **5.** egg-beating implement

whisker ('wɪskə) n. **1.** long stiff hair at side of mouth of cat or other animal **2.** any of hairs on a man's face —by a whisker *inf.* only just

whisky ('wɪskɪ) n. spirit distilled from fermented cereals (*Irish,* C, US '**whiskey**)

whisper ('wɪspə) v. **1.** speak in soft, hushed tones, without vibration of vocal cords **2.** rustle —n. **3.** such speech **4.** trace or suspicion **5.** rustle

whist (wɪst) n. card game

whistle ('wɪsəl) vi. **1.** produce shrill sound by forcing breath through rounded, nearly closed lips —vt. **2.** utter, summon *etc.* by whistle —n. **3.** such sound **4.** any similar sound **5.** instrument to make it —'**whistler** n. —**whistle stop 1.** US minor railway station where trains stop only on signal; small town having such a station **2.** brief appearance in town, *esp.* by political candidate

whit (wɪt) n. jot, particle (*esp.* in **not a whit**)

white (waɪt) a. **1.** of the colour of snow **2.** pale **3.** light in colour **4.** having a light-coloured skin —n. **5.** colour of snow **6.** white pigment **7.** white part **8.** clear fluid round yolk of egg **9.** (W-) white person —'**whiten** v. —'**whiteness** n. —'**whitish** a. —**white ant** termite —'**whitebait** n. small edible fish —**white blood cell** *see* LEUCOCYTE —'**whitecap** n. wave with white broken crest —**white-collar** a. denoting nonmanual salaried workers —**white dwarf** one of class of small faint stars of enormous density —**white elephant** useless, unwanted, gift or possession

—**white feather** symbol or mark of cowardice —'**whitefish** n. **1.** food fish having large silvery scales and small head **2.** in Brit. fishing industry, any edible marine fish or invertebrate excluding herrings but including trout, salmon and all shellfish —**white flag** white banner or cloth used as signal of surrender or truce —'**whitefly** n. insect typically having body covered with powdery wax —**white friar** Carmelite friar, so called because of white cloak that forms part of habit of this order —**white gold** white lustrous alloy containing gold together with platinum and palladium and sometimes smaller amounts of silver, nickel, or copper —**white goods 1.** household linen such as sheets, tablecloths *etc.* **2.** large household appliances, such as refrigerators *etc.* —**white heat 1.** intense heat characterized by emission of white light **2.** *inf.* state of intense excitement or activity —**white hope** one expected to bring honour or glory to his group, team *etc.* —**white horse 1.** outline of horse carved into side of chalk hill **2.** wave with white broken crest —**white-hot** a. **1.** at such high temperature that white light is emitted **2.** *inf.* in state of intense emotion —**white lead** (lɛd) n. **1.** white solid *usu.* regarded as mixture of lead carbonate and lead hydroxide used in paint and in making putty and ointments for treatment of burns **2.** either of two similar white pigments based on lead sulphate or lead silicate —**white lie** minor, unimportant lie —**white matter** whitish tissue of brain and spinal cord, consisting mainly of nerve fibres —**white meat** any meat that is light in colour, such as veal —**white noise** sound or electrical noise that has relatively wide continuous range of frequencies of uniform intensity —**white paper** government report on matter recently investigated —**white pepper** condiment made from husked dried beans of pepper plant —**white sale** sale of household linens at reduced prices —**white sauce** thick sauce made from flour, butter, seasonings, and milk or stock —**white slave** woman, child forced or enticed away for purposes of prostitution —**white spirit** colourless liquid obtained from petroleum, used as substitute for turpentine —**white tie 1.** white bow tie worn as part of man's formal evening dress **2.** formal evening dress for men —'**whitewash** n. **1.** substance for whitening walls *etc.* —vt. **2.** apply this to **3.** cover up, gloss over, suppress —**white whale** small white toothed whale of northern waters (*also* be'**luga**) —'**whitewood** n. **1.** white light-coloured wood, such as the tulip tree **2.** its wood —**show the white feather** act in cowardly manner —**the White House 1.** official Washington residence of president of U.S. **2.** U.S. presidency —**White man's burden** supposed duty of White race to bring education and Western culture to non-White inhabitants of their colonies

Whitehall (waɪt'hɔːl) *n.* **1.** street in London where main government offices are situated **2.** British Government

whither ('wɪðə) *adv. Poet.* **1.** to what place **2.** to which

whiting ('waɪtɪŋ) *n.* edible sea fish

whitlow ('wɪtləʊ) *n.* abscess on finger, *esp.* round nail

Whitsun ('wɪtsⁿn) *n.* week following **Whit Sunday,** seventh Sunday after Easter

whittle ('wɪtⁿl) *vt.* **1.** cut, carve with knife **2.** pare away —**whittle down** reduce gradually, wear (away)

whiz *or* **whizz** (wɪz) *n.* **1.** loud hissing sound **2.** *inf.* person skilful at something —*vi.* **3.** move with or make such sound **4.** *inf.* move quickly —**whiz kid, whizz kid,** *or* **wiz kid** *inf.* person who is outstandingly successful for his or her age

who (huː) *pron.* relative and interrogative pronoun, always referring to persons —**whodunnit** *or* **whodunit** (huː'dʌnɪt) *n. inf.* detective story —**who'ever** *pron.* who, any one or every one that —**whoso'ever** *pron. formal* whoever

W.H.O. World Health Organization

whoa (wəʊ) *interj.* command used, *esp.* to horses, to stop or slow down

whole (həʊl) *a.* **1.** complete **2.** containing all elements or parts **3.** entire **4.** not defective or imperfect **5.** healthy —*n.* **6.** complete thing or system —**'wholly** *adv.* —**'wholesome** *a.* producing good effect, physically or morally —**whole'hearted** *a.* **1.** sincere **2.** enthusiastic —**'wholemeal** *a.* of, pert. to flour which contains the whole of the grain —**whole number 1.** integer **2.** natural number —**'wholesale** *n.* **1.** sale of goods by large quantities to retailers —*a.* **2.** dealing by wholesale **3.** extensive —**'wholesaler** *n.* —**on the whole 1.** taking everything into consideration **2.** in general

whom (huːm) *pron.* objective case of WHO

whoop (wuːp) *n.* shout or cry expressing excitement *etc.*

whoopee ('wʊpiː) *n. inf.* gay, riotous time —**make whoopee 1.** participate in wild noisy party **2.** make love

whooping cough ('huːpɪŋ) infectious disease of mucous membrane lining air passages, marked by convulsive coughing with loud whoop or indrawing of breath

whoops (wʊps) *interj.* exclamation of surprise or of apology

whopper ('wɒpə) *n. inf.* **1.** anything unusually large **2.** monstrous lie —**'whopping** *a.*

whore (hɔː) *n.* prostitute —**'whorehouse** *n.* brothel

whorl (wɜːl) *n.* **1.** ring of leaves or petals **2.** turn of spiral **3.** anything forming part of circular pattern, *eg* lines of human fingerprint

whortleberry ('wɜːtⁿlberɪ) *n.* small Eurasian shrub of erica genus with edible sweet blackish berries (*also* **'bilberry, 'huckleberry, (UK) 'blaeberry)**

whose (huːz) *pron.* possessive case of WHO and WHICH

why (waɪ) *adv.* for what cause or reason

WI Wisconsin

W.I. 1. West Indian **2.** West Indies **3.** UK Women's Institute

wick (wɪk) *n.* strip of thread feeding flame of lamp or candle with oil, grease *etc.*

wicked ('wɪkɪd) *a.* **1.** evil, sinful **2.** very bad **3.** mischievous —**'wickedly** *adv.* —**'wickedness** *n.*

wicker(work) ('wɪkə(wɜːk)) *n.* woven cane *etc.,* basketwork

wicket ('wɪkɪt) *n.* **1.** small gate **2.** *Cricket* set of three stumps and bails **3.** cricket pitch —**'wicketkeeper** *n. Cricket* player on fielding side positioned directly behind wicket

wide (waɪd) *a.* **1.** having a great extent from side to side, broad **2.** having considerable distance between **3.** spacious **4.** liberal **5.** vast **6.** far from the mark **7.** opened fully —*adv.* **8.** to the full extent **9.** far from the intended target —*n.* **10.** *Cricket* ball bowled out of batsman's reach —**'widely** *adv.* —**'widen** *v.* —**width** (wɪdθ) *or* **'wideness** *n.* breadth —**wide-angle lens** lens system on camera that can cover angle of view of 60° or more —**wide-eyed** *a.* innocent or credulous —**'widespread** *a.* extending over a wide area **2.** common

widow ('wɪdəʊ) *n.* **1.** woman whose husband is dead and who has not married again —*vt.* **2.** make a widow of —**'widower** *n.* man whose wife is dead and who has not married again —**'widowhood** *n.*

wield (wiːld) *vt.* **1.** hold and use **2.** brandish **3.** manage

wife (waɪf) *n.* a man's partner in marriage, married woman (*pl.* **wives**) —**'wifely** *a.*

wig (wɪg) *n.* artificial hair for the head

wigeon *or* **widgeon** ('wɪdʒ᳚n) *n.* Eurasian duck of marshes, swamps *etc.*

wigging ('wɪgɪŋ) *n. UK sl.* reprimand

wiggle ('wɪgⁿl) *v.* **1.** (cause to) move jerkily from side to side —*n.* **2.** such movement —**'wiggly** *a.*

wigwam ('wɪgwæm) *n.* N *Amer.* Indian's hut or tent

wilco ('wɪlkəʊ) *interj.* expression in telecommunications *etc.* indicating that message just received will be complied with

wild (waɪld) *a.* **1.** not tamed or domesticated **2.** not cultivated **3.** savage **4.** stormy **5.**

uncontrolled **6.** random **7.** excited **8.** rash **9.** frantic **10.** *inf.* (of party *etc.*) rowdy, exciting —'**wildly** *adv.* —'**wildness** *n.* —'**wildcat** *n.* **1.** undomesticated European and Amer. feline animal **2.** *inf.* wild, savage person —*a.* **3.** unsound, irresponsible **4.** sudden, unofficial, unauthorized —**wild-goose chase** futile pursuit —'**wildlife** *n.* wild animals and plants collectively —**wild oats** *pl.* indiscretions of youth, *esp.* dissoluteness before settling down (*esp. in* **sow one's wild oats**) —**Wild West** western U.S., *esp.* with reference to its frontier lawlessness

wildebeest ('wɪldɪbiːst, 'vɪl-) *n.* gnu

wilderness ('wɪldənɪs) *n.* **1.** desert, waste place **2.** state of desolation or confusion

wildfire ('waɪldfaɪə) *n.* **1.** raging, uncontrollable fire **2.** anything spreading, moving fast

wile (waɪl) *n.* trick —'**wily** *a.* crafty, sly

wilful *or U.S.* **willful** ('wɪlful) *a.* **1.** obstinate, self-willed **2.** intentional —'**wilfully** *or U.S.* '**willfully** *adv.*

will (wɪl) *v. aux.* **1.** forms moods and tenses indicating intention or conditional result (**would** *pt.*) —*vi.* **2.** have a wish —*vt.* **3.** wish **4.** intend **5.** leave as legacy —*n.* **6.** faculty of deciding what one will do **7.** purpose **8.** volition **9.** determination **10.** wish **11.** directions written for disposal of property after death —'**willing** *a.* **1.** ready **2.** given cheerfully —'**willingly** *adv.* —'**willingness** *n.* —'**willpower** *n.* ability to control oneself, one's actions, impulses

willies ('wɪlɪz) *pl.n. sl.* nervousness, jitters, or fright (*esp. in* **give** (*or* **get**) **the willies**)

will-o'-the-wisp (wɪləðə'wɪsp) *n.* **1.** brief pale flame or phosphorescence sometimes seen over marshes **2.** elusive person or hope

willow ('wɪləʊ) *n.* **1.** tree, such as the weeping willow with long thin flexible branches **2.** its wood —'**willowy** *a.* lithe, slender, supple —'**willowherb** *n.* tall plant with mauve flowers

willy-nilly ('wɪlɪ'nɪlɪ) *adv./a.* **1.** (occurring) whether desired or not

wilt (wɪlt) *v.* (cause to) become limp, drooping or lose strength *etc.*

Wilts. (wɪlts) Wiltshire

wimple ('wɪmpəl) *n.* garment worn by nun, around face

win (wɪn) *vi.* **1.** be successful, victorious —*vt.* **2.** get by labour or effort **3.** reach **4.** allure **5.** be successful in **6.** gain the support, consent *etc.* of (**won**, '**winning**) —*n.* **7.** victory, *esp.* in games —'**winner** *n.* —'**winning** *a.* charming —'**winnings** *pl.n.* sum won in game, betting *etc.*

wince (wɪns) *vi.* **1.** flinch, draw back, as from pain *etc.* —*n.* **2.** this act

winceyette (wɪnsɪ'ɛt) *n.* cotton fabric with raised nap

winch (wɪntʃ) *n.* **1.** machine for hoisting or hauling using cable wound round drum —*vt.* **2.** move (something) by using a winch

wind¹ (wɪnd) *n.* **1.** air in motion **2.** breath **3.** flatulence **4.** idle talk **5.** hint or suggestion **6.** scent borne by air —*vt.* **7.** render short of breath, *esp.* by blow *etc.* **8.** get the scent of —'**windward** *n.* side against which wind is blowing —'**windy** *a.* **1.** exposed to wind **2.** flatulent **3.** *sl.* nervous, scared *etc.* —'**windbag** *n. sl.* voluble person who has little of interest to communicate —'**windbreak** *n.* fence, line of trees *etc.* serving as protection from wind —'**windcheater** *n.* warm jacket, usu. with close-fitting knitted neck, cuffs and waistband —'**windfall** *n.* **1.** unexpected good luck **2.** fallen fruit —**wind gauge 1.** *see* ANEMOMETER **2.** *Mus.* device for measuring wind pressure in bellows of organ —**wind instrument** musical instrument played by blowing or air pressure —'**windjammer** *n.* large merchant sailing ship —'**windmill** ('wɪndmɪl, 'wɪnmɪl) *n.* wind-driven apparatus with fanlike sails for raising water, crushing grain *etc.* —'**windpipe** *n.* passage from throat to lungs —'**windscreen** *n.* protective sheet of glass *etc.* in front of driver or pilot —**windscreen wiper** *UK* electrically operated blade with rubber edge that wipes windscreen clear of rain *etc.* —'**windsock** *n.* cone of material flown on mast at airfield to indicate wind direction —**wind tunnel** chamber for testing aerodynamic properties of aircraft *etc.* in which current of air can be maintained at constant velocity

wind² (waɪnd) *vi.* **1.** twine **2.** meander —*vt.* **3.** twist, coil **4.** wrap **5.** make ready for working by tightening spring (**wound**, '**winding**) —*n.* **6.** act of winding **7.** single turn of something wound **8.** a turn, curve —'**winding sheet** sheet in which corpse is wrapped for burial; shroud —**wind-up** *n. inf.*, *chiefly US* **1.** act of concluding **2.** end —**wind down 1.** lower or move down by cranking **2.** (of clock spring) become slack **3.** diminish gradually in force or power —**wind up 1.** bring to or reach a conclusion **2.** tighten spring of (clockwork mechanism) **3.** *inf.* make nervous, tense *etc.* **4.** *inf.* see LIQUIDATE (sense 2) **5.** *inf.* end up (in specified state)

windlass ('wɪndləs) *n.* winch, *esp.* simple one worked by a crank

window ('wɪndəʊ) *n.* **1.** hole in wall (with glass) to admit light, air *etc.* **2.** anything similar in appearance or function **3.** area for display of goods behind glass of shop front —**window box** long narrow box, placed on windowsill, in which plants are grown —**window-dressing** *n.* **1.** arrangement of goods in a shop window **2.** deceptive display —'**windowpane** *n.* sheet of glass in window —**window-shop** *vi.* look at goods in shop windows without buying them (-**pp**-) —'**windowsill** n. sill below window

Windsor chair ('wɪnzə) simple wooden chair, usu. having shaped seat, splayed legs, and back of many spindles

wine (waɪn) n. fermented juice of grape etc. —'**wino** n. person who habitually drinks wine as means of getting drunk —'**winepress** n. apparatus for extracting juice from grape —'**wineskin** n. skin of sheep or goat sewn up and used as holder for wine

wing (wɪŋ) n. 1. feathered limb a bird uses in flying 2. one of organs of flight of insect or some animals 3. main lifting surface of aircraft 4. lateral extension 5. side portion of building projecting from main central portion 6. one of sides of a stage 7. flank corps of army on either side 8. part of car body that surrounds wheels 9. Sport (player on) either side of pitch 10. faction, esp. of political party —pl. 11. insignia worn by qualified aircraft pilot 12. sides of stage —vi. 13. fly 14. move, go very fast —vt. 15. disable, wound slightly —**winged** a. having wings —**wing chair** chair having wings on each side of back —**wing commander** officer holding commissioned rank in certain air forces, such as Royal Air Force: junior to group captain and senior to squadron leader —**wing nut** threaded nut tightened by hand by means of two flat wings projecting from central body (also **butterfly nut**)

wink (wɪŋk) v. 1. close and open (an eye) rapidly, esp. to indicate friendliness or as signal —vi. 2. twinkle —n. 3. act of winking

winkle ('wɪŋk'l) n. shellfish, periwinkle —**winkle-pickers** pl.n. shoes or boots with very pointed narrow toes —**winkle out** extract

winnow ('wɪnəʊ) vt. 1. blow free of chaff 2. sift, examine

winsome ('wɪnsəm) a. charming, winning

winter ('wɪntə) n. 1. the coldest season —vi. 2. pass, spend the winter —'**wintry** or '**wintery** a. 1. of, like winter 2. cold —'**wintergreen** n. evergreen shrub, esp. subshrub of E N Amer., which has white, bell-shaped flowers and edible red berries —**winter solstice** time at which sun is at its southernmost point in sky appearing at noon at its lowest altitude above horizon. It occurs about Dec. 22nd. —**winter sports** sports held in open air on snow or ice —**oil of wintergreen** aromatic compound, formerly made from the shrub but now synthesized: used medicinally and for flavouring

wipe (waɪp) vt. 1. rub so as to clean —n. 2. wiping —'**wiper** n. 1. one that wipes 2. automatic wiping apparatus (esp. **windscreen wiper**) —**wipe out** 1. erase 2. annihilate 3. sl. kill

wire (waɪə) n. 1. metal drawn into thin, flexible strand 2. something made of wire, eg fence 3.

telegram —vt. 4. provide, fasten with wire 5. send by telegraph —'**wiring** n. system of wires —'**wiry** a. 1. like wire 2. lean and tough —**wire-gauge** n. 1. flat plate with slots in which standard wire sizes can be measured 2. standard system of sizes for measuring diameters of wires —**wire-haired** a. (of various breeds of dog) with short stiff hair —'**wiretap** v. tap (telephone wire etc.) to obtain information secretly —**wire wool** mass of fine wire, used esp. to clean kitchen articles

wireless ('waɪəlɪs) n. 1. old-fashioned term for radio, radio set —a. 2. of or for radio

wise[1] (waɪz) a. 1. having intelligence and knowledge 2. sensible —**wisdom** ('wɪzdəm) n. 1. (accumulated) knowledge, learning 2. erudition —'**wisely** adv. —'**wiseacre** n. one who wishes to seem wise —**wisdom tooth** third molar usu. cut about 20th year

wise[2] (waɪz) n. obs. manner

-**wise** (comb. form) 1. indicating direction or manner, as in clockwise, likewise 2. with reference to, as in businesswise

wisecrack ('waɪzkræk) n. inf. flippant, (would-be) clever remark

wish (wɪʃ) vi. 1. have a desire —vt. 2. desire —n. 3. desire 4. thing desired —'**wishful** a. 1. desirous 2. too optimistic —'**wishbone** n. V-shaped bone above breastbone of fowl —**wishful thinking** erroneous belief that one's wishes are in accordance with reality

wishy-washy ('wɪʃɪwɒʃɪ) a. inf. 1. lacking in substance, force, colour etc. 2. watery; thin

wisp (wɪsp) n. 1. light, delicate streak, as of smoke 2. twisted handful, as of straw etc. 3. stray lock of hair —'**wispy** a.

wisteria (wɪ'stɪərɪə) n. climbing shrub with usu. mauve flowers

wistful ('wɪstfʊl) a. 1. longing, yearning 2. sadly pensive —'**wistfully** adv.

wit[1] (wɪt) n. 1. ingenuity in connecting amusingly incongruous ideas 2. person gifted with this power 3. sense 4. intellect 5. understanding 6. ingenuity 7. humour —'**witless** a. foolish —'**witticism** n. witty remark —'**wittily** adv. —'**wittingly** adv. 1. on purpose 2. knowingly —'**witty** a.

wit[2] (wɪt) v. obs. be or become aware of (something) —**to wit** that is to say; namely

witch (wɪtʃ) n. 1. person, usu. female, believed to practise, practising, or professing to practise (black) magic, sorcery 2. ugly, wicked woman 3. fascinating woman —'**witchery** n. —'**witch-craft** n. —**witch doctor** in certain societies, man appearing to cure or cause injury, disease by magic —**witch-hunt** n. rigorous campaign to expose dissenters on pretext of safeguarding public welfare —**witch-hunting** n./a.

witch- (*comb. form*) *see* WYCH-

witch hazel *or* **wych-hazel** *n.* **1.** any of genus of trees and shrubs of N Amer. having medicinal properties **2.** astringent medicinal solution containing extract of bark and leaves of one of these shrubs, applied to treat bruises, *etc.*

with (wɪð, wɪθ) *prep.* **1.** in company or possession of **2.** against **3.** in relation to **4.** through **5.** by means of —**withal** (wɪˈθɔːl) *adv.* also, likewise —**within** (wɪˈðɪn) *prep./adv.* in, inside —**without** (wɪˈðaʊt) *prep.* **1.** lacking **2.** *obs.* outside

withdraw (wɪðˈdrɔː) *v.* draw back or out (-ˈdrew, -ˈdrawn, -ˈdrawing) —**with'drawal** *n.* —**with'drawn** *a.* reserved, unsociable

withe (wɪθ, wɪð, waɪð) *n.* **1.** strong flexible twig, *esp.* of willow, suitable for binding things together —*vt.* **2.** bind with withes

wither (ˈwɪðə) *v.* (cause to) wilt, dry up, decline —ˈ**withering** *a.* (of glance *etc.*) scornful

withers (ˈwɪðəz) *pl.n.* ridge between a horse's shoulder blades

withhold (wɪðˈhəʊld) *vt.* **1.** restrain **2.** keep back **3.** refrain from giving (-ˈheld, -ˈholding) —**with'holder** *n.*

withstand (wɪðˈstænd) *vt.* oppose, resist, *esp.* successfully (-ˈstood, -ˈstanding)

withy (ˈwɪðɪ) *n.* **1.** *see* WITHE (sense 1) **2.** willow tree

witness (ˈwɪtnɪs) *n.* **1.** one who sees something **2.** testimony **3.** one who gives testimony —*vi.* **4.** give testimony —*vt.* **5.** see **6.** attest to genuineness of **7.** see and sign as having seen —**witness box** *or esp. U.S.* **stand** place in court of law in which witnesses stand to give evidence

wives (waɪvz) *n., pl.* of WIFE —**old wives' tale** superstitious tradition

wizard (ˈwɪzəd) *n.* **1.** sorcerer, magician **2.** expert —ˈ**wizardry** *n.*

wizened (ˈwɪznd) *or* **wizen** *a.* shrivelled, wrinkled

wk. **1.** week (*pl.* **wks.**) **2.** work

WNW west-northwest

woad (wəʊd) *n.* blue dye from plant

wobble (ˈwɒbl) *vi.* **1.** move unsteadily, sway —*n.* **2.** an unsteady movement —ˈ**wobbly** *a.*

woe (wəʊ) *n.* grief —ˈ**woebegone** *a.* looking sorrowful —ˈ**woeful** *a.* **1.** sorrowful **2.** pitiful **3.** wretched —ˈ**woefully** *adv.*

wog (wɒg) *n. sl. offens.* foreigner, *esp.* one who is not White

wold (wəʊld) *n.* open downs, moorland

wolf (wʊlf) *n.* **1.** wild predatory doglike animal of northern countries **2.** *inf.* man who habitually tries to seduce women (*pl.* **wolves** (wʊlvz)) —*vt.* **3.** eat ravenously —ˈ**wolfhound** *n.* largest breed of dog, used formerly to hunt wolves —**wolf**

whistle whistle by man expressing admiration for a woman —**cry wolf** raise false alarm

wolfram (ˈwʊlfrəm) *n.* tungsten

wolverine (ˈwʊlvəriːn) *n.* carnivorous mammal inhabiting Arctic regions

woman (ˈwʊmən) *n.* **1.** adult human female **2.** women collectively (*pl.* **women** (ˈwɪmɪn)) —ˈ**womanhood** *n.* —ˈ**womanish** *a.* effeminate —ˈ**womanize** *or* **-ise** *vi. inf.* (of a man) indulge in many casual affairs with women —ˈ**womanizer** *or* **-iser** *n.* —ˈ**womankind** *n.* —ˈ**womanly** *a.* of, proper to woman —**Women's Institute** in Commonwealth countries, society for women interested in engaging in craft and cultural activities —**Women's Liberation** movement for removal of attitudes, practices that preserve social, economic *etc.* inequalities between women and men (*also* **women's lib**)

womb (wuːm) *n.* female organ of conception and gestation, uterus

wombat (ˈwɒmbæt) *n.* Aust. burrowing marsupial with heavy body, short legs and dense fur

won (wʌn) *pt./pp.* of WIN

wonder (ˈwʌndə) *n.* **1.** emotion excited by amazing or unusual thing **2.** marvel, miracle —*vi.* **3.** be curious **4.** feel amazement —ˈ**wonderful** *a.* **1.** remarkable **2.** very fine —ˈ**wonderfully** *adv.* —ˈ**wonderment** *n.* surprise —ˈ**wondrous** *a.* inspiring wonder **2.** strange

wonky (ˈwɒŋkɪ) *a. inf.* **1.** shaky, unsteady **2.** groggy **3.** askew **4.** unreliable

wont (wəʊnt) *n.* **1.** custom —*a.* **2.** accustomed —ˈ**wonted** *a.* habitual, established

woo (wuː) *vt.* court, seek to marry —ˈ**wooer** *n.* suitor

wood (wʊd) *n.* **1.** substance of trees, timber **2.** firewood **3.** tract of land with growing trees —ˈ**wooded** *a.* having (many) trees —ˈ**wooden** *a.* **1.** made of wood **2.** obstinate **3.** without expression —ˈ**woody** *a.* —ˈ**woodbine** *n.* honeysuckle —ˈ**woodcarver** *n.* —ˈ**woodcarving** *n.* act of carving wood **2.** work of art produced by carving wood —ˈ**woodchuck** *n.* Amer. burrowing marmot —ˈ**woodcock** *n.* game bird —ˈ**woodcut** *n.* **1.** engraving on wood **2.** impression from this —**woodland** (ˈwʊdlənd) *n.* woods, forest —ˈ**woodlark** *n.* Old World lark similar to skylark —ˈ**woodlouse** *n.* small grey land crustacean with seven pairs of legs (*pl.* **-lice**) —ˈ**woodpecker** *n.* bird which searches tree trunks for insects —**wood pigeon** large Eurasian pigeon —ˈ**woodpile** *n.* heap of firewood —**wood pulp** finely pulped wood that has been digested by chemical, such as caustic soda, used in making paper —ˈ**woodruff** *n.* plant, *esp.* sweet woodruff, which has small sweet-scented white flowers, used to flavour wine and in perfumery —**wood sorrel** Eurasian plant having trefoil leaves, underground creeping stem and white purple-veined flowers —**woodwind** ('wʊdwɪnd) *a./n.* (of) wind instruments of orchestra, *orig.* made of wood —'**woodwork** *n.* 1. art or craft of making things in wood 2. components made of wood, such as doors *etc.* —'**woodworm** *n.* insect larva that bores into wood

woof[1] (wuːf) *n.* the threads that cross the warp in weaving

woof[2] (wʊf) *interj.* 1. imitation of bark of dog —*vi.* 2. (of dog) bark

woofer ('wuːfə) *n.* loudspeaker for reproducing low-frequency sounds

wool (wʊl) *n.* 1. soft hair of sheep, goat *etc.* 2. yarn spun from this —'**woollen** *or U.S.* '**woolen** *a.* —'**woolly** *or U.S. (oft.)* '**wooly** *a.* 1. of wool 2. vague, muddled —*n.* 3. knitted woollen garment —'**woolgathering** *a./n.* daydreaming —'**woolsack** *n.* Lord Chancellor's seat in British House of Lords

woozy ('wuːzɪ) *a. inf.* 1. dazed or confused 2. experiencing dizziness, nausea *etc.* as result of drink —'**woozily** *adv.* —'**wooziness** *n.*

Worcs. (wɜːks) Worcestershire

word (wɜːd) *n.* 1. unit of speech or writing regarded by users of a language as the smallest separate meaningful unit 2. term 3. message 4. brief remark 5. information 6. promise 7. command —*vt.* 8. express in words, *esp.* in particular way —'**wordily** *adv.* —'**wording** *n.* choice and arrangement of words —'**wordy** *a.* using more words than necessary, verbose —**word blindness** *see* ALEXIA, DYSLEXIA —**word-perfect** *or U.S.* **letter-perfect** *a.* 1. correct in every detail 2. (of speaker *etc.*) knowing one's speech *etc.* perfectly —**word processing** storage and organization of language by electronic means, *esp.* for business purposes —**word processor** installation for word processing, typically consisting of keyboard and VDU incorporating microprocessor, storage and processing capabilities

wore (wɔː) *pt. of* WEAR

work (wɜːk) *n.* 1. labour 2. employment 3. occupation 4. task 5. toil 6. something made or accomplished 7. production of art or science 8. book 9. needlework —*pl.* 10. factory 11. total of person's deeds, writings *etc.* 12. *inf.* everything, full or extreme treatment 13. mechanism of clock *etc.* —*vt.* 14. cause to operate 15. make, shape —*vi.* 16. apply effort 17. labour 18. operate 19. be engaged in trade, profession *etc.* 20. turn out successfully 21. ferment —'**workable** *a.* —'**worker** *n.* —'**working** *n.* 1. operation or mode of operation of something 2. act or process of moulding something pliable 3. (*oft.*

pl.) part of mine or quarry that is being or has been worked —*a.* 4. of or concerned with person or thing that works 5. concerned with, used in, or suitable for work 6. capable of being operated or used —'**workaday** *a.* 1. ordinary 2. suitable for working days —**worka'holic** *n.* person obsessively addicted to work —**work force** 1. total number of workers employed by company on specific project *etc.* 2. total number of people who could be employed —'**workhouse** *n. Hist.* institution offering food, lodgings for unpaid menial work —**work-in** *n.* form of industrial action in which factory threatened with closure is occupied and run by its workers —**working class** social class consisting of wage earners, *esp.* manual —**working-class** *a.* —**working party** advisory committee studying specific problem, question —'**workman** *n.* manual worker —'**workmanlike** *or* '**workmanly** *a.* appropriate to or befitting a good workman —'**workmanship** *n.* 1. skill of workman 2. way thing is finished 3. style —**work-out** *n.* session of physical exercise, *esp.* for training or practice —'**workshop** *n.* place where things are made —'**workshy** *a.* not inclined to work —**work station** area in office *etc.* where one person works —**work in** 1. insert or become inserted 2. find space for —**work of art** 1. piece of fine art, as painting, sculpture 2. something that may be likened to piece of fine art, *esp.* in beauty *etc.* —**work out** 1. accomplish by effort 2. solve by reasoning or calculation 3. devise or formulate 4. prove satisfactory 5. happen as specified 6. take part in physical exercise, as in training 7. remove all mineral in (mine *etc.*) that can be profitably exploited —**work to rule** adhere strictly to all working regulations to reduce rate of work as form of protest

world (wɜːld) *n.* 1. the universe 2. the planet earth 3. sphere of existence 4. mankind, people generally 5. society —'**worldly** *a.* 1. earthly 2. mundane 3. absorbed in the pursuit of material gain, advantage 4. carnal —**World Bank** international organization established in 1945 to assist economic development, by advance of loans guaranteed by member governments (official name: **International Bank for Reconstruction and Development**) —**world-beater** *n.* person or thing that surpasses all others in its category; champion —**World Cup** international association football championship competition held every four years between national teams selected through preliminary tournaments —**world-shaking** *a.* of enormous significance; momentous —**world war** involving many countries

worm (wɜːm) *n.* 1. small limbless creeping snakelike creature 2. anything resembling worm in shape or movement 3. *inf.* weak, despised person —*pl.* **4.** (disorder caused by) infestation of worms, *esp.* in intestines —*vi.* **5.** crawl —*vt.* **6.** work (oneself) in insidiously **7.** extract (secret) craftily **8.** rid of worms —'**wormy** *a.* —'**wormcast** *n.* coil of earth excreted by earthworm —**worm-eaten** *a.* **1.** full of holes gnawed by worms **2.** old, antiquated —**worm gear 1.** device consisting of threaded shaft (**worm**) that mates with gear wheel (**worm wheel**) so that rotary motion can be transferred between two shafts at right angles to each other **2.** gear wheel driven by threaded shaft or worm (*also* **worm wheel**)

wormwood ('wɜːmwʊd) *n.* **1.** bitter herb **2.** bitterness

worn (wɔːn) *pp. of* WEAR —**worn-out** *a.* **1.** worn or used until threadbare, valueless or useless **2.** exhausted

worry ('wʌrɪ) *vi.* **1.** be (unduly) concerned —*vt.* **2.** trouble, pester, harass **3.** (of dog) seize, shake with teeth ('**worried,** '**worrying**) —*n.* **4.** (cause of) anxiety, concern —'**worrier** *n.* —'**worri-some** *a.* **1.** causing worry **2.** tending to worry —**worry beads** string of beads that when played with supposedly relieves nervous tension

worse (wɜːs) *a./adv.* **1.** *comp. of* BAD *or* BADLY —*n.* **2.** inferior or less good person, thing or state —'**worsen** *v.* **1.** make, grow worse —*vi.* **2.** impair —*vi.* **3.** deteriorate —**worst** *a./adv.* **1.** *sup. of* BAD *or* BADLY —*n.* **2.** least good or most inferior person, part or thing

worship ('wɜːʃɪp) *vt.* **1.** show religious devotion to **2.** adore **3.** love and admire (-**pp-**) —*n.* **4.** act of worshipping **5.** title used to address mayor, magistrate *etc.* —'**worshipful** *a.* —'**worshipper** *n.*

worsted ('wʊstɪd) *n.* **1.** woollen yarn —*a.* **2.** made of woollen yarn **3.** spun from wool

wort (wɜːt) *n.* **1.** *obs.* plant, herb **2.** infusion of malt before fermentation

worth (wɜːθ) *a.* **1.** having or deserving to have value specified **2.** meriting —*n.* **3.** excellence **4.** merit, value **5.** virtue **6.** usefulness **7.** price **8.** quantity to be had for a given sum —'**worthily** ('wɜːðɪlɪ) *adv.* —'**worthiness** ('wɜːðɪnɪs) *n.* —'**worthless** *a.* useless —'**worthy** ('wɜːðɪ) *a.* **1.** virtuous **2.** meriting —*n.* **3.** one of eminent worth **4.** (local) notable —**worth'while** *a.* worth the time, effort *etc.* involved

would (wʊd; *unstressed* wəd) *v. aux.* **1.** expressing wish, intention, probability —*v.* **2.** *pt. of* WILL —**would-be** *a.* wishing, pretending to be

wound[1] (wuːnd) *n.* **1.** injury, hurt from cut, stab *etc.* —*vt.* **2.** inflict wound on, injure **3.** pain

wound[2] (waʊnd) *pt./pp. of* WIND[2]

wove (wəʊv) *pt. of* WEAVE

woven ('wəʊvən) *pp. of* WEAVE

wow (waʊ) *interj.* **1.** exclamation of astonish-

ment, admiration *etc.* —*n.* **2.** *inf.* object of astonishment, admiration *etc.* **3.** variation, distortion in pitch in record player *etc.*

w.p.m. words per minute

W.R.A.C. Women's Royal Army Corps

wrack *or* **rack** (ræk) *n.* seaweed

W.R.A.F. Women's Royal Air Force

wraith (reɪθ) *n.* **1.** apparition of a person seen shortly before or after death **2.** spectre

wrangle ('ræŋgəl) *vi.* **1.** quarrel (noisily) **2.** dispute **3.** US, C herd cattle —*n.* **4.** noisy quarrel **5.** dispute —'**wrangler** *n.* US, C cowboy

wrap (ræp) *vt.* **1.** cover, *esp.* by putting something round **2.** put round (-**pp-**) —**wrap** *or* '**wrapper** *n.* loose garment **2.** covering —'**wrapping** *n.* material used to wrap —'**wrapover, 'wraparound** *or* '**wrapround** *a.* (of garment, *esp.* skirt) not sewn up at one side, but worn wrapped round body and fastened so that open edges overlap

wrasse (ræs) *n.* type of sea fish

wrath (rɒθ) *n.* anger —'**wrathful** *a.*

wreak (riːk) *vt.* **1.** inflict (vengeance) **2.** cause

wreath (riːθ) *n.* something twisted into ring form, *esp.* band of flowers *etc.* as memorial or tribute on grave *etc.* —**wreathe** *vt.* **1.** form into wreath **2.** surround **3.** wind round

wreck (rɛk) *n.* **1.** destruction of ship **2.** wrecked ship **3.** ruin **4.** something ruined —*vt.* **5.** cause the wreck of —'**wreckage** *n.* —'**wrecker** *n.* **1.** person or thing that destroys, ruins **2.** one whose job is to demolish houses, dismantle old cars *etc.*

wren (rɛn) *n.* kind of small songbird

Wren (rɛn) *n.* member of Women's Royal Naval Service

wrench (rɛntʃ) *vt.* **1.** twist **2.** distort **3.** seize forcibly **4.** sprain —*n.* **5.** violent twist **6.** tool for twisting or screwing **7.** spanner **8.** sudden pain caused *esp.* by parting

wrest (rɛst) *vt.* **1.** take by force **2.** twist violently

wrestle ('rɛsəl) *vi.* **1.** fight (*esp.* as sport) by grappling and trying to throw down **2.** strive **3.** struggle —*n.* **4.** struggle, tussle —'**wrestler** *n.* —'**wrestling** *n.*

wretch (rɛtʃ) *n.* **1.** despicable person **2.** miserable creature —**wretched** ('rɛtʃɪd) *a.* **1.** miserable, unhappy **2.** worthless —**wretchedly** ('rɛtʃɪdlɪ) *adv.* —**wretchedness** ('rɛtʃɪdnɪs) *n.*

wrick (rɪk) *n./vt.* strain; sprain

wriggle ('rɪgəl) *vi.* **1.** move with twisting action, as worm **2.** squirm —*n.* **3.** this action

wright (raɪt) *n.* *obs.* workman; maker; builder

wring (rɪŋ) *vt.* **1.** twist **2.** extort **3.** pain **4.** squeeze out (**wrung, 'wringing**) —'**wringer** *n.* machine consisting of two rollers between which wet clothes are run to squeeze out the water

wrinkle ('rɪŋkəl) *n.* **1.** slight ridge or furrow on

surface **2.** crease in the skin **3.** fold **4.** pucker **5.** *inf.* (useful) trick, hint —*v.* **6.** make, become wrinkled, pucker

wrist (rıst) *n.* joint between hand and arm —'**wristlet** *n.* band worn on wrist

writ (rıt) *n.* written command from law court or other authority

write (raıt) *vi.* **1.** mark paper *etc.* with the symbols which are used to represent words or sounds **2.** compose **3.** send a letter —*vt.* **4.** set down in words **5.** compose **6.** communicate in writing (**wrote, written** ('rıtən), '**writing**) —'**writer** *n.* **1.** one who writes **2.** author —**write-off** *n. inf.* something damaged beyond repair —**write-up** *n.* written (published) account of something

writhe (raıð) *vi.* **1.** twist, squirm in or as in pain *etc.* **2.** be acutely embarrassed (**writhed** *pt.,* **writhed,** *Poet.* **writhen** ('rıðən) *pp.,* '**writhing** *pr.p.*)

W.R.N.S. Women's Royal Naval Service

wrong (rɒŋ) *a.* **1.** not right or good **2.** not suitable **3.** wicked **4.** incorrect **5.** mistaken **6.** not functioning properly —*n.* **7.** that which is wrong **8.** harm **9.** evil —*vt.* **10.** do wrong to **11.** think badly of without justification —'**wrongful** *a.* —'**wrongfully** *adv.* —'**wrongly** *adv.* —'**wrongdoer** *n.* one who acts immorally or illegally —**wrong-foot** *vt. Tennis etc.* play shot in such a way as to cause (one's opponent) to be off balance —**wrong-headed** *a.* **1.** constantly wrong in judgment **2.** foolishly stubborn

wrote (rəʊt) *pt.* of WRITE

wrought (rɔːt) *v.* **1.** *pt./pp.* of WORK —*a.* **2.** (of metals) shaped by hammering or beating —**wrought iron** pure form of iron used *esp.* in decorative railings *etc.*

wrung (rʌŋ) *pt./pp.* of WRING

W.R.V.S. Women's Royal Voluntary Service

wry (raı) *a.* **1.** turned to one side, contorted, askew **2.** sardonic, dryly humorous —'**wryneck** *n.* type of woodpecker

WSW west-southwest

wt. weight

WV West Virginia

WWI World War One

WWII World War Two

WX women's extra (size)

WY Wyoming

wych- *or* **witch-** (*comb. form*) (of tree) with pliant branches

wych-elm *or* **witch-elm** ('wıtʃɛlm) *n.* **1.** Eurasian elm tree, having roundish shape, longish pointed leaves, clusters of small flowers and winged fruits **2.** wood of this tree

wynd (waınd) *n.* in Scotland, narrow lane, alley

X,x

x *or* **X** (ɛks) *n.* **1.** 24th letter of English alphabet **2.** speech sound sequence represented by this letter, pronounced as *ks* or *gz* or, in initial position, *z*, as in *xylophone* (*pl.* **x's, X's** *or* **Xs**)

x *Maths.* unknown quantity

X 1. Christ **2.** Christian **3.** Cross **4.** Roman numeral, 10 **5.** mark indicating something wrong, a choice, a kiss, signature *etc.* **6.** unknown, mysterious person, factor

xanthine ('zænθiːn, -θaın) *n.* **1.** crystalline compound found in urine, blood and certain plants **2.** any of three substituted derivatives of xanthine, which act as stimulants and diuretics

x-axis *n.* reference axis, usu. horizontal, along which *x*-coordinate is measured

X-chromosome *n.* sex-determining chromosome that occurs in pairs in homologically paired cells of females of many animals and as one of pair with Y-chromosome in those of males

Xe *Chem.* xenon

xeno- *or before vowel* **xen-** (*comb. form*) something strange, different or foreign, as in *xenogamy*

xenogamy (zɛ'nɒgəmı) *n.* **1.** pollination from another plant **2.** cross-fertilization —**xe'nogamous** *a.*

xenon ('zɛnɒn) *n.* colourless, odourless gas occurring in very small quantities in air

xenophobia (zɛnə'fəʊbıə) *n.* dislike, hatred, fear, of strangers or aliens

xerography (zı'rɒgrəfı) *n.* photocopying process —**Xerox** ('zıərɒks) *n.* **R** xerographic copying process, machine

xi (zaı, saı, ksaı, ksi:) *n.* 14th letter in Gr. alphabet (Ξ, ξ) (*pl.* -**s**)

Xmas ('ɛksməs, 'krısməs) Christmas

x-ray *or* **X-ray** *n.* **1.** radiation of very short wavelengths, capable of penetrating solid bodies, and printing on photographic plate shadow picture of objects not permeable by rays —*vt.* **2.** photograph by x-rays

xylem ('zaıləm, -lɛm) *n.* plant tissue that conducts water and mineral salts from roots to other parts

xylene ('zaıliːn) *n.* aromatic hydrocarbon existing in three isomeric forms, all three being colourless flammable volatile liquids used as solvents *etc.*

xylograph ('zaıləgrɑːf) *n.* **1.** wood engraving **2.** impression from wood block

xyloid ('zaılɔıd) *a.* **1.** pert. to wood **2.** woody, ligneous

xylophone ('zailəfəun) *n.* musical instrument of wooden bars which sound when struck

xylose ('zailəuz, -ləus) *n.* white crystalline sugar found in wood and straw and used in dyeing, tanning, diabetic diet *etc.*

Y,y

y *or* **Y** (wai) *n.* **1.** 25th letter of English alphabet **2.** speech sound represented by this letter, usu. semivowel, as in *yawn*, or vowel, as in *symbol, shy* **3.** something shaped like Y (*pl.* **y's, Y's** *or* **Ys**)

y *Maths.* **1.** *y*-axis or coordinate measured along *y*-axis in Cartesian coordinate system **2.** algebraic variable

Y 1. any unknown or variable factor, number or thing **2.** *Chem.* yttrium

-y¹ *or* **-ey** (*comb. form*) **1.** characterized by; consisting of; filled with; resembling, as in *sunny, sandy, smoky, classy* **2.** tending to; acting or existing as specified, as in *leaky, shiny*

-y², -ie, *or* **-ey** (*comb. form*) *inf.* **1.** denoting smallness and expressing affection and familiarity, as in *doggy, Jamie* **2.** person or thing concerned with or characterized by being, as in *groupie, goalie, fatty*

-y³ (*comb. form*) **1.** act of doing what is indicated by verbal element, as in *inquiry* **2.** state, condition, quality, as in *geography, jealousy*

yacht (jot) *n.* vessel propelled by sail or power, used for racing, pleasure *etc.* —'**yachtsman** *n.*

yahoo (jə'huː) *n.* crude, coarse person

yak¹ (jæk) *n.* shaggy-haired, long-horned ox of Central Asia

yak² (jæk) *sl. n.* **1.** noisy, continuous, trivial talk —*vi.* **2.** chatter or talk in this way (**-kk-**)

Yale lock (jeil) **R** cylinder lock using flat serrated key

yam (jæm) *n.* large edible tuber, sweet potato

Yang (jæŋ) *n. see* YIN AND YANG

yank (jæŋk) *vt.* **1.** jerk, tug; pull quickly —*n.* **2.** quick tug

Yank (jæŋk) *a./n. sl.* American

yap (jæp) *vi.* **1.** bark (as small dog) **2.** talk idly; gossip (**-pp-**) —*n.* **3.** sharp bark

yarborough ('jɑːbərə, -brə) *n. Bridge, whist* hand of 13 cards with no card higher than nine

yard¹ (jɑːd) *n.* **1.** unit of length, 0.915 metre **2.** spar slung across ship's mast to extend sails —'**yardstick** *n.* formula or standard of measurement or comparison

yard² (jɑːd) *n.* piece of enclosed ground, oft. attached to or adjoining building and used for some specific purpose, as garden, storage,

holding livestock *etc.* —'**yardage** *n.* **1.** use of yard **2.** charge made for this

yarmulke ('jɑːmɔlkə) *n. Judaism* man's skullcap worn at prayer, and by strongly religious Jews at all times

yarn (jɑːn) *n.* **1.** spun thread **2.** tale —*vi.* **3.** tell a tale

yarrow ('jærəu) *n.* plant with flat white flower clusters

yashmak *or* **yashmac** ('jæʃmæk) *n.* face veil worn by Muslim women

yaw (jɔː) *vi.* **1.** (of aircraft *etc.*) turn about vertical axis **2.** (of ship *etc.*) deviate temporarily from course

yawl (jɔːl) *n.* two-masted sailing vessel

yawn (jɔːn) *vi.* **1.** open mouth wide, *esp.* in sleepiness **2.** gape —*n.* **3.** a yawning

yaws (jɔːz) *pl.n.* contagious tropical skin disease

y-axis *n.* reference axis of graph or two- or three-dimensional Cartesian coordinate system along which *y*-coordinate is measured

Yb *Chem.* ytterbium

Y-chromosome *n.* sex chromosome that occurs as one of pair with X-chromosome in homologically paired cells of males of many animals

yd *or* **yd.** yard (measure)

ye (jiː, *unstressed* ji) *pron. obs.* you

yea (jei) *interj. obs.* yes

year (jiə) *n.* **1.** time taken by one revolution of earth round sun, about 365 days **2.** twelve months —'**yearling** *n.* animal one year old —'**yearly** *adv.* **1.** every year, once a year —*a.* **2.** happening *etc.* once a year —'**yearbook** *n.* reference book published annually and containing details of events of previous year

yearn (jɜːn) *vi.* **1.** feel longing, desire **2.** be filled with pity, tenderness —'**yearning** *n.*

yeast (jiːst) *n.* substance used as fermenting agent, *esp.* in raising bread —'**yeasty** *a.* **1.** of, like yeast **2.** frothy, fermenting

yell (jel) *v.* **1.** cry out in loud shrill tone **2.** *inf.* call —*n.* **3.** loud shrill cry **4.** *inf.* call

yellow ('jeləu) *a.* **1.** of the colour of lemons, gold *etc.* **2.** *inf.* cowardly —*n.* **3.** yellow colour —**yellow fever** acute infectious disease of (sub)tropical climates —'**yellowhammer** *n.* small European bunting —**yellow pages** classified telephone directory or section of directory that lists subscribers by business or service provided —**yellow streak** cowardly trait —'**yellowwood** *n. SA* **1.** type of conifer **2.** its rich yellow wood used *esp.* for furniture and building

yelp (jelp) *vi./n.* (produce) quick, shrill cry

yen¹ (jen) *n.* Japanese monetary unit (*pl.* **yen**)

yen² (jen) *n. inf.* longing, craving

yeoman ('jəumən) *n.* **1.** *Hist.* farmer cultivating his own land **2.** assistant, subordinate

—'**yeomanry** *n.* **1.** yeomen collectively **2.** Brit. volunteer cavalry force, organized in 1761 for home defence —**yeoman of the guard** member of ceremonial bodyguard (**Yeomen of the Guard**) of British monarch

yes (jɛs) *interj.* affirms or consents, gives an affirmative answer —**yes man** weak person willing to agree to anything

yesterday ('jɛstɔdi, -dei) *n.* **1.** day before today **2.** recent time —*adv.* **3.** on the day before today

yet (jɛt) *adv.* **1.** now **2.** still **3.** besides **4.** hitherto **5.** nevertheless —*conj.* **6.** but, at the same time, nevertheless

yeti ('jɛti) *n. see* **abominable snowman** *at* ABOMINABLE

yew (juː) *n.* **1.** evergreen tree with dark leaves **2.** its wood

Y.H.A. UK Youth Hostels Association

Yiddish ('jidiʃ) *a./n.* (of, in) dialect of mixed German and Hebrew spoken by many Jews in Europe —**yid** *n. sl. offens.* Jew

yield (jiːld) *vt.* **1.** give or return as food **2.** produce **3.** provide **4.** concede **5.** give up, surrender —*vi.* **6.** submit **7.** (*with* to) comply (with) **8.** surrender, give way —*n.* **9.** amount produced, result **10.** return, profit

Yin and Yang (jin) two complementary principles of Chinese philosophy: Yin is negative, dark and feminine; Yang is positive, bright and masculine

Y.M.C.A. Young Men's Christian Association

yob (jɒb) *or* **yobbo** ('jɒbəʊ) *n. sl.* aggressive, surly youth (*pl.* **-s**)

yodel ('jəʊdʲl) *v.* **1.** warble in falsetto tone (**-ll-**) —*n.* **2.** falsetto warbling as practised by Swiss mountaineers

yoga ('jəʊgə) *n.* Hindu philosophical system aiming at spiritual, mental and physical wellbeing by means of certain physical and mental exercises —**yogi** ('jəʊgi) *n.* one who practises yoga (*pl.* **-s, -gin** (-gin))

yoghurt *or* **yogurt** ('jɒgət) *n.* thick, custardlike preparation of curdled milk

yoicks (haik; *spelling pron.* jɔiks) *interj.* cry used by fox-hunters to urge on hounds

yoke (jəʊk) *n.* **1.** wooden bar put across necks of two animals to hold them together and to which plough *etc.* may be attached **2.** various objects like a yoke in shape or use **3.** fitted part of garment, *esp.* round neck, shoulders **4.** bond, tie **5.** domination —*vt.* **6.** put a yoke on **7.** couple, unite

yokel ('jəʊkʲl) *n. disparaging term for* (old-fashioned) country dweller

yolk (jəʊk) *n.* **1.** yellow central part of egg **2.** oily secretion of skin of sheep

Yom Kippur (jom 'kipɔ; *Hebrew* jɔm ki'pur) Jewish holiday celebrated as day of fasting, when prayers of penitence are recited in synagogue (*also* **Day of Atonement**)

yon (jɒn) *a. obs., dial.* that or those over there —'**yonder** *a.* **1.** yon —*adv.* **2.** over there, in that direction

yoo-hoo ('juːhuː) *interj.* call to attract attention

YOP (jɒp) Youth Opportunities Programme

yore (jɔː) *n. Poet.* the distant past

yorker ('jɔːkə) *n. Cricket* ball that pitches directly under bat —**york** *vt. Cricket* bowl (batsman) by pitching ball under or just beyond bat

Yorks. (jɔːks) Yorkshire

Yorkshire pudding ('jɔːkʃiə) savoury baked batter eaten with roast beef —**Yorkshire terrier** very small terrier with long straight coat

you (juː; *unstressed* jʊ) *pron.* referring to person(s) addressed, or to unspecified person(s)

young (jʌŋ) *a.* **1.** not far advanced in growth, life or existence **2.** not yet old **3.** immature **4.** junior **5.** recently formed **6.** vigorous —*n.* **7.** offspring —'**youngster** *n.* child

your (jɔː, juə; *unstressed* jə) *a.* belonging to you —**yours** *pron.* —**your**'**self** *pron.* (*pl.* **your**'**selves**)

youth (juːθ) *n.* **1.** state or time of being young **2.** state before adult age **3.** young man **4.** young people —'**youthful** *a.* —**youth hostel** inexpensive lodging place *esp.* for young people travelling cheaply (*also* '**hostel**)

yowl (jaul) *vi./n.* (produce) mournful cry

yo-yo ('jəʊjəʊ) *n.* toy consisting of a spool attached to a string, by which it can be spun out and reeled in while attached to the finger (*pl.* **-s**)

Y.S.T. US, C Yukon Standard Time

Y.T. C Yukon Territory

ytterbium (ɪ'tɜːbɪəm) *n.* silvery element of lanthanide series of metals, used to improve mechanical properties of steel

yttrium ('ɪtrɪəm) *n.* silvery metallic element used in various alloys

yucca ('jʌkə) *n.* tropical plant with stiff lancelike leaves

Yugoslav *or* **Jugoslav** ('juːgəʊslɑːv) *n.* **1.** native of Yugoslavia, federal republic in SE Europe **2.** Serbo-Croatian (language) —*a.* **3.** of Yugoslavia

yule (juːl) *n.* (*sometimes* Y-) the Christmas festival or season

Y.W.C.A. Young Women's Christian Association

Z,z

z or **Z** (zɛd; *U.S.* ziː) *n.* **1.** 26th letter of English alphabet **2.** speech sound represented by this letter **3.** something shaped like Z (*pl.* **z's, Z's** or **Zs**)

z *Maths.* **1.** z-axis or coordinate measured along z-axis in Cartesian or cylindrical coordinate system **2.** algebraic variable

zany ('zeɪnɪ) *a.* comical, funny in unusual way

zeal (ziːl) *n.* **1.** fervour **2.** keenness, enthusiasm —**zealot** ('zɛlət) *n.* **1.** fanatic **2.** enthusiast —**zealous** ('zɛləs) *a.* **1.** ardent **2.** enthusiastic **3.** earnest —**zealously** ('zɛləslɪ) *adv.*

zebra ('zɛbrə, 'ziːbrə) *n.* striped Afr. animal like a horse —**zebra crossing** pedestrian crossing marked by stripes on road

zebu ('ziːbuː) *n.* humped Indian ox or cow

Zen (zɛn) *n. Buddhism* Japanese school teaching contemplation, meditation

zenith ('zɛnɪθ) *n.* **1.** point of the heavens directly above an observer **2.** point opposite nadir **3.** summit, peak **4.** climax —**zenithal** *a.*

zephyr ('zɛfə) *n.* soft, gentle breeze

zeppelin ('zɛpəlɪn) *n.* large, cylindrical, rigid airship

zero ('zɪərəu) *n.* **1.** nothing **2.** figure 0 **3.** point on graduated instrument from which positive and negative quantities are reckoned **4.** the lowest point (*pl.* **-s, -es**) —**zero hour 1.** *Mil.* time set for start of attack *etc.* **2.** *inf.* critical time —**zero-rated** *a.* denoting goods on which buyer pays no value-added tax

zest (zɛst) *n.* **1.** enjoyment **2.** excitement, interest, flavour **3.** peel of orange or lemon

zeta ('ziːtə) *n.* sixth letter in Gr. alphabet (Z, ζ)

zigzag ('zɪgzæg) *n.* **1.** line or course characterized by sharp turns in alternating directions —*vi.* **2.** move along in zigzag course (**-zagged** *pt./pp.,* **-zagging** *pr.p.*)

zinc (zɪŋk) *n.* bluish-white metallic element with wide variety of uses, *esp.* in alloys as brass *etc.* —**'zincograph** *n.* —**zin'cographer** *n.* —**zin'cography** *n.* art or process of engraving zinc to form printing plate —**zinc ointment** medicinal ointment of zinc oxide, petrolatum and paraffin —**zinc oxide** white insoluble powder used as pigment in paints, cosmetics, glass *etc.* (*also* **flowers of zinc**)

zing (zɪŋ) *n. inf.* **1.** short high-pitched buzzing sound **2.** vitality; zest —*vi.* **3.** make or move with high-pitched buzzing sound

zinnia ('zɪnɪə) *n.* plant with daisylike, brightly-coloured flowers

Zion ('zaɪən) or **Sion** *n.* **1.** hill on which Jerusalem stands **2.** Judaism **3.** Christian Church **4.** heaven —'**Zionism** *n.* movement to found, support Jewish homeland in Palestine —'**Zionist** *n./a.*

zip (zɪp) *n.* **1.** device for fastening with two rows of flexible metal or nylon teeth, interlocked and opened by a sliding clip (*also* '**zipper, zip fastener**) **2.** short whizzing sound **3.** energy, vigour —*vt.* **4.** fasten with zip —*vi.* **5.** move with zip (**-pp-**)

zircon ('zɜːkɒn) *n.* mineral used as gemstone and in industry —**zir'conium** *n.* greyish-white metallic element, occurring chiefly in zircon, that is exceptionally corrosion-resistant and has low neutron absorption

zither ('zɪðə) *n.* flat stringed instrument

zloty ('zlɒtɪ) *n.* Polish coin (*pl.* **-s,** '**zloty**)

Zn *Chem.* zinc

zodiac ('zəudɪæk) *n.* imaginary belt of the heavens along which the sun, moon, and chief planets appear to move, divided crosswise into twelve equal areas, called **signs of the zodiac**, each named after a constellation —**zodiacal** (zəu'daɪəkəl) *a.*

zombie or **zombi** ('zɒmbɪ) *n.* **1.** person appearing lifeless, apathetic *etc.* **2.** corpse supposedly brought to life by supernatural spirit

zone (zəun) *n.* **1.** region with particular characteristics or use **2.** any of the five belts into which tropics and arctic and antarctic circles divide the earth —'**zonal** *a.*

zoo (zuː) *n.* place where wild animals are kept, studied, bred and exhibited (*in full* **zoological gardens**)

zoo- or *before vowel* **zo-** (*comb. form*) animals, as in *zooplankton*

zoogeography (zəuədʒɪ'ɒgrəfɪ) *n.* science of geographical distribution of animals

zoography (zəu'ɒgrəfɪ) *n.* descriptive zoology —**zo'ographer** or **zo'ographist** *n.* —**zoo'graphic(al)** *a.*

zooid ('zəuɔɪd) *n.* **1.** independent animal body, such as individual of coelenterate colony **2.** cell or body capable of spontaneous motion, produced by organism

zool. 1. zoological **2.** zoology

zoology (zəu'ɒlədʒɪ, zuː-) *n.* **1.** scientific study of animals **2.** characteristics of particular animals or of fauna of particular area —**zoo'logical** *a.* —**zo'ologist** *n.*

zoom (zuːm) *vi.* **1.** (cause to) make loud buzzing, humming sound **2.** (cause to) go fast or rise, increase sharply —*vi.* **3.** (*with* in *or* out) use camera lens of adjustable focal length to make subject appear closer or further away —**zoom lens** used in this way

zoophyte ('zəuəfaɪt) *n.* plantlike animal, *eg* sponge —**zoophytic** (zəu'fɪtɪk) *a.*

Zoroastrianism (zɒrəu'æstrɪənɪzəm) or **Zo-**

roastrism *n.* dualistic religion founded by Persian prophet Zoroaster, based on concept of continuous struggle between Ormazd, god of creation, light and goodness, and his archenemy, Ahriman, spirit of evil and darkness

Zr *Chem.* zirconium

Zulu ('zuːlʊ, -luː) *n.* member, language of native S Afr. tribes

zygote ('zaɪgəʊt, 'zɪg-) *n.* fertilized egg cell